GOODE'S
SCHOOL ATLAS

PHYSICAL, POLITICAL, and ECONOMIC

BY

J. PAUL GOODE, Ph. D.

LATE PROFESSOR OF GEOGRAPHY
UNIVERSITY OF CHICAGO

REVISED BY

EDWARD B. ESPENSHADE, JR.

ASSOCIATE PROFESSOR OF GEOGRAPHY
NORTHWESTERN UNIVERSITY

RAND McNALLY & COMPANY

NEW YORK   CHICAGO   SAN FRANCISCO

Printed in U. S. A.

Made in U. S. A.

TO

LIVINGSTON C. LORD, LLD.

IN RECOGNITION OF MY DEBT TO HIM
FOR INTELLECTUAL INSPIRATION
FOR UNCOMPROMISING STANDARDS OF SCHOLARSHIP
AND FOR THE RARE GIFT OF HIS FRIENDSHIP
AND
TO THE SACRED MEMORY OF

KATHERINE

THE CONTENTS

SOUTH AMERICA

COÖPERATING EXPERTS

R. G. HAINSWORTH
Office of Foreign Agricultural Relations
United States Department of Agriculture

A. W. KÜCHLER
Department of Geology and Geography
University of Rochester

THOBURN C. LYON
Consultant
Cartography and Air Navigation

A. C. ORVEDAL
Soil Scientist
Agricultural Research Administration
United States Department of Agriculture

GLENN T. TREWARTHA
Department of Geography
University of Wisconsin

J. PARKER VAN ZANDT
President
Aviation Research Institute

WALTER H. VOSKUIL
Mineral Economist
Illinois Geological Survey

DERWENT WHITTLESEY
Professor of Geography
Harvard University

PREFACE

Background. *Goode's School Atlas* was recognized as a notable contribution to cartography and education when it appeared more than a quarter of a century ago. The author was a distinguished cartographer and teacher. The atlas was an outgrowth of his long and rich experience. It was planned carefully to meet the needs of American students. This is apparent in the selection of materials for representation, in the projections and symbols employed, and even in the order of the maps.

The success of *Goode's School Atlas* was not only prompt but also enduring. It stood the test of time. Successive revisions kept it up-to-date. More maps were added as needed, the 96 pages of the first edition growing to 174 pages in later editions. In schoolrooms, offices, and libraries it became and remained the leading American atlas.

Looking forward. This book is issued as the eighth edition of *Goode's School Atlas*. The old name is retained with pride by the publishers and the editor. It suggests the high standards which all those who have participated in the preparation of the book have sought to attain.

The present atlas is more than a mere revision of the earlier work, however. The first 48 pages are entirely new. Some of the maps on those pages are issued here for the first time. All the others are the result of new design, new compilation, and new drafting. They were reproduced by a superior printing process perfected since *Goode's School Atlas* was first issued. All the maps that are not entirely new have been revised thoroughly, to the extent permitted by mechanical necessities and in the light of recent events throughout the world. The conversion of them to the new printing process will be completed in the near future.

Further systematic improvements in the atlas are envisaged. Doubtless many changes will be needed that are not now foreseen. The American public is becoming world-minded and map-minded. American interests and commitments are as wide as the continents and the seas. Backward peoples are on the march. Areas formerly of little importance to this country are becoming highly significant. As the world changes, *Goode's School Atlas* will change.

Coöperating experts. The variety and complexity of the problems involved in the preparation of a world atlas make highly desirable the participation of specialists in some of the problems. In the preparation of the new edition of *Goode's School Atlas* the editor has been ably assisted by several such experts. He expresses his deep appreciation and thanks to all of them. He is particularly indebted to the experts listed on the preceding page, who have assumed primary responsibility for certain maps.

Sources. Every effort has been made to assemble the latest and most authentic source materials for use in compiling the atlas. For the general physical-political maps, national and state surveys, recent military maps, and hydrographic charts, particularly those of the U.S. Hydrographic Office and the British Admiralty, have been utilized. For the specialized maps, the source materials are even more varied. They include both published and unpublished items in the form of maps, descriptions in articles and books, statistics, and correspondence with geographers and others. To the various agencies and organizations, official and unofficial, who have coöperated, appreciation and thanks are expressed. Noteworthy among these organizations and agencies are: Food and Agriculture Organization of The United Nations for production statistics on livestock, crop and forest products, and statistics on world trade; the Office of the Geographer, The Department of State, for the map of Surface Transport Facilities, and other items; the Office of Foreign Agricultural Relations, Department of Agriculture, for information on crop and livestock production and distribution; the Bureau of Mines, Department of the Interior, for information on mineral production; various branches of the National Military Establishment and the Weather Bureau, Department of Commerce, for information on temperature, wind, pressure, and ocean currents; the Maritime Commission and the Department of Commerce, for statistics on ocean trade; the American Geographical Society, for use of its library and permission to use the Miller cylindrical projection; the University of Chicago Press, owners of the copyright, for permission to use Goode's Homolosine equal-area projection; and McGraw-Hill Book Company, for coöperation in permitting the use of Glenn Trewartha's map of climatic regions and Petterson's diagram of zones of precipitation.

Other acknowledgments. In earlier editions of *Goode's School Atlas* acknowledgments are made of assistance rendered by various individuals. This assistance, in some if not in all instances, carries over to the present edition, and the earlier recognition and thanks are here renewed.

Finally, the editor's grateful thanks are due to the staff of Rand McNally and Company, and particularly to Miss Louise Elder, Mrs. Carol C. Bradley, Mrs. Ruth P. Schottroff, Mr. Adolph J. Bravi, and Mr. Paul T. Tiddens. Their faithful and careful work has contributed much to the final result.

EDWARD B. ESPENSHADE, JR.

NORTHWESTERN UNIVERSITY
SEPTEMBER, 1949

INTRODUCTION

Utility of maps. There are many kinds of maps, and they are useful in countless ways. It would be difficult to list all the ways in which even a simple road map, for example, is or may be useful. Three outstanding attributes may be noted in connection with the maps of this atlas. They are characteristics common to maps of the most varied kinds and utilities.

(1) The maps show facts of areal distribution, both qualitative and quantitative. For example, the world vegetation map (pp. 16–17) is based on observations made by many hundreds of individuals. The map shows hundreds of varied vegetative units and thirty-two types of vegetation. Thousands of words would be required to state the facts portrayed by the map. These facts can be presented best on a map and can be grasped quickly from a map. The information embodied in the world vegetation map is chiefly qualitative. It was reduced from a general, undefined form to a particular, classified form, and so its utility was greatly enhanced. The world rainfall map (pp. 14–15) provides quantitative facts concerning annual precipitation, by means of isohyets (lines connecting points of equal rainfall). Here again, a single map conveys factual information far better than could be done by volumes of words and tables.

(2) The maps in *Goode's School Atlas* also serve to illustrate innumerable facts of significance that are associated with location and areal distribution. For example, the climatic-regions map (pp. 8–9) shows the areal distribution of types of climate which are determined from a synthesis of thousands of rainfall and temperature statistics.

(3) Finally, many useful comparisons may be made between different maps, between two maps in some instances, between three or more in others, with a view to establishing relationships between the various types of information entered on the maps. Useful comparisons may also be made, of course, between different places on the same map as well as between different aspects of the same place as shown on two or more maps. For example, compare the areas of dense population (pp. 20–27) with areas which have an intensive subsistence rice or non-rice agriculture (pp. 24–25). There are few agricultural areas in the world, with the exception of those in Europe, which have similar population densities. Note also on the agricultural-regions map the absence of nomadic herding in the western hemisphere, whereas extensive areas exist in Asia and Africa.

The atlas habit. An atlas, like a dictionary, should be a constant companion of every student. To read without knowledge of the precise meaning of important words may easily result in confusion. Similarly, knowledge of location, relative size, direction, distance, or of other facts which are set down in an atlas is necessary to an understanding of much about which one reads today. Much of the material in this atlas is of fundamental importance in a liberal education. No reasonable device should go unused to fix these fundamental facts and relations in the mind of the critical reader and student.

The changing world and the widespread commitments of the United States place new emphasis on map study. An atlas has become a prime necessity for understanding the course of world events.

Reading maps. An ability to read maps is acquired through practice, in the same manner as the ability to read a written text. The effectiveness of any written text depends both on the skill of the writer and on that of the reader. Similarly, the value of a particular map depends both on the effectiveness of the cartography and on the map-reading ability of the user.

Effectiveness of the cartography. Accuracy is the chief test of the effectiveness of any map, but legibility is of almost equal importance. If the most accurate of maps cannot be read, its accuracy is of no value. Legibility is a question partly of the degree of detail employed and partly of the method used in presenting the data. In this atlas every effort has been made to eliminate useless detail. Instead of overloading one map with data of various types, there are included several maps, each carrying one type of data. And to increase the degree of practicable detail, the size of certain maps has been increased. Thus, the maps have been kept simple and readable. The facts presented for study are shown distinctly.

Other aids to legibility have been selected carefully. Unnecessary names and other nonessential items have been eliminated on all maps, after careful study and testing. The size and style of type likewise have been selected for their clarity and readability as well as to distinguish the class and size of features. The weight and use of lines, the arrangement of legends, and the complementary materials utilized, all have been planned for effectiveness.

Use of color. Color in map making is extremely important. It has not only a functional purpose in providing legibility but also an esthetic value of large significance. As an aid to legibility, its primary value is in distinguishing one region from another—lowland from highland, land from water, uninhabited lands from those densely populated.

Note on the map of the World Agricultural Regions (pp. 24–25) the use of deeper shades of green and red for regions of plantation and rudimental sedentary agriculture, areas of more intense occupance, which are interspersed throughout the region of shifting cultivation shown in a light green. Color, both in shades and in pattern, is used also to show relationships between classes of data. Note on the map World Natural Vegetation (pp. 16–17) the use of shades and patterns of brown to show decreasing size and spacing of deciduous vegetation. In other cases, certain color conventions have been followed. Thus, blue stands for cold and red for heat on maps showing temperatures of water and air. The grid and base of each specialized map have been subdued by printing them in gray. This increases the clarity of the regional patterns of phenomena depicted. The absence of color over the oceans on various maps increases the intensity of the colors over the land areas, and the contrasts among the colors.

The esthetic appeal of color harmony and intensity varies greatly with individuals. Most people, however, are susceptible to the element of beauty. Every effort, within technical limitations, has been made to select colors of pleasing intensity, and colors which in combinations are harmonious, so that they will contribute to a favorable impression of the maps.

Understanding scales. Maps are of little value to any individual unless he has some understanding of map reading. Of particular importance in reading maps is a knowledge of map scales, projections, and symbolism. Scale is a question of "How big is it?" Since part or all of the earth's surface is depicted on a single page of this atlas, the question also arises "What is the relation of map size to earth size?" The scale is given in three forms on most maps of this atlas to facilitate answering these questions.

To aid further in understanding scales, a comparison of scale is given in a series of maps on page 1. A comparison of diagrams A, B, C, and D illustrates how progressively smaller-scale maps (of constant page size) increase the size of the area covered but reduce the detail which can be expressed. On the second map and on each later map, the area covered by the previous map is outlined within the map, to provide a direct comparison of the areas covered. On the first map, individual buildings are shown. On the final map, even many cities are omitted.

To aid the student in acquiring accurate concepts of the relative size of continents and of some countries and regions, uniform scales for comparable areas are used as far as possible. Continental maps are given on a uniform scale of 1:40,000,000 (one inch to 640 miles). In similar fashion, series of regions comparable in area appear in groups of maps on uniform scales of 1:16,000,000 (one inch to 250 miles), 1:12,000,000 (one inch to 190 miles), 1:4,000,000 (one inch to 64 miles), and on larger scales. The maximum size of the scale utilized for any given region is a partial measure of the importance of the region and of interest in it.

Understanding projections. There is no way of representing the curved surface of the globe on a flat surface without some distortion of the useful features desired on flat maps. On large-scale maps covering areas of only a few square miles, this distortion is negligible. In maps representing large areas, as in maps of a large country, a continent, or the whole world, the distortion inevitably is considerable, and, unless understood, it may result in serious misconceptions. The distortion may involve distances, directions, or the shapes and sizes of areas.

A map projection is an orderly system of parallels and meridians on which a map can be drawn. There are hundreds of map projections in use, but none avoids distortion of the spatial relationships that only a globe map can show truthfully. It is not possible to have truth of area, shape, angle, and scale all in the same flat map. It is possible, however, to select from the many types of projections one which is accurate for a particular property or which is a compromise (limiting the distortion of one or more elements at the expense of the others) that is relatively satisfactory for a particular need.

Truth of area is of prime importance in many maps. Most of the maps made for geographical study, particularly those used to show the areal distribution of an item, are drawn on equal-area projections. In an equal-area projection any square inch on the map represents the same number of square miles on the earth's surface as any other square inch on the map. Continents, oceans, islands, states, all are shown in their true relative size. Close to the importance of equality of area is truth of shape. This characteristic is to some extent an esthetic quality, but it is also a practical one. The student becomes familiar with the true shape of a continent or an island or a body of water as it appears on a globe map. Distortion of these shapes almost beyond recognition on a flat map is incongruous and a source of bewilderment to the student. Truth of direction is especially important in the study of the distribution of factors of significance in world relations. To show the latitudinal or zonal distribution of such factors, it is obviously desirable that lines of latitude be parallel, or better, straight lines parallel with the equator.

Most of the maps used in this atlas are drawn on projections that give equality of area, good land and ocean shapes, and parallel latitudinal directions. To provide these and other qualities desired for particular maps, some distortion of other elements is inevitable. The student should make himself aware of the nature of such distortions and make allowances for them in his use of the maps. One of the more practical procedures is to compare the projection grid of the flat map with the grid of the globe map. He should first verify the fundamental characteristics of the globe grid as listed here:

(1) On the globe map all longitude lines are equal in length and meet at the poles.

(2) All latitude lines are parallel.

(3) The length of the latitude lines, that is, the circumference of latitude circles, decreases from the equator to the points representing the poles. At latitude 60°, the circumference of the latitude circle is one-half the circumference of the equatorial circle.

(4) Distances along lines of longitude between any two latitude lines are equal.

(5) All latitude and longitude lines meet at right angles.

With item (1) in mind, the student will observe that the projection used on pages 44–45 has latitude lines of equal length. This results in considerable exaggeration of areas in the higher latitudes. With item (5) in mind, he will note that the projection used on pages 6–7 has oblique angles at the junction of latitude and longitude lines in the higher latitudes, and that this partly causes distortion of land shapes in such areas as Alaska and Greenland. In this projection, however, truth of area has been maintained.

Some illustration of the construction of the more commonly used projections and indication of their properties are helpful in making clear the nature of inherent distortions. Pages 2 and 3 are designed to provide this help. They also illustrate the seven projections used in this atlas.

Few of the several hundred projections in use can be constructed graphically by methods of descriptive geometry. Most of them are derived from mathematical formulas designed to afford the properties desired. In some cases it is easier to visualize the general form and characteristics of a projection if the earth's surface is considered to be projected upon a plane, a cone, or a cylinder. The last two surfaces, when they are cut and unrolled, form a plane surface. These surfaces provide one general classification of projections: azimuthal (on a plane), conic, or cylindrical (fig. 1, 2, and 5, pp. 2 and 3). In each class the characteristics of the projections may be changed by varying the systematic arrangement or spacing of the latitude and longitude lines.

Figure 1, A (p. 2) is a true plane projection with the point of projection at the center of the globe. This geometrical projection of the earth grid on a tangent plane is called a gnomonic projection. In the illustration the plane is tangent to the equator, but it could be placed tangent to the poles, or to any other point on the earth's surface. Several other distinctive map projections can be obtained by changing the origin point of the projection. For example, the projection obtained from an origin point on the surface of the globe diametrically opposite the point of contact of the tangent plane is called a stereographic projection, and the projection from an origin point at infinity is called an orthographic projection. None of these perspective projections obtained from projection on a plane is used in this atlas, but the mathematically derived Lambert azimuthal equal-area projection (fig. 1, B, p. 2) may be considered in this general class. The polar aspect of the Lambert azimuthal equal-area projection is used for the map of the Northern Lands and Seas (p. 48); the oblique aspect is used for the series of continental maps. Besides its equal-area quality, the projection gives relatively good shapes to continental areas as a whole.

Conic projections may be thought of as derived from a tangent cone (fig. 2) or from an intersecting cone (fig. 3). In the latter case, the resulting projection is said to have "two standard parallels" along which the scale is exact (since the cone and the sphere coincide throughout the length of the parallels). In maps of areas covering a wide range of longitude, the projection used in this atlas is a modified conic of the latter type (De Lisle's). In this projection, as here used, the shapes are excellent, and the departure from the equal-area quality is almost negligible. (See Canada, pp. 54–55, and Siberia, pp. 138–139.) The scale between the two standard parallels is too small along the parallels, and outside the standard parallels is too great along the parallels. The use of two standard parallels, however, provides a much better opportunity of extending the area within which the scale is reasonably accurate than the use of a single standard parallel, as in the simple conic.

Another modification of the conic principle is the Bonne projection (fig. 3, C, p. 2), used on pages 112–113 for the map of the Mediterranean lands. It has a selected standard parallel, and other parallels are arcs of concentric circles truly divided for points of intersection with the meridians. The scale along all the parallels is true everywhere, but the central meridian is the only one along which it is true. By construction, however, it is equal-area, and reasonably correct representation of shape is obtained in narrow zones along the standard parallel and central meridian, where the intersections are at right angles or nearly so.

The polyconic projection (fig. 4, p. 2) is used for the United States and some other areas of similar position and size. In the case of the polyconic projection, the earth may be considered as made up of a series of tangent cones. As each base is developed, the result is as shown, somewhat exaggerated, in figure 4, B, page 2. The area of the projection used for the map of the United States (fig. 4, C, page 2) is the central portion of figure 4, B, beneath the word "Pole." In this projection the central meridian crosses all parallels at right angles, as on the globe; other intersections become noticeably oblique only at considerable distance from the central meridian. The scale is true on the central meridian and on each parallel. Shapes, as a result, are very good. Meridian-scale errors, however, increase rapidly with increasing distance from the central meridian. The projection is thus not well adapted to areas of wide longitudinal extent. The departure, however, from equality of area is slight where it has been used for maps in this atlas.

The cylindrical class of projections may be visualized as perspective projections on a tangent or intersecting cylinder

(fig. 5, page 3). Many of the cylindrical projections in use, however, are mathematical modifications of the true perspective forms. As a general class, the cylindrical projections have the following characteristics: (1) latitude lines which are straight, parallel, and equal in length; (2) longitude lines which are straight, parallel, equal in length, and equally spaced; (3) meridians and parallels which intersect at right angles (fig. 5, page 3). Since the latitude lines are all drawn equal in length, it is evident that increasing distortion of scale occurs along the parallels with increasing distance from the standard parallel or parallels of tangency.

Mercator's projection (fig. 5, C, page 3), which belongs to this general class, is one of the better-known projections. For nearly four hundred years it has been used widely for world distributional maps, in spite of the facts (1) that it is impossible with this projection to show the entire surface of the earth, the poles being at infinity; and (2) that distances and areas grow rapidly larger with increase of latitude, until the distortion becomes enormous in higher latitudes. This is made apparent by a comparison of the relative size of areas in figures 5, C, and 6. The distortion of area is so great that the use of the Mercator projection for world maps showing areal distributions of most kinds is pedagogically unsound and misleading. The projection was designed by Mercator primarily for use of navigators, and for that use it is incomparable. On it, the navigator can draw a straight line (called a rhumb line) between any two points, read the angle between the rhumb line and any meridian that it crosses, set his compass to that angle, and go direct to his destination without change of compass. This advantage is so great that no other projection has yet taken the place of the Mercator in marine navigation.

A variation of the Mercator is the transverse or oblique Mercator. The grid is derived from a cylinder tangent along a selected great circle (fig. 7). The resulting projection is conformal, but its grid bears no resemblance to that of the ordinary Mercator and may be mistaken for that of a conic projection. Although the transverse Mercator projection is not used in this atlas, it illustrates a special-purpose projection which is being used more and more because of its value in air navigation for maps of great-circle strips.

Miller's projection (fig. 5, D) is a recent "compromise projection." It has been used in the atlas (with permission of the American Geographical Society) for climatic maps showing barometric pressures, winds, and temperatures, and for the map of ocean communications. A continuous grid without interruptions, and straight-line parallels were desirable for the best presentation of the features listed above. Miller's projection meets these requirements and provides a compromise between the distortion of areas and shapes. Mercator's projection was not suitable because of its excessive area distortion, although shapes of areas are excellent. Use of continuous grids for the whole world which were strictly equal-area would result in considerable distortion of shapes. The student will note, however, that

even on the Miller projection there is still considerable distortion of areas and shapes in the higher latitudes (*cf.* fig. 5, D, 5, C, and 6). Changes in scale according to latitude are indicated in the legend of the map and should be carefully noted. For example, compare on the graphic scale (page 45) a distance of one thousand miles at the equator with the same distance at latitude 60° or 80°.

Figure 6 illustrates three projections which are purely conventional in design. They cannot be readily related to the three general classes just discussed. They are not projections in the sense of being projected on a plane, a cone, or a cylinder; rather, they all are based on mathematical formulas. The sinusoidal projection (fig. 6, C, page 3) is used for the large-scale sectional maps of South America and Africa and for the map showing world surface transport facilities. It is an equal-area projection. On these continental maps it is most accurate along the equator where the two continents are widest. The placement of the central meridian through the center of the continents results in relatively little distortion of scale or shapes in the narrower southern parts of the continents. The scale is true along all parallels and the central meridian, but it increases on other meridians in conformity with their increasing obliquity. On the world map (pp. 42–43) the extent of the distortion is reduced by the technique of interrupting the projection and of using a separate central meridian for different land masses.

Mollweide's equal-area projection (fig. 6, A, page 3), designed to show the entire globe as an uninterrupted unit, gives an elliptical picture of the earth. The ellipse is drawn to inclose an area equal to that of a globe on the same scale. The central meridian is divided so that the areas of the bands between the parallels are truthfully proportional. Mollweide's projection is thus an equal-area projection, but there is little uniformity in linear scale. So that the areas of greater distortion in the outer parts of the projection will be eliminated, it, like the sinusoidal projection, may be interrupted and a new central meridian established through each continent (*cf.* the two forms, fig. 6, A and B, page 3).

Most of the world distribution maps in this atlas are drawn on Goode's homolosine equal-area projection (fig. 6, D, page 3). This projection is derived by combining the sinusoidal projection for latitudes up to 40° north and south with the homolographic projection (Mollweide) for areas poleward of these latitudes. In this manner an equal-area projection is obtained which has some of the better qualities of both the sinusoidal and homolographic. Further improvement of shapes is obtained by application of the principle of interruption, so that extremely oblique intersections are eliminated. The result has a number of distinct advantages: (1) It presents the entire surface of the earth, which Mercator's projection cannot do. (2) It is strictly an equal-area projection, with no distortion of the size of areas. (3) On it the parallels of latitude are represented by straight lines trending with the equator, a real advantage in the study of

comparative latitudes. (4) On it the grid is interrupted in the oceans so as to give each continent in turn the advantage of being in the center of the projection, thus providing better shapes for the continents than any uninterrupted world map can give. No map projection has been devised which displays to better advantage the distribution of most world phenomena which are studied best from the equatorial aspect.

Symbolism. The signs, symbols, and conventions shown on maps are a form of "shorthand" indicating a variety of phenomena. Many of them are self-explanatory. Legends on the maps provide keys to others.

Two systems of measurement are used in connection with the maps in this atlas. The English system of measures, which is conventional in this country, is utilized, although admittedly it is somewhat irrational and cumbersome. Since much of the world uses the metric system of measurement and the centigrade thermometer, most measures are given also in these scientific terms, or conversion scales are provided. A linear scale in miles is placed alongside a linear scale in kilometers, with the zero points together. Heights and depths may be read in feet or in meters from opposite scales. Comparative scales in the margins permit ready conversion of temperature and precipitation values from one system to another.

Surface configuration on the physical maps is shown by means of colors described as layer tints. Note the Landscape and Physical Map on page 1. The color scheme is essentially the same as that for the International Map of the World, 1:1,000,000. The great lowlands, of prime importance to man, are in a striking green. To accentuate these areas further, the ocean blue has been omitted over the continental shelves. Thus, the lowlands end on the waterside against the white paper. Similarly, on the land side the lowlands are distinguished sharply from the areas adjacent to the 1000-foot contour, which are in bright yellow.

Although the layer-tint system is an effective way of representing surface configuration on medium- and small-scale maps, the reader should be conscious of its disadvantages. It indicates general elevations above sea level, but it does not indicate the detail of relative relief or the steepness of slopes. Differences in elevation having a value less than the value of the layer-tint interval are lost in many cases. In the lowlands, where the relative relief may be only a few hundred feet, significant features may be missed. Similarly, in the highlands, differences of several thousand feet in relief may exist within an elevation category. On the other hand, some high plateaus are nearly level, for the most part. Cartographers have not yet found a solution to these limiting problems in delineation that is completely satisfactory.

Place names. Place names are used to distinguish particular places and features—cities, towns, bays, peninsulas—from other similar features. Many place names consist of two parts—a specific and a generic part. For example, Lake Michigan consists of the specific term "Michigan" modifying the generic term "lake."

If the world used one alphabet and one language, no particular difficulty would arise in the use of place names. Unfortunately, people use many languages and various alphabets. Moreover, some of the people of the world, the Chinese and the Japanese, for example, use non-alphabet languages. In order to make some languages intelligible to American readers, their letters and symbols must be converted into the Roman alphabet. It has been the practice of many people to transform place names further by transcribing or translating part or all of them into English. The recent war, which brought far corners of the earth to our attention, and the increasing facilities for communication in recent years make this practice no longer desirable. In this atlas, a "local-name policy" has been used for the cities and towns shown and, on the maps that were redrafted, for all features. A glossary of "geographical equivalents" is given on pages 6 and 7.

A distinct feature of *Goode's School Atlas* is the pronouncing index. The variable vowel sounds of English and the differences among other languages make the correct pronunciation of place names difficult. The correct pronunciation of many names differs from the pronunciation that may seem natural. Under these circumstances, the pronouncing index of more than thirty thousand names should be very helpful to the student.

Economic maps and statistics. The statistics presented in this atlas are not intended to take the place of statistical reference works. Instead of having been planned to present an absolute index to production and trade, they were planned to give a picture of the relative importance of countries and regions in the particulars involved. The maps have been reserved to present facts of distribution. Marginal graphs show the relative importance of different areas by percentage values of world totals.

No single year affords, for this purpose, a satisfactory base for production and trade statistics. For this reason, the percentages and world totals used have been computed, with few exceptions, from averages of a period of five years. The base period of years was selected to present, as nearly as possible, normal as well as average conditions. The serious disruption of economic conditions by World War II and the absence of satisfactory statistics for a sufficiently long period since the war have precluded the use of a postwar statistical base. Numerous checks have been made of the statistics used. At the present time they provide for the student a more nearly accurate picture of the relative importance of areas than could the statistics for any other base period. One important exception has been made in the case of statistics for petroleum, where shifts in production having far more than temporary interest have occurred.

EDWARD B. ESPENSHADE, JR.

NORTHWESTERN UNIVERSITY
SEPTEMBER, 1949

SUN AND PLANETS

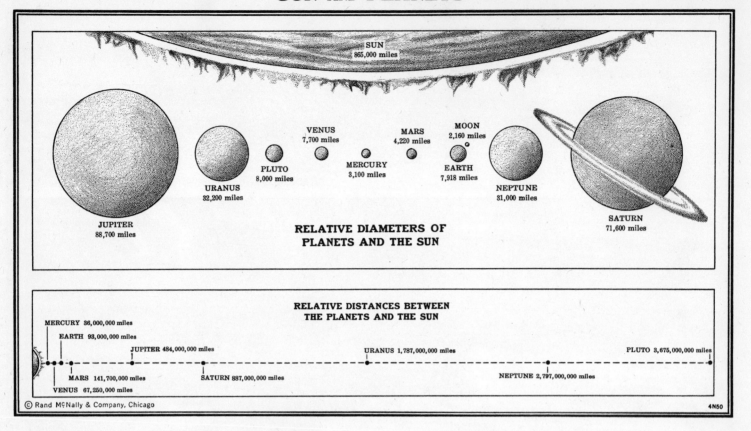

RELATIVE DIAMETERS OF PLANETS AND THE SUN

SUN
865,000 miles

JUPITER
88,700 miles

URANUS
32,200 miles

PLUTO
8,000 miles

VENUS
7,700 miles

MERCURY
3,100 miles

MARS
4,220 miles

MOON
2,160 miles

EARTH
7,918 miles

NEPTUNE
31,000 miles

SATURN
71,600 miles

RELATIVE DISTANCES BETWEEN THE PLANETS AND THE SUN

MERCURY 36,000,000 miles
EARTH 93,000,000 miles
JUPITER 484,000,000 miles
URANUS 1,787,000,000 miles
PLUTO 3,675,000,000 miles
MARS 141,700,000 miles
VENUS 67,250,000 miles
SATURN 887,000,000 miles
NEPTUNE 2,797,000,000 miles

4N50

EARTH, SUN, AND MOON.

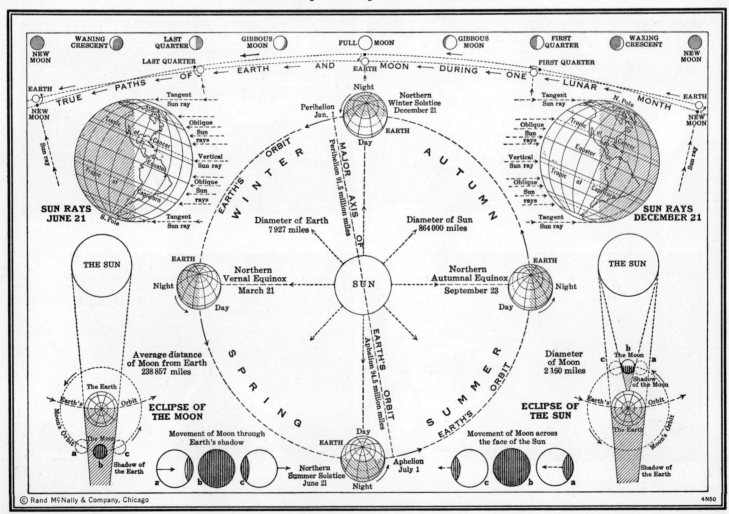

NEW MOON

WANING CRESCENT

LAST QUARTER

GIBBOUS MOON

FULL MOON

GIBBOUS MOON

FIRST QUARTER

WAXING CRESCENT

NEW MOON

TRUE PATHS OF EARTH AND MOON DURING ONE LUNAR MONTH

EARTH
NEW MOON
LAST QUARTER

FIRST QUARTER
EARTH
NEW MOON

Tangent Sun ray

Oblique Sun rays

Vertical Sun ray

Oblique Sun rays

Tangent Sun ray

Sun ray

Tropic of Cancer
Equator
Tropic of Capricorn
S. Pole

SUN RAYS JUNE 21

Tangent Sun ray

Oblique Sun rays

Vertical Sun ray

Oblique Sun rays

Tangent Sun ray

N. Pole

Tropic of Cancer
Equator
Tropic of Capricorn

Sun ray

SUN RAYS DECEMBER 21

WINTER

AUTUMN

SPRING

SUMMER

EARTH'S ORBIT

Perihelion Jan. 1

Northern Winter Solstice December 21

EARTH
Night
Day

MAJOR AXIS OF EARTH'S ORBIT
Perihelion 91.5 million miles

Diameter of Earth 7 927 miles

Diameter of Sun 864 000 miles

THE SUN

EARTH
Night
Day

Northern Vernal Equinox March 21

SUN

Northern Autumnal Equinox September 23

EARTH
Night
Day

THE SUN

Average distance of Moon from Earth 238 857 miles

EARTH'S ORBIT
Aphelion 94.5 million miles

Diameter of Moon 2 160 miles

The Moon
a
b
c
Shadow of the Moon

ECLIPSE OF THE MOON

The Earth
Earth's Orbit
Moon's Orbit
The Moon
a
b
c
Shadow of the Earth

ECLIPSE OF THE SUN

The Earth
Earth's Orbit
Moon's Orbit
Shadow of the Earth

Movement of Moon through Earth's shadow
a
b
c

Northern Summer Solstice June 21

EARTH
Day
Night

Aphelion July 1

Movement of Moon across the face of the Sun
c
b
a

4N50

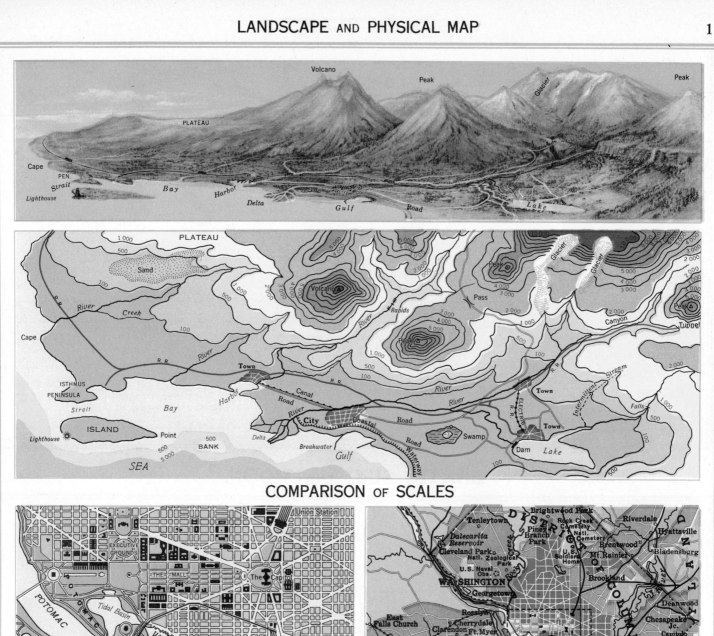

COMPARISON OF SCALES

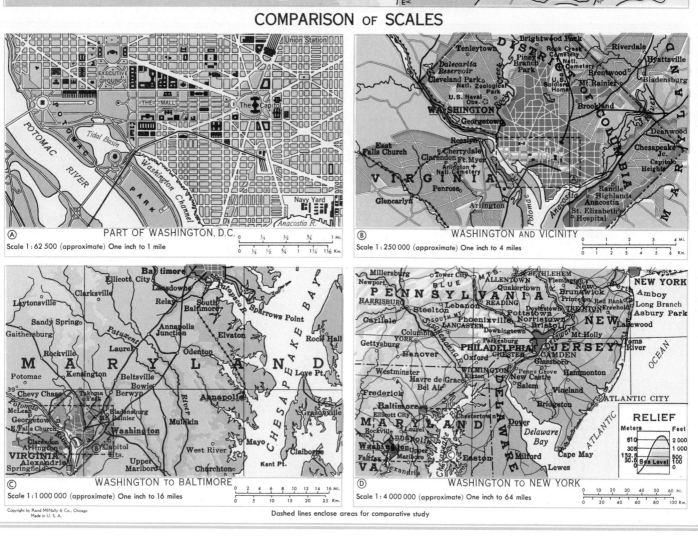

Ⓐ **PART OF WASHINGTON, D.C.**
Scale 1 : 62 500 (approximate) One inch to 1 mile

Ⓑ **WASHINGTON AND VICINITY**
Scale 1 : 250 000 (approximate) One inch to 4 miles

Ⓒ **WASHINGTON TO BALTIMORE**
Scale 1 : 1 000 000 (approximate) One inch to 16 miles

Ⓓ **WASHINGTON TO NEW YORK**
Scale 1 : 4 000 000 (approximate) One inch to 64 miles

Copyright by Rand McNally & Co., Chicago
Made in U.S.A.

Dashed lines enclose areas for comparative study

Elevations and depressions are given in feet

PROJECTIONS

A map projection is merely an orderly system of parallels and meridians on which a flat map can be drawn. There are hundreds of projections, but no one represents the earth's spherical surface without some distortion. The distortion is relatively small for most practical purposes when a small part of the sphere is projected. For larger areas, a sacrifice of some property is necessary.

Most projections are designed to preserve on the flat map some particular property of the sphere. By varying the systematic arrangement or spacing of the latitude and longitude lines, a projection may be made either equal-area or conformal. Although most projections are derived from mathematical formulas, some are easier to visualize if thought of as projected upon a plane, or upon a cone or cylinder which is then unrolled into a plane surface. Thus, many projections are classified as plane (azimuthal), conic, or cylindrical.

For a fuller discussion of map projections, see Preface. Figures with asterisks indicate projections used in this atlas.

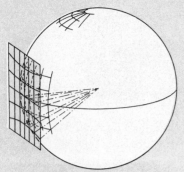

(A) GNOMONIC PROJECTION

A geometric or perspective projection on a tangent plane with the origin point at the center of the globe. Shapes and distances rapidly become increasingly distorted away from the center of the projection. Important in navigation, because all straight lines are great circles.

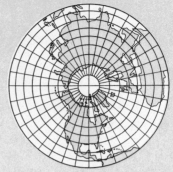

(B) LAMBERT EQUAL AREA PROJECTION*

A mathematically designed azimuthal equal-area projection. Excellent for continental areas. For larger areas away from the center, distortion of distances and shapes is appreciable.

FIGURE 1.–TYPICAL PLANE PROJECTIONS

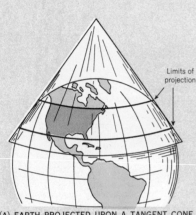

Limits of projection

(A) EARTH PROJECTED UPON A TANGENT CONE

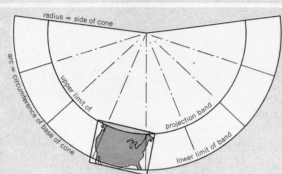

(B) CONE CUT FROM BASE TO APEX

A perspective projection on a tangent cone with the origin point at the center of the globe. At the parallel of tangency, all elements of the map are

radius = side of cone

arc = circumference of base of cone

upper limit of

projection band

lower limit of band

(C) CONE DEVELOPED INTO A PLANE SURFACE

true- angles, distances, shapes, areas. Away from the tangent parallel, distances increase rapidly, giving bad distortion of shapes and areas.

FIGURE 2.–SIMPLE CONIC PROJECTIONS

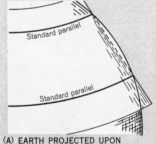

Standard parallel

Standard parallel

(A) EARTH PROJECTED UPON AN INTERSECTING CONE

This modification of the conic has two standard parallels, or lines of intersection. It is not an equal-area projection, the space being reduced in size between the standard parallels and

Standard parallel

Standard parallel

(B) CONIC PROJECTION WITH TWO STANDARD PARALLELS*

progressively enlarged beyond the standard parallels. Careful selection of the standard parallels provides, however, good representation for areas of limited latitudinal extent.

Standard parallel

(C) BONNE PROJECTION*

An equal-area modification of the conic principle. Distances are true along all parallels and the central meridian; but away from it, increasing obliqueness of intersections and longitudinal distances, with their attendant distortion of shapes, limits the satisfactory area.

FIGURE 3.–MODIFIED CONIC PROJECTIONS

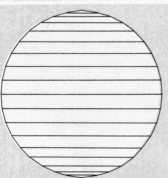

(A) EARTH CONSIDERED AS FORMED BY BASES OF CONES

Pole

(B) DEVELOPMENT OF THE CONICAL BASES

This variation is not equal-area. Parallels are nonconcentric circles truly divided. Distances along the straight central meridian are also true, but

(C) POLYCONIC PROJECTION*

along the curving meridians are increasingly exaggerated. Representation is good near the central meridian, but away from it there is marked distortion.

FIGURE 4.–POLYCONIC PROJECTION

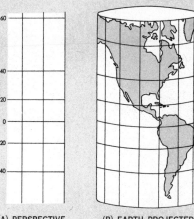

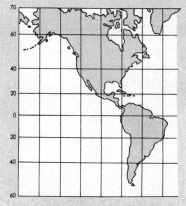

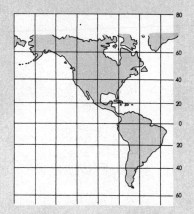

(A) PERSPECTIVE PROJECTION

A perspective projection on a tangent cylinder. Because of rapidly increasing distortion away from the line of tangency and the lack of any special advantage, it is rarely used.

(B) EARTH PROJECTED UPON A CYLINDER

(C) MERCATOR CONFORMAL PROJECTION

Mercator's modification increases the longitudinal distances in the same proportion as latitudinal distances are increased. Thus, at any point shapes are true, but areas become increasingly exaggerated. Of value in navigation, because a line connecting any two points gives the true direction between them.

(D) MILLER PROJECTION*

This recent modification is neither conformal nor equal-area. Whereas shapes are less accurate than on the Mercator, the exaggeration of areas has been reduced somewhat.

FIGURE 5.–CYLINDRICAL PROJECTIONS

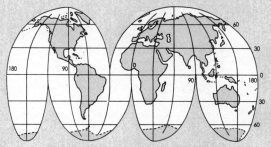

(A) MOLLWEIDE'S HOMOLOGRAPHIC PROJECTION

(B) GOODE'S INTERRUPTED HOMOLOGRAPHIC PROJECTION

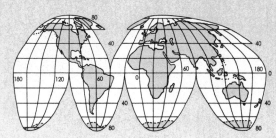

(C) SINUSOIDAL PROJECTION*

(D) GOODE'S INTERRUPTED HOMOLOSINE PROJECTION*

Although each of these projections is equal-area, differences in the spacing and arrangement of latitude and longitude lines result in differences in the distribution and relative degree of the shape and distance distortion within each grid. On the homolographic, there is no uniformity in scale. It is different on each parallel and each meridian. On the sinusoidal, only distances along all latitudes and the central meridian are true. The homolosine combines the homolographic, for areas poleward of 40°, with the sinusoidal. The principle of interruption permits each continent in turn the advantage of being in the center of the projection, resulting in better shapes.

FIGURE 6.–EQUAL AREA PROJECTIONS OF THE WORLD

A conformal projection in which a selected great circle of the globe is considered as the "equator" of the ordinary Mercator projection, with the cylinder tangent along the great circle. It is used chiefly for charts of great-circle air routes between distant cities.

FIGURE 7.–TRANSVERSE MERCATOR PROJECTION

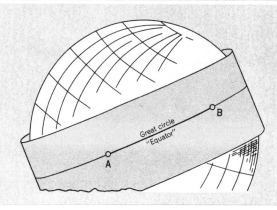

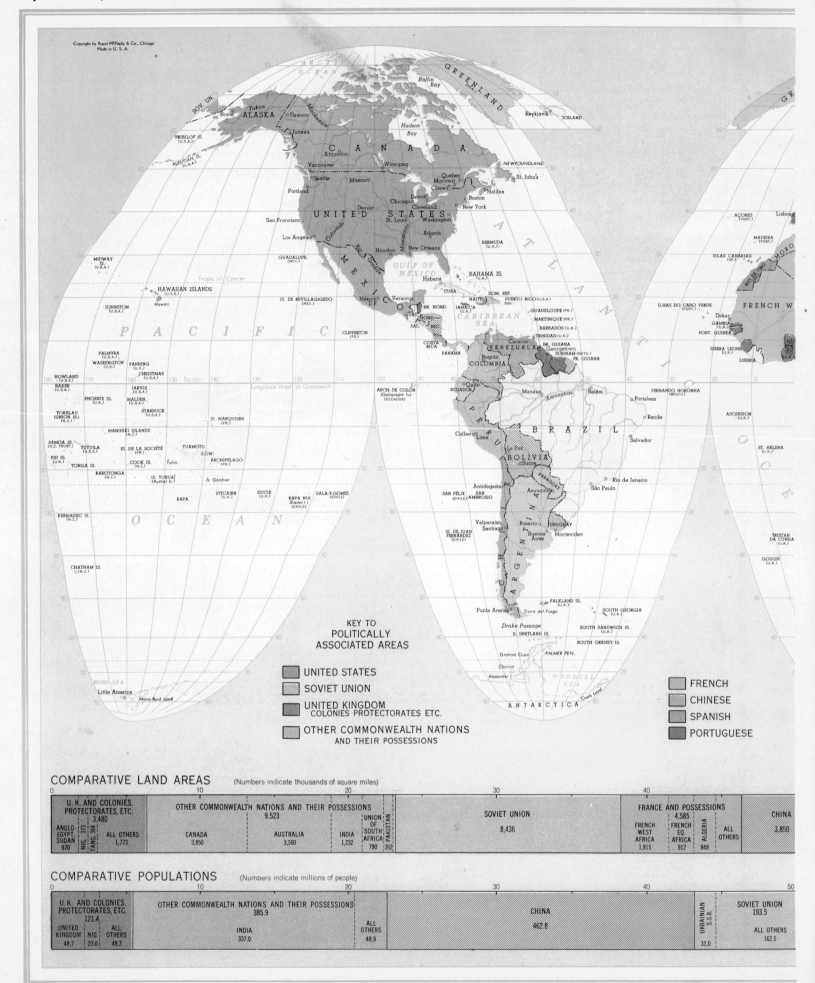

KEY TO POLITICALLY ASSOCIATED AREAS

- UNITED STATES
- SOVIET UNION
- UNITED KINGDOM COLONIES PROTECTORATES ETC.
- OTHER COMMONWEALTH NATIONS AND THEIR POSSESSIONS
- FRENCH
- CHINESE
- SPANISH
- PORTUGUESE

COMPARATIVE LAND AREAS   (Numbers indicate thousands of square miles)

U. K. AND COLONIES, PROTECTORATES, ETC. 3,480 — ANGLO-EGYPT. SUDAN 970 / NIG. 373 / TANG. 364 / ALL OTHERS 1,773	OTHER COMMONWEALTH NATIONS AND THEIR POSSESSIONS 9,523 — CANADA 3,850 / AUSTRALIA 3,160 / INDIA 1,232 / UNION OF SOUTH AFRICA 790 / PAKISTAN 362	SOVIET UNION 8,436	FRANCE AND POSSESSIONS 4,585 — FRENCH WEST AFRICA 1,815 / FRENCH EQ. AFRICA 912 / ALGERIA 848 / ALL OTHERS	CHINA 3,850

COMPARATIVE POPULATIONS   (Numbers indicate millions of people)

U. K. AND COLONIES, PROTECTORATES, ETC. 121.4 — UNITED KINGDOM 48.7 / NIG 23.0 / ALL OTHERS 49.7	OTHER COMMONWEALTH NATIONS AND THEIR POSSESSIONS 385.9 — INDIA 337.0 / ALL OTHERS 48.9	CHINA 462.8	UKRAINIAN S.S.R. 31.0	SOVIET UNION 193.5 — ALL OTHERS 162.5

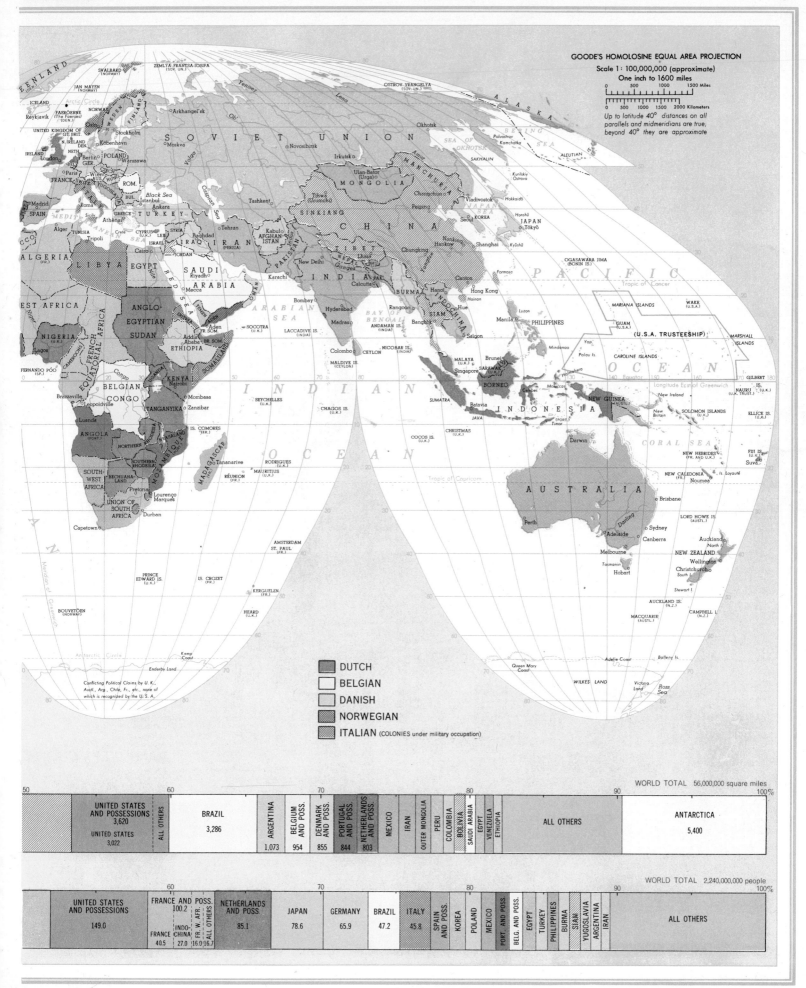

GOODE'S HOMOLOSINE EQUAL AREA PROJECTION

Scale 1 : 100,000,000 (approximate)

One inch to 1600 miles

Up to latitude 40° distances on all
parallels and midmeridians are true;
beyond 40° they are approximate

DUTCH

BELGIAN

DANISH

NORWEGIAN

ITALIAN (COLONIES under military occupation)

WORLD TOTAL   56,000,000 square miles

| | UNITED STATES AND POSSESSIONS 3,620 / UNITED STATES 3,022 | ALL OTHERS | BRAZIL 3,286 | ARGENTINA 1,073 | BELGIUM AND POSS. 954 | DENMARK AND POSS. 855 | PORTUGAL AND POSS. 844 | NETHERLANDS AND POSS. 803 | MEXICO | IRAN | OUTER MONGOLIA | PERU | COLOMBIA | BOLIVIA | SAUDI ARABIA | EGYPT | VENEZUELA | ETHIOPIA | ALL OTHERS | ANTARCTICA 5,400 |

WORLD TOTAL   2,240,000,000 people

| UNITED STATES AND POSSESSIONS 149.0 | FRANCE AND POSS. 100.2 / FRANCE 40.5 / INDO-CHINA 27.0 / FR. W. AFR. 16.0 / ALL OTHERS 16.7 | NETHERLANDS AND POSS. 85.1 | JAPAN 78.6 | GERMANY 65.9 | BRAZIL 47.2 | ITALY 45.8 | SPAIN AND POSS. | KOREA | POLAND | MEXICO | PORT. AND POSS. | BELG. AND POSS. | EGYPT | TURKEY | PHILIPPINES | BURMA | SIAM | YUGOSLAVIA | ARGENTINA | IRAN | ALL OTHERS |

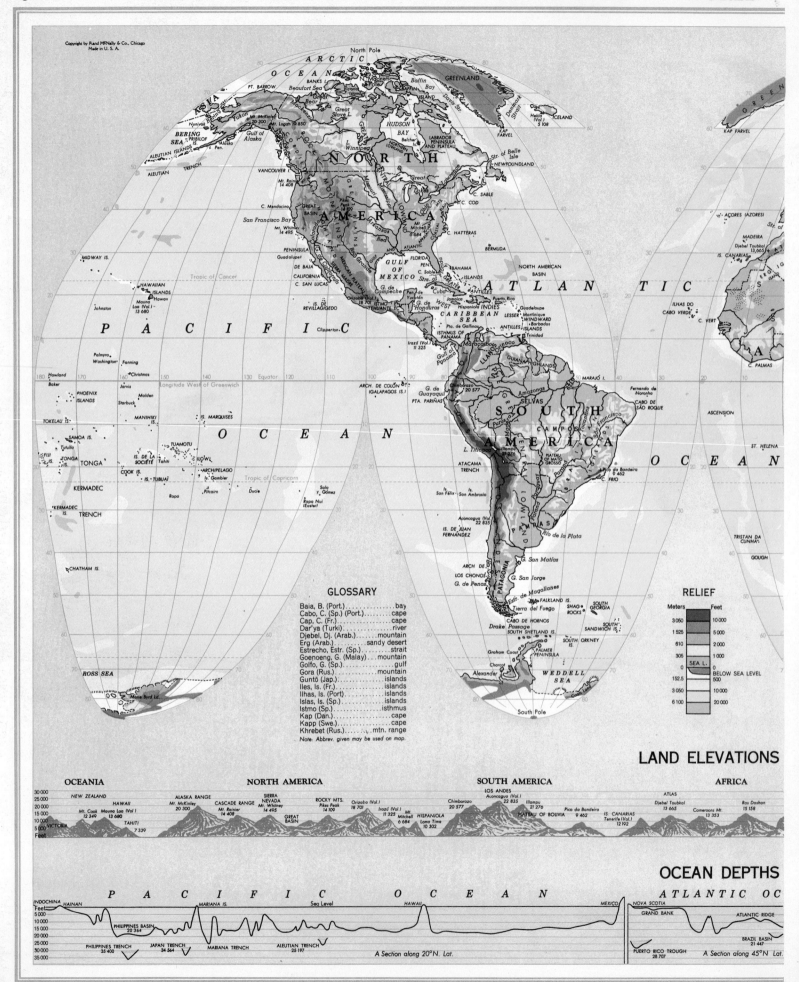

GLOSSARY

Baia, B. (Port.)	bay
Cabo, C. (Sp.) (Port.)	cape
Cap, C. (Fr.)	cape
Dar'ya (Turki)	river
Djebel, Dj. (Arab.)	mountain
Erg (Arab.)	sandy desert
Estrecho, Estr. (Sp.)	strait
Goenoeng, G. (Malay)	mountain
Golfo, G. (Sp.)	gulf
Gora (Rus.)	mountain
Guntō (Jap.)	islands
Iles, Is. (Fr.)	islands
Ilhas, Is. (Port)	islands
Islas, Is. (Sp.)	islands
Istmo (Sp.)	isthmus
Kap (Dan.)	cape
Kapp (Swe.)	cape
Khrebet (Rus.)	mtn. range

Note: Abbrev. given may be used on map.

RELIEF

Meters	Feet
3 050	10 000
1 525	5 000
610	2 000
305	1 000
0	SEA L.
	BELOW SEA LEVEL
152.5	500
3 050	10 000
6 100	20 000

LAND ELEVATIONS

OCEANIA	NORTH AMERICA
SOUTH AMERICA	AFRICA

OCEAN DEPTHS

A Section along 20°N. Lat.   *A Section along 45°N. Lat.*

Elevations and depressions

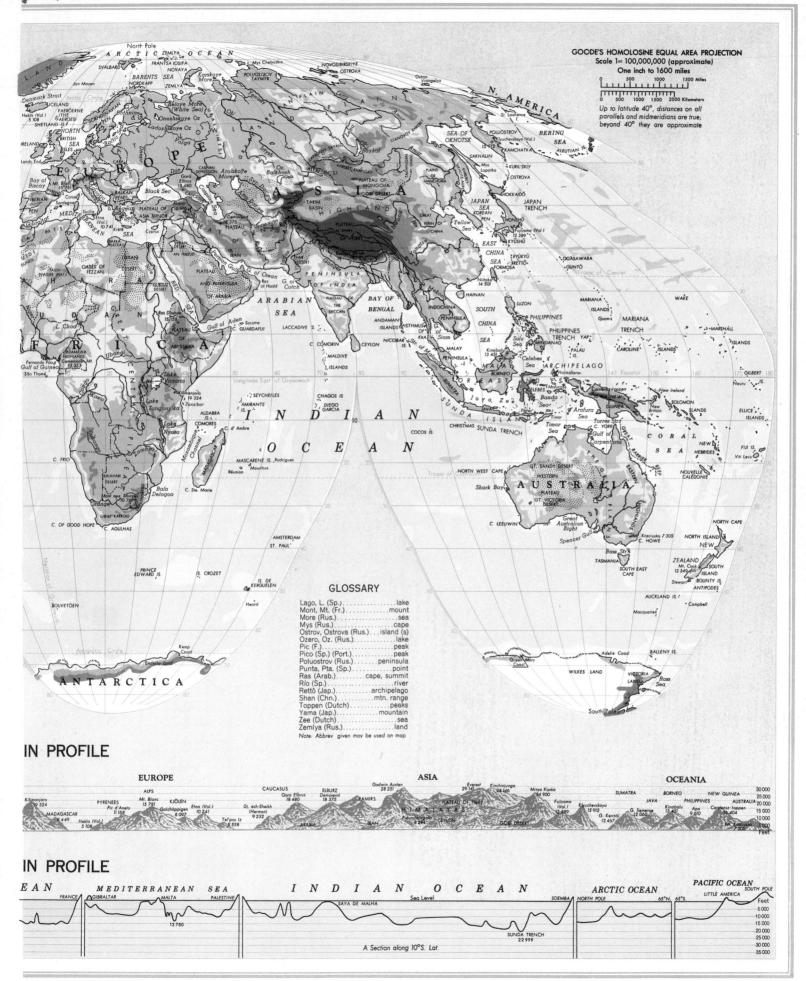

GOODE'S HOMOLOSINE EQUAL AREA PROJECTION
Scale 1= 100,000,000 (approximate)
One inch to 1600 miles

Up to latitude 40°, distances on all
parallels and midmeridians are true;
beyond 40° they are approximate

GLOSSARY

Lago, L. (Sp.)	lake
Mont, Mt. (Fr.)	mount
More (Rus.)	sea
Mys (Rus.)	cape
Ostrov, Ostrova (Rus.)	island (s)
Ozero, Oz. (Rus.)	lake
Pic (F.)	peak
Pico (Sp.) (Port.)	peak
Poluostrov (Rus.)	peninsula
Punta, Pta. (Sp.)	point
Ras (Arab.)	cape, summit
Río (Sp.)	river
Rettō (Jap.)	archipelago
Shan (Chn.)	mtn. range
Toppen (Dutch)	peaks
Yama (Jap.)	mountain
Zee (Dutch)	sea
Zemlya (Rus.)	land

Note: Abbrev. given may be used on map

IN PROFILE

EUROPE   ASIA   OCEANIA

IN PROFILE

MEDITERRANEAN SEA   INDIAN OCEAN   ARCTIC OCEAN   PACIFIC OCEAN

A Section along 10°S. Lat.

are given in feet

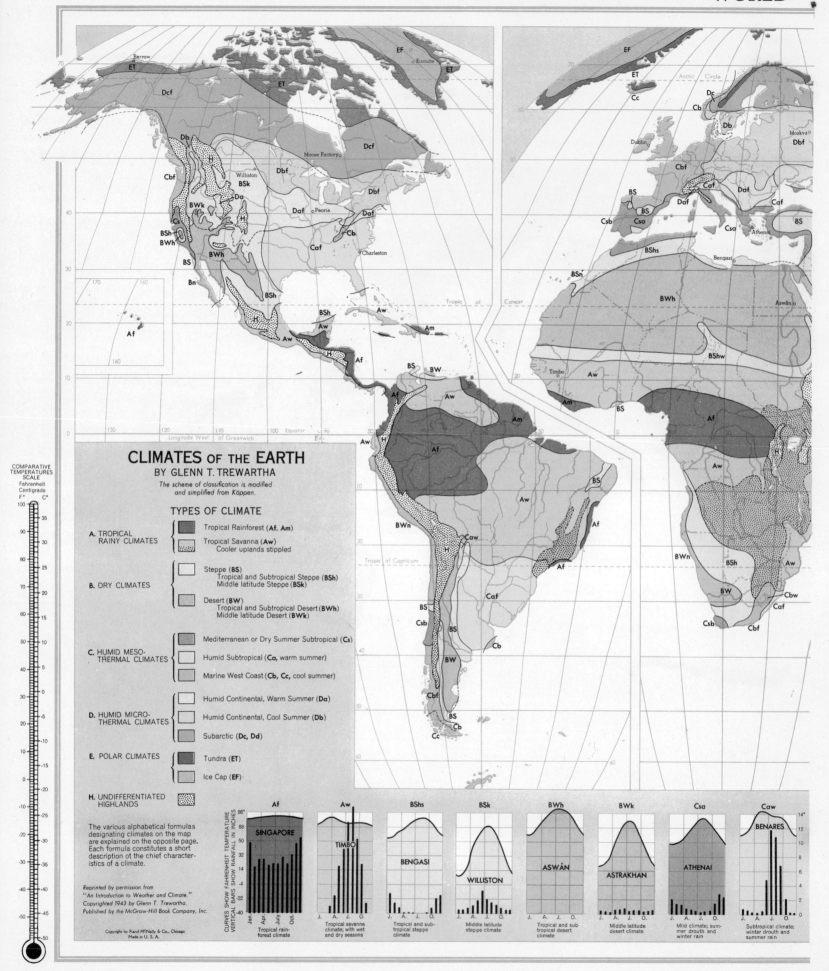

COMPARATIVE
TEMPERATURES
SCALE
Fahrenheit
Centigrade
F°   C°

CLIMATES OF THE EARTH
BY GLENN T. TREWARTHA

*The scheme of classification is modified
and simplified from Köppen.*

TYPES OF CLIMATE

**A. TROPICAL
RAINY CLIMATES**
- Tropical Rainforest (**Af, Am**)
- Tropical Savanna (**Aw**)
  Cooler uplands stippled

B. DRY CLIMATES
- Steppe (**BS**)
  Tropical and Subtropical Steppe (**BSh**)
  Middle latitude Steppe (**BSk**)
- Desert (**BW**)
  Tropical and Subtropical Desert (**BWh**)
  Middle latitude Desert (**BWk**)

**C. HUMID MESO-
THERMAL CLIMATES**
- Mediterranean or Dry Summer Subtropical (**Cs**)
- Humid Subtropical (**Ca**, warm summer)
- Marine West Coast (**Cb, Cc**, cool summer)

**D. HUMID MICRO-
THERMAL CLIMATES**
- Humid Continental, Warm Summer (**Da**)
- Humid Continental, Cool Summer (**Db**)
- Subarctic (**Dc, Dd**)

E. POLAR CLIMATES
- Tundra (**ET**)
- Ice Cap (**EF**)

**H. UNDIFFERENTIATED
HIGHLANDS**

The various alphabetical formulas
designating climates on the map
are explained on the opposite page.
Each formula constitutes a short
description of the chief characteristics of a climate.

*Reprinted by permission from
"An Introduction to Weather and Climate."
Copyrighted 1943 by Glenn T. Trewartha.
Published by the McGraw-Hill Book Company, Inc.*

Copyright by Rand M⁽N⁾ally & Co., Chicago
Made in U. S. A.

CURVES SHOW FAHRENHEIT TEMPERATURE
VERTICAL BARS SHOW RAINFALL IN INCHES

Af
SINGAPORE
Tropical rain-
forest climate

Aw
TIMBO
Tropical savanna
climate; with wet
and dry seasons

BShs
BENGASI
Tropical and sub-
tropical steppe
climate

BSk
WILLISTON
Middle latitude
steppe climate

BWh
ASWÂN
Tropical and sub-
tropical desert
climate

BWk
ASTRAKHAN
Middle latitude
desert climate

Csa
ATHENAI
Mild climate; sum-
mer drouth and
winter rain

Caw
BENARES
Subtropical climate;
winter drouth and
summer rain

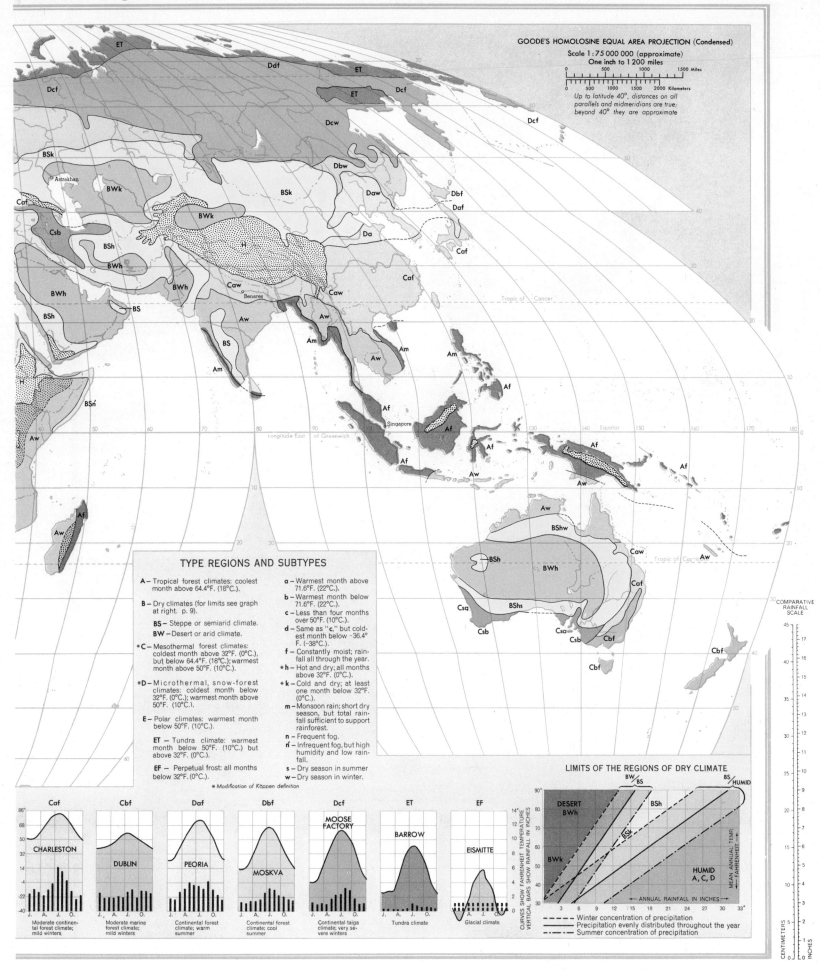

TYPE REGIONS AND SUBTYPES

A – Tropical forest climates: coolest month above 64.4°F. (18°C.).

B – Dry climates (for limits see graph at right. p. 9).

  BS – Steppe or semiarid climate.

  BW – Desert or arid climate.

***C** – Mesothermal forest climates: coldest month above 32°F. (0°C.), but below 64.4°F. (18°C.); warmest month above 50°F. (10°C.).

***D** – Microthermal, snow-forest climates: coldest month below 32°F. (0°C.); warmest month above 50°F. (10°C.).

E – Polar climates: warmest month below 50°F. (10°C.).

  ET – Tundra climate: warmest month below 50°F. (10°C.) but above 32°F. (0°C.).

  EF – Perpetual frost: all months below 32°F. (0°C.).

a – Warmest month above 71.6°F. (22°C.).

b – Warmest month below 71.6°F. (22°C.).

c – Less than four months over 50°F. (10°C.).

d – Same as "c," but coldest month below −36.4° F. (−38°C.).

f – Constantly moist; rainfall all through the year.

***h** – Hot and dry; all months above 32°F. (0°C.).

***k** – Cold and dry; at least one month below 32°F. (0°C.).

m – Monsoon rain; short dry season, but total rainfall sufficient to support rainforest.

n – Frequent fog.

n̄ – Infrequent fog, but high humidity and low rainfall.

s – Dry season in summer.

w – Dry season in winter.

* Modification of Köppen definition

LIMITS OF THE REGIONS OF DRY CLIMATE

- - - - Winter concentration of precipitation
——— Precipitation evenly distributed throughout the year
—·—·— Summer concentration of precipitation

Climate graphs (bottom)

Caf	Cbf	Daf	Dbf	Dcf	ET	EF
CHARLESTON	DUBLIN	PEORIA	MOSKVA	MOOSE FACTORY	BARROW	EISMITTE
Moderate continental forest climate; mild winters	Moderate marine forest climate; mild winters	Continental forest climate; warm summer	Continental forest climate; cool summer	Continental taiga climate; very severe winters	Tundra climate	Glacial climate

CURVES SHOW FAHRENHEIT TEMPERATURE
VERTICAL BARS SHOW RAINFALL IN INCHES

COMPARATIVE RAINFALL SCALE

GOODE'S HOMOLOSINE EQUAL AREA PROJECTION (Condensed)
Scale 1:75 000 000 (approximate)
One inch to 1 200 miles

Up to latitude 40°, distances on all parallels and midmeridians are true; beyond 40° they are approximate

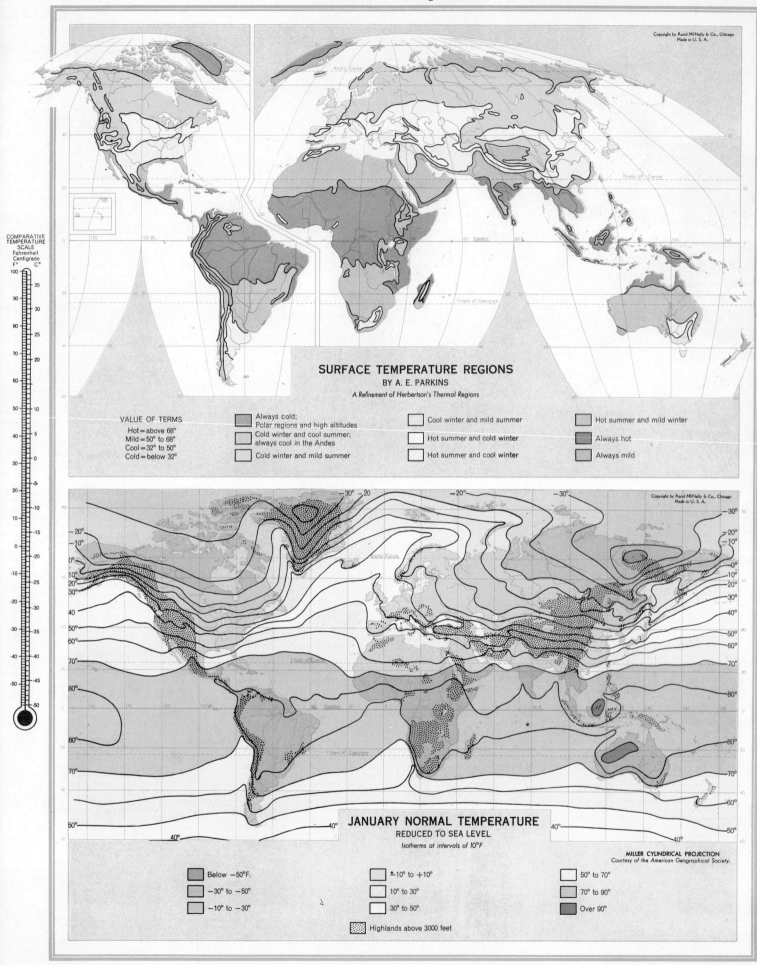

SURFACE TEMPERATURE REGIONS
BY A. E. PARKINS
A Refinement of Herbertson's Thermal Regions

VALUE OF TERMS

Hot = above 68°
Mild = 50° to 68°
Cool = 32° to 50°
Cold = below 32°

Always cold;
Polar regions and high altitudes

Cold winter and cool summer;
always cool in the Andes

Cold winter and mild summer

Cool winter and mild summer

Hot summer and cold winter

Hot summer and cool winter

Hot summer and mild winter

Always hot

Always mild

COMPARATIVE TEMPERATURE SCALE
Fahrenheit   Centigrade
F°   C°

JANUARY NORMAL TEMPERATURE
REDUCED TO SEA LEVEL
Isotherms at intervals of 10°F

MILLER CYLINDRICAL PROJECTION
Courtesy of the American Geographical Society.

Below −50°F.

−30° to −50°

−10° to −30°

−10° to +10°

10° to 30°

30° to 50°

50° to 70°

70° to 90°

Over 90°

Highlands above 3000 feet

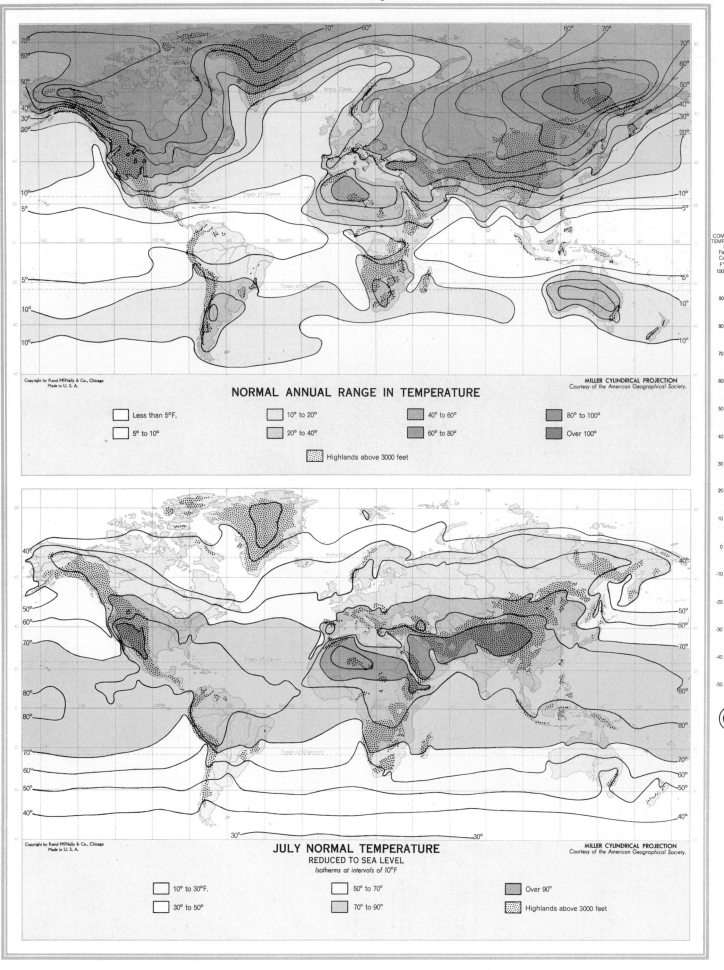

NORMAL ANNUAL RANGE IN TEMPERATURE

Copyright by Rand McNally & Co., Chicago
Made in U. S. A.

MILLER CYLINDRICAL PROJECTION
Courtesy of the American Geographical Society.

Less than 5°F.	10° to 20°	40° to 60°	80° to 100°
5° to 10°	20° to 40°	60° to 80°	Over 100°

Highlands above 3000 feet

JULY NORMAL TEMPERATURE
REDUCED TO SEA LEVEL
Isotherms at intervals of 10°F.

Copyright by Rand McNally & Co., Chicago
Made in U. S. A.

MILLER CYLINDRICAL PROJECTION
Courtesy of the American Geographical Society.

10° to 30°F.	50° to 70°	Over 90°
30° to 50°	70° to 90°	Highlands above 3000 feet

COMPARATIVE
TEMPERATURES
SCALE
Fahrenheit
Centigrade
F°   C°

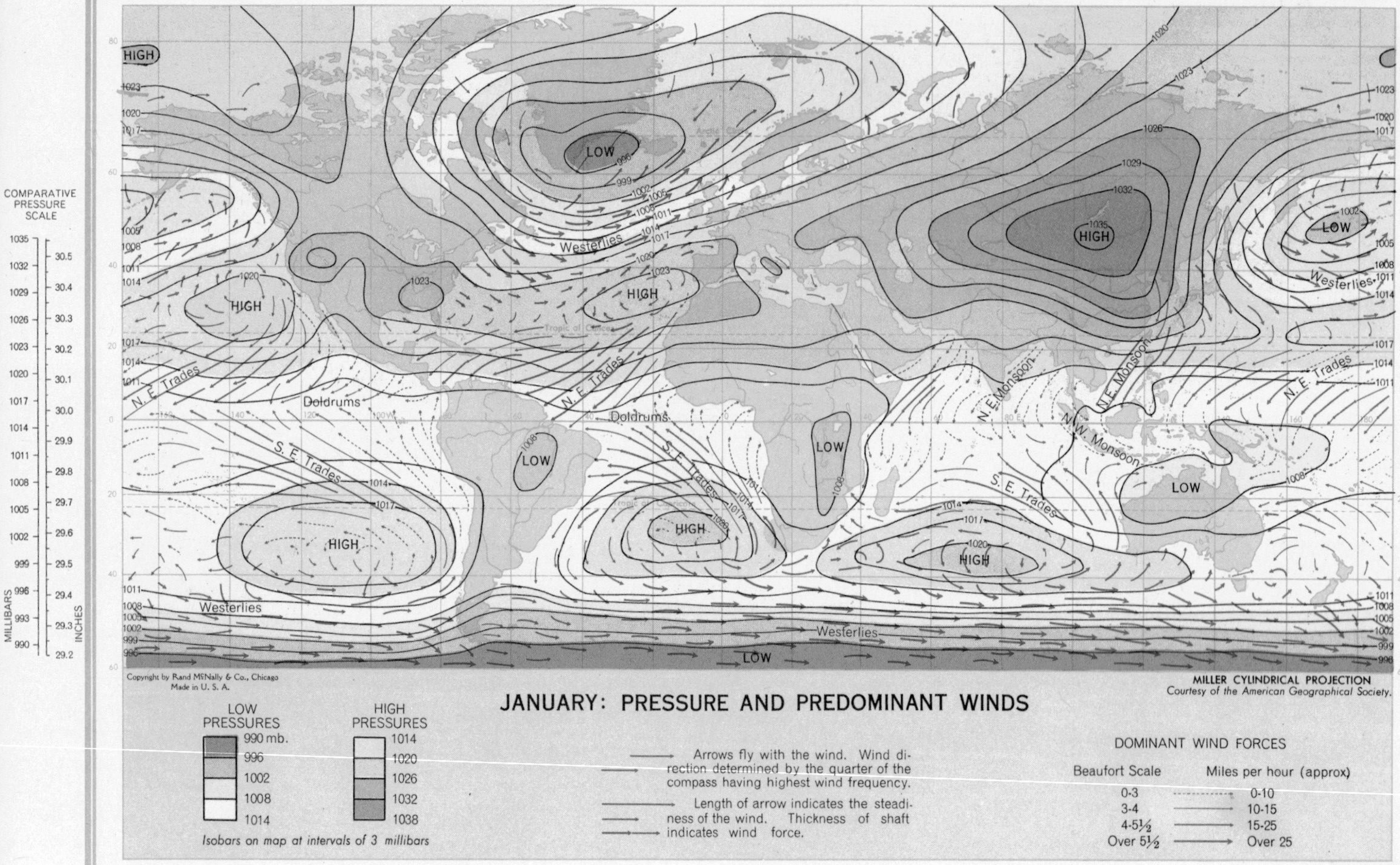

COMPARATIVE
PRESSURE
SCALE

MILLIBARS	INCHES
1035	30.5
1032	30.4
1029	30.3
1026	30.2
1023	30.1
1020	30.0
1017	29.9
1014	29.8
1011	29.7
1008	29.6
1005	29.5
1002	29.4
999	
996	29.3
993	
990	29.2

MILLER CYLINDRICAL PROJECTION
Courtesy of the American Geographical Society.

JANUARY: PRESSURE AND PREDOMINANT WINDS

LOW
PRESSURES

	990 mb.
	996
	1002
	1008
	1014

HIGH
PRESSURES

	1014
	1020
	1026
	1032
	1038

Isobars on map at intervals of 3 millibars

Arrows fly with the wind. Wind direction determined by the quarter of the compass having highest wind frequency.

Length of arrow indicates the steadiness of the wind. Thickness of shaft indicates wind force.

DOMINANT WIND FORCES

Beaufort Scale	Miles per hour (approx)
0-3	0-10
3-4	10-15
4-5½	15-25
Over 5½	Over 25

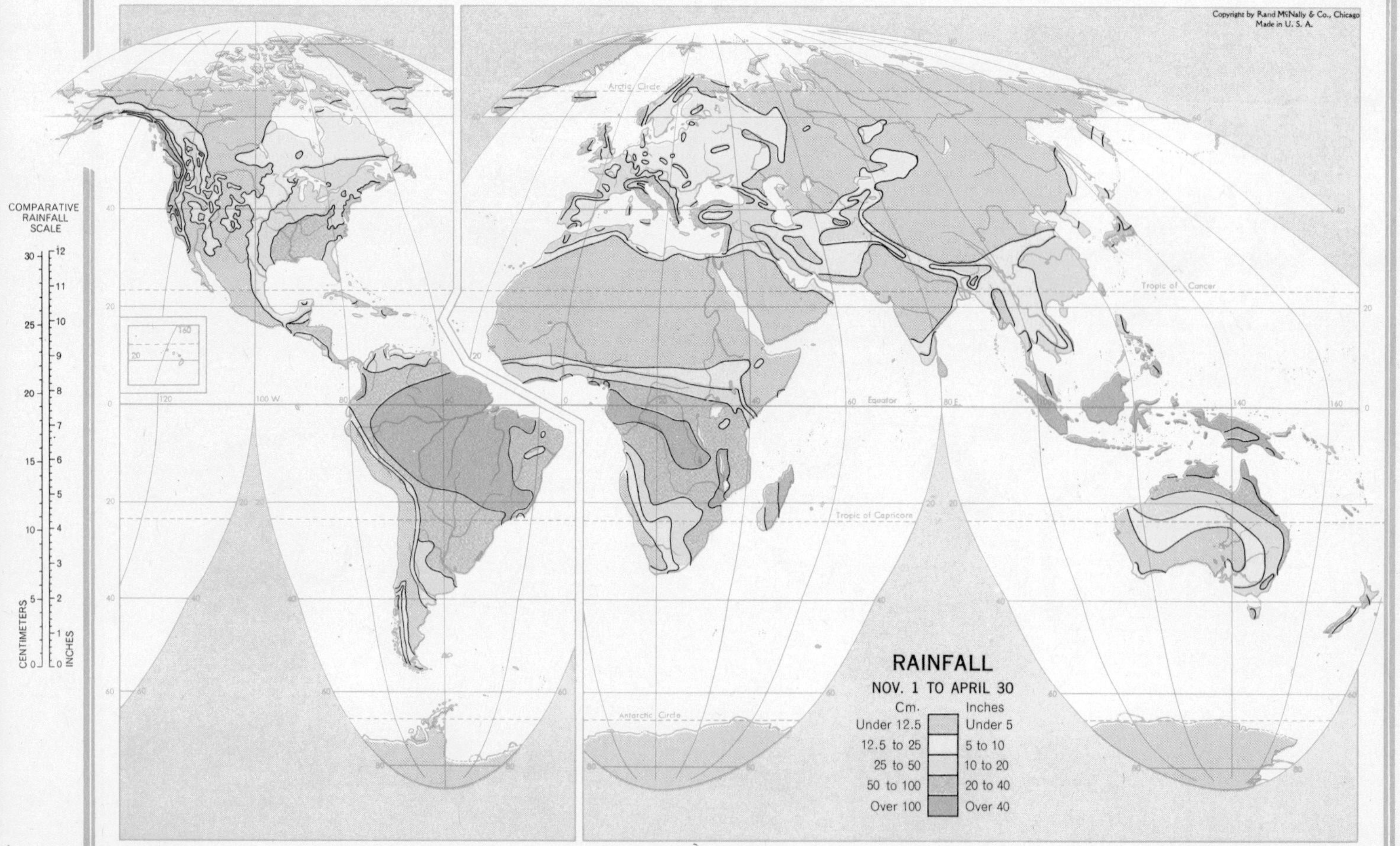

COMPARATIVE
RAINFALL
SCALE

CENTIMETERS | INCHES

30	12
	11
	10
25	9
	8
20	7
	6
15	5
	4
10	3
5	2
	1
0	0

RAINFALL

NOV. 1 TO APRIL 30

Cm.	Inches
Under 12.5	Under 5
12.5 to 25	5 to 10
25 to 50	10 to 20
50 to 100	20 to 40
Over 100	Over 40

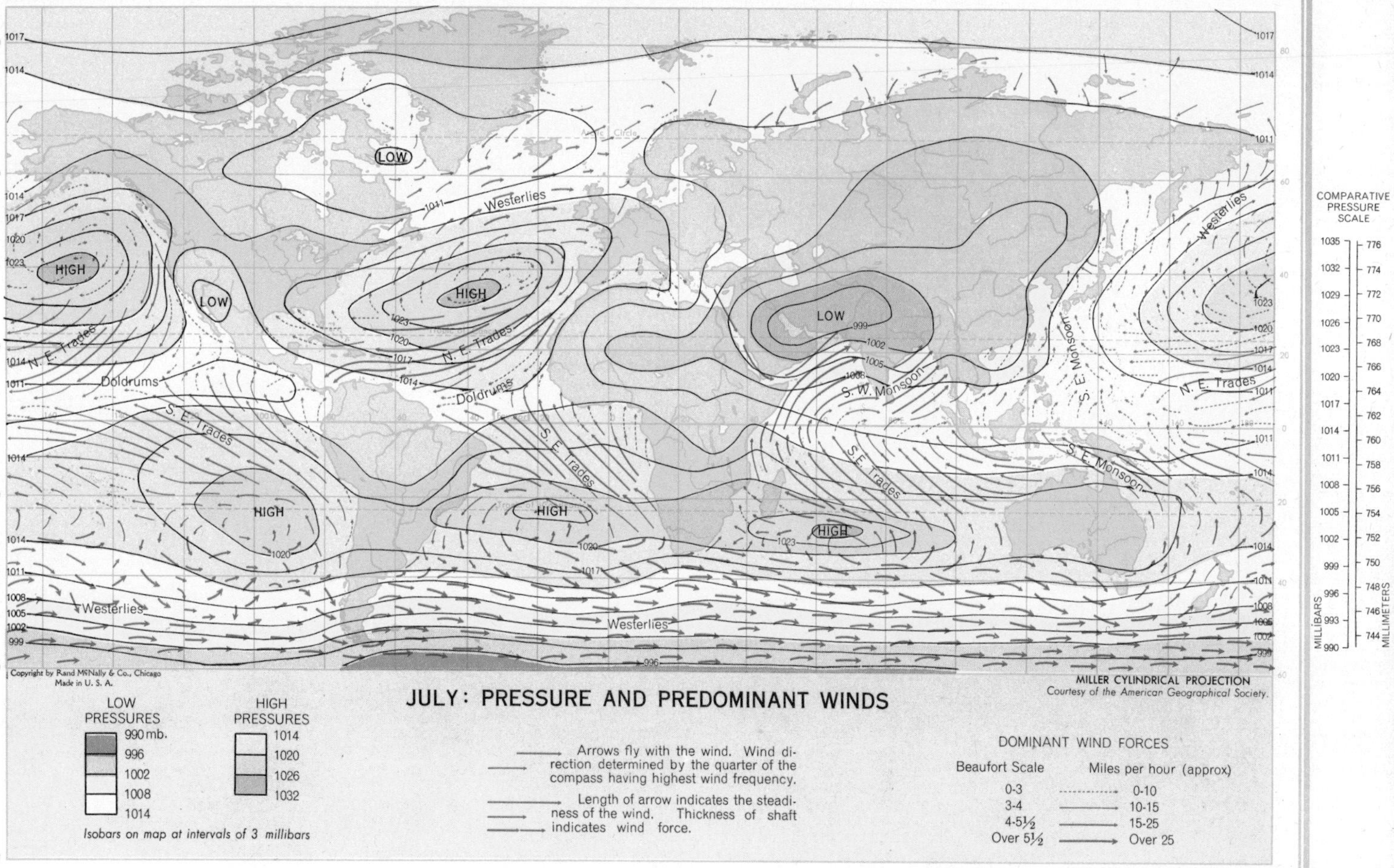

JULY: PRESSURE AND PREDOMINANT WINDS

MILLER CYLINDRICAL PROJECTION
Courtesy of the American Geographical Society.

LOW
PRESSURES

	mb.
	990
	996
	1002
	1008
	1014

HIGH
PRESSURES

	1014
	1020
	1026
	1032

Isobars on map at intervals of 3 millibars

Arrows fly with the wind. Wind direction determined by the quarter of the compass having highest wind frequency.

Length of arrow indicates the steadiness of the wind. Thickness of shaft indicates wind force.

DOMINANT WIND FORCES

Beaufort Scale	Miles per hour (approx)
0-3	0-10
3-4	10-15
4-5½	15-25
Over 5½	Over 25

COMPARATIVE
PRESSURE
SCALE

MILLIBARS	MILLIMETERS
1035	776
1032	774
1029	772
1026	770
1023	768
1020	766
1017	764
1014	762
1011	760
1008	758
1005	756
1002	754
999	752
996	750
993	748
990	746
	744

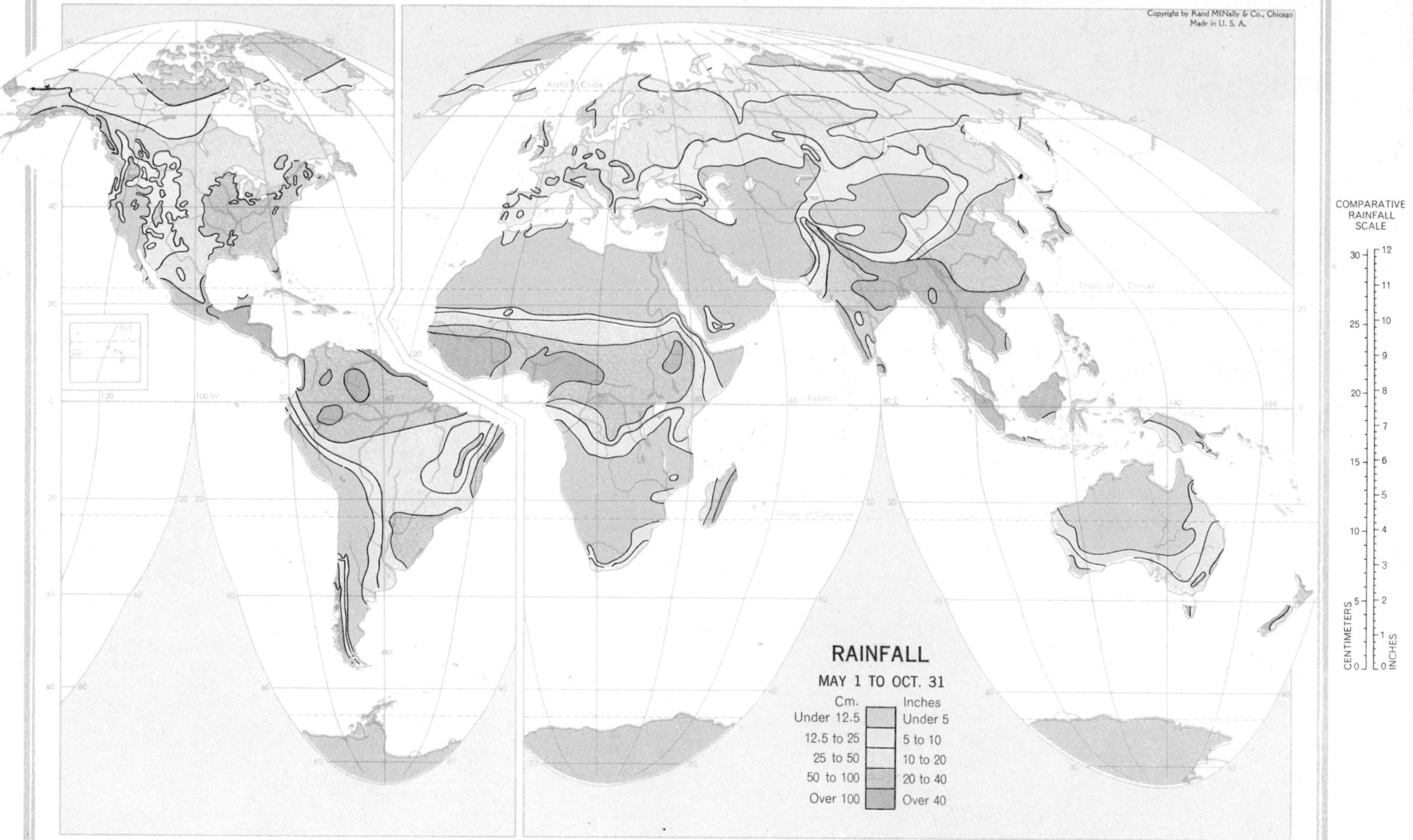

RAINFALL

MAY 1 TO OCT. 31

Cm.	Inches
Under 12.5	Under 5
12.5 to 25	5 to 10
25 to 50	10 to 20
50 to 100	20 to 40
Over 100	Over 40

COMPARATIVE
RAINFALL
SCALE

CENTIMETERS	INCHES
30	12
	11
	10
25	9
	8
20	7
	6
15	5
	4
10	3
	2
5	1
	0

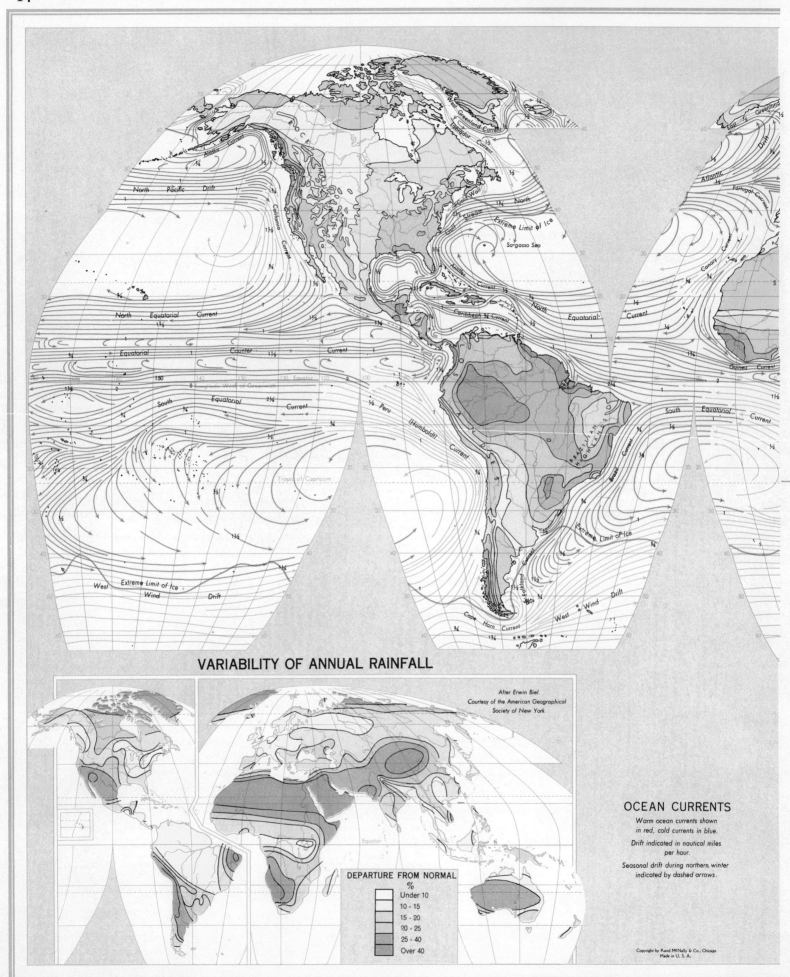

VARIABILITY OF ANNUAL RAINFALL

After Erwin Biel.
Courtesy of the American Geographical
Society of New York

OCEAN CURRENTS

Warm ocean currents shown
in red, cold currents in blue.

Drift indicated in nautical miles
per hour.

Seasonal drift during northern winter
indicated by dashed arrows.

DEPARTURE FROM NORMAL
%
- Under 10
- 10 - 15
- 15 - 20
- 20 - 25
- 25 - 40
- Over 40

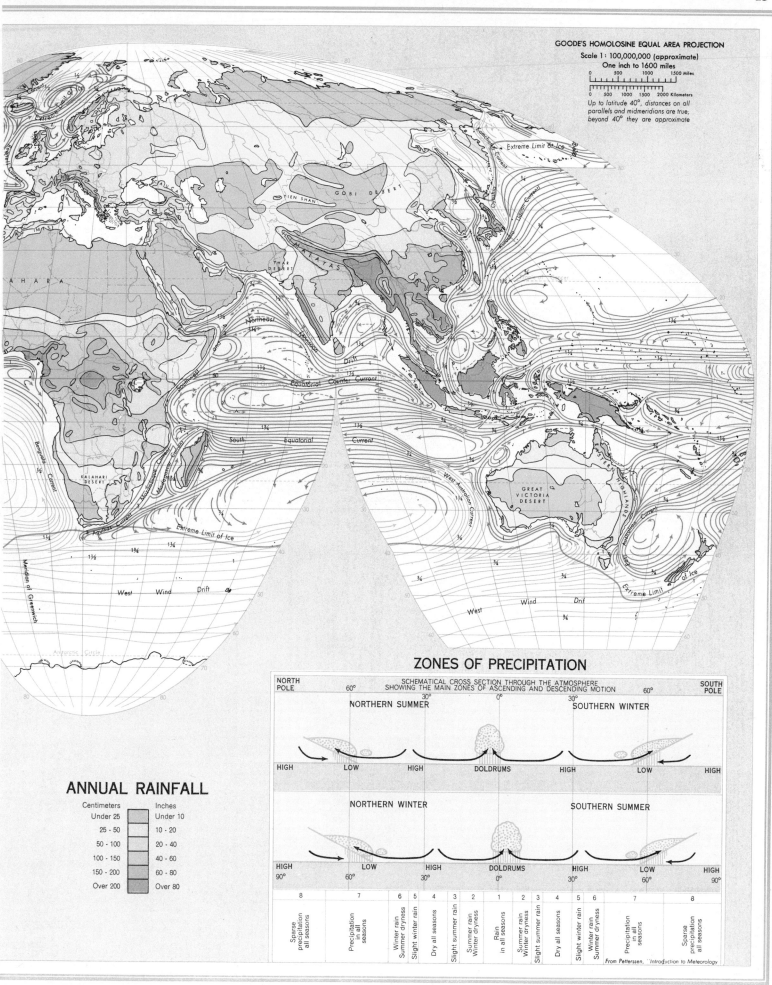

GOODE'S HOMOLOSINE EQUAL AREA PROJECTION
Scale 1 : 100,000,000 (approximate)
One inch to 1600 miles

Up to latitude 40°, distances on all
parallels and midmeridians are true;
beyond 40° they are approximate

ZONES OF PRECIPITATION

NORTH POLE	60°	SCHEMATICAL CROSS SECTION THROUGH THE ATMOSPHERE SHOWING THE MAIN ZONES OF ASCENDING AND DESCENDING MOTION		60°	SOUTH POLE
		30° 0° 30°			
		NORTHERN SUMMER	SOUTHERN WINTER		
HIGH	LOW	HIGH DOLDRUMS HIGH		LOW	HIGH
		NORTHERN WINTER	SOUTHERN SUMMER		
HIGH	LOW	HIGH DOLDRUMS HIGH		LOW	HIGH
90°	60°	30° 0° 30°		60°	90°

ANNUAL RAINFALL

Centimeters	Inches
Under 25	Under 10
25 - 50	10 - 20
50 - 100	20 - 40
100 - 150	40 - 60
150 - 200	60 - 80
Over 200	Over 80

8	7	6	5	4	3	2	1	2	3	4	5	6	7	8
Sparse precipitation all seasons	Precipitation in all seasons	Winter rain Summer dryness	Slight winter rain	Dry all seasons	Slight summer rain	Summer rain Winter dryness	Rain in all seasons	Summer rain Winter dryness	Slight summer rain	Dry all seasons	Slight winter rain	Winter rain Summer dryness	Precipitation in all seasons	Sparse precipitation all seasons

From Petterssen, "Introduction to Meteorology"

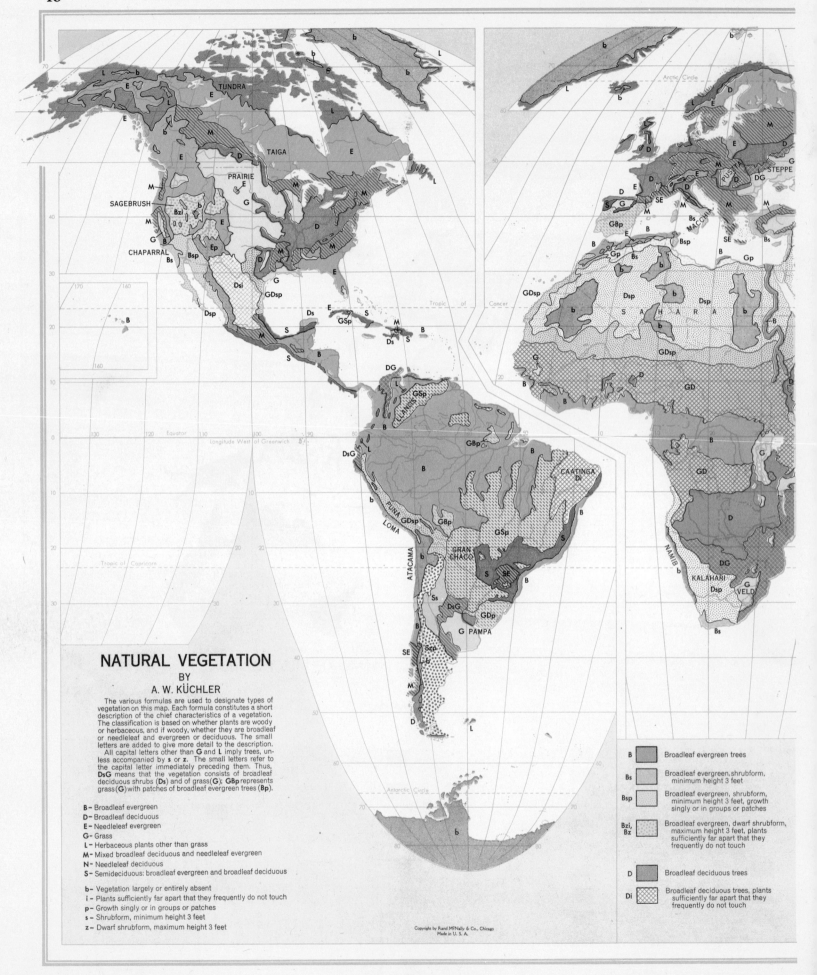

NATURAL VEGETATION

BY
A. W. KÜCHLER

The various formulas are used to designate types of vegetation on this map. Each formula constitutes a short description of the chief characteristics of a vegetation. The classification is based on whether plants are woody or herbaceous, and if woody, whether they are broadleaf or needleleaf and evergreen or deciduous. The small letters are added to give more detail to the description.

All capital letters other than **G** and **L** imply trees, unless accompanied by **s** or **z**. The small letters refer to the capital letter immediately preceding them. Thus, **DsG** means that the vegetation consists of broadleaf deciduous shrubs (**Ds**) and of grass (**G**); **GBp** represents grass (**G**) with patches of broadleaf evergreen trees (**Bp**).

B– Broadleaf evergreen
D– Broadleaf deciduous
E– Needleleaf evergreen
G– Grass
L– Herbaceous plants other than grass
M– Mixed broadleaf deciduous and needleleaf evergreen
N– Needleleaf deciduous
S– Semideciduous: broadleaf evergreen and broadleaf deciduous

b– Vegetation largely or entirely absent
i– Plants sufficiently far apart that they frequently do not touch
p– Growth singly or in groups or patches
s– Shrubform, minimum height 3 feet
z– Dwarf shrubform, maximum height 3 feet

B	Broadleaf evergreen trees
Bs	Broadleaf evergreen, shrubform, minimum height 3 feet
Bsp	Broadleaf evergreen, shrubform, minimum height 3 feet, growth singly or in groups or patches
Bzi, Bz	Broadleaf evergreen, dwarf shrubform, maximum height 3 feet, plants sufficiently far apart that they frequently do not touch
D	Broadleaf deciduous trees
Di	Broadleaf deciduous trees, plants sufficiently far apart that they frequently do not touch

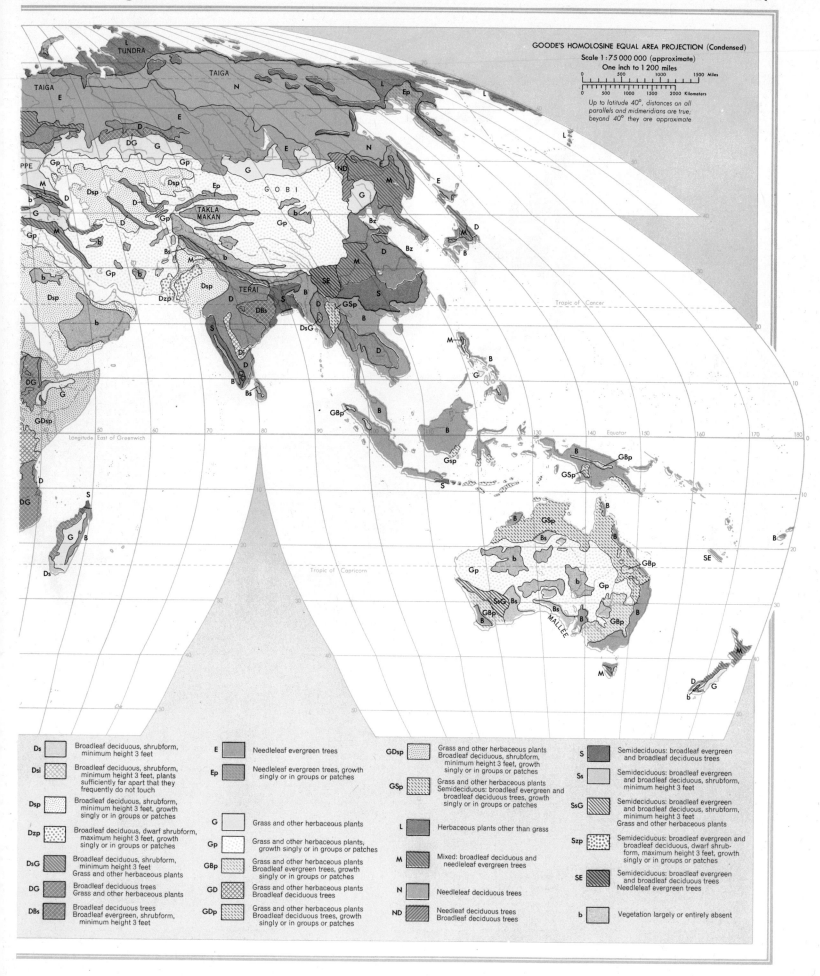

GOODE'S HOMOLOSINE EQUAL AREA PROJECTION (Condensed)
Scale 1:75 000 000 (approximate)
One inch to 1 200 miles

Up to latitude 40°, distances on all
parallels and midmeridians are true;
beyond 40° they are approximate

Ds		Broadleaf deciduous, shrubform, minimum height 3 feet
Dsi		Broadleaf deciduous, shrubform, minimum height 3 feet, plants sufficiently far apart that they frequently do not touch
Dsp		Broadleaf deciduous, shrubform, minimum height 3 feet, growth singly or in groups or patches
Dzp		Broadleaf deciduous, dwarf shrubform, maximum height 3 feet, growth singly or in groups or patches
DsG		Broadleaf deciduous, shrubform, minimum height 3 feet Grass and other herbaceous plants
DG		Broadleaf deciduous trees Grass and other herbaceous plants
DBs		Broadleaf deciduous trees Broadleaf evergreen, shrubform, minimum height 3 feet

E		Needleleaf evergreen trees
Ep		Needleleaf evergreen trees, growth singly or in groups or patches
G		Grass and other herbaceous plants
Gp		Grass and other herbaceous plants, growth singly or in groups or patches
GBp		Grass and other herbaceous plants Broadleaf evergreen trees, growth singly or in groups or patches
GD		Grass and other herbaceous plants Broadleaf deciduous trees
GDp		Grass and other herbaceous plants Broadleaf deciduous trees, growth singly or in groups or patches

GDsp		Grass and other herbaceous plants Broadleaf deciduous, shrubform, minimum height 3 feet, growth singly or in groups or patches
GSp		Grass and other herbaceous plants Semideciduous: broadleaf evergreen and broadleaf deciduous trees, growth singly or in groups or patches
G		Grass and other herbaceous plants
L		Herbaceous plants other than grass
M		Mixed: broadleaf deciduous and needleleaf evergreen trees
N		Needleleaf deciduous trees
ND		Needleaf deciduous trees Broadleaf deciduous trees

S		Semideciduous: broadleaf evergreen and broadleaf deciduous trees
Ss		Semideciduous: broadleaf evergreen and broadleaf deciduous, shrubform, minimum height 3 feet
SsG		Semideciduous: broadleaf evergreen and broadleaf deciduous, shrubform, minimum height 3 feet Grass and other herbaceous plants
Szp		Semideciduous: broadleaf evergreen and broadleaf deciduous, dwarf shrubform, maximum height 3 feet, growth singly or in groups or patches
SE		Semideciduous: broadleaf evergreen and broadleaf deciduous trees Needleleaf evergreen trees
b		Vegetation largely or entirely absent

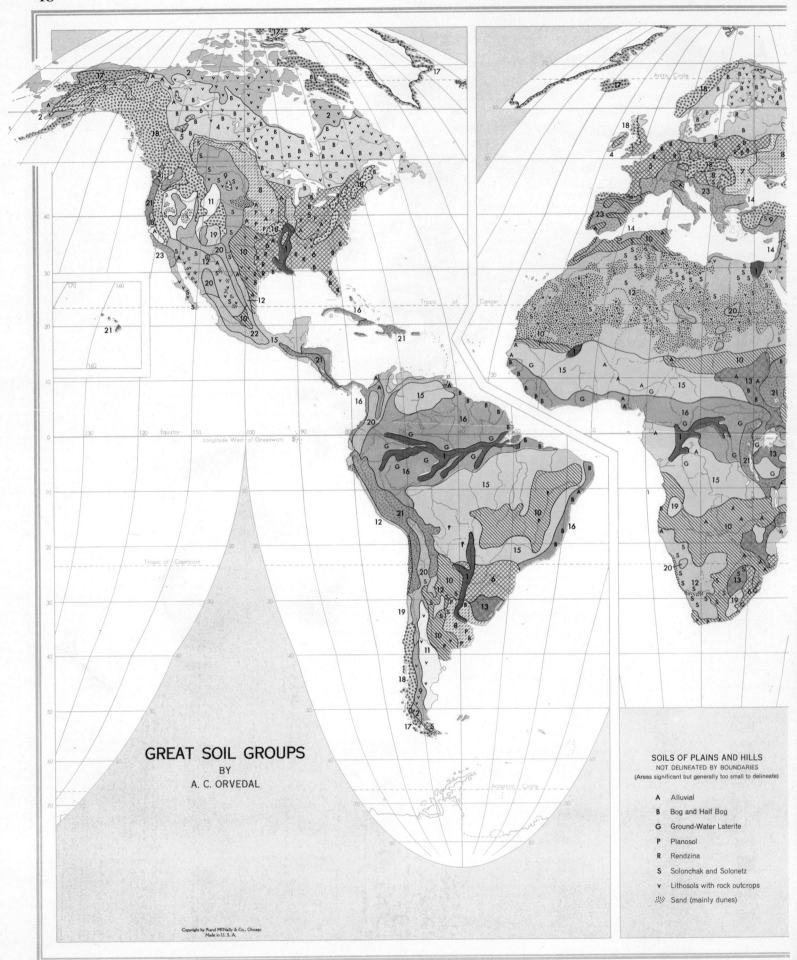

GREAT SOIL GROUPS

BY

A. C. ORVEDAL

SOILS OF PLAINS AND HILLS

NOT DELINEATED BY BOUNDARIES

(Areas significant but generally too small to delineate)

A Alluvial

B Bog and Half Bog

G Ground-Water Laterite

P Planosol

R Rendzina

S Solonchak and Solonetz

v Lithosols with rock outcrops

Sand (mainly dunes)

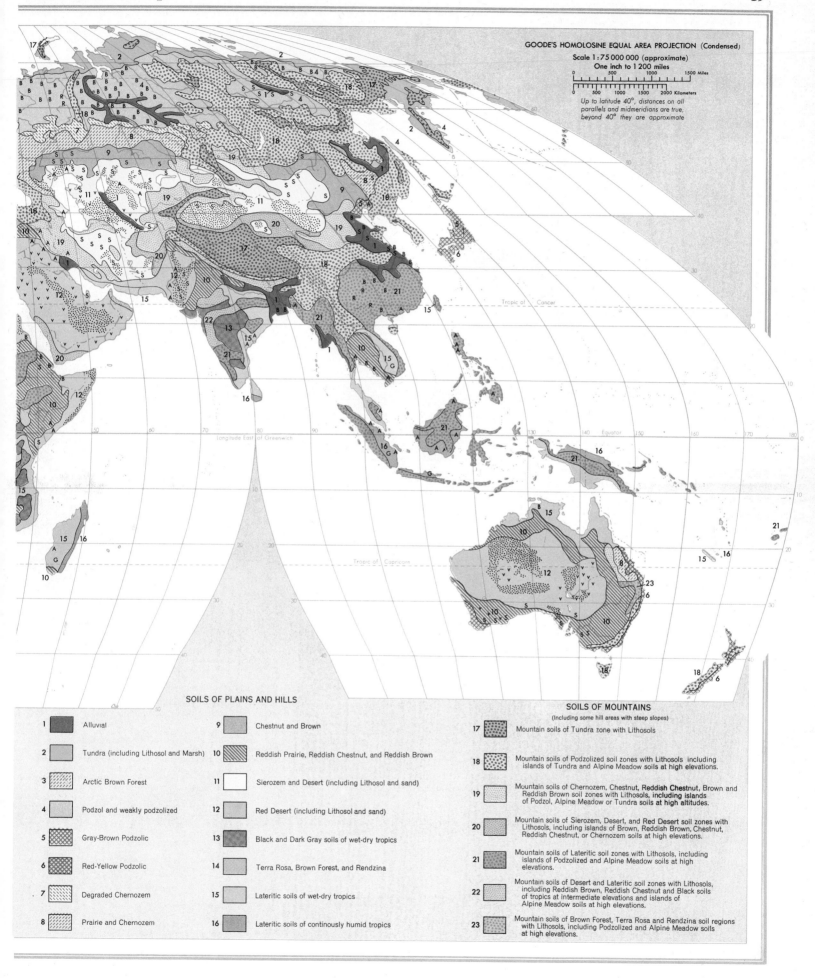

GOODE'S HOMOLOSINE EQUAL AREA PROJECTION (Condensed)
Scale 1:75 000 000 (approximate)
One inch to 1 200 miles

0   500   1000   1500 Miles

0   500   1000   1500   2000 Kilometers

Up to latitude 40°, distances on all
parallels and midmeridians are true;
beyond 40° they are approximate

SOILS OF PLAINS AND HILLS

1 Alluvial

2 Tundra (including Lithosol and Marsh)

3 Arctic Brown Forest

4 Podzol and weakly podzolized

5 Gray-Brown Podzolic

6 Red-Yellow Podzolic

7 Degraded Chernozem

8 Prairie and Chernozem

9 Chestnut and Brown

10 Reddish Prairie, Reddish Chestnut, and Reddish Brown

11 Sierozem and Desert (including Lithosol and sand)

12 Red Desert (including Lithosol and sand)

13 Black and Dark Gray soils of wet-dry tropics

14 Terra Rosa, Brown Forest, and Rendzina

15 Lateritic soils of wet-dry tropics

16 Lateritic soils of continuously humid tropics

SOILS OF MOUNTAINS
(Including some hill areas with steep slopes)

17 Mountain soils of Tundra zone with Lithosols

18 Mountain soils of Podzolized soil zones with Lithosols including islands of Tundra and Alpine Meadow soils at high elevations.

19 Mountain soils of Chernozem, Chestnut, Reddish Chestnut, Brown and Reddish Brown soil zones with Lithosols, including islands of Podzol, Alpine Meadow or Tundra soils at high altitudes.

20 Mountain soils of Sierozem, Desert, and Red Desert soil zones with Lithosols, including islands of Brown, Reddish Brown, Chestnut, Reddish Chestnut, or Chernozem soils at high elevations.

21 Mountain soils of Lateritic soil zones with Lithosols, including islands of Podzolized and Alpine Meadow soils at high elevations.

22 Mountain soils of Desert and Lateritic soil zones with Lithosols, including Reddish Brown, Reddish Chestnut and Black soils of tropics at intermediate elevations and islands of Alpine Meadow soils at high elevations.

23 Mountain soils of Brown Forest, Terra Rosa and Rendzina soil regions with Lithosols, including Podzolized and Alpine Meadow soils at high elevations.

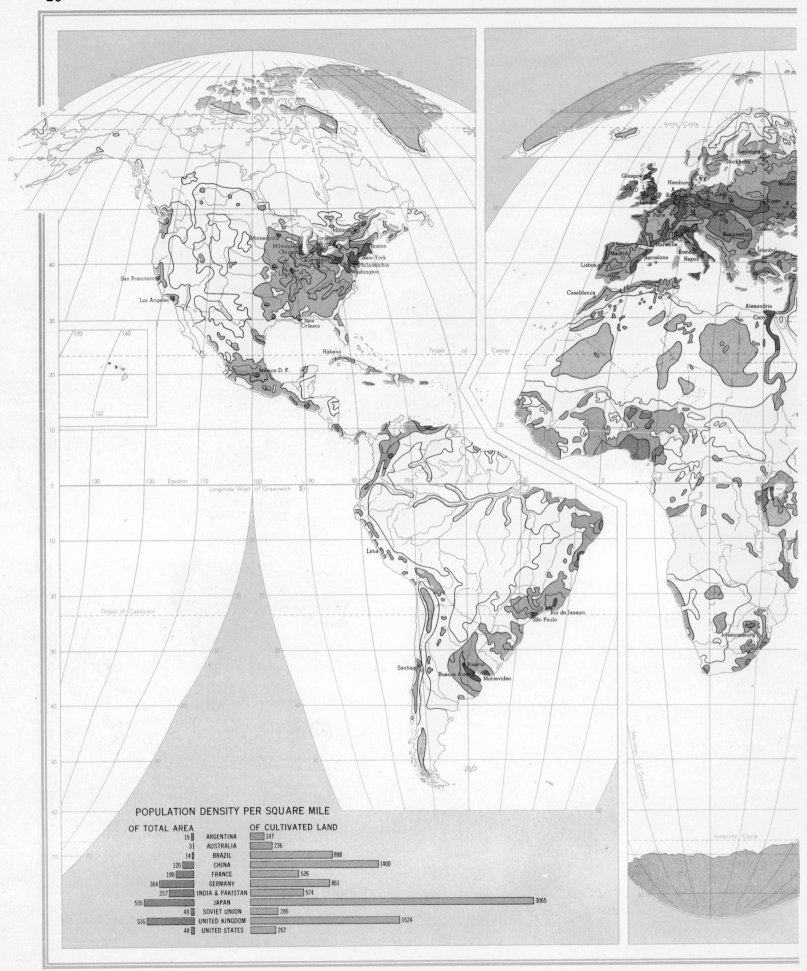

POPULATION DENSITY PER SQUARE MILE

OF TOTAL AREA		OF CULTIVATED LAND
15	ARGENTINA	147
3	AUSTRALIA	236
14	BRAZIL	898
120	CHINA	1400
190	FRANCE	526
364	GERMANY	861
257	INDIA & PAKISTAN	574
535	JAPAN	3065
48	SOVIET UNION	286
516	UNITED KINGDOM	1624
48	UNITED STATES	267

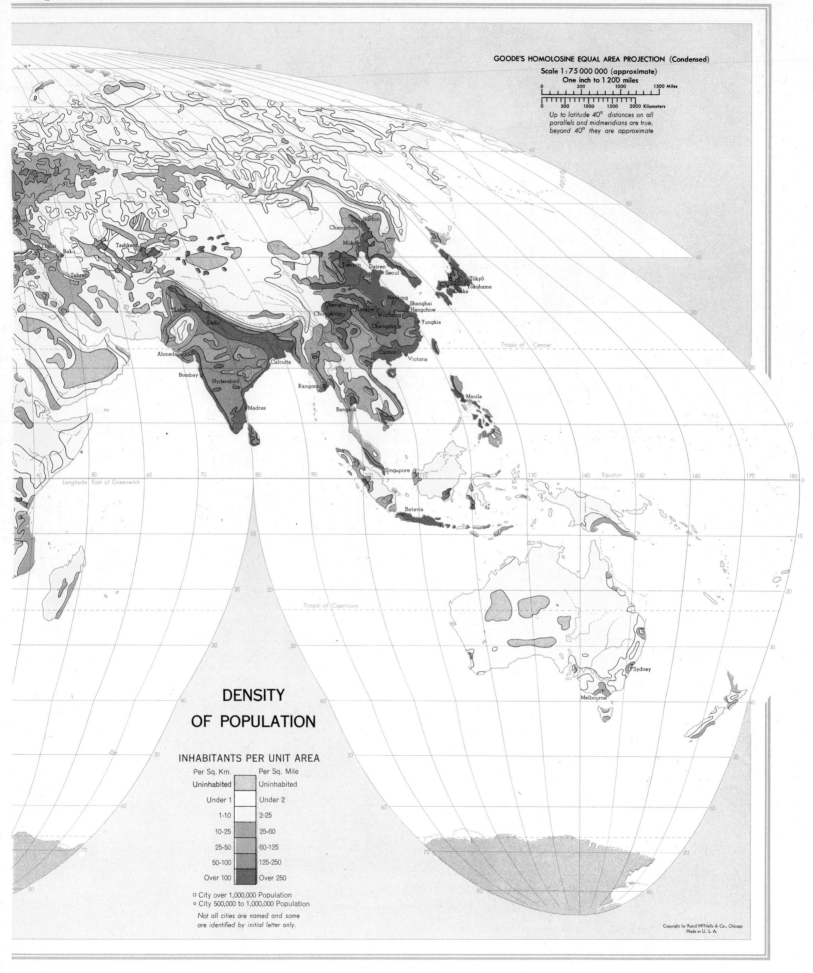

GOODE'S HOMOLOSINE EQUAL AREA PROJECTION (Condensed)
Scale 1 : 75 000 000 (approximate)
One inch to 1 200 miles

Up to latitude 40° distances on all
parallels and midmeridians are true;
beyond 40° they are approximate

DENSITY
OF POPULATION

INHABITANTS PER UNIT AREA

Per Sq. Km.	Per Sq. Mile
Uninhabited	Uninhabited
Under 1	Under 2
1-10	2-25
10-25	25-60
25-50	60-125
50-100	125-250
Over 100	Over 250

▫ City over 1,000,000 Population
○ City 500,000 to 1,000,000 Population

*Not all cities are named and some
are identified by initial letter only.*

Copyright by Rand McNally & Co., Chicago
Made in U. S. A.

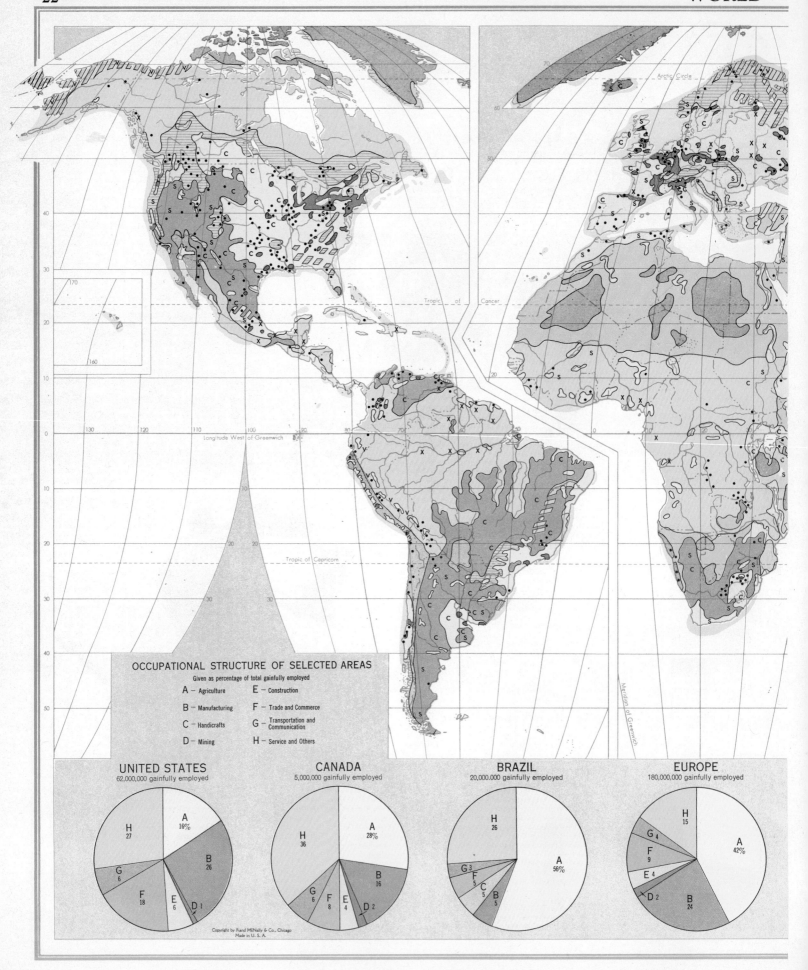

OCCUPATIONAL STRUCTURE OF SELECTED AREAS

Given as percentage of total gainfully employed

A – Agriculture   E – Construction

B – Manufacturing   F – Trade and Commerce

C – Handicrafts   G – Transportation and Communication

D – Mining   H – Service and Others

UNITED STATES
62,000,000 gainfully employed

H 27   A 16%   B 26   G 6   F 18   E 6   D 1

CANADA
5,000,000 gainfully employed

H 36   A 28%   B 16   G 6   F 8   E 4   D 2

BRAZIL
20,000,000 gainfully employed

H 26   A 56%   G 3   F 5   C 5   B 5

EUROPE
180,000,000 gainfully employed

H 15   A 42%   G 4   F 9   E 4   D 2   B 24

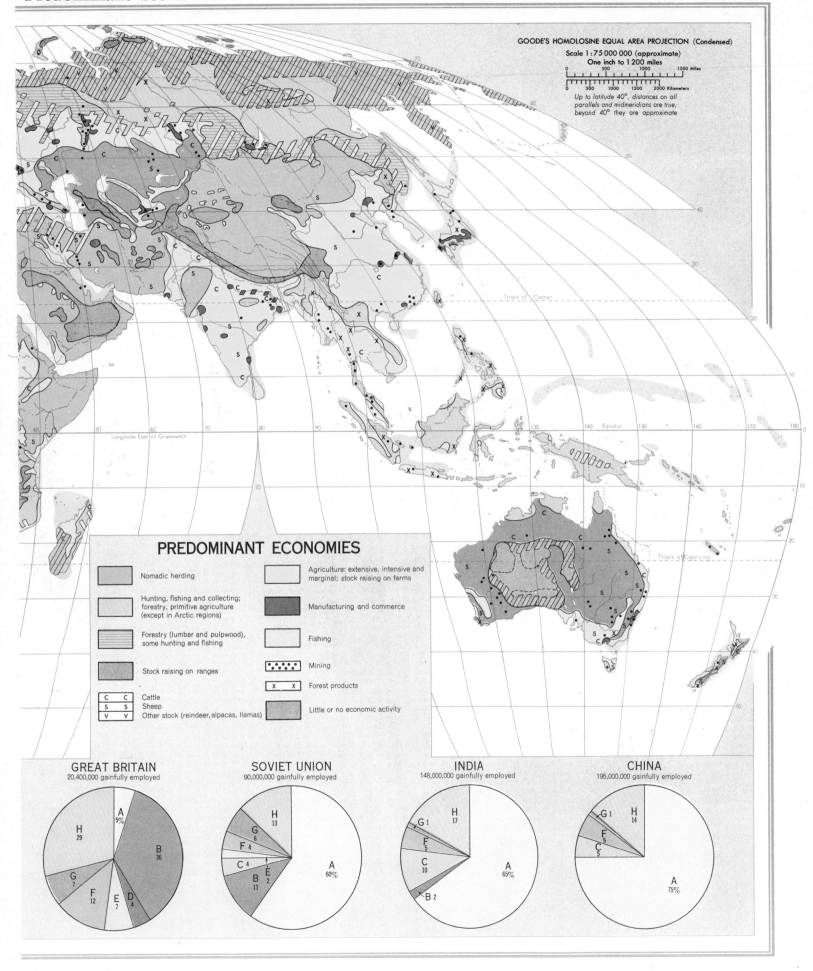

GOODE'S HOMOLOSINE EQUAL AREA PROJECTION (Condensed)

Scale 1:75 000 000 (approximate)

One inch to 1 200 miles

Up to latitude 40°, distances on all parallels and midmeridians are true; beyond 40° they are approximate

PREDOMINANT ECONOMIES

Nomadic herding

Hunting, fishing and collecting; forestry, primitive agriculture (except in Arctic regions)

Forestry (lumber and pulpwood), some hunting and fishing

Stock raising on ranges

C C Cattle
S S Sheep
V V Other stock (reindeer, alpacas, llamas)

Agriculture: extensive, intensive and marginal; stock raising on farms

Manufacturing and commerce

Fishing

Mining

X X Forest products

Little or no economic activity

GREAT BRITAIN
20,400,000 gainfully employed

A 5%
B 36
D 4
E 7
F 12
G 7
H 29

SOVIET UNION
90,000,000 gainfully employed

A 60%
B 11
C 4
E 2
F 4
G 6
H 13

INDIA
148,000,000 gainfully employed

A 65%
B 2
C 10
F 5
G 1
H 17

CHINA
195,000,000 gainfully employed

A 75%
C 5
F 5
G 1
H 14

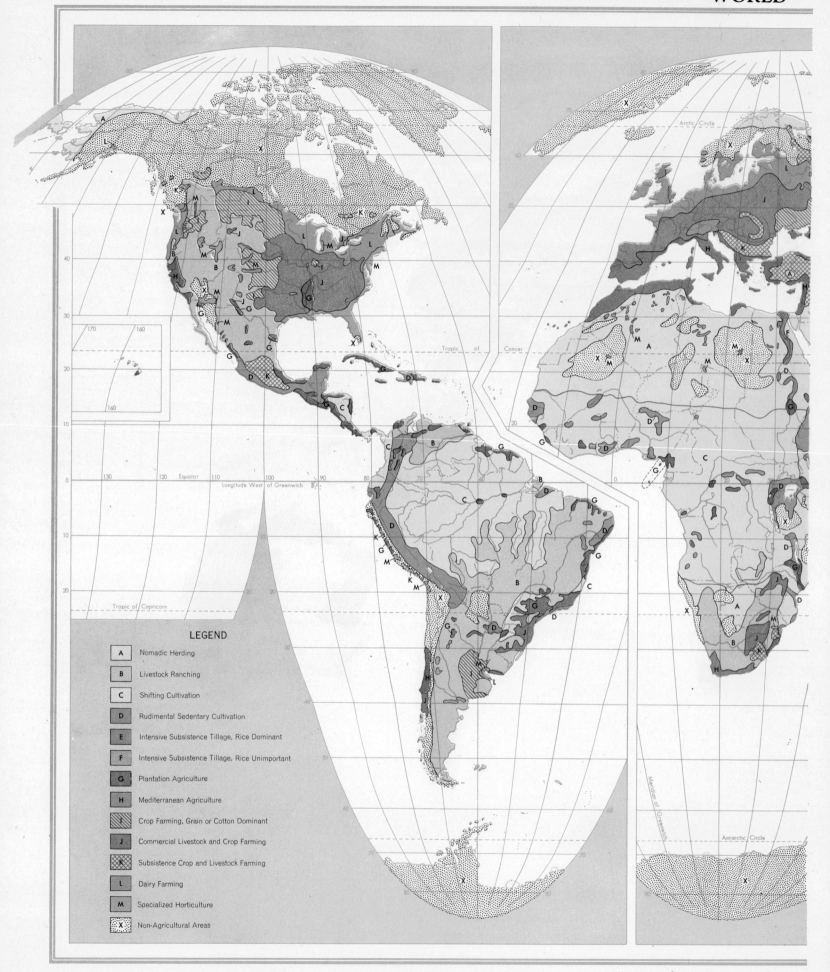

LEGEND

A	Nomadic Herding
B	Livestock Ranching
C	Shifting Cultivation
D	Rudimental Sedentary Cultivation
E	Intensive Subsistence Tillage, Rice Dominant
F	Intensive Subsistence Tillage, Rice Unimportant
G	Plantation Agriculture
H	Mediterranean Agriculture
I	Crop Farming, Grain or Cotton Dominant
J	Commercial Livestock and Crop Farming
K	Subsistence Crop and Livestock Farming
L	Dairy Farming
M	Specialized Horticulture
X	Non-Agricultural Areas

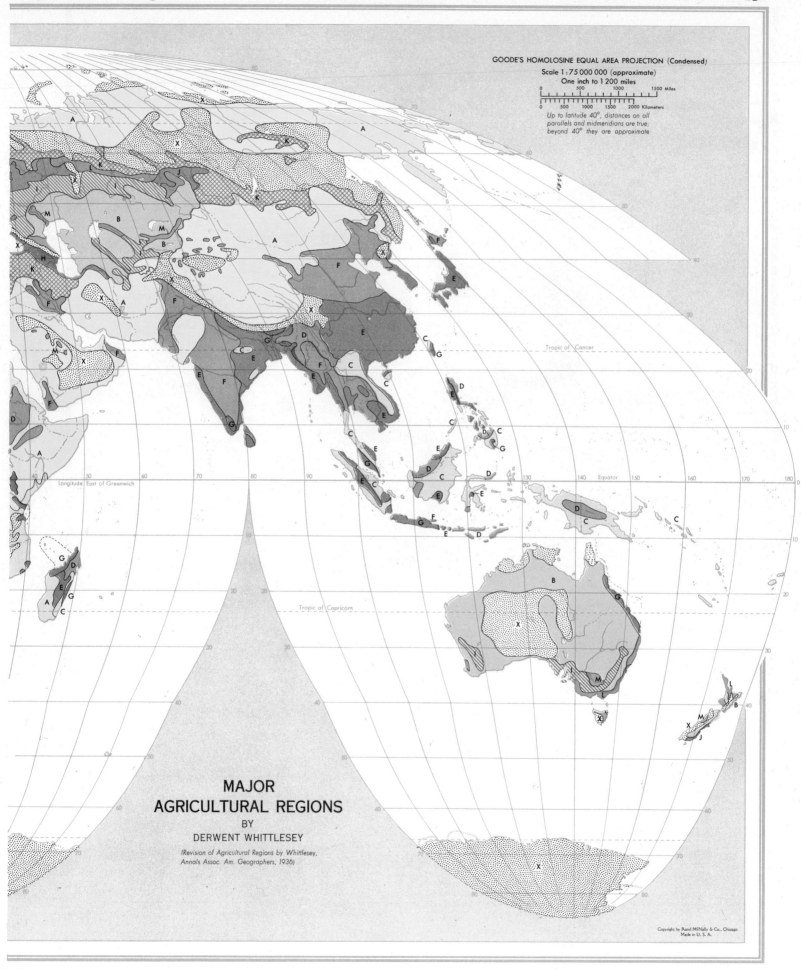

GOODE'S HOMOLOSINE EQUAL AREA PROJECTION (Condensed)

Scale 1 : 75 000 000 (approximate)

One inch to 1 200 miles

Up to latitude 40°, distances on all
parallels and midmeridians are true;
beyond 40° they are approximate

Tropic of Cancer

Equator

Longitude East of Greenwich

Tropic of Capricorn

MAJOR
AGRICULTURAL REGIONS
BY
DERWENT WHITTLESEY

(Revision of Agricultural Regions by Whittlesey,
Annals Assoc. Am. Geographers, 1936)

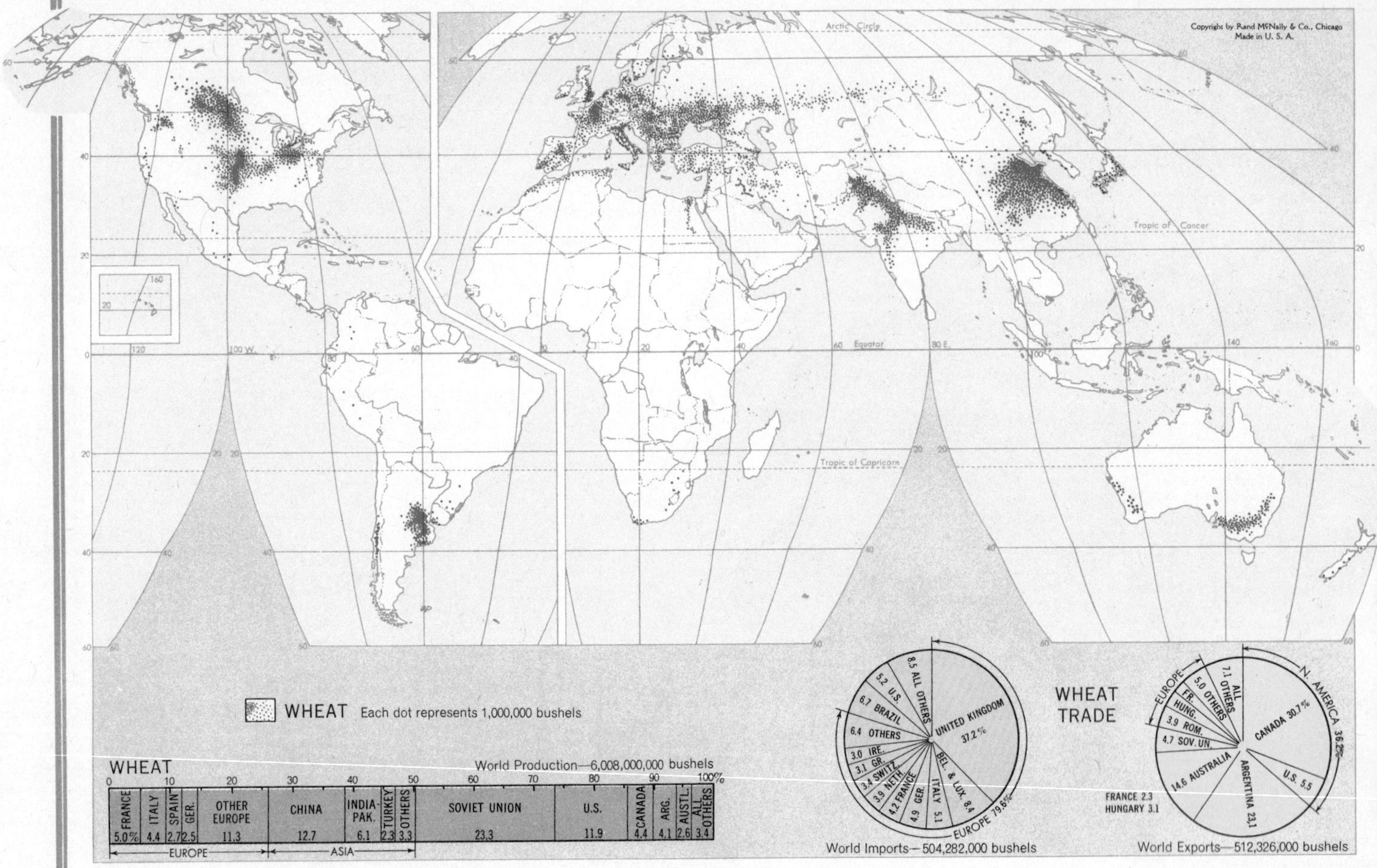

WHEAT Each dot represents 1,000,000 bushels.

WHEAT TRADE

WHEAT
World Production—6,008,000,000 bushels

FRANCE 5.0%	ITALY 4.4	SPAIN 2.7	GER. 2.5	OTHER EUROPE 11.3	CHINA 12.7	INDIA-PAK. 6.1	TURKEY 2.3	OTHERS 3.3	SOVIET UNION 23.3	U.S. 11.9	CANADA 4.4	ARG. 4.1	AUSTL. 2.6 ALL OTHERS 3.4

EUROPE — ASIA

World Imports—504,282,000 bushels

UNITED KINGDOM 37.2%
8.5 ALL OTHERS
5.2 U.S.
6.7 BRAZIL
6.4 OTHERS
3.0 IRE.
3.1 GR.
3.4 SWITZ.
3.9 NETH.
4.2 FRANCE
4.3 GER.
5.1 ITALY
8.1 BEL. & LUX.
EUROPE 79.6%

World Exports—512,326,000 bushels

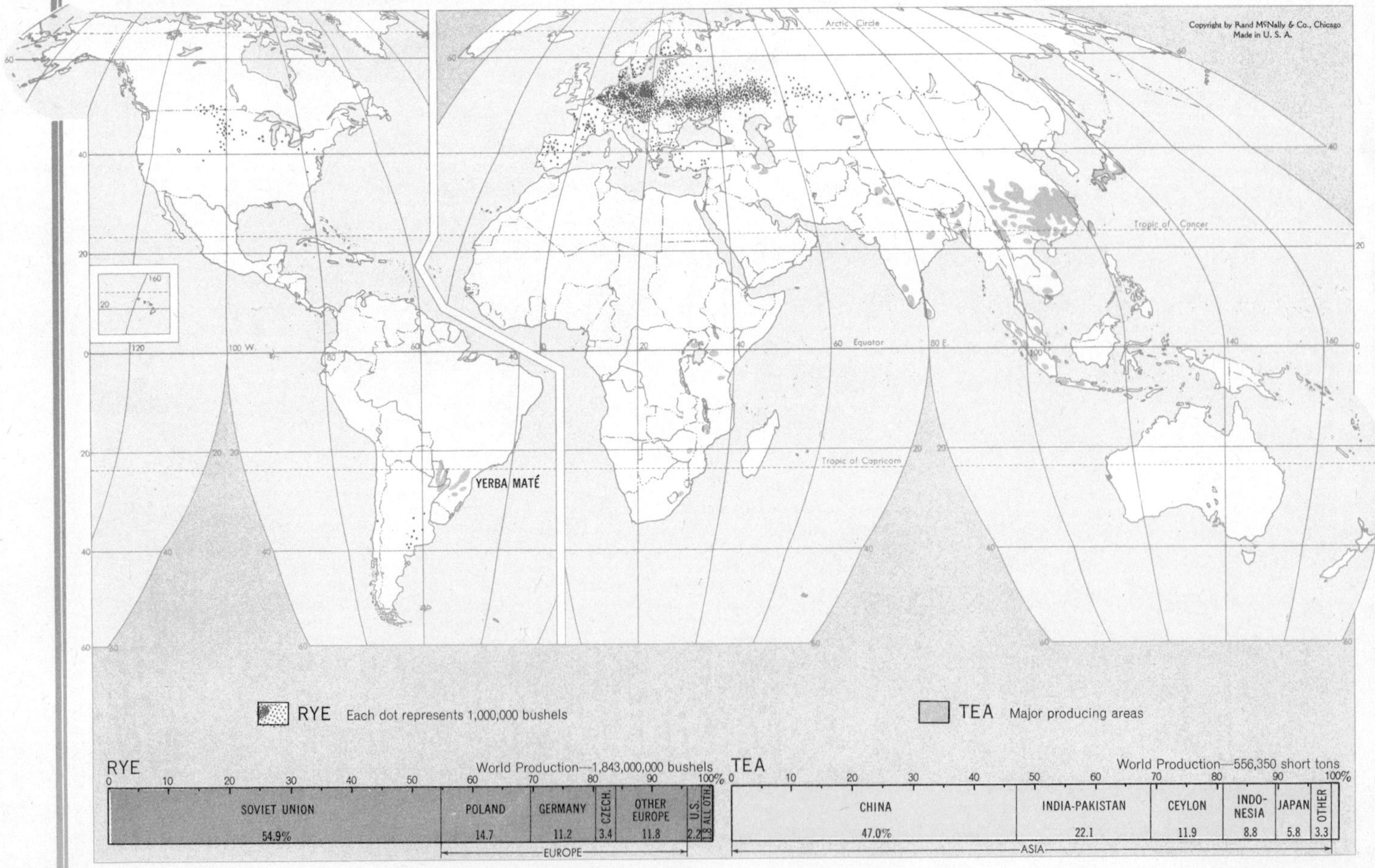

N. AMERICA 36.2%
CANADA 30.7%
U.S. 5.5
ARGENTINA 23.1
14.6 AUSTRALIA
4.7 SOV. UN.
3.9 ROM.
HUNG.
FR.
5.0 OTHERS
7.1 ALL OTHERS
EUROPE
FRANCE 2.3
HUNGARY 3.1

YERBA MATÉ

RYE Each dot represents 1,000,000 bushels.

TEA Major producing areas

RYE
World Production—1,843,000,000 bushels

SOVIET UNION 54.9%	POLAND 14.7	GERMANY 11.2	CZECH. 3.4	OTHER EUROPE 11.8	U.S. 2.2 ALL OTH.

EUROPE

TEA
World Production—556,350 short tons

CHINA 47.0%	INDIA-PAKISTAN 22.1	CEYLON 11.9	INDO-NESIA 8.8	JAPAN 5.8 OTHER 3.3

ASIA

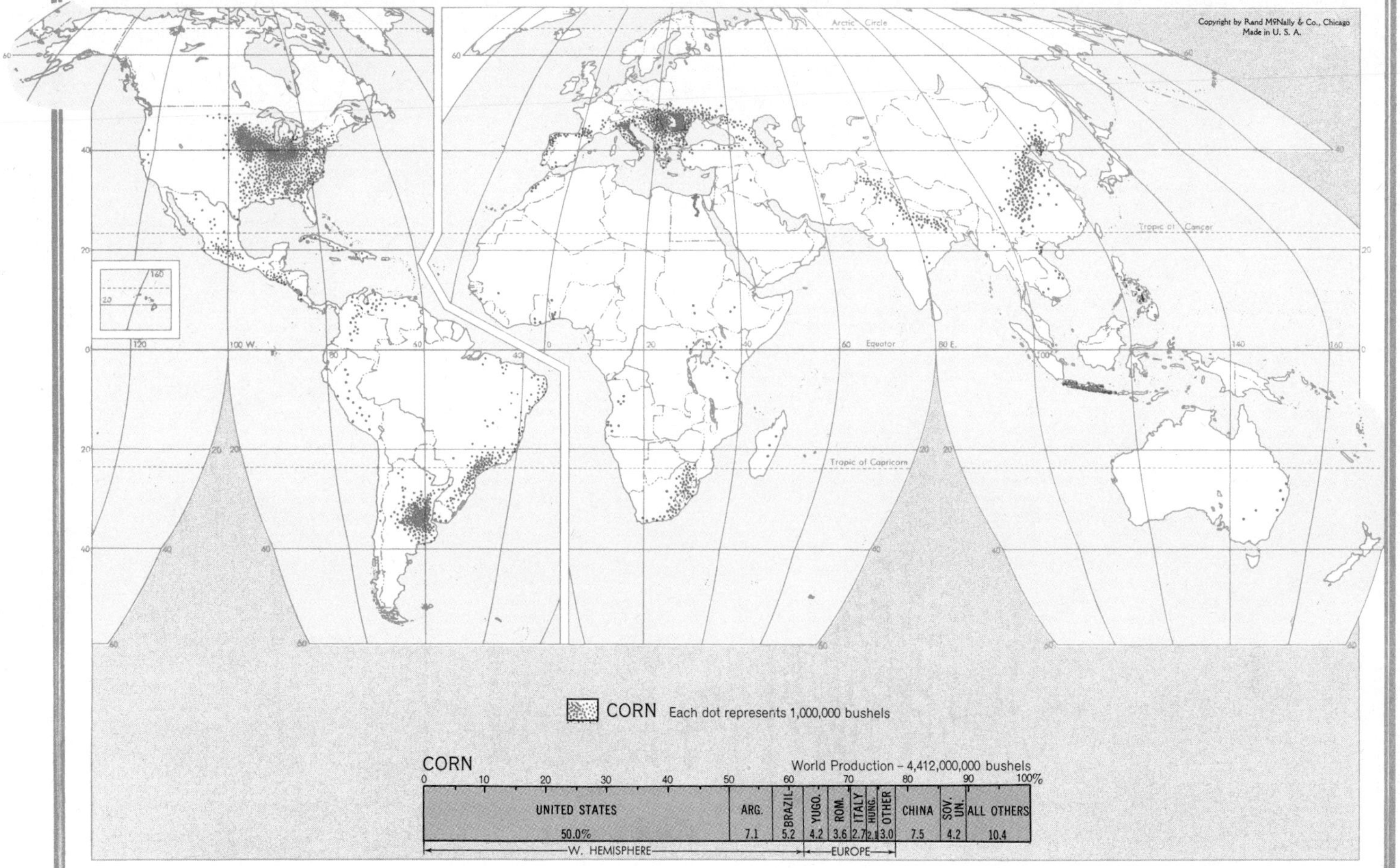

Copyright by Rand McNally & Co., Chicago
Made in U. S. A.

CORN Each dot represents 1,000,000 bushels

CORN

World Production – 4,412,000,000 bushels

| | | 0 | 10 | 20 | 30 | 40 | 50 | 60 | 70 | 80 | 90 | 100% |

UNITED STATES	ARG.	BRAZIL	YUGO.	ROM.	ITALY	HUNG.	OTHER	CHINA	SOV. UN.	ALL OTHERS
50.0%	7.1	5.2	4.2	3.6	2.7	2.	3.0	7.5	4.2	10.4

W. HEMISPHERE ←——— EUROPE ———→

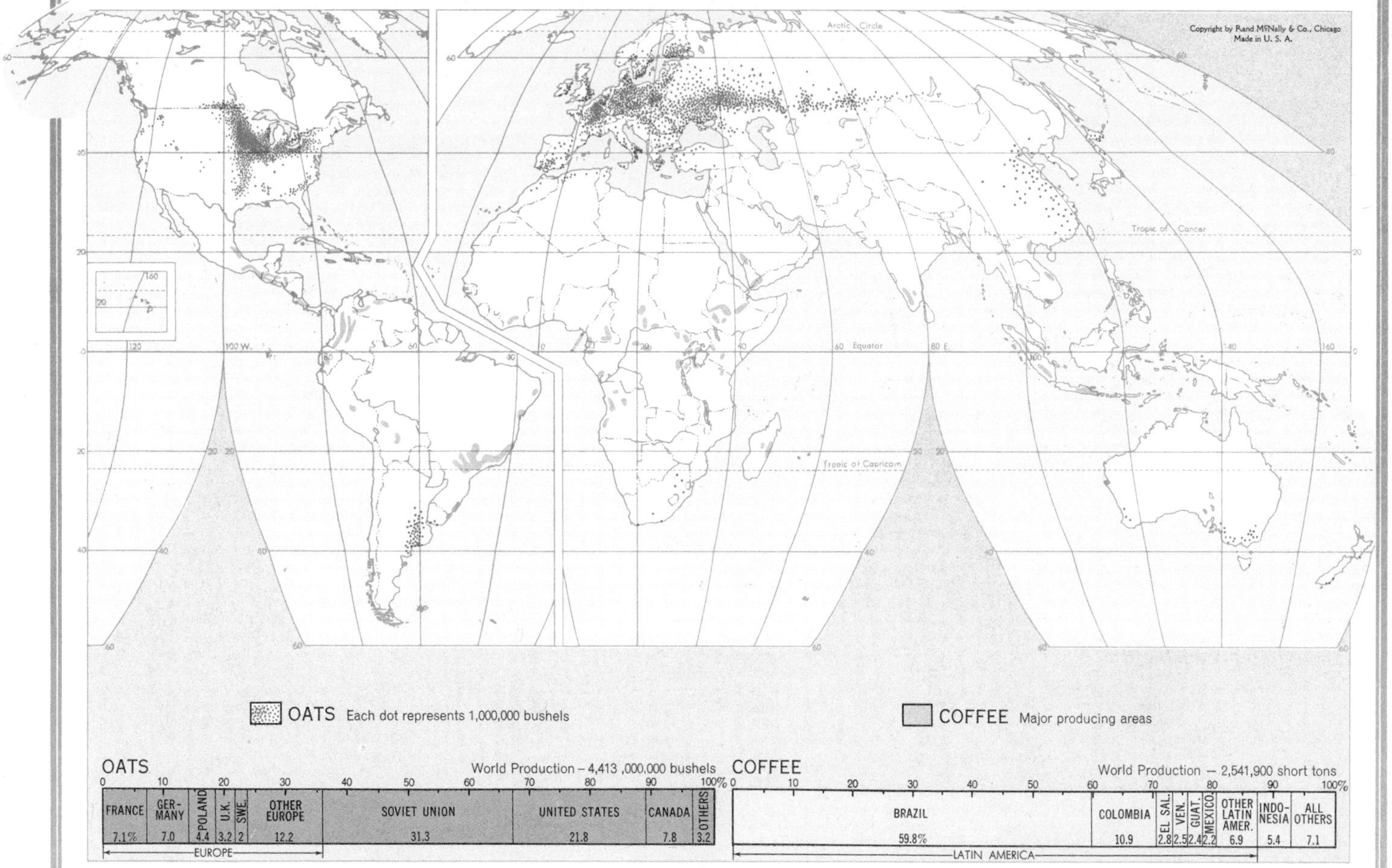

Copyright by Rand McNally & Co., Chicago
Made in U. S. A.

OATS Each dot represents 1,000,000 bushels

COFFEE Major producing areas

OATS

World Production – 4,413,000,000 bushels

| | | 0 | 10 | 20 | 30 | 40 | 50 | 60 | 70 | 80 | 90 | 100% |

FRANCE	GER-MANY	POLAND	U.K.	SWE.	OTHER EUROPE	SOVIET UNION	UNITED STATES	CANADA	OTHERS
7.1%	7.0	4.4	3.2	2	12.2	31.3	21.8	7.8	3.2

←——— EUROPE ———→

COFFEE

World Production — 2,541,900 short tons

| | 0 | 10 | 20 | 30 | 40 | 50 | 60 | 70 | 80 | 90 | 100% |

BRAZIL	COLOMBIA	EL SAL.	VEN.	GUAT.	MEXICO	OTHER LATIN AMER.	INDO-NESIA	ALL OTHERS
59.8%	10.9	2.8	2.5	2.4	2.2	6.9	5.4	7.1

←————————— LATIN AMERICA —————————→

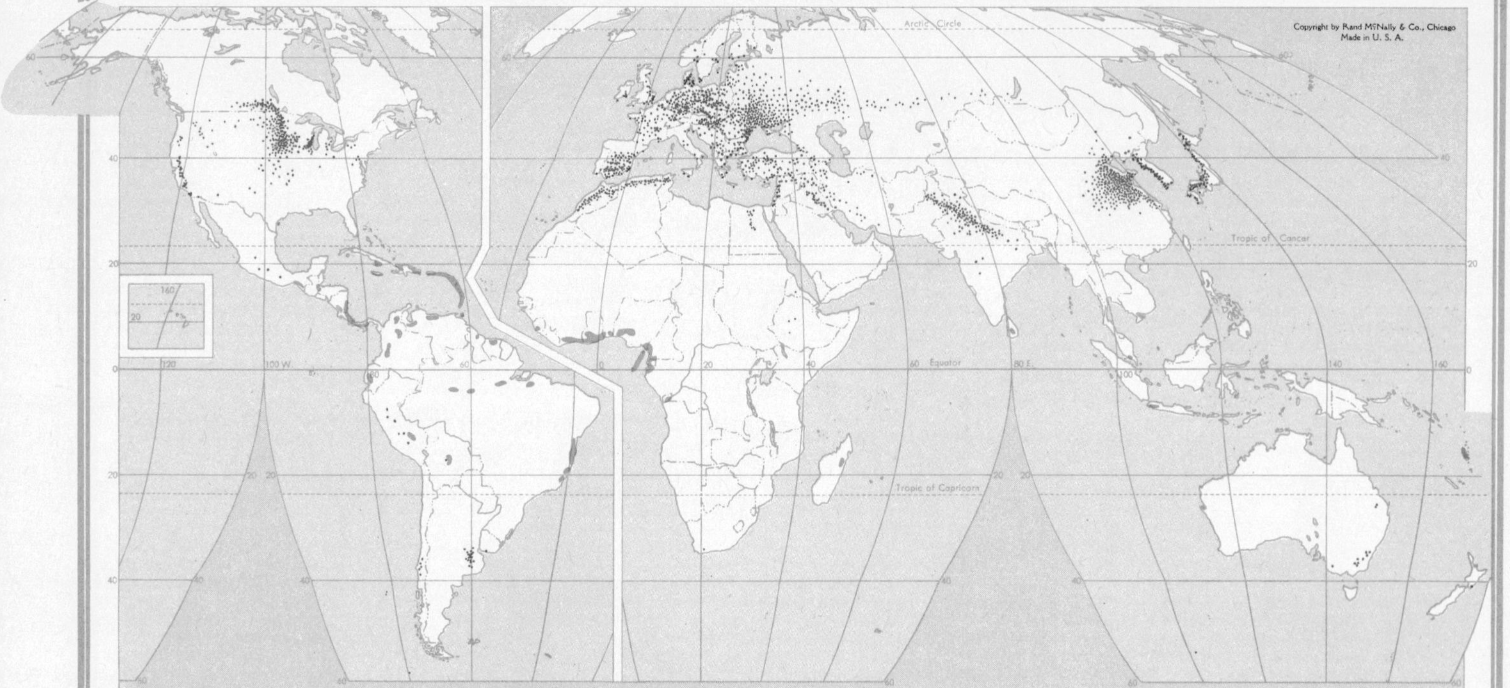

Copyright by Rand McNally & Co., Chicago
Made in U. S. A.

BARLEY Each dot represents 1,000,000 bushels

CACAO Major producing areas

BARLEY
World Production — 2,354,000,000 bushels

	0	10	20	30	40	50	60	70	80	90	100%

CHINA	INDIA & PAK.	TURKEY	JAPAN	OTHER ASIA	GER.	SPAIN	POLAND	OTHER EUROPE	SOVIET UNION	UNITED STATES	CAN.	ALL OTHERS
15.0%	4.6	4.1	3.0	5.8	5.3	4.7	3.2	15.1	20.0	8.8	3.4	7.0

—ASIA—   —EUROPE—

CACAO
World Production — 822,320 short tons

	0	10	20	30	40	50	60	70	80	90	100%

GOLD COAST	NIGERIA	IVORY COAST	FR.CAM.	OTHER AFRICA	BRAZIL	DOM. REP.	EC.	OTHER LATIN AMERICA
35.5%	12.0	6.7	3.5	7.7	17.4	3.9	2.6	9.6

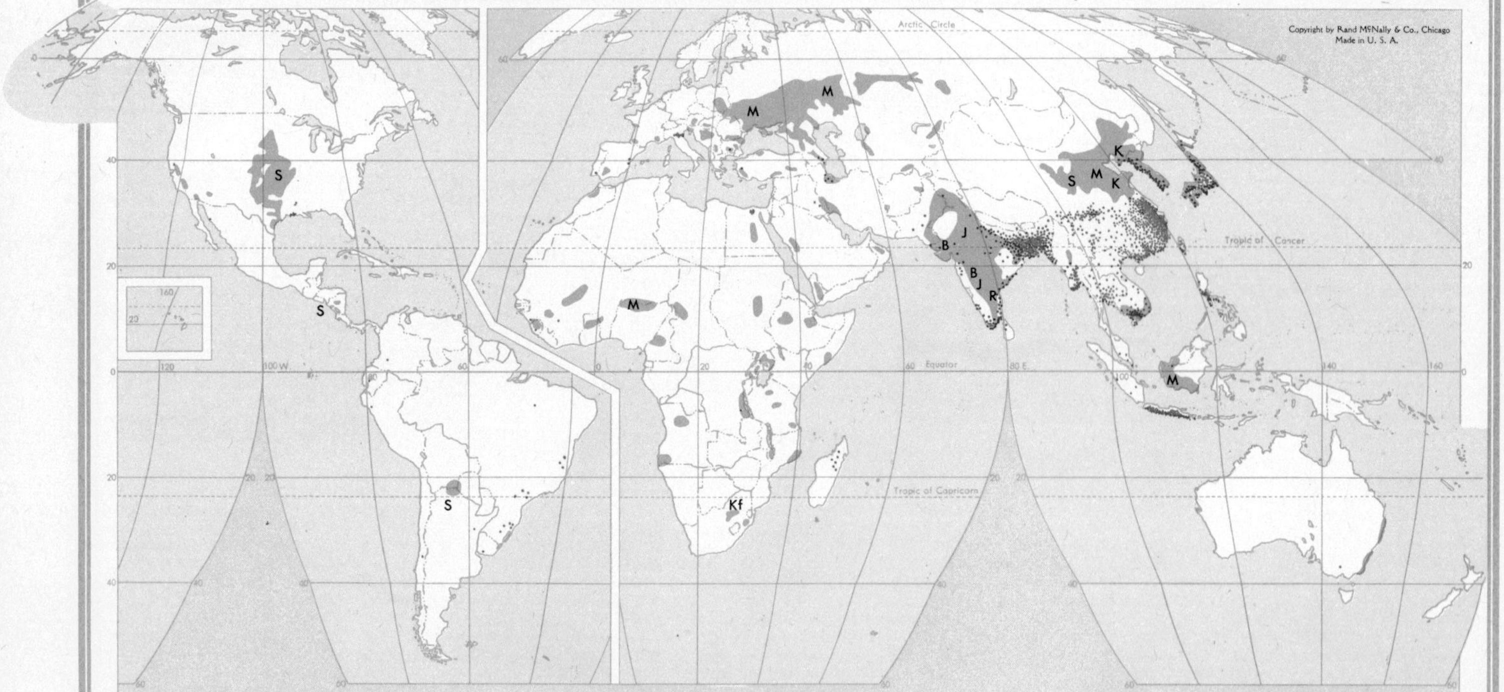

—AFRICA—   —LATIN AMERICA—

Copyright by Rand McNally & Co., Chicago
Made in U. S. A.

RICE Each dot represents 5,000,000 bushels

MILLET AND GRAIN SORGHUM
(primarily grown for grain)

B = BAJRA
J = JOWAR
K = KAOLIANG
Kf = KAFFIR CORN
M = MILLET, UNDIFFERENTIATED
R = RAGI
S = SORGHUM

RICE
World Production — 6,940,000,000 bushels

	0	10	20	30	40	50	60	70	80	90	100%

CHINA	INDIA & PAKISTAN	JAPAN	BURMA	INDO-NESIA	INDO-CHINA	SIAM	OTHER ASIA	ALL OTHERS
37.0%	27.4	8.1	5.2	4.9	4.4	3.1	5.5	4.4

—ASIA—

MILLET (FOR GRAIN)
World Production — 26,000,000 short tons

	0	10	20	30	40	50	60	70	80	90	100%

CHINA	INDIA & PAKISTAN	KOREA	OTHER	FR. W. AFRICA	EGYPT	OTHER AFRICA	SOVIET UNION	EUROPE
42.0%	19.8	2.4	2	6.6	2.4	7.9	11.7	3.5

—ASIA—   —AFRICA—

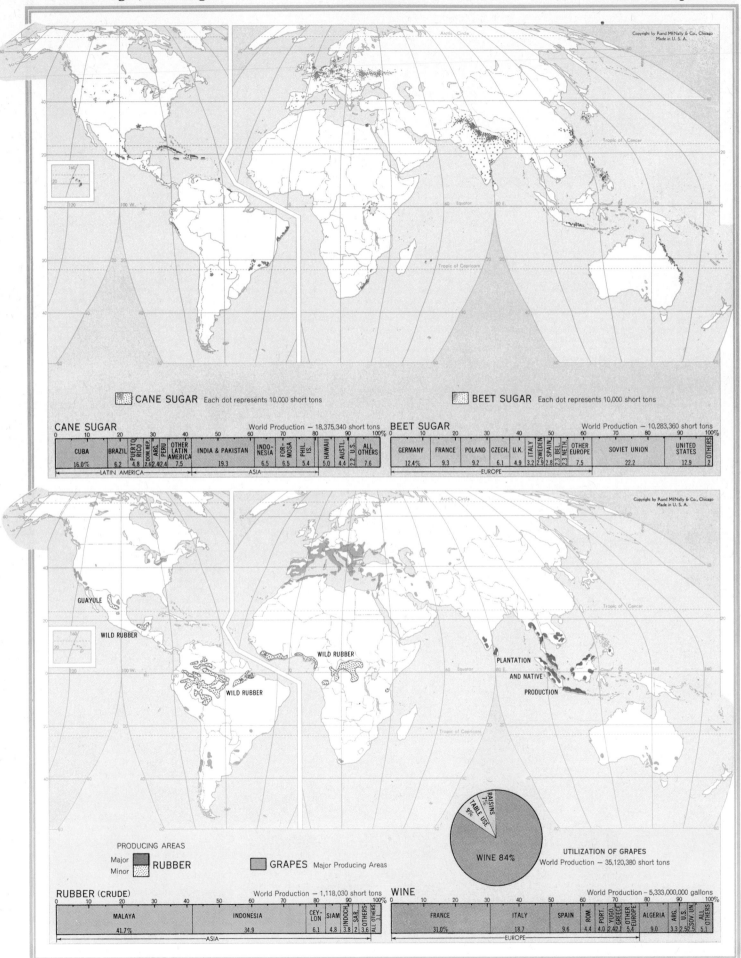

Copyright by Rand McNally & Co., Chicago
Made in U. S. A.

▨ CANE SUGAR   Each dot represents 10,000 short tons   ▨ BEET SUGAR   Each dot represents 10,000 short tons

CANE SUGAR
World Production — 18,375,340 short tons

CUBA	BRAZIL	PUERTO RICO	DOM. REP.	ARG.	PERU	OTHER LATIN AMERICA	INDIA & PAKISTAN	INDO-NESIA	FOR-MOSA	PHIL. IS.	HAWAII	AUSTL.	U.S.	ALL OTHERS
16.0%	6.2	4.8	2.6	2.4	2.4	7.5	19.3	6.5	6.5	5.4	5.0	4.4	2.2	7.6

←——— LATIN AMERICA ———→   ←——————— ASIA ———————→

BEET SUGAR
World Production — 10,283,360 short tons

GERMANY	FRANCE	POLAND	CZECH.	U.K.	ITALY	SWEDEN	SPAIN	BEL.	NETH.	OTHER EUROPE	SOVIET UNION	UNITED STATES	OTHERS
12.4%	9.3	9.2	6.1	4.9	3.2	2.9	2.8	2.3	2.3	7.5	22.2	12.9	2

←——————————— EUROPE ———————————→

Copyright by Rand McNally & Co., Chicago
Made in U. S. A.

GUAYULE

WILD RUBBER

WILD RUBBER

WILD RUBBER

WILD RUBBER

PLANTATION AND NATIVE PRODUCTION

PRODUCING AREAS
Major / Minor ▨ RUBBER   ▨ GRAPES   Major Producing Areas

UTILIZATION OF GRAPES
World Production — 35,120,380 short tons

Pie chart: WINE 84% · TABLE USE 9% · RAISINS 7%

RUBBER (CRUDE)
World Production — 1,118,030 short tons

MALAYA	INDONESIA	CEY-LON	SIAM	INDOCH.	SAR.	ALL OTHERS
41.7%	34.9	6.1	4.8	3.8	2	3.6 / 3.1

←——————————— ASIA ———————————→

WINE
World Production — 5,333,000,000 gallons

FRANCE	ITALY	SPAIN	ROM.	PORT.	YUGO.	GREECE	OTHER EUROPE	ALGERIA	ARG.	U.S.	SOV. UN.	ALL OTHERS
31.0%	18.7	9.6	4.4	4.0	2.4	2.1	5.4	9.0	3.3	2.9	2.3	5.1

←——————————— EUROPE ———————————→

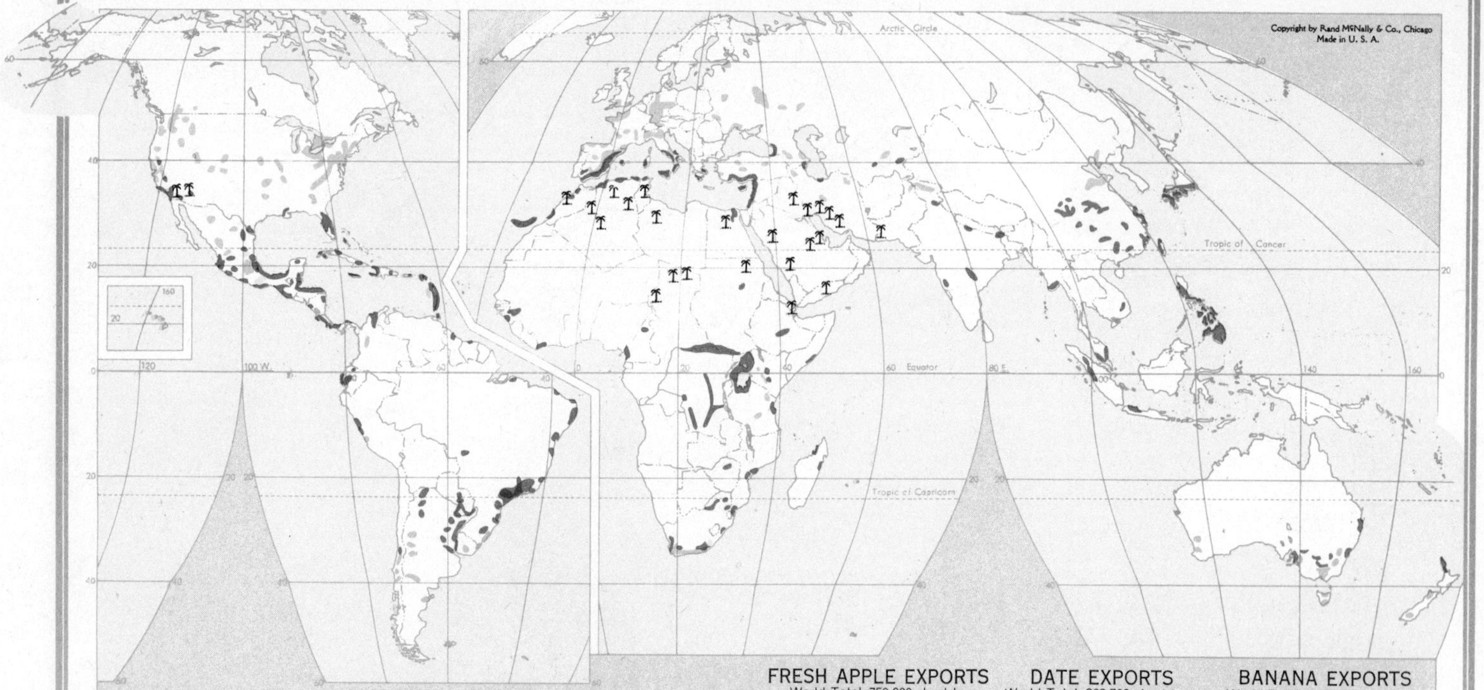

MAJOR PRODUCING AREAS

CITRUS FRUIT (Oranges, lemons, grapefruit)
DECIDUOUS FRUIT (Apples, peaches, pears, etc.)
BANANAS
PINEAPPLES
DATES

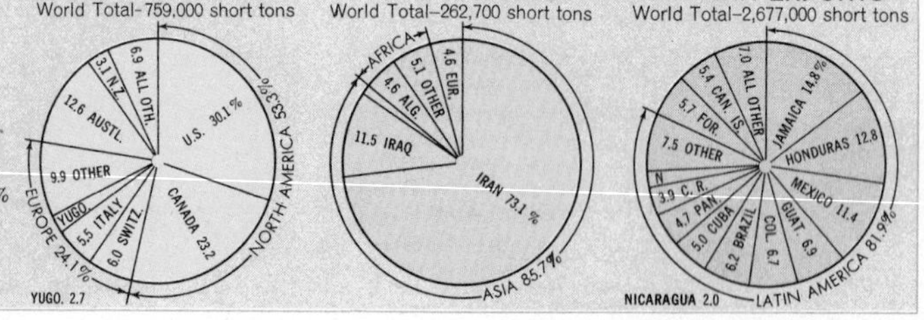

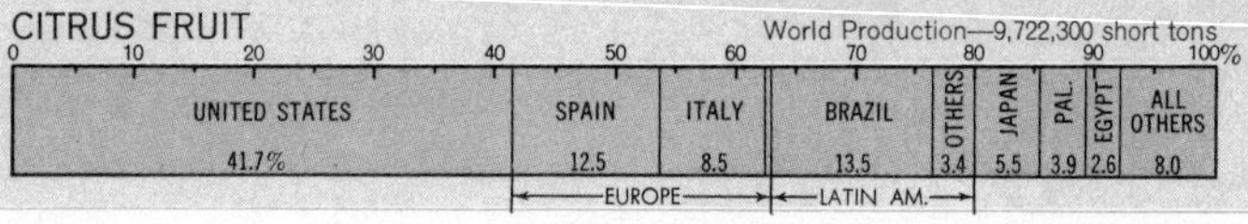

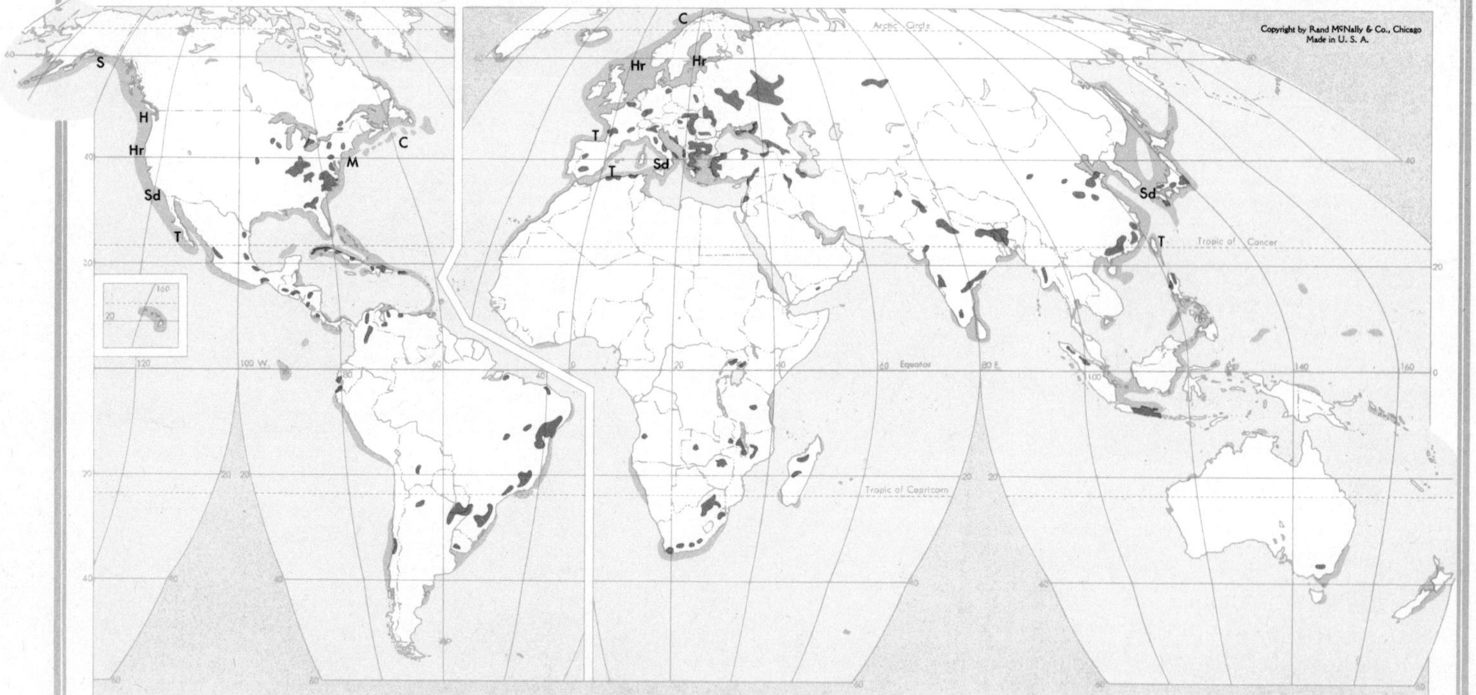

CITRUS FRUIT
World Production—9,722,300 short tons

UNITED STATES	SPAIN	ITALY	BRAZIL	OTHERS	JAPAN	PAL.	EGYPT	ALL OTHERS
41.7%	12.5	8.5	13.5	3.4	5.5	3.9	2.6	8.0

EUROPE   LATIN AM.

FRESH APPLE EXPORTS
World Total-759,000 short tons

6.9 ALL OTH.
3.1 N.Z.
12.5 AUSTL.
9.9 OTHER
U.S. 30.1%
NORTH AMERICA 53.3%
CANADA 23.2
EUROPE 24.1%
5.0 SWITZ.
6.0 ITALY
5.5 ITALY
YUGO. 2.7

DATE EXPORTS
World Total-262,700 short tons

AFRICA
4.6 EUR.
5.1 OTHER
4.6 ALG.
11.5 IRAQ
IRAN 73.1%
ASIA 85.7%

BANANA EXPORTS
World Total-2,677,000 short tons

7.0 ALL OTHER
5.4 CAN.
5.7 FOR.
7.5 OTHER
3.9 C.R.
4.7 PAN.
5.0 CUBA
6.2 BRAZIL
COL. 6.7
GUAT. 6.3
MEXICO 11.4
HONDURAS 12.8
JAMAICA 14.8%
LATIN AMERICA 81.9%
NICARAGUA 2.0

TOBACCO Major producing areas

FISHERIES Important areas

C – COD   M – MACKEREL
H – HALIBUT   S – SALMON
Hr – HERRING   Sd – SARDINE
T – TUNA

TOBACCO
World Production—3,243,950 short tons

CHINA	INDIA & PAKISTAN	INDON.	JAPAN	TURKEY	OTHER ASIA	UNITED STATES	SOV. UN.	BRAZIL	GREECE	ALL OTHERS
22.1%	17.0	3.8	2.2	2.1	5.0	20.1	8.0	3.2	2.2	14.5

ASIA

FISHERY PRODUCTION
World Production—18,390,000 short tons

JAPAN	CHINA	KOREA	OTHER ASIA	U.K.	NOR.	GER.	SPAIN	FRANCE	ICE.	OTHER EUR.	U. S. & ALASKA	CAN.	SOV. UN.	OTHERS
22.0%	7.9	6.3	7.0	6.4	5.6	4.3	2.6	2.1	2.2	5.5	11.0	4.5	9.3	3.5

ASIA   EUROPE   N. AMERICA

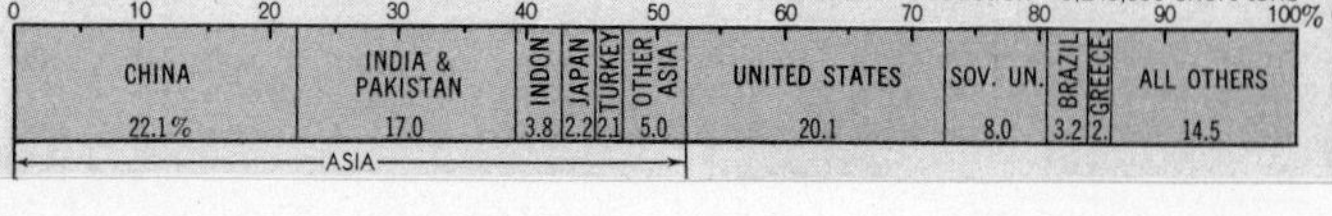

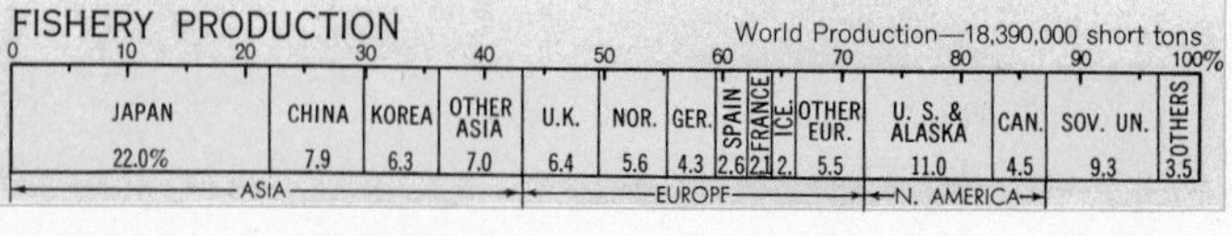

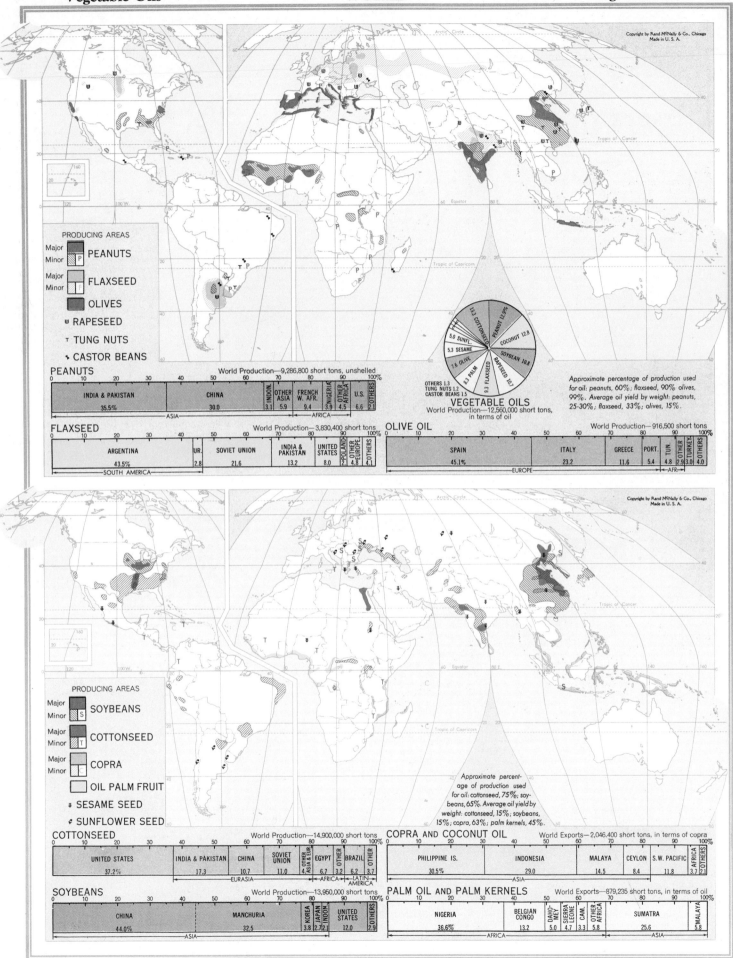

PRODUCING AREAS

Major / Minor   P   **PEANUTS**

Major / Minor   **FLAXSEED**

Major / Minor   **OLIVES**

w   **RAPESEED**

T   **TUNG NUTS**

⚷   **CASTOR BEANS**

VEGETABLE OILS
World Production—12,560,000 short tons, in terms of oil

13.3 COTTONSEED   PEANUT 12.5%   COCONUT 12.8   SOYBEAN 10.8   RAPESEED 10.7   9.3 FLAXSEED   8.3 PALM   7.5 OLIVE   5.3 SESAME   5.0 SUNFL.

OTHERS 1.3
TUNG NUTS 1.2
CASTOR BEANS 1.5

Approximate percentage of production used for oil: peanuts, 60%; flaxseed, 90%; olives, 99%. Average oil yield by weight: peanuts, 25-30%; flaxseed, 33%; olives, 15%.

PEANUTS
World Production—9,286,800 short tons, unshelled

INDIA & PAKISTAN 35.5%	CHINA 30.0	INDON. 3.1	OTHER ASIA 5.9	FRENCH W. AFR. 9.4	NIGERIA 3.9	OTHER AFRICA 4.5	U.S. 6.6	OTHERS 2.1

ASIA — AFRICA

FLAXSEED
World Production—3,830,400 short tons

ARGENTINA 43.5%	UR. 2.8	SOVIET UNION 21.6	INDIA & PAKISTAN 13.2	UNITED STATES 8.0	POLAND 2.1	OTHER EUROPE 4.8	OTHERS 4.1

SOUTH AMERICA

OLIVE OIL
World Production—916,500 short tons

SPAIN 45.1%	ITALY 23.2	GREECE 11.6	PORT. 5.4	TUN. 4.8	OTHER EUROPE 2.9	TURKEY 3.0	OTHERS 4.0

EUROPE — AFR.

PRODUCING AREAS

Major / Minor   S   **SOYBEANS**

Major / Minor   T   **COTTONSEED**

Major / Minor   C   **COPRA**

OIL PALM FRUIT

⚶   **SESAME SEED**

⚶   **SUNFLOWER SEED**

Approximate percentage of production used for oil: cottonseed, 75%; soybeans, 65%. Average oil yield by weight: cottonseed, 15%; soybeans, 15%; copra, 63%; palm kernels, 45%.

COTTONSEED
World Production—14,900,000 short tons

UNITED STATES 37.2%	INDIA & PAKISTAN 17.3	CHINA 10.7	SOVIET UNION 11.0	OTHER ASIA & EUR. 4.4	EGYPT 6.7	OTHER 3.2	BRAZIL 6.2	OTHER 3.7

EURASIA — AFRICA — LATIN AMERICA

SOYBEANS
World Production—13,950,000 short tons

CHINA 44.0%	MANCHURIA 32.5	KOREA 3.8	JAPAN 2.7	INDON. 2.1	UNITED STATES 12.0	OTHERS 2.9

ASIA

COPRA AND COCONUT OIL
World Exports—2,046,400 short tons, in terms of copra

PHILIPPINE IS. 30.5%	INDONESIA 29.0	MALAYA 14.5	CEYLON 8.4	S.W. PACIFIC 11.8	AFRICA 3.7	OTHERS 2.1

PALM OIL AND PALM KERNELS
World Exports—879,235 short tons, in terms of oil

NIGERIA 36.6%	BELGIAN CONGO 13.2	DAHO-MEY 5.0	SIERRA LEONE 4.7	CAM. 3.3	OTHER AFRICA 5.8	SUMATRA 25.6	MALAYA 5.8

AFRICA — ASIA

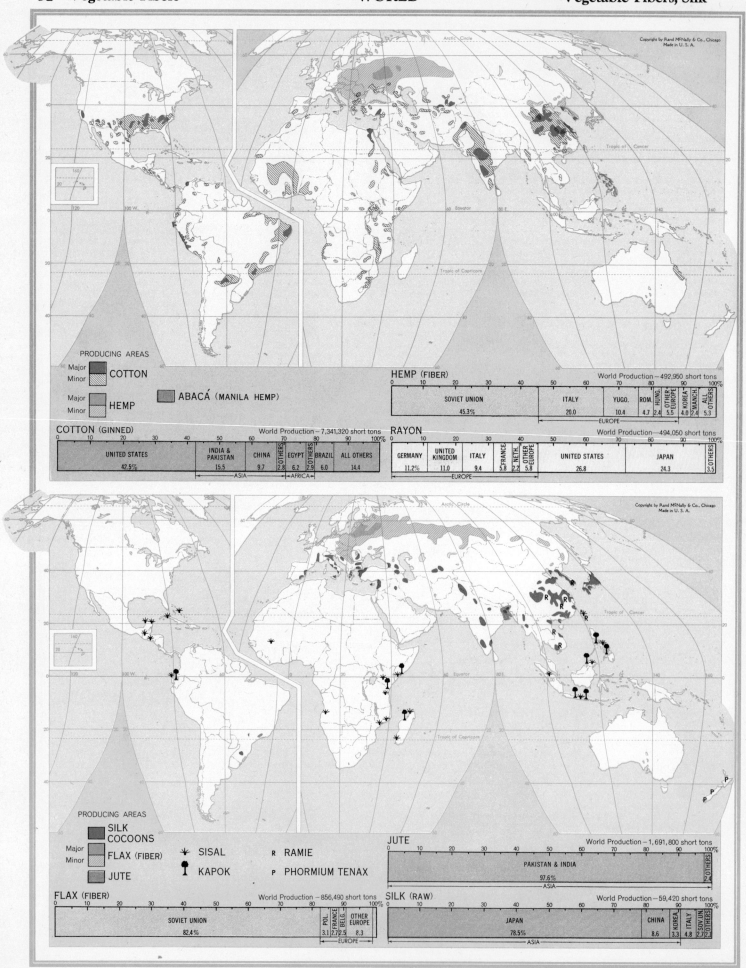

PRODUCING AREAS

Major / Minor — COTTON

Major / Minor — HEMP

ABACÁ (MANILA HEMP)

HEMP (FIBER)
World Production — 492,950 short tons

0	10	20	30	40	50	60	70	80	90	100%

SOVIET UNION 45.3%	ITALY 20.0	YUGO. 10.4	ROM. 4.7	HUNG. 2.4	OTHER EUROPE 5.5	KOREA 4.0	MANCH. 2.4	ALL OTHERS 5.3
— EUROPE —

COTTON (GINNED)
World Production — 7,341,320 short tons

0	10	20	30	40	50	60	70	80	90	100%

UNITED STATES 42.5%	INDIA & PAKISTAN 15.5	CHINA 9.7	OTHERS 2.8	EGYPT 6.2	OTHERS 2.9	BRAZIL 6.0	ALL OTHERS 14.4
	— ASIA —			— AFRICA —			

RAYON
World Production — 494,050 short tons

0	10	20	30	40	50	60	70	80	90	100%

GERMANY 11.2%	UNITED KINGDOM 11.0	ITALY 9.4	FRANCE 5.8	NETH. 2.2	OTHER EUROPE 5.8	UNITED STATES 26.8	JAPAN 24.3	OTHERS 3.5
	— EUROPE —							

PRODUCING AREAS

SILK COCOONS

Major / Minor — FLAX (FIBER)

JUTE

✳ SISAL   R RAMIE

♣ KAPOK   P PHORMIUM TENAX

JUTE
World Production — 1,691,800 short tons

0	10	20	30	40	50	60	70	80	90	100%

PAKISTAN & INDIA 97.6%	OTHERS 2.4
— ASIA —	

FLAX (FIBER)
World Production — 856,490 short tons

0	10	20	30	40	50	60	70	80	90	100%

SOVIET UNION 82.4%	POL. 3.1	FRANCE 2.7	BELG. 2.5	OTHER EUROPE 8.3
		— EUROPE —		

SILK (RAW)
World Production — 59,420 short tons

0	10	20	30	40	50	60	70	80	90	100%

JAPAN 78.5%	CHINA 8.6	KOREA 3.3	ITALY 4.8	SOV.UN. 2.7	OTHERS 2.1
— ASIA —					

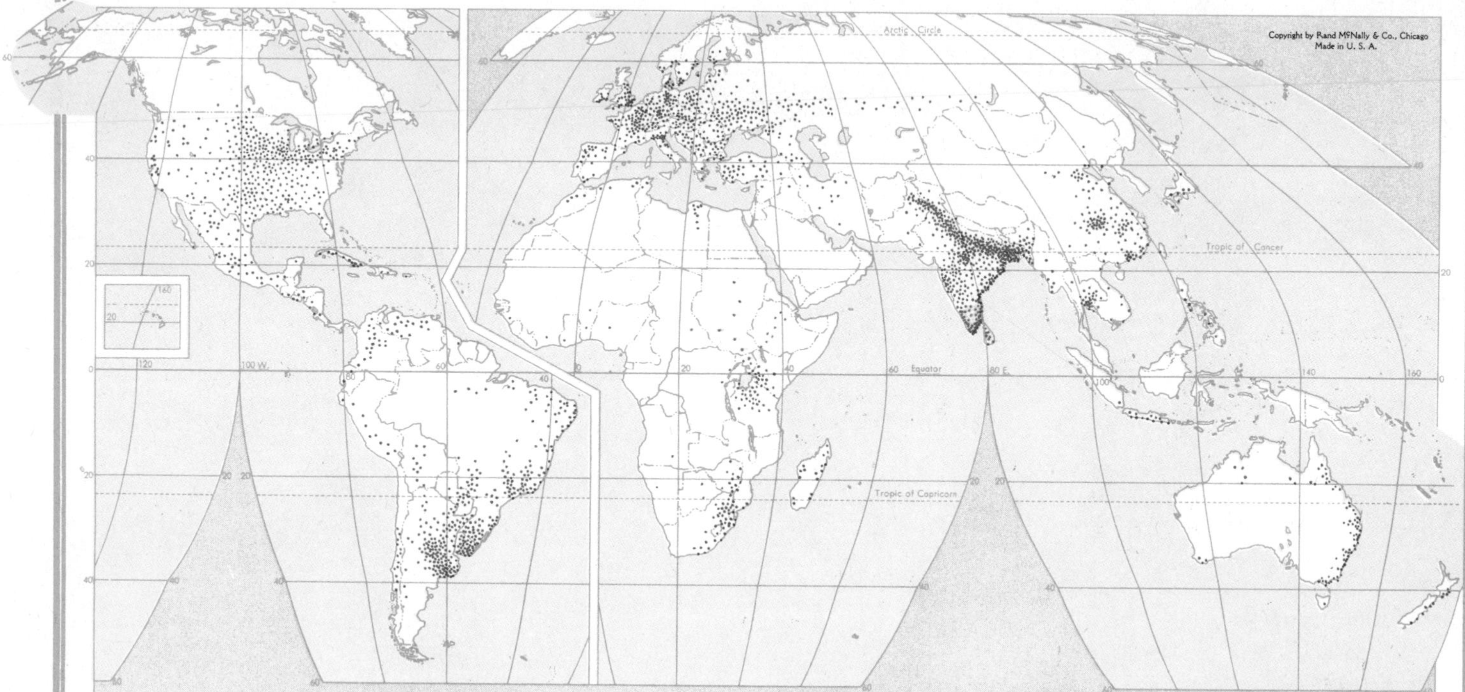

Copyright by Rand McNally & Co., Chicago
Made in U.S.A.

CATTLE Each dot represents 500,000 head

BEEF EXPORTS

World Total — 1,049,820 short tons

0	10	20	30	40	50	60	70	80	90	100%
ARGENTINA 50.8%					URUGUAY 9.9	BRAZIL 6.4	14 OTHERS	AUSTRALIA 11.7	N.Z. 5.4	U.K. 2.2	OTHER EUR. 6.1	ALL OTH. 6.1

SOUTH AMERICA — OCEANIA — EUR.

CATTLE

World Total — 723,000,000 head

0	10	20	30	40	50	60	70	80	90	100%
INDIA & PAKISTAN 28.5%			CHINA 3.4	OTHER ASIA 7.3	GER. 2.8	FR. 2.1	OTHER EUROPE 10.3	BRAZ. 5.6	ARG. 4.7	OTHER S. AM. 4.3	UNITED STATES 9.2	OTHER N. AM. 4.2	SOVIET UNION 6.7	ALL OTHERS 10.9

ASIA — EUROPE — S. AM. — N. AM.

BEEF IMPORTS

World Total — 935,300 short tons

0	10	20	30	40	50	60	70	80	90	100%
UNITED KINGDOM 73.7%							GER. 3.6	ITALY 3.1	OTHER EUR. 6.2	U.S. 4.3	ALL OTHERS 9.1

EUROPE

Copyright by Rand McNally & Co., Chicago
Made in U.S.A.

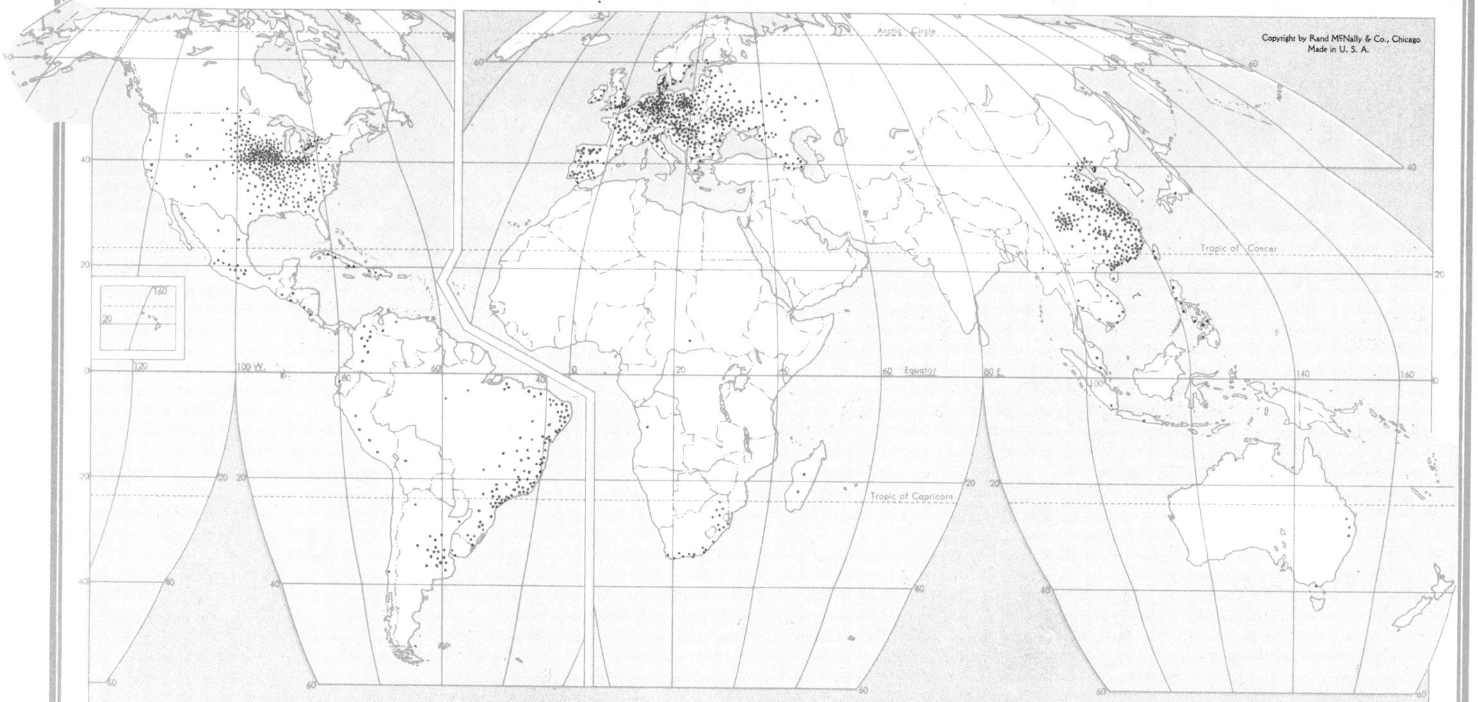

SWINE Each dot represents 500,000 head

SWINE

World Total — 288,700,000 head

0	10	20	30	40	50	60	70	80	90	100%
CHINA 22.4%		OTHER ASIA 6.2	GER. 6.5	POL. 3.4	FR. 2.4	OTHER EUROPE 13.9	UNITED STATES 16.7	OTHER N. AM. 4.5	SOV. UN. 11.2	BRAZIL 8.0	ALL OTHERS 4.8

ASIA — EUROPE — N. AMERICA

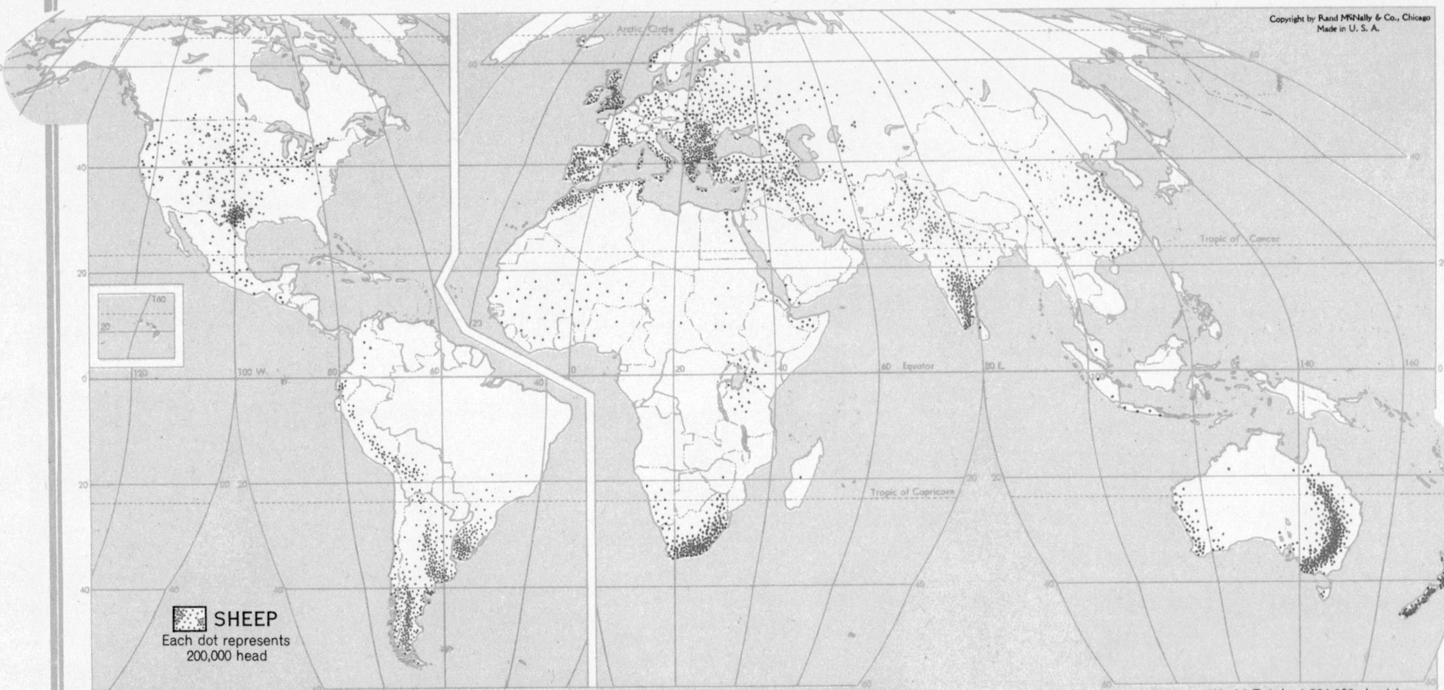

SHEEP
Each dot represents 200,000 head

SHEEP
World Total – 756,300,000 head

AUSTRALIA	N.Z.	INDIA & PAK.	CHINA	OTHER ASIA	U.K.	SPAIN	OTHER EUROPE	ARG.	OTHER S.A.	UN. OF S. AFR.	OTHER AFRICA	SOVIET UNION	U.S.
14.9%	4.1	5.8	3.4	9.5	3.4	2.6	11.3	5.9	7.5	5.3	7.9	10.5	6.8

OCEANIA — ASIA — EUROPE — S. AMERICA — AFRICA

WOOL EXPORTS
World Total – 1,224,000 short tons

AUSTRALIA	N.Z.	U.K. including re-exports	BEL. LUX.	FR.	ARGENTINA	UR.	OTHERS	UN. OF S. AFR.	IND.-PAK.	ALL OTH.
33.1%	10.9	12.6	4.2	2.3	11.8	3.9	2	9.4	2.3	4.5

OCEANIA — EUROPE — S. AMERICA — AFRICA

WOOL PRODUCTION
World Total – 1,888,000 short tons

AUSTRALIA	N.Z.	ARG.	UR.	OTHER	U.K.	OTHER EUROPE	UNITED STATES	UN. OF S. AFR.	SOV. UN.	CHINA	IND.-PAK.	ALL OTHERS
26.4%	7.9	9.6	2.9	3.0	2.9	11.9	11.8	6.6	5.6	3.2	2.6	5.6

OCEANIA — S. AMERICA — EUROPE

WOOL IMPORTS
World Total – 1,260,000 short tons

UNITED KINGDOM	GERMANY	BEL.- LUX.	ITALY	OTHER EUROPE	JAPAN	U.S.	SOV. UN.	OTH.
33.7%	14.3	8.9	3.8	18.6	8.1	8.0	2.5	2.1

EUROPE

FOREST REGIONS

- Conifers (softwoods)
- Temperate hardwoods
- Mixed hardwoods and softwoods
- Tropical hardwoods
- Commercial wood production

LUMBER EXPORTS
Estimated World Total – 504,933,000 cubic feet

CANADA	U.S.	SWEDEN	FINLAND	OTHER EUR.	ALL OTHERS
37.6%	12.3	13.9	11.4	5.7	19.1

N. AMERICA — EUROPE

USES OF WOOD

FUEL 53%
CONSTRUCTION 30%
PULP 7%
OTHER 6%
P.(?)
CROSSTIES 2%
PITPROPS 2%
INDUSTRIAL USES

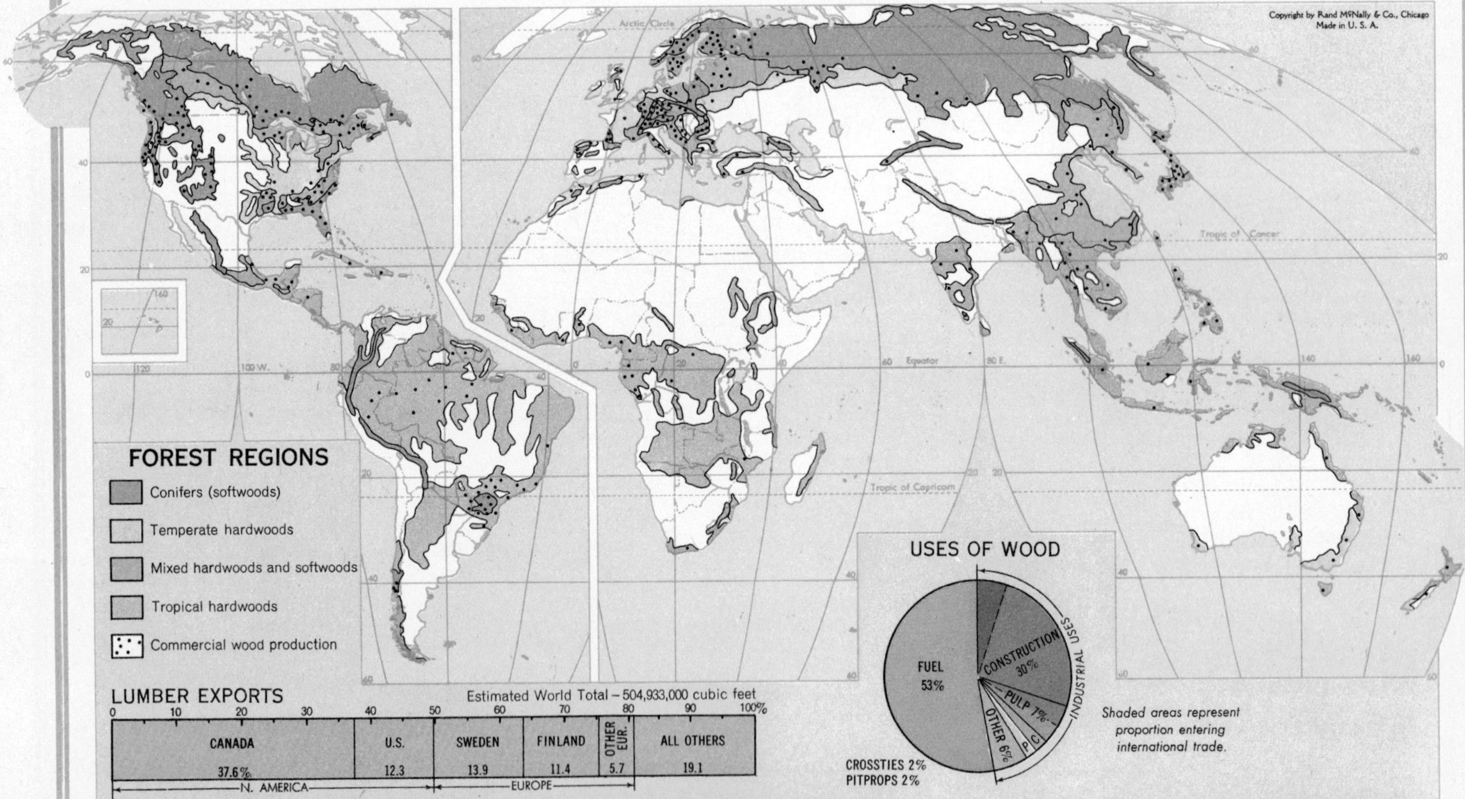

Shaded areas represent proportion entering international trade.

WOOD PULP & PULP PRODUCTS EXPORTS
Est. World Total – 10,520,000 short tons

CANADA	U.S.	SWEDEN	FINLAND	NOR.	OTHERS
56.8%	3.5	23.5	9.8	4.3	2

N. AMERICA — EUROPE

WOOD CUT
Estimated World Total – 49,787,000 cubic feet (round wood)

UNITED STATES	CAN.	GER.	SWE.	FIN.	OTHER EUROPE	SOVIET UNION	BRAZIL	JAPAN	CHINA	OTHER	AFRICA	UNKNOWN DISTRIBUTION
19.0%	5.9	4.3	2.7	2.1	11.3	17.7	7.8	4.9	2.7	3.1	2.9	13.2

N. AMERICA — EUROPE — LAT. AM. — ASIA — 1.1 AUSTL. & N.Z.

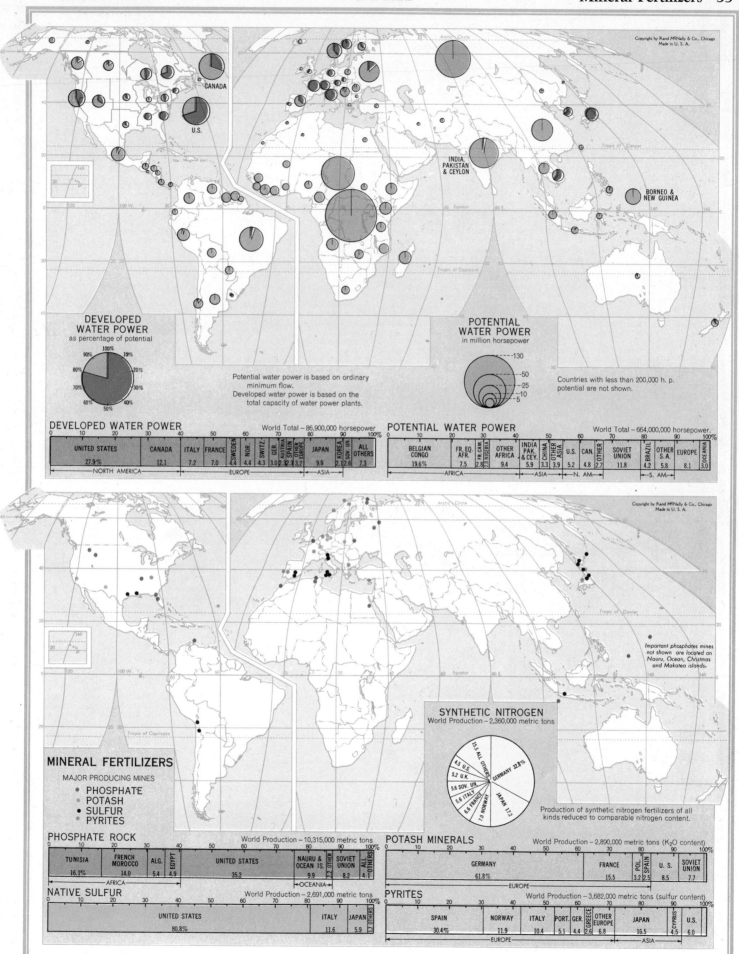

**DEVELOPED
WATER POWER**
as percentage of potential

**POTENTIAL
WATER POWER**
in million horsepower

Potential water power is based on ordinary
minimum flow.
Developed water power is based on the
total capacity of water power plants.

Countries with less than 200,000 h. p.
potential are not shown.

DEVELOPED WATER POWER

World Total – 86,900,000 horsepower

UNITED STATES	CANADA	ITALY	FRANCE	SWEDEN	NOR.	SWITZ.	GER.	AUSTRIA	SPAIN	OTHER EUROPE	JAPAN	KOREA	SOV. UN.	ALL OTHERS
27.9%	12.1	7.2	7.0	4.4	4.4	4.3	3.0	2.3	2.3	3.2	9.9	2.1	2.6	7.3

NORTH AMERICA — EUROPE — ASIA

POTENTIAL WATER POWER

World Total – 664,000,000 horsepower.

BELGIAN CONGO	FR. EQ. AFR.	FR. CAM. NIGERIA	OTHER AFRICA	INDIA PAK. & CEY.	CHINA	OTHER ASIA	U.S.	CAN.	SOVIET UNION	BRAZIL	OTHER S.A.	EUROPE	OCEANIA
19.6%	7.5	2.8 2.0	9.4	5.9	3.3	3.9	5.2	4.8	11.8	4.2	5.8	8.1	3.0

AFRICA — ASIA — N. AM. — S. AM.

Important phosphates mines
not shown are located on
Nauru, Ocean, Christmas
and Makatea islands.

MINERAL FERTILIZERS

MAJOR PRODUCING MINES

- PHOSPHATE
- POTASH
- SULFUR
- PYRITES

SYNTHETIC NITROGEN
World Production – 2,360,000 metric tons

- 15.5 ALL OTHERS
- 4.5 U.S.
- 5.2 U.K.
- 5.6 SOV. UN.
- 5.6 ITALY
- 6.6 FRANCE
- 7.0 NORWAY
- GERMANY 32.8%
- JAPAN 17.2

Production of synthetic nitrogen fertilizers of all
kinds reduced to comparable nitrogen content.

PHOSPHATE ROCK

World Production – 10,315,000 metric tons

TUNISIA	FRENCH MOROCCO	ALG.	EGYPT	UNITED STATES	NAURU & OCEAN IS.	OTHER	SOVIET UNION	ALL OTHERS
16.1%	14.0	5.4	4.9	35.2	9.9	2.7	8.2	4.1

AFRICA — OCEANIA

POTASH MINERALS

World Production – 2,890,000 metric tons (K$_2$O content)

GERMANY	FRANCE	POL.	SPAIN	U.S.	SOVIET UNION
61.8%	15.5	3.2	2.5	8.5	7.7

EUROPE

NATIVE SULFUR

World Production – 2,691,000 metric tons

UNITED STATES	ITALY	JAPAN	OTHERS
80.8%	11.6	5.9	1.7

PYRITES

World Production – 3,682,000 metric tons (sulfur content)

SPAIN	NORWAY	ITALY	PORT.	GER.	GREECE	OTHER EUROPE	JAPAN	CYPRUS	U.S.
30.4%	11.9	10.4	5.1	4.4	2.6	6.8	16.5	4.5	6.0

EUROPE — ASIA

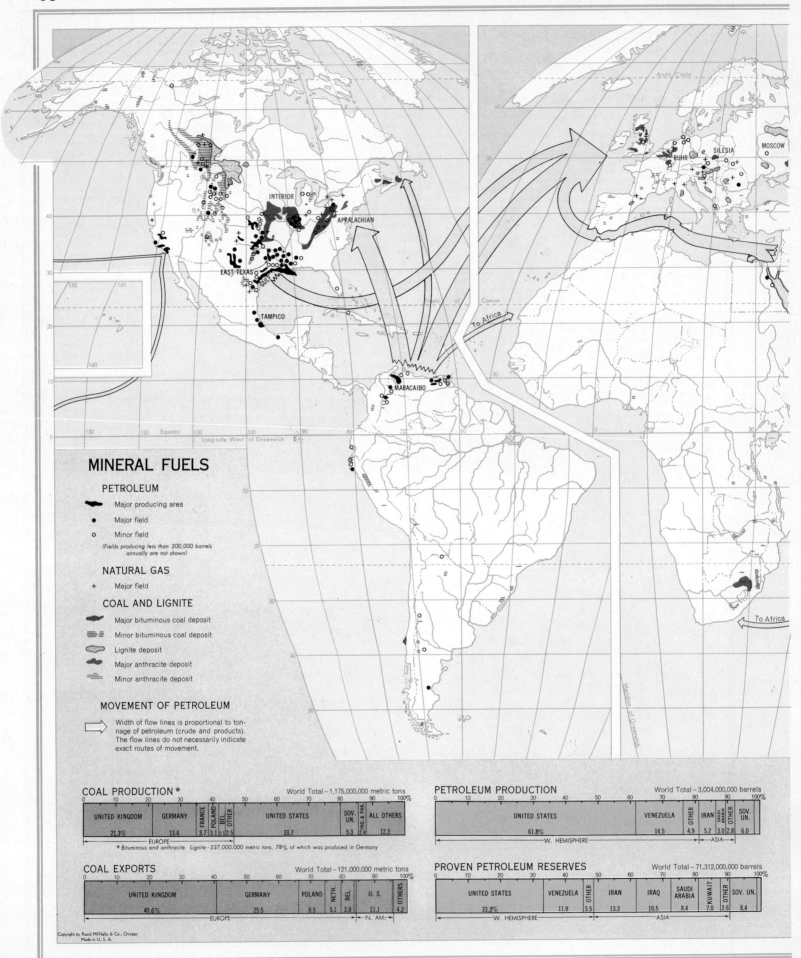

MINERAL FUELS

PETROLEUM

- ⬣ Major producing area
- ● Major field
- ○ Minor field

  (Fields producing less than 200,000 barrels annually are not shown)

NATURAL GAS

- + Major field

COAL AND LIGNITE

- ⬤ Major bituminous coal deposit
- ☰ Minor bituminous coal deposit
- ◯ Lignite deposit
- ⬛ Major anthracite deposit
- ☰ Minor anthracite deposit

MOVEMENT OF PETROLEUM

⇨ Width of flow lines is proportional to tonnage of petroleum (crude and products). The flow lines do not necessarily indicate exact routes of movement.

Map labels: INTERIOR, APPALACHIAN, EAST TEXAS, GULF, TAMPICO, MARACAIBO, To Africa, RUHR, SILESIA, MOSCOW, Arctic Circle, Tropic of Cancer, Equator, Longitude West of Greenwich, Meridian of Greenwich

COAL PRODUCTION *

World Total – 1,175,000,000 metric tons

UNITED KINGDOM	GERMANY	FRANCE	POLAND	BEL.	OTHER	UNITED STATES	SOV. UN.	IND. & PAK.	ALL OTHERS
21.3%	13.6	3.7	3.1	2	2.5	33.7	5.3	2.4	12.3

← EUROPE →

* Bituminous and anthracite. Lignite – 237,000,000 metric tons, 78% of which was produced in Germany

COAL EXPORTS

World Total – 121,000,000 metric tons

UNITED KINGDOM	GERMANY	POLAND	NETH.	BEL.	U. S.	OTHERS
40.6%	25.5	8.5	5.1	3.9	11.1	4.2

← EUROPE →   ← N. AM. →

PETROLEUM PRODUCTION

World Total – 3,004,000,000 barrels

UNITED STATES	VENEZUELA	OTHER	IRAN	SAUDI ARABIA	OTHER	SOV. UN.
61.8%	14.5	4.9	5.2	3.0	2.8	6.0

← W. HEMISPHERE →   ← ASIA →

PROVEN PETROLEUM RESERVES

World Total – 71,312,000,000 barrels

UNITED STATES	VENEZUELA	OTHER	IRAN	IRAQ	SAUDI ARABIA	KUWAIT	OTHER	SOV. UN.
33.3%	11.9	3.5	13.3	10.5	8.4	7.0	2.6	8.4

← W. HEMISPHERE →   ← ASIA →

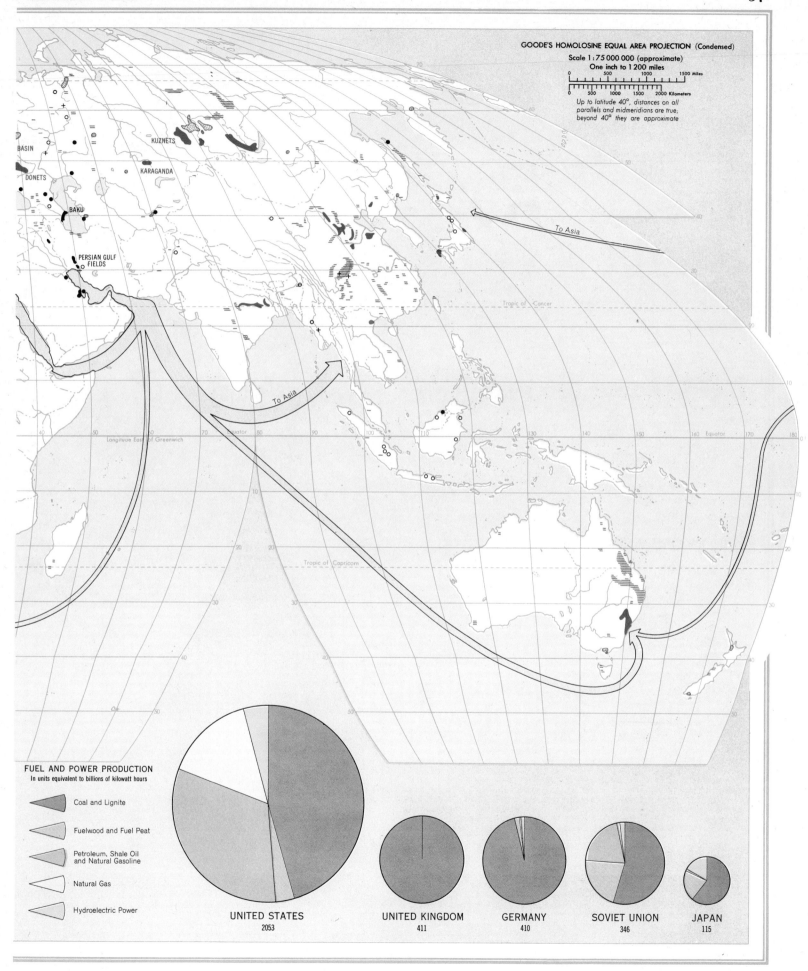

GOODE'S HOMOLOSINE EQUAL AREA PROJECTION (Condensed)

Scale 1:75 000 000 (approximate)
One inch to 1 200 miles

Up to latitude 40°, distances on all
parallels and midmeridians are true,
beyond 40° they are approximate

KUZNETS

BASIN

DONETS

KARAGANDA

BAKU

PERSIAN GULF
FIELDS

To Asia

To Asia

Tropic of Cancer

Longituae East of Greenwich

Equator

Equator

Tropic of Capricorn

FUEL AND POWER PRODUCTION
In units equivalent to billions of kilowatt hours

Coal and Lignite

Fuelwood and Fuel Peat

Petroleum, Shale Oil
and Natural Gasoline

Natural Gas

Hydroelectric Power

UNITED STATES
2053

UNITED KINGDOM
411

GERMANY
410

SOVIET UNION
346

JAPAN
115

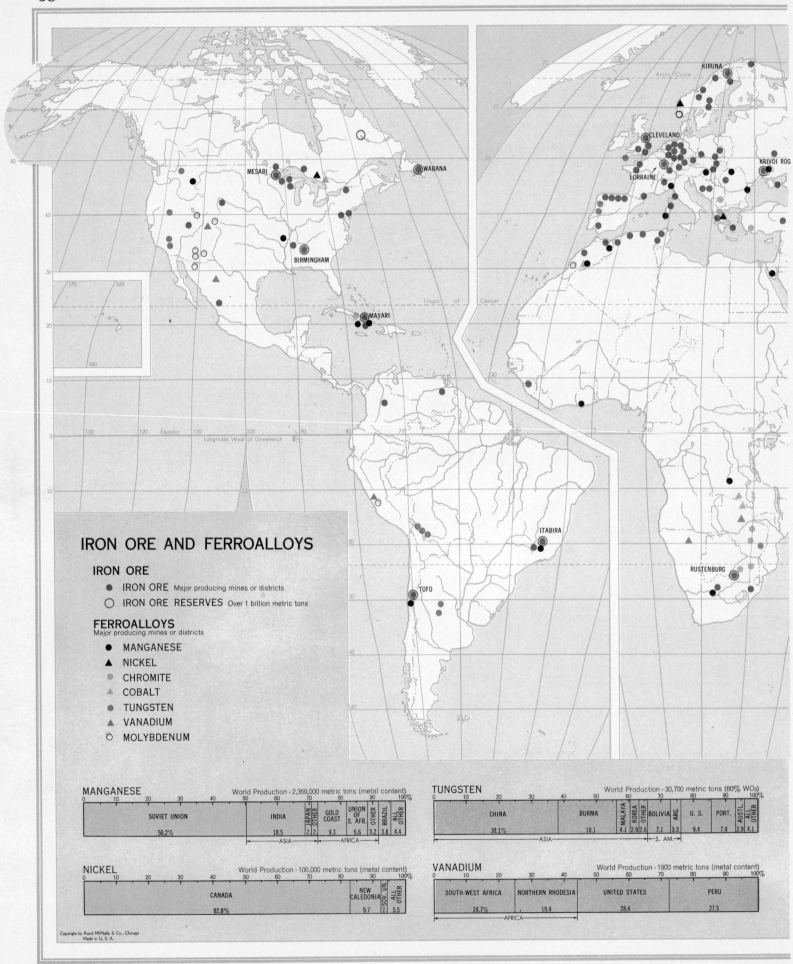

IRON ORE AND FERROALLOYS

IRON ORE

- ● IRON ORE Major producing mines or districts
- ○ IRON ORE RESERVES Over 1 billion metric tons

FERROALLOYS
Major producing mines or districts

- ● MANGANESE
- ▲ NICKEL
- ● CHROMITE
- ▲ COBALT
- ● TUNGSTEN
- ▲ VANADIUM
- ○ MOLYBDENUM

Map labels: KIRUNA, CLEVELAND, KRIVOI ROG, LORRAINE, MESABI, WABANA, BIRMINGHAM, MAYARI, ITABIRA, TOFO, RUSTENBURG

MANGANESE — World Production - 2,369,000 metric tons (metal content)

0	10	20	30	40	50	60	70	80	90	100%

SOVIET UNION 50.2%	INDIA 18.5	JAPAN 2.2	OTHER	GOLD COAST 9.3	UNION OF S. AFR. 6.6	OTHER 3.2	BRAZIL 3.8	ALL OTHER 4.4

— ASIA — — AFRICA —

NICKEL — World Production - 106,000 metric tons (metal content)

0	10	20	30	40	50	60	70	80	90	100%

CANADA 82.8%	NEW CALEDONIA 9.7	SOV. UN. 2.	ALL OTHER 5.5

TUNGSTEN — World Production - 30,700 metric tons (60% WO₃)

0	10	20	30	40	50	60	70	80	90	100%

CHINA 38.1%	BURMA 18.1	MALAYA 4.1	KOREA 2.9	OTHER 2.6	BOLIVIA 7.1	ARG. 3.3	U.S. 9.4	PORT. 7.4	AUSTL. 2.9	ALL OTHER 4.1

— ASIA — — S. AM. —

VANADIUM — World Production - 1900 metric tons (metal content)

0	10	20	30	40	50	60	70	80	90	100%

SOUTH-WEST AFRICA 24.7%	NORTHERN RHODESIA 19.4	UNITED STATES 28.4	PERU 27.5

— AFRICA —

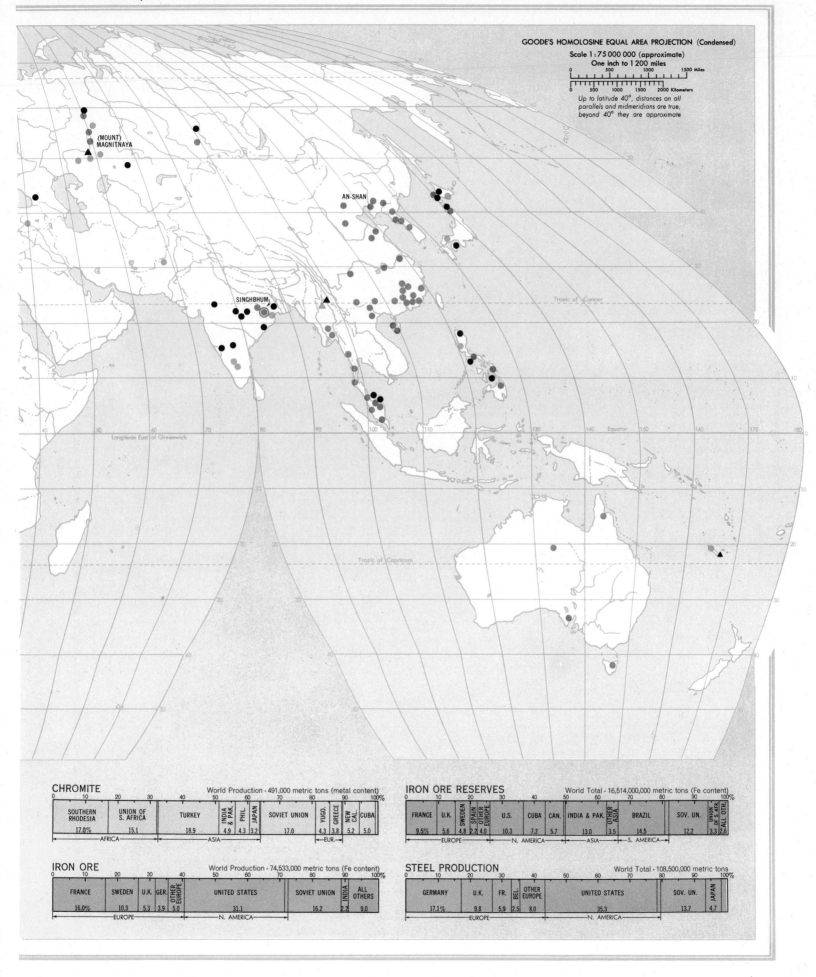

GOODE'S HOMOLOSINE EQUAL AREA PROJECTION (Condensed)
Scale 1 : 75 000 000 (approximate)
One inch to 1 200 miles

Up to latitude 40°, distances on all
parallels and midmeridians are true,
beyond 40° they are approximate

(MOUNT) MAGNITNAYA

AN-SHAN

SINGHBHUM

CHROMITE

World Production · 491,000 metric tons (metal content)

SOUTHERN RHODESIA	UNION OF S. AFRICA	TURKEY	INDIA & PAK.	PHIL.	JAPAN	SOVIET UNION	YUGO.	GREECE	NEW CAL.	CUBA
17.0%	15.1	18.9	4.9	4.3	3.2	17.0	4.3	3.8	5.2	5.0
←AFRICA→		←————————————ASIA————————————→					←————EUR.————→			

IRON ORE RESERVES

World Total · 16,514,000,000 metric tons (Fe content)

FRANCE	U.K.	SWEDEN	SPAIN	OTHER EUROPE	U.S.	CUBA	CAN.	INDIA & PAK.	OTHER ASIA	BRAZIL	SOV. UN.	UNION OF S. AFR.	ALL OTH.
9.5%	5.6	4.8	2.2	4.0	10.3	7.2	5.7	13.0	3.5	14.5	12.2	3.3	2.6
←————EUROPE————→					←——N. AMERICA——→			←——ASIA——→		←S. AMERICA→		

IRON ORE

World Production · 74,533,000 metric tons (Fe content)

FRANCE	SWEDEN	U.K.	GER.	OTHER EUROPE	UNITED STATES	SOVIET UNION	INDIA	ALL OTHERS
16.0%	10.3	5.3	3.9	5.0	31.1	16.2	2.2	9.0
←————EUROPE————→					←——N. AMERICA——→			

STEEL PRODUCTION

World Total · 108,500,000 metric tons

GERMANY	U.K.	FR.	BEL.	OTHER EUROPE	UNITED STATES	SOV. UN.	JAPAN
17.1%	9.8	5.9	2.5	8.0	35.3	13.7	4.7
←————EUROPE————→					←——N. AMERICA——→		

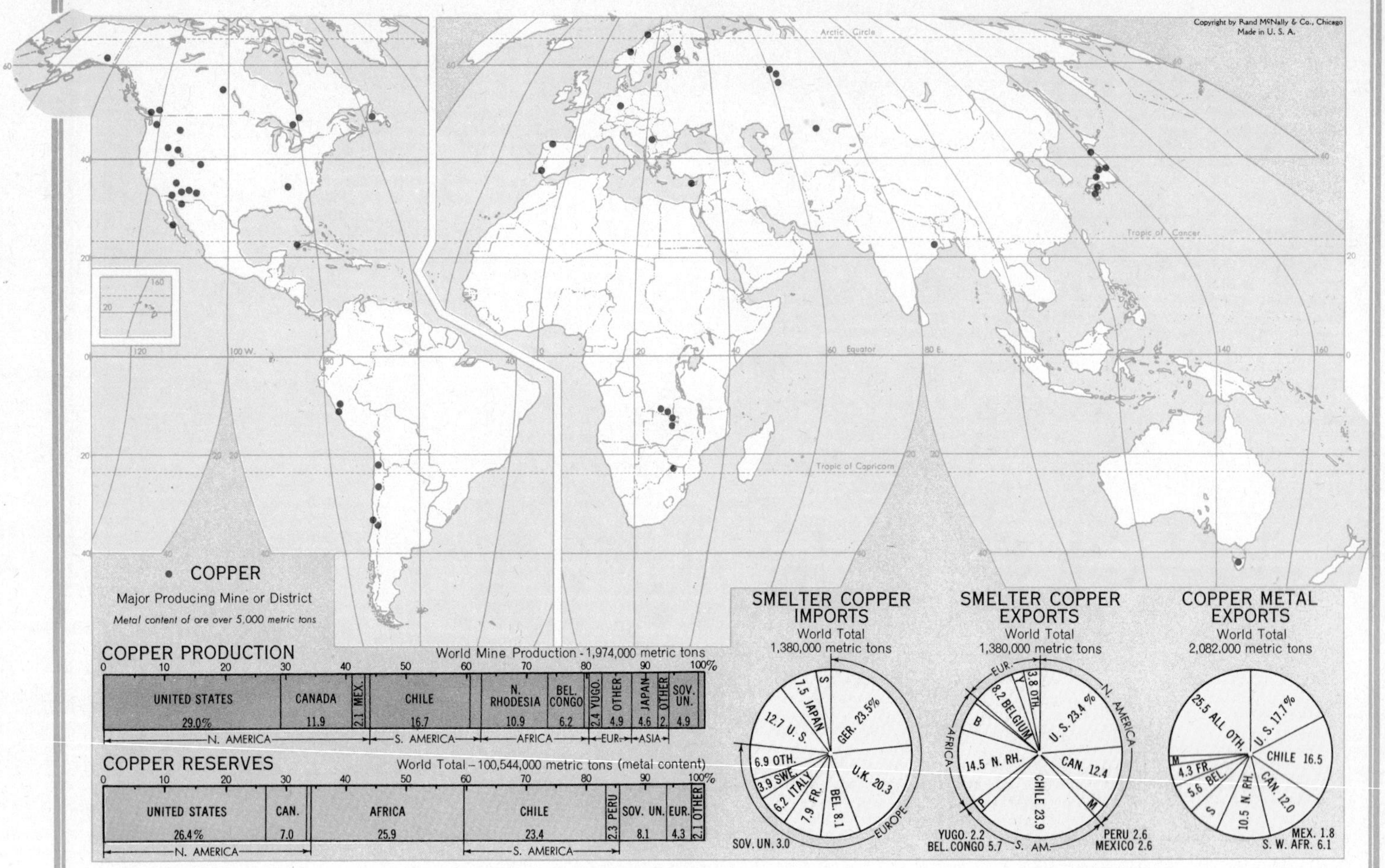

• COPPER

Major Producing Mine or District
Metal content of ore over 5,000 metric tons

COPPER PRODUCTION

World Mine Production – 1,974,000 metric tons

0	10	20	30	40	50	60	70	80	90	100%

| UNITED STATES 29.0% | CANADA 11.9 | MEX. 2.1 | CHILE 16.7 | N. RHODESIA 10.9 | BEL. CONGO 6.2 | YUGO. OTHER 2.4 | OTHER 4.9 | JAPAN 4.6 | OTHER 2 | SOV. UN. 4.9 |

← N. AMERICA →   ← S. AMERICA →   ← AFRICA →   ←EUR.→ ←ASIA→

COPPER RESERVES

World Total – 100,544,000 metric tons (metal content)

0	10	20	30	40	50	60	70	80	90	100%

| UNITED STATES 26.4% | CAN. 7.0 | AFRICA 25.9 | CHILE 23.4 | PERU 2.3 | SOV. UN. 8.1 | EUR. 4.3 | OTHER 2.1 |

← N. AMERICA →   ← S. AMERICA →

SMELTER COPPER IMPORTS
World Total
1,380,000 metric tons

S
7.5 JAPAN
12.7 U.S.
6.9 OTH.
3.9 SWE.
6.2 ITALY
7.3 FR.
BEL. 8.1
U.K. 20.3
GER. 23.5%
SOV. UN. 3.0

SMELTER COPPER EXPORTS
World Total
1,380,000 metric tons

EUR.
3.8 OTH.
8.2 BELGIUM
B
14.5 N. RH.
P
CHILE 23.9
MF
CAN. 12.4
U. S. 23.4%
N. AMERICA
YUGO. 2.2
BEL. CONGO 5.7
PERU 2.6
MEXICO 2.6
S. AM.
AFRICA
EUROPE

COPPER METAL EXPORTS
World Total
2,082,000 metric tons

25.5 ALL OTH.
M
4.3 FR.
5.6 BEL.
S
10.5 N. RH.
U. S. 17.1%
CHILE 16.5
CAN. 12.0
MEX. 1.8
S. W. AFR. 6.1

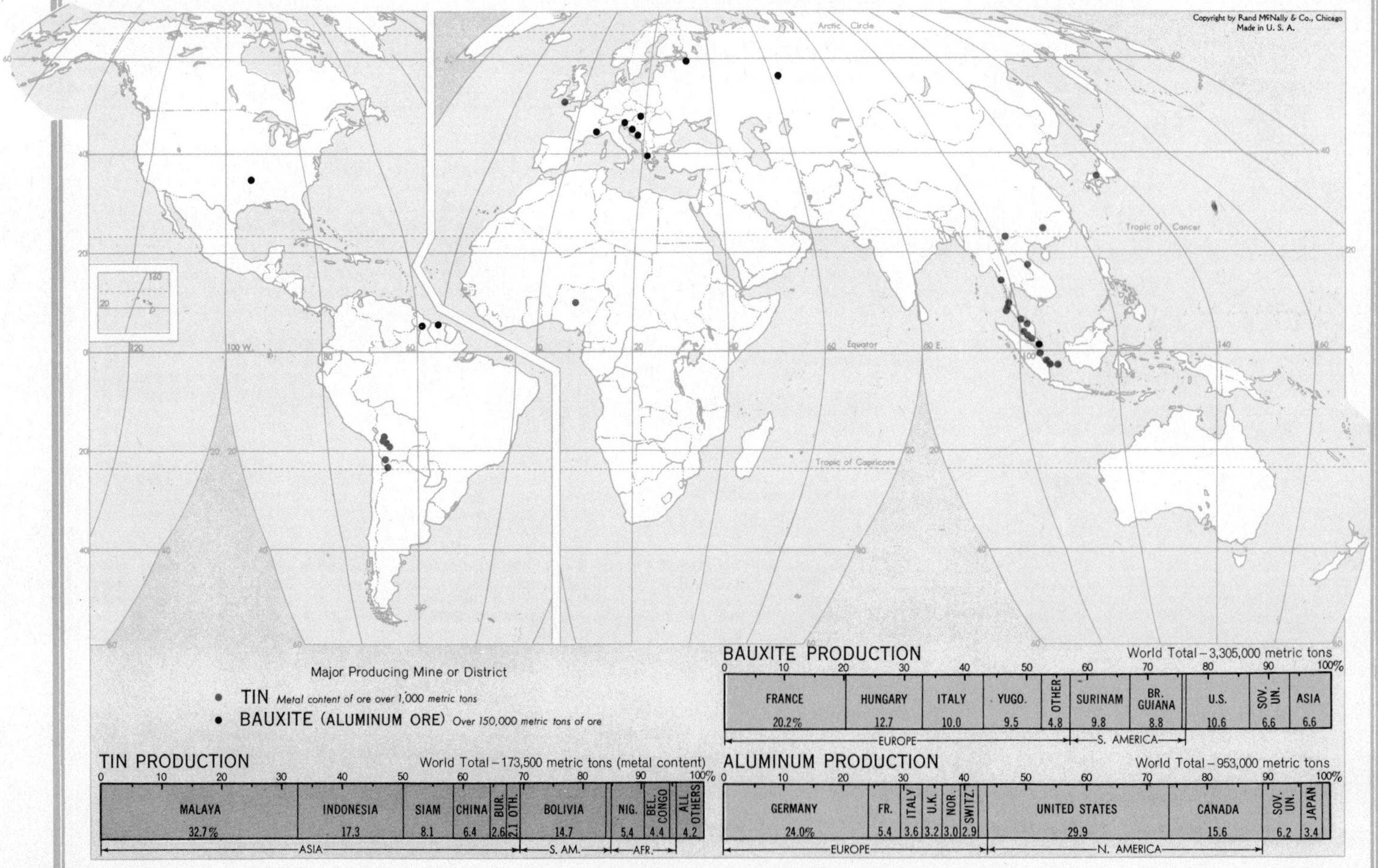

Major Producing Mine or District

• TIN *Metal content of ore over 1,000 metric tons*

• BAUXITE (ALUMINUM ORE) *Over 150,000 metric tons of ore*

BAUXITE PRODUCTION

World Total – 3,305,000 metric tons

0	10	20	30	40	50	60	70	80	90	100%

| FRANCE 20.2% | HUNGARY 12.7 | ITALY 10.0 | YUGO. 9.5 | OTHER 4.8 | SURINAM 9.8 | BR. GUIANA 8.8 | U.S. 10.6 | SOV. UN. 6.6 | ASIA 6.6 |

← EUROPE →   ← S. AMERICA →

TIN PRODUCTION

World Total – 173,500 metric tons (metal content)

0	10	20	30	40	50	60	70	80	90	100%

| MALAYA 32.7% | INDONESIA 17.3 | SIAM 8.1 | CHINA 6.4 | BUR. 2.1 | OTH. | BOLIVIA 14.7 | NIG. 5.4 | BEL. CONGO 4.4 | ALL OTHERS 4.2 |

← ASIA →   ← S. AM. →   ←AFR.→

ALUMINUM PRODUCTION

World Total – 953,000 metric tons

0	10	20	30	40	50	60	70	80	90	100%

| GERMANY 24.0% | FR. 5.4 | ITALY 3.6 | U.K. 3.2 | NOR. 3.0 | SWITZ. 2.9 | UNITED STATES 29.9 | CANADA 15.6 | SOV. UN. 6.2 | JAPAN 3.4 |

← EUROPE →   ← N. AMERICA →

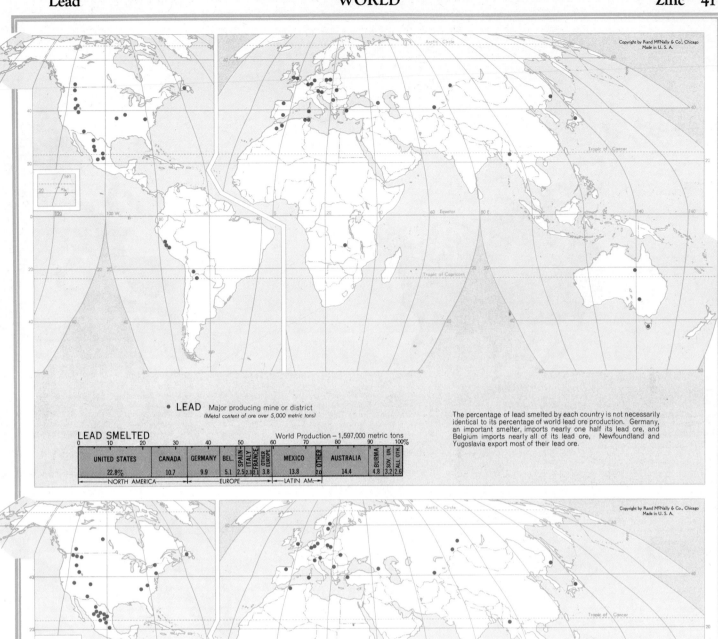

● **LEAD** Major producing mine or district
(Metal content of ore over 5,000 metric tons)

LEAD SMELTED   World Production – 1,597,000 metric tons

0	10	20	30	40	50	60	70	80	90				100%
UNITED STATES		CANADA	GERMANY	BEL.	SPAIN	ITALY	FRANCE	OTHER EUROPE	MEXICO	OTHER	AUSTRALIA	BURMA	SOV. UN.	ALL OTH.
22.8%		10.7	9.9	5.1	2.5	2.3	2.1	3.8	13.8	2.0	14.4	4.8	3.2	2.6

NORTH AMERICA ——— EUROPE ——— LATIN AM. ———

The percentage of lead smelted by each country is not necessarily identical to its percentage of world lead ore production. Germany, an important smelter, imports nearly one half its lead ore, and Belgium imports nearly all of its lead ore, Newfoundland and Yugoslavia export most of their lead ore.

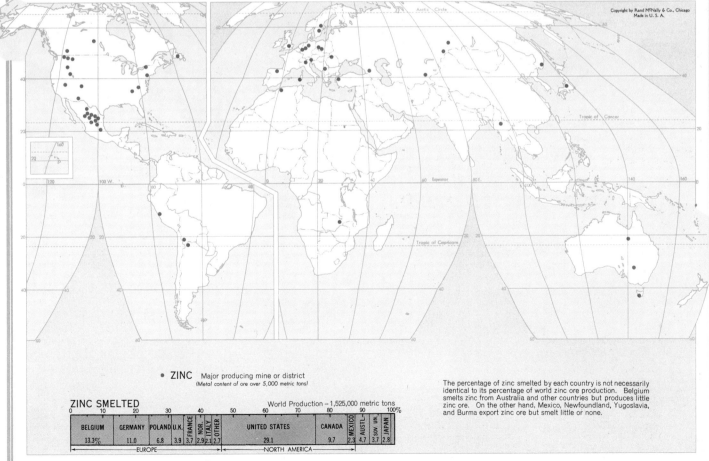

● **ZINC** Major producing mine or district
(Metal content of ore over 5,000 metric tons)

ZINC SMELTED   World Production – 1,525,000 metric tons

0	10	20	30	40	50	60	70	80	90			100%
BELGIUM	GERMANY	POLAND	U.K.	FRANCE	NOR.	ITALY	OTHER	UNITED STATES		CANADA	MEXICO	AUSTL.	SOV. UN.	JAPAN
13.3%	11.0	6.8	3.9	3.7	2.9	2.1	2.7	29.1		9.7	2.3	4.7	3.7	2.8

EUROPE ——— NORTH AMERICA ———

The percentage of zinc smelted by each country is not necessarily identical to its percentage of world zinc ore production. Belgium smelts zinc from Australia and other countries but produces little zinc ore. On the other hand, Mexico, Newfoundland, Yugoslavia, and Burma export zinc ore but smelt little or none.

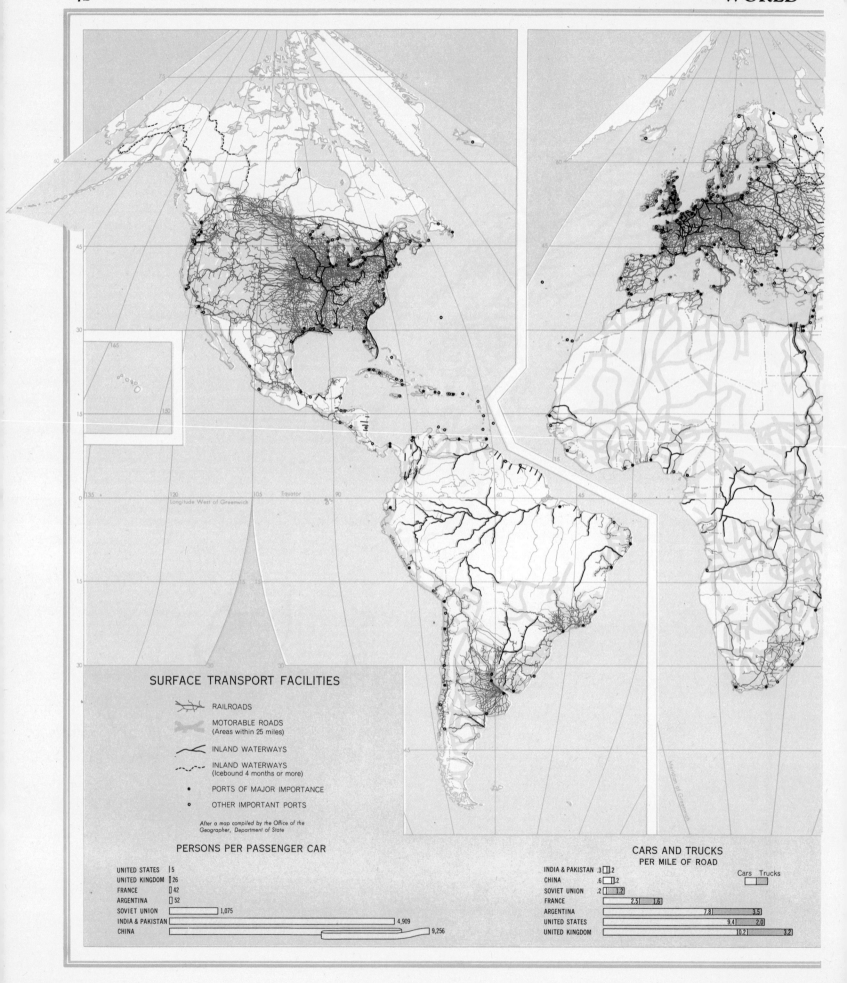

SURFACE TRANSPORT FACILITIES

RAILROADS

MOTORABLE ROADS
(Areas within 25 miles)

INLAND WATERWAYS

INLAND WATERWAYS
(Icebound 4 months or more)

● PORTS OF MAJOR IMPORTANCE

○ OTHER IMPORTANT PORTS

*After a map compiled by the Office of the
Geographer, Department of State*

PERSONS PER PASSENGER CAR

UNITED STATES	5
UNITED KINGDOM	26
FRANCE	42
ARGENTINA	52
SOVIET UNION	1,075
INDIA & PAKISTAN	4,909
CHINA	9,256

CARS AND TRUCKS
PER MILE OF ROAD

Cars   Trucks

	Cars	Trucks
INDIA & PAKISTAN	.3	.2
CHINA	.6	.2
SOVIET UNION	.2	1.2
FRANCE	2.5	1.6
ARGENTINA	7.8	3.5
UNITED STATES	9.4	2.0
UNITED KINGDOM	10.2	3.2

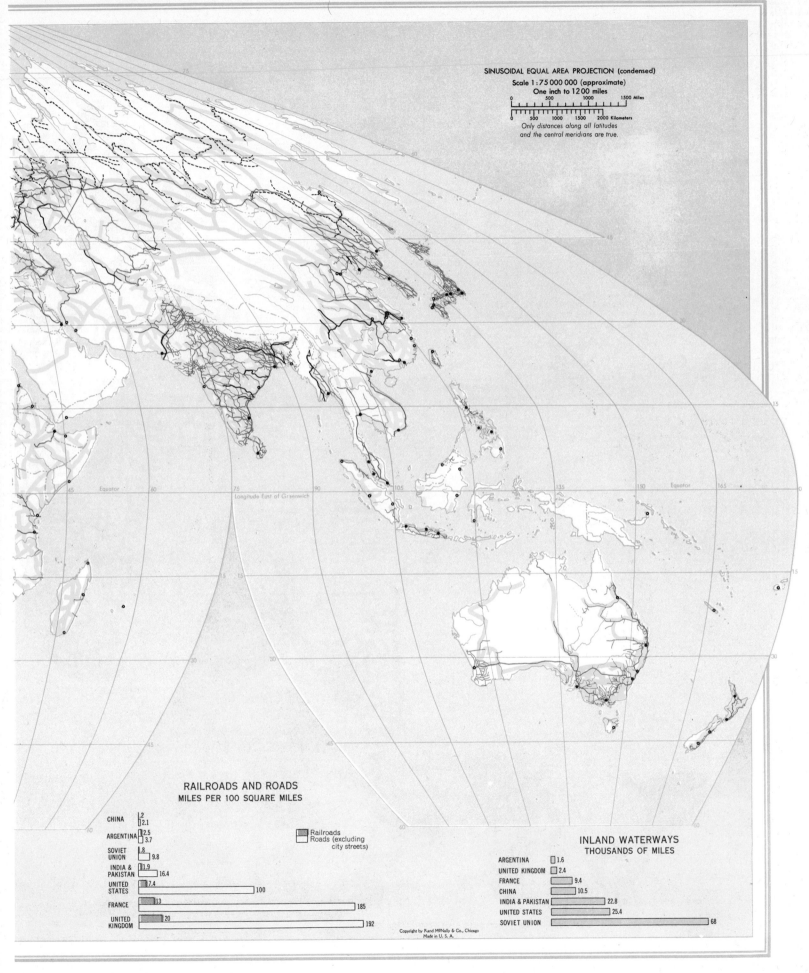

SINUSOIDAL EQUAL AREA PROJECTION (condensed)
Scale 1 : 75 000 000 (approximate)
One inch to 1200 miles

Only distances along all latitudes
and the central meridians are true.

RAILROADS AND ROADS
MILES PER 100 SQUARE MILES

CHINA	.2	
	2.1	
ARGENTINA	2.5	
	3.7	
SOVIET UNION	.8	
	9.8	
INDIA & PAKISTAN	1.9	
	16.4	
UNITED STATES	7.4	
	100	
FRANCE	13	
	185	
UNITED KINGDOM	20	
	192	

Railroads
Roads (excluding city streets)

INLAND WATERWAYS
THOUSANDS OF MILES

ARGENTINA	1.6
UNITED KINGDOM	2.4
FRANCE	9.4
CHINA	10.5
INDIA & PAKISTAN	22.8
UNITED STATES	25.4
SOVIET UNION	68

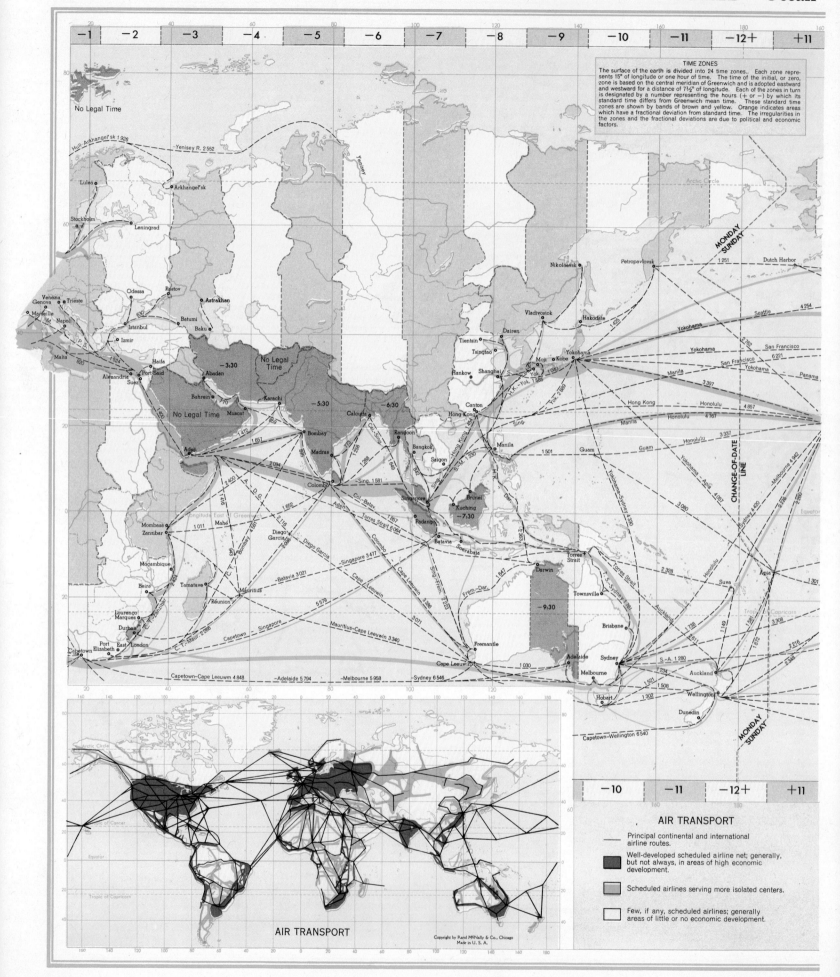

TIME ZONES
The surface of the earth is divided into 24 time zones. Each zone represents 15° of longitude or one hour of time. The time of the initial, or zero, zone is based on the central meridian of Greenwich and is adopted eastward and westward for a distance of 7½° of longitude. Each of the zones in turn is designated by a number representing the hours (+ or −) by which its standard time differs from Greenwich mean time. These standard time zones are shown by bands of brown and yellow. Orange indicates areas which have a fractional deviation from standard time. The irregularities in the zones and the fractional deviations are due to political and economic factors.

AIR TRANSPORT

—— Principal continental and international airline routes.

Well-developed scheduled airline net; generally, but not always, in areas of high economic development.

Scheduled airlines serving more isolated centers.

Few, if any, scheduled airlines; generally areas of little or no economic development.

AIR TRANSPORT

Copyright by Rand McNally & Co., Chicago
Made in U.S.A.

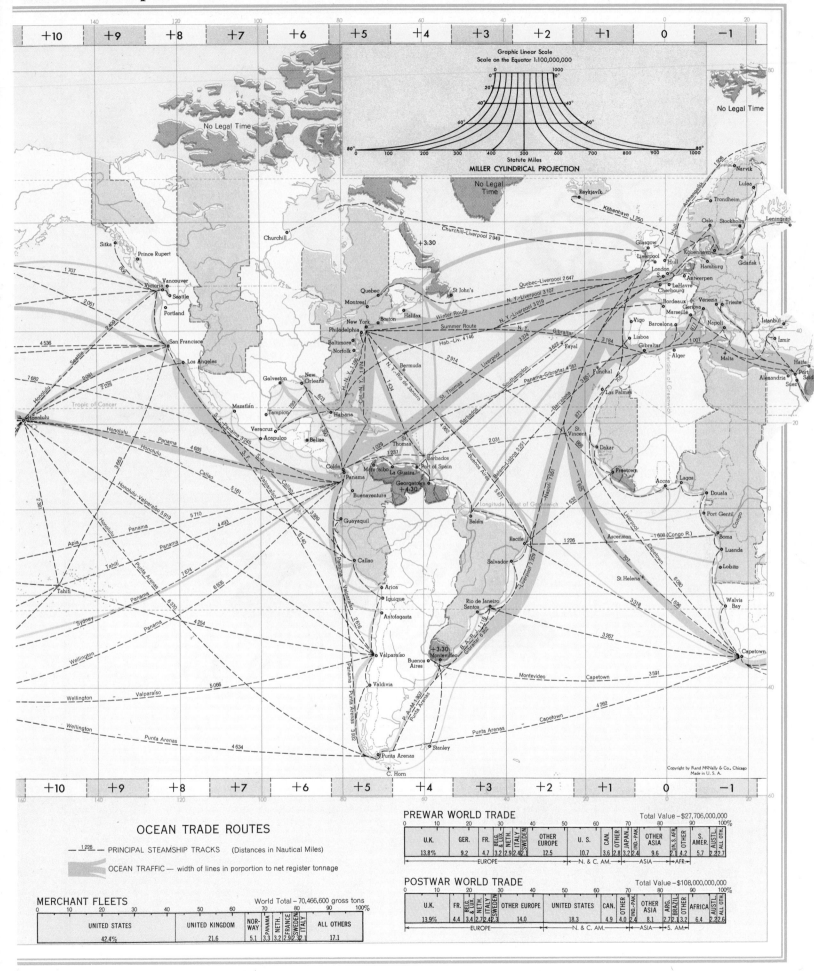

| +10 | +9 | +8 | +7 | +6 | +5 | +4 | +3 | +2 | +1 | 0 | −1 |

Graphic Linear Scale
Scale on the Equator 1:100,000,000

MILLER CYLINDRICAL PROJECTION

OCEAN TRADE ROUTES

1,226 — PRINCIPAL STEAMSHIP TRACKS (Distances in Nautical Miles)

OCEAN TRAFFIC — width of lines in porportion to net register tonnage

PREWAR WORLD TRADE

Total Value – $27,706,000,000

U.K.	GER.	FR.	BELG. & LUX.	NETH.	ITALY	SWEDEN	OTHER EUROPE	U.S.	CAN.	OTHER	JAPAN	IND.-PAK.	OTHER ASIA	UN. S. AFR.	OTHER	S. AMER.	AUSTL.	ALL OTH.
13.8%	9.2	4.7	3.2	2.9	2.4	2.1	12.5	10.7	3.6	2.8			9.6	7.1	4.2	5.7	2.2	2.7

EUROPE — N. & C. AM. — ASIA — AFR.

POSTWAR WORLD TRADE

Total Value – $108,000,000,000

U.K.	FR.	BELG. & LUX.	NETH.	ITALY	SWEDEN	OTHER EUROPE	UNITED STATES	CAN.	OTHER	IND.-PAK.	OTHER ASIA	ARG.	BRAZIL	OTHER	AFRICA	AUSTL.	ALL OTH.
13.9%	4.4	3.4	2.7	2.3	2.3	14.0	18.3	4.9	4.0	2.4	8.1	2.7	2.1	3.2	6.4	2.2	2.6

EUROPE — N. & C. AM. — ASIA — S. AM.

MERCHANT FLEETS

World Total – 70,466,600 gross tons

UNITED STATES	UNITED KINGDOM	NOR-WAY	PANAMA	NETH.	FRANCE	SWEDEN	ITALY	ALL OTHERS
42.4%	21.6	5.1	3.3	3.2	2.9	2.3	2.1	17.1

Copyright by Rand McNally & Co., Chicago
Made in U.S.A.

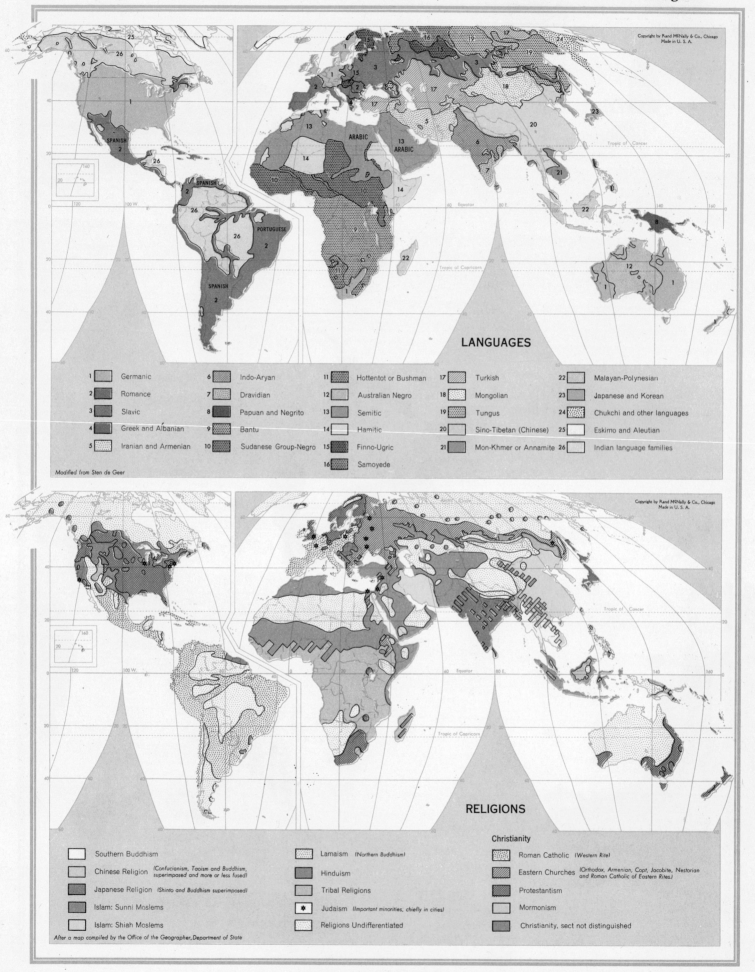

LANGUAGES

Copyright by Rand McNally & Co., Chicago
Made in U.S.A.

1	Germanic	6	Indo-Aryan	11	Hottentot or Bushman	17	Turkish	22	Malayan-Polynesian
2	Romance	7	Dravidian	12	Australian Negro	18	Mongolian	23	Japanese and Korean
3	Slavic	8	Papuan and Negrito	13	Semitic	19	Tungus	24	Chukchi and other languages
4	Greek and Albanian	9	Bantu	14	Hamitic	20	Sino-Tibetan (Chinese)	25	Eskimo and Aleutian
5	Iranian and Armenian	10	Sudanese Group-Negro	15	Finno-Ugric	21	Mon-Khmer or Annamite	26	Indian language families
				16	Samoyede				

Modified from Sten de Geer

RELIGIONS

Copyright by Rand McNally & Co., Chicago
Made in U.S.A.

			Christianity	
Southern Buddhism		Lamaism (Northern Buddhism)	Roman Catholic (Western Rite)	
Chinese Religion (Confucianism, Taoism and Buddhism, superimposed and more or less fused)		Hinduism	Eastern Churches (Orthodox, Armenian, Copt, Jacobite, Nestorian and Roman Catholic of Eastern Rites.)	
Japanese Religion (Shinto and Buddhism superimposed)		Tribal Religions	Protestantism	
Islam: Sunni Moslems		Judaism (Important minorities, chiefly in cities)	Mormonism	
Islam: Shiah Moslems		Religions Undifferentiated	Christianity, sect not distinguished	

After a map compiled by the Office of the Geographer, Department of State

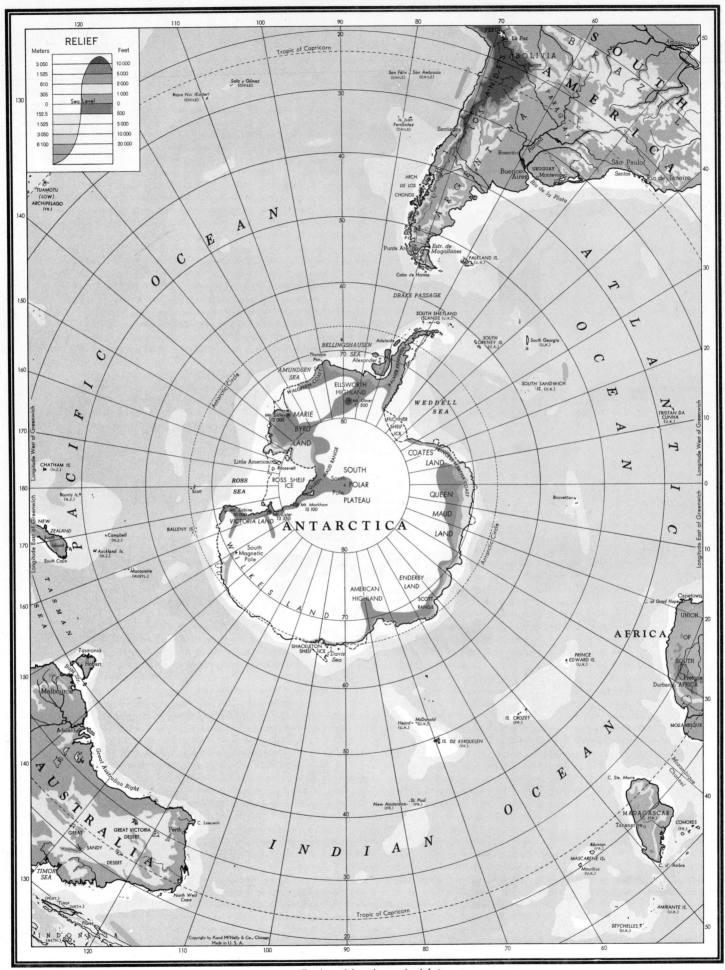

RELIEF

Meters		Feet
3 050		10 000
1 525		5 000
610		2 000
305		1 000
152.5	Sea Level	500
0		0
152.5		500
1 525		5 000
3 050		10 000
6 100		20 000

Elevations and depressions are given in feet
LAMBERTS AZIMUTHAL EQUAL-AREA PROJECTION
Scale 1:60,000,000 (approximate)

RELIEF

Meters		Feet
3 050		10 000
1 525		5 000
610		2 000
305		1 000
0	Sea Level	0
152.5		500
1 525		5 000
3 050		10 000
6 100		20 000

Copyright by Rand McNally & Co., Chicago
Made in U.S.A.

Elevations and depressions are given in feet
LAMBERT AZIMUTHAL EQUAL-AREA PROJECTION
Scale 1:60,000,000 (approximate)

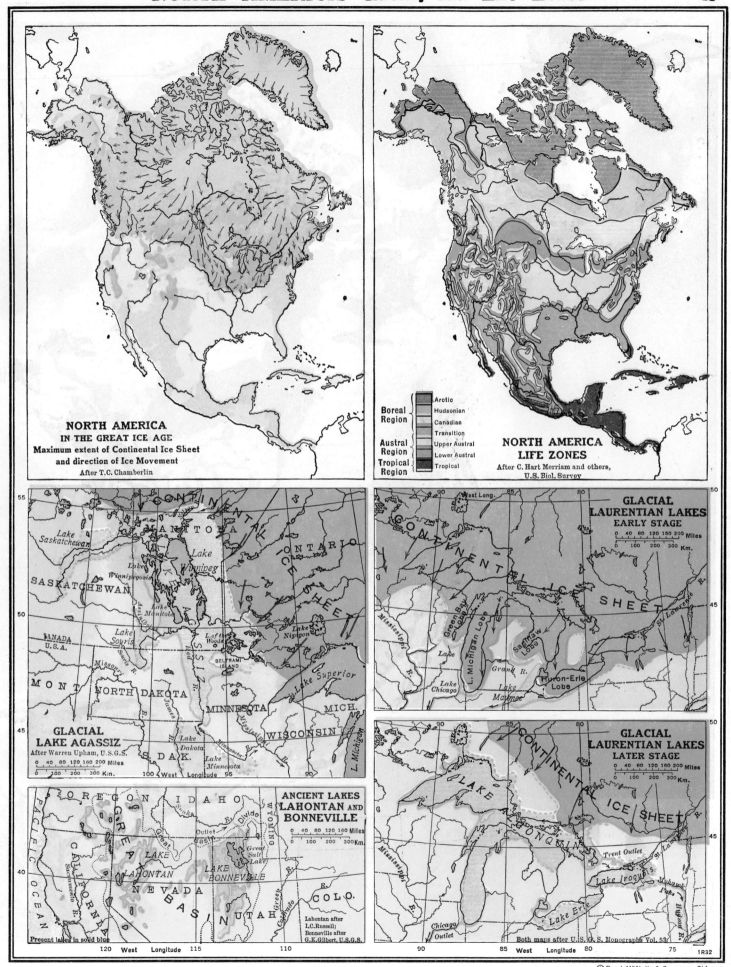

NORTH AMERICA
IN THE GREAT ICE AGE
Maximum extent of Continental Ice Sheet
and direction of Ice Movement
After T.C. Chamberlin

Boreal Region: Arctic, Hudsonian, Canadian
Austral Region: Transition, Upper Austral, Lower Austral
Tropical Region: Tropical

**NORTH AMERICA
LIFE ZONES**
After C. Hart Merriam and others,
U.S. Biol. Survey

**GLACIAL
LAKE AGASSIZ**
After Warren Upham, U.S.G.S.
0 40 80 120 160 200 Miles
0 100 200 300 Km.

**ANCIENT LAKES
LAHONTAN AND
BONNEVILLE**
0 40 80 120 160 Miles
0 100 200 300 Km.
Lahontan after
I.C. Russell;
Bonneville after
G.K. Gilbert, U.S.G.S.
Present lakes in solid blue

**GLACIAL
LAURENTIAN LAKES**
EARLY STAGE
0 40 80 120 160 200 Miles
0 100 200 300 Km.

**GLACIAL
LAURENTIAN LAKES**
LATER STAGE
0 40 80 120 160 200 Miles
0 100 200 300 Km.
Both maps after U.S.G.S. Monographs Vol. 53.

**Red arrows in glacial maps show the direction of ice movement
Present lakes and rivers in black**

© Rand McNally & Company, Chicago

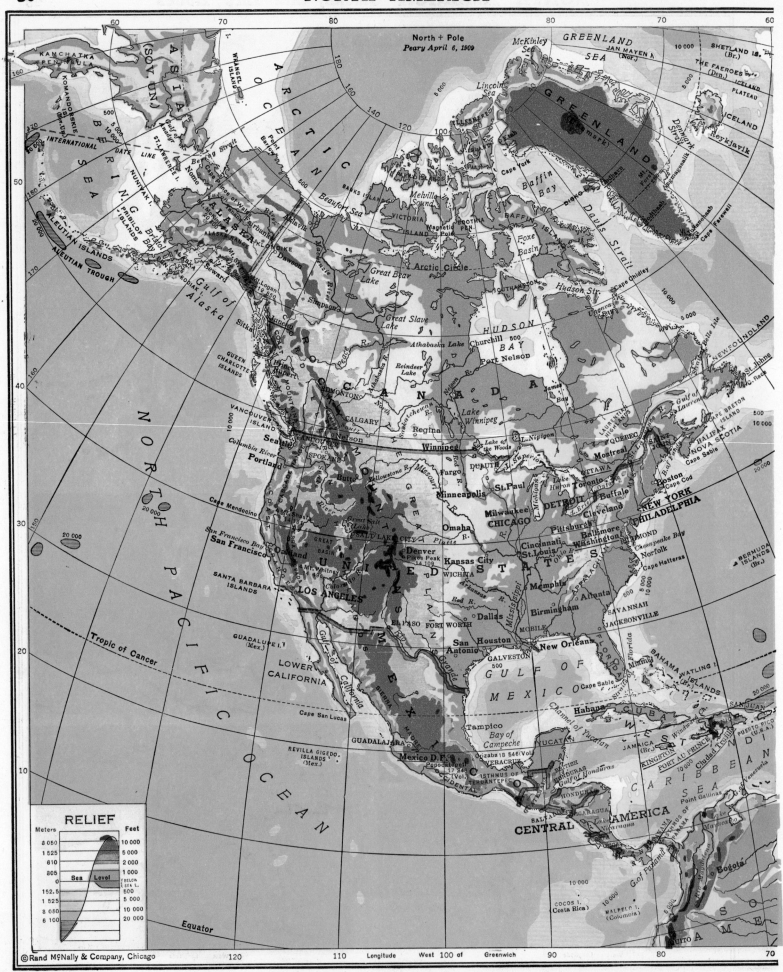

RELIEF

Meters		Feet
3 050		10 000
1 525		5 000
610		2 000
305		1 000
	Sea Level	BELOW SEA L.
152.5		500
1 525		5 000
3 050		10 000
6 100		20 000

© Rand McNally & Company, Chicago

0   200   400   600   800   1000 Miles

0   400   800   1200   1600 Kilometers

Scale 1:40 000 000; One inch to 630 miles.   Lambert's Azimuthal Equal Area Projection

Elevations and depressions are given in feet

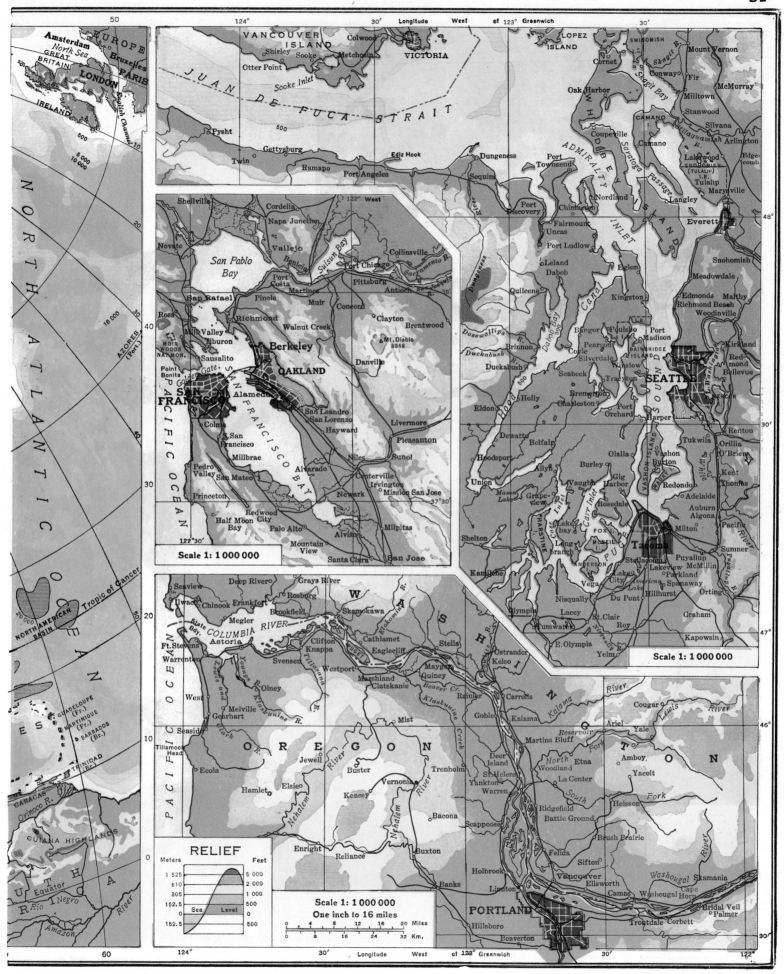

Scale 1: 1 000 000

Scale 1: 1 000 000

RELIEF

Meters		Feet
1 525		5 000
610		2 000
305		1 000
152.5		500
0	Sea Level	0
152.5		500

Scale 1: 1 000 000
One inch to 16 miles

0   4   8   12   16   20 Miles
0   8   16   24   32 Km.

Scale 1: 1 000 000

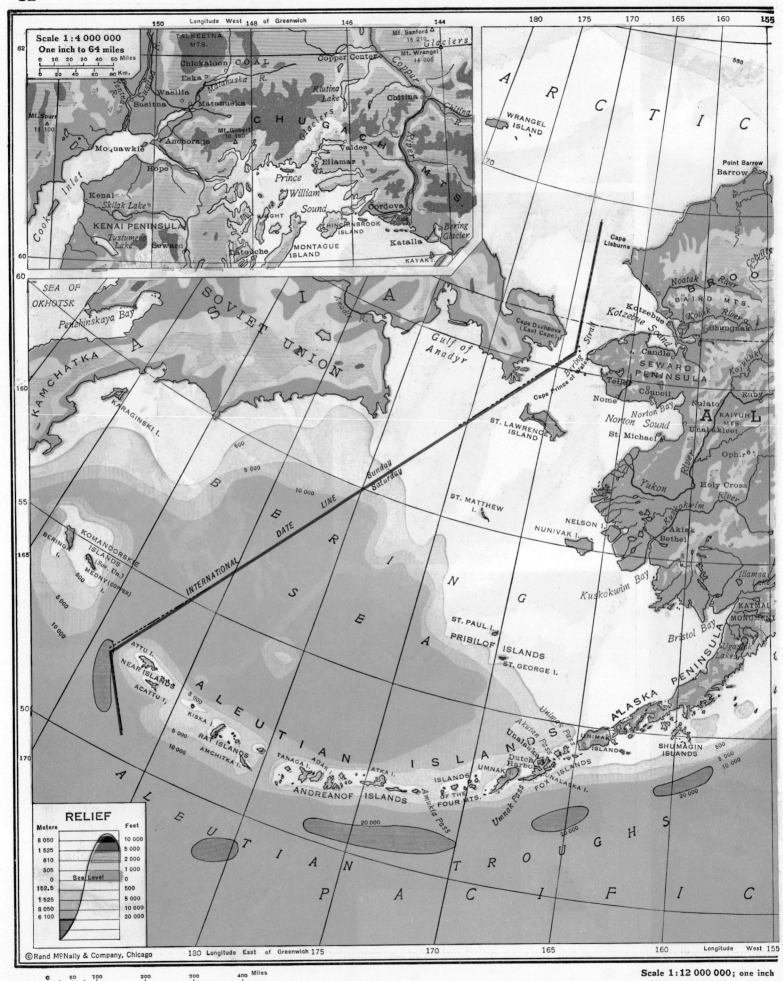

Scale 1:4 000 000
One inch to 64 miles
0 10 20 30 40 50 Miles
0   20   40   60   80 Km.

Longitude West 148 of Greenwich

TALKEETNA MTS.
Chickaloon COAL
Eska
Matanuska R.
Wasilla
Susitna
Matanuska
Mt. Spurr 11 100
Mohawkie
Anchorage
Hope
Kenai
Skilak Lake
Tustumena Lake
KENAI PENINSULA
Seward
Cook Inlet
CHUGACH
Mt. Gilbert 10 180
Prince William Sound
KNIGHT
Latouche
MONTAGUE ISLAND
Copper Center
Mt. Sanford 16 210
Mt. Wrangel 14 005
Glaciers
Copper R.
Klutina Lake
Chitina
Chitina R.
Valdez
Ellamar
Cordova
HINCHINBROOK ISLAND
Bering Glacier
Katalla
KAYAK I.

ARCTIC

Wrangel Island
Cape Lisburne
Point Barrow
Barrow
BROOKS
Noatak River
BAIRD MTS.
Kobuk River
Shungnak
Cape Dezhneva (East Cape)
Bering Strait
Kotzebue
Kotzebue Sound
SEWARD PENINSULA
Candle
Teller
Cape Prince of Wales
Nome
Council
Ruby
Nulato
KAIYUH MTS.
A L
Unalakleet
Ophir
Holy Cross
River

SEA OF OKHOTSK
Penzhinskaya Bay
KAMCHATKA
KARAGINSKI I.
Anadir R.
Gulf of Anadyr
St. Michael
Norton Bay
Norton Sound
Yukon River
Kuskokwim River
SOVIET UNION
A S I A

ST. LAWRENCE ISLAND
ST. MATTHEW I.
NELSON I.
NUNIVAK I.

Sunday
Saturday
5 000
10 000
INTERNATIONAL DATE LINE

KOMANDORSKIE ISLANDS (Sov. Un.)
BERING I.
MEDNY (COPPER)
600
5 000
10 000

B E R I N G   S E A

Kuskokwim Bay
Akiak
Bethel
Iliamna Lake
KATMAL MONUMENT

ST. PAUL I.
PRIBILOF ISLANDS
ST. GEORGE I.

Bristol Bay
Ugashik Lakes

ATTU I.
NEAR ISLANDS
ACATTU I.
KISKA I.
RAT ISLANDS
5 000
AMCHITKA I.
10 000
TANAGA I.
ADAK I.
ATKA I.
ANDREANOF ISLANDS

A L E U T I A N   I S L A N D S
Umnak Pass
Amukta Pass
ISLANDS OF THE FOUR MTS.
UMNAK
Akutan Pass
Unalaska
Dutch Harbor
FOX ISLANDS
Unalaska I.
UNIMAK ISLAND
Unimak Pass
ALASKA PENINSULA
SHUMAGIN ISLANDS
500
5 000
10 000
20 000

A L E U T I A N   T R O U G H S

20 000
20 000

P A C I F I C

RELIEF
Meters   Feet
8 050   10 000
1 525   5 000
610   2 000
305   1 000
0   Sea Level   0
152.5   500
1 525   5 000
8 050   10 000
6 100   20 000

© Rand McNally & Company, Chicago

180 Longitude East of Greenwich 175

0   50   100   200   300   400 Miles
0   100   200   300   400   500   600 Kilometers

Longitude West 155

Scale 1:12 000 000; one inch
Elevations and depressions

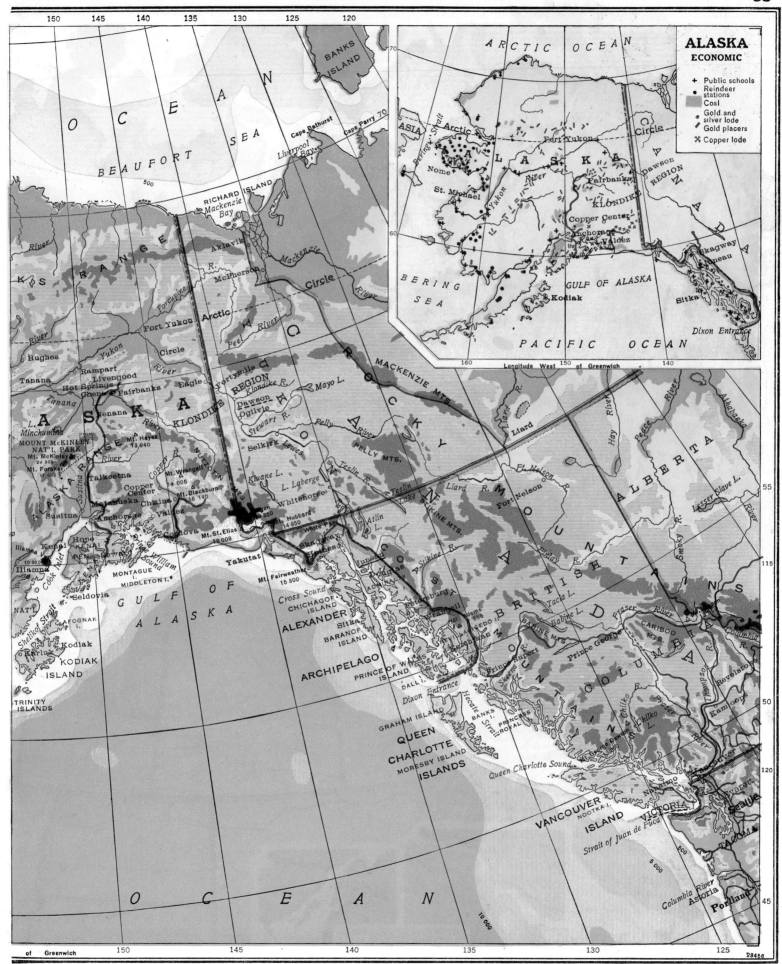

ALASKA
ECONOMIC

+ Public schools
• Reindeer stations
▨ Coal
◆ Gold and silver lode
╱ Gold placers
✕ Copper lode

Longitude West of Greenwich

to 190 miles. Conic Projection
are given in feet

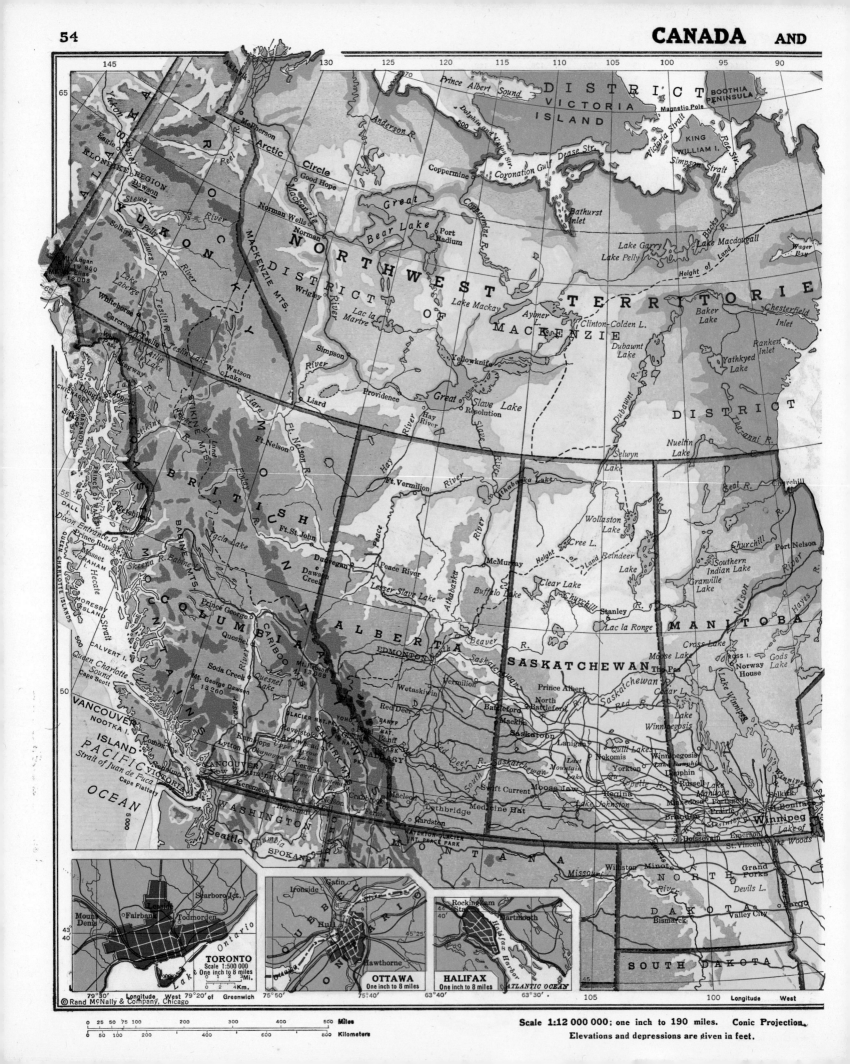

D I S T R I C T

VICTORIA
ISLAND

BOOTHIA
PENINSULA

Magnetic Pole

KING
WILLIAM I.

N O R T H W E S T   T E R R I T O R I E S

D I S T R I C T   OF   M A C K E N Z I E

D I S T R I C T

A L A S K A

KLONDIKE
REGION

Y U K O N

R O C K Y

M A C K E N Z I E   MTS.

Arctic   Circle

B R I T I S H   C O L U M B I A

M O U N T A I N S

QUEEN CHARLOTTE ISLANDS

PRINCE OF WALES I.

VANCOUVER ISLAND

PACIFIC

OCEAN

PACIFIC

WASHINGTON

A L B E R T A

EDMONTON

CALGARY

S A S K A T C H E W A N

M A N I T O B A

Winnipeg

M O N T A N A

N O R T H
D A K O T A

S O U T H   D A K O T A

Bismarck

Fargo

Grand
Forks

ATLANTIC OCEAN

TORONTO
Scale 1:500 000
One inch to 8 miles

OTTAWA
One inch to 8 miles

HALIFAX
One inch to 8 miles

© Rand McNally & Company, Chicago

Longitude   West 79°20' of Greenwich

| 0 25 50 75 100 | 200 | 300 | 400 | 500 Miles |
| 0 50 100 | 200 | 400 | 600 | 800 Kilometers |

Scale 1:12 000 000; one inch to 190 miles. Conic Projection.
Elevations and depressions are given in feet.

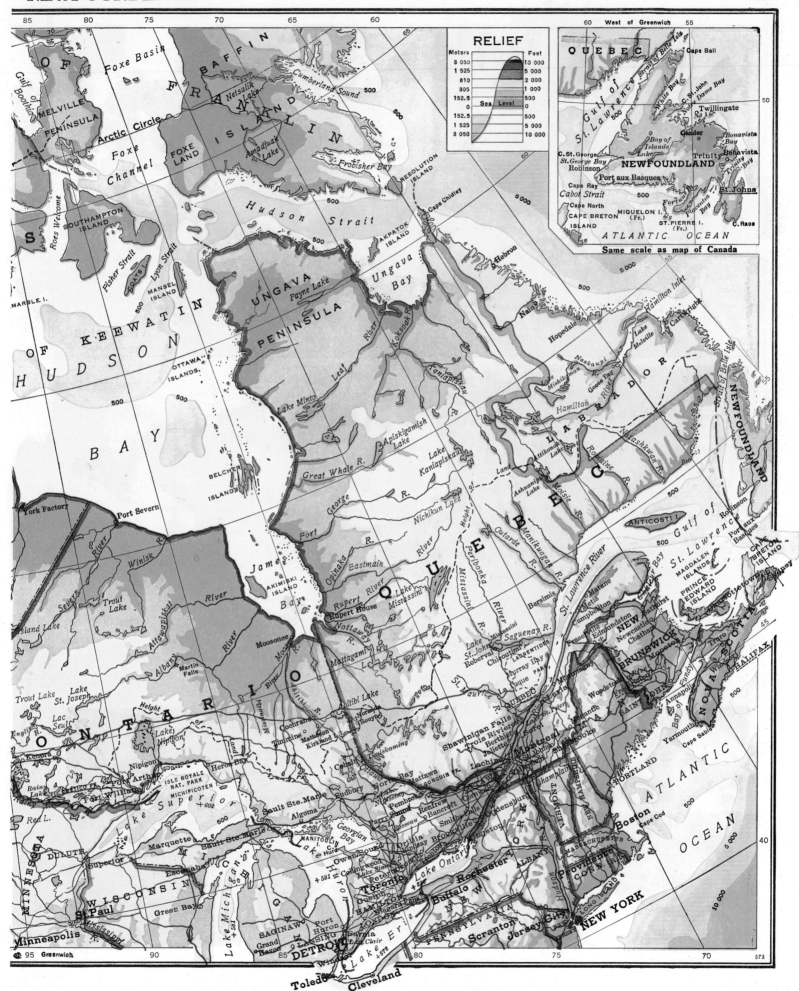

RELIEF

Meters		Feet
3 050		10 000
1 525		5 000
610		2 000
305		1 000
152.5		500
0	Sea Level	0
152.5		500
1 525		5 000
3 050		10 000

Same scale as map of Canada

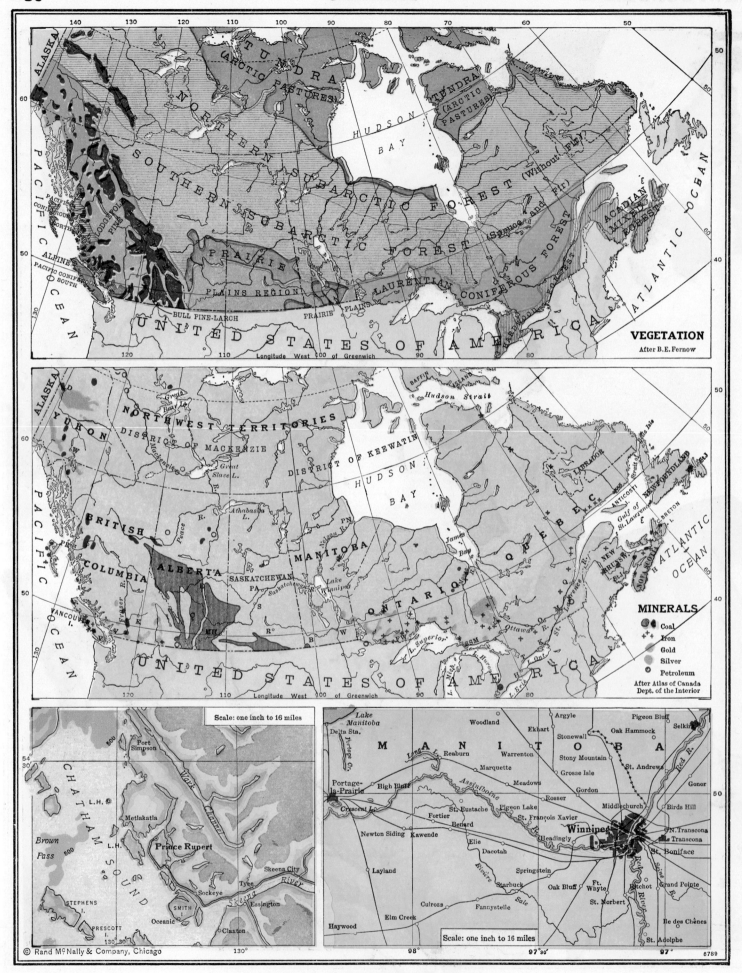

VEGETATION

After B.E. Fernow

MINERALS

- ⬤ Coal
- ✛ Iron
- ⬤ Gold
- ⬤ Silver
- ⬤ Petroleum

After Atlas of Canada
Dept. of the Interior

Scale: one inch to 16 miles

Scale: one inch to 16 miles

© Rand McNally & Company, Chicago

6789

For Canada: Conic Projection
Scale 1:30 000 000; one inch to 500 miles (approx.)

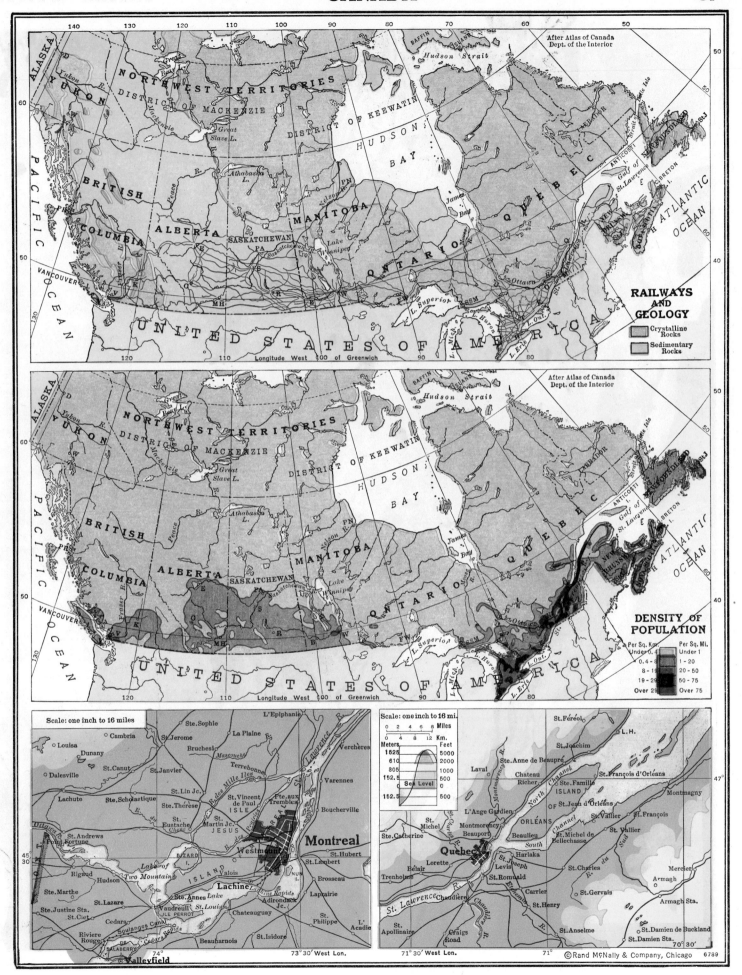

RAILWAYS AND GEOLOGY

Crystalline Rocks
Sedimentary Rocks

After Atlas of Canada
Dept. of the Interior

DENSITY OF POPULATION

Per Sq. Km.	Per Sq. Mi.
Under 0.4	Under 1
0.4 - 8	1 - 20
8 - 19	20 - 50
19 - 29	50 - 75
Over 29	Over 75

After Atlas of Canada
Dept. of the Interior

Scale: one inch to 16 miles

Scale: one inch to 16 mi.

© Rand McNally & Company, Chicago   6789

For Canada: Conic Projection
Scale 1:30 000 000; one inch to 500 miles (approx.)

UNITED STATES

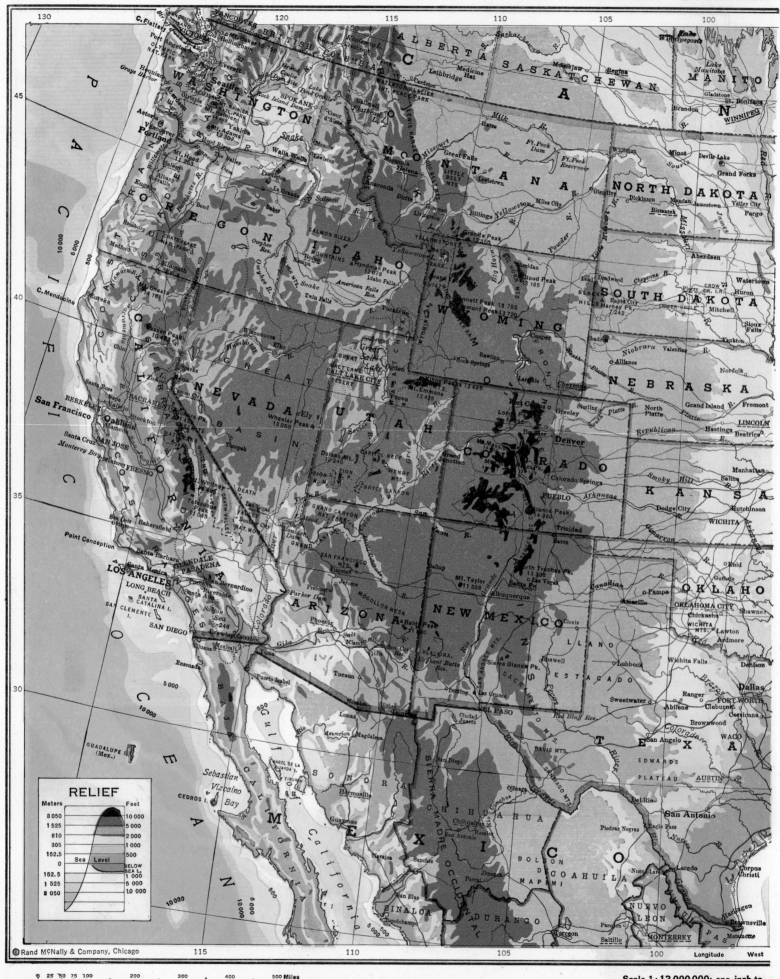

RELIEF

Meters		Feet
3 050		10 000
1 525		5 000
610		2 000
305		1 000
152.5		500
0	Sea Level	BELOW SEA L.
152.5		1 000
1 525		5 000
3 050		10 000

© Rand McNally & Company, Chicago

0 25 50 75 100   200   300   400   500 Miles
0   50 100   200   400   600   800 Kilometers

Scale 1: 12 000 000; one inch to

Elevations and depressions

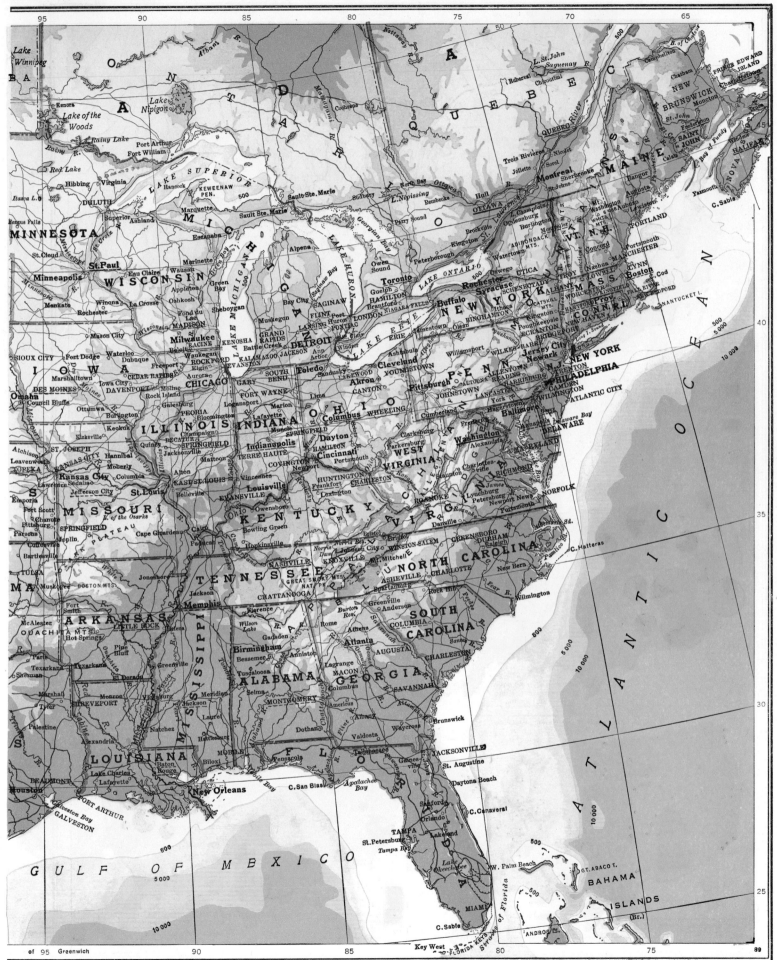

190 miles.   Polyconic Projection

are given in feet

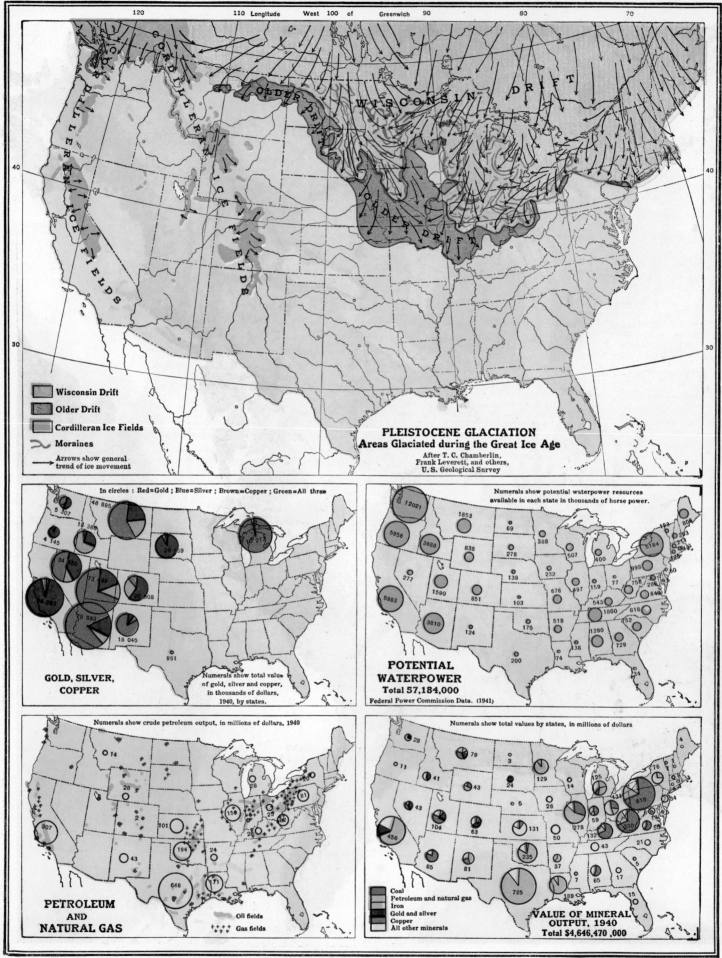

120　Longitude　West　100 of　Greenwich　90　80　70

Wisconsin Drift
Older Drift
Cordilleran Ice Fields
Moraines
Arrows show general
trend of ice movement

PLEISTOCENE GLACIATION
Areas Glaciated during the Great Ice Age
After T. C. Chamberlin,
Frank Leverett, and others,
U. S. Geological Survey

In circles : Red=Gold ; Blue=Silver ; Brown=Copper ; Green=All three

GOLD, SILVER,
COPPER

Numerals show total value
of gold, silver and copper,
in thousands of dollars,
1940, by states.

Numerals show potential waterpower resources
available in each state in thousands of horse power.

POTENTIAL
WATERPOWER
Total 57,184,000
Federal Power Commission Data. (1941)

Numerals show crude petroleum output, in millions of dollars, 1940

PETROLEUM
AND
NATURAL GAS

Oil fields
Gas fields

Numerals show total values by states, in millions of dollars

Coal
Petroleum and natural gas
Iron
Gold and silver
Copper
All other minerals

VALUE OF MINERAL
OUTPUT, 1940
Total $4,646,470,000

© Rand McNally & Company, Chicago

PHYSIOGRAPHIC DIVISIONS

The provinces are subdivided into sections, indicated by the letters, a, b, c, etc.

After Nevin M. Fenneman and others, Association of American Geographers

MAJOR DIVISIONS — **PROVINCES**

Pacific Mountain System { Sierra - Cascade Mts. / Pacific Border / Lower Californian

Intermontane Plateaus { Columbia Plateaus / Colorado Plateaus / Basin - and - Range

Rocky Mountain System { Southern Rocky Mts. / Wyoming Basin / Northern Rocky Mts.

Interior Plains { Interior Low Plateaus / Central Lowland / Great Plains

Interior Highlands { Ozark Plateaus / Ouachita

Appalachian Highlands { Piedmont / Blue Ridge / Appalachian Valley / St. Lawrence Valley / Appalachian Plateaus / New England / Adirondack

Laurentian Upland { Superior Upland

Atlantic Plain { Continental Shelf / Coastal Plain

RELIEF

Meters	Feet
1 525	5 000
610	2 000
305	1 000
0	Sea Level

Major Divisions
Provinces
Sections

VALUE OF LUMBER PRODUCTS

Numbers show annual values by states, in millions of dollars, 1942

Total $ 940 345 475

VALUE OF ALL FARM CROPS AND ANIMAL PRODUCTS

Numbers show annual values by states, in millions of dollars, 1942

Total $ 17 559 177 000

VALUE ADDED BY MANUFACTURE
VALUE OF PRODUCTS LESS COST OF MATERIALS

Numbers show annual values by states, in millions of dollars, 1940

Total $ 24 682 918 000

NATIONAL INCOME

Numbers show annual income payments, by states, in millions of dollars, 1940

Total $ 76 220 000 000

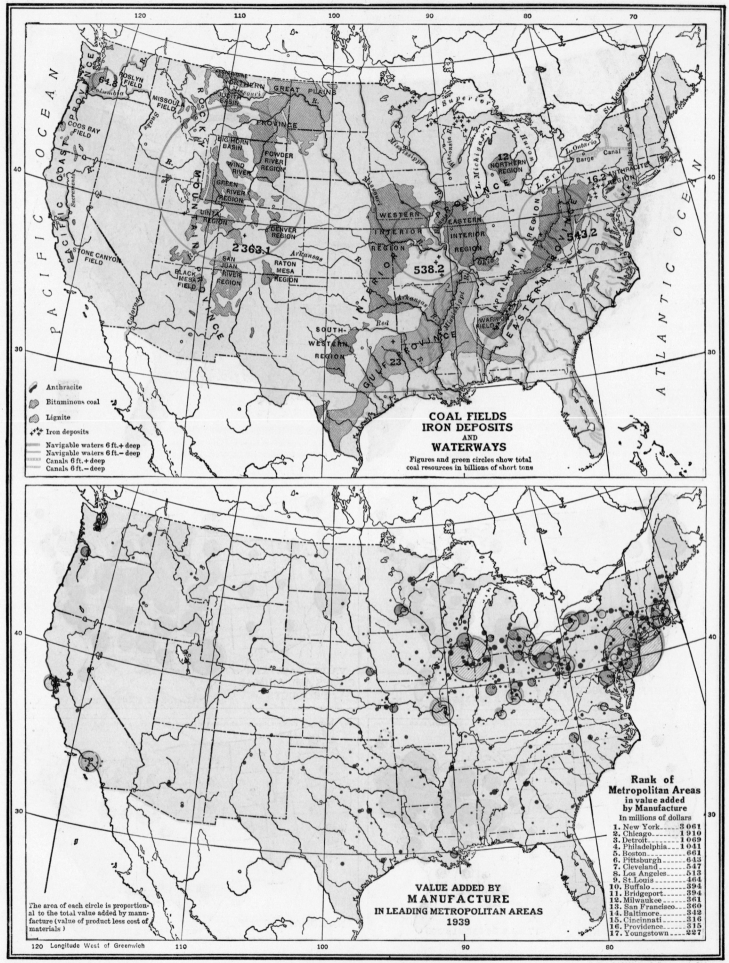

**COAL FIELDS
IRON DEPOSITS
AND
WATERWAYS**

Figures and green circles show total
coal resources in billions of short tons

Anthracite
Bituminous coal
Lignite
Iron deposits
Navigable waters 6 ft.+ deep
Navigable waters 6 ft.— deep
Canals 6 ft.+ deep
Canals 6 ft.— deep

**VALUE ADDED BY
MANUFACTURE**
IN LEADING METROPOLITAN AREAS
1939

The area of each circle is proportional to the total value added by manufacture (value of product less cost of
materials)

**Rank of
Metropolitan Areas**
in value added
by Manufacture
In millions of dollars

1.	New York	3 061
2.	Chicago	1 910
3.	Detroit	1 069
4.	Philadelphia	1 041
5.	Boston	661
6.	Pittsburgh	643
7.	Cleveland	547
8.	Los Angeles	513
9.	St. Louis	464
10.	Buffalo	394
11.	Bridgeport	394
12.	Milwaukee	361
13.	San Francisco	360
14.	Baltimore	342
15.	Cincinnati	316
16.	Providence	315
17.	Youngstown	227

Longitude West of Greenwich

Each Standard Time area keeps the sun time of some central meridian as standard.
Eastern keeps 75th
Central " 90th
Mountain " 105th
Pacific " 120th

RAILWAYS AND
STANDARD TIME
Total mileage 232,524 (1940)

Each Standard Time area keeps the sun time of some central meridian as standard.
Eastern keeps 75th
Central " 90th
Mountain " 105th
Pacific " 120th

AIRWAYS AND
STANDARD TIME

120 Longitude West of Greenwich

© Rand McNally & Company, Chicago

Scale for both maps ; one inch to 400 miles

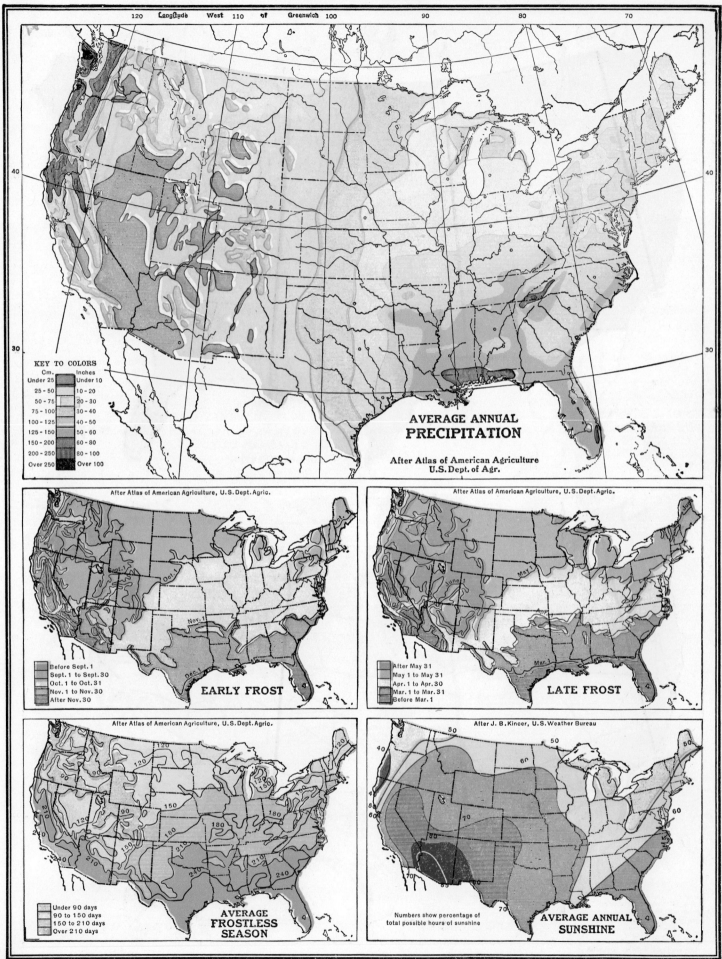

AVERAGE ANNUAL
PRECIPITATION

After Atlas of American Agriculture
U. S. Dept. of Agr.

KEY TO COLORS

Cm.	Inches
Under 25	Under 10
25 - 50	10 - 20
50 - 75	20 - 30
75 - 100	30 - 40
100 - 125	40 - 50
125 - 150	50 - 60
150 - 200	60 - 80
200 - 250	80 - 100
Over 250	Over 100

After Atlas of American Agriculture, U.S.Dept.Agric.

Before Sept. 1
Sept. 1 to Sept. 30
Oct. 1 to Oct. 31
Nov. 1 to Nov. 30
After Nov. 30

EARLY FROST

After Atlas of American Agriculture, U.S.Dept.Agric.

After May 31
May 1 to May 31
Apr. 1 to Apr. 30
Mar. 1 to Mar. 31
Before Mar. 1

LATE FROST

After Atlas of American Agriculture, U.S.Dept.Agric.

Under 90 days
90 to 150 days
150 to 210 days
Over 210 days

AVERAGE
**FROSTLESS
SEASON**

After J. B. Kincer, U.S. Weather Bureau

Numbers show percentage of
total possible hours of sunshine

AVERAGE ANNUAL
SUNSHINE

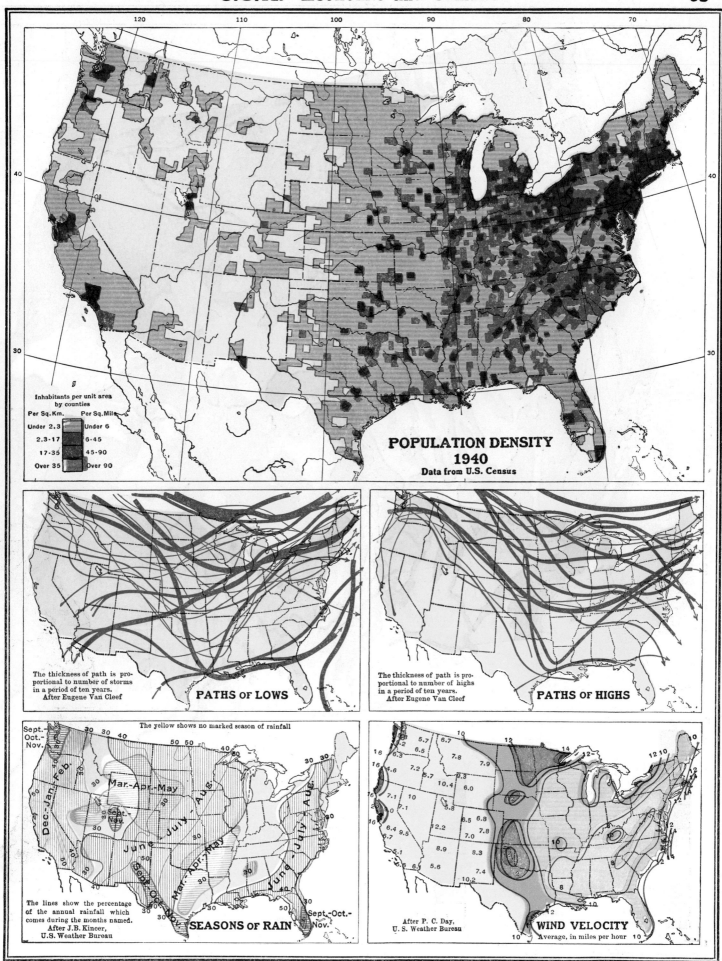

Inhabitants per unit area
by counties

Per Sq.Km.   Per Sq.Mile

Under 2.3   Under 6

2.3-17   6-45

17-35   45-90

Over 35   Over 90

POPULATION DENSITY
1940
Data from U.S. Census

The thickness of path is proportional to number of storms
in a period of ten years.
After Eugene Van Cleef

PATHS OF LOWS

The thickness of path is proportional to number of highs
in a period of ten years.
After Eugene Van Cleef

PATHS OF HIGHS

The yellow shows no marked season of rainfall

The lines show the percentage
of the annual rainfall which
comes during the months named.
After J.B. Kincer,
U.S. Weather Bureau

SEASONS OF RAIN

After P. C. Day,
U. S. Weather Bureau

WIND VELOCITY
Average, in miles per hour

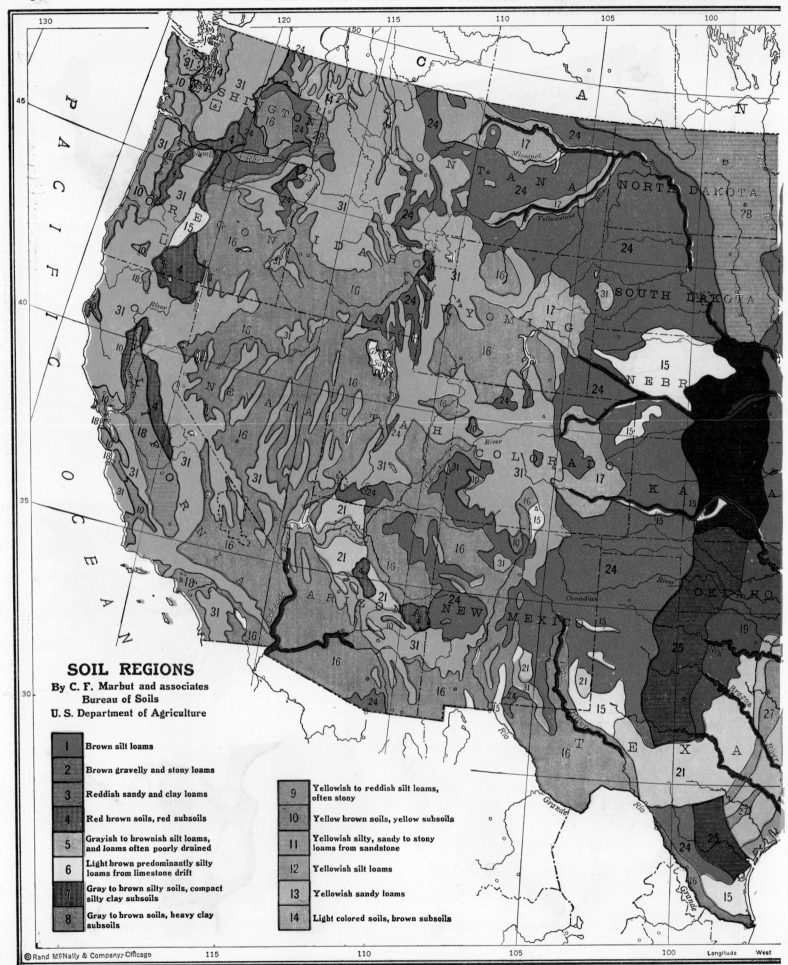

SOIL REGIONS

By C. F. Marbut and associates
Bureau of Soils
U. S. Department of Agriculture

1	Brown silt loams
2	Brown gravelly and stony loams
3	Reddish sandy and clay loams
4	Red brown soils, red subsoils
5	Grayish to brownish silt loams, and loams often poorly drained
6	Light brown predominantly silty loams from limestone drift
7	Gray to brown silty soils, compact silty clay subsoils
8	Gray to brown soils, heavy clay subsoils

9	Yellowish to reddish silt loams, often stony
10	Yellow brown soils, yellow subsoils
11	Yellowish silty, sandy to stony loams from sandstone
12	Yellowish silt loams
13	Yellowish sandy loams
14	Light colored soils, brown subsoils

© Rand McNally & Company, Chicago

Scale 1:12 000 000; one inch

0 25 50 75 100   200   300   400   500 Miles
0 50 100   200   300   400   500   600   700   800 Kilometers

Longitude West

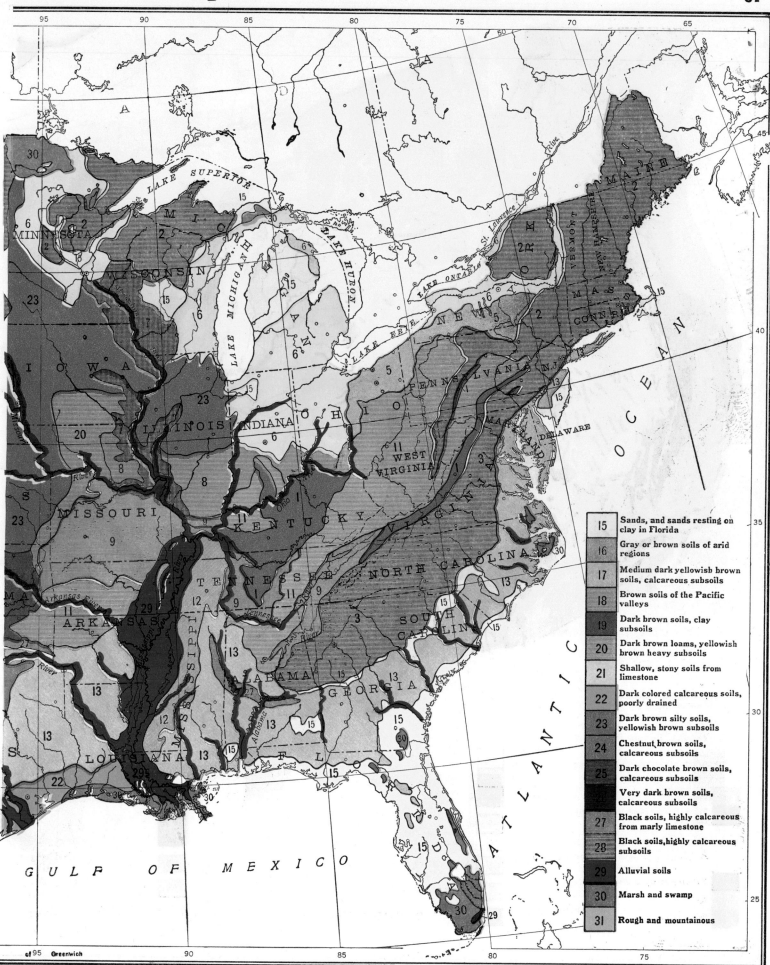

15	Sands, and sands resting on clay in Florida
16	Gray or brown soils of arid regions
17	Medium dark yellowish brown soils, calcareous subsoils
18	Brown soils of the Pacific valleys
19	Dark brown soils, clay subsoils
20	Dark brown loams, yellowish brown heavy subsoils
21	Shallow, stony soils from limestone
22	Dark colored calcareous soils, poorly drained
23	Dark brown silty soils, yellowish brown subsoils
24	Chestnut brown soils, calcareous subsoils
25	Dark chocolate brown soils, calcareous subsoils
26	Very dark brown soils, calcareous subsoils
27	Black soils, highly calcareous from marly limestone
28	Black soils, highly calcareous subsoils
29	Alluvial soils
30	Marsh and swamp
31	Rough and mountainous

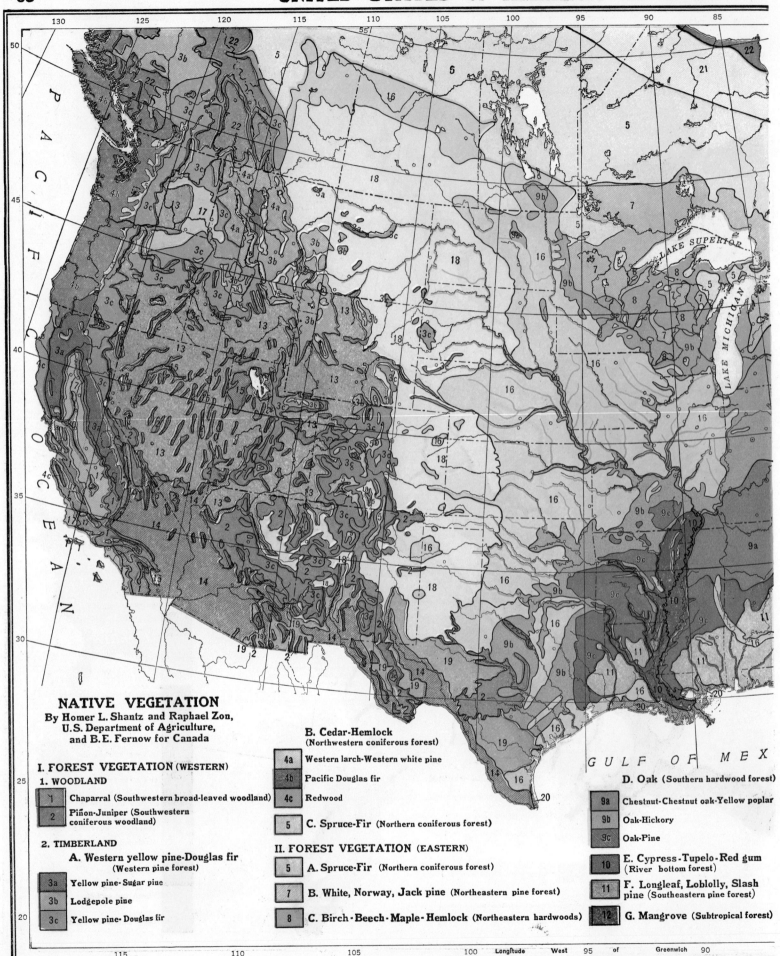

NATIVE VEGETATION

By Homer L. Shantz and Raphael Zon,
U.S. Department of Agriculture,
and B.E. Fernow for Canada

I. FOREST VEGETATION (WESTERN)

1. WOODLAND

1   Chaparral (Southwestern broad-leaved woodland)

2   Piñon-Juniper (Southwestern coniferous woodland)

2. TIMBERLAND

A. Western yellow pine-Douglas fir
(Western pine forest)

3a   Yellow pine-Sugar pine

3b   Lodgepole pine

3c   Yellow pine-Douglas fir

B. Cedar-Hemlock
(Northwestern coniferous forest)

4a   Western larch-Western white pine

4b   Pacific Douglas fir

4c   Redwood

5   C. Spruce-Fir (Northern coniferous forest)

II. FOREST VEGETATION (EASTERN)

5   A. Spruce-Fir (Northern coniferous forest)

7   B. White, Norway, Jack pine (Northeastern pine forest)

8   C. Birch-Beech-Maple-Hemlock (Northeastern hardwoods)

D. Oak (Southern hardwood forest)

9a   Chestnut-Chestnut oak-Yellow poplar

9b   Oak-Hickory

9c   Oak-Pine

10   E. Cypress-Tupelo-Red gum (River bottom forest)

11   F. Longleaf, Loblolly, Slash pine (Southeastern pine forest)

12   G. Mangrove (Subtropical forest)

Scale 1:16 000 000; one inch to 250 miles.   Polyconic Projection

0 50 100 200   300   400   500 Miles
0 50 100   200   400   600   800 Kilometers

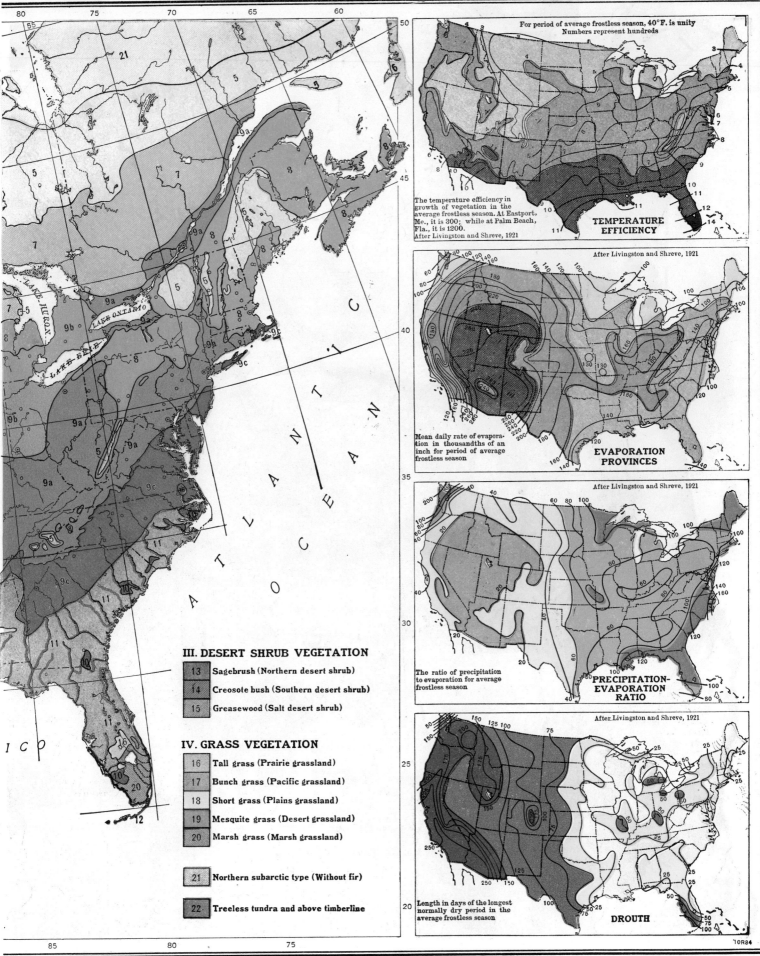

III. DESERT SHRUB VEGETATION

13	Sagebrush (Northern desert shrub)
14	Creosote bush (Southern desert shrub)
15	Greasewood (Salt desert shrub)

IV. GRASS VEGETATION

16	Tall grass (Prairie grassland)
17	Bunch grass (Pacific grassland)
18	Short grass (Plains grassland)
19	Mesquite grass (Desert grassland)
20	Marsh grass (Marsh grassland)

21	Northern subarctic type (Without fir)
22	Treeless tundra and above timberline

For period of average frostless season, 40°F. is unity
Numbers represent hundreds

The temperature efficiency in growth of vegetation in the average frostless season. At Eastport, Me., it is 300; while at Palm Beach, Fla., it is 1200.
After Livingston and Shreve, 1921

TEMPERATURE EFFICIENCY

After Livingston and Shreve, 1921

Mean daily rate of evaporation in thousandths of an inch for period of average frostless season

EVAPORATION PROVINCES

After Livingston and Shreve, 1921

The ratio of precipitation to evaporation for average frostless season

PRECIPITATION-EVAPORATION RATIO

After Livingston and Shreve, 1921

Length in days of the longest normally dry period in the average frostless season

DROUTH

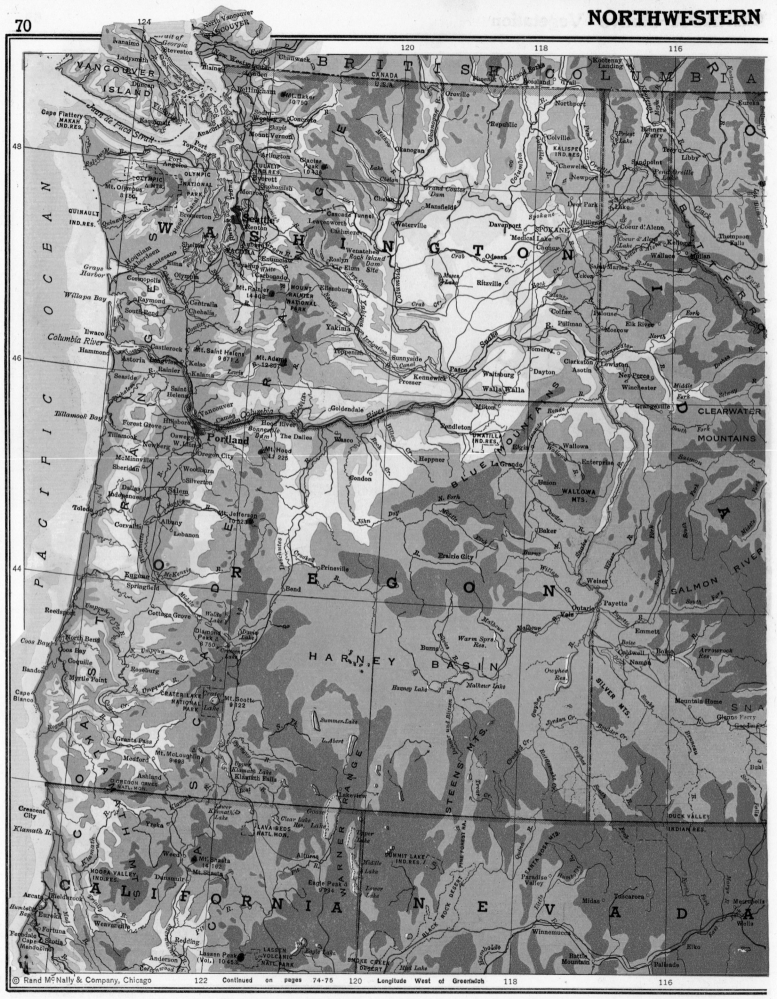

Continued on pages 74-75

Longitude West of Greenwich

Scale 1:4 000 000; one inch to

Elevations and depressions

| | 0 | 20 | 40 | 60 | 80 | 100 | 120 | Miles |
| 0 | 20 | 40 | 60 | 80 | 100 | 120 | 140 | 160 | 180 | 200 | Kilometers |

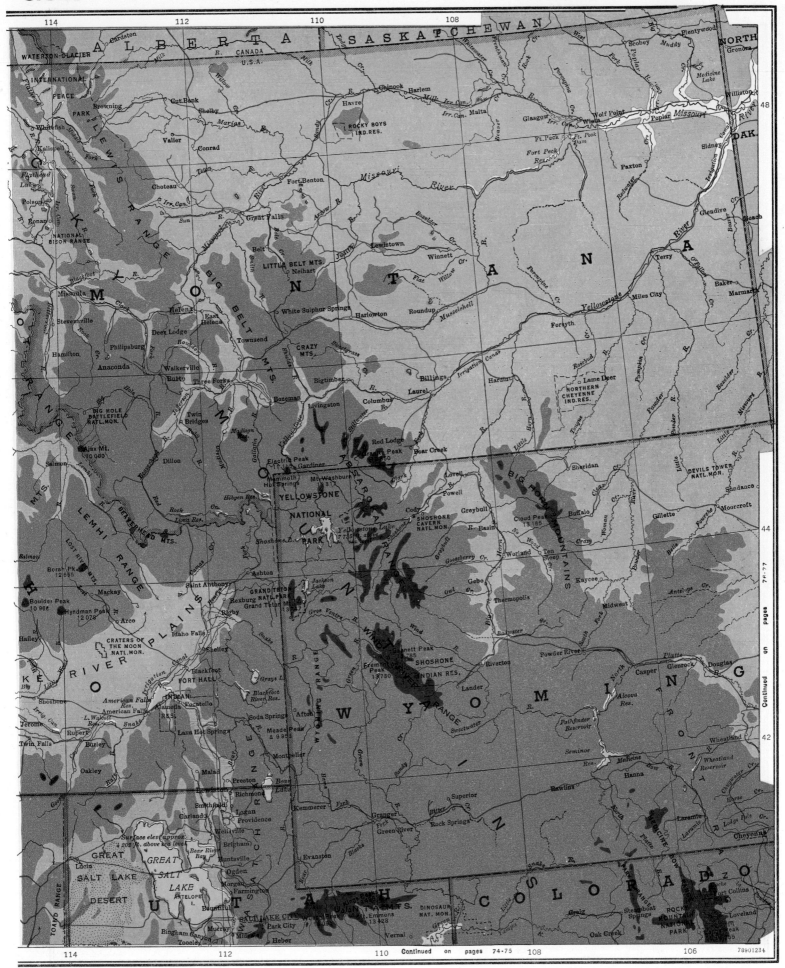

Continued on pages 74-75

64 miles. Conic Projection

are given in feet

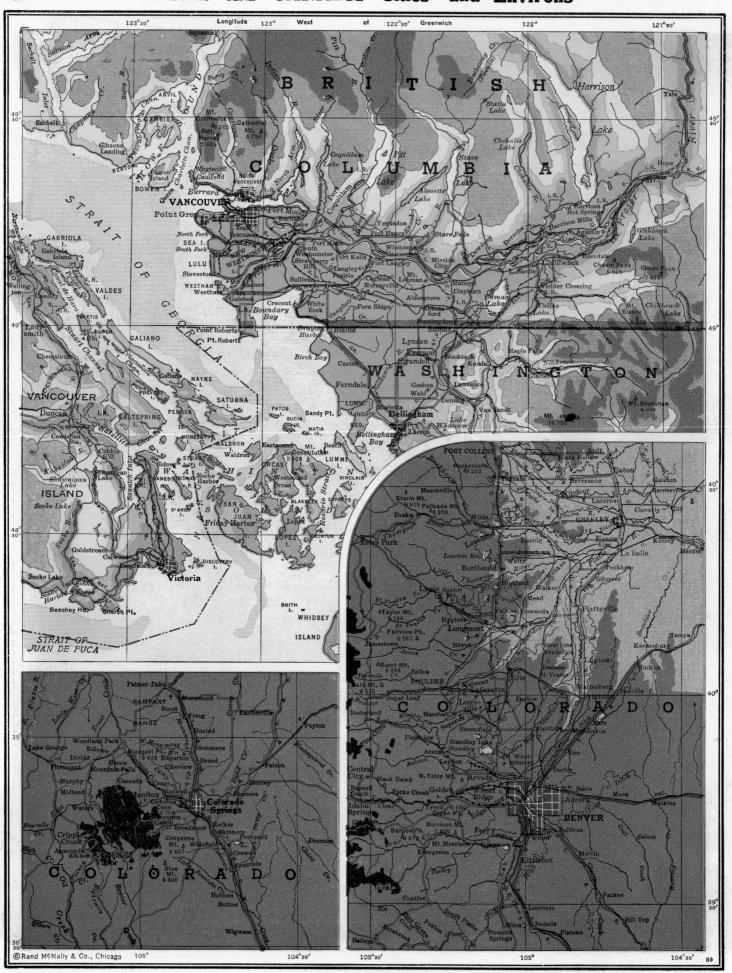

Scale 1:1 000 000; one inch to 16 miles
Elevations and depressions are given in feet

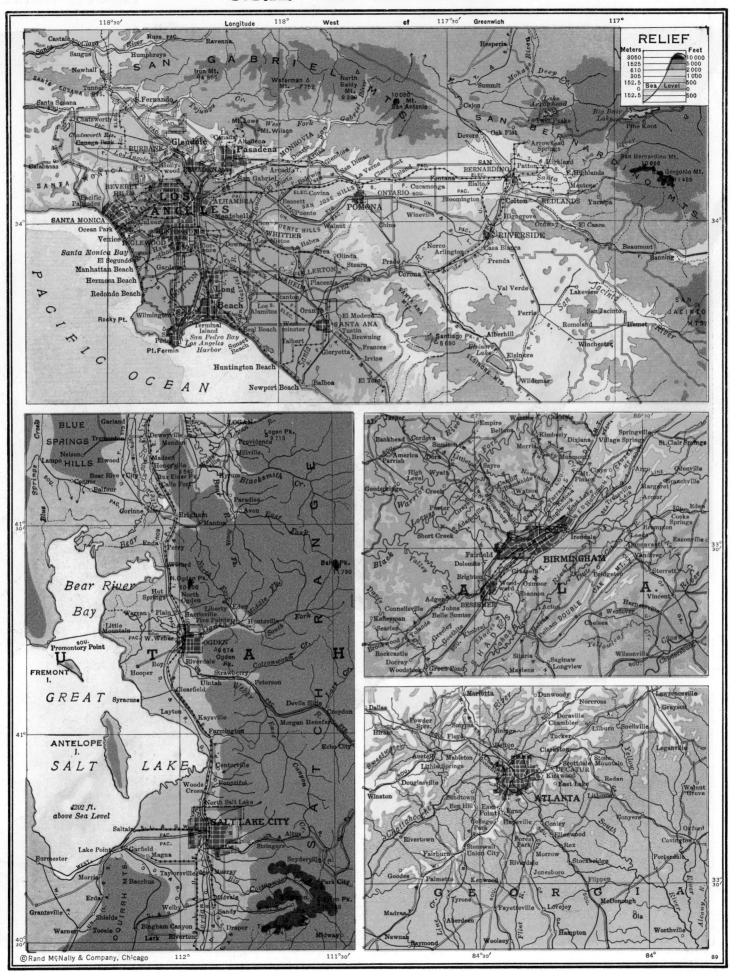

Scale 1:1 000 000; one inch to 16 miles

Elevations and depressions are given in feet

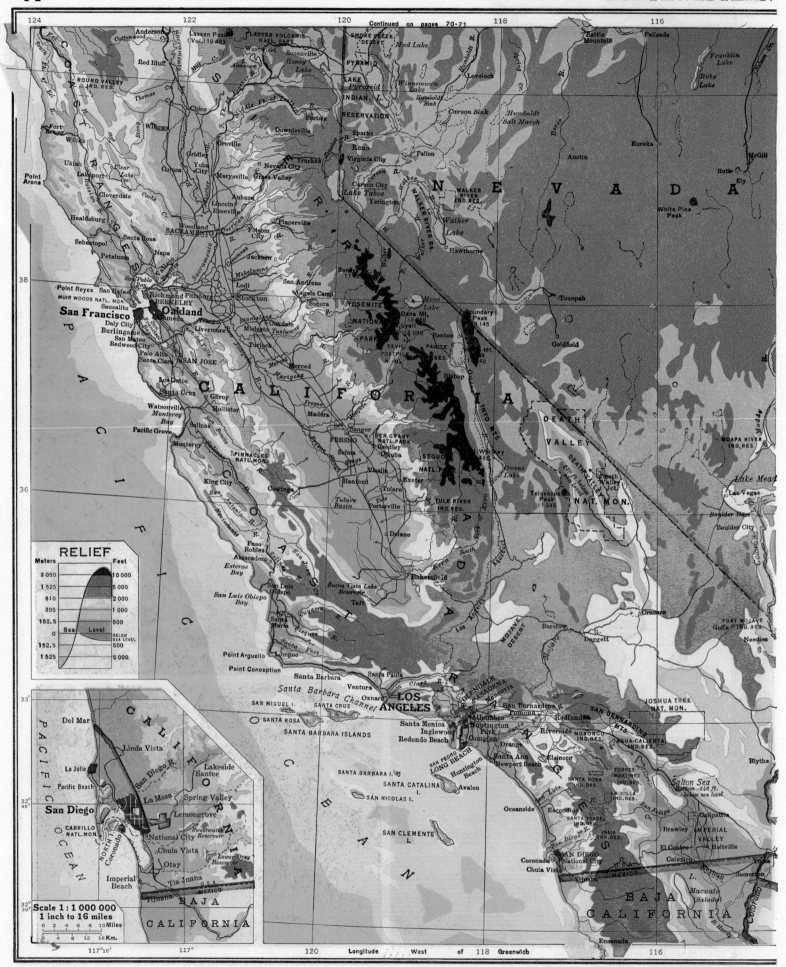

Continued on pages 70-71

RELIEF

Meters		Feet
3 050		10 000
1 525		5 000
610		2 000
305		1 000
152.5		500
0	Sea Level	
152.5	BELOW SEA LEVEL	500
1 525		5 000

Scale 1:1 000 000
1 inch to 16 miles

Longitude West of 118 Greenwich

Scale 1:4 000 000; one inch to

Elevations and depressions

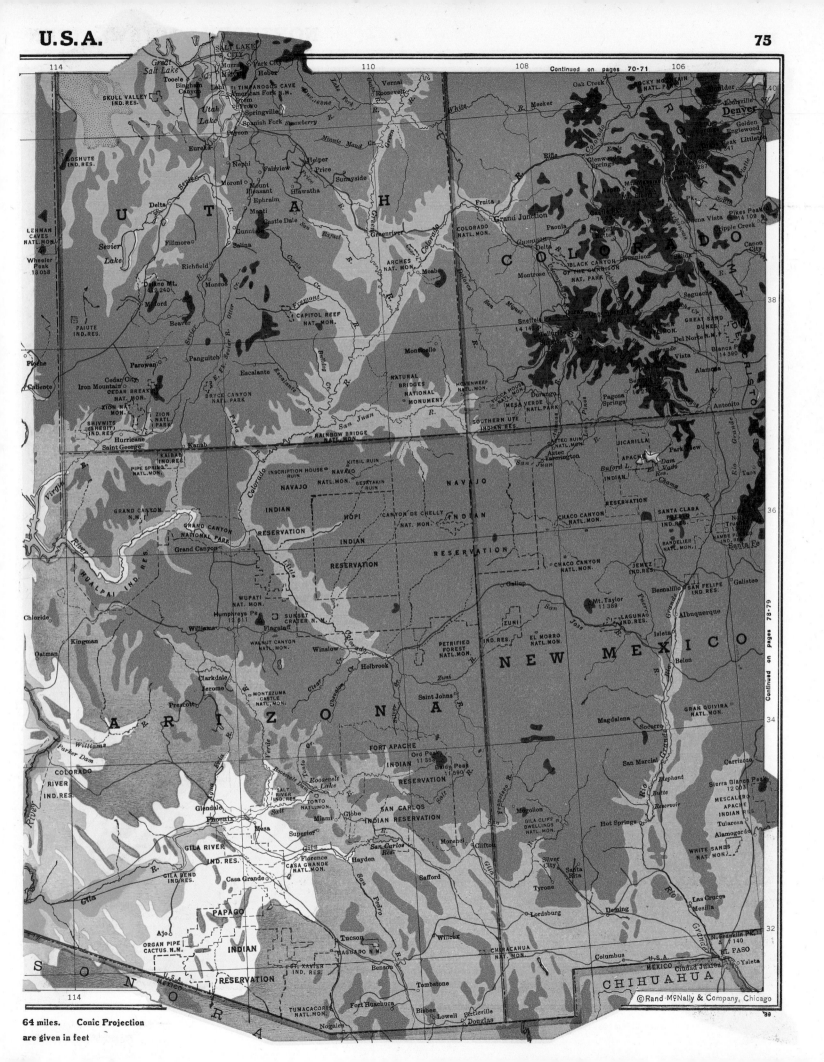

Continued on pages 70-71

Continued on pages 78-79

64 miles.   Conic Projection

are given in feet

©Rand McNally & Company, Chicago

NORTHERN

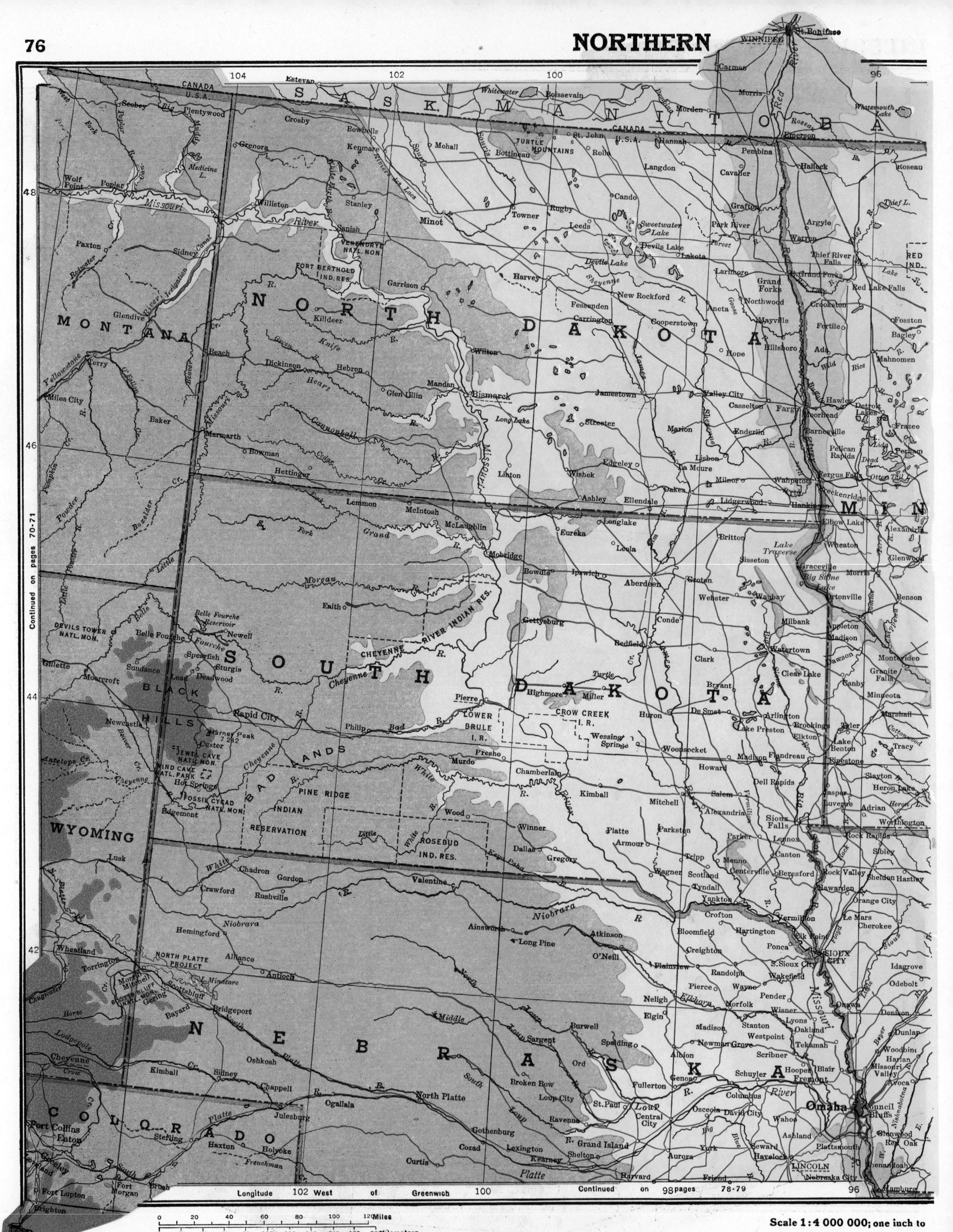
SASK.
MANITOBA
CANADA
U.S.A.
MONTANA
NORTH DAKOTA
SOUTH DAKOTA
WYOMING
NEBRASKA
COLORADO
MINN
BLACK HILLS
BAD LANDS
TURTLE MOUNTAINS
FORT BERTHOLD IND. RES.
VERENDRYE NATL. MON.
CHEYENNE RIVER INDIAN RES.
LOWER BRULE I. R.
CROW CREEK I. R.
PINE RIDGE INDIAN RESERVATION
ROSEBUD IND. RES.
DEVILS TOWER NATL. MON.
JEWEL CAVE NATL. MON.
WIND CAVE NATL. PARK
FOSSIL CYCAD NATL. MON.
SCOTTS BLUFF NATL. MON.
NORTH PLATTE PROJECT
Harney Peak 7 242
Winnipeg
St. Boniface
Estevan
Bismarck
Mandan
Minot
Williston
Devils Lake
Grand Forks
Fargo
Moorhead
Jamestown
Valley City
Pierre
Rapid City
Aberdeen
Watertown
Huron
Mitchell
Sioux Falls
Yankton
Sioux City
Omaha
Council Bluffs
Lincoln
Grand Island
North Platte
Kearney
Scottsbluff
Cheyenne
Fort Collins
Greeley
Denver
Missouri
Yellowstone
Platte
Niobrara
Cheyenne
James
Red
Miles City
Glendive
Sidney
Lusk
Torrington
Julesburg
Sterling
Fort Morgan
104
102
100
96
48
46
44
42
Longitude 102 West of Greenwich 100
0 20 40 60 80 100 120 Miles
0 20 40 60 80 100 120 140 160 180 200 Kilometers

Continued on pages 70-71

Continued on pages 78-79

Scale 1:4 000 000; one inch to

Elevations and depressions

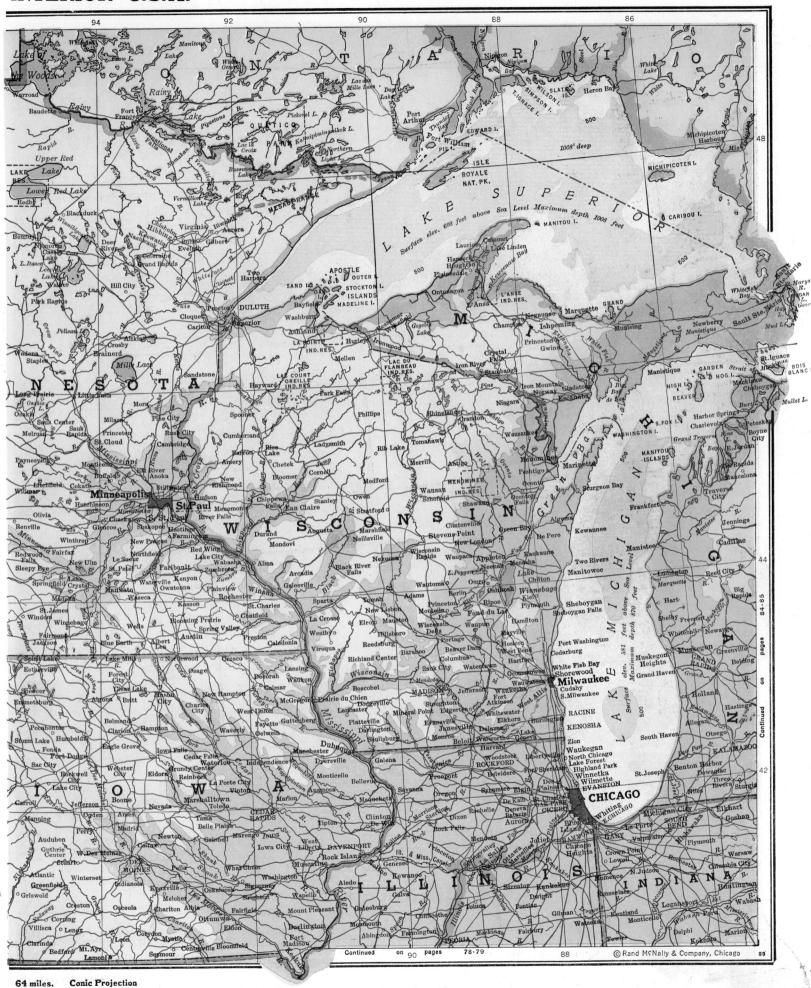

64 miles.   Conic Projection

are given in feet

© Rand McNally & Company, Chicago

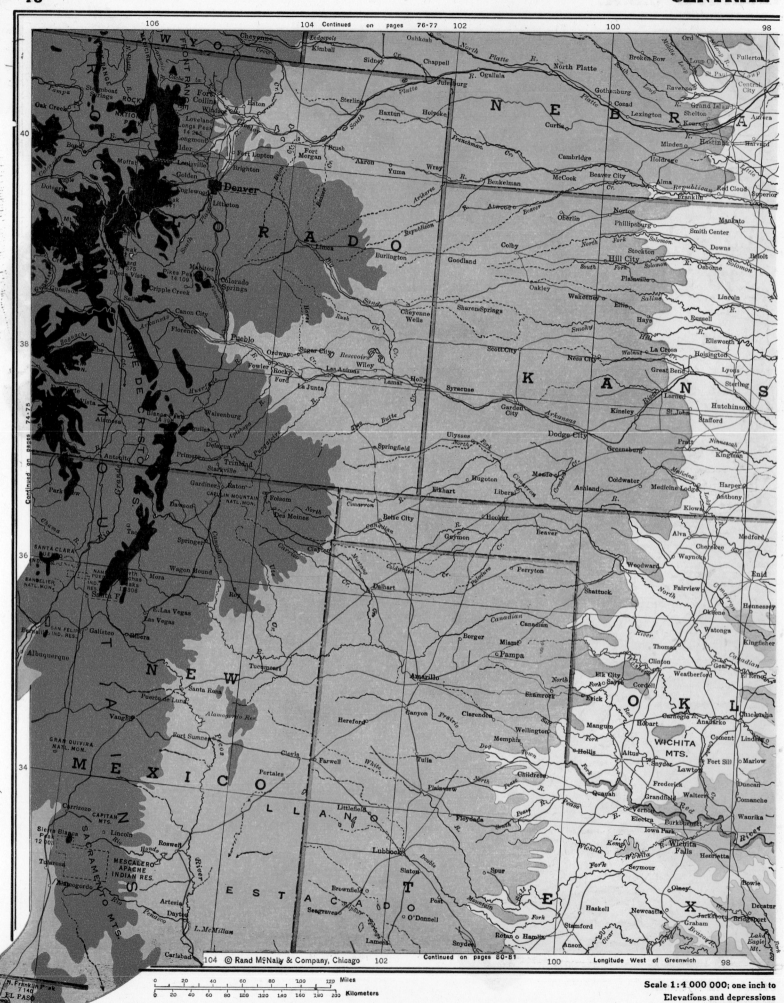

Continued on pages 76-77

Continued on pages 74-75

Continued on pages 80-81

© Rand McNally & Company, Chicago

Longitude West of Greenwich

Miles

Kilometers

Scale 1:4 000 000; one inch to
Elevations and depressions

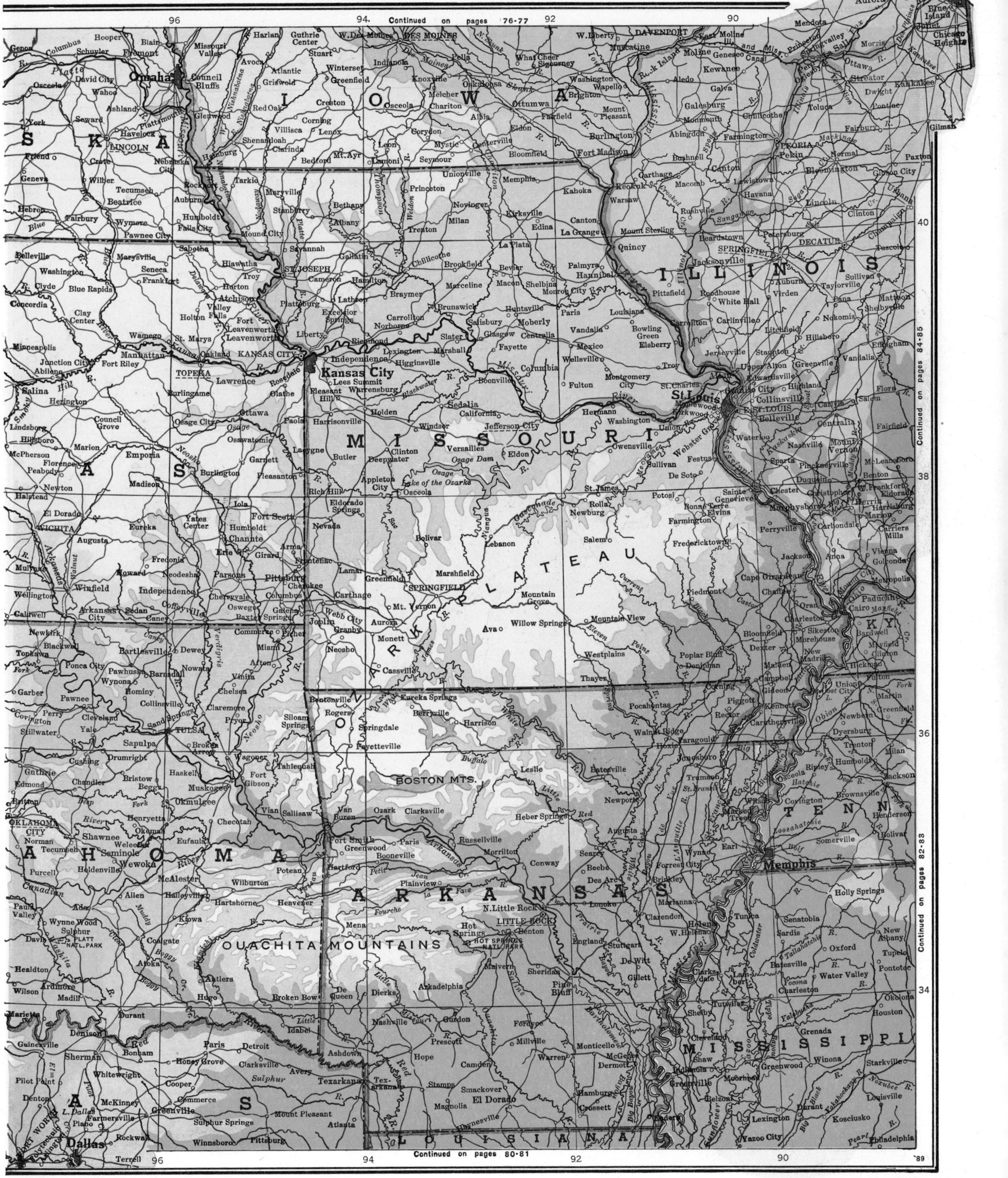

CHICAGO

Continued on pages 76-77

Continued on pages 80-81

Continued on pages 84-85

Continued on pages 82-83

IOWA

ILLINOIS

NEBRASKA

KANSAS

MISSOURI

OKLAHOMA

ARKANSAS

TENN

KY

MISSISSIPPI

LOUISIANA

OZARK PLATEAU

BOSTON MTS.

OUACHITA MOUNTAINS

DES MOINES

DAVENPORT

Omaha

Lincoln

St. Joseph

Kansas City

Lees Summit

TOPEKA

WICHITA

SPRINGFIELD

St. Louis

E. ST. LOUIS

SPRINGFIELD

DECATUR

PEORIA

Tulsa

OKLAHOMA CITY

LITTLE ROCK

N. Little Rock

Memphis

Dallas

40

38

36

34

96

94

92

90

64 miles. Conic Projection

are given in feet

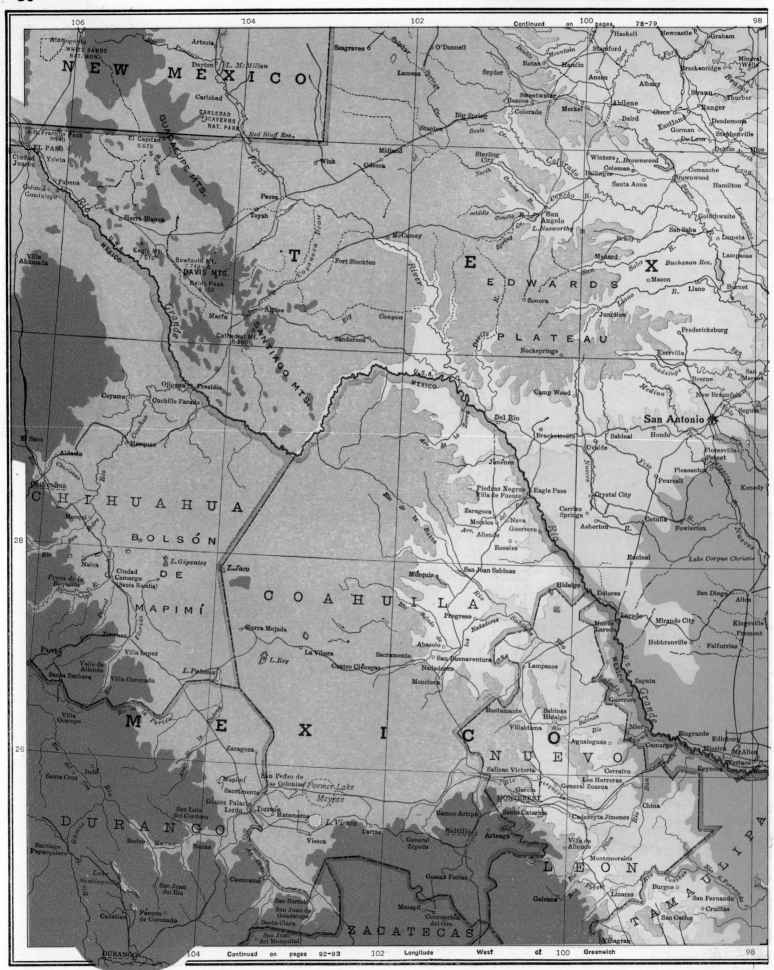

Continued on pages 78-79

Continued on pages 92-93

Longitude West of 100 Greenwich

Scale 1:4 000 000; one inch

Elevations and depressions

0   20   40   60   80   100   120 Miles

0   20   40   60   80   100 120 140 160 180 200 Kilometers

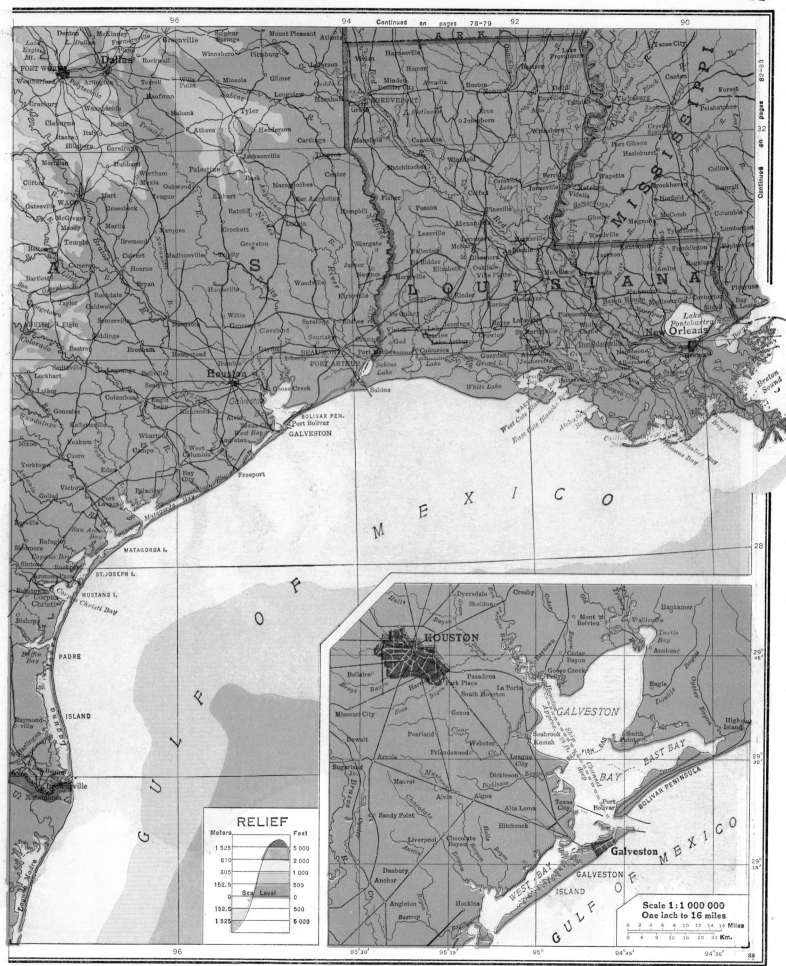

Continued on pages 78-79

Continued on pages 82-83

RELIEF

Meters		Feet
1 525		5 000
610		2 000
305		1 000
152.5		500
	Sea Level	0
152.5		500
1 525		5 000

Scale 1:1 000 000
One inch to 16 miles

0 2 4 6 8 10 12 14 16 Miles
0 4 8 12 16 20 24 Km.

to 64 miles.   Conic Projection

are given in feet

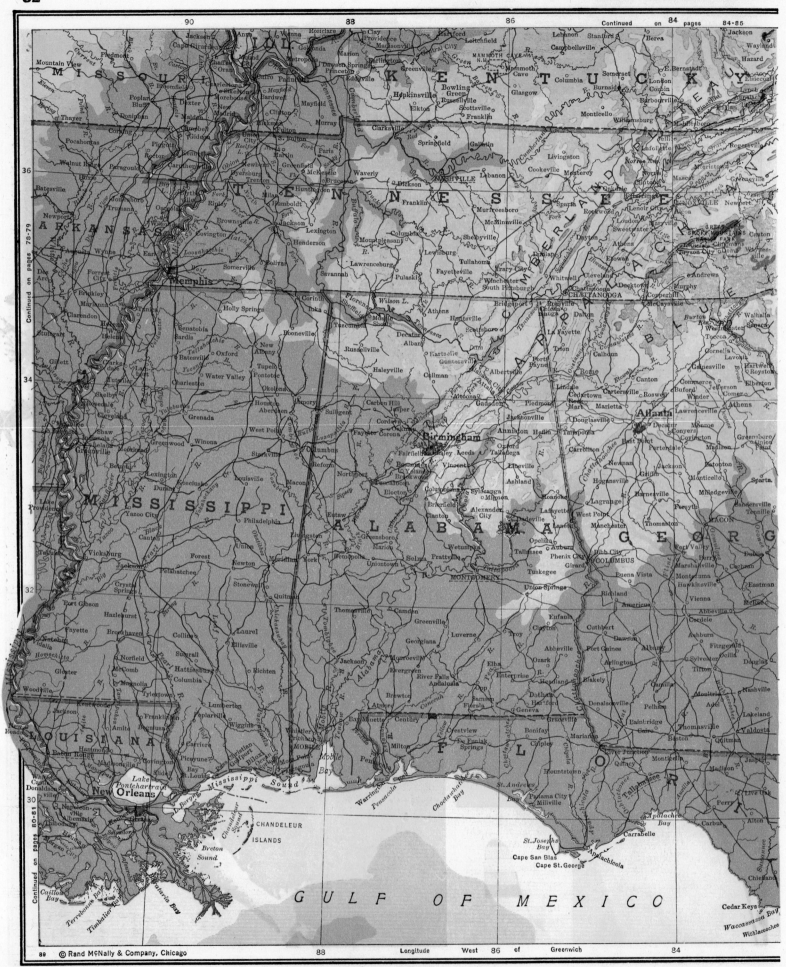

Scale 1:4 000 000; one inch to

Elevations and depressions

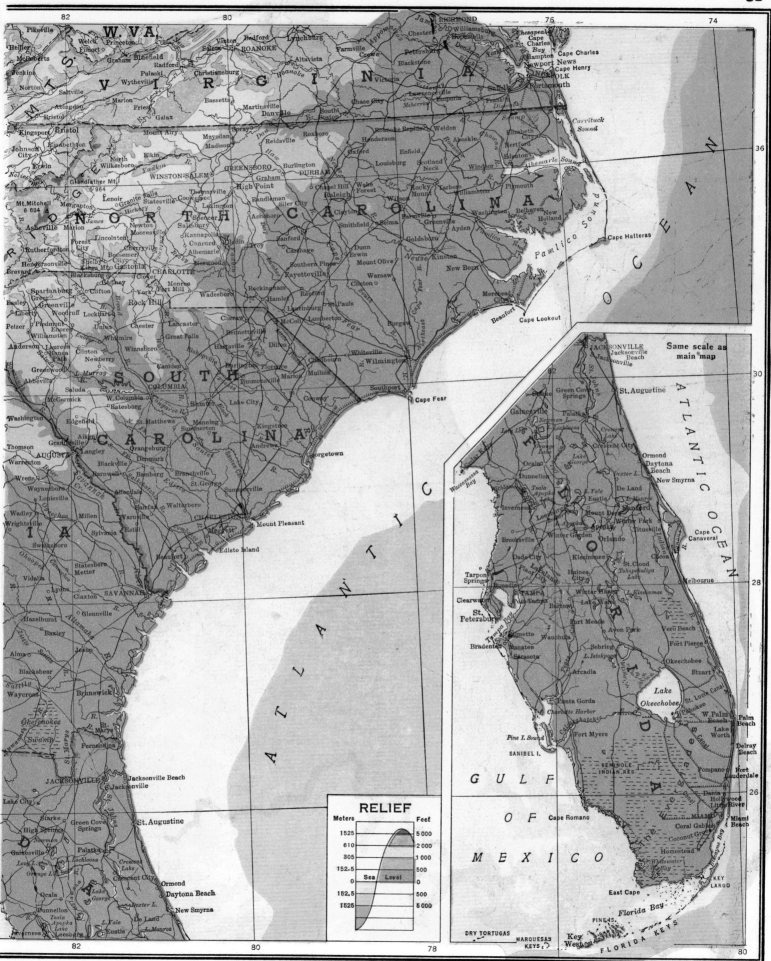

RELIEF

Meters		Feet
1525		5 000
610		2 000
305		1 000
152.5		500
0	Sea Level	0
152.5		500
1525		5 000

64 miles.   Conic Projection

are given in feet

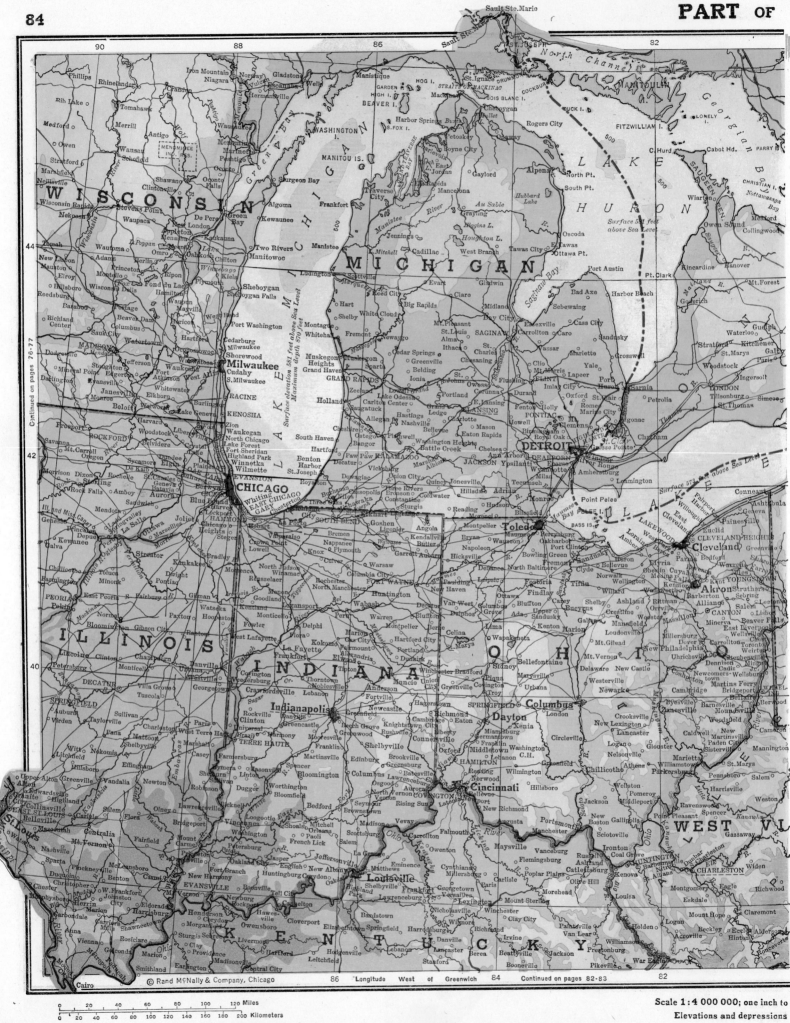

© Rand McNally & Company, Chicago

Continued on pages 82-83

Scale 1:4 000 000; one inch to

Elevations and depressions

0 20 40 60 80 100 120 Miles

0 20 40 60 80 100 120 140 160 180 200 Kilometers

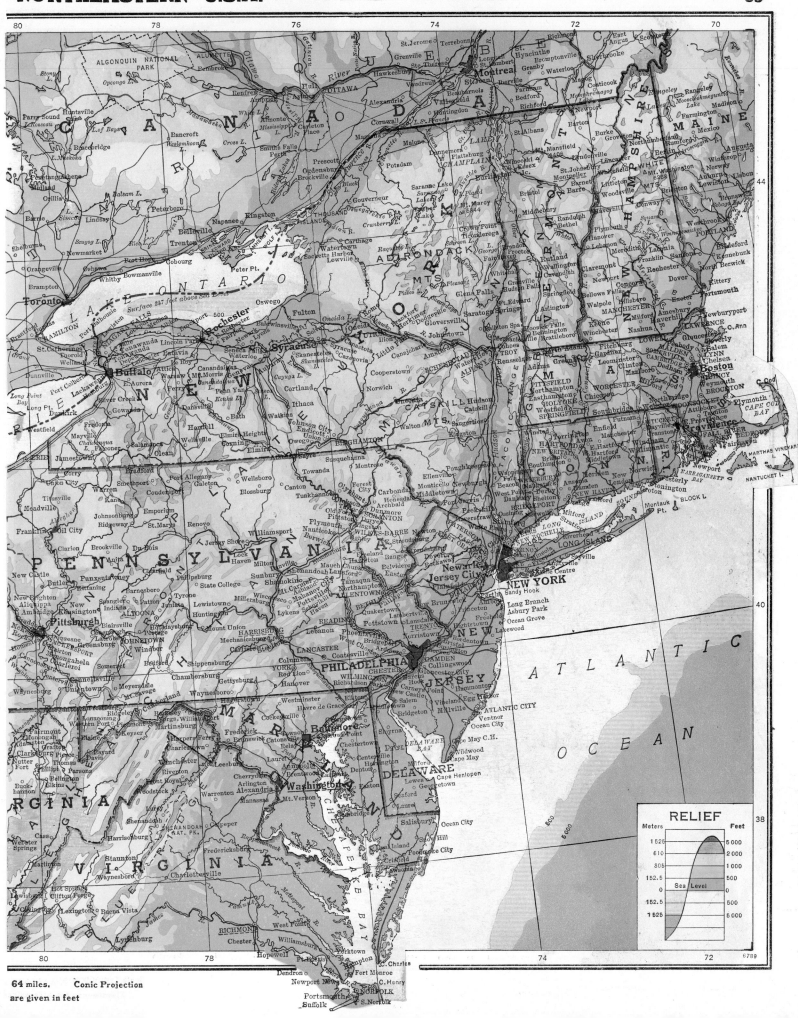

64 miles.   Conic Projection

are given in feet

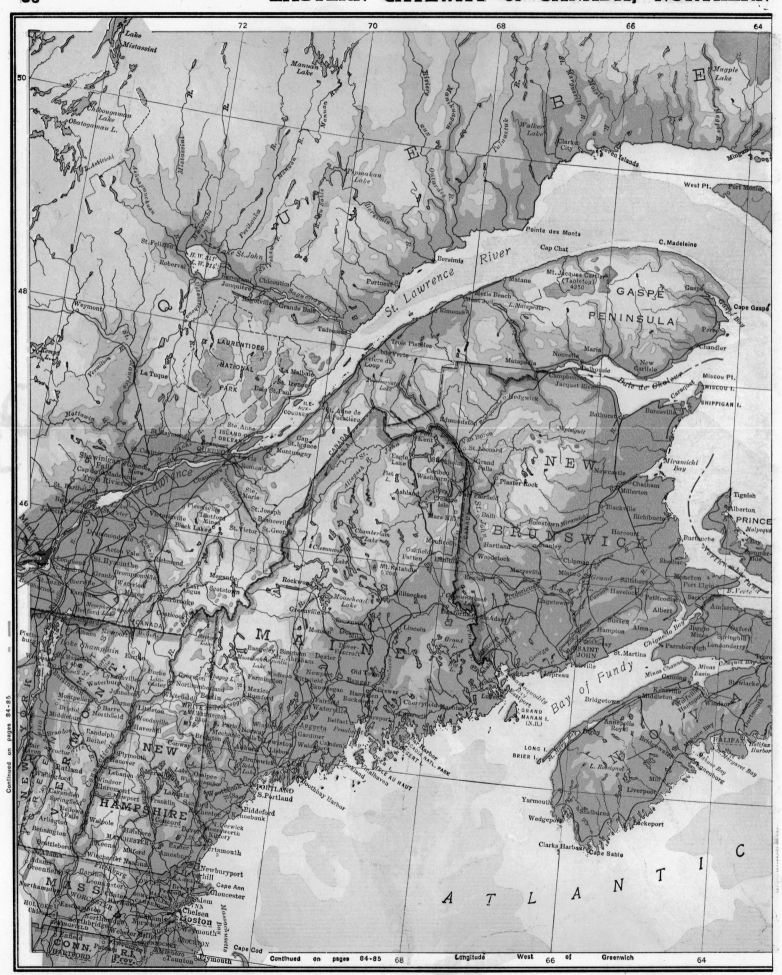

Continued on pages 84-85

Continued on pages 84-85

Longitude   West   of   Greenwich

ATLANTIC

0   20   40   60   80   100   120 Miles
0   20   40   60   80   100   120   140   160   180   200 Kilometers

Scale 1:4 000 000; one inch to

Elevations and depressions

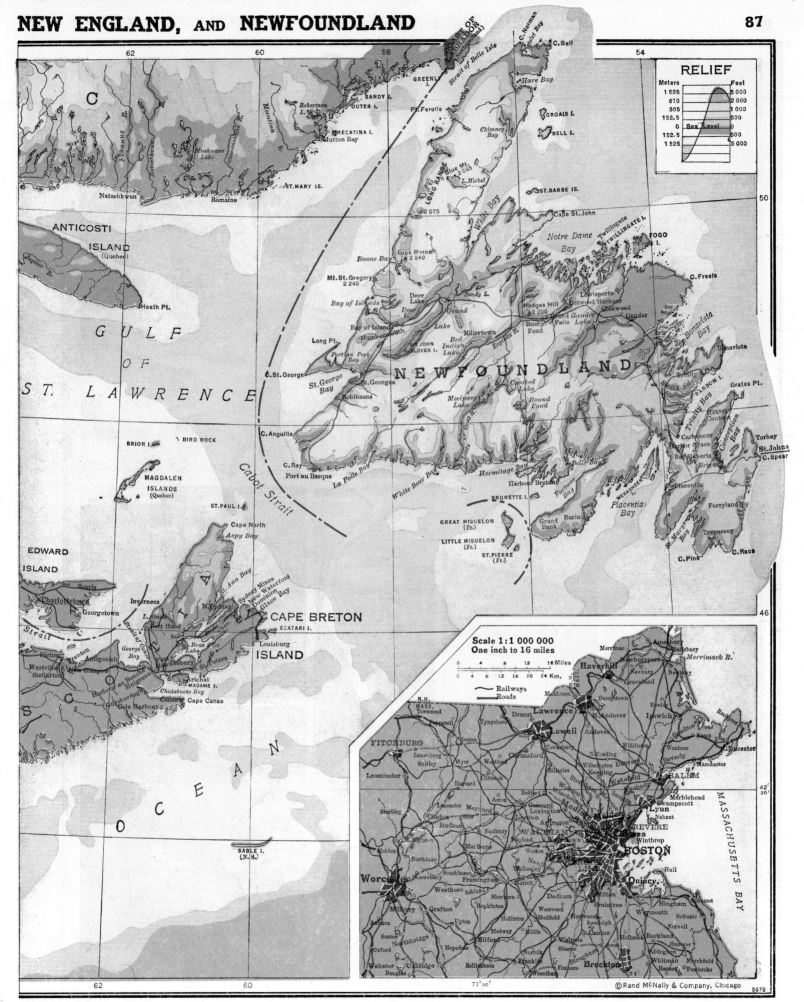

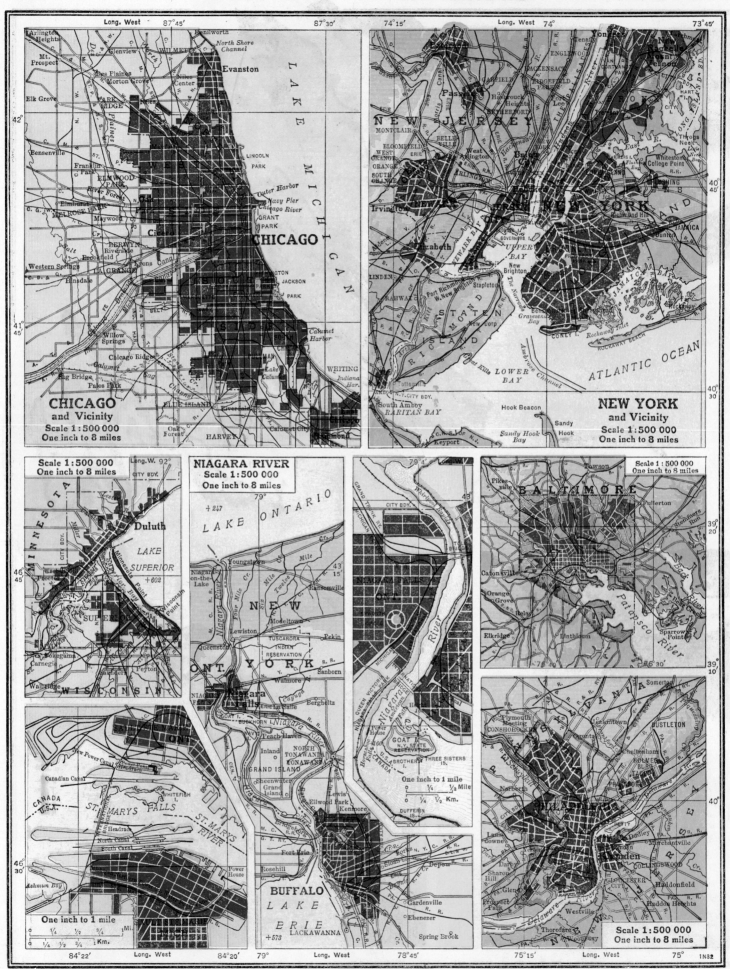

CHICAGO
and Vicinity
Scale 1:500 000
One inch to 8 miles

NEW YORK
and Vicinity
Scale 1:500 000
One inch to 8 miles

Scale 1:500 000
One inch to 8 miles

NIAGARA RIVER
Scale 1:500 000
One inch to 8 miles

Scale 1:500 000
One inch to 8 miles

BALTIMORE

One inch to 1 mile

BUFFALO

One inch to 1 mile

Scale 1:500 000
One inch to 8 miles

Scale 1:500 000; one inch to 8 miles
Elevations are given in feet

© Rand McNally & Company, Chicago

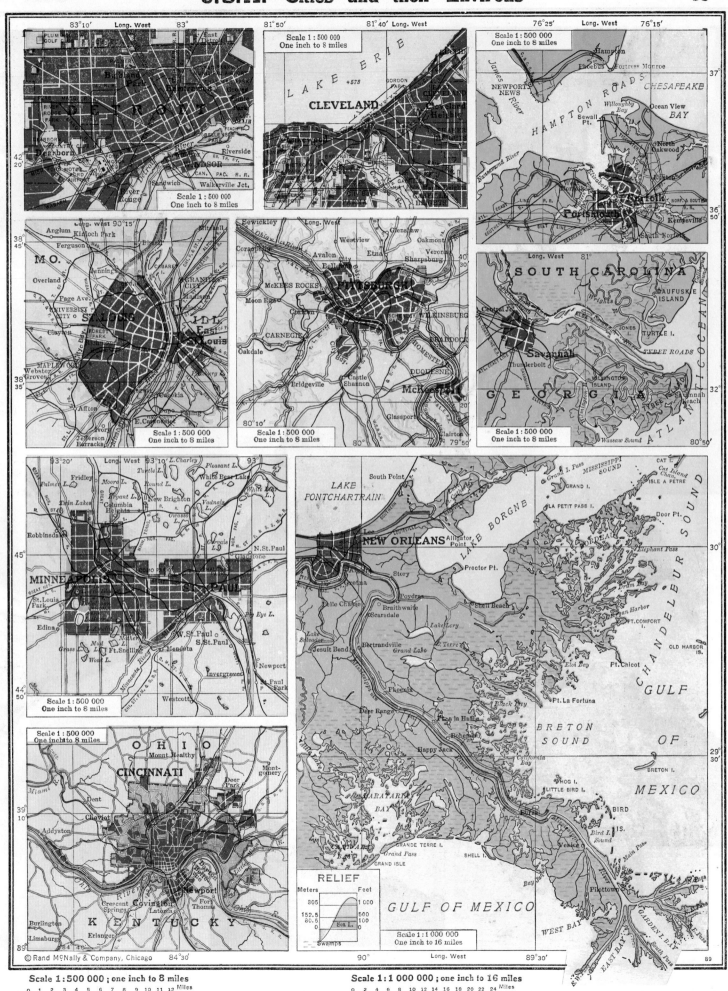

Scale 1 : 500 000
One inch to 8 miles

LAKE ERIE

CLEVELAND

Scale 1 : 500 000
One inch to 8 miles

HAMPTON ROADS   CHESAPEAKE

BAY

Scale 1 : 500 000
One inch to 8 miles

MO.

ST. LOUIS

PITTSBURGH

SOUTH CAROLINA

Savannah

GEORGIA

ATLANTIC OCEAN

Scale 1 : 500 000
One inch to 8 miles

Scale 1 : 500 000
One inch to 8 miles

Scale 1 : 500 000
One inch to 8 miles

MINNEAPOLIS   ST. PAUL

LAKE
PONTCHARTRAIN

MISSISSIPPI
SOUND

NEW ORLEANS

LAKE BORGNE

CHANDELEUR SOUND

GULF

BRETON
SOUND

OF

MEXICO

Scale 1 : 500 000
One inch to 8 miles

Scale 1 : 500 000
One inch to 8 miles

OHIO

CINCINNATI

KENTUCKY

RELIEF

Meters	Feet
305	1 000
152.5	500
80.5	100
	Sea L.

Swamps

GULF OF MEXICO

Scale 1 : 1 000 000
One inch to 16 miles

© Rand McNally & Company, Chicago

Scale 1 : 500 000 ; one inch to 8 miles

0 1 2 3 4 5 6 7 8 9 10 11 12 Miles
0 2 4 6 8 10 12 14 16 18 20 Km.

Scale 1 : 1 000 000 ; one inch to 16 miles

0 2 4 6 8 10 12 14 16 18 20 22 24 Miles
0 4 8 12 16 20 24 28 32 36 40 Km.

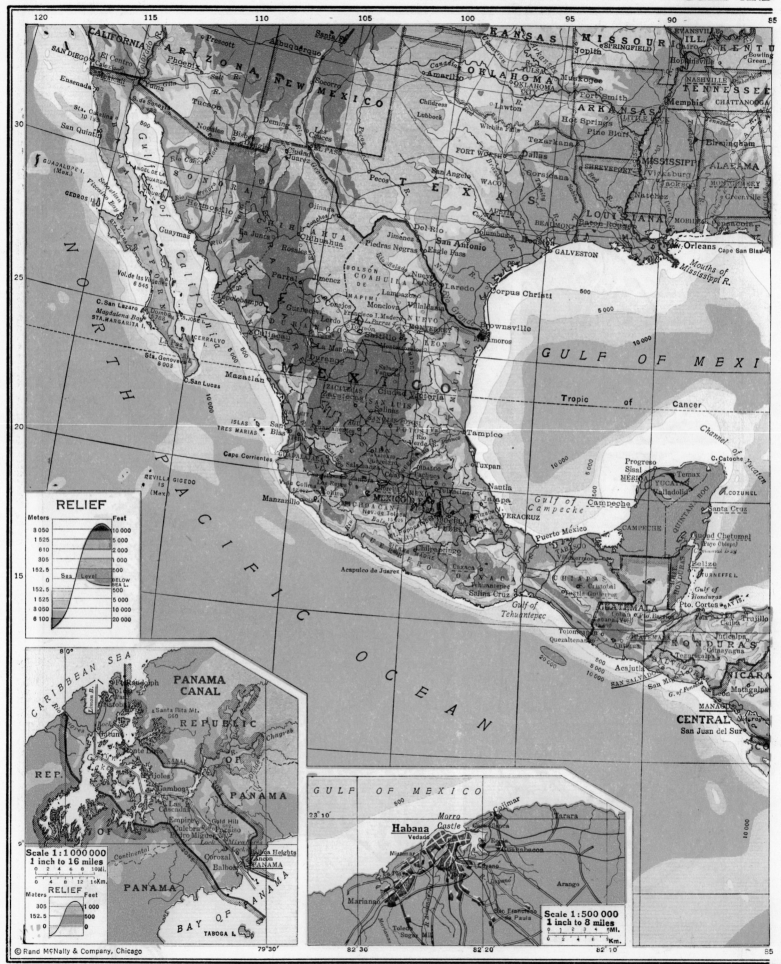

RELIEF

Meters		Feet
3 050		10 000
1 525		5 000
610		2 000
305		1 000
152.5		500
0	Sea Level	BELOW SEA L.
152.5		500
1 525		5 000
3 050		10 000
6 100		20 000

PANAMA CANAL

Scale 1:1 000 000
1 inch to 16 miles
0 2 4 6 8 10 Mi.
0 4 8 12 16 Km.

RELIEF

Maters	Feet
305	1 000
152.5	500
0	0

© Rand McNally & Company, Chicago

Habana

Scale 1:500 000
1 inch to 8 miles
0 1 2 3 4 5 Mi.
0 2 4 6 8 Km.

Scale 1 : 16 000 000; one inch to 250 miles.   Polyconic Projection

Elevations and depressions are given in feet

0   50   100   200   300   400   500 Miles

0   100   200   300   400   500   600   700   800 Kilometers

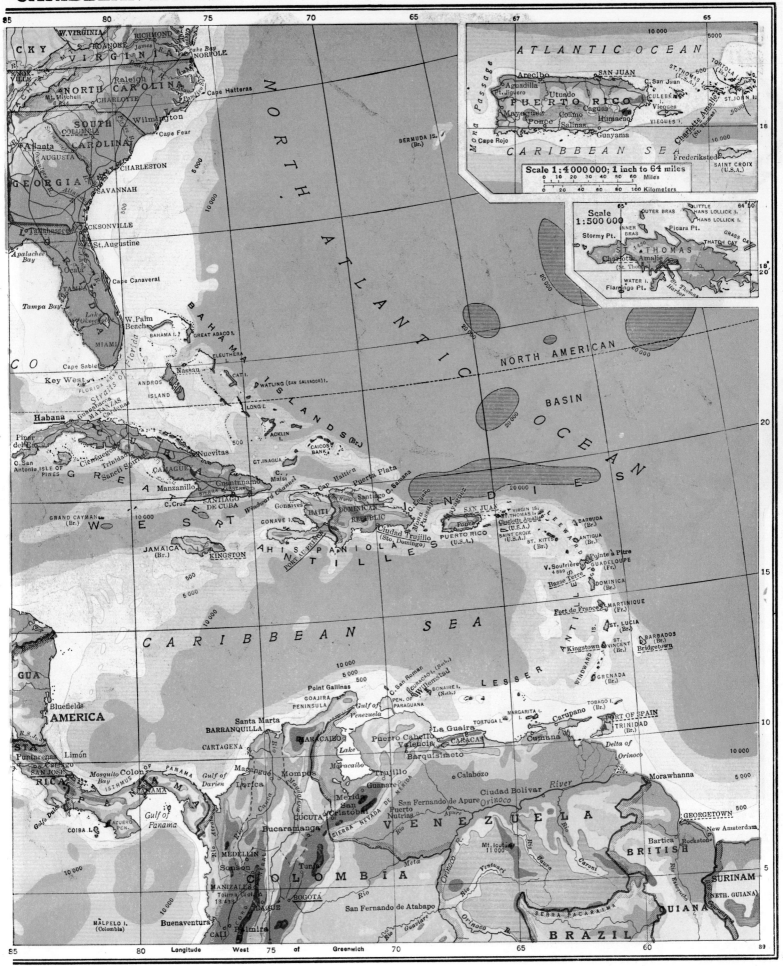

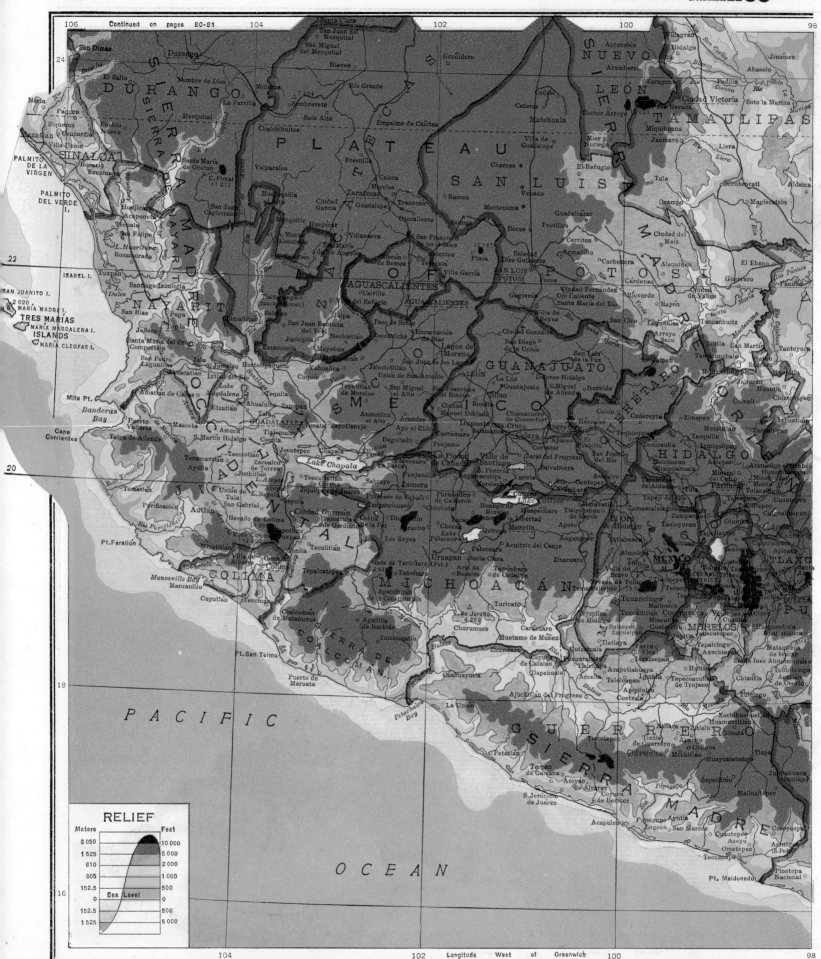

Continued on pages 80·81

RELIEF

Meters		Feet
3 050		10 000
1 525		5 000
610		2 000
305		1 000
152.5		500
0	Sea Level	0
152.5		500
1 525		5 000

PACIFIC

OCEAN

0 20 40 60 80 100 120 Miles
0 20 40 60 80 100 120 140 160 180 200 Kilometers

Longitude   West   of   Greenwich

Scale 1 : 4 000 000; one inch to

Elevations and depressions

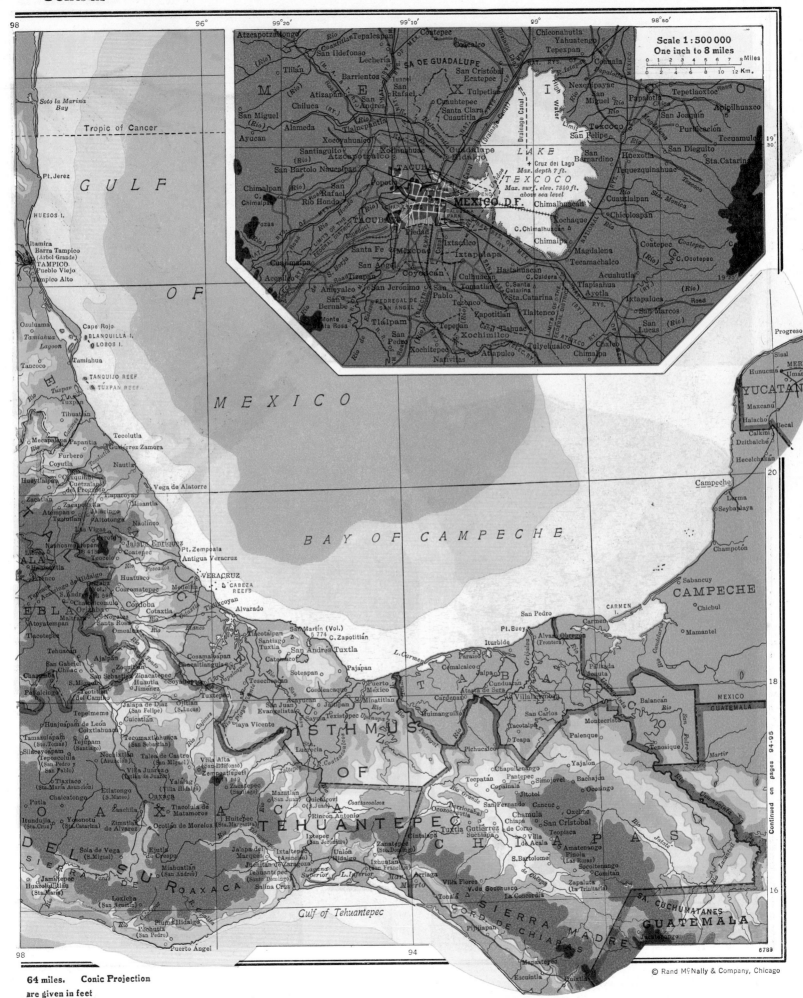

MEXICO D.F. (inset)

Scale 1 : 500 000
One inch to 8 miles

0 1 2 3 4 5 6 7 8 Miles
0 2 4 6 8 10 12 Km.

LAKE
TEXCOCO
+ Cruz del Lago
Max. depth 7 ft.
Max. surf. elev. 7340 ft.
above sea level

MEXICO D.F.

Main map labels

GULF

OF

MEXICO

Tropic of Cancer

Soto la Marina Bay

TAMPICO

BAY OF CAMPECHE

VERACRUZ

ISTHMUS OF TEHUANTEPEC

OAXACA

SIERRA DE OAXACA

SIERRA MADRE DEL SUR

CHIAPAS

TABASCO

CAMPECHE

YUCATAN

MERIDA

Progreso

GUATEMALA

SIERRA DE CHIAPAS

CORD DE CHIAPAS

Gulf of Tehuantepec

Oaxaca

Tuxtla Gutierrez

San Cristobal

Palenque

Campeche

Continued on pages 94-95

64 miles. Conic Projection
are given in feet

© Rand McNally & Company, Chicago

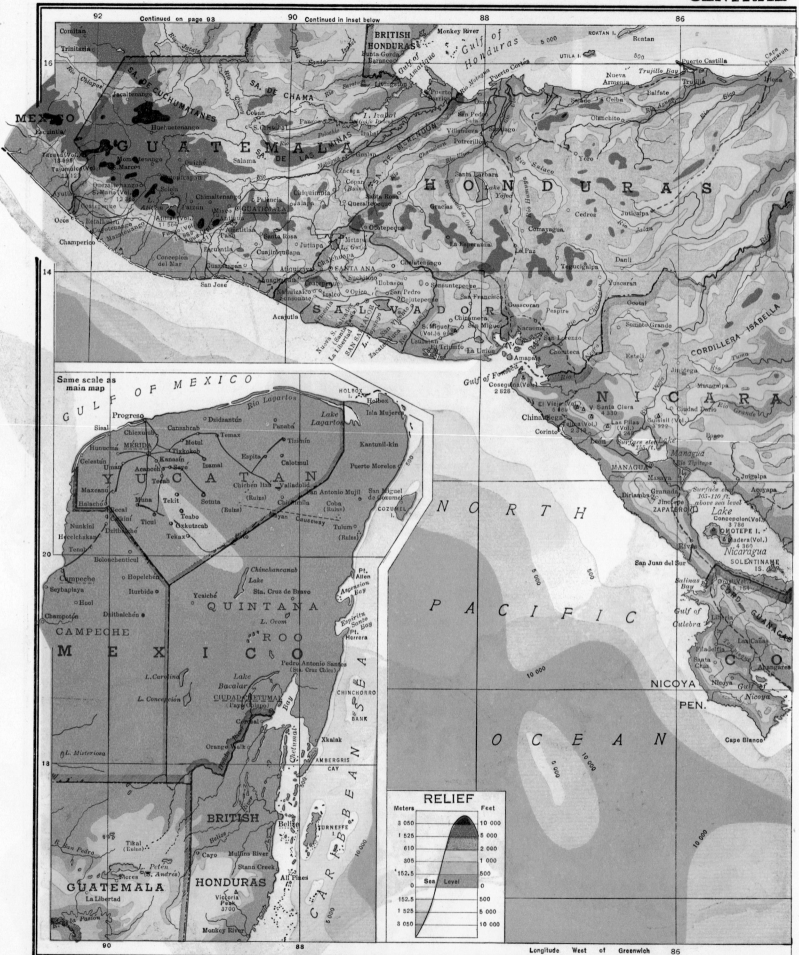

Continued on page 93   Continued in inset below

RELIEF

Meters		Feet
3 050		10 000
1 525		5 000
610		2 000
305		1 000
152.5		500
0	Sea Level	0
152.5		500
1 525		5 000
3 050		10 000

Same scale as main map

Longitude West of Greenwich

0 10 20 30 40 50 60 70 80 90 100 110 120 Miles
0 20 40 60 80 100 120 140 160 180 200 Kilometers

Scale 1:4 000 000; one inch

Elevations and depressions

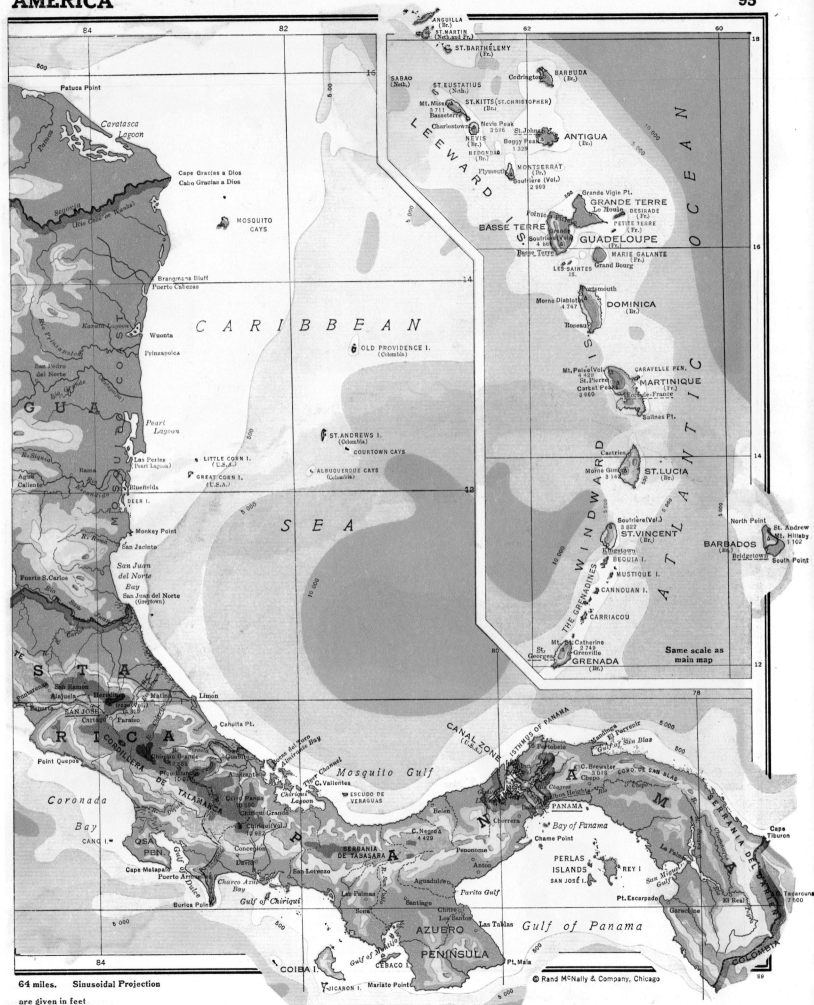

© Rand McNally & Company, Chicago

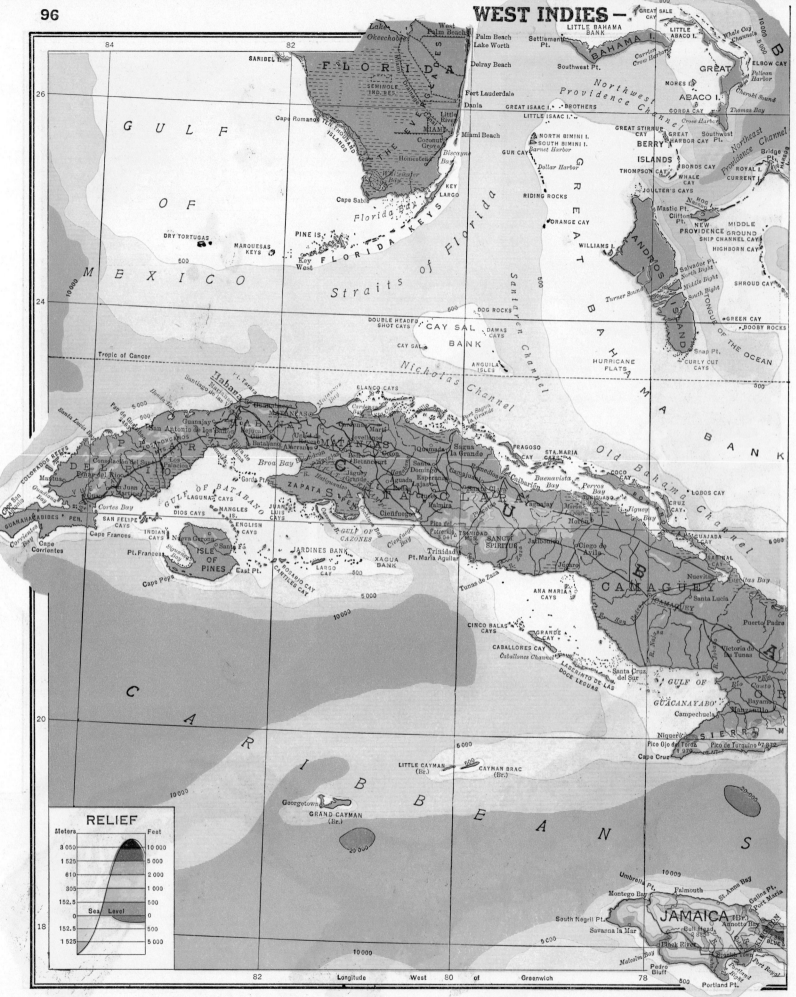

RELIEF

Meters		Feet
3 050		10 000
1 525		5 000
610		2 000
305		1 000
152.5		500
0	Sea Level	0
152.5		500
1 525		5 000

Scale 1 : 4 000 000; one inch

Elevations and depressions

0 10 20 30 40 50 60 70 80 90 100 110 120 Miles

0 20 40 60 80 100 120 140 160 180 200 Kilometers

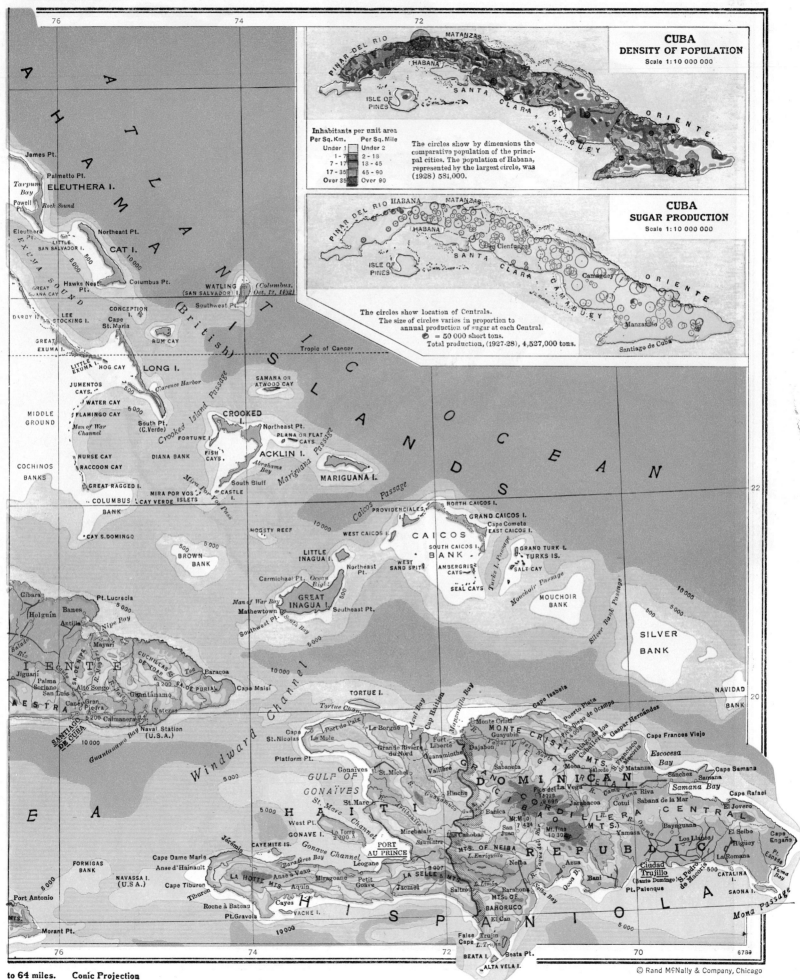

CUBA
DENSITY OF POPULATION
Scale 1:10 000 000

Inhabitants per unit area

Per Sq. Km.	Per Sq. Mile
Under 1	Under 2
1 - 7	2 - 18
7 - 17	18 - 45
17 - 35	45 - 90
Over 35	Over 90

The circles show by dimensions the comparative population of the principal cities. The population of Habana, represented by the largest circle, was (1928) 581,000.

CUBA
SUGAR PRODUCTION
Scale 1:10 000 000

The circles show location of Centrals. The size of circles varies in proportion to annual production of sugar at each Central.
⬡ = 50 000 short tons.
Total production, (1927-28), 4,527,000 tons.

to 64 miles.   Conic Projection
are given in feet

© Rand McNally & Company, Chicago

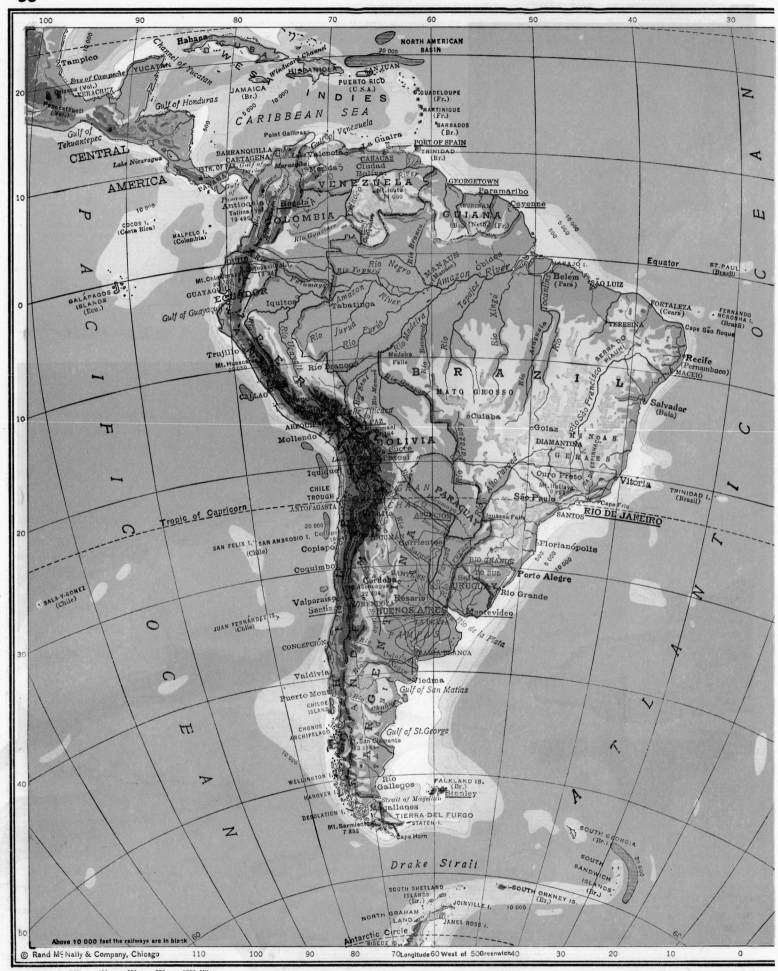

Above 10 000 feet the railways are in black

© Rand McNally & Company, Chicago

	200	400	600	800	1000 Miles
0	400	800	1200	1600 Kilometers	

Scale 1 : 40 000 000; One inch to 630 miles.   Lambert's Azimuthal, Equal Area Projection

Elevations and depressions are given in feet

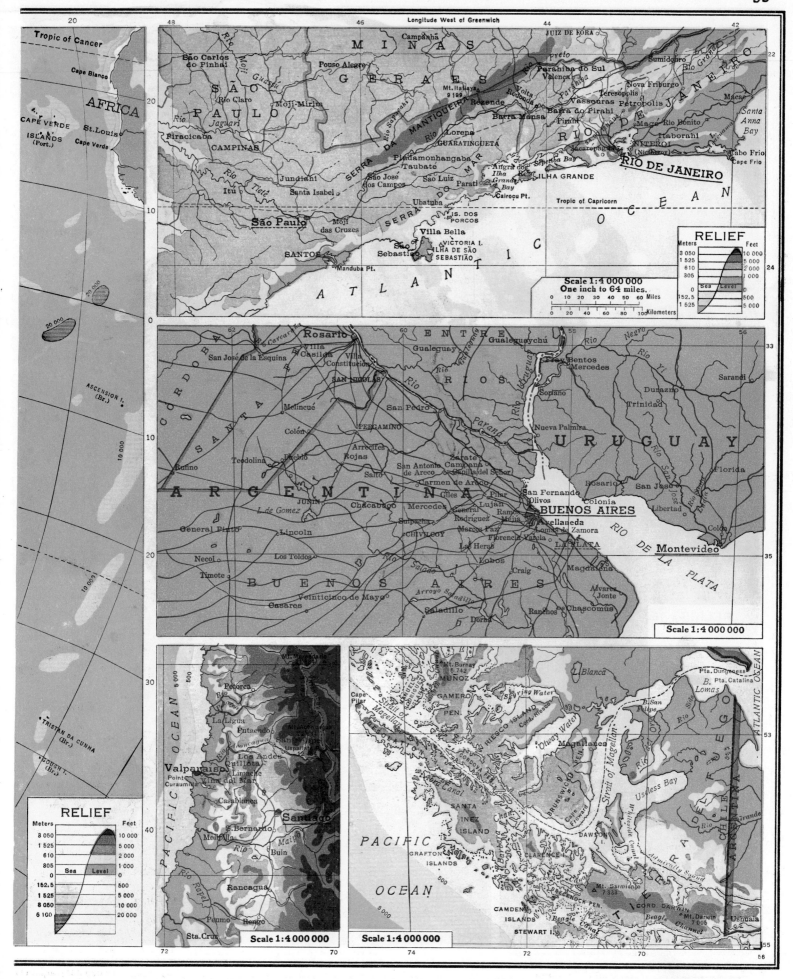

SOUTH AMERICA

Longitude West of Greenwich

Tropic of Cancer

Cape Blanco

AFRICA

CAPE VERDE
ISLANDS
(Port.)

St. Louis

Cape Verde

MINAS

GERAES

São Carlos
do Pinhal

Pouso Alegre

Campanha

JUIZ DE FORA

SÃO

PAULO

Rio Claro

Moji-Mirim

Mt. Itatiaya
9 199

Rezende

Volta
Redonda

Barra Mansa

Parahiba do Sul

Valença

Vassouras

Sumidouro

Nova Friburgo

Teresopolis

Petropolis

Rio Grande

Macae

Piracicaba

CAMPINAS

Lorena

GUARATINGUETA

Barra do Pirahi

Pirahi

Mage

Rio Bonito

Itaborahi

Santa
Anna
Bay

Pindamonhangaba

Taubaté

São José
dos Campos

São Luiz
Parati

Angra dos
Ilha
Grande
Bay

Jacarepagua

NITEROI
(Nichtevy)

RIO DE JANEIRO

Cabo
Frio
Cape Frio

Jundiahi

Santa Isabel

Ubatuba

Tropic of Capricorn

São Paulo

Moji
das Cruzes

Villa Bella

IS. DOS
PORCOS

OCEAN

SANTOS

São
Sebastião

VICTORIA I.
ILHA DE SÃO
SEBASTIÃO

ATLANTIC

Manduba Pt.

RELIEF

Scale 1:4 000 000
One inch to 64 miles.

Rosario

ENTRE

Gualeguay

Gualeguaychu

Rio Negro

San José de la Esquina

Villa
Casilda

Villa
Constitución

RIOS

Rey Bentos

Mercedes

Rio Yi

Sarandi

Melincué

SAN NICOLAS

San Pedro

Soriano

Durazno

Trinidad

Colón

PERGAMINO

Nueva Palmira

URUGUAY

Rufino

Teodolina

Pueblo

Arrecifes
Rojas

Salto

San Antonio
de Areco

Campana

Capilla del Señor

Rosario

San José

Florida

Chacabuco

Mercedes

Giles

Pilar

Zárate

Carmen de Areco

San Fernando
Olivos

Colonia

Libertad

ARGENTINA

Suipacha

General
Rodriguez

Lujan

Ramos
Mejia

BUENOS AIRES

Avellaneda

Colón

General Pinto

Lincoln

Marcos Paz

Florencio Varela

Lomas de Zamora

LA PLATA

Montevideo

RIO DE LA PLATA

Necol

Los Toldos

Las Heras

Lobos

Craig

Magdalena

Timote

BUENOS AIRES

Rio Salado

Arroyo Saladillo

Alvarez
Jonte

Veinticinco de Mayo

Casares

Saladillo

Dorha

Ranchos

Chascomus

Scale 1:4 000 000

RELIEF

Mt. Maravilla

Petorca

Mt. Burnay
6 742

L. Blanca

Pta. Dungeoss

B. Pta. Catalina

Lomas

PACIFIC OCEAN

La Ligua

Putaendo

MUÑOZ

GAMERO
PEN.

Skyring Water

B. San
Felipe

Mt. Aconcagua

San
Uspallata

Cape
Pilar

Strait of Magellan

Los Andes

Quillota

Limache

RIESCO ISLAND

Otway Water

Magallanes

Rio

Valparaiso
Point
Curaumilla

Viña del Mar

Casablanca

SANTA
INEZ
ISLAND

BRUNSWICK PEN.

Dawson

Useless Bay

ATLANTIC OCEAN

S. Bernardo

Melipilla

Santiago

DESOLATION

Cape Froward

ARGENTINA

Buin

CLARENCE I.

PACIFIC

Rio Maipo

GRAFTON
ISLANDS

Rancagua

CAMDEN
ISLANDS

OCEAN

CORD. DARWIN

Mt. Sarmiento
7 333

Mt. Darwin
7 005

Ushuaia

Penmo

Rengo

STEWART I.

Beagle Canal

Sta. Cruz

Scale 1:4 000 000

Scale 1:4 000 000

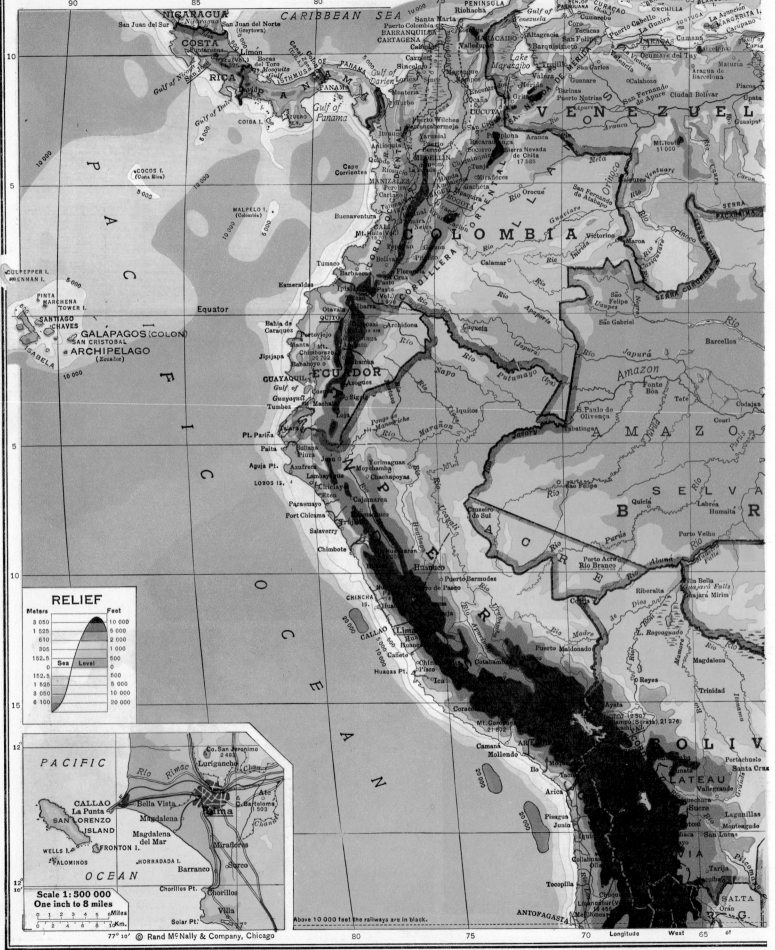

RELIEF

Meters		Feet
3 050		10 000
1 525		5 000
610		2 000
305		1 000
152.5		500
0	Sea Level	0
152.5		500
1 525		5 000
3 050		10 000
6 100		20 000

PACIFIC

Co. San Jeronimo 2 493
Lurigancho
Rio Rimac Chan
Co. Bartolome 1 503
Ate
CALLAO
La Punta
SAN LORENZO ISLAND
Bella Vista
Magdalena
Lima
Magdalena del Mar
Chann
WELLS I.
PALOMINOS
FRONTON I.
Miraflores
HORRADADA I.
Barranco
Surco
OCEAN
Chorillos Pt.
Chorillos
Villa
Solar Pt.

Scale 1 : 500 000
One inch to 8 miles

Miles
0 1 2 3 4 5
0 2 4 6 8 Km.

77° 10'
© Rand McNally & Company, Chicago

Above 10 000 feet the railways are in black.

0 50 100 200 300 400 500 Miles
0 100 200 400 600 800 Kilometers

Scale 1 : 16 000 000; one inch to
Elevations and depressions

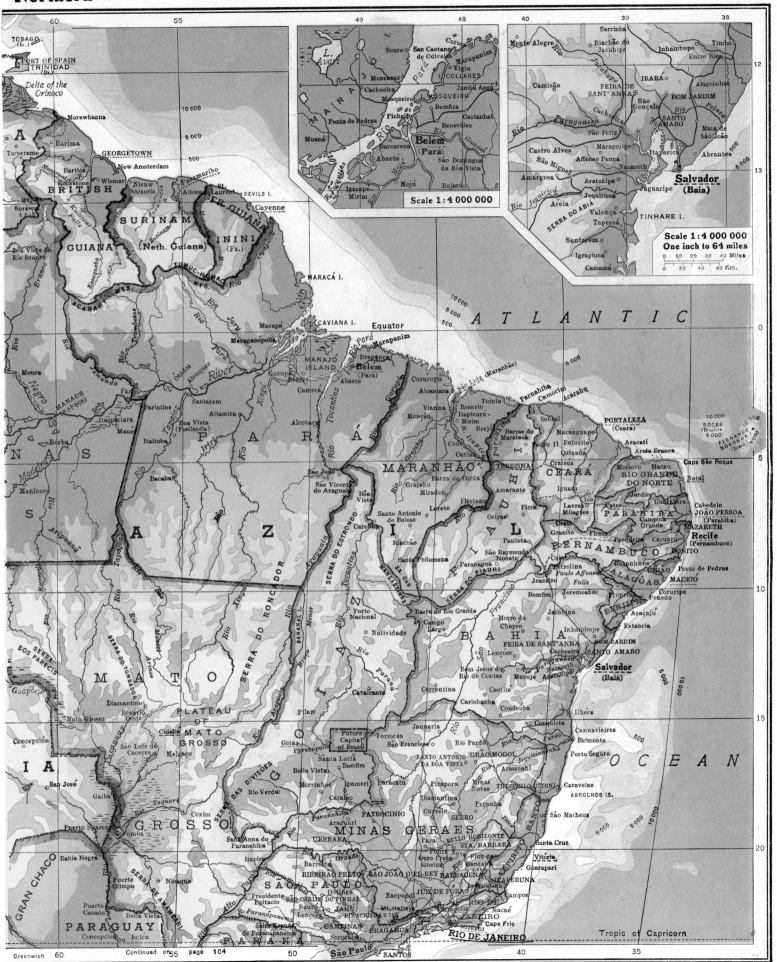

Belem
(Para)

Scale 1:4 000 000

Salvador
(Baia)

Scale 1:4 000 000
One inch to 64 miles

ATLANTIC

OCEAN

250 miles.   Sinusoidal Projection

are given in feet

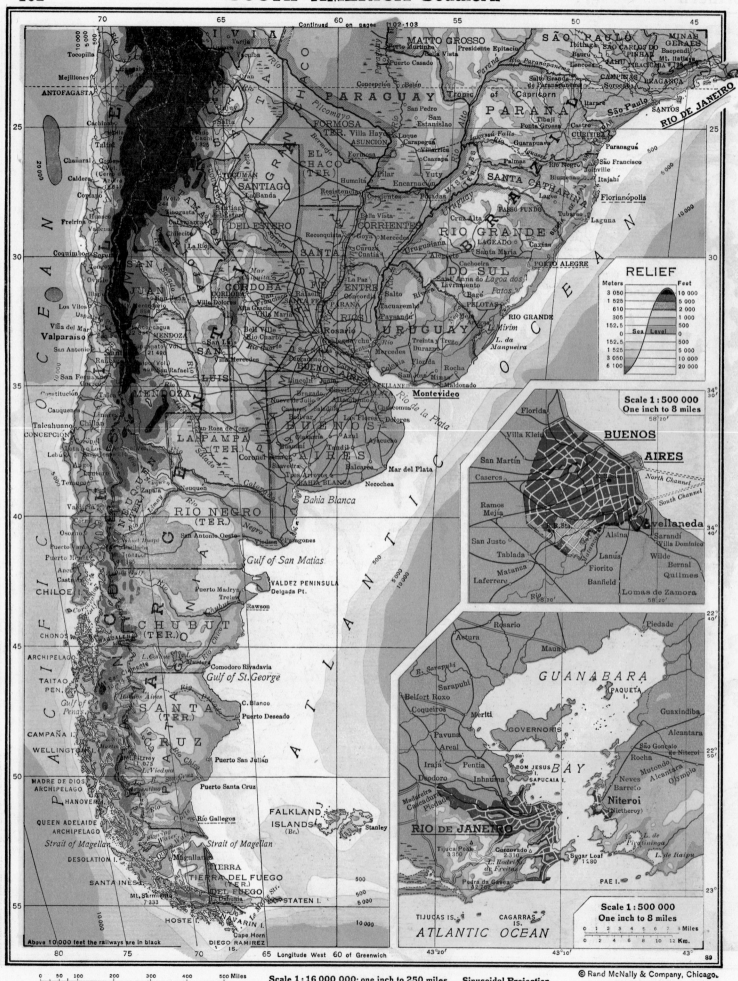

Scale 1:16 000 000; one inch to 250 miles.   Sinusoidal Projection
Elevations and depressions are given in feet

© Rand McNally & Company, Chicago.

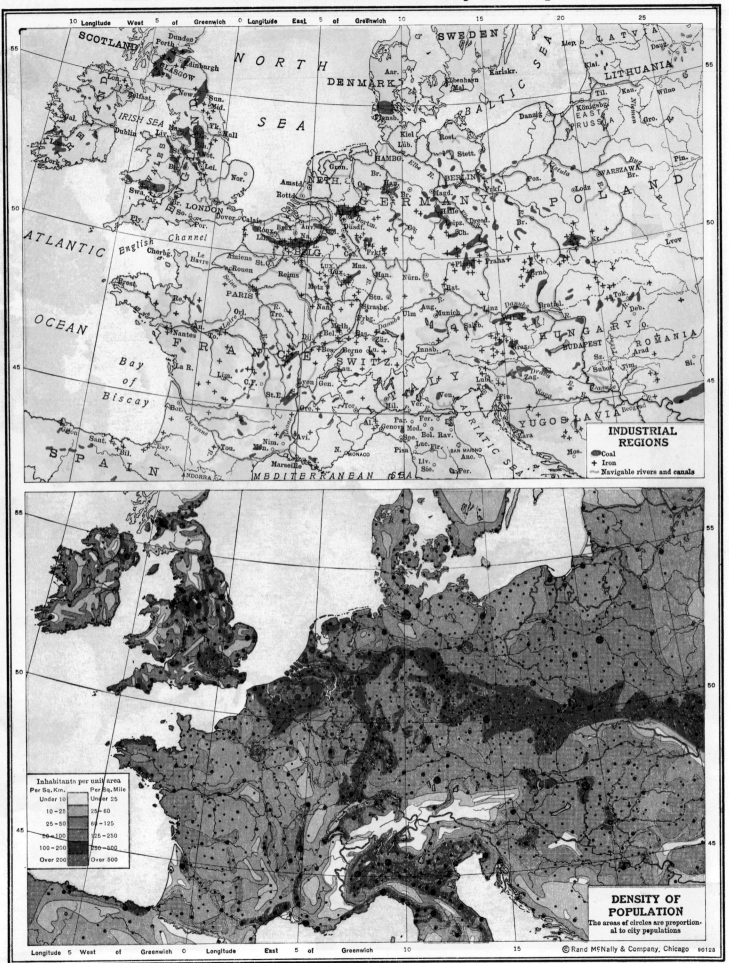

INDUSTRIAL REGIONS

- Coal
- † Iron
- Navigable rivers and canals

DENSITY OF POPULATION

The areas of circles are proportional to city populations

Inhabitants per unit area

Per Sq. Km.	Per Sq. Mile
Under 10	Under 25
10 - 25	25 - 60
25 - 50	60 - 125
50 - 100	125 - 250
100 - 200	250 - 500
Over 200	Over 500

© Rand McNally & Company, Chicago   90123

Scale for both maps: one inch to 216 miles

Conic Projection

Scale 1 : 16 000 000; one inch to 250 miles.   Conic Projection
Elevations and depressions are given in feet

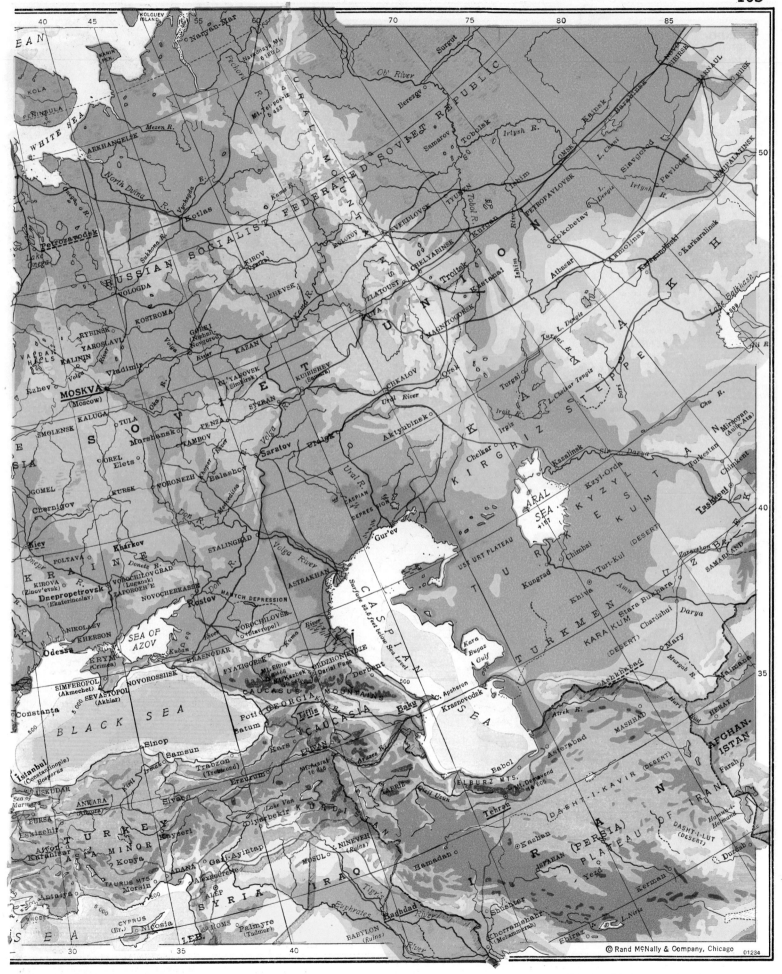

EUROPE–Languages

40   45   KOLGUEV ISLAND   55   Nar'yan-Mar   60   70   75   80   85

EAN

KOLA PENINSULA

KANIN PEN.

WHITE SEA

ARKHANGELSK   Mezen R.   Mt. Tel-pos-iz 5 433   Ob' River   Surgut   50

Pechora   Narodnaya Mt. 6 184

Onega R.   KOLA   Mezen R.

North Dvina R.   Sukhona R.   Bereg'y   Samarov   Tobolsk   Irtysh R.   NOVOSIBIRSK   BARNAUL   BIISK

Petrozavodsk   Lake Onega   Kotlas   Vychegda R.   Kama R.   L. Chani   Siavgorod   SEMIPALATINSK   OMSK

RUSSIAN   SOCIALIST   FEDERATED   SOVIET   REPUBLIC   Irtysh R.   Pavlodar

VOLOGDA   KIROV   SVERDLOVSK   TYUMEN   Tobol R.   PETROPAVLOVSK   L. Dengiz

VAGAN HILLS   YAROSLAVL   KOSTROMA   IZHEVSK   Kama R.   ZLATOUST   CHELYABINSK   Ishim R.   Akmolinsk   Karkaralinsk

RYBINSK   GORKI (Nizhni Novgorod)   KAZAN   UFA   MAGNITOGORSK   Atbasar   +899

KALININ   Vladimir   Volga River   KUIBISHEV (Samara)   CHKALOV   Orsk   Turgai R.   L. Chelkar Tengiz   Lake Balkhash

Rzhev   MOSKVA (Moscow)   Oka R.   SYZRAN   Ural River   Irgiz R.   KIRGHIZ   Ili R.

SMOLENSK   KALUGA   TULA   PENZA   Volga   Saratov   Uralsk   Aktyubinsk   Irgiz   S T E P P E   Miravoyan (Alma-Ata)

Morshansk   TAMBOV   CASPIAN DEPRESSION   Chelkar   L. Chelkar Tengiz   Kazalinsk   Turkestan   Chimkent

OREL   Elets   VORONEZH   Balashov   Don R.   KAZALINSK   Syr Darya   Tashkent   40

GOMEL   KURSK   Medveditsa R.   ARAL SEA +167   Kzyl-Orda   SAMARKAND

Chernigov   Kiev   Don R.   STALINGRAD   Volga River   Gur'ev   USTURT PLATEAU   Chimbai   Turt-Kul   KYZYL KUM (DESERT)   Zarafshan Br.

POLTAVA   KHARKOV   Donets R.   ASTRAKHAN   CASPIAN   Kungrad   Amu   Khiva   Stara Bukhara   Charjui   Darya

KIROVA (Zinov'evsk)   VOROSHILOVGRAD (Lugansk)   ZAPOROZH'E   Manych Depression   Kara Bugaz Gulf   TURKMEN   KARA KUM (DESERT)   Mary

Dnepropetrovsk (Ekaterinoslav)   NOVOCHERKASSK   VOROSHILOVSK (Stavropol)   Kuma River   Aktyubinsk

NIKOLAEV   Rostov   SEA OF AZOV   Kuban   KRASNODAR   Manych   PYATIGORSK   Mt. Elbrus 18 468   Mt. Kazbek   ORDZHONIKIDZE   Darial Pass   Derbent   500   C. Apsheron   Krasnovodsk   Ashkhabad   Atrek R.   Hari R.   MASHHAD   HERAT

ODESSA   KHERSON   SIMFEROPOL (Akmechet)   KRYM (Crimea)   CAUCASUS   MOUNTAINS   GEORGIA   Baku   SEA   AFGHAN-ISTAN

SEVASTOPOL (Akhtiar)   NOVOROSSIISK   Poti   Batum   Tiflis   CAUCASIA   Kars   ERIVAN   Araxes R.   ELBURZ MTS.   Mt. Demavend 18 605   Asterabad   Babol   DASHT-I-KAVIR (DESERT)   Farah

Constanţa   BLACK   SEA   Sinop   Samsun   Trabzon (Trebizond)   Erzurum   Mt. Ararat 16 946   TABRIZ   Tehran   Herat   Hamun-i-Helmand

Istanbul (Constantinople)   Bosporus   USKUDAR   Sea of Marmara   BURSA   Eskisehir   ANKARA (Angora)   Sivas   Kizil R.   Lake Van   Diyarbekir   KURDISTAN   Urmia L.   Veil Uzun   N   PLATEAU   OF   IRAN   DASHT-I-LUT (DESERT)   Duzdab

Afyon-Karahisar   TURKEY   Kayseri   ASIA MINOR   Konya   TAURUS MTS.   Mersin   ADANA   Gaji-Ayintap   MOSUL   NINEVEH (Ruins)   Hamadan   Kashan   ISFAHAN   Yezd   Kerman

Antalya   RHODES   CYPRUS (Br.)   Nicosia   ALEP   HOMS   Palmyra (Tadmor)   SYRIA   IRAQ   Euphrates   BABYLON (Ruins)   Baghdad   River   Tigris   Shushtar   Khorramshahr (Mohammerah)   Shiraz   L. Niriz

Alexandrette   LEB.   Tigris   Kizil R.

30   35   40   © Rand McNally & Company, Chicago   01234

I. INDO-EUROPEAN

1. Teutonic
English
Upper } High
Middle } German
Low German
Dutch
Flemish
Danish
Norwegian
Swedish
Icelandic and
  Faeroese
Frisian

2. Romanic
French
  (Langue d'oïl)
French
  (Langue d'oc)
Walloon
Italian
Rhaeto-Romanic
Ladinic
Friulian
Sardinian
Spanish
Catalan
Portuguese
Gallegan
Romanian
Vlach

3. Slavonic
Great Russian
Little Russian
White Russian
Polish
Serbo-Croatian
Slovenian
Czecho-Moravian
Slovakian
Bulgarian
Macedonian
Sorbian (Wendic)

4. Hellenic
Modern Greek

5. Baltic
Lettish
Lithuanian

6. Celtic
Irish
Gaelic
Welsh (Cymric)
Breton

7. Armenian
Armenian

8. Iranic
Persian
Tatic
Ossetic
Kurdic
Yezidic
Talyshinic

9. Thraco-Illyrian
Albanian

II. URAL-ALTAIC

1. Finno-Ugrian
Finnish (Suomi)
Estonian and
  Livonian
Lappish
Karelian
Syryenian
Permian
Cheremissian
Votiak
Mordvinian
Ostiak
Vogulic
Magyar

2. Samoyedic
Samoyedic

3. Turkish-Tataric
Turkish (Osmanli)
Kirghizic and
  Turkomanic
Bashkirian
Tataric
Kumykian
Chuvashian
Karachaic
Nogaic
Karapapakian
Kizilbashian
Tahtajic

4. Mongolian
Kalmuckian

III. SEMITIC
Arabic
Maltese
Syrian

IV. HAMITIC
Berber

V. CAUCASIC
Caucasian
  Northwest
  Northeast
  Southwest

VI. BASQUE
Basque

Scale 1:16 000 000; one inch to 250 miles.   Conic Projection.
After Language Map by Morris Jastrow

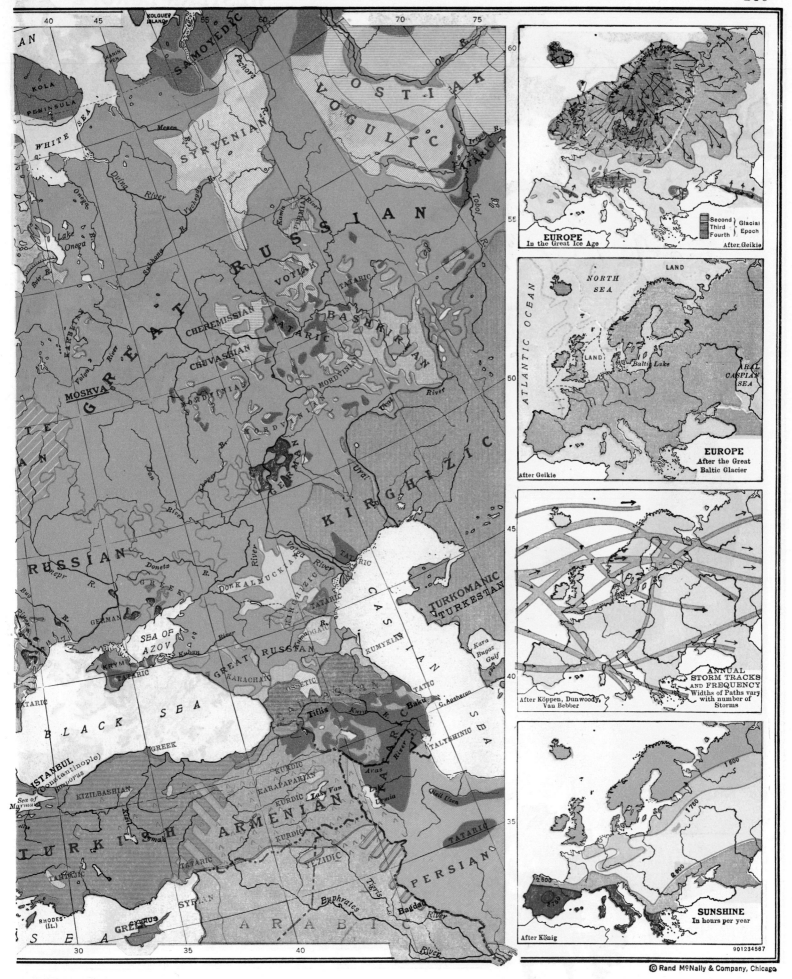

KOLA PENINSULA
WHITE SEA
KANIN PER.
SAMOYEDIC
KOLGUEV ISLAND
Ob
OSTIAK
VOGULIC
TATARIC
Pechora
Mesen
SYRYENIAN
Vychegda R.
Kama R.
Belaja R.
Onega
Svir R.
Lake Onega
Dwina River
Suchona
VOTIAK
CHEREMISSIAN
TATARIC
Volga River
BASHKIRIAN
GREAT RUSSIAN
Tobol R.
Irtysh R.
MOSKVA
CHUVASHIAN
MORDVINIAN
MORDVINIAN
GERMAN
Ural
KIRGHIZIC
RUSSIAN
Donetz R.
Dnepr R.
Don River
GREEK
KALMUCK
KIRGHIZIC
TATARIC
TURKOMANIC
Volga River
Ural River
TURKESTAN
Kara Bugaz Gulf
KUMYKIAN
SEA OF AZOV
GERMAN
KRYM
TATARIC
GREAT RUSSIAN
KARACHAI
OSSETIC
DAGHESTAN
Kuban River
Kuma River
Don R.
CASPIAN SEA
BLACK SEA
GREEK
Tiflis
Baku
C. Apsheron
TATARIC
Kura R.
Aras R.
TALYSHINIC
ISTANBUL (Constantinople)
Bosporus
KIZILBASHIAN
Sea of Marmara
KURDIC
KARAPAPAKIAN
Lake Van
Lake Urmia
Kizil Uzen
ARMENIAN
TURKISH
Smur
KURDIC
YEZIDIC
TATARIC
TATARIC
Tigris
Euphrates
Bagdad
PERSIAN
RHODES (It.)
CYPRUS
GREEK
SYRIAN
ARABIC
River

EUROPE
In the Great Ice Age
After Geikie

Second
Third
Fourth
} Glacial Epoch

NORTH SEA
LAND
ATLANTIC OCEAN
LAND
LAND
Baltic Lake
ARAL CASPIAN SEA
EUROPE
After the Great Baltic Glacier
After Geikie

ANNUAL STORM TRACKS AND FREQUENCY
Widths of Paths vary with number of Storms
After Köppen, Dunwoody, Van Bebber

SUNSHINE
In hours per year
After König
1 500
1 750
2 000
2 500
1 750

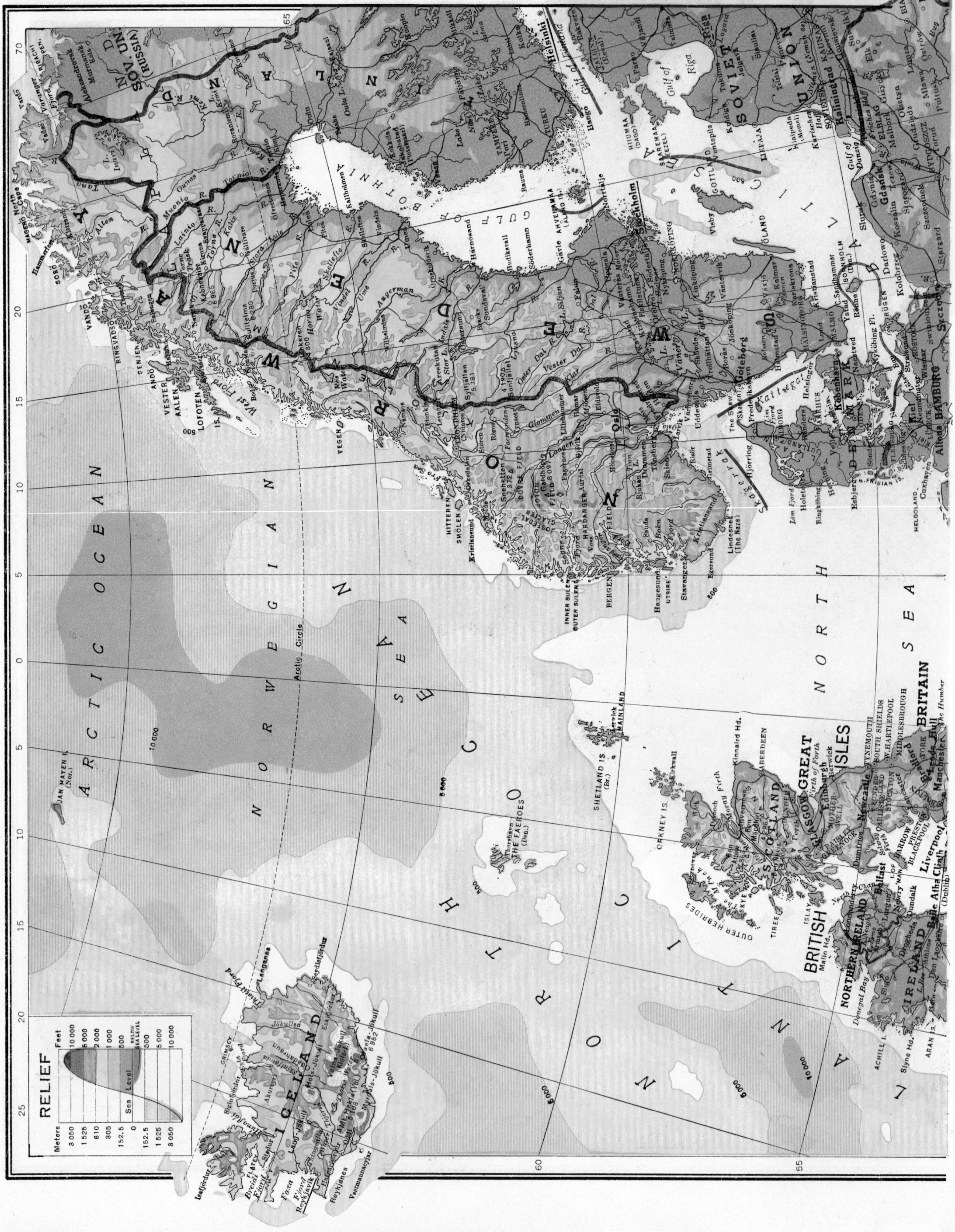

ARCTIC OCEAN

SOV. UN. (RUSSIA)

FINLAND

NORWAY

SWEDEN

DENMARK

SOVIET UNION

GULF OF BOTHNIA

Gulf of Finland

Helsinki

Stockholm

NORWEGIAN SEA

NORTH SEA

ATLANTIC OCEAN

Arctic Circle

ICELAND

Reykjavik

THE FAEROES (Den.)

SHETLAND IS. (Br.)

ORKNEY IS.

SCOTLAND

Glasgow
Edinburgh

GREAT BRITAIN

BRITISH ISLES

NORTHERN IRELAND
Belfast

IRELAND
Baile Átha Cliath (Dublin)

Liverpool
Manchester

JAN MAYEN I. (Nor.)

OUTER HEBRIDES

HAMBURG

Riga

RELIEF

Meters	Feet
3 050	10 000
1 525	5 000
610	2 000
305	1 000
152.5	500
0	Sea Level
152.5	500
1 525	5 000
3 050	10 000

BELOW SEA LEVEL

© Rand McNally & Company, Chicago

Scale 1:10 000 000; one inch to 160 miles.   Conic Projection

Elevations and depressions are given in feet

Miles

Kilometers

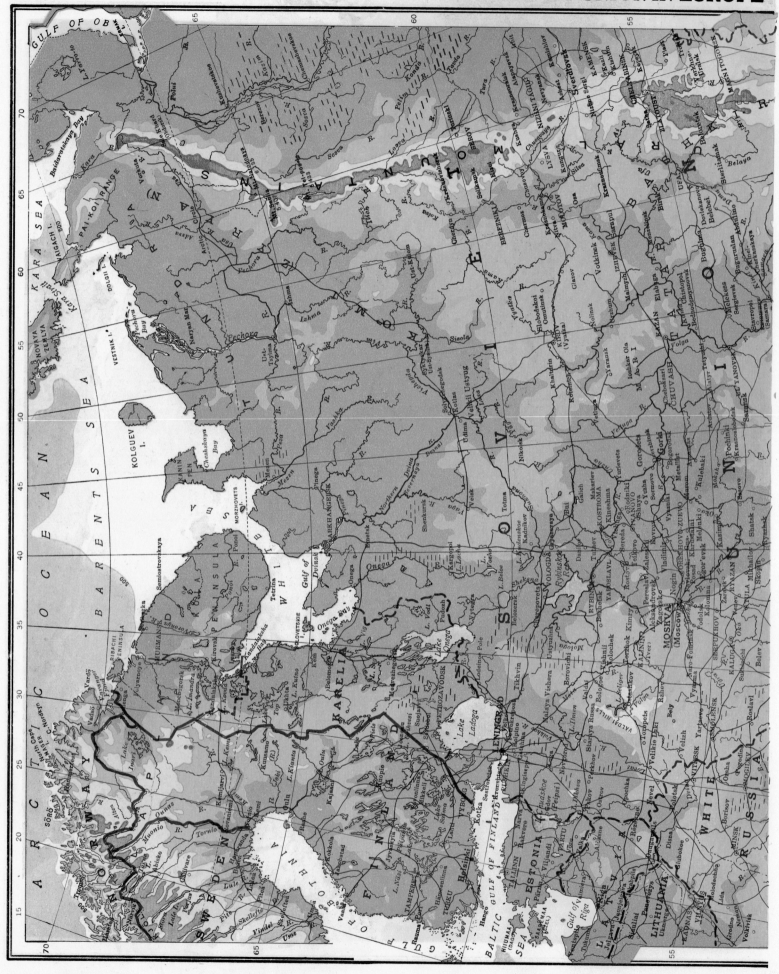

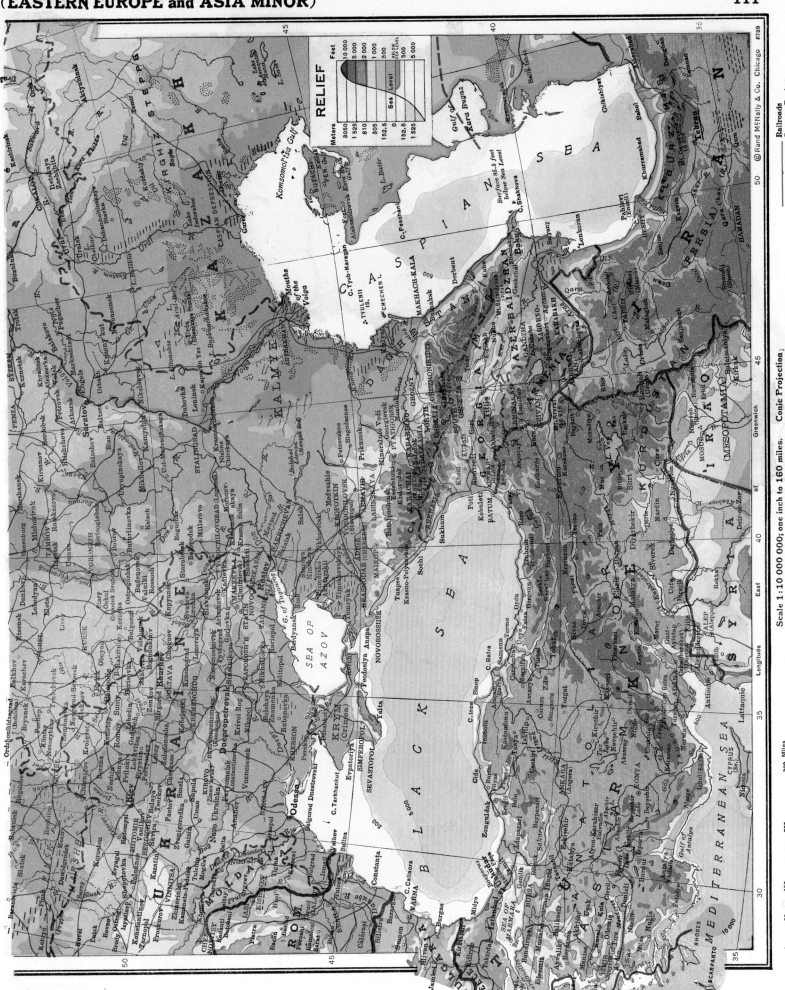

RELIEF

Feet		Meters
10 000		3050
5 000		1 525
2 000		610
500		152.5
Sea Level		0
BELOW SEA LEVEL		
500		152.5
5 000		1 525

© Rand McNally & Co. Chicago   6789

——————— Railroads
·················· Caravan Routes

Scale 1:10 000 000; one inch to 160 miles.   Conic Projection.
Elevations and depressions are given in feet

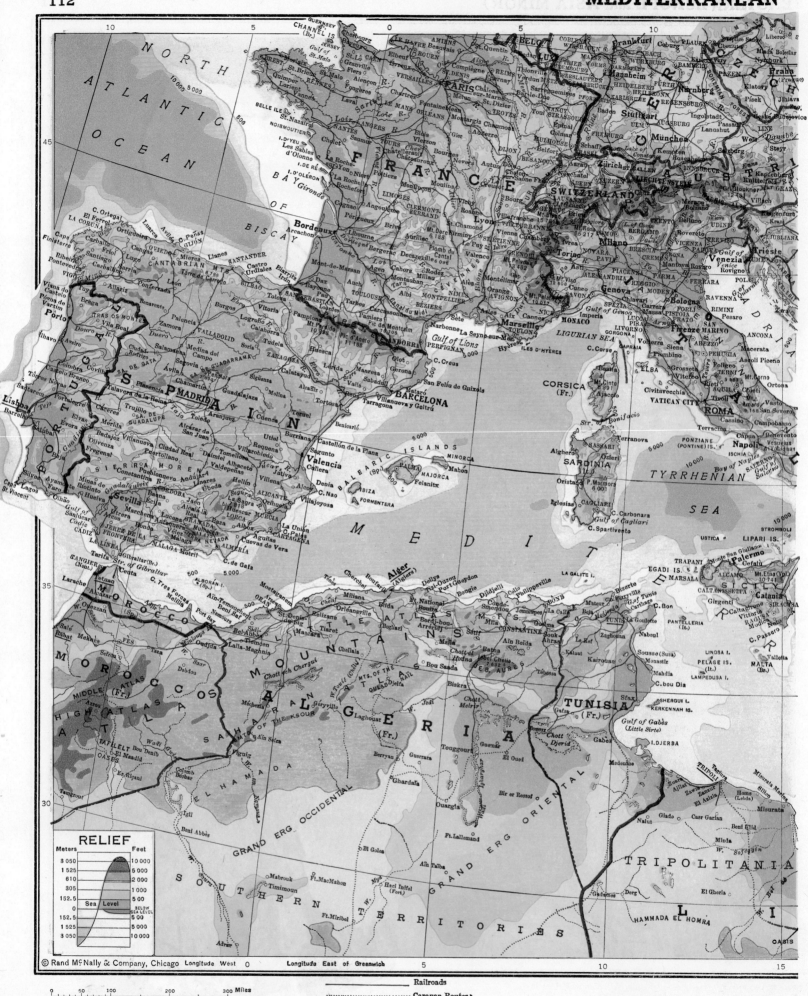

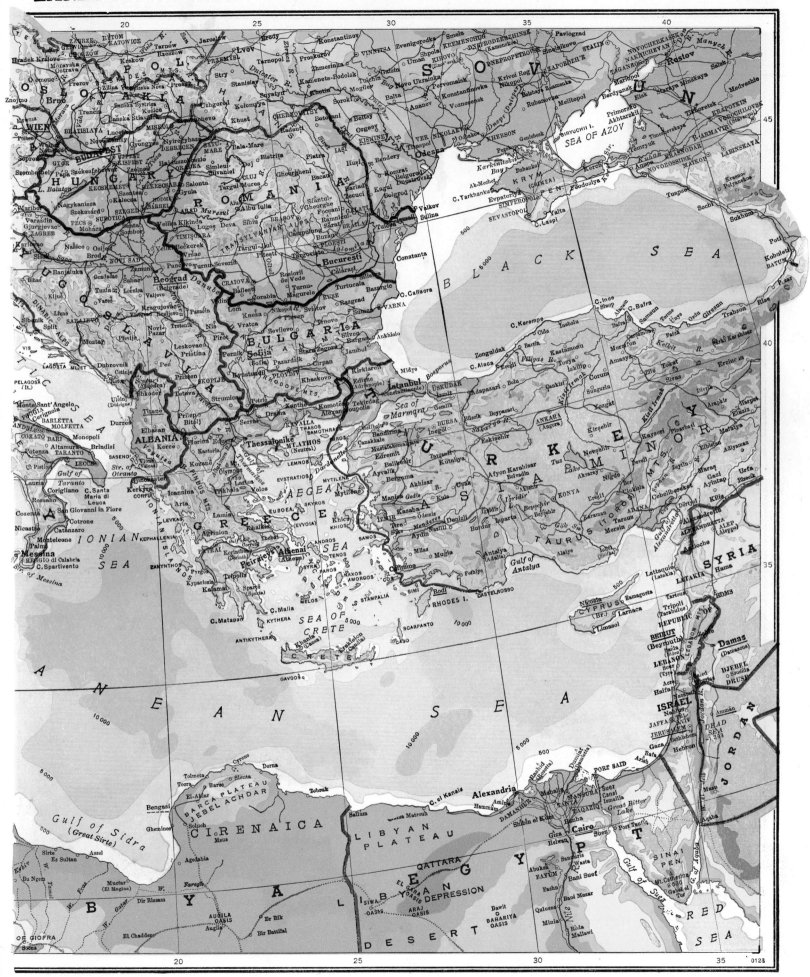

Scale 1:10 000 000; one inch to 160 miles.   **Bonne's Projection**

Elevations and depressions are given in feet

Same scale as main map

ATLANTIC

SHETLAND
ISLANDS
(Br.)

Herma Ness
UNST
YELL

St. Magnus Bay
MAINLAND

FOULA
"Edge of the World"
ss. Hirta photo.
here

OCEAN

Lerwick

Sumburgh Pt.

FAIR I.

WESTRAY
ROUSAY
N. RONALDSHAY
SANDAY
STRONSAY
ORKNEY
Kirkwall
POMONA OR MAINLAND
ISLANDS (Br.)
HOY
S. RONALDSHAY
Pentland
Firth
Thurso
Duncansby Hd.
SCOTLAND

© Rand McNally & Company, Chicago

Scale 1 : 4 000 000; one inch to 64 miles.   Conic Projection

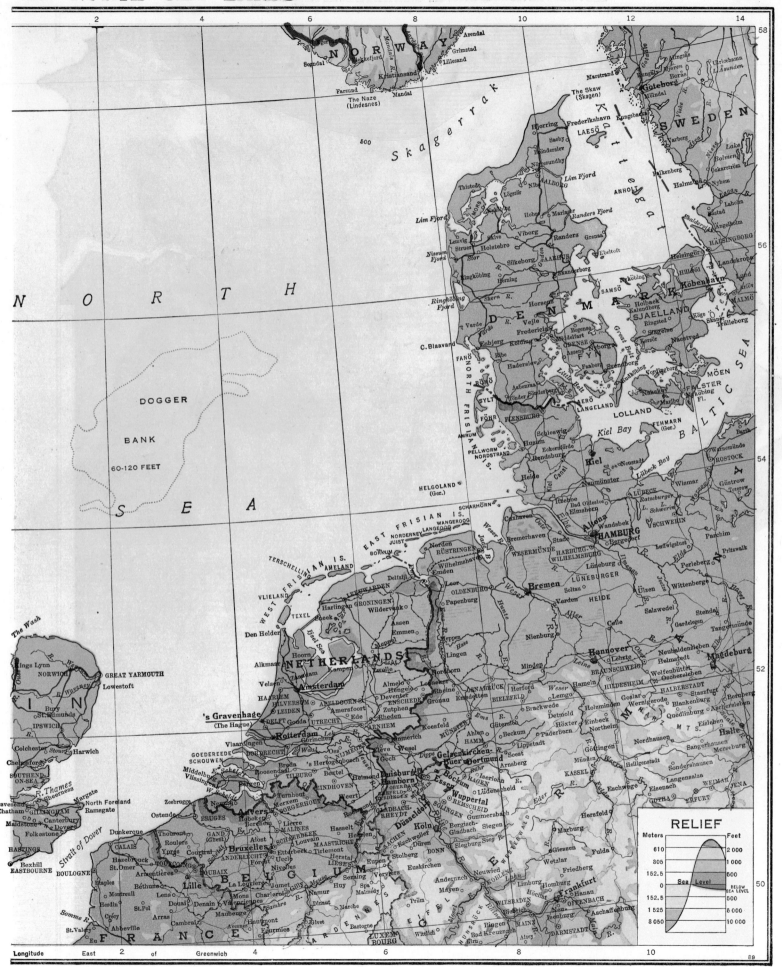

NORWAY
Sogndal · Flekkefjord · Arendal
Kristiansand · Grimstad · Lillesand
Farsund · Mandal
The Naze (Lindesnes)

SWEDEN
Marstrand · Goteborg
Mölndal · Kungsbacka
Varberg · Halmstad · Falkenberg
Lake Bolmen · Oskarström
HÄLSINGBORG · Landskrona
Helsingör · Hilleröd

Skagerrak
500

NORTH
SEA

DOGGER
BANK
60-120 FEET

DENMARK
Hjorring · Frederikshavn
Brönderslev · Saeby · LAESÖ
AALBORG · Norsundby
Thisted · Lögstör · Nibe
Hobro · Marlager · Randers Fjord
Skive · Viborg · Randers · Grena
Lemvig · Holstebro · GAARHUS
Struer · Silkeborg · Skanderborg
Ringköbing · Herning · Horsens
Ringköbing Fjord · Skern R.
Varde · Vejle · Fredericia
Esbjerg · Kolding
C. Blaavand · Ribe · Haderslev
FANÖ · RÖMÖ · SYLT
AMRUM · FÖHR
PELLWORM · NORDSTRAND
NORTH FRISIAN IS.
Husum · Schleswig · FLENSBURG
Eckernförde · Rendsburg
Heide · Neumünster · Kiel
Kiel Canal

SJAELLAND · FYN · Odense
Nyborg · Korsör · Slagelse · Ringsted
Holbaek · Kalundborg
Svendborg · Faaborg · Nakskov
AERÖ · LANGELAND · LOLLAND
Nykjöbing Fl. · Maribo
FALSTER · MÖEN
KÖBENHAVN · Köge · MALMÖ
Great Belt · Little Belt

BALTIC SEA
Warnemünde · ROSTOCK
Wismar · Güstrow · Teterow
LÜBECK · Lübeck Bay · Neustadt
FEHMARN (Ger.)

HELGOLAND (Ger.)
SCHARHÖRN

EAST FRISIAN IS.
NORDERNEY · LANGEOOG · WANGEROOG
JUIST · BORKUM · Norden
RÜSTRINGEN · Wilhelmshaven
Emden · Leer · Cuxhaven
Bremerhaven · Stade
WESERMÜNDE · HARBURG
WILHELMSBURG · HAMBURG
Altona · Wandsbek · Bergedorf
SCHWERIN · Ludwigslust · Parchim
Perleberg · Pritzwalk

Bremen · LÜNEBURG
LÜNEBURGER HEIDE
OLDENBURG · Papenburg
Verden · Soltau · Celle
Salzwedel · Stendal
Nienburg · Hannover · Lehrte
Helmstedt · Magdeburg
Neuhaldensleben · Oschersleben

TERSCHELLING · AMELAND
WEST FRISIAN IS.
VLIELAND · TEXEL
Den Helder · LEEUWARDEN
Harlingen · GRONINGEN · Wildervank
Assen · Emmen · Meppel
Hoorn · Alkmaar · Zaandam
NETHERLANDS · Kampen · Zwolle
Almelo · HENGELO · ENSCHEDE
Deventer · Zutphen · Rheine
Lingen · Meppen · Lingen
Minden · BRAUNSCHWEIG
HILDESHEIM · Goslar
HALBERSTAST · Wernigerode
Blankenburg · Quedlinburg
Eisleben · Halle

Velsen · HAARLEM
HILVERSUM · Amsterdam
LEIDEN · APELDOORN · Amersfoort
's Gravenhage (The Hague)
DELFT · Gouda · Ede · Rheden
UTRECHT · ARNHEM
Rotterdam · Lek R.
Vlaardingen · Gorinchem
OSNABRÜCK · Herford · Lemgo
Gronau · Emsdetten · BIELEFELD
Brackwede · Detmold · Höxter
Holzminden · Northeim
Einbeck · Nordhausen
Sangerhausen · Merseburg

GOEDEREEDE · DORDRECHT
SCHOUWEN · NIJMEGEN
Cleve · Wesel · Emmerich
Goch · Kleve
MÜNSTER · HAMM · Beckum
Paderborn · Lippstadt · Soest
Arnsberg · Göttingen
Münden · Heiligenstadt
KASSEL · Eschwege
Langensalza · Eisenach

Middelburg · W. Schelde
Vlissingen · Roosendaal · Breda
's Hertogenbosch · TILBURG
Boxtel · Helmond · Weert
EINDHOVEN · Duisburg · Hamborn
Essen · BOCHUM · Gelsenkirchen-Buer · Dortmund
Wuppertal · REMSCHEID
Solingen · Gummersbach
Düsseldorf · KÖLN
Siegburg · Siegen · BONN
Marburg · GOTHA · WEIMAR
JENA · ERFURT · Hersfeld
Fulda · Gieszen · Wetzlar
Friedberg · Homburg · Frankfurt
Hanau · OFFENBACH
WIESBADEN · MAINZ · DARMSTADT
Aschaffenburg · Bad Kreuznach

BELGIUM
Ostende · BRUGES · Zeebrugge
GAND (Ghent) · Antwers
SCHAERBEEK · Louvain
Bruxelles · ANDERLECHT · Forest
Etterbeek · Tirlemont · LIÈGE
Hasselt · Herstal · Verviers
Eupen · Stolberg · Düren
AACHEN · Eschweiler
Euskirchen · Andernach
Neuwied · KOBLENZ

Dunkerque · CALAIS
Thourout · Roulers · Ypres
Courtrai · ROUBAIX · TOURCOING
Mouscron · Lille · Hazebrouck
St. Omer · Armentieres
Béthune · Lens
BOULOGNE · Étaples
Hesdin · Montreuil
St. Pol · Arras · Douai
Denain · Valenciennes · Maubeuge
Cambrai · Avesnes · Fourmies

LUXEMBOURG
ARDENNES · EIFEL
HUNSRÜCK · Bingen · Simmern
Wittlich · Prüm · Bitburg

FRANCE
Somme R. · St. Valery
Eu · Abbeville · Crécy
Amiens

THE WASH
Kings Lynn · NORWICH
GREAT YARMOUTH · Lowestoft
Bury St. Edmunds · IPSWICH
Colchester · Harwich
Chelmsford · SOUTHEND-ON-SEA
Sheerness · Gravesend · Chatham
GILLINGHAM · Maidstone · Dover
Canterbury · Margate · Ramsgate
North Foreland · Folkestone
HASTINGS · Bexhill · EASTBOURNE

Strait of Dover

RELIEF

Meters		Feet
610		2 000
305		1 000
152.5		500
0	Sea Level	
152.5		500
	BELOW SEA LEVEL	
1 525		5 000
8 050		10 000

Elevations and depressions are given in feet

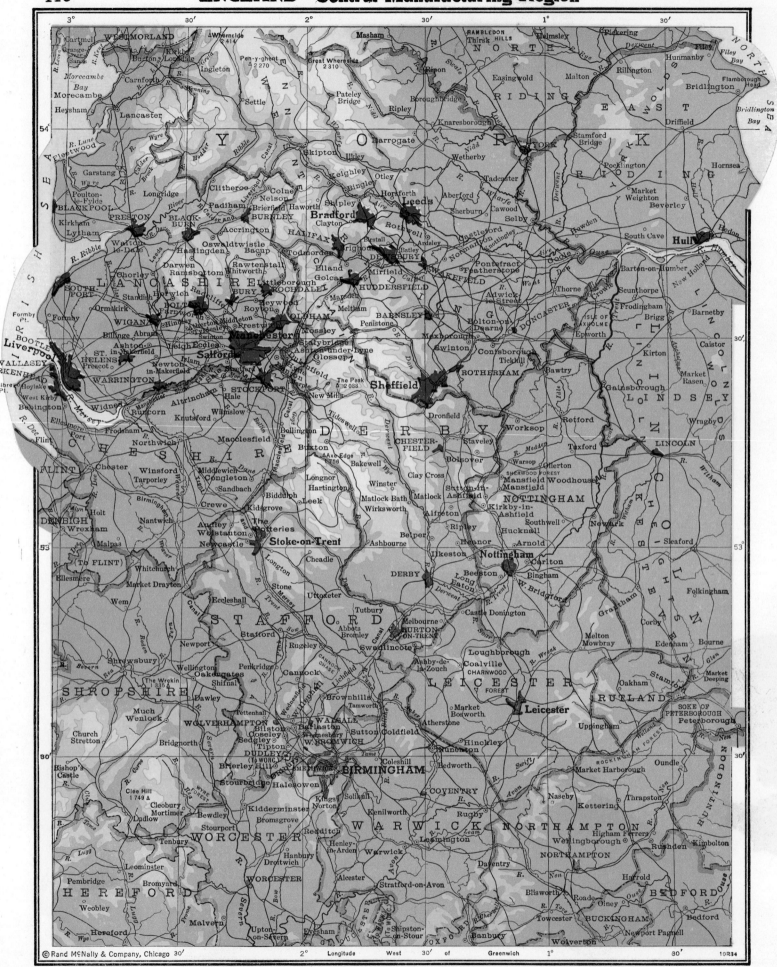

Scale 1:1 000 000; one inch to 16 miles.   Sinusoidal Projection
Elevations and depressions are given in feet

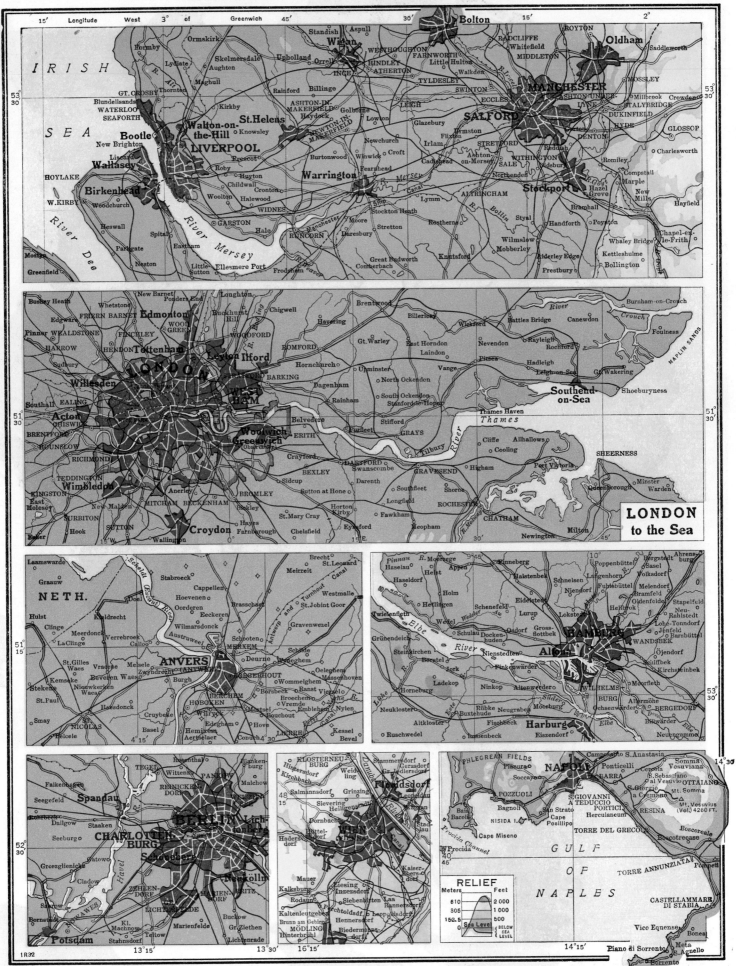

LONDON
to the Sea

RELIEF

Meters		Feet
610		2 000
305		1 000
152.5		500
	Sea Level	
	BELOW SEA LEVEL	

0 1 2 3 4 5 6 7 8 9 10 11 12 13 14 15 Miles
0 2 4 6 8 10 12 14 16 18 20 22 24 Kilometers

Scale 1:500 000; one inch to 8 miles

© Rand McNally & Company, Chicago

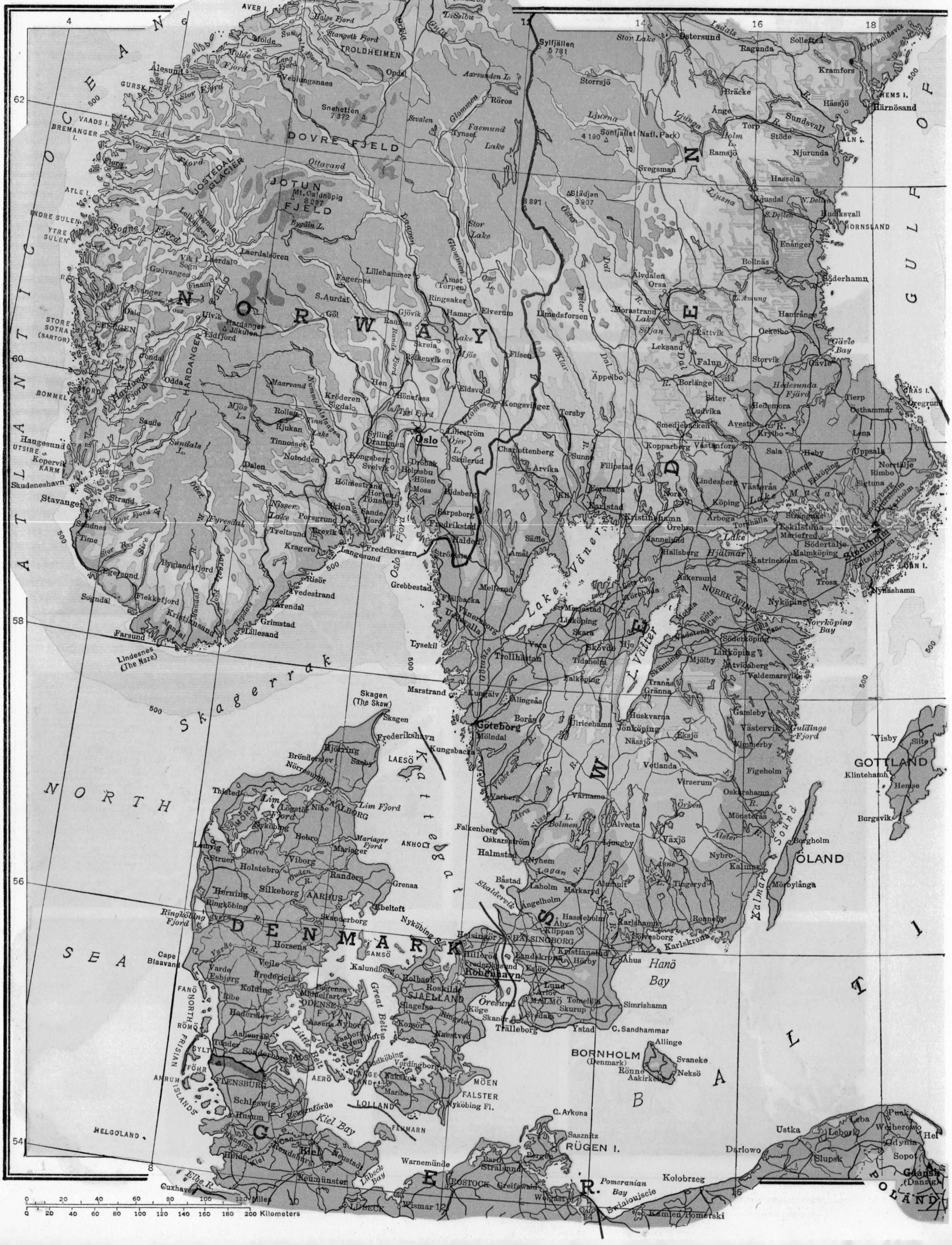

SOUTHERN SCANDINAVIA

NORWAY

SWEDEN

DENMARK

ATLANTIC OCEAN

NORTH SEA

GULF OF

Skagerrak

Kattegat

Kiel Bay

GOTTLAND

ÖLAND

BORNHOLM (Denmark)

RÜGEN I.

Lake Väner

L. Vätter

Hanö Bay

Oslo

Göteborg

Stockholm

København

MALMÖ

TRONDHEIM (Nidaros)

Kristiansund

Ålesund

Molde

Bergen

Stavanger

Haugesund

DOVRE FJELD

JOTUN FJELD

Mt. Galdhöpig 8,097

Snehetten 7,372

TROLDHEIMEN

Lillehammer

Hamar

Gjövik

Hönefoss

Drammen

Kongsberg

Skien

Fredrikstad

Halden

Östersund

Storsjö

Sundsvall

Härnösand

Kramfors

Hudiksvall

Söderhamn

Gävle

Falun

Uppsala

Västerås

Örebro

Karlstad

Kristinehamn

NORRKÖPING

Linköping

Jönköping

Borås

Växjö

Kalmar

Karlskrona

Karlshamn

Kristianstad

HÄLSINGBORG

HELSINGØR

Visby

Aalborg

Aarhus

Odense

Esbjerg

Roskilde

Skagen (The Skaw)

Frederikshavn

Randers

Horsens

Kolding

Flensburg

Schleswig

Kiel

Lübeck

ROSTOCK

Stralsund

Helgoland

Cuxhaven

Lindesnes (The Naze)

Lake Vänern

BALTIC

Pomeranian Bay

0 20 40 60 80 100 120 150 180 200 Miles
0 20 40 60 80 100 120 140 160 180 200 Kilometers

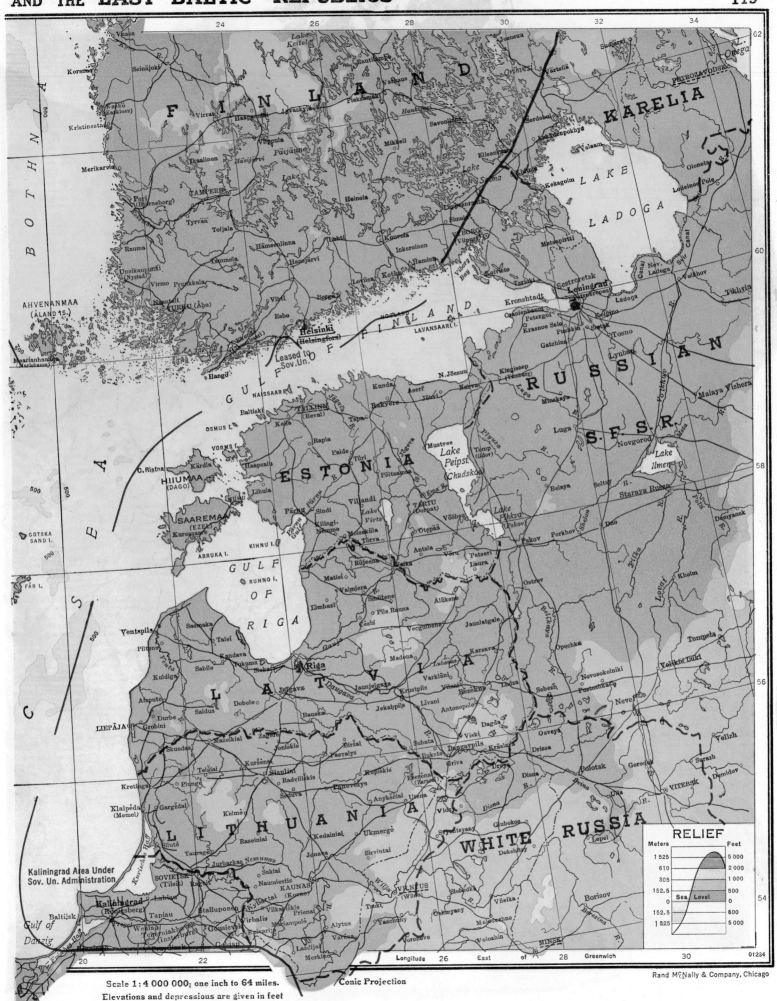

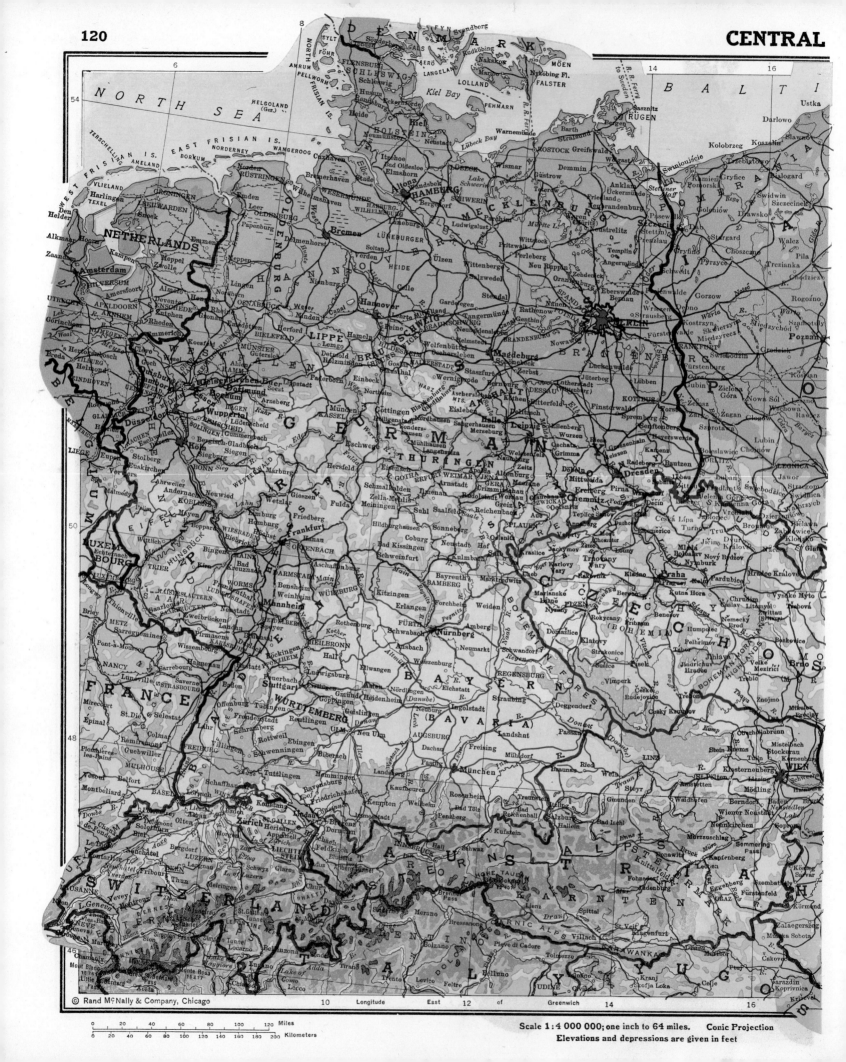

Scale 1:4 000 000; one inch to 64 miles.   Conic Projection

Elevations and depressions are given in feet

RELIEF

Meters		Feet
8 050		10 000
1 525		5 000
610		2 000
305		1 000
152.5		500
0	Sea Level	
		BELOW SEA LEVEL
152.5		500

LITHUANIA

BALTIC SEA

Gulf of Danzig

Kaliningrad (Königsberg)

SOVIETSK (Tilsit)

KAUNAS (Kovno)

VILNYUS

WHITE RUSSIA

MINSK

P O L A N D

WARSZAWA

Łódź

Wrocław (Breslau)

KRAKÓW

KATOWICE

CZĘSTOCHOWA

LUBLIN

RADOM

BIALYSTOK

S O V I E T   U N I O N

UKRAINE

Lvov

PRZEMYSL

BUCOVINA

BESSARABIA

CHERNOVITSY

PODKARPATSKA RUTHENIA

S L O V A K I A

BRATISLAVA

BUDAPEST

H U N G A R Y

DEBRECEN

R O M A N I A

TRANSYLVANIA

CLUJ

ORADEA

SATU-MARE

TIMIŞOARA

ARAD

Gdańsk (Danzig)

Pripyat (Pripet)

PRIPET MARSHES

Balaton Lake

BAŁKAN

CARPATHIANS

BESKIDS

TATRA MTS.

RODNEI MTS.

01234

FRANCE

RELIEF

Meters	Feet
3 050	10 000
1 525	5 000
610	2 000
305	1 000
152.5	500
0	Sea Level
152.5	500
1 525	5 000

On scale of main map

CORSICA

Scale 1:4 000 000; one inch to 64 miles. Conic Projection
Elevations and depressions are given in feet

0 10 20 30 40 50 60 70 80 90 100 110 120 Miles
0 20 40 60 80 100 150 180 200 Kilometers

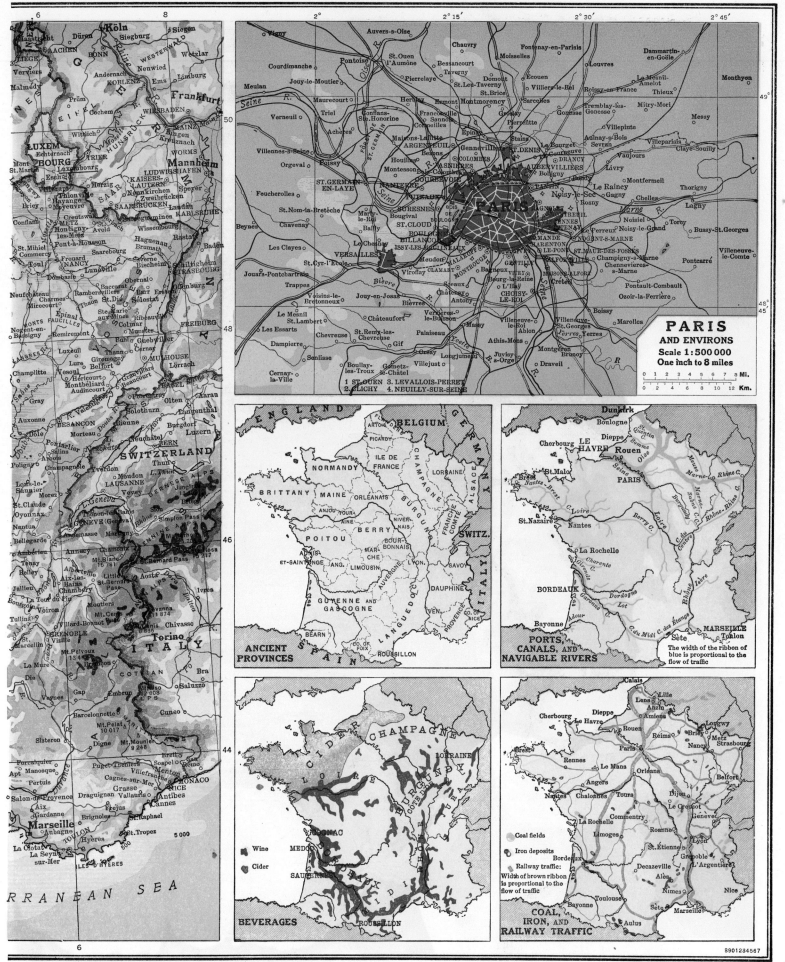

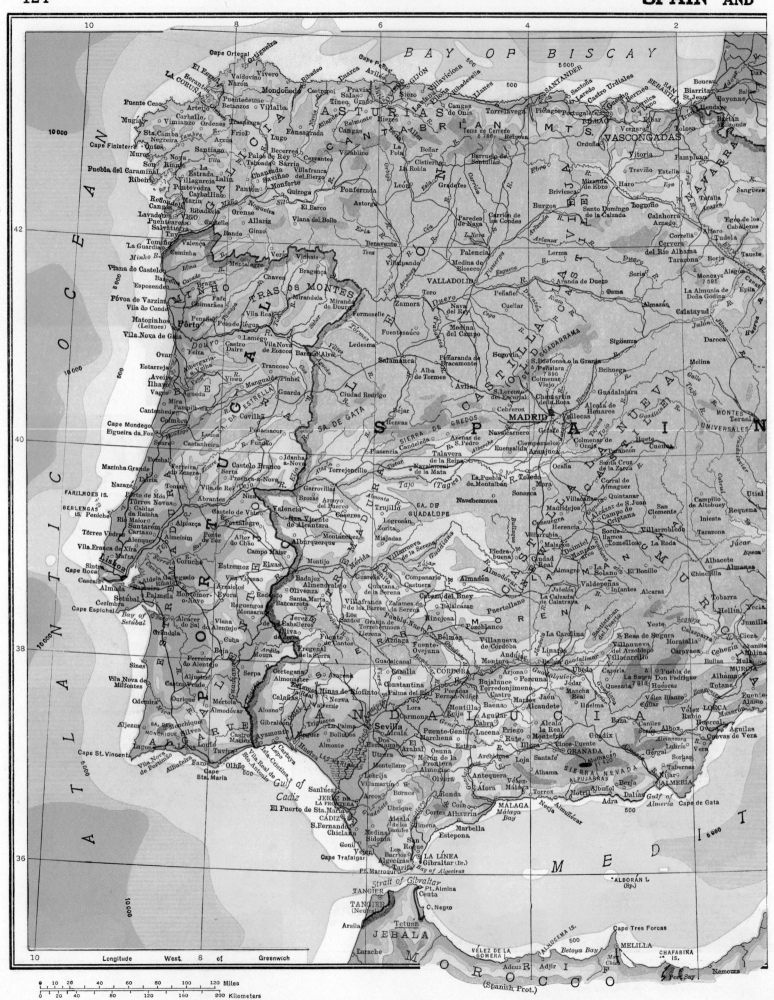

PORTUGAL

Scale 1:1 000 000 (Madrid inset)

Scale 1:1 000 000 (Barcelona inset)

Scale 1:1 000 000 (Lisboa inset)

Scale 1:1 000 000
One inch to 16 miles

RELIEF

Meters		Feet
6 050		10 000
1 525		5 000
610		2 000
305		1 000
152.5		500
	Sea Level	
152.5		500
1 525		5 000
3 050		10 000

Scale 1:4 000 000; one inch to 64 miles.   Conic Projection
Elevations and depressions are given in feet

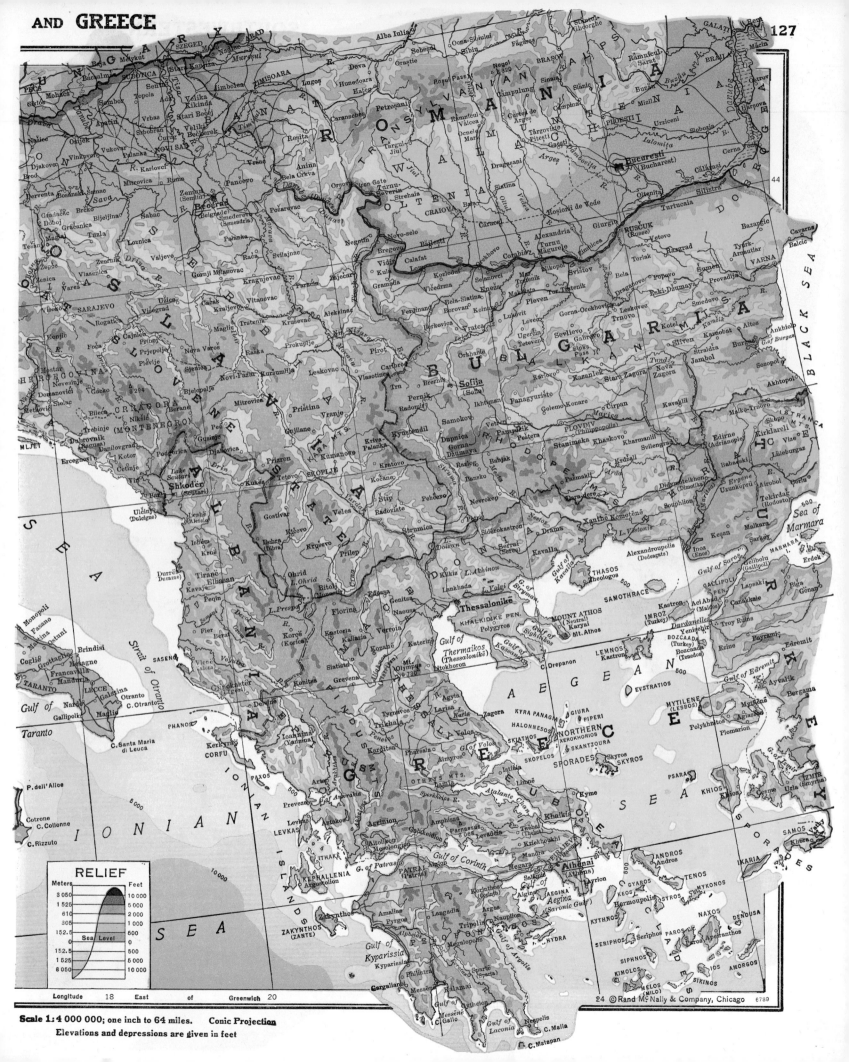

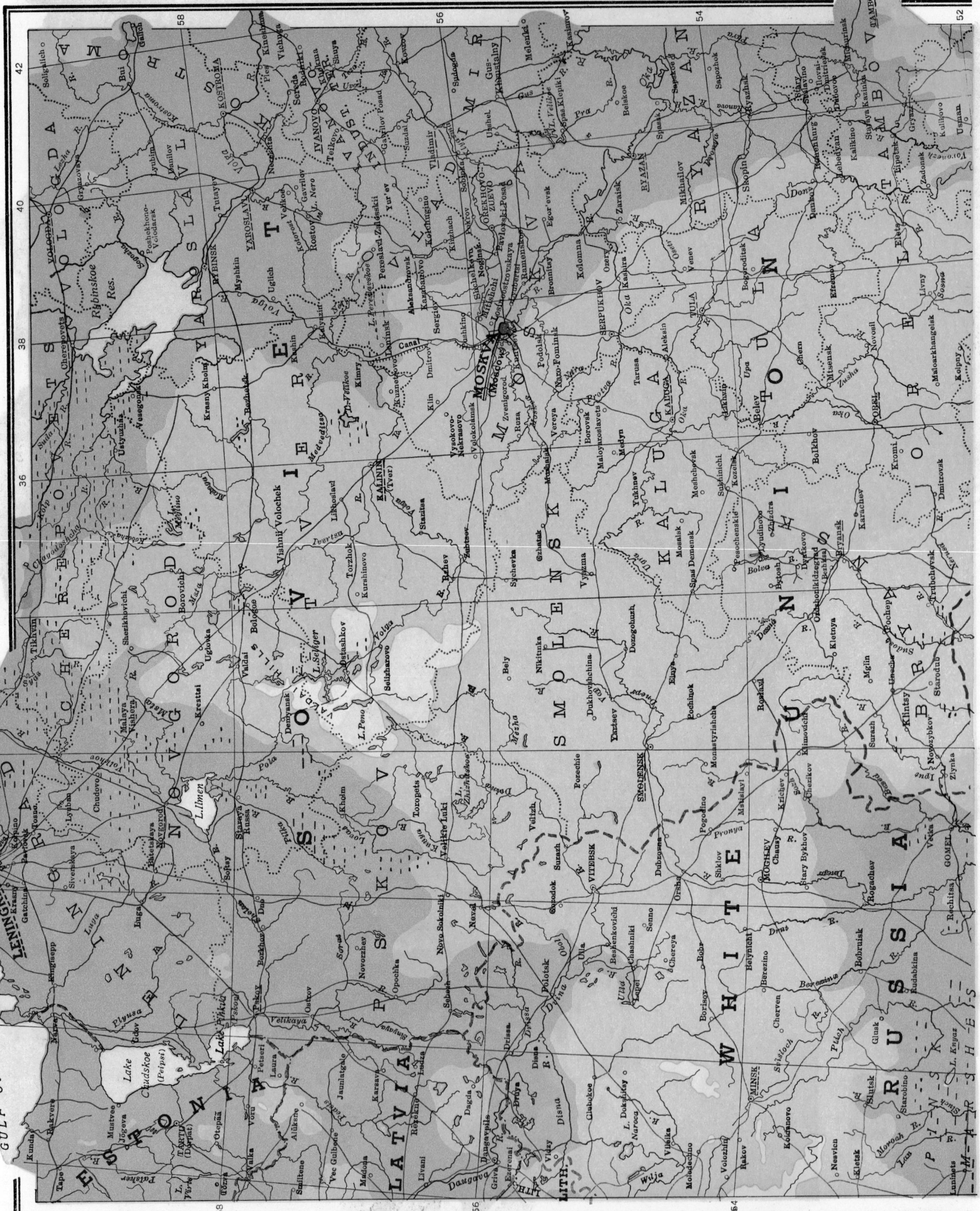

GULF OF FINLAND

ESTONIA

LATVIA

LITH.

WHITE RUSSIA

VOLOGDA

KOSTROMA

YAROSLAVL

IVANOVO

VLADIMIR

MOSKVA

MOSCOW

RYAZAN

TAMBOV

TULA

OREL

KALUGA

SMOLENSK

VITEBSK

SMOLENSK

GOMEL

MINSK

KALININ (Tver)

NOVGOROD

LENINGRAD

Kronshtadt

Leningrad

L. Ilmen

Lake Chudskoe (Peipus)

Rybinskoe Res.

Volga

Oka

Don

Pskov

Velikaya

Volkhov

Lake Ladoga

L. Seliger

L. Peno

VALDAI HILLS

PINSK MARSHES

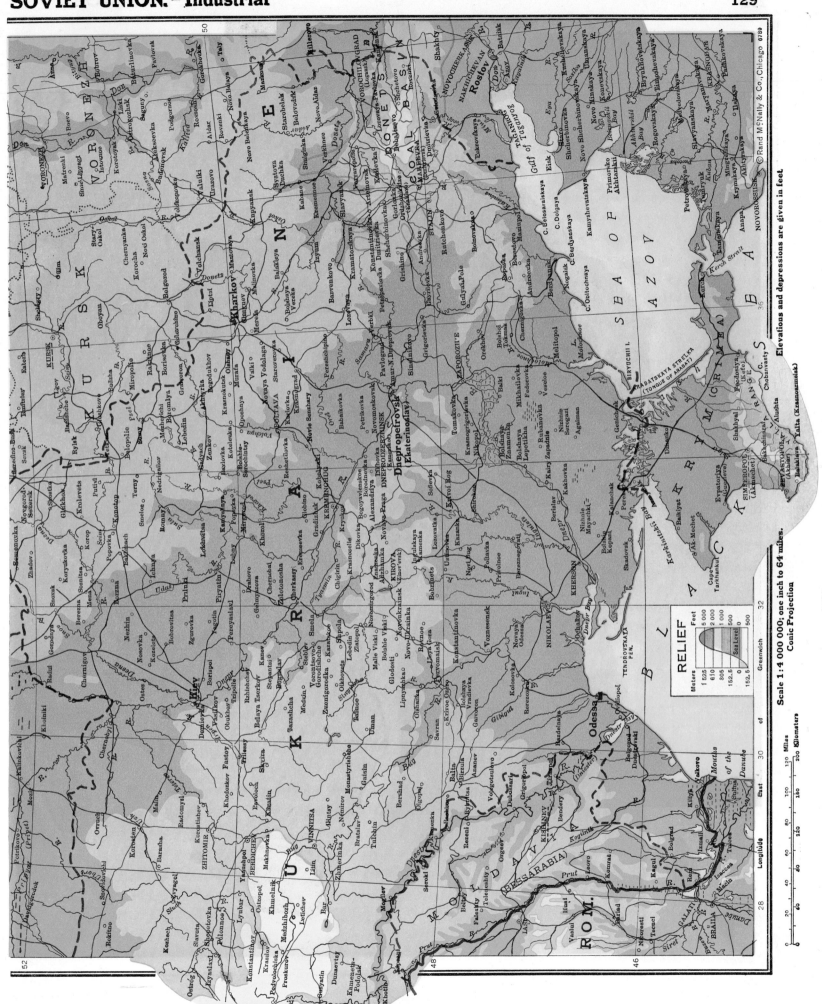

© Rand McNally & Co., Chicago 6789

Elevations and depressions are given in feet.

Scale 1:4 000 000; one inch to 64 miles.
Conic Projection

RELIEF

Meters	Feet
1 525	5 000
610	2 000
305	1 000
152.5	500
0	Sea Level
152.5	500

Miles

Kilometers

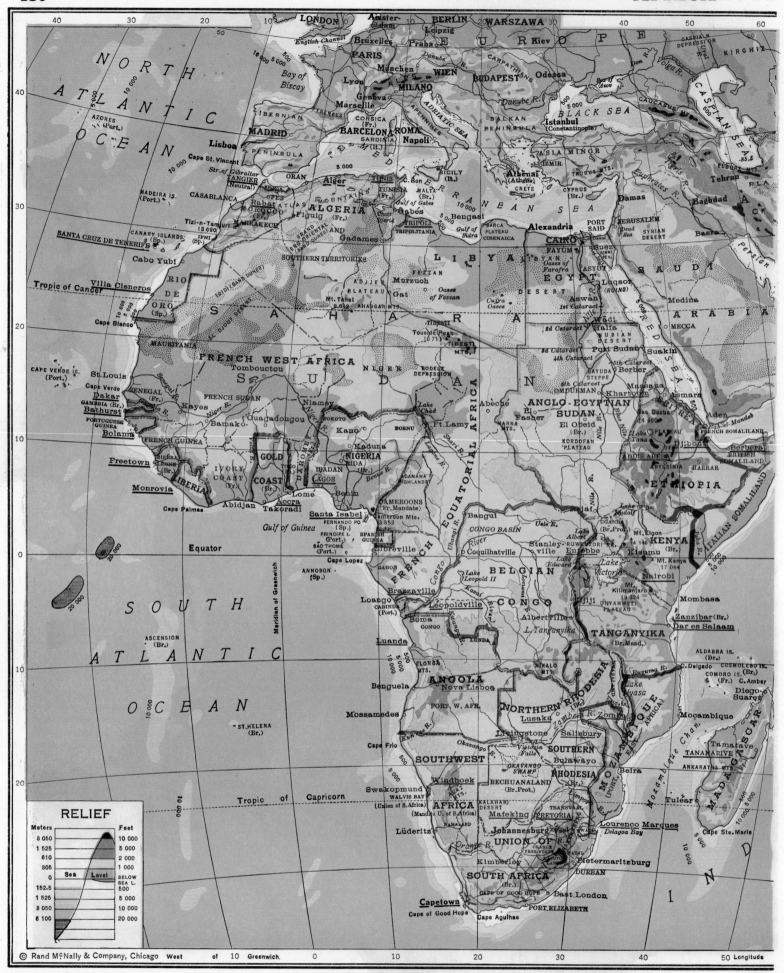

© Rand McNally & Company, Chicago   West of 10 Greenwich.

Scale 1 : 40 000 000; one inch to 630 miles.   Lambert's Azimuthal, Equal Area Projection
Elevations and depressions are given in feet

RELIEF

Meters			Feet
3 050			10 000
1 525			5 000
610			2 000
305			1 000
0	Sea	Level	BELOW SEA L.
152.5			500
1 525			5 000
3 050			10 000
6 100			20 000

| 0 | 200 | 400 | 600 | 800 | 1000 Miles |
| 0 | 400 | 800 | 1200 | 1600 Kilometers |

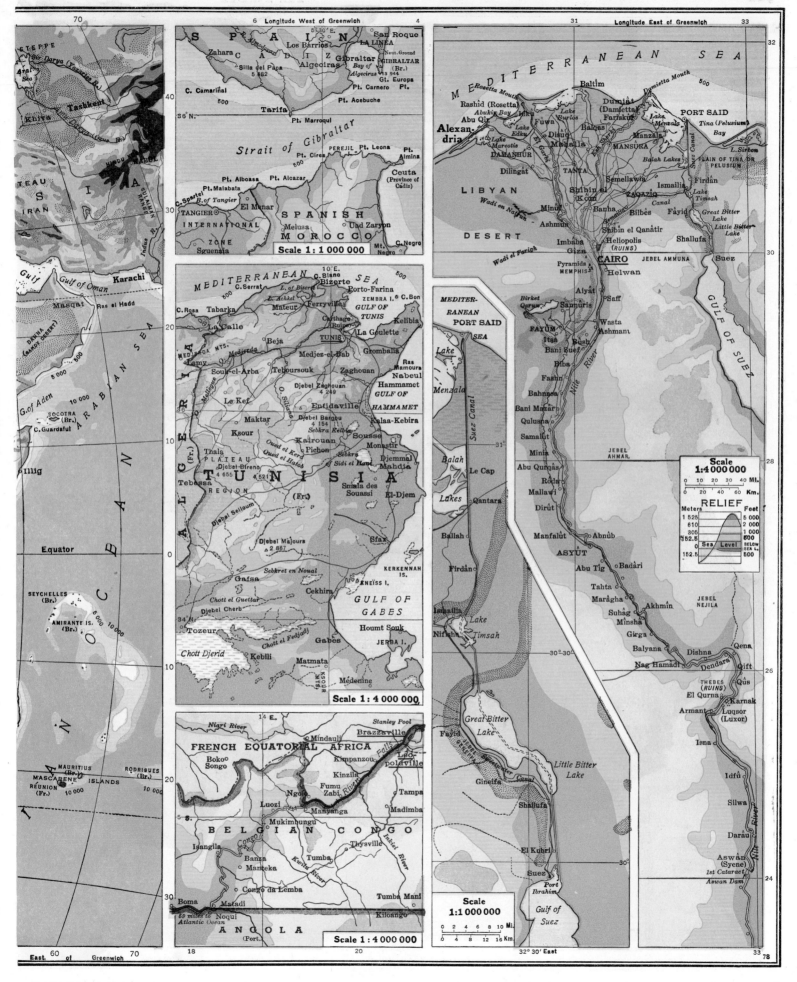

AFRICA—

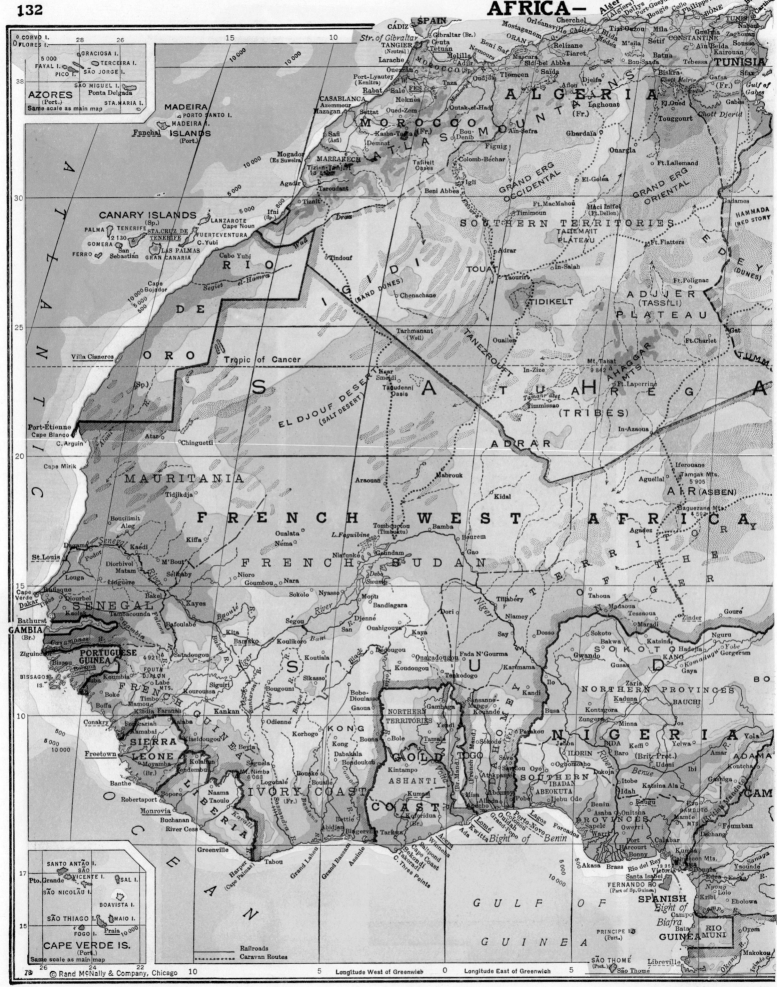

Railroads
Caravan Routes

Longitude West of Greenwich   Longitude East of Greenwich

0   50 100   200   300   500 Miles
0   100   200   400   600   800 Kilometers

Scale 1:16 000 000; one inch to

Elevations and depressions

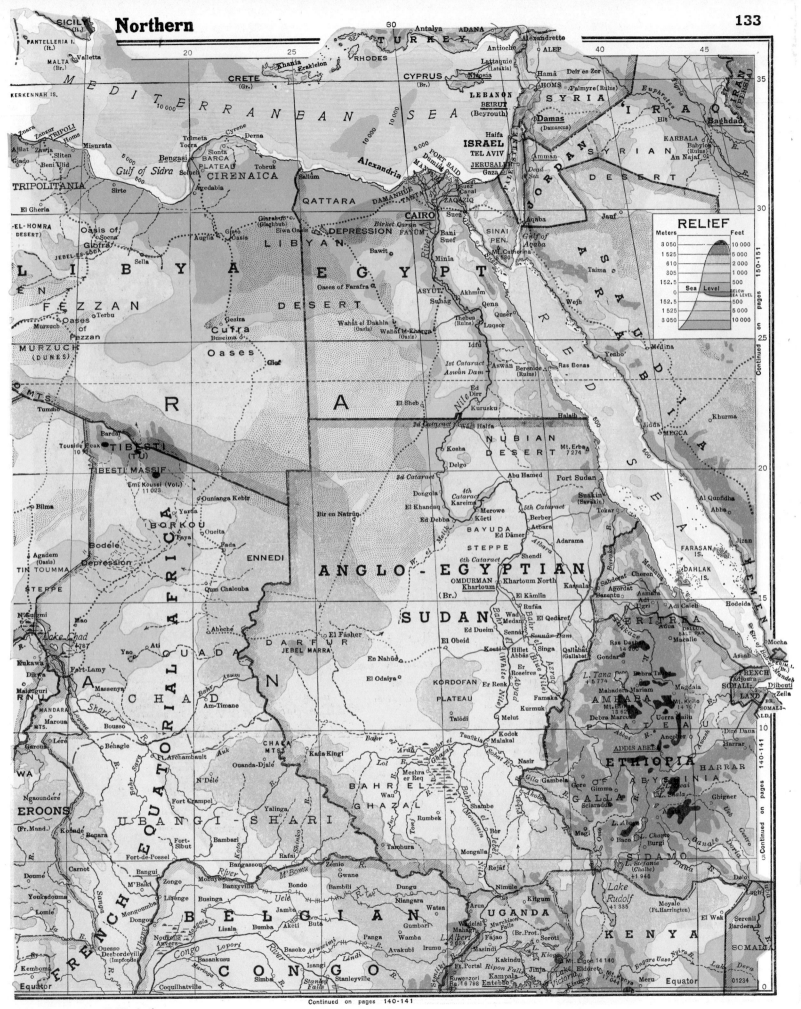

Continued on pages 140-141

250 miles. Sinusoidal Projection

are given in feet

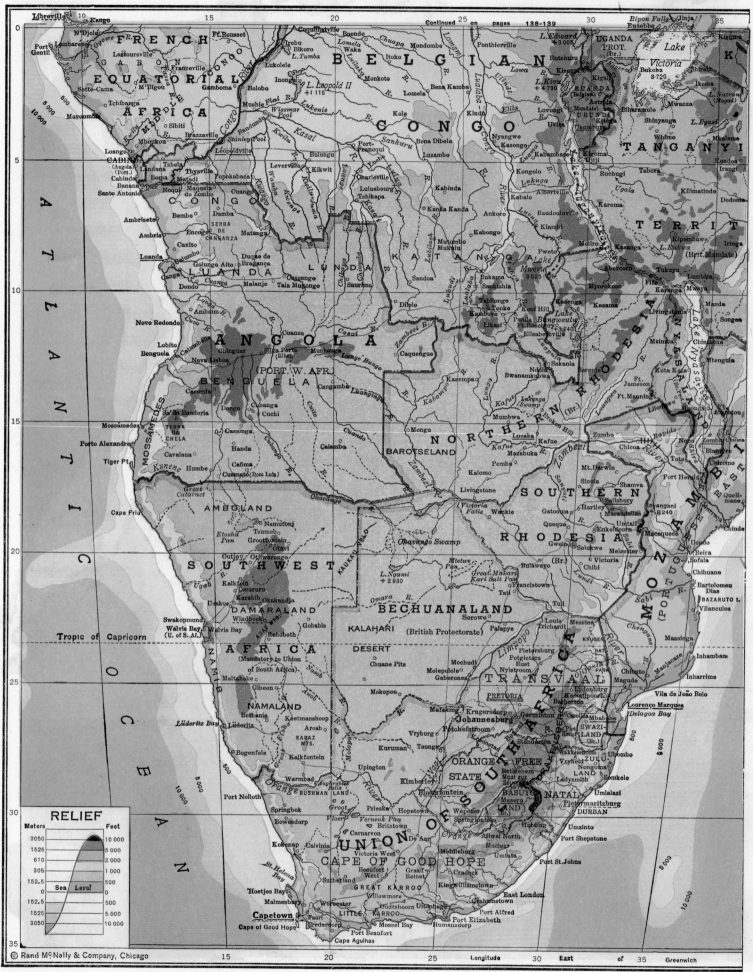

Continued on pages 138-139

RELIEF

Meters	Feet
3050	10 000
1525	5 000
610	2 000
305	1 000
152.5	500
0 Sea Level 0	
152.5	500
1525	5 000
3050	10 000

© Rand McNally & Company, Chicago

0   50   100   200   300   400   500   Miles
0   100   200   400   600   800   Kilometers

Longitude   30   East   of   35   Greenwich

Scale 1:16 000 000; one inch to

Elevations and depressions

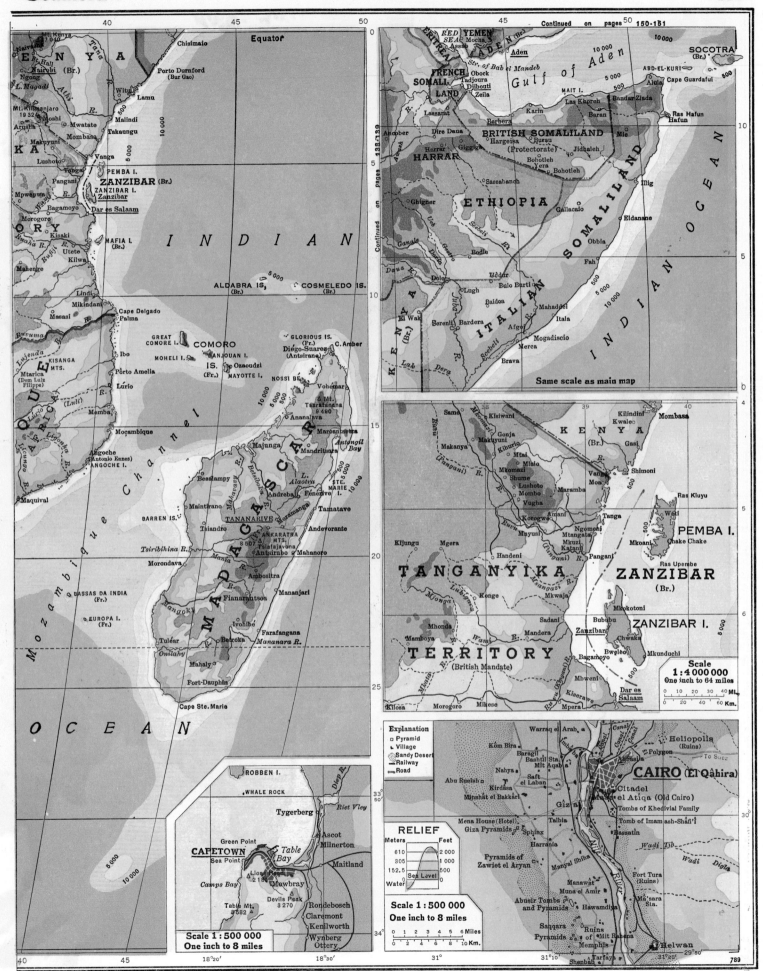

Southern

135

KENYA (Br.)
Mt. Kenya 17 040
Nairobi
Ngong
L. Magadi
Mt. Kilimanjaro 19 324
Moshi
Arusha
Makuyuni
Lushoto
Tanga
Pangani
Mpwapwa
Bagamoyo
Morogoro
Kisaki
Mahenge

Chisimaio
Porto Durnford (Bur Gao)
Equator
Lamu
Witu
Malindi
Takaungu
Mombasa
Vanga
PEMBA I.
ZANZIBAR (Br.)
ZANZIBAR I.
Zanzibar
Dar es Salaam
Utete
Kilwa
Lindi
Mikindani
Masasi
Cape Delgado
Palma

INDIAN
ALDABRA IS. (Br.)
COSMELEDO IS. (Br.)

GREAT COMORE I.
COMORO
MOHELI I.
ANJOUAN I. IS. (Fr.)
Ozoaudzi
MAYOTTE I.
GLORIOUS IS. (Fr.)
Diégo-Suarez (Antsirane)
C. Amber
NOSSI BÉ
Vohemar
Mt. Tsaratanana 9 490
Ananalava

Ibo
Pôrto Amelia
Lúrio
Memba
Moçambique
Angoche
Antonio Ennes
ANGOCHE I.
Maquival

KISANGA MTS.
Mtarica (Dom Luiz Filippe)

BARREN IS.
Tsiandro
Tsiribihina R.
Morondava

Besalampy
Maintirano
MADAGASCAR
TANANARIVE
ANKARATRA MTS. 8 507
Tsiafajavona 8 507
Antsirabe
Ambositra
Fianarantsoa
Ihosy
Betroka
Tuléar
Onilahy
Mahaly
Fort-Dauphin
Cape Ste. Marie

Majunga
Mandritsara
Maroantsetra
Antongil Bay
Andreba
L. Alaotra
Fenerive
STE. MARIE I.
Moramanga
Tamatave
Andevorante
Mahanoro
Mananjari
Ivohibe
Farafangana
Mananara R.

Mozambique Channel
AFRICA

BASSAS DA INDIA (Fr.)
EUROPA I. (Fr.)

OCEAN

Gulf of Aden
RED SEA
YEMEN
ERITREA
ADEN (Br.)
Assab
Mocha
Str. of Bab el Mandeb
Aden
SOCOTRA (Br.)
ABD-EL-KURI
Cape Guardafui
Alula
FRENCH SOMALILAND
Obock
Tadjoura
Djibouti
Zeila
Lassarat
MAIT I.
Karin
Las Khoreh
Bandar Ziada
Ras Hafun
Hafun
Ancober
Berbera
Baran
Dire Daua
BRITISH SOMALILAND (Protectorate)
Hargeisa
Burau
Giggiga
Jidhaleh
Mie
HARRAR
Harrar
Bohotleh
Yera
Bohotleh
Sassabaneh
Illig
ETHIOPIA
Ghigner
Gallacaio
Eldanane
ITALIAN SOMALILAND
Obbia
Fah
Uddur
Bodle
Dole
Lugh
Bulo Burti
Baidoa
Mahaddei
Itala
El Wak
Serenli
Bardera
Afgoi
Mogadiscio
Merca
Brava
Lake Dera

KENYA (Br.)
Ganale
Daua R.
Juba R.
Ueb
Scebeli R.

INDIAN OCEAN

Same scale as main map

KENYA (Br.)
Same
Kisiwani
Kilindini
Kwale
Mombasa
Gasi
Makanya
Makuyuni
Gonja
Kihurio
Mtai
Miala
Shimoni
Mkomazi
Shume
Lushoto
Mombo
Vugha
Korogwe
Amani
Ngomeni
Mtangata
Mkuzi
Katani
Tanga
Weti
Ras Kiuyu
PEMBA I.
Mkoani
Chake Chake
Kijungu
Mgera
Mpyusi
Pangani
Handeni
TANGANYIKA
ZANZIBAR (Br.)
Konge
Mkwaja
Mhonda
Sadani
Mandera
Bububu
Mkokotoni
ZANZIBAR I.
Mamboya
Zanzibar
Chwaka
Mkunduchi
Bweleo
TERRITORY (British Mandate)
Bagamoyo
Mbweni
Kilosa
Morogoro
Mikese
Kisarawe
Mpera
Mbwei
Dar es Salaam

Scale 1 : 4 000 000
One inch to 64 miles
0 10 20 30 40 ML
0 20 40 60 Km.

Explanation
□ Pyramid
▪ Village
Sandy Desert
Railway
Road

Warraq el Arab
Canal
Heliopolis (Ruins)
Kôm Bira
Baragil
Mit Aqaba
Bashtil Sta.
To Suez
Abu Rueish
Nahya
Saft el Laban
CAIRO (El Qâhira)
Minshât el Bakkâri
Gîza
Citadel
Masr el Atîqa (Old Cairo)
Tombs of Khedivial Family
Mena House (Hotel)
Giza Pyramids
Sphinx
Tomb of Imam ash-Shâfi'î
Bassatin
Harrania
Talbia
Pyramids of Zawiet el Aryan
Manyal Shiha
Manawat
Muna el Amir
Fort Tura (Ruins)
Wadi Tih
Ma'sara Sta.
Abusir Tombs and Pyramids
Hawamdiya
Ruins of Memphis
Saqqara Pyramids
Ruins of Mit Rahena
Shenbab
Tarfaya
Helwan

RELIEF
Meters	Feet
610	2 000
305	1 000
152.5	500
Sea Level	
Water	

Scale 1 : 500 000
One inch to 8 miles
0 1 2 3 4 5 6 Miles
0 2 4 6 8 10 Km.

CAPETOWN
ROBBEN I.
WHALE ROCK
Tygerberg
Riet Vley
Green Point
Sea Point
Ascot
Milnerton
Camps Bay
Lion's Head 2 195
Table Bay
Maitland
Mowbray
Rondebosch
Claremont
Kenilworth
Wynberg
Ottery
Devils Peak 3 270
Table Mt. 3 582

Scale 1 : 500 000
One inch to 8 miles

250 miles.   Sinusoidal Projection

are given in feet

RELIEF

Meters		Feet
8 050		10 000
1 525		5 000
610		2 000
305		1 000
0	Sea Level	0 Below Sea Level
152.5		500
1 525		5 000
8 050		10 000
6 100		20 000

©Rand McNally & Company, Chicago

Scale 1:40 000 000; One inch to 630 miles. Lambert's Azimuthal, Equal Area Projection

Elevations and depressions are given in feet

0	200	400	600	800	1000 Miles
0	400	800	1200	1600 Kilometers	

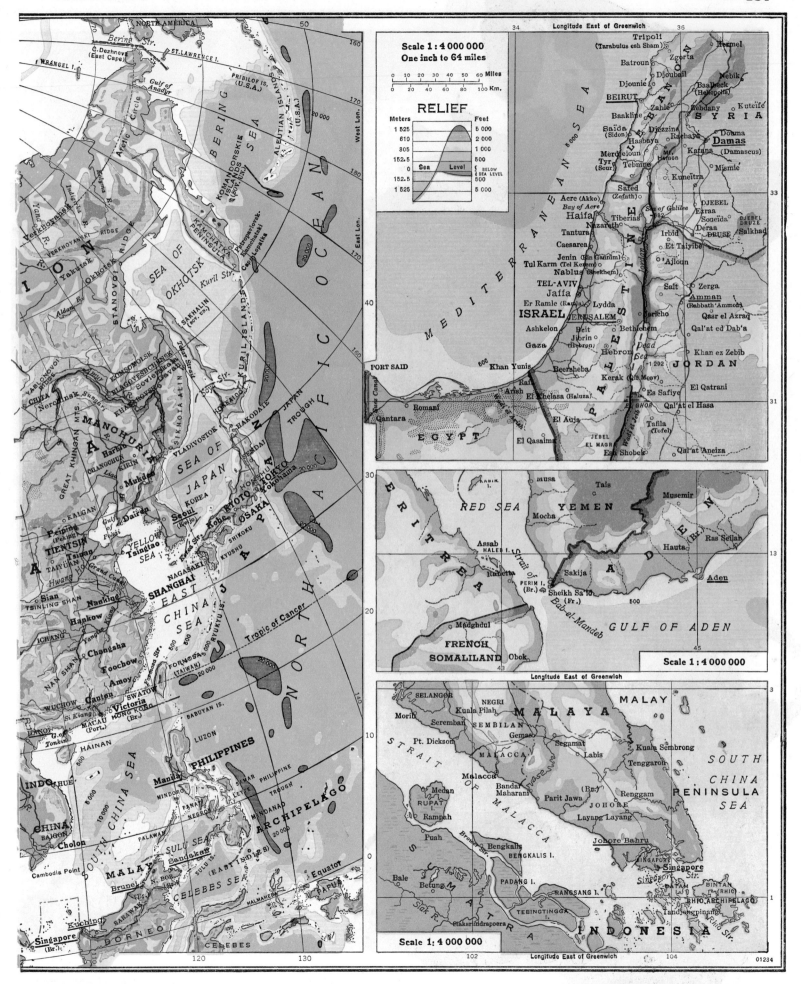

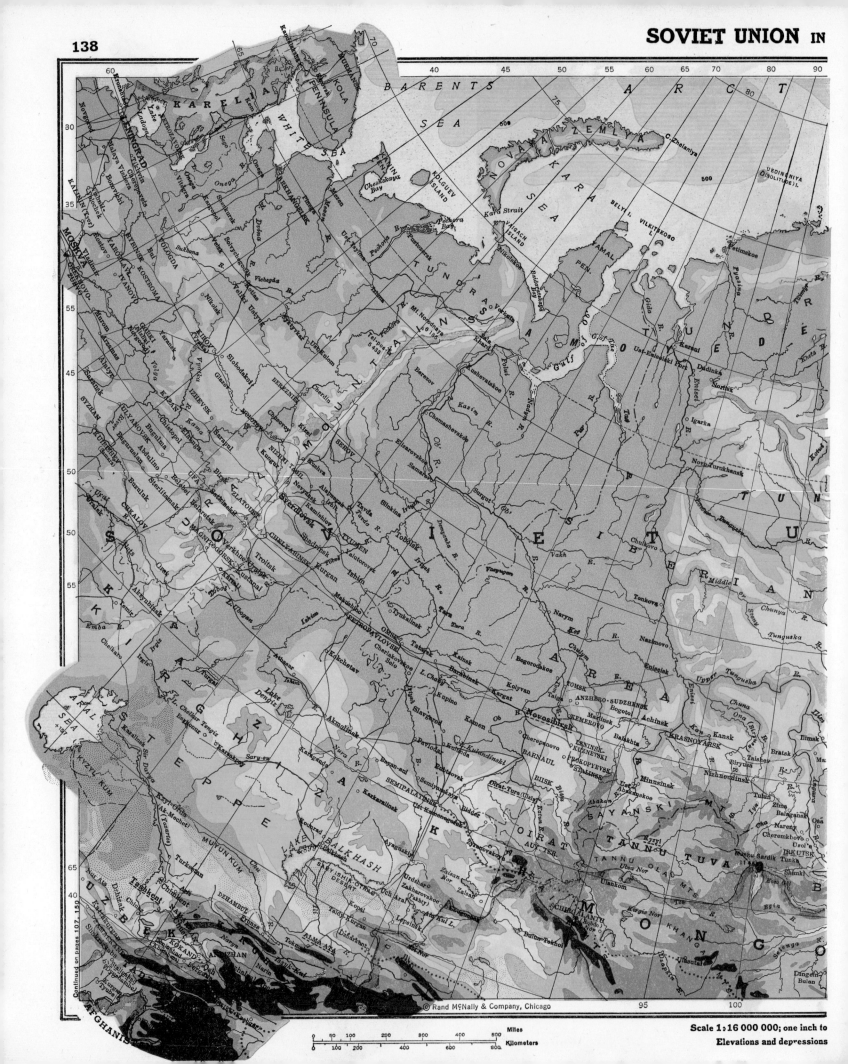

© Rand McNally & Company, Chicago

Scale 1:16 000 000; one inch to

Elevations and depressions

Miles
Kilometers

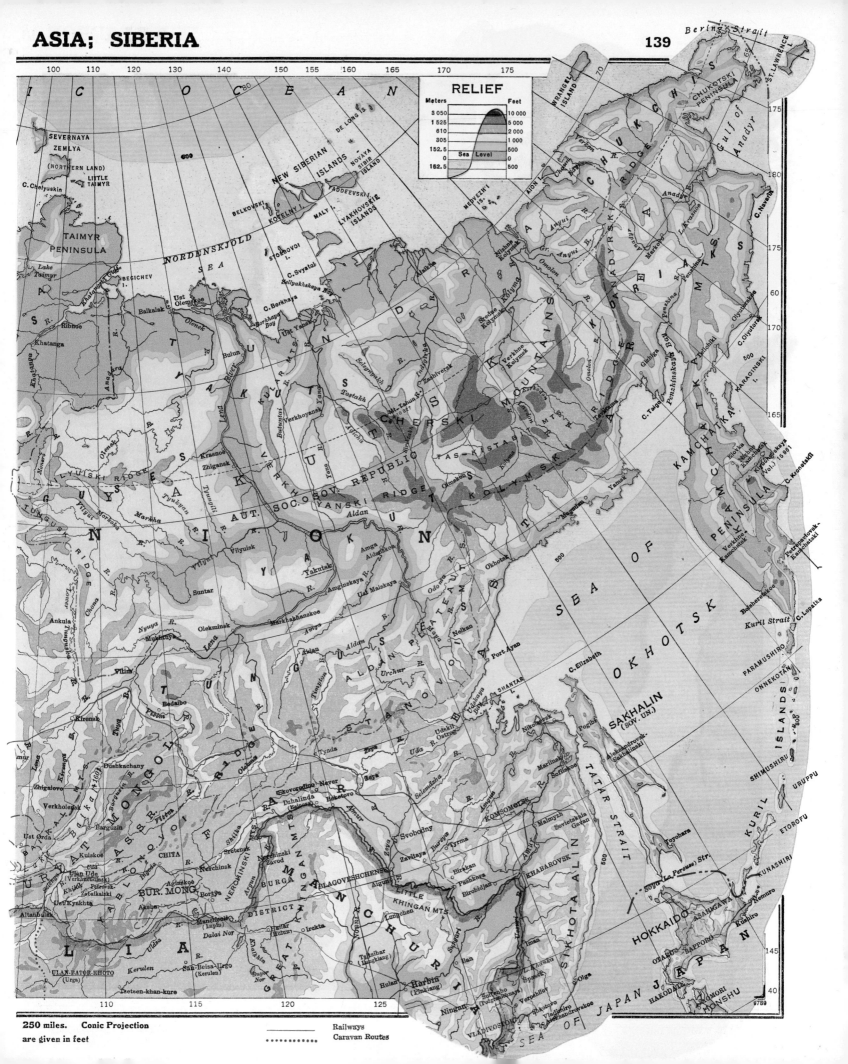

RELIEF

Meters		Feet
3 050		10 000
1 525		5 000
610		2 000
305		1 000
152.5		500
0	Sea Level	
152.5		500

250 miles.   Conic Projection

are given in feet

———————— Railways

· · · · · · · · · · Caravan Routes

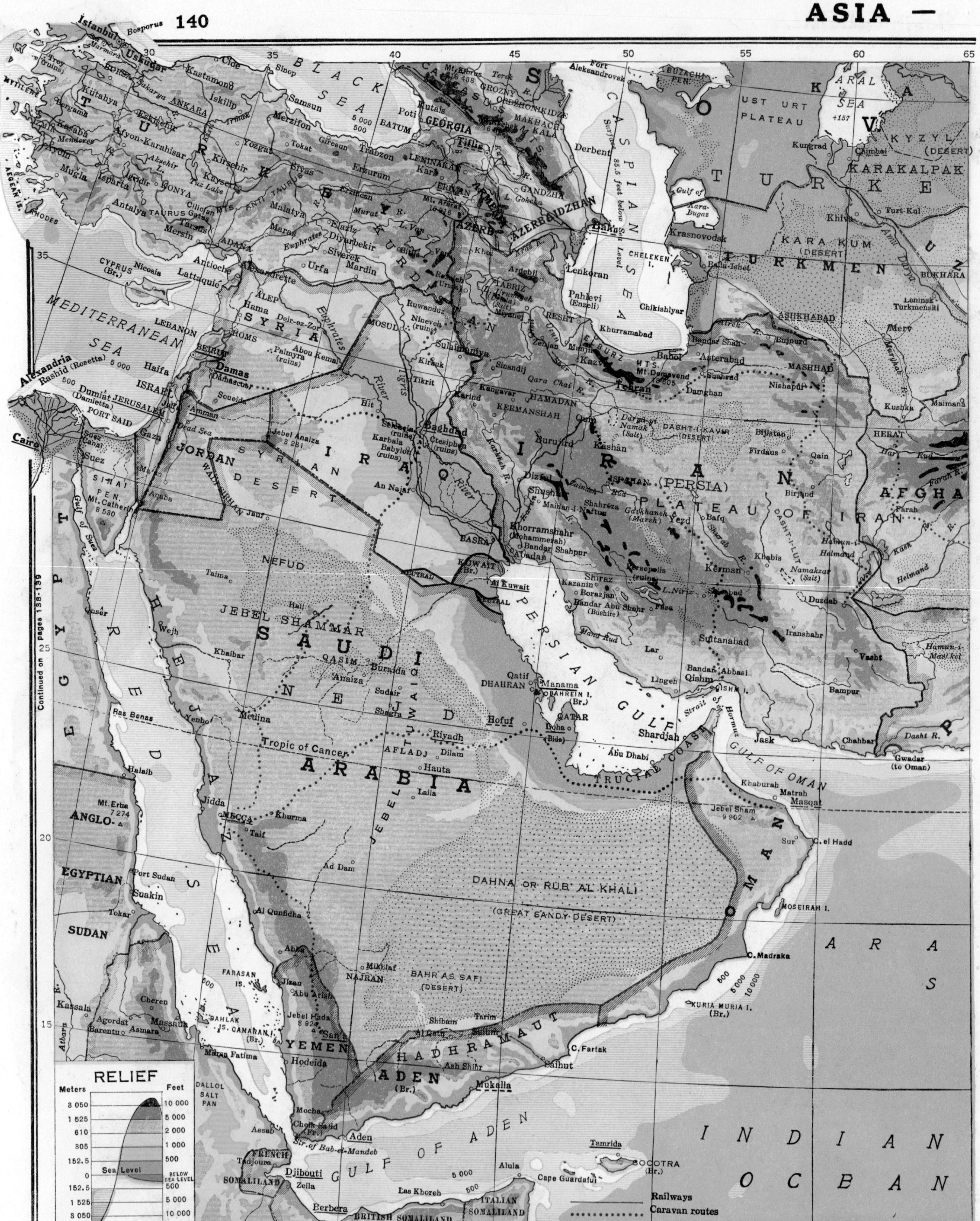

Istanbul Bosporus Uskudar
Troy (ruins)
MYTILENE
Bergama Kesaba
Menderes Aydin
Mugla Isparta
RHODES

Kütahya
Afyon-Karahisar
Akshehir
Egridir
KONYA
T U R K E Y

Cide Sinop
Kastamonu
Iskilip
Yozgat ANKARA
Kirshehir
Kaysu Tuz Lake
Niğde
Adana
TAURUS MTS. Tarsus
Mersin

BLACK SEA
Samsun
Merzifon
Sivas
Tokat
Giresun Trabzon
Erzincan
Malatya
Marag
Diyarbekir
Siverek
Mardin
Urfa

Terek R. GROZNY ORDSHONIKIDZE MAKHACH KALA
CAUCASUS Mt. Elbrus 18 488
Poti KUTAIS 5 000 500 BATUM
GEORGIA Tiflis LENINAKAN Kars
Murat R. Mt. Ararat 16 916
ERIVAN AZERB. BAKU
AZERBAIDZHAN

CASPIAN SEA
85.5 feet below sea level
Derbent
CHELEKEN I.
Gulf of Kara-Bugaz
Krasnovodsk

Fort Aleksandrovsk
BUZACHI PEN.
UST URT PLATEAU
+157
ARAL SEA
Kungrad
Chimbai
KARAKALPAK
Khiva Turt-Kul
KYZYL (DESERT)
T U R K E Z

MEDITERRANEAN SEA
CYPRUS (Br.) Nicosia
Lattaquie
Antioch ALEP
Alexandrette
Hama
HOMS
LEBANON
BEIRUT
SYRIA
Damas DAMASCUS
Deir-ez-Zor

Mt. Abrus
Ruwanduz Nineveh (ruins)
MOSUL
Kirkuk
Tikrit
Abou Kemah
Palmyra (ruins)
Hit
Baghdad
Ctesiphon (ruins)
Karbala (ruins)
Babylon (ruins)
An Najaf

TABRIZ
Khoi
Urmi
L. Gokcha
GANDZHA
Ardebil
RESHT
Pahlevi (Enzeli)
Khurramabad
Lenkoran
Chikishlyar

ELBURZ MTS. Mt. Demavend 18 605
Tehran
Babol Asterabad
Shahrud
Damghan
ASHKHABAD
Kizil Arvat
Bandar Shah
Bujnurd
Nishapur
MASHHAD
Merv
Leninsk Turkmenski
BUKHARA

KARA KUM (DESERT)
TURKMEN
Ashkhabad
HERAT
AFGHA

ALEXANDRIA
Rashid (Rosetta)
Haifa
ISRAEL Jaffa
JERUSALEM
Dumiat (Damietta)
PORT SAID
Gaza
Cairo
Suez Canal
Suez

Dead Sea
Amman
JORDAN
Soueida
Jebel Anaiza 3 281
SYRIAN DESERT
Wadi Hauran Jauf
An Najaf

Kirkuk
BAGHDAD
River Tigris
Euphrates River
BASRA
Karind
KERMANSHAH
HAMADAN
Burujird
Kashan
Qom
ISFAHAN (PERSIA)
Shahreza
Yezd

I R A N (PERSIA)
PLATEAU OF IRAN
Darya-yi Namak (Salt)
DASHT-I-KAVIR (DESERT)
Birjand
Qain
Firdaus
Bijistan
Namakzar (Salt)
DASHT-I-LUT
Kerman
Khabis
Bampur
Iranshahr
Duzdab
Vasht
Hamun-i Mashkel

SINAI PEN.
Mt. Catherine 8 530
Gulf of Suez
Aqaba

NEFUD
Taima
Jauf
Hail
JEBEL SHAMMAR
QASIM Buraida
Anaiza
Sudair
Shaqra
AFLADJ
Riyadh
Dilam
Hauta
Laila
NEJD
Hofuf
KUWAIT
Al Kuwait
KUWAIT
Abadan
Khorramshahr (Mohammerah)
Bandar Shahpur
Dizful
Shush (Susa)
Shushtar
Maidan-i-Naftun
Shiraz
Kazerun
Borazjan
Bandar Abu Shahr (Bushire)
Persepolis (ruins)
Fasa
L. Niriz
Sultanabad
Lar
Lingeh
Bandar Abbasi
Qishm
QISHM
Jask
Chahbar
Gwadar (to Oman)

SAUDI
ARABIA
HEJAZ
Medina
Yenbo
Khaibar
Ras Benas
Wejh
Taif
MECCA
Khurma
Jidda
Mt. Erba 7 274
ANGLO-
EGYPTIAN
SUDAN
Port Sudan
Suakin
Tokar

Tropic of Cancer
Ad Dam
Al Qunfidha
Mikhlaf
NAJRAN
Abu Arish
Jizan
FARASAN IS.
DAHLAK IS.
QAMARAN I. (Br.)
Jebel Hada 8 920
San'a
Shibam
Tarim
HADHRAMAUT
YEMEN
Mocha
Hodeida
Cheren
Agordat
Barentu
Asmara
Massaua
Mitsas Fatima
Sheikh Said
Aden
Str. of Bab-el-Mandeb
FRENCH SOMALILAND
Djibouti
Zeila
Tadjoura
Aessab
Berbera
BRITISH SOMALILAND

DAHNA OR RUB' AL KHALI
(GREAT SANDY DESERT)
BAHR AS SAFI (DESERT)
JEBEL TUWAIK
PERSIAN GULF
Qatif
DHAHRAN
Manama
BAHREIN I. (Br.)
QATAR
Doha (Bida)
Abu Dhabi
Shardjah
TRUCIAL COAST
Khaburah
Matrah
Masqat
Jebel Sham 9 902
Sur
C. el Hadd
O M A N
C. Madraka
MOSEIRAH I.
KURIA MURIA I. (Br.)

GULF OF OMAN
Strait of Hormuz
Bander Abbas
Qishm
Jask
Chahbar
Dasht R.
Gwadar (to Oman)
A R A B I A N

C. Fartak
Salhut
Ash Shir
Mukalla
ADEN (Br.)
GULF OF ADEN
Alula
C. Madraka
Las Khoreh
ITALIAN SOMALILAND
Cape Guardafui
Tamrida
SOCOTRA (Br.)

INDIAN OCEAN

RELIEF
Meters Feet
3 050 — 10 000
1 525 — 5 000
610 — 2 000
305 — 1 000
152.5 — 500
Sea Level — 0
152.5 — 500 BELOW SEA LEVEL
1 525 — 5 000
3 050 — 10 000

DALLOL SALT PAN

——— Railways
········· Caravan routes

© Rand McNally & Company, Chicago

0 50 100 200 300 400 500 Miles
0 100 200 400 600 800 Kilometers

Scale 1 : 16 000 000; one inch to
Elevations and depressions

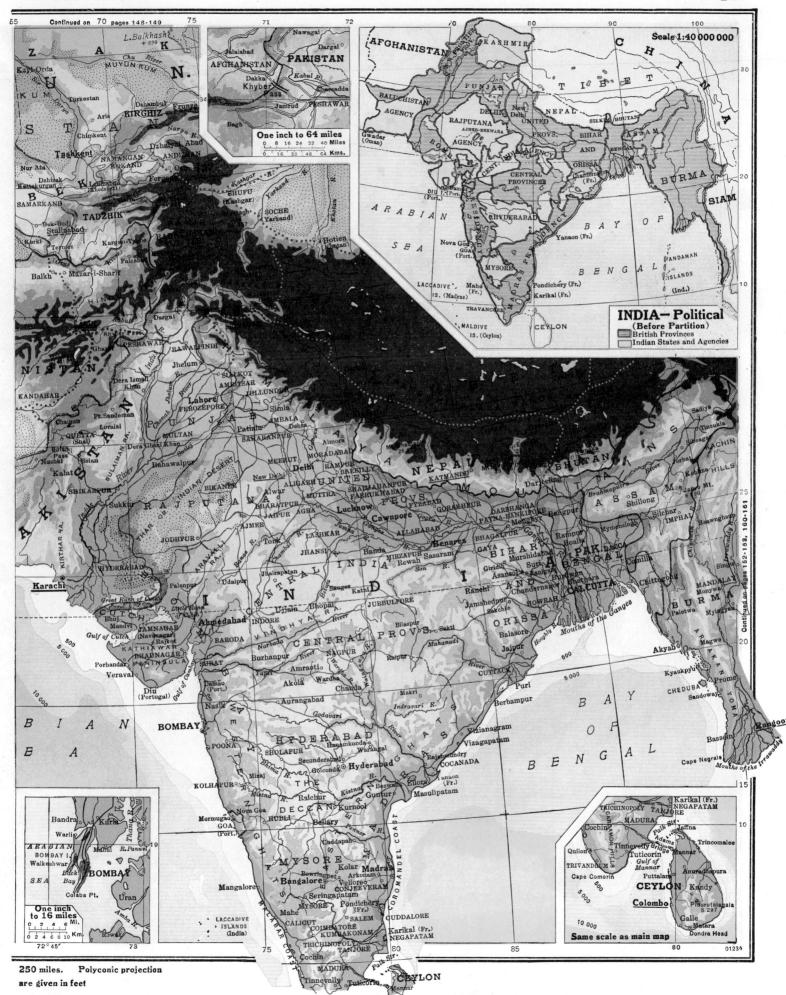

Continued on 70 pages 148-149

L. Balkhash
+899

ZAK.

MUYUN-KUM

CHU River

KIRGHIZ

AFGHANISTAN

PAKISTAN

Nawagai
Dargai

Jalalabad

Dakka
Khyber
Pass
Jamrud

PESHAWAR

Charsadda

Bagh

Kabul R.

One inch to 64 miles

0   8 16 24 32   40 Miles
0 16 32 48 64 Kms.

Scale 1:40 000 000

AFGHANISTAN

KASHMIR

CHINA

PUNJAB

BALUCHISTAN
AGENCY

DELHI
New
Delhi

NEPAL

SIKKIM BHUTAN

TIBET

RAJPUTANA
AGENCY

AJMER-MERWARA

UNITED
PROVS.

BIHAR
AND

ASSAM

Gwadar
(Oman)

CENT. IND.
AGENCY

ORISSA

Chandernagore
(Fr.)

BURMA

DIU I.
(Port.)
DAMAN
(Port.)

CENTRAL
PROVINCES

ARABIAN
SEA

HYDERABAD

Yanaon (Fr.)

BAY   OF

SIAM

Nova Goa
(Port.)

MYSORE

Pondichery (Fr.)

ANDAMAN
ISLANDS

Karikal (Fr.)

(Ind.)

BENGAL

LACCADIVE
IS. (Madras)

Mahé
(Fr.)

TRAVANCORE

MALDIVE
IS. (Ceylon)

CEYLON

INDIA— Political
(Before Partition)
British Provinces
Indian States and Agencies

TASHKENT

UZBEK

Samarkand

TADZHIK

Stalinabad

SHUFU
Kashgar

SOCHE
Yarkand

Hotien
Khotan

HINDU

PESHAWAR

RAWALPINDI

Dargai

NISTAN

KANDAHAR

Jhelum

SIALKOT

Amritsar

Lahore
FEROZEPORE

Jullundur

Simla

PUNJAB

Ambala

Dehra

NEPAL

Sadiya

Tinsukia

ASSAM

KACHIN

Multan

Patiala

SAHARANPUR

Almora

Katmandu

Shillong

Imphal

BHUTAN

Darjeeling

Bahawalpur

BIKANER

Meerut

Delhi

MORADABAD

RAMPUR
BAREILLY

GORAKHPUR

DARBHANGA

Rangpur

Brahmaputra

Silchar

PAKISTAN

New Delhi

Alwar

ALIGARH

UNITED

SHAHJAHANPUR

FYZABAD

PATNA-BANKIPORE

Mymensingh

RAJPUTANA

Jaipur

BHARATPUR

MUTTRA

Agra

Lucknow

PROVS.

FARRUKHABAD

Cawnpore

Ganges

Gaya

BHAGALPUR

Murshidabad

Comilla

DACCA

BENGAL

Jodhpur

AJMER

TONK

Son R.

Allahabad

Benares

MIRZAPUR

Giridih

Asansol

Suri

BURDWAN

Chittagong

JHANSI

Banda

Rewah

Sasaram

BIHAR

Ranchi

Jamshedpur

CALCUTTA

HOWRAH

Chandernagore

MANDALAY

Udaipur

Jhalrapatan

CENTRAL

INDIA

Bilaspur

Sakti

ORISSA

AND

Monywa

BURMA

Karachi

HYDERABAD

Palanpur

Ujjain

Bhopal

JUBBULPORE

Raipur

Balasore

Mahanadi

Akyab

CUTCH

Bhuj

JAMNAGAR
(Navanagar)

Ahmedabad

INDORE

VINDHYA RA.

Narbada

CENTRAL PROVS.

Nagpur

CUTTACK

Puri

CHEDUBA

Magwe

Gulf of Cutch

Rajkot

BARODA

Burhanpur

Tapti

Wardha

Chanda

Makri

Sandoway

Kyaukpyu

Porbandar

KATHIAWAR

BHAUNAGAR

SURAT

Amraoti

Akola

Indravari R.

Berhampur

BAY

Kyaukse

Prome

Veraval

PENINSULA

Damao
(Port.)

Godavari

Vizianagram

OF

Myingyan

Diu
(Portugal)

Nasik

Aurangabad

Rajahmundry

Vizagapatam

Bassein

ARABIAN

BOMBAY

POONA

HYDERABAD

Hasamkonda
Warangal

COCANADA

BENGAL

Rangoon

SEA

SHOLAPUR

Secunderabad

Golconda

Hyderabad

Yanaon
(Fr.)

Cape Negrais

KOLHAPUR

Miraj

Krishna R.

Raichur

Bezwada

Ellore

Masulipatam

Mouths of the Irrawaddy

Mormugao

GOA
(Port.)

Nova Goa

DECCAN

Kurnool

THE

Guntur

TRICHINOPOLY

Karikal (Fr.)
NEGAPATAM

Mangalore

HUBLI

Bellary

Penner

Cuddapah

Kolar

Arkonam

Madras

TANJORE

MADURA

Jaffna

Trincomalee

MYSORE

Bangalore

Vellore

CONJEEVERAM

Cochin

Tinnevelly Bridge

Tuticorin

Mannar

Seringapatam

CUDDALORE

Palk St.
Adam's

Quilon

Gulf of
Mannar

Anuradhapura

Mahé

Mysore

Pondichery
(Fr.)

Cape Comorin

TRIVANDRUM

Puttalam

Calicut

COIMBATORE

KUMBAKONAM

Karikal (Fr.)
NEGAPATAM

CEYLON

Kandy

MADURA

TRICHINOPOLY
TANJORE

Colombo

Galle

LACCADIVE
ISLANDS
(India)

Cochin

Matara
Dondra Head

Tinnevelly
Tuticorin

CEYLON
Mannar

BOMBAY

Bandra
Kurla
Warli

ARABIAN

BOMBAY I.

Mahul

SEA

Walkeshwar

Back
Bay

BOMBAY

Colaba Pt.

Uran

**One inch
to 16 miles**

0 2 4 6 Mi.
0 2 4 6 8 10 Km.

Same scale as main map

Continued on pages 152-153, 160-161

250 miles.   Polyconic projection
are given in feet

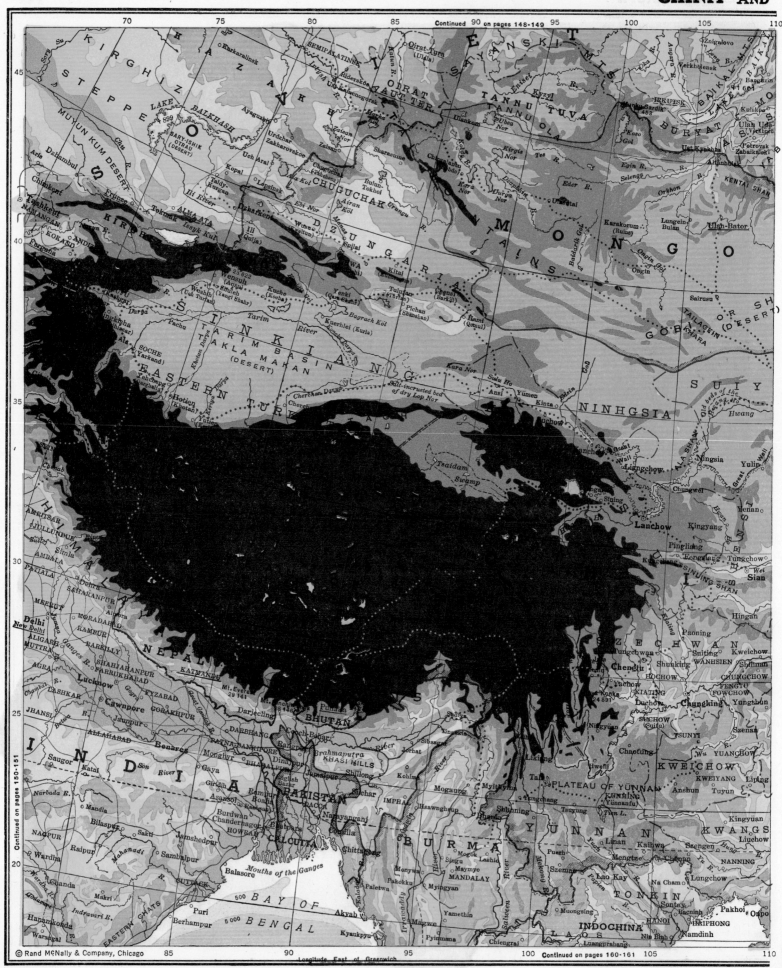

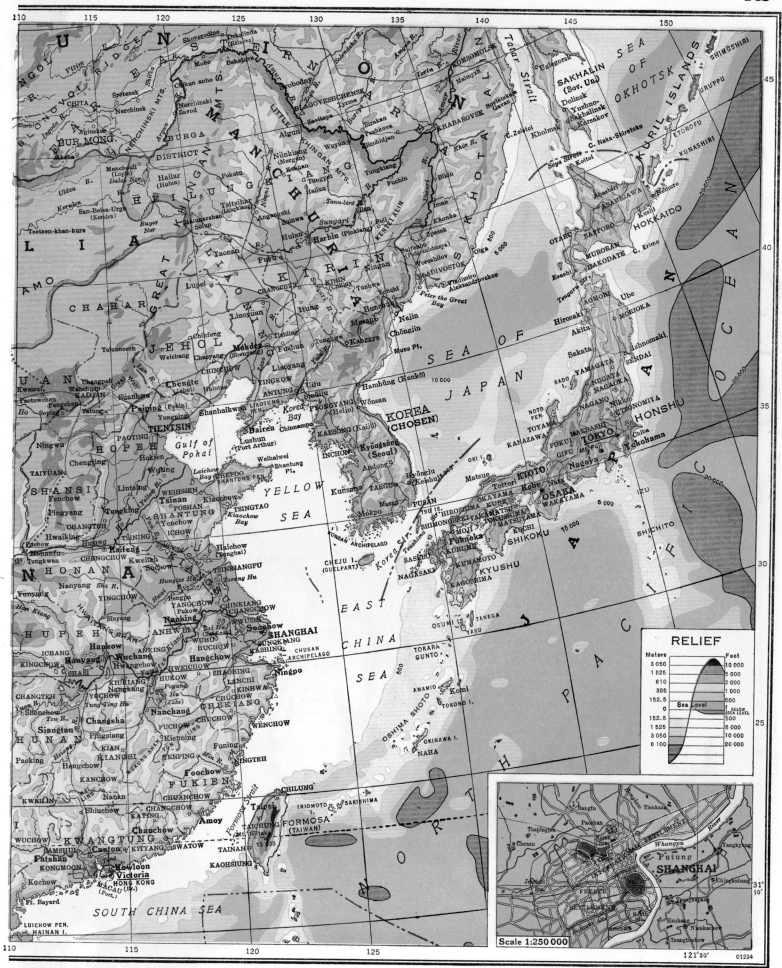

RELIEF

Meters		Feet
3 050		10 000
1 525		5 000
610		2 000
305		1 000
152.5		500
0	Sea Level	
152.5		BELOW SEA LEVEL 500
1 525		5 000
3 050		10 000
6 100		20 000

SHANGHAI

Scale 1:250 000

121°30'

01284

250 miles.   **Polyconic Projection**

are given in feet

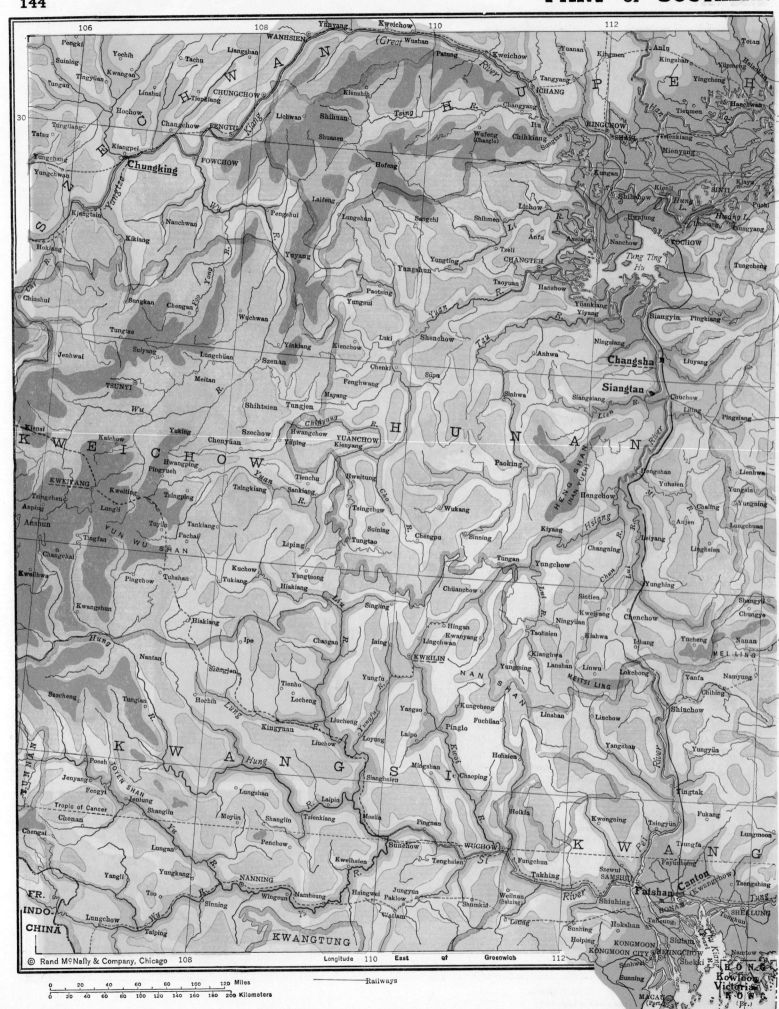

Longitude 110 East of Greenwich 112

Railways

20 0 20 40 60 80 100 120 Miles
20 0 20 40 60 80 100 120 140 160 180 200 Kilometers

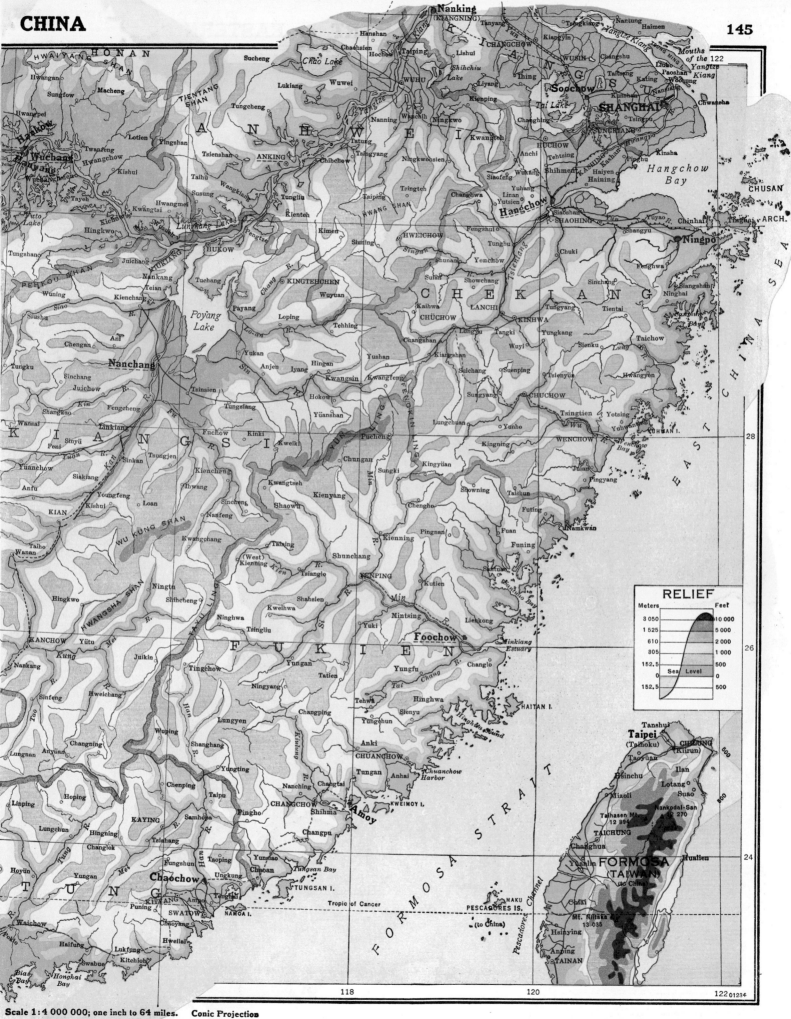

HONAN

HWAIYANG
HWAI

Hwangan
Sungfow
Macheng

Hankow
Wuchang
Hwangpei
Hwang
Hanyang
Wuchangkien

Lotien
Twanfeng
Hwangchow
Kishui

Tayeh
Hwangmen
Kwangtsi

Tungshan

Puto
Lake

Tungshan

Slushu

Chengan
Ani

Tungku
Sinchang
Juichow

Shangkao

Wansai

SHAN

TIENTANG
SHAN

Sucheng

Lukiang

Tungcheng

Taihu
Susung
Wangkiang

Hingkwo

PEHKOU
SHAN

Wuning
Siao

Juichang
Kienchang
Teian

Chengan

KIUKIANG
HUKOW

Poyang
Lake

Nanchang

Linkiang

KIANGSI

Hanshan
Chaohsien
Hochow

Taiping

Nanning
Tatung

ANKING

Tsienshan

Chihchow

Taihu

Tungliu

Kienteh

Kimen

Siuning

KINGTEHCHEN

Wuyuan

Payang
Loping

Tehhing

Yukan

Anjen
Iyang

Hingan

Kwangsin

Kweih

Hokow
Yuanshan

WUHU

Wuwei

Ningkwo

Kwangteh

Taiping
Tsingteh

Changhwa

HWEICHOW

Fengshui

Shunan

Sulan
Showchang

Yenchow

Chuki

Kaihwa
CHÜCHOW

LANCHI

Changshan
Lungyu
Tangki
KINHWA

Kiangshan

Suichang
Suenping

Yushan

Kwangfeng
Sungyang

CHEKIANG

Tungyang
Wuyi

Yungkang

Sienku
Taichow

Nanking
(KIANGNING)

Tanyang

CHANGCHOW
Lishui

Shihchiu
Lake

Kienping

Liyang
Ihing

Kiangyin

WUSIH

Soochow

SHANGHAI

Changshu
Kating
Paoshan
Woosung

Nanhiang

Chwansha

Tsingpu

Huchow

Kashan
Kiasing

Haiyen
Haining

Chaohing

Anchi

Tehtsing

Siaofeng
Wukang

Shihmen

Hangchow

Siaoshan
SHAOHING

Yuyao R.
Chinhai

Shangyu

Hangchow
Bay

CHUSAN

Ningpo

Fenghwa

Sinchang

Ninghai

Siangshan
Bay

TINGHAI ARCH.

EAST CHINA SEA

Yüanchow
Siakiang
Sinkan
Feni
Sinyü

Yungfeng

Kishui
Loan
Sincheng

KIAN

Anfu

Taiho
Wanan

Hingkwo

Ningtu

Shihcheng

Ninghwa

Tsingliu

Yütu

Nankang

KANCHOW

Kung

Juikin

Tingchow

WU KUNG SHAN

Kwangchang

Taning

(West)
Kienning

Shunchang

Kien R.

Shahsien

Kweihwa

Shaowu

Kienyang

Chengho

Pingnan

Kienning

KWANCHOW

Kutien

HWANGSHA SHAN

Ihwang

Nanfeng

Kwangtseh

Sungki

Chungan

Pucheng

Yüanshan

Kingyüan

Kingning

Lungchuan

Yunho

Yunhsiao

TEHWA SHAN

Tungku

Kingtehchen

Wuyuan

Jukin

Ningyang

Tatien

Yungan

FUKIEN

Yungfu

Yungchun

Sienyu

Tehwa

Changping

Hinghwa

Anki

CHUANCHOW

Tungan
Anhai

Nanching

Changtai

CHANGCHOW
Shihma

Amoy

Changpu

KWEIMOY I.

Chuanchow
Harbor

Chungan

Min R.

Shunchang

KIENPING

Yuki

Mintsing

Liehkong

Foochow

Minkiang
Estuary

Changlo

HAITAN I.

Tai Chang R.

Hinghwa
Sound

Futing

Fuan

Funing

Namkwan

Taishun

Showning

Yotsing

Wu R.

CHUCHOW

Tsingtien

Juian
Pingyang

Yuhwan

YUHWAN I.

Penghu
Bay

WENCHOW

WENCHOW R.

FORMOSA STRAIT

Tanshui

Taipei
(Taihoku)

KEELUNG
(Kirun)

Taoyüan

Ilan

Hsinchu

Lotang

Miaoli

Suao

Taihasen Mt.
12 994

Nankodai-San
12 270

TAICHUNG

Changhua

Yuanlin
FORMOSA
(TAIWAN)
(to China)

Hualien

Chiai

Mt. Niitaka
13 035

Hsinying

Anping
TAINAN

KIANGSI

KWANGTUNG

Yüanchow

Anfu

Sinfeng

Hweichang

Changning

Anyüan

Hoping

Lungnan

Linping

Lungchun

Hingning

KAYING

Tsishang

Changlok

Hoyün

Yungan

Chaochow

Puning
KITYANG

SWATOW

Chaoyang

Hwelai

Haifung

Lukfung
Kitchioh

Swabue

Bias
Bay

Honghai
Bay

Waichow

Pokio

Hingning

Ningyang

Wuping

Shanghang

Yungting

Chenping

Taipu

Pingho

Samhoa

Taoping

Chaoan

Ungkung

Tungsan Bay

TUNGSAN I.

NAMOA I.

MAKU

PESCADORES IS.
(to China)

Pescadores
Channel

Tropic of Cancer

Scale 1 : 4 000 000; one inch to 64 miles.   **Conic Projection**

Elevations and depressions are given in feet

RELIEF

Meters		Feet
3 050		10 000
1 525		5 000
610		2 000
305		1 000
152.5		500
Sea Level		0
152.5		500

GULF OF TUNG WAN

GULF OF POHAI

Strait of Pohai

Mouths of the Hwang Ho

Laichow Bay

MIAO-TAO I.

CHUNGSING I.

Society Bay

DAIREN (Free Port)

Loshan (Port Arthur) (China and Sov. Un.)

YINGKOW

Ningyuan · Hulutao

Suicheng

Funing

Shanhaikwan · Chinwangtao · Pehtaiho

Pochow · Machang

Pulantien

Kinchow · Talienwan

SHANTUNG PEN.

KUEN LUN SHAN

Chefoo · Weihaiwei

Ai Shan 3 200

Tengchow · Lungkow · Hwanghsien

Chaoyüan · Laichow

Ninghai · Tsieia

Haiyang · Wenteng

WEINSIEN · Pingtu · Leiyang

Kinkiakow · Shehfuchwang

Kiaochow · Tsimo

Changlo · Ankiu · Kaomi

Tsingtao · Kiaochow Bay

Tsangkow

PEIPING (Peking)

Tungchow · Tsienan

TIENTSIN · Tangku · Taku

Kichow · Yütien · Lwanchow · Fengjen · Kaiping · Loting

Shunyi · Paoti · Siangho · Ningho

Fengtai · Wuching · Kuan · Tungan

Paoting · PAOTING

HOPEH

Tsangchow · Yenshan

Tungkwang

Nanpi

Kingyün · Haifeng

Yangsin

SHANSI · WUTAI SHAN

Wutaishan 7,380

TAIHANG SHAN

Tsinan · TSINAN · POSHAN

TAI SHAN · Tai Shan 3,048 · TAIAN · Laiwu

SHANTUNG

MENG SHAN

Kufow · Yenchow · TSINING

Mengyin · Chüchow

ICHOW · Kanyü

Jihchao

SHANSI

Kaifeng · KAIFENG

HONAN

CHENGCHOW · CHENGCHOW

Kweiteh

Suichow · K · Suchow

Haichow (Tunghai)

Old mouth of the Hwang Ho before 1852

GREAT SAND BANK

Hungtze Lake

TSINGKIANGPU · Hwaiyin · Hwaian

Kaochow · Kaoyu L.

ANHWEI

HUPEH

Hwaiyang Shan

YINGCHOW

Chao Lake

LUCHOW

Nanking · NANKING (KIANGNING) · CHINKIANG · CHANGCHOW · WUSIH

Soochow · SHANGHAI

Tsung Ming I.

Mouths of the Yangtze Kiang

Yangtze Kiang

Tai Lake

Hwang Ho

Yellow R.

Grand Canal

0 20 40 60 80 100 120 Miles
0 20 40 60 80 100 120 140 160 180 200 Kilometers

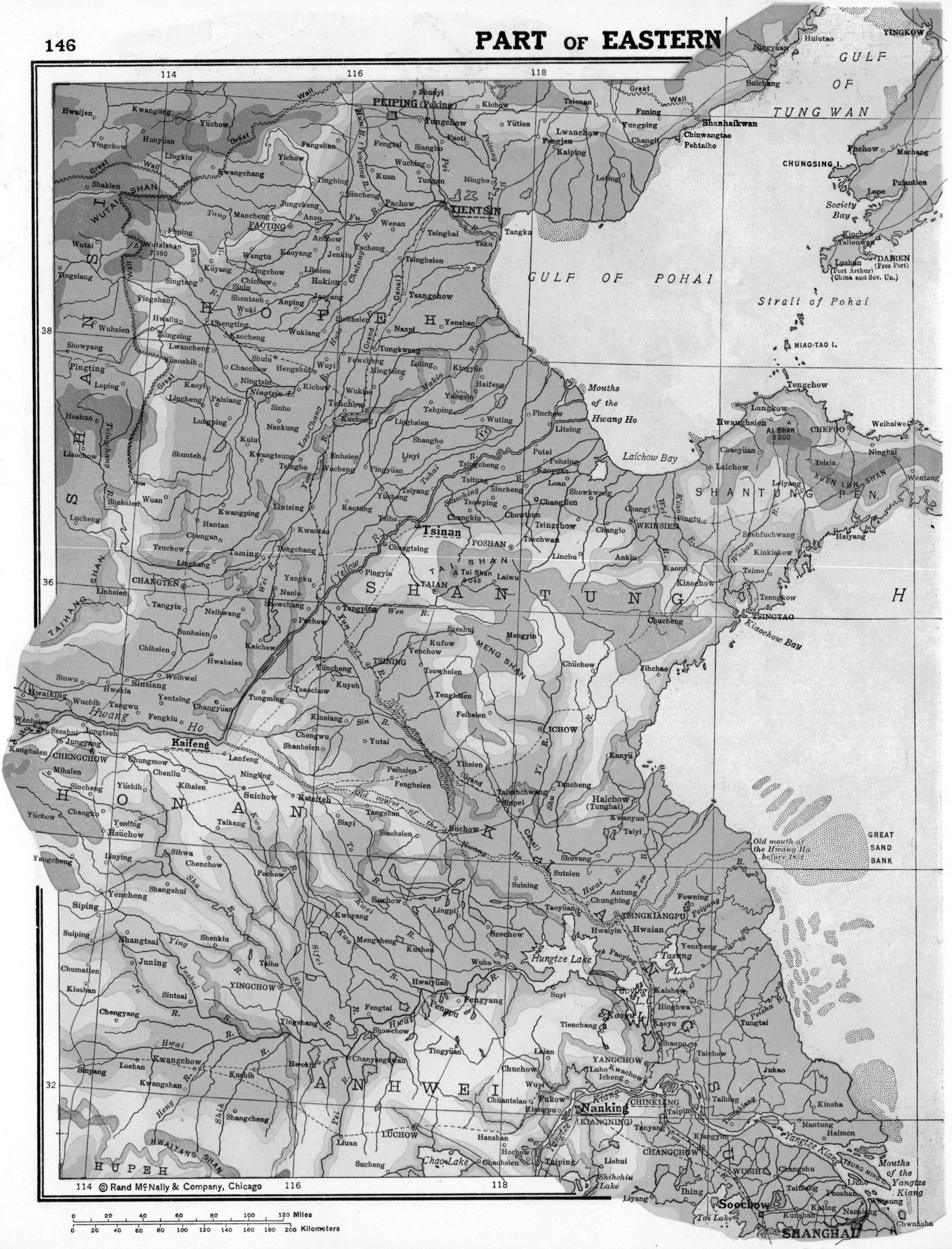

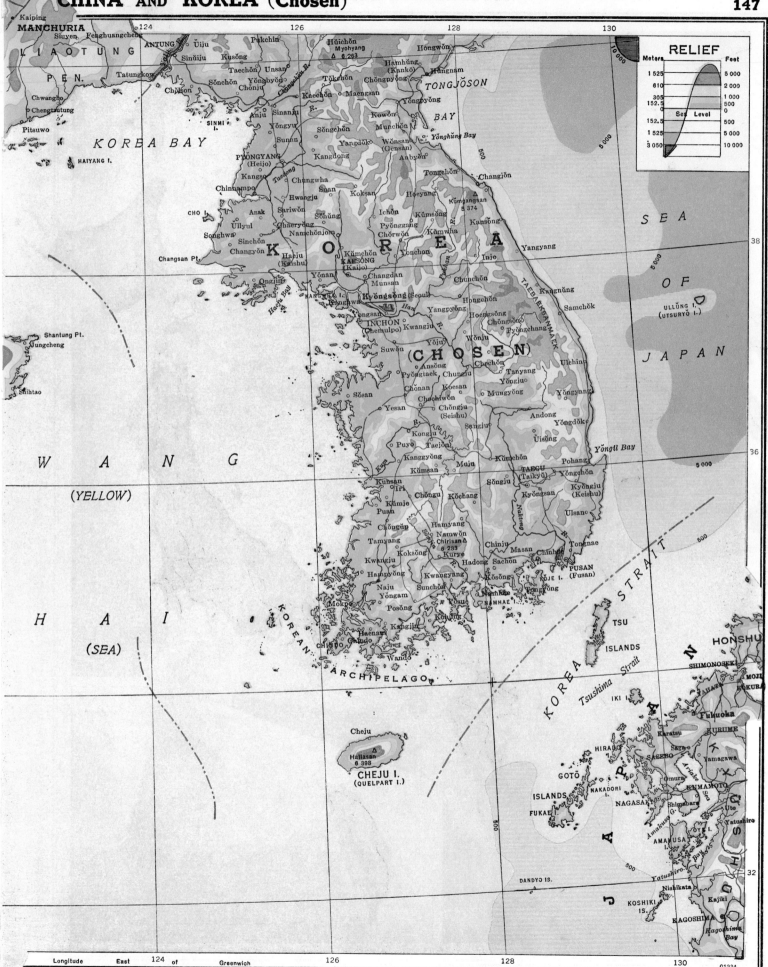

Scale 1:4 000 000; one inch to 64 miles.   **Conic Projection**

Elevations and depressions are given in feet

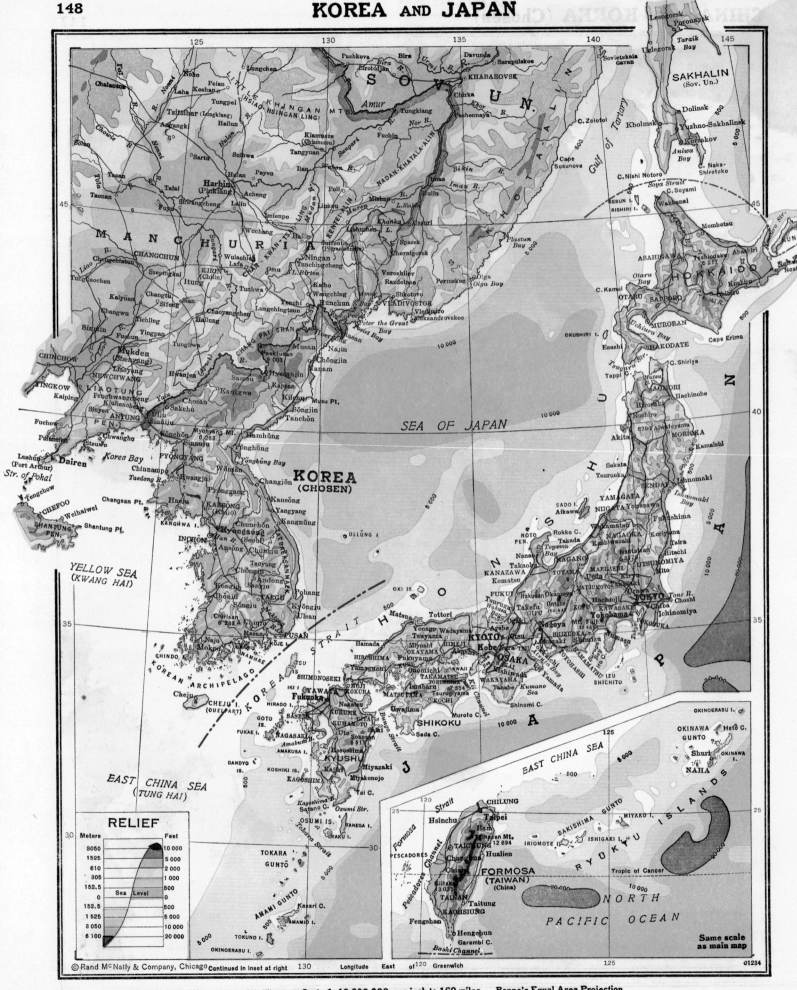

RELIEF

Meters	Feet
3050	10 000
1525	5 000
610	2 000
305	1 000
152.5	500
0 Sea Level	0
152.5	500
1 525	5 000
3 050	10 000
6 100	20 000

© Rand McNally & Company, Chicago   Continued in inset at right   130   Longitude   East   of   120   Greenwich   01234

Scale 1:10 000 000; one inch to 160 miles.   Bonne's Equal Area Projection

Elevations and depressions are given in feet

FORMOSA (TAIWAN) (China)

Same scale as main map

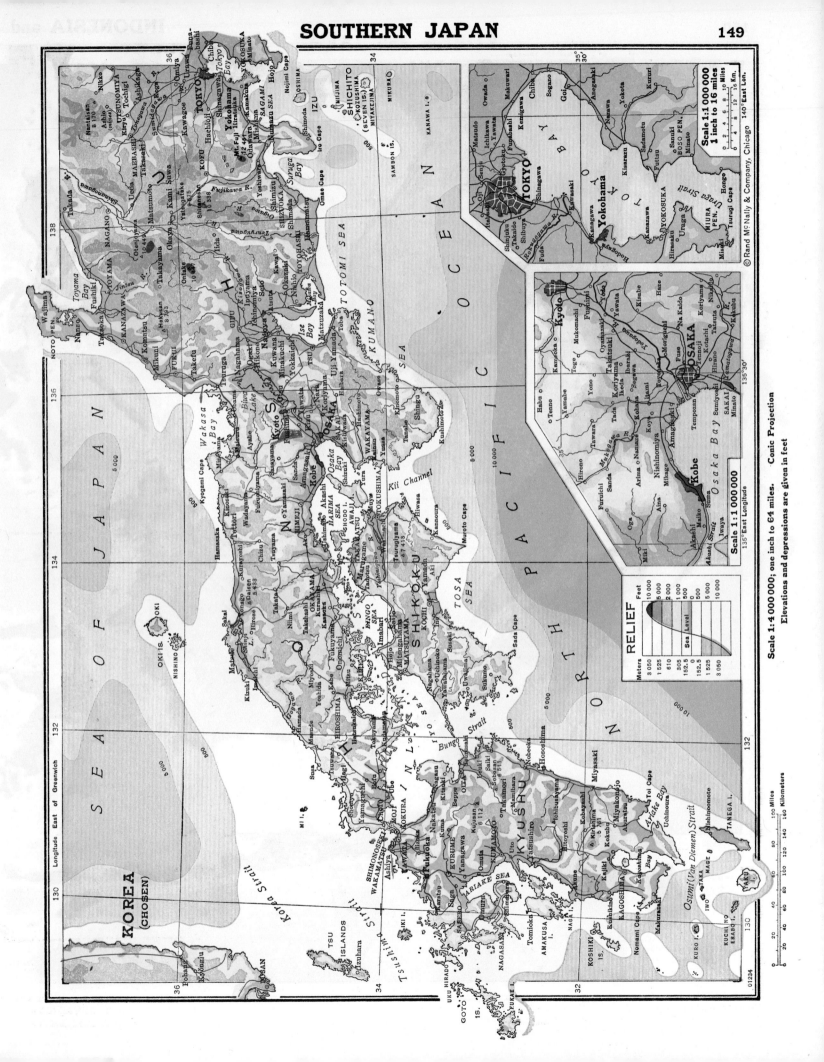

Scale 1:4 000 000; one inch to 64 miles.　Conic Projection

Elevations and depressions are given in feet

© Rand McNally & Company, Chicago

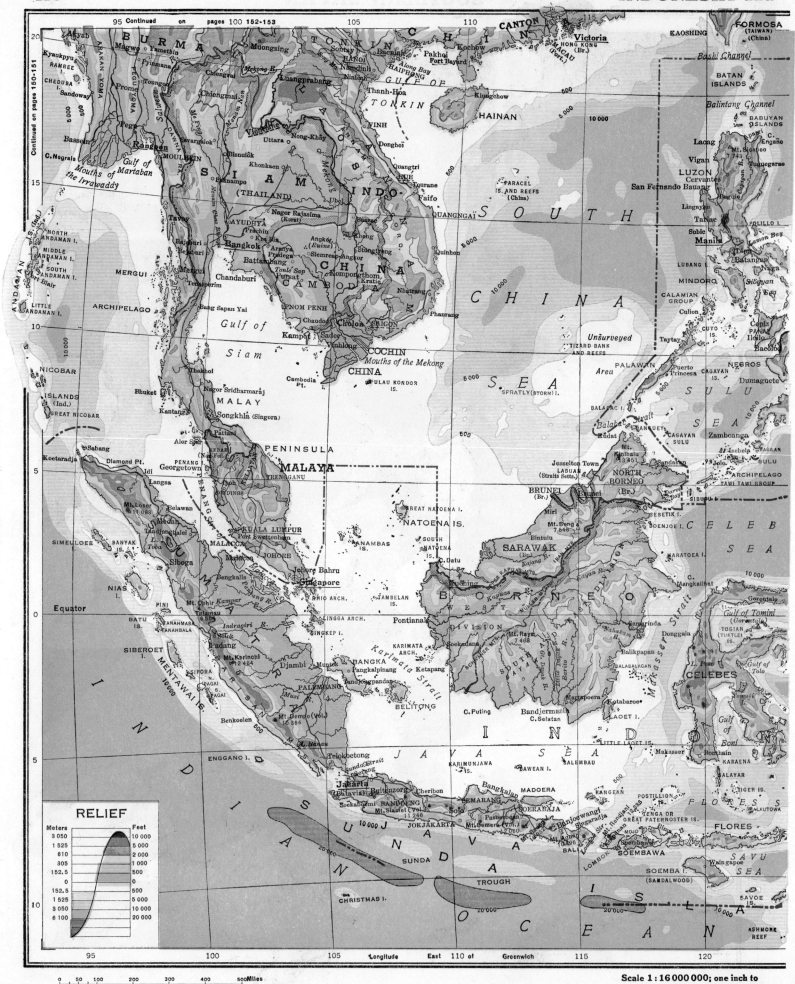

INDONESIA and

RELIEF

Meters		Feet
3 050		10 000
1 525		5 000
610		2 000
305		1 000
152.5		500
0		0
152.5		500
1 525		5 000
3 050		10 000
6 100		20 000

Scale 1 : 16 000 000; one inch to

Elevations and depressions

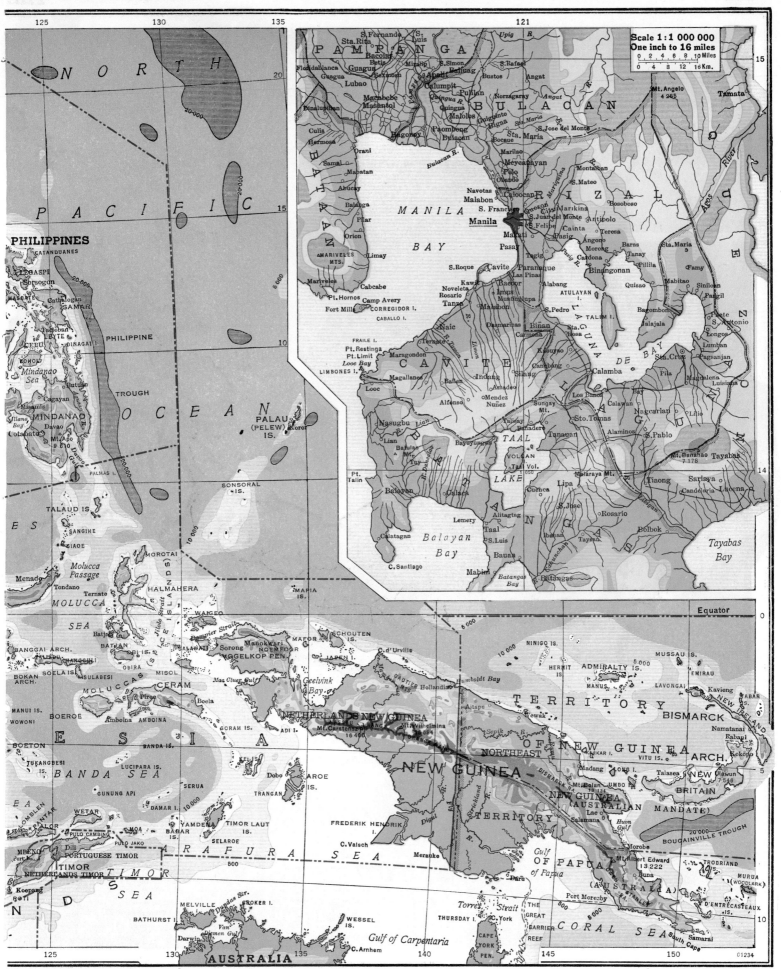

250 miles. **Polyconic Projection**

are given in feet

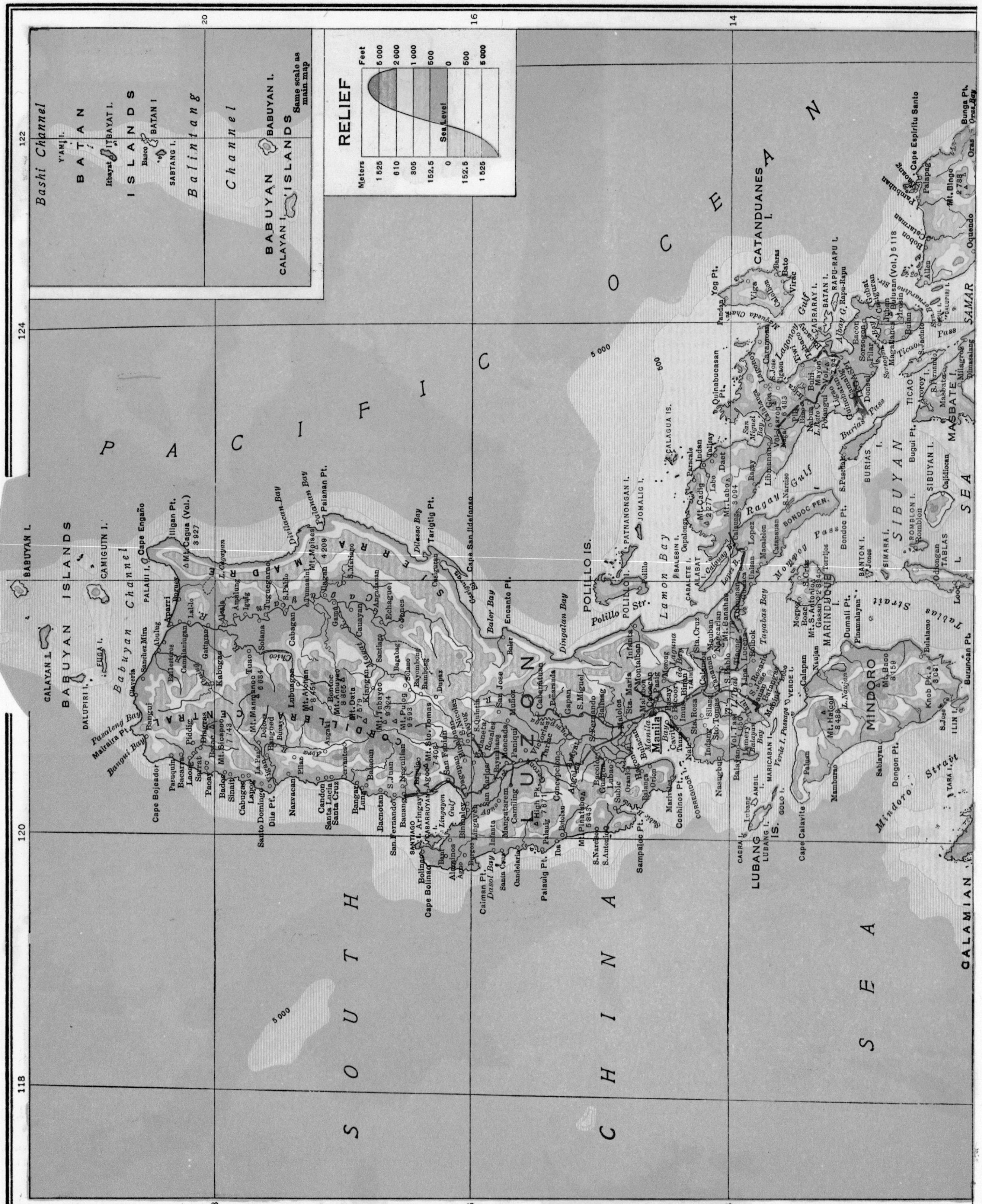

Bashi Channel

Y'AMI I.
ITBAYAT I.
BATAN ISLANDS
Ibayat BATAN I.
Basco
SABTANG I.

Balintang Channel

BABUYAN
CALAYAN ISLANDS

BABUYAN I.
CALAYAN I.
Same scale as main map

RELIEF

Feet	
5 000	
2 000	
1 000	
500	
0	Sea Level
500	
5 000	

Meters	
1 525	
610	
305	
152.5	
0	Sea Level
152.5	
1 525	

P A C I F I C   O C E A N

S O U T H   C H I N A   S E A

BABUYAN ISLANDS

BABUYAN I.
GALAYAN I.
CAMIGUIN I.
DALUPIRI I.
FUGA I.

Babuyan Channel

Cape Engaño
Aparri
Cape Bojeador

C O R D I L L E R A

S I E R R A   M A D R E

L U Z O N

Manila
Manila Bay
CORREGIDOR
Cavite
Batangas

MINDORO
Mt. Baco 8 159
Calapan

MINDORO
Mindoro Strait

LUBANG IS.

MARINDUQUE

Ragay Gulf

Lamon Bay

POLILLO IS.
Polillo
POLILLO STR.

CATANDUANES I.

SIBUYAN
ROMBLON
TABLAS

MASBATE I.
TICAO

BURIAS

SAMAR

Tayabas Bay

CALAMIAN

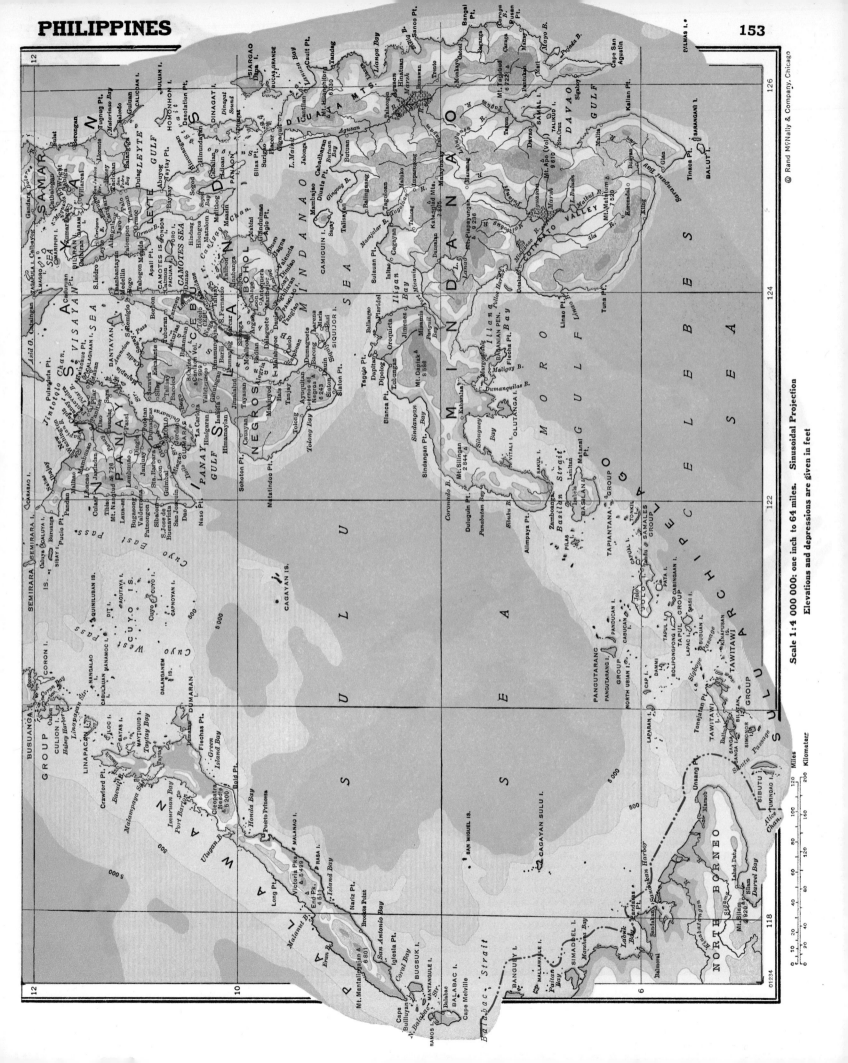

PHILIPPINES

© Rand McNally & Company, Chicago

Scale 1:4 000 000; one inch to 64 miles.   Sinusoidal Projection

Elevations and depressions are given in feet

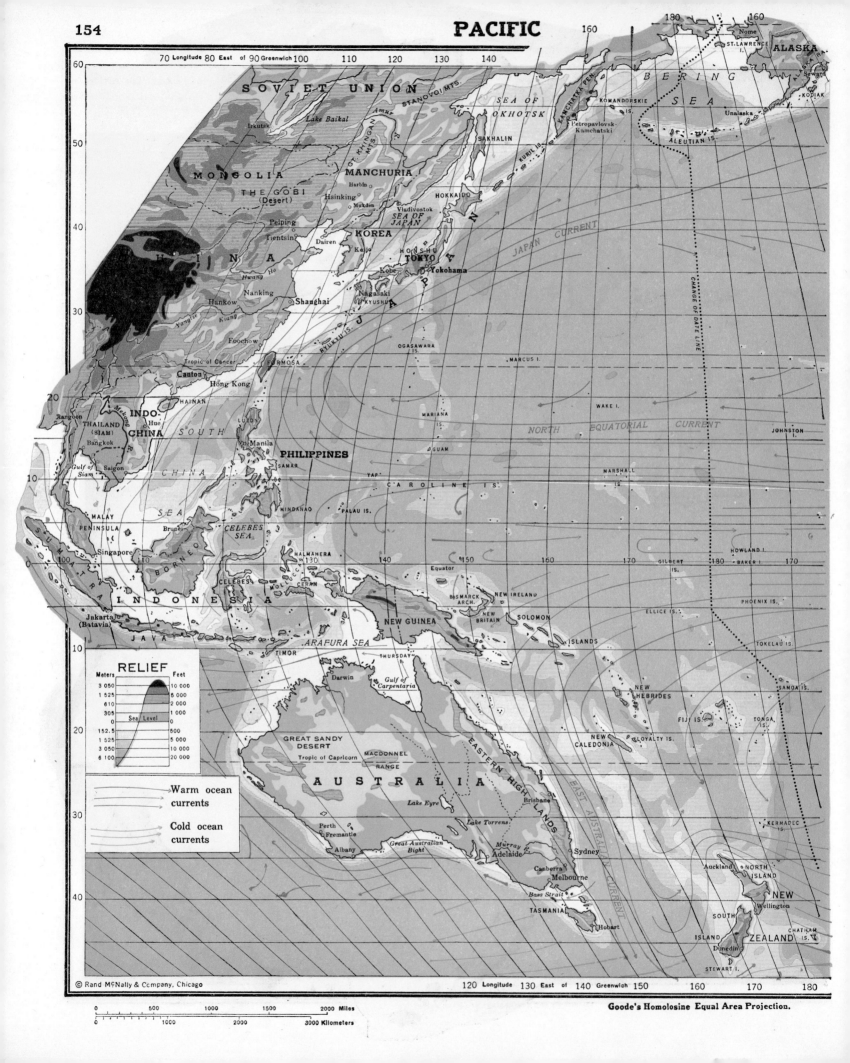

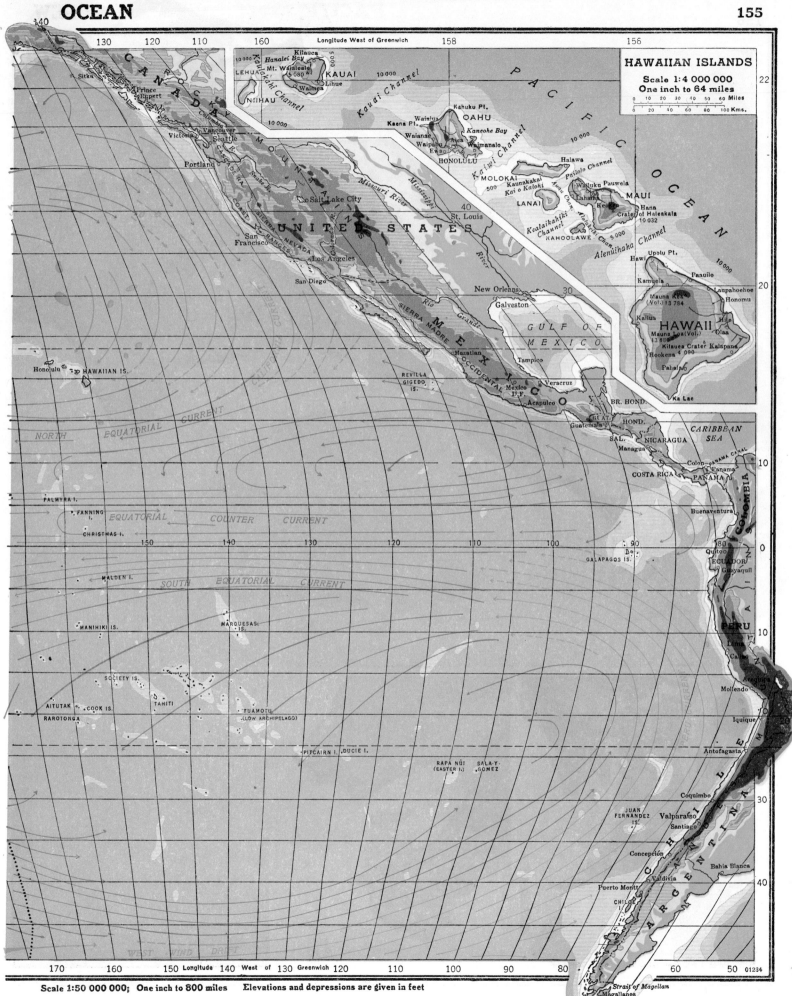

Scale 1:50 000 000; One inch to 800 miles   Elevations and depressions are given in feet

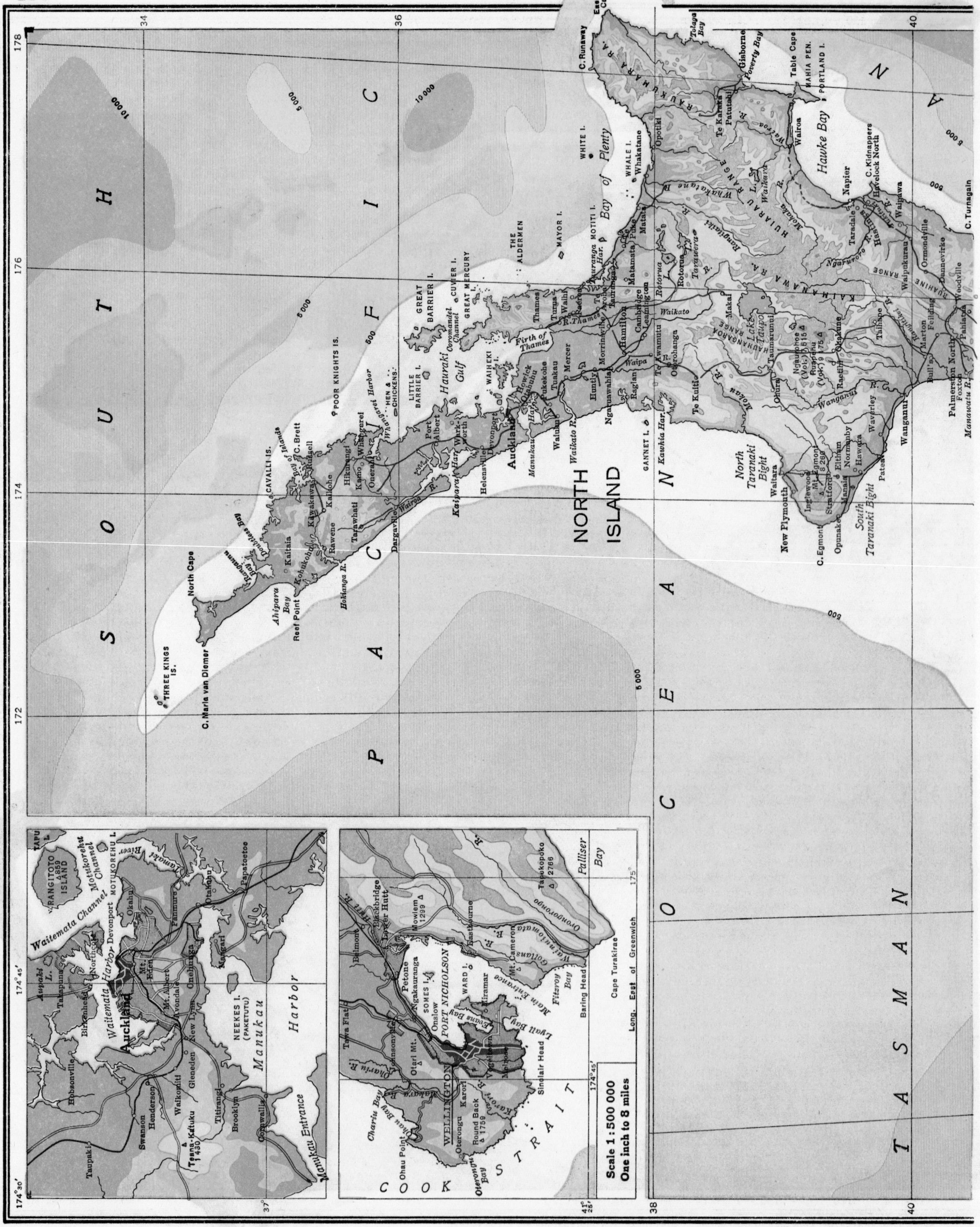

178
176
174
172

34
36
40

East
Cape

C. Runaway
Tolaga Bay
Gisborne
Poverty Bay
Table Cape
MAHIA PEN.
PORTLAND I.

WHITE I.
WHALE I.
Whakatane
Opotiki
Te Karaka
Patutahi
Wairoa
Hawke Bay
C. Kidnappers
Havelock North
Napier
Taradale
Hastings
Waipawa
Waipukurau
Ormondville
Dannevirke
Woodville
C. Turnagain

6 000
10 000
5 000
10 000

S O U T H

S O U T H   P A C I F I C   O C E A N

P A C I F I C

O C E A N

Bay of Plenty
THE ALDERMEN
MAYOR I.
MOTITI I.
Tauranga
Maketu
Te Puke
Matata
Whakatane
Rotorua
L. Rotorua
Taupo
Lake Taupo
KAIMANAWA RANGE
HUIARAU RANGE
RUAHINE RANGE
WHAKATANE R.
Rangitaiki R.

GREAT BARRIER I.
LITTLE BARRIER I.
CUVIER I.
GREAT MERCURY I.
Coromandel
Thames
Firth of Thames
Hauraki Gulf
WAIHEKI
HEN & CHICKENS
POOR KNIGHTS IS.
C. Brett
Bay of Islands
Russell
Whangarei
Whangarei Harbor
Hikurangi
Kaeo
Onerahi
Kaikohe
Tarawhati
Kaiwaka

CAVALLI IS.
North Cape
C. Maria van Diemen
THREE KINGS IS.
Ahipara Bay
Reef Point
Kaitaia
Kohukohu
Rawene
Hokianga R.
Dargaville
Kaipara Harbor
Helensville

NORTH ISLAND

Auckland
Manukau Harbor
Waikato R.
Mercer
Huntly
Ngaruawahia
Hamilton
Cambridge
Morrinsville
Te Aroha
Paeroa
Waihi
Raglan
Waipa
Te Awamutu
Otorohanga
Te Kuiti
Kawhia Har.
Kawhia
Mokau

North Taranaki Bight
New Plymouth
Inglewood
C. Egmont
Mt. Egmont
Stratford
Opunake
Eltham
Hawera
Manaia
Patea
Waverley
South Taranaki Bight
Wanganui
Wangaehu R.
Feilding
Palmerston North
Foxton
Pahiatua
Manawatu R.

GANNET I.
KAWHIA

5 000
500

T A S M A N

N

NORTH ISLAND

Inset left (Auckland):

TAPU
RANGITOTO ISLAND
Waitemata Channel
Motukorehu Channel
MOTUKOREHU I.
Devonport
Northcote
Birkenhead
Takapuna
Henderson
Swanson
Hobsonville
Waitakere L.
Mt. Eden
Mt. Albert
Avondale
New Lynn
Gleneden
Waikumiti
Titirangi
Brooklyn
Cornwallis
Auckland
Panmure
Onehunga
Otahuhu
Papatoetoe
Mangari
Oruari
NEEKES I. (PAKETUTU)
Manukau Harbor
Manukau Entrance
Taupaki
Puhinui
Tuakau
Waikaraka

174°30'
174°45'
37°

Inset right (Wellington):

Tapokopoko 2768
Pakuratahi R.
Tauherenikau R.
Otaki
Moumau 1209
Mt. Climie
Mangaroa
Upper Hutt
Belmont
Lower Hutt
Eastbourne
Petone
Ngakauranga
Onslow
Karori
SOMES I.
WARD I.
PORT NICHOLSON
WELLINGTON
Island Bay
Lyall Bay
Evans Bay
Miramar
Seatoun
Baring Head
Sinclair Head
Cape Turakirae
Fitzroy Bay
Palliser Bay
Otari Mt.
Tawa Flat
Johnsonville
Pukerua Bay
Round Back 1759
Plimmerton
Paremata
Paekakariki
Ohau Point
Otaki
Charta Bay
Otaki Bay
Cook Strait

174°45'
175°
41°25'
38

Long. East of Greenwich

C O O K   S T R A I T

Scale 1:500 000
One inch to 8 miles

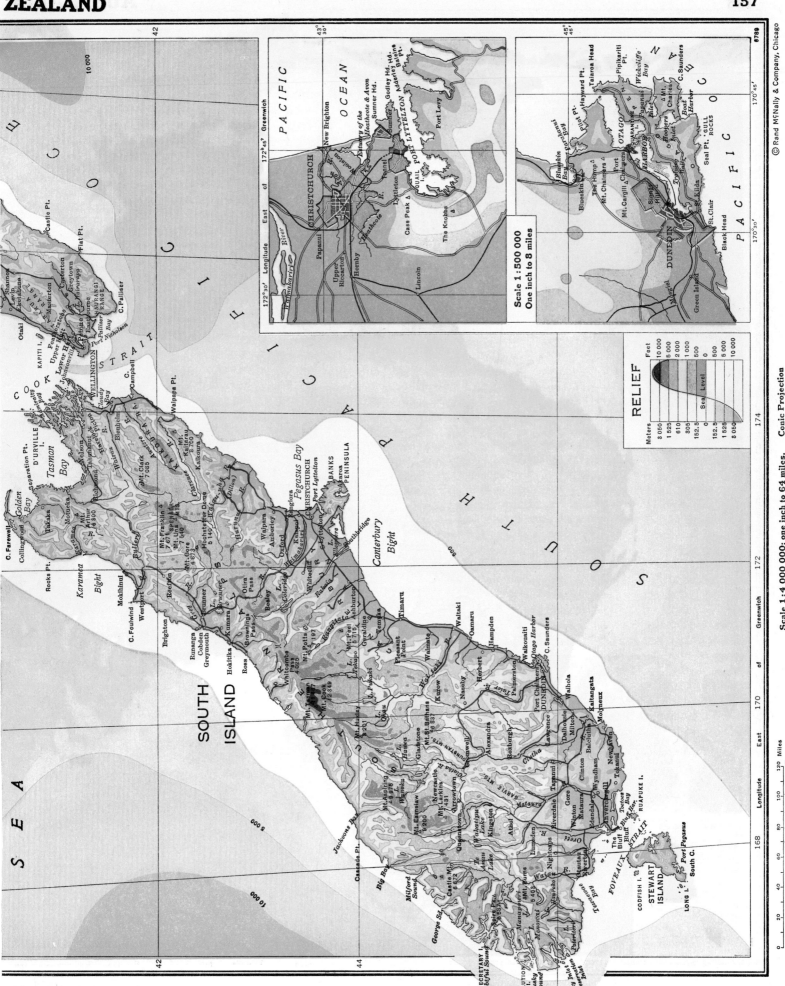

Scale 1:500 000
One inch to 8 miles

RELIEF

Scale 1:4 000 000; one inch to 64 miles.   Conic Projection
Elevations and depressions are given in feet

AUSTRALIA

NETHERLANDS
NEW GUINEA

INDONESIA

ARAFURA SEA

SUNDA ISLANDS

TIMOR SEA

ARNHEMLAND

GULF OF CARPENTARIA

NORTHERN TERRITORY

GREAT SANDY DESERT

WESTERN AUSTRALIA

GIBSON DESERT

SOUTH AUSTRALIA

GREAT VICTORIA DESERT

NULLARBOR PLAIN

GREAT AUSTRALIAN BIGHT

INDIAN OCEAN

Tropic of Capricorn

Perth

Adelaide

RELIEF

Meters		Feet
3 050		10 000
1 525		5 000
610		2 000
305		1 000
152.5		500
0	Sea Level	BELOW SEA LEVEL
152.5		500
1 525		5 000
3 050		10 000
6 100		20 000

© Rand McNally & Company, Chicago

0 50 100 200 300 400 500 600 Miles
0 100 200 400 600 800 1000 Kilometers

Scale 1:16 000 000; one inch to 250 miles.
Elevations and depressions

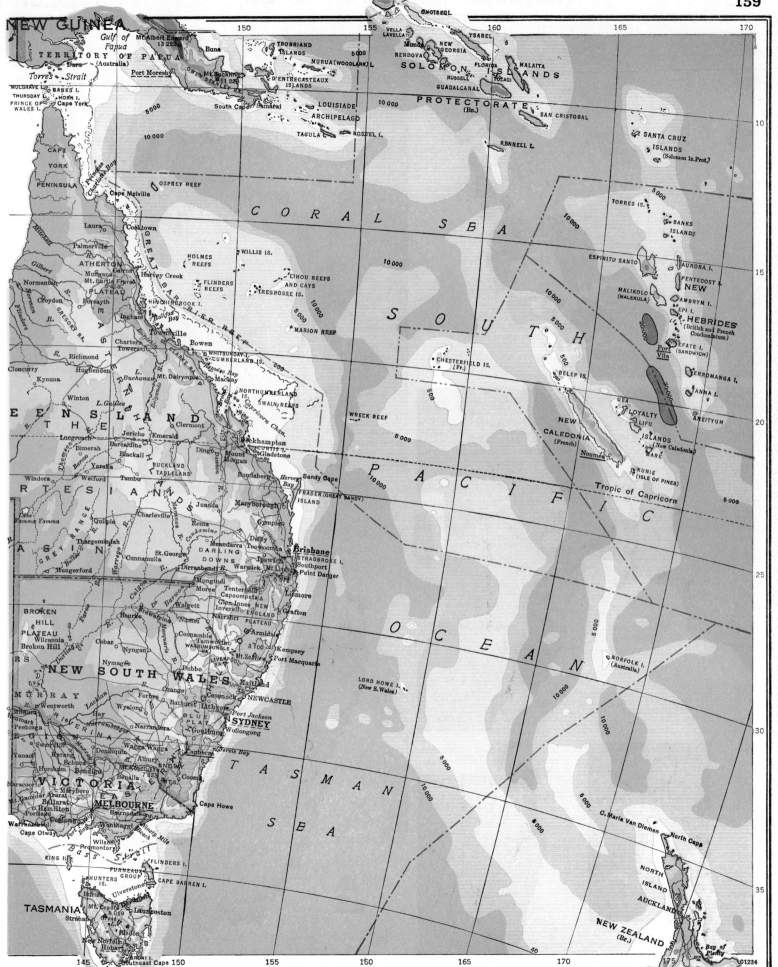

Lambert's Azimuthal, Equal Area Projection
are given in feet

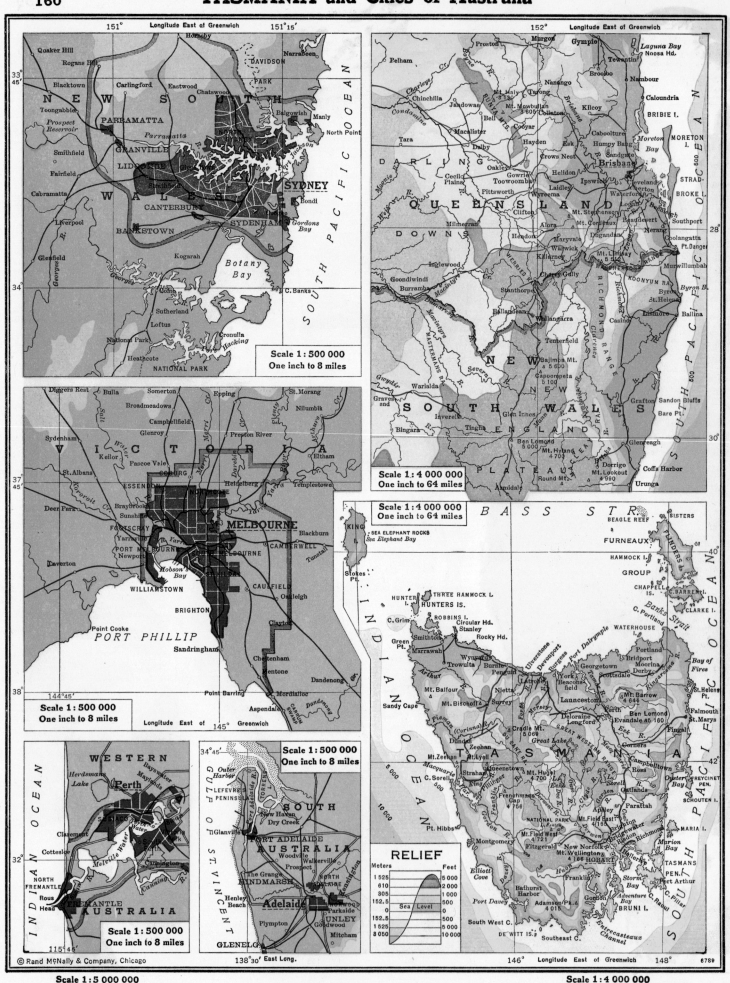

Scale 1 : 500 000
One inch to 8 miles

Scale 1 : 4 000 000
One inch to 64 miles

Scale 1 : 4 000 000
One inch to 64 miles

Scale 1 : 500 000
One inch to 8 miles

Scale 1 : 500 000
One inch to 8 miles

Scale 1 : 500 000
One inch to 8 miles

RELIEF

Meters		Feet
1 525		5 000
610		2 000
305		1 000
152.5		500
	Sea Level	0
152.5		500
1 525		5 000
3 050		10 000

© Rand McNally & Company, Chicago

Scale 1:5 000 000

Miles
0 1 2 3 4 5 6 7 8 9 10
Kilometers
0 2 4 6 8 10 12 14 16

Elevations and depressions are given in feet

Scale 1:4 000 000

Miles
0 20 40 60
Kilometers
0 20 40 60 80 100

WORLD COMPARISONS

Miscellaneous Dimensions

Equatorial Diameter of the Earth (miles)	7,926.68
Polar Diameter of the Earth (miles)	7,899.99
Equatorial Circumference of the Earth (mi.)	24,902.37
Polar Circumference of the Earth (miles)	24,860.44
Area of the Earth (square miles)	196,940,400.00
Diameter of the Mean Sphere of the Earth (mi.)	7,917.57
Land Area of the Earth (sq. miles)	56,000,000.00
Water Area of the Earth (sq. miles)	141,055,400.00
Greatest Altitude of Land (feet), Mt. Everest, Asia	29,141.00
Lowest Altitude on Land (feet), Dead Sea, Palestine	—1,292.00
Greatest Depth of the Ocean (feet), off Phil. Is., Pacific O.	35,400.00
Population of the Earth (estimated number)	2,240,000,000
Distance from Earth to Sun (mean miles)	92,900,000.00
Distance from Earth to Moon (mean miles)	238,857.00
Africa Area (square miles)	11,600,000.00
Antarctica Area (square miles)	5,362,626.00
Asia Area (square miles)	16,235,000.00
Australia Area (square miles)	2,974,581.00
Europe Area (square miles)	3,762,100.00
North America Area (square miles)	9,375,000.00
South America Area (square miles)	6,846,000.00

Principal Islands and Their Areas

Island	Area Sq. Miles
Baffin, Arctic Region	231,000
Banks, Arctic Region	25,000
Borneo, East Indies	282,416
Celebes, East Indies	72,679
Ceylon, Indian Ocean	25,332
Corsica, Mediterranean Sea	3,367
Crete, Mediterranean Sea	3,330
Cuba, West Indies	44,164
Cyprus, Mediterranean Sea	3,584
Devon, Arctic Region	24,000
Ellesmere, Arctic Region	41,000
Formosa, China Sea	13,836
Great Britain, North Atlantic O.	88,745
Greenland, Arctic Region	837,620
Hainan, South China Sea	13,000
Hawaii, Pacific O.	4,015
Hispaniola, West Indies	29,536
Hokkaido, Japan	30,000
Honshu, Japan	87,500
Iceland, Arctic Region	39,709
Ireland, North Atlantic O.	31,829
Jamaica, West Indies	4,450
Java, East Indies	50,745
Luzon, Philippines	40,814
Madagascar, Indian Ocean	228,707
Melville, Arctic Region	20,000
Mindanao, Philippines	36,906
Mindoro, Philippines	3,704
Negros, Philippines	4,903
New Britain, East Indies	10,000
New Caledonia, South Pacific O.	8,458
Newfoundland, North Atlantic O.	42,734
New Guinea, East Indies	342,232
New Ireland, East Indies	3,000
North Island (New Zealand), South Pacific O.	44,281
Novaya Zemlya, Arctic Region	35,150
Palawan, Philippines	4,500
Panay, Philippines	4,448
Prince Edward, Arctic Region	2,184
Prince of Wales, Arctic Region	15,000
Puerto Rico, West Indies	3,534
Sakhalin, Sov. Un.	29,100
Samar, Philippines	5,124
Sardinia, Mediterranean Sea	9,299
Sicily, Mediterranean Sea	9,935
Somerset, Arctic Region	12,000
South (New Zealand), South Pacific O.	58,092
Southampton, Hudson Bay	17,800
Sumatra, East Indies	163,138
Tasmania, Australia	26,215
Timor, East Indies	33,740
Vancouver, Canada	12,468
Victoria, Arctic Region	60,000
West Spitzbergen, Arctic Region	15,260
Wrangel, Arctic Region	1,806

Principal Lakes, Oceans, Seas, and Their Areas

Lake Country	Area Sq. Miles
Aral Sea, Soviet Union	26,166
Arctic O.	5,541,000
Athabaska, L., Canada	2,842
Atlantic O.	31,529,000
Baikal, L., Soviet Union	13,197
Balkhash, L., Soviet Union	7,115
Baltic Sea, Europe	158,000
Bering Sea, N. Pacific	878,000
Black Sea	168,500
Caribbean Sea, W. Indies	750,000
Caspian Sea, Asia	169,383
Chad, L., Africa	10,400
East China Sea, Asia	480,000
Erie, L., U. S.-Canada	9,940
Eyre, L., Australia	3,700
Gairdner, L., Australia	3,000
Great Bear L., Canada	14,000
Great Salt L., United States	2,560
Great Slave L., Canada	7,100
Hudson Bay, N. America	472,000
Huron, L., U. S.-Canada	23,010
Indian O.	28,357,000
Japan Sea, Asia	405,000
Koko-Nor (L.), Tibet-China	2,300
Ladoga, L., Soviet Union	7,000
Leopold II, L., Belgian Congo	1,700
Manitoba, L., Canada	1,817
Mediterranean Sea, Eur.	1,145,000
Mexico, G. of, N. America	700,000
Michigan, L., United States	22,400
Nicaragua, L., Nicaragua	2,975
North Sea, Europe	221,000
Nyasa, L., Africa	10,231
Okhotsk Sea, Asia	582,000
Onega, L., Soviet Union	3,800
Ontario, L., U. S.-Canada	7,540
Pacific O.	63,985,000
Red Sea, Africa-Asia	178,000
Rudolf, L., Kenya	3,500
Superior, L., U. S.-Canada	31,810
Tanganyika, L., Africa	12,355
Titicaca, L., Peru-Bolivia	3,261
Torrens, L., Australia	2,400
Van, L., Turkey	2,500
Vänern (L.), Sweden	2,150
Victoria, L., Africa	26,828
Winnipeg, L., Canada	9,400
Winnipegosis, L., Canada	2,085
Yellow Sea, Asia	480,000

Principal Mountains and Their Heights

Mountain Country	Height in Feet
Aconcagua, Argentina	22,835
Albaron, France	12,014
Albert Edward, New Guinea	13,222
Albert Markham, Antarctica	10,460
Alestschhorn, Switzerland	13,803
Altar, Ecuador	17,730
Ampato, Peru	21,702
Ancohuma, Bolivia	21,490
Antisana, Ecuador	18,885
Apo, Philippines	9,610
Ararat, Turkey	16,916
Arjias Dagh, Turkey	12,566
Aux Sources, Basutoland	10,761
Bear, Alaska	14,850
Blackburn, Alaska	16,140
Blanc, France-Italy	15,781
Blanca, Colorado, U. S	14,390
Bona, Canada	16,422
Bonete, Argentina	21,031
Borah, Idaho, U. S	12,655
Byelukha, Soviet Union	14,890
Caca Aca, Bolivia	20,329
Cachi, Argentina	21,326
Carstensz, New Guinea	16,404
Cayambe, Ecuador	19,023
Ceachuca, Bolivia	19,407
Chimborazo, Ecuador	20,577
Cincel, Bolivia	20,102
Colima, Mexico	13,572
Colorados, Argentina-Chile	19,846
Condori, Peru	18,045
Condoriri, Bolivia	20,043
Cook, New Zealand	12,349
Copiapo, Chile	19,947
Coropuna, Peru	22,802
Cotopaxi, Ecuador	19,498
Cuzco (Ausangate), Peru	20,187
Del Acay, Argentina	20,801
Demavend, Iran	18,375
Dos Conos, Argentina	22,507
Dykh-tau, Soviet Union	17,054
Elbert, Colorado, U. S	14,420
Elbrus, Soviet Union	18,480
Erebus, Antarctica	13,300
Etna, Sicily	10,741
Everest, Nepal	29,141
Fairweather, Alaska-Canada	15,399
Falso Azufre, Argentina-Chile	22,277
Foraker, Alaska	17,000
Forel, Greenland	11,286
Fremont, Wyoming, U. S	13,730
Fujiyama, Japan	12,389
Godwin Austen, India	28,251
Grand Teton, Wyo., U. S	13,747
Hekla, Iceland	5,108
Hood, Oregon, U. S	11,253
Huanacuni, Bolivia	19,829
Huascaran, Peru	22,188
Hubbard, Canada	14,950
Huelacalloc, Bolivia	19,082
Huila, Colombia	18,701
Illampú, Bolivia	21,276
Illimani, Bolivia	21,282
Incahuasu, Argentina-Chile	21,720
Ixtaccihuatl, Mexico	17,338
Juncal, Argentina-Chile	19,965
Jungfrau, Switzerland	13,671
Kaufmann, Soviet Union	23,386
Kazbek, Soviet Union	16,546
Kenya, Africa	17,044
Kilimanjaro, Africa	19,324
Kinchinjunga, India	28,146
King, Canada	16,971
Klyuchevskaya, Soviet Union	15,912
Koshtan-tau, Soviet Union	17,096
La Plata, Colorado, U. S	14,342
Lassen, California, U. S	10,453
Lincacabur, Chile-Bolivia	19,456
Llullaillaco, Argentina-Chile	22,015
Logan, Canada	19,850
Lucania, Canada	17,150
McKinley, Alaska	20,300
Maipo, Argentina-Chile	17,459
Matterhorn, Switz.-Italy	14,780
Mauna Kea, Hawaii	13,784
Mauna Loa, Hawaii	13,680
Mercedario, Argentina-Chile	21,884
Minya Konka, China	24,900
Misti, Peru	19,166
Mont Blanc, Italy	15,780
Monte Rosa, Italy-Switz	15,217
Mustagh Ata, China	24,357
Nanga Parbat, India	26,629
Niitaka, Formosa	14,501
Ojos del Salado, Argentina-Chile	22,573
Ollague, Bolivia-Chile	19,259
Orizaba, Mexico	18,701
Payachata, Bolivia	20,768
Pelée, Martinique	5,200
Pichu Pichu, Peru	18,373
Pikes, Colorado, U. S	14,109
Pili, Chile	19,850
Pissis, Argentina	22,245
Popocatepetl, Mexico	17,840
Porongos, Argentina-Chile	20,512
Pular, Chile	20,342
Quincy Adams, Alaska	15,560
Rainier, Washington, U. S	14,408
Ras Dashan, Ethiopia	15,158
Ruwenzori, Belgian Congo	16,798
St. Elias, Alaska-Canada	18,008
Sajama, Bolivia	21,390
Sanford, Alaska	16,210
San Francisco, Arizona, U. S	12,611
Sangay, Ecuador	17,465
San Jose, Argentina-Chile	20,067
Sarmiento, Chile	20,670
Semeroe, Java	12,060
Shasta, California, U. S	14,161
Socompa, Argentina-Chile	19,787
Steele, Canada	16,439
Taapaca, Bolivia	19,079
Tacora, Peru	19,521
Tengri Khan, Soviet Union	23,622
Tocorpuri, Bolivia-Chile	22,163
Tolima, Colombia	19,482
Toluca, Mexico	15,448
Tortolas, de las, Chile	20,018
Tres Cruces, Chile	21,720
Turpungato, Chile	21,490
Ushba, Soviet Union	15,409
Vancouver, Canada	15,700
Veladero, Argentina	20,735
Vesuvius, Italy	4,012
Vilcanota, Peru	17,998
Weisshorn, Switzerland	14,804
Wheeler, Nevada, U. S	13,058
White, California, U. S	14,242
Whitney, California, U. S	14,495
Wilhelmina, New Guinea	15,584
Wood, Canada	15,880
Wrangell, Alaska	14,005

Principal Rivers and Their Lengths

River Country	Length in Miles
Albany, North America	610
Amazon, South America	3,900
Amur, Asia	2,900
Araguaya, South America	1,550
Arkansas, North America	1,450
Athabaska, North America	750
Backs, North America	600
Brahmaputra, Asia	1,800
Branco, South America	580
Brazos, North America	950
Canadian, North America	760
Churchill, North America	1,000
Colorado, North America	1,650
Columbia, North America	1,270
Congo, Africa	2,900
Cumberland, North America	687
Danube, Europe	1,725
Dnieper, Europe	1,400
Dniester, Europe	800
Don, Europe	1,100
Donets, Europe	650
Dubawnt, North America	575
Dvina, Europe	1,100
Elbe, Europe	700
Euphrates, Asia	1,700
Fraser, North America	700
Ganges, Asia	1,455
Gila, North America	630
Green, North America	730
Hwang, Asia	2,700
Indus, Asia	2,000
Jurua, South America	1,200
Kama, Europe	1,115
Lena, Asia	2,860
Liard, North America	550
Loire, Europe	650
Mackenzie, North America	2,500
Madeira, South America	1,200
Magdalena, South America	950
Marañon, South America	1,000
Mekong, Asia	2,600
Meuse, Europe	575
Mississippi, North America	2,470
Mississippi-Missouri, N. A	3,988
Missouri, North America	2,723
Nelson, North America	1,660
Niemen, Europe	550
Niger, Africa	2,600
Nile, Africa	4,000
Ob, Asia	3,200
Oder, Europe	550
Ohio, North America	1,306
Oka, Europe	914
Orinoco, South America	1,600
Ottawa, North America	690
Paraná, South America	2,450
Parnahiba, South America	850
Peace, North America	1,050
Pechora, Europe	1,000
Pilcomayo, South America	1,000
Plata-Paraguay, S. America	2,300
Platte, North America	1,030
Purus, South America	1,500
Putumayo, South America	900
Red, North America	1,018
Rhine, Europe	700
Rhone, Europe	500
Rio Grande, North America	1,800
Rio Negro, South America	1,400
Roosevelt, South America	950
St. Lawrence, North America	2,150
Salado, South America	1,000
São Francisco, South America	1,800
Saskatchewan, North America	1,205
Sava, Europe	550
Snake, North America	1,038
Tagus, Europe	550
Tapajos, South America	1,150
Tennessee, North America	862
Theiss, Europe	800
Tocantins, South America	1,000
Ucayali, South America	1,100
Ural, Europe	1,400
Uruguay, South America	1,100
Vistula, Europe	630
Volga, Europe	2,300
Vyatka, Europe	680
White, North America	690
Xingu, South America	1,300
Yangtze, Asia	3,100
Yapura, South America	1,200
Yellowstone, North America	671
Yenisei, Asia	2,800
Yukon, North America	2,100
Zambezi, Africa	1,600

PRINCIPAL COUNTRIES OF THE WORLD

Political Division	Area in sq. miles	Population	Pop. per sq. mi.
Aden Colony & Prot. (Br.)	115,080	730,876	6.4
Afghanistan	245,000	12,000,000	48.9
Africa	11,600,000	175,500,000	15.1
Alabama (U. S.)	51,609	2,920,000	56.6
Alaska (U. S.)	586,400	85,000	0.1
Albania	11,100	1,175,000	105.9
Alberta (Can.)	255,285	871,000	3.4
Algeria (Fr.)	847,818	8,983,330	10.6
Andaman Is. (India)	2,508	21,545	8.6
Andora	191	6,000	31.4
Anglo-Egyp. Sudan (Br.)	969,600	7,931,150	8.2
Angola (Port.)	484,729	4,075,000	8.2
Argentina	1,074,209	16,105,626	15.0
Arizona (U. S.)	113,909	745,000	6.5
Arkansas (U. S.)	53,102	1,964,000	37.0
Ascension I. (Br.)	34	292	8.6
Asia	16,235,000	1,179,000,000	72.6
Australia	2,974,581	7,711,000	2.6
Austria	32,375	7,090,122	219.0
Azores Is. (Port.)	990	284,755	286.6
Bahama Is. (Br.)	4,404	68,846	15.6
Bahrein Is. (Br.)	250	120,000	480.0
Basutoland (Br.)	11,716	556,390	47.5
Bechuanaland (Br.)	275,000	294,232	1.1
Belgian Congo & Ruanda-Urundi (Bel.)	925,907	14,587,195	15.8
Belgium	11,779	8,557,000	726.5
Belgium & Poss.	953,561	19,112,106	20.0
Bermuda Is. (Br.)	19	35,560	1871.6
Bhutan	18,000	300,000	16.7
Bolivia	415,364	3,922,000	9.4
Brazil	3,286,111	50,700,000	15.4
British Columbia (Can.)	366,255	1,114,000	3.0
Br. Comm. of Nations	13,002,751	507,254,757	39.0
British Guiana (Br.)	82,997	388,288	4.7
British Honduras (Br.)	8,598	59,237	6.9
British Somaliland (Br.)	68,000	500,000	7.4
Brunei (Br.)	2,500	20,677	8.3
Bulgaria*	42,796	7,048,000	164.7
Bulgaria (1939)	39,814	6,319,232	159.2
Burma	261,610	17,700,000	67.7
California (U. S.)	158,693	10,665,000	67.2
Cameroons (Fr.)	166,489	2,801,455	16.8
Canada	3,843,144	13,549,000	3.5
Canal Zone (U. S.)	553	51,827	93.6
Canary Is. (Sp.)	2,807	777,027	276.8
Cape Verde Is. (Port.)	1,516	181,286	119.5
Ceylon	25,332	7,288,000	287.7
Chile	286,396	5,709,000	19.9
China*	3,850,000	462,800,000	120.2
China (1935)	2,903,475	424,795,000	149.7
Colombia	439,828	10,777,000	24.5
Colorado (U. S.)	104,247	1,215,000	11.7
Connecticut (U. S.)	5,009	2,019,000	403.1
Costa Rica	19,652	837,000	42.6
Cuba	44,217	5,194,779	117.5
Cyprus (Br.)	3,572	460,000	128.8
Czechoslovakia*	49,354	12,463,000	252.5
Czechoslovakia (1937)	54,192	15,215,000	280.7
Delaware (U. S.)	2,057	311,000	151.2
Denmark	16,576	4,190,000	252.8
Denmark & Poss.	854,736	4,240,582	5.0
Dist. of Columbia (U. S.)	69	870,000	12608.7
Dominican Republic	19,129	2,277,000	119.0
Ecuador	100,613	3,400,000	33.8
Egypt	386,000	19,528,000	50.6
England (Br.)	50,874	40,386,800	793.9
Eritrea (It.)	45,783	750,000	16.4
Ethiopia	350,000	7,500,000	21.4
Europe	3,762,100	534,327,000	142.0
Faeroes, The (Den.)	540	29,198	54.1
Falkland Is. (Br.)	4,618	2,440	0.5
Fiji Is. (Br.)	7,083	270,000	38.1
Finland*	130,159	3,958,000	30.4
Finland (1939)	149,954	3,834,662	25.6
Florida (U. S.)	58,560	2,494,000	42.6
Formosa (China)	13,836	6,384,019	461.4
France	213,009	41,850,000	196.5
France & Poss.	4,585,268	100,151,168	21.8
French Equat. Africa (Fr.)	965,250	4,127,808	4.3
French Guiana (Fr.)	35,135	28,537	0.8
French Somaliland (Fr.)	5,790	49,391	8.0
French West Africa (Fr.)	1,814,810	15,996,000	8.8
Gambia (Br.)	4,099	249,266	60.8
Georgia (U. S.)	58,876	3,196,000	54.3
Germany*	137,591	67,300,000	489.1
Germany (1937)	181,683	66,616,000	363.5
Gibraltar (Br.)	2	22,532	11266.0
Gold Coast (Br.)	91,843	4,500,000	49.0
Great Britain & N. Ire.	94,278	49,611,076	526.2
Great Britain & Poss. (Excluding Dominions)	3,479,874	121,359,297	32.0
Greece	51,182	7,840,000	153.2
Greece (1939)	50,147	7,020,000	140.0
Greenland (Den.)	837,620	21,384	0.03
Guadeloupe & Dep. (Fr.)	688	308,000	447.7
Guam (U. S.)	206	26,000	126.2
Guatemala	42,042	3,754,000	89.3
Haiti	11,069	3,700,000	334.3
Hawaii (U. S.)	6,433	533,000	82.9
Honduras	59,161	1,260,000	21.3
Hong Kong (Br.)	391	1,800,000	4603.6
Hungary	35,912	9,400,000	261.8
Iceland	39,698	139,000	3.5
Idaho (U. S.)	83,557	592,000	7.1
Ifni (Sp.)	741	35,000	47.2
Illinois (U. S.)	56,400	8,449,000	149.8
India	1,246,880	347,340,000	278.6
Indiana (U. S.)	36,291	3,994,000	110.1
Indochina (Fr.)	284,522	27,030,000	95.0
Indonesia	575,893	76,000,000	132.0
Iowa (U. S.)	56,280	2,643,000	47.0
Iran (Persia)	628,000	15,000,000	23.9
Iraq	168,243	4,799,500	28.5
Ireland	26,592	2,997,400	112.7
Israel & Palestine	10,425	1,677,000	166.2
Italy*	116,226	45,776,000	393.9
Italy (1939)	119,703	43,691,000	365.0
Jamaica (Br.)	4,470	1,340,000	299.8
Japan*	147,889	80,216,896	542.4
Japanese Empire (1937)	263,357	105,226,100	399.5
Jordan	35,326	491,365	139.1
Kansas (U. S.)	82,276	1,947,000	23.7
Kentucky (U. S.)	40,395	2,893,000	71.6
Kenya (Br.)	224,960	5,182,000	23.0
Korea	85,266	27,700,000	324.9
Kuwait (Br.)	1,930	80,000	41.5
Labrador (Newfd.)	110,000	5,528	0.05
Lebanon	3,926	1,186,145	302.1
Leeward Is. (Br.)	423	108,847	257.3
Liberia	43,000	1,500,000	34.9
Libya	633,040	888,401	1.4
Liechtenstein	65	11,218	172.4
Louisiana (U. S.)	48,523	2,630,000	54.2
Luxembourg	998	292,000	292.6
Madagascar (Fr.)	228,707	4,198,090	18.4
Madeira Is. (Port.)	307	251,798	820.2
Maine (U. S.)	33,215	909,000	27.4
Malaya (Br.)	52,100	5,000,000	96.0
Manchuria (China)	428,735	37,461,358	87.4
Manitoba (Can.)	246,512	778,000	3.2
Maryland (U. S.)	10,577	2,175,000	205.6
Massachusetts (U. S.)	8,257	4,713,000	570.8
Mauritius (Br.)	720	442,000	613.9
Mexico	760,373	24,602,313	32.4
Michigan (U. S.)	58,216	6,352,000	109.1
Minnesota (U. S.)	84,068	2,977,000	35.4
Mississippi (U. S.)	47,716	2,130,000	44.6
Missouri (U. S.)	69,674	3,935,000	56.5
Monaco	0.5	23,994	47988.0
Mongolia	558,054	880,000	1.6
Montana (U. S.)	147,138	521,000	3.5
Morocco (Fr.)	200,000	8,617,387	43.9
Mozambique (Port.)	297,731	6,258,000	21.0
Nebraska (U. S.)	77,237	1,285,000	16.6
Nepal	54,000	5,600,000	107.0
Netherlands	13,025	9,943,000	763.4
Netherlands & Poss.	227,909	10,634,861	46.7
Netherlands Indies, see Indonesia			
Neth. N. Guinea (Neth.)	159,375	333,631	2.1
Neth. W. Indies (Neth.)	366	148,530	405.8
Nevada (U. S.)	110,540	174,000	1.6
New Brunswick (Can.)	27,985	516,000	18.4
Newfoundland & Labrador (Can.)	152,734	348,000	2.3
New Gui. Ter. (Austl.)	91,000	755,882	8.3
New Hampshire (U. S.)	9,304	544,000	58.5
New Hebrides Is. (Br. & Fr.)	5,700	43,000	7.5
New Jersey (U. S.)	7,836	4,873,000	621.9
New Mexico (U. S.)	121,666	589,000	4.8
New York (U. S.)	49,576	14,392,000	290.3
New Zealand	103,416	1,842,000	17.8
Nicaragua	57,143	1,184,000	20.7
Nigeria (Br.)	372,674	24,000,000	64.4
North America	9,375,000	207,271,000	22.1
North Borneo (Br.)	31,106	314,850	10.1
North Carolina (U. S.)	52,712	3,864,000	73.3
North Dakota (U. S.)	70,665	605,000	8.6
Northern Ireland (Br.)	5,237	1,359,798	259.7
Northern Rhodesia (Br.)	290,320	1,720,320	5.9
Northwest Ter. (Can.)	1,304,903	16,000	0.01
Norway	125,182	3,198,274	25.5
Norway & Poss.	149,335	3,199,339	21.4
Nova Scotia (Can.)	21,068	645,000	30.6
Nyasaland (Br.)	37,596	2,150,000	57.2
Ohio (U. S.)	41,222	7,989,000	193.8
Oklahoma (U. S.)	69,919	2,302,000	32.9
Oman	82,000	500,000	6.1
Ontario (Can.)	412,582	4,411,000	10.7
Oregon (U. S.)	96,981	1,736,000	17.9
Pakistan	361,520	73,321,000	202.8
Palestine, see Israel & Palestine			
Panama	28,575	746,000	26.1
Papua Territory (Austl.)	90,540	301,500	3.3
Paraguay	157,047	1,270,000	8.1
Pennsylvania (U. S.)	45,333	10,633,000	234.6
Peru	482,258	8,132,793	16.9
Philippines	115,600	19,356,000	167.4
Poland*	120,359	23,900,000	198.6
Poland (1937)	149,915	34,220,000	228.3
Portugal	35,414	8,491,000	239.8
Portugal & Poss.	843,521	19,449,452	23.1
Portuguese Guinea (Port.)	13,944	351,089	25.2
Portuguese Timor (Port.)	7,330	438,338	59.8
Prince Edward I. (Can.)	2,184	94,000	43.0
Puerto Rico (U. S.)	3,435	2,185,000	636.1
Quebec (Can.)	594,860	3,887,000	6.5
Rhode Island (U. S.)	1,214	743,000	612.0
Rio de Oro & Adrar (Sp.)	109,200	37,000	0.3
Romania*	91,700	15,872,624	173.1
Romania (1937)	114,000	19,319,330	169.4
Salvador	13,176	2,100,000	159.4
San Marino	38	14,170	372.9
Sarawak (Br.)	48,300	546,361	11.3
Saskatchewan (Can.)	251,700	861,000	3.4
Saudi Arabia	413,792	5,500,000	13.3
Scotland (Br.)	30,405	5,169,217	170.0
Siam	198,271	17,987,000	90.7
Sierra Leone & Prot. (Br.)	31,000	2,000,000	64.5
Singapore (Br.)	281	800,000	2847.0
Solomon Is. (N. Guinea)	3,400	49,171	14.5
Solomon Is. (Br.)	11,458	100,000	8.8
Somaliland, Italian	190,000	1,210,000	6.4
South America	6,846,000	103,373,000	15.1
South Carolina (U. S.)	31,055	2,001,000	64.4
South Dakota (U. S.)	77,047	649,000	8.4
Southern Rhodesia (Br.)	150,354	1,979,000	13.2
Southwest Afr. (U. S. Afr.)	317,725	361,075	1.1
Soviet Union	8,436,000	193,500,000	22.9
Soviet Union (1938)	8,173,000	170,000,000	20.8
Spain	194,945	28,023,000	143.7
Spain & Poss.	325,191	29,489,509	90.7
Spanish Guinea (Sp.)	10,860	167,500	15.4
Spanish Morocco (Sp.)	8,880	1,082,009	121.9
Surinam (Neth.)	55,143	209,700	3.8
Svalbard (Nor.)	24,142	1,057	0.04
Swaziland (Br.)	6,705	184,781	27.6
Sweden	173,423	6,924,888	39.9
Switzerland	15,944	4,609,000	289.1
Syria	66,046	3,513,024	53.2
Tanganyika Ter. (Br.)	363,548	7,074,000	19.5
Tangier	147	130,000	884.3
Tennessee (U. S.)	42,246	3,234,000	76.6
Texas (U. S.)	267,339	7,532,000	28.2
Tibet (China)	469,194	1,000,000	2.1
Trieste Free Territory*	285	350,000	1228.1
Trinidad & Tobago (Br.)	1,980	590,000	298.0
Tunisia (Fr.)	63,616	3,230,952	50.8
Turkey	296,185	19,500,000	65.8
Uganda (Br.)	93,981	4,994,000	53.1
Ukraine* (Sov. Un.)	217,062	38,802,221	178.8
Union of South Africa	472,550	12,108,000	25.6
United States	3,022,387	150,588,000	49.8
United States & Poss.	3,619,644	153,530,935	42.4
Uruguay	72,172	2,350,000	32.6
Utah (U. S.)	84,916	682,000	8.0
Vatican City	0.2	1,025	5125.0
Venezuela	352,143	4,545,409	12.9
Vermont (U. S.)	9,609	369,000	38.4
Virgin Is. (U. S.)	133	27,000	203.0
Virginia (U. S.)	40,815	3,102,000	76.0
Wales (Br.)	7,466	2,552,200	341.8
Washington (U. S.)	68,192	2,582,000	37.9
West Virginia (U. S.)	24,181	1,941,000	80.3
White Russia* (Sov. Un.)	82,944	10,067,976	121.4
Windward Is. (Br.)	821	258,108	314.4
Wisconsin (U. S.)	56,154	3,355,000	59.7
Wyoming (U. S.)	97,914	284,000	2.9
Yemen	75,000	3,500,000	46.6
Yugoslavia*	99,181	15,751,935	158.8
Yugoslavia (1939)	95,551	15,630,129	163.6
Yukon (Can.)	207,076	8,000	0.04
Zanzibar (Br.)	640	244,000	381.3

*Figures shown are estimates based on postwar provisional boundaries.

GLOSSARY OF FOREIGN GEOGRAPHICAL TERMS

Annam ... Annamese
Arab ... Arabic
Bantu ... Bantu
Bur ... Burmese
Camb ... Cambodian
Celt ... Celtic
Chn ... Chinese
Czech ... Czech
Dan ... Danish
Du ... Dutch
Fin ... Finnish
Fr ... French
Ger ... German
Gr ... Greek
Hung ... Hungarian
Ice ... Icelandic
India ... India
Indian ... American Indian
It ... Italian
Jap ... Japanese
Kor ... Korean
Mal ... Malayan
Mong ... Mongolian
Nor ... Norwegian
Per ... Persian
Pol ... Polish
Port ... Portuguese
Rom ... Romanian
Rus ... Russian
Siam ... Siamese
So. Slav ... Southern Slavonic
Sp ... Spanish
Swe ... Swedish
Tib ... Tibetan
Tur ... Turkish

å, *Nor., Swe* ... brook, river
aa, *Dan., Nor* ... brook
aas, *Dan., Nor* ... ridge
ab, *Per* ... water, river
abad, *India, Per* ... town, city
ada, *Tur* ... island
adrar, *Arab* ... mountain
akrotírion, *Gr* ... cape
älf, *Swe* ... river
alp, *Ger* ... mountain
altipiano, *It* ... plateau
archipel, *Fr* ... archipelago
archipiélago, *Sp* ... archipelago
arquipélago, *Port* ... archipelago
arroyo, *Sp* ... brook, stream
ås, *Nor., Swe* ... ridge
austral, *Sp* ... southern
baai, *Du* ... bay
bab, *Arab* ... gate, port
bach, *Ger* ... brook, stream
backe, *Swe* ... hill
bad, *Ger* ... bath, spa
bahía, *Sp* ... bay, gulf
bahr, *Arab* ... sea, lake
baia, *It* ... bay, gulf
baía, *Port* ... bay
baie, *Fr* ... bay, gulf
bakke, *Dan., Nor* ... hill
balkan, *Tur* ... mountain range
bana, *Jap* ... point, cape
bandar, *Mal., Per.*
... town, port, harbor
bang, *Siam* ... village
bassin, *Fr* ... basin
batang, *Mal* ... river
ben, *Celt* ... mountain, summit
bender, *Arab* ... harbor, port
bereg, *Rus* ... coast, shore
berg, *Du., Ger., Nor., Swe.*
... mountain, hill
bir, *Arab* ... well
birket, *Arab* ... pond, pool
bit, *Arab* ... house
bjaerg, *Dan., Nor* ... mountain
boğaz, *Tur* ... strait
bois, *Fr* ... forest, wood
boloto, *Rus* ... marsh
bolsón, *Sp.*
... flat-floored desert valley
boreal, *Sp* ... northern
borg, *Dan., Nor., Swe.*
... castle, town
borgo, *It* ... town, suburb
bosch, *Du* ... forest, wood
bouche, *Fr* ... river mouth
bourg, *Fr* ... town, borough
bro, *Dan., Nor., Swe* ... bridge
brücke, *Ger* ... bridge
bucht, *Ger* ... bay, bight
bugt, *Dan., Nor., Swe* ... bay, gulf
burg, *Du., Ger* ... castle, town
buri, *Siam* ... town
burun, burnu, *Tur* ... cape
by, *Dan., Nor., Swe* ... village
caatinga, *Port. (Brazil)*
... open brushland
cabezo, *Sp* ... summit
cabo, *Port., Sp* ... cape
campo, *It, Port., Sp* ... field
campos, *Port. (Brazil)* ... plains
cañon, *Sp* ... canyon
cap, *Fr* ... cape
capo, *It* ... cape
casa, *It., Port., Sp* ... house
castello, *It., Port* ... castle, fort
castillo, *Sp* ... castle
çay, *Tur* ... stream, river
cayo, *Sp* ... rock, shoal, islet
cerro, *Sp* ... hill
champ, *Fr* ... field
chang, *Chn* ... village, middle
château, *Fr* ... castle
chen, *Chn* ... market town
chiang, *Chn* ... river
chott, *Arab* ... salt lake
chou, *Chn.*
... capital of district; island
chu, *Tib* ... water, stream
cidade, *Port* ... town, city
cima, *Sp* ... summit, peak
città, *It* ... town, city
ciudad, *Sp* ... town, city
col, *Fr* ... pass
colina, *Sp* ... hill
cordillera, *Sp* ... mountain chain
costa, *It., Port., Sp* ... coast
côte, *Fr* ... coast
cuchilla, *Sp* ... mountain ridge
dağ, *Tur* ... mountain
dake, *Jap* ... peak, summit
dal, *Dan., Du., Nor., Swe* ... valley
dan, *Kor* ... point, cape
dar, *Arab* ... house, abode, country
darya, *Per* ... river, sea
dasht, *Per* ... plain, desert
deniz, *Tur* ... sea
désert, *Fr* ... desert
deserto, *It* ... desert
desierto, *Sp* ... desert
détroit, *Fr* ... strait
dijk, *Du* ... dam, dike
djebel, *Arab* ... mountain
do, *Kor* ... island
dorf, *Ger* ... village
dorp, *Du* ... village
duin, *Du* ... dune
dzong, *Tib.*
... fort, administrative capital
eau, *Fr* ... water
ecuador, *Sp* ... equator
eiland, *Du* ... island
elv, *Dan., Nor* ... river, stream
erg, *Arab* ... dune, sandy desert
est, *Fr., It* ... east
estado, *Sp* ... state
este, *Port., Sp* ... east
estrecho, *Sp* ... strait
étang, *Fr* ... pond, lake
état, *Fr* ... state
eyjar, *Ice* ... islands
feld, *Ger* ... field, plain
festung, *Ger* ... fortress
fiume, *It* ... river
fjäll, *Swe* ... mountain
fjärd, *Swe* ... bay, inlet
fjeld, *Nor* ... mountain, hill
fjord, *Dan., Nor* ... fiord, inlet
fjördur, *Ice* ... fiord, inlet
fleuve, *Fr* ... river
flod, *Dan., Swe* ... river
flói, *Ice* ... bay, marshland
fluss, *Ger* ... river
foce, *It* ... river mouth
fontein, *Du* ... a spring
forêt, *Fr* ... forest
fors, *Swe* ... waterfall
forst, *Ger* ... forest
fos, *Dan., Nor* ... waterfall
fu, *Chn* ... town, residence
fuente, *Sp* ... spring, fountain
fuerte, *Sp* ... fort
furt, *Ger* ... ford
gang, *Kor* ... stream, river
gangri, *Tib* ... mountain
gat, *Dan., Nor* ... channel
gawa, *Jap* ... river
gebergte, *Du* ... mountain range
gebiet, *Ger* ... district, territory
gebirge, *Ger* ... mountains
ghat, *India*
... pass, mountain range
gobi, *Mong* ... desert
goenoeng, *Mal* ... mountain
gol, *Mong* ... river
göl, gölü, *Tur* ... lake
golf, *Du., Ger* ... gulf, bay
golfe, *Fr* ... gulf, bay
golfo, *It., Port., Sp* ... gulf, bay
gomba, gompa, *Tib* ... monastery
gora, *Rus., So. Slav* ... mountain
góra, *Pol* ... mountain
gorod, *Rus* ... town
grad, *Rus., So. Slav* ... town
guba, *Rus* ... bay, gulf
guntō, *Jap* ... archipelago
haf, *Swe* ... sea, ocean
hafen, *Ger* ... port, harbor
haff, *Ger* ... gulf, inland sea
hai, *Chn* ... sea, lake
hama, *Jap* ... beach, shore
hamada, *Arab* ... rocky plateau
hamn, *Swe* ... harbor
hamun, *Per* ... swampy lake, plain
hantō, *Jap* ... peninsula
hassi, *Arab* ... well, spring
haus, *Ger* ... house
haut, *Fr* ... summit, top
hav, *Dan., Nor* ... sea, ocean
havn, *Dan., Nor* ... harbor, port
havre, *Fr* ... harbor, port
háza, *Hung* ... house, dwelling of
heim, *Ger* ... hamlet, home
hem, *Swe* ... hamlet, home
higashi, *Jap* ... east
hisar, *Tur* ... fortress
hissar, *Arab* ... fort
ho, *Chn* ... river
hoek, *Du* ... cape
hof, *Ger* ... court, farm house
höfn, *Ice* ... harbor
hoku, *Jap* ... north
holm, *Dan., Nor., Swe* ... island
hora, *Czech* ... mountain
horn, *Ger* ... peak
hoved, *Dan., Nor* ... cape
hsien, *Chn.*
... district, district capital
hu, *Chn* ... lake
hügel, *Ger* ... hill
huk, *Dan., Swe* ... point
hus, *Dan., Nor., Swe* ... house
île, *Fr* ... island
ilha, *Port* ... island
indsö, *Dan., Nor* ... lake
insel, *Ger* ... island
insjö, *Swe* ... lake
irmak, irmaği, *Tur* ... river
isla, *Sp* ... island
isola, *It* ... island
istmo, *It., Sp* ... isthmus
järvi, jaur, *Fin* ... lake
jebel, *Arab* ... mountain
jima, *Jap* ... island
jökel, *Nor* ... glacier
joki, *Fin* ... river
jökull, *Ice* ... ice-covered mountain
kaap, *Du* ... cape
kai, *Jap* ... bay, gulf, sea
kaikyō, *Jap* ... channel, strait
kalat, *Per* ... castle, fortress
kale, *Tur* ... fort
kali, *Mal* ... river
kand, *Per* ... village
kang, *Chn.*
... mountain ridge; village
kap, *Dan., Ger* ... cape
kapp, *Nor., Swe* ... cape
kasr, *Arab* ... fort, castle
kawa, *Jap* ... river
kefr, *Arab* ... village
kei, *Jap* ... creek, river
ken, *Jap* ... prefecture
khor, *Arab* ... bay, inlet
khrebet, *Rus* ... mountain range
kiang, *Chn* ... large river
king, *Chn* ... capital city, town
kita, *Jap* ... north
ko, *Jap* ... lake
köbstad, *Dan* ... market-town
kol, *Mong* ... lake
kólpos, *Gr* ... gulf
kong, *Chn* ... river
kopf, *Ger* ... head, summit, peak
köpstad, *Swe* ... market-town
kou, *Chn* ... river mouth
köy, *Tur* ... village
kraal, *Du. (Africa)*
... native village
kšar, *Arab* ... fortified village
kuala, *Mal* ... river mouth
kuh, *Per* ... mountain
kum, *Tur* ... sand
kuppe, *Ger* ... summit
küste, *Ger* ... coast
kyo, *Jap* ... town, capital
la, *Tib* ... mountain pass
labuan, *Mal* ... anchorage, port
lac, *Fr* ... lake
lago, *It., Port., Sp* ... lake
lagoa, *Port* ... lake, marsh
laguna, *It., Port., Sp.*
... lagoon, lake
lahti, *Fin* ... bay, gulf
län, *Swe* ... county
landsby, *Dan., Nor* ... village
liehtao, *Chn* ... archipelago
liman, *Tur* ... bay, port
ling, *Chn* ... pass, ridge, mountain
llanos, *Sp* ... plains
loch, *Celt. (Scotland)* ... lake, bay
lough, *Celt. (Ireland)* ... lake, bay
machi, *Jap* ... town
man, *Kor* ... bay
mar, *Port., Sp* ... sea
mare, *It., Rom* ... sea
marisma, *Sp* ... marsh, swamp
mark, *Ger* ... boundary, limit
massif, *Fr* ... block of mountains
mato, *Port* ... forest, thicket
me, *Siam* ... river
meer, *Du., Ger* ... lake, sea
mer, *Fr* ... sea
mesa, *Sp* ... flat-topped mountain
mina, *Port., Sp* ... mine
minami, *Jap* ... south
minato, *Jap* ... harbor, haven
misaki, *Jap* ... cape, headland
mont, *Fr* ... mount, mountain
montagna, *It* ... mountain
montagne, *Fr* ... mountain
montaña, *Sp* ... mountain
monte, *It., Port., Sp.*
... mount, mountain
more, *Rus., So. Slav* ... sea
morro, *Port., Sp* ... hill, bluff
mühle, *Ger* ... mill
mund, *Ger* ... mouth, opening
mündung, *Ger* ... river mouth
mura, *Jap* ... township
myit, *Bur* ... river
mys, *Rus* ... cape
nada, *Jap* ... sea
nadi, *India* ... river, creek
naes, *Dan., Nor* ... cape
nafud, *Arab* ... desert of sand dunes
nagar, *India* ... town, city
nahr, *Arab* ... river
nam, *Siam* ... river, water
nan, *Chn., Jap* ... south
näs, *Nor., Swe* ... cape
nez, *Fr* ... point, cape
nishi, nisi, *Jap* ... west
njarga, *Fin* ... peninsula
nong, *Siam* ... marsh
noord, *Du* ... north
nor, *Mong* ... lake
nord, *Dan., Fr., Ger., It.,*
Nor., Swe ... north
norte, *Port., Sp* ... north
nos, *Rus* ... cape
nyasa, *Bantu* ... lake
ö, *Dan., Nor., Swe* ... island
occidental, *Sp* ... western
ocna, *Rom* ... salt mine
odde, *Dan., Nor* ... point, cape
oedjoeng, *Mal* ... point, cape
oeste, *Port., Sp* ... west
oka, *Jap* ... hill
oost, *Du* ... east
oriental, *Sp* ... eastern
óros, *Gr* ... mountain
ost, *Ger., Swe* ... east
öster, *Dan., Nor., Swe.*
... eastern
ostrov, *Rus* ... island
oued, *Arab* ... river, stream
ouest, *Fr* ... west
ozero, *Rus* ... lake
pää, *Fin* ... mountain
padang, *Mal* ... plain, field
pampas, *Sp. (Argentina)*
... grassy plains
pará, *Indian (Brazil)* ... river
pas, *Fr* ... channel, passage
paso, *Sp* ... passage
passo, *It., Port* ... passage, strait
patam, *India* ... city, town
pei, *Chn* ... north
pélagos, *Gr* ... open sea
peña, *Sp* ... rock
peresheyek, *Rus* ... isthmus
pertuis, *Fr* ... strait
pic, *Fr* ... mountain peak
pico, *Port., Sp* ... mountain peak
piedra, *Sp* ... stone, rock
ping, *Chn* ... plain, flat
planalto, *Port* ... plateau
playa, *Sp* ... shore, beach
pnom, *Camb* ... mountain
poelau, *Mal* ... island
pointe, *Fr* ... point
polder, *Du., Ger.*
... reclaimed marsh
polje, *So. Slav* ... field
poluostrov, *Rus* ... peninsula
pont, *Fr* ... bridge
ponta, *Port* ... point, headland
ponte, *It., Port* ... bridge
pore, *India* ... city, town
porthmós, *Gr* ... strait
porto, *It., Port* ... port, harbor
potamós, *Gr* ... river
prado, *Sp* ... field, meadow
presqu'île, *Fr* ... peninsula
proliv, *Rus* ... strait
pu, *Chn* ... commercial village
pueblo, *Sp* ... town, village
puerto, *Sp* ... port, harbor
pulau, *Mal* ... island
punkt, *Ger* ... point
punt, *Du* ... point
punta, *It., Sp* ... point
pur, *India* ... city, town
puy, *Fr* ... peak
qal'a, qal'at, *Arab* ... fort, village
qasr, *Arab* ... fort, castle
rann, *India* ... wasteland
ras, *Arab* ... cape, head
reka, *Rus., So. Slav* ... river
rettō, *Jap* ... island chain
ría, *Sp* ... estuary
ribeira, *Port* ... stream
riberão, *Port* ... river
rio, *It., Port* ... stream, river
río, *Sp* ... river
rivière, *Fr* ... river
roca, *Sp* ... rock
rud, *Per* ... river
saari, *Fin* ... island
sable, *Fr* ... sand
sahara, *Arab* ... desert, plain
saki, *Jap* ... cape
sal, *Sp* ... salt
san, *Jap., Kor* ... mountain, hill
sat, satul, *Rom* ... village
schloss, *Ger* ... castle
sebkha, *Arab* ... salt marsh
see, *Ger* ... lake, sea
sehir, *Tur* ... town, city
selvas, *Port. (Brazil)*
... tropical rain forests
serra, *Port* ... mountain chain
serranía, *Sp* ... mountain ridge
seto, *Jap* ... strait
severnaya, *Rus* ... northern
shahr, *Per* ... town, city
shan, *Chn.*
... mountain, hill, island
shatt, *Arab* ... river
shi, *Jap* ... city
shima, *Jap* ... island
shōtō, *Jap* ... archipelago
si, *Chn* ... west, western
sierra, *Sp* ... mountain range
sjö, *Nor., Swe* ... lake, sea
sö, *Dan., Nor* ... lake, sea
söder, södra, *Swe* ... south
soengai, soengei, *Mal* ... river
song, *Annam* ... river
sopka, *Rus* ... peak, volcano
source, *Fr* ... a spring
spitze, *Ger* ... summit, point
staat, *Ger* ... state
stad, *Dan., Du., Nor., Swe.*
... city, town
stadt, *Ger* ... city, town
stato, *It* ... state
step, *Rus* ... treeless plain, steppe
straat, *Du* ... strait
strand, *Dan., Du., Ger., Nor.,*
Swe ... shore, beach
stretto, *It* ... strait
strom, *Ger* ... river, stream
ström, *Dan., Nor., Swe.*
... stream, river
stroom, *Du* ... stream, river
su, suyu, *Tur* ... water, river
sud, *Fr., Sp* ... south
süd, *Ger* ... south
suidō, *Jap* ... channel
sul, *Port* ... south
sund, *Dan., Nor., Swe* ... sound
sungai, sungei, *Mal* ... river
sur, *Sp* ... south
syd, *Dan., Nor., Swe* ... south
tafelland, *Ger* ... plateau
take, *Jap* ... peak, summit
tal, *Ger* ... valley
tandjoeng, tanjong, *Mal* ... cape
tao, *Chn* ... island
târg, târgul, *Rom* ... market, town
tell, *Arab* ... hill
terra, *It* ... land
terre, *Fr* ... earth, land
thal, *Ger* ... valley
tierra, *Sp* ... earth, land
tō, *Jap* ... east; island
tonle, *Camb* ... river, lake
top, *Du* ... peak
torp, *Swe* ... hamlet, cottage
tsangpo, *Tib* ... river
tsi, *Chn* ... village, borough
tso, *Tib* ... lake
tsu, *Jap* ... harbor, port
tundra, *Rus.*
... treeless arctic plains
tung, *Chn* ... east
tuz, *Tur* ... salt
udde, *Swe* ... cape
ufer, *Ger* ... shore, river bank
umi, *Jap* ... sea, gulf
ura, *Jap* ... bay, coast, creek
ust'ye, *Rus* ... river mouth
valle, *It., Port., Sp* ... valley
vallée, *Fr* ... valley
vár, *Hung* ... fortress
város, *Hung* ... town
varoš, *So. Slav* ... town
veld, *Du* ... open plain, field
verkh, *Rus* ... top, summit
ves, *Czech* ... village
vest, *Dan., Nor., Swe* ... west
vik, *Swe* ... cove, bay
vila, *Port* ... town
villa, *Sp* ... town
villar, *Sp* ... village, hamlet
ville, *Fr* ... town, city
vostok, *Rus* ... east
wad, wadi, *Arab.*
... intermittent stream
wald, *Ger* ... forest, woodland
wan, *Chn., Jap* ... bay, gulf
weiler, *Ger* ... hamlet, village
westersch, *Du* ... western
wüste, *Ger* ... desert
yama, *Jap* ... mountain
yug, *Rus* ... south
zaki, *Jap* ... cape
zaliv, *Rus* ... bay, gulf
zapad, *Rus* ... west
zee, *Du* ... sea
zemlya, *Rus* ... land
zuid, *Du* ... south

ABBREVIATIONS OF GEOGRAPHICAL NAMES AND TERMS

A. E. Sud.
    Anglo-Egyptian Sudan
Afg...........Afghanistan
Afr................Africa
Ala...............Alabama
Alb...............Albania
Alg...............Algeria
Alsk..............Alaska
And...............Andorra
Ang...............Angola
Ant.............Antarctica
Arc. O.........Arctic O.
Arch...........Archipelago
Arg.............Argentina
Ariz.............Arizona
Ark...............Arkansas
A. S. S. R.
    Autonomous Socialist
    Soviet Republic
Atl. O.......Atlantic Ocean
Aus................Austria
Austl.............Australia
Aut..............Autonomous
Az. Is..........Azores Is.

B.............Bay, Bahia
Ba. Is.........Bahama Is.
Barb..............Barbados
Bas..............Basutoland
Bdy..............Boundary
Bech...........Bechuanaland
Bel...............Belgium
Bel. Cong...Belgian Congo
Bg..................Berg
Bhu...............Bhutan
Bk..................Bank
Bol................Bolivia
Br.................British
Braz...............Brazil
Br. Gu.....British Guiana
Br. Hond..British Honduras
Brit. Prot.
    British Protectorate
Br. Som.
    British Somaliland
Bru................Brunei
Bul...............Bulgaria
Bur.................Burma

C...........Cerro, Cape
Calif.............California
Cam............Cameroons
Can........Canal, Canada
Can. Is.......Canary Is.
Cen. Am..Central America
Cey................Ceylon
C. H........Court House

Chan...........Channel
Chl................Chile
Chn................China
Co.................County
Col..............Colombia
Colo.............Colorado
Conn..........Connecticut
Cor...............Corsica
C. R..........Costa Rica
Cr.................Creek
C. V. Is...Cape Verde Is.
Cyp...............Cyprus
C. Z.........Canal Zone
Czech.....Czechoslovakia

D. C..District of Columbia
Del..............Delaware
Den..............Denmark
Dept.........Department
Des................Desert
D. F....Distrito Federal
Dist..............District
Div..............Division
Dom. Rep......Dominica
Dom. Rep.
    Dominican Republic

E...................East
Ec..............Ecuador
Eg................Egypt
Elec.............Electric
Erit..............Eritrea
Eth..............Ethiopia
Eur..............Europe

Faer.........The Faeroes
Falk. Is....Falkland Is.
Fd................Fjord
Fin..............Finland
Fk.................Fork
Fla..............Florida
For.....Forest, Formosa
Fr.................France
Fr. Eq. Afr.
    French Equatorial Africa
Fr. Gu....French Guiana
Fr. Som.
    French Somaliland
Fr. W. Afr.
    French West Africa
Ft..................Fort

G...................Gulf
Ga...............Georgia
Gam..............Gambia
G. C...........Gold Coast
Ger..............Germany

Gib..............Gibraltar
Grc................Greece
Grnld...........Greenland
Gt..................Great
Gt. Brit...Great Britain
Guad...........Guadeloupe
Guat...........Guatemala

Hai................Haiti
Har., Hbr........Harbor
Haw..............Hawaii
Hd.................Head
Hond...........Honduras
Hts..............Heights
Hung............Hungary

I...................Island
Ia..................Iowa
Ice...............Iceland
Ida................Idaho
Ill...............Illinois
In...............Inset
Ind..............Indiana
Ind. O....Indian Ocean
Indoch........Indochina
Indon..........Indonesia
Ind. Res.
    Indian Reservation
Int., Intl....International
Ire...............Ireland
Is...............Islands
Isth.............Isthmus
It..................Italy

Jam.............Jamaica
Jap.............Japan
Jc.............Junction
Jor.............Jordan

Kan.............Kansas
Km..Kilometer, Kilometers
Kor..............Korea
Kuw.............Kuwait
Ky.............Kentucky

L.....Lake, Loch, Lough
La.............Louisiana
Lat.............Latitude
Leb............Lebanon
Le. Is......Leeward Is.
L. H........Lighthouse
Lib.............Liberia
Liech......Liechtenstein
Long..........Longitude
Lux.........Luxembourg

M............Mile, Miles
Madag......Madagascar

Mand..........Mandate
Mart..........Martinique
Mass.......Massachusetts
Max............Maximum
Max. surf. elev.
    Maximum surface
    elevation
Md.............Maryland
Me................Maine
Medit......Mediterranean
Mex..............Mexico
Mi..........Mile, Miles
Mich...........Michigan
Minn.........Minnesota
Miss.........Mississippi
Mo..............Missouri
Mong...........Mongolia
Mont...........Montana
Mor..............Morocco
Moz..........Mozambique
Mt.....Mount, Mountain
Mts...........Mountains

N...................North
N. A.....North America
Nat., Natl...National
Natl. Mon.
    National Monument
N. Bor....North Borneo
N. C.....North Carolina
N. Cal....New Caledonia
N. D......North Dakota
Neb...........Nebraska
Nep................Nepal
Neth.......Netherlands
Neth. N. Gui.
    Netherlands New Guinea
Nev..............Nevada
New Hebr...New Hebrides
N. Gui. Ter.
    New Guinea Ter.
N. H....New Hampshire
Nic............Nicaragua
Nig.............Nigeria
N. Ire...Northern Ireland
N. J.....New Jersey
N. M.....New Mexico
Nor..............Norway
N. Rh..Northern Rhodesia
N. Y............New York
Nya...........Nyasaland
N. Z.......New Zealand

O.................Ocean
Obs..........Observatory
Okla..........Oklahoma
Ore.............Oregon

P...................Pass
Pa...........Pennsylvania
Pac. O......Pacific Ocean
Pak..............Pakistan
Pal..............Palestine
Pan..............Panama
Pap. Ter......Papua Ter.
Par...........Paraguay
Pen.............Peninsula
Phil...........Philippines
Pk..........Peak, Park
Plat..............Plateau
Pol.................Poland
Port.............Portugal
Port. Gui.
    Portuguese Guinea
Port. Tim.
    Portuguese Timor
Poss...........Possession
P. R.........Puerto Rico
Prot...........Protectorate
Prov............Province
Pt..................Point
Pta..............Punta
Pte..............Pointe

R.....River, Rio, Rivière
Ra.................Range
R. de O......Rio de Oro
Reg...............Region
Rep.............Republic
Res.
    Reservation, Reservoir
Rf..................Reef
R. I.........Rhode Island
Rom............Romania
R. R............Railroad
Ry..............Railway
Rys.............Railways

S.....San, Santo, South
Sa....San, Santo, South
Sa.....Serra, Sierra
S. A.....South America
Sakh............Sakhalin
Sal...........Salvador
Sam..............Samoa
Sar...........Sarawak
Sard.............Sardinia
Sau. Ar.....Saudi Arabia
S. C.....South Carolina
S. D......South Dakota
Sd................Sound
S. F. S. R.
    Socialist Federated
    Soviet Republic
S. L.......Sierra Leone
Soc.............Socialist

Som....Italian Somaliland
Sov. Un.....Soviet Union
Sp..................Spain
Sp. Gui....Spanish Guinea
Sp. Mor..Spanish Morocco
Spr., Sprs..Spring, Springs
S. Rh....Southern Rhodesia
S. S. R....Socialistic Soviet
    Republic
St..........Station, Saint
Sta................Santa
Ste...............Sainte
Str.................Strait
Sur...............Surinam
S. W. Afr..Southwest Africa
Swaz...........Swaziland
Swe...............Sweden
Switz.........Switzerland
Syr...............Syria

Tan............Tanganyika
Tas.............Tasmania
Tenn..........Tennessee
Ter..............Territory
Tex...............Texas
Tr. F. Ter.
    Trieste Free Territory
Trin..............Trinidad
Tun...............Tunisia
Tur...............Turkey

Ug...............Uganda
U. K......United Kingdom
    of Gt. Brit. and N. Ire.
Ur.................Uruguay
U. S., U. S. A.
    United States of America
U. S. Afr.
    Union of South Africa

Va...............Virginia
Ven..........Venezuela
Vir. Is.......Virgin Is.
Vol..............Volcano
Vt...............Vermont

W...................West
Wash.........Washington
W. I.........West Indies
Wind. Is..Windward Islands
Wis............Wisconsin
W. Va....West Virginia
Wyo.............Wyoming

Yem...............Yemen
Yugo...........Yugoslavia

Zan............Zanzibar

PRONUNCIATION OF GEOGRAPHICAL NAMES

Key to the Sound Values of Letters and Symbols Used in the Index to Indicate Pronunciation

ă—ăt, căt, băttle
a̍—a̍ppeal, fina̍l
ā—rāte, elāte
â—anima̍te, senâte
ä—cälm, ärm
à—àsk, bàth
a̤—ma̤rine, sofa̤ (short neutral or indeterminate sound)
â—fâre, prepâre
ch—church, choose
dh—as th in other, either

ē—bē, ēve
ê—crêate, êvent
ĕ—bĕt, ĕnd
ẽ—recẽnt (short neutral or indeterminate sound)
ē—cratēr, cindēr
g—gō, gāme
gh—gutteral g
ĭ—wĭll, bĭt
ĭ—short neutral or indeterminate sound
ī—rīde, bīte
к—gutteral k as ch in German ich

ng—sing
ŋ—baŋk, liŋger
N—indicates nasalized preceding vowel
ŏ—nŏd, ŏdd
ŏ—cŏmmit, cŏnnect
ō—ōld, bōld
ȯ—ȯbey, hȯtel
ô—ôrder, nôrth
oi—boil
oo̅—foo̅d, roo̅t
o͝o—fo͝ot, wo͝od
ou—thou, out

s—as in soft, so, sane
sh—dish, finish
th—thin, thick
ū—pūre, cūre
u̍—u̍nite, u̍surp
û—ûrn, fûr
ŭ—stŭd, ŭp
ü—as in French tu or as "y" in study
ṳ—circṳs, sṳbmit
zh—as z in azure
'—indeterminate vowel sound

In many cases the spelling of foreign geographic names does not even remotely indicate the pronunciation to an American, i. e., Slupca in Poland is pronounced swoo̅p'tsà; Jujuy in Argentina is pronounced hoo̅-hwē'; Spezia in Italy is spât'sē-à.

This condition is hardly surprising, however, when we consider that in our own language Worcester, Massachusetts, is pronounced woo̅s'tēr; Sioux City, Iowa, soo̅ sĭ'tĭ; Schuylkill Haven, Pennsylvania, skoo̅l'kĭl; Poughkeepsie, New York, pȯ-kĭp'sĭ.

The indication of pronunciation of geographic names presents several peculiar problems:

(1) Many foreign tongues use sounds that are not present in the English language and which an American cannot normally articulate. Thus, though the nearest English equivalent sound has been indicated, only approximate results are possible.

(2) There are several dialects in each foreign tongue which cause variation in the local pronunciation of names. This also occurs in identical names in the various divisions of a great language group, as the Slavic or the Latin.

(3) Within the United States there are marked differences in pronunciation, not only of local geographic names, but also of common words, indicating that the sound and tone values for letters as well as the placing of the emphasis vary considerably from one part of the country to another.

(4) A number of different letter and diacritical combinations could be used to indicate essentially the same or approximate pronunciations.

Some variation in pronunciation other than that indicated in this index may be encountered, but such a difference does not necessarily indicate that either is in error, and in many cases it is a matter of individual choice as to which is preferred. In fact, an exact indication of pronunciation of many foreign names using English letters and diacriticals is extremely difficult and sometimes impossible.

A PRONOUNCING INDEX

of over 30,000 Geographical Names

Page	Name Pronunciation Region	Lat. °′	Long. °′
118	Aabenraa (ô'bĕn-rô) Den.	55.2 N	9.22 E
120	Aachen(ä'kĕn) Ger.	50.47 N	6.6 E
118	Aakirkeby (ô-kĭr'kĕ-bü) Den.	55.3 N	14.56 E
118	Aalborg (ôl'bŏr) Den.	57.0 N	9.55 E
120	Aalen (ä'lĕn) Ger.	48.50 N	10.6 E
118	Aaraals Fjord (ô'rôls fyōr') Nor.	58.40 N	7.55 E
120	Aarau (är'ou) Switz.	47.23 N	8.2 E
120	Aare R. (ä'rĕ) Switz.	47.14 N	7.43 E
118	Aarhus (ôr'hōōs) Den.	56.10 N	10.10 E
118	Aarsunden L. (ôr'sŏŏn-dĕn) Nor.	62.44 N	11.40 E
140	Abadan (ä-bŭ-dän') Iran	30.20 N	48.18 E
101	Abaeté (ä-bä-â-tā') Braz. (In.)	1.42 S	48.53 W
138	Abakan R. (ä-bä-kän') Sov. Un.	52.55 N	90.0 E
100	Abancay (ä-bän-kä'ê) Peru	13.52 S	72.45 W
94	Abangares (ä-bän-gä'rās) C. R.	10.10 N	85.2 W
124	Abanilla (ä-bä-nēl'yä) Sp.	38.14 N	1.5 W
148	Abashiri (ä-bä-shē'rê) Jap.	44.0 N	144.12 E
80	Abasolo (ä-bä-sō'lô) Mex.	27.11 N	101.25 W
92	Abasolo Mex.	24.4 N	98.23 W
133	Abaya, L. (ȧ-bä'yȧ) Eth.	6.15 N	37.55 E
133	Abbai R. (ȧ-bä'ê) Eth.	10.0 N	37.18 E
140	Abbasi (ä-bäs'ê) Iran	27.15 N	56.28 E
135	Abbasia (äb-bä'zē-ȧ) Eg.	30.4 N	31.16 E
82	Abbeville (ăb'ê-vĭl) Ala.	31.34 N	85.16 W
122	Abbeville (ȧb-vēl') Fr.	50.5 N	1.50 E
82	Abbeville (ăb'ê-vĭl) Ga.	31.59 N	83.22 W
81	Abbeville La.	29.59 N	92.7 W
83	Abbeville S. C.	34.11 N	82.23 W
126	Abbiategrasso (äb-byä'tâ-gräs'sō) It.	45.23 N	8.54 E
116	Abbots Bromley (ăb'ŭts brŭm'lê) Gt. Brit.	52.49 N	1.52 W
72	Abbotsford (ăb'ŭts-fērd) Can. (Vancouver In.)	49.3 N	122.17 W
135	Abd-El-Kuri (I.) (ăbd-ĕl-kōō'rê) Ind. O.	12.13 N	52.10 E
110	Abdulino (äb-dōō-lē'nō) Sov. Un.	53.40 N	53.35 E
133	Abèché (ȧ-bĕ-shā') Fr. Eq. Afr.	13.56 N	20.34 E
132	Abeokuta (ä-bâ-ô-kōō'tä) Nig.	7.12 N	3.21 E
114	Aberavon (ăb-ẽr-ā'vŏn) Gt. Brit.	51.35 N	3.45 W
134	Abercorn (ăb'ẽr-kôrn) N. Rh.	8.48 S	31.20 E
114	Aberdare (ăb-ẽr-dâr') Gt. Brit.	51.43 N	3.29 W
73	Aberdeen (ăb-ẽr-dēn') Ga. (Atlanta In.)	33.25 N	84.37 W
114	Aberdeen Gt. Brit.	57.9 N	2.9 W
82	Aberdeen Miss.	33.49 N	88.34 W
76	Aberdeen S. D.	45.28 N	98.29 W
70	Aberdeen Wash.	46.57 N	123.48 W
116	Aberford (ăb'ẽr-fẽrd) Gt. Brit.	53.51 N	1.21 W
114	Abergavenny (ăb-ẽr-gȧ-vĕn'ĭ) Gt. Brit.	51.50 N	3.0 W
70	Abert, L. (ā'bẽrt) Ore.	42.38 N	120.15 W
114	Aberystwith (ăb-ẽr-ĭst'wĭth) Gt. Brit.	52.25 N	4.5 W
140	Abha (äb-hä') Sau. Ar.	17.47 N	42.35 E
101	Abia, Serra do (sĕr'rȧ dōō ä-bē'ȧ) (Mts.) Braz. (In.)	13.25 S	39.35 W
113	Abiar, El (ĕl ä-bê-är') Libya	32.30 N	20.58 E
132	Abidjan (ä-bêd-zhäɴ') (ä-bê-jän') Fr. W. Afr.	5.27 N	4.3 W
79	Abilene (ăb'ĭ-lēn) Kan.	38.55 N	97.12 W
80	Abilene Tex.	32.26 N	99.45 W
79	Abingdon (ăb'ĭng-dŭn) Ill.	40.49 N	90.21 W
83	Abingdon Va.	36.43 N	81.59 W
87	Abington (ăb'ĭng-tŭn) Mass. (In.)	42.7 N	70.56 W
55	Abitibi L. (ăb-ĭ-tĭb'ĭ) Can.	48.48 N	79.45 W
55	Abitibi R. Can.	49.45 N	81.20 W
111	Abkhazia (Reg.) (ȧb-ᴋä'sê-ȧ) Sov. Un.	43.10 N	41.10 E
123	Ablon (ȧb-lôɴ') Fr. (In.)	48.43 N	2.25 E
131	Abnûb (ȧb-nōōb') Eg. (In.)	27.18 N	31.10 E
119	Åbo (Turku) (ô'bōō) (tōōr'kōō) Fin.	60.29 N	22.14 E
132	Abomey (ȧb-ô-mā') Fr. W. Afr.	7.12 N	2.1 E
121	Abony (ŏ'bô-ny') Hung.	47.11 N	20.0 E
140	Abou Kemal (ä'bōō kĕ'mȧl) Syr.	34.40 N	41.0 E
140	Abqaiq (ȧb-kīk) Sau. Ar.	25.55 N	49.40 E
99	Abra Canal (ä'brä) Chl. (Magallanes In.)	53.25 S	73.30 W
152	Abra R. Phil.	17.15 N	120.40 E
86	Abraham, Mt. (ā'brȧ-hăm) Me.	44.56 N	70.19 W
97	Abrahams B. Ba. Is.	22.25 N	73.55 W
116	Abram (ā'brăm) Gt. Brit.	53.31 N	2.36 W
101	Abrantes (ȧ-brän'tĕs) (Braz. In.)	12.51 S	38.19 W
124	Abrantes Port.	39.28 N	8.12 W
101	Abrolhos Is. (ä-brōl'yōs) Braz.	18.0 S	38.0 W
119	Abruka I. (ȧ-brōō'kȧ) Sov. Un.	58.8 N	22.32 E
126	Abruzzi and Molise (provinces) (ä-brōōt'sē, mô'lê-zā) It.	42.0 N	14.0 E
71	Absaroka Range (ȧb-sȧ-rō'kȧ) Wyo.	44.40 N	109.40 W
140	Abu Arish (ä'bōō ȧ-rēsh') Yemen	16.50 N	43.0 E
151	Abucay (ä-bōō-kī') Phil. (Manila In.)	14.42 N	120.27 E
140	Abu Dhabi (ä'bōō dä'bê) Sau Ar.	24.30 N	54.28 E
133	Abu Hamed (ä'bōō hä'mĕd) A. E. Sud.	19.34 N	33.22 E
131	Abukir B. (ă-bōō-kēr') Eg. (In.)	31.15 N	30.10 E
152	Abulug (ä-bōō'lōōg) Phil.	18.26 N	121.27 E
152	Abulug R. Phil.	18.10 N	121.21 E
100	Abunȧ, R. (ȧ-bōō-nä') Bol.-Braz.	10.0 S	66.30 W
131	Abu Qîr (ä'bōō kēr') Eg. (In.)	31.18 N	30.5 E
131	Abu Qurqâs (ä'bōō kōōr-käs') Eg. (In.)	27.57 N	30.51 E
149	Aburatsu (ä'bōō-rät'sōō) Jap.	31.36 N	131.22 E
135	Abu Rueish (ä'bōō rōō'wāsh) Eg.	30.3 N	31.4 E
135	Abusir Tombs and Pyramids (ä-bōō-sēr') Eg.	29.54 N	31.12 E
131	Abû Tîg (ä'bōō tēg') Eg. (In.)	27.3 N	31.20 E
153	Abuyog (ä-bōō'yôg) Phil.	10.44 N	125.0 E
118	Åby Klippan (ô'bü klĭp'pȧn) Swe.	56.9 N	13.20 E
133	Abyssinia, Plateau of Eth.	8.0 N	38.0 E
86	Acadia National Park (ȧ-kā'dĭ-ȧ) Me.	44.20 N	68.15 W
94	Acajutla (ä-kä-hōōt'lä) Sal.	13.37 N	89.50 W
92	Acámbaro (ä-käm'bä-rō) Mex.	20.2 N	100.42 W
92	Acapetlahuaya (ä-kä-pĕt'lä-hwä'-yä) Mex.	18.18 N	100.9 W
92	Acaponeta (ä-kä-pô-nā'tȧ) Mex.	22.30 N	105.23 W
92	Acaponeta, R. Mex.	22.40 N	105.21 W
92	Acapulco (ä-kä-pōōl'kō) Mex.	16.51 N	99.56 W
101	Acarahu (ä-kä-rä'ōō) Braz.	3.0 S	42.0 W
101	Acarahy Mts. (ä-kä-rä'ê) Br. Gu.-Braz.	1.30 N	58.0 W
92	Acatlán de Osorio (ä-kät-län'dā ô-sō'rē-ō) Mex.	18.12 N	98.3 W
52	Acattu I. (ä-kä'tū) Alsk.	52.30 N	173.30 E
93	Acatzingo de Hidalgo (ä-kät-zĭŋ'-gō dā ê-dhäl'gō) Mex.	18.59 N	97.48 W
93	Acayucan (ä-kä-yōō'kän) Mex.	17.56 N	94.55 W
84	Accoville (äk'kô-vĭl) W. Va.	37.47 N	81.50 W
132	Accra (ă'krȧ) G. C.	5.37 N	0.10 W
116	Accrington (ăk'rĭng-tŭn) Gt. Brit.	53.45 N	2.21 W
131	Acebuche, Pt. (ä-thā-bōō'chā) Sp. (Gibraltar In.)	36.3 N	5.33 W
100	Achacachi (ä-chä-kä'chê) Bol.	17.0 S	68.44 W
113	Achdar, Jebel (Mt.) (jĕb'ĕl äch-där') Libya	32.25 N	22.0 E
148	Acheng (ä'chĕng') Chn.	45.32 N	127.2 E
123	Achères (ä-shâr') Fr. (In.)	48.57 N	2.4 E
114	Achill (ă-chĭl') Ire.	53.55 N	9.55 W
114	Achill I. Ire.	54.0 N	10.0 W
138	Achinsk (ȧ-chênsk') Sov. Un.	56.10 N	90.25 E
131	Achkel, L. (äsh-kĕl') Tun. (In.)	37.8 N	9.43 E
127	Aci Abad (Maidos) (äd'zhê ä'bad) (mâ'dôs) Tur.	40.11 N	26.21 E
126	Acireale (ä-chê-râ-ä'lā) It.	37.36 N	15.9 E
97	Acklin I. (ăk'lĭn) Ba. Is.	22.29 N	73.55 W
73	Acmar (ăk'mȧr) Ala. (Birmingham In.)	33.37 N	86.30 W
102	Aconcagua, Mt. (ä-kôn-kä'gwä) Arg.	32.40 S	71.0 W
99	Aconcagua, R. Chl. (Valparaiso In.)	32.47 S	71.0 W
93	Acopilco (ä-kô-pēl'kō) Mex. (In.)	19.20 N	99.19 W
94	Acoyapa (ä-kô-yä'pä) Nic.	11.53 N	85.11 W
126	Acqui (äk'kwē) It.	44.40 N	8.30 E
100	Acre (State) (ä'krā) Braz.	9.0 S	70.30 W
137	Acre, B. of (ä'kẽr (ā'kẽr) Pal. (In.)	32.52 N	35.2 E
137	Acre (Akko) (ä'kẽr) (äk'kô) Pal. (In.)	32.57 N	35.3 E
73	Acton (ăk'tŭn) Ala. (Birmingham In.)	33.21 N	86.48 W
114	Acton Gt. Brit.	51.30 N	0.15 W
87	Acton Mass. (In.)	42.29 N	71.26 W
86	Acton Vale Que.	45.38 N	72.34 W
92	Actopan (äk-tô-pän') Mex.	20.16 N	98.57 W
102	Actura (äk-tōō'rȧ) Braz. (In.)	22.42 S	43.18 W
93	Acuahutla (ä-kwä-ōōt'lȧ) Mex. (In.)	19.21 N	98.52 W
92	Acuitzio del Canje (ä-kwēt'zê-ō dĕl kän'hâ) Mex.	19.30 N	101.12 W
97	Acul B. (ä-kōōl') Hai.	19.45 N	72.20 W
132	Ada (ā'dȧ) G. C.	5.52 N	0.32 E
76	Ada Minn.	47.18 N	96.30 W
84	Ada Ohio	40.47 N	83.43 W
79	Ada Okla.	34.45 N	96.43 W
127	Ada (ŏ'dŏ) Yugo.	45.48 N	20.8 E
52	Adak I. (ă-dăk') Alsk.	51.40 N	176.35 W
111	Adalia (Antalya) (ä-dä'lê-ä) (än-täl'yä) Tur.	36.55 N	30.50 E
132	Adamawa (Reg.) (ä-dä-mä'wä) Cam.	8.30 N	12.30 E
80	Adamo, R. (ä-dä'mō) Mex.	26.30 N	99.30 W
86	Adams (ăd'ămz) Mass.	42.35 N	73.10 W
77	Adams Wis.	43.55 N	89.48 W
141	Adams Bridge India-Cey. (Cey. In.)	9.10 N	79.30 E
53	Adams, Mt. Alsk.	55.55 N	130.30 W
70	Adams, Mt. Wash.	46.12 N	121.30 W
160	Adamson Peak (ăd'ăm-sŭn) Austl. (Tas. In.)	43.21 S	146.50 E
85	Adamstown W. Va.	39.18 N	80.2 W
73	Adamsville Ala. (Birmingham In.)	33.36 N	86.57 W
111	Adana (ä'dä-nä) Tur.	37.0 N	35.20 E
111	Adapazari (ä'dä-pä-zä'rê) Tur.	40.45 N	30.15 E
133	Adarama (ä-dä-rä'mä) A. E. Sud.	17.10 N	34.58 E
126	Adda R. (äd'dä) It.	45.36 N	9.30 E
140	Ad Dam (äd däm') Sau. Ar.	20.35 N	44.38 E
157	Adderley Head (ăd-ẽr-lĭ hĕd') N. Z. (In.)	43.36 S	172.51 E
133	Addis Abeba (äd'dĭs ä'bĕ-bȧ) Eth.	9.2 N	38.49 E
89	Addyston (ăd'ê-stŭn) Ohio (Cincinnati In.)	39.9 N	84.43 W
82	Adel (ā-dĕl') Ga.	31.7 N	83.27 W
158	Adelaide (ăd'ê-lād) Austl.	34.55 S	138.36 E
160	Adelaide Austl. (In.)		
51	Adelaide Wash. (In.)	47.19 N	122.22 W
47	Adelaide I. Ant.	67.15 S	68.40 W
7	Adélie Coast (Reg.) (ȧ-dâ-lē') Ant.	66.0 S	140.0 E
140	Aden (ä'dĕn) Aden	12.45 N	45.5 E
140	Aden Asia	14.30 N	47.0 E
140	Aden, G. of Asia	12.0 N	47.0 E
126	Aderno (ä-dĕr-nô') It.	37.40 N	14.50 E
73	Adger (ăj'ẽr) Ala. (Birmingham In.)	33.23 N	87.5 W
151	Adi I. (ä'dē) Neth. N. Gui.	4.15 S	133.30 E
133	Adi Caieh (ä'dē kī'ā) Erit.	14.50 N	39.20 E
139	Adicha R. (ä'dĭ-chȧ) Sov. Un.	66.0 N	136.30 E
126	Adige R. (ä'dê-jā) It.	45.40 N	10.54 E
111	Adige (Cherkess) (Reg.) (ä'dĭ-gā) Sov. Un.	45.0 N	40.5 E
57	Adirondack Junction Can. (Montreal In.)	45.24 N	73.39 W
85	Adirondack Mts. (ăd-ĭ-rŏn'dăk) N. Y.	43.40 N	74.30 W
110	Adisko (ä-dēs'kō) Swe.	68.30 N	18.55 E
133	Adi Ugri (ä-dē ōō'grē) Erit.	14.50 N	38.58 E
132	Adjjer (Tassili) Plat. (ä'jĕr tâs'ê-lê) Alg.	26.0 N	7.0 E
132	Adjir (äd-jēr') Sp. Mor.	35.10 N	3.55 W
121	Adjud (äd'zhōōd) Rom.	46.5 N	27.8 E
151	Admiralty B. (ăd'mĭ rȧl-tê) N. Z.	40.50 S	174.0 E
51	Admiralty Inlet Wash. (In.)	48.5 N	122.40 W
53	Admiralty I. Alsk.	57.40 N	135.30 W
151	Admiralty Is. N. Gui. Ter.	2.0 S	147.0 E
99	Admiralty Sd. Chl. (Magallanes In.)	54.20 S	69.30 W
122	Adour R. (ȧ-dōōr') Fr.	43.45 N	1.15 W
124	Adouz (ȧ-dōōz') Sp. Mor.	35.11 N	4.9 W
124	Adra (ä'drä) Sp.	36.46 N	3.1 W
132	Adrar (ä-drär') Alg.	27.55 N	0.19 W
132	Adrar (Reg.) Fr. W. Afr.-Alg.	20.30 N	2.0 E
126	Adria (ä'drê-ä) It.	45.4 N	12.8 E
84	Adrian (ā'drĭ-ăn) Mich.	41.55 N	84.3 W
76	Adrian Minn.	43.38 N	95.55 W
111	Adrianople (Edirne) (ā-drĭ-ăn-ō'pl) (ĕ-dĭr'nĕ) Tur.	41.40 N	26.35 E
126	Adriatic Sea (ā-drĭ-ăt'ĭk) It.-Yugo.	42.50 N	15.40 E
133	Adua (ä'dōō-ä) Eth.	14.6 N	39.0 E
160	Adventure B. Austl. (Tas. In.)	43.18 S	147.35 E
116	Adwick-le-Street (ăd'wĭk-lê-strēt') Gt. Brit.	53.34 N	1.11 W
129	Adzhamka (ȧd-zhäm'kȧ) Sov. Un.	48.33 N	32.26 E
111	Adzharistan (Reg.) (äd-zhär'ĭ-stȧn) Sov. Un.	41.45 N	42.15 E
110	Adzva R. (ädz'vȧ) Sov. Un.	67.0 N	59.45 E
126	Aegadian (Egadi) Is. (ê-gā'dĭ-ăn) (â'gä-dē) It.	38.55 N	12.20 E
111	Aegean Is. Medit. Sea	36.30 N	27.0 W
127	Aegean Sea (ê-jē'ăn) Gr.-Tur.	39.0 N	24.50 E
127	Aegina, G. of (Saronic G.) (ê-jī'nȧ) Gr.	37.35 N	23.40 E
127	Aegina (I.) Gr.	37.45 N	23.30 E
118	Aerö (I.) (âr'ö) Den.	54.48 N	10.25 E
117	Aertselaer (ärt'sĕ-lär) Bel. (Anvers In.)	51.8 N	4.23 E
101	Affonso Penna (ä-fōn'sōō pĕn'nȧ) Braz. (In.)	12.50 S	39.15 W
89	Affton (ăf'tŭn) Mo. (St. Louis In.)	38.33 N	90.20 W
140	Afghanistan (ăf-găn-ĭ-stăn') Asia	33.0 N	65.0 E
135	Afgoi (äf-gô'ĭ) Som.	2.5 N	45.5 E
140	Afladj (Reg.) (ä-flädj') Sau Ar.	24.0 N	46.0 E
132	Aflou (ä flōō') Alg.	34.2 N	2.2 E
53	Afognak I. (ä-fŏg-nȧk') Alsk.	58.15 N	152.30 W
130	Africa (ăf'rĭ-kȧ)		
79	Afton (ăf'tŭn) Okla.	36.41 N	94.56 W
111	Afyon-Karahisar (ä-fê-ōn-kä-rȧ-hê-sär') Tur.	38.45 N	30.20 E
133	Agedabia (ä-gä-dä'bê-ä) Libya	30.45 N	20.15 E
133	Agadem (Oasis) (ä'gȧ-dĕm) Fr. W. Afr.	16.52 N	13.15 E
132	Agadez (ä'gȧ-dĕz) Fr. W. Afr.	17.0 N	7.58 E
132	Agadir (ä-gä-dēr') Mor.	30.30 N	9.33 W
129	Agaiman (ȧ-gä-ê-män') Sov. Un.	46.40 N	34.16 E
72	Agassiz (ăg'ȧ-sê) Can. (Vancouver In.)	49.14 N	121.46 W
111	Agdam (äg'dȧm) Sov. Un.	39.59 N	46.58 E
122	Agde (ägd) Fr.	43.20 N	3.30 E
122	Agen (ȧ-zhäɴ') Fr.	44.12 N	0.35 E
127	Agiassos (ī'yä-sôs) Grc.	39.5 N	26.22 E
139	Aginskoe (ä-hĭn'skô-yĕ) Sov. Un.	51.15 N	114.59 E
153	Agio Pt. (ä-jē'ō) Phil.	9.43 N	124.32 E
139	Aion I. (ä'yōn) Sov. Un.	69.50 N	168.50 E
126	Agira (ä-jē'rä) It.	37.39 N	14.31 E
152	Agno (äg'nō) Phil.	16.8 N	119.48 E
152	Agno R. Phil.	15.47 N	120.20 E
126	Agnone (än-yō'nā) It.	41.48 N	14.22 E
152	Agoo (ä'gōō) Phil.	16.19 N	120.22 E
133	Agordat (ä-gōr'dät) Erit.	15.33 N	37.58 E
151	Agos R. (ä'gôs) Phil. (Manila In.)	14.47 N	121.37 E
122	Agout (ȧ-gōō') Fr.	43.40 N	2.0 E
141	Agra (ä'grä) India	27.10 N	78.8 E
	Agram, see Zagreb, Yugo.		
126	Agri R. (ä'grē) It.	40.16 N	16.10 E
127	Agrinion (ȧ-grē'nyôn) Grc.	38.37 N	21.26 E
94	Agua (Vol.) (ä'gwä) Guat.	14.28 N	90.44 W
74	Agua Calienta Ind. Res. (ä'gwä käl yĕn'tä) Calif.	33.50 N	116.32 W
95	Agua Caliente (ä'gwä kä-lyĕn'tā) Nic.	12.10 N	84.37 W
96	Aguada (ä-gwä'dȧ) Cuba	22.25 N	80.48 W
91	Aguadilla (ä-gwä-dēl'yä) P.R. (In.)	18.25 N	67.15 W
95	Aguadulce (ä-gwä-dōōl'sā) Pan.	8.15 N	80.32 W
75	Agua Fria R. (ä'gwä frē'ȧ) Ariz.	33.45 N	112.18 W
80	Agualegnas (ä-gwä lān'yäs) Mex.	26.18 N	99.33 W
94	Aguan, R. (ä-gwän') Hond.	15.34 N	86.10 W
80	Aguanaval, R. (ä-guä-nä-väl') Mex.	25.0 N	103.15 W
87	Aguanus R. (ȧ-gwā'nŭs) Que.	50.50 N	62.5 W
92	Aguascalientes (ä'gwäs-käl-yĕn'tās) Mex.	21.52 N	102.17 W
92	Aguascalientes (State) Mex.	22.0 N	102.30 W
124	Agueda (ä-gwā'dȧ) Port.	40.35 N	8.25 W
124	Agueda R. Sp.-Port.	40.40 N	6.40 W
132	Aguellal (ä-gĕl-yäl') Fr. W. Afr.	19.12 N	8.15 E
78	Aguilar (ä-gê-lär') Colo.	37.24 N	104.39 W
124	Aguilar Sp.	37.31 N	4.39 W

Aguilas PRONOUNCING INDEX Alexandriya

Page	Name Pronunciation	Region	Lat. °'	Long. °'
124	Aguilas (ä'gê-läs)	Sp.	37.25 N	1.35 W
100	Aguja Pt. (ȧ-gōō'hä)	Peru	5.58 S	81.10 W
134	Agulhas, C. (ä-gōōl'yäs)	U. S. Afr.	34.50 S	20.0 E
150	Agung, Mt. (ä-gŏŏng')	Indon.	8.28 S	115.22 E
153	Agusan Marsh (ä-gōō'sän)	Phil.	8.15 N	125.50 E
153	Agusan R	Phil.	8.40 N	125.37 E
153	Agutaya I. (ä-gōō-tä'yä)	Phil.	11.9 N	120.58 E
127	Agyia (äĭ-yȧ')	Grc.	39.41 N	22.45 E
132	Ahaggar Mts. (ȧ-hȧ-gär')	Alg.	23.30 N	6.30 E
156	Ahipara B. (ä-hĭ-pä'rȧ)	N. Z.	35.5 S	173.5 E
120	Ahlen (ä'lĕn)	Ger.	51.46 N	7.53 E
131	Ahmar, Jebel (Mts.) (jĕb'ĕl ä'-mär)	Eg. (In.)	28.5 N	31.30 E
141	Ahmedabad (ŭ-mĕd-ä-bäd'	India	23.0 N	72.44 E
83	Ahoskie (ā-hŏs'kē)	N. C.	36.17 N	76.59 W
117	Ahrensburg (ä'rĕns-bŏŏrg)	Ger. (Hamburg In.)	53.40 N	10.13 E
120	Ahrweiler (är'vī-lĕr)	Ger.	50.34 N	7.3 E
92	Ahuacatlan (ä-wä-kät-län')	Mex.	21.5 N	104.27 W
94	Ahuachapan (ä-wä-chä-pän')	Sal.	13.57 N	89.52 W
92	Ahualulco (ä-wä-lōōl'kō)	Mex.	20.43 N	103.58 W
118	Åhus (ô'hōōs)	Swe.	55.56 N	14.19 E
119	Ahvenanmaa (Åland Is.) (ä'vĕ-nȧn-mô) (ô'länd)	Fin.	60.20 N	20.0 E
129	Aidar (ä'ĭ-där)	Sov. Un.	50.2 N	38.52 E
129	Aidar R	Sov. Un.	49.8 N	38.56 E
155	Aiea (ȧēā'ä)	Haw.	21.20 N	157.55 W
127	Aigina (ȧ-yē'nȧ)	Grc.	37.45 N	23.26 E
127	Aigion (ȧ'yôn)	Grc.	38.14 N	22.5 E
122	Aiguesmortes (ĕg'-môrt)	Fr.	43.35 N	4.10 E
143	Aigun (ī-gŏŏn')	Chn.	49.50 N	127.28 E
148	Aikawa (ī-kä'wȧ)	Jap.	38.0 N	138.25 E
83	Aiken (ā'kĕn)	S. C.	33.34 N	81.44 W
149	Aina (ī'nä)	Jap. (Osaka In.)	34.45 N	135.6 E
132	Aïn Beida (ä'ên bā'ê-dȧ)	Alg.	35.51 N	7.27 E
132	Aïn Sefra (ä'ên sĕf'rä)	Alg.	32.50 N	0.40 W
87	Ainsle, L. (ān'slê)	Can.	46.10 N	61.10 W
76	Ainsworth (ānz'wûrth)	Neb.	42.33 N	99.51 W
112	Aïn Taïba (ä'ên tä'ê-bȧ)	Alg.	30.21 N	5.28 E
112	Aïn Temouchent (ä'ên tĕ-mōō-shäɴ')	Alg.	35.18 N	1.8 W
132	Aïr (Asben) (Reg.) (ä'êr) (äs'bĕn)	Fr. W. Afr.	18.35 N	9.0 E
142	Airan Köl (L.) (ä'ê-rän kûl')	Chn.	45.35 N	85.20 E
127	Airbol (ä-êr-bôl')	Tur.	41.12 N	27.6 E
122	Aire (âr)	Fr.	43.41 N	0.18 W
122	Aire	Fr.	50.41 N	2.22 E
116	Aire R	Gt. Brit.	53.50 N	1.42 W
146	Ai Shan (Mt.) (ī'shän')	Chn.	37.31 N	120.40 E
122	Aisne R. (ān)	Fr.	49.25 N	3.20 E
151	Aitape (ä-ê-tä'pȧ)	N. Gui. Ter.	3.12 S	142.10 E
77	Aitkin (āt'kĭn)	Minn.	46.32 N	93.42 W
127	Aitolikon (ȧ-tō'lĭ-kôn)	Grc.	38.27 N	21.22 E
127	Aitos (ä-ē'tōs)	Bul.	42.41 N	27.18 E
121	Aiud (ä'ê-ŏŏd)	Rom.	46.20 N	23.42 E
123	Aix (ĕks)	Fr.	43.32 N	5.28 E
	Aix-la-Chapelle, see Aachen, Ger.			
123	Aix-les-Bains (ĕks'-lā-baɴ')	Fr.	45.41 N	5.59 E
131	Aiyât (ä-ê-yät')	Eg. (In.)	29.38 N	31.18 E
119	Aizpute (ä'êz-pōō-tĕ)	Sov. Un.	56.44 N	21.40 E
122	Ajaccio (ä-yät'chō)	Cor. (In.)	41.55 N	8.42 E
122	Ajaccio, G. of	Cor. (In.)	41.55 N	8.40 E
93	Ajalpan (ä-häl'pän)	Mex.	18.21 N	97.15 W
71	Ajax Mt. (ā'jăks)	Mont.-Ida.	45.18 N	113.43 W
133	Ajilat (ä'jê-lät)	Libya	32.41 N	12.28 E
137	Ajloun (äj-lōōn')	Jor. (In.)	32.21 N	35.41 E
141	Ajmer (ŭj-mēr')	India.	26.31 N	74.32 E
75	Ajo (ä'hô)	Ariz.	32.22 N	112.53 W
92	Ajuchitlán del Progreso (ä-hōō-chet-lȧn')	Mex.	18.2 N	100.20 W
153	Ajuy (äj-wē')	Phil.	11.9 N	123.2 E
111	Ak L. (äk)	Tur.	37.30 N	33.45 E
157	Akaroa (ä-kä-rō'ä)	N. Z.	43.57 S	172.58 E
157	Akaroa Har	N. Z.	43.50 S	172.57 E
132	Akasa (ä-käs'ä)	Nig.	4.27 N	6.2 E
149	Akashi (ä'kä-shē)	Jap.	34.40 N	135.2 E
149	Akashi Str. (ä'kä-shē)	Jap. (Osaka In.)	34.38 N	135.0 E
133	Aketi (ä-kȧ-tē')	Bel. Cong.	2.46 N	24.0 E
111	Akhaltsikh (ȧ-ĸȧl-tsēĸ')	Sov. Un.	41.38 N	42.58 E
127	Akheloos R. (ä-hĕ'lô-ōs)	Grc.	39.0 N	21.25 E
129	Akhiar (Sevastopol) (äĸ'yȧr) (syĕ-väs'tô-pôl')	Sov. Un.	44.35 N	33.32 E
127	Akhinou L. (ä-ĸē'-nōō)	Grc.	40.55 N	23.40 E
111	Akhisar (äk-hĭs-sär')	Tur.	38.58 N	27.57 E
133	Akhmîm (äĸ-mēm')	Eg.	26.40 N	31.48 E
129	Akhtarskii B. (äĸ-tär'skĭ-ê)	Sov. Un.	45.53 N	38.16 E
127	Akhtopol (äĸ'tô-pōl)	Bul.	42.6 N	27.53 E
129	Akhtyrka (äĸ-tür'kȧ)	Sov. Un.	50.18 N	34.52 E
129	Akhtyrskaya (äĸ-tür'skȧ-yȧ)	Sov. Un.	44.52 N	38.11 E
149	Aki (ä'kê)	Jap.	33.30 N	133.50 E
52	Akiak (äk'yȧk)	Alsk.	61.0 N	161.30 W
55	Akimiski I. (ä-kĭ-mĭ'skĭ)	Can.	53.0 N	81.30 W
148	Akita (ä'kê-tä)	Jap.	39.45 N	140.10 E
	Akkerman, see Cetatea Alba, Rom.			
137	Akko (Acre) (äk'kô) (ä'kēr)	Pal. (In.)	32.57 N	35.3 E
53	Aklavik (äk'lä-vĭk)	Can.	68.20 N	135.30 W
129	Ak-Mechet (äk-mĕ'ch-ĕt)	Sov. Un.	45.30 N	32.39 E
138	Ak-Mechet (Kzyl-Orda) (kzêl'-ôr'dȧ)	Sov. Un.	44.50 N	65.30 E
129	Akmechet (Simferopol) (sêm-fĕ-rô'pôl')	Sov. Un.	44.57 N	34.4 E
138	Akmolinsk (ȧk'mô-lênsk)	Sov. Un.	51.15 N	71.25 E
149	Ako (ä'kô)	Jap.	34.45 N	134.21 E
133	Akobo R. (ȧ-kô'bô)	A. E. Sud.	7.0 N	34.30 E
141	Akola (ȧ-kô'lä)	India	20.40 N	77.0 E
55	Akpatok I. (ȧk'pȧ-tŏk)	Can.	60.30 N	68.0 W
78	Akron (ăk'rŭn)	Colo.	40.8 N	103.13 W
84	Akron	Ohio	41.5 N	81.30 W
111	Aksaray (äk-sȧ-rī')	Tur.	38.25 N	34.5 E
111	Akşehir (äk'shȧ-hēr)	Tur.	38.28 N	31.20 E
111	Akşehir L.	Tur.	38.33 N	31.30 E
139	Aksha (äk'shȧ)	Sov. Un.	50.20 N	113.25 E
138	Aktyubinsk (äk'tyōō-bênsk)	Sov. Un.	50.15 N	57.20 E
149	Akune (ä'kŏŏ-nȧ)	Jap.	32.1 N	130.12 E
108	Akureyri (ä-kŏŏ-rȧ'rê)	Ice.	65.40 N	18.14 W
52	Akutan Pass (ä-kōō-tän')	Alsk.	54.0 N	166.0 W
141	Akyab (ăk-yŭb')	Bur.	20.15 N	92.55 E
153	Ala R. (ä'lä)	Phil.	6.30 N	124.33 E
82	Alabama (State) (ăl-ȧ-băm'ȧ)	U. S.	32.45 N	86.45 W
82	Alabama R	Ala.	32.5 N	87.20 W
82	Alabama City	Ala.	34.1 N	86.3 W
151	Alabang (ä-lä-bäng')	Phil. (Manila In.)	14.27 N	121.3 E
152	Alabat I. (ä-lä-bät')	Phil.	14.7 N	122.4 E
111	Alaçam (ä-lä-chäm')	Tur.	41.35 N	35.40 E
96	Alacranes (ä-lä-krä'nȧs)	Cuba	22.42 N	81.35 W
101	Alagôas (State) (ä-lä-gō'äzh)	Braz.	9.30 S	37.0 W
101	Alagoinhas (ä-lä-gō-ēn'yäzh)	Braz. (In.)	12.7 S	38.18 W
124	Alagón (ä-lä-gōn')	Sp.	41.47 N	1.8 W
124	Alagón R	Sp.	40.0 N	6.17 W
111	Alaiye (ä-lī'yȧ)	Tur.	36.35 N	32.5 E
138	Ala Kul (L.) (ä'lä-kûl')	Sov. Un.	46.20 N	82.0 E
139	Alaikha (ä-lī'ĸȧ)	Sov. Un.	70.30 N	148.59 E
95	Alajuela (ä-lä-hwā'lä)	C. R.	10.1 N	84.13 W
155	Alalakeiki Chan. (ä-lä-lä-kā'kê)	Haw.	20.35 N	156.30 W
74	Alameda (ăl-ȧ-mā'dȧ)	Calif.	37.46 N	122.15 W
71	Alameda	Ida.	42.51 N	112.37 W
93	Alameda	Mex. (In.)	19.32 N	99.19 W
152	Alaminos (ä-lä-mē'nôs)	Phil.	16.10 N	119.58 E
151	Alaminos	Phil. (Manila In.)	14.5 N	121.15 E
75	Alamogordo (ăl-ȧ-mō-gôr'dō)	N. M.	32.54 N	105.58 W
78	Alamogordo Reservoir	N. M.	34.35 N	104.20 W
78	Alamosa (ăl-ȧ-mō'sȧ)	Colo.	37.27 N	105.51 W
119	Aland (Ahvenanmaa) Is. (ô'länd) (ä'vĕ-nȧn-mô)	Fin.	60.38 N	20.0 E
153	Alangalang (ä-läŋ-gä-läng')	Phil.	11.12 N	124.50 E
135	Alaotra, L. (ä-lä-ō'trȧ)	Madag.	16.25 S	48.35 E
138	Alapayevsk (ä'lȧ-pȧ-yĕfsk')	Sov. Un.	57.57 N	61.57 E
92	Alaquines (ȧ-lȧ-kē'nȧs)	Mex.	22.8 N	99.35 W
142	Ala Shan (Mts.) (ä'lä-shän')	Chn.	39.0 N	105.45 E
52	Alaska (Ter.) (ȧ-lăs'kȧ)	N. A.	65.0 N	150.0 W
53	Alaska, G. of	Alsk.	58.30 N	145.0 W
52	Alaska Pen	Alsk.	57.0 N	158.0 W
53	Alaska Ra. (Mts.)	Alsk.	62.40 N	150.30 W
110	Alatyr (ä'lä-tür)	Sov. Un.	54.48 N	46.35 E
126	Alba (äl'bä)	It.	44.40 N	8.2 E
124	Albacete (äl-bä-thā'tā)	Sp.	39.0 N	1.50 W
124	Alba de Tormes (äl'bä dā tôr'mās)	Sp.	40.49 N	5.29 W
121	Alba Iulia (äl-bä yōō'lyȧ)	Rom.	46.6 N	23.34 E
125	Albalate (äl-bä-lä'tā)	Sp.	41.7 N	0.31 W
127	Albania (ăl-bā'nĭ-ȧ)	Eur.	41.0 N	20.0 E
126	Albano Laziale (äl-bä'nō lät-zē-ä'lā)	It.	41.43 N	12.38 E
82	Albany (ôl'bȧ-nĭ)	Ala.	34.34 N	86.59 W
158	Albany	Austl.	34.57 S	117.58 E
82	Albany	Ga.	31.35 N	84.11 W
79	Albany	Mo.	40.15 N	94.20 W
85	Albany	N. Y.	42.42 N	73.46 W
70	Albany	Ore.	44.38 N	123.6 W
80	Albany	Tex.	32.43 N	99.18 W
55	Albany R	Can.	51.28 N	86.30 W
152	Albay G. (äl-bä'ê)	Phil.	13.10 N	124.0 E
81	Albemarle (ăl'bê-märl)	La.	29.53 N	91.2 W
83	Albemarle	N. C.	35.23 N	80.11 W
83	Albemarle Sd	N. C.	36.0 N	76.0 W
126	Albenga (äl-bĕn'gä)	It.	44.3 N	8.12 E
124	Alberche R. (äl-bĕr'chạ)	Sp.	40.20 N	4.15 W
158	Alberga (R.) (ăl-bûr'gȧ)	Austl.	27.0 S	135.0 E
124	Albergaria-a-Velha (äl-bĕr-gȧ-rē'-ȧ-ä-väl'yȧ)	Port.	40.41 N	8.29 W
73	Alberhill (ăl'bēr-hĭl)	Calif. (Los Angeles In.)	33.44 N	117.23 W
122	Albert (ȧl-bâr')	Fr.	50.0 N	2.40 E
86	Albert (ăl'bērt)	Can.	45.45 N	64.44 W
133	Albert, L. (ăl'bērt) (ȧl-bâr')	Bel. Cong.-Ug.	1.45 N	30.50 E
156	Albert, Mt	N. Z. (In.)	36.54 S	174.43 E
54	Alberta (Prov.) (ăl-bûr'tȧ)	Can.	54.15 N	115.0 W
151	Albert Edward, Mt. (ăl'bērt ĕd'wērd)	Pap. Ter.	8.25 S	147.15 E
77	Albert Lea (ăl'bērt lē')	Minn.	43.39 N	93.21 W
160	Alberton (ăl'bēr-tŭn)	Austl. (In.)	27.41 S	153.15 E
86	Alberton	Can.	46.50 N	64.4 W
82	Albertville (ăl'bērt-vĭl)	Ala.	34.17 N	86.12 W
134	Albertville (ȧl-bêr-vēl')	Bel. Cong.	5.55 S	29.12 E
123	Albertville	Fr.	45.40 N	6.28 E
122	Albi (äl-bē')	Fr.	43.55 N	2.10 E
77	Albia (ăl'bĭ-ȧ)	Ia.	41.1 N	92.48 W
79	Albia	Ia.	41.1 N	92.49 W
101	Albina (äl-bē'nä)	Sur.	5.29 N	54.2 W
84	Albion (ăl'bĭ-ŭn)	Mich.	42.16 N	84.50 W
76	Albion	Neb.	41.42 N	98.0 W
85	Albion	N. Y.	43.15 N	78.12 W
131	Alboasa, Pt. (äl-bō-ä'sä)	Sp. Mor. (Gibraltar In.)	35.50 N	5.19 E
124	Alborán I. (äl-bō-rän')	Sp.	35.58 N	3.0 W
124	Albox (äl-bōĸ')	Sp.	37.23 N	2.8 W
124	Albufeira (äl-bōō-fā'ê-rȧ)	Port.	37.6 N	8.15 W
124	Albuñol (äl-bōōn-yōl')	Sp.	36.48 N	3.12 W
78	Albuquerque (ăl-bû-kûr'kê)	N. M.	35.5 N	106.39 W
124	Albuquerque (äl-boo-kĕr'kā)	Sp.	39.14 N	7.0 W
95	Albuquerque Cays (Is.) (ăl-bû-kûr'kê kāz')	W. I.	12.12 N	81.50 W
159	Albury (ôl'bēr-ê)	Austl.	36.5 S	146.55 E
125	Alcabideche (äl-kȧ-bē-dā'chȧ)	Port. (In.)	38.43 N	9.24 W
124	Alcácer do Sal (äl-kä'sĕr dŏŏ säl')	Port.	38.22 N	8.31 W
152	Alcala (äl-kä-lä')	Phil.	17.56 N	121.39 E
124	Alcalá	Sp.	37.21 N	5.50 W
125	Alcalá de Chivert (äl-kä-lä' dā chē-vĕrt')	Sp.	40.18 N	0.12 E
125	Alcalá de Henares (äl-kä-lä' dā ā na'rās)	Sp. (In.)	40.29 N	3.22 W
124	Alcalá de los Gazules (äl-kä-lä' dā lōs gä-thōō'lȧs)	Sp.	36.29 N	5.43 W
124	Alcalá la Real (äl-kä-lä' lä rā-äl')	Sp.	37.27 N	3.55 W
126	Alcamo (äl'kȧ-mō)	It.	37.57 N	12.58 E
125	Alcanadre R. (äl-kä-nä'drȧ)	Sp.	41.45 N	0.10 W
125	Alcanar (äl-kä-när')	Sp.	40.34 N	0.29 E
125	Alcañiz (äl-kän-yēth')	Sp.	41.4 N	0.8 W
101	Alcantara (äl-kän'tȧ-rȧ)	Braz.	2.27 S	44.28 W
102	Alcantara	Braz. (In.)	22.48 S	43.2 W
124	Alcaraz (äl-kä-räth')	Sp.	38.39 N	2.29 W
124	Alcaudete (äl-kou-dhā'tā)	Sp.	37.35 N	4.5 W
112	Alcázar (äl-kä'thär)	Mor.	35.0 N	5.47 W
131	Alcázar Pt.	Sp. Mor. (Gibraltar In.)	35.50 N	5.27 E
124	Alcázar de San Juan (äl-kä'thär dā sän hwän')	Sp.	39.23 N	3.12 W
116	Alcester (ôl'stēr)	Gt. Brit.	52.13 N	1.52 W
152	Alchan, Mt. (äl-chän')	Phil.	17.15 N	121.0 E
125	Alcira (äl-thē'rä)	Sp.	39.9 N	0.26 W
82	Alcoa (ăl-kō'ȧ)	Tenn.	35.46 N	84.0 W
101	Alcobaça (äl-kō-bä'sä)	Braz.	3.33 S	49.34 W
125	Alcobendas (äl-kō-bĕn'dȧs)	Sp. (In.)	40.31 N	3.39 W
125	Alcochete (äl-kō-chā'tȧ)	Port. (In.)	38.45 N	8.58 W
73	Alcony R. (ăl-kō'nê)	Ga. (Atlanta In.)	33.25 N	83.50 W
125	Alcora (äl-kō'rä)	Sp.	40.6 N	0.13 W
125	Alcorcón (äl-kôr-kōn')	Sp. (In.)	40.21 N	3.50 W
125	Alcorisa (äl-kō-rē'sä)	Sp.	40.55 N	0.19 W
71	Alcova Reservoir (ăl-kō'vȧ)	Wyo.	42.35 N	106.45 W
125	Alcoy (äl-koi')	Sp.	38.42 N	0.27 W
125	Alcudia B. (äl-kōō-dhē'ä)	Sp.	39.45 N	3.15 E
135	Aldabra Is. (äl-dä'brä)	Ind. O.	9.20 S	46.20 E
92	Aldama (äl-dä'mä)	Mex.	22.56 N	98.3 W
80	Aldama	Mex.	28.50 N	105.53 W
139	Aldan (äl-dän')	Sov. Un.	58.45 N	125.20 E
139	Aldan R	Sov. Un.	61.50 N	135.50 E
139	Aldanskoe (äl-dän'skô-yĕ)	Sov. Un.	61.45 N	135.20 E
124	Aldeia Gallega do Ribatejo (äl-dā' yȧ gä-lā'gȧ dŏŏ rē-bā-tā'hŏŏ)	Port.	38.42 N	8.58 W
88	Aldene (ôl'dēn)	N. J. (N. Y. In.)	40.40 N	74.16 W
72	Aldergrove (ôl'dēr-grōv)	Can. (Vancouver In.)	49.3 N	122.28 W
117	Alderley Edge (ôl-dēr-lā ĕj')	Gt. Brit. (Liverpool In.)	53.18 N	2.14 W
156	Aldermen, The (Is.) (ôl-dēr-mĕn)	N. Z.	36.57 S	176.7 E
122	Alderney (I.) (ôl'dēr-nĭ)	Gt. Brit.	49.41 N	2.11 W
114	Aldershot (ôl'dēr-shŏt)	Gt. Brit.	51.15 N	0.50 W
85	Alderson (ôl-dēr-sŭn)	W. Va.	37.43 N	80.39 W
79	Aledo (ȧ-lē'dō)	Ill.	41.12 N	90.44 W
132	Aleg (ȧ-lĕg')	Fr. W. Afr.	17.10 N	14.0 W
102	Alegrete (ä-lȧ-grā'tā)	Braz.	29.45 S	55.51 W
153	Alegria (ä-lā-grē'ä)	Phil.	9.43 N	123.22 E
128	Aleksandrovsk (ä-lyĕk-sän'drôfsk)	Sov. Un.	56.25 N	38.41 E
139	Aleksandrovsk-Sakhalinski	Sakh.	50.55 N	142.10 E
121	Aleksandrów (ä-lĕk-sän'drŏŏf)	Pol.	52.44 N	18.45 E
129	Alekseevka (ä-lyĕk-sā-yĕf'kȧ)	Sov. Un.	50.38 N	38.40 E
128	Aleksin (ä-lyĕk-sēn)	Sov. Un.	54.31 N	37.5 E
127	Aleksinac (ȧ-lyĕk-sē-nȧk')	Yugo.	43.32 N	21.43 E
125	Alella (ä-lāl'yȧ)	Sp. (In.)	41.29 N	2.17 E
122	Alençon (ȧ-läɴ-sôɴ')	Fr.	48.25 N	0.5 E
101	Alenquer (ä-lĕŋ-kĕr')	Braz.	2.3 S	54.48 W
124	Alenquer	Port.	39.3 N	9.1 W
124	Alentejo (Prov.) (ä-lĕŋ-tā'zhŏŏ)	Port.	38.20 N	7.35 W
155	Alenuihaha Chan. (ä'lȧ-nōō-ê-hä'hä)	Haw.	20.25 N	156.0 W
140	Alep (Aleppo) (ȧ-lĕp') (ȧ-lĕp'ō)	Syr.	36.0 N	37.20 E
122	Aleria (ȧ-lā'rĭ-ȧ)	Cor. (In.)	42.5 N	9.30 E
122	Alès (ä-lĕs')	Fr.	44.8 N	4.5 E
126	Alessandria (ä-lĕs-sän'drê-ä)	It.	44.52 N	8.37 E
127	Alessio (Leshë) (ä-lĕs'syō) (lyĕsh)	Alb.	41.47 N	19.40 E
118	Ålesund (ô'lĕ-sŏŏn')	Nor.	62.28 N	6.12 E
52	Aleutian Is. (ȧ-lū'shăn)	Alsk.	52.40 N	175.0 W
52	Aleutian Troughs	Pac. O.	52.0 N	170.0 W
53	Alexander Archipelago (ăl-ĕg-zăn'dēr)	Alsk.	57.0 N	135.0 W
47	Alexander I	Ant.	71.0 S	71.0 W
82	Alexander City	Ala.	32.56 N	85.57 W
157	Alexandra (ăl-ĕg-zăn'drȧ)	N. Z.	45.13 S	169.25 E
140	Alexandrette (ä-lĕg-zäɴ-drĕt)	Syr.	36.35 N	36.15 E
85	Alexandria (ăl-ĕg-zăn'drĭ-ȧ)	Can.	45.17 N	74.35 W
133	Alexandria	Eg.	31.12 N	29.52 E
84	Alexandria	Ind.	40.17 N	85.41 W
81	Alexandria	La.	31.18 N	92.26 W
76	Alexandria	Minn.	45.53 N	95.21 W
127	Alexandria	Rom.	43.57 N	25.19 E
76	Alexandria	S. D.	43.39 N	97.44 W
85	Alexandria	Va.	38.49 N	77.4 W
129	Alexandriya (ä'lyĕk-sän'drē-yȧ)	Sov. Un.	48.41 N	33.9 E

ăt; finăl; rāte; senâte; ärm; ȧsk; sofȧ; fâre; ch-choose; dh-as th in other; bē; êvent; bĕt; recĕnt; cratēr; g-go; gh-gutteral g; bĭt; ĭ-short neutral; rīde; ĸ-gutteral k as ch in German ich;

Page	Name Pronunciation Region	Lat. °′	Long. °′
127	Alexandroupolis (Dedeagats) (ä-lĕk-sän-drōō'pō-lĭs) (dĕ'dĕ-ä-gäts). Grc.	40.51 N	25.51 E
	Alexandrovka (see Vladimiro Aleksandrovskoe)		
111	Alexeevka (ä-lyĕk-sā-yĕf'kä) Sov. Un.	52.15 N	48.0 E
124	Alfaro (äl-fä'rō) Sp.	42.10 N	1.45 W
151	Alfonso (äl-fōn'sō) Phil. (Manila In.)	14.10 N	120.50 E
116	Alfreton (ôl'fēr-tŭn) Gt. Brit.	53.6 N	1.24 W
124	Algarve (Prov.) (äl-gär'vĕ) Port.	37.15 N	8.5 W
124	Algeciras (äl-hā-thē'räs) Sp.	36.7 N	5.28 W
124	Algeciras, B. of Sp.	36.8 N	5.25 W
125	Algemesi (äl-hā-mä-sē') Sp.	39.12 N	0.27 W
132	Alger (Algiers) (äl-zhā') (ăl-jērz') Alg.	36.50 N	3.0 E
132	Algeria (ăl-gē'rĭ-ȧ) Afr.	30.0 N	4.0 E
125	Algete (äl-hā'tā) Sp. (In.)	40.36 N	3.30 W
126	Alghero (Sard.) (äl-gâ'rō) It.	40.34 N	8.22 E
89	Algiers (ăl-jērz') La. (New Orleans In.)	29.57 N	90.3 W
132	Algiers (Alger) (ăl-jērz') (äl-zhā') Alg.	36.50 N	3.0 E
81	Algoa (ăl-gō'ȧ) Tex. (In.)	29.24 N	95.10 W
55	Algoma (ăl-gō'mȧ) Can.	46.15 N	82.50 W
77	Algoma Wis.	44.37 N	87.28 W
77	Algona (ăl-gō'nȧ) Ia.	43.5 N	94.11 W
51	Algona Wash. (In.)	47.16 N	122.15 W
84	Algonac (ăl'gō-năk) Mich.	42.38 N	82.33 W
85	Algonquin Pk. (ăl-gŏŋ'kwĭn) Can.	45.50 N	78.20 W
124	Alhama (äl-hä'mä) Sp.	37.1 N	3.59 W
124	Alhama Sp.	37.54 N	1.24 W
74	Alhambra (ăl-hăm'brȧ) Calif.	34.5 N	118.9 W
125	Alhandra (äl-yän'drȧ) Port. (In.)	38.55 N	9.2 W
124	Alhaurín (ä-lou-rēn') Sp.	36.39 N	4.41 W
125	Alhos-Vedros (äl'yōs-vā'drōs) Port. (In.)	38.39 N	9.2 W
112	Alhucema Is. (äl-ōō-thā'mä) Mor.	35.15 N	4.0 W
127	Aliakmon (Vistritsa) R. (äl-ê-äk'-mōn) (vē-strēt'sä) Grc.	40.20 N	22.10 E
125	Alicante (ä-lê-kän'tā) Sp.	38.21 N	0.29 W
125	Alicante, G. of Sp.	38.15 N	0.23 W
80	Alice (ăl'ĭs) Tex.	27.45 N	98.4 W
127	Alice, Point dell' (dĕl ä-lē'chä) It.	39.24 N	17.8 E
158	Alice Sprs. (Stuart) (ăl'ĭs) (stū'ērt) Austl.	23.38 S	133.50 E
126	Alicudi (I.) (ä-lē-kōō'dē) It.	38.31 N	14.22 E
141	Aligarh (ä-lê-gŭr') India	27.45 N	78.15 E
153	Alimpaya Pt. (ä-lêm-pä'yä) Phil.	7.8 N	121.54 E
118	Alingsås (ä'lĭŋ-sōs) Swe.	57.57 N	12.32 E
85	Aliquippa (ăl-ĭ-kwĭp'ȧ) Pa.	40.38 N	80.15 W
151	Alitagtag (ä-lê-täg'täg) Phil. (Manila In.)	13.53 N	120.55 E
134	Aliwal North (ä-lê-wäl') U. S. Afr.	30.42 S	26.41 E
124	Aljezur (äl-zhā-zōōr') Port.	37.19 N	8.49 W
124	Aljustrel (äl-zhōō-strĕl') Port.	37.52 N	8.11 W
120	Alkmaar (älk-mär') Neth.	52.36 N	4.45 E
140	Al Kuwait (ăl-kōō-wīt') Kuw.	29.17 N	48.2 E
132	Allada (ä-lä'dä) Fr. W. Afr.	6.40 N	2.10 E
86	Allagash R. (ăl'ȧ-găsh) Me.	46.45 N	69.25 W
141	Allahabad (ŭl-ŭ-hä-bäd') India	25.30 N	81.58 E
124	Allande (äl-yän'dâ) Sp.	43.17 N	6.37 W
124	Allariz (äl-yä-rēth') Sp.	42.11 N	7.48 W
133	Allata (ä-lä'tä) Eth.	6.32 N	38.30 E
84	Allegan (ăl'ê-găn) Mich.	42.34 N	85.52 W
85	Allegheny Front (Mts.) (ăl-ê-gā'nĭ) U. S. A.	40.0 N	79.0 W
84	Allegheny Plat. U. S. A.	40.50 N	79.0 W
85	Allegheny R. Pa.	41.40 N	79.25 W
79	Allen (ăl'ĕn) Okla.	34.52 N	96.25 W
152	Allen Phil.	12.30 N	124.19 E
114	Allen, Lough (lŏĸ ăl'ĕn) Ire.	54.5 N	8.5 W
83	Allendale (ăl'ĕn-dāl) S. C.	33.0 N	81.18 W
80	Allende (äl-yĕn'dâ) Mex.	28.20 N	100.51 W
	Allenstein, see Olsztyn, Pol.		
85	Allentown (ăl'ĕn-toun) Pa.	40.36 N	75.30 W
124	Aller (äl-yâr') Sp.	43.11 N	5.36 W
120	Aller R. (äl'ēr) Ger.	52.35 N	10.10 E
117	Allermöhe (äl'ēr-mû'ĕ) Ger. (Hamburg In.)	53.29 N	10.7 E
117	Allhallows (ôl-hăl'ōs) Gt. Brit. (London In.)	51.28 N	0.38 E
76	Alliance (ȧ-lī'ăns) Neb.	42.5 N	102.51 W
84	Alliance Ohio	40.56 N	81.7 W
123	Allier R. (ȧ-lyā') Fr.	46.40 N	3.15 E
89	Alligator Pt. (ăl'ĭ-gā-tēr) La. (New Orleans In.)	30.1 N	89.43 W
118	Allinge (äl'ĭŋ-ĕ) Den.	55.14 N	14.50 E
114	Alloa (ăl'ō-ȧ) Gt. Brit.	56.5 N	3.45 W
88	Allouez R. (ăl-ōō-ā') Wis. (Duluth In.)	46.40 N	92.2 W
51	Allyn (ăl'ĭn) Wash. (Seattle In.)	47.23 N	122.51 W
83	Alma (ăl'mȧ) Ga.	31.31 N	82.30 W
84	Alma Mich.	43.24 N	84.38 W
78	Alma Neb.	40.8 N	99.21 W
86	Alma Can.	45.35 N	65.0 W
77	Alma Wis.	44.21 N	91.56 W
138	Alma Ata (Verny) (äl'mȧ ȧ'tȧ) (vyĕr'nē) Sov. Un.	43.30 N	77.0 E
125	Almada (äl-mä'dä) Port. (In.)	38.40 N	9.9 W
124	Almadén (äl-mȧ-dhän') Sp.	38.47 N	4.49 W
124	Almagro (äl-mä'grō) Sp.	38.53 N	3.42 W
153	Almagro I. Phil.	11.56 N	124.18 E
74	Almanor, L. (ăl-măn'ôr) Calif.	40.15 N	121.10 W
124	Almansa (äl-män'sä) Sp.	38.53 N	1.8 W
124	Almanzora R. (äl-män-thō'rä) Sp.	37.21 N	2.10 W
125	Almargen (äl-mär-zhän') Port. (In.)	38.51 N	9.16 W
124	Almazán (äl-mä-thän') Sp.	41.30 N	2.31 W
124	Almeirim (äl-mā̇-rēN') Port.	39.12 N	8.39 W
120	Almelo (äl'mē-lō) Neth.	52.21 N	6.43 E
90	Almendares, R. (äl-män-dä'räs) Cuba (Habana In.)	23.4 N	82.25 W
124	Almendralejo (äl-män-drä-lā'hō) Sp.	38.41 N	6.22 W
124	Almería (äl-mā-rē'ä) Sp.	36.51 N	2.28 W
124	Almería, G. of Sp.	36.45 N	2.25 W
124	Almería R. Sp.	37.5 N	2.40 W
118	Almhult (älm'hōōlt) Swe.	56.34 N	14.8 E
131	Almina, Pt. (äl-mē'nä) Sp. Mor. (Gibraltar In.)	35.52 N	5.43 E
95	Almirante (äl-mē-rän'tä) Pan.	9.17 N	82.23 W
95	Almirante B. Pan.	9.30 N	82.0 W
124	Almodóvar (äl-mō-dō'vär) Port.	37.33 N	8.3 W
124	Almodóvar (äl-mō-dhō'vär) Sp.	38.44 N	4.11 W
131	Almodóvar R. Sp. (Gibraltar In.)	36.10 N	5.21 E
124	Almogía (äl-mō-hē'ä) Sp.	37.0 N	5.0 W
92	Almoloya (äl-mō-lō'yä) Mex.	19.23 N	99.45 W
124	Almonaster (äl-mō-näs-tĕr') Sp.	37.53 N	6.47 W
85	Almonte (ăl-mŏn'tê) Can.	45.15 N	76.15 W
124	Almonte (äl-mōn'tā) Sp.	37.16 N	6.30 W
124	Almonte R. Sp.	39.25 N	5.28 W
141	Almora (ŭl-mō'rä) India	29.31 N	79.45 E
125	Almoradí (äl-mō-rä-dhē') Sp.	38.9 N	0.48 W
124	Almuñécar (äl-mōōn-yā'kär) Sp.	36.45 N	3.41 W
127	Almyros (äl'mê-rōs) Grc.	39.10 N	22.47 E
118	Aln I. (äln) Swe.	62.27 N	17.25 E
150	Along B. (ȧ-lông') Indoch.	20.50 N	107.15 E
151	Alor (I.) (ä'lôr) Indon.	8.20 S	124.45 E
160	Alora (ăl'ō-rä) Austl. (In.)	28.5 S	152.3 E
124	Alora (ä'lō-rä) Sp.	36.49 N	4.42 E
150	Alor Star (ä'lôr stär) Siam	6.30 N	100.10 E
124	Alosno (ä-lōs'nō) Sp.	37.33 N	7.8 W
115	Alost (ä'lôst) Bel.	51.0 N	4.5 E
72	Alouette L. (ä-lōō-ĕt') Can. (Vancouver In.)	49.19 N	122.25 W
84	Alpena (ăl-pē'nȧ) Mich.	45.4 N	83.26 W
127	Alpheios R. (äl'fā-ōs) Grc.	37.30 N	22.0 E
124	Alpiarca (äl-pyär'sȧ) Port.	39.17 N	8.35 W
80	Alpine (ăl'pīn) Tex.	30.21 N	103.40 W
126	Alps, The (Mts.) (ălps) Eur.	46.5 N	10.45 E
126	Alps, Bergamo (Mts.) (bĕr'gä-mō) It.	46.5 N	9.50 E
120	Alps, Bernese (bûr'nēz) Switz.	46.33 N	7.42 E
120	Alps, Carnic (Mts.) (kär'nĭk) Aus.-It.	46.43 N	12.50 E
126	Alps, Cottian (Mts.) (kŏt'ĭ-ăn) Fr.-It.	44.45 N	7.0 E
126	Alps, Dinaric (Mts.) (dĭ-năr'ĭk) Yugo.	43.40 N	16.30 E
120	Alps, Eastern (Mts.) Aus.-Switz.	47.17 N	12.10 E
126	Alps, Graian (Mts.) (grā'yăn) It.-Fr.	45.28 N	7.15 E
126	Alps, Julian (Mts.) (jōō'lyăn) Yugo.	46.0 N	14.0 E
126	Alps, Maritime (Mts.) (măr'ĭ-têm) It.-Fr.	44.10 N	7.5 E
126	Alps, Pennine (Mts.) (pĕn'ĭn) It.	46.5 N	9.50 E
120	Alps, Pennine (Mts.) (pĕn'ĭn) Switz.-Fr.	46.5 N	7.20 E
126	Alps, Rhaetian (Mts.) (rē'shăn) It.	46.30 N	11.0 E
127	Alps, Transylvanian (Mts.) (trăn-sĭl-vā'nĭ-ăn) Rom.	45.20 N	24.0 E
126	Alps, Venetian (Mts.) (vē-nē'shĭ-ăn) It.	46.5 N	12.30 E
120	Alps, Western (Mts.) Switz.-Fr.	46.25 N	7.45 E
124	Alpujarras (Mts.) (äl-pōō-här'räs) Sp.	36.56 N	3.15 W
140	Al Qatn (äl kät) Aden	16.00 N	43.30 E
140	Al Qunfidha (Qunfidha) (äl kün'fēd'hȧ) Sau. Ar.	18.59 N	41.29 E
118	Als (I.) (äls) Den.	54.57 N	9.54 E
102	Alsina (äl-sē'nä) Arg. (In.)	34.40 S	58.25 W
117	Alster R. (äl'stēr) Ger. (Hamburg In.)	53.37 N	10.0 E
118	Alster R. Swe.	57.0 N	16.0 E
117	Alt, R. (ält) Gt. Brit. (Liverpool In.)	53.31 N	2.58 W
73	Alta (ăl'tȧ) Utah (Salt Lake City In.)	40.36 N	111.38 W
73	Altadena (ăl-tȧ-dē'nȧ) Calif. (Los Angeles In.)	34.12 N	118.8 W
102	Alta Gracia (äl'tä grä'thê-ä) Arg.	31.45 S	64.15 W
100	Altagracia Ven.	10.32 N	71.30 W
142	Altai Mts. (äl'tī') Asia	47.0 N	92.0 E
81	Alta Loma (ăl'tȧ lō'mȧ) Tex. (In.)	29.22 N	95.5 W
83	Altamaha R. (ôl-tȧ-mȧ-hô') Ga.	31.30 N	81.40 W
101	Altamira (äl-tä-mē'rä) Braz.	3.2 S	52.46 W
93	Altamira Mex.	22.24 N	97.56 W
102	Altamirano (äl-tä-mê-rä'nō) Arg.	35.31 S	58.15 W
126	Altamura (äl-tä-mōō'rä) It.	40.49 N	16.33 E
142	Altanbulak (äl'tän-bōō-läk') Mong.	50.12 N	106.31 E
97	Alta Vela I. (äl'tä vä'lä) Hai.	17.28 N	71.40 W
83	Altavista (ăl-tȧ-vĭs'tȧ) Va.	37.7 N	79.17 W
108	Alten R. (äl'tĕn) Nor.	69.20 N	24.8 E
120	Altenburg (äl'tĕn-bōōrgh) Ger.	50.58 N	12.26 E
117	Altenwerder (äl-tĕn-vĕr'dĕr) Ger. (Hamburg In.)	53.31 N	9.55 E
124	Alter do Chão (äl-tĕr'dōō chä'ōō) Port.	39.14 N	7.39 W
117	Altkloster (ält-klō'stēr) Ger. (Hamburg In.)	53.28 N	9.41 E
120	Altmühl R. (ält'mül) Ger.	48.54 N	11.0 E
81	Alto (ăl'tō) La.	32.20 N	91.50 W
82	Alton (ôl'tŭn) Fla.	30.5 N	83.9 W
79	Alton Ill.	38.54 N	90.9 W
120	Altona (äl'tō-nä) Ger.	53.33 N	9.55 E
82	Altoona (ăl-tōō'nȧ) Ala.	34.2 N	86.19 W
85	Altoona Pa.	40.32 N	78.26 W
101	Alto Paraná, R. (äl'tō pä-rä-nä') Braz.	22.0 S	52.30 W
125	Altos de Garraf (Mts.) (äl'tōs dä gär-äf') Sp. (In.)	41.18 N	1.54 E
97	Alto Songo (äl'tō sôŋ'gō) Cuba	20.11 N	75.44 E
93	Altotonga (äl-tō-tôŋ'gä) Mex.	19.45 N	97.14 W
116	Altrincham (ôl'trĭng-ăm) Gt. Brit.	53.23 N	2.21 W
70	Alturas (ăl-tōō'rȧs) Calif.	41.29 N	120.32 W
78	Altus (ăl'tŭs) Okla.	34.37 N	99.21 W
73	Altus Utah (Salt Lake City In.)	40.45 N	111.37 W
142	Altyn Tagh (Mts.) (äl-tēn'täg') Chn.	37.30 N	88.0 E
119	Aluksne (ä'lŏŏks-nĕ) Sov. Un.	57.24 N	27.4 E
135	Alula (ä-lōō'lä) Som.	11.52 N	50.42 E
85	Alumette I. (ȧ-lü-mĕt') Can.	45.50 N	77.0 W
129	Alushta (ä'lŏŏsh-tȧ) Sov. Un.	44.39 N	34.21 E
78	Alva (ăl'vȧ) Okla.	36.47 N	98.40 W
51	Alvarado (ăl-vȧ-rä'dō) Calif. (San Francisco In.)	37.35 N	122.4 W
93	Alvarado (äl-vä-rä'dhō) Mex.	18.48 N	95.46 W
99	Alvarez Jonte (äl-vä'räth hōn'tä) Arg. (Buenos Aires In.)	35.21 S	57.21 W
93	Alvaro Obregon (Frontera) (äl-vä'-rō ô-brā-gōn') (frōn-tā'rä) Mex.	18.32 N	92.38 W
118	Alvdalen (ĕlv'dä-lĕn) Swe.	61.13 N	14.2 E
125	Alverca (äl-vĕr'kȧ) Port. (In.)	38.54 N	9.3 W
118	Alvesta (äl-vĕs'tä) Swe.	56.57 N	14.31 E
81	Alvin (ăl'vĭn) Tex. (In.)	29.26 N	95.15 W
51	Alviso (ăl-vī'sō) Calif. (San Francisco In.)	37.25 N	121.58 W
141	Alwar (ŭl'wŭr) India	27.32 N	76.40 E
116	Alyn, R. (ăl'ĭn) Gt. Brit.	53.6 N	2.57 W
119	Alytus (ä'lē-tōōs) Sov. Un.	54.24 N	24.4 E
92	Ama, R. (ä'mä) Mex.	21.0 N	99.0 W
151	Amadeo (ä-mä-dā'ō) Phil. (Manila In.)	14.12 N	120.54 E
158	Amadeus, L. (ăm-ȧ-dē'ŭs) Austl.	24.45 S	130.50 E
55	Amadjuak L. (ä-mädj'wäk) Can.	64.40 N	71.28 W
149	Amagasaki (ä'mä-gä-sä'kê) Jap.	34.44 N	135.23 E
148	Amakusa B. (ä-mä-kōō'sä) Jap.	32.32 N	130.0 E
149	Amakusa I. Jap.	32.28 N	130.8 E
118	Åmål (ô'môl) Swe.	59.3 N	12.42 E
127	Amalias (ȧ-mäl'yäs) Grc.	37.48 N	21.21 E
148	Amami Gunto (ä'mä'mē gōōn'tō') Jap.	28.15 N	129.15 E
135	Amani (ä-mä'nē) Tan.	5.5 S	38.39 E
94	Amapala (ä-mä-pä'lä) Hond.	13.16 N	87.38 W
132	Amar (ä-mär') Nig.	8.45 N	10.20 E
101	Amarante (ä-mȧ-rän'tĕ) Braz.	1.16 S	42.45 W
101	Amargosa (ä-mär-gō'sȧ) Braz. (In.)	13.2 S	39.41 W
78	Amarillo (ăm-ȧ-rĭl'ō) Tex.	35.13 N	101.49 W
126	Amaro, Mt. (ä-mä'rō) It.	42.5 N	14.4 E
111	Amasya (ä-mä'sê-ȧ) Tur.	40.40 N	35.55 E
93	Amatenango (ä-mä-tä-naŋ'gō) Mex.	16.31 N	92.27 W
94	Amatique, G. of (ä-mä-tē'kä) Br. Hond.-Guat.	16.0 N	88.45 W
94	Amatitlán (ä-mä-tê-tlän') Guat.	14.27 N	90.38 W
92	Amatlán de Cañas (ä-mät-län' dā kän-yäs) Mex.	20.50 N	104.28 W
101	Amazon R. (ăm'ȧ-zŏn) Braz.	3.1 S	60.0 W
100	Amazonas (State) (ä-mä-thō'-näs) Braz.	7.0 S	64.0 W
141	Amba R. (ŭm'bä) India (Bombay In.)	18.49 N	72.58 E
141	Ambala (ŭm-bä'lŭ) India	30.15 N	76.55 E
100	Ambalema (äm-bä-lā'mä) Col.	4.45 N	76.0 W
100	Ambato (äm-bä'tō) Ec.	1.29 S	78.33 W
151	Ambeno (Ter.) (äm-bā'nō) Tim.	9.20 S	124.20 E
135	Amber, Cape (ăm'bēr) Madag.	11.54 S	49.15 E
120	Amberg (äm'bĕrgh) Ger.	49.26 N	11.50 E
94	Ambergris Cay (I.) (ăm'bēr-grēs kā) Br. Hond. (In.)	18.0 N	87.56 W
97	Ambergris Cays (Is.) (ăm'bēr-grēs käz) Ba. Is.	21.18 N	71.38 W
123	Ambérieu (äN-bā-rē-û') Fr.	45.58 N	5.20 E
157	Amberley (ăm'bēr-lē) N. Z.	43.8 S	172.43 E
122	Ambert (äN-bĕr') Fr.	45.31 N	3.45 E
152	Ambil I. (äm'bēl) Phil.	13.48 N	120.18 E
134	Amboim (äm-bô-ēn') Ang.	10.45 S	14.13 E
151	Amboina (ăm-boi'nȧ) Indon.	3.47 S	128.16 E
151	Amboina (I.) Indon.	3.45 S	128.15 E
122	Amboise (äN-bwäz') Fr.	47.25 N	1.0 E
134	Amboland (Dist.) (ăm'bō-lănd) S. W. Afr.	18.15 S	16.15 E
135	Ambositra (äN-bô-sē'trä) Madag.	20.30 S	47.20 E
51	Amboy (ăm'boi) Wash. (Portland In.)	45.54 N	122.26 W
85	Ambridge (ăm'brĭdj) Pa.	40.37 N	80.14 W
134	Ambris (äm-brēzh') Ang.	7.47 S	13.13 E
134	Ambrisete (äm-brē-zā'tā) Ang.	7.13 S	12.58 E
88	Ambrose Chan. (ăm'brōz) N. Y. (N. Y. In.)	40.33 N	74.0 W
159	Ambrym I. (äm-brēm') New Hebr.	16.20 S	168.10 E
52	Amchitka I. (ăm-chĭt'kä) Alsk.	51.20 N	179.0 E
92	Amealco (ä-mā-äl'kō) Mex.	20.13 N	100.9 W
92	Ameca (ä-mā'kä) Mex.	20.32 N	104.2 W
92	Ameca, R. Mex.	20.40 N	104.30 W
92	Amecameca (ä-mȧ-kä-mä'kä) Mex.	19.7 N	98.45 W
120	Ameland (I.) (ä'mĕ-lănd) Neth.	53.27 N	5.45 E
89	Amelia, L. (ȧ-mē'lyȧ) Minn. (Minneapolis In.)	44.54 N	93.15 W
120	Amerfoort (ä'mĕr-fōōrt) Neth.	52.10 N	5.24 E
73	America (ȧ-mĕr'ĭ-kȧ) Ala. (Birmingham In.)	33.44 N	87.15 W
48	America, North (ȧ-mĕr'ĭ-kȧ)		
98	America, South		
71	American Falls (ȧ-mĕr'ĭ-kăn) Ida.	42.46 N	112.52 W
71	American Falls Reservoir Ida.	42.56 N	112.43 W
75	American Fork Utah	40.22 N	111.50 W
47	American Highland Ant.	72.0 S	79.0 E
51	American L. Wash. (Seattle In.)	47.7 N	122.34 W
74	American R. Calif.	38.37 N	121.15 W

ng-sing; ŋ-baŋk; N-nasalized n; nŏd; cŏmmit; ōld; ôbey; ôrder; fōōd; fŏŏt; ou-out; s-soft; sh-dish; th-thin; pūre; ûnite; ûrn; stŭd; circŭs; ü-as "y" in study; '-indeterminate vowel.

Americus PRONOUNCING INDEX **Apiskigamish**

Page	Name Pronunciation Region	Lat. °′	Long. °′
82	Americus (ȧ-mĕr′ĭ-kŭs)........Ga.	32.4 N	84.14 W
77	Amery (ā′mẽr-ê)............Wis.	45.19 N	92.21 W
77	Ames (āmz)..................Ia.	42.1 N	93.35 W
86	Amesbury (āmz′bẽr-ê)......Mass.	42.50 N	70.57 W
93	Ameyalco (ä-mā-yäl′kō). Mex. (In.)	19.20 N	99.16 W
139	Amga (äm-gä′).........Sov. Un.	62.0 N	134.10 E
139	Amga R..................Sov. Un.	60.0 N	129.0 E
139	Amginskaya (äm-gên′skȧ-yȧ) Sov. Un.	60.5 N	132.0 E
139	Amgun R. (äm-go͞on′)...Sov. Un.	52.0 N	136.0 E
133	Amhara (äm-hä′rä) (Division). Eth.	12.30 N	37.30 E
86	Amherst (ăm′hẽrst)........Can.	45.49 N	64.12 W
84	Amherst..................Ohio	41.22 N	82.14 W
85	Amherst I.................Can.	44.10 N	76.40 W
84	Amherstburg (ăm′hẽrst-bûrg). Can.	42.8 N	83.7 W
122	Amiens (ä-myăɴ′)............Fr.	49.55 N	2.20 E
81	Amite (ă-mēt′)..............La.	30.43 N	90.31 W
85	Amityville (ăm′ĭ-tĭ-vĭl).....N. Y.	40.42 N	73.25 W
140	Amman (Rabbath Ammon) (äm′-mȧn) (rä′bät äm′môn). Jor.	32.0 N	36.0 E
131	Ammuna, Jebel (Mts.) (jĕb′ĕl ä-mo͞o′nä). Eg. (In.)	29.57 N	32.0 E
127	Amorgos (I.) (ä-môr′gōs)....Grc.	36.50 N	25.55 E
82	Amory (ā′mô-rê)...........Miss.	33.58 N	88.28 W
118	Åmot (Torpen) (ô′mōt) (tôr′pĕn) Nor.	61.7 N	11.18 E
145	Amoy (ȧ-moi′).............Chn.	24.28 N	117.58 E
150	Ampenan (äm′pê-nän).....Indon.	8.45 S	116.7 E
127	Amphissa (ăm-fĭs′-ȧ)........Grc.	38.31 N	22.22 E
145	Ampo (äm′pō′)..............Chn.	23.27 N	116.25 E
125	Amposta (äm-pōs′tä).........Sp.	40.42 N	0.34 E
141	Amraoti (ŭm-rŭ-ô′tê).......India	20.59 N	77.50 E
141	Amritsar (ŭm-rĭt′sŭr).......India	31.45 N	74.58 E
120	Amrum (I.) (äm′ro͝om)......Ger.	54.38 N	8.20 E
120	Amsterdam (äm-stẽr-däm′). Neth.	52.22 N	4.56 E
85	Amsterdam (ăm′stẽr-dăm)..N. Y.	42.56 N	74.10 W
120	Amstetten (äm′stĕt-ĕn)......Aus.	48.9 N	14.53 E
133	Am-Timane (äm′tê-män′) Fr. Eq. Afr.	11.15 N	20.30 E
140	Amu Darya (Oxus) R. (ä-mo͞o dä′rēä). Asia	40.15 N	62.30 E
52	Amukta Pass (ä-mo͞ok′tȧ)...Alsk.	52.0 N	172.0 W
152	Amulung (ä′mo͞o′-lo͝ong).....Phil.	17.50 N	121.43 E
47	Amundsen Sea (ä′mŭn-sĕn). Pac. O.	72.0 S	110.0 W
118	Amung, L. (ä′mo͝ong).......Swe.	61.6 N	15.40 E
148	Amur B. (ä-mo͝or′).......Sov. Un.	43.15 N	131.56 E
139	Amur R. (ä-mo͝or′). Sov. Un.-Chn.	49.0 N	130.0 E
129	Amur-Novo Dneprovsk (ä-mo͞or′ nô′vô dnyĕ′-prôfsk). Sov. Un.	48.29 N	35.5 E
152	Amuyao, Mt. (ä-mo͞o-yä′ō)..Phil.	16.17 N	121.3 E
92	Amuzgos (San Pedro) (ä-mo͞oz′gōz) Mex.	16.38 N	98.6 W
127	Amvrakia, G. of (äm-vrä′kê-ȧ). Grc.	38.58 N	21.0 E
72	Anaconda (ăn-ȧ-kŏn′dȧ) Colo. (Colo. Sprs. In.)	38.44 N	105.10 W
71	Anaconda...................Mont.	46.7 N	112.58 W
70	Anacortes (ăn-ȧ-kôr′tĕz)...Wash.	48.29 N	122.38 W
139	Anadara R. (ăn-ȧ-där′ȧ). Sov. Un.	71.0 N	113.0 E
78	Anadarko (ăn-ȧ-där′kō).....Okla.	35.4 N	98.15 W
139	Anadyr, G. of..........Sov. Un.	64.35 N	178.0 E
139	Anadyr Ridge (Mts.)....Sov. Un.	67.0 N	170.0 E
139	Anadyr R..............Sov. Un.	65.0 N	172.0 E
73	Anaheim (ăn′ȧ-hīm) Calif. (Los Angeles In.)	33.50 N	117.55 W
81	Anahuac (ä-nä′wäk)....Tex. (In.)	29.41 N	94.40 W
140	Anaiza (ȧ-nī′zȧ).........Sau. Ar.	26.5 N	44.15 E
147	Anak (än′äk′)...............Kor.	38.32 N	125.27 E
96	Ana Maria Cays (Is.) (ä′nȧ mȧ-rē′ȧ kāz′). Cuba	21.25 N	78.45 W
101	Anambari, Serra de (Mts.) (sĕr′rȧ dā ä-män-bä′rê). Braz.	21.30 S	56.0 W
150	Anambas Is. (ä-näm′bäs)..Indon.	3.0 N	106.0 E
148	Anamio I. (ä-nä′myō).......Jap.	28.20 N	129.30 E
77	Anamosa (ăn-ȧ-mō′sȧ)........Ia.	42.8 N	91.17 W
135	Ananalava (ä-nä-nä-lä′vä). Madag.	14.35 S	47.43 E
129	Ananev (ȧ-nä′nyĕf)......Sov. Un.	47.42 N	29.59 E
129	Anapa (ȧ-nä′pä)........Sov. Un.	44.54 N	37.21 E
111	Anatolia (Reg.) (ăn-ȧ-tō′lĭ-ȧ). Tur.	39.15 N	33.45 E
147	Anbyŏn (än′byŭn′).........Kor.	39.4 N	127.33 E
122	Ancenis (äɴ-sē-nē′)...........Fr.	47.25 N	1.10 W
145	Anchi (än′chê)..............Chn.	30.39 N	119.43 E
116	Ancholme, R. (ăn′chŭm) Gt. Brit.	53.30 N	0.29 W
81	Anchor (ăŋ′kẽr)........Tex. (In.)	29.12 N	95.28 W
53	Anchorage (ăŋ′kẽr-âj).......Alsk.	61.10 N	149.45 W
146	Anchow (än′chō′)...........Chn.	38.58 N	115.41 E
90	Ancon (äŋ-kōn′).......C. Z. (In.)	8.58 N	79.33 W
126	Ancona (än-kō′nä)............It.	43.36 N	13.31 E
102	Ancud (äŋ-ko͞odh′)..........Chl.	41.58 S	73.45 W
102	Ancud G.....................Chl.	42.10 S	72.32 W
124	Andalucía (Reg.) (än-dä-lo͞o-thē′ä) Sp.	37.30 N	5.0 W
82	Andalusia (ăn-dȧ-lo͞o′zhĭ-ȧ)...Ala.	31.18 N	86.28 W
150	Andaman Is. (ăn-dȧ-măn′)..India	12.0 N	92.45 E
150	Andaman I., Little.........India	10.40 N	92.40 E
150	Andaman I., Middle........India	12.30 N	92.45 E
150	Andaman I., North........India	13.15 N	92.50 E
150	Andaman I., South.........India	12.0 N	92.45 E
115	Anderlecht (än′dẽr-lĕkt)......Bel.	50.49 N	4.15 E
120	Andernach (än′dẽr-näᴋ).....Ger.	50.25 N	7.23 E
74	Anderson (ăn′dẽr-sŭn)......Calif.	40.27 N	122.19 W
84	Anderson...................Ind.	40.5 N	85.31 W
83	Anderson...................S. C.	34.30 N	82.39 W
51	Anderson I....Wash. (Seattle In.)	47.10 N	122.42 W
54	Anderson R.................Can.	68.30 N	123.30 W
98	Andes Mts. (ăn′dēz) (än-dās′) S.A.		
135	Andevorante (än-dâ-vō-rän′tâ) Madag.	18.52 S	49.8 E
138	Andizhan (än-dê-zhän′)..Sov. Un.	40.45 N	72.25 E
108	Andö (I.) (änd′û)............Nor.	69.5 N	15.45 E
147	Andong (än′dŭng′)..........Kor.	36.34 N	128.44 E
125	Andorra (än-dôr′rä).........And.	42.29 N	1.29 E
125	Andorra.....................Eur.	42.32 N	1.30 E
87	Andover (ăn′dô-vẽr)..Mass. (In.)	42.39 N	71.8 W
125	Andraitx (än-drȧ-ĭtsh′).......Sp.	39.34 N	2.25 E
52	Andreanof Is. (än-drâ-ä′nôf). Alsk.	52.0 N	176.0 W
135	Andreba (än-drā′bȧ)......Madag.	17.35 S	48.39 E
129	Andreevka (än-drâ-yĕf′kȧ) Sov. Un.	47.4 N	36.34 E
129	Andreevka.............Sov. Un.	48.2 N	37.0 E
82	Andrews (ăn′dro͞oz)........N. C.	35.12 N	83.49 W
83	Andrews....................S. C.	33.26 N	79.33 W
126	Andria (än′drê-ä).............It.	41.13 N	16.18 E
127	Andros (ȧn′dhrôs)...........Grc.	37.50 N	24.55 E
96	Andros I. (ăn′drŏs).......Ba. Is.	24.21 N	77.55 W
127	Andros (I.) (ȧn′dhrôs).......Grc.	37.50 N	24.52 E
86	Androscoggin R. (ăn-drŭs-kŏg′ĭn) Me.	44.25 N	70.35 W
124	Andújar (än-do͞o′här).........Sp.	38.3 N	4.3 W
132	Anécho (ȧ-nā′chō)....Fr. W. Afr.	6.27 N	1.32 E
149	Anegasaki (ä′nâ-gä-sä′kê) Jap. (Tokyo In.)	35.28 N	140.3 E
117	Anerley (ăn′ẽr-lê) Gt. Brit. (London In.)	51.25 N	0.4 W
76	Aneta (ă-nē′tȧ).............N. D.	47.41 N	97.58 W
159	Aneityum (I.) (ä-nâ-ē′tê-ŭm) New Hebr.	20.8 S	169.45 E
144	Anfu (än′fo͞o′)..............Chn.	29.22 N	111.15 E
145	Anfu.......................Chn.	27.17 N	114.25 E
152	Angadanan (äŋ-gȧ-dä′nȧn)...Phil.	16.45 N	121.45 E
152	Angaki (än-gä′kê)...........Phil.	17.8 N	120.39 E
92	Angamacutiro (än′gä-mä-ko͞o-tē′rô) Mex.	20.7 N	101.44 W
142	Angangchi (än′gäng′kē′)....Chn.	47.8 N	123.54 E
92	Angangueo (än-gäŋ′gwâ-ō)..Mex.	19.37 N	100.17 W
151	Angat (än-gät′) Phil. (Manila In.)	14.57 N	121.1 E
151	Angat R.......Phil. (Manila In.)	14.55 N	121.5 E
118	Ånge (ông′ā)................Swe.	62.33 N	15.40 E
118	Angeland (I.) (äng′ĕ-länd)...Den.	54.54 N	10.45 E
158	Angeles (än′hâ-lās)..........Phil.	15.8 N	120.35 E
118	Angelholm (ĕng′ĕl-hôlm)....Swe.	56.14 N	12.51 E
81	Angelina R. (ăn-jê-lē′nȧ).....Tex.	31.30 N	94.50 W
151	Angelo, Mt. (ăn′jĕ-lō) (än′hâ-lō) Phil. (Manila In.)	14.56 N	121.23 E
74	Angels Camp (ān′jĕls kămp′). Calif.	38.3 N	120.33 W
108	Ångerman R. (ông′ĕr-män)...Swe.	64.10 N	17.20 E
120	Angermünde (äng′ẽr-mûn-dĕ). Ger.	53.2 N	14.0 E
122	Angers (äɴ-zhā′)..............Fr.	47.30 N	0.30 W
150	Angkor (Ruins) (ȧng-kōr′). Indoch.	13.40 N	103.55 E
114	Anglesey (ăŋ′g′l-sê).....Gt. Brit.	53.20 N	4.20 W
81	Angleton (ăŋ-g′l-tŭn)........Tex.	29.10 N	95.26 W
81	Angleton............Tex. (In.)	29.10 N	95.26 W
133	Anglo Egyptian Sudan (ăŋ′glō ê-jĭp′shȧn so͞o-dän′). Afr.	15.0 N	30.0 E
89	Anglum (ăŋ′glŭm) Mo. (St. Louis In.)	38.45 N	90.22 W
50	Angmagssalik (ȧŋ-mȧ′sȧ-lĭk) Grnld.	65.40 N	37.40 W
135	Angoche (Antonio Enes) (än-gō′-châ) (än-tō′nê-o͝o ĕn-nezh′). Moz.	16.10 S	39.55 E
135	Angoche I..................Moz.	16.15 S	39.50 E
102	Angol (äŋ-gōl′)..............Chl.	37.46 S	72.42 W
134	Angola (ăŋ-gō′lȧ)............Afr.	12.30 S	18.30 E
84	Angola......................Ind.	41.38 N	85.2 W
151	Angono (äŋ-gō′nō) Phil. (Manila In.)	14.33 N	121.10 E
111	Angora (Ankara) (ăŋ-gō′rȧ) (äŋ′kä-ra). Tur.	39.55 N	32.55 E
122	Angoulême (äŋ-go͞o-lâm′).....Fr.	45.40 N	0.15 E
99	Angra dos Reis (äŋ′grä dōs rā′ês) Braz. (Rio de Janeiro In.)	23.3 S	44.17 W
96	Anguila Isles (ăŋ-gwĭl′ȧ)....W. I.	23.30 N	79.35 W
95	Anguilla (I.) (ăŋ-gwĭl′ȧ). W. I. (In.)	18.13 N	63.0 W
87	Anguille, C, (äŋ-gē′yĕ)......Can.	47.55 N	59.25 W
145	Anhai (än′hī′)..............Chn.	24.43 N	118.23 E
120	Anhalt (State) (än′hält).....Ger.	51.45 N	11.45 E
118	Anholt (I.) (än′hŏlt)........Den.	56.42 N	11.35 E
144	Anhwa (än′hwä′)............Chn.	28.11 N	111.21 E
145	Anhwei (Prov.) (än′hwā′)...Chn.	30.50 N	117.20 E
145	Ani (ä′nê′)..................Chn.	28.46 N	115.16 E
75	Animas R. (ä′nê-mȧs). Colo.-N. M.	37.0 N	107.52 W
127	Anina (ä-nē′nä)............Rom.	45.2 N	21.49 E
85	Anita (ă-nē′tȧ)...............Pa.	41.3 N	79.0 W
148	Aniwa B. (ä′nê-wä′)........Sakh.	40.28 N	142.45 E
144	Anjen (än′jĕn′)..............Chn.	26.40 N	113.0 E
145	Anjen.......................Chn.	28.33 N	116.55 E
135	Anjouan I. (än-jo͞o-än′)...Ind. O.	12.10 S	44.18 E
147	Anju (än′jo͞o′)...............Kor.	39.36 N	125.40 E
111	Ankara (Angora) (äŋ′kä-rä) (ăŋ-gō′rȧ). Tur.	39.55 N	32.55 E
135	Ankaratra Mts. (äŋ-kȧ-rä′trä) Madag.	19.15 S	48.0 E
116	Anker R. (ăŋ′kẽr).......Gt. Brit.	52.36 N	1.34 W
127	Ankhiolo (än-ᴋē-ō′lō)........Bul.	42.33 N	27.41 E
145	Anki (än′kē′)................Chn.	25.0 N	118.3 E
145	Anking (än′kĭng′)...........Chn.	30.32 N	117.8 E
146	Ankiu (än′kê-o͞o′)...........Chn.	36.27 N	119.13 E
120	Anklam (än′kläm)...........Ger.	53.52 N	13.42 E
133	Ankober (äŋ-kō′bẽr).........Eth.	9.41 N	39.52 E
134	Ankoro (äŋ-kō′rō).....Bel. Cong.	6.46 S	26.45 E
139	Ankula (än′ko͝o-lȧ).......Sov. Un.	61.10 N	107.59 E
144	Anlu (än′lo͞o′)...............Chn.	31.10 N	112.28 E
147	Anmyon I. (än′myōn′)......Kor.	36.30 N	126.18 E
86	Ann, C. (ăn)...............Mass.	42.49 N	70.35 W
79	Anna (ăn′ȧ)...................Ill.	37.28 N	89.14 W
129	Anna (än′ä).............Sov. Un.	51.28 N	40.21 E
120	Annaberg (än′ä-bĕrgh).......Ger.	50.35 N	13.1 E
140	An Najaf (än nȧ-zhȧf′)......Iraq	31.40 N	44.38 E
150	Annam (State) (ȧn-näm′). Indoch.	15.0 N	108.0 E
150	Annamitic Cord. (Mts.) (ă-nȧ-mĭt′-ĭk kôr-dĭl-yā′rȧ. Indoch.	16.0 N	107.0 E
55	Annapolis (ă-năp′ô-lĭs)......Can.	44.45 N	65.35 W
85	Annapolis..................Md.	38.58 N	76.30 W
84	Ann Arbor (ăn är′bẽr)......Mich.	42.17 N	83.44 W
123	Annecy (ȧn′sē′)...............Fr.	45.55 N	6.5 E
123	Annemasse (än′mäs′).........Fr.	46.10 N	6.12 E
82	Anniston (ăn′ĭs-tŭn).........Ala.	33.38 N	85.50 W
125	Anneto, Pic d′ (Mt.) (pēk′dä-nā′tō) Sp.	42.38 N	0.38 W
122	Annonay (ȧ-nô-nĕ′)...........Fr.	45.15 N	4.41 E
96	Annotto B. (än-nō′tō)........Jam.	18.16 N	76.47 W
77	Anoka (ȧ-nō′kȧ)...........Minn.	45.11 N	93.21 W
144	Anping (än′pĭng′)...........Chn.	26.21 N	106.2 E
146	Anping.....................Chn.	38.20 N	115.31 E
145	Anping (än′pĭng′)...........For.	23.1 N	120.11 E
120	Ansbach (äns′bäᴋ)..........Ger.	49.18 N	10.34 E
97	Anse à Veau (äɴs′ä-vō′).....Hai.	18.30 N	73.22 W
97	Ansed′Hainault (äɴs′dĕnō′)..Hai.	18.30 N	74.27 W
144	Anshun (än-sho͞on′).........Chn.	26.10 N	105.47 E
142	Ansi (än′sē′).................Chn.	40.30 N	95.48 E
144	Ansiang (än′sê-äng′)........Chn.	29.20 N	111.58 E
80	Anson (ăn′sŭn)..............Tex.	32.45 N	99.54 W
158	Anson B. (ăn′sŭn).........Austl.	13.25 S	130.15 E
147	Ansŏng (än′sŭng′)...........Kor.	37.0 N	127.15 E
85	Ansonia (ăn-sō′nĭ-ȧ).......Conn.	41.23 N	73.5 W
146	Ansu (än′so͞o′)...............Chn.	39.6 N	115.30 E
111	Antalya (Adalia) (än-tä′lê-ä) (ä-dä′lê-ä). Tur.	36.55 N	30.50 E
111	Antalya, G. of..............Tur.	36.35 N	31.20 E
	Antananarivo, see Tananarive, Madag.		
47	Antarctica		
71	Antelope Cr. (ăn′tê-lōp)....Wyo.	43.30 N	105.30 W
71	Antelope I..................Utah	40.58 N	112.13 W
153	Antequera (än-tâ-kā′rä).....Phil.	9.47 N	123.54 E
124	Antequera....................Sp.	37.1 N	4.32 W
78	Anthony (ăn′thô-nê)........Kan.	37.8 N	98.3 W
123	Antibes (äɴ-tēb′)..............Fr.	43.35 N	7.10 E
87	Anticosti I. (ăn-tĭ-kŏs′tê)....Can.	49.50 N	6.30 W
77	Antigo (ăn′tĭ-gō).............Wis.	45.9 N	89.9 W
87	Antigonish (ăn-tĭ-gô-nêsh′)...Can.	45.39 N	61.59 W
94	Antigua (än-tē′gwä)........Guat.	14.33 N	90.43 W
91	Antigua (I.)................W. I.	17.5 N	61.37 W
93	Antigua Veracruz (än-tē′gwä vā-rä-kro͞oz′). Mex.	19.19 N	96.20 W
97	Antilla (än-tē′lyä)..........Cuba	20.50 N	75.44 W
51	Antioch (ăn′tĭ-ŏk) Calif. (San Francisco In.)	38.1 N	121.48 W
76	Antioch......................Neb.	42.3 N	102.34 W
140	Antioche (äɴ-tê-ôsh′)........Syr.	36.5 N	36.15 E
100	Antioquia (än-tê-ō′kêä)......Col.	6.20 N	76.3 W
7	Antipodes (ăn-tĭp′ô-dēz)..Pac. O.	49.0 S	180.0 E
151	Antipolo (än-tē′pô-lō) Phil. (Manila In.)	14.37 N	121.12 E
79	Antlers (ănt′-lẽrz)..........Okla.	34.13 N	95.38 W
102	Antofagasta (än-tô-fä-gäs′tä). Chl.	23.31 S	70.20 W
95	Antón (än-tōn′)..............Pan.	8.21 N	80.14 W
135	Antongil B. (äɴ-tôɴ-zhēl′). Madag.	15.30 S	49.50 E
135	Antonio Enes (Angoche) (än-tō′-nê-o͝o ĕn-nĕzh′) (äŋ-gō′châ). Moz.	16.10 S	39.55 E
78	Antonito (ăn-tô-nē′tō)......Colo.	37.4 N	106.1 W
119	Antonopole (än′tô-nô-pō′lyĕ) Sov. Un.	56.21 N	27.10 E
123	Antony (äɴ-tô-nē′)......Fr. (In.)	48.45 N	2.17 E
114	Antrim, Mts. of (ăn′trĭm)..N. Ire.	55.0 N	6.10 W
135	Antsirabe (änt-sê-rä′bā)..Madag.	19.50 S	47.10 E
135	Antsirane (Diégo-Suarez) (änt-sê-rä′nā) (dê-ā′gō-so͞o-ä′rās). Madag.	12.10 S	49.13 E
119	Antsla (änt′slȧ)..........Sov. Un.	57.50 N	26.35 E
102	Antuco (Vol.) (än-to͞o′kō)....Chl.	37.25 S	71.30 W
146	Antung (än′to͝ong′)..........Chn.	33.44 N	119.17 E
147	Antung......................Chn.	40.9 N	124.22 E
115	Antwerp (Anvers) (ănt′wẽrp) (äɴ-vâr′). Bel.	51.15 N	4.25 E
117	Antwerp and Turnhout Canal (ănt′wẽrp tŭrn′hout) Bel. (Anvers In.)	51.18 N	4.33 E
141	Anuradhapura (ŭ-no͞o′rä-dŭ-po͞o′rŭ). Cey.	8.25 N	80.25 E
115	Anvers (Antwerp) (äɴ-vâr′) (ănt′wẽrp). Bel.	51.15 N	4.25 E
117	Anvers (Antwerp)......Bel. (In.)		
72	Anvil I. (ăn′vĭl) Can. (Vancouver In.)	49.32 N	123.19 W
119	Anykščiai (ä-nĭksh′chê-ī). Sov. Un.	55.32 N	25.4 E
145	Anyüan (äɴ′yü-än′)........Chn.	24.50 N	114.56 E
139	Anyui R. (än′yo͞o-ĕ′)....Sov. Un.	68.0 N	165.0 E
138	Anzhero-Sudzhensk (än′zhâ-rô-so͞od′zhĕnsk). Sov. Un.	56.5 N	86.1 E
122	Anzin (äɴ-zăɴ′)..............Fr.	50.24 N	3.30 E
126	Anzio (änt′zê-ō)..............It.	41.27 N	12.38 E
148	Aomori (ä-ô-mō′rê)..........Jap.	40.45 N	140.45 E
126	Aosta (ä-ôs′tä)...............It.	45.44 N	7.19 E
82	Apalachee B. (ăp-ȧ-lăch′ē)....Fla.	30.0 N	84.10 W
82	Apalachicola (ăp-ȧ-lăch-ĭ-kō′lȧ) Fla.	29.44 N	85.0 W
82	Apalachicola R..............Fla.	30.10 N	85.2 W
153	Apali Pt. (ä-pä′lê)..........Phil.	10.50 N	124.30 E
151	Apalit (ä-pä′lêt). Phil. (Manila In.)	14.48 N	120.44 E
92	Apam (ä-päm′)..............Mex.	19.41 N	98.28 W
92	Apango (ä-päŋ′gō)..........Mex.	17.39 N	99.24 W
100	Apaporis, R. (ä-pä-pô′rĭs)....Col.	0.0	70.30 W
152	Aparri (ä-pär′rē)............Phil.	18.20 N	121.39 E
92	Apaseo (ä-pä′sâ-ō)..........Mex.	20.34 N	100.40 W
127	Apatin (ŏ′pŏ-tĭn)...........Yugo.	45.41 N	19.0 E
92	Apatzingán de la Constitución (ä-pät-zĭŋ-gän′ dā lä cōn-stĭ-to͞o-sê-ōn′). Mex.	19.5 N	102.15 W
127	Apeiranthos (ä-pĭr′än-thôs)...Grc.	37.4 N	25.32 E
120	Apeldoorn (ä′pĕl-do͞orn)....Neth.	52.12 N	5.56 E
126	Apennines (Mts.) (ăp′ĕ-nīnz)...It.	42.0 N	14.0 N
93	Apipilhuaxco (ä-pĭ-pĭl-hwȧz′kō) Mex. (In.)	19.32 N	98.45 W
92	Äpipilulco (ä-pĭ-pĭ-lo͞ol′kō)...Mex.	18.9 N	99.39 W
78	Apishapa R. (ăp-ĭ-shä′pȧ)...Colo.	37.35 N	104.15 W
55	Apiskıgamish L. (ȧ-pĭs-kĭ-gȧ-mēsh′). Can.	55.15 N	73.30 W

ăt; finăl; rāte; senâte; ärm; ȧsk; sofȧ; fâre; ch-choose; dh-as th in other; bē; êvent; bĕt; recĕnt; cratẽr; g-go; gh-gutteral g; bĭt; ĭ-short neutral; rīde; ᴋ-gutteral k as ch in German ich;

Apizaco PRONOUNCING INDEX Ashtabula

Page	Name Pronunciation Region	Lat. °'	Long. °'
92	Apizaco (ä-pê-zä'kō)........Mex.	19.25 N	98.7 W
153	Apo, Mt. (Vol.) (ä'-pō)......Phil.	6.59 N	125.17 E
120	Apolda (ä-pôl'dä)...........Ger.	51.2 N	11.31 E
83	Apopka (ȧ-pŏp'kȧ)......Fla. (In.)	28.38 N	81.30 W
83	Apopka, L............Fla. (In.)	28.38 N	81.35 W
92	Aporo (ä-pô'rō)...........Mex.	19.43 N	100.25 W
77	Apostle Is. (ă-pŏs'l)........Wis.	46.55 N	90.35 W
82	Appalachia (ăpȧ-lăch'ĭ-ȧ).....Va.	36.56 N	82.48 W
59	Appalachian Mts. (ăp-ȧ-lăch'ĭ-ăn) U. S.	38.0 N	80.30 W
118	Äppelbo (ĕp-ĕl-bŏŏ)........Swe.	60.30 N	14.0 E
117	Appen (äp'ĕn).Ger. (Hamburg In.)	53.40 N	9.44 E
120	Appenzell (äp'ĕn-tsĕl)......Switz.	47.19 N	9.24 E
76	Appleton (ăp''l-tŭn).......Minn.	45.11 N	96.1 W
77	Appleton.................Wis.	44.15 N	88.25 W
79	Appleton City.............Mo.	38.12 N	94.3 W
83	AppomattoxR. (ăp-ô-măt'ŭks).Va.	37.30 N	78.0 W
126	Aprilia (ȧ-prē'lĭȧ)...........It.	41.35 N	12.40 E
160	Apsley (ăps'lê)...Austl. (Tas. In.)	42.26 S	147.9 E
123	Apt (äpt)..................Fr.	43.55 N	5.20 E
126	Apulia (Prov.) (ȧ-pū'lĭ-ȧ)......It.	41.15 N	16.10 E
100	Apure, R. (ä-pōō'rä)........Ven.	8.0 N	69.30 W
100	Apurimac,R.(ä-pōō-rê-mäk').Peru	12.0 S	74.0 W
140	Aqaba (ä'kȧ-bȧ).............Jor.	29.30 N	35.5 E
142	Aqsu (Wensuh) (äk-sōō') (wĕn'sōō').Chn.	41.40 N	80.5 E
142	Aqsu R....................Chn.	40.45 N	78.0 E
126	Aquila (ä'kwê-lä)............It.	42.22 N	13.24 E
92	Aquililla de Iturbide (ä-kwê-lē'yȧ dä ê-tōōr-bē'dhä).Mex.	18.44 N	102.43 W
97	Aquin (ä-kăN')..............Hai.	18.15 N	73.24 W
129	Arabatskaya Strelka (Tongue of Arabat) (Pen.) (ä-rä-bät'-skä-yȧ strĕl'kȧ) (ä-rȧ-băt').Sov. Un.	45.50 N	35.0 E
140	ArabianPeninsula(ȧ-rā'bĭ-ăn).Asia	24.0 N	45.0 E
140	Arabian Sea...............Asia	19.0 N	65.0 E
101	Aracajú (ä-rä'kä-zhōō').....Braz.	10.59 S	37.1 W
101	Aracati (ä-rä'kä-tē')........Braz.	4.30 S	37.45 W
124	Aracena (ä-rä-thā'nä)........Sp.	37.54 N	6.35 W
122	Arachon (ä-rä-shôN')........Fr.	44.40 N	1.10 W
121	Arad (ŏ'rŏd)...............Rom.	46.11 N	21.19 E
124	Araduey R. (ä-rä-dōō-ā'ĭ)....Sp.	42.0 N	5.18 W
151	Arafura Sea (ä-rä-fōō'rä)..Indon.	9.0 S	134.0 E
125	Aragón (Reg.) (ä-rä-gōn')....Sp.	41.30 N	0.30 W
124	Aragón R...................Sp.	42.32 N	1.20 W
100	Aragua de Barcelona (ä-rä'gwä dā bär-thā-lō'nä).Ven.	9.29 N	64.58 W
101	Araguaia, R. (ä-rä-gwä'yä)..Braz.	9.0 S	50.0 W
101	Araguari (ä-rä-gwä'rê)......Braz.	18.45 S	48.2 W
141	Arakan Yoma (Mts.) (ŭ-rŭ-kŭn' yō'mä).Bur.	19.0 N	94.40 E
127	Arakhthos R. (är'äK-thôs)...Grc.	39.20 N	21.4 E
138	Aral Sea (ȧ-räl')........Sov. Un.	45.0 N	60.0 E
111	Aral-Sor, L. (ȧ-räl'sôr')..Sov. Un.	49.10 N	48.15 E
92	Aramberri (ä-räm-bĕr-rē')...Mex.	24.6 N	99.48 W
124	Aranda de Duero (ä-rän'dä dā dwā'rō).Sp.	41.41 N	3.41 W
92	Arandas (ä-rän'däs).........Mex.	20.44 N	102.17 W
90	Arango (ä-raŋ'gō) Cuba (Habana In.)	23.5 N	82.12 W
114	Aran I. (ăr'ăn)..............Ire.	55.0 N	8.25 W
114	Aran Is....................Ire.	53.5 N	9.45 W
124	Aranjuez (ä-rän-hwāth')......Sp.	40.2 N	3.36 W
81	Aransas Pass (ȧ-răn'sȧs)......Tex.	27.55 N	97.8 W
150	Aranya Pradega (ä-rän'yä prä-dā'gä).Siam	13.35 N	102.15 E
132	Araouan (ä-rou-äN')...Fr. W. Afr.	19.0 N	3.35 W
111	Arapkir (ä-räp-kēr')........Tur.	38.55 N	38.15 E
159	Ararat (ăr'ȧ-răt)..........Austl.	37.16 S	142.58 E
111	Ararat, Mt..................Tur.	39.45 N	44.18 E
99	Araruama, L. (ä-rä-rōō-ä'mä) Braz. (Rio De Janeiro In.)	22.54 S	42.15 W
111	Aras R. (ȧ-räs).....Sov. Un.-Iran	39.25 N	47.15 E
101	Aratuhipe (ä-rä-tōō-ē'pä) Braz. (In.)	13.5 S	39.5 W
100	Arauca (ä-rou'kä)...........Col.	7.0 N	70.30 W
100	Arauca, R..................Ven.	7.15 N	67.30 W
141	Aravalli Range (Mts.) (ä-rä'vŭ-lê).India	23.30 N	73.30 E
152	Arayat (ä-rä'yät)...........Phil.	15.9 N	120.45 E
118	Arboga (är-bō'gä)..........Swe.	59.24 N	15.41 E
123	Arbois (är-bwä')............Fr.	46.54 N	6.45 E
114	Arbroath (är-brōth')....Gt. Brit.	56.35 N	2.35 W
73	Arcadia (är-kā'dĭ-ȧ) Calif. (Los Angeles In.)	34.9 N	118.1 W
83	Arcadia..............Fla. (In.)	27.12 N	81.51 W
81	Arcadia....................La.	32.32 N	92.57 W
77	Arcadia...................Wis.	44.15 N	91.29 W
70	Arcata (är-kă'tȧ)..........Calif.	40.53 N	124.6 W
92	Arcelia (är-sā'lē-ä)........Mex.	18.17 N	100.22 W
110	Archangel (Arkhangelsk) (ärk'-ān-jĕl) (är-KäŋŊ'gĕlsk).Sov. Un.	64.30 N	40.40 E
85	Archbald (ärch'bôld).........Pa.	41.37 N	75.32 W
75	Arches Natl. Monument....Utah	38.42 N	109.35 W
100	Archidona (är-chê-do'nä).....Ec.	0.31 S	76.59 W
124	Archidona..................Sp.	37.7 N	4.22 W
122	Arcis-sur-Aube (är-sēs'sûr-ōb').Fr.	48.31 N	4.9 E
71	Arco (är'kō)...............Ida.	43.39 N	113.18 W
81	Arcola (är-kō'lȧ).......Tex. (In.)	29.30 N	95.27 W
124	Arcos (är'kōs)...............Sp.	36.45 N	5.49 W
48	Arctic Ocean (ärk'tĭk).......Arc.	74.0 N	
48	Arctic Regions		
127	Arda R. (är'dä).............Bul.	41.37 N	25.30 E
111	Ardahan (är-dȧ-hän')........Tur.	41.10 N	42.40 E
110	Ardatov (är-dȧ-tôf')....Sov. Un.	54.55 N	46.15 E
140	Ardebil (är-dē-bēl')..........Iran	38.20 N	48.2 E
115	Ardennes (är-dĕn')...........Bel.	50.20 N	5.30 E
124	Ardila R. (är-dē'lä).........Port.	38.12 N	7.0 W
79	Ardmore (ärd'mōr)........Okla.	34.11 N	97.8 W
85	Ardmore....................Pa.	40.1 N	75.20 W
116	Ardsley (ärdz'lê)........Gt. Brit.	53.42 N	1.26 W
102	Areal (ä-rā-äl')........Braz. (In.)	22.50 S	43.20 W

Page	Name Pronunciation Region	Lat. °'	Long. °'
91	Arecibo (ä-rā-sē'bō)...P. R. (In.)	18.27 N	66.43 W
101	Areia (ä-rā'yȧ)........Braz. (In.)	13.16 S	39.41 W
101	Areia Branca (bräŋ'kä).....Braz.	5.0 S	37.2 W
72	Arena (ȧ-rē'nȧ).Colo. (Denver In.)	39.52 N	105.15 W
74	Arena, Pt. (ä-rā'nȧ)........Calif.	38.57 N	123.44 W
124	Arenas de San Pedro (ä-rā'näs dā sän pā'drō).Sp.	40.13 N	5.4 W
118	Arendal (ä'rĕn-däl).........Nor.	58.29 N	8.43 E
100	Arequipa (ä-rā-kē'pä).......Peru	16.28 S	71.30 W
108	Areskutan (ä-rĕs'kōō-tă).....Swe.	63.28 N	13.5 E
122	Areyron R. (ä-rā-rôN')........Fr.	44.5 N	1.40 E
126	Arezzo (ä-rĕt'sō)............It.	43.29 N	11.53 E
124	Arga R. (är'gä)..............Sp.	42.30 N	1.50 W
125	Arganda (är-gän'dä).....Sp. (In.)	40.18 N	3.27 W
153	Argao (är-gä'ō).............Phil.	9.52 N	123.36 E
138	Argara R. (är-gä'rä).....Sov. Un.	54.0 N	103.10 E
122	Argelès-Gazost (är-zhĕ-lĕs'-gä-zō').Fr.	43.0 N	0.6 W
122	Argentan (är-zhäN-täN')......Fr.	48.45 N	0.1 E
122	Argentat (är-zhäN-tä')........Fr.	45.5 N	1.55 E
122	Argenteuil (är-zhäN-tû'y')....Fr.	48.56 N	2.15 E
102	Argentina (är-jĕn-tē'nȧ).....S. A.	35.30 S	67.0 W
102	Argentina, I................Arg.	50.15 S	72.30 W
122	Argenton (är-zhäN'tôN')......Fr.	46.35 N	1.30 E
125	Argentona (är-kĕn-tō'nä).Sp. (In.)	41.34 N	2.24 E
127	Argeș R. (är'zhĕsh).........Rom.	44.34 N	25.30 E
73	Argo (är'gō).Ala. (Birmingham In.)	33.42 N	86.32 W
127	Argolis, G. of (är'gô-lĭs).....Grc.	37.25 N	22.55 E
127	Argos (är'gōs)..............Grc.	37.37 N	22.44 E
127	Argostolion (är-gŏs-tô'lē-ōn)..Grc.	38.11 N	20.30 E
74	Arguello, Pt. (är-gwăl'yō)...Calif.	34.33 N	120.39 W
132	Arguin, C. (är-gōō-ēn') (är-găN') Fr. W. Afr.	20.32 N	16.30 W
139	Argun R. (är-gōōn').Chn.-Sov. Un.	51.45 N	120.0 E
56	Argyle (är'gīl).Can. (Winnipeg In.)	50.12 N	97.27 W
76	Argyle.....................Minn.	48.19 N	96.48 W
158	Argyle Downs.............Austl.	16.20 S	128.58 E
149	Ariake Bay (ä'rê-ä'kȧ).......Jap.	31.24 N	131.8 E
149	Ariake Sea..................Jap.	32.57 N	130.23 E
126	Ariano (ä-rē-ä'nō)............It.	41.8 N	15.6 E
100	Arica (ä-rē'kä)..............Chl.	18.30 S	70.20 W
87	Arichat (ä-rĭ-shät').........Can.	45.31 N	61.0 W
122	Ariège R. (ȧ-rê-ĕzh')..........Fr.	43.15 N	1.25 E
51	Ariel (ā'rĭ-ĕl).Wash. (Portland In.)	45.59 N	122.30 W
121	Arieșul R. (ä-rē-ä'shōōl)....Rom.	46.25 N	23.25 E
78	Arikaree R.(ă-rĭ-kȧ-rē').Colo.-Neb.	40.0 N	102.0 W
149	Arima (ä'rê-mä').Jap. (Osaka In.)	34.48 N	135.15 E
153	Aringay (ä-rĭŋ-gä'ê)........Phil.	16.24 N	120.21 E
101	Arinos, R. (ä-rē'nôzh)......Braz.	12.30 S	56.30 W
92	Ario de Rosales (ä'rê-ō dä (rō-sä'läs).Mex.	19.12 N	101.44 W
101	Aripuaña, R. (ä-rê-pwän'yȧ).Braz.	8.0 S	60.0 W
138	Ariz (ȧ-rēs')............Sov. Un.	42.35 N	69.20 E
137	Arîsh (ȧ-rēsh')..........Eg. (In.)	31.7 N	33.51 E
137	Arîsh, Wadi el (R.) (wä'dê ĕl ȧ-rēsh').Eg. (In.)	31.0 N	33.53 E
75	Arizona (State) (ăr-ĭ-zō'nȧ)..U. S.	34.25 N	111.40 W
124	Arjona (är-hō'nä)............Sp.	37.56 N	4.4 W
79	Arkadelphia (är-kȧ-dĕl'fĭ-ȧ)..Ark.	34.7 N	93.3 W
79	Arkansas (State) (är'kăn-sô) (är-kăn'sȧs).U. S.	34.50 N	93.0 W
79	Arkansas City.............Kan.	37.3 N	97.2 W
79	Arkansas R.................U. S.	37.30 N	97.15 W
79	Arkansas R., Salt Fk. of....Okla.	36.40 N	97.40 W
110	Arkhangelsk (Archangel) (är-Kän'-gĕlsk) (ärk'ān-jĕl).Sov. Un.	64.30 N	40.40 E
114	Arklow (ärk'lō)..............Ire.	52.45 N	6.10 W
141	Arkonam (är-kō-näm')......India	13.5 N	79.38 E
124	Arlanzá R. (är-län-thä')......Sp.	42.4 N	3.30 W
124	Arlanzón (är-län-thōn')......Sp.	42.20 N	4.10 W
120	Arlberg Tunnel (ärl'bĕrgh)...Aus.	47.8 N	10.12 E
122	Arles (ärl)...................Fr.	43.39 N	4.41 E
73	Arlington (är'lĭng-tŭn) Calif. (Los Angeles In.)	33.55 N	117.26 W
82	Arlington...................Ga.	31.26 N	84.43 W
87	Arlington............Mass. (In.)	42.25 N	71.11 W
88	Arlington.......N. J. (N. Y. In.)	40.46 N	74.9 W
76	Arlington...................S. D.	44.22 N	97.8 W
81	Arlington...................Tex.	32.44 N	97.6 W
86	Arlington....................Vt.	43.5 N	73.5 W
85	Arlington....................Va.	38.53 N	77.17 W
70	Arlington..................Wash.	48.11 N	122.8 W
88	Arlington Heights.Ill. (Chicago In.)	42.5 N	87.59 W
118	Arlöv (är'lûf)...............Swe.	55.37 N	13.5 E
158	Arltunga (ärl-tōōŋ'gä).......Austl.	23.20 S	134.45 E
79	Arma (är'mȧ)...............Kan.	37.34 N	94.43 W
92	Armadillo (är-mä-dēl'yō)....Mex.	22.15 N	100.39 W
57	Armagh (är-mä') (är-mäK') Can. (Que. In.)	46.45 N	70.36 W
114	Armagh...................N. Ire.	54.21 N	6.42 W
57	Armagh Station...Can. (Que. In.)	46.44 N	70.36 W
139	Arman (är-män')........Sov. Un.	59.45 N	149.50 E
131	Armant (är-mänt').......Eg. (In.)	25.37 N	32.30 E
111	Armavir (är-mȧ-vĭr')....Sov. Un.	44.58 N	41.5 E
94	Armenia (är-mā'nê-ä)..........Sal.	13.31 N	89.40 W
111	Armenia (Soviet Rep.) (är-mē'nĭ-ȧ) Sov. Un.	40.0 N	45.15 E
122	Armentières (är-mäN-tyâr')....Fr.	50.45 N	2.50 E
92	Armería, R. (är-mȧ-rē'ä)....Mex.	19.40 N	104.8 W
159	Armidale (är'mĭ-dāl)........Austl.	30.30 S	151.46 E
76	Armour (är'mēr)............S. D.	43.19 N	98.20 W
129	Armyansk (ärm'yánsk)..Sov. Un.	46.5 N	33.43 E
124	Arnedo (är-nā'dō)............Sp.	42.12 N	2.3 W
120	Arnhem (ärn'hĕm)..........Neth.	51.59 N	5.56 E
158	Arnhem, C.................Austl.	12.15 S	136.58 E
158	Arnhemland (ärn'hĕm-lănd).Austl.	13.15 S	134.0 E
116	Arnold (är'nŭld)..........Gt. Brit.	53.0 N	1.8 W
126	Arno R. (är'nō)...............It.	43.46 N	11.20 E
85	Arnprior (ärn-prī'ēr)........Can.	45.27 N	76.21 W
120	Arnsberg (ärns'bĕrgh)........Ger.	51.24 N	8.2 E
120	Arnstadt (ärn'shtät)..........Ger.	50.51 N	10.56 E
134	Aroab (är'ō-äb)........S. W. Afr.	26.47 S	19.43 E

Page	Name Pronunciation Region	Lat. °'	Long. °'
151	Aroe Is. (ä-rō'ē)..........Indon.	6.15 S	134.30 E
86	Aroostook R. (ȧ-rōōs'tŏŏk) Me.-Can.	46.40 N	68.18 W
152	Aroroy (ä-rô-rō'ê)..........Phil.	12.30 N	123.24 E
111	Arpaçay (är-pȧ-chä'ê)........Tur.	40.50 N	43.15 E
124	Arraiolos (är-rī-ō'lōzh)......Port.	38.45 N	7.59 W
114	Arran (I.) (ă'rȧn).......Gt. Brit.	55.35 N	5.15 W
122	Arras (ȧ-räs')................Fr.	50.20 N	2.45 E
101	Arrasuahi (är-rä-swä'ê).....Braz.	17.0 S	42.0 W
99	Arrecifes (är-rā-sē'fäs) Arg. (Buenos Aires In.)	34.0 S	60.8 W
122	Arrée Mts. (är-rā')...........Fr.	48.30 N	3.45 W
93	Arriaga (är-rê-ä'gä).........Mex.	16.14 N	93.56 W
54	Arrowhead (ăr'ō-hĕd).......Can.	50.47 N	117.47 W
73	Arrowhead, L. Calif. (Los Angeles In.)	34.16 N	117.12 W
73	Arrowhead Springs Calif. (Los Angeles In.)	34.12 N	117.15 W
71	Arrow R. (ăr'ō)............Mont.	47.29 N	110.0 W
70	Arrowrock Reservoir........Ida.	43.36 N	115.50 W
157	Arrowtown.................N. Z.	44.58 S	168.50 E
80	Arroyo de la Cadena (är-rō'yō dā lä kä-dā'nä).Mex.	26.15 N	104.0 W
80	Arroyo de la Zorro (är-rō'yō dā lä zôr'rō).Mex.	29.10 N	101.30 W
80	Arroyo del Bobo (är-rō'yō dĕl bō'bō).Mex.	28.25 N	101.0 W
124	Arroyo del Puerco (är-rō'yō dĕl pwĕr'kō).Sp.	39.27 N	6.32 W
92	Arroyo Seco (är-rō'yō sä'kō).Mex.	21.32 N	99.42 W
89	Arsenal I. (är'sē-nȧl) Ill. (St. Louis In.)	38.34 N	90.14 W
124	Arsila (är-sē'lä)............Mor.	35.29 N	6.2 W
127	Arta (är'tä).................Grc.	39.7 N	21.0 E
80	Arteaga (är-tā-ä'gä)........Mex.	25.28 N	100.50 W
124	Arteijo (är-tā'hō)............Sp.	43.18 N	8.29 W
96	Artemisa (är-tȧ-mē'sä)......Cuba	22.48 N	82.46 W
129	Artemovsk (är'tĕ-môfsk).Sov. Un.	48.36 N	38.0 E
78	Artesia (är-tē'sĭ-ȧ).........N. M.	32.52 N	104.23 W
159	Artesian Basin, The (är-tē'zhăn) Austl.	27.0 S	143.0 E
88	Arthur Kill (Inlet) N. J.-N. Y. (N. Y. In.)	40.36 N	74.12 W
157	Arthur Mt. (är'thŭr).......N. Z.	41.12 S	172.42 E
160	Arthur R..........Austl. (Tas. In.)	41.5 S	145.10 E
160	Arthurs Cr.Austl. (Melbourne In.)	37.42 S	145.9 E
97	Artibonite R. (är-tê-bô-nē'tä).Hai.	19.2 N	72.21 W
102	Artigas (är-tē'gäs)..........Ur.	32.40 S	53.24 W
133	Arua (ä'rōō-ä)...............Ug.	3.2 N	30.57 E
100	Aruba (I.) (ä-rōō'bȧ).......W. I.	12.30 N	70.0 W
158	Arunta Desert (ȧ-rōōn'tȧ)..Austl.	22.30 S	137.15 E
135	Arusha (ä-rōō'shȧ)..........Tan.	3.18 S	36.40 E
133	Aruwimi R. (ä-rōō-wē'mê) Bel. Cong.	1.30 N	27.15 E
72	Arvada (är-vă'dȧ) Colo. (Denver In.)	39.48 N	105.5 W
118	Arvika (är-vē'kȧ)............Swe.	59.39 N	12.36 E
110	Arzamas (är-zä-mäs')....Sov. Un.	55.20 N	43.45 E
112	Arzew (är-zȧ-ōō').............Alg.	35.52 N	0.19 W
124	Arzua (är-thōō'ä)............Sp.	42.55 N	8.10 W
120	Aš (ăsh')..................Czech.	50.12 N	12.12 E
132	Asaba (ä-sä'bä)..............Nig.	6.18 N	6.38 E
148	Asahigawa (ä-sä'hē-gä'wä)...Jap.	43.50 N	142.16 E
141	Asansol (ä-sän-sōl')........India	23.40 N	86.45 E
132	Asben (Air) (Reg.) (äs'bĕn) (ä'ēr) Fr. W. Afr.	18.35 N	9.0 E
110	Asbest (äs-bĕst')........Sov. Un.	57.2 N	61.30 E
85	Asbury Park (ăz'bĕr-ĭ)......N. J.	40.15 N	74.0 W
4	Ascension (I.) (ȧ-sĕn'shŭn).Atl. O.	7.57 S	14.22 W
92	Ascensión (äs-sĕn-sê-ōn')....Mex.	24.21 N	99.55 W
120	Aschaffenburg (ä-shäf'ĕn-bŏŏrgh) Ger.	49.59 N	9.10 E
120	Aschersleben (äsh'ĕrs-lā-bĕn).Ger.	51.45 N	11.27 E
126	AscoliPiceno(äs'kō-lēpē-chā'nō).It.	42.49 N	13.33 E
135	Ascot (ăs'kŏt).........U. S. Afr.	33.52 S	18.29 E
119	Aseri (ä'sĕ-rĭ)..........Sov. Un.	59.26 N	26.50 E
132	Asfi (Safi) (äs'fê) (sä'fê).....Mor.	32.24 N	9.12 W
132	Ashanti (Ter.) (ȧ-shăn'tê)...G. C.	7.30 N	1.30 W
116	Ashbourne (ăsh'bŭrn)...Gt. Brit.	53.1 N	1.44 W
82	Ashburn (ăsh'bŭrn)...........Ga.	31.42 N	83.41 W
157	Ashburton (ăsh'bûr-tŭn).....N. Z.	43.53 S	171.48 E
158	Ashburton R...............Austl.	23.15 S	116.30 E
116	Ashby-de-la-Zouch (ăsh-'bĭ-dē-lȧ-zōōsh').Gt. Brit.	52.45 N	1.28 W
79	Ashdown (ăsh'doun).........Ark.	33.41 N	94.7 W
83	Asheboro (ăsh'bŭr-ô).......N. C.	35.42 N	79.49 W
80	Asherton (ăsh'ēr-tŭn)........Tex.	28.26 N	99.46 W
83	Asheville (ăsh'vĭl)...........N. C.	35.35 N	82.34 W
149	Ashikaga (ä'shê-kä'gȧ).......Jap.	36.21 N	139.28 E
149	Ashio (Mines) (ä'shê-ō').....Jap.	36.48 N	139.28 E
149	Ashiya (ä'shē-yä')...........Jap.	33.55 N	130.40 E
137	Ashkelon (äsh'kȧ-lōn)...Pal. (In.)	31.40 N	34.33 E
140	Ashkhabad (ŭsh-Kä-bät').Sov. Un.	37.50 N	58.15 E
82	Ashland (ăsh'lănd)...........Ala.	33.16 N	85.50 W
78	Ashland....................Kan.	37.11 N	99.47 W
82	Ashland.....................Ky.	38.28 N	82.40 W
86	Ashland.....................Me.	46.37 N	68.25 W
87	Ashland...............Mass. (In.)	42.15 N	71.28 W
76	Ashland....................Neb.	41.2 N	96.22 W
84	Ashland....................Ohio	40.53 N	82.17 W
70	Ashland.....................Ore.	42.11 N	122.42 W
85	Ashland.....................Pa.	40.46 N	76.22 W
77	Ashland....................Wis.	46.35 N	90.54 W
76	Ashley (ăsh'lê)............N. D.	46.2 N	99.22 W
85	Ashley......................Pa.	41.12 N	75.54 W
131	Ashmant (äsh-mänt')....Eg. (In.)	29.17 N	31.15 E
150	Ashmore Reef (ăsh'mōr)..Indon.	12.15 S	122.30 E
131	Ashmûn (äsh-mōōn')....Eg. (In.)	30.19 N	30.59 E
88	Ashmun B. (ăsh'mŭn) Mich. (Sault Ste. Marie In.)	46.30 N	84.22 W
140	Ash Shihr (shēr)............Aden	14.50 N	44.50 E
84	Ashtabula (ăsh-tȧ-bū'lȧ).....Ohio	41.54 N	80.47 W

ng-sing; ŋ-baŋk; N-nasalized n; nŏd; cŏmmit; ōld; ôbey; ôrder; fōōd; fŏŏt; ou-out; s-soft; sh-dish; th-thin; pūre; ûnite; ûrn; stŭd; circŭs; ü-as "y" in study; '-indeterminate vowel.

Ashton PRONOUNCING INDEX **Bab-el-Mandeb**

Page	Name Pronunciation Region	Lat. °′	Long. °′
71	Ashton (ăsh'tŭn)....Ida.	44.4 N	111.29 W
116	Ashton-in-Makerfield (ăsh'tŭn-ĭn-māk'ēr-fēld). Gt. Brit.	53.29 N	2.39 W
117	Ashton-on-Mersey (ăsh'tŭn-ŏn-mûr'zĭ). Gt. Brit. (Liverpool In.)	53.25 N	2.18 W
116	Ashton-under-Lyne (ăsh'tŭn-ŭn-dēr-līn'). Gt. Brit.	53.29 N	2.4 W
55	Ashuanipi L. (ăsh-wȧ-nĭp'ĭ)..Can.	52.15 N	66.15 W
86	Ashuapmuchuan R. (ăsh-wăp-mōō-chwän'). Que.	49.8 N	73.6 W
136	Asia (ā'shȧ)		
111	Asia Minor (Reg.)....Asia	38.45 N	34.30 E
153	Asid G. (ä-sĭd')....Phil.	12.5 N	123.30 E
92	Asientos (ä-sê-ĕn'tōs)....Mex.	22.14 N	102.7 W
126	Asinara, G. of (ä-sē-nä'rä)...Sard.	40.55 N	8.35 E
126	Asinara I....Sard.	41.5 N	8.20 E
140	Asir (ä-sēr')....Sau. Ar.	17.30 N	43.0 E
118	Askersund (äs'kĕr-sōōnd)....Swe.	58.53 N	14.54 E
86	Askitichi, L. (ăs-kĭ-tĭ'chĭ)....Can.	49.12 N	74.8 W
111	Asmantai-Matai, L. (ăs-män-tä'ĭ-mä-tä'ĭ). Sov. Un.	45.45 N	57.15 E
133	Asmara (äs-mä'rä)....Erit.	15.20 N	39.0 .E
118	Asne L. (ôs'nĕ)....Swe.	56.35 N	14.45 E
123	Asnières (ä-nyâr')....Fr. (In.)	48.54 N	2.17 E
70	Asotin (ȧ-sō'tĭn)....Wash.	46.19 N	117.3 W
125	Aspe (äs'pā)....Sp.	38.21 N	0.45 W
78	Aspen (ăs'pĕn)....Colo.	39.11 N	106.50 W
160	Aspendale (ăs'pĕn-dāl) Austl. (Melbourne In.)	38.2 S	145.6 E
157	Aspiring Mt. (ăs-pīr'ĭng)....N. Z.	44.18 S	168.50 E
117	Aspull (ăs'pōōl) Gt. Brit. (Liverpool In.)	53.35 N	2.35 W
87	Aspy B. (ăs'pê)....Can.	46.55 N	60.28 W
133	Assab (ȧs-säb')....Erit.	13.0 N	42.35 E
141	Assam (Prov.) (ăs-săm')....India	25.30 N	92.0 E
113	Assel (äs-sĕl')....Libya	30.58 N	17.32 E
118	Assens (äs'sĕns)....Den.	55.15 N	9.53 E
54	Assiniboine R. (ă-sĭn'ĭ-boin). Can.	49.35 N	98.45 W
132	Assinie (ȧ-sê-nē')....Fr. W. Afr.	5.7 N	3.11 W
127	Astakos (äs'tä-kôs)....Grc.	38.41 N	20.58 E
140	Asterabad (äs'tĕ-rä-băd')....Iran	36.47 N	54.32 E
126	Asti (äs'tē)....It.	44.54 N	8.12 E
124	Astorga (äs-tôr'gä)....Sp.	42.27 N	6.5 W
70	Astoria (ăs-tō'rĭ-ȧ)....Ore.	46.10 N	123.49 W
111	Astrakhan (äs-trȧ-ĸän')..Sov. Un.	46.20 N	48.0 E
134	Astrida (äs-trē'dȧ)....Bel. Cong.	2.38 S	29.48 E
153	Asturias (äs-tōō'rê-äs)....Phil.	10.34 N	123.43 E
124	Asturias (Reg.)....Sp.	43.20 N	6.0 W
102	Asunción (ä-sōōn-syōn')....Par.	25.15 S	57.40 W
93	Asunción (Ixtaltepec)....Mex.	16.30 N	95.1 W
93	Asunción (Nochixtlan)....Mex.	17.27 N	97.13 W
153	Asuncion Pass....Phil.	11.5 N	123.30 E
133	Aswân Dam (ä-swän')....Eg.	23.45 N	32.50 E
133	Aswân (Syene) (ä-swän') (sê-ā'nĕ) Eg.	24.7 N	32.58 E
133	Asyût (ä-syōōt')....Eg.	27.10 N	31.10 E
132	Atakpamé (ä'tȧk-pȧ-mā') Fr. W. Afr.	7.36 N	1.05 E
127	Atalante Chan. (ä-tȧ-län'tê)..Grc.	38.40 N	23.20 E
82	Atalla (ă-tăl'ȧ)....Ala.	34.2 N	86.5 W
132	Atar (ä-tär')....Fr. W. Afr.	20.37 N	13.8 W
74	Atascadero (ăt-ăs-kȧ-dâ'rō). Calif.	35.27 N	120.41 W
80	Atascosa R. (ăt-ăs-kō'sȧ)....Tex.	29.0 N	98.30 W
93	Atasta de Sera (ä-täs'tä dā sā'rä) Mex.	17.58 N	92.57 W
133	Atbara (ät'bȧ-rä)....A. E. Sud.	17.45 N	34.0 E
133	Atbara R....A. E. Sud.	16.0 N	35.33 E
138	Atbasar (ät'bä-sär')....Sov. Un.	51.50 N	68.25 E
81	Atchafalaya B. (ăch-ȧ-fȧ-lī'ȧ). La.	29.25 N	91.15 W
81	Atchafalaya R....La.	30.40 N	91.45 W
79	Atchison (ăch'ĭ-sŭn)....Kan.	39.33 N	95.8 W
100	Ate (ä'tā)....Peru (In.)	12.4 S	76.58 W
93	Atempan (ä-tĕm-pän')....Mex.	19.50 N	97.26 W
92	Atenco, R. de (ä-tĕŋ'kō)....Mex.	22.30 N	104.6 W
54	Athabaska L. (ăth-ȧ-băs'kȧ). Can.	59.15 N	110.0 W
54	Athabaska R....Can.	55.45 N	112.45 W
127	Athēnai (Athens) (ȧ-thē'nā)..Grc.	37.54 N	23.52 E
82	Athens (ăth'ĕnz)....Ala.	34.48 N	86.59 W
82	Athens....Ga.	33.57 N	83.25 W
127	Athens (Athēnai)....Grc.	37.54 N	23.52 E
84	Athens....Ohio	39.23 N	82.9 W
85	Athens....Pa.	41.59 N	76.30 W
82	Athens....Tenn.	35.36 N	84.37 W
81	Athens....Tex.	32.13 N	95.51 W
116	Atherstone (ăth'ēr-stŭn). Gt. Brit.	52.34 N	1.32 W
117	Atherton (ăth'ēr-tŭn) Gt. Brit. (Liverpool In.)	53.31 N	2.29 W
116	Atherton....Gt. Brit.	53.32 N	2.30 W
159	Atherton Plat....Austl.	17.50 S	144.30 E
135	Athi R. (ä'tê)....Kenya	3.0 S	38.40 E
123	Athis-Mons (ȧ-tēs'môɴ'). Fr. (In.)	48.42 N	2.23 E
114	Athlone (ăth-lōn')....Ire.	53.25 N	7.55 W
157	Athol (ăth'ŏl)....N. Z.	45.30 S	108.38 E
127	Athos, Mt. (ăth'ŏs)....Grc.	40.7 N	24.19 E
114	Athy (ȧ-thī)....Ire.	52.55 N	6.55 W
133	Ati (ȧ-tē')....Fr. Eq. Afr.	13.16 N	18.6 E
152	Atimonan (ä-tê-mō'nän)....Phil.	14.0 N	121.55 E
94	Atiquizaya (ä'tê-kê-zä'yä)....Sal.	14.0 N	89.41 W
94	Atitlan, L. (ä-tê-tlän')....Guat.	14.40 N	91.10 W
94	Atitlan (Vol.)....Guat.	14.30 N	91.12 W
93	Atizapán (ä'tê-zȧ-pän'). Mex. (In.)	19.34 N	99.15 W
52	Atka I. (ăt'kȧ)....Alsk.	52.10 N	174.30 W
111	Atkarsk (ät'kȧrsk)....Sov. Un.	51.48 N	45.0 E
76	Atkinson (ăt'kĭn-sŭn)....Neb.	42.33 N	98.58 W
82	Atlanta (ăt-lăn'tȧ)....Ga.	33.45 N	84.25 W
73	Atlanta, Ga. (In.)		
79	Atlanta....Tex.	33.08 N	94.10 W
77	Atlantic (ăt-lăn'tĭk)....Ia.	41.24 N	95.0 W
85	Atlantic City....N. J.	39.21 N	74.27 W
4	Atlantic Ocean		
93	Atlapulco (ät-lä-pōōl'kô) Mex. (In.)	19.15 N	99.3 W
112	Atlas, High (Mts.) (ăt'lăs)...Mor.	32.30 N	4.35 W
112	Atlas, Little (Mts.)....Alg.	35.25 N	2.10 E
112	Atlas, Middle (Mts.)....Mor.	33.0 N	5.0 W
132	Atlas Mts....Mor.-Alg.	32.30 N	2.0 W
112	Atlas, Saharan (Mts.)....Mor.	34.0 N	1.0 E
118	Atle I. (ät'lĕ)....Nor.	61.22 N	5.0 E
92	Atliaca (ät-lê-ä'kä)....Mex.	17.42 N	99.23 W
54	Atlin L. (ăt'lĭn)....Can.	59.45 N	133.40 W
92	Atlixco (ät-lēz'kō)....Mex.	18.54 N	98.27 W
82	Atmore (ăt'mōr)....Ala.	31.1 N	87.32 W
79	Atoka (ȧ-tō'kȧ)....Okla.	34.23 N	96.8 W
92	Atotonilco el Alto (ä'tô-tô-nēl'kō ĕl äl'tō). Mex.	20.37 N	102.27 W
92	Atotonilco el Grande (ä'tô-tô-nēl'-kō ĕl grän'dā). Mex.	20.17 N	98.40 W
132	Atoui R. (ȧ-tōō-ē')....Fr. W. Afr.	21.0 N	15.40 W
92	Atoyac (ä-tô-yäk')....Mex.	20.0 N	103.29 W
92	Atoyac de Alvarez (ä-tô-yäk' dā äl'vä-rāz). Mex.	17.12 N	100.26 W
92	Atoyac, R....Mex.	18.40 N	98.0 W
93	Atoyatempan (ä-tō'yȧ-tĕm-pän') Mex.	18.48 N	97.55 W
118	Ätra R. (ĕt'rä)....Swe.	57.6 N	12.50 E
100	Atrato, R. (ä-trä'tō)....Colo.	7.30 N	77.0 W
140	Atrek R. (ä'trĕk)....Iran	37.45 N	56.30 E
149	Atsuta (ät'sōō-tä)....Jap.	35.7 N	136.54 E
148	Atsuta B....Jap.	34.45 N	136.45 E
55	Attawapiskat R. (ăt'ȧ-wȧ-pĭs'kăt) Can.	52.45 N	86.30 W
85	Attica (ăt'ĭ-kȧ)....N. Y.	42.55 N	78.17 W
55	Attikonak L. (ăt'ĭ-kō-năk'). Can..	52.45 N	64.32 W
86	Attleboro (ăt''l-bŭr-ô)....Mass.	41.55 N	71.15 W
52	Attu Is. (ät-tōō')....Alsk.	52.50 N	173.0 E
102	Atuel, R. (ä-tōō-ĕl')....Arg.	35.40 S	67.30 W
151	Atulayan I. (ä-tōō-lä-yän') Phil. (Manila In.)	14.25 N	121.13 E
118	Atvidaberg (ôt-vē'dȧ-bĕrgh)..Swe.	58.11 N	15.57 E
78	Atwood (ăt'wōōd)....Kan.	39.49 N	101.6 W
93	Atzcapotzalco (ät'zkä-pô-tzäl'kō) Mex. (In.)	19.29 N	99.11 W
93	Atzcapotzaltongo (ät'zkä-pô-tzäl-tôŋ'gō). Mex. (In.)	19.38 N	99.19 W
155	Auau Chan. (ä'ōō-ä'ōō)....Haw.	20.55 N	156.45 W
134	Auaz Mts. (ä'wäs)....S. W. Afr.	22.45 S	17.15 E
123	Aubagne (ō-bän'y')....Fr.	43.18 N	5.35 E
123	Aube R. (ōb)....Fr.	48.35 N	4.0 E
122	Aubenas (ōb'-näs')....Fr.	44.38 N	4.22 E
123	Aubervilliers (ō-bĕr-vē-yā') Fr. (In.)	48.54 N	2.24 E
122	Aubière (ō-byâr')....Fr.	45.44 N	3.5 E
122	Aubigny-sur-Nère (ō-bēn-yē' sür-nâr'). Fr.	47.30 N	2.28 E
122	Aubin (ō-băɴ')....Fr.	44.30 N	2.15 E
82	Auburn (ô'bŭrn)....Ala.	32.35 N	85.30 W
74	Auburn....Calif.	38.54 N	121.5 W
79	Auburn....Ill.	39.35 N	89.45 W
84	Auburn....Ind.	41.22 N	85.2 W
86	Auburn....Me.	44.12 N	70.15 W
87	Auburn....Mass. (In.)	42.11 N	71.50 W
79	Auburn....Neb.	40.24 N	95.51 W
85	Auburn....N. Y.	42.55 N	76.36 W
70	Auburn....Wash.	47.16 N	122.15 W
122	Aubusson (ō-bü-sôɴ')....Fr.	45.58 N	2.10 E
122	Auch (ōsh)....Fr.	43.39 N	0.35 E
82	Aucilla, R. (ô-sĭl'ȧ)....Fla.	30.25 N	83.45 W
156	Auckland (ôk'lănd)....N. Z. (In.)	36.52 S	174.45 E
47	Auckland Is....Pac. O.	50.30 S	166.30 E
122	Aude R. (ōd)....Fr.	43.5 N	2.15 E
122	Audierne (ō-dyĕrn')....Fr.	48.0 N	4.30 W
123	Audincourt (ō-dăɴ-kōōr')....Fr.	47.30 N	6.50 E
116	Audley (ôd'lĭ)....Gt. Brit.	53.3 N	2.18 W
77	Audubon (ô'dōō-bŏn)....Ia.	41.44 N	94.55 W
120	Aue (ou'ē)....Ger.	50.36 N	12.44 E
134	Aughrabies Falls (ô-grä'bês) U. S. Afr.	28.30 S	20.15 E
117	Aughton (ô'tŭn) Gt. Brit. (Liverpool In.)	53.32 N	2.55 W
133	Augila (ou-jē'lȧ)....Libya	29.6 N	21.11 E
113	Augila Oasis....Libya	29.15 N	21.15 E
120	Augsburg (ouks'bōōrgh)....Ger.	48.23 N	10.53 E
79	Augusta (ô-gŭs'tȧ)....Ark.	35.17 N	91.21 W
83	Augusta....Ga.	33.28 N	81.59 W
79	Augusta....Kan.	37.40 N	96.59 W
84	Augusta....Ky.	38.45 N	84.0 W
86	Augusta....Me.	44.19 N	69.50 W
77	Augusta....Wis.	44.41 N	91.8 W
121	Augustów (ou-gōōs'tōōf)....Pol.	53.50 N	22.59 E
133	Auk, R. (ouk)....Fr. Eq. Afr.	9.38 N	20.0 E
123	Aulnay-s-Bois (ō-nĕ'sōō-bwä') Fr. (In.)	48.56 N	2.30 E
72	Ault (ôlt)....Colo. (Denver In.)	40.35 N	104.44 W
122	Aune R. (ōn)....Fr.	48.15 N	4.0 W
134	Auob R. (ä'wŏb). S.W.Afr.-U.S.Afr.	25.45 S	19.43 E
156	Aupaki L. (ô-pä'kĭ)....N. Z. (In.)	36.47 S	174.46 E
141	Aurangabad (ou-rŭŋ-gä-bäd'). India	19.55 N	75.55 E
122	Auray (ō-rĕ')....Fr.	47.41 N	31.0 W
118	Aurdal, S. (our'däl)....Nor.	60.55 N	9.28 E
112	Aures, Jebel (Mts.) (jĕb'ĕl ō-rĕs') Alg.	35.25 N	6.30 E
122	Aurillac (ō-rē-yȧk')....Fr.	44.55 N	2.29 E
72	Aurora (ô-rō'rȧ). Colo. (Denver In.)	39.45 N	104.53 W
79	Aurora....Ill.	41.45 N	88.19 W
84	Aurora....Ind.	39.5 N	84.56 W
77	Aurora....Minn.	47.31 N	92.16 W
79	Aurora....Mo.	36.58 N	93.42 W
76	Aurora....Neb.	40.52 N	98.1 W
85	Aurora, E....N. Y.	42.49 N	78.39 W
159	Aurora I....New Hebr.	15.0 S	168.8 E
84	Au Sable R. (ô-sā'b'l)....Mich.	44.37 N	83.50 W
85	Ausable R....N. Y.	44.25 N	73.46 W
73	Austell (ôs-têl')..Ga. (Atlanta In.)	33.48 N	84.38 W
77	Austin (ôs'tĭn)....Minn.	43.40 N	92.58 W
74	Austin....Nev.	38.29 N	117.5 W
81	Austin....Tex.	30.16 N	97.43 W
81	Austin Bayou (ôs'tĭn bī-ōō') Tex. (In.)	29.15 N	95.20 W
158	Austin, L....Austl.	27.40 S	118.10 E
	Austral Is., see Tubuaï Is.		
158	Australia (ôs-trā'lĭ-ȧ)		
158	Australia, Western (State)..Austl.	25.0 S	120.0 E
120	Austria (ôs'trĭ-ȧ)....Eur.	47.20 N	13.20 E
117	Austruweel (ous-trû-vāl') Bel. (Anvers In.)	51.15 N	4.23 E
92	Autlán (ä-ōōt-län')....Mex.	19.47 N	104.21 W
122	Autun (ō-tŭɴ')....Fr.	46.59 N	4.19 E
122	Auvergne Mts. (ō-vĕrn'y')....Fr.	45.20 N	2.40 E
123	Auvers-s-Oise (ō-vâr'sūr-wäz') Fr. (In.)	49.4 N	2.11 E
122	Auxerre (ō-sâr')....Fr.	47.49 N	3.35 E
123	Auxonne (ō-sôn')....Fr.	47.15 N	5.25 E
79	Ava (ā'vȧ)....Mo.	36.57 N	92.39 W
133	Avakubi (ä-vȧ-kōō'bê). Bel. Cong.	1.21 N	27.32 E
156	Avalli I. (ȧ-văl'lê)....N. Z.	35.0 S	174.0 E
122	Avallon (ȧ-vȧ-lôɴ')....Fr.	47.29 N	3.53 E
74	Avalon (ăv'ȧ-lŏn)....Calif.	33.20 N	118.21 W
89	Avalon....Pa. (Pittsburgh In.)	40.30 N	80.4 W
101	Avari, L. (ȧ-vä'rê)....Braz. (In.)	0.40 S	49.20 W
124	Aveiro (ä-vā'rōō)....Port.	40.39 N	8.39 W
102	Avellaneda (ä-vĕl-yä-nā'dhä) Arg. (In.)	34.40 S	58.21 W
126	Avellino (ä-vĕl-lē'nō)....It.	40.55 N	14.50 E
118	Aver I. (ä'vēr)....Nor.	63.0 N	7.35 E
126	Aversa (ä-vĕr'sä)....It.	40.58 N	14.12 E
79	Avery (ā'vēr-ĭ)....Tex.	33.33 N	94.46 W
118	Avesta (ä-vĕs'tä)....Swe.	60.8 N	16.10 E
126	Avezzano (ä-vȧt-sä'nō)....It.	42.3 N	13.24 E
126	Avigliano (ä-vēl-yä'nō)....It.	40.44 N	15.43 E
122	Avignon (ȧ-vē-nyôɴ')....Fr.	43.55 N	4.50 E
124	Avila (ä'vê-lä)....Sp.	40.38 N	4.42 W
124	Avilés (ä-vê-lās')....Sp.	43.34 N	5.57 W
76	Avoca (ȧ-vō'kȧ)....Ia.	41.30 N	95.20 W
85	Avon (ā'vŏn)....Conn.	41.49 N	72.51 W
87	Avon....Mass. (In.)	41.8 N	71.2 W
73	Avon...Utah (Salt Lake City In.)	41.32 N	111.48 W
156	Avondale (ăv'ŏn-dāl)..N. Z. (In.)	36.54 S	174.42 E
83	Avon Park (ā'vŏn pärk'). Fla. (In.)	27.35 N	81.28 W
114	Avon, R....Gt. Brit.	51.0 N	1.50 W
157	Avon R....N. Z. (In.)	43.31 S	172.41 E
122	Avranches (ȧ-vräɴsh')....Fr.	48.40 N	1.20 W
149	Awaji I. (ä'wä-jê)....Jap.	34.20 N	134.52 E
133	Awash R. (ȧ-wäsh')....Eth.	10.0 N	40.22 E
157	Awatere R. (ä-wä-tā'rā)....N. Z.	41.53 S	173.40 E
116	Axe Edge (Mt.) (ăks'ĕj). Gt. Brit.	53.13 N	1.55 W
116	Axholme, Isle of (ăks'hōm). Gt. Brit.	53.33 N	0.48 W
122	Ax-les Thermes (äks'lā tĕrm')..Fr.	42.45 N	1.50 E
92	Axochiapan (äks-ō-chyä'pän). Mex.	18.30 N	98.45 W
122	Ay (ȧ'ê)....Fr.	49.5 N	4.0 E
149	Ayabe (ä'yä-bĕ)....Jap.	35.15 N	135.16 E
102	Ayacucho (ä-yä-kōō'chō)....Arg.	37.10 S	58.30 W
100	Ayacucho....Peru	13.0 S	74.16 W
138	Ayaguzkiy (ä-yȧ-gōōz'kĭ). Sov. Un.	48.5 N	80.20 E
118	Ayamonte (ä-yä-mōn'tā)....Sp.	37.14 N	7.25 W
100	Ayata (ä-yä'tä)....Bol.	15.5 S	68.45 W
83	Ayden (ā'dĕn)....N. C.	35.28 N	77.26 W
111	Aydin (ȧ'ĭ-dĭn)....Tur.	37.55 N	27.55 E
87	Ayer (âr)....Mass. (In.)	42.33 N	71.36 W
114	Aylesbury (ālz'bēr-ĭ)....Gt. Brit.	51.50 N	0.45 W
85	Aylmer (āl'mēr)....Can.	45.26 N	75.56 W
54	Aylmer L....Can.	64.15 N	108.30 W
92	Ayo el Chico (ä'yô ĕl chē'kō). Mex.	20.33 N	102.20 W
125	Ayora (ä-yō'rä)....Sp.	39.5 N	1.4 W
93	Ayotla (ä-yōt'lä)....Mex. (In.)	19.19 N	98.56 W
114	Ayr (âr)....Gt. Brit.	55.25 N	4.37 W
114	Ayr, R....Gt. Brit.	55.30 N	4.25 W
93	Ayucan (ä-yōō'kän)....Mex. (In.)	19.31 N	99.22 W
150	Ayudhyâ (ȧ-yōōt'hē'ä)....Siam	14.17 N	100.33 E
153	Ayuquitan (ä-yōō-kē'tän)....Phil.	9.24 N	123.14 E
94	Ayutla (ä-yōōt'lä)....Guat.	14.44 N	92.11 W
92	Ayutla....Mex.	16.51 N	99.15 W
92	Ayutla....Mex.	20.10 N	104.19 W
111	Ayvalik (ȧĭ-vä'lêk)....Tur.	39.18 N	26.50 E
132	Azemmour (ȧ-zē-mōōr')....Mor.	33.20 N	8.15 W
111	Azerbaidzhan (Soviet Rep.) (ä'zēr-bä-ê-jän'). Sov. Un.	40.50 N	47.0 E
100	Azogues (ä-sō'gās)....Ec.	2.45 S	78.32 W
132	Azores (Is.) (ȧ-zōrz'). Atl. O. (In.)	38.30 N	28.0 W
129	Azov (ȧ-zôf') (ä'zôf)....Sov. Un.	47.6 N	39.22 E
129	Azov, Sea of....Sov. Un.	45.50 N	36.22 E
92	Azoyú (ä-zô-yōō')....Mex.	16.37 N	98.39 W
112	Azrou (ȧz-rōō')....Mor.	32.28 N	5.12 W
75	Aztec (ăz'tĕk)....N. M.	36.48 N	108.1 W
75	Aztec Ruin Natl. Mon....N. M.	36.51 N	108.5 W
97	Azua (ä'swä)....Dom. Rep.	18.27 N	70.46 W
124	Azuaga (ä-thwä'gä)....Sp.	38.15 N	5.41 W
95	Azuero Pen. (ä-swā'rō)....Pan.	7.40 N	80.35 W
102	Azufre, Cerro del (Copiapó) (Vol.) (sĕr'rō dĕl ä-sōō'frā) (kō-pê-äpō'). Chl.	27.15 S	69.10 W
100	Azufrera (ä-sōō-frā'rä)....Peru	6.6 S	80.53 W
102	Azul (ä-sōōl')....Arg.	36.48 S	59.50 W
73	Azusa (ȧ-zōō'sȧ) Calif. (Los Angeles In.)	34.8 N	117.54 W
137	Baakline (bäk-lēn')....Leb. (In.)	33.43 N	34.34 E
137	Baalbeck (Heliopolis) (bäl'-bĕk) (hē-lĭ-ŏp'ô-lĭs). Leb. (In.)	33.59 N	36.9 E
152	Baao (bä'ō)....Phil.	13.27 N	123.22 E
127	Babaeski (bä'bä-ĕs'kĭ)....Tur.	41.24 N	27.5 E
100	Babahoyo (bä-bä-ō'yō)....Ec.	2.0 S	79.30 W
129	Babaikovka (bä'bȧ-ĭ-kôf'kȧ) Sov. Un.	49.0 N	34.30 E
151	Babar Is. (bä'bȧr)....Indon.	8.0 S	129.45 E
140	Bab-el-Mandeb (Str.) (bäb' ĕl män'dĕb). Asia	12.30 N	44.0 E

ăt; finăl; rāte; senâte; ärm; ȧsk; sofȧ; fâre; ch-choose; dh-as th in other; bē; êvent; bĕt; recĕnt; cratēr; g-go; gh-gutteral g; bĭt; ĭ-short neutral; rīde; ĸ-gutteral k as ch in German ich;

Page	Name Pronunciation Region	Lat. °′	Long. °′
80	Babia, R. de la (rē'ō dä lä bä'bē-ȧ). Mex.	28.36 N	102.0 W
54	Babine L. (băb'ēn) Can.	55.0 N	126.30 W
54	Babine Mts Can.	55.0 N	127.30 W
140	Babol (bä-bōl') Iran	36.30 N	52.50 E
152	BabuyanChan. (bä-bōō-yän'). Phil.	18.40 N	121.40 E
152	Babuyan I Phil.	19.30 N	121.55 E
152	Babuyan Is Phil.	19.10 N	121.30 E
127	Babjak (bäb'zhȧk) Bul.	41.58 N	23.41 E
140	Babylon (Ruins) (băb'ĭ-lŏn). Iraq	32.45 N	44.30 E
101	Bacabal (bä-kä-bäl') Braz.	5.20 S	56.14 W
152	Bacacay (bä-kä-kī') Phil.	13.17 N	123.47 E
94	Bacalar, L. (bä-kä-lär') Br. Hond.-Mex. (In.)	18.45 N	88.30 W
152	Bacarra (bä-kär'rä) Phil.	18.16 N	120.37 E
121	Bacău (bȧ'kȧ-ōō) Rom.	46.33 N	26.57 E
123	Baccarat (bȧ-kȧ-rȧ') Fr.	48.30 N	6.45 E
73	Bacchus (băk'ŭs) Utah (Salt Lake City In.)	40.40 N	112.6 W
93	Bachajón (bä-chä-hōn') Mex.	17.8 N	92.17 W
141	Back B. (băk). India (Bombay In.)	18.55 N	72.48 E
88	Back R Md. (Baltimore In.)	39.16 N	76.26 W
89	Back R S. C. (Savannah In.)	32.6 N	81.5 W
54	Backs R. (băks) Can.	66.30 N	97.0 W
158	Backstairs Passage (băk-stârs' păs'sĕj). Austl.	35.40 S	138.10 E
150	Bacninh (bäk'nēn'') Indoch.	21.7 N	106.8 E
152	Bacnotan (bäk-nō-tän') Phil.	16.42 N	120.22 E
152	Baco, Mt. (bä'kō) Phil.	12.51 N	121.12 E
117	Bacoli (bä-kō-lē'). It. (Napoli In.)	40.48 N	14.5 E
153	Bacolod (bä-kō'lōd) Phil.	10.39 N	122.57 E
152	Bacolor (bä-kō-lōr') Phil.	15.1 N	120.39 E
152	Bacon (bä-kōn') Phil.	13.2 N	124.2 E
51	Bacona (bä-kō'nȧ) Ore. (Portland In.)	45.46 N	123.8 W
153	Bacong (bä-kông') Phil.	9.14 N	123.17 E
152	Bacoor (bä-kō-ōr') Phil.	14.27 N	120.57 E
151	Bacoor Phil. (Manila In.)	14.28 N	120.55 E
121	Bacsalmás (bäch'ōl-mäs) Hung.	46.7 N	19.19 E
153	Bacuit (bä-kōō-ēt') Phil.	11.11 N	119.24 E
153	Bacuit B Phil.	11.7 N	119.22 E
116	Bacup (băk'ŭp) Gt. Brit.	53.42 N	2.12 W
76	Bad R. (băd) S. D.	44.5 N	101.0 W
125	Badalona (bä-dhä-lō'nä). Sp. (In.)	41.27 N	2.15 E
124	Badajoz (bä-dhä-hōth') Sp.	38.52 N	6.58 W
141	Badakhshan (Aut. Area) (bŭd-ŭk-shän'). Sov. Un.	37.30 N	73.15 E
131	Badâri (bä-dä'rē) Eg. (In.)	27.0 N	31.29 E
84	Bad Axe (băd' ăks) Mich.	43.48 N	82.56 W
120	Baden (bä'dĕn) Aus.	48.1 N	16.13 E
120	Baden (State) Ger.	48.48 N	8.18 E
120	Baden Switz.	47.27 N	8.17 E
153	Badian (bä-dē-än') Phil.	9.51 N	123.24 E
83	Badin (bă'dĭn) N. C.	35.24 N	80.6 W
120	Bad Ischl (bät ĭsh''l) Aus.	47.44 N	13.35 E
120	Bad Kissingen (bät kĭs'ĭng-ĕn) Ger.	50.12 N	10.4 E
120	Bad Kreuznach (bät kroits'näκ) Ger.	49.51 N	7.51 E
76	Bad Lands (băd' lănds) S. D.	43.43 N	102.30 W
152	Badoc (bä-dōk') Phil.	17.56 N	120.30 E
120	Bad Oldesloe (bät ōl'dĕs-lōē). Ger.	53.48 N	10.21 E
71	Badwater Cr. (băd'wô-tēr). Wyo.	43.16 N	107.50 W
124	Baena (bä-ā'nä) Sp.	37.37 N	4.19 W
101	Baependi (bä-pĕn'dĭ) Braz.	21.59 S	44.59 W
50	Baffin B. (băf'ĭn) Can.	72.0 N	65.0 W
81	Baffin Bay Tex.	27.15 N	97.35 W
55	Baffin I Can.	67.20 N	71.0 W
132	Bafoulabé (bȧ-fōō-lä-bā') Fr. W. Afr.	13.56 N	10.48 W
140	Bafq (bäfk) Iran	31.50 N	55.29 E
111	Bafra (bäf'rä) Tur.	41.31 N	35.58 E
111	Bafra, C Tur.	41.40 N	35.59 E
152	Bagabag (bä-gä-bäg') Phil.	16.37 N	121.15 E
135	Bagamoyo (bä-gä-mō'yō) Tan.	6.20 S	38.50 E
153	Baganga (bä-gäŋ'gä) Phil.	7.33 N	126.34 E
153	Baganian Pen. (bä-gä'nĭ-ȧn). Phil.	7.25 N	123.25 E
102	Bagé (bä-gā') Braz.	31.28 S	54.10 W
141	Bagh (bäκ) Pak.	33.48 N	70.45 E
140	Baghdad (bȧgh-dȧd') (băg'dăd) Iraq	33.15 N	44.30 E
126	Bagheria (bä-gȧ-rē'ä) It.	38.4 N	13.31 E
76	Bagley (băg'lē) Minn.	47.31 N	95.21 W
126	Bagnara (bän-yä'rä) It.	38.17 N	15.49 E
122	Bagnères-de-Biggorre (bän-yâr' dē bē-gōr'). Fr.	43.5 N	0.10 E
122	Bagnères-de-Luchon (bän-yâr' dē lü-chôN'). Fr.	42.45 N	0.35 E
122	Bagneux (bän-yû') Fr. (In.)	48.47 N	2.18 E
117	Bagnoli (bän'yō-lē). It. (Napoli In.)	40.49 N	14.10 E
122	Bagnols (bä-nyōl') Fr.	44.10 N	4.40 E
153	Bago (bä'gō) Phil.	10.31 N	122.51 E
132	Bagoe, R. (bȧ-gō'ā) Fr. W. Afr.	11.30 N	6.30 W
151	Bagombon (bä-gōm'bōn) Phil. (Manila In.)	14.23 N	121.27 E
86	Bagotville (bȧ-gō-vēl') Can.	48.19 N	70.54 W
142	Bagrach Kol (L.) (bä'grăch kûl') Chn.	42.0 N	87.0 E
132	Baguezane Mts. (bȧ-gē-zän') Fr. W. Afr.	17.50 N	8.40 E
152	Baguio (bä-gē-ō') Phil.	16.25 N	120.36 E
96	Bahama I. (bȧ-hā'mȧ) Ba. Is.	26.40 N	78.20 W
96	Bahama Is Atl. O.	23.30 N	75.0 W
113	Bahariya Oasis (bȧ-hä-rē'yä). Eg.	28.0 N	29.0 E
141	Bahawalpur (bŭ-hä'wŭl-pōōr) Pak.	29.15 N	71.33 E
101	Bahia (State) (bä-ē'ȧ) Braz.	12.30 S	42.0 W
102	Bahia Blanca (bä-ē'ä bläŋ'kä) Arg.	38.45 S	62.1 W
102	Bahia Blanca (B.) Arg.	39.28 S	61.45 W
100	Bahia de Caráquez (bä-ē'ä dā kä-rä'kĕz). Ec.	0.45 S	80.29 W
101	Bahia Negra (bä-ē'ä nä'grä). Par.	20.1 S	58.15 W

Page	Name Pronunciation Region	Lat. °′	Long. °′
131	Bahnasa (bä'nȧ-sȧ) Eg. (In.)	28.40 N	30.51 E
97	Bahoruco, Mts. of (bä-ō-rōō'kō) Hai.	18.5 N	71.25 W
140	Bahr As Safi (Des.) (bär' äs sä'-fē). Arabia	17.30 N	48.0 E
140	Bahrein I. (bä-rān') Asia	26.10 N	50.40 E
133	Bahr el Abyad (White Nile) (R.) (bär ĕl äb'yȧd). A. E. Sud.	13.0 N	32.45 E
133	Bahr el Arab (R.) (bär ĕl ä'rȧb) A. E. Sud.	9.45 N	27.30 E
133	Bahr el Azraq (Blue Nile) (R.) (äz-rȧk'). A. E. Sud.-Eth.	13.0 N	34.0 E
133	Bahr Azum (R.) (ä-zōōm') Fr. Eq. Afr.	11.20 N	20.30 E
133	Bahr el Ghazal (Reg.) (gȧ-zäl') A. E. Sud.	7.30 N	27.30 E
133	Bahr el Ghazal (R.) A. E. Sud.	9.25 N	30.0 E
133	Bahr el Jebel (Mountain Nile) (R.) (jĕb'ĕl). Afr.	7.0 N	31.0 E
133	Bahr Sara (R.) (sȧ-rä') Fr. Eq. Afr.	8.0 N	17.36 E
	Baia, see Salvador, Braz.		
117	Baia (bä'yä). It. (Napoli In.)	40.49 N	14.5 E
121	Baia-de-Cris (bä'yȧ dä krēs'). Rom.	46.10 N	22.40 E
121	Baia-Mare (bä'yȧ-mä'rā). Rom.	47.40 N	23.36 E
138	Baidaratskaya B. (bī-dȧ-rät-skȧ'yȧ). Sov. Un.	69.15 N	67.30 E
142	Baidarik Gol (R.) (bī'dȧ-rĭk gōl'). Mong.	46.0 N	99.10 E
135	Baidoa (bä-ĭ-dō'ä) Som.	3.7 N	43.38 E
86	Baie St. Paul (bā'sănt-pôl'). Can.	47.27 N	70.31 W
139	Baikal, L. (bī'kăl') (bī'kôl) Sov. Un.	54.0 N	108.40 E
139	Baikal Mts Sov. Un.	54.0 N	108.0 E
129	Baikiyat (bī-kē'ät) Sov. Un.	45.40 N	33.0 E
114	Baile Atha Cliath (Dublin) (bŏ'lĕ ô'hŏ clē'ŏh) (dŭb'lĭn). Ire.	53.20 N	6.15 W
151	Bailen (bä-ē-län') Phil. (Manila In.)	14.13 N	120.45 E
124	Bailén (bä-ē-lān') Sp.	38.7 N	3.38 W
127	Băilesti (bă-ĭ-lĕsh'tē). Rom.	44.1 N	23.21 E
72	Baileys (bā'lĭz). Colo. (Denver In.)	39.25 N	105.29 W
123	Bailly (bȧ-yē') Fr. (In.)	48.50 N	2.5 E
122	Bain (băN) Fr.	47.51 N	1.39 W
82	Bainbridge (bān'brĭj) Ga.	30.53 N	84.34 W
51	Bainbridge I. Wash. (Seattle In.)	47.40 N	122.30 W
127	Bairamiş (bȧ-ē-rä'mĭsh) Tur.	39.47 N	26.38 E
80	Baird (bârd) Tex.	32.22 N	99.23 W
52	Baird Mts Alsk.	67.40 N	160.0 W
159	Bairnsdale (bârnz'dāl) Austl.	37.47 S	147.35 E
153	Bais (bä-ēs') Phil.	9.35 N	123.8 E
122	Baïse R. (bä-ēz') Fr.	43.50 N	0.20 E
121	Baja (bŏ'yŏ) Hung.	46.11 N	18.58 E
74	Baja California (bä-hä). Mex.	32.20 N	116.0 W
160	Bajemba Mt. (bä-jĕm'bȧ) Austl. (In.)	29.20 S	152.4 E
132	Bakel (bȧ-kĕl') Fr. W. Afr.	14.52 N	12.30 W
71	Baker (bā'kēr) Mont.	46.23 N	104.17 W
70	Baker Ore.	44.47 N	117.50 W
54	Baker L Can.	64.15 N	96.25 W
70	Baker, Mt Wash.	48.47 N	121.49 W
74	Bakersfield (bā'kērz-fēld). Calif.	35.23 N	119.1 W
116	Bakewell (băk'wĕl) Gt. Brit.	53.12 N	1.40 W
129	Bakhchisarai (Bȧκ'chē-sȧ-rī') Sov. Un.	44.44 N	33.54 E
129	Bakhmach (bȧκ-mäch'). Sov. Un.	51.9 N	32.48 E
138	Bakhti (Zakarovskoe) (bȧκ-tē') (zȧ'kȧ-rôf-skō'yĕ). Sov. Un.	46.58 N	82.50 E
133	Bako (bä'kō) Eth.	5.46 N	36.37 E
121	Bakony Forest (Mts.) (bȧ-kōn'y') Hung.	47.10 N	17.55 E
132	Bakoy, R. (bȧ-kō'ē) Fr. W. Afr.	12.45 N	9.30 W
111	Baku (bä-kōō') Sov. Un.	40.28 N	49.45 E
132	Bakwa (bäk'wȧ) Nig.	12.42 N	5.58 E
153	Balabac (bä-lä'bäk) Phil.	7.59 N	117.3 E
153	Balabac I Phil.	7.57 N	117.0 E
150	Balabac Str N. Bor.	7.30 N	117.0 E
153	Balabac Str., N Phil.	7.35 N	117.0 E
150	Balabalagan (I.) (bä-lȧ-bä'lȧ-gän). Indon.	2.30 S	117.30 E
138	Balagansk (bä-lä-gänsk'). Sov. Un.	53.59 N	103.10 E
125	Balaguer (bä-lä-gĕr') Sp.	41.48 N	0.49 E
131	Balah Lakes (bä'lä) Eg. (Suez Can. In.)	30.54 N	32.18 E
138	Balakhta (bȧ'lȧκ-tȧ') Sov. Un.	55.25 N	91.35 E
129	Balaklava (bȧ-lȧ-klȧ'vȧ). Sov. Un.	44.29 N	33.40 E
129	Balakleya (bȧ'lȧ-klā'yȧ). Sov. Un.	49.28 N	36.51 E
111	Balakova (bȧ'lȧ-kō'vō). Sov. Un.	52.0 N	47.48 E
153	Balamban (bä-läm-bän') Phil.	10.29 N	123.44 E
93	Balancán (bä-läŋ-kän') Mex.	17.47 N	91.32 W
152	Balanga (bä-läŋ'gä) Phil.	14.40 N	120.32 E
153	Balangiga (bä-läŋ-hē'gä) Phil.	11.7 N	125.23 E
152	Balaoan (bä-lou'än) Phil.	16.49 N	120.24 E
153	Balasan (bä-lä'sän) Phil.	11.28 N	123.7 E
111	Balashov (bȧ'lȧ-shôf) Sov. Un.	51.28 N	43.15 E
141	Balasore (bä-lȧ-sōr') India	21.28 N	86.59 E
121	Balassagyarmat (bŏ'lŏsh-shô-dyôr'môt). Hung.	48.4 N	19.19 E
121	Balaton L. (bŏ'lô-tôn) Hung.	46.50 N	17.45 E
152	Balayan (bä-lä-yän') Phil.	13.57 N	120.43 E
152	Balayan B Phil.	13.50 N	120.48 E
73	Balboa (băl-bō'ȧ) Calif. (Los Angeles In.)	33.36 N	117.55 W
90	Balboa C. Z.	8.58 N	79.32 W
90	Balboa Heights C. Z.	8.58 N	79.33 W
73	Balbuena Park (bäl-bwā'nä) Mex. (In.)	19.25 N	99.7 W
102	Balcarce (bäl-kär'sā) Arg.	37.50 S	58.20 W
127	Balcic (bȧl-chĕk') Rom.	43.25 N	28.11 E
157	Balclutha (băl-clōō'thȧ) N. Z.	46.15 S	169.48 E
72	Bald, Mt. (bôld) Colo. (Denver In.)	40.2 N	105.28 W

Page	Name Pronunciation Region	Lat. °′	Long. °′
73	Baldwin Park (bôld'wĭn) Calif. (Los Angeles In.)	34.5 N	117.56 W
85	Baldwinsville (bôld'wĭns-vĭl). N. Y.	43.9 N	76.20 W
75	Baldy Peak (bôl'dē) Ariz.	33.53 N	109.35 W
80	Baldy Peak Tex.	30.39 N	104.12 W
73	Baldy Peak Utah (Salt Lake City In.)	41.24 N	111.29 W
137	Bale (bä'lȧ) Indon. (In.)	1.8 N	101.16 E
120	Bâle (Basel) (bäl) (bä'zĕl). Switz.	47.33 N	7.35 E
125	Balearic Is. (băl-ē-ăr'ĭk) Sp.	39.40 N	2.30 E
157	Baleine Point (bȧ-lān'). N. Z. (In.)	43.36 S	172.53 E
152	Baler (bä-lâr') Phil.	15.45 N	121.33 E
152	Baler B Phil.	15.50 N	121.36 E
152	Balesin I. (bä-lĕ-sēn') Phil.	14.25 N	122.2 E
94	Balfate (bĕl'făt) Hond.	15.50 N	86.17 W
73	Balfour. Utah (Salt Lake City In.)	41.35 N	112.17 W
160	Balfour Mt. (băl'fōōr) Austl. (Tas. In.)	41.22 S	144.57 E
160	Balgowish (băl'gō-wĭsh) Austl. (Sydney In.)	33.48 S	151.16 E
150	Bali (I.) (bä'lē) Indon.	8.30 S	115.0 E
153	Baliangao (bä'lē-äŋ-gä'ō) Phil.	8.38 N	123.38 E
111	Balikesir (bä-lĭ-kĕ-sēr') Tur.	39.42 N	28.0 E
150	Balikpapan (bä'lēk-pä'pän). Indon.	1.15 S	116.50 E
111	Balikta, L. (bȧ-lĕk'tȧ) Sov. Un.	50.0 N	50.45 E
153	Balimbing (bä-lĭm-bĕng') Phil.	5.6 N	119.57 E
153	Balingasag (bä-lĭŋ'gä-säg') Phil.	8.43 N	124.47 E
150	BalintangChan. (bä-lĭn-täng). Phil.	19.45 N	121.30 E
152	Baliuag (bä-lē'wäg) Phil.	14.58 N	120.54 E
139	Balkalakh (bäl-kä-läκ') Sov. Un.	72.50 N	119.40 E
127	Balkan Mts. (bô'kȧn) Bul.	42.40 N	25.25 E
141	Balkh (bälk) Afg.	36.44 N	66.58 E
138	Balkash (bȧl-kȧsh') Sov. Un.	46.5 N	75.2 E
138	Balkhash, L. (bȧl-κäsh'). Sov. Un.	46.35 N	76.0 E
129	Balki (bäl'kĭ) Sov. Un.	47.23 N	34.53 E
87	Ball, C. (bäl) Can.	51.35 N	55.25 W
131	Ballah (bä'lä). Eg. (Suez Can. In.)	30.47 N	32.21 E
111	Balla-Ishet (bä'lä-ĭsh-ĕt'). Sov. Un.	39.28 N	54.30 E
160	Ballandean (băl'ăn-dēn) Austl. (In.)	28.48 S	151.53 E
159	Ballarat (băl'ȧ-răt) Austl.	37.33 S	143.51 E
158	Ballard, L. (băl'ȧrd) Austl.	29.30 S	120.47 E
114	Ballater (băl'ȧ-tēr) Gt. Brit.	57.5 N	3.0 W
47	Balleny Is. (băl'ĕ-nē) Pac. O.	67.0 S	164.0 E
152	Ballesteros (bäl-yĕs-tā'rōs) Phil.	18.23 N	121.31 E
160	Ballina (băl-ĭ-nä') Austl. (In.)	28.49 S	153.32 E
114	Ballina Ire.	54.8 N	9.10 W
114	Ballinasloe (băl'ĭ-nȧ-slō') Ire.	53.20 N	8.0 W
80	Ballinger (băl'ĭn-jēr) Tex.	31.45 N	99.57 W
85	Ballston Spa (bôls'tŭn spä'). N. Y.	43.0 N	73.52 W
114	Ballycastle (bă-lĭ-căs''l) N. Ire.	55.10 N	6.15 W
121	Balmazújváros (bôl'môz-ōō'y'vä'-rōsh). Hung.	47.37 N	21.22 E
153	Balmoral (băl'mō-răl) N. Bor.	5.53 N	117.39 E
114	Balmoral Gt. Brit.	57.0 N	3.10 W
131	Balqas (bȧl-kȧs') Eg. (In.)	31.13 N	31.23 E
127	Bălş (bȧlsh) Rom.	44.20 N	24.6 E
85	Balsam L. (bôl'sȧm) Can.	44.30 N	78.30 W
92	Balsas R. (bäl'säs) Mex.	18.30 N	101.0 W
129	Balta (băl'tȧ) Sov. Un.	47.57 N	29.39 E
118	Baltic Sea (bôl'tĭk) Eur.	55.20 N	16.45 E
131	Baltîm (bȧl-tēm') Eg. (In.)	31.31 N	31.5 E
85	Baltimore (bôl'tĭ-môr) Md.	39.18 N	76.38 W
88	Baltimore, Md. (In.)		
119	Baltijsk (bȧl'tēzhk') Sov. Un.	54.40 N	19.54 E
119	Baltiski (bȧl'tē-skē) Sov. Un.	59.20 N	24.4 E
111	Baltser (bȧlt-sēr') Sov. Un.	51.0 N	45.40 E
141	Baluchistan (Dist.) (bȧ-lōō-chĭ-stän'). India (In.)	27.30 N	65.30 E
153	Balut I. (bȧ-lōōt') Phil.	5.24 N	125.23 E
131	Balyana (bäl'yȧ-nȧ) Eg. (In.)	6.12 N	32.2 E
132	Bamako (bä-mä-kō') Fr. W. Afr.	12.42 N	7.58 W
132	Bamba (bȧm-bä') Fr. W. Afr.	17.9 N	1.28 W
152	Bambang (bäm-bäng') Phil.	16.23 N	121.7 E
133	Bambari (bäm-bȧ-rē'). Fr. Eq. Afr.	5.37 N	20.36 E
120	Bamberg (bäm'bĕrgh) Ger.	49.55 N	10.52 E
83	Bamberg (băm'bûrg) S. C.	33.17 N	81.3 W
133	Bambili (bäm-bē-lē') Bel. Cong.	3.47 N	26.4 E
132	Bambuto Mts. (bäm-bōō'tō). Nig.	6.0 N	9.45 E
140	Bampur (bŭm-pōōr') Iran	27.27 N	60.28 E
151	Banadero (bä-nä-dā'rō) Phil. (Manila In.)	14.7 N	121.4 E
152	Banahao, Mt. (bä-nä-hä'ō) Phil.	14.4 N	121.30 E
134	Banana (bȧ-nä'nä) Bel. Cong.	5.55 S	12.23 E
83	Banana R. (bȧ-nă'nȧ) Fla. (In.)	28.30 N	80.35 W
101	Bananal I. (bä-nä-näl') Braz.	11.30 S	50.15 W
141	Banas R. (băn-äs') India	25.30 N	75.0 E
127	Banat(Prov.) (bȧ'nät). Rom.-Yugo.	45.25 N	22.0 E
95	Banbana, R. (bän-bän'ä) Nic.	13.35 N	84.0 W
116	Banbury (băn'bēr-ĭ) Gt. Brit.	52.44 N	1.20 W
55	Bancroft (băn'krŏft) Can.	45.5 N	77.50 W
141	Banda (bän'dä) India	25.27 N	80.25 E
151	Banda Is Indon.	4.38 S	129.55 E
151	Banda Sea Indon.	6.0 S	127.30 E
132	Bandama R. (bän-dä'mä) Fr. W. Afr.	6.30 N	5.30 W
140	Bandar 'Abbasi (bŭn'dȧr ȧb-bäs'ē). Iran	27.30 N	56.29 E
140	Bandar Abu Shehr (Bushire) (bŭn'dȧr ä'bōō shär'). Iran	28.47 N	50.47 E
137	Bandar Maharani (bŭn'dȧr mä-hä-rä'nē. Malaya (In.)	22.0 N	102.35 E
140	Bandar Shab (bŭn'dȧr shäb). Iran	37.0 N	54.25 E
140	Bandar Shapur (bŭn'dȧr shä-pōōr'). Iran	30.29 N	48.59 E
135	Bandar Ziada (bŭn-dȧr' zē-ä'dä) Br. Som.	11.8 N	48.52 E
124	Bande (bän'dhȧ) Sp.	42.2 N	7.58 W
101	Bandeira, Pico de (Mt.) (pē'kōō dä bän-dä'rä). Braz.	20.29 S	41.58 W
75	Bandelier Natl. Mon. (băn-dĕ-lēr') N. M.	35.45 N	106.18 W

ng-sing; ŋ-baŋk; N-nasalized n; nŏd; cŏmmit; ōld; ôbey; ôrder; fōōd; fŏŏt; ou-out; s-soft; sh-dish; th-thin; pūre; ûnite; ûrn; stŭd; circŭs; ü-as "y" in study; '-indeterminate vowel.

Banderas PRONOUNCING INDEX Batesburg

Page	Name Pronunciation Region	Lat. °′	Long. °′
92	Banderas B. (bän-dä'räs)....Mex.	20.35 N	105.30 W
132	Bandiagara (bän-dê-á-gä'rä) Fr. W. Afr.	14.26 N	3.40 W
111	Bandirma (bän-dĭr'mà)......Tur.	40.20 N	28.0 E
150	Bandjermasin (bän-jēr-mä'sĕn) Indon.	3.21 S	114.34 E
150	Bandoeng (bän'do͝ong).....Indon.	6.59 S	107.38 E
70	Bandon (băn'dŭn)..........Ore.	43.5 N	124.25 W
134	Bandundu (bän-do͞on'do͞o) Bel. Cong.	3.20 S	17.20 E
97	Banes (bä'nās)............Cuba	20.58 N	75.45 W
54	Banff (bănf)..............Can.	51.15 N	115.29 W
114	Banff..................Gt. Brit.	57.40 N	2.32 W
54	Banff National Park........Can.	51.0 N	116.0 W
102	Banfield (băn'fēld).....Arg. (In.)	34.44 S	58.23 W
153	Bangai Pt. (bäŋ-gī')........Phil.	7.42 N	126.35 E
141	Bangalore (băŋ-gȧ-lōr').....India	12.59 N	77.28 E
152	Bangar (bäŋ-gär')..........Phil.	16.54 N	120.25 E
133	Bangassou (bäɴ-gȧ-so͞o') Fr. Eq. Afr.	4.46 N	22.48 E
142	Bangfu (bäng'fo͞o') Chn. (Shanghai In.)	31.13 N	121.24 E
151	Banggai Arch. (bäng-gī')...Indon.	1.15 S	123.15 E
150	Bangka (I.) (bäŋ'kȧ)......Indon.	2.30 S	106.0 E
150	Bangkalan (bäng-kȧ-län')..Indon.	7.8 S	112.50 E
150	Bangkok (băng-kŏk')........Siam	13.45 N	100.30 E
114	Bangor (băŋ'gŏr) (băŋ'gēr) Gt. Brit.	53.12 N	4.5 W
86	Bangor (băn'gôr)...........Me.	44.47 N	68.47 W
84	Bangor...................Mich.	42.22 N	86.7 W
85	Bangor (băŋ'gēr)............Pa.	40.54 N	75.12 W
51	Bangor.......Wash. (Seattle In.)	47.43 N	122.45 W
150	Bang Sapan Yai (bäng'sä'pän-yī') Siam	11.15 N	99.32 E
152	Bangued (bän-gād')........Phil.	17.36 N	120.37 E
150	Banguey I. (bän-gā').......N. Bor.	7.15 N	117.10 E
133	Bangui (bäŋ-gē').....Fr. Eq. Afr.	4.28 N	18.33 E
152	Bangui (bän'gē)............Phil.	18.31 N	120.46 E
152	Bangui B..................Phil.	18.35 N	120.35 E
134	Bangweulu, L. (băng-wê-o͞o'lo͞o) N. Rh.	11.0 S	29.50 E
131	Banha (bän'hȧ).........Eg. (In.)	30.26 N	31.11 E
97	Bani (bä'nē)...............Hai.	18.16 N	70.24 W
152	Bani......................Phil.	16.12 N	119.51 E
97	Banica (bä'nê-kä)..........Hai.	18.59 N	71.37 W
131	Bani Mazâr (bä'nê-mȧ-zär') Eg. (In.)	28.30 N	30.49 E
132	Bani R. (bä'nê)......Fr. W. Afr.	13.30 N	5.0 W
129	Banishche (bá'nĭsh-chĕ)..Sov. Un.	51.42 N	35.2 E
133	Bani Suef (bä'nê so͞o-ĕf')......Eg.	29.12 N	31.2 E
126	Banjaluka (bän-yä-lo͞o'kä)..Yugo.	44.47 N	17.12 E
150	Banjoewangi (bän-jo͞o-wäŋ'gê) Indon.	8.15 S	114.18 E
73	Bankhead (bănk'hĕd) Ala. (Birmingham In.)	33.46 N	87.18 W
51	Banks (bănks).Ore. (Portland In.)	45.36 N	123.6 W
160	Banks, C.....Austl. (Sydney In.)	34.0 S	151.15 E
53	Banks I....................Can.	53.20 N	130.0 W
50	Banks I....................Can.	73.0 N	123.0 W
159	Banks I..............Pap. Ter.	10.10 S	142.10 E
159	Banks Is..................Austl.	13.40 S	167.30 E
157	Banks Pen.................N. Z.	43.45 S	173.0 E
160	Banks Str.......Austl. (Tas. In.)	40.38 S	148.5 E
160	Bankstown.................Austl.	33.57 S	151.1 E
114	Bann, R. (băn)..........N. Ire.	55.0 N	6.35 W
73	Banning (băn'ĭng) Calif. (Los Angeles In.)	33.55 N	116.53 W
125	Bañolas (bän-yō'läs).........Sp.	42.6 N	2.46 E
121	Banská Bystrica (bän'skä bê'strē-tzä).Czech.	48.45 N	19.9 E
121	Banská Stiavinica (bän'skä shtē'äv-nyē'tsä).Czech.	48.27 N	18.52 E
127	Bansko (bän'skō)...........Bul.	41.51 N	23.32 E
153	Bantayan I. (bän-tä-yän')...Phil.	11.14 N	123.44 E
132	Banthe (băn'thĕ)..........S. L.	7.32 N	12.36 W
152	Banton I. (bän-tōn')........Phil.	12.56 N	122.3 E
114	Bantry (băn'trĭ)............Ire.	51.37 N	9.28 W
114	Bantry B...................Ire.	51.35 N	9.50 W
150	Banyak Is. (bän'yäk)......Indon.	2.10 N	97.15 E
131	Banza Manteka (bän'zä män-tä'kä) Bel. Cong. (Brazzaville In.)	5.31 S	13.46 E
133	Banzyville (bäɴ-zē-vēl').Bel. Cong.	4.15 N	21.8 E
132	Baoulé R. (bȧ-o͞o-lā')..Fr. W. Afr.	14.0 N	9.0 W
129	Bar (bär)..............Sov. Un.	49.3 N	27.41 E
127	Bar......................Yugo.	42.4 N	19.8 E
138	Barabinsk (bä-rá'bĭnsk)..Sov. Un.	55.40 N	79.59 E
77	Baraboo (bâr'ȧ-bo͞o).........Wis.	43.30 N	89.44 W
97	Baracoa (bä-rä-kō'ä)........Cuba	20.20 N	74.28 W
97	Baradères B. (bä-rä-dâr')....Hai.	18.35 N	73.37 W
135	Baragil (bä-rä-gēl')..........Eg.	30.5 N	31.9 E
97	Barahona (bä-rä-hō'nä).......Hai.	18.12 N	71.5 W
125	Barajas de Madrid (bä-rä'häs dā mä-drēdh').Sp. (In.)	40.28 N	3.36 W
133	Baraka R. (bȧ-rä'kä) Erit.-A. E. Sud.	17.0 N	37.30 E
135	Baran (bä-rän')..........Br. Som.	10.40 N	48.30 E
94	Baranco (bä-räŋ'kō).....Br. Hond.	16.1 N	88.56 W
53	Baranof I. (bä-rä'nôf).......Alsk.	57.0 N	135.0 W
121	Baranovichi (bä'rä-nô-vē'chê) Sov. Un.	53.7 N	25.59 E
152	Baras (bä-räs')..............Phil.	13.39 N	124.22 E
151	Baras.........Phil. (Manila In.)	14.33 N	121.18 E
129	Barasha (bä'rä-shȧ).....Sov. Un.	50.45 N	28.2 E
81	Barataria B. (bä-rȧ-tä'rê-ȧ)...La.	29.20 N	89.55 W
101	Barbacena (bär-bä-sä'nȧ)...Braz.	21.15 S	43.50 W
100	Barbacoas (bär-bä-kō'äs).....Col.	1.40 N	78.1 W
91	Barbados (I.) (bär-bā'dōz)..W. I.	13.15 N	59.30 W
99	Barbara Chan. (bär'bȧ-rä) Chl. (Magallanes In.)	54.0 S	72.25 W
125	Barbastro (bär-bäs'trō)........Sp.	42.2 N	0.6 E
125	Barbate (bär-bä'tā).....Sp. (In.)	36.12 N	5.55 W
125	Barbate R..............Sp. (In.)	36.15 N	5.55 W

Page	Name Pronunciation Region	Lat. °′	Long. °′
84	Barberton (bär'bēr-tŭn).....Ohio	41.3 N	81.37 W
134	Barberton.............U. S. Afr.	25.47 S	31.2 E
122	Barbezieux (bärb'zyû')........Fr.	45.29 N	0.10 W
84	Barboursville (bär'bērs-vĭl).W. Va.	38.24 N	82.17 W
82	Barbourville (bär'bēr-vĭl).....Ky.	36.53 N	83.53 W
91	Barbuda (I.) (bär-bo͞o'dȧ)...W. I.	17.35 N	61.35 W
124	Barca d'Alva (bär'kä däl'vä).Port.	41.1 N	6.58 W
159	Barcaldine (bär'kôl-dīn)....Austl.	23.40 S	145.20 E
133	Barca Plat. (bär'kä).......Libya	32.0 N	21.30 E
101	Barcarena (bär-kä-rā'nä) Braz. (In.)	1.31 S	48.41 W
125	Barcarena...........Port. (In.)	38.44 N	9.18 W
124	Barcarrota (bär-kär-rō'tä).....Sp.	38.31 N	6.51 W
113	Barce (bär'chä)...........Libya	32.45 N	21.2 E
126	Barcellona (bär-chĕl-lō'nä).....It.	38.7 N	15.12 E
124	Barcellonnette (bär-sē-lō-nĕt').Fr.	44.25 N	6.41 E
100	Barcellos (bär-sāl'yōs).......Braz.	1.1 S	63.1 W
125	Barcelona (bär-thȧ-lō'nä).Sp.(In.)	41.23 N	2.11 E
125	Barcelona (Prov.)..........Sp. (In.)	41.27 N	1.57 E
100	Barcelona (bär-sȧ-lō'nä).....Ven.	10.10 N	64.45 W
124	Barcelos (bär-thä'lōs).......Port.	41.33 N	8.38 W
159	Barcoo (R.) (bär'ko͞o)......Austl.	28.0 S	139.15 E
133	Bardaï (bär-dä'ē)......Fr. W. Afr.	21.22 N	16.56 E
121	Bardějov (bär'dyĕ-yôf)....Czech.	49.17 N	21.17 E
133	Bardera (bär-dā'rä).........Som.	2.22 N	42.22 E
114	Bardsey I. (bärd'sê).....Gt. Brit.	52.45 N	4.45 W
84	Bardstown (bärds'town).......Ky.	37.48 N	85.29 W
82	Bardwell (bärd'wĕl).........Ky.	36.54 N	89.2 W
141	Bareilly (bŭ-rā'lē)..........India	28.15 N	79.25 E
122	Barentin (bȧ-räɴ-täɴ')........Fr.	49.35 N	0.59 E
110	Barents Sea (bä'rĕnts)......Asia	70.15 N	41.0 E
133	Barentu (bä-rĕn'to͞o)........Erit.	15.0 N	37.35 E
160	Bare Point (bâr).......Austl. (In.)	29.45 S	153.18 E
122	Barfleur, Pt. de (bär-flûr')......Fr.	49.45 N	1.15 W
	Barfrush, see Babol, Iran		
131	Bargou, Djebel (Mt.) (jĕb'ĕl bär-go͞o').Tun. (In.)	36.3 N	9.40 E
139	Barguzin (bär'go͞o-zĭn)...Sov. Un.	53.40 N	109.30 E
139	Barguzin R............Sov. Un.	54.35 N	110.20 E
86	Bar Harbor (bär här'bēr).....Me.	44.23 N	68.14 W
126	Bari (bä'rē)..................It.	41.6 N	16.52 E
153	Barili (bȧ-rē'lê).............Phil.	10.16 N	123.31 E
102	Bariloche (bä-rē-lō'chä)......Arg.	41.15 S	71.29 W
100	Barima (bä-rē'mä).......Br. Gu.	7.58 N	60.2 W
100	Barinas (bä-rē'näs)...........Ven.	8.31 N	70.13 W
156	Baring Head (C.) (bâr'ĭng hĕd) N. Z. (In.)	41.24 S	174.53 E
150	Barisan Mts. (bä-rê-sän')..Indon.	4.0 S	103.0 E
150	Barito R. (bä-rē'tō)........Indon.	1.0 S	114.50 E
117	Barking (bär'kĭng) Gt. Brit. (London In.)	51.32 N	0.5 E
158	Barkly Tableland (bär'klê).Austl.	19.0 S	137.30 E
142	Barköl (Chensi) (bär'kûl') (chĕn'sē').Chn.	43.32 N	93.0 E
121	Bârlad (bûr'lät)...........Rom.	46.16 N	27.39 E
122	Bar-le-Duc (bär-lē-dük')......Fr.	48.48 N	5.5 E
158	Barlee, L. (bär-lē')........Austl.	29.15 S	119.30 E
126	Barletta (bär-lĕt'tä)...........It.	41.18 N	16.28 E
138	Barnaul (bär-nä-o͞ol')....Sov. Un.	53.58 N	83.50 E
85	Barnesboro (bärnz'bēr-ô)......Pa.	40.44 N	78.50 W
72	Barnesville (bärnz'vĭl) Colo. (Denver In.)	40.29 N	104.28 W
82	Barnesville..................Ga.	33.3 N	84.10 W
76	Barnesville................Minn.	46.39 N	96.25 W
84	Barnesville................Ohio	38.58 N	81.10 W
86	Barnet (bär'nĕt)..............Vt.	44.15 N	72.5 W
116	Barnetby (bär'nĕt-bĭ)....Gt. Brit.	53.34 N	0.25 W
96	Barnet Har..............Ba. Is.	25.38 N	79.11 W
79	Barnsdall (bärnz'dôl).......Okla.	36.36 N	96.13 W
114	Barnsley (bärnz'lĭ).......Gt. Brit.	53.32 N	1.30 W
114	Barnstaple (bärn'stā-p'l).Gt. Brit.	5.15 N	4.5 W
83	Barnwell (bärn'wĕl)........S. C.	33.14 N	81.22 W
132	Baro (bä'rō)................Nig.	8.37 N	6.28 E
141	Baroda (bȧ-rō'dȧ)...........India	22.20 N	73.20 E
134	Barotseland (Dist.) (bȧ-rŏt'sē-lănd) N. Rh.	16.15 S	23.30 E
100	Barquisimeto (bär-kē-sê-mä'tō) Ven.	10.2 N	69.18 W
123	Barr (bär)....................Fr.	48.25 N	7.28 E
117	Barra (bär'rä)....It. (Napoli In.)	40.50 N	14.19 E
101	Barra do Corda (bär'rä do͞o cōr-dä) Braz.	5.30 S	45.15 W
99	Barra do Pirahi (bär'rä do͞o pê-rä'ē) Braz. (Rio de Janeiro In.)	22.30 S	43.52 W
101	Barra do Rio Grande (bär'rä do͞o rē'o͞o grän'dê).Braz.	11.2 S	43.2 W
114	Barra Head (C.) (băr'ȧ).Gt. Brit.	56.45 N	7.45 W
114	Barra Isles...............Gt. Brit.	56.55 N	7.30 W
99	Barra Mansa (bär'rä män'sä) Braz. (Rio de Janeiro In.)	22.32 S	44.14 W
100	Barrancabermeja (bär-räŋ'kä-bĕr-mä'hä).Col.	7.2 N	73.58 W
100	Barranco (bär-räŋ'kō...Peru (In.)	12.9 S	77.2 W
100	Barranquilla (bär-rän-kēl'yä).Col.	10.59 N	74.58 W
93	Barra Tampico (Arbol Grande) (bär'rä täm-pē'kō) (är-bōl' grän'dâ).Mex.	22.18 N	97.53 W
86	Barre (băr'ē)................Vt.	44.11 N	72.31 W
125	Barreiro (bär-rĕ'ê-ro͞o)..Port. (In.)	38.39 N	9.4 W
135	Barren Is. (băr'ĕn).........Madag.	18.20 S	43.45 E
82	Barren R....................Ky.	37.0 N	86.22 W
102	Barreto (bär-rā'to͞o)....Braz. (In.)	22.52 S	43.6 W
101	Barretos (bär-rā'tōs)........Braz.	20.32 S	48.32 W
85	Barrie (băr'ĭ)...............Can.	44.22 N	79.40 W
93	Barrientos (bär-rê-ĕn'tōs) Mex. (In.)	19.35 N	99.12 W
160	Barring, Pt. (bär'ĭng) Austl. (Melbourne In.)	38.0 S	145.2 E
72	Barr (bär).....Colo. (Denver In.)	39.57 N	104.46 W
97	Barron (băr'ŭn).............Wis.	45.25 N	91.51 W
52	Barrow (băr'ō)...............Alsk.	71.15 N	156.12 W
114	Barrow.................Gt. Brit.	54.10 N	3.10 W

Page	Name Pronunciation Region	Lat. °′	Long. °′
158	Barrow I..................Austl.	20.40 S	115.28 E
160	Barrow Mt......Austl. (Tas. In.)	41.23 S	147.25 E
52	Barrow, Pt..................Alsk.	71.20 N	156.0 W
114	Barrow, R...................Ire.	52.45 N	7.0 W
158	Barrows Creek (băr'ōz).....Austl.	21.20 S	133.50 E
124	Barruelo de Santullan (bär-ro͞o-ā-lō dā sän-to͞o-lyän').Sp.	42.55 N	4.17 W
117	Barsbüttel (bärs-büt"l) Ger. (Hamburg In.)	53.34 N	10.9 E
74	Barstow (bär'stō)..........Calif.	34.52 N	117.2 W
122	Bar-sur-Aube (bär'sür-ōb).....Fr.	48.15 N	4.40 E
120	Barth (bärt)..................Ger.	54.21 N	12.43 E
79	Bartholomew Bayou (bär-thŏl'ô-mū).Ark.	33.45 N	91.34 W
101	Bartica (bär'tĭ-kȧ).......Br. Gu.	6.18 N	57.33 W
111	Bartin (bär'tĭn)...............Tur.	41.42 N	32.18 E
159	Bartle Frere, Mt. (bärt"l frēr') Austl.	17.29 S	145.52 E
79	Bartlesville (bär'tlz-vĭl).....Okla.	36.46 N	95.58 W
81	Bartlett (bärt'lĕt)...........Tex.	30.48 N	97.26 W
100	Bartolomé, Cerro (Mt.) (bär-tō-lō-mā').Peru (In.)	12.4 S	77.0 W
134	Bartolomeu Dias (bär-tô-lô-mä'o͞o dē'äzh).Moz.	21.12 S	35.10 E
86	Barton (bär'tŭn)..............Vt.	44.45 N	72.10 W
116	Barton-on-Humber (bär'tŭn-ŏn-hŭm'bēr).Gt. Brit.	53.41 N	0.26 W
121	Bartoszyce (bär-tô-shĭ'tsȧ)...Pol.	54.15 N	20.50 E
83	Bartow (bär'tō)........Fla. (In.)	27.53 N	81.50 W
153	Barugo (bä-ro͞o'gō)..........Phil.	11.18 N	124.44 E
129	Barvenkovo (bär'vĕn-kô'vô) Sov. Un.	48.57 N	36.59 E
159	Barwon R. (bär'wŭn)......Austl.	29.0 S	148.45 E
120	Barycz (bä'rĭch)............Pol.	51.28 N	17.5 E
133	Basankusu (bä-sän-ko͞o'so͞o) Bel. Cong.	1.10 N	19.40 E
121	Basarabia (Bessarabia) (Reg.) (bäz-ȧ-rä'bê-ä) (bĕs-ȧ-rā'bĭ-ȧ) Sov. Un.	47.10 N	28.40 E
152	Basco (bäs'kō).........Phil. (In.)	20.28 N	121.59 E
117	Basel (bä-sĕl')...Bel. (Anvers In.)	51.9 N	4.18 E
120	Basel (Bâle) (bä'zĕl) (bäl)..Switz.	47.33 N	7.35 E
153	Basey (bä'sā)................Phil.	11.17 N	125.4 E
150	Bashi Chan. (bä'shē)........For.	21.30 N	121.0 E
152	Bashi Chan. (bäsh'ê)...Phil. (In.)	21.15 N	121.50 E
110	Bashkir (Soviet Rep.) bȧsh-kēr') Sov. Un.	54.12 N	57.15 E
135	Bashtil Station (bäsh'tĭl) Eg. (Cairo In.)	30.4 N	31.11 E
153	Basilan I. (bä-sē'län)........Phil.	6.35 N	122.0 E
153	Basilan Str.................Phil.	6.48 N	122.5 E
126	Basilicata (Prov.) (bä-zē-lê-kä'tä) It.	40.30 N	16.10 E
71	Basin (bā'sĭn)...............Wyo.	44.23 N	108.4 W
114	Basingstoke (bā'zĭng-stōk) Gt. Brit.	51.15 N	1.5 W
126	Bâska (bäsh'ka)............Yugo.	44.58 N	14.43 E
111	Başkale (bäsh-kä'lĕ)..........Tur.	38.10 N	44.5 E
111	Baskunchakskoe, L. (bäs'ko͝on-chäk-skō'yē).Sov. Un.	48.10 N	46.55 E
133	Basoko (bȧ-sō'-kō).....Bel. Cong.	1.21 N	23.40 E
81	Basque R. (bȧsk)............Tex.	31.40 N	97.30 W
140	Basra (bŭs'rȧ')...............Iraq	30.30 N	47.58 E
150	Bassac (bä-säk')..........Indoch.	14.55 N	105.38 E
126	Bassano (bäs-sän'ō)............It.	45.47 N	11.43 E
135	Bassas da India (I.) (bäs'säs dä ēn'dê-ȧ).Ind. O.	21.20 S	39.49 E
135	Bassatîn (bäs-sȧ-tēn')........Eg.	29.59 N	31.16 E
141	Bassein (bŭ-sēn')............Bur.	16.45 N	94.45 E
95	Basse Terre (bäs' târ').Guad. (In.)	17.19 N	62.43 W
95	Basse Terre (I.)......Guad. (In.)	16.10 N	26.10 W
73	Bassett (băs'sĕt) Calif. (Los Angeles In.)	34.3 N	118.0 W
83	Bassetts (băs'sĕts)............Va.	36.46 N	79.58 W
122	Bassin d'Arcachon (L.) (bȧ-säɴ' där-kȧ-shôɴ').Fr.	44.45 N	1.20 W
84	Bass Is. (băs)..............Mich.	41.40 N	82.48 W
159	Bass Str...................Austl.	39.15 S	146.0 E
77	Basswood L. (băs'wo͝od) Can.-U. S. A.	48.5 N	91.35 W
120	Båstad (bô'stät).............Swe.	56.26 N	12.48 E
122	Bastelica (bä-stä'lê-kä).Cor. (In.)	42.0 N	9.0 E
122	Bastia (bäs'tē-ä)........Cor. (In.)	42.40 N	9.28 E
115	Bastogne (bäs-tôn'y')..........Bel.	50.0 N	5.45 E
81	Bastrop (băs'trŭp)............La.	32.45 N	91.54 W
81	Bastrop......................Tex.	30.8 N	97.18 W
81	Bastrop Bayou.........Tex. (In.)	29.6 N	95.20 W
134	Basutoland (bȧ-so͞o'tō-lănd)..Afr.	29.32 S	28.20 E
132	Bata (bä'tä)............Sp. Gui.	1.57 N	9.50 E
151	Bataan (Prov.) (bä-tä-än') Phil. (Manila In.)	14.40 N	120.25 E
96	Batabanó (bä-tä-bä-nō')....Cuba	22.42 N	82.19 W
96	Batabanó, G. of..............Cuba	22.20 N	82.40 W
152	Batac (bä'täk)...............Phil.	18.4 N	120.34 E
129	Bataisk (bä-täsk')........Sov. Un.	47.8 N	39.46 E
111	Batalpashinsk (bȧ'täl-pȧ-shēnsk') Sov. Un.	44.15 N	42.2 E
137	Batam I. (bä-täm')...Indon. (In.)	15.0 N	104.2 E
152	Batan I. (bä-tän')...........Phil.	13.15 N	124.0 E
152	Batan I..............Phil. (In.)	20.25 N	122.0 E
150	Batan Is....................Phil.	20.45 N	122.0 E
142	Batang (bä'täng')............Chn.	30.4 N	99.4 E
152	Batangas (bä-tän'gäs)........Phil.	13.45 N	121.3 E
151	Batangas (Prov.) Phil. (Manila In.)	13.53 N	121.0 E
151	Batangas B....Phil. (Manila In.)	13.45 N	120.57 E
153	Batas I. (bä-täs')...........Phil.	11.10 N	119.35 E
121	Bátaszek (bä'tȧ-sĕk)........Hung.	46.11 N	18.43 E
79	Batavia (bȧ-tā'vĭ-ȧ)............Ill.	41.51 N	88.18 W
	Batavia, see Jakarta, Indon.		
85	Batavia (bȧ-tā'vĭ-ȧ)..........N. Y.	43.0 N	78.12 W
83	Batesburg (bāts'bûrg)........S. C.	33.54 N	81.32 W

ăt; finăl; rāte; senâte; ärm; àsk; sofȧ; fâre; ch-choose; dh-as th in other; bē; ēvent; bĕt; recĕnt; cratēr; g-go; gh-gutteral g; bĭt; ĭ-short neutral; rīde; ᴋ-gutteral k as ch in German ich;

Batesville PRONOUNCING INDEX **Belynichi**

Page	Name Pronunciation Region	Lat. °′	Long. °′
79	Batesville (bāts'vĭl)........Ark.	35.46 N	91.38 W
84	Batesville..................Ind.	39.15 N	85.17 W
82	Batesville.................Miss.	34.17 N	89.58 W
128	Batetskaya (bá'tĕt-skä'yȧ) Sov. Un.	58.35 N	30.20 E
114	Bath (bȧth)...........Gt. Brit.	51.25 N	2.25 W
86	Bath......................Me.	43.55 N	69.50 W
86	Bath.....................Can.	46.31 N	67.35 W
85	Bath....................N. Y.	42.23 N	77.21 W
159	Bathurst (bȧth'ŭrst).......Austl.	33.25 S	149.30 E
55	Bathurst..................Can.	47.33 N	65.33 W
132	Bathurst.................Gam.	13.28 N	16.42 W
53	Bathurst, C...............Can.	70.40 N	127.30 W
160	Bathurst Har....Austl. (Tas. In.)	43.19 S	146.1 E
54	Bathurst Inlet.............Can.	67.5 N	108.30 W
158	Bathurst I...............Austl.	11.40 S	130.15 E
111	Batir, L. (bä-tēr').......Sov. Un.	43.28 N	51.50 E
151	Batjan (bät-jän').........Indon.	0.41 S	127.32 E
151	Batjan (I.)...............Indon.	0.30 S	127.30 E
114	Batley (băt'lĭ)..........Gt. Brit.	53.45 N	1.40 W
132	Batna (bät'nä).............Alg.	35.37 N	6.15 E
152	Bato (bä'tō)...............Phil.	13.36 N	124.20 E
152	Bato, L...................Phil.	13.20 N	123.22 E
81	Baton Rouge (băt'ŭn rōōzh')..La.	30.28 N	91.10 W
137	Batroun (bȧ-trō-ŭN')...Leb. (In.)	34.15 N	35.40 E
150	Battambang (bȧt-tȧm-bäng') Indoch.	13.5 N	103.15 E
74	Battle Mountain (băt''l).....Nev.	40.38 N	116.58 W
85	Battle Creek (băt''l krēk')..Mich.	42.19 N	85.11 W
54	Battleford (băt''l-fērd)......Can.	52.47 N	108.30 W
51	Battle Ground (băt''l ground) Wash. (Portland In.)	45.46 N	122.31 W
117	Battles Bridge (băt''lz brĭj') Gt. Brit. (London In.)	51.37 N	0.34 E
121	Battonya (bät-tō'nyä).....Hung.	46.16 N	21.1 E
150	Batu Is. (bä'tōō).........Indon.	0.15 S	98.30 E
151	Batulao Mt. (bä-tōō-lä'ō) Phil. (Manila In.)	14.2 N	120.37 E
111	Batum (bȧ-tōōm')......Sov. Un.	41.40 N	41.35 E
101	Baturité (bä-tōō-rē-tā')....Braz.	4.20 S	38.55 E
152	Bauan (bä'wän)...........Phil.	13.47 N	121.0 E
152	Bauang (bä'wäng)..........Phil.	16.31 N	120.20 E
132	Bauchi (bȧ-ōō'chē)..........Nig.	10.25 N	9.50 E
77	Baudette (bô-dĕt').........Minn.	48.41 N	94.35 W
134	Baudouinville (bō-dwăN-vēl') Bel. Cong.	7.12 S	29.40 E
101	Baurú (bou-rōō')..........Braz.	22.28 S	49.1 W
119	Bauska (bou'skȧ).......Sov. Un.	56.25 N	24.11 E
120	Bautzen (bout'sĕn).........Ger.	51.10 N	14.26 E
120	Bavaria (Bayern) (State) (bȧ-vā'rĭ-ȧ) (bī'ĕrn).Ger.	48.47 N	11.55 E
150	Bawean I. (bá'vē-än)......Indon.	5.52 S	112.37 E
133	Bawit (bȧ-wēt')............Eg.	28.26 N	28.58 E
116	Bawtry (bô'trĭ).........Gt. Brit.	53.26 N	1.1 W
83	Baxley (băks'lĭ)............Ga.	31.46 N	82.22 W
79	Baxter Springs (băks'tēr springs') Kan.	37.2 N	94.45 W
151	Bay (bä'ē).....Phil. (Manila In.)	14.12 N	121.20 E
97	Bayaguana (bä-yä-gwä'nä)...Hai.	18.44 N	69.37 W
152	Bayambang (bä-yäm-bäng').Phil.	15.49 N	120.27 E
96	Bayamo (bä-yä'mō).........Cuba	20.22 N	76.39 W
138	Bayan-aul (bä'yän-oul').Sov. Un.	50.50 N	75.40 E
76	Bayard (bā'ērd)............Neb.	41.45 N	103.20 W
85	Bayard...................W. Va.	39.17 N	79.23 W
111	Bayazit (bä'yä-zēt')........Turk.	39.35 N	44.2 E
153	Baybay (bī'bī).............Phil.	10.40 N	124.48 E
111	Bayburt (bä'ī-bōōrt)........Tur.	40.20 N	40.8 E
84	Bay City..................Mich.	43.37 N	83.53 W
81	Bay City..................Tex.	28.59 N	95.58 W
120	Bayern (Bavaria) (State) (bī'ĕrn) (bȧ-vā'rĭ-ȧ).Ger.	48.47 N	11.55 E
122	Bayeux (bȧ-yû')............Fr.	49.19 N	0.40 W
77	Bayfield (bā'fēld)..........Wis.	46.48 N	90.50 W
138	Baykonur (bī-kô-nōōr')..Sov. Un.	45.50 N	66.2 E
82	Bay Minette (bā'mĭn-ĕt')....Ala.	30.52 N	87.47 W
152	Bayombong (bä-yôm-bông').Phil.	16.38 N	121.9 E
122	Bayonne (bȧ-yôn')...........Fr.	43.30 N	1.28 W
85	Bayonne (bā-yōn').........N. J.	40.40 N	74.7 W
120	Bayreuth (bī-roit')..........Ger.	49.57 N	11.35 E
87	Bay Roberts (bā rŏb'ērts)...Can.	47.35 N	53.15 W
85	Bays, L. of (bās)...........Can.	45.12 N	79.12 W
82	Bay St. Louis (bā' sânt lōō'ĭs).Miss.	30.19 N	89.21 W
160	Bayswater (bāz'wô-tēr) Austl. (Perth In.)	31.55 S	115.55 E
81	Baytown (bā'toun).....Tex. (In.)	29.44 N	95.0 W
133	Bayuda Steppe (bä-yōō'dȧ) A. E. Sud.	17.30 N	32.30 E
151	Bayuyungan (bä-yōō-yōōŋ'gän) Phil. (Manila In.)	14.5 N	120.55 E
124	Baza (bä'thä)...............Sp.	37.29 N	2.47 W
111	Bazardyuze, Mt. (bä'zär-dyōōz'ĕ) Sov. Un.	41.15 N	47.45 E
127	Bazargic (bä-zär'jĭk)........Bul.	43.34 N	27.51 E
134	Bazaruto I. (bä-zä-rōō'tō)....Afr.	21.40 S	35.25 E
124	Baztán (Elizonda) (bäth-tän') (ā-lē-thōn'dä).Sp.	43.11 N	1.32 W
76	Beach (bēch)..............N. D.	46.55 N	104.0 W
72	Beach.....Wash. (Vancouver In.)	48.43 N	122.41 W
85	Beacon (bē'kŭn)...........N. J.	41.29 N	73.58 W
160	Beaconsfield (bē'kŭnz-fēld) Austl. (Tas. In.)	41.12 S	146.50 E
99	Beagle Canal (bē'g'l)........Chl.	54.50 S	71.0 W
160	Beagle Reef.....Austl. (Tas. In.)	39.40 S	147.40 E
157	Bealey (bē'lĭ)..............N. Z.	43.2 S	171.38 E
80	Beals Cr. (bēls).............Tex.	32.13 N	101.15 W
72	Bear Cr.......Colo. (Denver In.)	39.38 N	105.25 W
88	Bear Creek...Md. (Baltimore In.)	39.15 N	76.29 W
71	Bear Creek................Mont.	45.9 N	109.8 W
79	Beardstown (bērds'toun).......Ill.	40.1 N	90.26 W
71	Bear L................Ida.-Utah	42.0 N	111.20 W
71	Bear R...................U. S.	42.20 N	111.44 W
71	Bear River Bay.............Utah	41.25 N	112.17 W
73	Bear River City Utah (Salt Lake City In.)	41.37 N	112.8 W
124	Beas de Segura (bā'äs dā sā-gōō'rä).Sp.	38.16 N	2.52 W
97	Beata I. (bā-ä'tȧ)...........Hai.	17.35 N	71.32 W
97	Beata Pt...................Hai.	17.36 N	71.26 W
79	Beatrice (bē'ȧ-trĭs)..........Neb.	40.15 N	96.45 W
84	Beattyville (bēt'ē-vĭl)........Ky.	37.35 N	83.42 W
122	Beaucaire (bō-kâr')...........Fr.	43.50 N	4.40 E
86	Beauceville (bōs'vēl)........Can.	46.13 N	70.45 W
123	Beaucourt (bō-kōōr')..........Fr.	47.30 N	6.55 E
160	Beaudesert (bō-dĕ-zĕrt') Austl. (In.)	27.58 S	153.1 E
83	Beaufort (bō'fērt) (bū'fērt)..N. C.	34.43 N	76.40 W
83	Beaufort..................S. C.	32.26 N	80.40 W
53	Beaufort Sea............Arc. O.	71.0 N	140.0 W
134	Beaufort West.........U. S. Afr.	32.20 S	22.32 E
122	Beaugency (bō-zhäN-sē')......Fr.	47.50 N	1.45 E
86	Beauharnois (bō-är-nwä')....Can.	45.18 N	73.51 W
57	Beaulieu (bō-lyû').Can. (Que. In.)	46.52 N	71.8 W
73	Beaumont (bō'mŏnt) Calif. (Los Angeles In.)	33.55 N	116.59 W
81	Beaumont..................Tex.	30.5 N	94.7 W
122	Beaune (bōn)................Fr.	47.0 N	4.50 E
86	Beauport (bō-pôr').........Can.	46.50 N	71.15 W
122	Beauvais (bō-vĕ')............Fr.	49.25 N	2.5 E
78	Beaver (bē'vēr)............Okla.	36.47 N	100.31 W
75	Beaver....................Utah	38.17 N	112.40 W
78	Beaver City................Neb.	40.9 N	99.51 W
78	Beaver Cr..................Colo.	39.50 N	103.35 W
78	Beaver Cr...........Kan.-Neb.	39.55 N	100.40 W
71	Beaver Cr..................Mont.	48.10 N	107.31 W
71	Beaver Cr..........Mont.-N. D.	47.0 N	104.11 W
51	Beaver Cr.....Ore. (Portland In.)	46.6 N	123.7 W
76	Beaver Cr...................Wyo.	43.45 N	104.20 W
77	Beaver Dam..................Wis.	43.30 N	88.49 W
85	Beaver Falls.................Pa.	40.47 N	80.22 W
71	Beaverhead Mts......Ida.-Mont.	44.34 N	113.0 W
71	Beaverhead R..............Mont.	45.10 N	112.42 W
84	Beaver I..................Mich.	45.40 N	85.35 W
54	Beaver R...................Can.	54.30 N	111.0 W
51	Beaverton (bē'vēr-tŭn) Ore. (Portland In.)	45.29 N	122.49 W
116	Bebington (bē'bĭng-tŭn).Gt. Brit.	53.20 N	3.0 W
93	Becal (bā-käl')..............Mex.	20.26 N	90.3 W
124	Becerrea (bā-thā'rē-ä)........Sp.	42.51 N	7.10 W
134	Bechuanaland (bĕch-ōō-ä'nȧ-lănd) Afr.	21.30 S	24.0 E
117	Beckenham (bĕk'ĕn-ăm) Gt. Brit. (London In.)	51.24 N	0.2 W
84	Beckley (bĕk'lĭ)..........W. Va.	37.44 N	81.17 W
122	Bédarieux (bā-dȧ-ryû')........Fr.	43.35 N	3.10 E
86	Bedford (bĕd'fērd)..........Can.	45.5 N	73.0 W
114	Bedford..................Gt. Brit.	52.12 N	0.28 W
84	Bedford....................Ind.	38.50 N	86.28 W
77	Bedford.....................Ia.	40.40 N	94.44 W
87	Bedford...............Mass. (In.)	42.29 N	71.16 W
84	Bedford...................Ohio	41.22 N	81.30 W
85	Bedford.....................Pa.	40.3 N	78.28 W
83	Bedford.....................Va.	37.20 N	79.32 W
116	Bedford Co...............Gt. Brit.	52.12 N	0.30 W
114	Bedlington (bĕd'lĭng-tŭn).Gt. Brit.	55.5 N	1.39 W
110	Bednodemyanovsk (byĕd'nô-dĕm-yä'nôfsk).Sov. Un.	55.2 N	49.28 E
116	Bedworth (bĕd'wērth)...Gt. Brit.	52.29 N	1.28 W
121	Będzin (băN'jēn)............Pol.	50.18 N	19.11 E
79	Beebe (bē'bē)................Ark.	35.2 N	91.52 W
72	Beechey Hd. (bē'chĭ hĕd) Can. (Vancouver In.)	48.19 N	123.39 W
84	Beech Grove (bēch grōv).....Ind.	39.42 N	86.6 W
160	Beenleigh (bīn'lā).......Austl. (In.)	27.42 S	153.12 E
137	Beersheba (bēr-shē'bȧ).Pal. (In.)	31.15 N	34.45 E
116	Beeston (bēs't'n).......Gt. Brit.	52.56 N	1.11 W
81	Beeville (bē'vĭl).............Tex.	28.25 N	97.43 W
79	Beggs (bĕgz)...............Okla.	35.46 N	96.6 W
139	Begichev I. (bĕg-ĭ-chĕf').Sov. Un.	74.25 N	112.50 E
122	Bègles (bĕ'gl')...............Fr.	44.48 N	0.30 W
123	Béhagle (bȧ-hä'gl')...Fr. Eq. Afr.	9.28 N	16.21 E
134	Beira (bā'ērȧ)...............Moz.	19.50 S	34.52 E
124	Beira (Prov.)...............Port.	40.30 N	8.0 W
140	Beirut (Beyrouth) (bā'rōōt) (bā-rōōt').Leb.	33.55 N	35.30 E
137	Beit Jibrin (Hebron) (bāt jē'brēn) Pal. (In.)	31.37 N	34.57 E
129	Beizugskii B. (bĕ-ĭ-zōōg'skĭ-yĕ) Sov. Un.	46.8 N	38.35 E
124	Beja (bā'zhȧ)...............Port.	38.2 N	7.52 W
131	Beja (bā-zhä')..........Tun. (In.)	36.42 N	9.18 E
150	Bejaburi (bā-jȧ-bōō'rē).......Siam	13.8 N	99.58 E
124	Béjar (bā'här)................Sp.	40.24 N	5.45 W
96	Bejucal (bā-hōō-käl').......Cuba	22.55 N	82.23 W
121	Békés (bā'kāsh).............Hung.	46.45 N	21.7 E
121	Bekescsaba (bā'kāsh-chô'bô) Hung.	46.40 N	21.5 E
139	Beketovo (bĕk'ĕ-tō'vō)..Sov. Un.	53.15 N	125.10 E
127	Bela (bä'lä).................Bul.	43.26 N	25.43 E
127	Bela Crkva (bĕ'lä tsĕrk'vä).Yugo.	44.53 N	21.24 E
57	Belair (bĕ-lâr')...Can. (Que. In.)	46.47 N	71.28 W
124	Belalcázar (bāl-äl-kä'thär)....Sp.	38.34 N	5.10 W
127	Bela-Slatina (bĕl'ȧ-slä-tē'nȧ).Bul.	43.27 N	23.57 E
150	Belawan (bȧ-lä'wän)......Indon.	3.45 N	98.44 E
110	Belaya R. (byĕ'lĭ-yȧ).Sov. Un.	53.15 N	55.50 E
129	Belaya Tserkov (byĕ'lĭ-yȧ tsĕr'kôf).Sov. Un.	49.48 N	30.9 E
117	Belcele (bĕl'sĕ-lĕ).Bel. (Anvers In.)	51.9 N	4.5 E
55	Belcher Is. (bĕl'chēr)........Can.	56.25 N	80.30 W
84	Belding (bĕl'dĭng)..........Mich.	43.5 N	85.21 W
110	Belebei (byĕ'lĕ-bā'ĭ).....Sov. Un.	54.2 N	54.2 E
112	Bel el Kebir, Wadi (R.) (wä'dē bĕl'ĕl kĕ-bēr').Libya	30.30 N	14.45 E
125	Belem (bȧ-lĕN').......Port. (In.)	38.42 N	9.12 W
101	Belèm (Pará) (bȧ-lĕN') (pä-rä') Braz. (In.)	1.28 S	48.29 W
75	Belen (bĕ-lăn')............N. M.	34.38 N	106.47 W
95	Belén (bā-lān')............Pan.	8.58 N	80.42 W
102	Belén......................Par.	23.27 S	57.15 W
159	Belep Is. (bĕl'ĕp)........N. Cal.	19.40 S	163.40 E
128	Belev (byĕl'yĕf)........Sov. Un.	53.49 N	36 8 E
51	Belfair (bĕl'fâr).Ore. (Portland In.)	46.12 N	123.28 W
86	Belfast (bĕl'fȧst)...........Me.	44.26 N	69.1 W
114	Belfast.................N. Ire.	54.42 N	6.15 W
114	Belfast Lough (L.)........N. Ire.	54.45 N	5.32 W
123	Belfort (bĕl-fôr')............Fr.	47.40 N	6.51 E
102	Belfort Roxo (bĕl'fôrt rō'shōō) Braz. (In.)	22.46 S	43.23 W
133	Belgian Congo (bĕl'jĭ-ăn kŏŋ'gō) Afr.	2.0 N	25.0 E
115	Belgium (bĕl'jĭ-ŭm).........Eur.	35.0 N	4.40 E
129	Belgorod (byĕl'gō-rôt)...Sov. Un.	50.36 N	36.35 E
129	Belgorod Dnestrovski (byĕl'gô-rôt dnyĕs-trŭf'skē).Sov. Un.	46.10 N	30.18 E
127	Belgrade (Beograd) (bĕl-grād') (bĕ-ō'gräd).Yugo.	44.52 N	20.32 E
83	Belhaven (bĕl'hā-vĕn)......N. C.	35.33 N	76.36 W
85	Belington (bĕl'ĭng-tŭn)....W. Va.	39.0 N	79.56 W
150	Belitong (bȧ-lē'tông)......Indon.	2.45 S	108.0 E
94	Belize (bĕ-lēz')........Br. Hond.	17.30 N	88.12 W
94	Belize R....Br. Hond.-Guat. (In.)	17.20 N	88.45 W
139	Belkovski I. (byĕl-kôf'skĭ) Sov. Un.	75.30 N	137.0 E
160	Bell (bĕl)...........Austl. (In.)	26.54 S	151.22 E
85	Bellaire (bĕl-âr')...........Ohio	40.2 N	80.46 W
81	Bellaire...............Tex. (In.)	29.42 N	95.27 W
141	Bellary (bĕ-lä'rē)............India	15.10 N	77.0 E
125	Bellas (bĕl'äs).........Port. (In.)	38.47 N	9.16 W
102	Bella Vista (bä'lyȧ vēs'tȧ)...Arg.	28.30 S	59.0 W
101	Bella Vista (bĕl'ȧ vēs'tȧ)....Braz.	17.0 S	49.0 W
102	Bella Vista (bä'lyȧ vēs'tȧ)...Par.	22.1 S	56.28 W
100	Bella Vista............Peru (In.)	12.4 S	77.8 W
87	Belle B. (bĕl)..............Can.	47.35 N	55.18 W
89	Belle Chasse (bĕl shäs') La. (New Orleans In.)	29.52 N	90.0 W
84	Bellefontaine (bĕl-fŏn'tān)...Ohio	40.25 N	83.48 W
76	Belle Fourche (bĕl'fōōrsh')..S. D.	44.39 N	103.40 W
76	Belle Fourche Reservoir.....S. D.	44.45 N	103.43 W
76	Belle Fourche R.......S. D.-Wyo.	44.40 N	103.30 W
123	Bellegarde (bĕl-gȧrd')........Fr.	46.4 N	5.50 E
122	Belle Ile (bĕl-ēl')............Fr.	47.20 N	3.10 W
87	Belle Isle, Str. of..........Can.	51.40 N	56.30 W
77	Belle Plaine (bĕl plān')........Ia.	41.54 N	92.18 W
160	Bellerive (bĕl'ĕ-rĭv) (bĕl-rēv') Austl. (Tas. In.)	42.51 S	147.24 E
73	Belle Sumter (bĕl sŭm'tēr) Ala. (Birmingham In.)	33.22 N	87.8 W
85	Belleville (bĕl'vĭl)..........Can.	44.10 N	77.21 W
122	Belleville (bĕl-vēl')..........Fr.	46.10 N	4.45 E
79	Belleville (bĕl'vĭl)...........Ill.	38.31 N	89.58 W
79	Belleville..................Kan.	39.49 N	97.37 W
88	Belleville.........N. J. (N. Y. In.)	40.48 N	74.10 W
77	Bellevue (bĕl'vū)..............Ia.	42.16 N	90.28 W
84	Bellevue....................Ky.	39.7 N	84.28 W
84	Bellevue...................Mich.	42.29 N	85.0 W
84	Bellevue...................Ohio	41.17 N	82.48 W
89	Bellevue.....Pa. (Pittsburgh In.)	40.29 N	80.3 W
51	Bellevue......Wash. (Seattle In.)	47.36 N	122.12 W
123	Belley (bĕ-lĕ')...............Fr.	45.45 N	5.41 E
87	Bell I. (bĕl)................Can.	50.45 N	55.33 W
87	Bellingham (bĕl'ĭng-hăm) Mass. (In.)	42.5 N	71.27 W
70	Bellingham.................Wash.	48.45 N	122.29 W
72	Bellingham B. Wash. (Vancouver In.)	48.44 N	122.35 W
47	Bellingshausen Sea (bĕl'ĭngz-hôz'n).Pac. O.	72.0 S	80.30 W
120	Bellinzona (bĕl-ĭn-tsō'nä)...Switz.	46.12 N	9.3 E
101	Bello Horizonte (bĕl'ōō ō-rē-zôn'tā) Braz.	19.59 S	43.59 W
86	Bellows Falls (bĕl'ōz fôls).....Vt.	43.10 N	72.30 W
126	Belluno (bĕl-lōō'nō)............It.	46.9 N	12.13 E
102	Bell Ville (bĕl vēl')..........Arg.	32.45 S	62.45 W
81	Bellville (bĕl'vĭl)............Tex.	29.57 N	96.17 W
124	Bélmez (bĕl'māth).............Sp.	38.17 N	5.13 W
77	Belmond (bĕl'mŏnd)...........Ia.	42.53 N	93.35 W
156	Belmont (bĕl'mŏnt)...N. Z. (In.)	41.12 S	174.56 E
101	Belmonte (bĕl-mōn'tȧ).......Braz.	15.45 S	38.59 W
124	Belmonte....................Sp.	43.17 N	6.11 W
110	Beloe, L. (bye'lō-yĕ).....Sov. Un.	60.15 N	37.45 E
78	Beloit (bē-loit')............Kan.	39.27 N	98.7 W
77	Beloit......................Wis.	42.31 N	89.1 W
110	Belomorsk (byĕl-ō-môrsk') Sov. Un.	64.32 N	34.45 E
129	Belopolie (byĕ'lô-pôl'yĕ).Sov. Un.	51.7 N	34.19 E
110	Beloretsk (byĕ'lō-rĕtsk)..Sov. Un.	53.58 N	58.28 E
129	Belosaraiskaya, C. (byĕ'lô-sȧ-rä'ĭ-skä'yȧ).Sov. Un.	46.52 N	37.20 E
129	Belovodsk (byĕ'lô-vôdsk).Sov. Un.	49.11 N	39.32 E
110	Belozersk (byĕ'lô-zyĕrsk).Sov. Un.	60.0 N	37.45 E
116	Belper (bĕl'pēr).......Gt. Brit.	53.1 N	1.28 W
128	Belskoe (byĕl'skō-yĕ).....Sov. Un.	54.41 N	40.21 E
71	Belt (bĕlt).................Mont.	47.10 N	110.57 W
71	Belt Cr....................Mont.	47.10 N	110.56 W
81	Belton (bĕl'tŭn).............Tex.	31.3 N	97.29 W
73	Beltona (bĕl-tō'nȧ) Ala. (Birmingham In.)	33.47 N	86.52 W
121	Beltsy (bĕl'tsē)..........Sov. Un.	47.57 N	29.39 E
117	Belvedere (bĕl-vĕ-dēr') Gt. Brit. (London In.)	51.29 N	0.9 E
77	Belvidere (bĕl-vĭ-dēr')........Ill.	42.15 N	88.50 W
85	Belvidere..................N. J.	40.49 N	75.6 W
128	Bely (byĕ'lĭ)..............Sov. Un.	55.51 N	33.09 E
159	Belyando R. (bĕl-yän'dō)...Austl.	21.30 S	146.45 E
138	Belyi (White) I. (bĕl'yē).Sov. Un.	73.20 N	71.0 E
128	Belynichi (byĕl-ĭ-nĭ'chĭ).Sov. Un.	54.0 N	29.42 E

ng-sing; ŋ-baŋk; N-nasalized n; nŏd; cŏmmit; ōld; ōbey; ôrder; fōōd; fŏŏt; ou-out; s-soft; sh-dish; th-thin; pūre; ūnite; ûrn; stŭd; circŭs; ü-as "y" in study; '-indeterminate vowel.

Page	Name Pronunciation Region	Lat. °′	Long. °′
82	Belzoni (bĕl-zō'nê).........Miss.	33.11 N	90.30 W
134	Bembe (bĕN'bĕ)...........Ang.	7.2 S	14.29 E
124	Bembezar R. (bĕm-bā-thär')..Sp.	38.0 N	5.20 W
101	Bemfica (bĕN-fē'kȧ)...Braz. (In.)	1.13 S	48.18 W
77	Bemidji (bê-mĭj'ĭ).........Minn.	47.28 N	94.51 W
125	Benabarre (bā-nȧ-bär'rȧ).....Sp.	42.5 N	0.29 E
134	Bena Dibele (bĕn'ȧ dē-bĕ'lĕ) Bel. Cong.	4.2 S	22.50 E
134	Bena Kamba (bĕn'ȧ käm'bȧ) Bel. Cong.	2.22 S	25.12 E
159	Benalla (bĕn-ăl'ȧ).........Austl.	36.32 S	145.59 E
56	Benard (bĕ-närd') Can. (Winnipeg In.)	49.55 N	97.51 W
141	Benares (bĕ-nä'rēz).........India	25.17 N	83.8 E
133	Benas, Ras (C.) (räs bȧ-näs').Eg.	23.56 N	35.52 E
114	Ben Attow (Mt.) (bĕn ăt'tō) Gt. Brit.	57.15 N	5.15 W
124	Benavente (bā-nä-vĕn'tā).....Sp.	42.1 N	5.41 W
70	Bend (bĕnd)...............Ore.	44.3 N	121.18 W
114	Ben Dearg (Mt.) (bĕn dĕrk) Gt. Brit.	57.48 N	4.55 W
129	Bendery (bĕn-dyĕ'rê)....Sov. Un.	46.48 N	29.28 E
159	Bendigo (bĕn'dĭ-gō)........Austl.	36.45 S	144.17 E
120	Benešov (bĕn'ĕ-shôf)......Czech.	49.47 N	14.42 E
126	Benevento (bā-nā-vĕn'tō)......It.	41.7 N	14.45 E
101	Benevides (bā-nȧ-vē'dĕzh) Braz. (In.)	1.21 S	48.15 W
141	Bengal (Presidency) (bĕn-gôl') India	23.30 N	89.45 E
141	Bengal, B. of..............India	18.0 N	90.0 E
133	Bengasi (bĕn-gä'sê).........Libya	32.6 N	20.4 E
150	Bengkalis (bĕng-kä'lĭs)....Indon.	1.35 N	102.7 E
137	Bengkalis I.........Indon. (In.)	1.25 N	102.20 E
134	Benguela (bĕn-gĕl'ȧ)........Ang.	12.32 S	13.28 E
134	Benguela (Dist.)...........Ang.	13.30 S	17.0 E
73	Ben Hill (bĕn hĭl) Ga. (Atlanta In.)	33.41 N	84.31 W
114	Ben Hope (Mt.) (bĕn hōp) Gt. Brit.	58.25 N	4.35 W
132	Beni Abbès (bā'nê ä-bās')....Alg.	30.6 N	2.12 W
125	Benicarló (bā-nē-kär-lō')......Sp.	40.26 N	0.25 E
74	Benicia (bê-nĭsh'ĭ-ȧ)........Calif.	38.4 N	122.11 W
132	Benin (bĕn-ēn')..............Nig.	6.27 N	5.34 E
132	Benin, Bight of.......Fr. W. Afr.	5.0 N	3.0 E
100	Beni, R. (bā'nê).............Bol.	12.30 S	67.18 W
125	Benisa (bā-nē'sä).............Sp.	38.42 N	0.1 E
132	Beni Saf (bā'nê säf').........Alg.	35.22 N	1.23 W
133	Beni Ulid (bā'nê ōō-lēd')...Libya	31.45 N	14.0 E
78	Benkelman (bĕn-kĕl-mȧn)...Neb.	40.4 N	101.33 W
150	Benkoelen (bĕn-kōō'lĕn)...Indon.	3.45 S	102.15 E
126	Benkovac (bĕn'kō-vȧts)....Yugo.	44.2 N	15.38 E
160	Ben Lomond (Mt.) (bĕn lō'mŭnd) Austl. (Tas. In.)	41.36 S	147.44 E
114	Ben Macdhui (Mt.) (bĕn măk-dōō'ê).Gt. Brit.	57.5 N	3.35 W
114	Ben More (Mt.) (bĕn mōr).Gt. Brit.	58.5 N	5.0 W
83	Bennettsville (bĕn'ĕts-vĭl)...S. C.	34.36 N	79.40 W
114	Ben Nevis (Mt.) (bĕn nĕ'vĭs) Gt. Brit.	56.55 N	4.55 W
86	Bennington (bĕn'ĭng-tŭn).....Vt.	42.52 N	73.10 W
134	Benoni (bĕ-nō'nī)......U. S. Afr.	26.11 S	28.19 E
88	Bensenville (bĕn'sĕn-vĭl) Ill. (Chicago In.)	41.57 N	87.56 W
120	Bensheim (bĕns-hīm)........Ger.	49.42 N	8.38 E
75	Benson (bĕn-sŭn)...........Ariz.	31.58 N	110.18 W
76	Benson...................Minn.	45.19 N	95.35 W
88	Bensonhurst (bĕn'sŭn-hûrst) N. Y.	40.36 N	74.0 W
79	Benton (bĕn'tŭn)...........Ark.	34.35 N	92.35 W
74	Benton...................Calif.	37.45 N	118.25 W
79	Benton.....................Ill.	38.0 N	88.55 W
86	Benton....................Can.	45.58 N	67.37 W
85	Benton Harbor............Mich.	42.5 N	86.28 W
79	Bentonville (bĕn'tŭn-vĭl).....Ark.	36.22 N	94.12 W
132	Benue R. (bā'nōō-ȧ)...Nig.-Cam.	8.30 N	10.0 E
127	Beograd (Belgrade) (bĕ-ō'grȧd) (bĕl-grād').Yugo.	44.52 N	20.32 E
149	Beppu (bĕ'pōō)..............Jap.	33.18 N	131.25 E
95	Bequia I. (bĕk-ē'ä)......Wind. Is.	13.0 N	61.15 W
127	Berane (bȧ-rä'nȧ)..........Yugo.	42.47 N	19.51 E
127	Berat (bā-rät')..............Alb.	40.43 N	19.59 E
151	Berau Pen (bȧ-rou').Neth. N. Gui.	1.30 S	133.0 E
133	Berber (bûr'bĕr).......A. E. Sud.	18.5 N	34.0 E
135	Berbera (bûr'bēr-ä).....Br. Som.	10.25 N	45.3 E
122	Berck (bĕrk).................Fr.	50.25 N	1.39 E
129	Berdichev (bĕr-dē'chĕf)..Sov. Un.	49.53 N	28.32 E
129	Berdyansk (bĕr-dyänsk').Sov. Un.	46.46 N	36.49 E
129	Berdyanskaya, C. (bĕr-dyän' skä-yä).Sov. Un.	46.37 N	36.48 E
84	Berea (bê-rē'ȧ)..............Ky.	37.35 N	84.21 W
84	Berea......................Ohio	41.24 N	81.49 W
121	Beregovo (bĕ'rĕ-gô-vô)...Sov. Un.	48.13 N	22.40 E
	Berenice, See Bengasi, Libya.		
133	Berenice (Ruins) (bĕr-ê-nī'sê)..Eg.	23.58 N	35.27 E
76	Beresford (bĕr'ĕs-fērd).......S. D.	43.6 N	96.46 W
121	Berestechko (bĕr-ĕs-tĕch'kô) Sov. Un.	50.20 N	25.7 E
129	Berestovo (bĕr'yĕs-tô'vô).Sov.Un.	47.7 N	36.44 E
121	Berettyóújfalu (bĕ'rĕt-tyō-ōō'y'fô-lōō).Hung.	47.13 N	21.33 E
121	Bereza (bĕ-rā'zȧ)........Sov. Un.	52.30 N	24.59 E
121	Berezhany (bĕr-yĕ'zhȧ-nê) Sov. Un.	49.27 N	24.57 E
128	Berezina R. (bĕr-yĕ'zē-nȧ) Sov. Un.	53.25 N	29.2 E
128	Berezino (bĕr-yä'zê-nô)..Sov. Un.	53.50 N	28.58 E
129	Berezna (bĕr-yôz'nȧ)....Sov. Un.	51.32 N	31.46 E
129	Bereznegovati (bĕr-yôz'nyĕ-gô'vä-tê).Sov. Un.	47.18 N	32.55 E
110	Berezniki (bĕr-yôz'nê-kê).Sov. Un.	59.24 N	56.44 E
138	Berezov (bĕr-yôz'ôf).....Sov. Un.	63.58 N	64.59 E
129	Berezovka (bĕr-yôz'ôf-kȧ) Sov. Un.	47.12 N	30.56 E
125	Berga (bĕr'gä)...............Sp.	42.7 N	1.50 E
111	Bergama (bĕr'gä-mä)........Tur.	39.10 N	27.15 E
126	Bergamo (bĕr'gä-mō).........It.	45.42 N	9.40 E
120	Bergedorf (bĕr'gē-dôrf)......Ger.	53.30 N	10.14 E
120	Bergen (bĕr'gĕn)............Ger.	54.26 N	13.25 E
115	Bergen...................Neth.	51.30 N	4.19 E
118	Bergen....................Nor.	60.24 N	5.22 E
72	Bergen Pk. (bûr'gĕn) Colo. (Denver In.)	39.39 N	105.24 W
122	Bergerac (bĕr-zhē-rȧk').......Fr.	44.50 N	0.30 E
88	Bergholz (bûrg'hŭls) N. Y. (Niagara Falls In.)	43.6 N	78.54 W
120	Bergisch-Gladbach (bĕrg'ĭsh-glät' bäK).Ger.	51.0 N	7.8 E
119	Bergstedt (bĕrg'shtĕt) Ger. (Hamburg In.)	53.40 N	10.7 E
141	Berhampur (bûr'ŭm-pōōr)...India	19.15 N	84.45 E
52	Bering Glacier (bē'rĭng) Alsk. (In.)	60.15 N	144.20 W
52	Bering Sea..............Pac. O.	58.0 N	175.0 W
52	Bering Str................Alsk.	65.40 N	169.0 W
129	Berislav (byĕr'ĭ-slȧf).....Sov. Un.	46.50 N	33.24 E
124	Berja (bĕr'hä)...............Sp.	36.51 N	2.57 W
74	Berkeley (bûrk'lĭ)..........Calif.	37.52 N	122.18 W
85	Berkeley Springs.........W. Va.	39.38 N	78.26 W
127	Berkovica (bĕr-kō'vê-tsȧ)....Bul.	43.14 N	23.7 E
124	Berlengas Is. (bĕr-lĕN'gäzh)..Port.	39.25 N	9.32 W
120	Berlin (bĕr-lēn')............Ger.	52.30 N	13.25 E
117	Berlin.................Ger. (In.)		
86	Berlin (bûr'lĭn)............N. H.	44.29 N	71.12 W
77	Berlin.....................Wis.	43.58 N	88.56 W
102	Bermejo, R. (bĕr-mā'hō).....Arg.	24.30 S	61.30 W
124	Bermeo (bĕr-mā'yō)..........Sp.	43.24 N	2.45 W
91	Bermuda Is. (bēr-mū'dȧ)...Atl. O.	32.20 N	64.55 W
120	Bern (bĕrn)...............Switz.	46.56 N	7.23 E
102	Bernal (bĕr-näl').......Arg. (In.)	34.42 S	57.17 W
78	Bernalillo (bĕr-nä-lē'yō)....N. M.	35.21 N	106.29 W
120	Bernau (bĕr'nou)............Ger.	52.41 N	13.36 E
122	Bernay (bĕr-nĕ')..............Fr.	49.5 N	0.35 E
120	Bernburg (bĕrn'bŏŏrgh)......Ger.	51.47 N	11.43 E
120	Berndorf (bĕrn'dôrf).........Aus.	47.57 N	16.6 E
84	Berne (bûrn)................Ind.	40.42 N	84.57 W
158	Bernier I. (bēr-nēr')........Austl.	24.47 S	113.5 E
115	Berohem (bĕ'rô-hĕm).........Bel.	51.9 N	4.10 E
120	Beroun (bā'rōn)...........Czech.	49.58 N	14.3 E
120	Berounka R. (bĕ-rōn'kȧ)...Czech.	50.1 N	13.50 E
93	Berriozabal (bā'rēō-zä-bäl')..Mex.	16.47 N	93.15 W
112	Berryan (bĕr-ê-äN').........Alg.	32.48 N	3.44 E
96	Berry Is................Ba. Is.	25.35 N	77.45 W
79	Berryville (bĕr'ê-vĭl)........Ark.	36.21 N	93.34 W
129	Bershad (byĕr'shät).....Sov. Un.	48.21 N	29.32 E
55	Bersimis (bĕr-sê-mē')........Can.	49.8 N	68.48 W
86	Bersimis R.................Can.	49.14 N	69.35 W
55	Berthier (bĕr-tyā')..........Can.	46.12 N	73.0 W
72	Berthould (bûr'thōld) Colo. (Denver In.)	40.18 N	105.5 W
89	Bertrandville (bûr'trȧnd-vĭl) La. (New Orleans In.)	29.45 N	90.0 W
114	Berwick (bûr'ĭk)........Gt. Brit.	55.45 N	2.0 W
85	Berwick.....................Pa.	41.5 N	76.13 W
84	Berwood (bûr'wŏŏd)......W. Va.	40.0 N	80.44 W
114	Berwyn Range (Mts.) (bûr'wĭn) Gt. Brit.	52.50 N	3.25 W
135	Besalampy (bĕz-ȧ-lȧm-pē') Madag.	16.40 S	44.30 E
123	Besançon (bē-säN-sôn)........Fr.	47.15 N	6.1 E
128	Besed R. (byĕ'syĕt).....Sov. Un.	52.55 N	31.22 E
128	Beshenkovichi (byĕ'shĕn-kō-vē'-chĭ).Sov. Un.	55.4 N	29.26 E
121	Beskides (Mts.) (bĕs'kēdz') Czech.-Pol.	49.30 N	19.20 E
123	Bessancourt (bĕs-säN-kōōr') Fr. (In.)	49.2 N	2.13 E
121	Bessarabia (Basarabia) (Reg.) (bĕs-ȧ-rā'bĭ-ȧ) (bäz-ȧ-rä'bê-ä) Sov. Un.	47.10 N	28.40 E
122	Besseges (bĕ-sĕzh').........Fr.	44.19 N	4.9 E
82	Bessemer (bĕs'ê-mēr)........Ala.	33.24 N	86.58 W
77	Bessemer.................Mich.	46.29 N	90.2 W
83	Bessemer City.............N. C.	35.17 N	81.17 W
124	Betánzos (bĕ-tän'thōs)........Sp.	43.17 N	8.14 W
75	Betatakin Ruin (bĕt-ȧ-tăk'ĭn) Ariz.	36.38 N	110.29 W
134	Bethanie (bĕth'ȧ-nĭ)...S. W. Afr.	26.29 S	17.7 E
79	Bethany (bĕth'ȧ-nĭ)..........Mo.	40.15 N	94.2 W
52	Bethel (bĕth'ĕl)............Alsk.	60.35 N	162.5 W
86	Bethel......................Vt.	43.50 N	72.39 W
145	Bethlehem (bĕth'lê-hĕm) Pal. (In.)	31.41 N	35.11 E
85	Bethlehem...................Pa.	40.39 N	75.23 W
134	Bethlehem............U. S. Afr.	28.8 S	28.23 E
122	Bethune (bā-tün')............Fr.	50.32 N	2.38 E
151	Betis (bā'tēs)...Phil. (Manila In.)	15.0 N	120.36 E
124	Betoya B. (bĕ-tō'yȧ)........Mor.	35.15 N	3.25 W
135	Betroka (bĕ-trōk'ȧ).......Madag.	23.5 S	46.10 E
135	Betsiboka R. (bĕt-sĭ-bō'kȧ) Madag.	17.15 S	47.15 E
132	Bettié (bĕt-tyā')......Fr. W. Afr.	6.1 N	3.31 W
137	Betung (bȧ-tŏŏng')...Indon. (In.)	1.4 N	101.37 E
141	Betwa R. (bĕt'wȧ).........India	25.0 N	78.30 E
117	Bevel (bā'vĕl)....Bel. (Anvers In.)	51.8 N	4.40 E
117	Beveren Waes (bā'vĕ-rĕn.vâs) Bel. (Anvers In.)	51.13 N	4.15 E
114	Beverley (bĕv'ēr-lĭ)......Gt. Brit.	53.48 N	0.25 W
86	Beverly...................Mass.	42.35 N	70.55 W
73	Beverly Hills Calif. (Los Angeles In.)	34.4 N	118.25 W
79	Bevier (bê-vēr')............Mo.	39.44 N	92.35 W
116	Bewdley (būd'lĭ)........Gt. Brit.	52.22 N	2.19 W
115	Bexhill (bĕks'hĭl)........Gt. Brit.	50.50 N	0.30 E
117	Bexley (bĕks'lĭ) Gt. Brit (London In.)	51.26 N	0.9 E
132	Beyla (bā'lȧ).........Fr. W. Afr.	8.44 N	8.32 W
123	Beynes (bȧn)................Fr.	48.51 N	1.53 E
111	Beypazari (bā-pȧ-zä'rĭ)......Tur.	40.12 N	31.45 E
140	Beyrouth (Beirut) (bā-rōōt') (bā'rōōt).Leb.	33.55 N	35.30 E
111	Beyşehir (bā-shĕ'h'r)........Tur.	37.40 N	31.45 E
111	Beyşehir L.................Tur.	37.45 N	31.30 E
128	Bezhetsk (byĕ-zhĕtsk')...Sov. Un.	57.47 N	36.41 E
	Bezhitsa (see Ordzhonikidzegrad) Sov. Un.		
122	Béziers (bā-zyā')............Fr.	43.21 N	3.15 E
123	Bezons (bē-zôN')........Fr. (In.)	48.55 N	2.13 E
141	Bezwada (bĕz-wä'dȧ).......India	16.38 N	80.38 E
141	Bhagalpur (bä'gŭl-pōōr)....India	25.20 N	86.30 E
142	Bhamo (bŭ-mō')............Bur.	24.16 N	97.11 E
141	Bharatpur (bŭrt'pōr).......India	27.8 N	77.32 E
141	Bhatpara (bŭt-pä'rȧ).......India	22.52 N	88.25 E
141	Bhaunagar (bäv-nŭg'ŭr)....India	21.45 N	72.8 E
141	Bhima R. (bē'mȧ)..........India	17.15 N	76.0 E
141	Bhopal (bô-päl')............India	23.15 N	77.30 E
141	Bhuj (bōōj)...............India	23.15 N	69.32 E
150	Bhuket (bōō-kĕt')..........Siam	7.59 N	98.26 E
129	Bhutan (bōō-tän')..........Asia	27.15 N	90.0 E
132	Biafra, Bight of (bê-ä'frä).Sp. Gu.	2.0 N	9.0 E
121	Biala Podlaska (byä'lä pŭd'läs-kä).Pol.	52.2 N	23.7 E
120	Bialogard (byä'lô-gärd)......Pol.	54.0 N	16.1 E
121	Bialystok (byȧ-wĭs'tôk)......Pol.	53.7 N	23.11 E
122	Biarritz (byä-rēts')...........Fr.	43.25 N	1.35 W
145	Bias B. (byäs).............Chn.	22.44 N	114.33 E
131	Biba (bē'bȧ)...........Eg. (In.)	28.55 N	31.0 E
82	Bibb City (bĭb' sĭ'tê).........Ga.	32.31 N	84.59 W
120	Biberach (bē'bēr-äK)........Ger.	48.7 N	9.48 E
117	Bickley (bĭk'lĭ) Gt. Brit. (London In.)	51.24 N	0.2 E
84	Bicknell (bĭk'nĕl)...........Ind.	38.47 N	87.18 W
121	Bicske (bĭsh'kê)...........Hung.	47.29 N	18.38 E
132	Bida (bē'dä)................Nig.	9.5 N	6.0 E
140	Bida (Doha) (bē'dȧ) (dō'hȧ) Sau. Ar.	25.15 N	51.45 E
86	Biddeford (bĭd'ê-fērd).......Me.	43.30 N	70.30 W
116	Biddulph (bĭd'ŭlf).......Gt. Brit.	53.7 N	2.10 W
120	Biebrich (bē'brĭK)..........Ger.	50.3 N	8.16 E
121	Biebrza R. (byĕb'zhȧ).......Pol.	53.26 N	22.35 E
117	Biedermannsdorf (bē'dĕr-mäns-dôrf).Aus. (Wien In.)	48.4 N	16.21 E
120	Biel (bēl)................Switz.	47.8 N	7.14 E
120	Bielawa (byĕ'lȧ-vä)..........Pol.	50.41 N	16.34 E
120	Bielefeld (bē'lē-fĕlt).........Ger.	52.2 N	8.32 E
126	Biella (byĕl'lä)...............It.	45.34 N	8.4 E
121	Bielsk Podlaski (byĕlsk pŭd-lä'skĭ).Pol.	52.45 N	23.12 E
123	Bièvre R. (byĕv'r')......Fr. (In.)	48.46 N	2.7 E
123	Bièvres.................Fr. (In.)	48.46 N	2.12 E
126	Biferno R. (bē-fĕr'nō).........It.	41.43 N	14.40 E
127	Biğa (bē'ghȧ)..............Tur.	40.13 N	27.13 E
151	Bigaa (bê-gä-ä').Phil. (Manila In.)	14.50 N	120.53 E
157	Big B.....................N. Z.	44.15 S	168.0 E
77	Big Bay de Noc (bĭg bā dê nŏk') Mich.	45.45 N	86.45 W
79	Big Bayou (bĭg' bī'yōō)......Ark.	33.15 N	91.25 W
73	Big Bear L. (bĭg bâr lāk) Calif. (Los Angeles In.)	34.15 N	116.55 W
71	Big Belt Mts.............Mont.	46.30 N	111.25 W
82	Big Black R..............Miss.	32.20 N	90.40 W
79	Big Blue R...........Neb.-Kan.	39.50 N	96.38 W
80	Big Canyon................Tex.	30.28 N	102.30 W
73	Big Cottonwood Cr. Utah (Salt Lake City In.)	40.38 N	111.45 W
89	Big Cr.......Ohio (Cleveland In.)	41.27 N	81.47 W
77	Big Fork R...............Minn.	48.20 N	93.50 W
71	Big Hole Battlefield Natl. Mon. Mont.	45.40 N	113.39 W
71	Big Hole R...............Mont.	45.40 N	113.2 W
71	Big Horn Mts..............Wyo.	44.30 N	107.20 W
71	Big Horn R..........Wyo.-Mont.	44.0 N	157.58 W
79	Big L......................Ark.	35.55 N	90.5 W
86	Big L......................Me.	45.10 N	67.42 W
71	Big Muddy Cr.............Mont.	48.52 N	105.0 W
79	Big Muddy R................Ill.	38.0 N	88.58 W
84	Big Rapids................Mich.	43.43 N	85.30 W
78	Big Sandy Cr..............Colo.	38.47 N	103.0 W
84	Big Sandy R.........Ky.-W. Va.	38.15 N	82.37 W
82	Big Sandy R...............Tenn.	36.10 N	88.10 W
76	Big Sioux R. (bĭg sōō)...S. D.-Ia.	44.0 N	96.36 W
80	Big Spring..................Tex.	32.15 N	101.28 W
82	Big Stone Gap...............Va.	36.53 N	82.50 W
76	Big Stone L.........Minn.-S. D.	45.25 N	96.40 W
71	Bigtimber (bĭg'tĭm-bēr)....Mont.	45.50 N	109.57 W
84	Big Vermilion R. (bĭg' vēr-mĭl' yŭn).Ill.-Ind.	40.10 N	87.38 W
71	Big Wood R.................Ida.	43.10 N	114.20 W
126	Bihać (bē'häch)...........Yugo.	44.48 N	15.51 E
134	Biharamulo (bê-hä-rä-mōō'lô) Tan.	2.38 S	31.20 E
141	Bihar and Orissa (Prov.) (bê-här'; ô-rĭs'ȧ).India	23.30 N	86.45 E
134	Bihe (Silva Porto) (bē'ĕ) (sēl'vȧ pôr'tŏŏ).Ang.	12.22 S	17.5 E
121	Bihor Mts. (bē'hôr)........Rom.	46.47 N	22.50 E
138	Biisk (bēsk)............Sov. Un.	52.40 N	85.15 E
127	Bijeljina (bē-yĕl'yê-nȧ).....Yugo.	44.45 N	19.13 E
140	Bijistan (bē-jĭ-stän').........Iran	34.29 N	58.28 E
78	Bijou Cr. (bē'zhōō)..........Colo.	40.0 N	104.5 W
141	Bikaner (bē-kȧ-nēr')........India	28.0 N	73.14 E
148	Bikin R. (bê-kēn')......Sov. Un.	46.30 N	135.0 E
134	Bikoro (bê-kō'rô)......Bel. Cong.	0.42 S	18.12 E
153	Bilaa Pt. (bē-lä-ä')..........Phil.	9.48 N	125.28 E
141	Bilaspur (bê-läs'pōōr).......India	22.10 N	82.10 E
153	Bilatan I. (bē-lä'tän)........Phil.	5.0 N	120.0 E

ăt; finăl; rāte; senȧte; ärm; ȧsk; sofȧ; fâre; ch-choose; dh-as th in other; bē; êvent; bĕt; recĕnt; cratēr; g-go; gh-gutteral g; bĭt; ĭ-short neutral; rīde; K-gutteral k as ch in German ich;

Bilbao PRONOUNCING INDEX **Bogoroditsk**

Page	Name Pronunciation Region	Lat. °′	Long. °′
124	Bilbao (bĭl-bä'ō) Sp.	43.16 N	2.55 W
131	Bilbês (bêl-bās') Eg. (In.)	30.26 N	31.37 E
127	Bileća (bê-lăt'yä) Yugo.	42.52 N	18.26 E
111	Bilecik (bē-lĕd-zhĕk') Tur.	40.10 N	29.59 E
121	Bilgoraj (bĭl-gō'rī) Pol.	50.31 N	22.43 E
153	Biliran I. (bē-lē'rän) Phil.	11.35 N	124.30 E
87	Billerica (bĭl'rĭk-à) Mass. (In.)	42.33 N	71.16 W
117	Billericay (bĭl'rĭk-â) Gt. Brit. (London In.)	51.37 N	0.25 E
116	Billinge (bĭl'ĭng) Gt. Brit.	53.30 N	2.41 W
71	Billings (bĭl'ĭngz) Mont.	45.47 N	108.30 W
117	Billwärder (bĕl'vĕr-dĕr) Ger. (Hamburg In.)	53.28 N	10.10 E
133	Bilma (bēl'mä) Fr. W. Afr.	18.42 N	13.25 E
82	Biloxi (bĭ-lŏk'sĭ) Miss.	30.24 N	88.53 W
116	Bilston (bĭl'stŭn) Gt. Brit.	52.34 N	2.4 W
150	Bima (bē'mä) Indon.	8.30 S	118.50 E
159	Bimerah (bĭm'ēr-à) Austl.	24.15 S	143.45 E
152	Binalonan (bē-nä-lō'nän) Phil.	16.3 N	120.36 E
152	Binan (bē'nän) Phil.	14.20 N	121.5 E
151	Binangonan (bē-näng-ō'nän) Phil. (Manila In.)	14.30 N	121.12 E
160	Bingara (bĭŋ-gä'rä) Austl. (In.)	29.53 S	150.36 E
120	Bingen (bĭng-ĕn) Ger.	49.57 N	7.54 E
132	Bingerville (băn-zhā-vēl') Fr. W. Afr.	5.25 N	3.58 W
116	Bingham (bĭng'ăm) Gt. Brit.	52.57 N	0.57 W
86	Bingham Me.	45.3 N	69.51 W
75	Bingham Canyon Utah	40.32 N	112.9 W
85	Binghamton (bĭng'ăm-tŭn) N. Y.	42.7 N	75.55 W
116	Bingley (bĭng'lĭ) Gt. Brit.	53.51 N	1.51 W
152	Bingo, Mt. (bĭn-gō') Phil.	12.12 N	125.8 E
149	Bingo, Sea (bĭn'gō) Jap.	34.10 N	133.25 E
152	Binmaley (bēn-mä-lā') Phil.	16.2 N	120.16 E
137	Bintan (Rhio) (I.) (bĭn'tän) (rē'ō). Indon.	1.3 N	104.20 E
150	Bintulu (bēn'tōō-lōō) Sar.	3.5 N	113.7 E
148	Bira (bē'rà) Sov. Un.	48.58 N	132.45 E
148	Bira R. Sov. Un.	49.0 N	132.30 E
139	Birakan (bē'rä-kän') Sov. Un.	49.30 N	130.45 E
113	Bir Battifal (bêr bä-tē-fäl') Libya	28.31 N	22.0 E
89	Bird Is. La. (New Orleans In.)	29.21 N	89.17 W
89	Bird I. Sd. La. (New Orleans In.)	29.18 N	89.18 W
87	Bird Rock Can.	47.52 N	61.10 W
56	Birds Hill Can. (Winnipeg In.)	49.58 N	97.0 W
158	Birdsville (bûrdz'vĭl) Austl.	26.0 S	138.25 E
158	Birdum (bûrd'ŭm) Austl.	15.42 S	133.20 E
111	Birecik (bē-rĕd-zhĕk') Tur.	37.5 N	38.2 E
133	Bir en Natrūn (bēr' ĕn nä'trōōn) A. E. Sud.	18.12 N	26.45 E
131	Bireno, Djebel (Mt.) (jĕb'ĕl bē-rā'nō). Tun. (In.)	35.27 N	8.49 E
112	Bir er Ressof (bēr ĕr rĕ-sŏf'). Alg.	32.18 N	7.57 E
133	Birhan, Mt. (bēr'hän) Eth.	10.40 N	37.55 E
140	Birjand (bēr'jänd) Iran	33.2 N	59.29 E
114	Birkenhead (bûr'kĕn-hĕd). Gt. Brit.	53.25 N	3.0 W
156	Birkenhead N. Z. (In.)	36.49 S	174.44 E
133	Birket Qarun (Pond) (bēr'kĕt ĕl kä-rōōn'). Eg.	29.30 N	30.30 E
82	Birmingham (bûr'mĭng-ăm). Ala.	33.30 N	86.50 W
73	Birmingham Ala. (In.)		
114	Birmingham Gt. Brit.	52.25 N	1.55 W
84	Birmingham Mich.	42.32 N	83.16 W
116	Birmingham Can Gt. Brit.	53.0 N	2.31 W
139	Birobidjan (bē'rō-bē-jän'). Sov. Un.	48.0 N	133.20 E
110	Birsk (bĭrsk) Sov. Un.	55.25 N	55.32 E
116	Birstall (bûr'stôl) Gt. Brit.	53.44 N	1.39 W
129	Biryughii I. (bĭr-yōō'gĭ-ē) Sov. Un.	46.7 N	35.10 E
138	Biryusa (bĭr-yōō'sä) Sov. Un.	55.40 N	97.27 E
138	Biryusa (Ona) R. (ō'nä) Sov. Un.	56.30 N	98.35 E
119	Biržai (bêr-zhä'ê) Sov. Un.	56.10 N	24.45 E
129	Birzula (bĭr'zōō-lä) Sov. Un.	47.49 N	29.28 E
75	Bisbee (bĭz'bē) Ariz.	31.27 N	109.55 W
122	Biscay, B. of (bĭs'kā) Atl. O.	45.0 N	2.30 W
83	Biscayne B. (bĭs-kān') Fla. (In.)	25.30 N	80.15 W
126	Bisceglie (bê-shā'lyā) It.	41.14 N	16.30 E
123	Bischeim (bĭsh'hīm) Fr.	48.39 N	7.49 E
160	Bischoff, Mt. (bĭsh'ŏf) Austl. (Tasmania In.)	42.16 S	145.34 E
126	Biševo (I.) (bē'shĕ-vō) Yugo.	42.58 N	16.1 E
74	Bishop (bĭsh'ŭp) Calif.	37.21 N	118.24 W
81	Bishop Tex.	27.35 N	97.45 W
116	Bishop's Castle Gt. Brit.	52.29 N	2.57 W
83	Bishopville S. C.	34.13 N	80.13 W
132	Biskra (bĕs'krä) Alg.	34.50 N	5.45 E
153	Bislig B. (bĭs'lĭg) Phil.	8.15 N	126.25 E
76	Bismarck (bĭz'märk) N. D.	46.49 N	100.46 W
151	Bismarck Arch. N. Gui. Ter.	4.0 S	151.30 E
151	Bismarck Ra. N. Gui. Ter.	5.45 S	145.0 E
150	Bisnulôk (bĭs-nōō-lōk') Siam	16.52 N	100.10 E
132	Bissago Is. (bĭ-sä'gōō). Port. Gui.	11.20 N	16.10 W
132	Bissau (bē-sä'ōō) Port. Gui.	11.56 N	15.40 W
89	Bissell (bĭs'ĕl). Mo. (St. Louis In.)	38.45 N	90.13 W
81	Bistineau L. (bĭs-tĭ-nō') La.	32.20 N	93.26 W
121	Bistrita (bĭs'trĭt-sà) Rom.	47.9 N	24.29 E
121	Bistrita R. Rom.	46.53 N	26.10 E
111	Bitlis (bĭt-lēs') Tur.	38.28 N	42.2 E
127	Bitolj (Monastir) (bê-tôl'y'). Yugo.	41.2 N	21.22 E
126	Bitonto (bē-tôn'tō) It.	41.6 N	16.42 E
71	Bitter Cr. (bĭt'ēr) Wyo.	41.41 N	108.50 W
120	Bitterfeld (bĭt'ēr-fĕlt) Ger.	51.39 N	12.18 E
70	Bitter Root Mts. (bĭt'ēr-ōōt) Ida.-Mont.	47.0 N	115.0 W
71	Bitterroot R. Mont.	46.35 N	114.7 W
128	Bityug R. (bĭt'yōōg) Sov. Un.	51.18 N	40.12 E
148	Biwa L. (bē'wä) Jap.	35.15 N	136.10 E
77	Biwabik (bê-wä'bĭk) Minn.	47.32 N	92.21 W
138	Biya R. (bĭ'yà) Sov. Un.	52.25 N	87.0 E
57	Bizard I. (bĭz'ērd) Can. (Montreal In.)	45.30 N	73.53 W
132	Bizerte (bê-zĕrt') Tun.	37.22 N	9.55 E
131	Bizerte, L. of Tun. (In.)	37.10 N	9.50 E
127	Bjelopolje (byĕ-lō-pôl'yĕ). Yugo.	43.2 N	19.45 E
126	Bjelovar (byĕ-lō'vär) Yugo.	45.53 N	16.51 E
119	Björneborg (Pori) (byûr-nĕ-bôr'y') (pō'rē). Fin.	61.30 N	21.48 E
118	Björne Fjord (byûr'nĕ fyôrd). Nor.	60.8 N	5.30 E
118	Blaavand, C. (blô'vänd) Den.	55.34 N	8.5 E
159	Blackall (blăk'ŭl) Austl.	24.25 S	145.35 E
77	Black B. Can.	48.40 N	88.28 W
89	Black B. La. (New Orleans In.)	29.37 N	89.37 W
156	Blackbridge (blăk'brĭj). N. Z. (In.)	41.12 S	174.56 E
160	Blackburn (blăk'bûrn) Austl. (Melbourne In.)	37.49 S	145.7 E
114	Blackburn Gt. Brit.	53.45 N	2.30 W
53	Blackburn, Mt. Alsk.	61.50 N	142.15 W
75	Black Canyon of the Gunnison Nat'l Mon. Colo.	38.35 N	107.45 W
114	Blackdown Hills (blăk'doun) Gt. Brit.	50.55 N	3.0 W
77	Blackduck (blăk'dŭk) Minn.	47.42 N	94.32 W
71	Blackfoot (blăk'fŏŏt) Ida.	43.10 N	112.20 W
71	Blackfoot R. Mont.	46.56 N	113.40 W
71	Blackfoot R. Reservoir Ida.	42.55 N	111.35 W
120	Black Forest Ger.	48.5 N	8.0 E
72	Black Hawk (blăk' hôk) Colo. (Denver In.)	39.48 N	105.29 W
157	Black Head N. Z. (In.)	45.56 S	170.28 E
76	Black Hills S. D.-Wyo.	44.5 N	104.0 W
72	Black Hollow. Colo. (Denver In.)	40.34 N	104.54 W
86	Black Lake Can.	46.2 N	71.21 W
85	Black L. N. Y.	44.30 N	75.35 W
114	Blackpool (blăk'pōōl) Gt. Brit.	53.50 N	3.0 W
79	Black R. Ark.-Mo.	36.30 N	90.25 W
96	Black R. Jam.	18.1 N	77.51 W
85	Black R. N. Y.	43.40 N	75.20 W
83	Black R. S. C.	33.52 N	80.0 W
77	Black R. Wis.	44.28 N	90.40 W
77	Black River Falls Wis.	44.18 N	90.50 W
70	Black Rock Desert Nev.	41.0 N	118.50 W
83	Blacksburg (blăks'bûrg) S. C.	35.7 N	81.31 W
111	Black Sea Eur.-Asia	43.30 N	35.0 E
71	Black Fork (R.) Wyo.	41.22 N	110.15 W
83	Blackshear (blăk'shĭr) Ga.	31.18 N	82.16 W
114	Blacksod B. (blăk'sŏd) Ire.	54.5 N	10.0 W
72	Blacksquirrel Cr. Colo. (Colo. Sprs. In.)	38.58 N	104.27 W
83	Blackstone (blăk'stôn) Va.	37.4 N	77.59 W
77	Black Sturgeon R. (blăk stûr'jŭn) Can.	49.0 N	88.30 W
160	Blacktown (blăk'toun) Austl. (Sydney In.)	33.46 S	150.54 E
86	Blackville (blăk'vĭl) Can.	46.45 N	65.51 W
83	Blackville S. C.	33.21 N	81.18 W
132	Black Volta R. (vŏl'tà) Fr. W. Afr.	10.0 N	2.45 W
82	Black Warrior R. Ala.	33.0 N	87.47 W
114	Blackwater Ire.	52.5 N	8.15 W
79	Blackwater R. Mo.	38.55 N	93.30 W
83	Blackwater R. Va.	37.0 N	76.50 W
79	Blackwell (blăk'wĕl) Okla.	36.48 N	97.18 W
72	Bladgett Pk. (blă'jĕt pēk) Colo. (Colo. Spgs. In.)	38.58 N	104.54 W
111	Blagodarnoe (blä'gō-där-nō'yĕ) Sov. Un.	45.2 N	43.30 E
139	Blagoveshchensk (blä'gŏ-vyĕsh'-chĕnsk). Sov. Un.	50.20 N	127.40 E
122	Blain (blăN) Fr.	47.30 N	1.45 W
70	Blaine (blān) Wash.	48.59 N	122.44 W
85	Blaine W. Va.	39.24 N	79.12 W
76	Blair (blâr) Neb.	41.33 N	96.9 W
114	Blairgowrie (blâr-gou'rē). Gt. Brit.	56.35 N	3.20 W
85	Blairsville (blârs'vĭl) Pa.	40.27 N	79.14 W
82	Blakely (blāk'lē) Ga.	31.23 N	84.57 W
72	Blakeley I. Wash. (Vancouver In.)	48.33 N	122.48 W
99	Blanca, L. (blăŋ'kä) Chl. (Magallanes In.)	52.25 S	71.10 W
78	Blanca Pk. (blăŋ'kà) Colo.	37.33 N	105.29 W
75	Blanca Pk., Sierra N. M.	33.21 N	105.48 W
153	Blanca Pt. Phil.	8.30 N	123.3 E
80	Blanca, Sierra (Mts.) (sĭ-ĕr'à blăŋ'kà). Tex.	31.10 N	105.21 W
131	Blanc, Cape (blăN) Tun. (In.)	37.14 N	9.50 E
123	Blanc, Mt. (môN blăN) Fr.	45.50 N	6.50 E
102	Blanco, C. (blăŋ'kō) Arg.	47.10 S	65.45 W
94	Blanco, C. C. R.	9.33 N	85.7 W
132	Blanco, C. Fr. W. Afr.	20.45 N	17.7 W
70	Blanco, C. (blăŋ'kō) Ore.	42.50 N	124.32 W
96	Blanco Cays (Is.) Cuba	23.15 N	81.0 W
95	Blanco, Pico (Mt.) (pē'kō blăŋ'kō). C. R.	9.18 N	83.2 W
93	Blanco, R. (blăŋ'kō) Mex.	18.43 N	96.30 W
92	Blanco, R. Mex.	24.9 N	99.20 W
117	Blankenburg (blăŋ'kĕn-bōōrgh) Ger. (Berlin In.)	52.36 N	13.27 E
120	Blankenburg Ger.	51.48 N	10.57 E
93	Blanquilla I. (blän-kē'lyä). Mex.	21.30 N	97.17 W
100	Blanquilla I. Ven.	11.50 N	64.45 W
134	Blantyre (blăn-tīr') Nya.	15.50 S	35.3 E
126	Blato (blä'tō) Yugo.	42.55 N	16.47 E
122	Blaye-et-Ste.-Luce (blā'-ā-sănt-lüs'). Fr.	45.7 N	0.41 W
121	Blażowa (bwä-zhō'vä) Pol.	49.52 N	22.6 E
157	Blenheim (blĕn'ĕm) N. Z.	41.32 S	174.0 E
160	Blicks, R. (blĭks) Austl. (In.)	30.5 S	152.45 E
132	Blida (blē'dä) Alg.	36.32 N	2.50 E
84	Blissfield (blĭs-fēld) Mich.	41.48 N	83.50 W
116	Blisworth (blĭz'wûrth) Gt. Brit.	52.10 N	0.56 W
116	Blithe, R. (blĭth) Gt. Brit.	52.36 N	1.41 W
85	Block I. (blŏk) R. I.	41.20 N	71.35 W
82	Blocton (blŏk'tŭn) Ala.	33.6 N	87.7 W
134	Bloemfontein (blōōm'fŏn-tān) U. S. Afr.	29.6 S	26.11 E
122	Blois (blwä) Fr.	47.35 N	1.21 E
121	Blonie (bwôn'yĕ) Pol.	52.11 N	20.39 E
77	Bloomer (blōōm'ēr) Wis.	45.8 N	91.30 W
84	Bloomfield (blōōm'fēld) Ind.	39.0 N	86.56 W
77	Bloomfield Ia.	40.45 N	92.25 W
79	Bloomfield Mo.	36.54 N	89.55 W
76	Bloomfield Neb.	42.36 N	97.39 W
88	Bloomfield N. J. (N. Y. In.)	40.48 N	74.12 W
77	Blooming Prairie (blōōm'ĭng prâ'rĭ). Minn.	43.53 N	93.3 W
73	Bloomington (blōōm'ĭng-tŭn) Calif. (Los Angeles In.)	34.4 N	117.24 W
79	Bloomington Ill.	40.29 N	88.59 W
84	Bloomington Ind.	39.9 N	86.32 W
85	Bloomsburg (blōōmz'bûrg) Pa.	40.48 N	76.28 W
73	Blossburg (blŏs'bûrg) Ala. (Birmingham In.)	33.38 N	86.58 W
85	Blossburg Pa.	41.43 N	77.1 W
82	Blountstown (blŭnts'tun) Fla.	30.26 N	85.3 W
120	Bludenz (blōō-dĕnts') Aus.	47.10 N	9.50 E
83	Bluefield (blōō'fēld) W. Va.	37.35 N	81.15 W
95	Bluefields (blōō'fēldz) Nic.	12.0 N	83.43 W
77	Blue Earth Minn.	43.38 N	94.5 W
77	Blue Earth R. Minn.	43.50 N	94.10 W
79	Blue Island Ill.	41.39 N	87.40 W
72	Blue Mt. Colo. (Colo. Spgs. In.)	38.42 N	104.55 W
87	Blue Mt. Can.	50.20 N	57.11 W
96	Blue Mts. Jam.	18.2 N	76.33 W
70	Blue Mts. Ore.	45.30 N	118.20 W
158	Blue Mud B. Austl.	13.30 S	136.15 E
133	Blue Nile (Bahr el Azraq) (R.) (bär ĕl äz-räk'). A. E. Sud.-Eth.	13.0 N	34.0 E
159	Blue Plat Austl.	33.40 S	149.40 E
79	Blue Rapids Kan.	39.40 N	96.41 W
59	Blue Ridge Mts. U. S.	36.30 N	80.30 W
157	Blueskin (blōō'skĭn) N. Z. (In.)	45.46 S	170.36 E
157	Blueskin B. N. Z. (In.)	45.44 S	170.36 E
73	Blue Spgs. Cr. Utah (Salt Lake City In.)	41.35 N	112.28 W
73	Blue Spgs. Hills Utah (Salt Lake City In.)	41.42 N	112.21 W
157	Bluff (blŭf) N. Z.	46.37 S	168.19 E
157	Bluff Har. N. Z.	46.33 S	168.22 E
157	Bluff, The N. Z.	46.33 S	168.15 E
84	Bluffton (blŭf-tŭn) Ind.	40.45 N	85.12 W
84	Bluffton Ohio	40.53 N	83.53 W
102	Blumenau (blōō'mĕn-ou) Braz.	26.50 S	49.2 W
117	Blundellsands (blŭn'dĕl-sănds) Gt. Brit. (Liverpool In.)	53.29 N	3.3 W
114	Blyth (blīth) Gt. Brit.	55.5 N	1.32 W
74	Blythe Calif.	33.36 N	114.37 W
79	Blytheville (blīth'vĭl) Ark.	35.55 N	89.54 W
152	Boac (bō'äk) Phil.	13.27 N	121.50 E
94	Boaco (bô-ä'kō) Nic.	12.27 N	85.47 W
157	Boat Har. N. Z. (In.)	45.53 S	170.43 E
101	Bôa Vista (bō'ä vēsh'tà) Braz.	6.15 S	47.30 W
101	Boa Vista (Fordlandia) Braz.	3.50 S	55.25 W
101	Boa Vista do Rio Branco (bō'ä vēsh'tä dōō rē'ōō brän'kōō). Braz.	2.48 N	60.45 W
132	Boavista I. (bō-ä-vēsh'tä) C. V. Is. (In.)	16.0 N	22.50 W
121	Boberka (bō'bēr-kà) Sov. Un.	49.37 N	24.17 E
123	Bobigny (bô-bē-nyē') Fr. (In.)	48.54 N	2.26 E
132	Bobo-Dioulasso (bō'bō-dyōō lȧs-sō'). Fr. W. Afr.	11.15 N	4.15 W
152	Bobon (bō-bōn') Phil.	12.30 N	124.34 E
128	Bobr (bô'b'r) Sov. Un.	54.18 N	29.12 E
120	Bobr (bŭ'br) Pol.	51.20 N	15.33 E
129	Bobrinets (bŏ-brĭ-nyĕts'). Sov. Un.	48.4 N	32.8 E
129	Bobrov (bŏb'rôf) Sov. Un.	51.5 N	40.1 E
129	Bobrovitsa (bŏb'rō-vĕt-sȧ) Sov. Un.	50.43 N	31.25 E
128	Bobruisk (bŏ-brōō'ĭsk) Sov. Un.	53.6 N	29.12 E
92	Bocas (bō'käs) Mex.	22.31 N	101.0 W
95	Bocas del Toro (bō'käs dĕl tō'rō) Pan.	9.20 N	82.16 W
151	Bocaue (bō-kä'wä) Phil. (Manila In.)	14.48 N	120.54 E
121	Bochnia (bōK'nyä) Pol.	49.58 N	20.28 E
120	Bochum (bō'Kōōm) Ger.	51.28 N	7.12 E
120	Böckingen (bûk'ĭng-ĕn) Ger.	49.9 N	9.11 E
139	Bodaibo (bō-dī'bō) Sov. Un.	57.55 N	114.20 E
133	Bodélé Depression (Reg.) (bō-dā-lā'). Fr. Eq. Afr.-Fr. W. Afr.	17.0 N	17.0 E
120	Bodenbach (Podmokly) (bō'dĕn-bäk) (pŏd'mōk-lē). Czech.	50.47 N	14.10 E
114	Boderg, L. (bō'dûrg) Ire.	53.50 N	7.55 W
135	Bodle (bŏd'lē) Eth.	5.5 N	42.53 E
114	Bodmin (bŏd'mĭn) Gt. Brit.	50.27 N	4.42 W
114	Bodmin Moor (bŏd'mĭn mōōr) Gt. Brit.	50.35 N	4.30 W
108	Bodö (bōd'û) Nor.	67.13 N	14.20 E
151	Boela (bōō'lä) Indon.	3.12 S	130.30 E
122	Boën (bō-äN') Fr.	45.45 N	4.5 E
134	Boende (bō-ĕn'dä) Bel. Cong.	0.24 S	21.12 E
150	Boenjoe I. (bō-ĕn'jō-ē) Indon.	3.35 N	117.51 E
80	Boerne (bō'ērn) Tex.	29.47 N	98.44 W
151	Boeroe (I.) (bō-ē'rō-ē) Indon.	3.30 S	126.40 E
151	Boeton (I.) (bō'tŏn) Indon.	5.0 S	122.50 E
81	Boeuf R. (bĕf) La.	32.30 N	91.48 W
129	Boevo (bō'yĕ-vō) Sov. Un.	51.24 N	39.12 E
132	Boffa (bŏf'ä) Fr. W. Afr.	10.12 N	14.8 W
149	Bofu (bō'fōō) Jap.	34.3 N	131.37 E
81	Bogalusa (bō-gȧ-lōō'sȧ) La.	30.48 N	89.51 W
134	Bogenfels (bō'ghĕn-fĕls). S. W. Afr.	37.20 S	15.22 E
118	Bogense (bō'gĕn-sĕ) Den.	55.33 N	10.9 E
95	Boggy Pk. (bŏg'ĭ-pĕk). Le. Is. (In.)	17.3 N	61.51 W
112	Boghari (bō-gä-rē') (bō-gä'rē). Alg.	35.50 N	2.49 E
153	Bogo (bō-gō') Phil.	11.3 N	124.0 E
129	Bogodukhov (bŏ-gŏ-dōō'kôf) Sov. Un.	50.10 N	35.31 E
128	Bogoroditsk (bŏ-gŏ'rô-dĭtsk) Sov. Un.	53.47 N	38.7 E

ng-sing; ŋ-baŋk; N-nasalized n; nŏd; cŏmmit; ōld; ôbey; ôrder; fōōd; fŏŏt; ou-out; s-soft; sh-dish; th-thin; pūre; ûnite; ûrn; stŭd; circŭs; ü-as "y" in study; '-indeterminate vowel.

Bogorodskoe PRONOUNCING INDEX Bowling Green

Page	Name Pronunciation Region	Lat. °′	Long. °′
138	Bogorodskoe (bŏ'gŏ-rôd-skō'yĕ) Sov. Un.	56.40 N	84.20 E
100	Bogotá (bō-gō-tä') . . . . Col.	4.32 N	74.15 W
138	Bogotol (bŏ'gô-tŏl) . . . . . . Sov. Un.	56.10 N	89.30 E
129	Bogoyavlenskoe (bŏ'gô-yäf'lĕn-skō'yĕ) . Sov. Un.	48.46 N	33.17 E
111	Boguchar (bō'gŏŏ-chär) . . Sov. Un.	49.42 N	41.0 E
121	Bogumin (Bohumín) (bō'gōō-mēn) (bōō'hōō-mēn) . Pol.	49.55 N	18.21 E
129	Boguslav (bō'gŏŏ-släf) . . . Sov. Un.	49.34 N	30.54 E
122	Bohain (bō-ăN') . . . . Fr.	49.55 N	3.25 E
89	Bohemia . . . La. (New Orleans In.)	29.33 N	89.45 W
120	Bohemia (Čechy) (Prov.) (bô-hē'mĭ-à) (chĕK'ê) . Czech.	49.44 N	14.15 E
120	Bohemian For. (bô-hē'mĭ-ăn) Ger.-Czech.	49.15 N	12.55 E
120	Bohemian-Moravian Highlands (bô-hē'mĭ-ăn-mō-rā'vĭ-ăn) . Czech.	49.20 N	15.40 E
153	Bohol (I.) (bô-hôl') . . . . Phil.	9.50 N	124.15 E
153	Bohol Str . . . . Phil.	9.50 N	123.35 E
135	Bohotleh (bô-hŏt'lĕ) . . . . . Br. Som.	8.15 N	46.15 E
135	Bohotleh Yera (bô-hŏt'lĕ yĕ'rà) Br. Som.	8.55 N	45.57 E
	Bohumin, see Bogumin, Pol.		
86	Boiestown (boiz'toun) . . . . Can.	46.25 N	66.25 W
84	Bois Blanc I. (boi' blăŋk) . . Mich.	45.47 N	84.30 W
123	Bois de Boulogne (bwä dē bōō-lôn'y') . Fr. (In.)	48.51 N	2.15 E
70	Boise (boi'zå) . . . . Ida.	43.38 N	116.12 W
78	Boise City . . . . Okla.	36.43 N	102.28 W
70	Boise R . . . . Ida.	43.41 N	116.30 W
54	Boissevain (bois'vān) . . . . Can.	49.17 N	100.2 W
123	Boissy (bwä-sē') . . . . Fr. (In.)	48.0 N	2.30 E
132	Bojador, C. (bō-hä-dōr') (bŏj-à-dōr') . R. de O.	26.15 N	14.30 W
152	Bojeador, C. (bô-hā-à-dōr') . . Phil.	18.30 N	120.33 E
151	Bokan Arch. (bô-kän') . . . . . Indon.	2.0 S	123.40 E
132	Boké (bō-kā') . . . . Fr. W. Afr.	10.58 N	14.18 W
118	Bokn Fd. (bôk''n) . . . . Nor.	59.15 N	5.50 E
131	Boko Songo (bō'kō sôŋ'gō) Fr. Eq. Afr. (Brazzaville In.)	4.22 S	13.37 E
132	Bolama (bô-lä'mä) . . . . . Port. Gui.	11.37 N	15.32 W
141	Bolan (bô-län') . . . . Pak.	29.30 N	67.55 E
151	Bolan, Mt. (bô-län') . . N. Gui. Ter.	6.10 S	146.52 E
141	Bolan P . . . . Pak.	29.50 N	67.30 E
92	Bolaños (bō-län'yôs) . . . . Mex.	21.37 N	103.50 W
92	Bolaños, R . . . . Mex.	21.40 N	103.55 W
122	Bolbec (bôl-bĕk') . . . . Fr.	49.35 N	0.30 E
152	Bolbok (bôl-bôk') . . . . Phil.	13.48 N	121.23 E
153	Bold Pt. (bōld) . . . . Phil.	10.3 N	119.12 E
132	Bole (bō'lå) . . . . G. C.	9.2 N	2.28 W
120	Boleslawiec (bō-lĕ-slä'vyĕts) . . Pol.	51.15 N	15.35 E
129	Bolgrad (bŏl-gråt') . . . . . . Sov. Un.	45.40 N	28.39 E
152	Bolinao (bō-lē-nä'ô) . . . . Phil.	16.22 N	119.53 E
152	Bolinao, C . . . . Phil.	16.20 N	119.46 E
153	Bolipongpong I. (bō-lĭ-pông'pông) Phil.	5.40 N	120.50 E
102	Bolívar (bô-lē'vär) . . . . Arg.	36.20 S	61.10 W
100	Bolívar . . . . Col.	1.48 N	76.50 W
79	Bolivar (bŏl'ĭ-vår) . . . . Mo.	37.36 N	93.24 W
82	Bolivar . . . . Tenn.	35.44 N	88.59 W
81	Bolivar Pen . . . . Tex.	29.27 N	94.37 W
100	Bolivia (bô-lĭv'ĭ-à) . . . . S. A.	17.0 S	64.0 W
100	Bolivia, Plat. of . . . . Bol.	19.0 S	66.0 W
128	Bolkhov (bŏl-Kôf') . . . . . . Sov. Un.	53.28 N	35.59 E
117	Bollin, R. (bŏl'ĭn) Gt. Brit. (Liverpool In.)	53.22 N	2.20 W
116	Bollin, R . . . . Gt. Brit.	53.19 N	2.12 W
116	Bollington (bôl'ĭng-tŭn) . . Gt. Brit.	53.18 N	2.6 W
118	Bollnas (bôl'nĕs) . . . . Swe.	61.22 N	16.20 E
124	Bollullos (bō-lyōō'lyōs) . . . . Sp.	37.20 N	6.32 W
118	Bolmen, L. (bôl'mĕn) . . . . Swe.	56.55 N	13.40 E
129	Bolnovakna (bŏl-nô-väk'nà) Sov. Un.	47.32 N	37.30 E
134	Bolobo (bō'lô-bô) . . . . . . Bel. Cong.	2.12 S	16.20 E
126	Bologna (bô-lōn'yä) . . . . It.	44.30 N	11.21 E
128	Bologoe (bŏ-lŏ-gô'yĕ) . . . . Sov. Un.	57.52 N	34.4 E
96	Bolondrón (bô-lôn-drōn') . . . . Cuba	22.43 N	81.28 W
126	Bolseno, L. of (bôl-sā'nô) . . . . . . It.	42.35 N	11.56 E
129	Bolshaya Lepetikha (bŏl-shà'yà lyĕ'pyĕ-tē'Kà) . Sov. Un.	47.9 N	33.54 E
129	Bolshaya Vereka (bŏl-shà'yà vyĕr-yĕ'kà) . Sov. Un.	49.27 N	36.9 E
129	Bolshaya Vradievka (bŏl-shà'yà vrà-dyĕf'kà) . Sov. Un.	47.51 N	30.33 E
129	Bolshaya Znamenka (bŏl-shà'yà znà-myĕŋ'kà) . Sov. Un.	47.26 N	34.18 E
139	Bolsheretskoe (bôl-shyĕ'ryĕt-skô'yĕ) . Sov. Un.	52.40 N	156.50 E
129	Bolshie Kopani (bôl'shyĕ kô-pä'nĭ) . Sov. Un.	46.27 S	32.55 E
129	Bolshie-Sorochintsy (bôl'shyĕ-sô-rô-chĭnt'sĭ) . Sov. Un.	49.59 N	33.55 E
129	Bolshie Viski (bôl'shyĕ vĭs'kĭ) Sov. Un.	48.35 N	31.49 E
116	Bolsover (bōl'zô-vĕr) . . . . Gt. Brit.	53.14 N	1.17 W
73	Bolton (bōl'tŭn) . Ga. (Atlanta In.)	33.49 N	84.28 W
114	Bolton . . . . Gt. Brit.	53.35 N	2.25 W
116	Bolton-on-Dearne (bōl'tŭn-ŏn-dûrn) . Gt. Brit.	53.31 N	1.18 W
111	Bolu (bō'lŏŏ) . . . . Tur.	40.46 N	31.46 E
128	Bolva R. (bôl'vä) . . . . Sov. Un.	53.55 N	34.22 E
111	Bolvadin (bŏl-vä-dēn') . . . . . . Tur.	38.45 N	31.0 E
126	Bolzano (bôl-tsä'nō) . . . . It.	46.31 N	11.23 E
134	Boma (bō'mä) . . . . Bel. Cong.	5.47 S	13.5 E
141	Bombay (bŏm-bā') . . . . India	19.0 N	72.48 E
141	Bombay (Presidency) . . . . India	22.0 N	73.0 E
141	Bombay I . . . . India (In.)	18.58 N	72.50 E
101	Bomfim (bôN-fēN') . . . . Braz.	10.29 S	40.2 W
101	Bomfim (bôN-fēN') . . . . Braz.	16.47 S	48.32 W
101	Bom Jardim (bôN zhär-dēN') Braz. (In.)	12.18 S	38.34 W
101	Bom Jesus do Rio de Contas (bôN zha'zōōsh dōō rē'ōō dā Kôn'tàzh) . Braz.	13.5 S	41.59 W
102	Bom Jesus I. (bôN zhā'zōōsh) Braz. (In.)	22.51 S	43.13 W
118	Bommel I. (bôm'mĕl) . . . . Nor.	59.48 N	5.15 E
100	Bonaire (I.) bô-nâr') . . . . W. I.	12.5 N	68.20 W
125	Bonanza (bō-nän'thà) . . . . Sp. (In.)	36.48 N	6.20 W
124	Boñar (bō-nyär') . . . . Sp.	42.54 N	5.18 W
87	Bonavista (bŏ-nà-vĭs'tà) . . . . . Can.	48.36 N	53.8 W
87	Bonavista B . . . . Can.	48.40 N	53.40 W
131	Bon C. (bŏn) . . . . Tun. (In.)	37.5 N	10.50 E
78	Bond (bŏnd) . . . . Colo.	39.53 N	106.43 W
160	Bondi (bŏn'dê) . Austl. (Sydney In.)	33.54 S	151.16 E
133	Bondo (bôn'dô) . . . . Bel. Cong.	3.50 N	23.45 E
152	Bondoc Pen. (bôn-dŏk') . . . . . Phil.	13.30 N	122.30 E
152	Bondoc Pt . . . . Phil.	13.10 N	122.35 E
132	Bondoukou (bŏn-dōō'kōō) Fr. W. Afr.	8.8 N	2.48 W
96	Bonds Cay (I.) (bŏnds kē) . Ba. Is.	25.30 N	77.43 W
123	Bondy (bôN-dê') . . . . Fr. (In.)	48.54 N	2.28 E
132	Bône (bōn) . . . . Alg.	36.58 N	7.45 E
117	Bonea (bō'nā-à) . . . It. (Napoli In.)	40.40 N	14.27 E
79	Bonham (bŏn'ăm) . . . . Tex.	33.35 N	96.11 W
122	Bonifacio (bō-nê-fä'chō) . Cor. (In.)	41.25 N	9.10 E
126	Bonifacio, Str. of . . . . Cor.	41.20 N	9.20 E
82	Bonifay (bŏn-ĭ-fā') . . . . Fla.	30.47 N	85.42 W
150	Boni, G. of (bō'nê) . . . . Indon.	4.30 S	121.0 E
51	Bonita, Pt. (bô-nē'tà) Calif. (San Francisco In.)	37.48 N	122.32 W
101	Bonito (bô-nē'tō) . . . . Braz.	8.28 S	35.40 W
120	Bonn (bôn) . . . . Ger.	50.45 N	7.6 E
87	Bonne B. (bŏn) . . . . Can.	49.35 N	58.0 W
70	Bonners Ferry (bŏn'ērz) . . . . . Ida.	48.41 N	116.19 W
122	Bonnétable (bôn-å-tàb'l') . . . . . Fr.	48.11 N	0.25 E
79	Bonne Terre (bŏn târ') . . . . . . Mo.	37.55 N	90.33 W
70	Bonneville Dam . . . . Ore.-Wash.	45.40 N	121.55 W
132	Bonny (bŏn'ê) . . . . Nig.	4.30 N	7.11 E
126	Bonorva (bô-nôr'vä) . . . . Sard.	40.26 N	8.46 E
150	Bonthain (bôn-tīn') . . . . Indon.	5.29 S	119.58 E
152	Bontoc (bôn-tŏk') . . . . Phil.	17.9 N	121.2 E
96	Booby Rocks (bōō'bĭ rŏks) . Ba. Is.	23.58 N	77.2 W
77	Boone (bōōn) . . . . Ia.	42.5 N	93.51 W
79	Booneville (bōōn'vĭl) . . . . Ark.	35.8 N	93.53 W
84	Booneville . . . . Ky.	37.38 N	83.42 W
82	Booneville . . . . Miss.	34.37 N	88.36 W
84	Boonville . . . . Ind.	38.3 N	87.14 W
79	Boonville . . . . Mo.	38.57 N	92.45 W
86	Boothbay Harbor (bōōth'bā här'bēr) . Me.	43.52 N	69.38 W
55	Boothia, G. of (bōō'thĭ-à) . . . . Can.	68.30 N	87.0 W
54	Boothia Pen . . . . Can.	70.30 N	95.0 W
114	Bootle (bōō't'l) . . . . Gt. Brit.	53.30 N	3.0 W
132	Boporo (bô-pō'rō) . . . . Lib.	7.10 N	10.42 W
120	Boppard (bôp'ärt) . . . . Ger.	50.14 N	7.35 E
133	Bor (bôr) . . . . A. E. Sud.	6.9 N	31.36 E
111	Bor (bōr) . . . . Tur.	37.58 N	34.35 E
71	Borah Peak (bō'rä) . . . . Ida.	44.12 N	113.41 W
118	Borås (bŏŏ'rōs) . . . . Swe.	57.43 N	12.57 E
140	Borazjan (bō-räz-jän') . . . . Iran	29.15 N	51.15 E
101	Borba (bôr'bä) . . . . Braz.	4.29 S	59.32 W
153	Borbon (bôr-bōn') . . . . Phil.	10.49 N	124.1 E
122	Bordeaux (bôr-dō') . . . . Fr.	44.40 N	0.30 W
89	Bordeau, B. (bôr-dō') La. (New Orleans In.)	30.0 N	89.21 W
85	Bordentown (bôr'dĕn-toun) . . N. J.	40.7 N	74.43 W
112	Bordj-bou-Arréridj (bôrj-bōō-à-rå-rēj') . Alg.	36.3 N	4.49 E
119	Borgå (Porvoo) (bôr'gŏŏ pôr'vō) Fin.	60.26 N	25.44 E
78	Borger (bôr'gēr) . . . . Tex.	35.39 N	101.22 W
115	Borgerhout (bôr'gēr-hout) . . . . Bel.	51.11 N	4.25 E
118	Borgholm (bôrg-hŏlm') . . . . . . Swe.	56.53 N	16.41 E
81	Borgne, L. (bôrn'y') . . . . La.	30.0 N	89.40 W
126	Borgo (bôr'gō) . . . . It.	44.51 N	10.2 E
126	Borgomanero(bôr'gō-mä-nâ'rō) . It.	45.41 N	8.28 E
126	Borgo San Donnino (bôr'gō sän dôn-nē'nō) . It.	44.45 N	10.8 E
126	Borgotaro (bôr-gō-tä'rō) . . . . It.	44.29 N	9.45 E
121	Borislav (bô'rĭs-lôf) . . . . . Sov. Un.	49.16 N	23.25 E
111	Borisoglebsk (bŏ-rē'sô-glyĕpsk') Sov. Un.	51.18 N	42.5 E
128	Borisov (bŏ-rē'sôf) . . . . . . Sov. Un.	54.14 N	28.34 E
129	Borisovka (bŏ-rē-sôf'kà) . . Sov. Un.	50.37 N	36.0 E
129	Borispol (bŏ-rĭs'pôl) . . . . . Sov. Un.	50.21 N	30.53 E
124	Borja (bôr'hä) . . . . Sp.	41.50 N	1.32 W
125	Borjas Blancas (bôr'häs bläŋ'käs) . Sp.	41.31 N	0.53 E
139	Borkhaya, C. (bŏr-Kä'yä) . Sov. Un.	71.50 N	133.20 E
139	Borkhaya B . . . . Sov. Un.	71.25 N	131.0 E
133	Borkou (Reg.) (bôr-kōō') Fr. Eq. Afr.	18.0 N	19.30 E
120	Borkum (I.) (bôr'kŏŏm) . . . . Neth.	53.36 N	6.45 E
118	Borlänge (bôr-lĕŋ'gĕ) . . . . Swe.	60.29 N	15.25 E
150	Borneo (I.) (bôr'nê-ō) . . . . Pac. O.	1.0 N	114.0 E
118	Bornholm (I.) (bôrn-hôlm') . . Den.	55.10 N	14.50 E
124	Bornos (bôr'nōs) . . . . Sp.	36.49 N	5.45 W
117	Bornstädt (bôrn'stĕt) Ger. (Berlin In.)	52.25 N	13.2 E
133	Bornu (Prov.) (bôr-nōō) . . . . . Nig.	11.30 N	13.0 E
129	Borodnevka (bŏ-rŏd-nyĕf'kà) Sov. Un.	48.44 N	34.6 E
129	Boromlya (bŏ-rôm''l-yä) . Sov. Un.	50.35 N	34.56 E
111	Borona R. (bô'rô-nà) . . . . Sov. Un.	51.45 N	42.20 E
153	Borongan (bô-rŏng'än) . . . . . . Phil.	11.36 N	125.27 E
116	Boroughbridge (bŭr'ô-brĭj) Gt. Brit.	54.5 N	1.23 W
127	Borovan (bŏ-rô-vän') . . . . Bul.	43.24 N	23.45 E
128	Borovichi (bŏ-rô-vē'chê) . Sov. Un.	58.22 N	33.56 E
128	Borovsk (bô'rŏvsk) . . . . . Sov. Un.	55.12 N	36.29 E
158	Borroloola (bŏr-rô-lōō'là) . . . Austl.	16.15 S	136.15 E
117	Borsbeck (bôrs'bĕk) Bel. (Anvers In.)	51.12 N	4.29 E
121	Borshchov (bôrsh'chŏŏf) . Sov. Un.	48.48 N	26.4 E
72	Borst (bôrst) . Colo. (Colo. Sprs. In.)	39.4 N	104.52 W
117	Borstel (bôr'stĕl) Ger. (Hamburg In.)	53.32 N	9.42 E
122	Bort-es-Orgues (bôr-tĕs-ôrg') . . Fr.	45.25 N	2.30 E
129	Borzna (bôrz'nà) . . . . Sov. Un.	51.15 N	32.22 E
139	Borzya (bôrz'yà) . . . . Sov. Un.	50.25 N	116.37 E
126	Bosa (bō'sä) . . . . Sard.	40.19 N	8.33 E
126	Bosanska Dubica (bō'sän-skä dōō'bĭt-sä) . Yugo.	45.10 N	16.49 E
126	Bosanska Gradiška (bō'sän-skä grä-dĭsh'kä) . Yugo.	45.7 N	17.17 E
126	Bosanski Novi (bō'sän-skĭ nō'vē) Yugo.	45.2 N	16.23 E
126	Bosanski Petrovac (bō'sän-skĭ pĕt'rō-väts) . Yugo.	44.34 N	16.23 E
127	Bosanski Šamac (bō'sän-skĭ shä'mäts) . Yugo.	45.3 N	18.29 E
77	Boscobel (bŏs'kô-bĕl) . . . . Wis.	43.8 N	90.41 W
117	Boscoreale (bôs'kô-rā-ä'lā) It. (Napoli In.)	40.46 N	14.28 E
117	Boscotrecase (bŏs'kô-trā-kä'sā) It. (Napoli In.)	40.46 N	14.26 E
120	Boskovice (bŏs'kō-vē-tsĕ) . . Czech.	49.29 N	16.40 E
127	Bosna R. (bŏs'nà) . . . . Yugo.	44.30 N	18.10 E
126	Bosnia (Prov.) (bŏs'nĭ-à) . . . Yugo.	44.0 N	17.35 E
149	Boso Pen. (bō'sō') . Jap. (Tokyo In.)	35.15 N	140.10 E
151	Bosoboso (bō-sô-bō'sô) Phil. (Manila In.)	14.39 N	121.15 E
111	Bosporus (Str.) (bŏs'pô-rŭs) . . Tur.	41.10 N	29.10 E
81	Bossier City (bŏsh'ēr) . . . . La.	32.32 N	93.41 W
82	Boston (bôs'tŭn) . . . . Ga.	30.47 N	83.50 W
114	Boston . . . . Gt. Brit.	53.0 N	0.0
86	Boston . . . . Mass.	42.15 N	71.7 W
87	Boston . . . . Mass. (In.)		
79	Boston Mts . . . . Ark.	35.45 N	93.30 W
160	Botany B. (bŏt'à-nĭ bā) . . . . Austl.	33.58 S	151.13 E
108	Bothnia, G. of (bŏth'nĭ-à) . . . . Eur.	63.10 N	20.30 E
152	Botolan (bō-tō-län') . . . . Phil.	15.17 N	120.1 E
121	Botosani (bô-tô-shàn'ĭ) . . . . . Rom.	47.46 N	26.41 E
76	Bottineau (bŏt-ĭ-nō') . . . . N. D.	48.50 N	100.27 W
87	Botwood Harbour (bŏt'wŏŏd) . Can.	49.6 N	55.22 W
132	Bouaflé (bōō-å-flā') . . . Fr. W. Afr.	7.20 N	5.31 W
132	Bouaké (bōō-å-kā') . . . Fr. W. Afr.	7.46 N	5.3 W
133	Bouara (bōō-å-rä') (bōō-är'ä) Fr. Eq. Afr.	5.59 N	15.33 E
57	Boucherville (bōō-shā-vēl') Can. (Montreal In.)	45.37 N	73.26 W
117	Bouchout (bōō-shōō') Bel. (Anvers In.)	51.10 N	4.29 E
132	Bou-Denib (bōō-dĕ-nēb') . . . . Mor.	32.12 N	3.7 W
112	Bou Dia, C. (bōō dē'à) . . . . . . Tun.	35.15 N	11.10 E
112	Boufarik (bōō-fà-rēk') . . . . Alg.	36.35 N	2.55 E
151	Bougainville Trough (bōō-găN-vēl') N. Gui. Ter.	7.0 S	151.0 E
132	Bougie (bōō-zhē') . . . . Alg.	36.38 N	5.0 E
132	Bougouni (bōō-gōō-nē') . Fr. W. Afr.	11.22 N	7.30 W
125	Bouira (boo-ē'rà) . . . . Alg.	36.22 N	3.54 E
158	Boulder (bōl'dēr) . . . . Austl.	30.47 S	121.30 E
78	Boulder . . . . Colo.	40.2 N	105.18 W
74	Boulder City . . . . Nev.	36.1 N	114.53 W
72	Boulder Cr . . . . . Colo. (Denver In.)	40.8 N	104.58 W
70	Boulder Cr . . . . Ida.	42.50 N	116.50 W
74	Boulder Dam . . . . Ariz.	36.4 N	114.45 W
71	Boulder Pk . . . . Ida.	43.51 N	114.32 W
71	Boulder R . . . . Mont.	46.10 N	112.0 W
132	Boulé R. (bōō-lā') . . . . Fr. W. Afr.	11.30 N	7.20 W
123	Boullay-les Troux (bōō-lĕ'-lā trōō') . Fr. (In.)	48.41 N	2.3 E
122	Boulogne (bōō-lôn'y') . . . . Fr.	50.45 N	1.40 E
122	Boulogne-Billancourt (bōō-lôn'y'-bē-yäN-kōōr') . Fr.	48.50 N	2.20 E
132	Bouna (bōō-nä') . . . . . . Fr. W. Afr.	9.18 N	2.57 W
72	Boundary B. (boun'dà-rĭ bā) Can. (Vancouver In.)	49.2 N	122.58 W
74	Boundary Pk . . . . Nev.	37.51 N	118.21 W
71	Bountiful (boun'tĭ-fŏŏl) . . . . . Utah	40.54 N	111.54 W
132	Bourem (bōō-răN') . . . . Fr. W. Afr.	16.51 N	0.15 W
122	Bourg (bōōr) . . . . Fr.	46.15 N	5.15 E
122	Bourg-de-Péage (bōōr-dē-pā-äzh') Fr.	45.0 N	5.5 E
122	Bourges (bōōrzh) . . . . Fr.	47.5 N	2.25 E
123	Bourgival (bōōr-zhē-vål') . Fr. (In.)	48.52 N	2.7 E
123	Bourg-la-Reine (bōōr-lå-rān') Fr. (In.)	48.46 N	2.19 E
122	Bourgoin (bōōr-gwăN') . . . . Fr.	45.35 N	5.20 E
122	Bourg-St. Andéol (bōōr'-săN täN-dā-ôl') . Fr.	44.25 N	4.39 E
159	Bourke (bōrk) . . . . Austl.	30.14 S	145.59 E
116	Bourne (bōrn) . . . . Gt. Brit.	52.46 N	0.21 W
114	Bournemouth (bôrn'mŭth) Gt. Brit.	50.44 N	1.55 W
132	Bou-Saada (bōō-sä'dä) . . . . Alg.	35.12 N	4.7 E
133	Bousso (bōō-sô') . . . . . Fr. Eq. Afr.	10.30 N	16.42 E
132	Boutilimit (bōō-tê-lê-mē') Fr. W. Afr.	17.30 N	14.52 W
47	Bouvetöen (Bouvet Is.) (bōō-vĕ') Atl. O.	54.0 S	5.0 E
126	Bovino (bō-vē'nō) . . . . It.	41.15 N	15.21 E
54	Bow R. (bō) . . . . Can.	51.15 N	114.0 W
116	Bow, R . . . . Gt. Brit.	52.12 N	2.5 W
76	Bowbells (bō'bĕls) . . . . N. D.	48.47 N	102.1 W
76	Bowdle (bōd''l) . . . . S. D.	45.28 N	99.37 W
159	Bowen (bō'ĕn) . . . . Austl.	20.0 S	148.8 E
72	Bowen I . . . . Can. (Vancouver In.)	49.22 N	123.23 W
134	Bowesdorp (bōz'dôrp) . . U. S. Afr.	30.9 S	17.55 E
78	Bowie (bōō'ĭ) (bō'ê) . . . . Tex.	33.33 N	97.50 W
82	Bowling Green (bō'lĭng grēn) . . Ky.	37.0 N	86.27 W
79	Bowling Green . . . . Mo.	39.19 N	91.12 W
84	Bowling Green . . . . Ohio	41.25 N	83.39 W

ăt: finăl; rāte; senåte; ärm; åsk; sofà; fâre; ch-choose; dh-as th in other; bē; êvent; bĕt; recĕnt; cratēr; g-go; gh-gutteral g; bĭt; ĭ-short neutral; rīde; K-gutteral k as ch in German ich;

Bowman PRONOUNCING INDEX **Brozas**

Page	Name Pronunciation Region	Lat. °'	Long. °'
76	Bowman (bō'măn) N. D.	46.11 N	103.23 W
85	Bowmanville (bō'măn-vĭl) Can.	43.52 N	78.40 W
141	Bowringpet (bō'rĭng-pĕt') India	13.5 N	78.5 E
72	Boxelder Cr. (bŏks'ĕl-dẽr) Colo. (Denver In.)	40.10 N	104.37 W
71	Boxelder Cr. Mont.	47.20 N	108.43 W
71	Boxelder Cr. Mont.	45.30 N	104.36 W
73	Box Elder Pk. Utah (Salt Lake City In.)	41.38 N	112.1 W
76	Boyer R. (boi'ẽr) Ia.	41.45 N	95.40 W
114	Boyle (boil) Ire.	53.55 N	8.20 W
73	Boyles (boilz) Ala. (Birmingham In.)	33.33 N	86.47 W
84	Boyne City (boin) Mich.	45.13 N	85.1 W
160	Boyne, R. Austl. (In.)	26.25 S	151.20 E
114	Boyne, R. Ire.	53.40 N	6.40 W
127	Bozcaada (I.) (bōz-cä'dä) Tur.	39.47 N	26.2 E
127	Bozcaada (Tenedos) (bōz-cä'dä) Tur.	39.48 N	26.4 E
71	Bozeman (bōz'măn) Mont.	45.41 N	111.1 W
	Bozen, see Bolzano, It.		
126	Bra (brä) It.	44.41 N	7.52 E
126	Brač (I.) brăch) Yugo.	43.18 N	16.40 E
126	Bracciano, L. of (brä-chä'nō) It.	42.7 N	12.15 E
85	Bracebridge (brās'brĭj) Can.	45.3 N	79.19 W
118	Bräcke (brĕk'kĕ) Swe.	62.44 N	15.26 E
80	Brackettville (brăk'ĕt-vĭl) Tex.	29.18 N	100.25 W
101	Braço Menor, (R.) (brä'sō mä-nôr') Braz.	12.0 S	50.2 W
126	Bradano R. (brä-dä'nō) It.	40.40 N	16.20 E
85	Braddock (brăd'ŭk) Pa.	40.26 N	79.52 W
83	Bradenton (brā'dĕn-tŭn) Fla. (In.)	27.28 N	82.35 W
114	Bradford (brăd'fẽrd) Gt. Brit.	53.48 N	1.35 W
84	Bradford Ohio	40.10 N	84.28 W
85	Bradford Pa.	41.58 N	78.41 W
84	Bradley (brăd'lĭ) Ill.	41.10 N	87.52 W
80	Brady (brā'dĭ) Tex.	31.8 N	99.21 W
124	Braga (brä'gä) Port.	41.32 N	8.26 W
102	Bragado (brä-gä'dō) Arg.	35.18 S	60.30 W
101	Bragança (brä-gän'sä) Braz.	23.0 S	46.32 W
101	Bragança Braz.	2.1 S	46.58 W
124	Braganca Port.	41.47 N	6.48 W
142	Brahmaputra (Tsang Po) R. (brä'mȧ-pōō'trȧ) tsäng'-pō') Chn.-India	29.30 N	95.0 E
127	Brăila (brē'ē-lȧ) Rom.	45.15 N	27.59 E
77	Brainerd (brān'ẽrd) Minn.	46.22 N	94.9 W
87	Braintree (brān'trē) Mass. (In.)	42.13 N	71.0 W
117	Bramfeld (brăm'fĕlt) Ger. (Hamburg In.)	53.37 N	10.5 E
117	Bramhall (brăm'hôl) Gt. Brit. (Liverpool In.)	53.22 N	2.9 W
85	Brampton (brămp'tŭn) Can.	43.40 N	79.45 W
73	Branchville (brănch'vĭl) Ala. (Birmingham In.)	33.39 N	86.26 W
83	Branchville S. C.	33.16 N	80.49 W
101	Branco, R. (brăŋ'kō) Braz.	0.0	61.45 W
120	Brandenburg (brän'dĕn-bōōrgh) Ger.	52.24 N	12.33 E
120	Brandenburg (Prov.) Ger.	52.12 N	13.55 E
54	Brandon (brăn'dŭn) Can.	49.50 N	99.59 W
86	Brandon Vt.	43.47 N	73.5 W
114	Brandon Hill Ire.	52.15 N	10.10 W
85	Branford (brăn'fẽrd) Conn.	41.16 N	72.50 W
95	Brangmans Bluff (brăng'mȧnz blŭf) Nic.	14.5 N	83.20 W
121	Braniewo (brä-nyĕ'vō) Pol.	54.23 N	19.51 E
121	Bránsk (brän''sk) Pol.	52.44 N	22.53 E
85	Brantford (brănt'fẽrd) Can.	43.10 N	80.12 W
87	Bras d' Or L. (brä-dôr') Can.	45.53 N	60.58 W
121	Braşov (brä'shôf) Rom.	45.40 N	25.35 E
132	Brass (brăs) Nig.	4.26 N	6.27 E
117	Brasschaet (brăs'kät) Bel. (Anvers In.)	51.18 N	4.29 E
126	Bratello P. (brä-tel'lō) It.	44.25 N	10.0 E
121	Bratislava (brä-tĭ-slä'vä) Czech.	48.8 N	17.7 E
138	Bratsk (brätsk) Sov. Un.	56.10 N	101.59 E
129	Bratslav (brät'slâf) Sov. Un.	48.49 N	28.55 E
86	Brattleboro (brăt''l-bŭr-ō) Vt.	42.50 N	72.35 W
120	Braunau (broun'äu) Aus.	48.15 N	13.2 E
	Braunsberg, see Braniewo, Pol.		
120	Braunschweig (State) (broun'shvīgh) Ger.	52.10 N	10.10 E
120	Braunschweig (Brunswick) (brŭnz'wĭk) Ger.	52.16 N	10.31 E
135	Brava (brä'vä) Som.	1.10 N	44.2 E
74	Brawley (brô'lĭ) Calif.	32.59 N	115.31 W
114	Bray (brā) Ire.	53.10 N	6.5 W
160	Braybrook (brā'brŏŏk) Austl. (Melbourne In.)	37.47 S	144.52 E
79	Braymer (brā'mẽr) Mo.	39.34 N	93.47 W
81	Brays Bayou (brās' bī'yōō) Texas (In.)	29.42 N	95.28 W
84	Brazil (brȧ-zĭl') Ind.	39.32 N	87.7 W
100	Brazil S. A.	9.0 S	53.0 W
81	Brazos R. (brä'zōs) Tex.	30.50 N	96.40 W
80	Brazos R., Clear Fork of Tex.	33.0 N	99.15 W
78	Brazos R., Double Mt. Fork of Tex.	33.8 N	101.0 W
78	Brazos R., Salt Fork of Tex.	33.34 N	99.30 W
134	Brazzaville (brȧ-zȧ-vēl') Fr. Eq. Afr.	4.10 S	15.18 E
127	Brčko (bĕrch'kō) Yugo.	44.53 N	18.46 E
121	Brda R. (bẽr-dä') Pol.	53.30 N	17.53 E
73	Brea (brē'ȧ) Calif. (Los Angeles In.)	33.55 N	117.54 W
114	Brechin (brē'kĭn) Gt. Brit.	56.45 N	2.40 W
117	Brecht (brĕkt) Bel. (Anvers In.)	51.21 N	4.38 E
76	Breckenridge (brĕk'ĕn-rĭj) Minn.	46.17 N	96.34 E
80	Breckenridge Tex.	32.45 N	98.54 W
99	Brecknock Pen. (brĕk'nŏk) Chl. (Magallanes In.)	54.30 S	71.20 W
120	Brclav (brzhĕl'läf) Czech.	48.47 N	16.53 E
114	Brecon Beacons (brĕk'ŭn bē'kŭns) Gt. Brit.	51.50 N	3.20 W
120	Breda (brā-dä') Neth.	51.36 N	4.49 E
134	Bredasdorp (brā'das-dôrp) U. S. Afr.	34.32 S	20.2 E
72	Breed (brēd) Colo. (Colo. Spgs. In.)	38.57 N	104.49 W
120	Bregenz (brā'gĕnts) Aus.	47.31 N	9.46 E
127	Bregovo (brĕ-gō'vō) Bul.	44.8 N	22.40 E
108	Breidi Fd. (brā'dĭ) Ice.	65.10 N	23.0 W
123	Breil (brĕ'y') Fr.	43.59 N	7.30 E
101	Brejo (brå'zhōō) Braz.	3.37 S	42.48 W
118	Bremanger I. (brĕ'măŋ-gẽr) Nor.	61.50 N	5.5 E
120	Bremen (brā-mĕn) Ger.	53.5 N	8.49 E
84	Bremen (brē'mĕn) Ind.	41.27 N	86.8 W
120	Bremerhaven (brām-ẽr-hä'fĕn) Ger.	53.34 N	8.34 E
70	Bremerton (brĕm'ẽr-tŭn) Wash.	47.33 N	122.40 W
81	Bremond (brĕm'ŭnd) Tex.	31.10 N	96.40 W
81	Brenham (brĕn'ăm) Tex.	30.10 N	96.23 W
120	Brenner Pass (brĕn'ẽr) Aus.-It.	47.0 N	11.30 E
117	Brentford (brent'fẽrd) Gt. Brit. (London In.)	51.29 N	0.19 W
51	Brentwood (brĕnt'wŏŏd) Calif. (In.)	37.56 N	121.43 W
117	Brentwood Gt. Brit. (London In.)	51.38 N	0.18 E
85	Brentwood Md.	8.57 N	6.58 W
126	Brescia (brā'shä) It.	45.32 N	10.13 E
	Breslau, see Wroclaw, Pol.		
126	Bressanone (brĕs-sä-nō'nā) It.	46.44 N	11.37 E
122	Bressuire (brĕ-swēr') Fr.	46.50 N	0.30 W
122	Brest (brĕst) Fr.	48.25 N	4.30 W
121	Brest (brĕst) Sov. Un.	52.5 N	23.43 E
89	Breton I. (brĕt'ŭn) La. (New Orleans In.)	29.29 N	80.10 W
81	Breton Sd. La.	29.30 N	89.20 W
156	Brett C. (brĕt) N. Z.	35.10 S	174.20 E
83	Brevard (brē-värd') N. C.	35.15 N	82.43 W
101	Breves (brā'vĕzh) Braz.	1.45 S	50.15 W
118	Brevik (brĕ'vêk) Nor.	59.4 N	9.41 E
159	Brewarrina (brōō-ẽr-rē'nȧ) Austl.	30.0 S	146.48 E
86	Brewer (brōō'ẽr) Me.	44.45 N	68.45 W
95	Brewster, Cerro (Mt.) (brōō'stẽr) Pan.	9.20 N	79.15 W
82	Brewton (brōō'tŭn) Ala.	31.6 N	87.4 W
126	Brezice (brĕ'zhē-tsĕ) Yugo.	45.54 N	15.36 E
127	Breznik (brĕz'nĕk) Bul.	42.44 N	22.54 E
121	Brezno (bräz'nô) Czech.	48.49 N	19.39 E
123	Briançon (brē-äN-sôN') Fr.	44.55 N	6.40 E
122	Briare (brē-är') Fr.	47.40 N	2.48 E
160	Bribie (I.) (brī'bē) Austl. (In.)	26.55 S	153.7 E
51	Bridal Veil (brīd'ăl vāl) Ore. (Portland In.)	45.33 N	122.10 W
88	Bridgeburg (brĭj'bĕrg) Can. (Niagara Falls In.)	42.55 N	78.55 W
96	Bridge Pt. (brĭj) Ba. Is.	25.33 N	76.43 W
82	Bridgeport (brĭj'pōrt) Ala.	34.56 N	85.42 W
85	Bridgeport Conn.	41.12 N	73.12 W
84	Bridgeport Ill.	38.41 N	87.47 W
76	Bridgeport Neb.	41.40 N	103.7 W
84	Bridgeport Ohio	40.4 N	80.46 W
85	Bridgeport Pa.	40.7 N	75.22 W
79	Bridgeport Tex.	33.13 N	97.45 W
73	Bridgeton (brĭj'tŭn) Ala. (Birmingham In.)	33.28 N	86.38 W
85	Bridgeton N. J.	39.27 N	75.17 W
91	Bridgetown (brĭj'toun) Barb.	13.14 N	59.38 W
86	Bridgetown (brĭj'tŭn) Can.	44.52 N	65.19 W
89	Bridgeville (brĭj'vĭl) Pa. (Pittsburgh In.)	40.21 N	80.7 W
160	Bridgewater (brĭj'wô-tẽr) Austl. (Tas. In.)	42.45 S	147.13 E
86	Bridgewater Can.	44.22 N	64.31 W
114	Bridgewater Gt. Brit.	51.10 N	3.0 W
116	Bridgnorth (brĭj'nôrth) Gt. Brit.	52.32 N	2.25 W
86	Bridgton (brĭj'tŭn) Me.	44.3 N	70.45 W
114	Bridlington (brĭd'lĭng-tŭn) Gt. Brit.	54.5 N	0.15 W
116	Bridlington B. Gt. Brit.	54.3 N	0.9 W
160	Bridport (brĭd'pōrt) Austl. (Tas. In.)	41.1 S	147.24 E
83	Brier Cr. (brī'ẽr) Ga.	33.7 N	82.0 W
82	Brierfield (brī'ẽr-fēld) Ala.	33.2 N	86.55 W
116	Brierfield Gt. Brit.	53.49 N	2.14 W
86	Brier I. (brī'ẽr) Can.	44.15 N	66.25 W
116	Brierley Hill (brī'ẽr-lē hĭl) Gt. Brit.	52.29 N	2.7 W
123	Briey (brē-ĕ') Fr.	49.15 N	5.55 E
120	Brig (brēg) Switz.	46.18 N	7.59 E
116	Brigg (brĭg) Gt. Brit.	53.33 N	0.29 W
71	Brigham (brĭg'ăm) Utah	41.31 N	112.1 W
116	Brighouse (brĭg'hous) Gt. Brit.	53.42 N	1.47 W
73	Brighton (brīt'ŭn) Ala. (Birmingham In.)	33.25 N	86.58 W
160	Brighton Austl.	37.56 S	144.59 E
160	Brighton (brī'tŭn) Austl. (Tas. In.)	42.41 S	147.17 E
78	Brighton Colo.	39.57 N	104.49 W
114	Brighton Gt. Brit.	50.50 N	0.10 W
77	Brighton Ia.	41.11 N	91.49 W
157	Brighton N. Z.	42.5 S	171.30 E
73	Brighton Utah (Salt Lake City In.)	40.37 N	111.36 W
123	Brignoles (brēn-yôl') Fr.	43.25 N	6.5 E
87	Brigus (brĭg'ŭs) Can.	47.30 N	53.14 W
124	Brihuega (brê-wä'gä) Sp.	40.47 N	2.52 W
127	Brindisi (brēn'dē-zē) It.	40.38 N	18.0 E
126	Brinje (brēn'yĕ) Yugo.	45.1 N	15.7 E
79	Brinkley (brĭŋk'lĭ) Ark.	34.54 N	91.11 W
51	Brinnon (brĭn'ŭn) Wash. (Seattle In.)	47.41 N	122.54 W
87	Brion I. (brē-ôN') Can.	47.47 N	61.30 W
122	Brioude (brē-ōōd') Fr.	45.18 N	3.21 E
159	Brisbane (brĭz'bān) Austl.	27.29 S	153.8 E
160	Brisbane R. Austl. (In.)	27.0 S	152.23 E
85	Bristol (brĭs'tŭl) Conn.	41.40 N	72.58 W
114	Bristol Gt. Brit.	51.25 N	2.40 W
85	Bristol Pa.	40.7 N	74.52 W
85	Bristol R. I.	41.38 N	71.18 W
83	Bristol Tenn.	36.35 N	82.10 W
86	Bristol Vt.	44.10 N	73.5 W
83	Bristol Va.	36.36 N	82.10 W
52	Bristol B. Alsk.	58.20 N	158.0 W
114	Bristol Chan. Gt. Brit.	51.20 N	4.0 W
79	Bristow (brĭs'tō) Okla.	35.50 N	96.25 W
54	British Columbia (Prov.) Can.	56.50 N	125.0 W
101	British Guiana (gē-ä'nȧ) S. A.	5.0 N	59.0 W
94	British Honduras (hŏn-dōō'rȧs) Cen. Am. (In.)	17.10 N	88.40 W
135	British Somaliland (sō-mä'lē-lănd) Afr. (In.)	9.30 N	46.0 E
134	Britstown (brĭts'toun) U. S. Afr.	30.35 S	23.32 E
77	Britt (brĭt) Ia.	43.5 N	93.47 W
122	Brittany, Hills of (brĭt'ȧ-nĭ) Fr.	48.25 N	3.19 W
79	Britton (brĭt'ŭn) Okla.	35.34 N	97.33 W
76	Britton S. D.	45.48 N	97.44 W
117	Britz (brĕts) Ger. (Berlin In.)	52.27 N	13.27 E
122	Brive (brēv) Fr.	45.9 N	1.31 E
124	Briviesca (brē-vyās'kȧ) Sp.	42.33 N	3.20 W
120	Brno (Brünn) (b'r'nō) Czech.	49.13 N	16.35 E
96	Broa B. (brō'ȧ-bä) Cuba	22.30 N	81.55 W
159	Broad B. (brôd) Austl.	22.15 S	149.45 E
160	Broadmeadows (brôd'mĕd-ōz) Austl. (Melbourne In.)	37.40 S	144.56 E
72	Broadmoor (brôd'mŏŏr) Colo. (Colo. Sprs. In.)	38.48 N	104.51 W
82	Broad R. (brôd) Ga.	34.4 N	83.0 W
83	Broad R. S. C.	34.34 N	81.26 W
116	Brock R. (brŏk) Gt. Brit.	53.53 N	2.42 W
85	Brockport (brŏk'pōrt) N. Y.	43.13 N	77.57 W
86	Brockton (brŏk'tŭn) Mass.	42.5 N	71.0 W
51	Brockville (brŏk'vĭl) Can.	44.29 N	76.0 W
127	Brod (brōt) Yugo.	45.9 N	18.1 E
121	Brodnica (brôd'nĭt-sȧ) Pol.	53.16 N	19.26 E
121	Brody (brô'dĭ) Sov. Un.	50.4 N	25.11 E
117	Broechem (brû'kĕm) Bel. (Anvers In.)	51.11 N	4.36 E
79	Broken Arrow Okla.	36.3 N	95.46 W
76	Broken Bow Neb.	41.24 N	99.38 W
79	Broken Bow Okla.	34.1 N	94.44 W
134	Broken Hill N. Rh.	14.25 S	28.27 E
159	Broken Hill Austl.	31.58 S	141.37 E
159	Broken Hill Plat Austl.	30.45 S	142.30 E
159	Broken Hill (Willyama) (brōk'ĕn hĭl) (wĭl'yăm-ȧ) Austl.	31.57 S	141.28 E
117	Bromley (brŭm'lĭ) Gt. Brit. (London In.)	51.24 N	0.1 E
73	Brompton (brŏmp'tŭn) Ala. (Birmingham In.)	33.34 N	86.29 W
86	Bromptonville (brŭmp'tŭn-vĭl) Can.	45.38 N	71.59 W
116	Bromsgrove (brŏmz'grōv) Gt. Brit.	52.20 N	2.3 W
114	Bromwich, W. (brŭm'ĭch) Gt. Brit.	52.30 N	2.0 W
116	Bromyard (brŏm'yẽrd) Gt. Brit.	52.11 N	2.30 W
118	Brönderslev (brûn'dẽr-slĕv) Den.	57.17 N	9.57 E
128	Bronnitsy (brô-nyĭ'tsĭ) Sov. Un.	55.25 N	38.14 E
84	Bronson (brŏn'sŭn) Mich.	41.55 N	85.14 W
88	Bronx R. (brŏnks) N. Y. (New York In.)	40.53 N	73.52 W
153	Brookes Pt. (brŏŏks) Phil.	8.47 N	117.50 E
88	Brookfield (brŏŏk'fēld) Ill. (Chicago In.)	41.49 N	87.51 W
79	Brookfield Mo.	39.47 N	93.3 W
51	Brookfield Wash. (Portland In.)	46.15 N	123.34 W
82	Brookhaven (brŏŏk'hāv'n) Miss.	31.35 N	90.28 W
76	Brookings (brŏŏk'ĭngs) S. D.	44.18 N	96.47 W
87	Brookline (brŏŏk'lĭn) Mass. (In.)	42.19 N	71.6 W
88	Brooklyn (brŏŏk'lĭn) N. Y. (In.)	40.40 N	73.58 W
156	Brooklyn N. Z. (In.)	36.58 S	174.37 E
73	Brookside (brŏŏk'sīd) Ala. (Birmingham In.)	33.38 N	86.55 W
53	Brooks Ra. (brŏŏks) Alsk.	68.20 N	150.0 W
83	Brooksville (brŏŏks'vĭl) Fla. (In.)	28.32 N	82.28 W
84	Brookville (brŏŏk'vĭl) Ind.	39.25 N	85.0 W
85	Brookville Pa.	41.10 N	79.3 W
82	Brookwood (brŏŏk'wŏŏd) Ala.	33.17 N	87.20 W
160	Brooloo (brōō'lōō) Austl. (In.)	26.28 S	152.39 E
114	Broom, L. (brōōm) Gt. Brit.	57.28 N	5.30 W
158	Broome (brōōm) Austl.	17.57 S	122.5 E
72	Broomfield (brōōm'fēld) Colo. (Denver In.)	39.55 N	105.5 W
57	Brosseau (brôs-sō') Can. (Montreal In.)	45.27 N	73.27 W
88	Brother I. N. Y. (Niagara Falls In.)	43.5 N	79.4 W
96	Brothers (Is.) Ba. Is.	26.3 N	79.2 W
120	Broumov (brōō'môf) Czech.	50.31 N	16.10 E
137	Brower Str. (brou'ẽr) Indon.	1.30 N	102.0 E
97	Brown Bank Ba. Is.	21.30 N	74.32 W
78	Brownfield (broun'fēld) Tex.	33.11 N	102.15 W
116	Brownhills (broun'hĭlz) Gt. Brit.	52.38 N	1.55 W
73	Browning (broun'ĭng) Calif. (Los Angeles In.)	33.43 N	117.47 W
71	Browning Mont.	48.33 N	113.1 W
157	Brownings Pass N. Z.	42.57 S	171.22 E
56	Brown Pass. Can. (Prince Rupert In.)	54.18 N	130.48 W
84	Brownstown (brounz'toun) Ind.	38.51 N	86.2 W
82	Brownsville (brounz'vĭl) Tenn.	35.36 N	89.16 W
81	Brownsville Tex.	25.55 N	97.30 W
86	Brownville (broun'vĭl) Me.	45.19 N	69.2 W
80	Brownwood (broun'wŏŏd) Tex.	31.43 N	98.59 W
80	Brownwood L. Tex.	31.55 N	99.5 W
124	Brozas (brō'thäs) Sp.	39.37 N	6.47 W

ng-sing; ŋ-baŋk; N-nasalized n; nŏd; cŏmmit; ōld; ôbey; ôrder; fōōd; fŏŏt; ou-out; s-soft; sh-dish; th-thin; pūre; ûnite; ûrn; stŭd; circŭs; ü-as "y" in study; '-indeterminate vowel.

Bruce PRONOUNCING INDEX **Bytow**

Page	Name Pronunciation Region	Lat. °′	Long. °′
158	Bruce, Mt. (brōōs) Austl.	22.40 S	118.5 E
82	Bruceton (brōōs'tŭn) Tenn.	36.4 N	88.17 W
125	Bruch (brōōch) Sp. (In.)	41.35 N	1.48 E
57	Bruchesi (brōō-chē'sĭ) Can. (Montreal In.)	45.46 N	73.48 W
120	Bruchsal (brōōκ'zäl) Ger.	49.8 N	8.42 E
120	Bruck (brŏŏk) Aus.	47.25 N	15.15 E
120	Bruck Aus.	48.2 N	16.44 E
115	Bruges (brōō'jĕz; brüzh) Bel.	51.12 N	3.12 E
123	Brumath (brü-mät') Fr.	48.45 N	7.41 E
70	Bruneau R. (brōō-nō') Ida.	42.45 N	115.42 W
150	Brunei (brōō-nī') Bru.	5.0 N	115.0 E
150	Brunei Borneo	4.30 N	114.30 E
125	Brunete (brōō-nā'tā) Sp. (In.)	40.24 N	4.0 W
158	Brunette Downs (brōō-nĕt' dounz') Austl.	18.45 S	136.0 E
87	Brunette I. Can.	47.18 N	55.55 W
160	Bruni I. (brōō'nē) Austl. (Tas. In.)	43.25 S	147.18 E
	Brünn, see Brno, Czech.		
117	Brunn am Gebirge (brōōn' äm gĕ-bĭr'gĕ) Aus. (Wien In.)	48.7 N	16.17 E
157	Brunner (brŭn'ĕr) N. Z.	42.27 S	171.22 E
157	Brunner L. N. Z.	42.38 S	171.28 E
123	Brunoy (brü-nwä') Fr. (In.)	48.42 N	2.30 E
	Brunswick, see Braunschweig, Ger.		
83	Brunswick (brŭnz'wĭk) Ga.	31.8 N	81.29 W
86	Brunswick Me.	43.55 N	69.59 W
85	Brunswick Md.	39.18 N	77.38 W
79	Brunswick Mo.	39.25 N	93.7 W
72	Brunswick, Mt. Can. (Vancouver In.)	49.29 N	123.12 W
99	Brunswick Pen. Chl. (Magallanes In.)	53.30 S	71.30 W
78	Brush (brŭsh) Colo.	40.14 N	103.38 W
51	Brush Prairie. Wash. (Portland In.)	45.44 N	122.32 W
	Brussels, see Bruxelles, Bel.		
115	Bruxelles (Brussels) (brü-sĕl'; brŭs'ĕls) Bel.	50.52 N	4.22 E
84	Bryan (brī'ăn) Ohio	41.28 N	84.29 W
81	Bryan Tex.	30.40 N	96.22 W
128	Bryansk (b'r-yänsk') Sov. Un.	53.12 N	34.21 E
128	Bryansk (Dist.) Sov. Un.	52.45 N	33.50 E
76	Bryant (brī'ănt) S. D.	44.36 N	97.26 W
89	Bryant L. Minn. (Minneapolis In.)	45.4 N	93.12 W
75	Bryce Canyon Natl. Park (brīs) Utah	37.38 N	112.10 W
82	Bryson City (brīs'ŭn) N. C.	35.26 N	83.27 W
129	Bryukhovetskaya (b'ryŭk'ô-vyĕt-skä'yä) Sov. Un.	45.48 N	38.58 E
121	Brzeg (bzhĕg) Pol.	50.52 N	17.29 E
121	Brzeziny (bzhĕ-zhē'nĭ) Pol.	51.48 N	19.47 E
153	Buayan (bōō-ä'yän) Phil.	6.3 N	125.15 E
132	Buba (bōō'bȧ) Port. Gui.	11.42 N	14.58 W
153	Bubuan I. (bōō-bwän') Phil.	5.24 N	120.35 E
135	Bububu (bōō-bōō-bōō') Zan.	6.5 S	39.16 E
100	Bucaramanga (bōō-kä'rä-mäŋ'gä) Col.	7.0 N	73.28 W
153	Bucas Grande I. (bōō'kȧs grän'dē) Phil.	9.40 N	125.58 E
152	Bucay (bōō-kī') Phil.	17.32 N	120.42 E
158	Buccaneer Arch. (bŭk-ȧ-nēr') Austl.	16.15 S	123.15 E
121	Buchach (bōō'chȧch) Sov. Un.	49.3 N	25.24 E
132	Buchanan (bû-kăn'ăn) Lib.	6.0 N	10.6 W
84	Buchanan (bû-kăn'ăn) Mich.	41.49 N	86.25 W
159	Buchanan, L. Austl.	21.30 S	145.50 E
80	Buchanan Reservoir Tex.	30.45 N	98.25 W
127	Bucharest (Bucureşti) (bōō-kȧ-rĕst') (bōō-kōō-rĕsh'tĭ) Rom.	44.25 N	26.7 E
85	Buckhannon (bŭk-hăn'ŭn) W. Va.	39.0 N	80.14 W
114	Buckhaven (bŭk-hā'v'n) Gt. Brit.	56.10 N	3.0 W
72	Buckhorn Cr. (bŭk'hôrn) Colo. (Denver In.)	40.30 N	105.14 W
88	Buckhorn I. N. Y. (Niagara Falls In.)	43.4 N	79.0 W
117	Buckhurst Hill (bŭk'hûrst) Gt. Brit. (London In.)	51.38 N	0.2 E
114	Buckie (bŭk'ĭ) Gt. Brit.	57.40 N	3.0 W
116	Buckingham Co. (bŭk'ĭng-ăm) Gt. Brit.	52.7 N	0.45 W
159	Buckland Tableland (buk'lănd) Austl.	24.45 S	147.40 E
117	Buckow (bōō'kou) Ger. (Berlin In.)	52.25 N	13.26 E
86	Bucksport (bŭks'pôrt) Me.	44.36 N	68.46 W
121	Bucovina (Reg.) (bōō-kō-vē'nȧ) Sov. Un.	48.7 N	25.35 E
86	Buctouche (bük-tōōsh') Can.	46.29 N	64.42 W
127	Bucureşti (Bucharest) (bōō-kōō-rĕsh'tĭ) (bōō-kȧ-rĕst') Rom.	44.25 N	26.7 E
84	Bucyrus (bū-sī'rŭs) Ohio	40.50 N	82.48 W
121	Budapest (bōō'dȧ-pĕsht') Hung.	47.30 N	19.5 E
129	Budenovsk (bōō'dĕ-nôfsk) Sov. Un.	50.38 N	38.22 E
	Budweis, see České Budějovice, Czech.		
132	Buea (bōō-ā'ä) Nig.	4.12 N	9.15 E
100	Buenaventura (bwā'nä-vĕn-tōō'rä) Col.	3.58 N	77.5 W
78	Buena Vista (bū'nȧ vĭs'tȧ) Colo.	38.51 N	106.9 W
82	Buena Vista Ga.	32.16 N	84.31 W
85	Buena Vista Va.	37.44 N	79.21 W
96	Buenavista B. (bwā'nä-vēs'tä) Cuba	22.25 N	79.0 W
74	Buena Vista L. Reservoir, (bū'nȧ vĭs'tȧ) Calif.	35.12 N	119.18 W
102	Buenos Aires (bwā'nōs ī'rās) Arg.	34.35 S	58.22 W
99	Buenos Aires Arg. (In.)		
102	Buenos Aires (State) Arg.	36.30 S	60.0 W
102	Buenos Aires, L. Chl.-Arg.	46.32 S	72.0 W
93	Buey, Pt. (bōō-ā') Mex.	18.36 N	92.42 W
77	Buffalo (buf'ȧ-lō) Minn.	45.10 N	93.50 W
85	Buffalo N. Y.	42.55 N	78.55 W
88	Buffalo N. Y. (In.)		
71	Buffalo Wyo.	44.21 N	106.41 W
81	Buffalo Bayou (bŭf'ȧ-lō bī'ōō) Tex. (In.)	29.45 N	95.17 W
77	Buffalo Cr. Minn.	44.46 N	94.3 W
88	Buffalo Cr. N. Y. (Niagara Falls In.)	42.53 N	78.45 W
54	Buffalo L. Can.	56.0 N	109.0 W
79	Buffalo R. Ark.	35.57 N	92.50 W
76	Buffalo R. Minn.	46.52 N	96.20 W
82	Buffalo R. Tenn.	35.35 N	87.50 W
82	Buford (bū'fērd) Ga.	34.6 N	84.1 W
75	Buford Lake N. M.	36.35 N	106.55 W
129	Bug R. (bōōk) Sov. Un.-Pol.	48.10 N	30.0 E
153	Bugasong (bōō-gȧ-sông') Phil.	11.2 N	122.4 E
126	Bugojno (bōō-gō-ĭ-nô) Yugo.	44.3 N	17.27 E
153	Bugsuk I. (bōōg-sōōk') Phil.	8.15 N	117.18 E
152	Buguey (bōō'gā') Phil.	18.16 N	121.51 E
152	Bugui Pt. (bōō'gē) Phil.	12.36 N	123.14 E
110	Bugulma (bōō-gōōl'mȧ) Sov. Un.	54.40 N	52.40 E
110	Buguruslan (bōō-gōō-rōōs-lȧn') Sov. Un.	53.33 N	52.28 E
152	Buhi (bōō'ē) Phil.	13.26 N	123.31 E
123	Buhl (būl) Fr.	47.45 N	7.11 E
70	Buhl (būl) Ida.	42.46 N	114.46 W
77	Buhl Minn.	47.29 N	92.49 W
128	Bui (bwē) Sov. Un.	58.27 N	41.32 E
99	Buin (bōō-ēn') Chl. (Valparaiso In.)	33.44 S	70.48 W
111	Buinaksk (bōō'ē-näksk) Sov. Un.	42.44 N	47.10 E
150	Buitenzorg (bûē'tĕn-zôrgh) Indon.	6.45 S	106.45 E
124	Bujalance (bōō-hä-län'thā) Sp.	37.53 N	4.22 W
101	Bujaru (bōō-hȧ-rōō) Braz. (In.)	1.59 S	39.59 W
111	Bujnurd (bōōj-nōōrd') Iran	37.25 N	57.5 E
134	Bukama (bōō-kä'mȧ) Bel. Cong.	9.10 S	25.55 E
140	Bukhara (bōō-κä'rä) Sov. Un.	39.50 N	64.15 E
152	Bulacan (bōō-lä-kän') Phil.	14.47 N	120.53 E
151	Bulacan (Prov.) (bōō-lä-kän') Phil. (Manila In.)	14.54 N	121.0 E
151	Bulacan R. Phil. (Manila In.)	14.47 N	120.48 E
153	Bulacaue Pt. (bōō-lä-kou'ā) Phil.	11.35 N	123.10 E
152	Bulalacao (bōō-lȧ-lȧ'kä-ô) Phil.	12.31 N	121.26 E
152	Bulan (bōō'län) Phil.	12.40 N	123.53 E
134	Bulawayo (bōō-lȧ-wä'yō) S. Rh.	20.13 S	28.38 E
127	Bulgaria (bŏŏl-gā'rĭ-ȧ) Eur.	43.0 N	25.0 E
153	Buliluyan, C. (bōō-lĭ-lōō'yän) Phil.	8.20 N	117.11 E
160	Bulla (bŏŏl'ȧ) Austl. (Melbourne In.)	37.39 S	144.49 E
124	Bullaque R. (bōō-lä'kȧ) Sp.	39.15 N	4.15 W
124	Bullas (bōōl'yäs) Sp.	38.5 N	1.40 W
75	Bulldog Cr. Utah	37.40 N	110.50 W
157	Buller R. (bŏŏl'ĕr) N. Z.	41.50 S	172.10 E
96	Bull Head (Mt.) Jam.	18.9 N	77.17 W
153	Bulloo R. (bŭ-lōō') Austl.	27.30 S	144.0 E
156	Bulls N. Z.	40.8 S	175.25 E
135	Bulo Burti (bōō'lō bōōr'tĭ) Som.	3.55 N	45.28 E
153	Buluan, L. (bōō-lōō'än) Phil.	6.40 N	124.48 E
139	Bulun (bōō-lōōn') Sov. Un.	70.40 N	127.10 E
134	Bulungu (bōō-lōōŋ'gōō) Bel. Cong.	5.0 S	19.0 E
142	Bulun-Tokhoi (bōō-lōōn'-tô-κoi') Chn.	46.55 N	87.17 E
152	Bulusan (Vol.) (bōō-lōō'sän) Phil.	12.46 N	124.4 E
133	Bumba (bōōm'bȧ) Bel. Cong.	2.12 N	22.31 E
151	Buna (bōō'nȧ) Pap. Ter.	8.45 S	148.25 E
153	Bunawan (bōō-na'wän) Phil.	8.11 N	125.57 E
159	Bundaberg (bŭn'dȧ-bûrg) Austl.	24.45 S	152.10 E
113	Bu Ngem (bōō 'n-gĕm) Libya	30.30 N	15.30 E
149	Bungo Str. (bōōŋ'gō) Jap.	33.10 N	132.10 E
81	Bunkie (bŭŋ'kĭ) La.	30.58 N	92.10 W
160	Bunya Mts. (bŭn'yȧ) Austl. (In.)	26.50 S	151.30 E
140	Buraida (bōō-rī'dȧ) Sau. Ar.	26.28 N	44.15 E
89	Buras (bûr'ȧs) La. (New Orleans In.)	29.21 N	89.33 W
135	Burau (bōō-rä'ōō) Br. Som.	9.37 N	45.37 E
73	Burbank (bûr'bănk) Calif. (Los Angeles In.)	34.11 N	118.19 W
159	Burdekin R. (bûr'dē-kĭn) Austl.	20.30 S	147.10 E
111	Burdur (bōōr-dōōr') Tur.	37.45 N	30.18 E
141	Burdwan (bōōrd-wän') India	23.15 N	87.58 E
139	Bureya R. (bōō-rā'yȧ) Sov. Un.	50.45 N	131.0 E
135	Bur Gao (Porto Durnford) (bûr gä'ô) Som.	1.10 S	41.47 E
127	Burgas (bōōr-gäs') Bul.	42.29 N	27.29 E
127	Burgas, G. of Bul.	42.30 N	27.40 E
83	Burgaw (bûr'gô) N. C.	34.33 N	77.56 W
120	Burgdorf (bōōrg'dôrf) Switz.	47.3 N	7.37 E
160	Burgess (bûr'jĕs) Austl. (Tas. In.)	41.10 S	146.32 E
117	Burgh (bōōrg) Bel. (Anvers In.)	51.12 N	4.20 E
133	Burgi (bōōr'gē) Eth.	5.28 N	38.0 E
80	Burgos (bōōr'gōs) Mex.	24.57 N	98.48 W
152	Burgos Phil.	16.3 N	119.52 E
124	Burgos Sp.	42.22 N	3.43 W
118	Burgsvik (bōōrgs'vĭk) Swe.	57.3 N	18.20 E
141	Burhanpur (bōōr'hän-pōōr) India	21.15 N	76.15 E
153	Burias I. (bōō'rē-äs) Phil.	13.0 N	123.5 E
152	Burias Pass Phil.	13.0 N	123.15 E
95	Burica Pt. (bōō'rē-kä) C. R.-Pan.	8.3 N	82.55 W
87	Burin (bûr'ĭn) Can.	47.5 N	55.11 W
79	Burkburnett (bûrk-bûr'nĕt) Tex.	34.5 N	98.34 W
86	Burke (bûrk) Vt.	44.38 N	71.59 W
158	Burketown (bûrk'toun) Austl.	17.48 S	139.30 E
71	Burley (bûr'lĭ) Ida.	42.31 N	113.48 W
51	Burley Wash. (Seattle In.)	47.24 N	122.38 W
74	Burlingame (bûr'lĭn-găm) Calif.	37.34 N	122.24 W
79	Burlingame Kan.	38.45 N	95.49 W
78	Burlington (bûr'lĭng-tŭn) Colo.	39.17 N	102.26 W
77	Burlington Ia.	40.49 N	91.8 W
79	Burlington Kan.	38.12 N	95.45 W
89	Burlington Ky. (Cincinnati In.)	39.2 N	84.44 W
85	Burlington N. J.	40.3 N	74.57 W
83	Burlington N. C.	36.5 N	79.26 W
86	Burlington Vt.	44.30 N	73.15 W
77	Burlington Wis.	42.41 N	88.18 W
72	Burlington Ditch Colo. (Denver In.)	39.53 N	104.55 W
131	Burlos, L. (bōōr'lōs) Eg. (In.)	31.25 N	30.55 E
141	Burma (bûr'mȧ) Asia	21.30 N	94.30 E
73	Burmester (bûr'mĕs-tēr) Utah (Salt Lake City In.)	40.42 N	112.27 W
72	Burnaby L. (bûrn'ȧ-bĭ) Can. (Vancouver In.)	49.15 N	122.57 W
99	Burnay, Mt. (bōōr-nī') Chl. (Magallanes In.)	52.19 S	73.20 W
80	Burnet (bûrn'ĕt) Tex.	30.45 N	98.15 W
19	Burnham-on-Crouch (bûrn'ăm-ŏn-krouch) Gt. Brit. (London In.)	51.38 N	0.48 E
160	Burnie (bûr'nē) Austl. (Tas. In.)	41.4 S	145.55 E
114	Burnley (bûrn'lē) Gt. Brit.	53.48 N	2.20 W
70	Burns (bûrnz) Ore.	43.35 N	119.4 W
82	Burnside (bûrn'sīd) Ky.	36.59 N	84.36 W
157	Burns Mt. N. Z.	45.40 S	167.28 E
86	Burnsville (bûrnz'vĭl) Can.	47.43 N	65.8 W
72	Burnt Mt. (bûrnt) Colo. (Denver In.)	40.4 N	105.29 W
70	Burnt R. Ore.	44.30 N	117.43 W
	Burra, see Kooringa.		
160	Burramba (bû-răm'bȧ) Austl. (In.)	28.38 S	150.36 E
72	Burrard Inlet (bûr'ȧrd) Can. (Vancouver In.)	49.18 N	123.13 W
72	Burrard Inlet, N. Arm Can. (Vancouver In.)	49.22 N	122.55 W
125	Burriana (bōōr-rē-ä'nä) Sp.	39.54 N	0.5 W
111	Bursa (bōōr'sȧ) Tur.	40.10 N	29.10 E
114	Burton (bûr'tŭn) Gt. Brit.	52.50 N	1.40 W
116	Burton Gt. Brit.	54.11 N	2.43 W
51	Burton Wash. (Seattle In.)	47.23 N	122.28 W
59	Burton Reservoir Ga.	34.45 N	83.30 W
117	Burtonwood (bûr'tŭn-wŏŏd) Gt. Brit. (Liverpool In.)	53.26 N	2.39 W
84	Burts L. (bûrts) Mich.	45.27 N	84.40 W
153	Buruanga (bōō-rōō-äŋ'gä) Phil.	11.50 N	121.53 E
140	Burujird (bōō-rōō-jērd') Iran	33.50 N	49.0 E
152	Buruncan Pt. (bōō-rōōn'kän) Phil.	12.13 N	121.13 E
76	Burwell (bûr'wĕl) Neb.	41.46 N	99.8 W
114	Bury (bĕr'ĭ) Gt. Brit.	53.35 N	2.20 W
139	Buryat-Mongol (Soviet Rep.) (bōōr'yät'-mŏŋ'gôl) Sov. Un.	53.0 N	110.0 E
115	Bury St. Edmunds (bĕr'ĭ-sānt ĕd'mŭndz) Gt. Brit.	52.12 N	0.42 E
132	Busa (bōō'sȧ) Nig.	10.12 N	4.30 E
133	Buseima (Well) (bōō-zā'mȧ) Libya	25.7 N	22.10 E
131	Bûsh (bōōsh) Eg. (In.)	29.12 N	31.10 E
117	Bushey Heath (bŏŏsh'ĭ hēth) Gt. Brit. (London In.)	51.39 N	0.22 W
140	Bushire (Bandar Abu Shehr) (bōō-shēr') (bŭn'dăr-ä'bōō-shĕr') Iran	28.47 N	50.47 E
134	Bushman Land (bŏŏsh-măn lănd) U. S. Afr.	29.20 S	19.30 E
79	Bushnell (bŏŏsh'nĕl) Ill.	40.33 N	90.29 W
133	Businga (bōō-sĭŋ'gȧ) Bel. Cong.	3.15 N	20.33 E
158	Busselton (bŭs''l-tŭn) Austl.	33.31 S	115.29 E
123	Bussy-St. Georges (bü-sē'săn zhôrzh') Fr. (In.)	48.50 N	2.42 E
80	Bustamante (bōōs-tȧ-män'tȧ) Mex.	26.34 N	100.30 W
51	Buster (bŭs'tēr) Ore. (Portland In.)	45.54 N	123.24 W
88	Bustleton (bŭs''l-tŭn) Pa. (Philadelphia In.)	40.5 N	75.1 W
126	Busto Arsizio (bōōs'tō är-sēd'zē-ō) It.	45.35 N	8.54 E
151	Bustos (bōōs'tōs) Phil. (Manila In.)	14.58 N	120.53 E
152	Busuanga I. (bōō-swäŋ'gä) Phil.	12.10 N	120.5 E
133	Buta (bōō'tȧ) Bel. Cong.	2.47 N	24.45 E
84	Butler (bŭt'lĕr) Ind.	41.26 N	84.53 W
79	Butler Mo.	38.16 N	94.19 W
85	Butler Pa.	40.52 N	79.54 W
	Buton (I.) see Boeton.		
121	Bütow (bü'tou) Pol.	54.9 N	17.30 E
82	Buttahatchie R. (bŭt-ȧ-hăch'ē) Miss.	33.54 N	88.10 W
71	Butte (būt) Mont.	46.0 N	112.31 W
72	Buttes (būts) Colo. (Colo. Spgs. In.)	38.36 N	104.40 W
153	Butuan (bōō-tōō'än) Phil.	8.56 N	125.32 E
153	Butuan B. Phil.	9.5 N	125.24 E
139	Butuntai R. (bōō-tōōn-tī') Sov. Un.	68.25 N	130.0 E
129	Buturlinovka (bōō-tōōr'lē-nôf'kȧ) Sov. Un.	50.47 N	40.38 E
117	Buxtehude (bŏŏks-tĕ-hōō'dĕ) Ger. (Hamburg In.)	53.29 N	9.43 E
116	Buxton (bŭks't'n) Gt. Brit.	53.15 N	1.55 W
51	Buxton Ore. (Portland In.)	45.41 N	123.11 W
143	Buyer Nor (L.) (bōō'yĕr nôr) Chn.	47.45 N	117.40 E
111	Buzachi Pen. (bōō-zä'che) Sov. Un.	45.0 N	53.40 E
127	Buzău (bōō-zĕ'ōō) Rom.	45.8 N	26.51 E
127	Buzău R. Rom.	45.5 N	27.0 E
121	Buzhsk (bōōzhk) Sov. Un.	49.57 N	24.39 E
111	Buzuluk (bōō-zōō-lōōk') Sov. Un.	52.45 N	52.15 E
134	Bwanamkubwa (bwä-näm-kōōb'wȧ) N. Rh.	13.10 S	28.45 E
135	Bweleo (bwā'lä-ô) Zan.	6.18 S	39.18 E
121	Bydgoszcz (bĭd'gôshch) Pol.	53.8 N	18.0 E
84	Byesville (bīz-vĭl) Ohio	39.58 N	81.33 W
118	Bygdin L. (bügh-dēn') Nor.	61.23 N	8.30 E
118	Byglandsfjord (bügh'länds-fyôr) Nor.	58.40 N	7.50 E
160	Byrun (bī'rŭn) Austl. (In.)	28.36 S	153.33 E
160	Byron B. Austl. (In.)	28.34 S	153.35 E
121	Bytom (bĭ'tŭm) Pol.	50.21 N	18.55 E
128	Bytosh (bĭ-tôsh') Sov. Un.	53.46 N	34.2 E
121	Bytow (bĭ'tŭf) Pol.	54.9 N	17.30 E

ăt; finăl; rāte; senâte; ärm; ȧsk; sofȧ; fâre; ch-choose; dh-as th in other; bē; êvent; bĕt; recĕnt; cratĕr; g-go; gh-gutteral g; bĭt; ĭ-short neutral; rīde; κ-gutteral k as ch in German ich;

Caazapá PRONOUNCING INDEX **Campechuela**

Page	Name Pronunciation Region	Lat. °′	Long. °′
102	Caazapá (kä-zä-pä′)........Par.	26.10 S	56.28 W
153	Cabadbaran (kä′bäd-bä-rän′). Phil.	9.6 N	125.33 E
152	Cabagan (kä-bä-gän′........Phil.	17.26 N	121.46 E
152	Cabalete I. (kä-bä-lā′tå).....Phil.	14.18 N	121.50 E
153	Cabalian (kä-bä-lē′än)......Phil.	10.16 N	125.12 E
96	Caballones Cay (I.) (kä-bä-lyō′ nås). Cuba	20.51 N	79.0 W
96	Caballones Channel........Cuba	20.48 N	78.57 W
152	Cabanatuan (kä-bä-nä-twän′) Phil.	15.29 N	120.58 E
89	Cabaret I. (kă′bȧ-rĕt) Ill. (St. Louis In.)	38.43 N	90.11 W
152	Cabarruyan I. (kä-bä-rōō′yän) Phil.	16.17 N	119.58 E
151	Cabcabe (käb-kä′bå) Phil. (Manila In.)	14.27 N	120.30 E
101	Cabedelo (kä-bē-dā′lōō).....Braz.	6.59 S	34.55 W
124	Cabeza del Buey (kä-bā′thä dĕl bwā′). Sp.	38.43 N	5.14 W
93	Cabeza Reefs (kä-bā′thä)...Mex.	19.5 N	95.53 W
100	Cabija (kä-bē′hä)...........Bol.	11.1 S	68.59 W
134	Cabinda (kä-bĭn′dȧ)........Ang.	5.40 S	12.12 E
134	Cabinda (Prov.)............Ang.	5.0 S	12.15 E
153	Cabingaan I. (kä-bĭng-ä′än)..Phil.	5.40 N	121.3 E
95	Cabo Gracias a Dias (kä′bō grä′sê-äs ä dyōs′). Nic.	14.57 N	83.17 W
160	Caboolture (kȧ-bōōl′tûr) Austl. (In.)	27.3 S	152.57 E
84	Cabot Head (C.) (kăb′ŭt)...Can.	45.15 N	81.17 W
87	Cabot Str..................Can.	47.40 N	59.59 W
132	Cabo Yubi (că′bō yōō′bē). R. de O.	27.55 N	12.46 W
124	Cabra (käb′rä)..............Sp.	37.28 N	4.26 W
152	Cabra I....................Phil.	13.52 N	120.2 E
160	Cabramatta (kă-brȧ-măt′ȧ) Austl. (Sydney In.)	33.54 S	150.56 E
125	Cabrera I. (kä-brā′rä)........Sp.	39.8 N	2.57 E
124	Cabriel R. (kä-brē-ĕl′)........Sp.	39.35 N	1.38 W
74	Cabrillo Natl. Mon. (kä-brēl′yō) Calif. (In.)	32.40 N	117.15 W
101	Cabrodó (kä-brō-dōō′)..... Braz.	8.47 S	38.59 W
153	Cabucan I. (kä-bōō′kän).....Phil.	6.8 N	120.54 E
152	Cabugao (kä-bōō′gä-ô)......Phil.	17.47 N	120.27 E
153	Cabulauan I. (kä-bōō-lä′wän) Phil.	11.22 N	120.7 E
127	Čačak (chä′chȧk)..........Yugo.	43.51 N	20.22 E
124	Caceres (kä′thå-rās)..........Sp.	39.28 N	6.21 W
74	Cache Cr. (kăsh)..........Calif.	38.50 N	122.13 W
78	Cache Cr..................Okla.	34.35 N	98.23 W
78	Cache la Poudre R. (kȧsh lȧ pōōd′r′). Colo.	40.33 N	105.0 W
79	Cache R....................Ark.	35.20 N	91.12 W
102	Cachinal (kä-chē-näl′).......Chl.	24.40 S	69.35 W
101	Cachoeira (kä-shô-ā′rä). Braz.(In.)	1.2 S	48.59 W
102	Cachoeira.................Braz.	30.1 S	53.0 W
101	Cachoeira...........Braz. (In.)	12.34 S	39.1 W
134	Caconda (kä-kōn′dä).........Ang.	13.42 S	15.8 E
81	Caddo L. (kăd′ō)........La.-Tex.	32.41 N	94.0 W
92	Cadereyta (kä-dâ-rā′tä).....Mex.	20.41 N	99.48 W
80	Cadereyta Jiménez (kä-dä-rā′tä hê-mā′nāz). Mex.	25.36 N	100.0 W
152	Cadig, Mt. (kä′dêg).........Phil.	14.11 N	122.27 E
84	Cadillac (kăd′ĭ-lăk)........Mich.	44.15 N	85.25 W
117	Cadishead (kăd′ĭs-hĕd) Gt. Brit. (Liverpool In.)	53.25 N	2.26 W
84	Cadiz (kā′dĭz)..............Ohio	40.18 N	81.0 W
153	Cadiz (kā′dēz)..............Phil.	10.57 N	123.19 E
125	Cadiz (kä′dhēth)........Sp. (In.)	36.32 N	6.17 W
125	Cadiz (Prov.)..........Sp. (In.)	36.36 N	6.6 W
125	Cadiz B...............Sp. (In.)	36.33 N	6.12 W
124	Cadiz, G. of.................Sp.	36.50 N	7.0 W
153	Caduruan Pt. (kä-dōō-rōō-än′) Phil.	11.43 N	124.4 E
122	Caen (käɴ)...................Fr.	49.10 N	0.20 W
137	Caesarea (sĕs-ȧ-rē′ȧ)....Pal. (In.)	32.29 N	34.54 E
101	Caetité (kä-â-tê-tā′)........Braz.	14.2 S	42.32 W
134	Cafima (kä-fē′mä)..........Ang.	16.52 S	16.25 E
102	Cagarras Is. (kä-gär′rȧs) Atl. O. (In.)	23.2 S	43.12 W
153	Cagayan (kä-gä-yän′).......Phil.	8.29 N	124.40 E
153	Cagayan Is.................Phil.	9.35 N	121.15 E
152	Cagayan, L.................Phil.	18.2 N	121.58 E
152	Cagayan R..................Phil.	17.25 N	121.50 E
153	Cagayan Sulu I. (kä-gä-yän′ sōō′lōō). Phil.	7.0 N	118.30 E
126	Cagli (käl′yē)..................It.	43.32 N	12.38 E
126	Cagliari (käl′yä-rē).........Sard.	39.14 N	9.6 E
126	Cagliari, G. of.............Sard.	39.5 N	9.15 E
123	Cagnes-sur-Mer (kän′y′-sûr-mâr) Fr.	43.40 N	7.5 E
152	Cagraray I. (kä-grä-rī′)......Phil.	13.20 N	123.52 E
152	Cagua, Mt. (Vol.) (kä′gwä)..Phil.	18.13 N	122.7 E
91	Caguas (kä′gwäs)......P. R. (In.)	18.10 N	66.0 W
73	Cahaba Mt. (kȧ-hô′bȧ) Ala. (Birmingham In.)	33.43 N	86.33 W
82	Cahaba R....................Ala.	32.45 N	87.15 W
89	Cahokia (kȧ-hō′kĭ-ȧ) Ill. (St. Louis In.)	38.34 N	90.12 W
122	Cahors (kȧ-ôr′)...............Fr.	44.28 N	1.30 E
95	Cahuita Pt. (kä-wē′tȧ).....C. R.	9.45 N	82.50 W
151	Cahunchan, R. (kä-hōōn′chän) Phil. (Manila In.)	13.47 N	121.5 E
134	Caiambo (kä-yäm′bō).......Ang.	15.47 S	20.15 E
96	Caibarién (kī-bä-rê-ĕn′).....Cuba	22.29 N	79.31 W
153	Caibiran (kī-bê′rän).........Phil.	11.33 N	124.34 E
97	Caicos Bank (kī′kōs)......Ba. Is.	21.25 N	72.0 W
97	Caicos Passage...........Ba. Is.	22.0 N	72.40 W
81	Caillou B. (kȧ-yōō′)..........La.	29.15 N	90.55 W
97	Caimanera (kī-mä-nā′rä)....Cuba	19.58 N	75.10 W
152	Caiman Pt. (kī′mȧn)........Phil.	15.57 N	119.45 E
151	Cainta (kä-ēn-tä′) Phil. (Manila In.)	14.35 N	121.7 E
159	Cairns (kârnz)............Austl.	17.0 S	145.47 E
133	Cairo (kī′rō)................Eg.	30.2 N	31.21 E
135	Cairo, Eg. (In.)		
82	Cairo (kā′rō)................Ga.	30.52 N	84.14 W
79	Cairo.......................Ill.	37.0 N	89.10 W
99	Cairoçu Pt. (kī′rō-sōō) Braz. (Rio de Janeiro In.	23.22 S	44.35 W
135	Cairo, Old (Masr el Atîqa) (kī′rō) (mäz″r ĕl ȧ-tē′kä). Eg.	30.1 N	31.15 E
116	Caistor (kâs′tēr)........Gt. Brit.	53.30 N	0.20 W
100	Cajamarca (kä-hä-mär′kä)...Peru	7.2 S	78.30 W
152	Cajidiocan (kä-hē-dyô′kän)..Phil.	12.21 N	122.41 E
127	Cajniče (chī′nĭ-chĕ).........Yugo.	43.32 N	19.5 E
73	Cajon (kȧ-hōn′) Calif. (Los Angeles In.)	34.17 N	117.28 W
93	Cajones, R. (kȧ-hō′nås).....Mex.	17.35 N	96.10 W
126	Cakovec (chä′kō-vĕts).....Yugo.	46.25 N	16.27 E
152	Calabanga (kä-lä-bäŋ′gä)....Phil.	13.41 N	123.12 E
132	Calabar (kăl-ȧ-bär′).........Nig.	4.58 N	8.21 E
73	Calabasas (kä-lä-bäs′äs) Calif. (Los Angeles In.)	34.9 N	118.40 W
100	Calabozo (kä-lä-bō′zō)......Ven.	9.0 N	67.28 W
92	Calabozo, R...............Mex.	21.30 N	98.24 W
126	Calabria (Prov.) (kä-lä′brê-ä)..It.	39.20 N	16.30 E
151	Calaca (kä-lä′kä) Phil. (Manila In.)	13.57 N	120.46 E
127	Calafat (kȧ-lȧ-fȧt′).........Rom.	43.59 N	22.57 E
153	Calagnaan I. (kä-läg-nȧ-än′). Phil.	11.27 N	123.15 E
152	Calagua Is. (kä-läg′wä).....Phil.	14.28 N	122.58 E
124	Calahorra (kä-lä-ôr′rä).......Sp.	42.18 N	1.58 W
122	Calais (kȧ-lĕ′)...............Fr.	50.55 N	1.50 E
86	Calais (kăl′ĭs)...............Me.	45.9 N	67.15 W
100	Calamar (kä-lä-mär′)........Col.	2.1 N	71.68 W
100	Calamar....................Col.	10.15 N	74.59 W
152	Calamba (kä-läm′bä).......Phil.	14.13 N	121.9 E
152	Calamian Group (Is.) (kä-lä-myän′). Phil.	12.0 N	120.0 E
124	Calañas (kä-län′yäs).........Sp.	37.41 N	6.52 W
125	Calanda (kä-län′dä)..........Sp.	40.57 N	0.14 W
152	Calapan (kä-lä-pän′)........Phil.	13.24 N	121.10 E
153	Calape (kä-lä′pā)...........Phil.	9.52 N	123.53 E
127	Călăraşi (kŭ-lŭ-rȧsh′ĭ)......Rom.	44.11 N	27.22 E
129	Călăraşi-Târg (kŭ-lŭ-rȧsh′ĭ-tărg) Rom.	47.14 N	28.12 E
124	Calasparra (kä-lä-spär′rä).....Sp.	38.14 N	1.42 W
151	Calatagan (kä-lä-tä-gän′) Phil. (Manila In.)	13.50 N	120.34 E
124	Calatayud (kä-lä-tä-yōōdh′)...Sp.	41.23 N	1.38 W
152	Calauag (kä-lä-wäg′)........Phil.	13.58 N	122.17 E
152	Calauag B..................Phil.	14.15 N	122.10 E
152	Calavite, C. (kä-lä-vē′tā)....Phil.	13.27 N	120.18 E
151	Calawan (kä-lä′wän) Phil. (Manila In.)	14.10 N	121.21 E
152	Calayan I. (kä-lä-yän′)......Phil.	19.20 N	121.23 E
153	Calbayog (käl-bä′yōg).......Phil.	12.4 N	124.37 E
153	Calbiga (käl-bē′gä)..........Phil.	11.37 N	125.1 E
81	Calcasieu L. (kăl′kȧ-shū).....La.	29.55 N	93.17 W
81	Calcasieu R..................La.	30.28 N	93.0 W
141	Calcutta (kăl-kŭt′ȧ).......India	22.30 N	88.30 E
124	Caldas da Rainha (käl′däs dä rīn′yă). Port.	39.24 N	9.8 W
125	Caldas de Mombúy (käl′däs dā môm-bōō′ê). Sp. (In.)	41.36 N	21.11 E
116	Calder, R. (kôl′dēr).....Gt. Brit.	53.40 N	1.36 W
102	Caldera (käl-dā′rä)..........Chl.	27.1 S	70.40 W
93	Caldera, Cerro (Mt.) (käl-dā′rä, sĕr′rō). Mex. (In.)	19.20 N	98.58 W
70	Caldwell (kôld′wĕl)..........Ida.	43.40 N	116.41 W
79	Caldwell...................Kan.	37.3 N	97.36 W
80	Caldwell...................Ohio	39.43 N	81.32 W
81	Caldwell....................Tex.	30.33 N	96.42 W
77	Caledonia (kăl-ê-dō′nĭ-ȧ)...Minn.	43.38 N	91.30 W
114	Caledonian Canal.......Gt. Brit.	57.10 N	4.30 W
125	Calella (kä-lĕl′yä)............Sp.	41.36 N	2.40 E
122	Calenzana (kä-lĕnt-sä′nä) Cor. (In.)	42.30 N	8.50 E
92	Calera (kä-lā′rä)...........Mex.	22.57 N	102.40 W
74	Calexico (kȧ-lĕk′sĭ-kō)......Calif.	32.40 N	115.30 W
54	Calgary (kăl′gȧ-rĭ)..........Can.	51.1 N	114.1 W
125	Calha Pt. (käl′yä).....Port. (In.)	38.40 N	9.16 W
82	Calhoun (kăl-hōōn′).........Ga.	34.30 N	84.57 W
89	Calhoun, L. Minn. (Minneapolis In.)	44.56 N	93.18 W
100	Cali (kä′lē).................Col.	3.20 N	76.33 W
111	Caliacra, C. (kä-lyä-krä′)...Rom.	43.28 N	28.30 E
89	Calibogue Sd. (kă-lĭ-bō′gū) S. C. (Savannah In.)	32.8 N	80.50 W
153	Calicoan I. (kä-lê-kô′än).....Phil.	11.0 N	125.48 E
141	Calicut (kăl′ĭ-kŭt)..........India	11.15 N	75.47 E
75	Caliente (käl-yĕn′tā).......Nev.	37.38 N	114.29 W
79	California (kăl-ĭ-fôr′nĭ-ȧ).....Mo.	38.37 N	92.37 W
74	California (State)..........U. S.	37.5 N	119.50 W
89	California B. La. (New Orleans In.)	29.0 N	89.33 W
74	Calipatria (kăl-ĭ-pȧt′rĭ-ȧ)...Calif.	33.8 N	115.30 W
93	Calkiní (käl-kê-nē′).........Mex.	20.23 N	90.3 W
72	Calkins L. (kô′kĭnz) Colo. (Denver In.)	40.11 N	105.3 W
100	Callao (käl-yä′ô)...........Peru	12.2 S	77.1 W
117	Calloo (kä-lōō′)..Bel. (Anvers In.)	51.15 N	4.17 E
73	Calls Fort (kôlz fôrt) Utah (Salt Lake City In.)	41.36 N	112.4 W
77	Calmar (käl′mȧr).............Ia.	43.11 N	91.43 W
92	Calnali (käl-nä-lē′).........Mex.	20.53 N	98.34 W
152	Calolbon (kä-lôl-bōn′).......Phil.	13.37 N	124.7 E
152	Caloocan (kä-lô-ō′kän)......Phil.	14.38 N	120.59 E
83	Caloosahatchee R. (kȧ-lōō-sȧ-hăch′ê). Fla. (In.)	26.40 N	81.50 W
160	Caloundria (kȧ-lōōn′drĭ-ȧ) Austl. (In.)	26.45 S	153.6 E
92	Calpulálpam (käl-pōō-läl′päm) Mex.	19.35 N	98.34 W
126	Caltagirone (käl-tä-jē-rō′nå)...It.	37.15 N	14.30 E
126	Caltanissetta (käl-tä-nê-sĕt′tä). It.	37.29 N	14.2 E
122	Caluire (kȧ-lwēr′)............Fr.	45.50 N	4.50 E
134	Calumbo (kä-lōōm′bō)......Ang.	9.2 S	13.32 E
77	Calumet (kă-lū-mĕt′)......Mich.	47.15 N	88.26 W
88	Calumet City....Ill. (Chicago In.)	41.38 N	87.32 W
88	Calumet Har....Ill. (Chicago In.)	41.44 N	87.31 W
88	Calumet, L......Ill. (Chicago In.)	41.41 N	87.35 W
88	Calumet Sag Chan. (Canal) Ill. (Chicago In.)	41.41 N	87.48 W
151	Calumpit (kä-lōōm-pēt′) Phil. (Manila In.)	14.57 N	120.42 E
153	Caluya (kä-lōō′yȧ)..........Phil.	11.56 N	121.33 E
153	Caluya I...................Phil.	11.55 N	121.33 E
81	Calvert (kăl′vērt)...........Tex.	30.58 N	96.40 W
54	Calvert I...................Can.	51.31 N	128.0 W
122	Calvi (käl′vē)..........Cor. (In.)	42.30 N	8.42 E
92	Calvillo (käl-vēl′yō).........Mex.	21.53 N	102.48 W
134	Calvinia (kăl-vĭn′ĭ-ȧ)...U. S. Afr.	31.28 S	19.45 E
96	Camagüey (kä-mä-gwā′)....Cuba	21.21 N	77.59 W
96	Camagüey (State)..........Cuba	21.28 N	78.0 W
96	Camajuani (kä-mä-hwä′nê)..Cuba	22.25 N	79.46 W
152	Camalig (kä-mä′lêg)........Phil.	13.10 N	123.39 E
100	Camana (kä-mä′nä).........Peru	16.32 S	72.47 W
51	Camano (kä-mä′nō) Wash. (Seattle In.)	48.10 N	122.31 W
51	Camano I.....Wash. (Seattle In.)	48.14 N	122.30 W
80	Camargo (kä-mär′gō).......Mex.	26.17 N	98.50 W
131	Camariñal, C. (kä-mä-rê-nyäl′) Sp. (Gibraltar In.)	36.5 N	5.14 E
94	Camarón, C. (kä-mä-rōn′)..Hond.	15.58 N	85.8 W
125	Camarón, Pt...........Sp. (In.)	36.44 N	6.27 W
70	Camas (kăm′ȧs)...........Wash.	45.35 N	122.25 W
51	Camas......Wash. (Portland In.)	45.35 N	122.25 W
71	Camas Cr...................Ida.	44.12 N	112.0 W
141	Cambay, G. of (kăm-bā′)...India	21.30 S	72.15 E
160	Camberwell (kăm′bēr-wĕl) Austl. (Melbourne In.)	37.50 S	145.4 E
150	Cambodia (State) (kăm-bō′dĭ-ȧ) Indoch.	12.15 N	105.0 E
150	Cambodia Pt............Indoch.	8.37 N	104.38 E
114	Camborne (kăm′bôrn)...Gt. Brit.	50.15 N	5.15 W
122	Cambrai (käɴ-brĕ′)..........Fr.	50.10 N	3.11 E
57	Cambria (kăm′brĭ-ȧ) Can. (Montreal In.)	45.48 N	74.11 W
114	Cambrian Mts. (kăm′brĭ-ăn) Gt. Brit.	52.20 N	3.30 W
114	Cambridge (kām′brĭj)...Gt. Brit.	52.12 N	0.0
85	Cambridge...................Md.	38.34 N	76.7 W
86	Cambridge.................Mass.	42.25 N	71.10 W
77	Cambridge.................Minn.	45.35 N	93.12 W
78	Cambridge..................Neb.	40.17 N	100.11 W
156	Cambridge..................N. Z.	37.55 S	175.30 E
84	Cambridge..................Ohio	40.2 N	81.35 W
84	Cambridge City.............Ind.	39.46 N	85.12 W
82	Camden (kăm′dĕn)...........Ala.	31.59 N	87.18 W
79	Camden.....................Ark.	33.35 N	92.49 W
86	Camden.....................Me.	44.12 N	69.4 W
85	Camden.....................N. J.	39.53 N	75.9 W
83	Camden.....................S. C.	34.15 N	80.37 W
99	Camden Is..Chl. (Magallanes In.)	54.45 S	72.0 W
79	Cameron (kăm′ēr-ŭn)........Mo.	39.45 N	94.14 W
81	Cameron....................Tex.	30.51 N	97.0 W
84	Cameron................W. Va.	39.45 N	80.47 W
72	Cameron Cone Colo. (Colo. Sprs. In.)	38.50 N	104.57 W
156	Cameron Mt.........N. Z. (In.)	41.21 S	174.53 E
132	Cameroon Mts. (kăm-ēr-ōōn′). Nig.	4.15 N	9.6 E
132	Cameroons (kăm-ēr-ōōnz′)....Afr.	5.0 N	12.30 E
101	Cametá (kä-mȧ-tä′)........Braz.	2.15 S	44.30 W
152	Camiguin I. (kä-mê-gēn′)....Phil.	18.55 N	121.55 E
153	Camiguin I.................Phil.	9.10 N	124.43 E
152	Camiling (kä-mê-lĭng′)......Phil.	15.41 N	120.24 E
82	Camilla (kȧ-mĭl′ȧ)...........Ga.	31.14 N	84.13 W
89	Caminada B. (kȧ-mĭ-nȧ′dȧ) La. (New Orleans In.)	29.15 N	90.3 W
124	Caminha (kä-mĭn′yȧ).......Port.	41.52 N	8.50 W
101	Camisão (kä-mē-souɴ′). Braz. (In.)	12.12 S	39.43 W
101	Cammamú (käm-mä-mōō′) Braz. (In.)	13.57 S	39.9 W
101	Camocim (kä-mô-sēɴ′)......Braz.	2.59 S	40.58 W
158	Camooweal (kȧ′mōō-wēl)...Austl.	19.59 S	138.10 E
153	Camotes Is. (kä-mō′tās).....Phil.	10.40 N	124.25 E
153	Camotes Sea...............Phil.	10.30 N	124.30 E
99	Campana (käm-pä′nä) Arg. (Buenos Aires In.)	34.9 S	59.0 W
102	Campaña I. (käm-pän′yä)....Chl.	48.28 S	75.20 W
124	Campanario (käm-pä-nä′rê-ō). Sp.	38.53 N	5.36 W
99	Campanhã (käm-pän-yăɴ′) Braz. (Rio de Janeiro In.)	21.49 S	45.20 W
126	Campania (Prov.) (käm-pän′yä) It.	40.45 N	15.0 E
151	Camp Avery (ā′vēr-ê) Phil. (Manila In.)	14.24 N	120.31 E
79	Campbell (kăm′bĕl).........Mo.	36.28 N	90.5 W
157	Campbell C................N. Z.	41.45 S	174.20 E
72	Campbell Cr. Can. (Vancouver In.)	49.3 N	122.42 W
47	Campbell I.............Pac. O.	52.30 S	169.0 E
160	Campbellfield (kăm′bĕl-fēld) Austl. (Melbourne In.)	37.41 S	144.57 E
82	Campbellsville (kăm′bĕlz-vĭl). Ky.	37.20 N	85.20 W
55	Campbellton (kăm′bĕl-tŭn)..Can.	48.0 N	66.35 W
160	Campbelltown (kăm′bĕl-toun) Austl. (Tas. In.)	41.56 S	147.31 E
114	Campbeltown..........Gt. Brit.	55.25 N	5.40 W
72	Camp Cr. (kămp) Colo. (Colo. Sprs. In.)	38.54 N	104.55 W
93	Campeche (käm-pā′chā)....Mex.	19.50 N	90.31 W
93	Campeche (State)..........Mex.	19.0 N	90.45 W
93	Campeche, B. of............Mex.	19.0 N	94.0 W
96	Campechuela (käm-pȧ-chwā′lä) Cuba	20.13 N	77.15 W

ng-sing; ŋ-baŋk; ɴ-nasalized n; nŏd; cŏmmit; ōld; ôbey; ôrder; fōōd; fŏŏt; ou-out; s-soft; sh-dish; th-thin; pūre; ûnite; ûrn; stŭd; circŭs; ü-as "y" in study; ′-indeterminate vowel.

Campillo PRONOUNCING INDEX Carrara

Page	Name Pronunciation Region	Lat. °′	Long. °′
124	Campillo de Altobuey (käm-pēl′yō dā äl-tō-bōō′å) . Sp.	39.37 N	1.48 W
127	Câmpina (kûm′pê-nä) . . . . . . Rom.	45.7 N	25.45 E
101	Campina Grande (käm-pē′nä grän′dě) . Braz.	7.10 S	35.50 W
101	Campinas (käm-pē′näzh) . . . . Braz.	22.58 S	47.2 W
101	Campo (käm′pōō) . . . . Braz.	21.45 S	41.28 W
132	Campo (käm′pō) . . . . Cam.	2.28 N	9.58 E
126	Campobasso (käm′pô-bäs′sō) . . It.	41.34 N	14.37 E
124	Campo de Criptana (käm′pō dā krêp-tä′nä) . Sp.	39.25 N	3.7 W
101	Campo Largo (käm-pōō lär′gōō) Braz.	11.47 S	44.25 W
124	Campo Maior (käm-pōō mä-yôr′) Port.	39.1 N	7.5 W
132	Campo R . . . . Cam.	2.30 N	10.30 E
125	Campo Real (käm′pō rå-äl′) Sp. (In.)	40.21 N	3.23 W
117	Camposanto (käm′pō-sän′tō) It. (Napoli In.)	40.52 N	14.17 E
135	Camps B. (kămps) . . . . . U. S. Afr.	33.56 S	18.22 E
127	Câmpulung (kûm-pōō-lōōng′) Rom.	45.17 N	25.2 E
121	Câmpulungul (kûm-pōō-lōōŋ′gōōl) Rom.	47.32 N	25.37 E
80	Camp Wood . . . . Tex.	29.42 N	100.0 W
114	Cam, R. (kăm) . . . . Gt. Brit.	52.15 N	0.10 E
97	Camu R. (kä′mōō) . . . . Hai.	19.8 N	70.20 E
86	Canaan R. (kā′năn) . . . . Can.	45.55 N	65.45 W
54	Canada . . . . N. A.	55.0 N	95.0 W
78	Canadian (kȧ-nā′dĭ-ăn) . . . . . . Tex.	35.54 N	100.23 W
79	Canadian R . . . . U. S.	35.0 N	97.22 W
79	Canadian R., Deep Fork of . . Okla.	35.37 N	96.20 W
78	Canadian R., North . . . . Okla.	35.20 N	97.0 W
85	Canajoharie (kăn-ȧ-jô-hăr′ê) . N. Y.	42.55 N	74.32 W
111	Canakkale (chä-näk-kä′lĕ) . . . Tur.	40.10 N	26.32 E
95	Canal Zone . . . . Cen. Am.	9.40 N	80.20 W
90	Canal Zone, Central America (In.)		
85	Canandaigua (kăn-ăn-dā′gwȧ) N. Y.	42.55 N	77.19 W
85	Canandaigua L . . . . N. Y.	42.45 N	77.20 W
132	Canary Is. (kȧ-nā′rê) . . . . . . Atl. O.	28.30 N	15.0 W
85	Canastota (kăn-ȧs-tō′tȧ) . . . . N. Y.	43.3 N	75.45 W
80	Canatlan (kä-nät-län′) . . . . . . Mex.	24.31 N	104.46 W
83	Canaveral, C. (kȧ-năv′ẽr-ăl) Fla. (In.)	28.28 N	80.32 W
159	Canberra (kăn′bĕr-ȧ) . . . . . . Austl.	35.28 S	149.9 E
159	Canberra . . . . Austl.	35.28 S	149.9 E
76	Canby (kăn′bĭ) . . . . Minn.	44.43 N	96.15 W
122	Cancale (käɴ-kål′) . . . . Fr.	48.40 N	1.50 W
93	Cancue (kän-kōō′å) . . . . Mex.	16.53 N	92.28 W
152	Candelaria (kän-då-lä′rê-ä) . . Phil.	15.38 N	119.55 E
151	Candelaria . . . . . Phil. (Manila In.)	13.57 N	121.28 E
93	Candelaria, R . . . . Mex.	18.20 N	91.18 W
124	Candeleda (kän-dhå-lā′dhä) . . . Sp.	40.10 N	5.15 W
126	Candia (Erakleion) (kăn′dĭ-ȧ) (hê-răk′lĭ-ŏn) . Grc. (In.)	35.19 N	25.8 E
52	Candle (kăn′d′l) . . . . Alsk.	65.50 N	162.0 W
76	Cando (kăn′dō) . . . . N. D.	48.28 N	99.12 W
152	Candon (kän-dōn′) . . . . Phil.	17.12 N	120.27 E
125	Candor, Pt. (kän-dôr′) . . . Sp. (In.)	36.37 N	6.21 W
126	Canea (Khania) (kä-nĕ′ä) . Grc. (In.)	35.27 N	24.4 E
100	Cañete (kän-yā′tā) . . . . Peru	13.2 S	76.28 W
117	Canewdon (kȧ-nū′dŭn) . . Gt. Brit.	51.37 N	0.44 E
97	Caney (kä-nā′) (kā′nĭ) . . . . . . Cuba	20.3 N	75.46 W
79	Caney . . . . Kan.	37.1 N	95.57 W
79	Caney R . . . . Okla.	36.40 N	96.7 W
134	Canga (käŋ′gä) . . . . Ang.	9.17 S	13.47 E
134	Cangamba (kän-gôm′bä) . . . . Ang.	13.30 S	19.55 E
134	Canganza, Serra de (Mts.) (sĕr′rȧ dā kän-gän′zȧ) . Ang.	7.45 S	15.30 E
124	Cangas (kän′gäs) . . . . Sp.	43.6 N	6.38 W
124	Cangas . . . . Sp.	42.6 N	8.47 W
124	Cangas de Onís (kaŋ′gäs dā ô-nēs′) . Sp.	43.22 N	5.9 W
124	Canha R. (kän′yä) . . . . Port.	38.45 N	8.35 W
126	Canicatti (kä-nê-kät′tē) . . . . It.	37.22 N	13.51 E
153	Canigao Chan. (kä-nê-gä′ô) . . Phil.	10.10 N	124.40 E
124	Caniles (kä-nē′lås) . . . . Sp.	37.27 N	2.42 W
125	Canillejas (kä-nē-lā′häs) . Sp. (In.)	40.27 N	3.37 W
111	Cankiri (chäŋ-kē′rē) . . . . Tur.	40.40 N	33.35 E
153	Canlaon (Vol.) (kän-lä-ōn′) . . Phil.	10.25 N	123.85 E
114	Canna (I.) (kăn′nȧ) . . . . . Gt. Brit.	57.5 N	6.38 W
101	Cannavieiras (kä-nä-vyā′räzh) Braz.	15.30 S	39.1 W
84	Cannelton (kăn′ĕl-tŭn) . . . . Ind.	37.55 N	86.45 W
123	Cannes (kån) . . . . Fr.	43.35 N	7.0 E
86	Canning (kăn′ĭng) . . . . Can.	45.10 N	64.25 W
160	Canning R . . . . . . Austl. (Perth In.)	32.1 S	115.54 E
160	Cannington (kăn′ĭng-tŭn) Austl. (Perth In.)	32.0 S	115.55 E
116	Cannock (kăn′ŭk) . . . . Gt. Brit.	52.41 N	2.2 W
116	Cannock Chase (kăn′ŭk chās) Gt. Brit.	52.43 N	1.55 W
76	Cannonball R . . . . N. D.	46.21 N	102.0 W
77	Cannon R. (kăn′ŭn) . . . . Minn.	44.20 N	93.14 W
85	Cannonsburg (kăn′ŭnz-bûrg) . . Pa.	40.13 N	80.17 W
95	Cannouan I. (kä-nōō-äɴ′) Wind. Is. (In.)	12.42 N	61.20 W
95	Cano I. (kä′nō) . . . . C. R.	8.40 N	83.53 W
73	Canoga (kä-nō′gȧ) Park . . . . Calif.	34.12 N	118.36 W
78	Cañon City (kăn′yŭn) . . . . . . Colo.	38.27 N	105.15 W
83	Canoochee R. (kȧ-nōō′chē) . . . Ga.	32.20 N	82.5 W
126	Canosa (kä-nō′sä) . . . . It.	41.13 N	16.4 E
87	Canso (kăn′sō) . . . . Can.	45.19 N	61.0 W
87	Canso, C . . . . Can.	45.20 N	61.0 W
87	Canso, Str. of . . . . Can.	45.40 N	61.20 W
124	Cantabrian Mts. (kăn-tā′brĭ-ăn) Sp.	43.10 N	5.0 W
124	Cantanhede (kän-täɴ-yā′då) . Port.	40.20 N	8.35 W
160	Canterbury (kăn′tẽr-bẽr-ê) Austl. (Sydney In.)	33.55 S	151.7 E
115	Canterbury . . . . Gt. Brit.	51.15 N	1.0 E
157	Canterbury Bight . . . . N. Z.	44.10 S	172.0 E
157	Canterbury Plains . . . . N. Z.	43.50 S	171.30 E
153	Cantilan (kän-tē′län) . . . . Phil.	9.20 N	125.58 E
96	Cantiles Cay (I.) (kän-tē′lås) . Cuba	21.38 N	82.0 W
82	Canton (kăn′tŏn) . . . . Ga.	34.14 N	84.29 W
79	Canton . . . . Ill.	40.33 N	90.2 W
87	Canton . . . . Mass. (In.)	42.9 N	71.8 W
82	Canton . . . . Miss.	32.46 N	90.3 W
79	Canton . . . . Mo.	40.7 N	91.31 W
82	Canton . . . . N. C.	35.32 N	82.52 W
84	Canton . . . . Ohio	40.50 N	81.22 W
85	Canton . . . . Pa.	41.43 N	76.43 W
76	Canton . . . . S. D.	43.18 N	96.35 W
144	Canton (Kwangchow) (kăn′tŏn′) (kwäng′chō′) . Chn.	23.7 N	113.15 E
126	Cantù (kän-tōō′) . . . . It.	45.44 N	9.8 E
151	Canubang (kä-nōō-bäng′) Phil. (Manila In.)	14.15 N	121.8 E
78	Canyon (kăn′yŭn) . . . . Tex.	34.58 N	101.57 W
75	Canyon de Chelly (shĕl′lĭ) Nat. Mon. Ariz.	36.7 N	109.15 W
152	Capalonga (kä-pä-lôŋ′gä) . . . . Phil.	14.20 N	122.30 E
126	Capannori (kä-pän′nô-rē) . . . . . . It.	43.51 N	10.36 E
125	Caparica (kä-pä-rē′kä) . Port. (In.)	38.40 N	9.12 W
86	Cap Chat (kȧp shä′) . . . . Can.	49.6 N	66.42 W
86	Cap de la Madeleine (kȧp dē lȧ mȧ-d′lĕn′) . Can.	46.23 N	72.29 W
122	Capdenac-Gare (kȧ-dē-näk-gär′) Fr.	44.35 N	2.5 E
160	Cape Barren I. (kāp băr′ĕn) Austl. (Tas. In.)	40.23 S	148.15 E
55	Cape Breton I. (kāp brĕt′ŭn) . Can.	46.0 N	61.0 W
132	Cape Coast . . . . G. C.	5.10 N	1.15 W
85	Cape Cod B . . . . Mass.	41.50 N	70.20 W
83	Cape Fear R . . . . N. C.	35.10 N	78.50 W
79	Cape Girardeau (jē-rär-dō′) . . Mo.	37.17 N	89.33 W
51	Cape Horn . . Wash. (Portland In.)	45.35 N	122.11 W
125	Capellades (kä-pål-yä′dās) . Sp. (In.)	41.33 N	1.42 E
85	Cape May . . . . N. J.	38.56 N	74.56 W
85	Cape May C. H . . . . N. J.	39.4 N	74.53 W
134	Cape of Good Hope (Prov.) U. S. Afr.	31.35 S	24.0 E
132	Cape Palmas (Harper) (päl′mäs) (här′pẽr) . Lib.	4.30 N	7.54 W
122	Capestan (kȧ-pē-stäɴ′) . . . . Fr.	43.20 N	3.0 E
134	Capetown . . . . U. S. Afr.	33.55 S	18.22 E
135	Capetown . . . . U. S. Afr. (In.)		
132	Cape Verde Is. (kāp vûrd) Atl. O. (In.)	16.0 N	24.0 W
159	Cape York Pen. (kāp yôrk) . Austl.	13.0 S	142.30 E
97	Cap Haitien (kȧp ȧ-ē-syăɴ′) . . Hai.	19.47 N	72.13 W
153	Cap I. (käp) . . . . Phil.	5.57 N	120.10 E
72	Capilano Cr. (kă-pĭ-lā′nō) Can. (Vancouver In.)	49.28 N	123.7 W
99	Capilla del Señor (kä-pēl′yä dĕl sān-yôr′) . Arg. (Buenos Aires In.)	34.16 S	59.8 W
78	Capitan Mts. (kä-pê-tän′) . . N. M.	33.38 N	105.25 W
75	Capitol Reef (kăp′ĭ-tŏl) Natl. Mon . Utah	38.15 N	111.30 W
153	Capiz (kä′pêz) . . . . Phil.	11.36 N	122.46 E
153	Capnoyan I. (käp-nō′yän) . . . Phil.	10.40 N	120.55 E
159	Capoompeta (Mt.) (kȧ-pōōm-pē′tȧ) . Austl.	29.20 S	152.10 E
126	Caporetto (kä-pô-rĕt′tō) . . . . Yugo.	46.15 N	13.34 E
117	Cappellen (kä-pĕl′ĕn) Bel. (Anvers In.)	51.19 N	4.26 E
126	Capraia (I.) (kä-prä′yä) . . . . It.	43.3 N	9.48 E
126	Caprara Pt. (kä-prä′rä) . . . . . Sard.	41.8 N	8.22 E
126	Caprera (I.) (kä-prā′rä) . . . . . Sard.	41.15 N	9.25 E
126	Capri (I.) (kä′prē) . . . . It.	40.33 N	14.13 E
159	Capricorn Chan. (kăp′rĭ-kôrn) Austl.	22.30 S	151.30 E
86	Cap St. Ignace (käp săɴ-tê-nyȧs′) (sānt ĭg′nȧs) . Can.	47.2 N	70.26 W
126	Capua (kä′pwä) . . . . It.	41.7 N	14.12 E
153	Capual I. (kä-pwäl′) . . . . Phil.	6.3 N	121.25 E
132	Capuchinos (kä-pōō-chē′nōs) Az. Is. (In.)	38.34 N	28.48 W
152	Capul (kä-pōōl′) . . . . Phil.	12.25 N	124.10 E
92	Capulhuac (kä-pōōl-hwäk′) . . Mex.	19.28 N	99.32 W
78	Capulin Mountain Natl. Mon. (kȧ-pū′lĭn) . N. M.	36.53 N	103.57 W
134	Caquengue (kä-kĕŋ′gĕ) . . . . . . Ang.	12.20 S	22.28 E
100	Caquetá (Japura), R. (kä-kā-tä′) (hä-pōō′rȧ) . Col.	1.0 S	72.2 W
125	Carabaña (kä-rä-bän′yä) . Sp. (In.)	40.16 N	3.15 W
125	Carabanchel Alto (kä-rä-bän-chĕl′ äl′tō) . Sp. (In.)	40.23 N	3.45 W
125	Carabanchel Bajo (kä-rä-bän-chĕl′ bä′hō) . Sp. (In.)	40.23 N	3.45 W
153	Carabao I. (kä-rä-bä′ō) . . . . . Phil.	12.5 N	121.56 E
127	Caracál (kȧ-rȧ-kål′) . . . . Rom.	44.6 N	24.22 E
100	Caracas (kä-rä′käs) . . . . Ven.	10.30 N	66.58 W
92	Carácuaro (kä-rä′kwä-rō) . . . Mex.	18.45 N	101.0 W
153	Caraga (kä-rä′gä) . . . . Phil.	7.19 N	126.34 E
153	Caraga B . . . . Phil.	7.20 N	126.35 E
152	Caramoan (kä-rä-mō′än) . . . . Phil.	13.46 N	123.51 E
127	Caransebeș (kȧ-rȧn-sā′bĕsh) . Rom.	45.24 N	22.13 E
102	Carapeguá (kä-rä-på-gwä′) . . . Par.	25.40 S	57.15 W
86	Caraquet (kă-rȧ-kĕt′) . . . . Can.	47.47 N	64.56 W
95	Caratasca Lagoon (kä-rä-täs′kä) . Hond.	15.30 N	83.40 W
124	Caravaca (kä-rä-vä′kä) . . . . Sp.	38.6 N	1.52 W
101	Caravelas (kä-rä-vĕl′äzh) . . . . Braz.	17.47 S	39.18 W
95	Caravelle Pen. (kä-rä-vĕl′) Mart. (In.)	14.50 N	60.50 W
124	Carballino (kär-bäl-yē′nō) . . . . . Sp.	42.36 N	8.5 W
124	Carballo (kär-bäl′yō) . . . . Sp.	43.13 N	8.42 W
95	Carbet Peaks (kär-bā′) . Mart. (In.)	14.43 N	61.6 W
70	Carbonado (kȧr-bō-nā′dō) . . Wash.	47.4 N	122.3 W
126	Carbonara, C. (kär-bō-nä′rä) . Sard.	39.7 N	9.31 E
79	Carbondale (kär′bŏn-dāl) . . . . . Ill.	37.44 N	89.13 W
85	Carbondale . . . . Pa.	41.32 N	75.30 W
87	Carbonear (kär-bô-nēr′) . . . . . Can.	47.42 N	53.15 W
92	Carbonera (kär-bö-nā′rä) . . . . Mex.	22.15 N	100.14 W
82	Carbon Hill (kär′bŏn) . . . . Ala.	33.53 N	87.33 W
82	Carbur (kär′bûr) . . . . Fla.	29.56 N	83.28 W
125	Carcagente (kär-kä-hĕn′tā) . . . . Sp.	39.7 N	0.28 W
153	Carcar (kär′kär) . . . . Phil.	10.7 N	123.39 E
99	Carcaraña, R. (kär-kä-rän′yä) Arg. (Buenos Aires In.)	33.0 S	61.25 W
122	Carcassone (kȧr-kȧ-sôn′) . . . . . . Fr.	43.11 N	2.21 E
54	Carcross (kär′krôs) . . . . Can.	60.14 N	134.31 W
141	Cardamon Hills (kär′dȧ-mŭn) India (Cey. In.)	9.30 N	77.30 E
96	Cárdenas (kär′då-näs) . . . . . . Cuba	23.1 N	81.11 W
93	Cárdenas . . . . Mex.	17.59 N	93.23 W
92	Cárdenas . . . . Mex.	22.0 N	99.38 W
96	Cárdenas B . . . . Cuba	23.5 N	81.8 W
73	Cardiff (kär′dĭf) Ala. (Birmingham In.)	33.39 N	86.56 W
114	Cardiff . . . . Gt. Brit.	51.30 N	3.10 W
114	Cardigan (kär′dĭ-găn) . . . Gt. Brit.	52.5 N	4.35 W
114	Cardigan B . . . . Gt. Brit.	52.30 N	4.30 W
151	Cardona (kär-dō′nä) Phil. (Manila In.)	14.30 N	121.15 E
54	Cardston (kärds′tŭn) . . . . Can.	49.10 N	113.6 W
121	Careii (kä-rĕ′ê) . . . . Rom.	47.42 N	22.27 E
122	Carentan (kä-rôɴ-täɴ′) . . . . Fr.	49.18 N	1.11 W
84	Carey (kā′rê) . . . . Ohio	40.57 N	83.27 W
158	Carey, L . . . . Austl.	29.0 S	122.25 E
157	Cargill, Mt. (kär′gĭl) . . . N. Z. (In.)	45.49 S	170.35 E
122	Carhaix (kär-ĕ′) . . . . Fr.	48.20 N	3.35 W
91	Caribbean S. (kăr-ĭ-bē′ăn) Cen. Am.	15.0 N	75.0 W
54	Cariboo Mts. (kă′rĭ-bōō) . . . . Can.	53.15 N	121.30 W
86	Caribou . . . . Me.	46.52 N	68.0 W
77	Caribou I . . . . Can.	47.20 N	85.47 W
127	Çaribrod (tsär′ĭ-brôd) . . . . . . Yugo.	43.1 N	22.46 E
153	Carigara (kä-rê-gä′rä) . . . . Phil.	11.17 N	124.42 E
153	Carigara B . . . . Phil.	11.20 N	124.40 E
101	Carinhanha (kä-rĭ-nyăn′yä) . . Braz.	14.32 S	43.58 W
126	Carini (kä-rē′nē) . . . . It.	38.8 N	13.10 E
85	Carleton Place (kärl′tŭn) . . . . Can.	45.7 N	76.7 W
160	Carlingford (kär′lĭng-fẽrd) Austl. (Sydney In.)	33.46 S	151.1 E
79	Carlinville (kär′lĭn-vĭl) . . . . Ill.	39.17 N	89.54 W
114	Carlisle (kär-lil′) . . . . Gt. Brit.	54.55 N	3.0 W
84	Carlisle . . . . Ky.	38.18 N	84.2 W
85	Carlisle . . . . Pa.	40.12 N	77.10 W
126	Carloforte (kär′lō-fôr-tȧ) . . . . Sard.	39.9 N	8.19 E
114	Carlow (kär′lō) . . . . Ire.	52.50 N	6.55 W
	Carlsbad, see Karlovy Vary, Czech.		
78	Carlsbad (kärlz′băd) . . . . N. M.	32.24 N	104.14 W
80	Carlsbad Caverns Nat. Pk . . N. M.	32.5 N	104.10 W
116	Carlton (kärl′tŭn) . . . . Gt. Brit.	52.58 N	1.5 W
77	Carlton . . . . Minn.	46.40 N	92.26 W
84	Carlton Center . . . . Mich.	42.47 N	85.18 W
79	Carlyle (kär-lil′) . . . . Ill.	38.36 N	89.22 W
126	Carmagnola (kär-mä-nyô′lä) . . . It.	44.49 N	7.45 E
76	Carman (kär′mȧn) . . . . Can.	49.34 N	98.1 W
114	Carmarthen (kär-mär′thĕn) Gt. Brit.	51.50 N	4.20 W
114	Carmarthen B . . . . Gt. Brit.	51.45 N	4.30 W
122	Carmaux (kȧr-mō′) . . . . Fr.	44.5 N	2.10 E
100	Carmen (kär′mĕn) . . . . Col.	9.45 N	75.30 W
93	Carmen . . . . Mex.	18.38 N	91.48 W
153	Carmen . . . . Phil.	10.34 N	124.1 E
99	Carmen de Areco (kär′mĕn′ dā ä-rā′kô) . Arg. (Buenos Aires In.)	34.20 S	59.50 W
93	Carmen I . . . . Mex.	18.41 N	91.40 W
93	Carmen, L . . . . Mex.	18.16 N	93.47 W
84	Carmi (kär′mī) . . . . Ill.	38.6 N	88.10 W
97	Carmichael (kär′mĭ-kāl) . . . Ba. Is.	21.14 N	73.25 W
151	Carmona (kär-mō′nä) Phil. (Manila In.)	14.20 N	121.5 E
124	Carmona . . . . Sp.	37.28 N	5.38 W
158	Carnarvon (kär-när′-vŭn) . . Austl.	24.47 S	113.40 E
114	Carnarvon . . . . Gt. Brit.	53.8 N	4.15 W
134	Carnarvon . . . . U. S. Afr.	30.59 S	22.9 E
114	Carnarvon B . . . . Gt. Brit.	53.8 N	4.30 W
125	Carnaxide (kär-nä-shē′dě) Port. (In.)	38.43 N	9.15 W
114	Carndonagh (kärn-dō-nä′) . . . . Ire.	55.15 N	7.15 W
78	Carnegie (kär-nĕg′ĭ) . . . . Okla.	35.6 N	98.36 W
89	Carnegie . . . . . Pa. (Pittsburgh In.)	40.24 N	80.5 W
88	Carnegie . . . . Wis. (Duluth In.)	46.38 N	92.11 W
158	Carnegie, L . . . . Austl.	26.10 S	122.45 E
131	Carnero, Pt. (kär-nā′rō) Sp. (Gibraltar In.)	36.5 N	5.35 E
85	Carneys Point (kär′nês) . . . . . N. J.	39.42 N	75.27 W
116	Carnforth (kärn′fûrth) . . . Gt. Brit.	54.7 N	2.47 W
125	Carnot (kär-nō′) . . . . Alg.	36.16 N	1.41 E
133	Carnot . . . . Fr. Eq. Afr.	4.57 N	15.58 E
114	Carnoustie (kär-nōōs′tĭ) . . Gt. Brit.	56.30 N	2.40 W
114	Carnsore Pt. (kärn′sôr) . . . . Ire.	52.10 N	6.20 W
84	Caro (kâ′rō) . . . . Mich.	43.28 N	83.24 W
101	Carolina (kä-rô-lē′nä) . . . . Braz.	7.27 S	47.29 W
134	Carolina (kăr-ô-lī′nȧ) . . . U. S. Afr.	26.5 S	30.9 E
5	Caroline Is. (kăr′ô-līn) . . . . Pac. O.	8.0 N	150.0 E
100	Caroni, R. (kä-rō′nē) . . . . Ven.	5.30 N	62.48 W
120	Carouge (kȧ-rōōzh′) . . . . Switz.	46.11 N	6.11 E
121	Carpathians (Mts.) (kär-pā′thĭ-ăn) Eur.	48.35 N	23.55 E
121	Carpathians, Little (Mts.) . . Czech.	48.30 N	17.20 E
121	Carpathians, White (Mts.) . Czech.	49.0 N	18.0 E
158	Carpentaria, G. of (kär-pĕn-târ′ĭȧ) Austl.	14.0 S	138.30 E
122	Carpentras (kȧr-päɴ-träs′) . . . . Fr.	44.4 N	5.2 E
126	Carpi (kär′pē) . . . . It.	44.46 N	10.53 E
82	Carrabelle (kăr′å-bĕl) . . . . Fla.	29.52 N	84.40 W
126	Carrara (kä-rä′rä) . . . . It.	44.4 N	10.5 E

ăt; finăl; rāte; senåte; ärm; ȧsk; sofȧ; fâre; ch-choose; dh-as th in other; bē; ėvent; bĕt; recĕnt; cratẽr; g-go; gh-gutteral g; bĭt; ĭ-short neutral; rīde; ᴋ-gutteral k as ch in German ich;

Carriacou PRONOUNCING INDEX Centralia

Page	Name Pronunciation Region	Lat. °′	Long. °′
95	Carriacou (I.) (kăr-ê-ȧ-kōō′) Wind. Is. (In.)	12.30 N	61.26 W
114	Carrick (kăr′ĭk) .... Ire.	52.20 N	7.25 W
82	Carriere (kȧ-rēr′) .... Miss.	30.37 N	89.40 W
57	Carrier (kăr′ĭ-ēr) . . Can. (Que. In.)	46.44 N	71.6 W
79	Carriers Mills (kăr′ĭ-ērs) ..... Ill.	37.41 N	88.37 W
76	Carrington (kăr′ĭng-tŭn) .... N. D.	47.26 N	99.8 W
51	Carr Inlet (kär) . Wash. (Seattle In.)	47.17 N	122.43 W
96	Carrion Crow Har. (kăr′ĭ-ŭn krō) Ba. Is.	26.38 N	77.52 W
124	Carrión de los Condes (kär-rê-ōn′ dā lōs kōn′dȧs) . Sp.	42.21 N	4.35 W
124	Carrión R. (kär-rê-ōn′) .... Sp.	42.30 N	4.44 W
78	Carrizo Cr. (kär-rē′zō) ..... N. M.	36.14 N	103.10 W
80	Carrizo Springs .... Tex.	28.32 N	99.53 W
75	Carrizozo (kär-rê-zō′zō) .... N. M.	33.38 N	105.52 W
77	Carroll (kăr′ŭl) .... Ia.	42.3 N	94.50 W
51	Carrolls (kăr′ŭlz) Wash. (Portland In.)	46.4 N	122.52 W
82	Carrollton (kăr-ŭl-tŭn) .... Ga.	33.34 N	85.4 W
79	Carrollton .... Ill.	39.19 N	90.23 W
84	Carrollton .... Ky.	38.39 N	85.11 W
84	Carrollton .... Mich.	43.29 N	83.57 W
79	Carrollton .... Mo.	39.22 N	93.28 W
84	Carrollton .... Ohio	40.34 N	81.8 W
114	Carron, Loch (L.) (kȧ′rŭn, lŏĸ) Gt. Brit.	57.20 N	5.30 W
160	Carrum Swamp Austl. (Melbourne In.)	38.2 S	145.7 E
111	Carsamba (chär-shäm′bä) .... Tur.	41.10 N	36.50 E
74	Carson City (kär′sŭn) .... Nev.	39.10 N	119.45 W
74	Carson R .... Nev.	39.12 N	119.35 W
74	Carson Sink .... Nev.	39.50 N	118.25 W
151	Carstensz, Mt. (kärs′tĕns) Neth. N. Gui.	3.57 S	137.3 E
100	Cartagena (kär-tä-hā′nä) ..... Col.	10.30 N	75.30 W
125	Cartagena .... Sp.	37.35 N	1.0 W
100	Cartago (kär-tä′gō) .... Col.	4.40 N	76.2 W
95	Cartago .... C. R.	9.52 N	83.51 W
124	Cartaxo (kär-tä′shō) .... Port.	39.10 N	8.48 W
124	Cartaya (kär-tä′yä) .... Sp.	37.16 N	7.9 W
124	Cartelle (kär-tĕl′yȧ) .... Sp.	42.15 N	8.4 W
122	Carteret (kär-tē-rĕ′) .... Fr.	49.25 N	1.45 W
82	Cartersville (kär′tērs-vĭl) ..... Ga.	34.10 N	84.48 W
157	Carterton (kär′tēr-tŭn) ..... N. Z.	41.2 S	175.32 E
79	Carthage (kär′thȧj) .... Ill.	40.26 N	91.8 W
79	Carthage .... Mo.	37.10 N	94.19 W
85	Carthage .... N. Y.	43.59 N	75.39 W
83	Carthage .... N. C.	35.22 N	79.26 W
81	Carthage .... Tex.	32.9 N	94.20 W
132	Carthage (Ruins) .... Tun.	37.0 N	10.20 E
116	Cartmel (kärt′mĕl) ...... Gt. Brit.	54.12 N	2.57 W
55	Cartwright (kärt′rīt) .... Can.	53.48 N	56.59 W
101	Caruarú (kä-rōō-ȧ-rōō′) ..... Braz.	8.16 S	35.58 W
100	Carúpano (kä-rōō′pä-nō) .... Ven.	10.33 N	63.28 W
79	Caruthersville (kȧ-rŭdh′ērz-vĭl) Mo.	36.11 N	89.39 W
73	Casa Blanca (kä′sä bläŋ′kä) Calif. (Los Angeles In.)	33.56 N	117.24 W
99	Casablanca (kä-sä-bläŋ′kä) Chl. (Valparaiso In.)	33.19 S	71.25 W
90	Casa Blanca . . . Cuba (Habana In.)	23.9 N	82.21 W
132	Casablanca .... Mor.	33.38 N	7.36 W
75	Casa Grande (kä′sä grän′dā) . Ariz.	32.51 N	11.45 W
75	Casa Grande Natl. Mon ..... Ariz.	33.0 N	111.31 W
134	Casai R. (kä-sī′) . . Bel. Cong.-Ang.	11.20 S	20.30 E
126	Casale (kä-sä′lā) .... It.	45.7 N	8.28 E
126	Casalmaggiore (kä-säl-mäd-jō′rā) It.	45.0 N	10.24 E
132	Casamance R. (kä-sä-mäɴs′) Fr. W. Afr.	12.50 N	15.30 W
102	Casares (kä-sä′rĕs) .... Arg.	35.45 S	61.28 W
72	Cascade (kăs-kād′) Colo. (Colo. Sprs. In.)	38.54 N	104.58 W
157	Cascade Pt .... N. Z.	43.58 S	168.25 E
58	Cascade Range .... U. S.	42.0 N	122.0 W
70	Cascade Tunnel .... Wash.	47.43 N	121.0 W
102	Cascadura (käs-kä-dōō′rä) Braz. (In.)	22.53 S	43.20 W
125	Cascais (käs-kȧ-ēzh′) . . . Port. (In.)	38.42 N	9.25 W
125	Cascais B .... Port. (In.)	38.40 N	9.22 W
51	Case Inlet (kās) . Wash. (Seattle In.)	47.15 N	122.51 W
102	Caseros (kä-sā′rȯs) ..... Arg. (In.)	34.36 S	58.34 W
126	Caserta (kä-zĕr′tä) .... It.	41.4 N	14.19 E
84	Casey (kā′sĭ) .... Ill.	39.19 N	7.59 W
70	Cashmere (kăsh′mĭr) .... Wash.	47.30 N	120.29 W
152	Casiguran (kä-sē-gōō′rän) .... Phil.	12.52 N	124.2 E
152	Casiguran .... Phil.	16.16 N	122.9 E
152	Casiguran Sd .... Phil.	16.5 N	122.0 E
160	Casino (kȧ-sē′nō) ..... Austl. (In.)	28.52 S	153.2 E
100	Casiquiare, R. (kä-sê-kyä′rā) . Ven.	2.0 N	66.30 W
120	Čáslav (chä′slȧf) .... Czech.	49.54 N	15.24 E
125	Caspe (käs′pȧ) .... Sp.	41.15 N	0.2 W
71	Casper (kăs′pēr) .... Wyo.	42.51 N	106.18 W
111	Caspian Sea (kăs′pĭ-ăn) . . . Eurasia	42.0 N	50.0 E
112	Casr Garian (käs″r gä′rê-än) . Libya	32.41 N	13.4 E
85	Cass (kăs) .... W. Va.	38.27 N	79.53 W
125	Cassá (käs-sä′) .... Sp.	41.53 N	2.52 E
134	Cassangi (kä-säŋ′gē) .... Ang.	9.15 S	17.45 E
84	Cass City (kăs) .... Mich.	43.36 N	83.10 W
76	Casselton (kăs″l-tŭn) ...... N. D.	46.54 N	97.12 W
72	Cassidy (käs′ĭ-dĭ) Can. (Vancouver In.)	49.4 N	123.52 W
134	Cassinga (kä-sĭŋ′gȧ) .... Ang.	15.8 S	16.12 E
126	Cassino (käs-sē′nō) .... It.	41.29 N	13.48 E
77	Cass Lake (kăs) .... Minn.	47.22 N	94.35 W
77	Cass L .... Minn.	47.25 N	94.30 W
84	Cassopolis (kăs-ŏ′pō-lĭs) .... Mich.	41.56 N	86.0 W
157	Cass Pk .... N. Z. (In.)	43.36 S	172.40 E
79	Cassville (kăs′vĭl) .... Mo.	36.41 N	93.53 W
73	Castaic (kăs-tā′ĭk) Calif. (Los Angeles In.)	34.26 N	118.37 W
101	Castanhal (käs-tä-nyäl′) Braz. (In.)	115.0 S	47.58 W
124	Castanheira (käs-tän-yā′rä) . . Port.	40.0 N	8.8 W
122	Casteljaloux (käs-tĕl-zhä-lōō′) . Fr.	44.20 N	0.5 E
126	Castellammare (käs-tĕl-läm-mä′rā) It.	40.42 N	14.28 E
125	Castellar (käs-tĕl-yär′) . . . Sp. (In.)	41.36 N	2.5 E
125	Castellón de la Plana (käs-tĕl-lyōn′ dā lä plä′nä) . Sp.	39.59 N	0.3 W
122	Castelnaudary (kȧs′tĕl-nō-dȧ-rē′) Fr.	43.20 N	1.58 E
124	Castelo Branco (käs-tā′lo͝o bräŋ′ko͝o) . Port.	39.49 N	7.29 W
124	Castelo de Vide (käs-tā′lo͝o dĭ vē′dĭ) . Port.	39.25 N	7.27 W
122	Castelsarraisin (kȧs′tĕl-sȧ-rȧ-zăɴ′) Fr.	44.1 N	1.10 E
126	Castelvetrano (käs′tĕl-vê-trä′nō) It.	37.43 N	12.47 E
124	Castilla la Nueva (New Castile) (Prov.) (käs-tē′lyä lä nwā′vȧ) . Sp.	39.50 N	3.0 W
124	Castilla La Vieja (Old Castile) (Prov.) (käs-tēl′yä lä vyā′hä) . Sp.	41.40 N	3.40 W
114	Castlebar (kȧs″l-bär) .... Ire.	53.55 N	9.19 W
75	Castle Dale .... Utah	39.13 N	111.1 W
116	Castle Donington (dŏn′ĭng-tŭn) Gt. Brit.	52.50 N	1.21 W
116	Castleford (kȧs″l-fērd) . . . Gt. Brit.	53.43 N	1.21 W
97	Castle I. (kȧs″l) .... Ba. Is.	22.8 N	74.19 W
157	Castle, Mt .... N. Z.	44.50 S	167.50 E
78	Castle Pk .... Colo.	39.0 N	106.51 W
157	Castle Pt .... N. Z.	40.55 S	176.15 E
70	Castlerock (kȧs″l-rŏk) ..... Wash.	46.16 N	122.54 W
89	Castle Shannon (shăn′ŭn) ..... Pa.	40.22 N	80.1 W
79	Castor R. (kăs′tôr) .... Mo.	36.55 N	89.50 W
122	Castres (kȧs′tr′) .... Fr.	43.35 N	2.11 E
95	Castries (kȧs-trē′) ...... Wind. Is.	14.0 N	61.0 W
102	Castro (käs′tro͝o) .... Braz.	24.50 S	50.0 W
102	Castro (käs′tro) .... Chl.	42.28 S	73.48 W
124	Castro .... Sp.	37.42 N	4.27 W
101	Castro Alves (käs′tro͝o ȧl′vĕzh) Braz. (In.)	12.46 S	39.32 W
126	Castrogiovanni (käs′trō-jô-vän′nē) It.	37.35 N	14.16 E
124	Castro Daire (käs′tro͝o dīr′ĭ) . Port.	40.56 N	7.58 W
124	Castro Marim (käs′tro͝o mä-rĭɴ′) Port.	37.15 N	7.29 W
124	Castropol (käs-trō-pōl′) .... Sp.	43.30 N	7.5 W
124	Castro Urdiales (käs′trō o͝or-dyä′lās) . Sp.	43.23 N	3.13 W
124	Castro Verde (käs-trō vĕr′dĕ) . Port.	37.44 N	8.4 W
126	Castrovillari (käs′trō-vēl-lyä′rē) It.	39.47 N	16.13 E
124	Castuera (käs-to͝o-ā′rä) .... Sp.	38.43 N	5.32 W
81	Catahoula L. (kăt-ȧ-ho͝o′lȧ) . . . La.	31.30 N	92.8 W
153	Cataingan (kä-tä-ēŋ′gän) .... Phil.	12.0 N	123.29 E
101	Catalão (kä-tä-louɴ′) .... Braz.	18.10 S	47.59 W
97	Catalina I. (kä-tä-lē′nä) ..... Hai.	18.21 N	69.0 W
99	Catalina Punta Chl. (Magallanes In.)	52.32 S	68.45 W
125	Catalonia (Cataluña (Prov.) (kăt-ȧ-lō′nĭ-ȧ) (kä-tä-lo͝on′yä) . Sp.	41.30 N	1.0 E
102	Catamarca (State) (kä-tä-mär′kä) . Arg.	28.0 S	66.30 W
102	Catamarca .... Arg.	28.29 S	65.59 W
152	Catanauan (kä-tä-nä′wän) . . . Phil.	13.37 N	122.19 E
152	Catanduanes I. (kä-tän-dwä′nās) Phil.	13.45 N	124.15 E
126	Catania (kȧ-tä′nyä) .... It.	37.31 N	15.4 E
126	Catania, G. of .... It.	37.25 N	15.15 E
126	Catanzaro (kä-tän-dzä′rō) ..... It.	38.53 N	16.36 E
152	Catarman (kä-tär-män′) ..... Phil.	12.29 N	124.39 E
125	Catarroja (kä-tär-rō′hä) .... Sp.	39.24 N	0.25 W
83	Catawba R. (kȧ-tô′bȧ) . N. C.-S. C.	35.0 N	81.0 W
153	Catbalogan (kät-bä-lō′gän) . . Phil.	11.46 N	124.53 E
153	Cateel (kä-tā-ĕl′) .... Phil.	7.47 N	126.27 E
93	Catemaco (kä-tā-mä′kō) .... Mex.	18.25 N	95.8 W
72	Cathedral Mt. (kȧ-thē′drăl) Can. (Vancouver In.)	49.28 N	12.31 W
80	Cathedral, Mt .... Tex.	30.9 N	103.45 W
133	Catherina, Mt. (kă-thēr-ē′nä) . . Eg.	28.32 N	33.52 E
51	Cathlamet (kăth-lăm′ĕt) . . . Wash.	46.10 N	123.20 W
97	Cat I .... Ba. Is.	24.25 N	75.31 W
89	Cat I ..... Miss. (New Orleans In.)	30.13 N	89.6 W
89	Cat Island Chan. La.-Miss. (New Orleans In.)	30.11 N	89.7 W
84	Catlettsburg (kăt′lĕts-bûrg) . . Ky.	38.24 N	82.37 W
153	Catmon (kät-mōn′) .... Phil.	10.42 N	124.1 E
85	Catonsville (kā′tŭnz-vĭl) ..... Md.	39.16 N	76.42 W
92	Catorce (kä-tôr′sȧ) .... Mex.	23.41 N	100.52 W
85	Catskill (kăts′kĭl) .... N. Y.	42.15 N	73.51 W
85	Catskill Mts .... N. Y.	42.15 N	74.35 W
134	Catumbella (kä′tŭm-bĕl′ä) . . . Ang.	12.30 S	13.40 E
153	Cauayan (kou-ä′yän) .... Phil.	9.58 N	122.38 E
152	Cauayan .... Phil.	16.57 N	121.46 E
100	Cauca, R. (kou′kä) .... Col.	7.30 N	75.30 W
111	Caucasus Mts. (kô′kȧ-sŭs) . Sov. Un.	43.10 N	43.45 E
122	Caudebec-St. Pierre (kōd-bĕk′-săɴ pyâr′) . Fr.	49.16 N	1.2 E
122	Caudéran (kō-dā-räɴ′) .... Fr.	44.52 N	0.35 W
125	Caudete (kou-dā′tȧ) .... Sp.	38.43 N	0.59 W
122	Caudry (kō-drē′) .... Fr.	50.10 N	3.30 E
153	Cauit, Pt. (kä′wêt) .... Phil.	9.18 N	126.12 E
72	Caulfeild (kôl′fēld) Can. (Vancouver In.)	49.20 N	123.15 W
160	Caulfield (kôl′fēld) Austl. (Melbourne In.)	37.53 S	145.3 E
126	Caulonia (kou-lō′nyä) .... It.	38.24 N	16.24 E
102	Cauquenes (kou-kā′nās) ..... Chl.	36.0 S	72.28 W
152	Cauralaningan (kou′rä-lä-nĭŋ′gän) Phil.	18.16 N	121.40 E
100	Caura, R. (kou′rä) .... Ven.	6.0 N	64.30 W
96	Cauto, R. (kou′tō) .... Cuba	20.33 N	76.30 W
124	Cavado, R. (kä-vä′dō) ...... Port.	41.40 N	8.11 W
134	Cavalaua (kä-vä-lou′ä) ...... Ang.	16.12 S	14.15 E
101	Cavalcante (kä-väl-kän′tā) . . Braz.	13.47 S	47.30 W
76	Cavalier (kăv-ȧ-lēr′) .... N. D.	48.47 N	97.37 W
114	Cavan (kăv′ăn) .... Ire.	54.0 N	7.20 W
127	Cavarna (kä-vär′nä) .... Bul.	43.25 N	28.22 E
126	Cavarzere (kä-vär′dzȧ-rā) ..... It.	45.8 N	12.5 E
86	Cavendish (kăv′ĕn-dĭsh) ...... Vt.	43.25 N	72.35 W
101	Caviana I. (kä-vyä′nä) ...... Braz.	0.15 N	50.0 W
152	Cavite (kä-vē′tā) .... Phil.	14.29 N	120.54 E
151	Cavite (Prov.) . . Phil. (Manila In.)	14.16 N	120.50 E
141	Cawnpore (kôn-pōr′) .... India	26.29 N	80.20 E
116	Cawood (kā′wo͝od) ...... Gt. Brit.	53.50 N	1.7 W
101	Caxias (kä′shê-äzh) .... Braz.	4.50 S	43.18 W
102	Caxias .... Braz.	29.14 S	51.15 W
134	Caxito (kä-shē′to͝o) .... Ang.	8.22 S	13.33 E
80	Cayanosa Draw (kä-yä-nō′sȧ drô) Tex.	31.0 N	103.10 W
97	Cayemite Is. (kī-mēt′) .... Hai.	18.38 N	73.46 W
101	Cayenne (kā-ĕn′) .... Fr. Gu.	4.58 N	52.18 W
97	Cayes (kī′ĕs) .... Hai.	18.12 N	73.46 W
100	Cay Grande (I.) (kī grän′dȧ) . Ven.	11.56 N	66.42 W
96	Cayman Is. (kī-män′) ...... W. I.	19.30 N	80.0 W
96	Cayman Brac (I.) (kī-män′ brȧk) W. I.	19.43 N	79.46 W
96	Cay Sal Bank .... W. I.	23.50 N	80.10 W
96	Cay Sal (I.) (kī säl) .... W. I.	23.41 N	80.25 W
85	Cayuga L. (kā-yōō′gȧ) ..... N. Y.	42.45 N	76.43 W
88	Cayuga R. N. Y. (Niagara Falls In.)	43.6 N	78.57 W
124	Cazalla (kä-thäl′yä) .... Sp.	37.56 N	5.46 W
85	Cazenovia (kăz-ê-nō′vĭ-ă) . . . N. Y.	42.55 N	75.50 W
88	Cazenovia Cr. N. Y. (Niagara Falls In.)	42.50 N	78.47 W
126	Čazma (chäz′mä) .... Yugo.	45.45 N	16.38 E
96	Cazones B. (kä-zō′nȧs) ..... Cuba	22.10 N	81.25 W
96	Cazones, G. of .... Cuba	21.55 N	81.10 W
93	Cazones, R .... Mex.	20.30 N	97.28 W
124	Cazorla (kä-thôr′lä) .... Sp.	37.55 N	3.0 W
126	Cazza (I.) (kät′sä) .... Yugo.	42.46 N	16.31 E
124	Céa R. (thā′ä) .... Sp.	42.15 N	5.10 W
101	Ceará (State) (sā-ä-rä′) ..... Braz.	5.0 S	39.30 W
101	Ceará (Fortaleza) (fôr-tä-lā′zä) Braz.	3.40 S	38.32 W
95	Cebaco I. (sȧ-bä′kō) .... Pan.	7.29 N	81.10 W
111	Cebelibereket (sĕ′bĕl-ĭ-bĕr′ĕ-kĕt) Tur.	37.5 N	37.30 E
75	Cebolla Cr. (sē-bōl′yä) ...... Colo.	38.20 N	107.5 W
124	Cebreros (thā-brā′rōs) .... Sp.	40.28 N	4.28 W
153	Cebu (sā-bōō′) .... Phil.	10.18 N	123.53 E
153	Cebu (I.) .... Phil.	10.25 N	123.50 E
120	Čechy (Bohemia) (Prov.) (chĕ′ĸē) . Czech.	49.44 N	14.15 E
160	Cecil Plains (sē′sĭl) .... Austl. (In.)	27.31 S	151.11 E
81	Cedar Bayou (R.) (sē′dēr) Tex. (In.)	29.51 N	94.55 W
81	Cedar Bayou .... Tex. (In.)	29.45 N	94.55 W
75	Cedar Breaks Natl. Mon .... Utah	37.38 N	112.45 W
77	Cedarburg .... Wis.	43.18 N	88.0 W
75	Cedar City .... Utah	37.41 N	113.3 W
76	Cedar Cr .... N. D.	46.3 N	102.0 W
77	Cedar Falls .... Ia.	42.32 N	92.25 W
81	Cedar Grove .... La.	32.25 N	93.46 W
82	Cedar Keys .... Fla.	29.7 N	83.3 W
54	Cedar L .... Can.	53.20 N	100.2 W
89	Cedar Lake Minn. (Minneapolis In.)	44.58 N	93.19 W
77	Cedar Rapids .... Ia.	42.0 N	91.41 W
77	Cedar R .... Ia.	42.25 N	92.12 W
77	Cedar R.. West Fork of .... Ia.	42.45 N	92.58 W
57	Cedars .... Can. (Montreal In.)	45.21 N	74.6 W
57	Cedars Rapids . Can. (Montreal In.)	45.17 N	74.0 W
84	Cedar Springs .... Mich.	43.14 N	85.37 W
82	Cedartown .... Ga.	34.0 N	85.15 W
92	Cedral (sā-dräl′) .... Mex.	23.48 N	100.42 W
94	Cedros (sā′drōs) .... Hond.	14.35 N	87.25 W
158	Ceduna (sê-do͝o′nȧ) .... Austl.	32.5 S	133.50 E
126	Cefalù (chā-fä-lo͝o′) .... It.	38.2 N	14.1 E
124	Cega R. (thā′gä) .... Sp.	41.20 N	4.15 W
121	Cegléd (tsă′glād) .... Hung.	47.10 N	19.48 E
124	Cehegín (thā-ȧ-hēn′) .... Sp.	38.5 N	1.48 W
131	Cekhira (sĕ′ĸē-rä) ..... Tun. (In.)	34.17 N	10.5 E
92	Celaya (sā-lä′yä) .... Mex.	20.32 N	100.49 W
150	Celebes (Is.) (sĕl′ê-bēz) (sĕl-ā′bĕs) . Indon.	2.30 S	120.30 E
150	Celebes Sea .... Indon.	3.0 N	122.0 E
84	Celina (sê-lī′nȧ) .... Ohio	40.34 N	84.37 W
126	Celje (tsĕl′yĕ) .... Yugo.	46.14 N	15.15 E
120	Celle (tsĕl′ĕ) .... Ger.	52.37 N	10.4 E
78	Cement (sê-mĕnt′) .... Okla.	34.55 N	98.7 W
126	Cenis, Mt. (sẽ-nē′) .... It.-Fr.	45.15 N	6.53 E
123	Cenis Pass, Mt .... Fr.-It.	45.15 N	6.50 E
122	Cenon (sẽ-nôɴ′) .... Fr.	44.50 N	0.30 W
81	Center (sĕn′tēr) .... Tex.	31.49 N	94.11 W
51	Centerville Calif. (San Francisco In.)	37.33 N	122.0 W
77	Centerville .... Ia.	40.42 N	92.51 W
85	Centerville .... Md.	39.2 N	76.5 W
85	Centerville .... Pa.	40.3 N	79.57 W
76	Centerville .... S. D.	43.7 N	96.56 W
73	Centerville Utah (Salt Lake City In.)	40.55 N	111.53 W
94	Central America (ȧ-mĕr′ĭ-kȧ) . N. A.		
72	Central City . . . Colo. (Denver In.)	39.48 N	105.31 W
84	Central City .... Ky.	37.16 N	86.8 W
78	Central City .... Neb.	41.8 N	98.00 W
152	Central, Cordillera (Mts.) (sĕn′träl) . Phil.	17.0 N	121.0 E
79	Centralia (sĕn-trā′lĭ-ȧ) .... Ill.	38.31 N	89.8 W
79	Centralia .... Mo.	39.12 N	92.7 W

ng-sing; ŋ-baŋk; ɴ-nasalized n: nŏd; cŏmmit; ōld; ôbey; ôrder; fōōd; fo͝ot; ou-out; s-soft; sh-dish; th-thin; pūre; ûnite; ûrn; stŭd; circŭs; ü-as "y" in study; ′-indeterminate vowel.

Centralia PRONOUNCING INDEX Chazumba

Page	Name Pronunciation Region	Lat. °′	Long. °′
70	Centralia . . . Wash.	46.42 N	122.58 W
141	Central India (Agency) . . . India	24.30 N	78.30 E
89	Central Junction Ga. (Savannah In.)	32.5 N	81.8 W
141	Central Provinces . . . India	22.0 N	80.0 E
82	Century . . . Fla.	30.58 N	87.18 W
151	Ceram (I.) (sē'räm) . . . Indon.	3.0 S	129.0 E
122	Cerberus, C. (sûr'bēr-ŭs') (sĕr-bĕ-rüs') . Fr.	42.25 N	3.10 E
117	Cercola (chĕr'kō-lä) . It. (Napoli In.)	40.51 N	14.21 E
118	Céret (sā-rĕ') . . . Fr.	42.29 N	2.46 E
126	Cerignola (chā-rē-nyô'lä) . . . It.	41.15 N	15.54 E
126	Cerknica (tsĕr'knē-tsà) . . . Yugo.	45.47 N	14.21 E
	Cernăuti, see Chernovitsy, Sov. Un.		
127	Cerna Vodă (chĕr-nȧ vō'dȧ) . Rom.	44.21 N	28.4 E
123	Cernay (sĕr-nĕ') . . . Fr.	47.50 N	7.10 E
123	Cernay-la-Ville (sĕr-nĕ'-lä-vēl') Fr. (In.)	48.40 N	1.57 E
80	Cerralvo (sĕr-räl'vō) . . . Mex.	26.5 N	99.37 W
92	Cerritos (sĕr-rē'tōs) . . . Mex.	22.26 N	100.17 W
100	Cerro de Pasco (sĕr'rō dā päs'kō) Peru	10.45 S	76.15 W
92	Cerro La Gallina (Mt.) (gä'lē-nä) Mex.	22.18 N	101.30 W
92	Cerro Peña Nevada (Mt.) (pē'ŋä nĕ-vä'dä) . Mex.	23.45 N	99.53 W
152	Cervantes (sĕr-vän'täs) . . . Phil.	17.0 N	120.42 E
124	Cervantes (thĕr-vän'täs) . . . Sp.	42.53 N	7.4 W
124	Cervera del Río (thĕr-vā'rä dĕl rē'ō) . Sp.	42.2 N	1.57 W
122	Cervione (sĕr-vē-ōn') (chĕr-vē-ō'nä) . Cor. (In.)	40.22 N	9.80 E
126	Cesena (chā-zā'nä) . . . It.	44.9 N	12.15 E
119	Cēsis (sä'sis) . . . Sov. Un.	57.18 N	25.19 E
120	Česka Lipa (chĕs'kä lē'pa) . Czech.	50.41 N	14.31 E
120	České Budejovice (chĕs'kā bōō'dyĕ-yô-vēt-sĕ) . Czech.	48.59 N	14.28 E
120	Český Krumlov (ches'kē krōōm'lôf) . Czech.	48.48 N	14.18 E
127	Cesme (chĕsh'mĕ) . . . Tur.	38.19 N	26.19 E
159	Cessnock (sĕs'nŏk) . . . Austl.	32.58 S	151.35 E
127	Cetinje (tsĕt'in-yĕ) . . . Yugo.	42.24 N	18.56 E
132	Ceuta (thā-ōō'tä) . . . Sp. Mor.	35.58 N	5.23 W
122	Cévennes (Mts.) (sā-vĕn') . . . Fr.	44.30 N	4.0 E
141	Ceylon (sē-lŏn') . . . Asia (In.)	9.30 N	80.15 E
125	Cezimbra (sĕ-zēm'brȧ) . Port. (In.)	38.27 N	9.6 W
99	Chacabuco (chä-kä-bōō'kō) Arg. (Buenos Aires In.)	34.31 S	60.27 W
92	Chacala R. (chä-kä'lä) . . . Mex.	19.16 N	104.20 W
93	Chacaltianguis (chä-käl-tē-äŋ'-gwēs) . Mex.	18.20 N	95.51 W
100	Chachapoyas (chä-chä-poi'yäs) Peru	6.15 S	77.45 W
75	Chaco Canyon Natl. Mon. (chä'kō) . N. M.	36.5 N	107.55 W
133	Chad (Colony) (chăd) . Fr. Eq. Afr.	11.20 N	19.0 E
83	Chadbourn (chăd'bŭrn) . . . N. C.	34.18 N	78.54 W
133	Chad L. (chăd) . . . Afr.	13.30 N	14.30 E
76	Chadron (chăd'rŭn) . . . Neb.	42.50 N	103.0 W
147	Chaeryŏng (chàr-yŭng') . . . Kor.	38.24 N	125.36 E
124	Chafarina Is. (chä-fä-rē'nä) . . Mor.	35.12 N	2.25 W
79	Chaffee (chăf'ē) . . . Mo.	27.10 N	89.38 W
122	Chagny (shä-nyē') . . . Fr.	46.55 N	4.48 E
128	Chagodoshcha R. (chä-gō-dôsh-chä) . Sov. Un.	59.25 N	34.45 E
95	Chagres, R. (chä'grĕs) . . . C. Z.	9.10 N	79.40 W
143	Chahar (Prov.) (chä'här) . . . Chn.	44.15 N	115.0 E
140	Chahbar (chä'bär) . . . Iran	25.20 N	60.45 E
134	Chai-Chai (Vila Nova de Gaza) (chī-chī) (vē-lä nō'vä dä gä'zä) . Moz.	25.3 S	33.40 E
135	Chake Chake (chä'kĕ chä'kĕ) . Zan.	5.17 S	39.46 E
133	Chala Mts. (chä'lä) . . Fr. Eq. Afr.	9.30 N	23.20 E
158	Chalantun (chä'län-tōōn') . . . Chn.	47.59 N	122.45 E
94	Chalatenango (chäl-ä-tĕ-näŋ'gō) Sal.	14.6 N	89.0 W
133	Chalbe (Stefanie) L. (chäl'bĕ) (stĕf-ȧ-nē') . Eth.	4.45 N	36.50 E
93	Chalcatongo (chäl-kä-tôŋ'gō) . Mex.	17.2 N	97.34 W
93	Chalchicomula (chäl-chē-kō-mōō'-lä) . Mex.	18.58 N	97.27 W
92	Chalchihuites (chäl-chē-wē'tās) Mex.	23.30 N	103.54 W
94	Chalchuapa (chäl-chwä'pä) . . . Sal.	14.2 N	89.39 W
127	Chalcidice (Khalkidike) Pen. (kăl-sĭd'ĭ-sē) (käl-kē-dē-kĕ') . Grc.	40.25 N	23.25 E
127	Chalcis (Khalkis) (kăl'sĭs) (käl'kĭs) . Grc.	38.27 N	23.38 E
93	Chalco (chäl-kō) . . . Mex. (In.)	19.16 N	98.54 W
55	Chaleur B. (shȧ-lûr') . . . Can.	48.0 N	65.0 W
144	Chaling (chä'lĭng') . . . Chn.	26.47 N	113.17 E
157	Chalky Inlet (chôk'ĭ) . . . N. Z.	46.0 S	166.35 E
157	Chalmers, Mt. (chäl'mērs) N. Z. (In.)	45.47 S	170.38 E
122	Chalon-sur-Saône (shȧ-lôN'-sür-sōn') . Fr.	46.52 N	4.55 E
122	Chalons-sur-Marne (shȧ-lôN'-sür-märn) . Fr.	48.55 N	4.20 E
92	Chamacuero de Comonfort (chä-mä-kwä'rō dā kō-mōn-fôrt') . Mex.	20.42 N	100.44 W
122	Chamalières (shä-mä-lyâr') . . . Fr.	45.45 N	3.1 E
141	Chaman (chŭm-än') . . . Pak.	30.50 N	66.40 E
75	Chama R. (chä'mä) . . . N. M.	36.22 N	106.36 W
125	Chamartín de la Rosa (chä-mär-tēn'dä lä rō'sä) . Sp. (In.)	40.28 N	3.42 W
94	Chama, Sierra de (Mts.) . . . Guat.	15.45 N	90.0 W
141	Chambal R. (chŭm-bäl') . . . India	26.00 N	77.0 E
76	Chamberlain (chām'bēr-lĭn) . S. D.	43.49 N	99.20 W
86	Chamberlain L. . . . Me.	46.13 N	69.20 W
85	Chambersburg (chām'bērz-bûrg) Pa.	39.57 N	77.41 W
123	Chambéry (shäm-bā-rē') . . . Fr.	45.35 N	5.55 E
73	Chamblee (chăm-blē') Ga. (Atlanta In.)	33.53 N	84.18 W
94	Chameleón, R. (kä-mȧ-lā-ōn') Hond.	15.14 N	88.40 W
95	Chame Pt. (chä'mȧ) . . . Pan.	8.38 N	79.40 W
133	Chamo, L. (chä'mō) . . . Eth.	5.50 N	37.35 E
123	Chamonix (shȧ-mô-nē') . . . Fr.	45.55 N	6.50 E
123	Champagnole (shäN-pȧ-nyŭl') . Fr.	46.45 N	5.52 E
79	Champaign (shăm-pān') . . . Ill.	40.7 N	88.15 W
94	Champerico (chăm-pȧ-rē'kō) Guat.	14.18 N	91.56 W
123	Champigny-sur-Marne (shäN-pē-nyē'-sür-märn') . Fr. (In.)	48.48 N	2.31 E
77	Champion (chăm'pĭ-ŭn) . . . Mich.	46.31 N	87.59 W
86	Champlain L. (shăm-plān') Vt.-N. Y.	44.35 N	73.20 W
123	Champlitte (shäN-plēt') . . . Fr.	47.38 N	5.30 E
93	Champotón (chäm-pō-tōn') . . Mex.	19.21 N	90.43 W
93	Chamula (chä-mōō'lä) . . . Mex.	16.46 N	92.41 W
102	Chañaral (chän-yä-räl') . . . Chl.	26.20 S	70.46 W
124	Chanca R. (chäŋ'kä) . . . Sp.-Port.	38.0 N	7.10 W
141	Chanda (chän'dŭ) . . . India	19.59 N	79.29 E
150	Chandaburi (chän-dŭ-bōō'rē) Siam	12.35 N	102.0 E
82	Chandeleur Is. (shăn-dē-lōōr') . La.	29.50 N	88.50 W
82	Chandeleur Sd. . . . G. of Mex.	29.54 N	89.6 W
141	Chandernagor (chŭn-dēr-nȧ-gōr') India	22.45 N	88.20 E
86	Chandler (chăn'dlēr) . . . Can.	48.23 N	64.38 W
79	Chandler . . . Okla.	35.41 N	96.52 W
144	Changan (chän'gän') . . . Chn.	25.17 N	109.26 E
144	Changchai (chäng'chī') . . . Chn.	25.56 N	106.14 E
145	Changchow (chäng'chō') . . . Chn.	24.30 N	117.36 E
144	Changchow . . . Chn.	30.2 N	107.7 E
145	Changchow . . . Chn.	31.45 N	119.55 E
143	Changchun (Hsinking) (chäng'chōōn') (hsĭn'kĭng) . . Chn.	44.2 N	123.29 E
147	Changdan (chäng'dän') . . . Kor.	37.56 N	126.45 E
145	Changhing (chäng'hĭng') . . . Chn.	30.57 N	119.50 E
145	Changhua (chäng'hwä') . . . For.	24.5 N	120.32 E
145	Changhwa (chäng'hwä') . . . Chn.	30.16 N	119.18 E
146	Changi (chäng'ē') . . . Chn.	36.53 N	119.21 E
146	Changi . . . Chn.	36.53 N	119.21 E
147	Changjŏn (chäng'jŭn') . . . Kor.	38.45 N	128.11 E
146	Changko (chäng'kō') . . . Chn.	34.13 N	113.55 E
146	Changku (chäng'kōō') . . . Chn.	36.48 N	117.27 E
146	Changli (chäng'lē') . . . Chn.	39.46 N	119.11 E
145	Changlo (chäng'lō') . . . Chn.	25.53 N	119.28 E
146	Changlo . . . Chn.	36.44 N	118.53 E
145	Changlok (chäng'lōk') . . . Chn.	24.1 N	115.24 E
145	Changning (chäng'nĭng') . . . Chn.	24.52 N	115.15 E
144	Changning . . . Chn.	26.25 N	112.12 E
148	Chang Pai Shan (Mts.) (chäng' pī shän') . Chn.	42.15 N	128.15 E
143	Changpeh (chäng'pĕ') . . . Chn.	41.7 N	114.34 E
145	Changping (chäng'pĭng') . . . Chn.	25.18 N	117.23 E
145	Changpu (chäng-pōō') . . . Chn.	24.7 N	117.31 E
145	Chang R. (chäng) . . . Chn.	29.24 N	116.58 E
147	Changsan Pt. (chäng'sän') . . . Kor.	38.10 N	124.45 E
145	Changsha (chäng'shä') . . . Chn.	28.12 N	112.45 E
146	Changshan (chäng'shän') . . . Chn.	36.55 N	118.3 E
145	Changshu (chäng'shōō') . . . Chn.	31.33 N	120.40 E
145	Changtai (chäng'tī') . . . Chn.	24.36 N	117.42 E
147	Changtan (chäng'tän') . . . Kor.	37.57 N	126.44 E
146	Changte (chäng'tĕ') . . . Chn.	36.4 N	114.32 E
146	Changteh . . . Chn.	29.0 N	111.22 E
146	Changtsing (chäng'tsĭng') . . . Chn.	36.30 N	116.34 E
146	Changtu (chäng'tōō') . . . Chn.	43.0 N	123.59 E
144	Changyang (chäng'yäng') . . . Chn.	30.29 N	111.4 E
148	Changwu (chäng'wōō') . . . Chn.	42.26 N	122.54 E
147	Changyŏn (chäng'yŭn') . . . Kor.	38.17 N	125.5 E
146	Changyüan (chäng'yü-än') . . . Chn.	35.9 N	114.58 E
148	Chan-Kwan-Tsai-Ling (Mts.) (chän'kwän'-tsī'lĭng') . Chn.	44.30 N	128.30 E
122	Channel Is. (chăn'ĕl) . . . Gt. Brit.	49.35 N	2.30 W
124	Chantada (chän-tä'dä) . . . Sp.	42.36 N	7.46 W
122	Chantilly (shäN-tē-yē') . . . Fr.	49.12 N	2.28 E
79	Chanute (shȧ-nōōt') . . . Kan.	37.41 N	95.28 W
138	Chany, L. (chä'nē) . . . Sov. Un.	54.45 N	77.30 E
146	Chanyangkwan (chän'yäng'kwän') Chn.	32.22 N	116.28 E
146	Chao L. (chä'ō) . . . Chn.	31.34 N	117.25 E
145	Chaoan (chä'ō-än') . . . Chn.	23.45 N	117.0 E
145	Chaochow (chä'ō-chō') . . . Chn.	23.41 N	116.25 E
146	Chaochow . . . Chn.	37.50 N	114.50 E
145	Chaohsien (chä'ō-hsyĕn') . . . Chn.	31.38 N	117.48 E
144	Chaoping (chä'o-pĭng') . . . Chn.	24.7 N	110.46 E
148	Chaotung (chä'ō-tōōng) . . . Chn.	27.26 N	103.48 E
148	Chaoyang (chä'ō-yäng') . . . Chn.	41.35 N	120.25 E
145	Chaoyang (chä'ō-yäng') . . . Chn.	23.18 N	116.20 E
148	Chaoyangchen (chou'yäng'chĕn') Chn.	42.45 N	126.2 E
146	Chaoyüan (chä'ō-yü-än') . . . Chn.	37.20 N	120.23 E
92	Chapala (chä-pä'lä) . . . Mex.	20.18 N	103.11 W
92	Chapala L. . . . Mex.	20.15 N	103.0 W
143	Chapei (chä'pä'ē) Chn. (Shanghai In.)	31.11 N	121.25 E
117	Chapel-en-le-Frith (chăp''l-ĕn-lē-frĭth) Gt. Brit. (Liverpool In.)	53.20 N	1.54 W
83	Chapel Hill (chăp''l hĭl) . . . N. C.	35.55 N	79.3 W
72	Chapman Cr. (chăp'măn) Can. (Vancouver In.)	49.28 N	123.43 W
76	Chappell (chă-pĕl') . . . Neb.	41.6 N	102.27 W
160	Chappell I. . . . Austl. (Tas. In.)	40.18 S	147.53 E
93	Chapultenango (chä-pōōl-tē-näŋ'gō) . Mex.	17.16 N	93.6 W
92	Charcas (chär'käs) . . . Mex.	23.9 N	101.7 W
95	Charco Azul B. (chär'kō ä-zōōl') Pan.	8.15 N	82.40 W
4	Charcot I. (shär-kō') . . . Pac. O.	70.0 S	74.0 W
122	Charente R. (shȧ-räNt') . . . Fr.	45.45 N	0.30 W
123	Charenton-le-Pont (shȧ-räN-tôN'-lē-pôN') . Fr. (In.)	48.48 N	2.25 E
77	Chariton (chăr'ĭ-tŭn) . . . Ia.	41.1 N	93.19 W
79	Chariton R. . . . Mo.	39.55 N	92.40 W
156	Chariu B. (chär'yōō) . . N. Z. (In.)	41.13 S	174.44 E
115	Charleroi (shȧr-lē-rwä') . . . Bel.	50.25 N	4.31 E
85	Charleroi . . . Pa.	40.18 N	79.55 W
85	Charles, C. (chärlz) . . . Md.	37.5 N	75.58 W
77	Charles City . . . Ia.	43.4 N	92.39 W
157	Charles, Mt. . . . N. Z. (In.)	45.52 S	170.44 E
84	Charleston (chärlz'tŭn) . . . Ill.	39.30 N	88.12 W
82	Charleston . . . Miss.	34.0 N	90.3 W
79	Charleston . . . Mo.	36.55 N	89.20 W
83	Charleston . . . S. C.	32.47 N	79.57 W
51	Charleston . . . Wash. (Seattle In.)	47.33 N	122.41 W
84	Charleston . . . W. Va.	38.22 N	81.38 W
84	Charleston, South . . . W. Va.	38.22 N	81.42 W
95	Charlestown . . . Le. Is. (In.)	17.8 N	62.37 W
85	Charlestown . . . W. Va.	39.15 N	77.55 W
117	Charlesworth Gt. Brit. (Liverpool In.)	53.26 N	1.59 W
159	Charleville (chär'lē-vĭl) . . . Austl.	26.15 S	146.29 E
134	Charleville (shärl-vēl') . Bel. Cong.	5.25 S	21.0 E
122	Charleville . . . Fr.	49.48 N	4.42 E
85	Charlevoix (shär'lē-voi) . . . Mich.	45.18 N	85.17 W
89	Charley, L. Minn. (Minneapolis In.)	45.6 N	93.8 W
160	Charleys Cr. . . . Austl. (In.)	25.40 S	150.40 E
122	Charlieu (shär-lyû') . . . Fr.	46.11 N	4.10 E
84	Charlotte (shär'lŏt) . . . Mich.	42.37 N	84.50 W
83	Charlotte . . . N. C.	35.14 N	80.50 W
91	Charlotte Amalia (St. Thomas) (shär-lŏt'ĕ ȧ-mä'lĭ-ȧ) St. Thomas I. (In.)	18.20 N	64.54 W
83	Charlotte Har. . . . Fla. (In.)	26.50 N	82.5 W
118	Charlottenberg (shär-lŭt'ĕn-bĕrg) Swe.	59.54 N	12.18 E
117	Charlottenburg (shär-lŭt'ĕn-bōōrgh) . Ger. (Berlin In.)	52.32 N	13.18 E
85	Charlottesville (shär'lŏtz-vĭl) . Va.	38.2 N	78.29 W
55	Charlottetown (shär'lŏt-toun) Can.	46.21 N	63.20 W
158	Charlotte Waters (shär'lŏt) . Austl.	26.5 S	134.59 E
123	Charmes (shärm) . . . Fr.	48.25 N	6.15 E
116	Charnwood Forest (chärn'wŏŏd) . Gt. Brit.	52.42 N	1.15 W
141	Charsadda (chŭr-sä'dä) Pak. (Peshawar In.)	34.8 N	71.43 E
159	Charters Towers (chär'tērz) . Austl.	20.5 S	146.27 E
122	Chartres (shärt'r') . . . Fr.	48.25 N	1.30 E
102	Chascomus (chäs-kō-mōōs') . . Arg.	35.40 S	58.2 W
83	Chase City (chās) . . . Va.	36.47 N	78.39 W
128	Chashniki (chäsh'nyē-kē) . Sov. Un.	54.50 N	29.10 E
77	Chaska (chăs'kȧ) . . . Minn.	44.48 N	93.33 W
122	Châteaubriant (shȧ-tō-brē-äN') . Fr.	47.42 N	1.21 W
122	Château-Chinon (shȧ-tō'-shē-nôN') . Fr.	47.5 N	3.57 E
122	Château-du-Loir (shȧtō'-dü-lwär') . Fr.	47.40 N	0.27 E
122	Châteaudun (shä-tō-dăN') . . . Fr.	48.5 N	1.20 E
123	Châteaufort (shȧ-tō-fôr') . Fr. (In.)	48.45 N	2.6 E
122	Château Gontier (shȧ-tō' gôN'-tyā') . Fr.	47.50 N	0.49 W
57	Châteauguay (shȧ-tō-gā') Can. (Montreal In.)	45.23 N	73.46 W
122	Châteauneuf-sur-Loire (shȧ-tō-nûf'-sür-lwär') . Fr.	47.52 N	2.11 E
122	Châteaurenault (shȧ-tō-rē-nō') . Fr.	47.35 N	1.0 E
57	Château Richer (shȧ-tō' rē-shā') Can. (Que. In.)	46.59 N	71.2 W
122	Châteauroux (shȧ-tō-rōō') . . . Fr.	46.48 N	1.40 E
122	Château-Thierry (shȧ-tō'-tyĕr-rē') . Fr.	49.2 N	3.22 E
122	Châtellerault (shä-tĕl-rō') . . . Fr.	46.49 N	0.31 E
123	Châtenay (shät-nĕ') . . . Fr. (In.)	48.46 N	2.17 E
77	Chatfield (chăt'fēld) . . . Minn.	43.51 N	92.10 W
55	Chatham (chăt'ăm) . . . Can.	47.0 N	65.28 W
84	Chatham . . . Can.	42.25 N	82.15 W
115	Chatham . . . Gt. Brit.	51.20 N	0.35 E
4	Chatham Is. . . . Pac. O.	44.0 S	176.0 W
56	Chatham Sd. Can. (Prince Rupert In.)	54.20 N	130.35 W
122	Châtillon-sur-Seine (shä-tē-yôN'-sür-sän') . Fr.	47.50 N	4.35 E
160	Chatswood (chăts'wŏŏd) Austl. (Sydney In.)	33.47 S	151.11 E
73	Chatsworth (chătz'wûrth) Calif. (Los Angeles In.)	34.15 N	118.36 W
73	Chatsworth Res. . . . Calif.	34.18 N	118.29 E
73	Chattahoochee (chăt-ȧ-hōō'chē) Ga. (Atlanta In.)	33.48 N	84.29 W
82	Chattahoochee R. . . . Ala.-Ga.	32.30 N	85.0 W
82	Chattanooga (chăt-ȧ-nōō'gȧ) Tenn.	35.2 N	85.18 W
82	Chattanooga, East . . . Tenn.	35.5 N	85.14 W
82	Chattooga R. (chă-tōō'gȧ) Ga.-S. C.	34.50 N	83.17 W
57	Chaudière (shō-dyĕr') Can. (Que. In.)	46.42 N	71.18 W
86	Chaudière R. . . . Can.	46.0 N	70.50 W
150	Chaudoc (shō-dŏk') . . . Indoch.	10.45 N	105.5 E
122	Chaumont (shō-môN') . . . Fr.	48.9 N	5.9 E
139	Chaun B. (choun) . . . Sov. Un.	69.25 N	170.0 E
122	Chauny (shō-nē') . . . Fr.	49.39 N	3.10 E
128	Chausy (chou'sĭ) . . . Sov. Un.	53.48 N	31.0 E
85	Chautauqua L. (shȧ-tô'kwȧ) . N. Y.	42.10 N	79.23 W
123	Chauvry (shō-vrē') . . . Fr. (In.)	49.3 N	2.17 E
123	Chavenay (shäv-nĕ') . . . Fr. (In.)	48.51 N	1.58 E
124	Chaves (chä'vĕzh) . . . Port.	41.45 N	7.29 W
101	Chaves (I.) (chä'vĕs) . . . Ec.	0.40 S	90.15 W
122	Chazelles (shä-zĕl') . . . Fr.	45.45 N	4.15 E
93	Chazumba (chä-zōōm'bä) . . . Mex.	18.13 N	97.39 W

ăt; finăl; rāte; senāte; ärm; åsk; sofȧ; fâre; ch-choose; dh-as th in other; bē; ēvent; bĕt; recĕnt; cratēr; g-go; gh-gutteral g; bĭt; ĭ-short neutral; rīde; K-gutteral k as ch in German ich;

Cheadle PRONOUNCING INDEX **China Sea**

Page	Name Pronunciation Region	Lat. °′	Long. °′
18	Cheadle (chē'd'l) Gt. Brit.	52.59 N	1.59 W
72	Cheam Pk. (chēm) Can. (Vancouver In.)	49.9 N	121.40 W
85	Cheat R. (chēt) W. Va.	39.30 N	79.38 W
120	Cheb, (kĕb) Czech.	50.4 N	12.23 E
110	Cheboksari (chyĕ-bôk-sä'rê) Sov. Un.	56.8 N	47.12 E
84	Cheboygan (shê-boi'găn) Mich.	45.38 N	84.29 W
111	Chechen I. (chyĕch'ĕn) Sov. Un.	44.0 N	47.45 E
147	Chechŏn (chĕ'chŭn') Kor.	37.8 N	128.12 E
79	Checotah (chê-kō'tȧ) Okla.	35.27 N	95.32 W
87	Chedabucto B. (chĕd-ȧ-bŭk-tō) Can.	45.25 N	61.25 W
141	Cheduba (I.) (chê-dōō'bȧ) Bur.	18.45 N	93.45 E
146	Chefoo (chē-fōō') Chn.	37.32 N	121.20 E
70	Chehalis (chê-hā'lĭs) Wash.	46.39 N	122.58 W
72	Chehalis L. Can. (Vancouver In.)	49.25 N	122.2 W
72	Chehalis R. Can. (Vancouver In.)	49.22 N	122.0 W
70	Chehalis R. Wash.	46.55 N	123.18 W
147	Cheju (chĕ'jōō') Kor.	33.30 N	126.32 E
147	Cheju I. (Quelpart I.) (kwĕl'pärt) Kor.	33.24 N	126.34 E
145	Chekiang (Prov.) (chĕ'kyäng') Chn.	29.20 N	119.48 E
70	Chelan (chê-lăn') Wash.	47.48 N	119.59 W
70	Chelan, L. Wash.	48.0 N	120.20 W
134	Chela, Serra da (Mts.) (sĕr'rȧ dä shä'lȧ) Ang.	15.30 S	13.30 E
125	Cheleiros (shĕ-lā'rōzh) Port. (In.)	38.53 N	9.20 W
140	Cheleken I. (chĕ-lyĕ-kĕn') Sov. Un.	39.30 N	53.15 E
112	Chelia, Jebel (Mt.) (jĕb'ĕl shȧl'yȧ) Alg.	35.29 N	6.35 E
112	Chelif (Touil) Wadi (R.) (wä'dê shȧ-lēf') (tōō-ēl') Alg.	34.30 N	2.12 E
138	Chelkar (chyĕl'kär) Sov. Un.	48.0 N	59.40 E
111	Chelkar, L. Sov. Un.	50.30 N	51.35 E
138	Chelkar Tengiz, L. (tĕn'yēz) Sov. Un.	48.15 N	63.15 E
112	Chellala (chĕl-ȧ'lȧ) Alg.	35.5 N	2.22 E
123	Chelles (shĕl) Fr. (In.)	48.52 N	2.35 E
121	Chelm (kĕlm) Pol.	51.7 N	23.30 E
121	Chelmno (kĕlm'nō) Pol.	53.20 N	18.26 E
115	Chelmsford (chĕmz'fĕrd) Gt. Brit.	51.45 N	0.27 E
87	Chelmsford Mass. (In.)	42.36 N	71.21 W
121	Chelmza (kĕlm'zhȧ) Pol.	53.9 N	18.37 E
73	Chelsea (chĕl'sê) Ala. (Birmingham In.)	33.20 N	86.36 W
86	Chelsea Mass.	42.25 N	71.0 W
84	Chelsea Mich.	42.22 N	84.2 W
79	Chelsea Okla.	36.32 N	95.20 W
117	Chelsfield (chĕls'fēld) Gt. Brit. (London In.)	51.21 N	0.8 E
160	Cheltenham (chĕlt'nȧm) Austl. (Melbourne In.)	37.58 S	145.3 E
114	Cheltenham Gt. Brit.	51.55 N	2.5 W
88	Cheltenham Pa. (Philadelphia In.)	40.3 N	75.3 W
125	Chelva (chĕl'vä) Sp.	39.44 N	0.58 W
138	Chelyabinsk (chĕl-yä-bênsk') Sov. Un.	55.15 N	61.30 E
139	Chelyuskin, C. (chĕl-yōōs'kĭn) Sov. Un.	77.35 N	105.0 E
72	Chemainus (chĕ-mā'nŭs) Can. (Vancouver In.)	48.55 N	123.43 W
138	Chemashevskoe (chĕm'ȧ-shyĕf-skō'yĕ) Sov. Un.	62.55 N	65.10 E
122	Chemillé (shē-mê-yā') Fr.	47.17 N	0.42 W
120	Chemnitz (kĕm'nĭts) Ger.	50.50 N	12.54 E
147	Chemulpo (Inchŏn) (che-mŭl'pō) (ĭn'chŭn) Kor.	37.28 N	126.38 E
83	Chemung, R. (shê-mŭng') N. Y.	42.20 N	77.29 W
53	Chena (chē'nȧ) Alsk.	64.44 N	147.45 W
141	Chenab R. (chê-näb') Pak.	31.0 N	72.0 E
132	Chenachane (shē-nȧ-shän') Alg.	26.8 N	4.10 W
144	Chenan (chĕn'än') Chn.	23.20 N	106.46 E
144	Chenchow (chĕn'chō') Chn.	25.48 N	112.54 E
146	Chenchow Chn.	33.54 N	114.59 E
57	Chene, R. du (dü shĕn) Can. (Montreal In.)	45.35 N	74.0 W
70	Cheney (chē'nȧ) Wash.	47.29 N	117.34 W
144	Chengan (chĕŋ'gän') Chn.	28.18 N	107.29 E
145	Chengan Chn.	28.45 N	115.2 E
146	Chengan Chn.	36.27 N	114.53 E
134	Chengane R. (chĕn-gä'nĕ) Moz.	23.30 S	33.47 E
143	Chengchiatun (Liaoyuan) (chĕng'-chyä-tōōn') (lē-ou'yōō-än') Chn.	43.44 N	123.28 E
146	Chengchow (chĕng'chō') Chn.	34.42 N	113.45 E
145	Chengho (chĕng'hō') Chn.	26.23 N	118.40 E
144	Chengpu (chĕng-pōō') Chn.	26.20 N	110.12 E
144	Chengsi (chĕng-sē') Chn.	23.10 N	106.23 E
143	Chengte (Jehol) (chĕng'tĕ') (rē-hōl') Chn.	40.59 N	117.37 E
142	Chengtu (chĕng'tōō') Chn.	30.40 N	104.15 E
147	Chengtzutung (chĕng'tsōō-tōōng') Chn.	39.35 N	122.25 E
146	Chengwu (chĕng'wōō') Chn.	34.59 N	115.58 E
146	Chengyang (chĕng'yäng') Chn.	32.34 N	114.12 E
144	Chenki (chĕŋ-kē') Chn.	27.58 N	109.50 E
146	Chenliu (chĕn'lyōō') Chn.	34.37 N	114.40 E
123	Chennevières-sur-Marne (shĕn-nĕ-vyâr'-sür-märn') Fr. (In.)	48.47 N	2.32 E
145	Chenping (chĕn-pĭng') Chn.	24.36 N	115.58 E
142	Chensi (Barköl) (chĕn'sē) (bär-kûl') Chn.	43.32 N	93.0 E
146	Chenting (chĕn'tĭng) Chn.	38.12 N	114.35 E
144	Chenyüan (chĕn'yü-än') Chn.	27.4 N	108.10 E
143	Chenzu (chĕn'zōō') Chn. (Shanghai In.)	31.11 N	121.21 E
95	Chepo (chā'pō) Pan.	9.12 N	79.6 W
95	Chepo, R. Pan.	9.10 N	78.44 W
92	Cherán (chā-rän') Mex.	19.41 N	101.55 W
83	Cheraw (chē'rô) S. C.	34.40 N	79.52 W
131	Cherb, Djebel (Mts.) (jĕb'ĕl chĕrb) Tun. (In.)	34.7 N	8.50 E
122	Cherbourg (shär-bōōr') Fr.	49.38 N	1.35 W
132	Cherchel (shĕr-shĕl') Alg.	36.40 N	2.5 E
142	Cherchen (chĕr-chĕn') Chn.	37.58 N	85.30 E
142	Cherchen Darya (R.) (chĕr-chĕn' där'yä) Chn.	39.0 N	87.0 E
138	Cherdin (chĕr-dyēn') Sov. Un.	60.30 N	56.30 E
138	Cheremkhovo (chĕr'yĕm-kô-vō) Sov. Un.	52.55 N	103.20 E
133	Cheren (chĕr'ĕn) Erit.	15.41 N	38.30 E
138	Cherepanovo (chĕr'yĕ-pä-nô'vō) Sov. Un.	54.15 N	83.10 E
128	Cherepovets (chĕr-yĕ-pô'vyĕtz) Sov. Un.	59.7 N	37.56 E
128	Cherepovets (Dist.) Sov. Un.	59.20 N	35.13 E
128	Chereya (chĕr-ā'yä) Sov. Un.	54.36 N	29.16 E
112	Chergui, Chott ech (chĕr gē) Alg.	34.15 N	0.30 E
150	Cheribon (chĕr-ĭ-bŏn') Indon.	6.47 S	108.36 E
128	Cherikov (chĕ'rē-kôf) Sov. Un.	53.34 N	31.22 E
129	Cherkassy (chĕr-käs'sĭ) Sov. Un.	49.27 N	32.2 E
111	Cherkess (Adige) (Reg.) (chĕr-kĕs') (ä'dĭ-gā) Sov. Un.	45.0 N	40.5 E
111	Cherkess (Karachai) (Auton. Reg.) (chĕr'kĕs) (kä-rȧ-chī') Sov. Un.	43.45 N	42.0 E
138	Cherlakovskoe Selo (chĕr-läk-ôf'-skō-yĕ syĕ'lō) Sov. Un.	54.10 N	74.55 E
110	Chermoz (chĕr-môz') Sov. Un.	58.50 N	56.5 E
128	Chern (chĕrn) Sov. Un.	53.26 N	36.49 E
129	Chernigov (chĕr-nē'gôf) Sov. Un.	51.29 N	31.19 E
129	Chernigovka (chĕr-nê-gôf'kȧ) Sov. Un.	47.7 N	36.15 E
148	Chernigovsk (chĕr-nê'gôfsk) Sov. Un.	44.18 N	132.19 E
129	Chernobai (chĕr-nō-bī') Sov. Un.	49.39 N	32.19 E
129	Chernobyl (chĕr-nō-bĭl') Sov. Un.	51.17 N	30.11 E
111	Chernovitsy (Cernăuti) (chĕr-nôf'-ĭ-tsê) (chĕr-nou'tsê) Sov. Un.	48.18 N	25.56 E
129	Chernyanka (chĕrn-yäŋ'kȧ) Sov. Un.	50.57 N	37.48 E
76	Cherokee (chĕr-ô-kē') Ia.	42.45 N	95.32 W
79	Cherokee Kan.	37.19 N	94.49 W
78	Cherokee Okla.	36.45 N	98.22 W
96	Cheroki Sd. (chĕr-ô-kē') Ba. Is.	26.16 N	77.8 W
122	Cher R. (shâr) Fr.	47.20 N	1.10 E
86	Cherrifield (chĕr'ĭ-fēld) Me.	44.37 N	67.57 W
72	Cherry Cr. (chĕr'ĭ) Colo. (Denver In.)	39.34 N	104.46 W
85	Cherrydale Va.	38.56 N	77.8 W
160	Cherry Gully Austl. (In.)	28.29 S	151.58 E
79	Cherryvale Kan.	37.16 N	95.34 W
83	Cherryville N. C.	35.22 N	81.22 W
139	Cherski Mts. (chĕrs'kĭ) Sov. Un.	64.35 N	149.0 E
126	Cherso (kĕr'sō) Yugo.	44.58 N	14.23 E
126	Cherso (I.) Yugo.	44.55 N	14.23 E
121	Chertkov (chĕrt-kôf') Sov. Un.	49.1 N	25.51 E
128	Cherven (chĕr'vyĕn) Sov. Un.	53.42 N	28.28 E
116	Cherwell, R. (chär'wĕl) Gt. Brit.	52.7 N	1.15 W
84	Chesaning (chĕs'ȧ-nĭng) Mich.	43.12 N	84.10 W
85	Chesapeake B. (chĕs'ȧ-pēk) Md.	38.0 N	76.10 W
84	Cheshire (chĕsh'ĭr) Mich.	42.30 N	85.58 W
116	Cheshire Co. Gt. Brit.	53.15 N	2.30 W
110	Cheshskaya B. (chĕsh-skä'yä) Sov. Un.	67.30 N	46.30 E
114	Chester (chĕs'tĕr) Gt. Brit.	53.12 N	2.55 W
79	Chester Ill.	37.55 N	89.48 W
84	Chester Ohio	40.36 N	80.33 W
85	Chester Pa.	39.50 N	75.20 W
83	Chester S. C.	34.42 N	81.13 W
85	Chester Va.	37.21 N	77.27 W
88	Chester Cr. Minn. (Duluth In.)	46.49 N	92.6 W
114	Chesterfield Gt. Brit.	53.15 N	2.25 W
54	Chesterfield Inlet Can.	64.0 N	92.30 W
159	Chesterfield Is. Pac. O.	19.45 S	158.30 E
84	Chesterton Ind.	41.37 N	87.5 W
85	Chestertown Md.	39.12 N	76.5 W
86	Chesuncook L. (chĕs'ŭn-kŏŏk) Me.	46.2 N	69.22 W
77	Chetek (chĕ'tĕk) Wis.	45.19 N	91.40 W
94	Chetumal B. (chĕt-ōō-mäl') Br. Hond.-Mex. (In.)	18.20 N	88.0 W
75	Chevalon Cr. (shĕv'ȧ-lŏn) Ariz.	34.35 N	110.50 W
84	Cheviot (shĕv'ĭ-ŭt) Ohio	39.7 N	84.39 W
114	Cheviot Hills Gt. Brit.	55.20 N	2.30 W
123	Chevreuse (shĕ-vrûz') Fr. (In.)	48.42 N	2.3 E
70	Chewelah (chê-wē'lȧ) Wash.	48.16 N	117.43 W
71	Cheyenne (shī-ĕn') Wyo.	41.9 N	104.48 W
72	Cheyenne Canon Colo. (Colo. Sprs. In.)	38.48 N	104.52 W
72	Cheyenne Cr. Colo. (Colo. Sprs. In.)	38.48 N	104.55 W
72	Cheyenne Mt. Colo. (Colo. Sprs. In.)	38.44 N	104.52 W
76	Cheyenne R. S. D.	44.20 N	102.20 W
76	Cheyenne River Indian Res. S. D.	44.55 N	101.0 W
78	Cheyenne Wells Colo.	38.47 N	102.21 W
145	Chiai (chĭ'ī') For.	23.32 N	120.32 E
142	Chiamdo (chē'äm'dô) Chn.	30.52 N	96.33 E
	Chiangkiakow, see Kalgan, Chn.		
93	Chiapa de Corzo (chê-ä'pȧ dä kôr'zō) Mex.	16.41 N	93.1 W
93	Chiapas (State) (chê-ä'päs) Mex.	16.35 N	92.0 W
93	Chiapas, Cordillera de (Mts.) (chê-ä'päs) Mex.	15.45 N	93.0 W
126	Chiari (kyä'rē) It.	45.32 N	9.55 E
126	Chiasso (kyäs'sō) It.	45.49 N	9.1 E
120	Chiasso Switz.	45.51 N	9.1 E
92	Chiautla (chyä-ōōt'lä) Mex.	18.16 N	98.36 W
126	Chiavara (kyä'vä-rē) It.	44.18 N	9.19 E
149	Chiba (chē'bä) Jap.	35.32 N	140.10 E
134	Chibi (chē'bē) S. Rh.	20.17 S	30.17 E
86	Chibougamau L. (chē-bōō'gȧ-mou) Can.	49.50 N	74.15 W
134	Chibuto (chê-bōō'tō) Moz.	24.40 S	33.35 E
84	Chicago (shĭ-kô'gō; chĭ-kȧ'gō) Ill.	41.50 N	87.40 W
88	Chicago Ill. (In.)		
88	Chicago Drainage Can. Ill. (Chicago In.)	41.48 N	87.48 W
79	Chicago Hts. Ill.	41.29 N	87.38 W
88	Chicago Ridge Ill. (Chicago In.)	41.42 N	87.49 W
88	Chicago R., N. Ill. (Chicago In.)	42.0 N	87.47 W
124	Chica, Mar (Sea) (mär chē'kä) Mor.	35.10 N	2.50 W
93	Chica, R. (chē'kâ) Mex. (In.)	19.33 N	98.51 W
93	Chicbul (chĭk-bōōl') Mex.	18.45 N	90.56 W
53	Chichagof (I.) (chê-chä'gôf) Alsk.	58.0 N	136.0 W
114	Chichester (chĭch'ĕs-tĕr) Gt. Brit.	50.50 N	0.50 W
146	Chichow (chĭ'chō') Chn.	38.31 N	115.17 E
52	Chickaloon (chĭk'ȧ-lōōn) Alsk. (In.)	61.50 N	148.30 W
82	Chickamauga (chĭk-ȧ-mô'gȧ) Ga.	34.53 N	85.18 W
82	Chickasawhay R. (chĭk-ȧ-sô'wā) Miss.	31.30 N	88.32 W
78	Chickasha (chĭk'ȧ-shā) Okla.	35.3 N	97.58 W
125	Chiclana de la Frontera (chê-klä'nä dā lä frôn-tā'rä) Sp. (In.)	36.25 N	6.9 W
100	Chiclayo (chê-klä'yō) Peru	6.45 S	79.58 W
74	Chico (chē'kō) Calif.	39.43 N	121.51 W
134	Chicoa (chē-kō'ä) Moz.	15.40 S	32.23 E
72	Chico Cr. Colo. (Colo. Sprs. In.)	38.43 N	104.27 W
93	Chicoloapan (chê-kō-lwä'pän) Mex. (In.)	19.25 N	98.54 W
93	Chiconahutla (chê-kō-nä-ōō'tlä) Mex. (In.)	19.38 N	99.0 W
92	Chicontepec (chê-kōn'tĕ-pĕk') Mex.	20.58 N	98.9 W
86	Chicopee (chĭk'ô-pē) Mass.	42.10 N	72.35 W
102	Chico, R. Arg.	44.32 S	67.0 W
152	Chico, R. Phil.	17.30 N	121.27 E
55	Chicoutimi (shē-kōō'tē-mē') Can.	48.30 N	71.0 W
55	Chidley, C. (chĭd'lĭ) Can.	60.33 N	64.25 W
82	Chiefland (chēf'lănd) Fla.	29.29 N	82.53 W
72	Chief Mt. (chēf) Colo. (Denver In.)	39.40 N	105.32 W
150	Chiengmai (chĭ-ĕng-mī') Siam	18.45 N	98.55 E
150	Chiengrai (chĭ-ĕng-rī') Siam	19.50 N	99.45 E
126	Chieri (kyä'rē) It.	45.1 N	7.50 E
126	Chieti (kyĕ'tē) It.	42.21 N	14.9 E
129	Chigirin (chê-gē'rĕn) Sov. Un.	49.2 N	32.38 E
92	Chignahuapan (chĕn-yä-wä'pän) Mex.	19.50 N	98.2 W
86	Chignecto B. (shĭg-nĕk'tō) Canada	45.40 N	64.35 W
117	Chigwell (chĭg'wĕl) Gt. Brit. (London In.)	51.38 N	0.5 E
145	Chihchow (chĭ-chō) Chn.	30.38 N	117.32 E
143	Chihfeng (chĭ'fŭng') Chn.	43.0 N	119.0 E
144	Chihing (chĭ'hĭng') Chn.	25.7 N	113.38 E
144	Chihkiang (chĭ-kyäng') Chn.	30.18 N	111.19 E
146	Chihsien (chĭ'hsyĕn') Chn.	35.31 N	114.29 E
80	Chihuahua (chê-wä'wä) Mex.	28.37 N	106.5 W
80	Chihuahua (State) Mex.	28.30 N	105.0 W
134	Chihuane (chē-wä'nȧ) Moz.	20.47 S	34.52 E
143	Chikan (chĕ'kän) Chn.	52.15 N	120.57 E
134	Chikapa R. (chē-kä'pä) Ang.	9.0 S	20.30 E
140	Chikishlyar (chê-kêsh-lyär') Iran	37.46 N	54.2 E
92	Chilapa (chê-lä'pä) Mex.	17.35 N	99.15 W
92	Chilchota (chêl-chō'tä) Mex.	19.50 N	102.3 W
73	Childersburg (chĭl'dērz-bûrg) Ala. (Birmingham In.)	33.17 N	86.21 W
78	Childress (chĭld'rĕs) Tex.	34.25 N	100.12 W
117	Childwall (chĭld'wȯl) Gt. Brit. (Liverpool In.)	53.24 N	2.53 W
102	Chile (chē'lā) S. A.	39.0 S	72.0 W
102	Chilecito (chê-lâ-sē'tō) Arg.	29.15 S	67.40 W
143	Chilin (Kirin) (chĭl'ĭn') (kĭr'ĭn) Chn.	43.50 N	126.36 E
53	Chilko L. (chĭl'kō) Can.	51.0 N	124.15 W
53	Chilko R. Can.	51.50 N	124.0 W
102	Chillán (chêl-yän') Chl.	36.35 S	72.5 W
79	Chillicothe (chĭl-ĭ-kŏth'ê) Ill.	40.55 N	89.31 W
79	Chillicothe Mo.	39.47 N	93.33 W
84	Chillicothe Ohio	39.20 N	82.58 W
70	Chiliwack (chĭl'ĭ-wăk) Can.	49.9 N	121.55 W
72	Chilliwack L. Can. (Vancouver In.)	49.3 N	121.25 W
102	Chiloé I. (chē-lō-ā') Chl.	42.30 S	73.45 W
92	Chilpancingo (chēl-pän-sēŋ'gō) Mex.	17.32 N	99.30 W
77	Chilton (chĭl'tŭn) Wis.	44.2 N	88.11 W
93	Chiluca (chê-lōō'kä) Mex. (In.)	19.33 N	99.17 W
145	Chilung (Kiirun) (chĭ'lŭng) (kĭ'ĭ-rŭn') For.	25.6 N	121.45 E
134	Chilwa, L. (chĭl'wä) Nya.-Moz.	15.15 S	35.45 E
51	Chimacum (chĭm'ȧ-kŭm) Wash. (Seattle In.)	48.0 N	122.46 W
93	Chimalhuacán (chê-mäl-wä-kän') Mex. (In.)	19.25 N	98.56 W
93	Chimalhuacán Cerro (Mt.) Mex. (In.)	19.24 N	98.57 W
93	Chimalpa (chē-mäl'pä) Mex. (In.)	19.14 N	98.56 W
93	Chimalpan (chē-mäl'pän) Mex. (In.)	19.26 N	99.20 W
93	Chimalpan Cerro (Mt.) Mex. (In.)	19.26 N	99.21 W
94	Chimaltenango (chê-mäl-tȧ-näŋ'-gō) Guat.	14.40 N	90.48 W
92	Chimaltitán (chêmäl-tē-tän') Mex.	21.33 N	103.50 W
140	Chimbai (chĭm-bī') Sov. Un.	43.14 N	59.58 E
100	Chimborazo, Mt. (chêm-bô-rä'zō) Ec.	1.32 S	78.48 W
100	Chimbote (chêm-bō'tä) Peru	9.1 S	78.31 W
138	Chimkent (chĭm-kĕnt) Sov. Un.	42.25 N	69.40 E
87	Chimney B. (chĭm'nĭ) Can.	50.45 N	56.15 W
94	Chinameca (chê-nä-mā'kä) Sal.	13.33 N	88.18 W
94	Chinandega (chê-nän-dā'gä) Nic.	12.37 N	87.8 W
142	China (chī'nȧ) Asia	35.0 N	110.0 E
143	China Sea, E. Asia	30.0 N	125.0 E
150	China Sea, S. Asia	15.0 N	115.0 E

ng-sing; ŋ-baŋk; n-nasalized n; nŏd; cŏmmit; ōld; ôbey; ôrder; fōōd; fŏŏt; ou-out; s-soft; sh-dish; th-thin; pūre; ûnite; ûrn; stŭd; circŭs; ü-as "y" in study; '-indeterminate vowel.

Chinaz PRONOUNCING INDEX Clarion

Page	Name Pronunciation Region	Lat. °′	Long. °′
138	Chinaz (chĭn-äz′) . . . . Sov. Un.	40.55 N	68.55 E
100	Chincha Alta (chĭn′chä äl′tä) . Peru	30.29 S	76.5 W
100	Chincha Is. (chĭn′chä) . . . . Peru	11.28 S	77.45 W
160	Chinchilla (chĭn-chĭl′ȧ) . Austl. (In.)	26.45 S	150.35 E
124	Chinchilla (chên-chē′lyä) . . . . . . Sp.	38.55 N	1.44 W
143	Chinchow (chĭn′chō′) . . . . Chn.	41.4 N	120.58 E
134	Chinde (shên′dĕ) . . . . Moz.	18.38 S	36.23 E
147	Chindo (chĭn′dô) . . . . Kor.	34.29 N	120.16 E
147	Chindo I. . . . . Kor.	34.28 N	126.16 E
141	Chindwin R. (chĭn-dwĭn) . . . . . Bur.	23.30 N	94.0 E
143	Chingkahang (chĭng′kä-häng′) Chn. (Shanghai In.)	31.10 N	121.32 E
145	Ching San Yuen (Kinsha) (chĭng sän yōō′ĕn) (kēn-shä′) . . . Chn.	30.43 N	121.20 E
134	Chinguar (chĭng-gär) . . . . Ang.	12.30 S	16.18 E
132	Chinguetti (chêŋ-gĕt′ê) . Fr.W.Afr.	20.35 N	12.32 W
147	Chinhae (chĭn′hȧ) . . . . Kor.	35.8 N	128.40 E
145	Chinhai (chĭn′hī′) . . . . Chn.	29.58 N	121.45 E
147	Chinju (chĭn′jōō) . . . . Kor.	35.12 N	128.4 E
146	Chinkiang (chĭn′kyäng′) . . . . . Chn.	32.11 N	119.28 E
147	Chinnampo (chĭn-nȧm′pō) . . . Kor.	38.44 N	125.24 E
73	Chino (chē′nō) Calif. (Los Angeles In.)	34.0 N	117.42 W
80	Chino . . . . Mex.	25.42 N	99.15 W
122	Chinon (shē-nôɴ′) . . . . Fr.	47.10 N	0.11 E
71	Chinook (shĭn-ŏŏk′) . . . . Mont.	48.35 N	109.15 W
51	Chinook . . . . . Wash. (Portland In.)	46.17 N	123.56 W
142	Chinshui (chĭn′shwē′) . . . . Chn.	28.18 N	105.38 E
134	Chinteche (chĭn-tĕ′chĕ) . . . . . Nya.	11.47 S	34.8 E
146	Chinwangtao (chĭn′wäng′tou′) Chn.	39.55 N	119.36 E
144	Chinyang, R. (chĭn′yäng′) . . . Chn.	27.23 N	109.5 E
126	Chioggia (kyôd′jä) . . . . It.	45.13 N	12.16 E
127	Chios (Khios) (kĭ′ōs) . . . . Grc.	38.22 N	26.9 E
125	Chipiona (chē-pê-ō′nä) . . . Sp. (In.)	36.44 N	6.26 W
82	Chipley (chĭp′lĭ) . . . . Fla.	30.45 N	85.32 W
86	Chipman (chĭp′măn) . . . . Can.	46.11 N	65.53 W
82	Chipola R. (chĭ-pō′lȧ) . . . . Fla.	30.30 N	85.10 W
77	Chippewa Falls (chĭp′ê-wä) . . Wis.	44.53 N	91.54 W
76	Chippewa R. . . . . Minn.	45.30 N	95.42 W
77	Chippewa R. . . . . Wis.	45.0 N	91.21 W
86	Chiputneticook L. (chĭ-pŏŏt-nĕt′ĭ-kŏŏk) . Me.-Can.	45.45 N	67.50 W
94	Chiquimula (chē-kê-mōō′lä) . Guat.	14.47 N	89.32 W
100	Chiquinquirá (chê-kēŋ′kê-rä′) . Col.	5.29 N	74.2 W
102	Chiquita, Mar (L.) (mär chê-kē′tä) . Arg.	31.50 S	62.35 W
144	Chi R. (chē) . . . . Chn.	28.23 N	105.42 E
75	Chiracahua Natl. Mon. (chĭ-rā-cä′hwä) . Ariz.	32.1 N	109.12 W
142	Chirgalantu (Kobdo) (chêr-gä-län′tōō) (kôb′dō) . Mong.	49.0 N	91.0 E
95	Chiriquí (Vol.) (chē-rê-kē′) . . Pan.	8.47 N	82.37 W
95	Chiriquí Grande (grän′dā) . . . Pan.	9.57 N	82.8 W
95	Chiriquî, G. of . . . . Pan.	8.0 N	82.20 W
95	Chiriquí Lagoon . . . . Pan.	9.5 N	82.0 W
147	Chirisan (Mt.) (chĭ′rĭ-sän′) . . . Kor.	35.20 N	127.44 E
148	Chirka (chĭr′kȧ) . . . . Sov. Un.	48.23 N	134.58 E
134	Chiromo (chê-rō′mō) . . . . Moz.	16.33 S	35.9 E
95	Chirripo, R. (chêr-rē′pō) . . . . C. R.	9.50 N	83.24 W
95	Chirripo Grande (Mt.) (grän′dā) . C R.	9.28 N	83.32 W
	Chishima, see Kuril Is., Sov. Un.		
77	Chisholm (chĭz′ŭm) . . . . Minn.	47.29 N	92.51 W
135	Chisimaio (kē-sē-mī′ō) . . . . . . Som.	0.15 S	42.30 E
	Chişinău, see Kishinev, Sov. Un.		
110	Chistopol (chĭs-tô′pôl-y′) . Sov. Un.	55.20 N	50.35 E
117	Chiswick (chĭz′ĭk) Gt. Brit. (London In.)	51.29 N	0.17 W
139	Chita (chê-tȧ′) . . . . Sov. Un.	52.10 N	113.30 E
100	Chita, Sierra Nevada de (Mt.) (chē′tä) . Col.	6.15 N	72.28 W
53	Chitina (chĭ-tē′nȧ) . . . . Alsk.	61.35 N	143.30 W
52	Chitina R. . . . . Alsk. (In.)	61.20 N	144.0 W
141	Chitral (chē-träl′) . . . . Pak.	35.55 N	71.50 E
95	Chitre (chē′trȧ) . . . . Pan.	7.58 N	80.26 W
141	Chittagong (chĭt-ȧ-gông′) . . . . Pak.	22.15 N	91.55 E
134	Chiumbe R. (chê-ŏŏm′bȧ) . . . Ang.	8.15 S	21.0 E
126	Chivasso (kê-väs′sō) . . . . It.	45.11 N	7.52 E
102	Chivilcoy (chē-vêl-koi′) . . . . . . Arg.	34.50 S	60.1 W
94	Chixoy, R. (chē-ĸoi′) . Guat.-Mex.	15.40 N	90.40 W
149	Chizu (chê-zōō′) . . . . Jap.	35.16 N	134.15 E
111	Chkalov (Orenburg) (chkä′lŏf) (ô-rĕn-bŏŏrgh′) . Sov. Un.	51.48 N	55.10 E
75	Chloride (klō′rīd) . . . . Ariz.	35.24 N	114.12 W
121	Chmielnik (ĸmyĕl′nêk) . . . . Pol.	50.36 N	20.46 E
129	Chobanvasty (chō′bän-väs′tê) Sov. Un.	44.47 N	35.8 E
147	Chochiwŏn (chô′chĭ-wŭn′) . . . Kor.	36.36 N	127.18 E
81	Chocolate Bayou . . . . . . Tex. (In.)	29.19 N	95.16 W
82	Choctawhatchee B. (chôk-tô-hăch′ê) . Fla.	30.25 N	86.20 W
82	Choctawhatchee R. . . . . Fla.	31.0 N	85.50 W
120	Chodziez (ĸōj′yĕsh) . . . . Pol.	52.59 N	16.52 E
149	Chofu (chō′fōō′) . . . . Jap.	34.0 N	131.0 E
147	Cho I. (chō) . . . . Kor.	38.33 N	124.47 E
159	Choiseul I. (shwä-zûl′) Solomon Is. (Prot.)	7.0 S	156.45 E
123	Choizy-le-Roi (schwä-zê-lû rwä′) Fr. (In.)	48.46 N	2.25 E
121	Chojnice (ĸōĭ-nē′tsĕ) . . . . Pol.	53.41 N	17.34 E
120	Chojnow (khoi′nŭf) . . . . Pol.	51.16 N	15.56 E
122	Cholet (shô-lĕ′) . . . . Fr.	47.5 N	0.56 W
150	Cholon (shô-lôɴ′) . . . . Indoch.	10.45 N	106.31 E
147	Chŏlsan (chŭl′sän) . . . . Kor.	39.48 N	124.38 E
92	Cholula (chō-lōō′lä) . . . . Mex.	19.3 N	98.20 W
94	Choluteca (chō-lōō-tā′kä) . . Hond.	13.18 N	87.12 W
94	Choluteca, R. . . . . Hond.	13.30 N	87.0 W
120	Chomutov (kō′mŏŏ-tôf) . . . . Czech.	50.27 N	13.25 E
147	Chŏnan (chŭ′nän) . . . . Kor.	36.48 N	127.10 E
139	Chona R. (chō′nä) . . . . . . Sov. Un.	62.0 N	110.0 E
147	Chŏngchŏn R. (chŭng-chŭn′) . Kor.	39.50 N	126.0 E
148	Chŏngjin (chŭng-jĭn′) . . . . Kor.	41.46 N	129.49 E
147	Chŏngju (chŭng-jōō′) . . . . Kor.	39.43 N	125.13 E
147	Chŏngju (Seishū) (chŭng-jōō′) (sȧ-shōō′) . Kor.	36.38 N	127.30 E
147	Chŏngpyŏng (chŭng-pyŭng′) . Kor.	39.48 N	127.22 E
147	Chŏngsŏn (chŭng-sŭn′) . . . . . . Kor.	37.27 N	128.38 E
147	Chŏngŭp (chŭng-ŭp′) . . . . Kor.	35.36 N	126.52 E
147	Chŏnju (chŭn-jōō′) . . . . Kor.	35.48 N	127.8 E
102	Chonos Arch. (chō′nōs) . . . . . . Chl.	45.0 S	74.0 W
144	Cho R. (chō) . . . . Chn.	26.45 N	109.50 E
100	Chorillos (chô-rēl′yōs) . . Peru (In.)	12.10 S	77.2 W
100	Chorillos Pt. . . . . Peru (In.)	12.10 S	77.3 W
116	Chorley (chôr′lĭ) . . . . Gt. Brit.	53.39 N	2.38 W
95	Chorrera (chôr-rā′rä) . . . . Pan.	8.54 N	79.49 W
147	Chŏrwŏn (chŭr-wŭn′) . . . . Kor.	38.14 N	127.12 E
121	Chorzów (kô-zhŏŏf′) . . . . Pol.	50.18 N	18.58 E
148	Chosan (chō-sän′) . . . . Kor.	40.50 N	125.48 E
	Chosen, see Korea.		
148	Choshi (chō′shē) . . . . Jap.	35.40 N	140.48 E
120	Choszczno (chôsh′chnô) . . . . . . Pol.	53.10 N	15.26 E
71	Choteau (shō′tō) . . . . Mont.	47.50 N	112.10 W
83	Chowan R. (chô-wän′) . . . . . . N. C.	36.10 N	76.45 W
148	Chowie R. (chō′wê-ĕ′) . . . . Chn.	47.0 N	122.0 E
146	Chowtsun (chō′tsōōn′) . . . . . . Chn.	36.50 N	117.49 E
157	Christchurch (krīst′chûrch) N. Z. (In.)	43.29 S	172.40 E
84	Christian I. (krĭs′chăn) . . . . . . Can.	44.50 N	80.15 W
83	Christiansburg (krĭs′chănz-bûrg) Va.	37.8 N	80.26 W
150	Christmas I. . . . . Asia	11.0 S	105.35 E
6	Christmas I. . . . . Pac. O.	1.55 N	157.20 W
79	Christopher (krĭs′tô-fēr) . . . . . . Ill.	37.57 N	89.4 W
120	Chrudim (ĸrōō′dyêm) . . . . . Czech.	49.57 N	15.48 E
121	Chrzanów (ĸzhä′nŏŏf) . . . . Pol.	50.8 N	19.24 E
145	Chuanchow (chwän′chō′) . . . . Chn.	24.55 N	118.35 E
144	Chüanchow (chü-än′chō′) . . . . Chn.	25.54 N	110.56 E
145	Chuanchow Har. (chwän′chō′) Chn.	24.47 N	118.45 E
134	Chuane Pits (chŏŏ-än′ĕ) . . . . Bech.	23.57 S	21.50 E
146	Chüantsiao (chü-än′tsê-ou′) . . Chn.	32.7 N	118.17 E
134	Chuapa R. (chwä′pä) . . Bel. Cong.	1.4 S	23.30 E
102	Chubut (State) (chŏŏ-bōōt′) . . Arg.	44.0 S	69.0 W
102	Chubut R. . . . . Arg.	43.50 S	68.28 W
146	Chucheng (chōō′chĕng′) . . . . . Chn.	36.2 N	119.21 E
144	Chuchow (chŏŏ′chō′) . . . . Chn.	27.51 N	112.52 E
145	Chuchow . . . . Chn.	28.24 N	119.50 E
146	Chuchow . . . . Chn.	32.18 N	118.19 E
145	Chüchow (chü′chō′) . . . . Chn.	29.3 N	119.2 E
146	Chüchow . . . . Chn.	35.34 N	118.46 E
95	Chucunaque R. (chōō-kōō-nä′kȧ) Pan.	8.35 N	77.50 W
128	Chudovo (chŏŏ′dô-vô) . . . Sov. Un.	59.2 N	31.42 E
119	Chudskoe (Peipsi) L. (chŏŏt′skô-yĕ) (pī′psĭ) . Sov. Un.	58.40 N	27.30 E
143	Chuerhkanho (chōō′ĕr-kän′hō) Chn.	52.15 N	120.57 E
52	Chugach Mts. (chōō′gȧch) Alsk. (In.)	61.10 N	146.0 W
138	Chuguchak (chōō′gōō-chäk′) . Chn.	46.55 N	83.0 E
142	Chuguchak (Prov.) . . . . Chn.	46.0 N	85.0 E
142	Chuguchak (Tahcheng) (tä′chĕng′) . Chn.	46.48 N	83.5 E
129	Chuguev (chōō′gwĕf) . . . . Sov. Un.	49.50 N	36.41 E
71	Chugwater Cr. (chŭg′wô-tēr) . Wyo.	41.40 N	105.0 W
145	Chuki (chōō′kê) . . . . Chn.	29.43 N	120.12 E
144	Chu Kiang (Pearl R.) (chōō′ kyäng′) (pērl) . Chn.	22.38 N	113.38 E
139	Chukotski Pen. (chōō-kôtsk′) Sov. Un.	66.0 N	175.0 W
74	Chula Vista (chōō′lȧ vĭs′tȧ) Calif. (In.)	32.37 N	117.5 W
138	Chulym R. (chŏŏ-lĭm′) . . . Sov. Un.	57.0 N	86.10 E
138	Chulkovo (chōōl′kō-vô) . . Sov. Un.	62.40 N	88.30 E
143	Chultzuchien (Yenchi) (chōōl′-tzōō-chê-ĕn′) (yĕn′kē′) . Chn.	43.0 N	129.32 E
146	Chulung R. (chōō′lōōng′) . . . . Chn.	38.45 N	116.4 E
146	Chumatien (chōō′mä-tyĕn′) . . Chn.	32.59 N	113.53 E
138	Chuna R. (chōō′nȧ) . . . . . Sov. Un.	57.0 N	99.10 E
147	Chunchŏn (chŏŏn-chŭn′) . . . . Kor.	37.52 N	127.44 E
145	Chungan (chŏŏng′än′) . . . . . . Chn.	27.44 N	117.47 E
144	Chungchow (chŏŏng′chō′) . . . Chn.	30.26 N	108.6 E
146	Chunghing (chŏŏng′hĭng′) . . . Chn.	33.42 N	118.47 E
147	Chunghwa (chŭng′hwä′) . . . . . Kor.	38.53 N	125.47 E
147	Chungju (chŭng′jōō′) . . . . Kor.	36.58 N	127.56 E
144	Chungking (chŏŏng′kĭng′) . . . Chn.	29.46 N	106.34 E
	Chungming I., see Tsung Ming I.		
146	Chungmow (chŏŏng′mō′) . . . . Chn.	34.40 N	114.4 E
146	Chungsing I. (chŏŏng′sĭng′) . . Chn.	39.35 N	121.15 E
142	Chungwei (chŏŏng′wā) . . . . . . Chn.	37.37 N	105.20 E
144	Chungye (chŏŏng′yĕ′) . . . . Chn.	25.53 N	113.52 E
144	Chun R. (chŏŏn) . . . . Chn.	26.8 N	112.20 E
138	Chunya R. (chŏŏn′yä′) . . Sov. Un.	61.35 N	100.0 E
102	Chuquicamata (chōō-kê-kä-mä′tä) Chl.	21.12 S	68.50 W
120	Chur (kōōr) . . . . Switz.	46.52 N	9.32 E
138	Chu R. (chŏŏ) . . . . Sov. Un.	44.45 N	72.0 E
54	Churchill (chûrch′ĭl) . . . . Can.	58.50 N	94.0 W
54	Churchill R. . . . . Can.	57.15 N	96.30 W
72	Church Pt. . . Can. (Vancouver In.)	48.19 N	123.32 W
116	Church Stretton (chûrch strĕt′ŭn) Gt. Brit.	52.32 N	2.49 W
92	Churumuco (chōō-rōō-mōō′kō) Mex.	18.38 N	101.42 W
110	Chusovaya R. (chŏŏ-sô-vä′yȧ) Sov. Un.	58.0 N	58.30 E
110	Chusovoy (chōō-sô-voi′) . Sov. Un.	58.25 N	57.59 E
138	Chust (chŏŏst) . . . . Sov. Un.	41.0 N	71.20 E
110	Chuvash (chōō′vȧsh) . . . . Sov. Un.	55.30 N	47.0 E
80	Chuviscar R. (chōō-vês-kär′) . Mex.	28.40 N	106.0 W
135	Chwaka (chwä′kä) . . . . Zan.	6.9 S	39.25 E
147	Chwangho (chwäng′hō′) . . . . . Chn.	39.39 N	122.56 E
145	Chwansha (chwän′shä) . . . . . . Chn.	31.8 N	121.46 E
97	Cibao Mts. (Gran Cordillera Cen.) (sê-bä′ô) (grän kôr-dēl-yā′rȧ sĕn-träl′) . Hai.	18.53 N	70.30 W
80	Cibolo Cr. (sē′bô-lō) . . . . Tex.	29.30 N	98.10 W
79	Cicero (sĭs′ēr-ō) . . . . Ill.	41.51 N	87.46 W
111	Cide (jē′dĕ) . . . . Tur.	41.50 N	32.58 E
121	Ciechanów (tsyĕ-ĸä′nŏŏf) . . . . Pol.	52.53 N	20.40 E
96	Ciego de Ávila (syā′gō dā ä′vê-lä) Cuba	21.50 N	78.46 W
124	Ciempozuelos (thyĕm-pô-thwā′lōs) Sp.	40.9 N	3.36 W
100	Cienaga (syā′nä-gä) . . . . Col.	11.0 N	74.30 W
96	Cienfuegos (syĕn-fwā′gōs) . . . Cuba	22.8 N	80.28 W
96	Cienfuegos B. . . . . Cuba	22.5 N	80.26 W
121	Cieszyn (tsyĕ′shên) . . . . Pol.	49.44 N	18.40 E
124	Cieza (thyā′thä) . . . . Sp.	38.15 N	1.25 W
111	Cilician Gates (P.) (sĭ-lĭsh′ăn) . Tur.	37.17 N	34.50 E
114	Cill Cainnig (Kilkenny) (kĭl′kä′nĭ) (kĭl-kĕn′ê) . Ire.	52.39 N	7.15 W
114	Cill Mantainn (Wicklow) (kĭl män′tän) (wĭk′lō) . Ire.	53.0 N	6.5 W
78	Cimarron R. (sĭm-ȧ-rōn′) N. M.-Okla.	36.0 N	98.0 W
78	Cimarron R., N. Fork Colo.-Kan.-Okla.	37.25 N	101.5 W
125	Cinca R. (thēŋ′kä) . . . . Sp.	42.0 N	0.8 E
84	Cincinnati (sĭn-sĭ-năt′ĭ) . . . . . Ohio	39.6 N	84.30 W
89	Cincinnati . . . . Ohio (In.)		
96	Cinco Balas Cays (Is.) (thēŋ′kō bä′läs) . Cuba	21.5 N	79.22 W
93	Cintalapa (sên-tä-lä′pä) . . . . . Mex.	16.41 N	93.45 W
122	Cinto Mt. (chēn′tō) . . . . Cor. (In.)	42.25 N	8.55 E
53	Circle (sûr′k′l) . . . . Alsk.	65.48 N	144.30 W
84	Circleville . . . . Ohio	39.36 N	82.57 W
160	Circular Hd . . . . . Austl. (Tas. In.)	40.42 S	145.16 E
133	Cirenaica (Prov.) (sĭr-ê-nā′ĭ-kȧ) Libya	31.30 N	22.0 E
131	Cires, Pt. (thē′rȧs) Sp. Mor. (Gib. In.)	35.54 N	5.31 E
123	Cirey (sē-rĕ′) . . . . Fr.	48.35 N	6.55 E
127	Čirpan (chĭr-pȧn′) . . . . Bul.	42.12 N	25.19 E
80	Cisco (sĭs′kō) . . . . Tex.	32.22 N	98.58 W
124	Cistierna (thês-tyĕr′nä) . . . . Sp.	42.48 N	5.8 W
126	Cittadella (chēt-tä-dĕl′lä) . . . . . . It.	45.39 N	12.47 E
126	Città del Vaticano (Vatican City) (chēt-tä′ dĕl vä-tê-kä′nō) (văt′ĭ-kăn sĭt′ê) . It.	41.53 N	12.28 E
126	Città di Castello (chēt-tä′ dē käs-tĕl′lō) . It.	43.27 N	12.17 E
88	City I. . . . . N. Y. (In.)	41.51 N	73.48 W
100	Ciuadad Bolivar (syōō-dhädh′ bô-lē′vär) . Ven.	8.1 N	63.32 W
80	Ciudad Camargo (Santa Rosalia) (syōō-dhädh′ kä-mär′gō) (sän′tȧ rō-sä′lēȧ) . Mex.	27.40 N	105.10 W
94	Ciudad Chetumal (Payo Obispo) (syōō-dhädh′ chĕt-ōō-mäl) (pä′yō ō-bēs′pō) . Mex. (In.)	18.30 N	88.18 W
94	Ciudad Dario (syōō-dhädh′ dä′rê-ō) Nic.	12.53 N	86.1 W
92	Ciudad del Maíz (syōō-dhädh′ dĕl mä-ēz′) . Mex.	22.24 N	99.36 W
92	Ciudad de Valles (syōō-dhädh′ dā vä′lyās) . Mex.	21.59 N	99.1 W
125	Ciudadela (thyōō-dhä-dhā′lä) . Sp.	40.0 N	3.50 E
92	Ciudad Fernández (syōō-dhädh′ fĕr-nän′dĕz) . Mex.	21.57 N	100.1 W
92	Ciudad García (gär-sē′ä) . . . . Mex.	22.42 N	103.2 W
92	Ciudad Gonzáles (gôn-zä′lȧs) . Mex.	21.30 N	101.16 W
92	Ciudad Guzmán (gŏŏz-män′) . Mex.	19.41 N	103.25 W
80	Ciudad Juárez (hwä′rāz) . . . . Mex.	31.45 N	106.20 W
92	Ciudad Manuel Doblado (män-wāl′ dō-blä′dō) . Mex.	20.46 N	101.55 W
124	Ciudad Real (thyōō-dhädh′ rā-äl′) Sp.	38.59 N	3.55 W
124	Ciudad Rodrigo (thyōō-dhädh′ rô-drē′gō) . Sp.	40.37 N	6.32 W
97	Ciudad Trujillo (Santo Domingo) (syōō-dhädh′ trōō-hē′yō) (sän′tô dô-mĭŋ′gô) . Dom. Rep.	18.28 N	69.53 W
92	Ciudad Victoria (syōō-dhädh′ vêk-tō′rê-ä) . Mex.	23.43 N	99.7 W
126	Cividale (chē-vê-dä′-lā) . . . . It.	46.6 N	13.4 E
126	Civitavecchia (chē′vê-tä-vĕk′kyä) It.	42.6 N	11.48 E
111	Civril (jĭv-rĭl′) . . . . Tur.	38.15 N	29.45 E
111	Cizre (jĭz′rĕ) . . . . Tur.	37.20 N	42.0 E
117	Cladow (klä′dou) . Ger. (Berlin In.)	52.27 N	13.9 E
85	Clairton (klâr′tŭn) . . . . Pa.	40.18 N	79.54 E
123	Clamart (klȧ-mȧr′) . . . . . . Fr. (In.)	48.47 N	2.15 E
122	Clamecy (kläm-sē′) . . . . Fr.	47.28 N	3.31 E
82	Clanton (klăn′tŭn) . . . . Ala.	32.50 N	86.38 W
84	Clare (klâr) . . . . Mich.	43.48 N	84.48 W
114	Clare I. Ire.	53.50 N	9.50 W
160	Claremont . . . . . . Austl. (Perth In.)	31.58 S	115.47 E
73	Claremont . Calif. (Los Angeles In.)	34.6 N	117.43 W
86	Claremont . . . . N. H.	43.23 N	72.22 W
135	Claremont . . . . U. S. Afr.	33.59 S	18.28 E
84	Claremont . . . . W. Va.	37.57 N	81.3 W
79	Claremore . . . . Okla.	36.17 N	95.37 W
114	Claremorris (klâr-mŏr′ĭs) . . . . . Ire.	53.45 N	9.0 W
97	Clarence Har. (klăr′ĕns) . . . Ba. Is.	23.5 N	74.58 W
99	Clarence I. . . Chl. (Magallanes In.)	54.10 S	71.40 W
160	Clarence R. . . . . Austl. (In.)	29.10 S	152.33 E
157	Clarence R. . . . . N. Z.	42.20 S	173.15 E
158	Clarence Str. . . . . Austl.	11.50 S	131.15 E
79	Clarendon (klăr′ĕn-dŭn . . . . . . Ark.	34.42 N	91.18 W
78	Clarendon . . . . Tex.	34.56 N	100.52 W
77	Clarinda (klȧ-rĭn′dȧ) . . . . Ia.	40.44 N	95.2 W
77	Clarion (klăr′i-ŭn) . . . . Ia.	42.44 N	93.43 W
85	Clarion . . . . Pa.	41.10 N	79.23 W

ăt; finăl; rāte; senâte; ärm; ȧsk; sofȧ; fâre; ch-choose; dh-as th in other; bē; êvent; bĕt; recĕnt; cratēr; g-go; gh-gutteral g; bĭt; ĭ-short neutral; rīde; ĸ-gutteral k as ch in German ich;

Clark PRONOUNCING INDEX **Columbia**

Page	Name Pronunciation Region	Lat. °′	Long. °′
76	Clark (klärk) . . . . S. D.	44.54 N	97.44 W
75	Clarkdale . . . . Ariz.	34.45 N	112.5 W
86	Clarke City . . . . Can.	50.13 N	66.41 W
160	Clarke I. (klärk) . Austl. (Tas. In.)	40.32 S	148.10 E
159	Clarke Ra . . . . Austl.	20.30 S	148.0 E
71	Clark Fork . . . . Mont.-Wyo.	45.0 N	109.0 W
70	Clark Fork (R.) . . . . Mont.	47.47 N	115.30 W
157	Clark Mt . . . . N. Z.	41.50 S	173.5 E
84	Clark, Pt . . . . Can.	44.2 N	81.45 W
85	Clarksburg . . . . W. Va.	39.16 N	80.21 W
82	Clarksdale . . . . Miss.	34.01 N	90.31 W
86	Clarks Har . . . . Can.	43.35 N	65.45 W
73	Clarkston . . . . Ga. (Atlanta In.)	33.48 N	88.14 W
70	Clarkston . . . . Wash.	46.25 N	117.3 W
79	Clarksville . . . . Ark.	35.28 N	93.28 W
82	Clarksville . . . . Tenn.	36.32 N	87.22 W
79	Clarksville . . . . Tex.	33.36 N	95.1 W
157	Clatha R. (klă'thȧ) . . . . N. Z.	45.0 S	169.15 E
51	Clatskanie (klăt-skā'nė) Ore. (Portland In.)	46.6 N	123.13 W
120	Clausthal (klous'täl) . . . . Ger.	51.48 N	10.20 E
152	Claveria (klä-vȧ-rē'ä) . . . . Phil.	18.37 N	121.6 E
56	Claxton (klăks'tŭn) Can. (Prince Rupert In.)	54.6 N	130.5 W
83	Claxton . . . . Ga.	32.7 N	81.55 W
84	Clay (klā) . . . . Ky.	37.29 N	87.50 W
72	Clayburn (klā'bûrn) Can. (Vancouver In.)	49.5 N	122.17 W
79	Clay Center . . . . Kan.	39.24 N	97.8 W
84	Clay City . . . . Ky.	37.54 N	83.56 W
116	Clay Cross . . . . Gt. Brit.	53.10 N	1.25 W
123	Claye-Souilly (klā'-soo-yē') Fr. (In.)	48.56 N	2.42 E
73	Clays (klāz) . Ala. (Birmingham In.)	33.41 N	86.36 W
82	Clayton (klā'tŭn) . . . . Ala.	31.52 N	85.28 W
160	Clayton . . . Austl. (Melbourne In.)	37.55 S	145.7 E
51	Clayton . Calif. (San Francisco In.)	37.56 N	121.56 W
116	Clayton . . . . Gt. Brit.	53.47 N	1.49 W
89	Clayton . . . . Mo. (St. Louis In.)	38.39 N	90.20 W
78	Clayton . . . . N. M.	36.26 N	103.11 W
83	Clayton . . . . N. C.	35.39 N	78.28 W
73	Clayton Pk. Utah (Salt Lake City In.)	40.36 N	111.34 W
79	Clear Boggy Cr. (klēr bŏg'ĭ krēk) Okla.	34.20 N	96.20 W
114	Clear, C. (klēr) . . . . Ire.	51.25 N	9.25 W
75	Clear Cr . . . . Ariz.	34.40 N	111.5 W
72	Clear Cr . . . . Colo. (Denver In.)	39.44 N	105.27 W
81	Clear Cr . . . . Tex. (In.)	29.34 N	95.12 W
70	Clear Cr . . . . Wyo.	44.35 N	106.30 W
85	Clearfield . . . . Pa.	41.0 N	78.27 W
73	Clearfield . Utah (Salt Lake City In.)	41.7 N	112.1 W
74	Clear L . . . . Calif.	39.5 N	122.50 W
54	Clear L . . . . Can.	56.20 N	108.30 W
77	Clear L . . . . Ia.	43.9 N	93.21 W
76	Clear L . . . . S. D.	44.48 N	96.40 W
70	Clear Lake Reservoir . . . . Calif.	41.50 N	121.10 W
73	Clearwater . Calif. (Los Angeles In.)	33.54 N	118.10 W
82	Clearwater . . . . Fla. (In.)	27.57 N	82.47 W
70	Clearwater Mts . . . . Ida.	45.55 N	115.10 W
70	Clearwater R . . . . Ida.	46.30 N	116.43 W
70	Clearwater R., Middle Fork of . Ida.	46.8 N	115.50 W
70	Clearwater R., N. Fork of . . . . Ida.	46.50 N	115.40 W
70	Clearwater R., S. Fork of . . . . Ida.	45.45 N	115.50 W
81	Cleburne (klē'bŭrn) . . . . Tex.	32.21 N	97.23 W
116	Clee Hill (klē) . . . . Gt. Brit.	52.24 N	2.38 W
70	Cle Elum (klē ĕl'ŭm) . . . . Wash.	47.11 N	120.57 W
116	Cleobury Mortimer (klē'ō-bĕr'ĭ môr'tĭ-mēr) . Gt. Brit.	52.22 N	2.28 W
153	Cleopatra Needle (Mt.) (klē-ô-pä'trȧ) . Phil.	10.8 N	119.0 E
159	Clermont (klĕr'mŏnt) . . . . Austl.	22.58 S	147.38 E
122	Clermont-Ferrand (klĕr-môɴ'-fĕr-räɴ') . Fr.	45.45 N	3.5 E
122	Clermont l'Herault (klĕr-môɴ' lā-rō') . Fr.	43.38 N	3.22 E
120	Cleve (klā'vē) . . . . Ger.	51.48 N	6.8 E
160	Cleveland (klēv'lănd) . Austl. (In.)	27.31 S	153.16 E
82	Cleveland . . . . Miss.	33.45 N	90.42 W
84	Cleveland . . . . Ohio	41.30 N	81.42 W
89	Cleveland . . . . Ohio (In.)		
79	Cleveland . . . . Okla.	36.17 N	96.28 W
82	Cleveland . . . . Tenn.	35.8 N	84.52 W
81	Cleveland . . . . Tex.	30.20 N	95.5 W
84	Cleveland, East . . . . Ohio	41.33 N	81.33 W
84	Cleveland Hts . . . . Ohio	41.30 N	81.34 W
114	Clew B. (kloo) . . . . Ire.	53.50 N	9.40 W
123	Clichy (klē-shē') . . . . Fr. (In.)	48.53 N	2.18 E
114	Clifden (klĭf'dĕn) . . . . Ire.	53.25 N	10.10 W
117	Cliffe (klĭf) . Gt. Brit. (London In.)	51.28 N	0.30 E
75	Clifton (klĭf'tŭn) . . . . Ariz.	33.3 N	109.19 W
160	Clifton . . . . Austl. (In.)	27.54 S	151.57 E
85	Clifton . . . . N. J.	40.54 N	74.8 W
83	Clifton . . . . S. C.	35.0 N	81.48 W
81	Clifton . . . . Tex.	31.45 N	97.32 W
51	Clifton . . . . Wash. (Seattle In.)	47.26 N	122.50 W
85	Clifton Forge . . . . Va.	37.50 N	79.50 W
96	Clifton Pt . . . . Ba. Is.	25.1 N	77.36 W
82	Clinch R. (klĭnch) . . . . Tenn.-Va.	36.25 N	83.0 W
117	Clinge (klĭŋ'gĕ) (klăɴzh) Neth. (Anvers In.)	51.16 N	4.5 E
82	Clingmans Dome (Mt.) (klĭng'măns dōm) . N. C.	35.33 N	83.30 W
79	Clinton (klĭn-tŭn) . . . . Ill.	40.9 N	88.57 W
84	Clinton . . . . Ind.	39.40 N	87.23 W
77	Clinton . . . . Ia.	41.50 N	90.11 W
79	Clinton . . . . Ky.	36.39 N	88.59 W
86	Clinton . . . . Mass.	42.25 N	71.41 W
79	Clinton . . . . Mo.	38.23 N	93.46 W
157	Clinton . . . . N. Z.	46.13 S	169.22 E
83	Clinton . . . . N. C.	34.59 N	78.18 W
78	Clinton . . . . Okla.	35.31 N	98.57 W
83	Clinton . . . . S. C.	34.28 N	81.53 W
82	Clinton . . . . Tenn.	36.6 N	84.9 W
54	Clinton-Colden L. (klĭn'tŭn-kōl'dĕn) . Can.	64.0 N	107.30 W
77	Clintonville (klĭn'tŭn-vĭl) . . . . Wis.	44.37 N	88.44 W
84	Clio (klē'ō) . . . . Mich.	43.10 N	83.3 W
4	Clipperton I. (klĭp'ĕr-tŭn) . Pac. O.	11.0 N	109.20 W
116	Clitheroe (klĭdh'ĕr-ō) . . . . Gt. Brit.	53.53 N	2.23 W
158	Cloates, Pt. (klōts) . . . . Austl.	22.45 S	113.40 E
114	Clonakilty B. (klŏn'ȧ-kĭl'tė) . . . . Ire.	51.35 N	8.55 W
158	Cloncurry (klŏn-kŭr'ė) . . . . Austl.	21.5 S	140.40 E
114	Clonmel (klŏn-mĕl') . . . . Ire.	52.20 N	7.45 W
77	Cloquet (klō-kā') . . . . Minn.	46.45 N	92.29 W
77	Cloquet R . . . . Minn.	47.2 N	92.5 W
71	Cloud Pk . . . . Wyo.	44.23 N	107.11 W
157	Cloudy B . . . . N. Z.	41.25 S	174.10 E
83	Clover (klō'vēr) . . . . S. C.	35.7 N	81.12 W
74	Cloverdale . . . . Calif.	38.49 N	123.4 W
72	Cloverdale . . Can. (Vancouver In.)	49.6 N	122.45 W
72	Cloverly (klō'vēr-lė) Colo. (Denver In.)	40.27 N	104.38 W
84	Cloverport (klō'vēr-pôrt) . . . . Ky.	37.48 N	86.39 W
78	Clovis (klō'vĭs) . . . . N. M.	34.24 N	103.11 W
121	Cluj (kloozh) . . . . Rom.	46.46 N	23.35 E
116	Clun R. (klŭn) . . . . Gt. Brit.	52.24 N	2.53 W
122	Cluny (klü-nē') . . . . Fr.	46.28 N	4.42 E
157	Clutha R. (kloo'thȧ) . . . . N. Z.	45.45 S	169.30 E
79	Clyde (klīd) . . . . Kan.	39.35 N	97.23 W
84	Clyde . . . . Ohio	41.17 N	82.59 W
114	Clydebank . . . . Gt. Brit.	55.55 N	4.20 W
114	Clyde, Firth of . . . . Gt. Brit.	55.30 N	5.0 W
160	Clyde R . . . . Austl. (Tas. In.)	42.25 S	147.0 E
114	Clyde (R.) . . . . Gt. Brit.	55.40 N	4.0 W
93	Coacalco (kō-ä-käl'kō) . Mex. (In.)	19.38 N	99.6 W
92	Coahuay R., (kō-ä-wī') . . . . Mex.	19.0 N	103.32 W
92	Coahuayutla (kō'ä-wī-yoot'lä) Mex.	18.18 N	101.49 W
80	Coahuila (State) (kō-ä-wē'lä) . Mex.	27.20 N	102.0 W
92	Coalcoman de Matamoros (kō-äl-kō-män' dā mä-tä-mō'rōs) . Mex.	18.48 N	103.8 W
92	Coalcomán, Sierra de (Mts.) (syĕr'rä dā kō-äl-kō-män') . Mex.	18.30 N	103.0 W
72	Coal Creek . . . . Colo. (Denver In.)	39.40 N	104.40 W
73	Coaldale . . . Ala. (Birmingham In.)	33.49 N	86.47 W
79	Coalgate . . . . Okla.	34.32 N	96.14 W
84	Coal Grove . . . . Ohio	38.29 N	82.39 W
74	Coalinga (kō-ȧ-lĭŋ'gȧ) . . . . Calif.	36.9 N	120.22 W
160	Coal R . . . . Austl. (Tas. In.)	42.35 S	147.26 E
116	Coalville . . . . Gt. Brit.	52.43 N	1.21 W
91	Coamo (kō-ä'mō) . . . . P. R. (In.)	18.4 N	66.22 W
93	Coanala (kō-ä-nä'lä) . . . Mex. (In.)	19.36 N	98.55 W
124	Coa R. (kō'ä) . . . . Port.	40.40 N	6.55 W
100	Coari (kō-är'ė) . . . . Braz.	4.5 S	63.10 W
54	Coast Mts . . . . Can.	54.30 N	129.0 W
58	Coast Ranges . . . . U. S.	40.0 N	123.30 W
114	Coatbridge (kōt'brĭj) . . . . Gt. Brit.	55.50 N	4.0 W
92	Coatepec (kō-ä-tä-pĕk') . . . . Mex.	19.24 N	98.45 W
93	Coatepec . . . . Mex.	19.26 N	96.57 W
93	Coatepec, R . . . . Mex. (In.)	19.24 N	98.52 W
94	Coatepeque (kō-ä-tā-pā'kȧ) . Guat.	14.41 N	91.53 W
94	Coatepeque . . . . Sal.	13.56 N	89.30 W
85	Coatesville (kōts'vĭl) . . . . Pa.	39.59 N	75.49 W
92	Coatetelco (kō-ä-tȧ-tĕl'kō) . . . Mex.	18.43 N	99.19 W
86	Coaticook (kō'tĭ-kook) . . . . Can.	45.9 N	71.50 W
55	Coats I. (kōts) . . . . Can.	62.35 N	82.30 W
47	Coats Land (Reg.) . . . . Ant.	74.0 S	12.0 W
93	Coatzacoalcos R. (kō-ät'zä-kō-äl'kōs) . Mex.	16.57 N	94.40 W
55	Cobalt (kō'bôlt) . . . . Can.	47.12 N	79.47 W
94	Cobán (kō-bän') . . . . Guat.	15.28 N	90.20 W
159	Cobar (kō'bär) . . . . Austl.	31.28 S	145.50 E
72	Cobble Hill (kŏb''l) Can. (Vancouver In.)	48.42 N	123.37 W
88	Cobbs Cr. (kŏbz) Pa. (Philadelphia In.)	39.57 N	75.15 W
86	Cobequid B. (kŏb'ė-kwĭd) . . . . Can.	45.25 N	63.45 W
114	Cobh (kôv) . . . . Ire.	51.55 N	8.15 W
85	Cobourg (kō'boorgh) . . . . Can.	43.57 N	78.4 W
96	Cobre R. (kō'brā) . . . . Jam.	18.5 N	76.58 W
160	Coburg (kō'bûrg) Austl. (Melbourne In.)	37.45 S	144.57 E
120	Coburg (kō'boorgh) . . . . Ger.	50.16 N	10.57 E
158	Coburg Pen . . . . Austl.	11.30 S	133.0 E
141	Cocanada (kō-kō-nä'dȧ) . . . . India	16.50 N	82.15 E
125	Cocentaina (kō-thān-tä-ē'nä) . . Sp.	38.44 N	0.25 W
100	Cochabamba (kō-chä-bäm'bä) . Bol.	17.29 S	66.30 W
141	Cochin (kō-chĭn') . . . . India	9.58 N	76.14 E
150	Cochin-China (State) . . . . Indoch.	10.0 N	105.30 E
97	Cochinos Banks (kō-chē'nōs) Ba. Is.	22.20 N	76.15 W
96	Cochinos B . . . . Cuba	22.8 N	81.3 W
152	Cochinos Pt . . . . Phil.	14.25 N	120.30 E
82	Cochran (kŏk'răn) . . . . Ga.	32.23 N	83.25 W
55	Cochrane . . . . Can.	49.0 N	80.55 W
99	Cockburn Canal Chl. (Magallanes In.)	54.20 S	71.30 W
84	Cockburn I . . . . Can.	45.55 N	83.22 W
85	Cockeysville (kŏk'ĭz-vĭl) . . . . Md.	39.29 N	76.40 W
83	Cocoa (kō'kō) . . . . Fla. (In.)	28.20 N	80.44 W
96	Coco Cay (I.) . . . . Cuba	22.28 N	78.22 W
83	Coconut Grove (kō'kō-nŭt grōv) Fla. (In.)	25.43 N	80.14 W
94	Coco, R . . . . Hond.-Nic.	14.30 N	85.0 W
5	Cocos I . . . . Ind. O.	12.0 S	96.0 E
93	Cocula (kō-koo'lä) . . . . Mex.	20.23 N	103.47 W
100	Codajaz (kō-dä-häzh') . . . . Braz.	3.56 S	62.2 W
86	Cod, C. (kŏd) . . . . Mass.	42.0 N	70.15 W
157	Codfish I . . . . N. Z.	46.48 S	167.42 E
101	Codo (kō'dō) . . . . Braz.	4.32 S	43.38 W
126	Codogno (kō-dō'nyō) . . . . It.	45.9 N	9.42 E
95	Codrington (kŏd'rĭng-tŭn) Le. Is. (In.)	17.38 N	61.50 W
71	Cody (kō'dĭ) . . . . Wyo.	44.31 N	109.2 W
92	Coeneo de la Libertad (kō-ā'nā-ō dä lä lē-bĕr-tädh') . Mex.	19.47 N	101.32 W
70	Coeur d'Alene (kûr dȧ-lān') . . Ida.	47.41 N	116.48 W
70	Coeur d'Alene L . . . . Ida.	47.30 N	116.40 W
70	Coeur d'Alene R . . . . Ida.	47.28 N	116.32 W
79	Coffeyville (kŏf'ĭ-vĭl) . . . . Kan.	37.3 N	95.37 W
160	Coffs Harbour (kŏfs) . . . . Austl.	30.18 S	153.10 E
129	Cogalnic R. (kō-gäl'nĭk) . . . . Rom.	46.35 N	28.45 E
126	Coghinas R. (kō'gē-nás) . . . . Sard.	40.45 N	9.0 E
72	Coghlan (kŏg'lăn) Can. (Vancouver In.)	49.7 N	122.31 W
127	Coglie (kôl'yā) . . . . It.	40.48 N	17.31 E
122	Cognac (kōn-yăk') . . . . Fr.	45.40 N	0.20 W
87	Cohasset (kō-hăs'ĕt) . . Mass. (In.)	42.14 N	70.48 W
85	Cohoes (kō-hōz') . . . . N. Y.	42.43 N	73.43 W
95	Coiba I. (kō-ē'bä) . . . . Pan.	7.25 N	81.45 W
102	Coile, R. (kō-ē'lä) . . . . Arg.	51.15 S	70.30 W
141	Coimbatore (kō-ēm-bȧ-tōr') . India	11.0 N	76.59 E
124	Coimbra (kō-ēm'brä) . . . . Port.	40.13 N	8.26 W
124	Coín (kō-ēn') . . . . Sp.	36.39 N	4.45 W
125	Coina (kō-ē'nȧ) . . . . Port. (In.)	38.36 N	9.3 W
93	Coixtlahuaca (kō-ēks'tlä-wä'kä) Mex.	17.40 N	97.18 W
90	Cojimar (kō-hē-mär') Cuba (Habana In.)	23.10 N	82.19 W
94	Cojutepeque (kō-hoo-tĕ-pā'kȧ) Sal.	13.46 N	88.52 W
77	Cokato (kō-kā'tō) . . . . Minn.	45.5 N	94.11 W
141	Colaba Pt. (kō-lä'bä) India (Bombay In.)	18.53 N	72.50 E
78	Colby (kōl'bĭ) . . . . Kan.	39.24 N	101.3 W
115	Colchester (kōl'chĕs-tēr) . Gt. Brit.	51.52 N	0.52 E
78	Coldwater (kōld'wô-tēr) . . . . Kan.	37.14 N	99.19 W
84	Coldwater . . . . Mich.	41.56 N	85.0 W
78	Coldwater Cr . . . . Okla.-Tex.	36.20 N	102.10 W
79	Coldwater R . . . . Miss.	34.30 N	90.10 W
82	Coldwater R . . . . Miss.	34.32 N	90.0 W
86	Cole Harbour (kōl) . . . . Can.	45.15 N	61.11 W
80	Coleman (kōl'măn) . . . . Tex.	31.48 N	99.26 W
160	Colenton (kōl'ĕn-tŭn) . Austl. (In.)	26.54 S	152.18 E
77	Coleraine (kōl-rān') . . . . Minn.	47.18 N	93.28 W
114	Coleraine . . . . N. Ire.	55.5 N	6.40 W
157	Coleridge L. (kōl'rĭj) . . . . N. Z.	43.15 S	171.32 E
116	Coleshill (kōlz'hĭl) . . . . Gt. Brit.	52.29 N	1.42 W
77	Colfax (kōl'făks) . . . . Ia.	41.41 N	93.14 W
81	Colfax . . . . La.	31.31 N	92.42 W
70	Colfax . . . . Wash.	46.52 N	117.12 W
102	Colhue, L. (kōl-wā') . . . . Arg.	45.28 S	69.0 W
92	Colima (kō-lē'mä) . . . . Mex.	19.13 N	103.44 W
92	Colima (State) . . . . Mex.	19.0 N	104.0 W
92	Colima, Vol. de . . . . Mex.	19.30 N	103.37 W
100	Collahuasi (kō-lyä-wä'sė) . . . . Chl.	20.58 S	68.58 W
125	Collares (kō-lär'äzh) . . . Port. (In.)	38.48 N	9.27 W
101	Collares (I.) . . . . Braz. (In.)	0.55 S	48.12 W
73	College Pk . . . . Ga. (Atlanta In.)	33.39 N	84.27 W
88	College Pt . . N. Y. (New York In.)	40.47 N	73.51 W
114	Coll (I.) (kōl) . . . . Gt. Brit.	56.35 N	6.30 W
158	Collie (kōl'ė) . . . . Austl.	33.12 S	116.12 E
158	Collier B. (kōl-yēr) . . . . Austl.	16.15 S	124.15 E
85	Collingswood (kōl'ĭngz-wood) . N. J.	39.50 N	75.6 W
55	Collingwood (kōl'ĭng-wood) . . Can.	44.32 N	80.29 W
157	Collingwood . . . . N. Z.	40.40 S	172.40 E
82	Collins (kŏl'ĭns) . . . . Miss.	31.38 N	89.34 W
51	Collinsville (kōl'ĭnz-vĭl) Calif. (San Francisco In.)	38.5 N	121.51 W
79	Collinsville . . . . Ill.	38.40 N	89.59 W
79	Collinsville . . . . Okla.	36.21 N	95.50 W
132	Collo (kōl'ō) . . . . Alg.	37.0 N	6.30 E
127	Collonne, C. (kōl-lō'nä) . . . . It.	39.2 N	17.13 E
51	Colma (kōl'mä) Calif. (San Francisco In.)	37.40 N	122.28 W
123	Colmar (kōl'mär) . . . . Fr.	48.5 N	7.22 E
124	Colmenar de Oreja (kōl-mā-när' dā ō-rā'hä) . Sp.	40.6 N	3.23 W
125	Colmenar Viejo (kōl-mā-när' vyā'hō) . Sp. (In.)	40.39 N	3.47 W
	Cöln, see Köln, Ger.		
116	Colne (kōln) . . . . Gt. Brit.	53.52 N	2.10 W
132	Colomb-Béchar (kō-lôɴ' bā-shär') Alg.	31.41 N	2.12 W
123	Colombes (kō-lôɴb') . . . . Fr. (In.)	48.56 N	2.17 E
100	Colombia (kō-lôm'bē-ä) . . . . S. A.	3.30 N	72.30 W
141	Colombo (kō-lŏm'bō) . . . . Cey.	6.55 N	79.50 E
99	Colón (kō-lōn') Arg. (Buenos Aires In.)	33.50 S	61.8 W
100	Colon (Galapagos) Arch. (kō-lōn') (gä-lä-pä-gōs) . Ec.	0.1 S	90.30 W
96	Colón . . . . Cuba	22.42 N	80.52 W
92	Colón . . . . Mex.	20.47 N	100.2 W
95	Colon . . . . Pan.	9.22 N	79.54 W
99	Colón . . . . Ur. (Buenos Aires In.)	34.47 S	56.10 W
102	Colonia (kō-lō'nē-ä) . . . . Ur.	34.30 S	57.45 W
80	Colonia Guadalupe (kō-lō'nē-ä gwä-dä-loo'pä) . Mex.	31.23 N	106.6 W
114	Colonsay (I.) (kŏl-ŏn-sā') . Gt. Brit.	56.5 N	6.10 W
80	Colorado (kŏl-ō-rä'dō) . . . . Tex.	32.34 N	100.51 W
75	Colorado (State) . . . . U. S.	38.40 N	107.0 W
75	Colo. Natl. Mon . . . . Colo.	39.3 N	108.42 W
102	Colorado R . . . . Arg.	38.42 S	66.30 W
58	Colorado R . . . . U. S.-Mex.	32.15 N	114.50 W
96	Colorados Rfs. (kō-lō-rä'dōs) . Cuba	22.30 N	84.21 W
75	Colorado R. Ind. Res . Ariz.-Calif.	33.55 N	114.25 W
78	Colorado Springs . . . . Colo.	38.49 N	104.49 W
72	Colorado Springs . . . . Colo. (In.)		
93	Colotepec R. (kō-lō-tĕ-pĕk') . Mex.	16.0 N	96.45 W
92	Colotlan (kō-lō-tlän') . . . . Mex.	22.11 N	103.17 W
92	Colotlan, R . . . . Mex.	22.15 N	103.35 W
100	Colquechaca (kōl-kā-chä'kä) . Bol.	18.47 S	66.0 W
73	Colton (kōl'tŭn) Calif. (Los Angeles In.)	34.4 N	117.20 W
82	Columbia (kō-lŭm'bĭ-ȧ) . . . . Ky.	37.7 N	85.18 W

ng-sing; ŋ-baŋk; ɴ-nasalized n; nŏd; cŏmmit; ōld; ôbey; ôrder; fōōd; fŏŏt; ou-out; s-soft; sh-dish; th-thin; pūre; ůnite; ûrn; stŭd; circŭs; ü-as "y" in study; '-indeterminate vowel.

Page	Name Pronunciation Region	Lat. °′	Long. °′
82	Columbia . . . . . Miss.	31.15 N	89.50 W
79	Columbia . . . . . Mo.	38.57 N	92.19 W
85	Columbia . . . . . Pa.	40.2 N	76.30 W
83	Columbia . . . . . S. C.	34.0 N	81.2 W
82	Columbia . . . . . Tenn.	35.37 N	87.3 W
84	Columbia City . . . . . Ind.	41.9 N	85.30 W
89	Columbia Hts. Minn. (Minneapolis In.)	45.3 N	93.14 W
82	Columbiana (kô-lŭm-bĭ-ă'nȧ) . Ala.	33.10 N	86.37 W
70	Columbia R. . . . . U. S.-Can.	45.52 N	121.40 W
82	Columbus (kô-lŭm'bŭs) . . . . . Ga.	32.29 N	84.58 W
84	Columbus . . . . . Ind.	39.13 N	85.56 W
79	Columbus . . . . . Kan.	37.11 N	94.50 W
82	Columbus . . . . . Miss.	33.29 N	88.26 W
71	Columbus . . . . . Mont.	45.39 N	109.17 W
76	Columbus . . . . . Neb.	41.25 N	97.21 W
75	Columbus . . . . . N. M.	31.50 N	107.38 W
84	Columbus . . . . . Ohio	39.56 N	83.0 W
81	Columbus . . . . . Tex.	29.43 N	96.33 W
77	Columbus . . . . . Wis.	43.21 N	89.0 W
97	Columbus Bank . . . . . Ba. Is.	22.2 N	75.42 W
84	Columbus Grove . . . . . Ohio	40.55 N	84.5 W
97	Columbus Pt. . . . . . Ba. Is.	24.9 N	75.17 W
74	Colusa (kô-lū'sȧ) . . . . . Calif.	39.13 N	122.2 W
70	Colville (kŏl'vĭl) . . . . . Wash.	48.33 N	117.53 W
52	Colville R. . . . . . Alsk.	69.0 N	154.0 W
70	Colville R. . . . . . Wash.	48.20 N	117.50 W
72	Colwood (kŏl'wŏŏd) Can. (Vancouver In.)	48.27 N	123.29 W
119	Comacchio (kô-mäk'kyō) . . . . . It.	44.40 N	12.10 E
92	Comalá (kō-mä-lä') . . . . . Mex.	19.16 N	103.45 E
93	Comalcalco (kō-mäl-käl'kō) . . Mex.	18.15 N	93.14 W
78	Comanche (kō-măn'chē) . . . . Okla.	34.21 N	97.58 W
80	Comanche . . . . . Tex.	31.54 N	98.36 W
94	Comayagua (kō-mä-yä'gwä) . Hond.	14.30 N	87.45 W
83	Combahee R. (kŏm-bȧ-hē') . . S. C.	32.40 N	80.40 W
117	Comberbach (kō'mẽr-băk) Gt. Brit. (Liverpool In.)	53.17 N	2.32 W
82	Comer (kŭm'ẽr) . . . . . Ga.	34.4 N	83.10 W
97	Comete C. (kō-mä'tȧ) . . . . . Ba. Is.	21.43 N	71.28 W
141	Comilla (kō-mĭl'ȧ) . . . . . Pak.	23.29 N	91.15 E
126	Comino, C. (kō-mē'nō) . . . . . Sard.	40.23 N	9.46 E
93	Comitán (kō-mē-tän') . . . . . Mex.	16.15 N	92.8 W
122	Commentry (kō-mäɴ-trē') . . . . . Fr.	46.15 N	2.15 E
82	Commerce (kŏm'ẽrs) . . . . . Ga.	34.12 N	83.28 W
79	Commerce . . . . . Okla.	36.56 N	94.54 W
79	Commerce . . . . . Tex.	33.15 N	95.54 W
123	Commercy (kô-mĕr-sē') . . . . . Fr.	48.45 N	5.35 E
160	Como (kō'mō) . Austl. (Sydney In.)	34.0 S	151.4 E
126	Como . . . . . It.	45.47 N	9.5 E
102	Comodoro Rivadavia (kō-mō-dō'rō rē-vä-dä'vē-ä) . Arg.	45.45 S	67.28 W
132	Comoé R. (kô-mô-ā') . Fr. W. Afr.	7.0 N	4.50 W
126	Como, L. . . . . . It.-Switz.	46.0 N	9.15 E
141	Comorin, C. (kŏ'mô-rĭn) . . . . India	7.37 N	77.28 E
135	Comoro Is. (kŏm'ô-rō) . . . . Ind. O.	12.10 S	44.15 E
55	Comox (kŭm'ŏks) . . . . . Can.	49.40 N	129.1 W
122	Compiegne (kôɴ-pyĕn'y') . . . . . Fr.	49.25 N	2.50 E
125	Comporta (kôm-pôr'tȧ) . Port. (In.)	38.24 N	8.49 W
92	Compostela (kōm-pō-stä'lä) . Mex.	21.15 N	104.54 W
117	Compstall (kŏmps'tôl) Gt. Brit. (Liverpool In.)	53.25 N	2.3 W
74	Compton (kŏmp'tŭn) . . . . . Calif.	33.51 N	118.15 W
132	Conakry (kô-nȧ-krē') . Fr. W. Afr.	9.30 N	13.45 W
82	Conasauga (kō-nȧ-sô'gȧ) . . . . Ga.	34.52 N	84.50 W
122	Concarneau (kôɴ-kär-nō') . . . . . Fr.	47.55 N	3.56 W
101	Concepción (kōn-sĕp-syōn') . . Bol.	15.58 S	61.28 W
102	Concepción . . . . . Chl.	36.45 S	72.59 W
95	Concepción . . . . . Pan.	8.31 N	82.38 W
102	Concepción . . . . . Par.	23.28 S	57.29 W
152	Concepcion . . . . . Phil.	15.19 N	120.39 E
94	Concepcion (Vol.) . . . . . Nic.	11.33 N	85.38 W
94	Concepción del Mar (dĕl mär') Guat.	14.7 N	91.22 W
80	Concepción del Oro (dĕl ō'rō) . Mex.	24.39 N	101.24 W
87	Conception B. (kŏn-sĕp'shŭn) . Can.	47.40 N	53.5 W
97	Conception I. . . . . . Ba. Is.	23.50 N	75.7 W
74	Conception, Pt. . . . . . Calif.	34.27 N	120.29 W
80	Concho R. (kŏn'chō) . . . . . Tex.	31.31 N	100.0 W
80	Conchos R. (kōn'chōs) . . . . . Mex.	25.5 N	99.0 W
80	Conchos R. . . . . . Mex.	28.0 N	105.15 W
51	Concord (kŏŋ'kẽrd) Calif. (San Francisco In.)	37.58 N	122.1 W
87	Concord . . . . . Mass. (In.)	42.27 N	71.21 W
83	Concord . . . . . N. C.	35.24 N	80.36 W
86	Concord . . . . . N. H.	43.12 N	71.32 W
102	Concordia (kŏn-kôr'dĭ-ȧ) . . . . Arg.	31.28 S	58.1 W
79	Concordia . . . . . Kan.	39.34 N	97.39 W
92	Concordia . . . . . Mex.	23.17 N	106.5 W
70	Concrete (kŏn'krēt) . . . . . Wash.	48.33 N	121.44 W
159	Condamine R. (kŏn'dȧ-mīn) . Austl.	27.0 S	150.0 E
76	Conde (kŏn-dē') . . . . . S. D.	45.9 N	98.5 W
157	Conden (kŏn'dĕn) . . . . . N. Z.	42.25 S	171.15 E
112	Condé-Smendou (kôɴ-dā'-smäɴ-dōō') . Alg.	36.52 N	6.36 E
122	Condé-sur-Noireau (kôɴ-dā'-sür-nwä-rō') . Fr.	45.50 N	0.32 W
101	Condeúba (kōn-dā-ōō'bä) . . Braz.	14.57 S	41.58 W
122	Condom (kôɴ-dôɴ') . . . . . Fr.	43.38 N	0.22 E
70	Condon (kŏn'dŭn) . . . . . Ore.	45.14 N	120.11 W
82	Conecuh R. (kō-nē'kū) . . . . . Ala.	31.30 N	86.20 W
126	Conegliano (kō-nāl-yä'nō) . . . . It.	45.53 N	12.18 E
78	Conejos R. (kō-nā'hōs) . . . . Colo.	37.5 N	106.20 W
85	Conemaugh (kŏn'ē-mô) . . . . . Pa.	40.22 N	78.50 W
88	Coney I. (kō'nĭ) . . . . . N. Y. (In.)	40.34 N	73.58 W
122	Confalens (kôɴ-fȧ-läɴ') . . . . . Fr.	46.1 N	0.40 E
123	Conflans (kôɴ-fläɴ') . . . . . Fr.	49.10 N	5.50 E
123	Conflans-Ste. Honorine (kôɴ'fläɴ'-săɴt'ô-nō-rēn') . Fr. (In.)	48.58 N	2.5 E
83	Congaree R. (kŏŋ-gȧ-rē') . . S. C.	33.50 N	80.55 W
116	Congleton (kŏŋ'g'l-tŭn) . . Gt. Brit.	53.10 N	2.13 W
134	Congo (Dist.) (kŏŋ'gō) . . . . . Ang.	6.30 S	15.15 E
131	Congo da Lemba (kôŋ'gō dȧ lĕm'-bȧ) . Bel. Cong. (Brazzaville In.)	5.47 S	13.42 E
133	Congo R. (kŏŋ'gō) . . . . . Afr.	2.15 N	22.0 E
131	Congo River Falls Bel. Cong. (Brazzaville In.)	4.50 S	14.30 E
72	Conifer (kō'nĭ-fẽr) Colo. (Denver In.)	39.30 N	105.18 W
125	Conil (kō-nēl') . . . . . Sp. (In.)	36.16 N	6.6 W
116	Conisborough (kŏn'ĭs-bŭr-ō) Gt. Brit.	53.29 N	1.13 W
141	Conjeeveram (kŏn-jē-vẽr-ŭm') India	12.47 N	79.45 E
73	Conley (kŏn'lĭ) . . Ga. (Atlanta In.)	33.39 N	84.19 W
84	Conneaut (kŏn-ē-ôt') . . . . . Ohio	41.57 N	80.34 W
85	Connecticut (State) (kŏ-nĕt'ĭ-kŭt) U. S.	41.30 N	72.40 W
86	Connecticut R. . . . . . U. S.	43.50 N	72.30 W
73	Connellsville (kŏn'ĕlz-vĭl) Ala. (Birmingham In.)	33.21 N	87.11 W
85	Connellsville . . . . . Pa.	40.2 N	79.36 W
114	Connemara, Mts. of (kŏn-nē-mȧ'rȧ) . Ire.	53.40 N	9.30 W
84	Connersville (kŏn'ẽrz-vĭl) . . . . Ind.	39.37 N	85.10 W
114	Conn, Lough (L.) (lŏĸ kŏn) . . . Ire.	54.0 N	9.20 W
73	Connor (kŏn'ẽr) Utah (Salt Lake City In.)	41.37 N	112.21 W
101	Conquista (kōn-kēs'tä) . . . . . Braz.	15.10 S	40.45 W
71	Conrad (kŏn'răd) . . . . . Mont.	48.10 N	111.48 W
81	Conroe (kŏn'rō) . . . . . Tex.	30.18 N	95.28 W
85	Conshohocken (kŏn-shō-hŏk'ĕn) Pa.	40.5 N	75.20 W
96	Consolación del Sur (kōn-sō-lä-syōn' dĕl sōōr') . Cuba	22.27 N	83.28 W
120	Constance, L. of (kŏn'stȧns) Switz.-Ger.	47.38 N	9.20 E
111	Constanța (kōn-stän'tsȧ) . . . . Rom.	44.12 N	28.38 E
124	Constantina (kōn-stän-tē'nä) . . Sp.	37.53 N	5.38 W
132	Constantine (kôɴ-stäɴ'tēn') . . Alg.	36.28 N	6.35 E
84	Constantine (kŏn'stȧn-tēn) . Mich.	41.51 N	85.40 W
111	Constantinople (Istanbul) (kŏn-stăn-tĭ-nō'p'l) (ē-stän-bōōl') . Tur.	41.2 N	29.0 E
102	Constitución (kōn'stĭ-tōō-syōn') Chl.	35.28 S	72.30 W
72	Constitution, Mt. (kŏn-stĭ-tū'shŭn) Wash. (Vancouver In.)	48.41 N	122.50 W
124	Consuegra (kōn-swā'grä) . . . . . Sp.	39.27 N	3.36 W
92	Contepec (kōn-tĕ-pĕk') . . . . . Mex.	20.3 N	100.7 W
117	Contich (kŏn'tĭĸ) . Bel. (Anvers In.)	51.7 N	4.27 E
79	Conway (kŏn'wā) . . . . . Ark.	35.6 N	92.26 W
86	Conway . . . . . N. H.	43.59 N	71.10 W
83	Conway . . . . . S. C.	33.50 N	79.3 W
51	Conway . . . . . Wash. (Seattle In.)	48.20 N	122.22 W
82	Conyers (kŏn'yẽrz) . . . . . Ga.	33.42 N	84.4 W
160	Coogee (kōō-gē') Austl. (Sydney In.)	33.55 S	151.15 E
160	Cooke, Pt. . Austl. (Melbourne In.)	37.56 S	144.48 E
82	Cookeville (kŏŏk'vĭl) . . . . . Tenn.	36.9 N	85.31 W
53	Cook Inlet (kŏŏk) . . . . . Alsk.	60.0 N	152.30 W
6	Cook Is. . . . . . Pac. O.	19.30 S	158.30 W
157	Cook, Mt. . . . . . N. Z.	43.33 S	170.10 E
73	Cooks Sprs. Ala. (Birmingham In.)	33.35 N	86.24 W
157	Cook, Str. . . . . . N. Z.	41.0 S	174.30 E
159	Cooktown . . . . . Austl.	15.38 S	145.25 E
160	Coolangatta (kōō-lȧŋ-gă'tȧ) Austl. (In.)	28.9 S	153.27 E
83	Cooleemee (kōō-lē'mē) . . . . . N. C.	35.49 N	80.31 W
158	Coolgardie (kōōl-gär'dē) . . . . Austl.	30.52 S	121.15 E
117	Cooling (kōōl'ĭng) Gt. Brit. (London In.)	51.28 N	0.32 E
159	Cooma (kōō'mȧ) . . . . . Austl.	36.15 S	149.18 E
159	Coonamble (kōō-năm'b'l) . . . Austl.	30.56 S	148.22 E
79	Cooper (kōōp'ẽr) . . . . . Tex.	33.22 N	95.40 W
85	Cooperstown . . . . . N. Y.	42.43 N	74.55 W
76	Cooperstown . . . . . N. D.	47.27 N	98.6 W
82	Coosa R. (kōō'sȧ) . . . . . Ala.-Ga.	34.0 N	86.0 W
82	Coosawattee R. (kōō-sȧ-wôt'ē) Ga.	34.35 N	84.40 W
70	Coos B. (kōōs) . . . . . Ore.	43.20 N	124.20 W
160	Cooyar (kōō'yär) . . . . . Austl. (In.)	26.59 S	151.51 E
93	Copainalá (kō-pī-nä-lä') . . . . . Mex.	17.5 N	93.10 W
93	Copalita, R. (kō-pä-lē'tä) . . . . Mex.	16.0 N	96.17 W
94	Copán (Ruins) (kō-pän') . . Guat.	14.50 N	89.20 W
81	Copano B. (kō-pän'ō) . . . . . Tex.	28.8 N	97.5 W
	Copenhagen, see København, Den.		
102	Copiapó (Cerro del Azufre) (Vol.) (kō-pyä-pō') (sẽr'rō dĕl ä-zōō'frā) . Chl.	27.15 S	69.10 W
126	Copparo (kôp-pä'rō) . . . . . It.	44.54 N	11.49 E
53	Copper Center (kŏp'ẽr) . . . . . Alsk.	61.57 N	145.18 W
82	Copperhill . . . . . Tenn.	35.0 N	84.22 W
54	Coppermine . . . . . Can.	67.49 N	115.6 W
54	Coppermine R. . . . . . Can.	66.30 N	115.0 W
53	Copper R. . . . . . Alsk.	62.20 N	145.0 W
102	Coqueiros (kô-kā'rōzh) . Braz. (In.)	22.47 S	43.22 W
134	Coquilhatville (kô-kē'yȧ-vēl') Bel. Cong.	0.0	18.18 E
70	Coquille (kô-kēl') . . . . . Ore.	43.10 N	124.11 W
102	Coquimbo (kô-kēm'bō) . . . . . Chl.	29.59 S	71.29 W
72	Coquitlam L. (kō-kwĭt-lȧm) Can. (Vancouver In.)	49.24 N	122.46 W
127	Corabia (kô-rä'bĭ-ȧ) . . . . . Rom.	43.45 N	24.29 E
100	Coracora (kō'rä-kō'rä) . . . . . Peru	15.30 S	73.32 W
153	Coral B. (kŏr'ăl) . . . . . Phil.	8.25 N	117.25 E
83	Coral Gables . . . . . Fla. (In.)	25.44 N	80.14 W
159	Coral Sea . . . . . Austl.	15.0 S	155.0 E
89	Coraopolis (kŏ-rȧ-ŏp'ô-lĭs) Pa. (Pittsburgh In.)	40.31 N	80.10 W
126	Corato (kō'rä-tō) . . . . . It.	41.9 N	16.25 E
122	Corbeil (kôr-bĕ'y') . . . . . Fr.	48.38 N	2.31 E
51	Corbett (kôr'bĕt) Wash. (Seattle In.)	45.32 N	122.17 W
122	Corbie (kôr-bē') . . . . . Fr.	49.55 N	2.31 E
82	Corbin (kôr'bĭn) . . . . . Ky.	36.56 N	84.7 W
72	Corboia Cr. (kôr-boi'ȧ) Can. (Vancouver In.)	49.38 N	122.38 W
116	Corby (kôr'bĭ) . . . . . Gt. Brit.	52.50 N	0.32 W
102	Corcovado (Mt.) (kôr-kô-vä'dōō) Braz. (In.)	22.57 S	43.12 W
102	Corcovado G. (kôr-kô-vä'dhō) . Chl.	43.30 S	73.30 W
160	Cordeaux, Mt. (kôr-dō') Austl. (In.)	27.59 S	152.23 E
82	Cordele (kôr-dēl') . . . . . Ga.	31.57 N	83.50 W
51	Cordelia (kôr-dē'lyȧ) Calif. (San Francisco In.)	38.11 N	122.10 W
78	Cordell (kôr-dĕl') . . . . . Okla.	35.18 N	98.59 W
102	Córdoba (kôr'dô-vä) . . . . . Arg.	31.28 S	64.10 W
102	Córdoba (State) . . . . . Arg.	31.0 S	64.0 W
93	Córdoba . . . . . Mex.	18.55 N	96.55 W
124	Córdoba . . . . . Sp.	37.54 N	4.46 W
82	Cordova . . . . . Ala.	33.45 N	87.12 W
53	Cordova . . . . . Alsk.	60.30 N	145.45 W
99	Cordova Pen. Chl. (Magallanes In.)	53.20 S	72.50 W
127	Corfu (I.) (kôr'fū) . . . . . Grc.	39.35 N	19.52 E
127	Corfu (kerkyra) (kĕr'kē-rȧ) . . Grc.	39.36 N	19.55 E
126	Corigliano (kō-rē-lyä'nō) . . . . . It.	39.36 N	16.32 E
160	Corinna (Pieman) R. (kô-rĭn'ȧ) Austl. (Tas. In.)	41.45 S	145.20 E
73	Corinne (kô-rēn') Utah (Salt Lake City In.)	41.32 N	112.6 W
82	Corinth (kŏr'ĭnth) . . . . . Miss.	34.56 N	88.32 W
127	Corinth (Korinthos) (kô'rĭn-thôs) Grc.	37.55 N	22.55 E
127	Corinth, G. of . . . . . Grc.	38.10 N	22.40 E
94	Corinto (kŏr-ĭn'tō) . . . . . Nic.	12.30 N	87.12 W
126	Corizia (kō-rēd'zē-ä) . . . . . It.	45.57 N	13.37 E
114	Cork (kôrk) . . . . . Ire.	51.55 N	8.30 W
114	Cork Har. . . . . . Ire.	51.45 N	8.15 W
126	Corleone (kôr-lā-ō'nā) . . . . . It.	37.48 N	13.18 E
127	Çorlu (chôr'lōō) . . . . . Tur.	41.8 N	27.48 E
123	Cormeilles (kôr-mā'y') . . . Fr. (In.)	48.58 N	2.12 E
82	Cornelia (kôr-nē'lyȧ) . . . . . Ga.	34.32 N	83.33 W
77	Cornell (kôr-nĕl') . . . . . Wis.	45.10 N	91.10 W
169	Corners (kôr'nẽrz) . Austl. (Tas. In.)	41.50 S	147.23 E
51	Cornet (kôr'nĕt) Wash. (Seattle In.)	48.23 N	122.37 W
126	Corneto (Tarquinia) (kôr-nā'tō) (tär-kwē'nyä) . It.	42.16 N	11.45 E
79	Corning (kôr'nĭng) . . . . . Ark.	36.25 N	90.35 W
79	Corning . . . . . Ia.	40.59 N	94.42 W
85	Corning . . . . . N. Y.	42.9 N	77.5 W
95	Corn I., Gt. . . . . . W. I.	12.12 N	83.2 W
95	Corn I., Little . . . . . W. I.	12.18 N	82.58 W
126	Corno, Mt. (kôr'nō) . . . . . It.	42.27 N	13.33 E
55	Cornwall (kôrn'wôl) . . . . . Can.	45.3 N	74.45 W
156	Cornwallis (kôrn-wŏl'ĭs) N. Z. (In.)	37.0 S	174.37 E
100	Coro (kō'rō) . . . . . Ven.	11.28 N	69.32 W
100	Corocoro (kō-rō-kō'rō) . . . . . Bol.	17.15 S	68.31 W
156	Coromandel Chan. (kŏr-ô-măn'dĕl) N. Z.	36.25 S	175.30 E
141	Coromandel Coast . . . . . India	13.0 N	80.30 E
153	Coron (kō-rōn') . . . . . Phil.	12.1 N	120.13 E
82	Corona (kô-rō'nȧ) . . . . . Ala.	33.42 N	87.28 W
73	Corona . . . Calif. (Los Angeles In.)	33.53 N	117.34 W
92	Corona, R. . . . . . Mex.	24.0 N	99.10 W
95	Coronado B. (kō-rō-nä'dō) . . C. R.	9.0 N	84.0 W
74	Coronado (kŏr-ô-nä'dō) . Calif. (In.)	32.41 N	117.11 W
153	Coronado B. . . . . . Phil.	7.55 N	122.10 E
54	Coronation G. (kŏr-ô-nā'shŭn) Can.	68.0 N	112.30 W
153	Coron B. (kô-rōn') . . . . . Phil.	11.55 N	120.10 E
102	Coronel (kō-rō-nĕl') . . . . . Chl.	37.5 S	73.12 W
102	Coronel Suárez (swä'räs) . . . . . Arg.	37.32 S	62.5 W
153	Coron I. . . . . . Phil.	11.55 N	120.15 E
100	Coropuna, Mt. (kō-rô-pōō'nä) Peru	15.58 S	72.2 W
90	Corozal (kō-rō-zäl') . . . . C. Z. (In.)	8.58 N	7.35 W
81	Corpus Christi (kôr'pŭs krĭs'tē) Tex.	27.48 N	97.24 W
81	Corpus Christi B. . . . . . Tex.	27.50 N	97.15 W
80	Corpus Christi, L. . . . . . Tex.	28.10 N	97.50 W
102	Corral (kôr-räl') . . . . . Chl.	39.59 S	73.28 W
124	Corral de Almaguer (kô-räl' dā äl-mä-gär') . Sp.	39.47 N	3.8 W
96	Corralillo (kō-rä-lē'lyō) . . . . . Cuba	22.58 N	80.38 W
152	Corregidor I. (kō-rā-hē-dōr') . Phil.	14.22 N	120.35 E
124	Correlia (kō-rĕl'yȧ) . . . . . Sp.	42.8 N	1.48 W
101	Correntina (kō-rĕn-tē'nȧ) . . . Braz.	13.45 S	44.45 W
114	Corrib, Lough (L.) (lŏĸ kŏr'ĭb) . Ire.	53.30 N	9.10 W
102	Corrientes (kō-ryĕn'tās) . . . . . Arg.	27.28 S	58.45 W
102	Corrientes (State) . . . . . Arg.	28.45 S	58.0 W
96	Corrientes B. . . . . . Cuba	21.50 N	84.35 W
100	Corrientes, C. . . . . . Col.	5.30 N	77.30 W
96	Corrientes, C. . . . . . Cuba	21.45 N	84.28 W
92	Corrientes, C. . . . . . Mex.	20.22 N	105.43 W
85	Corry (kŏr'ĭ) . . . . . Pa.	41.56 N	79.39 W
122	Corse, C. (kôrs) . . . . . Cor. (In.)	44.0 N	9.25 E
122	Corsica (I.) (kôr'sĭ-kȧ) . . . Fr. (In.)	42.0 N	9.0 E
81	Corsicana (kôr-sĭ-kăn'ȧ) . . . . . Tex.	32.6 N	96.28 W
92	Cortazar (kôr-tä-zär') . . . . . Mex.	20.28 N	100.57 W
122	Corte (kôr'tā) . . . . . Cor. (In.)	42.20 N	9.11 E
124	Cortegana (kôr-tā-gä'nä) . . . . . Sp.	37.55 N	6.49 W
124	Cortes (kôr-tās') . . . . . Sp.	36.38 N	5.20 W
96	Cortes B. . . . . . Cuba	22.5 N	83.51 W
85	Cortland (kôrt'lȧnd) . . . . . N. Y.	42.36 N	76.9 W
126	Cortona (kôr-tō'nä) . . . . . It.	43.27 N	11.59 E
124	Coruche (kô-rōō'she) . . . . . Port.	38.57 N	8.32 W
111	Çoruh R. (chō-rōōĸ') . . . . . Tur.	40.40 N	41.30 E
111	Çorum (chō-rōōm') . . . . . Tur.	40.30 N	34.47 E
101	Corumbá (kō-rōōm-bä') . . . . . Braz.	19.0 S	57.45 W
84	Corunna (kō-rŭn'ȧ) . . . . . Mich.	42.57 N	84.8 W
101	Coruripe (kō-rōō-rē'pĭ) . . . . . Braz.	10.1 N	36.1 W
70	Corvallis (kŏr-văl'ĭs) . . . . . Ore.	44.34 N	123.17 W

ăt; finȧl; rāte; senâte; ärm; àsk; sofȧ; fâre; ch-choose; dh-as th in other; bē; ēvent; bĕt; recĕnt; cratẽr; g-go; gh-gutteral g; bĭt; ĭ-short neutral; rīde; ĸ-gutteral k as ch in German ich;

Corve PRONOUNCING INDEX Cumberland

Page	Name Pronunciation Region	Lat. °′	Long. °′
116	Corve, R. (kôr'vê) . . . . . . Gt. Brit.	52.28 N	2.42 W
132	Corvo I. (kôr'vōō) . . . . Azores (In.)	39.40 N	31.8 W
84	Corydon (kŏr'ĭ-dŭn) . . . . Ind.	38.12 N	86.8 W
79	Corydon . . . . Ia.	40.49 N	93.21 W
84	Corydon . . . . Ky.	37.45 N	87.42 W
93	Cosamaloápan (kô-sä-mä-lwä'pän) Mex.	18.21 N	95.49 W
93	Coscomatepec (kôs'kō-mä-tĕ-pĕk') Mex.	19.4 N	97.2 W
94	Coseguina (Vol.) (kô-sâ-gē'nä) Nic.	12.58 N	87.34 W
116	Coseley (kōz'lĭ) . . . . Gt. Brit.	52.33 N	2.5 W
126	Cosenza (kô-zĕnt'sä) . . . . It.	39.15 N	16.16 E
84	Coshocton (kô-shŏk'tŭn) . . . . . Ohio	40.17 N	81.53 W
135	Cosmoledo Is. (kŏs-mô-lā'dō) Ind. O.	9.40 S	47.40 E
70	Cosmopolis (kŏz-mŏp'ô-lĭs) . Wash.	46.57 N	123.48 W
122	Cosne (kōn) . . . . Fr.	47.25 N	2.59 E
93	Cosamaloapan (kô-sô-mä-lwä'pän) Mex.	18.1 N	94.36 W
92	Cosoyoapa (kô-sô-yô-ä'pä) . . Mex.	16.45 N	98.25 W
94	Costa Rica (kŏs'tȧ rē'kȧ) Cen. Am.	10.0 N	84.0 W
74	Cosumnes R. (kō-sŭm'nĕz) . . Calif.	38.20 N	121.15 W
100	Cotabambas (kô-tä-bàm'bäs) . Peru	13.40 S	72.20 W
153	Cotabato (kō-tä-bä'tō) . . . . . . Phil.	7.12 N	124.16 E
153	Cotabato Valley . . . . Phil.	7.0 N	124.30 E
93	Cotaxtla (kō-täs'tlä) . . . . Mex.	18.48 N	96.23 W
93	Cotaxtla, R. . . . . Mex.	18.50 N	96.23 W
122	Côte d'Or (kōt dôr') . . . . Fr.	47.10 N	4.50 E
92	Cotija de la Paz (kō-tē'hä dā lä päz) . Mex.	19.45 N	102.38 W
132	Cotonou (kô-tô-nōō') . . Fr. W. Afr.	6.28 N	2.28 E
100	Cotopaxi (Vol.) (kō-tô-păk'sê) . Ec.	0.45 S	78.29 W
127	Cotrone (kô-trō'nâ) . . . . It.	39.4 N	17.5 E
114	Cotswold Hills (kŏtz'wōld) Gt. Brit.	51.40 N	2.10 W
70	Cottage Grove (kŏt'āj grōv) . . Ore.	43.47 N	123.5 W
160	Cottesloe (kŏt'ĕs-lō) . . . . Austl.	32.0 S	115.46 E
74	Cottonwood Cr. (kŏt'ŭn-wŏŏd) Calif.	40.20 N	122.50 W
73	Cottonwood Cr. Utah (Salt Lake City In.)	41.10 N	111.41 W
76	Cottonwood R. . . . . Minn.	44.12 N	95.0 W
97	Cotui (kō-twē') . . . . Hai.	19.4 N	70.11 W
80	Cotulla (kŏ-tŭl'lȧ) . . . . Tex.	28.27 N	99.15 W
85	Coudersport (koŭ'dērz-pōrt) . . . Pa.	41.45 N	78.1 W
124	Couéron (kōō-ā-rôN') . . . . Fr.	45.15 N	1.41 W
51	Cougar (kōō'gȧr) Wash. (Seattle In.)	46.3 N	122.17 W
122	Coulommiers (kōō-lô-myā') . . . . Fr.	48.50 N	3.5 E
52	Council (koun'sĭl) . . . . Alsk.	64.55 N	163.30 W
79	Council Bluffs . . . . Ia.	41.18 N	95.55 W
79	Council Grove . . . . Kan.	39.39 N	96.30 W
51	Coupeville (kōōp'vĭl) Wash. (Seattle In.)	48.12 N	122.41 W
101	Courantyne R. (kôr'ăn-tĭn) Br. Gu.-Sur.	4.0 N	58.0 W
123	Courbevoie (kōōrb-vwä') . Fr. (In.)	48.54 N	2.16 E
123	Courdimanche (kōōr-dē-mänsh') Fr. (In.)	49.2 N	2.0 E
122	Coursan (kōōr'säN) . . . . Fr.	43.15 N	3.5 E
95	Courtown Cays (Is.) (kōōr'toun) W. I.	12.24 N	81.38 W
115	Courtrai (kōōr-trĕ') . . . . Bel.	50.49 N	3.15 E
81	Coushatta (kou-shăt'ȧ) . . . . La.	32.2 N	93.21 W
122	Coutances (kōō-täNs') . . . . Fr.	49.4 N	1.28 W
122	Coutras (kōō-trà') . . . . Fr.	45.2 N	0.9 W
114	Coventry (kŭv'ĕn-trĭ) . . . . Gt. Brit.	52.25 N	1.35 W
124	Covilhã (kô-vēl'yăN) . . . . Port.	40.18 N	7.31 W
73	Covina (kô-vē'nȧ) Calif. (Los Angeles In.)	34.5 N	117.54 W
82	Covington (kŭv'ĭng-tŭn) . . . . . . Ga.	33.36 N	83.51 W
84	Covington . . . . Ind.	40.8 N	87.25 W
84	Covington . . . . Ky.	39.5 N	84.32 W
81	Covington . . . . La.	30.30 N	90.7 W
84	Covington . . . . Ohio	40.9 N	84.23 W
79	Covington . . . . Okla.	36.18 N	97.32 W
82	Covington . . . . Tenn.	35.34 N	89.40 W
85	Covington . . . . Va.	37.48 N	79.59 W
72	Cowan (kou'ăn) . Colo. (Denver In.)	39.38 N	105.7 W
158	Cowan, L. . . . . Austl.	31.45 S	121.47 E
70	Cow Cr. . . . . Ore.	42.45 N	123.30 W
114	Cowes (kouz) . . . . Gt. Brit.	50.45 N	1.20 W
72	Cowichan Station (kou-ĭch'ăn) Can. (Vancouver In.)	48.44 N	123.40 W
70	Cowlitz R. (kou'lĭts) . . . . Wash.	46.30 N	122.40 W
101	Coxim (kō-shēN') . . . . Braz.	18.30 S	54.58 W
93	Coxquihui (kōz-kē-wē') . . . . . . Mex.	20.11 N	97.34 W
80	Coyame (kō-yä'mä) . . . . Mex.	29.27 N	105.5 W
51	Coyle (koil) . . . Wash. (Seattle In.)	47.41 N	122.47 W
93	Coyoacán (kô-yô-ȧ-kän') Mex. (In.)	19.21 N	99.10 W
73	Coyote Cr. (kī-ō'tê) Calif. (Los Angeles In.)	33.50 N	118.4 W
74	Coyote R. . . . . Calif.	37.26 N	121.58 W
92	Coyuca de Benítez (kō-yōō'kä dā bä-nē'tāz) . Mex.	17.2 N	100.14 W
92	Coyuca de Catalán (dā kä-tä-län') Mex.	18.20 N	100.39 W
93	Coyutla (kō-yōō'tlä) . . . . Mex.	20.14 N	97.39 W
78	Cozad (kō'zăd) . . . . Neb.	40.51 N	99.59 W
70	Crab Cr. (krăb) . . . . Wash.	47.20 N	118.50 W
160	Cradle Mt. (krā'd'l) Austl. (Tas. In.)	41.42 S	145.57 E
134	Cradock (krā'dŭk) . . . . . U. S. Afr.	32.11 S	25.36 E
89	Crafton (krăf'tŭn) Pa. (Pittsburgh In.)	40.26 N	80.4 W
72	Crags (krăgz) . . . . Colo. (In.)	38.53 N	104.57 W
99	Craig (krāg) Arg. (Buenos Aires In.)	35.10 S	58.41 W
71	Craig . . . . Colo.	40.33 N	107.33 W

Page	Name Pronunciation Region	Lat. °′	Long. °′
57	Craigs Road (krāgz) Can. (Que. In.)	46.37 N	71.23 W
127	Craiova (krȧ-yō'vȧ) . . . . Rom.	44.18 N	23.49 E
85	Cranberry L. (krăn'bĕr-ĭ) . . . N. Y.	44.10 N	74.50 W
54	Cranbrook (krăn'brŏŏk) . . . . . Can.	49.28 N	115.32 W
77	Crandon (krăn'dŭn) . . . . Wis.	45.35 N	88.54 W
122	Cransac (kräN-zȧk') . . . . Fr.	44.28 N	2.20 E
85	Cranston (krăns'tŭn) . . . . R. I.	41.45 N	71.27 W
70	Crater L. (krā'tĕr) . . . . Ore.	42.55 N	122.7 W
70	Crater L. Natl. Pk. . . . . Ore.	42.58 N	122.10 W
71	Craters of the Moon Natl. Mon. Ida.	43.25 N	113.30 W
101	Crateús (krä-tâ-ōōzh') . . . . . . Braz.	5.10 S	40.32 W
101	Crato (krä'tōō) . . . . Braz.	7.27 S	39.29 W
76	Crawford (krô'fērd) . . . . Neb.	42.41 N	103.25 W
153	Crawford Pt. . . . . Phil.	11.20 N	119.25 E
84	Crawfordsville . . . . Ind.	40.2 N	86.55 W
81	Crawley (krô'lê) . . . . La.	30.14 N	92.22 W
117	Crayford (krā'fērd) Gt. Brit. (London In.)	51.27 N	0.11 E
71	Crazy Mts. . . . . Mont.	46.10 N	110.30 W
71	Crazy Woman Cr. . . . . Wyo.	44.10 N	106.26 W
73	Creek (krēk) Ala. (Birmingham In.)	33.39 N	87.6 W
54	Cree L. (krē) . . . . Can.	57.35 N	107.0 W
76	Creighton (krā'tŭn) . . . . Neb.	42.27 N	97.54 W
122	Creil (krĕ'y') . . . . Fr.	49.18 N	2.31 E
126	Crema (krā'mä) . . . . It.	45.16 N	9.52 E
126	Cremona (krā-mō'nä) . . . . It.	45.8 N	10.1 E
72	Crescent (krĕs'ĕnt) Can. (Vancouver In.)	49.3 N	122.52 W
70	Crescent City . . . . Calif.	41.45 N	124.13 W
83	Crescent City . . . . Fla.	29.26 N	81.33 W
56	Crescent L. . . Can. (Winnipeg In.)	49.58 N	98.18 W
83	Crescent L. . . . . Fla.	29.25 N	81.30 W
70	Crescent L. . . . . Ore.	43.28 N	122.0 W
89	Crescent Sprs. Ky. (Cincinnati In.)	39.3 N	84.35 W
77	Cresco (krĕs'kō) . . . . Ia.	43.23 N	92.7 W
122	Crest (krĕst) . . . . Fr.	44.42 N	5.1 E
78	Crested Butte (krĕst'ĕd bŭt) . Colo.	38.50 N	106.40 W
84	Crestline (krĕst-līn) . . . . Ohio	40.48 N	82.44 W
77	Creston (krĕs'tŭn) . . . . Ia.	41.3 N	94.21 W
82	Crestview (krĕst'vū) . . . . Fla.	30.46 N	86.34 W
79	Crete (krēt) . . . . Neb.	40.37 N	96.57 W
126	Crete (I.) . . . . Grc. (In.)	35.10 N	25.0 E
123	Créteil (krā-tĕ'y') . . . . Fr. (In.)	48.47 N	2.30 E
126	Crete, Sea of . . . . Grc.	35.40 N	24.55 E
125	Creus, C. (krā'ōōs) . . . . Sp.	42.18 N	3.18 E
122	Creuse R. (krûz) . . . . Fr.	46.45 N	0.50 E
123	Creutzwald (kroits'väld) . . . . . . Fr.	49.11 N	6.41 E
125	Crevillente (krā-vê-lyĕn'tâ) . . . Sp.	38.14 N	0.49 W
114	Crewe (krōō) . . . . Gt. Brit.	53.15 N	2.30 W
83	Crewe . . . . Va.	37.10 N	78.8 W
72	Crews (krōōs) . Colo. (Colo. Sprs. In.)	38.43 N	104.43 W
120	Crimmitschau (krĭm'ĭt-shou) . Ger.	50.49 N	12.22 E
78	Cripple Creek . . . . Colo.	38.45 N	105.12 W
85	Crisfield (krĭs-fēld) . . . . Md.	38.0 N	75.51 W
90	Cristoval (krēs-tô-bäl') . C. Z. (In.)	9.21 N	79.54 W
121	Crişul Alb R. (krē'shōōl älb) . Rom.	46.20 N	22.10 E
127	Crnagora (Montenegro) (Prov.) (ts'r-nä-gō'rä) (mōn-tâ-nā'grō) (mōn-tê-nē'grō) . Yugo.	42.45 N	19.25 E
127	Crna R. (ts'r'nä) . . . . Yugo.	41.10 N	21.47 E
126	Crnomelj (ch'r'nō-māl') . . . . Yugo.	45.36 N	15.13 E
126	Croatia (Prov.) (krō-ā'shȧ) . Yugo.	45.15 N	15.40 E
81	Crockett (krŏk'ĕt) . . . . Tex.	31.19 N	95.28 W
117	Croft (krŏft) Gt. Brit. (Liverpool In.)	53.26 N	2.33 W
76	Crofton (krŏf'tŭn) . . . . Neb.	42.43 N	97.29 W
122	Croix (krwä) . . . . Fr.	50.40 N	3.19 E
158	Croker I. (krōk'ēr) . . . . Austl.	11.5 S	132.40 E
114	Cromarty (krŏm'ȧr-tĭ) . . . Gt. Brit.	57.40 N	4.0 W
157	Cromwell (krŏm'wĕl) . . . . . . N. Z.	45.2 S	169.15 E
117	Cronton (krōn'tŭn) Gt. Brit. (Liverpool In.)	53.23 N	2.45 W
160	Cronulla (krō-nŭl'ȧ) Austl. (Sydney In.)	34.4 S	151.9 E
79	Crooked Cr. (krŏŏk'ĕd) . . . . Ill.	40.15 N	90.45 W
78	Crooked Cr. . . . . Kan.	37.15 N	100.20 W
70	Crooked Cr. . . . . Ore.	42.35 N	118.0 W
97	Crooked I. . . . . Ba. Is.	22.45 N	74.12 W
97	Crooked I. Passage . . . . Ba. Is.	22.55 N	74.30 W
52	Crooked L. . . . . Can.	48.25 N	56.15 W
70	Crooked R. . . . . Ore.	44.20 N	121.0 W
96	Crookston (krŏŏks'tŭn) . . . . Minn.	47.45 N	96.36 W
84	Crooksville (krŏŏks'vĭl) . . . . . . Ohio	39.47 N	82.7 W
77	Crosby (krôz'bĭ) . . . . Minn.	46.30 N	93.58 W
76	Crosby . . . . N. D.	48.55 N	103.18 W
81	Crosby . . . . Tex. (In.)	30.0 N	95.3 W
79	Crossett (krôs'ĕt) . . . . Ark.	33.7 N	91.57 W
96	Cross Har. . . . . Ba. Is.	25.55 N	77.18 W
55	Cross L. . . . . Can.	44.55 N	76.50 W
54	Cross L. . . . . Can.	54.40 N	98.15 W
81	Cross L. . . . . La.	32.30 N	93.55 W
53	Cross Sd. . . . . Alsk.	58.20 N	136.30 W
84	Crosswell (krŏz'wĕl) . . . . Mich.	43.15 N	82.36 W
117	Crouch, R. (krouch) Gt. Brit. (London In.)	51.37 N	0.48 E
78	Crow Cr. (krō) . . . . Wyo.-Colo.	40.40 N	104.20 W
76	Crow Creek Indian Res. . . . . S. D.	44.10 N	99.23 W
117	Crowden (krō'dĕn) Gt. Brit. (Liverpool In.)	53.30 N	1.54 W
77	Crow L. . . . . Can.	49.12 N	93.50 W
116	Crowle (kroul) . . . . Gt. Brit.	53.36 N	0.49 W
84	Crown Point (kroun point') . Ind.	41.25 N	81.22 W
85	Crown Point . . . . N. Y.	43.58 N	73.27 W
77	Crow R. . . . . Minn.	45.10 N	93.38 W
160	Crows Nest . . . . Austl. (In.)	27.15 S	152.3 E
77	Crow Wing R. . . . . Minn.	46.40 N	94.51 W
159	Croydon (kroi'dŭn) . . . . Austl.	18.8 S	142.5 E
114	Croydon . . . . Gt. Brit.	51.25 N	0.5 W

Page	Name Pronunciation Region	Lat. °′	Long. °′
73	Croydon Utah (Salt Lake City In.)	41.4 N	111.31 W
5	Crozet Is. (krō-zĕ') . . . . Ind. O.	46.20 S	51.30 E
74	Crucero (krōō-sē'rō) . . . . Calif.	35.3 N	116.11 W
96	Cruces (krōō'sâs) . . . . Cuba	22.19 N	80.18 W
80	Cruillas (krōō-ēl'yäs) . . . . Mex.	24.45 N	98.31 W
117	Cruybeke (kroi'bĕ-kĕ) Bel. (Anvers In.)	51.10 N	4.18 E
102	Cruz Alta (krōōz äl'tä) . . . . . Braz.	28.40 S	53.40 W
96	Cruz, C. (krōōz) . . . . Cuba	19.50 N	77.43 W
96	Cruz Cay (I.) (krōōz) . . . . Cuba	22.12 N	77.48 W
100	Cruzeiro do Sul (krōō-zā'rōō dōō sōōl) . Braz.	7.31 S	72.33 W
80	Crystal City . . . . Tex.	28.40 N	99.50 W
77	Crystal Falls . . . . Mich.	46.7 N	88.20 W
82	Crystal Sprs. . . . . Miss.	31.59 N	90.22 W
121	Csongrad (chôn'gräd) . . . . . . Hung.	46.43 N	20.10 E
121	Csorna (chôr'nä) . . . . Hung.	47.40 N	17.11 E
140	Ctesiphon (Ruins) (tĕs'ĭ-fŏn) . Iraq	33.0 N	44.45 E
93	Cuajimalpa (kwä-hê-mäl'pä) Mex. (In.)	19.21 N	99.18 W
94	Cuajiniquilapa (kwä'hê-nê-kê-lä'-pä) . Guat.	14.16 N	90.19 W
134	Cuamato (Dom Luiz) (kwä-mä'tō) (dōN lōō-ēzh') . Ang.	17.5 S	15.10 E
134	Cuando R. (kwän'dō) . Ang.-N. Rh.	16.12 S	22.0 E
134	Cuango (kwäŋ'gō) . . . . Ang.	6.17 S	16.58 E
134	Cuanza (kwän'zä) . . . . Ang.	11.52 S	18.40 E
102	Cuareim, R. (kwä-rāN') . Braz.-Ur.	30.30 S	56.30 W
102	Cuarto, R. (kwär'tō) . . . . Arg.	33.30 S	63.0 W
80	Cuatro Ciénegas (kwä'trō syā'nā-gäs) . Mex.	26.58 N	102.4 W
93	Cuauhtepec (kwä-ōō-tĕ-pĕk') Mex. (In.)	19.33 N	99.8 W
92	Cuautepec . . . . Mex.	16.44 N	99.3 W
92	Cuautepec . . . . Mex.	19.59 N	98.19 W
93	Cuautitlan, R. (kwä-ōō-têt-län') Mex. (In.)	19.38 N	99.15 W
92	Cuautla (kwä-ōō'tlä) . . . . Mex.	18.47 N	98.58 W
93	Cuautlalpan (kwä-ōō-tläl-pän') Mex. (In.)	19.26 N	98.54 W
96	Cuba (kū'bȧ) . . . . W. I.	22.0 N	79.0 W
124	Cuba (kōō'bȧ) . . . . Port.	38.10 N	7.54 W
134	Cubango (kōō-bäŋ'gō) . . . . Ang.	14.35 S	16.33 E
72	Cub Mt. (kŭb) . Colo. (Denver In.)	39.34 N	105.28 W
73	Cucamonga (kōō-kȧ-mŏŋ'gȧ) Calif. (Los Angeles In.)	34.6 N	117.34 W
134	Cuchi (kōō'chē) . . . . Ang.	14.47 S	16.55 E
97	Cuchillas de Toar (Mts.) (kōō-chē'lyäs dā twär') . Cuba	20.30 N	75.0 W
80	Cuchillo Parado (kōō-chē'lyô pä-rä'dō) . Mex.	29.27 N	104.59 W
94	Cuchumatanes, Sierra de (Mts.) kōō-chōō-mä-tä'nâs) . Guat.	15.40 N	91.20 W
100	Cúcuta (kōō'kōō-tä) . . . . Col.	7.58 N	72.29 W
77	Cudahy (kŭd'ȧ-hī) . . . . Wis.	42.57 N	87.52 W
141	Cuddalore (kŭd-ȧ-lōr') . . . . . . India	11.35 N	79.45 E
141	Cuddapah (kŭd'ȧ-pä) . . . . India	14.30 N	78.45 E
158	Cue (kū) . . . . Austl.	27.28 S	118.2 E
124	Cuellar (kwā-lyär') . . . . Sp.	41.25 N	4.18 W
100	Cuenca (kwĕn'kä) . . . . Ec.	2.58 S	79.20 W
151	Cuenca . . . . Phil. (Manila In.)	13.56 N	121.3 E
124	Cuenca . . . . Sp.	40.5 N	2.8 W
80	Cuencamé (kwĕn-kä-mā') . . . Mex.	24.52 N	103.40 W
92	Cuerámaro (kwā-rä'mä-rô) . . Mex.	20.35 N	101.41 W
92	Cuernavaca (kwĕr-nä-vä'kä) . Mex.	18.55 N	99.14 W
153	Cuernos of Negros (Mt.) (kwĕr'-nōs) . Phil.	9.15 N	123.12 E
81	Cuero (kwā'rō) . . . . Tex.	29.5 N	97.18 W
92	Cuetzalá (kwĕt-zä-lä') . . . . . . Mex.	17.58 N	99.54 W
93	Cuetzalán del Progreso (kwĕt-zä-län dĕl prō-grā'sō) . Mex.	20.1 N	97.32 W
124	Cuevas de Vera (kwā'väs dā vā'rä) Sp.	37.18 N	1.52 W
125	Cuevas de Vinromá (vēn-rō-mä') Sp.	40.17 N	0.2 E
133	Cufra, Oases of (kōō'frä) . . . Libya	25.0 N	22.0 E
126	Cuglieri (kōō-lyâ'rē) . . . . Sard.	40.13 N	8.38 E
101	Cuiabá (kōō-yä-bä') . . . . Braz.	15.30 S	56.10 W
93	Cuicatlán (kwē-kä-tlän') . . . . . Mex.	17.48 N	96.57 W
114	Cuillan Sd. (kool'ăn) . . . . Gt. Brit.	57.5 N	6.0 W
134	Cuito R. (kōō-ē'tō) . . . . Ang.	15.30 S	19.17 E
92	Cuitzeo (kwēt'zä-ō) . . . . Mex.	19.57 N	101.9 W
92	Cuitzeo, L. . . . . Mex.	19.55 N	101.0 W
153	Culasi (kōō-lä'sê) . . . . Phil.	11.25 N	122.4 E
90	Culebra (kōō-lā'brä) . . . C. Z. (In.)	9.2 N	79.40 W
94	Culebra, G. of . . . . C. R.	10.45 N	85.50 W
91	Culebra I. . . . . P. R. (In.)	18.19 N	65.17 W
159	Culgoa R. (kŭl-gō'ȧ) . . . . Austl.	29.5 S	147.0 E
93	Culhuacán (kōōl-wä-kän') Mex. (In.)	19.20 N	99.7 W
153	Culion (kōō-lê-ōn') . . . . Phil.	11.52 N	120.0 E
153	Culion I. . . . . Phil.	11.50 N	120.0 E
151	Culis (kōō'lês) . . Phil. (Manila In.)	14.50 N	120.25 E
124	Cúllar (kōō'lyär) . . . . Sp.	37.36 N	2.35 W
125	Cullera (kōō-lyā'rä) . . . . Sp.	39.11 N	0.15 W
82	Cullman (kŭl'mȧn) . . . . Ala.	34.10 N	86.50 W
85	Culpeper (kŭl'pĕp-ēr) . . . . Va.	38.30 N	7.58 W
100	Culpepper I. . . . . Ec.	1.45 N	92.0 W
56	Culross (kŭl'rôs) Can. (Winnipeg In.)	49.43 N	97.52 W
72	Cultus L. (kŭl'tŭs) Can. (Vancouver In.)	49.3 N	121.59 W
73	Culver (kŭl'vēr) Calif. (Los Angeles In.)	34.1 N	118.25 W
84	Culver . . . . Ind.	41.16 N	86.27 W
100	Cumana (kōō-mä-nä') . . . . Ven.	10.28 N	64.15 W
100	Cumarebo (kōō-mä'rē-bō) . . . . Ven.	11.28 N	69.20 W
85	Cumberland (kŭm'bēr-lȧnd) . . Md.	39.40 N	78.44 W
77	Cumberland . . . . Wis.	45.31 N	92.1 W
159	Cumberland Is. . . . . Austl.	20.30 S	149.0 E

ng-sing; ŋ-baŋk; N-nasalized n; nŏd; cŏmmit; ōld; ôbey; ôrder; fōōd; fŏŏt; ou-out; s-soft; sh-dish; th-thin; pūre; ûnite; ûrn; stŭd; circŭs; ü-as "y" in study; '-indeterminate vowel.

Cumberland PRONOUNCING INDEX Dead Sea

Page	Name Pronunciation Region	Lat. °′	Long. °′
82	Cumberland Plat..........Tenn.	35.55 N	85.0 W
82	Cumberland R.........Ky.-Tenn.	36.20 N	86.10 W
55	Cumberland Sd............Can.	65.30 N	66.0 W
93	Cunduacán (kōōn-dōō-ä-kän') Mex.	18.4 N	93.10 W
126	Cuneo (kōō'nā-ō).............It.	44.23 N	7.32 E
159	Cunnamulla (kŭn-à-mŭl-à). Austl.	28.0 S	145.58 E
92	Cuquio (kōō-kē'ō)..........Mex.	21.4 N	103.9 W
100	Curaçao (kōō-rä-sä'ō).......W. I.	12.2 N	69.0 W
99	Curaumilla, Pt. (kōō-rou-mē'lyä) Chl. (Valparaiso In.)	33.5 S	71.46 W
102	Curicó (kōō-rē-kō')..........Chl.	34.57 S	71.20 W
102	Curitiba (kōō-rē-tē'bà).......Braz.	25.20 S	49.15 W
96	Curly Cut Cays (Is.).......Ba. Is.	23.40 N	77.40 W
96	Current I................Ba. Is.	25.22 N	77.50 W
79	Current R.............Ark.-Mo.	37.0 N	91.2 W
83	Currituck Sd. (kûr'ĭ-tŭk)...N. C.	36.24 N	75.54 W
127	Curtea de Argeş (kōōr'tē-ä dĕ är'zhĕsh). Rom.	45.8 N	24.39 E
76	Curtis (kûr'tĭs).............Neb.	40.37 N	100.30 W
75	Curtis Cr.................Utah	38.45 N	111.5 W
159	Curtis I...................Austl.	23.45 S	151.28 E
101	Curuca (kōō-rōō'kä)...Braz. (In.)	0.39 S	47.55 W
127	Čurug (chōō'rōōg).........Yugo.	45.27 N	20.4 E
100	Curupira, Serra (Mts.) (sĕr'rà kōō-rōō-pē'rà). Braz.-Ven.	1.0 N	65.0 W
101	Cururupú (kōō-rōō-rōō-pōō'). Braz.	1.45 S	44.48 W
102	Curuzú Cuatiá (kōō-rōō-zōō' kwä-tē-ä'). Arg.	29.50 S	58.0 W
101	Curvêlo (kōōr-vĕl'ōō).......Braz.	18.45 S	44.29 W
79	Cushing (kŭsh'ĭng).........Okla.	35.58 N	96.47 W
122	Cusset (kü-sĕ')..............Fr.	46.9 N	3.30 E
76	Custer (kŭs'tēr).............S. D.	43.46 N	103.36 W
72	Custer....Wash. (Vancouver In.)	48.55 N	122.38 W
71	Cut Bank................Mont.	48.38 N	112.19 W
140	Cutch (State) (kŭch).........India	23.30 N	70.0 E
141	Cutch, Great Rann of (rŭn)..India	24.0 N	70.0 E
141	Cutch, G. of...............India	22.30 N	69.0 E
141	Cutch, Little Rann of......India	23.30 N	72.00 E
82	Cuthbert (kŭth'bērt).........Ga.	31.47 N	84.48 W
141	Cuttack (kŭ-tăk')...........India	20.25 N	85.47 E
92	Cutzamalá (kōō-tzä-mä-lä'). Mex.	18.26 N	100.31 W
92	Cutzamalá, R.............Mex.	19.0 N	100.20 W
156	Cuvier I. (kü-vyā')..........N. Z.	36.27 S	175.50 E
134	Cuvo R. (kōō'vō)............Ang.	11.15 S	14.45 E
120	Cuxhaven (kōōks'hä-fĕn).......Ger.	53.53 N	8.42 E
84	Cuyahoga Falls (kī-à-hō'gà). Ohio	41.8 N	81.27 W
89	Cuyahoga R..Ohio (Cleveland In.)	41.26 N	81.40 W
74	Cuyama R. (kōō-yä'mà)....Calif.	35.0 N	120.10 W
153	Cuyo (kōō'yō)..............Phil.	10.50 N	121.1 E
153	Cuyo East Pass............Phil.	11.0 N	121.30 E
153	Cuyo I....................Phil.	10.50 N	121.3 E
153	Cuyo Is...................Phil.	11.5 N	121.0 E
94	Cuyotenango (kōō-yō-tĕ-näŋ'gō) Guat.	14.30 N	91.36 W
153	Cuyo West Pass...........Phil.	11.0 N	120.30 E
92	Cuyutlán (kōō-yōō-tlän')....Mex.	18.55 N	104.3 W
100	Cuzco (kōōz'kō).............Peru	13.30 S	72.0 W
127	Cyclades (Is.) (sĭk'là-dēz)....Grc.	37.20 N	24.55 E
84	Cynthiana (sĭn-thĭ-ăn'à)......Ky.	38.22 N	84.18 W
81	Cypress Cr. (sī'prĕs)........Tex.	32.50 N	94.43 W
72	Cypress I..Wash. (Vancouver In.)	48.34 N	122.43 W
113	Cyprus (I.) (sī'prŭs) Mediterranean Sea	35.0 N	33.30 E
	Cyrenaica, see Cirenaica, Libya		
133	Cyrene (Ruins) (sī-rē'nē)...Libya	32.55 N	21.50 E
120	Czechoslovakia (chĕκ'ō-slō-vä'kĭ-à). Eur.	49.5 N	18.35 E
121	Czersk (chĕrsk)..............Pol.	53.47 N	17.57 E
121	Czestochowa (chĕN-stō-κô'và). Pol.	50.49 N	19.8 E
153	Daanbantayan (dä-än'bän-tä-yän') Phil.	11.14 N	124.0 E
120	Dąb (dônb)................Pol.	53.24 N	14.41 E
132	Dabakala (dä-bà-kä'lä). Fr. W. Afr.	8.21 N	4.30 W
51	Dabob (dā'bŏb) Wash. (Seattle In.)	47.51 N	122.49 W
51	Dabob B.....Wash. (Seattle In.)	47.43 N	122.51 W
121	Dąbrowa (dŏN-brō'và).......Pol.	50.18 N	19.15 E
121	Dąbrowa...................Pol.	53.37 N	23.20 E
141	Dacca (dä'kä) (dăk'à).......Pak.	23.45 N	90.25 E
120	Dachau (dä'κou).............Ger.	48.17 N	11.25 E
72	Dacono (dà-kō'nō) Colo. (Denver In.)	40.5 N	104.57 W
56	Dacotah (dà-kō'tà) Can. (Winnipeg In.)	49.53 N	97.38 W
83	Dade City (dād).......Fla. (In.)	28.22 N	82.12 W
82	Dadeville (dād'vĭl)...........Ala.	32.49 N	85.47 W
152	Daet (dä'ĕt)................Phil.	14.7 N	122.59 E
132	Dagama (dä-gä'mä)...Fr. W. Afr.	16.30 N	15.28 W
119	Dagda (dăg'dà)..........Sov. Un.	56.5 N	27.32 E
117	Dagenham (dăg'ĕn-ăm) Gt. Brit. (London In.)	51.32 N	0.10 E
74	Daggett (dăg'ĕt)...........Calif.	34.51 N	116.52 W
111	Daghestan (Soviet Republic) (dä-gĕs-tän'). Sov. Un.	44.0 N	47.0 E
119	Dago (Hiiumaa) (I.) (dägh'ū) (hē'ōō-mä). Sov. Un.	58.50 N	22.40 E
152	Dagupan (dä-gōō'pän).......Phil.	16.2 N	120.20 E
133	Dahlak Is. (dä-läk')..........Erit.	15.45 N	40.15 E
140	Dahna (Great Sandy Desert) (dä'nä). Asia	20.0 N	52.0 E
132	Dahomey (Colony) (dà-hō'mā) (dä-hô-mā'). Fr. W. Afr.	0.0 N	2.0 E
124	Daimiel (dī-myĕl')...........Sp.	39.4 N	3.36 W
146	Dairen (dī'rĕn')............Chn.	38.55 N	121.33 E
149	Daisen (Mt.) (dī'sĕn').......Jap.	35.21 N	133.2 E
97	Dajabon (dä-hä-bōn').......Hai.	19.34 N	71.42 W
158	Dajarra (dà-jăr'à)..........Austl.	21.40 S	139.28 E
132	Dakar (dà-kär')......Fr. W. Afr.	14.40 N	17.28 W
141	Dakka (dăk'ä). Afg. (Peshawar In.)	34.13 N	71.2 E
153	Dalaguete (dä-lä-gā'tä)......Phil.	9.45 N	123.32 E
143	Dalai Nor (L.) (dä-lī' nōr)....Chn.	49.0 N	117.40 E
153	Dalanganem Is. (dä-läŋ-gä'nĕm) Phil.	10.40 N	120.15 E
159	Dalby (dôl'bē)............Austl.	27.8 S	151.10 E
118	Dale (dä'lĕ)................Nor.	60.34 N	5.51 E
118	Dalen (dä'lĕn)..............Nor.	59.28 N	8.2 E
57	Dalesville (dālz'vĭl) Can. (Montreal In.)	45.43 N	74.24 W
78	Dalhart (dăl'härt)..........Tex.	36.4 N	102.32 W
86	Dalhousie (dăl-hōō'zē).......Can.	48.3 N	66.23 W
157	Dalhousie.................N. Z.	46.2 S	169.32 E
124	Dalías (dä-lē'äs).............Sp.	36.50 N	2.51 W
73	Dallas (dăl'ăs)..Ga. (Atlanta In.)	33.55 N	84.51 W
70	Dallas....................Ore.	44.55 N	123.20 W
76	Dallas....................S. D.	43.14 N	99.33 W
81	Dallas....................Tex.	32.47 N	96.48 W
81	Dallas, L..................Tex.	33.0 N	97.7 W
70	Dalles, The (dălz)..........Ore.	45.35 N	121.11 W
117	Dallgow (dal'go). Ger. (Berlin In.)	52.32 N	13.5 E
133	Dallol Salt Pan (dä-lôl').....Eth.	13.45 N	40.30 E
126	Dalmatia (Prov.) (dăl-mā'shĭ-à) Yugo.	43.30 N	16.40 E
159	Dalrymple, Mt. (dăl'rĭm-p'l). Austl.	21.15 S	148.40 E
160	Dalrymple, Port..Austl. (Tas. In.)	41.4 S	146.46 E
82	Dalton (dôl'tŭn)..............Ga.	34.46 N	84.59 W
152	Dalupiri I. (dä-lōō-pē'rē)....Phil.	19.4 N	121.13 E
152	Dalupiri I..................Phil.	12.25 N	124.15 E
74	Daly City (dā'lē)..........Calif.	37.40 N	122.30 W
158	Daly R...................Austl.	14.15 S	131.30 E
158	Daly Waters..............Austl.	16.19 S	133.28 E
101	Dam (däm)................Sur.	4.45 N	55.0 W
133	Damanhûr (dä-män-hōōr')....Eg.	30.57 N	30.58 E
141	Damão (dä-mouN').........India	20.20 N	72.45 E
134	Damaraland (Dist.) (dă'mà-rà-lănd). S. W. Afr.	22.15 S	17.30 E
151	Damar I. (dä'mär)........Indon.	7.5 S	128.45 E
96	Damas Cays (Is.) (dä'mäs)..W. I.	23.52 N	79.48 W
140	Damas (Damascus) (dà-mä') (dà-măs'kŭs). Syr.	33.35 N	36.28 E
134	Damba (däm'bä)............Ang.	6.48 S	15.22 E
127	Dâmbovița R. (dûm'bô-vē'tsà) Rom.	44.35 N	25.40 E
97	Dame Marie, C. (däm mà-rē'). Hai.	18.36 N	74.26 W
140	Damghan (däm-gän')........Iran	35.50 N	54.29 E
133	Damietta (Dumiât) (dăm-ĭ-ĕt'à) (dōōm-yät'). Eg.	31.27 N	31.48 E
123	Dammartin-en-Goële (däN-mär-tăN-äN-gō-ĕl'). Fr. (In.)	49.3 N	2.42 E
153	Dammi I. (däm'mē).........Phil.	5.48 N	120.26 E
158	Dampier Arch. (dăm'pēr)...Austl.	20.40 S	116.45 E
151	Dampier Str......Neth. N. Gui.	0.30 S	131.30 E
123	Dampierre (däN-pyâr')...Fr. (In.)	48.43 N	1.58 E
74	Dana Mt. (dā'nà)...........Calif.	37.53 N	119.12 W
153	Danao (dä-nä'ō)............Phil.	10.30 N	124.10 E
85	Danbury (dăn'bēr-ĭ).......Conn.	41.24 N	73.27 W
81	Danbury...............Tex. (In.)	29.13 N	95.21 W
151	Dancolao, R. (dän-kō-lä'ō) Phil. (Manila In.)	14.0 N	120.43 E
160	Dandenong (dăn'dē-nông)..Austl.	37.59 S	145.12 E
160	Dandenong Cr. Austl. (Melbourne In.)	38.0 S	145.12 E
148	Dandyo Is. (dän'dyō)........Jap.	32.0 N	128.20 E
116	Dane, R. (dān).........Gt. Brit.	53.11 N	2.15 W
86	Danforth (dăn'fŭrth).........Me.	45.37 N	67.53 W
159	Danger, Pt.................Austl.	28.10 S	153.35 E
83	Dania (dā'nĭ-à).........Fla. (In.)	26.2 N	8.8 W
128	Danilov (dä'nē-lôf)......Sov. Un.	58.10 N	40.9 E
127	Danilovgrad (dä'nē-lôf'gräd) Yugo.	42.32 N	19.6 E
128	Dankov (däŋ'kôf).......Sov. Un.	53.16 N	39.7 E
94	Danli (dän'lē)..............Hond.	13.57 N	86.29 W
85	Dannemora (dăn-ē-mō'rà)..N. Y.	44.44 N	43.47 W
156	Dannevirke (dän'nĕ-vĭrk-ĕ)..N. Z.	40.15 S	176.3 E
83	Dan R. (dăn)..........N. C.-Va.	36.30 N	79.40 W
153	Dansalan (dän-sä'län).......Phil.	8.1 N	124.19 E
85	Dansville (dănz'vĭl).........N. Y.	42.34 N	77.40 W
117	Danube Canal (dăn'ūb) Aus. (Wien In.)	48.13 N	16.22 E
127	Danube R..................Eur.	45.0 N	27.50 E
87	Danvers (dăn'vērz)....Mass. (In.)	42.34 N	70.57 W
51	Danville (dăn'vĭl) Calif. (San Francisco In.)	37.49 N	121.59 W
84	Danville....................Ill.	40.9 N	87.37 W
84	Danville...................Ind.	39.45 N	86.30 W
84	Danville...................Ky.	37.48 N	84.48 W
85	Danville...................Pa.	40.57 N	76.37 W
83	Danville...................Va.	36.36 N	79.23 W
121	Danzig (Gdańsk) (dän'tsĭk) (gdänsk). Pol.	54.10 N	18.50 E
121	Danzig, G. of...............Pol.	54.33 N	19.14 E
153	Dao (dä'ō).................Phil.	10.30 N	121.57 E
153	Dao.......................Phil.	11.23 N	122.41 E
153	Dapa (dä-pä')..............Phil.	9.46 N	126.3 E
153	Dapiak, Mt. (däp-yäk')......Phil.	8.5 N	123.27 E
153	Dapitan (dä-pē'tän).........Phil.	8.38 N	123.27 E
121	Dărăbani (dă-rā-băn'ĭ).....Rom.	48.13 N	26.39 E
127	Dara-dere (dä'rà-dĕr'ĕ)......Bul.	41.23 N	25.20 E
153	Daram I. (dä-räm')..........Phil.	11.35 N	124.48 E
131	Darâu (dà-rä'ōō)........Eg. (In.)	24.24 N	32.59 E
141	Darbhanga (dŭr-bŭŋ'gä).....India	26.10 N	85.59 E
88	Darby (där'bĭ) Pa. (Philadelphia In.)	39.55 N	75.16 W
88	Darby C....Pa. (Philadelphia In.)	39.55 N	75.16 W
97	Darby I.................Ba. Is.	23.50 N	76.15 W
72	D'Arcy I. (där'sē) Can. (Vancouver In.)	48.34 N	123.17 W
113	Dardanelles (Str.) (där-dà-nĕlz'). Tur.	40.15 N	26.40 E
160	Darebin Cr. (dă'rē-bĭn) Austl. (Melbourne In.)	37.42 S	145.20 E
117	Darenth (dăr'ĕnt) Gt. Brit. (London In.)	51.25 N	0.15 E
117	Daresbury (dârz'bēr-ĭ) Gt. Brit. (Liverpool In.)	53.20 N	2.38 W
135	Dar es Salaam (där ĕs sà-läm'). Tan.	6.47 S	39.15 E
133	Darfur (Reg.) (där-fōōr'). A. E. Sud.	13.30 N	24.30 E
141	Dargai (dŭr-gä'ê)............Pak.	34.44 N	71.28 E
156	Dargaville (där'gà-vĭl)......N. Z.	35.59 S	173.54 E
100	Darien, G. of (dā-rĭ-ĕn').....Col.	9.0 N	77.0 W
95	Darien, Serrania del (Mts.) (sĕr-ä-nē'ä dĕl dä-rê-ĕn'). Pan.-Col.	8.40 N	77.30 W
141	Darjeeling (dŭr-jē'lĭng).....India	26.58 N	88.29 E
116	Darlaston (där'làs-tŭn)..Gt. Brit.	52.34 N	2.2 W
159	Darling Downs (där'lĭng) (Reg.) Austl.	27.45 S	150.0 E
159	Darling R.................Austl.	31.30 S	144.0 E
158	Darling Scarp.............Austl.	31.30 S	116.0 E
114	Darlington.............Gt. Brit.	54.30 N	1.40 W
83	Darlington.................S. C.	34.17 N	79.52 W
77	Darlington.................Wis.	42.45 N	90.30 W
72	Darlow (där'lō). Colo. (Denver In.)	39.59 N	104.57 W
120	Darlowo (där-lô'vô).........Pol.	54.26 N	16.23 E
120	Darmstadt (därm'shtät).....Ger.	49.53 N	8.39 E
122	Darnétal (där-nā-täl')........Fr.	49.25 N	1.10 E
124	Daroca (dä-rō'kä)............Sp.	41.8 N	1.25 W
117	Dartford (därt'fērd) Gt. Brit. (London In.)	51.27 N	0.13 E
114	Dartmoor (därt'mōōr)...Gt. Brit.	50.35 N	4.0 W
54	Dartmouth (därt'mŭth). Can. (In.)	44.40 N	63.34 W
114	Dartmouth..............Gt. Brit.	50.20 N	3.30 W
151	Daru (dä'rōō).........Pap. Ter.	9.10 S	143.10 E
126	Daruvar (dä'rōō-vär)......Yugo.	45.35 N	17.17 E
150	Darvel B. (där'vĕl).......N. Bor.	4.45 N	118.30 E
116	Darwen (där'wĕn).......Gt. Brit.	53.41 N	2.28 W
116	Darwen, R.............Gt. Brit.	53.46 N	2.36 W
158	Darwin (där'wĭn)...........Austl.	12.20 S	130.59 E
99	Darwin, Cordillera (Mts.) Chl. (Magallanes In.)	54.40 S	69.40 W
99	Darwin, Mt. Chl. (Magallanes In.)	54.43 S	69.22 W
134	Darwin, Mt..............S. Rh.	16.47 S	31.35 E
140	Darya-yi Namak (Des.) (där'yä-yĭ nà-màk'). Iran	34.45 N	51.45 E
140	Dasht-i-Kavir (Des.) (dŭsht-ê-kà-vēr'). Iran	34.30 N	55.0 E
140	Dasht-i-Lut (Des.) (dŭsht-ê-lōōt'). Iran	31.30 N	58.30 E
140	Dasht R. (dŭsht)............Pak.	26.0 N	63.30 E
151	Dasmarinas (däs-mä-rē'näs) Phil. (Manila In.)	14.20 N	120.55 E
152	Dasol B. (dä-sōl')..........Phil.	15.53 N	119.50 E
152	Data, Mt. (dä-tä')..........Phil.	16.50 N	120.53 E
150	Datu, C. (dä-tōō')...........Sar.	2.5 N	109.36 E
133	Daua R. (dä'wä).....Eth.-Kenya	4.45 N	40.0 E
125	Dauera (dä-ü-ĕ'rà)..........Alg.	36.41 N	2.58 E
89	Daufuskie I. (dô-fōō'skê) S. C. (Savannah In.)	32.7 N	80.52 W
119	Daugava R. (dä'vōō-gä-vä) Sov. Un.	56.38 N	24.45 E
119	Daugavpils (dä'ōō-gäv-pêls) Sov. Un.	55.53 N	26.32 E
153	Dauin (dä'wēn).............Phil.	9.11 N	123.16 E
153	Dauis (dä'wēs)..............Phil.	9.37 N	123.52 E
54	Dauphin (dô'fĭn).............Can.	51.5 N	100.1 W
54	Dauphin, L.................Can.	51.15 N	99.45 W
153	Davao (dä'vä-ō)............Phil.	7.4 N	125.37 E
153	Davao G...................Phil.	6.35 N	125.45 E
77	Davenport (dăv'ĕn-pōrt)......Ia.	41.31 N	90.33 W
70	Davenport.................Wash.	47.38 N	118.9 W
116	Daventry (dăv'ĕn-trĭ)...Gt. Brit.	52.15 N	1.9 W
160	Davey R. (dā-vē). Austl. (Tas. In.)	43.0 S	145.58 E
160	Davey, Port.......Austl. (Tas. In.)	43.20 S	145.55 E
95	David (dà-vēdh')............Pan.	8.27 N	82.27 W
76	David City (dā'vĭd)..........Neb.	41.15 N	97.6 W
129	Davidgorodok (dà-vĕt'gô-rō'dôk) Sov. Un.	52.2 N	27.14 E
160	Davidson Pk. (dā'vĭd-sŭn) Austl. (Sydney In.)	33.45 S	151.12 E
79	Davis (dā'vĭs)..............Okla.	34.33 N	97.8 W
85	Davis.....................W. Va.	39.10 N	79.28 W
73	Davis Cr...Ala. (Birmingham In.)	33.23 N	87.18 W
70	Davis L...................Ore.	43.38 N	121.51 W
80	Davis Mts.................Tex.	30.40 N	104.20 W
47	Davis Sea...............Ind. O.	66.0 S	92.0 E
48	Davis Str..................Can.	66.0 N	60.0 W
120	Davos (dä'vōs)............Switz.	46.48 N	9.59 E
148	Davunda (dà-vōōn'dà)...Sov. Un.	48.55 N	138.55 E
116	Dawley (dô'lĭ).........Gt. Brit.	52.38 N	2.28 W
150	Dawna Ra. (dô'nà).....Bur.-Siam	17.0 N	98.15 E
54	Dawson (dô'sŭn)............Can.	64.5 N	139.31 W
82	Dawson.....................Ga.	31.46 N	84.28 W
76	Dawson....................Minn.	44.56 N	96.2 W
78	Dawson....................N. M.	36.41 N	104.47 W
54	Dawson Creek..............Can.	55.54 N	120.16 W
99	Dawson I...Chl. (Magallanes In.)	54.0 S	70.40 W
159	Dawson R..................Austl.	25.0 S	150.0 E
82	Dawson Sprs................Ky.	37.10 N	87.41 W
122	Dax (dàks)...................Fr.	43.42 N	1.2 W
150	Dayak R., Gt. (dī'yăk)....Indon.	2.15 S	113.58 E
150	Dayak R., Little...........Indon.	2.0 S	114.15 E
89	Dayton (dā'tŭn) Ky. (Cincinnati In.)	39.7 N	84.28 W
78	Dayton....................N. M.	32.44 N	104.22 W
84	Dayton....................Ohio	39.45 N	84.12 W
82	Dayton....................Tenn.	35.30 N	85.1 W
81	Dayton.....................Tex.	30.3 N	94.54 W
70	Dayton....................Wash.	46.17 N	117.59 W
83	Daytona Beach (dā-tō'nà)...Fla.	29.12 N	81.12 W
85	Dayville (dā'vĭl)...........Conn.	41.49 N	71.53 W
134	De Aar (dē-är').........U. S. Afr.	30.30 S	34.1 E
76	Dead L....................Minn.	46.30 N	95.45 W
137	Dead Sea..........Pal.-Jor. (In.)	31.25 N	35.25 E

ăt; finăl; rāte; senāte; ärm; ȧsk; sofȧ; fâre; ch-choose; dh-as th in other; bē; ėvent; bĕt; recĕnt; cratēr; g-go; gh-gutteral g; bĭt; ĭ-short neutral; rīde; κ-gutteral k as ch in German ich;

Deadwood PRONOUNCING INDEX **Disko**

Page	Name	Pronunciation	Region	Lat. °′	Long. °′
76	Deadwood		S. D.	44.23 N	103.42 W
85	Deal Island		Md.	38.10 N	75.57 W
84	Dearborn	(dēr′bŭrn)	Mich.	42.20 N	83.13 W
54	Dease Str.	(dēz)	Can.	68.40 N	108.30 W
74	Death Valley		Calif.	36.25 N	116.55 W
74	Death Valley Jc		Calif.	36.19 N	116.25 W
74	Death Valley Natl. Mon		Calif.	36.0 N	117.0 W
122	Deauville	(dō-vēl′)	Fr.	49.20 N	0.1 E
129	Debaltsevo	(dyĕb′ȧl-tsyĕ′vô)	Sov. Un.	48.16 N	38.25 E
112	Debdou	(dĕb-do͞o′)	Mor.	34.0 N	2.58 W
121	Dęblin	(dăɴ′blĭn)	Pol.	51.35 N	21.50 E
120	Dębno	(dăɴ′bnô)	Pol.	52.44 N	14.43 E
132	Debo Swamp	(dā′bō)	Fr. W. Afr.	15.30 N	3.30 W
127	Debra (Dibra)	(dā′brä)	Yugo.	41.31 N	20.32 E
133	Debra Marcos	(dĕ′brȧ mär′kôs)	Eth.	10.17 N	37.41 E
133	Debra Tabor	(dĕ′brȧ tä′bôr)	Eth.	11.58 N	38.6 E
121	Debreçen	(dĕ′brĕ-tsĕn)	Hung.	47.32 N	21.38 E
82	Decatur	(dē-kā′tŭr)	Ala.	34.35 N	87.0 W
82	Decatur		Ga.	33.47 N	84.17 W
79	Decatur		Ill.	39.51 N	88.58 W
84	Decatur		Ind.	40.47 N	84.57 W
84	Decatur		Mich.	42.11 N	85.58 W
79	Decatur		Tex.	33.14 N	97.34 W
72	Decatur I.		Wash. (Vancouver In.)	48.30 N	122.48 W
122	Decazeville	(dē-käz′vēl′)	Fr.	44.32 N	2.17 E
141	Deccan, The (Plat.)	(dĕk′ăn)	India	15.45 N	77.0 E
120	Děčín	(dyĕ′chēn)	Czech.	50.47 N	14.13 E
122	Decize	(dē-sēz′)	Fr.	46.55 N	3.30 E
77	Decorah	(dē-kō′rȧ)	Ia.	43.18 N	91.48 W
127	Dedeagats (Alexandroupolis)	(dĕ-dĕ-ä-gäts′) (ä-lĕk-zän-dro͞o′-pō-lĭs)	Grc.	40.51 N	25.51 E
86	Dedham	(dĕd′ăm)	Mass.	42.15 N	71.11 W
132	Dédougou	(dā-do͞o-go͞o′)	Fr. W. Afr.	12.30 N	3.25 W
73	Deep Cr.		Calif. (Los Angeles In.)	34.21 N	117.10 W
83	Deep R		N. C.	35.30 N	79.25 W
51	Deep R		Wash. (Portland In.)	46.20 N	123.41 W
79	Deepwater		Mo.	38.15 N	93.46 W
158	Deep Well		Austl.	24.10 S	134.10 E
160	Dee R.	(dē)	Austl. (Tas. In.)	42.20 S	146.39 E
114	Dee, R		Gt. Brit.	52.55 N	3.10 W
86	Deer I.	(dēr)	Me.	44.15 N	68.40 W
95	Deer I		Nic.	11.56 N	83.40 W
51	Deer I		Ore. (Portland In.)	45.56 N	122.51 W
87	Deer L		Can.	49.8 N	57.25 W
71	Deer Lodge		Mont.	46.23 N	112.44 W
160	Deer Park		Austl. (Melbourne In.)	37.47 S	114.47 E
89	Deer Park		Ohio (Cincinnati In.)	39.12 N	84.24 W
70	Deer Park		Wash.	47.57 N	117.29 W
89	Deer Range		La. (New Orleans In.)	29.36 N	89.54 W
77	Deer R		Minn.	47.20 N	93.48 W
84	Defiance	(dē-fī′ăns)	Ohio	41.17 N	84.21 W
82	De Funiak Springs	(dē fū′nĭ-ăk)	Fla.	30.42 N	86.7 W
120	Deggendorf	(dĕ′ghĕn-dôrf)	Ger.	48.51 N	12.58 E
92	Degollado	(dā-gô-lyä′dō)	Mex.	20.27 N	102.9 W
158	De Grey R.	(dē grā′)	Austl.	21.0 S	120.58 E
141	Dehra	(dā′rŭ)	India	30.15 N	78.5 E
140	Deir-ez-zor	(dâ-ēr′-ĕz-zôr′)	Syr.	35.25 N	40.14 E
121	Dej	(dāzh)	Rom.	47.8 N	23.53 E
77	De Kalb	(dē kălb′)	Ill.	41.55 N	88.43 W
134	Delagoa B.	(dĕl-ȧ-gō′ȧ)	Moz.	26.0 S	32.45 E
78	Delagua	(dĕl-ä′gwä)	Colo.	37.19 N	104.40 W
83	De Land	(dē lănd′)	Fla.	29.2 N	81.18 W
74	Delano	(dĕl′ȧ-nō)	Calif.	35.46 N	119.17 W
75	Delano Mt		Utah	38.28 N	112.28 W
121	Delatin	(dĕ-lä′tĭn)	Sov. Un.	48.31 N	24.38 E
77	Delavan	(dĕl′ȧ-văn)	Wis.	42.39 N	88.35 W
84	Delaware	(dĕl′ȧ-wâr)	Ohio	40.17 N	83.3 W
85	Delaware (State)		U. S.	39.0 N	75.20 W
85	Delaware B		Del.-N. J.	39.0 N	75.10 W
79	Delaware R		Kan.	39.30 N	95.34 W
85	Delaware R		U. S.	41.30 N	75.0 W
120	Delémont	(dē-lā-môɴ′)	Switz.	47.21 N	7.20 E
80	De Leon	(dē lē-ŏn′)	Tex.	32.7 N	98.32 W
115	Delft	(dĕlft)	Neth.	52.0 N	4.21 E
135	Delgado, C.	(dĕl-gä′dō)	Moz.	10.30 S	40.30 E
102	Delgado Pt		Arg.	42.50 S	63.40 W
133	Delgo	(dĕl′gô)	A. E. Sud.	20.5 N	30.36 E
141	Delhi	(dĕl′hī)	India	28.29 N	77.15 E
81	Delhi		La.	32.27 N	91.30 W
120	Delitzsch	(dā′lĭch)	Ger.	51.32 N	12.17 E
111	Delizhan	(dyĕ′lĭ-zhän′)	Sov. Un.	40.47 N	45.0 E
118	Dellen L., N.	(dĕl′ĕn)	Swe.	61.54 N	16.40 E
118	Dellen L., S		Swe.	61.48 N	16.32 E
76	Dell Rapids	(dĕl)	S. D.	43.51 N	96.41 W
132	Dellys	(dĕ-lēs′)	Alg.	37.0 N	3.52 E
74	Del Mar	(dĕl mär′)	Calif. (In.)	32.57 N	117.16 W
120	Delmenhorst	(dĕl′mĕn-hôrst)	Ger.	53.2 N	8.38 E
78	Del Norte	(dĕl nôrt′)	Colo.	37.40 N	106.22 W
139	Delong Is.	(dyĕ-lōŋ′)	Sov. Un.	76.40 N	158.59 E
160	Deloraine	(dĕl-ô-rān′)	Austl. (Tas. In.)	41.32 S	146.42 E
84	Delphi	(dĕl′fī)	Ind.	40.36 N	86.41 W
84	Delphos	(dĕl′fŏs)	Ohio	40.50 N	84.22 W
83	Delray Beach	(dĕl-rā′)	Fla. (In.)	26.27 N	80.4 W
80	Del Rio	(dĕl rē′ō)	Tex.	29.21 N	100.54 W
75	Delta	(dĕl′tȧ)	Colo.	38.44 N	108.5 W
75	Delta		Utah	39.21 N	112.35 W
56	Delta Station		Can. (Winnipeg In.)	50.10 N	98.21 W
133	Delvinë	(dĕl′vē-nȧ)	Alb.	39.57 N	20.9 E
110	Dema R.	(dyĕm′ä)	Sov. Un.	53.50 N	54.40 E
140	Demavend, Mt.	(dĕm-ȧ-vĕnd′)	Iran	36.0 N	52.2 E
129	Demievka	(dyĕm-yĕf′kȧ)	Sov. Un.	50.24 N	30.30 E
75	Deming	(dĕm′ĭng)	N. M.	32.16 N	107.46 W
72	Deming		Wash. (Vancouver In.)	48.50 N	122.13 W
120	Demmin	(dĕ-mēn′)	Ger.	53.55 N	13.2 E
132	Demnat	(dĕm-nät′)	Mor.	31.48 N	7.0 W
82	Demopolis	(dē-mŏp′ô-lĭs)	Ala.	32.30 N	87.50 W
150	Dempo, Mt. (Vol.)	(dĕm′pô)	Indon.	3.47 S	103.7 E
138	Demyanka R.	(dyĕm-yän′kä)	Sov. Un.	59.0 N	72.0 E
128	Demyansk	(dyĕm-yänsk′)	Sov. Un.	47.38 N	32.28 E
122	Denain	(dē-năɴ′)	Fr.	50.22 N	3.25 E
114	Denbigh	(dĕn′bĭ)	Gt. Brit.	53.12 N	3.20 W
131	Dendara	(dĕn′dȧ-rȧ)	Eg. (In.)	26.8 N	32.40 E
85	Dendron	(dĕn′drŭn)	Va.	37.2 N	76.52 W
138	Dengiz, L.	(dĕŋ-gĭz′)	Sov. Un.	50.30 N	64.0 E
120	Den Helder	(dĕn hĕl′dēr)	Neth.	52.57 N	4.45 E
125	Denia	(dā′nyä)	Sp.	38.50 N	0.5 E
159	Deniliquin	(dĕ-nĭl′ĭ-kwĭn)	Austl.	35.35 S	144.59 E
76	Denison	(dĕn′ĭ-sŭn)	Ia.	42.1 N	95.20 W
79	Denison		Tex.	33.45 N	96.32 W
111	Denizli	(dĕn-ĭz-lē′)	Tur.	37.47 N	29.12 E
118	Denmark	(dĕn′märk)	Eur.	56.0 N	10.10 E
83	Denmark		S. C.	33.19 N	81.90 W
48	Denmark Str		Grnld.	66.30 N	27.0 W
84	Dennison	(dĕn′ĭ-sŭn)	Ohio	40.25 N	81.18 W
127	Denousa (I.)	(dĕ-no͞o′sȧ)	Grc.	37.5 N	25.50 E
89	Dent	(dĕnt)	Ohio (Cincinnati In.)	39.11 N	84.39 W
116	Denton	(dĕn′tŭn)	Gt. Brit.	53.27 N	2.70 W
85	Denton		Md.	38.54 N	75.50 W
81	Denton		Tex.	33.11 N	97.8 W
169	D′Entrecasteaux Chan.	(däɴ-tr′-kȧs-tō′)	Austl. (Tas. In.)	43.25 S	147.5 E
161	D′Entrecasteaux Is		Pap. Ter.	9.30 S	150.45 E
164	D′Entrecasteaux Pt		Austl.	34.48 S	116.0 E
78	Denver	(dĕn′vēr)	Colo.	39.45 N	105.0 W
72	Denver		Colo. (In.)		
102	Deodoro	(dā-o͝o-dō′ro͝o)	Braz. (In.)	22.52 S	43.22 W
77	De Pere	(dē pēr′)	Wis.	42.26 N	88.2 W
85	Depew	(dē-pū′)	N. Y.	42.56 N	78.42 W
79	De Queen	(dē kwēn′)	Ark.	34.2 N	94.21 W
81	De Quincy	(dē kwĭn′sĭ)	La.	30.27 N	93.27 W
137	Déraa	(dā-rä′)	Syr. (In.)	32.37 N	36.7 E
141	Dera Ghazi Khan	(dā′rū gä-zē′ ᴋän′)	Pak.	30.8 N	70.38 E
141	Dera Ismail Khan	(dā′rŭ ĭs-mä-ēl′ ᴋän′)	Pak.	31.59 N	70.59 E
111	Derbent	(dĕr-bĕnt′)	Sov. Un.	42.0 N	48.15 E
111	Derbeziye	(dēr-bā′zē-yȧ)	Tur.	37.10 N	40.1 E
158	Derby	(där′bē) (dûr′bē)	Austl.	17.17 S	123.31 E
160	Derby		Austl. (Tas. In.)	41.9 S	147.50 E
72	Derby	(dûr′bē)	Colo. (Denver In.)	39.49 N	104.55 W
85	Derby		Conn.	41.20 N	73.6 W
114	Derby	(där′bē)	Gt. Brit.	52.55 N	1.30 W
116	Derby (Co.)		Gt. Brit.	53.18 N	1.30 W
112	Derg	(dĕrg)	Libya	30.10 N	10.29 E
114	Dergh, Lough (L.)	(lŏᴋ dĕrg)	Ire.	52.55 N	8.20 W
81	De Ridder	(dē rĭd′ēr)	La.	30.50 N	93.18 W
79	Dermott	(dûr′mŏt)	Ark.	33.32 N	91.25 W
133	Derna	(dĕr′nä)	Libya	32.45 N	22.32 E
72	Deroche	(dē-rōsh′)	Can. (Vancouver In.)	49.11 N	122.4 W
114	Derravaragh, L.	(dâr-rä-vä′rä)	Ire.	53.40 N	7.20 W
127	Derventa	(dĕr′vĕn-tȧ)	Yugo.	44.58 N	17.55 E
160	Derwent R.	(dûr′wĕnt)	Austl. (Tas. In.)	42.33 S	146.45 E
116	Derwent, R		Gt. Brit.	53.4 N	1.30 W
57	De Salaberry I.	(dē să-lȧ-bĕr′ĭ)	Can. (Montreal In.)	45.16 N	74.8 W
79	Des Arc	(dāz ärk′)	Ark.	34.58 N	91.31 W
133	Desbordeville (Impfondo)	(dā-bôrd-vēl′) (ĭmp-fōn′dô)	Fr. Eq. Afr.	1.41 N	18.2 E
70	Deschutes R.	(dā-sho͞ot′)	Ore.	44.30 N	121.18 W
80	Desdemona	(dĕz-dē-mō′nȧ)	Tex.	32.17 N	98.32 W
102	Deseado, R.	(dā-sā-ä′dhō)	Arg.	47.0 S	68.0 W
95	Désirade	(dā-zē-rȧd′)	Guad. (In.)	16.20 N	61.3 W
76	De Smet	(dē smĕt′)	S. D.	44.23 N	97.32 W
79	Des Moines	(dē moin′)	Ia.	41.32 N	93.32 W
78	Des Moines		N. M.	36.44 N	103.47 W
79	Des Moines R		Ia.	41.25 N	93.20 W
128	Desna R.	(dyĕs-nȧ′)	Sov. Un.	53.50 N	33.40 E
102	Desolation I		Chl.	53.0 S	74.0 W
153	Desolation Pt		Phil.	10.29 N	125.40 E
79	De Soto	(dē sō′tō)	Mo.	38.7 N	90.32 W
77	Des Plaines	(dĕs plānz′)	Ill.	42.5 N	87.55 W
77	Des Plaines R		Ill.	42.0 N	87.53 W
120	Dessau	(dĕs′ou)	Ger.	51.50 N	12.13 E
120	Detmold	(dĕt′mōld)	Ger.	51.56 N	8.53 E
84	Detroit	(dē-troit′)	Mich.	42.20 N	83.0 W
89	Detroit		Mich. (In.)		
79	Detroit		Tex.	33.40 N	95.15 W
76	Detroit Lakes		Minn.	46.50 N	95.50 W
89	Detroit R		Mich. (Detroit In.)	42.20 N	83.2 W
121	Detva	(dyĕt′vȧ)	Czech.	48.34 N	19.23 E
117	Deurne	(dûrn)	Bel. (Anvers In.)	51.14 N	4.27 E
127	Deva	(dā′vä)	Rom.	45.52 N	22.53 E
121	Dévaványa	(dā′vô-vän-yô)	Hung.	47.2 N	20.57 E
111	Develi	(dĕ′vȧ-lē)	Tur.	38.25 N	35.15 E
120	Deventer	(dĕv′ĕn-tēr)	Neth.	52.15 N	6.10 E
101	Devils I		Fr. Gu.	5.18 N	52.33 W
76	Devils L		N. D.	48.3 N	99.0 W
76	Devils Lake		N. D.	48.7 N	98.51 W
135	Devils Pk		U. S. Afr.	33.57 S	18.27 E
74	Devil Postpile Natl. Mon		Calif.	37.40 N	119.6 W
80	Devils R		Tex.	30.10 N	101.0 W
73	Devils Slide		Utah (Salt Lake City In.)	41.4 N	111.33 W
71	Devils Tower Natl. Mon		Wyo.	44.37 N	104.42 W
160	Devonport	(dĕv′ŭn-pôrt)	Austl. (Tas. In.)	41.10 S	146.11 E
156	Devonport		N. Z. (In.)	36.51 S	174.48 E
73	Devore	(dē-vôr′)	Calif. (Los Angeles In.)	34.14 N	117.27 W
81	Dewalt	(dū′ȧlt)	Tex. (In.)	29.32 N	95.33 W
51	Dewatto	(dē-wȧt′ô)	Wash. (Seattle In.)	47.27 N	123.3 W
72	Dewdney	(dūd′nĭ)	Can. (Vancouver In.)	49.9 N	122.12 W
79	Dewey	(dū′ĭ)	Okla.	36.47 N	95.55 W
73	Deweyville	(dū′ĭ-vĭl)	Utah (Salt Lake City In.)	41.43 N	112.6 W
79	De Witt	(dē wĭt′)	Ark.	34.16 N	91.21 W
77	De Witt		Ia.	41.47 N	90.32 W
160	De Witt I		Austl. (Tas. In.)	43.38 S	146.16 E
114	Dewsbury	(dūz′bēr-ĭ)	Gt. Brit.	53.45 N	1.40 W
86	Dexter	(dĕks′tēr)	Me.	45.1 N	69.18 W
79	Dexter		Mo.	36.47 N	89.57 W
83	Dexter L		Fla.	29.7 N	81.25 W
52	Dezhneva, (East), C.	(dyĕzh-nyôf′ȧ)	Sov. Un.	66.0 N	170.0 W
140	Dhahran	(dä-rän′)	Sau. Ar.	26.19 N	50.7 E
141	Dhaulagiri, Mt.	(dou-lȧ-gē′rē)	Nep.	28.45 N	83.30 E
126	Dia (I.)	(dē′ä)	Grc.	35.26 N	25.13 E
51	Diablo, Mt.	(dyä′blô)	Calif. (San Francisco In.)	37.53 N	121.55 W
101	Diamantina	(dē-ȧ-män-tē′nȧ)	Braz.	18.12 S	43.32 W
158	Diamantina R.	(dī′man-tē′nȧ)	Austl.	25.42 S	140.0 E
101	Diamantino	(dē-ȧ-män-tē′no͝o)	Braz.	14.28 S	56.30 W
70	Diamond Pk		Ore.	43.32 N	122.10 W
150	Diamond Pt.	(dī′mŭnd)	Indon.	5.15 N	97.30 E
97	Diana Bank	(dī-ăn′ȧ)	Ba. Is.	22.28 N	74.45 W
127	Dibra (Debra)	(dē′brȧ) (dā′brȧ)	Yugo.	41.31 N	20.32 E
142	Dichu (Yangtze Kiang) (R.)	(dē′cho͞o′) (yäng′tsĕ kyäng′)	Chn.	33.0 N	97.30 E
76	Dickinson	(dĭk′ĭn-sŭn)	N. D.	46.52 N	102.48 W
81	Dickinson		Tex. (In.)	29.27 N	95.2 W
81	Dickinson Bayou		Tex. (In.)	29.27 N	95.3 W
85	Dickson	(dĭk′sŭn)	Pa.	41.26 N	75.41 W
82	Dickson		Tenn.	36.4 N	87.23 W
111	Dicle R.	(dĭj′lȧ)	Tur.	37.50 N	41.0 E
117	Didsbury	(dĭds′bēr-ĭ)	Gt. Brit. (Liverpool In.)	53.25 N	2.13 W
127	Didymoteikhon (Dimotika)	(dē-dü-mō′tā-ᴋōn) (dē-mŏt′ĭ-kȧ)	Grc.	41.20 N	26.28 E
123	Die	(dē)	Fr.	44.45 N	5.23 E
97	Diego de Ocampo, Pico (Pk.)	(pē′kō dē ā′gō dā ô-käm′pō)	Hai.	19.38 N	70.42 W
102	Diego Ramirez Is.	(dē ā′gō rä-mē′rāz)	Pac. O.	56.32 S	68.40 W
135	Diégo-Suarez (Antsirane)	(dē-ā′gō-swȧ′rāz) (änt-sē-rän′)	Madag.	12.10 S	49.13 E
122	Dieppe	(dē-ĕp′)	Fr.	49.55 N	1.7 E
135	Diep R.	(dē-ĕp′)	U. S. Afr.	33.48 S	18.32 E
79	Dierks	(dērks)	Ark.	34.7 N	94.1 W
86	Digby	(dĭg′bĭ)	Can.	44.38 N	65.45 W
160	Diggers Rest		Austl. (Melbourne In.)	37.38 S	144.44 E
123	Digne	(dēn′y′)	Fr.	44.6 N	6.18 E
122	Digoin	(dē-gwăɴ′)	Fr.	46.28 N	4.9 E
151	Digul R.	(dē-go͞ol′)	Neth. N. Gui.	6.30 S	140.22 E
122	Dijon	(dē-zhôɴ′)	Fr.	47.20 N	5.4 E
129	Dikovka	(dē-kôf′kä)	Sov. Un.	48.47 N	32.51 E
133	Dikwa	(dē′kwȧ)	Nig.	12.4 N	13.57 E
140	Dilam	(dē-läm′)	Sau. Ar.	23.59 N	47.8 E
152	Dilasac B.	(dĭ-lä′säk)	Phil.	16.25 N	122.15 E
152	Dile Pt.	(dē′lā)	Phil.	17.34 N	120.20 E
151	Dili	(dĭl′ē)	Port. Tim.	8.37 S	125.34 E
131	Dillingât	(dĭl-lĭŋ-gât′)	Eg. (In.)	30.49 N	30.31 E
71	Dillon	(dĭl′ŭn)	Mont.	45.12 N	112.38 W
83	Dillon		S. C.	34.24 N	79.22 W
134	Dilolo	(dē-lō′lō)	Bel. Cong.	10.24 S	22.28 E
152	Dimasalang	(dē-mä-sä-läng′)	Phil.	12.11 N	123.52 E
153	Dimiao	(dē-mē-ä′ō)	Phil.	9.37 N	124.10 E
127	Dimotika (Didymoteikhon)	(dē-mŏt′ĭ-kȧ) (dē-dü-mō′tā-ᴋōn)	Grc.	41.20 N	26.28 E
153	Dinagat	(dē-nā′gät)	Phil.	10.0 N	125.34 E
153	Dinagat I		Phil.	10.10 N	125.35 E
153	Dinagat Sd		Phil.	10.5 N	125.50 E
151	Dinalupihan	(dē-nȧ-lo͞o-pē′hän)	Phil. (Manila In.)	14.53 N	120.24 E
122	Dinan	(dē-näɴ′)	Fr.	48.28 N	2.5 W
115	Dinant	(dē-näɴ′)	Bel.	50.15 N	4.55 E
122	Dinard-St. Enogat	(de-nȧr′săɴ-té-nō-gä′)	Fr.	48.35 N	2.0 W
150	Dindings	(dĭn-dĭngz′)	Malaya	4.30 N	100.45 E
152	Dingalan B.	(dĭŋ-gä′län)	Phil.	15.18 N	121.25 E
114	Dingle	(dĭng″l)	Ire.	52.10 N	10.15 W
153	Dingle	(dĭng′lā)	Phil.	11.0 N	122.40 E
114	Dingle B.	(dĭng″l)	Ire.	52.0 N	10.20 W
159	Dingo	(dĭŋ′gō)	Austl.	23.44 S	149.27 E
152	Dingras	(dĭn-grȧs′)	Phil.	18.6 N	120.40 E
114	Dingwall	(dĭng′wôl)	Gt. Brit.	57.35 N	4.25 W
71	Dinosaur Nat′l. Mon.	(dī′nô-sôr)	Utah-Colo.	40.30 N	109.0 W
74	Dinuba	(dĭ-nū′bȧ)	Calif.	36.32 N	119.22 W
132	Diorbivol	(dē-ôr-bē-vôl′)	Fr. W. Afr.	16.8 N	13.20 W
96	Dios Cays (Is.)	(dē-ōs′)	Cuba	22.5 N	83.2 W
121	Diósgyör	(dē′ōsh-dyûr)	Hung.	48.6 N	20.42 E
132	Diourbel	(dē-o͞or-bĕl′)	Fr. W. Afr.	14.36 N	16.20 W
153	Dipolog	(dē-pô′lŏg)	Phil.	8.34 N	123.23 E
95	Diquis, R.	(dē-kēs′)	C. R.	8.57 N	83.25 W
133	Dire Daua	(dē-rȧ dȧ′wȧ)	Eth.	9.34 N	41.48 E
94	Diriamba	(dēr-yäm′bä)	Nic.	11.52 N	86.16 W
158	Dirk Hartog I.	(dûrk här′tōg)	Austl.	25.50 S	113.0 E
159	Dirranbandi	(dĭ-rȧ-băn′dē)	Austl.	28.30 S	148.18 E
113	Dir Rissam	(dēr rē-säm′)	Libya	30.3 N	18.57 E
131	Dirût	(dē-ro͞ot′)	Egypt	27.35 N	30.50 E
158	Disappointment, L		Austl.	23.30 S	122.45 E
72	Discovery I.		Can. (Vancouver In.)	48.26 N	123.14 W
131	Dishna	(dēsh′nȧ)	Eg. (In.)	26.6 N	32.28 E
50	Disko I.	(dĭs′kō)	Grnld.	70.0 N	54.0 W

ng-sing; ŋ-baŋk; ɴ-nasalized n; nŏd; cŏmmit; ōld; ôbey; ôrder; fo͞od; fo͝ot; ou-out; s-soft; sh-dish; th-thin; pūre; ûnite; ûrn; stŭd; circŭs; ü-as "y" in study; ′-indeterminate vowel.

ăt; fĭnăl; rāte; senāte; ârm; ȧsk; sofȧ; fâre; ch-choose; dh-as th in other; bē; ĕvent; bĕt; recĕnt; crātĕr; g-go; gh-guttural g; bĭt; ĭ-short neutral; rīde; ᴋ-guttural k as ch in German ich;

ng-sing; ŋ-baŋk; N-nasalized n; nȏd; cȏmmit; ōld; ȏbey; ȏrder; fōōd; fŏŏt; ou-out; s-soft; sh-dish; th-thin; pūre; únite; ûrn; stŭd; circŭs; ü-as "y" in study; ′-indeterminate vowel.

191

Edmond PRONOUNCING INDEX **Emirau**

Page	Name Pronunciation Region	Lat. °'	Long. °'
79	Edmond (ĕd'mŭnd)........Okla.	35.38 N	97.29 W
51	Edmonds (ĕd'mŭndz) Wash. (Seattle In.)	47.48 N	122.22 W
54	Edmonton (ĕd'mŭn-tŭn).....Can.	53.45 N	113.30 W
117	Edmonton..Gt. Brit. (London In.)	51.37 N	0.9 W
55	Edmundston (ĕd'mŭn-stŭn)..Can.	47.27 N	68.8 W
81	Edna (ĕd'nȧ)..............Tex.	28.58 N	96.38 W
111	Edremit (ĕd-rĕ-mēt')........Tur.	39.40 N	27.2 E
127	Edremit, G. of.............Tur.	39.25 N	26.40 E
142	Edsin Gol (ĕd'sĕn gôl)......Chn.	40.45 N	100.0 E
77	Edward I. (ĕd'wērd)........Can.	48.23 N	88.37 W
134	Edward, L..................Afr.	0.20 S	29.40 E
80	Edwards Plat. (ĕd'wērdz)....Tex.	30.30 N	100.30 W
79	Edwardsville................Ill.	38.48 N	89.58 W
117	Eeckeren (āk'ēr-ĕn) Bel. (Anvers In.)	51.17 N	4.25 E
70	Eel R. (ēl)................Calif.	40.35 N	124.10 W
84	Eel R......................Ind.	40.52 N	86.0 W
74	Eel R., South Fork.........Calif.	40.0 N	123.48 W
159	Efate (Sandwich) I. (ȧ-fä'tä) (sand-wich).New Hebr.	17.50 S	168.15 E
79	Effingham (ĕf'ĭng-hăm).......Ill.	39.5 N	88.32 W
128	Efremov (yĕf'rĕ-môf)....Sov. Un.	53.8 N	38.5 E
126	Egadi (Aegadian) Is. (ĕ'gä-dē) (ē-gā'dĭ-ăn).It.	38.55 N	12.20 E
73	Egan (ē'gȧn)....Ga. (Atlanta In.)	33.40 N	84.26 W
124	Ega R. (ā'gä)..............Sp.	42.40 N	2.0 W
124	Egéa de los Caballeros (ȧ-Kā'ȧ dā lōs kä-bäl-yä'rōs).Sp.	42.8 N	1.7 W
121	Eger (ĕ'gĕr)..............Hung.	47.54 N	20.23 E
120	Eger (Ohře) R. (ā'gĕr) (ōr'zhĕ) Czech.	50.23 N	13.15 E
118	Egersund (ĕ'ghĕr-sŏŏn').....Nor.	58.29 N	6.1 E
120	Eggenberg (ĕg'ĕn-bĕrgh).....Aus.	47.6 N	15.22 E
85	Egg Harbor (City).........N. J.	39.32 N	74.40 W
142	Egin R. (ȧ-gēn')..........Mong.	49.40 N	102.30 E
51	Eglon (ĕg'lŭn).Wash. (Seattle In.)	47.53 N	122.31 W
156	Egmont, C. (ĕg'mŏnt)......N. Z.	39.17 S	173.45 E
156	Egmont, Mt.................N. Z.	39.18 S	174.2 E
128	Egor'evsk (yĕ-gôr-yĕfsk).Sov. Un.	55.21 N	39.1 E
133	Egypt (ē'jĭpt)..............Afr.	28.0 N	30.0 E
124	Eibar (ā'ē-bär)..............Sp.	43.11 N	2.22 W
120	Eichstatt (īk'shtät).........Ger.	48.55 N	11.13 E
118	Eid (īdh)...................Nor.	61.55 N	6.0 E
117	Eidelstedt (ī'dĕl-shtĕt) Ger. (Hamburg In.)	53.36 N	9.54 E
118	Eidfjord (īdh'fyōr').........Nor.	60.29 N	7.5 E
118	Eidsberg (īdhs'bĕrgh).......Nor.	59.31 N	11.16 E
118	Eidsvold (īdhs'vôl).........Nor.	60.20 N	11.15 E
120	Eifel (Reg.) (ī'fĕl)..........Ger.	50.7 N	6.40 E
114	Eigg (I.) (ĕg).........Gt. Brit.	56.55 N	6.5 W
72	Eightmile Cr. (āt'mīl) Colo. (Colo. Sprs. In.)	38.37 N	105.8 W
158	Eighty Mile Beach........Austl.	19.25 S	121.15 E
120	Eilenburg (ī'lĕn-bŏŏrgh).....Ger.	51.27 N	12.37 E
120	Einbeck (īn'bĕk)............Ger.	51.48 N	9.52 E
120	Eindhoven (īnd'hō-vĕn).....Neth.	51.26 N	5.28 E
137	Ein Gannim (Jenin) (ān gä-nēm') (jĕ-nēn').Pal. (In.)	32.22 N	35.18 E
120	Eisenach (ī'zĕn-äk).........Ger.	50.59 N	10.18 E
129	Eisk (yĕ'ĕsk)...........Sov. Un.	46.42 N	38.18 E
120	Eisleben (īs'lā'bĕn).........Ger.	51.32 N	11.32 E
117	Eiszendorf (īs'ĕn-dôrf) Ger. (Hamburg In.)	53.28 N	9.57 E
93	Ejutla de Crespo (ȧ-hōōt'lä dā krās'pō).Mex.	16.33 N	96.43 W
	Ekaterinburg, see Sverdlovsk, Sov. Un.		
	Ekaterinodar, see Krasnodar, Sov. Un.		
129	Ekaterinoslav (Dnepropetrovsk) (yĕ-kȧ-tyĕ-rĕ'nô-slâf') (d'nyĕp'-rō-pyĕ-trôfsk').Sov. Un.	48.28 N	35.2 E
119	Ekenäs (Tammisaari) (ĕ'kĕ-nâs tȧm'ĭ-sä'rĭ).Fin.	59.58 N	23.28 E
157	Eketahuna (ĕk-ĕ-tȧ-hōō'nȧ).N. Z.	40.35 S	175.43 E
56	Ekhart (ĕk'ȧrt) Can. (Winnipeg In.)	50.10 N	97.26 W
118	Eksjö (ĕk'shû)..............Swe.	57.41 N	14.59 E
110	Elabuga (yĕ-lä'bŏŏ-gȧ)...Sov. Un.	55.45 N	52.5 E
125	El Affraun (ĕl áf-froun')....Alg.	36.28 N	2.38 E
111	Elan (yĕ-län')..........Sov. Un.	50.50 N	43.58 E
124	El Arahal (ĕl ä-rä-äl')........Sp.	37.16 N	5.33 W
137	El Auja (äl ou'jȧ)......Pal. (In.)	30.52 N	34.25 E
111	Elâziz (ĕl-ā'zēz)............Tur.	38.35 N	39.12 E
112	El Azizia (ĕl ä-zē'zē-ä).....Libya	32.40 N	13.12 E
82	Elba (ĕl'bȧ)................Ala.	31.36 N	86.4 W
89	Elba I........Ga. (Savannah In.)	32.5 N	81.0 W
126	Elba (I.)....................It.	42.45 N	10.18 E
124	El Barco (ĕl bär'kō)..........Sp.	42.25 N	6.59 W
127	Elbasan (ĕl-bä-sän')..........Alb.	41.7 N	20.4 E
120	Elbe (Labe) R. (ĕl'bĕ) (läb'ĕ).Eur.	50.10 N	15.0 E
78	Elbert, Mt. (ĕl'bĕrt)........Colo.	39.7 N	106.27 W
82	Elberton (ĕl'bĕr-tŭn)..........Ga.	34.6 N	82.53 W
111	Elbistan (ĕl-bē-stän')........Tur.	38.15 N	37.15 E
121	Elbląg (ĕl'blăng).............Pol.	54.10 N	19.24 E
122	Elboeuf (ĕl-bûf')..............Fr.	49.17 N	1.0 E
124	El Bonillo (ĕl bō-nēl'yō)......Sp.	38.58 N	2.32 W
96	Elbow Cay..............Ba. Is.	26.30 N	77.0 W
76	Elbow Lake.................Minn.	45.59 N	95.58 W
111	Elbrus, Mt. (ĕl'brŏŏs')...Sov. Un.	43.28 N	42.30 E
140	Elburz Mts. (ĕl'bŏŏrz')........Iran	36.15 N	52.0 E
81	El Campo (ĕl kăm'pō).........Tex.	29.12 N	96.17 W
97	El Can (ĕl kän).......Dom. Rep.	17.57 N	71.15 W
80	El Capitan (Mt.) (ĕl kȧ-pĭ-tăn') Tex.	31.58 N	104.55 W
73	El Casco (ĕl kăs'kō) Calif. (Los Angeles In.)	33.59 N	117.6 W
74	El Centro (ĕl sĕn'trō).......Calif.	32.48 N	115.32 W
102	El Chaco (State) (chä'kō)....Arg.	26.30 S	61.0 W
113	El Chadder (ĕl chăd'ĕr).....Libya	28.48 N	19.24 E
125	Elche (ĕl'chā)...............Sp.	38.16 N	0.41 W
125	Elda (ĕl'dä).................Sp.	38.29 N	0.46 W
135	Eldanane (ĕl-dä-nä'nä)......Som.	6.30 N	49.0 E
120	Elde R. (ĕl'dē)..............Ger.	53.25 N	11.34 E
131	El Djem (ĕl jĕm')...........Tun.	35.18 N	10.35 E
132	El Djouf (Salt) Desert (ĕl djōōf) Fr. W. Afr.	22.0 N	6.0 W
77	Eldon (ĕl-dŭn)................Ia.	40.55 N	92.12 W
79	Eldon........................Mo.	38.19 N	92.35 W
51	Eldon........Wash. (Seattle In.)	47.32 N	123.3 W
77	Eldora (ĕl-dō'rȧ)..............Ia.	42.21 N	93.5 W
79	El Dorado (ĕl dō-rä'dō)......Ark.	33.13 N	92.38 W
79	Eldorado.....................Ill.	37.49 N	88.25 W
79	El Dorado...................Kan.	37.48 N	96.51 W
79	Eldorado Springs............Mo.	37.52 N	94.2 W
133	Eldoret (ĕl-dō-rĕt').........Kenya	0.32 N	35.18 E
92	El Ebano (ĕl ā-bä'nō).......Mex.	22.13 N	98.25 W
78	Electra (ē-lĕk'trȧ)...........Tex.	34.2 N	98.55 W
71	Electric Pk.................Mont.	45.1 N	110.52 W
75	Elephant Butte Reservoir..N. M.	33.25 N	107.10 W
89	Elephant Pass La. (New Orleans In.)	30.0 N	89.9 W
128	Elets (yĕ-lyĕts').........Sov. Un.	52.38 N	38.30 E
97	Eleuthera I. (ē-lū'thēr-ȧ)..Ba. Is.	25.10 N	76.12 W
97	Eleuthera Pt............Ba. Is.	24.40 N	76.10 W
79	Eleven Point R.........Mo.-Ark.	36.40 N	91.12 W
133	El Fāsher (ĕl fȧ'shĕr)..A. E. Sud.	13.42 N	25.22 E
124	El Ferrol (ĕl fā-rōl')..........Sp.	43.29 N	8.14 W
113	El Gara Oasis (ĕl gä'rä)......Eg.	29.30 N	26.30 E
131	El Garbi (R.) (ĕl gär'bē).Eg. (In.)	31.0 N	30.43 E
133	El Gheria (ĕl gä'rē-ä)......Libya	30.27 N	13.21 E
137	El Ghor (ĕl gōr)....Pal.-Jor. (In.)	39.55 N	35.23 E
114	Elgin (ĕl'jĭn)..........Gt. Brit.	57.40 N	3.20 W
77	Elgin........................Ill.	42.2 N	88.18 W
76	Elgin.......................Neb.	41.59 N	98.4 W
70	Elgin.......................Ore.	45.34 N	117.54 W
81	Elgin.......................Tex.	30.20 N	97.22 W
132	El Goléa (ĕl gō-lā-ä').......Alg.	30.38 N	2.51 E
133	Elgon, Mt. (ĕl'gŏn).......Kenya	1.5 N	34.35 E
112	El Hamada (Plat.) (ĕl häm'ȧ-dä) Alg.	31.45 N	0.30 W
131	El Hatob, Oued (R.) (ĕl hȧ'tôb) Tun. (In.)	35.30 N	9.30 E
56	Elie (ē'lē)....Can. (Winnipeg In.)	49.54 N	97.47 W
134	Elila R. (ĕ-lē'lȧ).......Bel. Cong.	3.28 S	27.30 E
119	Elisenvaara (ā-lē'sĕn-vä'rȧ)...Fin.	61.29 N	29.40 E
81	Elizabeth (ē-lĭz'ȧ-bĕth)........La.	30.53 N	92.48 W
85	Elizabeth...................N. J.	40.40 N	74.12 W
139	Elizabeth, C..............Sakh.	54.30 N	142.50 E
83	Elizabeth City.............N. C.	36.17 N	76.14 W
89	Elizabeth R.....Va. (Norfolk In.)	36.52 N	76.19 W
89	Elizabeth R. South Branch Va. (Norfolk In.)	36.49 N	76.17 W
89	Elizabeth R. Western Branch Va. (Norfolk In.)	36.51 N	76.21 W
83	Elizabethton..............Tenn.	36.20 N	82.12 W
84	Elizabethtown...............Ky.	37.42 N	85.54 W
134	Elizabethville.........Bel. Cong.	11.40 S	27.28 E
138	Elizarovskoe (yĕ-lē-zä-rôf'skô-yĕ) Sov. Un.	61.25 N	68.15 E
	Elisavetgrad, see Zinovievsk, Sov. Un.		
124	Elizonda (Baztán) (ā-lē-thōn'dä) (bäth-tän').Sp.	43.11 N	1.32 W
124	Elja R. (ĕl'zhä)..........Port.-Sp.	40.0 N	6.53 W
97	El Jovero (ĕl hō-vä'rō).......Hai.	18.59 N	69.4 W
121	Elk (ĕlk)....................Pol.	53.50 N	22.22 E
133	El Kamlin (ĕl kăm-lēn').A. E. Sud.	15.3 N	33.10 E
113	El Kanais, C. (ĕl kȧ'nīs)......Eg.	31.25 N	27.25 E
78	Elk City (ĕlk)...............Okla.	35.24 N	99.23 W
72	Elk Cr........Colo. (Denver In.)	39.29 N	105.27 W
88	Elk Grove.......Ill. Chicago (In.)	42.1 N	87.58 W
133	El Khandaq (ĕl kän-dȧk') A. E. Sud.	18.36 N	30.30 E
84	Elkhart (ĕlk'härt)............Ind.	41.41 N	85.57 W
78	Elkhart.....................Kan.	37.1 N	101.54 W
81	Elkhart.....................Tex.	31.38 N	95.33 W
137	El Khelasa (Haluza) (ĕl kĕ-lä'sȧ) (hȧ-lōō'zȧ).Pal. (In.)	31.6 N	34.37 E
77	Elkhorn (ĕlk'hôrn)..........Wis.	42.40 N	88.30 W
76	Elkhorn R...................Neb.	42.0 N	97.0 W
83	Elkin (ĕl'kĭn)...............N. C.	36.15 N	80.50 W
85	Elkins (ĕl'kĭnz)...........W. Va.	38.54 N	79.50 W
70	Elko (ĕl'kō)................Nev.	40.50 N	115.45 W
76	Elk Point...................S. D.	42.42 N	96.40 W
84	Elk Rapids..................Mich.	44.53 N	85.25 W
88	Elkridge.....Md. (Baltimore In.)	39.12 N	76.43 W
82	Elk R..................Ala.-Tenn.	35.5 N	86.45 W
70	Elk R.......................Ida.	46.47 N	116.11 W
77	Elk R......................Minn.	45.18 N	93.32 W
84	Elk R......................W. Va.	38.30 N	81.15 W
72	Elkton.....Colo. (Colo. Sprs. In.)	38.43 N	105.9 W
82	Elkton......................Ky.	36.50 N	87.10 W
85	Elkton......................Md.	39.36 N	75.52 W
76	Elkton......................S. D.	44.16 N	96.27 W
131	El Kubri (ĕl kōō'brē) Eg. (Suez Can. In.)	30.2 N	32.35 E
52	Ellamar (ĕl'ȧ-mär).....Alsk. (In.)	60.56 N	146.40 W
116	Elland (el'ănd).........Gt. Brit.	53.40 N	1.50 W
76	Ellendale (ĕl'ĕn-dāl).........N. D.	46.0 N	98.31 W
70	Ellensburg (ĕl'ĕnz-bûrg)....Wash.	47.0 N	120.33 W
85	Ellenville (ĕl'ĕn-vĭl).........N. Y.	41.38 N	74.27 W
73	Ellenwood (ĕl'ĕn-wŏŏd) Ga. (Atlanta In.)	33.37 N	84.17 W
116	Ellesmere (ĕlz'mēr)......Gt. Brit.	52.55 N	2.54 W
48	Ellesmere I.................Can.	81.0 N	80.0 W
157	Ellesmere, L................N. Z.	43.45 S	172.30 E
116	Ellesmere Port..........Gt. Brit.	53.17 N	2.54 W
5	Ellice Is. (ĕl'ĕs)..........Pac. O.	8.31 S	179.8 E
160	Elliott Cove (ĕl'ĭ-ŭt) Austl. (Tas. In.)	43.3 S	145.35 E
78	Ellis (ĕl'ĭs).................Kan.	38.56 N	99.34 W
82	Ellisville..................Miss.	31.36 N	89.12 W
141	Ellore (ĕl-lōr')..............India	16.38 N	81.5 E
78	Ellsworth (ĕlz'wûrth)........Kan.	38.34 N	98.14 W
86	Ellsworth...................Me.	44.33 N	68.25 W
51	Ellsworth....Wash. (Portland In.)	45.36 N	122.34 W
47	Ellsworth Highland.........Ant.	77.0 S	90.0 W
120	Ellwangen (ĕl'väng-gĕn)......Ger.	48.58 N	10.8 E
88	Ellwood Park (ĕl'wŏŏd) N. Y. (Niagara Falls In.)	42.58 N	78.51 W
72	Elm (ĕlm).....Colo. (Denver In.)	40.22 N	104.46 W
70	Elma (ĕl'mȧ)...............Wash.	47.1 N	123.20 W
112	El Maadid (ĕl mȧ-ä-dēd')....Mor.	31.30 N	4.31 W
79	Elm Cr......................Tex.	33.20 N	97.3 W
56	Elm Cr................Can. (In.)	49.42 N	97.59 W
131	El Menar (ĕl mā-när') Sp. Mor. (Gibraltar In.)	35.47 N	5.17 E
88	Elmhurst (ĕlm'hûrst).........Ill.	41.59 N	87.59 W
85	Elmira (ĕl-mī'rȧ)..........N. Y.	42.6 N	76.50 W
85	Elmira Heights.............N. Y.	42.9 N	76.49 W
73	El Modeno (ĕl mō-dē'nō) Calif. (Los Angeles In.)	33.46 N	117.49 W
73	El Monte (ĕl mŏn'tā) Calif. (Los Angeles In.)	34.5 N	118.2 W
75	El Morro Natl. Mon. (ĕl môr'rō) N. M.	35.3 N	108.21 W
76	Elm R.......................S. D.	45.50 N	98.24 W
120	Elmshorn (ĕlms'hôrn)........Ger.	53.46 N	10.38 E
113	El Mugtaa (Muctar) (ĕl mōōg'tȧ) (mōōk'tär).Libya	30.25 N	18.42 E
88	Elmwood Park (ĕlm'wŏŏd) Ill. (Chicago In.)	41.55 N	87.50 W
122	Elne (ĕln)...................Fr.	42.37 N	3.0 E
128	Elnya (yĕl'nyȧ).........Sov. Un.	54.33 N	33.12 E
133	El Obeid (ĕl ō-bād')....A. E. Sud.	13.12 N	30.15 E
133	El Odaiya (ĕl ō-dī'yȧ)..A. E. Sud.	12.6 N	28.17 E
89	Eloi B. (ē'loi) La. (New Orleans In.)	29.43 N	89.23 W
51	Elokomin R. (ē-lō'kō-mĭn) Wash. (Seattle In.)	46.15 N	123.18 W
92	El Oro de Hidalgo (ĕl ō'rō dā ē-däl'gō).Mex.	19.48 N	100.5 W
132	El Oued (ĕl wĕd')...........Alg.	33.28 N	6.52 E
139	Elovka (Yelovka) (yĕ-lôf'kȧ) Sov. Un.	56.59 N	160.45 E
125	El Panadés (ĕl pä-nä-dās') Sp. (In.)	41.17 N	1.42 E
125	El Pardo (ĕl pär'dō).....Sp. (In.)	40.31 N	3.47 W
80	El Paso (ĕl păs'ō)...........Tex.	31.46 N	106.28 W
95	El Porvenir (ĕl pôr-vȧ-nēr')..Pan.	9.35 N	78.55 W
92	El Pueblito (ĕl pwĕ-blē'tō)..Mex.	20.32 N	100.25 W
125	El Puerto de Sta. María (ĕl pwĕr'tō dā sän'tä mä-rē'ä).Sp. (In.)	36.36 N	6.13 W
137	El Qasaima (ĕl kȧ-sä'ē-mȧ) Eg. (In.)	30.41 N	34.21 E
137	El Qatrani (ĕl kä-trä'nē).Jor. (In.)	31.9 N	35.59 E
133	El Qedāref (ĕl kȧ-dȧ'rĕf) A. E. Sud.	14.5 N	35.26 E
131	El Qurna (ĕl kōōr'nȧ)...Eg. (In.)	25.42 N	32.38 E
95	El Real (ĕl rā-äl')...........Pan.	8.7 N	77.42 W
92	El Refugio (ĕl rā-fōō'hē-ō)...Mex.	23.3 N	100.28 W
78	El Reno (ĕl rē'nō)...........Okla.	35.32 N	97.58 W
77	Elroy (ĕl'roi)................Wis.	43.44 N	90.16 W
124	Elsa R. (ĕl'sä)...............Sp.	42.10 N	5.33 W
92	El Salto (ĕl säl'tō)..........Mex.	23.48 N	105.20 W
80	El Sauz (ĕl sous')...........Mex.	29.3 N	106.14 W
79	Elsberry (ĕlz'bĕr-ĭ)..........Mo.	39.9 N	90.45 W
73	El Segundo (ĕl sĕgŭn'dō) Calif. (Los Angeles In.)	33.55 N	118.25 W
97	El Seibo (ĕl sā'bō)...........Hai.	18.45 N	69.2 W
133	El Sheb (ĕl shĕb)..............Eg.	22.30 N	29.57 E
51	Elsie (ĕl'sē).....Ore. (Portland In.)	45.51 N	123.35 W
84	Elsiecoal (ĕl'sē-kōl)..........Ky.	37.8 N	82.56 W
	Elsinore, see Helsingör, Den.		
74	Elsinore (ĕl'sĭ-nōr)..........Calif.	33.40 N	117.20 W
73	Elsinore L. Calif. (Los Angeles In.)	33.40 N	117.20 W
73	Elsinore Mts. Calif. (Los Angeles In.)	33.39 N	117.25 W
72	Elsmere (ĕlz'mēr) Colo. (Colo. Sprs. In.)	38.52 N	104.43 W
160	Eltham (ĕl'thȧm) Austl. (Melbourne In.)	37.43 S	145.9 E
156	Eltham......................N. Z.	39.25 S	174.15 E
111	Eltonskoe, L. (yĕl-tôn'skô-yĕ) Sov. Un.	49.5 N	46.45 E
73	El Toro (ĕl tō'rō) Calif. (Los Angeles In.)	33.37 N	117.41 W
94	El Triumfo (ĕl trē-ōōm'fō)....Sal.	13.16 N	88.32 W
75	El Vado Reservoir (ĕl vä'dō).N. M.	36.35 N	106.45 W
124	Elvas (ĕl'väzh)...............Port.	38.54 N	7.10 W
118	Elverum (ĕl'vĕ-rŏŏm).........Nor.	60.54 N	11.32 E
92	El Vieja (Taxco) (ĕl vyā'hä) (täs'kō).Mex.	18.32 N	99.36 W
79	Elvins (ĕl'vĭnz)..............Mo.	37.47 N	90.32 W
133	El Wak (ĕl wäk')............Kenya	2.58 N	40.58 E
84	Elwood (ĕl'wŏŏd)............Ind.	40.17 N	85.51 W
73	Elwood.Utah (Salt Lake City In.)	41.40 N	112.11 W
114	Ely (ē'lĭ)...............Gt. Brit.	52.25 N	0.20 E
77	Ely.........................Minn.	47.54 N	91.52 W
74	Ely.........................Nev.	39.15 N	114.53 W
84	Elyria (ē-lĭr'ĭ-ȧ)..............Ohio	41.22 N	82.7 W
119	Ema R. (ā'mȧ).........Sov. Un.	58.25 N	27.0 E
111	Emba R. (yĕm'bȧ)......Sov. Un.	47.0 N	55.0 E
84	Embarras R. (ĕm-băr'ăs)......Ill.	39.20 N	88.10 W
117	Emblehem (ĕm'blĕ-hĕm) Bel. (Anvers In.)	51.10 N	4.36 E
123	Embrun (äN-brăN')............Fr.	44.35 N	6.30 E
120	Emden (ĕm'dĕn)..............Ger.	53.22 N	7.12 E
159	Emerald (ĕm'ēr-ăld).........Austl.	23.35 S	148.0 E
54	Emerson (ĕm'ēr-sŭn)........Can.	49.1 N	97.1 W
110	Emetsk (yĕ-myĕtsk')....Sov. Un.	63.30 N	41.45 E
133	Emi Koussi (Vol.) (ā'mē kōō-sē') Fr. Eq. Afr.	19.50 N	18.30 E
126	Emilia (Prov.) (ā-mēl'yä)......It.	44.40 N	11.0 E
84	Eminence (ĕm'ĭ-nĕns)........Ky.	38.25 N	85.11 W
151	Emirau (I.) (ā-mē-rä'ōō) N. Gui. Ter.	1.45 S	150.0 E

ăt; finȧl; rāte; senâte; ärm; ȧsk; sofȧ; fâre; ch-choose; dh-as th in other; bē; ēvent; bĕt; recĕnt; cratēr; g-go; gh-gutteral g; bĭt; ĭ-short neutral; rīde; K-gutteral k as ch in German ich;

Page	Name Pronunciation Region	Lat. °'	Long. °'
120	Emmen (ĕm'ĕn) . . . Neth.	52.47 N	6.57 E
120	Emmerich (ĕm'ĕr-ĭk) . . . Ger.	51.51 N	6.13 E
77	Emmetsburg (ĕm'ĕts-bûrg) . . . Ia.	43.5 N	94.40 W
70	Emmett (ĕm'ĕt) . . . Ida.	43.52 N	116.30 W
71	Emmons, Mt. (ĕm'ŭnz) . . . Utah	40.44 N	110.19 W
92	Empalme de Cañitas (ĕm-päl'mā dā kä-nyē'täs) . Mex.	23.33 N	102.37 W
73	Empire (ĕm'pīr) Ala. (Birmingham In.)	33.48 N	86.59 W
90	Empire . . . C. Z. (In.)	9.3 N	79.41 W
126	Empoli (äm'pô-lē) . . . It.	43.43 N	10.57 E
79	Emporia (ĕm-pō'rĭ-ȧ) . . . Kan.	38.24 N	96.11 W
83	Emporia . . . Va.	36.41 N	77.33 W
85	Emporium (ĕm-pō'rĭ-ŭm) . . . Pa.	41.28 N	78.14 W
118	Em R. (ĕm) . . . Swe.	57.25 N	15.50 E
120	Emsdetten (ĕms'dĕt-ĕn) . . . Ger.	52.10 N	7.30 E
120	Ems R. (ĕms) . . . Ger.	52.30 N	7.18 E
	Enakievo, see Ordzhonikidze, Sov. Un.		
118	Enånger (ĕn-ôŋ'gĕr) . . . Swe.	61.35 N	16.59 E
152	Encanto Pt. (ĕn-kän'tō) . . . Phil.	15.44 N	121.38 E
102	Encarnación (ĕn-kär-nä-syōn') Par.	27.15 S	55.59 W
92	Encarnación de Díaz (ĕn-kär-nä-syōn dā dē'äz) . Mex.	21.31 N	102.14 W
80	Encinal (ĕn'sĭ-nôl) . . . Tex.	28.3 N	99.21 W
134	Encoge (ĕn-kō'zhā) . . . Ang.	7.42 S	15.2 E
100	Encontrados (ĕn-kōn-trä'dōs) . Ven.	9.0 N	75.0 W
158	Encounter B. (ĕn-koun'tēr) . Austl.	35.38 S	138.42 E
73	Enda (ĕn'dä) Utah (Salt Lake City In.)	41.28 N	112.4 W
47	Enderby Land (Reg.) (ĕn'dēr-bĭ) Ant.	69.0 S	52.0 E
76	Enderlin (ĕn'dēr-lĭn) . . . N. D.	46.38 N	97.36 W
85	Endicott (ĕn'dĭ-kŏt) . . . N. Y.	42.7 N	76.4 W
153	End Pk . . . Phil.	9.19 N	118.12 E
131	Enfidaville (äN-fē-dȧ-vēl') Tun. (In.)	36.8 N	10.18 E
85	Enfield (ĕn'fēld) . . . Conn.	41.55 N	72.35 W
114	Enfield . . . Gt. Brit.	51.35 N	0.10 W
83	Enfield . . . N. C.	36.12 N	77.41 W
97	Engaño, C. (ĕn-gän'yō) . . . Hai.	18.38 N	68.20 W
152	Engaño, C . . . Phil.	18.31 N	122.15 E
133	Engare Uaso Nyiro R. (ĕn-gä'rä wä'sô nyē'rō) . Kenya	0.48 N	38.0 E
111	Engels (ĕŋ'gĕls) . . . Sov. Un.	51.25 N	46.10 E
150	Enggano (Telanjang I.) (ĕng-gä'-nō) (tĕ-län-yäng') . Indon.	5.25 S	102.15 E
79	England (ĭŋ'glănd) . . . Ark.	34.33 N	91.58 W
114	England . . . Gt. Brit.	52.40 N	1.0 W
78	Englewood (ĕn'g'l-wŏŏd) . . . Colo.	39.38 N	105.0 W
88	Englewood . . . Ill. (Chicago In.)	41.47 N	87.38 W
88	Englewood . . . N. J. (N. Y. In.)	40.54 N	73.58 W
84	English (ĭn'glĭsh) . . . Ind.	38.18 N	86.26 W
96	English Cays (Is.) . . . Cuba	21.55 N	82.25 W
114	English Chan . . . Gt. Brit.	50.20 N	2.0 W
55	English R . . . Can.	50.35 N	94.0 W
125	Enguera (ān'gārä) . . . Sp.	38.58 N	0.41 W
146	Enhsien (ĕn'hsyĕn') . . . Chn.	37.9 N	116.14 E
78	Enid (ē'nĭd) . . . Okla.	36.24 N	97.54 W
138	Enisei (Yenisei) R. (yĕ-nê-sĕ'ē) Sov. Un.	61.30 N	90.0 E
138	Eniseisk (yĕ-nĭ-sā'ĭsk) . . . Sov. Un.	58.30 N	92.10 E
134	Enkeldoorn (ĕŋ'k'l-dōōrn) . . S. Rh.	19.5 S	30.50 E
118	Enköping (ēn'kû-pĭng) . . . Swe.	59.38 N	17.5 E
133	En Nahud (ĕn nä'hōōd) . A. E. Sud.	12.41 N	28.26 E
133	Ennedi (Reg.) (ĕn-nĕd'ē) Fr. Eq. Afr.	16.45 N	23.0 E
114	Ennell, L. (ĕn'ĕl) . . . Ire.	53.25 N	7.25 W
114	Ennis (ĕn'ĭs) . . . Ire.	52.55 N	9.0 W
81	Ennis . . . Tex.	32.20 N	96.38 W
114	Enniscorthy (ĕn-ĭs-kôr'thĭ) . . . Ire.	52.40 N	6.40 W
114	Enniskillen (ĕn-ĭs-kĭl'ĕn) . . . N. Ire.	54.20 N	7.40 W
120	Enns R. (ĕns) . . . Aus.	47.36 N	14.30 E
72	Eno (ē'nō) . . . Colo. (Denver In.)	39.52 N	104.52 W
83	Enoree (ē-nō'rē) . . . S. C.	34.39 N	81.58 W
83	Enoree R . . . S. C.	34.35 N	81.50 W
127	Enos (Inoz) (ā'nôs) (ē'nōz) . . . Tur.	40.42 N	46.3 E
51	Enright (ĕn'rīt) . Ore. (Portland In.)	45.43 N	123.31 W
97	Enriquillo L. (ĕn-rē-kēl'yō) . . . Hai.	18.25 N	71.35 W
120	Enschede (ĕns'kȧ-dĕ) . . . Neth.	52.13 N	6.53 E
74	Ensenada (ĕn-sĕ-nä'dä) . . . Mex.	31.50 N	116.38 W
82	Ensley (ĕnz'lĭ) . . . Ala.	33.32 N	86.51 W
133	Entebbe (ĕn-tĕb'ĕ) . . . Ug.	0.2 N	32.28 E
82	Enterprise (ĕn'tēr-prīz) . . . Ala.	31.19 N	85.52 W
70	Enterprise . . . Ore.	45.25 N	117.17 W
122	Entraygues (ĕN-trĕg') . . . Fr.	44.39 N	2.35 E
102	Entre Rios (State) (ĕn'trä rē'ōs) . Arg.	31.30 S	59.0 W
101	Entre Rios (ĕn'trä rē'ōōzh) Braz. (In.)	11.55 S	38.1 W
132	Enugu (ĕ-nōō'gōō) . . . Nig.	6.38 N	7.22 E
70	Enumclaw (ĕn'ŭm-klô) . . . Wash.	47.11 N	121.59 W
140	Enzeli (Pahlevi) (ĕn'zĕ-lē) (pä'lĕ-vē) . Iran	37.28 N	49.28 E
122	Epernay (ā-pĕr-nĕ') . . . Fr.	49.3 N	3.55 E
75	Ephraim (ē'frā-ĭm) . . . Utah	39.22 N	111.35 W
159	Epi I. (ā'pē) . . . New Hebr.	16.45 S	168.15 E
124	Épila (ā'pê-lä) . . . Sp.	41.38 N	1.16 W
123	Épinal (ā-pē-nàl') . . . Fr.	48.11 N	6.28 E
123	Épinay (ā-pē-nĕ') . . . Fr. (In.)	48.57 N	2.18 E
127	Epirus (Prov.) (ē-pī'rŭs) . . . Grc.	39.30 N	20.50 E
160	Epping (ĕp'ĭng) . . . Austl.	37.39 S	145.2 E
116	Epworth (ĕp'wûrth) . . . Gt. Brit.	53.31 N	0.50 W
122	Équeurdreville (ā-kûr-dr'-vēl') . Fr.	49.39 N	1.38 W
126	Erakleion (Candia) (hē-räk'lĭ-ŏn) (kăn'dĭ-ȧ) . Grc. (In.)	35.19 N	25.8 E
153	Eran B. (ā'rän) . . . Phil.	9.5 N	117.42 E
133	Erba, Mt. (ĕr'bȧ) . . . A. E. Sud.	20.48 N	36.48 E
127	Ercegnovi (ĕr-tsăg-nō'vē) . . . Yugo.	42.27 N	18.32 E

Page	Name Pronunciation Region	Lat. °'	Long. °'
73	Erda (ĕr'dä) Utah (Salt Lake City In.)	40.37 N	112.15 W
127	Erdek (ĕr'dĕk) . . . Tur.	40.24 N	27.47 E
111	Ereğli (ĕ-rā'ĭ-lē) . . . Tur.	37.32 N	34.0 E
111	Ereğli . . . Tur.	41.20 N	31.30 E
129	Eremeevka (yĕ'rĕ-mĕ-yĕf'kä) Sov. Un.	49.23 N	32.31 E
120	Erfurt (ĕr'fōōrt) . . . Ger.	50.59 N	11.1 E
127	Ergene R. (ĕr'gĕ-nĕ) . . . Tur.	41.21 N	27.0 E
127	Ergeri (Gjinocastro) (ĕr-gĕ-rē') (jē-nô-käs'trō) . Alb.	40.4 N	20.8 E
124	Eria R. (ā-rē'ä) . . . Sp.	42.11 N	6.10 W
78	Erick (âr'ĭk) . . . Okla.	35.13 N	99.52 W
72	Erie (ē'rĭ) . . . Colo. (Denver In.)	40.3 N	105.3 W
79	Erie . . . Kan.	37.35 N	95.17 W
85	Erie . . . Pa.	42.6 N	80.4 W
84	Erie, L . . . U. S.-Can.	42.0 N	81.0 W
148	Erimo C. (ā'rē-mō) . . . Jap.	42.0 N	143.5 E
117	Erith (ē'rĭth) Gt. Brit. (London In.)	51.29 N	0.11 E
133	Eritrea (ā-rê-trā'ä) . . . Afr.	13.30 N	39.0 E
111	Erivan (ĕr-ê-vän') . . . Sov. Un.	40.10 N	44.32 E
120	Erlangen (ĕr'läng-ĕn) . . . Ger.	49.37 N	11.1 E
89	Erlanger (ĕr'läng-ĕr) Ky. (Cincinnati In.)	39.1 N	84.36 W
110	Ermak I. (yĕr-mäk') . . . Sov. Un.	66.40 N	71.15 E
123	Ermont (ĕr-môN') . . . Fr. (In.)	48.58 N	2.16 E
122	Ernée (ĕr-nā') . . . Fr.	48.19 N	0.51 W
114	Erne, Lough (L.) (lŏk ûrn) . . N. Ire.	54.30 N	7.50 W
81	Eros (ē'rōs) . . . La.	32.23 N	92.27 W
137	Er Ramle (Ramla) (ĕr răm'lĕ) (răm'lä) . Pal. (In.)	31.55 N	34.51 E
133	Er Renk (ĕr rĕnk') . . . A. E. Sud.	11.47 N	32.50 E
114	Errigal, Mt. (ĕr-ĭ-gôl') . . . Ire.	55.0 N	8.5 W
113	Er Rik (ĕr rêk') . . . Libya	29.7 N	22.22 E
114	Erris Head (ĕr'ĭs) . . . Ire.	54.20 N	10.0 W
159	Erromanga I. (ĕr-ô-mäŋ'gä) New Hebr.	18.45 S	169.15 E
133	Er Roseires (ĕr rô-sā'rĕs) A. E. Sud.	12.2 N	32.51 E
123	Erstein (ĕr'shtīn) . . . Fr.	48.25 N	7.42 E
83	Erwin (ûr'wĭn) . . . N. C.	35.16 N	78.40 W
83	Erwin . . . Tenn.	36.8 N	82.25 W
111	Erzincan (ĕr-zĭn-jän') . . . Tur.	39.45 N	39.30 E
111	Erzurum (ĕrz'-rōōm') . . . Tur.	39.55 N	41.15 E
148	Esashi (ĕs'ä-shē) . . . Jap.	41.52 N	140.10 E
118	Esbjerg (ĕs'byĕrgh) . . . Den.	55.28 N	8.27 E
119	Esbo (ĕs'bô) . . . Fin.	60.14 N	24.45 E
153	Escalante (ĕs-kä-län'tä) . . . Phil.	10.48 N	123.33 E
75	Escalante (ĕs-kȧ-lăn'tē) . . . Utah	37.47 N	111.37 W
75	Escalante R . . . Utah	47.40 N	111.15 W
82	Escambia R. (ĕs-kăm'bĭ-ȧ) . . . Fla.	30.45 N	87.19 W
77	Escanaba (ĕs-kȧ-nô'bȧ) . . . Mich.	45.45 N	87.5 W
77	Escanaba R . . . Mich.	45.48 N	87.30 W
95	Escarpado, Pt. (ĕs-kär-pä'dō) . Pan.	8.5 N	78.30 W
123	Esch (ĕsh) . . . Lux.	49.30 N	6.0 E
120	Eschwege (ĕsh'vā-gĕ) . . . Ger.	51.11 N	10.2 E
120	Eschweiler (ĕsh'vī-lĕr) . . . Ger.	50.49 N	6.16 E
97	Escocesa B. (ĕs-kō-sā'sä) . . . Hai.	19.20 N	69.40 W
74	Escondido (ĕs-kŏn-dē'dō) . . . Calif.	33.6 N	117.7 W
95	Escondido (ĕs-kŏn-dē'dō) R . . Nic.	12.7 N	84.6 W
125	Escorial (ĕs-kō-rê-äl') . . . Sp. (In.)	40.35 N	4.8 W
95	Escuda de Veraguas (I.) (ĕs-kōō'dä dā vä-rä'gwäs) . Pan.	9.5 N	81.33 W
92	Escuinapa (ĕs-kwē-nä'pä) . . . Mex.	22.51 N	105.46 W
94	Escuintla (ĕs-kwēn'tlä) . . . Guat.	14.16 N	90.48 W
93	Escuintla . . . Mex.	15.18 N	92.41 W
132	Eséka (ĕ-sā'kä) . . . Cam.	3.45 N	11.2 E
124	Esgueva R. (ĕs-gā'vä) . . . Sp.	41.50 N	4.0 W
117	Esher (ēsh'ĕr) Gt. Brit. (London In.)	51.22 N	0.23 W
137	Esh Shobek (ĕsh shō-bĕk') Jor. (In.)	30.31 N	35.32 E
160	Esk (ĕsk) . . . Austl. (In.)	27.13 S	152.25 E
52	Eska (ĕs'kȧ) . . . Alsk. (In.)	61.49 N	148.56 W
84	Eskdale (ĕsk'dāl) . . . W. Va.	38.7 N	81.27 W
127	Eski-Džumaya (ĕs'kē-dzhōō-mä'-yä) . Bul.	43.14 N	26.33 E
108	Eskifjördur (ĕs'kê-fyûr'dōōr) . . Ice.	65.4 N	13.50 W
118	Eskilstuna (å'shĕl-stü-nä) . . . Swe.	59.21 N	16.29 E
111	Eskişehir (ĕs-kê-shĕ'h'r) . . . Tur.	39.45 N	30.30 E
160	Esk R . . . Austl. (Tas. In.)	41.45 S	147.27 E
93	Eslava, R. de (ĕs-lä'vä, rē'ō dä) Mex. (In.)	19.17 N	99.14 W
118	Eslöv (ĕs'lûv) . . . Swe.	55.50 N	13.19 E
100	Esmeraldas (ĕs-mä-räl'däs) . . . Col.	0.59 N	79.45 W
97	Espada Pt. (ĕs-pä'dä) . . . Hai.	18.22 N	68.28 W
125	Esparraguera (ĕs-pär-rä-gā'rä) Sp. (In.)	41.32 N	1.52 E
95	Esparta (ĕs-pär'tä) . . . C. R.	9.59 N	84.40 W
158	Esperance (ĕs'pê-rȧns) . . . Austl.	33.40 S	121.58 E
96	Esperanza (ĕs-pâ-ränd'zä) . . . Cuba	22.26 N	80.7 W
125	Espichel, C. (ĕs-pē-shĕl') Port. (In.)	38.25 N	9.13 W
100	Espinal (ĕs-pê-näl') . . . Col.	3.58 N	75.10 W
101	Espirito Santo (State) . . . Braz.	20.0 S	41.0 W
152	Espiritu Santo, C. (ĕs-pē'rê-tōō sänt'ō) . Phil.	12.35 N	125.9 E
159	Espiritu Santo I. (ĕs-pē'rê-tōō sän'tō) . New Hebr.	15.15 S	167.0 E
124	Esposende (ĕs-pō-zĕn'dā) . . . Port.	41.32 N	8.48 W
70	Esquimalt (ĕs-kwī'mŏlt) . . . Can.	48.25 N	123.35 W
137	Es Safiye (ĕs sä'fē-yĕ) . . . Jor. (In.)	31.6 N	35.29 E
120	Essen (ĕs'sĕn) . . . Ger.	51.28 N	7.0 E
160	Essendon (ĕs'ĕn-dŭn) Austl. (Melbourne In.)	37.45 S	144.55 E
111	Essentuki (yĕs'ĕn-tōō'kē) Sov. Un.	44.5 N	42.45 E
101	Essequibo R. (ĕs-ä-kē'bō) . Br. Gu.	3.0 N	58.15 W
87	Essex (ĕs'ĕks) . . . Mass. (In.)	42.38 N	70.47 W
86	Essex Jc . . . Vt.	44.31 N	73.8 W
84	Essexville (ĕs'ĕks-vĭl) . . . Mich.	43.36 N	83.49 W

Page	Name Pronunciation Region	Lat. °'	Long. °'
56	Essington (ĕs'ĭng-tŭn) Can. (Prince Rupert In.)	54.9 N	129.58 W
113	Es Sultan (ĕs sōōl-tän') . . . Libya	31.2 N	17.17 E
132	Es Suweira (Mogador) (ĕs sōō-wā' rä) (mō-gȧ-dōr') . Mor.	31.32 N	9.42 W
72	Estabrook (ĕs'tȧ-brŏŏk) Colo. (Denver In.)	39.24 N	105.22 W
101	Estancia (ĕs-tän'sĭ-ä) . . . Braz.	11.27 S	37.28 W
92	Estanzuela (ĕs-tän-zwā'lä) . . . Mex.	21.17 N	103.31 W
124	Estarreja (ĕs-tär-rā'zhä) . . . Port.	40.45 N	8.39 W
126	Este (ĕs'tā) . . . It.	45.14 N	11.38 E
94	Estelí (ĕs-tā-lē') . . . Nic.	13.14 N	86.17 W
124	Estella (ĕs-tāl'yä) . . . Sp.	42.41 N	2.1 W
124	Estepa (ĕs-tā'pä) . . . Sp.	37.18 N	4.53 W
124	Estepona (ĕs-tâ-pō'nä) . . . Sp.	36.26 N	5.9 W
117	Este R. (ĕs'tē) . Ger. (Hamburg In.)	53.29 N	9.42 E
74	Esteros B. (ĕs-tā'rōs) . . . Calif.	35.25 N	120.55 W
72	Estes Park (ĕs'tĭz) Colo. (Denver In.)	40.23 N	105.32 W
76	Estevan (ĕ-stē'vȧn) . . . Can.	49.10 N	103.0 W
77	Estherville (ĕs'tēr-vĭl) . . . Ia.	43.25 N	94.49 W
83	Estill (ĕs'tĭl) . . . S. C.	32.45 N	81.15 W
119	Estonia (ĕs-tō'nĭ-ȧ) . . . Sov. Un.	58.45 N	25.20 E
124	Estrella, Serra da (Mts.) (sĕr'rä dä ĕs-trā'lȧ) . Port.	40.25 N	7.45 W
124	Estremadura (Prov.) (ĕs-trā-mä-dōō'rȧ) . Port.	39.0 N	8.30 W
124	Estremoz (ĕs-trā-mōzh') . . . Port.	38.50 N	7.35 W
101	Estrondo, Serra do (Mts.) (sĕr'rȧ dōō ĕs-trôn'dōō) . Braz.	8.0 S	49.0 W
120	Eszlingen (ĕs'lĭng-ĕn) . . . Ger.	48.46 N	9.19 E
121	Esztergom (ĕs'tĕr-gōm) . . . Hung.	47.45 N	18.44 E
48	Etah (ē'tȧ) . . . Grnld.	78.20 N	72.42 W
122	Étampes (ā-täNp') . . . Fr.	48.25 N	2.9 E
122	Étang de Carcans (L.) (ā-täN dē kär-käN') . Fr.	45.5 N	1.5 W
122	Étang de Cazau (L.) (ā-täN' dē kä-zō') . Fr.	44.30 N	1.10 W
122	Étaples (ā-täp'l') . . . Fr.	50.31 N	1.41 E
57	Etchemin R. (ĕch'ĕ-mĭn) Can. (Quebec In.)	46.42 N	71.5 W
100	Eten (ā-tān') . . . Peru	7.0 S	79.45 W
130	Ethiopia (Abyssinia) (ē-thē-ō'-pē-ȧ) (ă-bĭ-sĭn'ē-ȧ) . Afr.	10.0 N	40.0 E
93	Etlatongo (San Mateo) (ĕt-lä-tôŋ'-gō) (sän-mä-tā'ō) . Mex.	17.1 N	97.1 W
89	Etna (ĕt'nȧ) . . Pa. (Pittsburgh In.)	40.30 N	79.57 W
126	Etna (Mt.) . . . It.	37.44 N	14.59 E
139	Etorofu (I.) (ĕ'tō-rō'fōō) . . Kur. Is.	45.0 N	147.45 E
134	Etosha Pan (Dry L.) (ĕtō'shä) S. W. Afr.	18.50 S	16.20 E
82	Etowah (ĕt'ô-wä) . . . Tenn.	35.18 N	84.32 W
82	Etowah, R . . . Ga.	34.15 N	84.30 W
137	Et Taiyibe (ĕt tī-yē'bĕ) . . Jor. (In.)	32.29 N	35.44 E
115	Etterbeek (ĕt'ĕr-bāk) . . . Bel.	50.50 N	4.20 E
92	Etzatlán (ĕt-zä-tlän') . . . Mex.	20.45 N	104.4 W
122	Eu (ü) . . . Fr.	50.1 N	1.29 E
127	Euboea (I.) (ū-bē'ȧ) . . . Grc.	38.30 N	23.55 E
158	Eucla (ū'klȧ) . . . Austl.	31.40 S	128.46 E
84	Euclid (ū'klĭd) . . . Ohio	41.36 N	81.29 W
79	Eudora (ū-dō'rȧ) . . . Ark.	33.5 N	91.17 W
82	Eufaula (ū-fô'lȧ) . . . Ala.	31.54 N	85.9 W
79	Eufaula . . . Okla.	35.16 N	95.34 W
70	Eugene (ū-jēn') . . . Ore.	44.3 N	123.6 W
80	Eunice (ū'nĭs) . . . La.	30.30 N	92.25 W
115	Eupen (oi'pĕn) . . . Bel.	50.35 N	6.5 E
140	Euphrates (Firat) R. (ū-frā'tēz) (fĭ-rät') . Asia	38.0 N	39.5 E
70	Eureka (ū-rē'kȧ) . . . Calif.	40.47 N	124.10 W
79	Eureka . . . Kan.	37.48 N	96.17 W
70	Eureka . . . Mont.	48.52 N	115.3 W
74	Eureka . . . Nev.	39.33 N	115.58 W
76	Eureka . . . S. D.	45.47 N	99.38 W
81	Eureka . . . Tex. (In.)	29.48 N	95.23 W
75	Eureka . . . Utah	39.56 N	112.8 W
79	Eureka Springs . . . Ark.	36.24 N	93.44 W
122	Eure R. (ûr) . . . Fr.	49.1 N	1.10 E
135	Europa I. (ū-rō'pȧ) . . . Ind. O.	22.20 S	40.25 E
104	Europe (ū'rŭp)		
120	Euskirchen (ois'kĭrk-ĕn) . . . Ger.	50.40 N	6.48 E
83	Eustis (ūs'tĭs) . . . Fla.	28.51 N	81.41 W
82	Eutaw (ū'tô) . . . Ala.	32.49 N	87.53 W
160	Evandale (ĕv'ăn-dāl) . . . Austl.	41.35 S	147.17 E
118	Evanger (ĕ-väŋ'gĕr) . . . Nor.	60.39 N	6.8 E
72	Evans (ĕv'ănz) . Colo. (Denver In.)	40.22 N	104.41 W
156	Evans B . . . N. Z. (In.)	41.18 S	174.49 E
77	Evanston . . . Ill.	42.2 N	87.42 W
71	Evanston . . . Wyo.	41.16 N	110.58 W
84	Evansville . . . Ind.	38.0 N	87.33 W
77	Evansville . . . Wis.	42.38 N	89.18 W
84	Evart (ĕv'ērt) . . . Mich.	43.57 N	85.10 W
77	Eveleth (ĕv'ē-lĕth) . . . Minn.	47.26 N	92.32 W
158	Everard, L. (ĕv'ēr-ărd) . . . Austl.	31.15 S	135.5 E
158	Everard Ranges (Mts.) . . . Austl.	37.15 S	132.30 E
141	Everest, Mt. (ĕv'ēr-ĕst) . . . Nep.	27.58 N	87.5 E
87	Everett (ĕv'ēr-ĕt) . . . Mass. (In.)	42.24 N	71.3 W
70	Everett . . . Wash.	47.59 N	122.12 W
83	Everglades, The (Swamp) (ĕv'ēr-glādz) . Fla. (In.)	26.0 N	80.40 W
82	Evergreen (ĕv'ēr-grēn) . . . Ala.	31.36 N	86.58 W
72	Evergreen . . . Colo. (Denver In.)	39.38 N	105.20 W
72	Everson (ĕv'ēr-sŭn) Wash. (Vancouver In.)	48.55 N	122.20 W
116	Evesham (ēv'shăm) . . . Gt. Brit.	52.5 N	1.56 W
124	Évora (ĕv'ô-rä) . . . Port.	38.34 N	7.55 W
129	Evpatoriya (Guesleve) (yĕf-pä-tō'-rē-yȧ) (gwĕs'lyĕ-vĕ) . Sov. Un.	45.11 N	32.22 E
122	Évreux (ā-vrû') . . . Fr.	49.1 N	1.10 E
127	Evros (Maritsa) R. (ĕv'rōs) (mä'rêt-sä) . Tur.	41.0 N	26.21 E
127	Evrotas R. (ĕv-rō'täs) . . . Grc.	37.0 N	22.30 E

ng-sing; ŋ-baŋk; N-nasalized n; nŏd; cŏmmit; ōld; ôbey; ôrder; fōōd; fŏŏt; ou-out; s-soft; sh-dish; th-thin; pūre; ůnite; ûrn; stŭd; circŭs; ü-as "y" in study; '-indeterminate vowel.

Page	Name Pronunciation Region	Lat. °′	Long. °′
127	Evstratios (I.) (ĕv-strä'tĭ-ōs). Grc.	39.30 N	25.0 E
155	Ewa (ē'wä)... Haw.	21.18 N	158.2 W
79	Excelsior Springs (ĕk-sĕl'sĭ-ŏr) Mo.	39.20 N	94.13 W
114	Exe (R.) (ĕks)... Gt. Brit.	51.5 N	3.30 W
74	Exeter (ĕk'sē-tēr)... Calif.	36.17 N	119.9 W
114	Exeter... Gt. Brit.	50.45 N	3.30 W
86	Exeter... N. H.	42.55 N	70.58 W
114	Exmoor (ĕks'mo͝or)... Gt. Brit.	51.10 N	3.45 W
114	Exmouth (ĕks'mŭth)... Gt. Brit.	50.40 N	3.22 E
158	Exmouth G... Austl.	22.0 S	114.15 E
87	Exploits R. (ĕks-ploits')... Can.	48.45 N	56.25 W
124	Extremadura (Prov.) (ĕks-trā-mä-doo'rä). Sp.	39.0 N	6.20 W
97	Exuma (ĕk-so͞o'mä)... Ba. Is.	24.15 N	76.5 W
129	Eya R. (ĕ-yȧ')... Sov. Un.	46.38 N	38.54 E
134	Eyasi, L. (ȧ-yä'sē)... Tan.	3.38 S	35.0 E
108	Eyla Fjord (ī'lȧ)... Ice.	66.0 N	18.15 W
117	Eynsford (ānz'fērd) Gt. Brit. (London In.)	51.22 N	0.13 E
119	Ezel (Saaremaa) (I.) (ā'zĕl) (sä'rĕ-mä'). Sov. Un.	58.26 N	22.36 E
119	Ežerenai (Zarasai) ă-zhă'rē-nī') (zä-rä-sī'). Sov. Un.	55.44 N	26.17 E
127	Ezine (ȧ'zĭ-nȧ)... Tur.	39.46 N	26.20 E
158	Eyre (âr)... Austl.	32.10 S	126.10 E
158	Eyre, L... Austl.	28.30 S	137.15 E
158	Eyre's Pen. (ârz)... Austl.	33.28 S	136.40 E
137	Ezraa (ĕz-rä')... Syr. (In.)	32.53 N	36.8 E
132	Ezu (ĕ-zo͞o')... Nig.	6.40 N	10.3 E
118	Faaborg (fô'bôrg)... Den.	55.5 N	10.18 E
80	Fabens (fā'bĕnz)... Tex.	31.30 N	106.8 W
126	Fabriano (fä-brē-ä'nô)... It.	43.19 N	12.55 E
133	Fada (fä'dä)... Fr. Eq. Afr.	17.3 N	21.20 E
132	Fada N'Gourma (fä'dä 'n go͞or'mȧ) Fr. W. Afr.	12.12 N	0.23 E
139	Faddeevski (Thaddaeus) I. (fä-dyā'-yĕf-skĭ) (thăd-ē-ŭs). Sov. Un.	75.20 N	144.0 E
118	Faemund L. (fȧ'mo͞on')... Nor.	62.10 N	11.54 E
126	Faenza (fä-ĕnd'zä)... It.	44.27 N	11.52 E
108	Faeroes, The (Is.) (fā'rōz).. Atl. O.	61.55 N	6.45 W
124	Fafe (fä'fā)... Port.	41.30 N	8.10 W
121	Făgăraş (fȧ-gä'räsh)... Rom.	45.50 N	24.58 E
118	Fagernes (fä'ghēr-nĕs)... Nor.	61.0 N	9.15 E
132	Faguibine, L. (fä-gē-bē'nā) Fr. W. Afr.	16.50 N	4.0 W
135	Fah (fä)... Som.	4.58 N	48.3 E
150	Faifo (fä'ē-fō')... Indoch.	15.58 N	108.10 E
54	Fairbank (fâr'bănk).... Can. (In.)	43.42 N	79.28 W
53	Fairbanks (fâr'bănks)... Alsk.	64.44 N	147.39 W
73	Fairbûrn (fâr'bürn) Ga. (Atlanta In.)	33.34 N	84.35 W
79	Fairbury (fâr'bĕr-ĭ)... Ill.	40.43 N	88.30 W
79	Fairbury... Neb.	40.8 N	97.11 W
77	Fairfax (fâr'făks)... Minn.	44.31 N	94.42 W
83	Fairfax... S. C.	32.57 N	81.15 W
82	Fairfield (fâr'fēld)... Ala.	33.29 N	86.57 W
160	Fairfield (fâr'fēld)... Austl.	33.52 S	150.57 E
79	Fairfield... Ill.	38.23 N	88.22 W
77	Fairfield... Ia.	41.0 N	91.58 W
86	Fairfield... Me.	44.36 N	69.37 W
85	Fairhaven (fâr-hā'vĕn)... Mass.	41.35 N	70.57 W
86	Fair Haven... Vt.	43.37 N	73.15 W
114	Fair I. (fâr)... Gt. Brit. (In.)	59.30 N	1.30 W
84	Fairmont (fâr'mŏnt)... Ind.	40.26 N	85.42 W
76	Fairmont... Minn.	43.39 N	94.25 W
51	Fairmont..... Wash. (Seattle In.)	47.59 N	122.51 W
85	Fairmont... W. Va.	39.29 N	80.11 W
85	Fairport (fâr'pōrt)... N. Y.	43.7 N	77.26 W
84	Fairport Har... Ohio	41.44 N	81.16 W
89	Fairview (fâr'vū) Ohio (Cleveland In.)	41.27 N	81.50 W
78	Fairview... Okla.	36.16 N	98.29 W
75	Fairview... Utah	39.38 N	111.28 W
72	Fairview Pk... Colo. (Denver In.)	40.8 N	105.21 W
86	Fairville (fâr'vĭl)... Can.	45.16 N	66.7 W
53	Fairweather, Mt. (fâr-wĕdh'ēr) Alsk.	59.0 N	134.30 W
76	Faith (fāth)... S. D.	45.1 N	102.2 W
141	Faizabad (fī-zä-bäd')... Afg.	37.15 N	70.31 E
133	Fajao (fä-jä'ō)... Ug.	2.9 N	31.41 E
122	Falaise (fȧ-lâz')... Fr.	48.56 N	0.11 W
72	Falcon (fô'k'n) Colo. (Colo. Sprs. In.)	38.56 N	104.36 W
85	Falconer (fô'k'n-ēr)... N. Y.	42.7 N	79.11 W
132	Falémé R. (fȧ-lā-mā'). Fr. W. Afr.	13.30 N	12.0 E
129	Faleshty (fä-lȧsh'tĭ)... Sov. Un.	47.33 N	27.43 E
80	Falfurrias (făl'fo͞o-rē'ȧs)... Tex.	27.13 N	98.9 W
118	Falkenberg (fäl'kĕn-bĕrgh)... Swe.	56.55 N	12.29 E
117	Falkenhagen (fäl'kĕn-hä-gĕn) Ger. (Berlin In.)	52.34 N	13.7 E
114	Falkirk (fôl'kûrk)... Gt. Brit.	55.59 N	3.45 W
102	Falkland Is. (fôk'lănd)... Atl. O.	51.45 S	59.0 W
4	Falkland Is. Dependencies. Atl. O.	65.0 S	50.0 W
118	Falköping (fäl'chûp-ĭng)... Swe.	58.9 N	13.32 E
89	Falling (fôl'ĭng). Ill. (St. Louis In.)	38.33 N	90.10 W
74	Fallon (făl'ŭn)... Nev.	39.29 N	118.47 W
85	Fall River... Mass.	41.40 N	71.10 W
79	Falls City... Neb.	40.3 N	95.36 W
160	Falmouth (făl'mŭth) Austl. (Tas. In.)	41.31 S	148.16 E
114	Falmouth... Gt. Brit.	50.10 N	5.5 W
96	Falmouth... Jam.	18.31 N	77.41 W
84	Falmouth... Ky.	38.40 N	84.22 W
97	False C... Hai.	17.45 N	71.40 W
118	Falster (I.) (fäls'tĕr)... Den.	54.50 N	12.0 E
121	Fălticeni (fŭl-tē-chȧn'y')... Rom.	47.28 N	26.17 E
118	Falun (fä-lo͞on')... Swe.	60.38 N	15.38 E
113	Famagusta (fä-mä-go͞os'tä).. Cyp.	35.18 N	34.0 E
133	Famaka (fä-mä'kä).... A. E. Sud.	11.24 N	34.47 E
151	Famy (fä'mē).. Phil. (Manila In.)	14.30 N	121.30 E
146	Fangshan (fäng'shän')... Chn.	39.42 N	115.52 E
4	Fanning I. (făn'ĭng)... Pac. O.	3.51 N	159.21 W
56	Fannystelle (făn'ĭ-stĕl) Can. (Winnipeg In.)	49.45 N	97.45 W
126	Fano (fä'nō)... It.	43.50 N	13.1 E
118	Fanö (I.) (fän'û)... Den.	55.22 N	8.25 E
135	Farafangana (fä-rä-fäŋ-gä'nä) Madag.	22.47 S	47.50 E
133	Farafra, Oases of (fä-rä'frä)... Eg.	27.8 N	28.2 E
140	Farah (fä-rä')... Afg.	32.20 N	62.12 E
140	Farah R... Afg.	32.45 N	63.0 E
92	Farallón, Pt. (fä-rä-lōn')... Mex.	19.23 N	105.3 W
132	Faranah (fä-rä'nä).... Fr. W. Afr.	10.2 N	10.37 W
140	Farasan Is. (fä-rȧ-sän')... Asia	16.45 N	41.45 E
139	Far East Area... Sov. Un.	60.0 N	145.0 E
113	Faregh Wadi (R.) (wä'dē fä-rĕg') Libya	30.3 N	20.0 E
50	Farewell, C. (fâr-wĕl')... Grnld.	60.0 N	44.0 W
157	Farewell C... N. Z.	40.32 S	172.32 E
76	Fargo (fär'gō)... N. D.	46.53 N	96.47 W
119	Fâr, I. (fôr)... Swe.	57.54 N	19.10 E
77	Faribault (fâ'rĭ-bō)... Minn.	44.18 N	93.15 W
131	Farigh, Wadi el (R.) (wädē ĕl fä-rēg'). Eg. (In.)	30.0 N	30.20 E
124	Farilhões Is. (fä-rē-lyôɴzh').. Port.	39.28 N	9.32 W
158	Farina (fȧ-rē'nȧ)... Austl.	30.2 S	138.27 E
131	Fariskûr (fä-rēs-ko͞or')... Eg. (In.)	31.19 N	31.45 E
121	Farkašd (fär'käsht)... Czech.	42.2 N	17.56 E
84	Farmersburg (fär'mērz-bûrg). Ind.	39.15 N	87.25 W
79	Farmersville... Tex.	33.11 N	96.38 W
87	Farmingham... Mass. (In.)	42.17 N	71.25 W
79	Farmington... Ill.	40.41 N	90.1 W
86	Farmington... Me.	44.49 N	70.18 W
77	Farmington... Minn.	44.38 N	93.4 W
79	Farmington... Mo.	37.46 N	90.26 W
75	Farmington... N. M.	36.41 N	108.10 W
71	Farmington... Utah	41.0 N	111.55 W
83	Farmville... N. C.	35.36 N	77.36 W
83	Farmville... Va.	37.17 N	78.25 W
117	Farnborough (färn'bŭr-ô) Gt. Brit. (London In.)	51.21 N	0.4 E
114	Farne Is. (färn)... Gt. Brit.	55.39 N	1.35 W
86	Farnham (fär'năm)... Can.	45.15 N	72.55 W
116	Farnworth (färn'wŭrth).. Gt. Brit.	53.33 N	2.23 W
101	Faro (fä'ro͞o)... Braz.	2.15 S	56.45 W
124	Faro... Port.	37.1 N	7.57 W
158	Farquhar C. (fär'kwȧr)... Austl.	23.45 S	113.28 E
84	Farrell (făr'ĕl)... Ohio	41.12 N	80.30 W
141	Farukhabad (fŭ-ro͞ok-hä-bäd') India	27.15 N	79.38 E
118	Farsund (fär'so͞on)... Nor.	58.5 N	6.50 E
140	Fartak, C. (fär-täk')... Aden	15.40 N	52.15 E
78	Farwell (fär'wĕl)... Tex.	34.24 N	103.1 W
140	Fasa (fŭ-sä')... Iran	29.0 N	53.59 E
127	Fasano (fä-zä'nō)... It.	40.50 N	17.21 E
131	Fashn (fäsh'n)... Eg. (In.)	28.48 N	30.55 E
114	Fastnet Light House (făst'nĕt). Ire.	51.22 N	9.35 W
129	Fastov (fäs'tôf)... Sov. Un.	50.4 N	29.55 E
129	Fatezh (fät'yĕzh)... Sov. Un.	52.5 N	35.53 E
111	Fatsa (fät'sä)... Tur.	40.58 N	37.32 E
144	Fatshan (fät'shän')... Chn.	23.5 N	113.3 E
123	Faucilles, Monts (Mts.) (môɴ' fō-sēl'). Fr.	48.10 N	6.0 E
126	Favara (fä-vä'rä)... It.	37.19 N	13.39 E
117	Fawkham (fôk'ăm) Gt. Brit. (London In.)	51.23 N	0.18 W
108	Faxa Fjord (fäk'sä fyôr')... Ice.	64.27 N	23.0 W
133	Faya (fȧ-yä')... Fr. Eq. Afr.	17.47 N	19.30 E
132	Fayal I. (fȧ-yäl')... Az. Is. (In.)	38.33 N	28.42 W
132	Fayal I... Az. Is. (In.)	38.30 N	28.40 W
82	Fayette (fȧ-yĕt')... Ala.	33.40 N	87.50 W
77	Fayette... Ia.	42.51 N	91.49 W
82	Fayette... Miss.	31.42 N	91.4 W
79	Fayette... Mo.	39.8 N	92.40 W
79	Fayetteville... Ark.	36.3 N	94.9 W
73	Fayetteville..... Ga. (Atlanta In.)	33.27 N	84.27 W
83	Fayetteville... N. C.	35.3 N	78.55 W
82	Fayetteville... Tenn.	35.10 N	86.32 W
131	Fâyid (fä-yēd'). Eg. (Suez Can. In.)	30.20 N	32.19 E
133	Fayûm (fä-ē-o͞om')... Eg.	29.21 N	30.47 E
144	Fayünhsing (fä'yün'hsĭng').. Chn.	23.29 N	113.12 E
83	Fear, C... S. C.	33.50 N	77.58 W
117	Fearnhead (fērn'hĕd) Gt. Brit. (Liverpool In.)	53.24 N	2.34 W
74	Feather R. (fĕth'ēr)... Calif.	38.55 N	121.37 W
74	Feather R. Middle Fk... Calif.	39.47 N	121.15 W
74	Feather R. North Fk... Calif.	39.50 N	121.30 W
116	Featherstone (fĕdh'ēr-stŭn) Gt. Brit.	53.40 N	1.21 W
157	Featherstone... N. Z.	41.7 S	175.20 E
122	Fécamp (fā-käɴ')... Fr.	49.45 N	0.21 E
101	Federal Dist... Braz.	16.15 S	48.15 W
92	Federal Dist... Mex.	19.15 N	99.10 W
	Federated Malay States, see Malaya		
131	Fedjadj, Chott el (L.) (shŏt ĕl fä'jäj). Tun. (In.)	33.55 N	9.20 E
129	Fedorovka (fyĕ-dô-rôf'kȧ). Sov. Un.	47.3 N	35.19 E
120	Fehmarn (I.) (fā'märn)... Ger.	54.27 N	11.5 E
146	Feihsien (fā'ē-hsyĕn')... Chn.	35.12 N	117.44 E
156	Feilding (fēld'ĭng)... N. Z.	40.12 S	175.40 E
124	Feira (fĕ'ē-rä)... Port.	40.57 N	8.32 W
101	Feira de Sant-Anna (dā sänt-än'ä). Braz. (In.)	12.15 S	38.55 W
125	Felanitx (fā-lä-nēch')... Sp.	39.38 N	3.9 E
120	Feldkirch (fĕlt'kĭrĸ)... Aus.	47.15 N	9.38 E
51	Felida (fĕ-lē'dȧ) Wash. (Portland In.)	45.42 N	122.42 W
121	Felsögalla (fĕl'shû-gäl'lä)... Hung.	47.33 N	18.26 E
124	Feltre (fĕl'trā)... It.	46.2 N	11.53 E
143	Fenchow (fûn'chō')... Chn.	37.4 N	111.40 E
135	Fénérive (fē-nȧ-rēv')... Madag.	17.17 S	49.25 E
143	Fengchen (fûng'chĕn')... Chn.	40.30 N	113.28 E
145	Fengcheng (fûng'chûng')... Chn.	28.7 N	115.37 E
146	Fenghsien (fûng'hsyĕn')... Chn.	34.39 N	116.47 E
145	Fenghwa (fûng'hwä')... Chn.	29.38 N	121.27 E
144	Fenghwang (fûng'hwäng')... Chn.	27.52 N	109.18 E
147	Fenghwangcheng (fûng-hwäng'-chĕng'). Chn.	40.21 N	123.58 E
146	Fengjen (fûng'jûn')... Chn.	39.48 N	118.2 E
145	Fengkin Ling (Mts.) (fûng'-kĭn' lĭng'). Chn.	28.15 N	118.32 E
146	Fengkiu (fûng'kyo͞o')... Chn.	34.58 N	114.38 E
145	Fengshui (fûng'shwē)... Chn.	29.59 N	119.31 E
148	Fengshan (fĕng'shän')... For. (In.)	22.30 N	120.31 E
142	Fengsiang (fûng'syäng')... Chn.	34.32 N	107.21 E
146	Fengtai (fûng'tī')... Chn.	32.45 N	116.39 E
146	Fengtai... Chn.	39.45 N	116.19 E
144	Fengtu (fûng'to͞o')... Chn.	30.2 N	107.48 E
146	Fengyang (fûng'yäng')... Chn.	32.53 N	117.32 E
144	Fengyi (fûng'yē')... Chn.	23.43 N	107.0 E
145	Feni (fû-nĭ')... Chn.	27.43 N	114.42 E
84	Fenton (fĕn-tŭn)... Mich.	42.48 N	83.41 W
160	Fenton, L... Austl. (Tas. In.)	42.37 S	146.39 E
129	Feodosiya (Kefe) (fĕ-ô-dō'sē'yȧ) (kyĕ'fĕ). Sov. Un.	45.1 N	35.23 E
127	Ferdinand (fûr'dĭ-nănd)... Bul.	43.24 N	23.13 E
132	Fernando Po (I.) (fēr-năn'dō pō') (fĕr-nän'dō-pō'ō). Sp. Gui.	3.30 N	8.40 E
126	Ferentino (fā-rĕn-tē'nō)... It.	41.41 N	13.15 E
76	Fergus Falls (fûr'gŭs)... Minn.	46.17 N	96.4 W
89	Ferguson (fûr-gŭ-sŭn) Mo. (St. Louis In.)	38.45 N	90.18 W
81	Feriday (fĕr'ĭ-dā)... La.	31.37 N	91.33 W
73	Fermin, Pt. (fēr'mĭn) Calif. (Los Angeles In.)	33.43 N	118.17 W
126	Fermo (fĕr'mō)... It.	43.10 N	13.41 E
124	Fermoselle (fĕr-mō-sāl'yȧ)... Sp.	41.20 N	6.22 W
114	Fermoy (fēr-moi')... Ire.	52.5 N	8.15 W
83	Fernandina (fûr-năn-dē'nȧ)... Fla.	30.39 N	81.29 W
101	Fernando Noronha, I. (fĕr-nȧn'do͞o nȯ-rō'nyä). Braz.	3.58 S	32.30 W
124	Fernan-Nuñez (fĕr-nän' no͞on'yȧth). Sp.	37.41 N	4.42 W
70	Ferndale (fûrn'dāl)... Calif.	40.35 N	124.15 W
72	Ferndale... Wash. (Vancouver In.)	48.52 N	122.36 W
54	Fernie (fûr'nĭ)... Can.	49.27 N	115.5 W
72	Fern Ridge (fûrn) Can. (Vancouver In.)	49.3 N	122.39 W
87	Ferolle, Pt. (fē-rōl')... Can.	51.0 N	57.0 W
141	Ferozepore (fē-rōz-pōr')... India	30.59 N	74.31 E
126	Ferrara (fĕr-rä'rä)... It.	44.50 N	11.37 E
125	Ferrat, C. (fĕr-rät')... Alg.	35.54 N	0.28 W
124	Ferreira do Alentejo (fĕr-rĕ'ē-rä do͞o ä-lĕɴ-tā'zho͞o). Port.	38.3 N	8.8 W
124	Ferreira do Zezere (do͞o zȧ-zā'rĕ) Port.	39.44 N	8.17 W
132	Ferro (I.) (fĕr'rō)... Can. Is.	27.45 N	18.0 W
87	Ferryland (fĕr'ē-lănd)... Can.	47.5 N	52.58 W
131	Ferryville (fĕr-ē-vēl')... Tun. (In.)	37.8 N	9.48 E
76	Fertile (fûr'tĭl)... Minn.	47.32 N	96.18 W
126	Fertilia (fĕr-tē'lē-ȧ)... Sard.	40.38 N	8.19 E
132	Fès (Fez) (fĕs) (fĕz)... Mor.	34.10 N	4.59 W
76	Fessenden (fĕs'ĕn-dĕn)... N. D.	47.35 N	99.37 W
114	Festiniog (fĕs-tĭn'ĭ-ŏg)... Gt. Brit.	52.57 N	3.55 W
79	Festus (fĕst'ŭs)... Mo.	38.13 N	90.23 W
111	Fethiye (fĕt-hē'yĕ)... Tur.	36.42 N	29.10 E
123	Feucherolles (fû-shē-rōl') Fr. (Paris In.)	48.53 N	1.58 E
120	Feuerbach (foi'ēr-bäĸ)... Ger.	48.49 N	9.11 E
122	Feurs (fûr)... Fr.	45.45 N	4.15 E
133	Fezzan (Reg.) (fĕz-zän')... Libya	26.30 N	15.30 E
133	Fezzan, Oases of... Libya	25.30 N	15.0 E
135	Fianarantsoa (fyȧ-nä'rȧn-tsō'ȧ) Madag.	21.25 S	47.8 E
54	Field (fēld)... Can.	51.28 N	116.35 W
70	Fieldbrook (fēld'bro͝ok)... Calif.	40.59 N	124.2 W
160	Field East, Mt... Austl. (Tas. In.)	42.36 S	146.49 E
160	Field West, Mt.. Austl. (Tas. In.)	42.38 S	146.30 E
127	Fier (fyĕr)... Alb.	40.43 N	19.33 E
134	Fife (fīf)... N. Rh.	9.22 S	32.32 E
114	Fife Ness (fīf' nes')... Gt. Brit.	56.15 N	2.25 W
122	Figeac (fē-zhȧk')... Fr.	44.38 N	2.1 E
118	Figeholm (fē-ghĕ-hōlm)... Swe.	57.23 N	16.36 E
124	Figueira da Foz (fē-gā'ē-rȧ dä fōzh). Port.	40.9 N	8.51 W
125	Figueras (fē-gā'räs)... Sp.	42.17 N	2.57 W
132	Figuig (fē-gēg')... Mor.	32.12 N	1.20 E
5	Fiji Is. (fē'jē)... Pac. O.	18.0 S	178.0 E
95	Filadelfia (fĭl-ȧ-dĕl'fĭ-ȧ)... C. R.	10.27 N	85.37 W
83	Filbert (fĭl'bērt)... W. Va.	37.17 N	81.33 W
47	Filchner Shelf Ice (fĭlĸ'nēr) Atl. O.	77.30 S	38.0 W
116	Filey (fī'lĭ)... Gt. Brit.	54.13 N	0.17 W
116	Filey Bay... Gt. Brit.	54.12 N	0.15 W
126	Filicudi, (I.) (fē'lē-ko͞o'dē)... It.	38.34 N	14.33 E
118	Filipstad (fĭl'ĭps-städh)... Swe.	59.41 N	14.9 E
75	Fillmore (fĭl'môr)... Utah	38.59 N	112.20 W
111	Filyas (fĭl'yȧs)... Tur.	41.32 N	3.28 E
111	Filyas R... Tur.	41.12 N	32.45 E
117	Finchley (fĭnsh'lĭ) Gt. Brit. (London In.)	51.35 N	0.10 W
84	Findlay (fĭnd'lȧ)... Ohio	41.5 N	83.29 W
160	Fingal (fĭŋ'găl)... Austl. (Tas. In.)	41.38 S	148.2 E
134	Fini R. (fē-nē')... Bel. Cong.	2.45 S	17.45 E
124	Finisterre C. (fĭn-ĭs-târ')... Sp.	42.52 N	9.18 W
117	Finkenwärder (fĭŋ'kĕn-vĕr-dēr) Ger. (Hamburg In.)	53.32 N	9.52 E
158	Finke R. (fĭŋ'kē)... Austl.	26.0 S	135.30 E
119	Finland (fĭn'lănd)... Eur.	62.20 N	27.0 E
119	Finland, G. of... Eur.	60.0 N	27.0 E
54	Finlay R. (fĭn'lȧ)... Can.	57.30 N	125.30 W
120	Finsterwalde (fĭn'stēr-väl-dĕ). Ger.	51.37 N	13.42 E
102	Fiorito (fyô-rē'tô)... Arg. (In.)	34.43 S	58.26 W
51	Fir (fûr)... Wash. (Seattle In.)	48.21 N	122.20 W

ăt; finăl; rāte; senȧte; ärm; ȧsk; sofȧ; fâre; ch-choose; dh-as th in other; bē; ēvent; bĕt; recĕnt; cratēr; g-go; gh-gutteral g; bĭt; ĭ-short neutral; rīde; ĸ-gutteral k as ch in German ich;

194

Page	Name Pronunciation Region	Lat. °′	Long. °′
111	Firat (Euphrates) (R.) (fē-rät') (ū-frā'tēz). Asia	38.0 N	39.5 E
131	Firdân (fēr-dän') Eg. (Suez Can. In.)	30.42 N	32.21 E
140	Firdaus (fēr-dȧ'o͞os) Iran	34.5 N	58.14 E
126	Firenze (Florence) (fē-rĕnt'sä) It.	43.47 N	11.15 E
126	Firenzuola (fē-rĕnt-swô'lä) It.	44.6 N	11.24 E
160	Fires, B. of Austl. (Tas. In.)	41.2 S	148.20 E
72	Firestone (fīr'stōn) Colo. (Denver In.)	40.8 N	104.57 W
122	Firminy (fēr-mē-nē') Fr.	45.22 N	4.15 E
117	Fischbeck (fĭsh'bĕk) Ger. (Hamburg In.)	53.28 N	9.50 E
97	Fish Cays (Is.) Ba. Is.	22.30 N	74.15 W
81	Fisher (fĭsh'ēr) La.	31.28 N	93.30 W
54	Fisher Str. Can.	62.45 N	84.15 W
86	Fish L. Me.	46.48 N	68.48 W
86	Fitchburg (fĭch'bûrg) Mass.	42.35 N	71.50 W
160	Fitzgerald (fĭts-jĕr'ăld) Austl. (Tas. In.)	42.47 S	146.36 E
82	Fitzgerald Ga.	31.42 N	83.18 W
158	Fitzroy (fĭts-roi') Austl.	18.0 S	125.45 E
156	Fitzroy B. N. Z. (In.)	41.23 S	174.53 E
102	Fitzroy, Mt. Arg.	49.15 S	73.0 W
158	Fitzroy R. Austl.	18.30 S	125.0 E
84	Fitzwilliam I. (fĭts-wĭl'yŭm) Can.	45.30 N	81.45 W
126	Fiume (fyo͞o'mä) Yugo.	45.20 N	14.26 E
73	Five Points Utah (Salt Lake City In.)	41.17 N	111.57 W
118	Fjällbacka (fyĕl'băk-ȧ) Swe.	58.36 N	11.18 E
118	Flaam (flôm) Nor.	60.52 N	7.9 E
75	Flagstaff Ariz.	35.12 N	111.39 W
77	Flambeau R. (flăm-bō') Wis.	45.42 N	90.48 W
114	Flamborough Hd. (flăm'bŭr-ô) Gt. Brit.	54.10 N	0.0
97	Flamingo Cay (I.) (flȧ-mĭŋ'gô) Ba. Is.	22.53 N	75.51 W
91	Flamingo Pt. St. Thomas (In.)	18.19 N	64.58 W
76	Flandreau (flăn'drō) S. D.	44.2 N	96.34 W
114	Flannan (Is.) (flăn'ăn) Gt. Brit.	58.15 N	7.35 W
108	Flatey (I.) (flăt'ā) Ice.	65.18 N	22.45 W
71	Flathead L. (flăt'hĕd) Mont.	47.57 N	114.6 W
71	Flathead R. Mont.	48.40 N	114.10 W
71	Flathead R., Middle Fork Mont.	48.20 N	113.40 W
71	Flathead R., South Fork Mont.	48.50 N	113.50 W
157	Flat Pt. N. Z.	41.13 S	176.0 E
70	Flattery, C. (flăt'ēr-ĭ) Wash.	48.23 N	124.44 W
71	Flat Willow Cr. Mont.	46.45 N	108.43 W
153	Flecha Pt. (flä'chä) Phil.	7.21 N	123.26 E
153	Flechas Pt. (flä'chäs) Phil.	10.22 N	119.34 E
116	Fleetwood (flēt'wo͝od) Gt. Brit.	53.55 N	3.1 W
118	Flekkefjord (flĕk'kē-fyôr) Nor.	58.18 N	6.40 E
84	Flemingsburg (flĕm'ĭngz-bûrg) Ky.	38.26 N	83.48 W
120	Flensburg (flĕns'bo͝orgh) Ger.	54.44 N	9.25 E
122	Flers (flâr) Fr.	48.43 N	0.35 W
159	Flinders I. (flĭn'dērz) Austl.	40.0 S	148.0 E
159	Flinders-Murray Reg. (mûr'ĭ) Austl.	34.0 S	142.0 E
158	Flinders Ra. (flĭn'dērz) Austl.	31.25 S	138.48 E
159	Flinders Rfs. Austl.	17.45 S	148.30 E
116	Flint (flĭnt) Gt. Brit.	53.15 N	3.7 W
84	Flint Mich.	43.2 N	83.40 W
116	Flint Co. Gt. Brit.	53.12 N	3.0 W
82	Flint R. Ga.	30.52 N	84.0 W
73	Flippen (flĭp'ĕn) Ga. (Atlanta In.)	33.30 N	84.11 W
118	Flisen (flē'sĕn) Nor.	60.35 N	12.3 E
117	Flixton (flĭks'tŭn) Gt. Brit. (Liverpool In.)	53.26 N	2.24 W
79	Flora (flō'rȧ) Ill.	38.39 N	88.29 W
84	Flora Ind.	40.32 N	86.30 W
82	Florala (flŏr-ăl'ȧ) Ala.	31.1 N	86.19 W
82	Florence (flŏr'ĕns) Ala.	34.47 N	87.40 W
75	Florence Ariz.	33.3 N	111.23 W
73	Florence Calif. (Los Angeles In.)	33.58 N	118.14 W
78	Florence Colo.	38.23 N	105.8 W
126	Florence (Firenze) It.	43.47 N	11.15 E
79	Florence Kan.	38.14 N	96.56 W
83	Florence S. C.	34.11 N	79.46 W
100	Florencia (flō-rĕn'sē-ȧ) Col.	1.45 N	75.15 W
99	Florencia Varela (flō-rĕn'sē-ȧ vä-rā'lä) Arg. (Buenos Aires In.)	34.51 S	58.14 W
101	Flores (flō'rĕzh) Braz.	7.58 S	37.58 W
94	Flores (flō'rĕs) Guat. (In.)	16.53 N	89.54 W
132	Flores I. (flō'rĕzh) Az. Is. (In.)	39.30 N	31.10 W
150	Flores (I.) (flō'rĕs) Indon.	8.40 S	121.30 E
150	Flores Sea Indon.	7.15 S	122.30 E
80	Floresville Tex.	29.8 N	98.9 W
101	Floriano (flō-rē-ä'no͞o) Braz.	6.47 S	43.1 W
102	Florianópolis (flō-rē-ä-nō'pô-lēs) Braz.	27.35 S	48.30 W
102	Florida (flô-rē'dhä) Arg. (In.)	34.32 S	58.30 W
102	Florida Ur.	34.10 S	56.25 W
82	Florida (State) (flŏr'ĭ-dȧ) U. S.	30.20 N	84.0 W
83	Florida B. Fla. (In.)	24.55 N	81.0 W
151	Floridablanca (flō-rē'dä-bläŋ'kä) Phil. (Manila In.)	14.59 N	120.26 E
159	Florida (I.) Solomon Is. (Prot.)	9.5 S	160.8 E
83	Florida Keys Fla. (In.)	24.40 N	81.10 W
80	Florido, R. (flô-rē'dō) Mex.	27.0 N	105.0 W
117	Floridsdorf (flō'rĭds-dôrf) Aus. (Wien In.)	48.16 N	16.24 E
127	Florina (flô-rē'nä) Grc.	40.47 N	21.24 E
72	Florissant (flŏr'ĭ-sănt) Colo. (Colo. Sprs. In.)	38.57 N	105.17 W
118	Florö (flôr'ü) Nor.	61.36 N	5.2 E
73	Floyd (floid) Ga. (Atlanta In.)	33.51 N	84.33 W
78	Floydada (floi-dā'dȧ) Tex.	33.59 N	101.19 W
96	Floyd R. Ia.	42.50 N	96.10 W
126	Flumendosa R. (flo͞o-mĕn-dō'sä) Sard.	39.40 N	9.18 E
	Flushing, see Vlissingen, Neth.		
84	Flushing (flŭsh'ĭng) Mich.	43.4 N	83.52 W

Page	Name Pronunciation Region	Lat. °′	Long. °′
88	Flushing N. Y. (In.)	40.45 N	73.50 W
88	Flushing B. N. Y. (In.)	40.46 N	73.51 W
151	Fly R. Neth. N. Gui.-Pap. Ter.	7.0 S	141.0 E
127	Foča (fō'chä) Yugo.	43.29 N	18.48 E
121	Focşani (fôk-shä'nē) Rom.	45.41 N	27.13 E
126	Foggia (fôd'jä) It.	41.27 N	15.33 E
87	Fogo (fô'gō) Can.	49.38 N	54.12 W
132	Fogo I. (fō'gō) C. V. Is. (In.)	14.55 N	24.25 W
87	Fogo I. Can.	49.35 N	54.10 W
120	Fohnsdorf (fōns'dôrf) Aus.	47.13 N	14.41 E
120	Föhr (I.) (fûr) Ger.	54.53 N	8.30 E
122	Foix (fwä) Fr.	42.59 N	1.38 E
126	Foligno (fô-lēn'yō) It.	42.57 N	12.41 E
115	Folkestone (fōk'stŭn) Gt. Brit.	51.5 N	1.8 E
116	Folkingham (fō'kĭng-ăm) Gt. Brit.	52.53 N	0.24 W
78	Folsom (fōl'sŭm) N. M.	36.49 N	103.55 W
74	Folsom City Calif.	38.39 N	121.10 W
77	Fonda (fŏn'dȧ) Ia.	42.35 N	94.51 W
77	Fond du Lac (fŏn dū lăk') Wis.	43.48 N	88.28 W
126	Fondi (fōn'dē) It.	41.23 N	13.27 E
124	Fonsagrada (fôn-sä-grä'dhä) Sp.	43.7 N	7.6 W
94	Fonseca, G. of (fôn-sā'kä) Cen. Am.	13.0 N	87.50 W
122	Fontainebleau (fôN-tĕn-blō') Fr.	48.25 N	2.45 E
73	Fontana (fŏn-tă'nȧ) Calif. (Los Angeles In.)	34.6 N	117.28 W
100	Fonte Boa (fōn'tȧ bō'ȧ) Braz.	2.31 S	66.2 W
123	Fontenay-en-Parisis (fôNt-nĕ'-äN-pȧ-rē-sē') Fr. (In.)	49.3 N	2.27 E
122	Fontenay-le-Comte (fôNt-nĕ'-lē-kôNt') Fr.	46.28 N	0.50 W
145	Foochow (fo͞o'chō') Chn.	26.5 N	119.12 E
160	Footscray (fo͝ots'krā) Austl. (Melbourne In.)	37.49 S	144.53 E
144	Foo Yong R. (fo͞o-yông') Chn.	28.25 N	107.34 E
53	Foraker, Mt. (fôr'ȧ-kēr) Alsk.	63.0 N	151.30 W
123	Forbach (fôr'bäk) Fr.	49.11 N	6.55 E
159	Forbes (fôrbz) Austl.	33.28 S	148.0 E
159	Forbes Austl.	33.22 S	148.2 E
132	Forcados (fôr-kä'dōs) Nig.	5.21 N	5.28 E
123	Forcalquier (fôr-kȧl-kyā') Fr.	43.38 N	5.49 E
120	Forchheim (fôrk'hĭm) Ger.	49.43 N	11.3 E
79	Fordyce (fôr'dīs) Ark.	33.47 N	92.25 W
132	Forecariah (fōr-kȧ-rē'ȧ') Fr. W. Afr.	9.32 N	13.12 W
115	Forest (fô-rĕ') (fŏrĕst) Bel.	50.45 N	4.20 E
82	Forest (fŏr'ĕst) Miss.	32.22 N	89.28 W
77	Forest City Ia.	43.15 N	93.56 W
83	Forest City N. C.	35.20 N	81.52 W
85	Forest City Pa.	41.35 N	75.30 W
70	Forest Grove Ore.	45.30 N	123.6 W
73	Forest Park Ga. (Atlanta In.)	33.37 N	84.21 W
76	Forest R. N. D.	48.10 N	97.40 W
50	Foret, Mt. (fô-rĕ') Grnld.	65.50 N	37.41 W
122	Forez Mts. (fô-rĕ') Fr.	45.55 N	3.45 E
114	Forfar (fôr'fȧr) Gt. Brit.	56.35 N	2.51 W
82	Forked Deer R. Tenn.	35.56 N	89.30 W
82	Forked Deer R., North Fork Tenn.	35.52 N	89.0 W
82	Forked Deer R., South Fork Tenn.	35.30 N	88.44 W
88	Forks N. Y. (Niagara Falls In.)	42.54 N	78.46 W
72	Forks Creek Colo. (Denver In.)	39.45 N	105.24 W
126	Forli (fôr-lē') It.	44.14 N	12.2 E
116	Formby (fôrm'bē) Gt. Brit.	53.33 N	3.3 W
116	Formby Pt. Gt. Brit.	53.33 N	3.7 W
125	Formentera I. (fôr-mĕn-tā'rä) Sp.	38.45 N	1.25 E
97	Formigas Bk. (fōr-mē'gäs) W. I.	18.32 N	75.42 W
102	Formosa (State) (fôr-mō'sä) Arg.	24.45 S	60.0 W
102	Formosa Arg.	26.10 S	58.14 W
101	Formosa Braz.	15.28 S	47.15 W
148	Formosa (Taiwan) (fŏr-mō'sȧ) (tī-wän') Chn. (In.)	24.0 N	121.0 E
148	Formosa Str. Chn. (For. In.)	25.0 N	120.0 E
79	Forrest City (fŏr'ĕst) Ark.	35.1 N	90.46 W
159	Forsayth (fôr-sīth') Austl.	18.29 S	143.35 E
118	Forshaga (fôrs'hä'gä) Swe.	59.32 N	13.29 E
120	Forst (fōrst) Ger.	51.45 N	14.38 E
82	Forsyth (fôr-sīth') Ga.	33.3 N	83.57 W
71	Forsyth Mont.	46.15 N	106.40 W
101	Fortaleza (Ceará) (fôr-tä-lā'zȧ) (sä-ȧ-rä') Braz.	3.40 S	38.32 W
140	Fort Aleksandrovsk (Ft. Uritskogo) (ȧ-lyĕk-sän'drôfsk) (o͞o'rĭts-kō-gō) Sov. Un.	44.30 N	50.15 E
75	Fort Apache Ind. Res. (ȧ-păch'ē) Ariz.	34.0 N	110.15 W
133	Fort Archambault (fôr är-chäN-bō') Fr. Eq. Afr.	9.7 N	18.21 E
77	Fort Atkinson (ăt'kĭn-sŭn) Wis.	42.55 N	88.50 W
150	Fort Bayard (fôr bȧ-yär') Indoch.	21.15 N	110.15 E
71	Fort Benton (bĕn'tŭn) Mont.	47.50 N	110.40 W
76	Fort Berthold Ind. Res. (bērth'ōld) N. D.	47.40 N	102.30 W
74	Fort Bragg (fôr brăg) Calif.	39.27 N	123.48 W
84	Fort Branch (fôr brănch) Ind.	38.16 N	87.34 W
132	Fort Charlet (fôr shȧr-lĕ') Alg.	24.37 N	9.36 E
78	Fort Collins (fôr kŏl'ĭns) Colo.	40.35 N	105.6 W
133	Fort Crampel (fôr krȧm-pĕl') Fr. Eq. Afr.	7.6 N	19.10 E
135	Fort Dauphin (fôr dō-făN') Madag.	25.0 S	46.58 E
91	Fort de France (fôr dē fräNs) Mart.	14.40 N	61.8 W
132	Fort Delion (Haci Inifel) (fôr dē-lē-ôN') (hȧ'sē ē-nē-fĕl') Alg.	29.47 N	3.57 E
133	Fort de Possell (dē pô-sĕl') Fr. Eq. Afr.	5.2 N	19.11 E
158	Fortescue R. (fôr'tĕs-kū) Austl.	22.0 S	118.0 E
77	Fort Dodge (dŏj) Ia.	42.30 N	94.10 W
85	Fort Edward (ĕd'wērd) N. Y.	43.16 N	73.35 W
88	Fort Erie (ē'rĭ) Can. (Niagara Falls In.)	42.54 N	78.55 W
85	Fort Eustis (ūs'tĭs) Va.	37.10 N	76.35 W
86	Fort Fairfield (fâr'fēld) Me.	46.47 N	68.5 W

Page	Name Pronunciation Region	Lat. °′	Long. °′
132	Fort Flatters (fôr flȧ-târ') Alg.	28.4 N	6.31 E
77	Fort Frances (frăn'cĕz) Can.	48.35 N	93.25 W
82	Fort Gaines (gānz) Ga.	31.36 N	85.3 W
55	Fort George R. (jôrj) Can.	54.0 N	78.0 W
79	Fort Gibson (gĭb'sŭn) Okla.	35.47 N	95.15 W
114	Forth, Firth of (fûrth ŭv fōrth') Gt. Brit.	56.10 N	2.40 W
160	Forth R. (fôrth) Austl. (Tas. In.)	41.25 S	146.10 E
135	Fort Hall (hôl) Kenya	0.40 S	37.3 E
71	Fort Hall Ind. Res. Ida.	43.0 N	112.30 W
133	Fort Harrington (Moyale) (hăr'ĭng-tŭn) (mō-yä'lĕ) Kenya	3.28 N	39.6 E
75	Fort Huachuca (wä-cho͞o'kä) Ariz.	31.32 N	110.21 W
56	Fortier (fôr-tyā') Can. (Winnipeg In.)	49.56 N	97.55 W
134	Fort Jameson (jām'sŭn) N. Rh.	13.39 S	32.39 E
134	Fort Johnston Nya.	14.21 S	35.12 E
86	Fort Kent (kĕnt) Me.	47.14 N	68.37 W
132	Fort Lallemand (fôr lȧ-lē-mäN') Alg.	31.17 N	6.12 E
133	Fort Lamy (fôr lȧ-mē') Fr. Eq. Afr.	12.12 N	15.3 E
72	Fort Langley (lăng'lĭ) Can. (Vancouver In.)	49.10 N	122.34 W
132	Fort Lapperrine (fôr lȧ-pē-rēn') Alg.	22.45 N	5.45 E
83	Fort Lauderdale (lô'dēr-dāl) Fla. (In.)	26.8 N	80.9 W
79	Fort Leavenworth (lĕv'ĕn-wûrth) Kan.	39.21 N	94.55 W
88	Fort Lee N. J. (New York In.)	40.51 N	73.48 W
97	Fort Liberte (lē-bĕr-tā') Hai.	19.40 N	71.52 W
72	Fort Logan (lō'găn) Colo. (Denver In.)	39.38 N	105.3 W
78	Fort Lupton (lŭp'tŭn) Colo.	40.4 N	104.48 W
132	Fort Mac Mahon (fôr măk mȧ-ôN') Alg.	29.50 N	1.48 E
79	Fort Madison (măd'ĭ-sŭn) Ia.	40.38 N	91.19 W
134	Fort Manning (măn'ĭng) Nya.	13.45 S	32.58 E
83	Fort Meade (mēd) Fla. (In.)	27.45 N	81.47 W
83	Fort Mill S. C.	35.2 N	80.58 W
151	Fort Mills (mĭlz) Phil. (Manila In.)	14.24 N	120.30 E
112	Fort Miribel (fôr mē-rē-bĕl') Alg.	28.58 N	2.57 E
74	Fort Mohave Ind. Res. (mô-hä'vä) Ariz.-Nev.	35.0 N	114.38 W
85	Fort Monroe (mŏn-rō') Va.	37.0 N	76.22 W
78	Fort Morgan (môr'găn) Colo.	40.13 N	103.48 W
83	Fort Myers (mī'ērz) Fla. (In.)	26.37 N	81.51 W
112	Fort National (fôr nȧ-syô-nȧl') Alg.	36.43 N	4.15 E
54	Fort Nelson (nĕl'sŭn) Can.	58.46 N	123.20 W
54	Fort Nelson R. Can.	59.0 N	123.0 W
82	Fort Payne (pān) Ala.	34.36 N	85.42 W
71	Fort Peck (pĕk) Mont.	47.58 N	106.30 W
71	Fort Peck Dam Site Mont.	47.58 N	106.25 W
83	Fort Pierce (pērs) Fla. (In.)	27.26 N	80.20 W
132	Fort Polignac (fôr pô-lē-nyȧk') Alg.	26.30 N	8.35 E
133	Fort Portal (pôr'tȧl) Ug.	0.40 N	30.17 E
90	Fort Randolph (răn'dŏlf) C. Z. (In.)	9.23 N	79.53 W
89	Fortress Monroe Va. (Norfolk In.)	37.0 N	76.19 W
79	Fort Riley (rī'lĭ) Kan.	39.4 N	96.46 W
134	Fort Rosebery (rōz'bēr-ĭ) N. Rh.	11.12 S	28.52 E
134	Fort Rousset (fôr ro͞o-sĕ') Fr. Eq. Afr.	0.29 S	15.46 E
54	Fort St. John Can.	56.18 N	120.50 W
141	Fort Sandeman (săn'dā-măn) Pak.	31.15 N	69.29 E
79	Fort Scott (skŏt) Kan.	37.51 N	94.42 W
55	Fort Severn (sĕv'ērn) Can.	55.58 N	87.35 W
77	Fort Sheridan (shĕr'ĭ-dăn) Ill.	42.14 N	87.49 W
133	Fort Sibut (fôr sē-bü') Fr. Eq. Afr.	5.45 N	19.3 E
78	Fort Sill (sĭl) Okla.	34.38 N	98.23 W
79	Fort Smith Ark.	35.23 N	94.24 W
89	Fort Snelling (snĕl'ĭng) Minn. (Minneapolis In.)	44.53 N	93.12 W
51	Fort Stevens (stē-vĕnz) Ore. (Portland In.)	46.12 N	123.57 W
80	Fort Stockton (stŏk'tŭn) Tex.	30.54 N	102.53 W
78	Fort Sumner (sŭm'nēr) N. M.	34.29 N	104.15 W
89	Fort Thomas (tŏm'ȧs) Ky. (Cincinnati In.)	39.4 N	84.27 W
135	Fort Tura (Ruins) (to͞o'rä) Eg.	29.56 N	31.17 E
70	Fortuna (fŏr-tū'nȧ) Calif.	40.36 N	124.8 W
87	Fortune B. (fôr'tūn) Can.	47.25 N	55.25 W
97	Fortune I. Ba. Is.	22.38 N	74.20 W
82	Fort Valley (văl'ĭ) Ga.	32.33 N	83.53 W
54	Fort Vermilion (vēr-mĭl'yŭn) Can.	58.28 N	115.44 W
84	Fortville Ind.	39.38 N	85.48 W
84	Fort Wayne (wān) Ind.	41.4 N	85.10 W
56	Fort Whyte (whīt) Can. (Winnipeg In.)	49.46 N	97.14 W
55	Fort William (wĭl'yăm) Can.	48.20 N	89.15 W
114	Fort William Gt. Brit.	56.48 N	5.5 W
81	Fort Worth (wûrth) Tex.	32.45 N	97.18 W
53	Fortymile (fôr'tĭ-mīl) Can.	64.20 N	140.35 W
53	Fort Yukon (yo͞o'kŏn) Alsk.	66.28 N	145.15 W
126	Fossano (fōs-sä'nō) It.	44.33 N	7.43 E
76	Fossil Cycad Natl. Mon. (fŏs-ĭl sī'kăd) S. D.	43.23 N	103.42 W
126	Fossombrone (fôs-sôm-brō'nā) It.	43.42 N	12.47 E
76	Fosston (fŏs'tŭn) Minn.	47.35 N	95.42 W
84	Fostoria (fŏs-tō'rĭ-ȧ) Ohio	41.10 N	83.24 W
122	Fougères (fo͞o-zhâr') Fr.	48.22 N	1.11 W
114	Foula (I.) (fou'lȧ) Gt. Brit. (In.)	60.5 N	2.5 W
117	Foulness (foul-nĕs') Gt. Brit. (London In.)	51.36 N	0.52 E
157	Foulwind C. (foul'wĭnd) N. Z.	41.45 S	171.35 E
132	Foumban (fo͞om-bän') Cam.	5.48 N	10.48 E
72	Fountain (foun'tĭn) Colo. (Colo. Sprs. In.)	38.41 N	104.42 W
78	Fountain Cr. Colo.	38.40 N	104.43 W
122	Fourchambaut (fo͞or-shäN-bō') Fr.	47.0 N	3.9 E

ng-sing; ŋ-baŋk; N-nasalized n; nŏd; cŏmmit; ōld; ôbey; ôrder; fo͞od; fo͝ot; ou-out; s-soft; sh-dish; th-thin; pūre; ûnite; ûrn; stŭd; circŭs; ü-as "y" in study; '-indeterminate vowel.

Fourche PRONOUNCING INDEX Galapagar

Page	Name Pronunciation Region	Lat. °′	Long. °′
79	Fourche la Fave R. (fo͞orsh lä fȧv′) Ark.	34.57 N	93.20 W
122	Fourmies (fo͞or-mē′)..........Fr.	50.0 N	4.5 E
72	Fourmile Cr. (fōr′mīl) Colo. (Colo. Sprs. In.)	38.47 N	105.20 W
72	Fourmile Cr...Colo. (Denver In.)	40.3 N	105.30 W
88	Four Mile Cr. N. Y. (Niagara Falls In.)	43.14 N	79.2 W
132	Fouta Djalon Mts. (fo͞o′tä shä-lŏŋ) Fr. W. Afr.	11.30 N	17.0 W
157	Foveaux Str. (fô-vō′)........N. Z.	46.40 S	168.0 E
146	Fowcheng (fō′chĕng′).......Chn.	37.59 N	116.4 E
144	Fowchow (fō-chō′).........Chn.	29.47 N	107.24 E
78	Fowler (foul′ẽr)............Colo.	38.6 N	104.3 W
84	Fowler....................Ind.	40.38 N	87.21 W
80	Fowlerton..................Tex.	28.27 N	98.50 W
146	Fowning (fō′nĭng′)..........Chn.	33.43 N	119.49 E
87	Foxboro (fŏks′bŭr-ô)..Mass. (In.)	42.4 N	71.15 W
55	Foxe Channel (fŏks)........Can.	66.10 N	81.0 W
55	Foxe Land.................Can.	65.30 N	77.0 W
84	Fox I....................Mich.	45.25 N	85.50 W
51	Fox I........Wash. (Seattle In.)	47.14 N	122.37 W
52	Fox Is....................Alsk.	54.0 N	166.0 W
77	Fox R.....................Wis.	44.0 N	88.3 W
77	Fox R......................Ill.	41.50 N	88.18 W
72	Foxton........Colo. (Denver In.)	39.25 N	105.15 W
156	Foxton...................N. Z.	40.25 S	175.18 E
114	Foyle Lough (L.) (lŏκ foil′). N. Ire.	55.5 N	7.10 W
125	Fraga (frä′gä)...............Sp.	41.32 N	0.21 E
96	Fragoso Cay (I.) (frä-gō′sô). Cuba	22.40 N	79.25 W
151	Fraile I. (frä-ē′lā) Phil. (Manila In.)	14.18 N	120.34 E
127	Francavilla (fräŋ-kä-vēl′lä)....It.	40.31 N	17.36 E
122	France (frȧns)..............Eur.	48.0 N	2.0 E
73	Frances (frȧn′sĕz) Calif. (Los Angeles In.)	33.42 N	117.45 W
96	Frances C.................Cuba	21.52 N	83.55 W
96	Frances, Pt..........Isle of Pines	21.38 N	83.10 W
97	Frances Viejo, C. (frän′sȧs vyā′hô) Dom. Rep.	19.37 N	69.51 W
134	Franceville (fräɴs-vēl′). Fr. Eq. Afr.	1.40 S	13.36 E
134	Francistown (frȧn′sĭs-toun)..Bech.	21.15 S	27.28 E
123	Franconville (fräɴ-kôɴ-vēl′) Fr. (In.)	48.58 N	2.13 E
120	Frankenthal (fräŋk′ĕn-täl)...Ger.	49.32 N	8.22 E
88	Frankford (frăŋk′fŭrd) Pa. (Philadelphia In.)	40.1 N	75.5 W
88	Frankford Cr. Pa. (Philadelphia In.)	40.4 N	75.6 W
84	Frankfort (frăŋk′fŭrt).......Ind.	40.15 N	86.32 W
79	Frankfort.................Kan.	39.41 N	96.21 W
84	Frankfort..................Ky.	38.11 N	84.55 W
84	Frankfort.................Mich.	44.39 N	86.13 W
85	Frankfort.................N. Y.	43.6 N	75.6 W
51	Frankfort...Wash. (Portland In.)	46.16 N	123.45 W
120	Frankfurt (fräŋk′fo͝ort)......Ger.	52.20 N	14.30 E
120	Frankfurt..................Ger.	50.7 N	8.41 E
160	Franklin (frăŋk′lĭn) Austl. (Tas. In.)	43.4 S	147.0 E
84	Franklin...................Ind.	39.37 N	86.3 W
82	Franklin...................Ky.	36.44 N	86.34 W
81	Franklin...................La.	29.46 N	91.30 W
87	Franklin............Mass. (In.)	42.5 N	71.23 W
78	Franklin..................Neb.	40.5 N	98.58 W
86	Franklin..................N. H.	43.25 N	71.40 W
84	Franklin..................Ohio	39.34 N	84.19 W
85	Franklin...................Pa.	41.25 N	79.50 W
82	Franklin..................Tenn.	35.55 N	86.55 W
83	Franklin...................Va.	36.40 N	76.57 W
55	Franklin Dist. of...........Can.	69.0 N	84.0 W
74	Franklin L................Nev.	40.25 N	115.20 W
157	Franklin, Mt..............N. Z.	42.2 S	172.48 E
88	Franklin Park...Ill. (Chicago In.)	41.56 N	87.52 W
160	Franklin R......Austl. (Tas. In.)	42.20 S	145.47 E
81	Franklinton.................La.	30.51 N	90.9 W
	Franz Josef Land, see Fridtjof Nansen Land, Arc. O.		
126	Frascati (fräs-kä′tē)...........It.	41.48 N	12.41 E
114	Fraserburgh (frā′zẽr-bûrg) Gt. Brit.	57.40 N	2.0 W
159	Fraser (Great Sandy) I. (frā′zẽr) Austl.	25.0 S	153.5 E
70	Fraser R..................Can.	49.10 N	122.20 W
72	Fraser R. North Arm Can. (Vancouver In.)	49.12 N	123.6 W
72	Fraser R. North Arm, North Fork. Can. (Vancouver In.)	49.13 N	123.12 W
72	Fraser R. North Arm, South Fork Can. (Vancouver In.)	49.10 N	123.12 W
55	Fraserville (frā′zẽr-vĭl)......Can.	48.59 N	69.10 W
113	Fras, Wadi (R.) (wä′dē fräs′). Libya	30.24 N	17.30 E
102	Fray Bentos (frī bĕn′tōs).....Ur.	33.15 S	58.15 W
76	Frazee (frȧ-zē′)...........Minn.	46.42 N	95.44 W
118	Fredericia (frĕdh-ĕ-rē′tsē-ȧ)..Den.	55.33 N	9.45 E
72	Frederick (frĕd′ẽr-ĭk) Colo. (Denver In.)	40.6 N	104.56 W
85	Frederick..................Md.	39.26 N	77.27 W
78	Frederick.................Okla.	34.23 N	99.0 W
80	Fredericksburg.............Tex.	30.16 N	98.52 W
85	Fredericksburg..............Va.	38.18 N	77.38 W
79	Fredericktown..............Mo.	37.32 N	90.17 W
55	Fredericton (frĕd′ẽr-ĭk-tŭn)..Can.	45.46 N	66.35 W
151	Frederik Hendrik I. (hĕn′drēk) Neth. N. Gui.	7.40 S	138.20 E
118	Frederikshavn (frĕdh′ĕ-rēks-houn) Den.	57.28 N	10.31 E
118	Frederikssund (frĕdh′ĕ-rēks-so͝on) Den.	55.49 N	12.2 E
91	Frederiksted (frĕd′rĭk-stĕd) St. Croix I. (P. R. In.)	17.44 N	64.54 W
79	Fredonia (frē-dō′nĭ-ȧ).......Kan.	37.32 N	95.49 W
85	Fredonia..................N. Y.	42.27 N	79.20 W
	Fredrikshald, see Halden, Nor.		
118	Fredrikstad (frȧdh′rēks-stȧd). Nor.	59.12 N	10.59 E
118	Fredriksvaern (frȧdh′rēks-vĕrn) Nor.	58.59 N	10.1 E
85	Freehold (frē′hōld).........N. J.	40.16 N	74.15 W
85	Freeland (frē′lănd)...........Pa.	41.0 N	75.52 W
87	Freels, C. (frēlz)............Can.	49.15 N	52.25 W
77	Freeport (frē′pōrt)...........Ill.	42.18 N	89.37 W
85	Freeport.................N. Y.	40.41 N	73.36 W
81	Freeport..................Tex.	28.56 N	95.22 W
132	Freetown (frē′toun).........S. L.	8.32 N	13.15 W
124	Fregenal de la Sierra (frā-hȧ-näl′ dā lä syĕr′rä). Sp.	38.11 N	6.39 W
120	Freiberg (frī′bĕrgh).........Ger.	50.56 N	13.19 E
120	Freiburg (frī′bo͞orgh)........Ger.	48.0 N	7.50 E
120	Freienwalde (frī′ĕn-vȧl-dĕ)...Ger.	52.48 N	14.2 E
102	Freirina (frȧ-ĭ-rē′nä).........Chl.	28.29 S	71.25 W
120	Freising (frī′zĭng)...........Ger.	48.24 N	11.44 E
123	Frejus (frā-zhüs′).............Fr.	43.28 N	6.45 E
158	Fremantle (frē′măn-t′l).....Austl.	32.0 S	115.47 E
84	Fremont (frē-mŏnt′).......Mich.	43.27 N	85.58 W
76	Fremont..................Neb.	41.27 N	96.29 W
84	Fremont..................Ohio	41.20 N	83.6 W
73	Fremont I. Utah (Salt Lake City In.)	41.9 N	112.22 W
71	Fremont Peak.............Wyo.	43.5 N	109.36 W
75	Fremont R................Utah	38.23 N	111.0 W
82	French Broad R......Tenn.-N. C.	35.55 N	83.0 W
133	French Equatorial Africa.....Afr.	10.0 N	19.0 E
132	French Guinea (Colony) (gĭ′nē) Fr. W. Afr.	10.30 N	11.0 W
101	French Guiana (gē-ä′nä).....S.A.	4.50 N	52.30 W
	French Indo-China, see Indochina		
84	French Lick................Ind.	38.35 N	86.37 W
78	Frenchman Cr.........Colo.-Neb.	40.24 N	101.30 W
71	Frenchman Cr.............Mont.	48.50 N	107.15 W
160	Frenchmans Cap (Mt.) Austl. (Tas. In.)	42.17 S	145.53 E
133	French Somaliland..........Afr.	12.0 N	42.30 E
132	French Sudan (Colony) (so͞o-dăn′) Fr. W. Afr.	16.0 N	5.0 W
132	French West Africa..........Afr.	17.0 N	2.0 W
92	Fresnillo (frȧs-nēl′yô).......Mex.	23.12 N	102.50 W
74	Fresno (frĕz′nō)...........Calif.	36.44 N	119.48 W
74	Fresno R..................Calif.	36.58 N	120.15 W
74	Fresno Slough..............Calif.	36.35 N	120.10 W
120	Freudenstadt (froi′dĕn-shtät). Ger.	48.27 N	8.25 E
122	Frévent (frā-väɴ′).............Fr.	50.18 N	2.21 E
160	Freycinet Pen. (frā-sē-nĕ′) Austl. (Tas. In.)	42.10 S	148.21 E
120	Fribourg (frē-boor′)........Switz.	46.48 N	7.9 E
72	Friday Harbor Wash. (Vancouver In.)	48.32 N	123.1 W
89	Fridley (frĭd′lĭ) Minn. (Minneapolis In.)	45.5 N	93.17 W
136	Fridtjof Nansen Land (frĕt′yôf nän′sĕn). Arc. O.	80.0 N	50.0 E
120	Friedberg (frēd′bĕrgh).......Ger.	50.20 N	8.46 E
120	Friedland (frēt′länt).........Ger.	53.40 N	13.33 E
	Friedland, see Pravdinsk, Sov. Un.		
120	Friedrichshafen (frē-drĭκs-häf′ĕn) Ger.	47.39 N	9.29 E
79	Friend (frĕnd)..............Neb.	40.38 N	97.16 W
81	Friendswood..........Tex. (In.)	29.31 N	95.11 W
117	Friern Barnet (frī′ẽrn bär′nĕt) Gt. Brit. (London In.)	51.37 N	0.11 W
83	Fries (frēz)..................Va.	36.43 N	80.58 W
90	Frijoles (frē-hō′lȧs) Canal Zone (In.)	9.11 N	79.49 W
101	Frio, C. (frē′ō)............Braz.	22.50 S	42.0 W
134	Frio, C..............S. W. Afr.	18.30 S	12.5 E
124	Friol (frē-ōl′)...............Sp.	43.2 N	7.47 W
80	Frio R....................Tex.	28.30 N	98.55 W
121	Frisches Haff (Sea) (frĭsh′ĕs häf) Pol.	54.30 N	19.50 E
120	Frisian Is., East (frē′zhăn)..Neth.	53.40 N	7.0 E
120	Frisian Is., North...........Ger.	54.40 N	8.30 E
120	Frisian Is., West...........Neth.	53.22 N	4.57 E
55	Frobisher B. (frŏb′ĭsh-ẽr)....Can.	63.0 N	67.0 W
116	Frodingham (frŏd′ĭng-ăm) Gt. Brit.	53.36 N	0.38 W
116	Frodsham (frŏdz′ăm)....Gt. Brit.	53.18 N	2.43 W
158	Frome, L. (fro͞om).........Austl.	30.45 S	139.50 E
116	Frome, R.............Gt. Brit.	52.7 N	2.29 W
79	Frontenac (frŏn′tē-năk).....Kan.	37.27 N	94.40 W
93	Frontera (Alvaro Obregón) (frôn-tā′rä) (äl′vä-rō ō-brā-gōn′). Mex.	18.32 N	92.38 W
122	Frontignan (frôɴ-tē-nyäɴ′)....Fr.	43.36 N	3.47 E
100	Fronton I. (frôn-tōn′)...Peru (In.)	12.7 S	77.12 W
58	Front Range.........Wyo.-Colo.	41.0 N	105.15 W
85	Front Royal..................Va.	38.56 N	78.11 W
126	Frosinone (frō-zē-nō′nȧ).......It.	41.37 N	13.22 E
85	Frostburg (frôst′bûrg).......Md.	39.41 N	78.57 W
123	Frouard (fro͞o-ȧr′)...........Fr.	48.45 N	6.9 E
99	Froward, C. (frō′wẽrd) Chl. (Magallanes In.)	53.55 S	71.10 W
75	Fruita (fro͞ot-ȧ)...........Colo.	39.8 N	108.45 W
138	Frunze (fro͞on′zĕ).......Sov. Un.	42.45 N	74.40 E
121	Frýdek (frē′dĕk)..........Czech.	49.42 N	18.23 E
120	Frýdlant (frēd′länt).......Czech.	50.56 N	15.6 E
120	Frývaldov (frē′väl-dôf)....Czech.	50.13 N	17.13 E
145	Fu R. (fo͞o)................Chn.	28.7 N	115.55 E
146	Fu R.....................Chn.	39.4 N	116.5 E
145	Fuan (fo͞o′än′).............Chn.	27.5 N	119.33 E
143	Fuchin (fo͞o′chĭn′)..........Chn.	47.10 N	131.59 E
145	Fuchow (fo͞o′chō′).........Chn.	27.55 N	116.15 E
146	Fuchow....................Chn.	39.45 N	121.41 E
144	Fuchüan (fo͞o′chü-än′)......Chn.	24.41 N	111.14 E
149	Fuda (fo͞o′dä)....Jap. (Tokyo In.)	35.36 N	139.37 E
94	Fuego (Vol.) (fwā′gō)......Guat.	14.27 N	90.53 W
125	Fuencarral (fuān-kär-räl′). Sp. (In.)	40.29 N	3.41 W
124	Fuensalida (fwān-sä-lē′dä)....Sp.	40.4 N	4.15 W
124	Fuente Álamo (fwĕn′tȧ äl′ä-mō) Sp.	37.45 N	1.14 W
124	Fuente de Cantos (dā kän′tōs). Sp.	38.14 N	6.18 W
125	Fuente el Saz (ēl säth′)...Sp. (In.)	40.38 N	3.30 W
124	Fuente Ovejuna (ōvȧ-ho͞o′nä)..Sp.	38.15 N	5.25 W
124	Fuentesaúco (fwĕn-tȧ-sä-o͞o′kō) Sp.	41.14 N	5.28 W
101	Fuerte Olimpo (fwĕr′tȧ ô-lēmpō) Par.	21.0 S	58.0 W
95	Fuerte San Carlos (fwĕr′tȧ sän kär′lōs). Nic.	11.8 N	84.48 W
132	Fuerteventura (I.) (fwĕr′tȧ-vĕn-to͞o′rä). Can. Is.	28.30 N	14.0 W
152	Fuga I. (fo͞o′gä)............Phil.	18.52 N	121.22 E
117	Fuhlsbüttel (fo͞ols′büt-ĕl) Ger. (Hamburg In.)	53.38 N	10.1 E
149	Fujikawa R. (fo͞o′jē-kä′wä)...Jap.	35.30 N	138.27 E
149	Fuji, Mt. (fo͞o′jē)...........Jap.	35.18 N	138.46 E
149	Fukae (I.) (fo͞o′kä-ĕ)........Jap.	32.44 N	128.45 E
144	Fukang (fo͞o′käng′).........Chn.	23.51 N	113.30 E
145	Fukien (Prov.) (fo͞o′kyĕn′)..Chn.	25.58 N	117.38 E
149	Fukuchiyama (fo͞o′ko͞o-chē-yä′mä) Jap.	35.17 N	135.7 E
149	Fukui (fo͞o′ko͞o-ē)...........Jap.	36.5 N	136.15 E
149	Fukuoka (fo͞o′ko͞o-ō′kȧ).....Jap.	33.31 N	130.29 E
148	Fukushima (fo͞o′ko͞o-shē′mȧ)..Jap.	37.46 N	140.29 E
149	Fukuyaam (fo͞o′ko͞o-yä′mȧ)...Jap.	34.29 N	133.21 E
120	Fulda (fo͝ol′dä).............Ger.	50.34 N	9.42 E
120	Fulda R..................Ger.	50.50 N	9.41 E
73	Fullerton (fo͝ol′ẽr-tŭn) Calif. (Los Angeles In.)	33.52 N	117.55 W
81	Fullerton...................La.	31.0 N	93.0 W
88	Fullerton....Md. (Baltimore In.)	39.22 N	76.31 W
76	Fullerton..................Neb.	41.22 N	97.58 W
82	Fulton.....................Ky.	36.31 N	88.53 W
79	Fulton.....................Mo.	38.51 N	91.56 W
85	Fulton...................N. Y.	43.18 N	76.26 W
131	Fumu Zabi (fü-mü′ zȧ-bē′) (fo͞o′-mo͞o zä′bē). Fr. Eq. Afr. (Brazzaville In.)	4.47 S	14.50 E
149	Funabashi (fo͞o′nȧ-bä′shē)....Jap.	35.43 N	140.0 E
132	Funchal (fo͞on-shäl′)..Madeira Is.	32.36 N	16.58 W
124	Fundão (fo͞on-douɴ′).......Port.	40.8 N	7.30 W
55	Fundy, B. of (fŭn′dĭ).......Can.	45.10 N	65.30 W
144	Fungchun (fo͞ong′cho͞on′)....Chn.	23.21 N	111.27 E
145	Fungshun (fo͞ong′sho͞on′)....Chn.	23.53 N	116.3 E
145	Funing (fo͞o′nĭng′).........Chn.	26.55 N	119.54 E
146	Funing....................Chn.	39.58 N	119.19 E
146	Fuping (fo͞o′pĭng′).........Chn.	38.52 N	114.5 E
93	Furpero (fo͞or-bā′rô)........Mex.	20.25 N	97.32 W
160	Furneaux Group (Is.) (fûr′nō) Austl. (Tas. In.)	40.0 S	148.0 E
72	Furry Cr. (fûr′ĭ)...........Can.	49.35 N	123.10 W
120	Fürstenburg (für′stĕn-bo͞orgh). Ger.	52.8 N	14.39 E
120	Fürstenfeld (für′stĕn-fĕlt)....Aus.	47.3 N	16.3 E
120	Fürstenwalde (für′stĕn-väl-dĕ) Ger.	52.22 N	14.4 E
120	Fürth (fürt)...............Ger.,	49.28 N	10.59 E
149	Furuichi (fo͞o′ro͞o-ē′chē) Jap. (Osaka In.)	34.53 N	135.6 E
147	Fusan (Pusan) (fo͞o′sän′) (po͞o′sän′) Kor.	35.6 N	129.3 E
149	Fuse (fo͞o′sȧ)....Jap. (Osaka In.)	34.40 N	135.34 E
149	Fushiki (fo͞o′shē-kē).........Jap.	36.47 N	137.1 E
149	Fushimi (fo͞o′shē-mē)........Jap.	34.57 N	135.45 E
143	Fushun (fo͞o′sho͞on′)........Chn.	42.0 N	124.5 E
145	Futing (fo͞o′tĭng′)..........Chn.	27.16 N	120.4 E
145	Futo L. (fo͞o′tō′)..........Chn.	29.57 N	114.18 E
149	Futtsu (fo͞ot′tso͞o′). Jap. (Tokyo In.)	35.19 N	139.48 E
131	Fûwa (fo͞o′wȧ)..........Eg. (In.)	31.11 N	30.33 E
143	Fuyu (fo͞o′yo͞o′)............Chn.	45.18 N	125.4 E
118	Fyn (I.) (fü″n).............Den.	55.20 N	10.30 E
114	Fyne (L.) (fīn)..........Gt. Brit.	56.10 N	5.10 W
118	Fyresdal L. (fü′rĕs-däl)......Nor.	59.2 N	8.15 E
141	Fyzabad (fī-zä-bäd′)........India	26.38 N	82.10 E
134	Gaberones (gă-bē-rō′nēz)...Bech.	24.40 S	25.55 E
132	Gabés (gä′bĕs).............Tun.	33.58 N	10.3 E
132	Gabés, G. of...............Tun.	34.15 N	10.45 E
121	Gąbin (gŏɴ′bēn)............Pol.	52.23 N	19.48 E
134	Gabon (Colony) (gȧ-bôɴ′) Fr. Eq. Afr.	1.30 S	12.15 E
72	Gabriola I. (gă-brĭ-ō′lȧ) Can. (Vancouver In.)	49.10 N	123.45 W
127	Gabrovo (gäb′rô-vō).........Bul.	42.50 N	25.20 E
100	Gacheta (gä-chā′tä).........Col.	4.55 N	73.58 W
127	Gacko (gäts′kô)...........Yugo.	43.10 N	18.32 E
132	Gadames (gä-dä′mĕs)......Libya	30.3 N	9.30 E
82	Gadsden (gădz′dĕn).........Ala.	34.1 N	86.1 W
129	Gadyach (gäd-yäch′)....Sov. Un.	50.21 N	33.59 E
127	Gaeşti (gä-yĕsh′tē).........Rom.	44.43 N	25.21 E
126	Gaeta (gä-ȧ′tä)...............It.	41.13 N	13.34 E
126	Gaeta, G. of..................It.	41.12 N	13.40 E
83	Gaffney (găf′nĭ)............S. C.	35.4 N	81.39 W
132	Gafsa (gäf′sä)..............Tun.	34.24 N	8.40 E
86	Gagetown (gāj′toun)........Can.	45.47 N	66.8 W
123	Gagny (gȧ-nyē′)........Fr. (In.)	48.53 N	2.32 E
101	Gaiba (gä-ē′bä).............Bol.	18.0 S	57.45 W
126	Gaidaronisi (I.) (gȧ′ē-dä-rô-nē′sē) Grc. (Crete In.)	34.52 N	25.42 E
122	Gaillac (gȧ-yȧk′)..............Fr.	43.55 N	1.51 E
114	Gaillimh (Galway) (gŏl′lĭv) (gôl′wā). Ire.	53.15 N	9.0 W
83	Gainesville (gānz′vĭl)........Fla.	29.38 N	82.18 W
82	Gainesville.................Ga.	34.17 N	83.48 W
79	Gainesville.................Tex.	33.37 N	97.8 W
114	Gainsborough (gānz′bŭr-ô) Gt. Brit.	53.25 N	0.45 W
158	Gairdner, L. (gȧrd′nẽr).....Austl.	31.30 S	136.0 E
129	Gaisin (gä′ĭ-sēn)........Sov. Un.	48.47 N	29.22 E
129	Gaivoron (gä′ĭ-vô-rôn′)..Sov. Un.	47.39 N	30.11 E
125	Galapagar (gä-lä-pä-gär′). Sp. (In.)	40.35 N	3.59 W

ăt; finăl; rāte; senȧte; ärm; ȧsk; sofȧ; fâre; ch-choose; dh-as th in other; bē; ēvent; bĕt; recĕnt; cratẽr; g-go; gh-gutteral g; bĭt; ĭ-short neutral; rīde; κ-gutteral k as ch in German ich;

Page	Name Pronunciation Region	Lat. °′	Long. °′
100	Galapagos (Colon) Arch. (gä-lä'pä-gôs) (kō-lōn'). Ec.	0.1 S	90.30 W
114	Galashiels (găl-ȧ-shēlz)...Gt. Brit.	55.35 N	1.50 W
127	Galati (gà-lätz'ĭ)...Rom.	45.25 N	28.1 E
127	Galatina (gä-lä-tē'nä)...It.	40.11 N	18.11 E
83	Galax (gā'lăks)...Va.	36.40 N	80.56 W
127	Galaxeidion (gä-läks-ē'dĭ-ŏn). Grc.	38.22 N	22.22 E
118	Galdhöpig (Mt.) (gäl-hû-pēgh') Nor.	61.38 N	8.15 E
80	Galeana (gä-lā-ä'nä)...Mex.	24.50 N	100.4 W
77	Galena (gȧ-lē'nȧ)...Ill.	42.25 N	90.16 W
79	Galena...Kan.	37.5 N	94.38 W
79	Galesburg (gālz'bûrg)...Ill.	40.56 N	90.22 W
77	Galesville (gālz'vĭl)...Wis.	44.5 N	91.22 W
72	Galeton (gāl'tŭn) Colo. (Denver In.)	40.31 N	104.35 W
85	Galeton...Pa.	41.44 N	77.40 W
72	Galiano (găl-ĭ-ä'nō) Can. (Vancouver In.)	48.52 N	123.22 W
128	Galich (gàl'ĭch)...Sov. Un.	58.21 N	42.21 E
121	Galicia (Prov.) (gà-lĭsh'ĭ-à)...Pol.	49.37 N	22.20 E
124	Galicia (Prov.) (gä-lē'thyä)...Sp.	42.50 N	7.50 W
159	Galilee, L. (găl'ĭ-le)...Austl.	22.30 S	145.45 E
137	Galilee, Sea of...Pal.-Syria (In.)	32.50 N	35.35 E
96	Galina Pt. (gä-lē'nä)...Jam.	18.25 N	76.55 W
84	Galion (găl'ĭ-ŭn)...Ohio	40.44 N	82.46 W
133	Galla (gäl'lä) (Division)...Eth.	7.30 N	36.0 E
133	Gallabat (Qallabat) (găl'ȧ-băt) (kà-lä-bät). A. E. Sud.	12.58 N	36.6 E
135	Gallacaio (gäl-lä-kī'ō)...Som.	7.0 N	47.22 E
126	Gallarate (gäl-lä-rä'tä)...It.	45.39 N	8.49 E
79	Gallatin (găl'ȧ-tĭn)...Mo.	39.55 N	93.58 W
82	Gallatin...Tenn.	36.24 N	86.26 W
71	Gallatin R...Mont.	45.15 N	111.15 W
141	Galle (gäl)...Cey.	6.10 N	80.12 E
125	Gallego R. (gäl-yā'gō)...Sp.	42.0 N	0.46 W
100	Gallinas, Pt. (gä-lyē'näs)...Col.	12.15 N	71.45 W
127	Gallipoli (gäl-lē'pō-lē)...It.	40.43 N	17.58 E
127	Gallipoli (Gelibolu) (gȧ-lĭp'ō-lē) (gĕ-lĭb'ō-lōō). Tur.	40.25 N	26.40 E
127	Gallipoli Pen...Tur.	40.20 N	26.30 E
84	Gallipolis (găl-ĭ-pō-lēs')...Ohio	38.50 N	82.15 W
78	Galisteo (gȧ-lĭst'ê-ō)...N. M.	35.23 N	105.58 W
108	Gällivare (yĕl-ĭ-vär'ĕ)...Swe.	20.28 N	67.5 E
127	Gallo, C. (gäl'lō)...Grc.	36.33 N	21.54 E
124	Gallo R. (gäl'yō)...Sp.	40.46 N	1.45 W
75	Gallup (găl'ŭp)...N. M.	35.31 N	108.45 W
85	Galt (gôlt)...Can.	43.18 N	80.18 W
114	Galtee Mts. (gôl'tē)...Ire.	52.20 N	8.15 W
79	Galva (găl'vä)...Ill.	41.10 N	90.2 W
81	Galveston...Tex.	29.19 N	94.49 W
81	Galveston B...Tex. (In.)	29.30 N	94.50 W
81	Galveston I...Tex. (In.)	29.15 N	94.54 W
114	Galway B. (gôl'wā)...Ire.	53.10 N	9.10 W
132	Gambaga (gäm-bä'gä)...G. C.	10.33 N	0.25 W
133	Gambela (găm-bā'lȧ)...Eth.	8.16 N	34.34 E
132	Gambia (găm'bē-ȧ)...Afr.	13.30 N	16.0 W
132	Gambia R...Fr. W. Afr.-Gam.	13.30 N	13.45 W
72	Gambier I. (găm'bēr) Can. (Vancouver In.)	49.30 N	123.24 W
4	Gambier Is...Pac. O.	23.8 S	134.58 W
90	Gamboa (gäm-bō'ä) Canal Zone (In.)	9.7 N	79.43 W
134	Gamboma (gäm-bō'mä) Fr. Eq. Afr.	2.10 S	16.3 E
118	Gamleby (gäm'lĕ-bü)...Swe.	57.54 N	16.21 E
152	Gamu (gä-mōō')...Phil.	17.4 N	121.50 E
115	Gand (Ghent) (gäN) (gĕnt)...Bel.	51.5 N	3.41 W
153	Gandara (gän-dä'rä)...Phil.	12.1 N	124.49 E
87	Gander (găn'dēr)...Can.	48.58 N	54.30 W
87	Gander L...Can.	48.55 N	54.45 W
87	Gander R...Can.	48.45 N	55.15 W
125	Gandia (gän-dē'ä)...Sp.	38.58 N	0.11 W
111	Gandzha (gänd'zhä)...Sov. Un.	40.40 N	46.25 E
122	Ganges (gäNzh)...Fr.	43.55 N	3.42 E
141	Ganges R. (găn'jēz)...India	26.0 N	80.15 E
126	Gangi (gän'jē)...It.	37.47 N	14.12 E
122	Gannat (gän-nä')...Fr.	46.5 N	3.11 E
156	Gannet I. (găn'ĕt)...N. Z.	37.57 S	174.40 E
71	Gannett Peak...Wyo.	43.10 N	109.39 W
132	Gao (gä'ō)...Fr. W. Afr.	16.20 N	0.0
132	Gaoua (gà-ōō-ä')...Fr. W. Afr.	10.20 N	3.8 W
123	Gap (gàp)...Fr.	44.35 N	6.6 E
152	Gapan (gä-pän')...Phil.	15.18 N	120.57 E
95	Garachine (gä-rä-chē'nä)...Pan.	8.3 N	78.21 W
121	Garam (Hron) R. (gŏ'rŏm) (hrōn) Czech.-Hung.	48.35 N	18.40 E
148	Garambi C. (gä-räm'bē). For. (In.)	22.0 N	120.45 E
101	Garanhuns (gä-rän-yōōNsh'). Braz.	8.48 S	36.31 W
79	Garber (gär'bēr)...Okla.	36.26 N	97.32 W
80	Garcia (gär-sē'ä)...Mex.	25.49 N	100.36 W
126	Garda, L. of (gär'dä)...It.	45.45 N	10.45 E
123	Gardanne (gär-dàn')...Fr.	43.27 N	5.28 E
120	Gardelegen (gär-dē-lā'ghĕn)...Ger.	52.32 N	11.21 E
73	Gardena (gär-dē'nȧ) Calif. (Los Angeles In.)	33.54 N	118.17 W
78	Garden City...Kan.	37.57 N	100.53 W
84	Garden I. (gär'd'n)...Mich.	45.48 N	85.40 W
89	Garden Island B. La. (New Orleans In.)	29.5 N	89.9 W
88	Gardenville N. Y. (Niagara Falls In.)	42.51 N	78.45 W
86	Gardiner (gärd'nēr)...Me.	44.13 N	69.47 W
71	Gardiner...Mont.	45.4 N	110.45 W
78	Gardiner...N. M.	36.52 N	104.30 W
86	Gardner...Mass.	42.35 N	72.0 W
88	Garfield (gär'fēld) N. J. (New York In.)	40.52 N	74.6 W
73	Garfield. Utah (Salt Lake City In.)	40.44 N	112.11 W
89	Garfield Heights Ohio (Cleveland In.)	41.24 N	81.36 W
127	Gargalianoi (gär-gä-lyä'nē)...Grc.	37.4 N	21.39 E

Page	Name Pronunciation Region	Lat. °′	Long. °′
119	Gargždai (gärgzh'dī)...Sov. Un.	55.42 N	21.23 E
71	Garland (gär'lănd)...Utah	41.45 N	112.12 W
79	Garnett (gär'nĕt)...Kan.	38.16 N	95.15 W
122	Garonne R. (gà-rôn')...Fr.	44.32 N	0.0
133	Garoua (gär'wä)...Cam.	9.20 N	13.28 E
84	Garrett (găr'ĕt)...Ind.	41.22 N	85.8 W
76	Garrison (găr'ĭ-sŭn)...N. D.	47.38 N	101.25 W
124	Garrovillas (gä-rō-vēl'yäs)...Sp.	39.42 N	6.32 W
54	Garry, L. (găr'ĭ)...Can.	66.10 N	100.30 W
116	Garstang (gär'stăng)...Gt. Brit.	53.55 N	2.47 W
117	Garston (gärs'tŭn) Gt. Brit. (Liverpool In.)	53.21 N	2.54 W
142	Gartok (gär-tŏk')...Chn.	32.0 N	80.27 E
157	Garvie Mts. (gär'vĭ)...N. Z.	45.20 S	169.0 E
121	Garwolin (gär-vō'lēn)...Pol.	51.56 N	21.38 E
84	Gary (gā'rĭ)...Ind.	41.35 N	87.20 W
100	Garzón (gär-thōn')...Col.	2.30 N	75.29 W
152	Gasan (gä-sän')...Phil.	13.19 N	121.52 E
84	Gas City...Ind.	40.30 N	85.42 W
79	Gasconade R. (găs-kō-nād')...Mo.	38.0 N	91.58 W
158	Gascoyne R. (găs-koin')...Austl.	25.0 S	116.28 E
132	Gashiga (gä-shē'gä)...Nig.	7.30 N	11.27 E
135	Gasi (gä'sē)...Kenya	4.25 S	39.31 E
97	Gaspar Hernández (gäs-pär' ĕr-nän'däth). Hai.	19.38 N	70.15 W
86	Gaspé (gàs'pā) (gäs-pā')...Can.	48.51 N	64.31 W
86	Gaspé B...Can.	48.45 N	64.15 W
86	Gaspé, C...Can.	48.45 N	64.10 W
86	Gaspé Pen...Can.	48.48 N	65.30 W
84	Gassaway (găs'ȧ-wā)...W. Va.	38.40 N	80.48 W
83	Gastonia (găs-tō'nĭ-ȧ)...N. C.	35.16 N	81.12 W
132	Gat (gät)...Libya	24.57 N	10.18 E
124	Gata, C. de (gä'tä)...Sp.	36.44 N	2.8 W
113	Gatar, Wadi (R.) (wä'dē gä'tär) Libya	29.43 N	18.30 E
124	Gata, Sierra de (Mt.) (syĕr'rȧ dā gä'tä). Sp.	40.20 N	6.30 W
119	Gatchina (gä-chē'nȧ)...Sov. Un.	59.38 N	30.6 E
114	Gateshead (gāts'hĕd)...Gt. Brit.	54.55 N	1.35 W
81	Gatesville (gāts'vĭl)...Tex.	31.26 N	97.45 W
54	Gatin (găt'ĭn)...Can. (In.)	45.31 N	75.42 W
85	Gatineau R. (gà'tē-nō)...Can.	45.40 N	75.55 W
134	Gatooma (gä-tōō'mä)...S. Rh.	18.27 S	29.50 E
117	Gatow (gä'tō)...Ger. (Berlin In.)	52.29 N	13.11 E
152	Gattaran (gä-tä-rän')...Phil.	18.3 N	121.39 E
90	Gatun (gä-tōōn'). Canal Zone (In.)	9.17 N	79.55 W
95	Gatun L...Pan.	9.5 N	80.0 W
119	Gauja R. (gou'yȧ)...Sov. Un.	57.36 N	25.40 E
151	Gautier Mts. (gō-tyā') Neth. N. Gui.	2.30 S	139.0 E
125	Gavá (gä-vä')...Sp. (In.)	41.18 N	2.1 E
114	Gava, Lough (L.) (lŏK gä'vȧ)...Ire.	53.55 N	8.30 W
126	Gavdos (I.) (gäv'dôs)...Grc.	34.48 N	24.5 E
122	Gave de Pau R. (gäv' dē pō')...Fr.	43.35 N	0.50 W
122	Gave d'Ossau R. (gäv' dôs-sō') Fr.	43.20 N	0.50 W
140	Gavkhaneh (Marsh) (gäv-Kä'nä) Iran	31.45 N	53.30 E
118	Gävle (yĕv'lĕ)...Swe.	60.40 N	17.8 E
118	Gävle B...Swe.	60.43 N	17.20 E
128	Gavrilov (gà-vrē-lôf')...Sov. Un.	57.13 N	39.49 E
129	Gavrilovka (gà'vrē-lôf'ka) Sov. Un.	48.4 N	36.24 E
128	Gavrilov Posad (pô-sàt)...Sov. Un.	56.33 N	40.9 E
158	Gawler (gô'lēr)...Austl.	34.35 S	138.45 E
158	Gawler Ranges...Austl.	32.30 S	136.0 E
141	Gaya (gŭ'yä) (gī'ȧ)...India	24.45 N	84.58 E
132	Gaya (gä'yä)...Nig.	12.0 N	9.10 E
84	Gaylord (gā'lôrd)...Mich.	45.1 N	84.46 W
137	Gaza (gä'zä)...Pal. (In.)	31.29 N	34.27 E
111	Gazi-Ayintap (gä-zĭ ȧ-yĭn-tăp') Tur.	37.5 N	37.32 E
121	Gdańsk (Danzig) (g'dänsk) (dän'tsĭk). Pol.	54.10 N	18.50 E
128	Gdov (g'dôf)...Sov. Un.	58.44 N	27.51 E
121	Gdynia (g'dēn'yä)...Pol.	54.28 N	18.32 E
51	Gearhart (gēr'härt) Ore. (Portland In.)	46.1 N	123.55 W
78	Geary (gē'rĭ)...Okla.	35.36 N	98.18 W
71	Gebo (gĕb'ō)...Wyo.	43.47 N	108.15 W
81	Ged (gĕd)...La.	30.8 N	93.35 W
159	Geelong (jē-lông')...Austl.	38.8 S	144.18 E
151	Geelvink B. (gāl'vĭŋk) Neth. N. Gui.	2.30 S	135.30 E
158	Geikie Range (gē'kē)...Austl.	18.15 S	126.45 E
120	Geislingen (gīs'lĭng-ĕn)...Ger.	48.37 N	9.52 E
127	Gelibolu (Gallipoli) (gĕ-lĭb'ō-lōō) Tur.	40.25 N	26.40 E
125	Gelida (hȧ-lē'dȧ)...Sp. (In.)	41.26 N	1.53 E
129	Gelmyazova (gyĕl'myä-zō'vȧ) Sov. Un.	49.49 N	31.50 E
120	Gelsenkirchen-Buer (gĕl-zĕn-kĭrK-ĕn-bōōr'). Ger.	51.38 N	7.6 E
137	Gemas (jĕm'ȧs)...Malaya (In.)	2.33 N	102.37 E
111	Gemlik (gĕm'lĭk)...Tur.	40.30 N	29.12 E
131	Geneffa, Jebel (Mts.) (jĕ-nĕf'ȧ) Eg. (Suez Canal In.)	30.16 N	32.20 E
74	General Grant Natl. Park...Calif.	36.44 N	118.58 W
99	General Pinto (gā-nā-räl' pēn'tō) Arg. (Buenos Aires In.)	34.44 S	61.57 W
99	General Rodriguez (rô-drē'gāz) Arg. (Buenos Aires In.)	34.37 S	58.58 W
80	General Zepeda (zȧ-pä'dä)...Mex.	25.25 N	101.30 W
80	General Zuazua (zwä'zwä)...Mex.	25.55 N	100.8 W
85	Genesee R. (jĕn-ē-sē')...N. Y.	42.30 N	77.55 W
79	Geneseo (jĕn-ē-sē'ō)...Ill.	41.26 N	90.9 W
82	Geneva (jē-nē'vȧ)...Ala.	31.3 N	85.52 W
79	Geneva...Neb.	40.33 N	97.35 W
85	Geneva...N. Y.	42.52 N	77.0 W
84	Geneva...Ohio	41.57 N	80.47 W
120	Geneva (Génève) (zhä-nĕv'). Switz.	46.13 N	6.11 E
120	Geneva, L...Switz.	46.25 N	6.40 E

Page	Name Pronunciation Region	Lat. °′	Long. °′
120	Généve (Geneva) (zhā-nĕv') Switz.	46.13 N	6.11 E
129	Genichesk (gĕ'nē-chyĕsk'). Sov. Un.	46.11 N	34.49 E
124	Genil R. (hȧ-nēl')...Sp.	37.15 N	4.30 W
127	Genitsa (yĕ-nēt'sä)...Grc.	40.46 N	22.25 E
123	Gennevilliers (zhĕn-vē-yā') Fr. (In.)	48.56 N	2.17 E
76	Genoa (jĕn'ō-ȧ)...Neb.	41.28 N	97.42 W
81	Genoa...Tex. (In.)	29.37 N	95.11 W
126	Genoa (Genova) (jĕn'ō-vä)...It.	44.24 N	8.55 E
126	Genoa, G. of...It.	44.10 N	9.0 E
126	Genova (Genoa) (jĕn'ō-vä) (jen'ō-ȧ). It.	44.24 N	8.55 E
120	Genthin (gĕn-tēn')...Ger.	52.24 N	12.10 E
123	Gentilly (zhäN-tē-yē')...Fr. (In.)	48.48 N	2.21 E
147	Genzan (Wŏnsan) (jĕn'zän) (wŭn'sän). Kor.	39.11 N	127.38 E
158	Geographe B. (jē-ô-grăf')...Austl.	33.25 S	115.15 E
158	Geographe Chan...Austl.	24.45 S	113.15 E
111	Geokchai (gĕ-ôk'chī)...Sov. Un.	40.40 N	47.45 E
87	George B...Can.	45.45 N	61.40 W
54	George Dawson, Mt. (dô'sŭn) Can.	51.27 N	124.32 W
83	George, L...Fla.	29.17 N	81.37 W
85	George, L...N. Y.	43.40 N	73.30 W
157	George Sd...N. Z.	44.50 S	167.25 E
160	Georges R...Austl. (Sydney In.)	33.57 S	150.58 E
160	Georgetown...Austl. (Tas. In.)	41.5 S	146.50 E
101	Georgetown...Br. Gu.	6.45 N	58.15 W
87	Georgetown...Can.	46.10 N	62.30 W
85	Georgetown...Del.	38.42 N	75.22 W
84	Georgetown...Ill.	39.59 N	87.39 W
96	Georgetown...Grand Cayman I.	19.18 N	81.24 W
84	Georgetown...Ky.	38.12 N	84.34 W
85	Georgetown...Md.	39.23 N	75.53 W
87	Georgetown...Mass. (In.)	42.43 N	71.0 W
83	Georgetown...S. C.	33.23 N	79.18 W
150	Georgetown...Malaya	5.21 N	100.15 E
81	Georgetown...Tex.	30.37 N	97.40 W
82	Georgia (State)...U. S.	32.40 N	83.20 W
111	Georgia (Soviet Rep.)...Sov. Un.	41.50 N	44.0 E
82	Georgiana...Ala.	31.38 N	86.44 W
55	Georgian B...Can.	45.30 N	81.0 W
70	Georgia, Str. of...Can.	49.0 N	123.25 W
111	Georgievsk (gyôr-gyĕfsk'). Sov. Un.	44.8 N	43.30 E
158	Georgina R. (jôr-jē'nȧ)...Austl.	22.0 S	138.30 E
120	Gera (gā'rä)...Ger.	50.53 N	12.4 E
157	Geraldine (jĕr'ăl-dēn)...N. Z.	44.4 S	171.17 E
158	Geraldton (jĕr'ăld-tŭn)...Austl.	28.32 S	114.31 E
102	Geral, Serra (Mts.) (sĕr'rȧ zhȧ-räl') Braz.	28.0 S	49.30 W
117	Gerasdorf (gĕ'räs-dôrf)...Ger.	48.18 N	16.28 E
124	Gérgal (gĕr'gäl)...Sp.	37.8 N	2.29 W
76	Gering (gē'rĭng)...Neb.	41.49 N	103.40 W
84	Germantown (jûr'mȧn-toun). Ohio	39.38 N	84.23 W
120	Germany (jûr'mȧ-nĭ)...Eur.	51.0 N	13.0 E
134	Germiston (jûr'mĭs-tŭn). U. S. Afr.	26.13 S	28.11 E
152	Gerona (hä-rō'nä)...Phil.	15.36 N	120.36 E
125	Gerona...Sp.	41.57 N	2.49 E
89	Gervais L. (jûr'vās) Minn. (Minneapolis In.)	45.1 N	93.4 W
112	Géryville (zhā-rē-vēl')...Alg.	33.42 N	1.2 E
133	Gesira (Well) (jĕ'zē-rä)...Libya	25.45 N	21.28 E
125	Getafe (hä-tä'fā)...Sp. (In.)	40.19 N	3.44 W
85	Gettysburg (gĕt'ĭs-bûrg)...Pa.	39.52 N	77.13 W
76	Gettysburg...S. D.	45.1 N	99.59 W
51	Gettysburg...Wash. (Seattle In.)	48.9 N	123.50 W
112	Ghardaïa (gär-dä'ē-ä)...Alg.	32.30 N	3.35 E
141	Ghats, Eastern (Mts.)...India	17.0 N	80.30 E
141	Ghats, Western (Mts.)...India	16.30 N	74.15 E
141	Ghazni (gŭz'nē)...Afg.	33.32 N	68.30 E
133	Ghemines (gȧ-mē'nȧs)...Libya	31.35 N	20.0 E
115	Ghent (Gand) (gĕnt) (gäN)...Bel.	51.5 N	3.41 W
121	Gheorgheni (gyôr-gän'ĭ)...Rom.	46.49 N	25.31 E
121	Gherla (gĕr'lä)...Rom.	47.2 N	23.55 E
133	Ghigner (gĕn-yĕr')...Eth.	7.7 N	40.35 E
133	Giado (jä'dō)...Libya	31.58 N	12.2 W
133	Giaghbub (Giarabub) (jäg'bōōb) (jä'rä-bōōb). Libya	29.47 N	24.32 E
133	Gialo, Oasis (jä'lō)...Libya	29.15 N	22.5 E
126	Giannutri (I.) (jän-nōō'trē)...It.	42.15 N	11.7 E
133	Giarabub (Giaghbub) (jä'rä-bōōb) (jäg'bōōb). Libya	29.47 N	24.32 E
97	Gibara (hē-bä'rä)...Cuba	21.6 N	76.10 W
134	Gibeon (gĭb'ē-ŭn)...S. W. Afr.	25.13 S	17.35 E
124	Gibraleón (hē-brä-lā-ōn')...Sp.	37.24 N	6.59 W
124	Gibraltar (jĭ-brôl'tēr)...Gib.	36.8 N	5.21 W
131	Gibraltar...Eur. (In.)	36.7 N	5.21 W
79	Gibson City (gĭb'sŭn)...Ill.	40.28 N	88.21 W
158	Gibson Desert (gĭb'sŭn)...Austl.	24.45 S	125.0 E
72	Gibsons Landing Can. (Vancouver In.)	49.24 N	123.31 W
138	Gida R. (gē'dä)...Sov. Un.	70.35 N	79.0 E
81	Giddings (gĭd'ĭngz)...Tex.	30.11 N	96.57 W
79	Gideon (gĭd'ē-ŭn)...Mo.	36.26 N	89.57 W
122	Gien (zhē-ăN')...Fr.	47.42 N	2.38 E
120	Gieszen (gēs'ĕn)...Ger.	50.35 N	8.40 E
123	Gif (zhēf)...Fr. (In.)	48.42 N	2.8 E
149	Gifu (gē'fōō)...Jap.	35.30 N	136.45 E
80	Gigantes, L. (hē-gän'tȧs)...Mex.	27.55 N	104.35 W
153	Gigaquit (hē-gä'kēt)...Phil.	9.35 N	125.42 E
135	Giggiga (jē-jē'gä)...Eth.	9.28 N	42.48 E
51	Gig Harbor (gĭg) Wash. (Seattle In.)	47.20 N	122.36 W
126	Giglio (Il) (jēl'yō)...It.	42.22 N	10.55 E
124	Giguela R. (hē-gā'lä)...Sp.	39.40 N	3.4 W
152	Gihulngan (hē-ōōl'ny'gän)...Phil.	10.8 N	123.16 E
124	Gijon (hē-hōn')...Sp.	43.32 N	5.38 W
75	Gila Bend Ind. Res...Ariz.	33.0 N	112.50 W
75	Gila Cliff Dwellings Nat'l Mon. N. M.	33.14 N	108.16 W
75	Gila R. (hē'lȧ)...Ariz.	33.5 N	111.15 W

ng-sing; ŋ-baŋk; N-nasalized n; nŏd; cŏmmit; ōld; ôbey; ôrder; fōōd; fŏŏt; ou-out; s-soft; sh-dish; th-thin; pūre; ûnite; ûrn; stŭd; circŭs; ü-as "y" in study; '-indeterminate vowel.

Page	Name Pronunciation Region	Lat. °′	Long. °′
133	Gila R. (gē'lä) Eth.	7.45 N	34.0 E
75	Gila River Ind. Res. Ariz.	33.10 N	112.0 W
77	Gilbert (gĭl'bẽrt) Minn.	47.28 N	92.28 W
5	Gilbert Is. Pac. O.	1.0 S	175.0 E
52	Gilbert, Mt. Alsk. (In.)	61.12 N	148.20 W
159	Gilbert R. Austl.	17.18 S	142.0 E
72	Gilcrest (gĭl'krĕst) Colo. (Denver In.)	40.17 N	104.46 W
99	Giles (hē'lås) Arg. (Buenos Aires In.)	34.23 S	59.29 W
141	Gilgit (gĭl'gĭt) India	35.59 N	74.14 E
72	Gill (jĭl) Colo. (Denver In.)	40.27 N	104.32 W
79	Gillett (jĭ-lĕt') Ark.	34.7 N	91.23 W
72	Gillett Colo. (Colo. Sprs. In.)	38.47 N	105.7 W
71	Gillette Wyo.	44.18 N	105.29 W
115	Gillingham (gĭl'ĭng-ăm) Gt. Brit.	51.20 N	0.35 E
158	Gillon, L. (gĭl'ŭn) Austl.	26.10 S	124.45 E
115	Gilly (zhē-yē') Bel.	50.25 N	4.35 E
79	Gilman (gĭl'măn) Ill.	40.46 N	88.0 W
81	Gilmer (gĭl'mẽr) Tex.	32.43 N	94.58 W
74	Gilroy (gĭl-roi') Calif.	37.0 N	121.33 W
122	Gimone R. (zhē-mōn') Fr.	43.35 N	0.45 E
131	Gineifa (jê-nā'fá) Eg. (Suez Can. In.)	30.12 N	32.26 E
153	Gingoog B. (hēn-gō'ôg) Phil.	9.0 N	125.5 E
126	Ginosa (jê-nō'zä) It.	40.34 N	16.46 E
124	Ginzo (hēn-thō') Sp.	42.4 N	7.45 W
133	Giof (jôf) Libya	24.15 N	23.36 E
133	Giofra, Oasis of (jôf'rä) Libya	29.0 N	15.30 E
126	Gioja del Colle (jô'yä dĕl kôl'lā) It.	40.47 N	16.57 E
160	Gipps Town (gĭps' toun) Austl. (Sydney In.)	33.52 S	151.8 E
82	Girard (jĭ-rärd') Ala.	32.26 N	85.1 W
79	Girard Kan.	37.31 N	94.51 W
100	Girardot (hē-rär-dōt') Col.	4.15 N	69.59 W
111	Giresun (ghĕr'ĕ-sōōn') Tur.	40.55 N	38.28 E
131	Girga (jĕr'gȧ) Eg. (In.)	26.20 N	31.53 E
126	Girgenti (jēr-jĕn'tē) It.	37.19 N	13.34 E
141	Giridih (jē'rē-dê) India	24.8 N	86.7 E
123	Giromagny (zhē-rô-mȧn-yē') Fr.	47.45 N	6.59 E
122	Gironde R. (zhē-rôɴd') Fr.	45.25 N	0.50 W
114	Girvan (gûr'văn) Gt. Brit.	55.15 N	4.50 W
156	Gisborne (gĭz'bŭrn) N. Z.	38.40 S	178.3 E
122	Gisors (zhē-zôr') Fr.	49.18 N	1.49 E
127	Giura (I.) (yōō'rä) Grc.	39.22 N	24.10 E
127	Giurgiu (jōōr'jōō) Rom.	43.53 N	25.57 E
115	Givet (zhē-vĕ') Bel.	51.8 N	4.49 E
122	Givors (zhē-vôr') Fr.	45.35 N	4.48 E
135	Giza (gē'zȧ) Eg.	30.1 N	31.13 E
135	Giza Pyramids Eg.	29.59 N	31.7 E
139	Gizhiga (gē'zhĭ-gȧ) Sov. Un.	61.55 N	160.30 E
121	Giżycko (gĭ'zhĭ-ko) Pol.	54.3 N	21.49 E
127	Gjinocastër (Ergeri) (gyē-nô-käs'tĕr) (ĕr-gĕ-rē') Alb.	40.5 N	20.8 E
118	Gjövik (gyû'vĕk) Nor.	60.48 N	10.40 E
126	Gjurgjevac (dyōōr'dyĕ-väts) Yugo.	46.2 N	17.3 E
87	Glace B. (glȧs) Can.	46.15 N	59.57 W
54	Glacier (glā'shẽr) Can.	51.10 N	117.16 W
72	Glacier Wash. (Vancouver In.)	48.54 N	121.57 W
54	Glacier Natl. Park Can.	51.15 N	117.15 W
71	Glacier Natl. Park (Waterton-Glacier Internat'l Peace Park) Mont.	48.50 N	114.0 W
70	Glacier Peak Wash.	48.7 N	121.8 W
120	Gladbach-Rheydt (glät'bäĸ-rīt') Ger.	51.13 N	6.27 E
159	Gladstone (glăd'stōn) Austl.	23.50 S	151.15 E
158	Gladstone Austl.	33.16 S	138.21 E
77	Gladstone Mich.	45.51 N	87.1 W
89	Gladstone Minn. (Minneapolis In.)	45.0 N	93.2 W
157	Gladstone N. Z.	44.35 S	169.23 E
84	Gladwin (glăd'wĭn) Mich.	43.59 N	84.27 W
126	Glamoč (gläm'ôch) Yugo.	44.2 N	16.51 E
153	Glan (glän) Phil.	5.46 N	125.12 E
160	Glanville (glăn'vĭl) Austl. (Adelaide In.)	34.50 S	138.29 E
120	Glarus (glä'rōōs) Switz.	47.2 N	9.2 E
114	Glasgow (glȧs'gō) Gt. Brit.	55.50 N	4.15 W
82	Glasgow Ky.	37.1 N	85.56 W
79	Glasgow Mo.	39.14 N	92.48 W
71	Glasgow Mont.	48.13 N	106.39 W
89	Glassport (glȧs'pōrt) Pa. (Pittsburgh In.)	40.19 N	79.54 W
120	Glauchau (glou'kou) Ger.	50.49 N	12.34 E
117	Glazebury (glāz'bẽr-ĭ) Gt. Brit. (Liverpool In.)	53.28 N	2.30 W
110	Glazov (glä'zôf) Sov. Un.	58.5 N	52.45 E
120	Glda R. (g'l'dȧ) Pol.	53.30 N	16.55 E
	Gleiwitz, see Gliwice, Pol.		
123	Glénans, Iles de (Is.) (glā-nȧɴ') Fr.	47.40 N	4.0 W
77	Glencoe (glĕn'kō) Minn.	44.46 N	94.8 W
75	Glendale (glĕn'dāl) Ariz.	33.31 N	112.13 W
74	Glendale Calif.	34.9 N	118.18 W
71	Glendive (glĕn'dīv) Mont.	47.7 N	104.41 W
73	Glendora (glĕn-dō'rȧ) Calif. (Los Angeles In.)	34.9 N	117.52 W
156	Gleneden (glĕn-ē'dĕn) N. Z. (In.)	36.55 S	174.40 E
160	Glenelg (glĕn-ĕlg') Austl.	34.59 S	138.32 E
160	Glenfield (glĕn'fēld) Austl. (Sydney In.)	33.58 S	150.53 E
159	Glen Innes (glĕn ĭn'ĕs) Austl.	29.45 S	151.45 E
81	Glenmora (glĕn-mō'rȧ) La.	30.58 N	92.35 W
70	Glenns Ferry (glĕnz fĕr'ĭ) Ida.	42.59 N	115.18 W
83	Glennville (glĕn'vĭl) Ga.	31.55 N	81.56 W
88	Glen Olden (glĕn ōl'd'n) Pa. (Philadelphia In.)	39.54 N	75.17 W
116	Glen, R. (glĕn) Gt. Brit.	52.44 N	0.18 W
160	Glenreagh (glĕn-rā') Austl.	30.2 S	153.1 E
71	Glenrock (glĕn'rŏk) Wyo.	42.52 N	105.51 W
160	Glenroy (glĕn-roi') Austl. (Melbourne In.)	37.42 S	144.55 E
85	Glens Falls (glĕnz) N. Y.	43.18 N	73.38 W
89	Glenshaw (glĕn'shô) Pa. (Pittsburgh In.)	40.32 N	79.57 W
76	Glen Ullin (glĕn ŭl'ĭn) N. D.	46.48 N	101.49 W
88	Glenview (glĕn'vū) Ill. (Chicago In.)	42.4 N	87.48 W
79	Glenwood (glĕn'wŏŏd) Ia.	41.3 N	95.41 W
76	Glenwood Minn.	45.39 N	95.21 W
87	Glenwood Can.	48.58 N	54.50 W
75	Glenwood Springs Colo.	39.33 N	107.19 W
121	Gliwice (gwĭ-wĭt'sĕ) Pol.	50.17 N	18.41 E
75	Globe (glōb) Ariz.	33.23 N	110.47 W
129	Globino (glôb'ē-nô) Sov. Un.	49.19 N	33.12 E
129	Glodosti (glô-dôst'yĭ) Sov. Un.	48.28 N	31.16 E
120	Glogów (glō'gŭf) Pol.	51.40 N	16.3 E
118	Glommen R. (glôm'ĕn) Nor.	61.10 N	11.20 E
135	Glorious Is. Ind. O.	11.30 S	47.20 E
73	Gloryetta (glô-rĭ-et'ȧ) Calif. (Los Angeles In.)	33.42 N	117.51 W
116	Glossop (glŏs'ŭp) Gt. Brit.	53.27 N	1.57 W
82	Gloster (glŏs'tẽr) Miss.	31.11 N	91.3 W
114	Gloucester (glŏs'tẽr) Gt. Brit.	51.55 N	2.15 W
86	Gloucester Mass.	42.35 N	70.40 W
84	Gloucester Ohio	39.35 N	82.58 W
85	Gloucester City N. J.	39.52 N	75.10 W
116	Gloucester County Gt. Brit.	52.6 N	1.48 W
85	Gloversville (glŭv'ẽrz-vĭl) N. Y.	43.4 N	74.20 W
121	Glubczyce (gwŭb-chĭ'tsĕ) Pol.	50.12 N	17.48 E
128	Glubokoe (glōō-bô-kō'yĕ) Sov. Un.	55.8 N	27.44 E
121	Glucholazy (glŭ-kô-lä'zĭ) Pol.	50.19 N	17.23 E
129	Glukhov (glōō'kôf') Sov. Un.	51.42 N	33.52 E
129	Glushkovo (glōōsh'kô-vō) Sov. Un.	51.21 N	34.42 E
128	Glusk (glōōsk) Sov. Un.	52.55 N	28.39 E
120	Gmünd (g'münt) Ger.	48.48 N	9.49 E
120	Gmunden (g'mōōn'dĕn) Aus.	47.57 N	13.48 E
120	Gniezno (g'nyȧz'nô) Pol.	52.33 N	17.36 E
127	Gnjilane (gnyē'lä-nĕ) Yugo.	42.27 N	21.27 E
141	Goa (gō'ȧ) India	15.15 N	74.0 E
152	Goa (gō'ä) Phil.	13.41 N	123.29 E
100	Goajira Pen. (gō-ä-ĸē'rä) Col.	11.30 N	72.45 W
94	Goascoran (gō-äs'kō-rän') Hond.	13.39 N	87.46 W
88	Goat Is. N. Y. (Niagara Falls In.)	43.5 N	79.4 W
134	Gobabis (gō-bä'bĭs) S. W. Afr.	22.32 S	18.58 E
142	Gobi, The (Shamo) (Desert) (gō'bē) Mong.-Chn.	43.0 N	130.0 E
51	Goble (gō'b'l) Ore. (Portland In.)	45.1 N	122.53 W
120	Goch (gôĸ) Ger.	51.42 N	6.12 E
141	Godavari R. (gô-dä'vŭ-rê) India	19.0 N	79.0 E
158	Goddards Cr. (gŏd'ȧrdz) Austl.	31.18 S	124.15 E
84	Goderich (gŏd'rĭch) Can.	43.44 N	81.42 W
50	Godhavn (gōdh'hȧvn) Grnld.	69.15 N	53.30 W
157	Godley Head (gŏd'lĭ) N. Z. (In.)	43.35 S	172.50 E
54	Gods L. (gŏdz) Can.	54.20 N	95.0 W
50	Godthaab (gŏt'hōōb) Grnld.	64.10 N	51.32 W
141	Godwin Austen, Mt. (gŏd'wĭn ôs'tĕn) India	35.58 N	76.30 E
115	Goedereede (I.) (ĸōō'dē-rā-dē) Neth.	51.45 N	4.10 E
73	Goethite (gō'thĭt) Ala. (Birmingham In.)	33.16 N	87.6 W
74	Goffs (gôfs) Calif.	34.56 N	115.4 W
149	Gogawa, R. (gō-gä'wä) Jap.	35.2 N	132.40 E
77	Gogebic L. (gō-gē'bĭk) Mich.	46.30 N	89.34 W
92	Gogorrón (gō-gō-rōn') Mex.	21.50 N	100.54 W
141	Gogra R. (gŏ'grä) India	26.15 N	83.0 E
149	Goi (gō'ē) Jap. (Tokyo In.)	35.30 N	140.6 E
101	Goiaz (State) (gô-yäzh') Braz.	14.0 S	49.0 W
101	Goiaz Braz.	15.58 S	50.5 W
111	Gökcha, L. (gûk-chä) (gûk'chȧ) Sov. Un.	40.25 N	46.15 E
111	Gök Su (R.) (gûk'sōō') Tur.	37.0 N	33.0 E
118	Göl (gûl) Nor.	60.44 N	9.1 E
117	Golborne (gōl'bŭrn) Gt. Brit. (Liverpool In.)	53.28 N	2.36 W
116	Golcar (gŏl'kȧr) Gt. Brit.	53.38 N	1.52 W
79	Golconda (gŏl-kŏn'dȧ) Ill.	37.22 N	88.29 W
141	Golconda India	17.15 N	78.15 E
121	Goldap (gōl'däp) Pol.	54.17 N	22.18 E
132	Gold Coast Afr.	8.0 N	1.30 W
75	Golden Colo.	39.45 N	105.13 W
157	Golden B. N. Z.	40.40 S	172.50 E
70	Goldendale Wash.	45.48 N	120.50 W
51	Golden Gate Calif. (San Francisco In.)	37.47 N	122.28 W
72	Goldfield Colo. (Colo. Sprs. In.)	38.43 N	105.7 W
74	Goldfield Nev.	37.42 N	117.13 W
90	Gold Hill (Mt.) C. Z. (In.)	9.3 N	79.38 W
83	Goldsboro N. C.	35.23 N	77.59 W
72	Goldstream Can. (Vancouver In.)	48.27 N	123.34 W
80	Goldthwaite (gōld'thwāt) Tex.	31.27 N	98.33 W
127	Golemo-Konare (gō'lȧ-mō-kō'nä-rĕ) Bul.	42.16 N	24.31 E
120	Goleniów (gô-lĕ-nyŭf') Pol.	53.33 N	14.51 E
81	Goliad (gō-lĭ-ăd') Tex.	28.40 N	97.22 W
156	Gollans R. (gŏl'ănz) N. Z. (In.)	41.22 S	174.53 E
129	Golodaevka (gô'lô-dä-yĕf'kȧ) Sov. Un.	47.51 N	38.53 E
152	Golo I. (gō'lō) Phil.	13.39 N	120.22 E
129	Golovchino (gô-lôf'chē-nō) Sov. Un.	50.31 N	35.51 E
134	Golungo Alto (gô-lōōŋ'gō äl'tō) Ang.	9.10 S	14.40 E
128	Gomel (gô'mĕl') Sov. Un.	52.25 N	31.1 E
132	Gomera I. (gô-mā'rä) Canary Is.	28.10 N	17.15 W
123	Gometz-le-Châtel (gō-mĕts'-lĕ-shä-tĕl') Fr. (In.)	48.41 N	2.8 E
80	Gómez Farias (gō'māz fä-rē'äs) Mex.	24.59 N	101.2 W
99	Gómez, L. de (gō'māz) Arg. (Buenos Aires In.)	34.35 S	61.5 W
80	Gómez Palacio (gō'māz pä-lä'syō) Mex.	25.34 N	103.30 W
97	Gonaïves (gō-nȧ-ēv') Hai.	19.27 N	72.42 W
97	Gonaïves, G. of Hai.	19.20 N	73.10 W
127	Gönan (gû'năn) Tur.	40.6 N	27.41 E
97	Gonave Chan. (gô-näv') Hai.	18.40 N	73.10 W
97	Gonave I. Hai.	18.50 N	73.5 W
133	Gondar (gŏn'dȧr) Eth.	12.36 N	37.28 E
123	Gonesse (gō-nĕs') Fr. (In.)	48.58 N	2.28 E
135	Gonja (gŏn'jä) Tan.	4.16 S	38.4 E
56	Gonor (gō'nŏr) Can. (Winnipeg In.)	50.3 N	96.54 W
81	Gonzales (gŏn-zä'lĕz) Tex.	29.31 N	97.27 W
73	Goodes (gŏŏdz) Ga. (Atlanta In.)	33.32 N	84.44 W
54	Good Hope Can.	66.9 N	128.35 W
134	Good Hope, C. of U. S. Afr.	34.21 S	18.25 E
70	Gooding (gŏŏd'ĭng) Ida.	42.56 N	114.44 W
84	Goodland (gŏŏd'lănd) Ind.	40.52 N	87.14 W
78	Goodland Kan.	39.20 N	101.42 W
73	Goodsprings (gŏŏd'sprĭngz) Ala. (Birmingham In.)	33.39 N	87.14 W
160	Goodwood (gŏŏd'wŏŏd) Austl. (Adelaide In.)	34.57 S	138.36 E
116	Goole (gōōl) Gt. Brit.	53.42 N	0.52 W
160	Goondiwindi (gōōn-dē-wĭn'dê) Austl. (In.)	28.33 S	150.22 E
55	Goose Bay Can.	53.32 N	60.25 W
71	Gooseberry Cr. Wyo.	44.1 N	108.30 W
71	Goose Cr. Nev.-Ida.	42.0 N	114.0 W
81	Goose Creek Tex.	29.42 N	95.0 W
70	Goose L. Calif.	41.56 N	120.25 W
76	Goose R. N. D.	47.30 N	97.20 W
120	Göppingen (gûp'ĭng-ĕn) Ger.	48.43 N	9.40 E
121	Góra-Kalwaria (gŭ'rȧ-kȧl-vär'yȧ) Pol.	51.58 N	21.13 E
141	Gorakhpur (gō'rŭk-pōōr) India	26.35 N	83.29 E
151	Goram Is. (gō'räm) Indon.	4.0 S	131.29 E
96	Gorda Cay (I.) (gôr'dä) Ba. Is.	26.5 N	77.33 W
96	Gorda Pt. Cuba	22.23 N	82.5 W
160	Gordon (gôr'dŭn) Austl. (Tas. In.)	43.16 S	147.13 E
56	Gordon Can. (Winnipeg In.)	50.0 N	97.21 W
76	Gordon Neb.	42.48 N	102.11 W
160	Gordon R. Austl. (Tas. In.)	42.40 S	145.58 E
160	Gordona B. Austl. (Sydney In.)	33.56 S	151.16 E
133	Gore (gō'rē) Eth.	8.12 N	35.32 E
157	Gore (gōr) N. Z.	46.5 S	168.55 E
157	Gore, Mt. N. Z.	42.17 S	172.0 E
132	Gorgeram (gôr'gȧ-räm) Nig.	12.40 N	10.45 E
126	Gorgona (I.) (gôr-gō'nä) It.	43.27 N	9.53 E
111	Gori (gō'rē) Sov. Un.	42.0 N	44.5 E
120	Gorinchem (gō'rĭn-ĸĕm) Neth.	51.50 N	5.0 E
110	Gorki (Nizhni Novgorod) (gôr'kĭ) (nêzh'nĭ-ē nôv'gô-rŏt) Sov. Un.	56.15 N	43.58 E
121	Gorlice (gôr-lē'tsĕ) Pol.	49.39 N	21.10 E
120	Görlitz (gûr'lĭts) Ger.	51.9 N	15.1 E
129	Gorlovka (gôr'lôf-kȧ) Sov. Un.	48.18 N	38.2 E
80	Gorman (gôr'măn) Tex.	32.13 N	98.40 W
127	Gorna-Džumaya (gôr'nä-dzhōō-mä'yȧ) Bul.	42.1 N	23.5 E
127	Gorna-Orekhovica (gôr'nä-ôr-yĕĸ'ô-vē-tsȧ) Bul.	43.7 N	25.41 E
127	Gornji-Milanovac (gôrn'yē-mē'lȧ-nô-väts) Yugo.	44.2 N	20.29 E
121	Gorodenka (gō-rô-deŋ'kä) Sov. Un.	48.41 N	25.31 E
110	Gorodets (gôr'ô-dyĕts) Sov. Un.	56.40 N	43.30 E
129	Gorodnya (gō-rôd'nyä) Sov. Un.	51.53 N	31.31 E
128	Gorodok (gō-rô-dôk') Sov. Un.	55.27 N	29.58 E
121	Gorodok Sov. Un.	49.46 N	23.40 E
129	Gorokhovka (gô'rô-ĸôf'kȧ) Sov. Un.	50.7 N	40.5 E
150	Gorontalo (gō-rōn-tä'lō) Indon.	0.51 N	123.0 E
150	Gorontalo (Tomini) G. of (tō-mē'nê) Indon.	0.0	122.0 E
117	Gorton (gôr'tŭn) Gt. Brit. (Liverpool In.)	53.28 N	2.8 W
121	Goryn R. (gō'rĕn') Sov. Un.	51.20 N	26.22 E
120	Gorzów (gôr-zŭf') Pol.	48.3 N	10.54 E
84	Goshen (gō'shĕn) Ind.	41.36 N	85.49 W
72	Goshen Wash. (Vancouver In.)	48.51 N	122.20 W
75	Goshute Ind. Res. (gō-shōōt') Utah	39.50 N	114.0 W
120	Goslar (gôs'lär) Ger.	51.55 N	10.25 E
126	Gospić (gôs'pĭch) Yugo.	44.32 N	15.23 E
127	Gostivar (gôs'tê-vär) Yugo.	41.46 N	20.57 E
121	Gostyń (gôs'tĭn-y') Pol.	51.52 N	17.1 E
121	Gostynin (gôs-tē'nĭn) Pol.	52.25 N	19.31 E
118	Götaälv (R.) (yû'tȧ-ĕlv) Swe.	58.10 N	12.8 E
118	Göta Canal (yû'tȧ) Swe.	58.38 N	15.25 E
118	Göteborg (yû'tĕ-bôrgh) Swe.	57.41 N	11.58 E
94	Gotera (San Francisco) (gō-tā'rä) Sal.	13.47 N	88.7 W
120	Gotha (gō'tȧ) Ger.	50.57 N	10.42 E
78	Gothenburg (gŏth'ĕn-bûrg) Neb.	40.56 N	100.9 W
149	Gotō Is. (gō'tō) Jap.	32.50 N	128.50 E
119	Gotska Sand I. (gŏt'skȧ sänd') Swe.	58.23 N	19.15 E
120	Göttingen (gût'ĭng-ĕn) Ger.	51.32 N	9.55 E
118	Gottland (I.) (gŏt'lănd) Swe.	57.30 N	18.30 E
115	Gouda (gou'dä) Neth.	52.0 N	4.45 E
4	Gough I. (gŏf) Atl. O.	39.20 S	11.10 W
159	Goulburn (gōl'bŭrn) Austl.	34.46 S	149.42 E
132	Goumbou (gōōm-bōō') Fr. W. Afr.	15.2 N	7.34 W
132	Goundam (gōōn-dăɴ') Fr. W. Afr.	16.30 N	3.40 W
132	Gouré (gōō-rā') Fr. W. Afr.	13.57 N	10.40 E
122	Gournay (gōōr-nĕ') Fr.	49.28 N	1.45 E
121	Gousievsk (Gumbinnen) (gō-ōō-syĕfsk') (gŭm-bĕn'nĕn) Sov. Un.	54.35 N	22.12 E
85	Gouverneur (gŭv-ẽr-nōōr') N. Y.	44.20 N	75.28 W
102	Governor's I. (gŭv'ẽr-nẽrz) Braz. (In.)	22.48 S	43.12 W
88	Governors I. N. Y. (N. Y. In.)	40.41 N	74.1 W
72	Gowanda (gô-wŏn'dȧ) Colo. (Denver In.)	40.12 N	104.55 W
85	Gowanda N. Y.	42.30 N	78.56 W

ăt; finăl; rāte; senâte; ärm; åsk; sofȧ; fâre; ch-choose; dh-as th in other; bē; êvent; bĕt; recĕnt; cratẽr; g-go; gh-gutteral g; bĭt; ĭ-short neutral; rīde; ĸ-gutteral k as ch in German ich;

Gowna PRONOUNCING INDEX Greenville

Page	Name Pronunciation Region	Lat. °′	Long. °′
114	Gowna, L. (gō'nȧ) Ire.	53.50 N	7.35 W
160	Gowrie (gou'rē) Austl. (In.)	27.28 S	151.53 E
102	Goya (gō'yä) Arg.	29.10 S	59.15 W
116	Goyt, R. (goit) Gt. Brit.	53.21 N	2.0 W
134	Graaff-Reinet (gräf'-rī'nĕt) U. S. Afr.	32.14 S	24.32 E
117	Graauw (grou). Neth. (Anvers In.)	51.20 N	4.6 E
126	Gračac (grä'chäts) Yugo.	44.17 N	15.51 E
127	Gračanica (grä-chän'ĭ-tsä) Yugo.	44.42 N	18.20 E
76	Graceville (grās'vĭl) Minn.	45.33 N	96.27 W
82	Graceville Fla.	30.59 N	85.32 W
94	Gracias (grä'sē-äs) Hond.	14.32 N	88.44 W
95	Gracias a Dios, C. Nic.	15.0 N	83.0 W
132	Graciosa I. (grä-sē-ōzȧ) Az. Is. (In.)	39.0 N	28.0 W
127	Gradačac (gra-dä'chats) Yugo.	44.52 N	18.28 E
124	Gradefes (grä-dhā'fās') Sp.	42.38 N	5.16 W
129	Gradizhsk (grä-dēzhsk') Sov. Un.	49.11 N	33.2 E
124	Grado (grä'dō) Sp.	43.23 N	6.5 W
159	Grafton (graf'tŭn) Austl.	29.42 S	152.58 E
87	Grafton Mass. (In.)	42.12 N	71.41 W
76	Grafton N. D.	48.25 N	97.23 W
85	Grafton W. Va.	39.19 N	80.1 W
99	Grafton Is. Chl. (Magallanes In.)	54.10 S	73.20 W
83	Graham (grā'ăm) N. C.	36.4 N	79.24 W
78	Graham Tex.	33.8 N	98.35 W
83	Graham Va.	37.34 N	81.18 W
51	Graham Wash. (Seattle In.)	47.3 N	122.16 W
54	Graham I. Can.	53.30 N	130.15 W
134	Grahamstown U. S. Afr.	33.19 S	26.31 E
126	Graian Alps (Mts.) (grā'yăn) It.-Fr.	45.28 N	7.15 E
129	Graivoron (grä'ĭ-vô-rōn') Sov. Un.	50.28 N	35.41 E
101	Grajahu (grä-zhä'ōō) Braz.	5.58 S	43.29 W
101	Grajahu, R. Braz.	5.0 S	46.0 W
121	Grajewo (grä-yä'vō) Pol.	53.38 N	22.27 E
127	Gramada (grä'mä-dä) Bul.	43.46 N	22.41 E
126	Grammichele (gräm-mê-kĕ'lā) It.	37.14 N	14.37 E
114	Grampians (Mts.) (grăm'pĭ-ănz) Gt. Brit.	56.50 N	4.20 W
94	Granada (grä-nä'dhä) Nic.	11.56 N	85.58 W
124	Granada Sp.	37.11 N	3.36 W
81	Granbury (grăn'bĕr-ĭ) Tex.	32.27 N	97.46 W
86	Granby (grăn'bĭ) Can.	45.25 N	72.45 W
79	Granby Mo.	36.55 N	94.15 W
132	Gran Canaria (I.) (grän' kä-nä'rē-ä) Can. Is.	28.0 N	15.30 W
101	Gran Chaco (Mts.) (grän chä'kō) Par.	22.0 S	61.45 W
97	Gran Cordillera Central (Cibao Mts.) (grän côr-dêl-yä'rȧ sĕn-träl') (sê-bä'ō) Hai.	18.53 N	70.30 W
86	Grande Baie (gränd bā') Can.	48.17 N	70.51 W
87	Grand Bank Can.	47.5 N	55.45 W
132	Grand Bassam (grän bȧ-säN') Fr. W. Afr.	5.15 N	3.47 W
95	Grand Bourg (grän bōōr') Guad. (In.)	15.54 N	61.19 W
97	Grand Caicos I. (grănd kä-ē'kōs) Ba. Is.	21.48 N	71.44 W
146	Grand Canal (Yun R.) (yōōn) Chn.	35.50 N	116.10 E
75	Grand Canyon Ariz.	36.3 N	112.8 W
75	Grand Canyon Natl. Mon. Ariz.	36.20 N	112.55 W
75	Grand Canyon Natl. Park Ariz.	36.15 N	112.20 W
96	Grand Cayman (I.) (kä'mȧn) W. I.	19.18 N	81.15 W
96	Grande Cay (I.) (grän'dā) Cuba	20.59 N	79.11 W
70	Grand Coulee Dam (kōō'lē) Wash.	47.58 N	118.58 W
93	Grande de Chiapas, R. (grän'dā dā chê-ä'päs) (chê-äp'ä) Mex.	16.40 N	93.0 W
94	Grande de Otoro (grän'dā dā ô-tō'rō) Hond.	14.36 N	88.14 W
101	Grande, R. (grän'dĕ) Braz.	20.0 S	48.0 W
99	Grande, R. (grän'dā) Chl.-Arg. (Magallanes In.)	53.55 S	68.40 W
58	Grande, R. U. S.-Mex.	30.0 N	104.45 W
132	Grand Erg Occidental (ûrg) Alg.	30.0 N	1.0 E
132	Grand Erg Oriental Alg.	30.0 N	7.0 E
97	Grande Rivière du Nord (gräNd' rē-vyâr' dü nôr') Hai.	19.35 N	72.10 W
70	Grande Ronde R. (grănd rŏnd') Ore.	45.45 N	117.45 W
95	Grande Terre (I.) (gränd tĕr') Guad. (In.)	16.20 N	61.28 W
89	Grande Terre I. La. (New Orleans In.)	29.18 N	89.51 W
95	Grande Vigie Point (Gränd vē-gē') Guad. (In.)	16.30 N	61.28 W
86	Grand Falls Can.	47.0 N	67.47 W
87	Grand Falls Can.	48.58 N	55.39 W
83	Grandfather Mt. N. C.	36.6 N	81.49 W
78	Grandfield (grănd'fēld) Okla.	34.14 N	98.41 W
70	Grand Forks Can.	49.3 N	118.28 W
76	Grand Forks N. D.	47.55 N	97.2 W
122	Grand-Fougeray (gräN-fōōzh'-rā') Fr.	47.44 N	1.41 W
84	Grand Haven (grănd hā'v'n) Mich.	43.3 N	86.14 W
89	Grand I. (grănd) La. (New Orleans In.)	30.9 N	89.26 W
77	Grand I. Mich.	46.30 N	86.40 W
78	Grand Island Neb.	40.56 N	98.20 W
88	Grand I. N. Y. (Niagara Falls In.)	43.1 N	78.57 W
88	Grand Island N. Y. (Niagara Falls In.)	42.59 N	78.57 W
89	Grand I. Pass La.-Miss. (New Orleans In.)	30.10 N	89.26 W
89	Grand Isle La. (New Orleans In.)	29.14 N	89.57 W
75	Grand Junction Colo.	39.3 N	108.32 W
132	Grand Lahou (grän lȧ-ōō') Fr. W. Afr.	58.0 N	5.0 W
86	Grand L. Can.	45.58 N	66.2 W
89	Grand L. La. (New Orleans In.)	29.45 N	89.51 W
81	Grand L. La.	29.55 N	92.45 W
81	Grand L. La.	30.0 N	91.30 W
86	Grand L. Me.	45.15 N	67.52 W
87	Grand L. Can.	48.50 N	57.35 W
84	Grand Ledge Mich.	42.45 N	84.47 W
122	Grand-Lieu, L. de (gräN'-lyû') Fr.	47.5 N	1.40 W
86	Grand Manan I. (mȧ-năn) Can.	44.45 N	66.48 W
86	Grand Mère (gräN mâr') Can.	46.34 N	72.41 W
124	Grândola (grăN'dō-lȧ) Port.	38.11 N	8.36 W
89	Grand Pass. La. (New Orleans In.)	29.16 N	89.54 W
56	Grand Pointe (grănd point') Can. (Winnipeg In.)	49.47 N	97.2 W
132	Grand-Popo (gräN'-pō-pō') Fr. W. Afr.	6.28 N	1.56 E
84	Grand Rapids (răp'ĭdz) Mich.	43.0 N	85.42 W
77	Grand Rapids Minn.	47.15 N	93.32 W
85	Grand R. Can.	43.7 N	80.0 W
77	Grand R. Ia.	41.0 N	94.5 W
84	Grand R. Mich.	43.0 N	85.0 W
79	Grand R. Mo.	39.44 N	93.30 W
94	Grand, R. (Matagalpa) (mä-tä-gäl'pä) Nic.	13.0 N	84.10 W
76	Grand R. S. D.	45.40 N	101.20 W
76	Grand R., North Fork S. D.	45.56 N	102.50 W
76	Grand R., South Fork S. D.	45.40 N	102.50 W
71	Grand Teton Mt. (grănd tē'tŏn) Wyo.	43.45 N	110.48 W
71	Grand Teton Natl. Park Wyo.	43.45 N	110.48 W
84	Grand Traverse B. (trăv'ērs) Mich.	45.0 N	85.30 W
97	Grand Turk I. (tûrk) Ba. Is.	21.28 N	71.8 W
116	Grange-over-Sands (grānj) Gt. Brit.	54.11 N	2.55 W
160	Grange, The Austl. (Adelaide In.)	34.54 S	138.30 E
71	Granger (grān'jēr) Wyo.	41.37 N	109.59 W
70	Grangeville (grānj'vĭl) Ida.	45.56 N	116.9 W
79	Granite City Ill.	38.43 N	90.9 W
76	Granite Falls Minn.	44.48 N	95.32 W
83	Granite Falls N. C.	35.48 N	81.25 W
71	Granite Peak (grăn'ĭt) Mont.	45.12 N	109.46 W
83	Graniteville S. C.	33.33 N	81.49 W
101	Granito (grä-nē'tō) Braz.	7.38 S	39.45 W
124	Granja de Torrehermosa (grän'hä dā tôr'rā-ĕr-mō'sä) Sp.	38.21 N	5.35 W
118	Gränna (grĕn'ä) Swe.	58.1 N	14.28 E
125	Granollérs (grä-nôl-yĕrs') Sp.	41.37 N	2.28 E
75	Gran Quivira Natl. Mon. (grän kē-vē'rä) N. M.	34.11 N	106.5 W
114	Grantham (grăn'tăm) Gt. Brit.	52.55 N	0.40 W
70	Grants Pass Ore.	42.27 N	123.20 W
73	Grantsville Utah (Salt Lake City In.)	40.36 N	112.28 W
123	Granvillars (gräN-vē-yär') Fr.	47.35 N	7.0 E
160	Granville (grăn'vĭl) Austl.	33.50 S	151.1 E
122	Granville (gräN-vēl') Fr.	48.51 N	1.32 W
85	Granville (grăn'vĭl) N. Y.	43.26 N	73.18 W
54	Granville L. Can.	56.30 N	100.30 W
101	Grão Mogol (grouN'mōō-gôl') Braz.	16.32 S	42.48 W
51	Grapeview (grāp'vu) Wash. (Seattle In.)	47.20 N	122.50 W
118	Gräs I. (grĕs) Swe.	60.24 N	18.25 E
91	Grass Cay (I.) St. Thomas (In.)	18.22 N	64.50 W
123	Grasse (gräs) Fr.	43.40 N	6.55 E
73	Grasselli (grä-sĕl'ĭ) Ala. (Birmingham In.)	33.27 N	86.54 W
89	Grass L. Minn. (Minneapolis In.)	44.53 N	93.15 W
85	Grass R. N. Y.	44.40 N	75.10 W
74	Grass Valley Calif.	39.12 N	121.4 W
87	Grates Pt. (grāts) Can.	48.10 N	52.55 W
122	Graulhet (grō-lĕ') Fr.	43.45 N	1.59 E
117	Gravenwezel (Kräv'ĕn-vā'zĕl) Bel. (Anvers In.)	51.16 N	4.33 E
160	Gravesend (grāvz'ĕnd) Austl.	29.35 S	150.22 E
115	Gravesend Gt. Brit.	51.25 N	0.20 E
88	Gravesend B. N. Y. (New York In.)	40.35 N	74.0 W
126	Gravina (grä-vē'nä) It.	40.48 N	16.27 E
97	Gravois, Pt. (grȧ-vwä') Hai.	18.2 N	73.53 W
123	Gray (grā) Fr.	47.27 N	5.37 E
84	Grayling (grā'lĭng) Mich.	44.40 N	84.40 W
87	Gray (Little) R. Can.	48.0 N	56.55 W
117	Grays (grāz) Gt. Brit. (London In.)	51.28 N	0.20 E
70	Grays Harbor Wash.	46.55 N	124.10 W
71	Grays L. Ida.	43.3 N	111.25 W
73	Grayson (grā'sŭn) Ga. (Atlanta In.)	33.55 N	83.58 W
78	Grays Peak (grāz) Colo.	39.30 N	105.52 W
51	Grays River. Wash. (Portland In.)	46.21 N	123.36 W
73	Graysville Ala. (Birmingham In.)	33.37 N	86.59 W
120	Graz (gräts) Aus.	47.4 N	15.25 E
96	Great Abaco I. (ä'bä-kō) Ba. Is.	26.20 N	77.10 W
158	Great Australian Bight Austl.	33.30 S	130.0 E
96	Great Bahama Bank (bȧ-hā'mȧ) Atl. O.	24.0 N	78.40 W
156	Great Barrier I. (băr'ĭ-ēr) N. Z.	36.12 S	175.25 E
159	Great Barrier Reef Austl.	18.0 S	147.30 E
58	Great Basin Nev.	39.0 N	116.30 W
54	Great Bear L. Can.	66.0 N	120.30 W
118	Great Belt (Str.) Den.	55.25 N	10.55 E
78	Great Bend Kan.	38.21 N	98.47 W
131	Great Bitter L. Eg. (Suez Canal In.)	30.21 N	32.24 E
114	Great Blasket I. (blăs'kĕt) Ire.	52.5 N	10.35 W
114	Great Britain (brĭt''n) Eur.	54.0 N	2.0 W
117	Great Budworth (bŭd'wûrth) Gt. Brit. (Liverpool In.)	53.18 N	2.30 W
134	Great Cataract (Waterfall) (căt'ȧ-răkt) S. W. Afr.	17.18 S	14.30 E
85	Great Chazy R. (shā-sē') N. Y.	44.55 N	73.40 W
135	Great Comoro I. (kŏm'ō-rō) Ind. O.	11.40 S	43.15 E
117	Great Crosby (krôz'bĭ) Gt. Brit. (Liverpool In.)	53.30 N	3.1 W
132	Great Eastern Dunes, The (El Erg) Alg.	30.0 N	7.0 E
131	Great Europa Pt. (û-rō'pȧ) Gib. (In.)	36.7 N	5.40 E
97	Great Exuma I. (ĕk-sōō'mä) Ba. Is.	23.35 N	75.55 W
71	Great Falls Mont.	47.31 N	111.18 W
83	Great Falls S. C.	34.33 N	80.54 W
134	Great Fish R. S. W. Afr.	27.20 S	17.41 E
97	Great Guana Cay (I.) (gwä'nä) Ba. Is.	24.3 N	76.22 W
96	Great Harbor Cay (I.) Ba. Is.	25.45 N	77.53 W
97	Great Inagua I. (ē-nä'gwä) Ba. Is.	21.5 N	73.20 W
96	Great Isaac I. (ī'zȧk) Ba. Is.	26.3 N	79.6 W
88	Great Kills (Inlet) N. Y. (New York In.)	40.33 N	74.8 W
160	Great L. Austl. (Tas. In.)	41.54 S	146.46 E
134	Great Makari Kari Salt Pan (Dry L.) (mä-kä'rē kä'rē) Bech.	20.45 S	26.15 E
156	Great Mercury I. (mûr'kū-rĭ) N. Z.	36.35 S	175.50 E
87	Great Miquelon I. (mĭk-ē-lôN') N. A.	47.5 N	56.20 W
150	Great Paternoster (Tenga) Is. (pä'tēr-nŏs-tēr) (tĕn'gä) Indon.	7.35 S	117.30 E
97	Great Ragged I. Ba. Is.	22.11 N	75.44 W
126	Great St. Bernard Pass (sănt bĕr-närd') It.	45.50 N	7.10 E
96	Great Sale Cay (I.) Ba. Is.	27.1 N	78.11 W
71	Great Salt L. Utah	41.15 N	112.40 W
71	Great Salt Lake Des. Utah	41.20 N	113.30 W
75	Great Sand Dunes Natl. Mon. Colo.	37.45 N	105.45 W
158	Great Sandy Des. Austl.	21.30 S	125.0 E
140	Great Sandy Des. (Dahna or Rub al Khali) (dä'nä; rōōb äl Kä'lē) Asia	20.0 N	52.0 E
159	Great Sandy (Fraser) I. (frā'zēr) Austl.	25.0 S	153.5 E
125	Great Sebkha (Basin) (sĕb'Kȧ) Alg.	35.35 N	0.50 W
54	Great Slave L. Can.	61.30 N	114.30 W
82	Great Smoky Mountains Natl. Park N. C.	35.35 N	83.30 W
96	Great Stirrup Cay (I.) (stĭr-ŭp) Ba. Is.	25.49 N	77.55 W
158	Great Victoria Des. (vĭk-tō'rĭ-ȧ) Austl.	29.30 S	127.0 E
117	Great Wakering (wāk'ēr-ĭng) Gt. Brit. (London In.)	51.35 N	0.48 E
143	Great Wall Chn.	41.0 N	115.30 E
117	Great Warley (wôr'lĭ) Gt. Brit. (London In.)	51.36 N	0.17 E
132	Great Western Dunes, The (El Erg) (ĕl ĕrg') Alg.	30.0 N	1.0 E
160	Great Western Range Austl. (Tas. In.)	41.50 S	147.0 E
55	Great Whale R. Can.	55.15 N	7.6 W
116	Great Whernside (Mt.) (whērn'sīd) Gt. Brit.	54.11 N	1.59 W
115	Great Yarmouth (yär'mŭth) Gt. Brit.	52.35 N	1.45 E
118	Grebbestad (grĕb-bĕ-städh) Swe.	58.42 N	11.14 E
124	Gredos, Sierra de (Mt.) (syĕr'rä dā grā'dōs) Sp.	40.15 N	5.10 W
127	Greece (grēs) Eur.	39.30 N	22.30 E
73	Greeley (grē'lĭ) Ala. (Birmingham In.)	33.17 N	87.8 W
78	Greeley Colo.	40.26 N	104.43 W
77	Green B. Wis.-Mich.	45.0 N	87.30 W
77	Green Bay Wis.	44.31 N	88.1 W
81	Green Bayou Tex. (In.)	29.48 N	95.12 W
96	Green Cay (I.) Ba. Is.	24.1 N	77.12 W
84	Greencastle Ind.	39.38 N	86.49 W
83	Green Cove Springs Fla.	29.57 N	81.41 W
82	Greeneville Tenn.	36.9 N	82.52 W
117	Greenfield Gt. Brit. (Liverpool In.)	53.18 N	31.9 W
84	Greenfield Ind.	39.46 N	85.42 W
77	Greenfield Ia.	41.15 N	94.29 W
86	Greenfield Mass.	42.35 N	72.38 W
79	Greenfield Mo.	37.24 N	93.49 W
84	Greenfield Ohio	39.20 N	83.26 W
82	Greenfield Tenn.	36.8 N	88.48 W
157	Green I. N. Z. (In.)	45.54 S	170.25 E
153	Green Island B. Phil.	10.15 N	119.22 E
50	Greenland (grēn'lȧnd) N. A.	74.0 N	40.0 W
50	Greenland Sea Grnld.	75.30 N	10.0 W
87	Greenly I. (grēn'lē) Can.	51.22 N	57.5 W
72	Green Mt. Colo. (Denver In.)	39.43 N	105.11 W
72	Green Mountain Falls Colo. (Colo. Sprs. In.)	38.56 N	105.1 W
86	Green Mts. Vt.	44.10 N	72.50 W
114	Greenock (grēn'ŭk) Gt. Brit.	55.55 N	4.45 W
114	Greenore Pt. (grē-nôr') Ire.	52.15 N	6.20 W
160	Green Pt. Austl. (Tas. In.)	40.53 S	144.40 E
135	Green Point U. S. Afr.	33.53 S	18.24 E
73	Green Pond. Ala. (Birmingham In.)	33.14 N	87.8 W
82	Green R. Ky.	37.15 N	86.0 W
76	Green R. N. D.	47.0 N	103.0 W
58	Green R. U. S.	40.0 N	109.45 W
71	Green R. Wash.	47.15 N	121.40 W
75	Greenriver Utah	38.59 N	110.9 W
71	Green River Wyo.	41.33 N	109.28 W
82	Greensboro Ala.	32.42 N	87.36 W
82	Greensboro Ga.	33.34 N	83.12 W
83	Greensboro N. C.	36.4 N	79.46 W
84	Greensburg Ind.	39.18 N	85.30 W
78	Greensburg Kan.	37.36 N	99.18 W
85	Greensburg Pa.	40.18 N	79.32 W
82	Greenville Ala.	31.49 N	86.39 W
79	Greenville Ill.	38.53 N	89.24 W
82	Greenville Ky.	37.13 N	87.12 W
132	Greenville Lib.	5.3 N	8.45 W
86	Greenville Me.	45.27 N	69.36 W
84	Greenville Mich.	43.11 N	85.22 W
82	Greenville Miss.	33.25 N	91.3 W
83	Greenville N. C.	35.35 N	77.22 W

ng-sing; ŋ-baŋk; N-nasalized n; nŏd; cŏmmit; ōld; ôbey; ôrder; fōōd; fŏŏt; ou-out; s-soft; sh-dish; th-thin; pūre; ûnite; ûrn; stŭd; circŭs; ü-as "y" in study; '-indeterminate vowel.

ăt; fĭnăl; rāte; senāte; ärm; àsk; sofà; fâre; ch-choose; dh-as th in other; bē; ēvent; bĕt; recĕnt; cratēr; g-go; gh-gutteral g; bĭt; ĭ-short neutral; rīde; ĸ-gutteral k as ch in German ich;

Habana PRONOUNCING INDEX **Hartford**

Page	Name Pronunciation Region	Lat. °′	Long. °′
90	Habana . . . . Cuba (In.)		
125	Habibas I. (hä-bē'bȧs) . . . . Alg.	35.45 N	0.53 W
149	Habu (hä'bōō') . . . Jap. (Osaka In.)	35.3 N	135.27 E
148	Hachinoche (hä'chē-nō'chĕ) . . Jap.	40.30 N	141.29 E
149	Hachioji (hä'chē-ō'jē) . . . . Jap.	35.44 N	139.20 E
85	Hackensack (hăk'ĕn-săk) . . . . N. J.	40.53 N	74.3 W
88	Hackensack R. N. J. (New York In.)	40.52 N	74.2 W
140	Hadd, C. el (ĕl häd') . . . . Oman	22.35 N	59.48 E
88	Haddonfield (hăd'ŭn-fēld) Pa. (Philadelphia In.)	39.54 N	75.2 W
88	Haddon Heights Pa. (Philadelphia In.)	39.53 N	75.3 W
132	Hadeija (hä-dā'jä) . . . . Nig.	12.32 N	10.3 E
117	Hadersdorf (hä'dĕrs-dôrf) Aus. (Wien In.)	48.13 N	16.14 E
118	Haderslev (hä'dhĕrs-lĕv) . . . . Den.	55.16 N	9.28 E
140	Hadhramaut (Reg.) (hä-drä-môt') Aden	16.0 N	51.0 E
117	Hadleigh (hăd'lĭ) Gt. Brit. (London In.)	51.34 N	0.36 E
147	Hadong (hä'dông') . . . . Kor.	35.6 N	127.47 E
147	Haeju (Kaishū) (hä'ĕ-jŭ) (kī'shōō) Kor.	38.2 N	125.42 E
147	Haeju Bay . . . . Kor.	37.30 N	120.30 E
147	Haenam (hä'ĕ-nām) . . . . Kor.	34.35 N	126.36 E
117	Haesdonck (häs'dônk) Bel. (Anvers In.)	51.11 N	4.14 E
108	Hafnafjördur (häf'nä-fyûr-dōōr) Ice.	64.2 N	21.55 W
135	Hafun (hä-fōōn') . . . . . . Som. (In.)	10.30 N	51.15 E
120	Hagen (hä'gĕn) . . . . Ger.	51.22 N	7.27 E
84	Hagerstown (hā'gẽrz-toun) . . . Ind.	39.54 N	85.11 W
85	Hagerstown . . . . Md.	39.39 N	77.45 W
149	Hagi (hä'gĭ) . . . . Jap.	34.25 N	131.45 E
152	Hagonoy (hä-gō-noi') . . . . Phil.	14.49 N	120.43 E
122	Hague, C. de la (dē lä äg') . . . . Fr.	49.45 N	1.55 W
123	Haguenau (äg'nō') . . . . Fr.	48.48 N	7.49 E
149	Haibara (hä'ē-bä'rä) . . . . Jap.	34.28 N	135.57 E
146	Haichow (Tunghai) (hä'ē-chō') (tōōng'hī') . Chn.	34.32 N	119.13 E
111	Haidar Pasa (hī'där pä-shä') . . Tur.	40.58 N	29.15 E
137	Haifa (hä'ē-fȧ) . . . . Pal. (In.)	32.48 N	34.59 E
146	Haifeng (hä'ē-fĕng') . . . . Chn.	37.52 N	117.31 E
145	Haifung (hī'fōōng') . . . . Chn.	23.0 N	115.13 E
140	Hail (hāl) . . . . Sau. Ar.	27.45 N	41.55 E
143	Hailar (Hulun) (hä-ē-lär') (hōō'lōōn') . Chn.	49.8 N	119.34 E
71	Hailey (hā'lĭ) . . . . Ida.	43.31 N	114.19 W
79	Haileyville (hā'lĭ-vĭl) . . . . Okla.	34.53 N	95.34 W
148	Hailin (hä'ē-lēn') . . . . Chn.	44.35 N	129.15 E
148	Hailun (hä'ē-lōōn') . . . . Chn.	47.44 N	127.0 E
148	Hailung (hä'ē-lōōng') . . . . Chn.	42.40 N	125.53 E
146	Haimen (hä'ē-mĕn') . . . . Chn.	31.51 N	121.6 E
150	Hainan (I.) (hä'e-nän') . . . . . Chn.	19.0 N	110.0 E
120	Hainburg (hīn'bōōrgh) . . . . . . Aus.	48.8 N	16.54 E
53	Haines (hānz) . . . . Alsk.	59.20 N	135.30 W
83	Haines City . . . . Fla. (In.)	28.7 N	81.37 W
145	Haining (hī'nĭng') . . . . Chn.	30.24 N	120.32 E
150	Haiphong (hī'fông') (hä'ēp-hŏng) Indoch.	20.58 N	106.40 E
145	Haitan I. (hī'tän') . . . . Chn.	25.26 N	119.58 E
97	Haiti (Hispaniola) (I.) (hā'tĭ) . W. I.	19.10 N	72.10 W
97	Haiti . . . . W. I.	19.0 N	71.0 W
146	Haiyang (hä'ē-yäng') . . . . Chn.	36.44 N	121.11 E
147	Haiyang I. . . . . Chn.	39.5 N	123.5 E
145	Haiyen (hī'yĕn') . . . . Chn.	30.31 N	120.53 E
121	Hajdubószörmény (hôl'dōō-bŭ'sûr-mān') . Hung.	47.42 N	21.32 E
121	Hajduhadház (hô'ĭ-dōō-hôd'häz) . Hung.	47.42 N	21.43 E
121	Hajdunánás (hô'ĭ-dōō-nä'näsh) . Hung.	47.51 N	21.28 E
121	Hajduszoboszió (hô'ĭ-dōō-sô'bôs-lō) . Hung.	47.27 N	21.25 E
148	Hakodate (hä-kō-dä'tȧ) . . . . . Jap.	41.46 N	140.46 E
149	Hakusan (Mt.) (hä'kōō-sän') . Jap.	36.7 N	136.46 E
93	Halachó (ä-lä-chō') . . . . Mex.	20.20 N	90.4 W
133	Halaib (hä-lä'ēb) . . . . Eg.	22.2 N	36.10 E
155	Halawa (hä-lä'wä) . . . . Haw.	21.10 N	156.45 W
120	Halberstadt (häl'bĕr-shtät) . . . Ger.	51.54 N	11.4 E
152	Halcon, Mt. (häl-kōn') . . . . . . Phil.	13.17 N	121.0 E
118	Halden (häl'dĕn) . . . . Nor.	59.9 N	11.20 E
116	Hale (hāl) . . . . Gt. Brit.	53.23 N	2.21 W
155	Haleakala, Crater of (hä'lā-ä'kä-lä) . Haw.	20.43 N	156.14 W
116	Halesowen (hälz'ō-wĕn) . . Gt. Brit.	52.27 N	2.3 W
117	Halewood (hāl'wŏŏd) Gt. Brit. (Liverpool In.)	53.22 N	2.49 W
82	Haleyville (hā'lĭ-vĭl) . . . . Ala.	34.13 N	87.37 W
51	Halfmoon B. (häf'mōōn) Calif. (San Francisco In.)	37.28 N	122.26 W
55	Halifax (hăl'ĭ-făks) . . . . Can.	44.8 N	63.47 W
54	Halifax . . . . Can. (In.)		
114	Halifax . . . . Gt. Brit.	53.45 N	1.55 W
159	Halifax B. . . . . Austl.	19.0 S	146.50 E
86	Halifax Harbor . . . . Can.	44.40 N	63.45 W
120	Hall (hôl) . . . . Ger.	47.18 N	11.30 E
120	Hall . . . . Ger.	49.7 N	9.44 E
147	Hallasan (Mt.) (häl'lä-sän) . . Kor.	33.22 N	126.32 E
120	Halle (häl'lĕ) . . . . Ger.	51.30 N	11.57 E
120	Hallein (häl-līn') . . . . Aus.	47.41 N	13.3 E
81	Halletsville (hăl'ĕts-vĭl) . . . . . . Tex.	29.27 N	96.55 W
76	Hallock (hăl'ŭk) . . . . Minn.	48.48 N	96.55 W
81	Halls Bayou . . . . Tex. (In.)	29.52 N	95.20 W
118	Hallsberg (häls'bĕrgh) . . . . . . Swe.	59.3 N	15.5 E
158	Halls Creek (hôlz) . . . . Austl.	18.15 S	127.45 E
86	Halls Stream (R.) . . . . . N. H.-Can.	45.10 N	71.30 W
122	Halluin (äl-lü-ăN') . . . . Fr.	50.48 N	3.9 E
151	Halmahera (I.) (häl-mä-hä'rä) Indon.	0.40 N	128.0 E
118	Halmstad (hälm'städ) . . . . Swe.	56.40 N	12.49 E
127	Halonnesos (I.) (ȧ-lô-nä'sōs) . . Grc.	39.10 N	23.55 E
118	Halse Fjord (häl'sĕ) . . . . Nor.	63.0 N	8.12 E
153	Halsey Harbor (hôl'zĭ) . . . . . . Phil.	11.47 N	119.55 E
118	Hälsingborg (hĕl'sĭng-bôrgh) . Swe.	56.3 N	12.41 E
79	Halstead (hôl'stĕd) . . . . Kan.	38.3 N	97.31 W
117	Halstenbek (häl'stĕn-bĕk) Ger. (Hamburg In.)	53.38 N	9.51 E
143	Halunarshan (hä'lōō-nar-shän') Chn.	47.30 N	119.50 E
137	Haluza (El Khelasa) (hȧ-lōō'zȧ) (ĕl Kĕ-lä'zȧ) . Pal. (In.)	31.6 N	34.37 E
160	Haly, Mt. (hā'lē) . . . . . Austl. (In.)	26.46 S	151.31 E
140	Hama (hä'mä) . . . . Syr.	35.15 N	36.50 E
149	Hamada (hä-mä'dä) . . . . Jap.	34.50 N	132.2 E
140	Hamadan (hŭ-mŭ-dän') . . . . . Iran	34.45 N	48.15 E
149	Hamamatsu (hä'mä-mät'sōō) . Jap.	34.45 N	137.45 E
118	Hamar (hä'mär) . . . . Nor.	60.49 N	11.5 E
149	Hamasaka (hă'mä-sä'kȧ) . . . . . Jap.	35.37 N	134.28 E
116	Hambledon Hills (hăm'b'l-dŭn) Gt. Brit.	54.15 N	1.18 W
79	Hamburg (hăm'bûrg) . . . . Ark.	33.14 N	91.48 W
120	Hamburg (häm'bōōrgh) . . . . . . Ger.	53.33 N	10.2 E
117	Hamburg . . . . Ger. (In.)		
79	Hamburg (hăm'bûrg) . . . . Ia.	40.35 N	95.40 W
85	Hamburg . . . . N. Y.	42.47 N	78.52 W
85	Hamden (hăm'dĕn) . . . . Conn.	41.22 N	72.58 W
119	Hämeenlinna (hĕ'mān-lĭn-nä) . Fin.	61.1 N	24.30 E
120	Hameln (hä'mĕln) . . . . Ger.	52.6 N	9.23 E
158	Hamersley Plat. (hăm'ẽrz-lē) Austl.	22.15 S	118.15 E
147	Hamhŭng (Kankō) (häm'hōōng') (kän'kō') . Kor.	39.54 N	127.32 E
142	Hami (Qomul) (hä'mē) (kô-mōōl') Chn.	42.47 N	93.29 E
159	Hamilton (hăm'ĭl-tŭn) . . . . . Austl.	37.45 S	142.8 E
55	Hamilton . . . . Can.	43.13 N	79.48 W
114	Hamilton . . . . Gt. Brit.	56.45 N	4.5 W
87	Hamilton . . . . Mass. (In.)	42.37 N	70.51 W
71	Hamilton . . . . Mont.	46.15 N	114.10 W
79	Hamilton . . . . Mo.	39.45 N	94.0 W
156	Hamilton . . . . N. Z.	37.46 S	175.22 E
84	Hamilton . . . . Ohio	39.24 N	84.36 W
80	Hamilton . . . . Tex.	31.41 N	98.8 W
77	Hamilton . . . . Wis.	43.43 N	88.28 W
55	Hamilton Inlet . . . . Can.	54.30 N	56.45 W
55	Hamilton R. . . . . Can.	53.0 N	62.0 W
119	Hamina (hä'mē-nä) . . . . Fin.	60.35 N	27.18 E
83	Hamlet (hăm'lĕt) . . . . N. C.	34.52 N	79.42 W
51	Hamlet . . . . . . Ore. (Portland In.)	45.50 N	123.41 W
80	Hamlin (hăm'lĭn) . . . . Tex.	32.52 N	100.8 W
120	Hamm (häm) . . . . Ger.	51.40 N	7.50 E
132	Hammada-el-Homra (Red Stony Desert) (häm'ä-dä-ĕl-hôm'rä) Libya	29.30 N	12.0 E
131	Hammamet (hä-mä-mĕt') Tun. (In.)	36.22 N	10.30 E
131	Hammamet, G. of . . . . . Tun. (In.)	36.10 N	10.40 E
108	Hammerfest (häm'mĕr-fĕst) . . Nor.	70.38 N	23.38 E
160	Hammock I. . . . . Austl. (Tas. In.)	40.4 S	147.45 E
84	Hammond (hăm'ŭnd) . . . . Ind.	41.37 N	87.28 W
81	Hammond . . . . La.	30.31 N	90.28 W
70	Hammond . . . . Ore.	46.10 N	123.58 W
85	Hammonton (hăm'ŭn-tŭn) . . N. J.	39.37 N	74.46 W
86	Hampden (hăm'dĕn) . . . . Me.	44.45 N	68.51 W
157	Hampden . . . . N. Z.	45.19 S	170.52 E
114	Hampshire Downs (hămp'shĭr dounz) . Gt. Brit.	51.5 N	1.0 W
86	Hampton (hămp'tŭn) . . . . Can.	45.32 N	65.50 W
73	Hampton . . . . Ga. (Atlanta In.)	33.23 N	84.17 W
77	Hampton . . . . Ia.	42.45 N	93.12 W
85	Hampton . . . . Va.	37.0 N	76.22 W
89	Hampton Roads (Inlet) Va. (Norfolk In.)	36.58 N	76.21 W
147	Hampyŏng (häm'pyŭng) . . . . . Kor.	35.7 N	126.32 E
118	Hamrange (häm'rông'ĕ) . . . . . Swe.	60.58 N	17.1 E
71	Hams Fork (R.) (hămz) . . . . Wyo.	42.0 N	110.40 W
84	Hamtramck (hăm-trăm'ĭk) . Mich.	42.22 N	83.2 W
140	Hamun-i-Helmand (L.) (hä-mōōn'ē-hĕl'mŭnd) . Iran-Afg.	31.0 N	61.15 E
141	Hamun-i Mashkel (L.) (hä-mōōn'ē mäsh-kĕl') . Pak.	28.15 N	63.5 E
147	Hamyang (häm'yäng') . . . . . . Kor.	35.35 N	127.46 E
144	Han R. (hän) . . . . Chn.	30.55 N	112.35 E
147	Han R. . . . . Kor.	37.30 N	127.30 E
155	Hana (hä'nä) . . . . Haw.	20.43 N	155.59 W
96	Hanabana, R. (hä-nä-bä'nä) . Cuba	22.30 N	80.35 W
155	Hanalei B. (hä-nä-lä'ē) . . . . . Haw.	22.12 N	159.33 W
141	Hanamkonda (hŭ-näm-kōn'dŭ) India	18.5 N	79.38 E
120	Hanau (hä'nou) . . . . Ger.	50.9 N	8.57 E
116	Hanbury (hăn'bẽr-ĭ) . . . . . Gt. Brit.	52.17 N	2.4 W
144	Hanchwan (hän'chwän') . . . . . Chn.	30.38 N	113.40 E
77	Hancock (hăn'kŏk) . . . . Mich.	47.8 N	88.35 W
134	Handa (hän'dä) . . . . Ang.	15.52 S	15.55 E
135	Handeni (hän-dā'nē) . . . . Tan.	5.27 S	38.4 E
117	Handforth (hăn'fẽrth) Gt. Brit. (Liverpool In.)	53.21 N	2.13 W
74	Hanford (hăn'fẽrd) . . . . Calif.	36.19 N	119.39 W
145	Hangchow (häng'chō') . . . . . . Chn.	30.15 N	120.10 E
145	Hangchow B. . . . . Chn.	30.32 N	121.30 E
119	Hangö (häŋ'gû) . . . . Fin.	59.50 N	22.57 E
81	Hankamer (hăŋ'kȧ-mẽr) . Tex. (In.)	29.52 N	94.37 W
76	Hankinson (hăŋ'kĭn-sŭn) . . . N. D.	46.5 N	96.54 W
145	Hankow (hän'kō') . . . . Chn.	30.35 N	114.8 E
71	Hanna (hăn'ȧ) . . . . Wyo.	41.52 N	106.34 W
76	Hannah . . . . N. D.	48.58 N	98.42 W
79	Hannibal (hăn'ĭ-bȧl) . . . . Mo.	39.42 N	91.21 W
158	Hann, Mt. (hän) . . . . Austl.	16.0 S	125.47 E
120	Hannover (hän-ō'vẽr) . . . . Ger.	52.29 N	9.20 E
120	Hannover (Prov.) . . . . Ger.	52.50 N	9.20 E
118	Hanö B. (hän'û) . . . . Swe.	55.50 N	15.0 E
150	Hanoi (hä-noi') . . . . Indoch.	21.0 N	105.51 E
84	Hanover (hăn'ō-vẽr) . . . . Can.	40.10 N	81.4 W
87	Hanover . . . . Mass. (In.)	42.7 N	70.48 W
86	Hanover . . . . N. H.	43.42 N	72.18 W
85	Hanover . . . . Pa.	39.48 N	76.59 W
102	Hanover I. . . . . Chl.	51.0 S	74.30 W
147	Han R. (hän) . . . . Kor.	37.35 N	127.10 E
146	Hanshan (hän'shän') . . . . Chn.	31.45 N	118.3 E
144	Hanshow (hän'shō') . . . . Chn.	28.53 N	111.39 E
91	Hans Lollick I. (häns' lŏl ĭk) St. Thomas (In.)	18.24 N	64.55 W
87	Hanson (hăn'sŭn) . . . . . Mass. (In.)	42.3 N	70.53 W
146	Hantan (hän'tän') . . . . Chn.	36.36 N	114.38 E
86	Hantsport (hănts'pōrt) . . . . . . Can.	45.5 N	64.12 W
145	Hanyang (hän'yäng') . . . . Chn.	30.32 N	114.6 E
108	Haparanda (hä-pä-rän'dä) . . . Swe.	65.55 N	24.0 E
73	Hapeville (hăp'vĭl) Ga. (Atlanta In.)	33.39 N	84.24 W
89	Happy Jack . La. (New Orleans In.)	29.30 N	89.45 W
143	Harbin (Pinkiang) (här-bēn') (pĭn'kyäng') . Chn.	45.40 N	126.31 E
84	Harbor Beach . . . . Mich.	43.50 N	82.40 W
87	Harbor Grace . . . . Can.	47.39 N	53.15 W
96	Harbor I. . . . . Ba. Is.	25.26 N	76.35 W
84	Harbor Springs . . . . Mich.	45.27 N	85.0 W
87	Harbour au Bouche (här'bẽr ō bōōsh') . Can.	45.39 N	61.31 W
87	Harbour Breton (brĕt'ŭn) (brē-tôN') . Can.	47.28 N	55.51 W
120	Harburg-Wilhelmsburg (här'-bōōrgh-vēl'hĕlms-bōōrgh) . Ger.	53.27 N	9.57 E
86	Harcourt (här'côrt) (är-kōōr') . Can.	46.28 N	65.15 W
118	Hardanger Fjeld (Plat.) (här-däng'ẽr fyĕl') . Nor.	60.15 N	7.0 E
118	Hardanger Fd. . . . . Nor.	59.58 N	5.57 E
118	Hardanger Jökulen (Mt.) (yû'kōōl-ĕn) . Nor.	60.32 N	7.25 E
72	Hardin (här'dĭn) Colo. (Denver In.)	40.21 N	104.26 W
71	Hardin . . . . Mont.	45.45 N	107.37 W
134	Harding (här'dĭng) . . . . . U. S. Afr.	30.35 S	29.51 W
74	Hardy, R. (här'dĭ) . . . . Mex.	32.0 N	115.12 W
87	Hare B. (hâr) . . . . Can.	51.15 N	55.55 W
122	Harfleur (är-flûr') . . . . Fr.	49.31 N	0.11 E
135	Hargeisa (här-gā'ē-sä) . . Br. Som.	9.35 N	43.55 E
121	Harghitei Mts. (Kär-gē'tȧ) . . Rom.	46.26 N	25.40 E
149	Harima Sea (hä'rē-mä) . . . . . . Jap.	34.33 N	134.36 E
140	Hari Rud (R.) (hŭ'rē rōōd') . . Afg.	34.20 N	63.0 E
57	Harlaka (här'lä-kȧ) Can. (Quebec In.)	46.49 N	71.8 W
76	Harlan (här'lăn) . . . . Ia.	41.40 N	95.19 W
82	Harlan . . . . Ky.	36.53 N	83.19 W
71	Harlem (här'lĕm) . . . . Mont.	48.32 N	108.50 W
88	Harlem R. . N. Y. (New York In.)	40.50 N	73.56 W
120	Harlingen (här'lĭng-ĕn) . . . . . Neth.	53.10 N	5.27 E
81	Harlingen . . . . Tex.	26.12 N	97.41 W
71	Harlowton (här'lō-tŭn) . . . . . Mont.	46.27 N	109.50 W
84	Harmony (här'mō-nĭ) . . . . Ind.	39.33 N	87.3 W
70	Harney Basin (här'nĭ) . . . . Ore.	43.25 N	120.0 W
70	Harney L. . . . . Ore.	43.13 N	119.10 W
76	Harney Peak . . . . S. D.	43.52 N	103.30 W
118	Härnösand (hĕr-nû-sänd) . . . . Swe.	62.39 N	18.0 E
124	Haro (ä'rō) . . . . Sp.	42.35 N	2.50 W
72	Haro, Canal de (hä'rō, cȧ-näl dē) Can. (Vancouver In.)	49.5 N	123.35 W
72	Haro Str. (hă'rō) Wash.-Can. (Vancouver In.)	48.37 N	123.14 W
78	Harper (här'pẽr) . . . . Kan.	37.18 N	98.2 W
51	Harper . . . . . . Wash. (Seattle In.)	47.30 N	122.31 W
132	Harper (Cape Palmas) (päl'mȧs) . Lib.	4.30 N	7.54 W
85	Harpers Ferry . . . . W. Va.	39.18 N	77.47 W
73	Harpersville . Ala. (Birmingham In.)	33.21 N	86.27 W
111	Harput (Kär-pōōt') . . . . Tur.	38.45 N	39.15 E
135	Harrania (hȧr-rä'nyȧ) . . . . Eg.	29.58 N	31.10 E
135	Harrar (hȧ-rär') (Division) . . . Eth.	8.30 N	42.0 E
133	Harrar (hȧ-rär') . . . . Eth.	9.17 N	42.3 E
89	Harriet, L. (hăr'ĭ-ĕt) Minn. (Minneapolis In.)	44.55 N	93.18 W
82	Harriman (hăr'ĭ-măn) . . . . . . Tenn.	35.56 N	84.33 W
85	Harrington (hăr'ĭng-tŭn) . . . . . Del.	38.55 N	75.37 W
79	Harrisburg (hăr'ĭs-bûrg) . . . . Ill.	37.45 N	88.32 W
85	Harrisburg . . . . Pa.	40.16 N	76.50 W
81	Harrisburg . . . . Tex. (In.)	29.43 N	95.16 W
114	Harris (I.) . . . . Gt. Brit.	57.48 N	7.0 W
83	Harris, L. . . . . Fla. (In.)	28.46 N	81.50 W
79	Harrison . . . . Ark.	36.14 N	93.5 W
88	Harrison . . . . N. J. (New York In.)	40.45 N	74.10 W
85	Harrisonburg . . . . Va.	38.28 N	78.52 W
72	Harrison Hot Springs Can. (Vancouver In.)	49.18 N	121.47 W
72	Harrison L. . Can. (Vancouver In.)	49.35 N	121.50 W
72	Harrison Mills Can. (Vancouver In.)	49.14 N	121.56 W
79	Harrisonville . . . . Mo.	38.39 N	94.20 W
73	Harrisville Utah (Salt Lake City In.)	41.17 N	112.0 W
84	Harrisville . . . . W. Va.	39.11 N	81.3 W
84	Harrodsburg (hăr'ŭdz-bûrg) . . Ky.	37.42 N	84.50 W
116	Harrogate (hăr'ō-gāt) . . . . Gt. Brit.	53.59 N	1.33 W
116	Harrold (hăr'ŭld) . . . . Gt. Brit.	52.12 N	0.37 W
117	Harrow (hăr'ō) Gt. Brit. (London In.)	51.35 N	0.21 W
127	Hârsova (Kär-sō'vȧ) . . . . Rom.	44.41 N	27.58 E
108	Harstad (här'städh) . . . . Nor.	68.45 N	16.27 E
51	Harstine I. (här'stĭn) Wash. (Seattle In.)	47.14 N	122.54 W
84	Hart (härt) . . . . Mich.	43.41 N	86.23 W
82	Hartford (härt'fẽrd) . . . . Ala.	31.5 N	85.42 W
79	Hartford . . . . Ark.	35.3 N	94.22 W
85	Hartford . . . . Conn.	41.45 N	72.40 W
84	Hartford . . . . Ky.	37.27 N	86.53 W
84	Hartford . . . . Mich.	42.16 N	86.16 W

ng-sing; ŋ-baŋk; N-nasalized n; nŏd; cŏmmit; ōld; ôbey; ôrder; fōōd; fŏŏt; ou-out; s-soft; sh-dish; th-thin; pūre; ūnite; ûrn; stŭd; circŭs; ü-as "y" in study; '-indeterminate vowel.

Hartford PRONOUNCING INDEX Hidalgo

Page	Name Pronunciation Region	Lat. °′	Long. °′
77	Hartford ..... Wis.	43.19 N	88.22 W
84	Hartford City ..... Ind.	40.30 N	40.27 W
88	Hart I. ..... N. Y. (In.)	40.51 N	73.46 W
116	Hartington (härt'ĭng-tŭn). Gt. Brit.	53.8 N	1.48 W
76	Hartington ..... Neb.	42.38 N	97.17 W
86	Hartland (härt'lănd) ..... Can.	46.19 N	67.31 W
114	Hartland Pt. ..... Gt. Brit.	51.5 N	4.35 W
114	Hartlepool (här't'l-pōōl). Gt. Brit.	54.40 N	1.12 W
76	Hartley (härt'lĭ) ..... Ia.	43.11 N	95.28 W
134	Hartley ..... S. Rh.	18.12 S	30.9 E
82	Hartselle (härt'sĕl) ..... Ala.	34.37 N	86.57 W
79	Hartshorne (härts'hôrn) ..... Okla.	34.51 N	95.33 W
83	Hartsville (härts'vĭl) ..... S. C.	34.21 N	80.3 W
82	Hartwell (härt'wĕl) ..... Ga.	34.21 N	82.57 W
77	Harvard (här'vărd) ..... Ill.	42.25 N	88.38 W
87	Harvard ..... Mass. (In.)	42.30 N	71.35 W
78	Harvard ..... Neb.	40.36 N	98.5 W
78	Harvard, Mt. ..... Colo.	38.56 N	106.21 W
84	Harvey (här'vĭ) ..... Ill.	41.42 N	87.36 W
76	Harvey ..... N. D.	47.47 N	99.56 W
159	Harvey Creek ..... Austl.	17.27 N	146.5 E
72	Harvey Mt. Can. (Vancouver In.)	49.28 N	123.14 W
115	Harwich (här'wĭch) ..... Gt. Brit.	51.55 N	1.15 E
120	Harz Mts. (härts) ..... Ger.	51.43 N	10.55 E
137	Hasbaya (häs'bä'yȧ) ... Leb. (In.)	33.27 N	35.42 E
88	Hasbrouck Heights (hăz'brŏŏk) N. J. (N. Y. In.)	40.52 N	74.4 W
117	Haselau (häs'ĕ-lou) Ger. (Hamburg In.)	53.40 N	9.37 E
117	Haseldorf (häs'ĕl-dōrf) Ger. (Hamburg In.)	53.38 N	9.36 E
149	Hashimoto (hä'shē-mō'tō) ..... Jap.	34.20 N	135.37 E
119	Häsijarvi (L.) (hĕ'sē-yĕr'vē) .. Fin.	61.40 N	23.50 E
79	Haskell (hăs'kĕl) ..... Okla.	35.49 N	95.39 W
78	Haskell ..... Tex.	33.9 N	99.45 W
116	Haslingden (hăz'lĭng-dĕn). Gt. Brit.	53.42 N	2.20 W
118	Hassela (häs'ĕl-ô) ..... Swe.	62.6 N	16.49 E
115	Hasselt (häs'ĕlt) ..... Bel.	50.59 N	5.25 E
118	Hässjö (hĕs'shû) ..... Swe.	62.36 N	17.31 E
118	Hassleholm (häs'lĕ-hōlm) ..... Swe.	56.10 N	13.45 E
93	Hastahuacán (ä-stä-hwä-kän') Mex. (In.)	19.21 N	99.2 W
115	Hastings (hās'tĭngz) ..... Gt. Brit.	50.51 N	0.35 E
84	Hastings ..... Mich.	42.42 N	85.20 W
77	Hastings ..... Minn.	44.45 N	92.51 W
78	Hastings ..... Neb.	50.35 N	98.24 W
156	Hastings ..... N. Z.	39.40 S	176.52 E
82	Hatchie R. (hăch'ē) ..... Tenn.	35.25 N	89.5 W
127	Hațeg (kät-säg') ..... Rom.	45.36 N	22.57 E
96	Hatiguanico R. (ä-tē-gwä-nē'kō) Cuba	22.22 N	81.20 W
149	Hatsukaichi (hät'sōō-kä'ē-chē) Jap.	34.22 N	132.19 E
83	Hatteras, C. (hăt'ēr-ås) ..... N. C.	35.15 N	75.32 W
82	Hattiesburg (hăt'ĭz-bûrg) ... Miss.	31.19 N	89.19 W
121	Hatvan (hôt'vôn) ..... Hung.	47.39 N	19.43 E
118	Haugesund (hou'gĕ-sōōn') ... Nor.	59.27 N	5.20 E
156	Hauhangaroa Ra. (hä'ōō-häŋ-gä-rō'ä). N. Z.	38.40 S	175.30 E
119	Haukivesi (L.) (hou'kē-vĕ'sē). Fin.	62.2 N	28.35 E
156	Hauraki G. (hä-ōō-rä'kē) .. N. Z.	36.25 S	175.5 E
157	Haurangi Ra. (hä-ōō-räŋ'gē). N. Z.	41.25 S	175.25 E
157	Hauroko L. (hä-ōō-rō'kō) .. N. Z.	46.0 S	167.20 E
119	Hausjärvi (hä'ōōs-yĕr'vē) .... Fin.	60.46 N	24.48 E
137	Hauta (hou'tȧ) ..... Aden (In.)	13.3 N	44.54 E
140	Hauta ..... Sau. Ar.	23.35 N	46.35 E
122	Hautmont (ō-môN') ..... Fr.	50.15 N	3.52 E
79	Havana (hȧ-vă'nȧ) ..... Ill.	40.17 N	90.2 W
76	Havelock (hăv'lŏk) ..... Neb.	40.51 N	96.38 W
86	Havelock ..... Can.	45.59 N	65.20 W
157	Havelock ..... N. Z.	41.15 S	173.48 E
120	Havel R. (hä'fĕl) ..... Ger.	53.0 N	13.20 E
86	Haverhill (hā'vēr-hĭl) ..... Mass.	42.47 N	71.5 W
86	Haverhill ..... N. H.	44.1 N	72.5 W
117	Havering (hā'vēr-ĭng) Gt. Brit. (London In.)	51.37 N	0.11 E
85	Haverstraw (hā'vēr-strô) ... N. Y.	41.12 N	73.59 W
71	Havre (hăv'ēr) ..... Mont.	48.33 N	109.41 W
85	Havre de Grace (hăv'ēr dē gràs') Md.	39.33 N	76.7 W
155	Hawaiian Is. (hä-wī'ăn) ... Pac. O.	21.0 N	157.0 W
155	Hawaii (I.) (hä-wī'ē) ..... Haw.	19.30 N	155.30 W
155	Hawaii (Ter.) ..... Pac. O.	21.0 N	157.0 W
135	Hawamdiya (hä'wäm-dē-yȧ) .. Eg.	29.54 N	31.15 E
76	Hawarden (hā'wär-dĕn) ..... Ia.	43.0 N	96.5 W
157	Hawea L. (hä'wē-ȧ) ..... N. Z.	44.30 S	169.22 E
156	Hawera (hä'wȧ-rä) ..... N. Z.	39.35 S	174.15 E
84	Hawesville (hôz'vĭl) ..... Ky.	37.53 N	86.46 W
155	Hawi (hä'wē) ..... Haw.	20.15 N	155.48 W
114	Hawick (hô'ĭk) ..... Gt. Brit.	55.25 N	2.50 W
156	Hawke B. (hôk) ..... N. Z.	39.20 S	177.30 E
85	Hawkesbury (hôks'bēr-ĭ) ..... Can.	45.35 N	74.37 W
82	Hawkinsville (hô'kĭnz-vĭl) .... Ga.	32.17 N	83.29 W
97	Hawks Nest Pt. ..... Ba. Is.	24.9 N	75.33 W
76	Hawley (hô'lĭ) ..... Minn.	46.54 N	96.18 W
116	Haworth (hô'ŭrth) ..... Gt. Brit.	53.50 N	1.57 W
83	Haw River (hô) ..... N. C.	35.55 N	79.18 W
73	Hawthorne (hô'thôrn) Calif. (Los Angeles In.)	33.55 N	118.21 W
54	Hawthorne ..... Can. (In.)	45.23 N	75.36 W
74	Hawthorne ..... Nev.	38.31 N	118.38 W
78	Haxtun (hăks'tŭn) ..... Colo.	40.37 N	102.38 W
159	Hay ..... Austl.	34.28 S	144.52 E
123	Hayange (hä-yäNzh') ..... Fr.	49.20 N	6.5 E
75	Hayden (hā'dĕn) ..... Ariz.	33.1 N	110.49 W
160	Hayden ..... Austl. (In.)	27.14 S	151.52 E
117	Haydock (hā'dŏk) Gt. Brit. (Liverpool In.)	53.28 N	2.39 W
117	Hayes (hāz). Gt. Brit. (London In.)	51.22 N	0.1 E
53	Hayes, Mt. ..... Alsk.	63.40 N	146.30 W
54	Hayes R. ..... Can.	55.30 N	94.0 W
117	Hayfield. Gt. Brit. (Liverpool In.)	53.22 N	1.56 W
77	Hay L. ..... Mich.	46.22 N	84.12 W
79	Haynesville (hānz'vĭl) ..... Ark.	32.59 N	93.8 W
81	Haynesville ..... La.	32.57 N	93.10 W
158	Hay R. ..... Austl.	23.30 S	137.10 E
54	Hay River ..... Can.	60.58 N	116.19 W
78	Hays ..... Kan.	38.52 N	99.20 W
77	Hayward (hā'wērd) ..... Wis.	46.1 N	91.29 W
157	Hayward Pt. ..... N. Z. (In.)	45.46 S	170.43 E
51	Haywards Calif. (San Francisco In.)	37.40 N	122.5 W
56	Haywood ... Can. (Winnipeg In.)	49.40 N	98.14 W
82	Hazard (hăz'ȧrd) ..... Ky.	37.15 N	83.12 W
149	Haze (hä'zē) ..... Jap. (Osaka In.)	34.45 N	135.47 E
122	Hazebrouck (àz-brōōk') ..... Fr.	50.45 N	2.35 E
117	Hazel Grove (hā'z'l) Gt. Brit. (Liverpool In.)	53.23 N	2.8 W
83	Hazelhurst (hā'z'l-hûrst) ..... Ga.	31.51 N	82.36 W
82	Hazlehurst ..... Miss.	31.52 N	90.24 W
85	Hazleton (hā'z'l-tŭn) ..... Pa.	40.58 N	75.58 W
56	Headingly (hĕd'ĭng-lĭ) Can. (Winnipeg In.)	49.53 N	97.22 W
82	Headland (hĕd'lănd) ..... Ala.	31.21 N	85.32 W
74	Healdsburg (hēldz'bûrg) .... Calif.	38.37 N	122.53 W
79	Healdton (hēld'tŭn) ..... Okla.	34.14 N	97.29 W
116	Heanor (hēn'ōr) ..... Gt. Brit.	53.1 N	1.22 W
5	Heard I. (hûrd) ..... Ind. O.	53.10 S	74.35 E
81	Hearne (hûrn) ..... Tex.	30.52 N	96.36 W
76	Heart R. (härt) ..... N. D.	46.38 N	102.0 W
87	Hearts Content ..... Can.	47.52 N	53.22 W
160	Heathcote (hĕth'kŏt) Austl. (Sydney In.)	34.5 S	151.1 E
157	Heathcote R. ..... N. Z.	43.33 S	172.37 E
87	Heath Pt. (hēth) ..... Can.	49.5 N	61.45 W
79	Heavener (hēv'nēr) ..... Okla.	34.53 N	94.36 W
80	Hebbronville (hē'brŭn-vĭl) ... Tex.	27.18 N	98.41 W
75	Heber (hē'bēr) ..... Utah	40.31 N	111.27 W
79	Heber Springs ..... Ark.	35.28 N	91.59 W
71	Hebgen Reservoir (hĕb'gĕn). Mont.	44.48 N	111.15 W
114	Hebrides, G. of the (hĕb'rĭ-dēz) Gt. Brit.	56.50 N	6.50 W
55	Hebron (hĕb'rŭn) ..... Can.	58.10 N	62.45 W
79	Hebron ..... Neb.	40.10 N	97.35 W
76	Hebron ..... N. D.	46.54 N	102.3 W
137	Hebron ..... Pal. (In.)	31.32 N	35.5 E
137	Hebron (Beit Jibrin) (bāt' zhē-brēn'). Pal. (In.)	31.37 N	34.57 E
118	Heby (hĭ'bü) ..... Swe.	59.57 N	16.50 E
54	Hecate Str. (hĕk'ȧ-tē) ..... Can.	53.15 N	131.0 W
93	Hecelchakán (ā-sĕl-chä-kän'). Mex.	20.11 N	90.7 W
118	Hedemora (hĭ-dĕ-mō'rä) .... Swe.	60.17 N	15.55 E
118	Hedesunda Fjörd (hĭ-dĕ-sōōn'dä) Swe.	60.26 N	17.10 E
116	Hedon (hĕd-ŭn) ..... Gt. Brit.	53.44 N	0.12 W
115	Heerlen (hār'lĕn) ..... Neth.	50.54 N	5.57 E
82	Heflin (hĕf'lĭn) ..... Ala.	33.39 N	85.36 W
120	Heide (hī'dē) ..... Ger.	54.12 N	9.6 E
160	Heidelberg (hī'dĕl-bûrg) Austl. (Melbourne In.)	37.45 S	145.4 E
120	Heidelberg (hī'dĕl-bĕrgh) ..... Ger.	49.25 N	8.43 E
120	Heidenheim (hī'dĕn-hīm) ..... Ger.	48.42 N	10.9 E
147	Heijō (Pyŏngyang) (hā'jō') (pyŭng'yäng'). Kor.	39.1 N	125.44 E
120	Heilbronn (hīl'brōn) ..... Ger.	49.9 N	9.14 E
117	Heiligenstadt (hī'lĭ-gĕn-shtät) Aus. (Wien In.)	48.15 N	16.22 E
120	Heiligenstadt ..... Ger.	51.22 N	10.0 E
143	Heilungkiang (Prov.) (hā-lōōng'kyăng'). Chn.	48.10 N	122.0 E
119	Heinola (hā-nō'lä) ..... Fin.	61.14 N	26.4 E
51	Heisson (hī'sŭn) Wash. (Portland In.)	45.49 N	122.28 W
117	Heist (hīst) ... Ger. (Hamburg In.)	53.39 N	9.40 E
140	Hejaz (State) (hē-jăz') (hĕ-zhăz') Sau. Ar.	25.0 N	38.0 E
108	Hekla, Mt. (Vôl.) (hĕk'lȧ) .... Ice.	64.0 N	19.45 W
121	Hel (hāl) ..... Pol.	54.36 N	18.48 E
73	Helena (hĕl'ē-nȧ) Ala. (Birmingham In.)	33.18 N	86.50 W
79	Helena ..... Ark.	34.32 N	90.36 W
71	Helena ..... Mont.	46.36 N	112.1 W
114	Helensburgh (hĕl'ĕnz-bŭr-ō) Gt. Brit.	56.0 N	4.40 W
156	Helensville (hĕl'ĕnz-vĭl) ..... N. Z.	36.40 S	174.27 E
118	Helge R. (hĕl'gĕ) ..... Swe.	56.20 N	14.2 E
120	Helgoland (I.) (hĕl'gô-länd) North Sea	54.12 N	7.53 E
160	Helidon (hĕl'ĭ-dŏn) .... Austl. (In.)	27.31 S	152.8 E
135	Heliopolis (Ruins) (hē-lĭ-ŏp'ō-lĭs). Eg.	30.6 N	31.20 E
137	Heliopolis (Baalbeck) (bäl'bĕk) Leb. (In.)	33.59 N	36.9 E
117	Hellbrok (hĕl'brōk) Ger. (Hamburg In.)	53.36 N	10.4 E
83	Hellier (hĕl'yēr) ..... Ky.	37.17 N	82.29 W
124	Hellin (ĕl-yēn') ..... Sp.	38.31 N	1.41 W
140	Helmand R. (hĕl'mŭnd) ..... Afg.	31.0 N	64.0 E
120	Helmond (hĕl'mônt) (ĕl'môN') Neth.	51.30 N	5.42 E
116	Helmsley (hĕlmz'lĭ) ..... Gt. Brit.	54.15 N	1.3 W
120	Helmstedt (hĕlm'shtĕt) ..... Ger.	52.14 N	11.1 E
75	Helper (hĕlp'ēr) ..... Utah	39.41 N	110.55 W
119	Helsingfors (Helsinki) (hĕl-sĭng-fôrs') (hĕl'sēn-kē). Fin.	60.10 N	24.58 E
118	Helsingör (hĕl-sĭng-ûr') ..... Den.	56.3 N	12.35 E
119	Helsinki (Helsingfors) (hĕl'sēn-kē). Fin.	60.10 N	23.58 E
135	Helwan (hĕl'wän) ..... Eg.	29.50 N	31.19 E
73	Hemet (hĕm'ĕt) Calif. (Los Angeles In.)	33.45 N	116.58 W
76	Hemingford (hĕm'ĭng-fērd) .. Neb.	42.19 N	103.2 W
117	Hemixem (hĕm'ĭk-sĕm) Bel. (Anvers In.)	51.9 N	4.20 E
81	Hemphill (hĕmp'hĭl) ..... Tex.	31.20 N	93.49 W
81	Hempstead (hĕmp'stĕd) ..... Tex.	30.7 N	96.5 W
118	Hemse (hĕm'sē) ..... Swe.	57.16 N	18.28 E
118	Hems I. (hĕms) ..... Swe.	62.45 N	18.5 E
118	Hen (hĭn) ..... Nor.	60.15 N	10.13 E
156	Hen and Chickens Is. ..... N. Z.	36.0 S	174.45 E
124	Henares R. (ā-nä'rås) ..... Sp.	40.40 N	3.10 W
122	Hendaye (äN-dā') ..... Fr.	43.25 N	1.38 W
72	Henderson (hĕn'dēr-sŭn) Colo. (Denver In.)	39.55 N	104.51 W
84	Henderson ..... Ky.	37.50 N	87.33 W
156	Henderson ..... N. Z.	36.53 S	174.38 E
83	Henderson ..... N. C.	36.18 N	78.22 W
82	Henderson ..... Tenn.	35.27 N	88.40 W
81	Henderson ..... Tex.	32.9 N	94.49 W
83	Hendersonville ..... N. C.	35.18 N	82.28 W
160	Hendon (hĕn'dŭn) .... Austl. (In.)	28.5 S	151.59 E
114	Hendon ..... Gt. Brit.	51.35 N	0.15 W
73	Henefer (hĕn'ĕ-fēr) Utah (Salt Lake City In.)	41.2 N	111.30 W
144	Hengchow (hĕng'chō') ..... Chn.	26.56 N	112.30 E
148	Hengchun (hĕng'chŭn') ..... For.	22.1 N	120.44 E
120	Hengelo (hĕng'ĕ-lō) ..... Neth.	52.16 N	6.47 E
146	Heng R. (hĕng) ..... Chn.	31.56 N	114.50 E
144	Hengshan (hĕng'shän') ..... Chn.	27.10 N	112.32 E
144	Heng Shan (Nan Yueh) (Mts.) (nän'yōō-ā'). Chn.	26.55 N	111.48 E
146	Hengshui (hĕng'shōō-ē') ..... Chn.	37.51 N	115.46 E
122	Hénin-Liétard (ā-năN'lyā-târ'). Fr.	50.25 N	2.59 E
160	Henley Beach (hĕn'lē) Austl. (Adelaide In.)	34.56 S	138.30 E
116	Henley-in-Arden (hĕn'lĭ-ĭn-är'dĕn) Gt. Brit.	52.17 N	1.47 W
85	Henlopen, C. (hĕn-lō'pĕn) .... Del.	38.48 N	75.6 W
122	Hennebont (ĕn-bôN') ..... Fr.	47.48 N	3.15 W
117	Hennersdorf (hĕn'ĕrs-dōrf) Aus. (Wien In.)	48.7 N	16.22 E
78	Hennessey (hĕn'ĕ-sĭ) ..... Okla.	36.6 N	97.53 W
78	Henrietta (hĕn-rĭ-ĕt'ȧ) ..... Tex.	33.47 N	98.13 W
85	Henry, C. (hĕn'rĭ) ..... Va.	36.53 N	76.0 W
79	Henryetta ..... Okla.	35.26 N	95.58 W
71	Henrys Fork (R.) ..... Ida.	43.50 N	111.55 W
70	Heppner (hĕp'nēr) ..... Ore.	45.22 N	119.33 W
140	Herat (hĕ-rät') ..... Afg.	34.30 N	62.15 E
157	Herbert (hēr'bērt) ..... N. Z.	45.15 S	170.50 E
123	Herblay (ĕr-blĕ') ..... Fr. (In.)	49.0 N	2.10 E
126	Hercegovina (Prov.) (hĕr-tsĕ-gô'vē-nȧ). Yugo.	43.20 N	18.10 E
117	Herculaneum (hĕr-kōō-lā'nā-ōōm) (hûr-kū-lā'nē-ŭm). It. (Napoli In.)	40.48 N	14.20 E
92	Hércules (ĕr'kōō-lâs) ..... Mex.	20.38 N	100.19 W
160	Herdsmans L. (hûrdz'mănz) Austl. (Perth In.)	31.55 S	115.48 E
95	Heredia (ā-rā'dhē-ä) ..... C. R.	10.3 N	84.7 W
114	Hereford (hĕr'ĕ-fērd) .... Gt. Brit.	52.5 N	2.45 W
78	Hereford ..... Tex.	34.47 N	102.25 W
116	Hereford Co. ..... Gt. Brit.	52.12 N	2.45 W
124	Herencia (ā-rän'thē-ä) ..... Sp.	39.23 N	3.21 W
120	Herford (hĕr'fôrt) ..... Ger.	52.7 N	8.40 E
123	Héricourt (ā-rē-kōōr') ..... Fr.	47.35 N	6.45 E
79	Herington (hĕr'ĭng-tŭn) ..... Kan.	38.41 N	96.47 W
120	Herisau (hā'rē-zou) ..... Switz.	47.23 N	9.17 E
85	Herkimer (hûr'kĭ-mēr) ..... N. Y.	43.3 N	74.58 W
114	Herma Ness (hûr'mȧ nĕs) Gt. Brit. (In.)	60.50 N	1.0 W
79	Hermann (hûr'măn) ..... Mo.	38.41 N	91.27 W
137	Hermel (hûr'mĕl) ..... Leb. (In.)	34.24 N	36.22 E
87	Hermitage B. (hûr'mĭ-tĕj) ... Can.	47.40 N	56.0 W
151	Hermit Is. (hûr'mĭt) .. N. Gui. Ter.	1.30 S	145.0 E
137	Hermon, Mt. (hûr'mŭn) .. Leb. (In.)	33.25 N	35.48 E
151	Hermosa (ĕr-mō'sä) Phil. (Manila In.)	14.48 N	120.27 E
73	Hermosa Beach (hēr-mō'sȧ) Calif. (Los Angeles In.)	33.52 N	118.25 W
127	Hermoupolis (ĕr-mōō'pô-lyēs). Grc.	37.28 N	24.55 E
118	Herning (hĕr'nĭng) ..... Den.	56.8 N	8.59 E
55	Heron Bay (hĕr'ŭn) ..... Can.	48.35 N	86.0 W
76	Heron Lake ..... Minn.	43.45 N	95.15 W
160	Herries Ra. (hĕr'ēz) ... Austl. (In.)	28.23 S	151.47 E
79	Herrin (hĕr'ĭn) ..... Ill.	37.47 N	89.1 W
120	Hersfeld (hĕrs'fĕlt) ..... Ger.	50.54 N	9.42 E
115	Herstal (hĕr'stäl) ..... Bel.	50.40 N	5.40 E
114	Hertford (hûrt'fērd) ..... Gt. Brit.	51.50 N	0.10 W
83	Hertford ..... N. C.	36.11 N	76.28 W
124	Hervas (ĕr'väs) ..... Sp.	40.17 N	5.51 W
159	Hervey B. (hûr'vē) ..... Austl.	25.0 S	152.45 E
73	Hesperia (hĕs-pē'rĭ-ȧ) Calif. (Los Angeles In.)	34.25 N	117.19 W
120	Hessen (State) (hĕs'ĕn) ..... Ger.	50.20 N	8.46 E
117	Heswall (hĕz'wôl) Gt. Brit. (Liverpool In.)	53.21 N	3.8 W
117	Hetlingen (hĕt'lĭng-ĕn) Ger. (Hamburg In.)	53.37 N	9.38 E
148	Heto C. (hĕ'tō'). Ryukyu Is. (In.)	26.48 N	128.15 E
76	Hettinger (hĕt'ĭn-jēr) ..... N. D.	46.6 N	102.38 W
158	Heughlin, Mt. (hoi'glĭn) .... Austl.	23.5 S	133.59 E
116	Heysham (hā'shăm) .... Gt. Brit.	54.2 N	2.54 W
116	Heywood (hā'wŏŏd) .... Gt. Brit.	53.35 N	2.12 W
144	Hiakiang (hyä'kyăng') ..... Chn.	25.45 N	108.42 E
144	Hiakiang ..... Chn.	25.23 N	107.44 E
79	Hiawatha (hī-ȧ-wô'thȧ) ..... Kan.	39.51 N	95.34 W
75	Hiawatha ..... Utah	39.29 N	111.4 W
77	Hibbing (hĭb'ĭng) ..... Minn.	47.27 N	92.55 W
160	Hibbs, Pt. (hĭbz). Austl. (Tas. In.)	42.37 S	145.14 E
82	Hickman (hĭk'măn) ..... Ky.	36.33 N	89.10 W
83	Hickory (hĭk'ō-rĭ) ..... N. C.	35.43 N	81.21 W
84	Hicksville (hĭks'vĭl) ..... Ohio	41.17 N	84.46 W
80	Hico (hī'kō) ..... Tex.	31.59 N	98.1 W
92	Hidalgo (State) (ē-dhäl'gō) .. Mex.	20.25 N	99.0 W
92	Hidalgo ..... Mex.	24.13 N	99.27 W
80	Hidalgo ..... Mex.	27.48 N	99.53 W

ăt; finăl; rāte; senâte; ärm; àsk; sofȧ; fâre; ch-choose; dh-as th in other; bē; ēvent; bĕt; recĕnt; cratēr; g-go; gh-gutteral g; bĭt; ĭ-short neutral; rīde; K-gutteral k as ch in German ich;

Hierapetra PRONOUNCING INDEX **Horton**

Page	Name Pronunciation Region	Lat. °′	Long. °′
126	Hierapetra (yä'rä-pä'trä) Grc. (Crete In.)	35.1 N	25.45 E
84	Higgins L. (hĭg'ĭnz) Mich.	44.28 N	84.42 W
79	Higginsville (hĭg'ĭnz-vĭl) Mo.	39.4 N	93.44 W
117	Higham (hĭg'ăm) Gt. Brit. (London In.)	51.26 N	0.29 E
116	Higham Ferrers (fĕr'ĕrz). Gt. Brit.	52.19 N	0.34 W
56	High Bluff...Can. (Winnipeg In.)	50.2 N	98.10 W
96	Highborn Cay (I.) (hī'bôrn) Ba. Is.	24.42 N	76.50 W
72	High Cr....Colo. (Colo. Sprs. In.)	38.43 N	105.20 W
73	Highgrove. Calif. (Los Angeles In.)	34.1 N	117.20 W
84	High I. Mich.	45.44 N	85.42 W
81	High Island Tex. (In.)	29.34 N	94.25 W
73	Highland..Calif. (Los Angeles In.)	34.8 N	117.13 W
72	Highland......Colo. (Denver In.)	40.15 N	105.5 W
79	Highland Ill.	38.45 N	89.39 W
77	Highland Park Ill.	42.11 N	87.47 W
84	Highland Park Ky.	38.12 N	85.50 W
84	Highland Park Mich.	42.23 N	83.5 W
73	High Level. Ala. (Birmingham In.)	33.39 N	87.12 W
76	Highmore S. D.	44.31 N	99.27 W
152	High Peak Phil.	15.30 N	120.7 E
83	High Point N. C.	35.57 N	80.0 W
83	High Springs Fla.	29.51 N	82.37 W
85	Hightstown (hīts'toun) N. J.	40.15 N	74.32 W
97	Higüey (ē-gwā') Hai.	18.37 N	68.42 W
119	Hiiumaa (Dago) (I.) (hē'ōōm-ô) (däg'ö). Sov. Un.	58.50 N	22.40 E
119	Hiitola (hē-ē'tô-lä) Fin.	61.15 N	29.35 E
149	Hikone (hē'kô-nĕ) Jap.	35.15 N	136.14 E
156	Hikurangi (hē-kōō-räŋ'gē)...N. Z.	35.37 S	174.20 E
116	Hilbre Pt. (hĭl'brē) Gt. Brit.	53.23 N	3.11 W
120	Hildburghausen (hĭld'bōōrg-hou-zĕn). Ger.	50.26 N	10.44 E
120	Hildesheim (hĭl'dĕs-hīm) Ger.	52.9 N	9.56 E
95	Hillaby, Mt. (hĭl'à-bĭ)..Barb. (In.)	13.14 N	59.36 W
78	Hill City Kan.	39.22 N	99.55 W
77	Hill City Minn.	46.59 N	93.35 W
118	Hilleröd (hē'lĕ-rûdh) Den.	55.55 N	12.19 E
133	Hillet Abbas (hēl'ĕt à-bäs') A. E. Sud.	13.6 N	32.41 E
51	Hillhurst (hĭl'hûrst) Wash. (Seattle In.)	47.5 N	122.31 W
79	Hillsboro (hĭlz'bŭr-ō) Ill.	39.8 N	89.28 W
79	Hillsboro Kan.	38.22 N	97.11 W
86	Hillsboro N. H.	43.5 N	71.55 W
76	Hillsboro N. D.	47.24 N	97.3 W
84	Hillsboro Ohio	39.11 N	83.40 W
70	Hillsboro Ore.	45.31 N	122.59 W
81	Hillsboro Tex.	32.1 N	97.7 W
77	Hillsboro Wis.	43.38 N	90.20 W
84	Hillsdale Mich.	41.55 N	84.37 W
72	Hill Top......Colo. (Denver In.)	39.28 N	104.41 W
70	Hillyard (hĭl'yàrd) Wash.	47.42 N	117.22 W
155	Hilo (hē'lō) Haw.	19.42 N	155.3 W
153	Hilonghilong, Mt. (hē-lông-hē'lông). Phil.	9.7 N	125.43 E
153	Hilongos (hē-lôŋ'gôs) Phil.	10.22 N	124.46 E
120	Hilversum (hĭl'vēr-sŭm) Neth.	52.12 N	5.10 E
141	Himalaya Mts. (hĭ-mä'lȧ-yȧ). Asia	28.0 N	81.0 E
153	Himamaylan (hē-mä-mī'län). Phil.	10.7 N	122.53 E
149	Himeji (hē'mà-jē) Jap.	34.45 N	134.46 E
153	Hinatuan (hē-nä-tōō'än) Phil.	8.22 N	126.20 E
97	Hinche (hēn'chà) (äNsh) Hai.	19.9 N	72.0 W
52	Hinchinbrook I. (hĭn'chĭn-brŏŏk) Alsk. (In.)	60.20 N	146.25 W
159	Hinchinbrook I. Austl.	18.15 S	146.15 E
116	Hinckley (hĭnk'lĭ) Gt. Brit.	52.32 N	1.21 W
153	Hindang (hēn-däng') Phil.	10.27 N	124.44 E
	Hindenburg, see Zabrze, Pol.		
117	Hindley (hĭnd'lĭ) Gt. Brit. (Liverpool In.)	53.32 N	2.34 W
116	Hindley Gt. Brit.	53.32 N	2.36 W
160	Hindmarsh (hīnd'märsh)...Austl.	34.54 S	138.34 E
141	Hindu Kush Mts. (hĭn'dōō kōōsh') Asia	35.45 N	70.30 E
142	Hingan (hĭn'gän') Chn.	32.42 N	109.29 E
144	Hingan Chn.	25.32 N	110.32 E
145	Hingan Chn.	27.37 N	117.39 E
87	Hingham (hĭng'ăm)...Mass. (In.)	42.14 N	70.54 W
145	Hinghwa (hĭng'hwä') Chn.	25.26 N	118.58 E
146	Hinghwa Chn.	32.55 N	119.50 E
145	Hinghwa Sound Chn.	25.18 N	119.18 E
145	Hingkwo (hĭng'kwō) Chn.	29.46 N	115.8 E
145	Hingkwo Chn.	26.18 N	115.1 E
145	Hingning (hĭng'nĭng') Chn.	24.4 N	115.32 E
153	Hinigaran (hē-nē-gä'rän) Phil.	10.16 N	122.52 E
124	Hinojosa (ē-nô-hō'sä) Sp.	38.30 N	5.9 W
88	Hinsdale (hĭnz'dāl) Ill. (Chicago In.)	41.48 N	87.54 W
117	Hinterbrühl (hĭn'tēr-brül) Aus. (Wien In.)	48.4 N	16.14 E
117	Hintersdorf (hĭn'tērs-dôrf) Aus. (In.)	48.18 N	16.13 E
84	Hinton (hĭn'tŭn) W. Va.	37.42 N	80.55 W
153	Hinunangan (hē-nōō-nän'gän) Phil.	10.24 N	125.12 E
153	Hinundayan (hē-nōōn-dä'yän) Phil.	10.21 N	125.15 E
148	Hirado (I.) (hē'rä-dō) Jap.	33.16 N	129.30 E
73	Hiram (hī'răm). Ga. (Atlanta In.)	33.52 N	84.46 W
149	Hirano (hē'rä-nō). Jap. (Osaka In.)	34.37 N	135.33 E
149	Hirasaki (hē'rä-sä'kē) Jap. (Tokyo In.)	35.15 N	139.38 E
149	Hiratsuka (hē-rät-sōō'kä)....Jap.	35.20 N	139.22 E
148	Hirosaki (hē'rô-sä'kē) Jap.	40.33 N	140.30 E
149	Hirose (hē'rô-sä) Jap.	35.20 N	133.10 E
149	Hiroshima (hē-rô-shē'mà)....Jap.	32.29 N	132.28 E
122	Hirson (ēr-sôN') Fr.	4.8 N	49.53 W
97	Hispaniola (Haiti) (I.) (hĭs'păn-ĭ-ō-là). W. I.	19.10 N	72.10 W
138	Hissar (hĭ-sär') Sov. Un.	38.35 N	68.40 E
140	Hit (hĭt) Iraq	33.38 N	42.45 E
148	Hitachi (hē-tä'chē) Jap.	39.36 N	140.40 E
81	Hitchcock (hĭch'kŏk)...Tex. (In.)	29.21 N	95.1 W
149	Hitoyoshi (hē'tô-yō'shē) Jap.	32.14 N	130.44 E
118	Hitteren (I.) (hĭt'tēr-ĕn) Nor.	53.30 N	8.40 E
149	Hiwasa (hē'wà-sä) Jap.	33.45 N	134.30 E
82	Hiwassee R. (hī-wôs'sē)....Tenn.	35.20 N	84.50 W
118	Hjälmar, L. (yĕl'mär) Swe.	59.16 N	15.45 E
118	Hjo (yō) Swe.	58.19 N	14.13 E
118	Hjörring (jûr'ĭng) Den.	57.27 N	10.0 E
121	Hlohovec (hlō'hô-vĕts) Czech.	48.25 N	17.48 E
160	Hobart (hō'bȧrt). Austl. (Tas. In.)	42.52 S	147.19 E
84	Hobart Ind.	41.34 N	87.17 W
78	Hobart Okla.	35.1 N	99.6 W
115	Hoboken (hō'bō-kĕn) Bel.	51.11 N	4.21 E
88	Hoboken N. J. (N. Y. In.)	40.45 N	74.2 W
118	Hobro (hô-brô') Den.	56.38 N	9.47 E
160	Hobsons B. (hŏb'sŭnz) Austl.	37.51 S	144.55 E
156	Hobsonville N. Z. (In.)	36.48 S	174.40 E
144	Hochih (hō'chē') Chn.	24.40 N	107.52 E
144	Hochow (hō'chō') Chn.	30.10 N	106.22 E
145	Hochow Chn.	31.40 N	118.18 E
146	Hochow Chn.	31.38 N	118.17 E
120	Höchst (hûKst) Ger.	50.7 N	8.32 E
157	Hochstetter Dome Mt. (hōK'stĕt-ēr). N. Z.	42.30 S	172.12 E
116	Hodder, R. (hŏd'ēr) Gt. Brit.	53.56 N	2.30 W
140	Hodeida (hô-dā'ē-dà) Yem.	14.45 N	43.0 E
84	Hodgenville (hŏj'ĕn-vĭl) Ky.	37.33 N	85.46 W
87	Hodges Hill (hŏj'ĕz) Can.	49.0 N	55.55 W
121	Hodmezövasarhely (hōd'mĕ-zû-vô'shôr-hĕl-y'). Hung.	46.25 N	20.20 E
112	Hodna, Chott el (L.) (shŏt ĕl hŏd'nȧ). Alg.	35.25 N	4.45 E
149	Hodogawa R. (hō'dô-gä'wä) Jap. (Tokyo In.)	35.24 N	139.36 E
121	Hodonín (hô'dô-nēn) Czech.	48.51 N	17.6 E
147	Hoengsŏng (hwĕng'sŭng') Kor.	37.27 N	127.58 E
148	Hoeryŏng (hwĕr'yŭng') Kor.	42.30 N	129.40 E
134	Hoetjes Bay (hōōt'yĕz). U. S. Afr.	32.59 S	17.55 E
117	Hoevenen (hōō'vē-nĕn) Bel. (Anvers In.)	51.18 N	4.24 E
147	Hoeyang (hwā'yäng') Kor.	38.44 N	127.40 E
120	Hof (hōf) Ger.	50.19 N	11.54 E
147	Hofeng (hō'fĕng') Chn.	29.54 N	109.42 E
89	Hoffman Cr. (hŏf'măn) Ohio (Cleveland In.)	41.26 N	81.45 W
108	Hofs-Jökull (Glacier) (hôfs'-yû'kŏŏl). Ice.	64.50 N	17.30 W
140	Hofuf (hô-fōōf') Sau. Ar.	25.25 N	49.45 E
82	Hogansville (hō'gănz-vĭl)....Ga.	33.11 N	84.55 W
97	Hog Cay (I.) Ba. Is.	23.23 N	75.30 W
96	Hog I. Ba. Is.	25.5 N	77.22 W
89	Hog I......La. (New Orleans In.)	29.27 N	89.26 W
84	Hog I. Mich.	45.48 N	85.22 W
119	Hogland (I.) Fin.	60.5 N	27.0 E
97	Hogsty Reef Ba. Is.	21.42 N	73.50 W
120	Hohe Tauern (Mts.) (hō'ĕ tou'ērn) Aus.	47.10 N	12.20 E
144	Hohsien (hō'syĕn') Chn.	24.19 N	111.28 E
144	Hoikin (hoi'kĭn') Chn.	23.52 N	111.23 E
144	Hoiping (hoi'pĭng') Chn.	22.36 N	112.22 E
78	Hoisington (hoi'zĭng-tŭn)....Kan.	38.31 N	98.46 W
149	Hojo (hō'jō) Jap.	33.58 N	132.49 E
149	Hojo Jap.	35.0 N	139.53 E
144	Hokiang (hō'kyäng') Chn.	28.49 N	105.45 E
156	Hokianga R. (hō-kē-äŋ'gä)..N. Z.	35.30 S	173.20 E
146	Hokien (hō'kē-ĕn') Chn.	38.34 N	116.2 E
157	Hokitika (hō-kĭ-tē'kä)......N. Z.	42.42 S	171.3 E
148	Hokkaido I. (hôk'kī-dō)....Jap.	43.30 N	143.0 E
145	Hokow (hō'kō') Chn.	28.19 N	117.42 E
144	Hokshan (hōk'shän') Chn.	22.45 N	112.36 E
118	Holbaek (hôl'bĕk) Den.	55.41 N	11.42 E
75	Holbrook (hōl'brŏŏk) Ariz.	34.54 N	110.11 W
87	Holbrook Mass. (In.)	42.9 N	71.1 W
51	Holbrook.....Ore. (Portland In.)	45.39 N	122.51 W
87	Holden (hōl'dĕn)......Mass. (In.)	42.21 N	71.56 W
79	Holden Mo.	38.42 N	94.0 W
84	Holden W. Va.	37.48 N	82.5 W
79	Holdenville Okla.	35.4 N	96.25 W
78	Holdrege (hōl'drĕj) Neb.	40.25 N	99.24 W
118	Hölen (hûl'ĕn) Nor.	59.33 N	10.41 E
97	Holguin (ôl-gēn') Cuba	20.53 N	76.18 W
84	Holland (hŏl'ănd) Mich.	42.46 N	86.8 W
151	Hollandia (hôl-län'dĭ-ä) Neth. N. Gui.	2.30 S	140.35 E
85	Hollidaysburg (hŏl'ĭ-dāz-bûrg). Pa.	40.28 N	78.26 W
78	Hollis (hŏl'ĭs) Okla.	34.40 N	99.55 W
74	Hollister (hŏl'ĭs-tēr) Calif.	36.51 N	121.24 W
87	Holliston (hŏl'ĭs-tŭn). Mass. (In.)	42.15 N	71.25 W
78	Holly (hŏl'ĭ) Colo.	38.3 N	102.7 W
84	Holly Mich.	42.49 N	83.33 W
51	Holly........Wash. (Seattle In.)	47.33 N	122.58 W
82	Holly Springs Miss.	34.46 N	89.28 W
73	Hollywood (hŏl'ĭ-wŏŏd) Calif. (Los Angeles In.)	34.8 N	118.20 W
83	Hollywood Fla. (In.)	26.1 N	80.10 W
117	Holm (hōlm). Ger. (Hamburg In.)	53.37 N	9.41 E
159	Holmes Reefs (hōmz) Austl.	16.50 S	148.0 E
72	Holmes....Colo. (Colo. Sprs. In.)	38.38 N	104.42 W
88	Holmesburg (hōmz'bûrg) Pa. (Philadelphia In.)	40.3 N	75.3 W
118	Holmestrand (hôl'mĕ-strän)..Nor.	59.29 N	10.18 E
118	Holm I. (hôlm) Swe.	62.26 N	15.20 E
118	Holmsbu (hôlms'bōō) Nor.	59.36 N	10.30 E
118	Holstebro (hôl'stĕ-brô') Den.	56.22 N	8.40 E
82	Holston R. (hōl'stŭn) Tenn.	36.10 N	83.30 W
116	Holt (hōlt) Gt. Brit.	53.4 N	2.53 W
79	Holton (hōl'tŭn) Kan.	39.28 N	95.44 W
74	Holtville Calif.	32.49 N	115.24 W
52	Holy Cross Alsk.	62.10 N	160.0 W
114	Holyhead (hŏl'ē-hĕd)....Gt. Brit.	53.19 N	4.35 W
114	Holyhead I. Gt. Brit.	53.15 N	4.45 W
114	Holy I. (hō'lĭ) Gt. Brit.	55.42 N	1.50 W
78	Holyoke (hōl'yōk) Colo.	40.36 N	102.19 W
86	Holyoke Mass.	42.12 N	72.40 W
120	Holzminden (hôlts'mĭn-dĕn)..Ger.	51.51 N	9.27 E
120	Homburg (hôm'bōōrgh) Ger.	50.14 N	8.37 E
123	Homécourt (ô-mā-kōōr') Fr.	49.14 N	5.59 E
81	Homer (hō'mēr) La.	32.47 N	93.5 W
83	Homestead (hōm'stĕd)..Fla. (In.)	25.27 N	80.28 W
85	Homestead Pa.	40.24 N	79.54 W
79	Hominy (hŏm'ĭ-nĭ) Okla.	36.25 N	96.24 W
82	Homochitto R. (hō-mō-chĭt'ō) Miss.	31.20 N	91.0 W
153	Homonhon I. (hō-môn-hōn'). Phil.	10.43 N	125.43 E
140	Homs (hōms) Syr.	34.45 N	36.50 E
133	Homs (Lebda) (lĕb'dȧ) Libya	32.36 N	14.12 E
144	Honam (hō'näm') Chn.	23.4 N	113.15 E
145	Honan (Prov.) (hō'nän') Chn.	31.33 N	115.12 E
143	Honanfu (hō'nän-fōō') Chn.	34.44 N	112.26 E
100	Honda (hŏn'dȧ) Col.	5.12 N	74.58 W
96	Honda B. Cuba	22.58 N	83.9 W
153	Honda B. Phil.	9.55 N	118.48 E
80	Hondo (hŏn'dō) Tex.	29.20 N	99.9 W
94	Hondo R....Br. Hond.-Mex. (In.)	18.10 N	88.40 W
73	Hondo, R. Calif. (Los Angeles In.)	34.2 N	118.4 W
93	Hondo, R. Mex. (In.)	19.26 N	99.15 W
78	Hondo, R. N. M.	33.20 N	105.0 W
94	Honduras (hŏn-dōō'răs). Cen. Am.	14.50 N	87.10 W
94	Honduras, G. of Cen. Am.	16.10 N	88.0 W
83	Honea Path (hŭn'ĭ păth)....S. C.	34.24 N	82.27 W
118	Hönefoss (hē'nē-fōs) Nor.	60.10 N	10.13 E
85	Honesdale (hōnz'dāl) Pa.	41.30 N	75.16 W
79	Honey Grove Tex.	33.35 N	95.55 W
74	Honey L. Calif.	40.15 N	120.20 W
73	Honeyville Utah (Salt Lake City In.)	41.38 N	112.5 W
122	Honfleur (ôN-flûr') Fr.	49.25 N	0.15 E
147	Hongchŏn (hŏng'chŭn') Kor.	37.40 N	127.53 E
145	Honghai B. (hŏng'hī') Chn.	22.43 N	115.2 E
144	Hong Kong (I.) (hŏng'kŏng'). Asia	22.16 N	114.12 E
143	Hongkow Cr. (hŏng'kō') Chn. (Shanghai In.)	31.13 N	121.26 E
149	Hongo (hôŋ'gô)..Jap. (Tokyo In.)	35.9 N	139.51 E
147	Hongwŏn (hŏng'wŭn') Kor.	40.4 N	127.57 E
155	Honolulu (hŏn-ō-lōō'lōō)....Haw.	21.18 N	157.51 W
155	Honomu (hŏn'ō-mōō) Haw.	19.51 N	155.4 W
148	Honshu I. (hŏn'shōō) Jap.	36.0 N	138.0 E
70	Hood Canal (hŏŏd) Wash.	47.30 N	123.3 W
70	Hood, Mt. Ore.	45.22 N	121.42 W
70	Hood River Ore.	45.43 N	121.30 W
51	Hoodsport (hŏŏdz'pōrt) Wash. (Seattle In.)	47.25 N	123.8 W
141	Hooghly R. (hōōg'lĭ) India	21.30 N	88.0 E
117	Hook (hŏŏk). Gt. Brit. (London In.)	51.22 N	0.19 W
78	Hooker (hŏŏk'ēr) Okla.	36.51 N	101.13 W
155	Hookeng (hō-ô-kĕng') Haw.	19.22 N	155.51 W
70	Hoopa Valley Ind. Res. (hōō'pȧ) Calif.	41.5 N	123.40 W
76	Hooper (hōōp'ēr) Neb.	41.37 N	96.31 W
73	Hooper. Utah (Salt Lake City In.)	41.10 N	112.8 W
157	Hoopers Inlet N. Z. (In.)	45.51 S	170.42 E
84	Hoopeston (hōōps'tŭn) Ill.	40.28 N	87.40 W
120	Hoorn (hōrn) Neth.	52.38 N	5.4 E
85	Hoosick Falls (hōō'sĭk)....N. Y.	42.55 N	73.20 W
53	Hope (hōp) Alsk.	60.45 N	144.30 W
79	Hope Ark.	33.39 N	93.35 W
72	Hope......Can. (Vancouver In.)	49.23 N	121.27 W
76	Hope N. D.	47.18 N	97.46 W
55	Hopedale (hōp dāl) Can.	55.29 N	60.32 W
87	Hopedale Mass. (In.)	42.7 N	71.32 W
146	Hopeh (Prov.) (hō'pā') Chn.	38.20 N	116.0 E
158	Hopetoun (hōp'toun) Austl.	33.45 S	120.10 E
134	Hopetown U. S. Afr.	29.35 S	24.5 E
85	Hopewell (hōp'wĕl) Va.	37.16 N	77.13 W
75	Hopi Ind. Res. (hō'pē) Ariz.	36.18 N	110.30 W
145	Hoping (hō'pĭng') Chn.	24.23 N	114.53 E
82	Hopkinsville Ky.	36.53 N	87.28 W
87	Hopkinton Mass. (In.)	42.13 N	71.31 W
70	Hoquiam (hō'kwĭ-ăm) Wash.	46.59 N	123.52 W
118	Hörby (hûr'bü) Swe.	55.50 N	13.39 E
120	Horgen (hôr'gĕn) Switz.	47.15 N	8.34 E
77	Horicon (hŏr'ĭ-kŏn) Wis.	43.29 N	88.38 W
140	Hormuz, Str. of (hôr'mŭz)...Asia	26.30 N	56.30 E
102	Horn, C. (hôrn) S. A.	56.0 S	67.30 W
108	Horna Water (L.) (hôr'nȧ)...Swe.	66.0 N	17.50 E
157	Hornby (hôrn'bē)....N. Z. (In.)	43.32 S	172.32 E
117	Hornchurch (hôrn'chûrch) Gt. Brit. (London In.)	51.34 N	0.13 E
117	Horneburg (hôr'nĕ-bōōrgh) Ger. (Hamburg In.)	53.31 N	9.35 E
85	Hornell (hôr-nĕl') N. Y.	42.21 N	77.40 W
159	Horn I. Pap. Ter.	10.42 S	142.30 E
151	Hornos, Pt. (ôr'nōs) Phil. (Manila In.)	14.25 N	120.25 E
160	Hornsby (hôrnz'bĭ) Austl.	33.43 S	151.6 E
116	Hornsea (hôrn'zē) Gt. Brit.	53.55 N	0.10 W
114	Hornsey Gt. Brit.	51.35 N	0.10 W
118	Hornsland (Pen.) (hōrns'lănd) Swe.	61.40 N	17.28 E
100	Horrodada I. (hôr-rä-dhä'dhä) Peru (In.)	12.8 S	77.8 W
78	Horse Cr. (hôrs) Colo.	38.30 N	103.40 W
71	Horse Cr. Wyo.	41.25 N	105.10 W
118	Horsens (hôrs'ĕns) Den.	55.50 N	9.50 E
72	Horsetooth (Mt.) (hôrs'tōōth) Colo. (Denver In.)	40.33 N	105.12 W
116	Horsforth (hôrs'fŭrth)...Gt. Brit.	53.50 N	1.39 W
159	Horsham (hôr'shăm) (hôrs'ăm) Austl.	36.35 S	142.15 E
118	Horten (hôr'tĕn) Nor.	59.25 N	10.30 E
79	Horton (hôr'tŭn) Kan.	39.38 N	95.32 W

ng-sing; ŋ-baŋk; N-nasalized n; nŏd; cŏmmit; ōld; ôbey; ôrder; fōōd; fŏŏt; ou-out; s-soft; sh-dish; th-thin; pūre; ûnite; ûrn; stŭd; circŭs; ü-as "y" in study; '-indeterminate vowel.

Page	Name Pronunciation	Region	Lat. °′	Long. °′
117	Horton Kirby (kûr'bĭ)	Gt. Brit. (London In.)	51.23 N	0.15 E
116	Horwich (hŏr'ĭch)	Gt. Brit.	53.35 N	2.33 W
146	Hoshun (hō'shoon')	Chn.	37.19 N	113.32 E
81	Hoskins (hŏs'kĭnz)	Tex. (In.)	29.8 N	95.12 W
148	Hososhima (hō'sô-shē'mä)	Jap.	32.29 N	131.40 E
125	Hospitalet (ôs-pē-tä-lĕt')	Sp. (In.)	41.22 N	2.6 E
102	Hoste I. (ôs'tā)	Chl.	55.15 S	69.0 W
92	Hostotipaquillo (ôs-tō'tĭ-pä-kēl'yô)	Mex.	21.11 N	104.4 W
142	Hotien (Khotan) (hō'tyĕn') (kō-tän')	Chn.	37.2 N	79.52 E
53	Hot Springs	Alsk.	65.0 N	150.35 W
79	Hot Springs	Ark.	34.30 N	93.2 W
75	Hot Springs	N. M.	33.8 N	107.19 W
76	Hot Springs	S. D.	43.26 N	103.30 W
73	Hot Springs	Utah (Salt Lake City In.)	41.20 N	112.2 W
85	Hot Springs	Va.	38.0 N	79.52 W
79	Hot Springs Natl. Park	Ark.	34.30 N	93.0 W
77	Houghton (hŏ'tŭn)	Mich.	47.6 N	88.32 W
84	Houghton L	Mich.	44.20 N	84.45 W
123	Houilles (ōō-yĕs')	Fr. (In.)	48.55 N	5.11 E
86	Houlton (hōl'tŭn)	Me.	46.8 N	67.50 W
81	Houma (hōō'mȧ)	La.	29.35 N	90.43 W
131	Houmt Souk (hōōmt sōōk')	Tun. (In.)	33.53 N	10.43 E
117	Hounslow (hounz'lō)	Gt. Brit. (London In.)	51.28 N	0.23 W
85	Housatonic R. (hōō-sȧ-tŏn'ĭk)	Conn.-Mass.	42.0 N	73.23 W
82	Houston (hūs'tŭn)	Miss.	33.54 N	89.2 W
81	Houston	Tex.	29.45 N	95.22 W
81	Houston	Tex. (In.)		
81	Houston Ship Channel	Tex. (In.)	29.35 N	94.56 W
158	Houtman Rocks (hout'män)	Austl.	28.5 S	112.28 E
117	Hove (hō'vĕ)	Bel. (Anvers In.)	51.9 N	4.28 E
114	Hove (hōv)	Gt. Brit.	50.50 N	0.10 W
75	Hovenweep Natl. Mon. (hō'v'n-wēp)	Utah	37.22 N	109.5 W
79	Howard (hou'ȧrd)	Kan.	37.26 N	96.14 W
76	Howard	S. D.	44.2 N	97.31 W
159	Howe, C. (hou)	Austl.	37.30 S	149.56 E
116	Howeden (hou'dĕn)	Gt. Brit.	53.45 N	0.52 W
84	Howell (hou'ĕl)	Mich.	42.40 N	83.57 W
72	Howe Sound	Can. (Vancouver In.)	49.25 N	123.25 W
156	Howick (hou'ĭk)	N. Z.	36.54 S	174.56 E
4	Howland I. (hou'lănd)	Pac. O.	0.48 N	176.38 W
141	Howrah (hou'rä)	India	22.30 N	88.25 E
114	Howth (hōth)	Ire.	53.20 N	6.5 W
79	Hoxie (hŏk'sĭ)	Ark.	36.3 N	91.0 W
120	Hoyerswerda (hoi'ĕrs-vĕr'dȧ)	Ger.	51.27 N	14.13 E
114	Hoy (I.) (hoi)	Gt. Brit. (In.)	58.50 N	3.15 W
116	Hoylake (hoi-lāk')	Gt. Brit.	53.23 N	3.10 W
125	Hoyo, Sierra del (Mt.) (syĕr'rȧ dĕl hō'yō)	Sp. (In.)	40.38 N	3.55 W
145	Hoyün (hō'yün')	Chn.	23.40 N	114.37 E
120	Hradec Králové (hrȧ'dĕts krä'lô-vā)	Czech.	50.12 N	15.51 E
121	Hranice (hrän'yê-tsĕ)	Czech.	49.33 N	17.44 E
121	Hriňová (hrēn'yô-vä)	Czech.	48.36 N	19.33 E
121	Hrubieszów (hrōō-byā'shōōf)	Pol.	50.47 N	23.53 E
141	Hsawnghsup (sông'sŭp')	Bur.	24.25 N	94.40 E
144	Hsiang R. (hsē'äng')	Chn.	26.38 N	112.10 E
144	Hsiaokan (hsē-ä'ō-kän')	Chn.	30.54 N	113.47 E
148	Hsifeng (Taulu) (hsē'fĕng') (tou'lōō')	Chn.	43.26 N	124.15 E
145	Hsinchu (hsĭn'chōō')	For.	24.45 N	121.0 E
	Hsinking, see Changchung, Chn.			
145	Hsinying (hsĭn'yĭng')	For.	23.18 N	120.18 E
144	Hsingwei (hsĭng'wā')	Chn.	22.53 N	109.59 E
146	Hsüchow (hsü'chō')	Chn.	34.4 N	113.56 E
143	Hsuhang (hsōō'häng')	Chn. (Shanghai In.)	31.9 N	121.28 E
100	Huacas Pt. (wä'käs)	Peru	13.45 S	76.30 W
100	Huacho (wä'chō)	Peru	11.10 S	77.31 W
92	Huajicori (wä-jê-kō'rê)	Mex.	22.39 N	105.22 W
93	Huajuápam de León (wäj-wä'päm dā lā-ōn')	Mex.	17.48 N	97.47 W
145	Hualien (hwä'lyĕn')	For.	24.1 N	121.31 E
100	Huallaga R. (wäl-yä'gä)	Peru	8.30 S	76.0 W
75	Hualpai Ind. Res. (wäl'pī)	Ariz.	35.45 N	113.35 W
100	Huamachuco (wä-mä-chōō'kō)	Peru	7.32 S	78.2 W
93	Huamantla (wä-män'tlȧ)	Mex.	19.19 N	97.55 W
134	Huambo (Nova Lisboa) (wäm'bō) (nō'vȧ lêzh-bō'ȧ)	Ang.	12.45 S	15.47 E
92	Huamuxtitlán (wä-mōōs-tē-tlän')	Mex.	17.49 N	98.36 W
100	Huancavelica (wän'kä-vā-lē'kä)	Peru	12.58 S	75.0 W
100	Huancayo (wän-kä'yô)	Peru	12.2 S	75.3 W
100	Huanchaca (wän-chä'kä)	Bol.	20.15 S	66.40 W
92	Huango de Morelos (wäŋ'gō dā mô-rā'lōs)	Mex.	19.55 N	101.25 W
100	Huanuco (wä-nōō'kô)	Peru	9.57 S	76.12 W
92	Huaquechula (wä-kä-chōō'lä)	Mex.	18.44 N	98.36 W
100	Huaráz (wä-räz')	Peru	9.30 S	77.30 W
92	Huaritura, L. (wä-rê-tōō'rȧ)	Mex.	22.15 N	105.30 W
100	Huascarán, Mt. (wäs-kä-rän')	Peru	9.0 S	77.40 W
102	Huasco (wäs'kō)	Chl.	28.35 S	71.5 W
92	Huatlatlauca (wä'tlä-tlä-ōō'kä)	Mex.	18.40 N	98.4 W
93	Huatusco (wä-tōōs'kô)	Mex.	19.8 N	96.58 W
92	Huauchinango (wä-ōō-chê-näŋ'gô)	Mex.	20.10 N	98.3 W
93	Huautla (wä-ōō'tlä)	Mex.	18.9 N	96.51 W
92	Huautla	Mex.	21.1 N	98.18 W
92	Huaycatenango (wī'kä-tĕ-näŋ'gô)	Mex.	17.30 N	99.4 W
93	Huazolotlitlán (Sta. María) (wä'zô-lô-tlē-tlän')	Mex.	16.18 N	97.54 W
81	Hubbard (hŭb'ērd)	Tex.	31.51 N	96.47 W
84	Hubbard L	Mich.	44.50 N	83.30 W
53	Hubbard, Mt	Can.	60.20 N	139.0 W
141	Hubli (hōō'blê)	India	15.20 N	75.12 E
145	Huchow (hōō'chō')	Chn.	30.50 N	120.3 E
116	Hucknall (hŭk'năl)	Gt. Brit.	53.2 N	1.12 W
114	Huddersfield (hŭd'ērz-fēld)	Gt. Brit.	53.40 N	1.50 W
118	Hudiksvall (hōō'dĭks-väl)	Swe.	61.46 N	17.5 E
57	Hudson (hŭd'sŭn)	Can. (Montreal In.)	45.28 N	74.9 W
72	Hudson	Colo. (Denver In.)	40.4 N	104.39 W
87	Hudson	Mass. (In.)	42.24 N	71.33 W
84	Hudson	Mich.	41.50 N	84.19 W
85	Hudson	N. Y.	42.27 N	73.47 W
77	Hudson	Wis.	44.59 N	92.45 W
55	Hudson B	Can.	60.30 N	85.30 W
85	Hudson Falls	N. Y.	43.19 N	73.32 W
85	Hudson R	N. Y.	42.0 N	73.55 W
55	Hudson Str	Can.	62.50 N	73.0 W
150	Hué (ü-ā')	Indoch.	16.29 N	107.28 E
94	Huehuetenango (wā-wȧ-tȧ-näŋ'gô)	Guat.	15.20 N	91.26 W
92	Huejotzingo (wā-hô-tzĭŋ'gō)	Mex.	19.9 N	98.25 W
92	Huejúcar (wā-hōō'kär)	Mex.	22.26 N	103.22 W
92	Huejutla (wā-hōō'tlä)	Mex.	21.8 N	98.25 W
92	Huejuquilla el Alto (wā-hōō-kēl'yä ĕl äl'tō)	Mex.	22.41 N	103.55 W
124	Huelma (wĕl'mä)	Sp.	37.39 N	3.26 W
124	Huelva (wĕl'vä)	Sp.	37.16 N	6.56 W
124	Huercal-Overa (wĕr-käl' ō-vā'rä)	Sp.	37.23 N	1.57 W
78	Huerfano R. (wâr'fȧ-nō)	Colo.	37.45 N	104.50 W
124	Huerva R. (wĕr'vä)	Sp.	41.20 N	1.5 W
125	Huesca (wĕs'kä)	Sp.	42.8 N	0.25 W
124	Huéscan (wās'kän)	Sp.	37.49 N	2.32 W
93	Huesos I. (wā'sōs)	Mex.	22.43 N	97.52 W
92	Huetamo de Múñez (wȧ-tä'mō dā mōōn'yĕz)	Mex.	18.33 N	100.52 W
124	Huete (wā'tȧ)	Sp.	40.8 N	2.41 W
93	Huexotla (wāks-ō'tlä)	Mex. (In.)	19.29 N	98.52 W
93	Hueytlalpan (wā'ĭ-tläl'pän)	Mex.	20.4 N	97.40 W
73	Huffman (hŭf'măn)	Ala. (Birmingham In.)	33.36 N	86.39 W
160	Hugel, Mt. (hŭg'ĕl)	Austl. (Tas. In.)	42.6 S	146.8 E
159	Hughenden (hū'ĕn-dĕn)	Austl.	20.45 S	144.8 E
53	Hughes (hūz)	Alsk.	66.0 N	154.0 W
158	Hughes	Austl.	30.32 S	129.30 E
79	Hugo (hū'gō)	Okla.	34.1 N	95.31 W
78	Hugoton (hū'gō-tŭn)	Kan.	37.11 N	101.26 W
156	Huiarau Ra. (hwē'ȧ-rä'ōō)	N. Z.	38.45 S	176.50 E
92	Huichapan (wē-chä-pän')	Mex.	20.22 N	99.38 W
147	Hŭichŏn (hwĭ'chŭn)	Kor.	40.10 N	126.16 E
100	Huila, Mt. (Vol.) (wē'lä)	Col.	3.0 N	77.0 W
93	Huimanguillo (wē-män-gēl'yō)	Mex.	17.50 N	93.24 W
93	Huitepec (Sta. Margarita) (wē-tȧ-pĕk')	Mex.	16.54 N	95.43 W
92	Huitzitziling (wē-tsê-tzê-lĭng')	Mex.	21.10 N	98.41 W
92	Huitzuco (wê-tzōō'kō)	Mex.	18.19 N	99.18 W
93	Huixtla (wēs'tlä)	Mex.	15.12 N	92.26 W
148	Hukae I. (hōō'kä-ȧ)	Jap.	32.40 N	128.45 E
145	Hukow (hōō'kō')	Chn.	29.46 N	116.15 E
143	Hulan (hōō'län')	Chn.	45.58 N	126.28 E
148	Hulan R	Chn.	46.52 N	126.30 E
148	Hulin (hōō'lĭn')	Chn.	46.0 N	133.30 E
85	Hull (hŭl)	Can.	45.27 N	75.56 W
114	Hull	Gt. Brit.	53.45 N	0.25 W
87	Hull	Mass. (In.)	42.18 N	70.54 W
116	Hull, R	Gt. Brit.	53.51 N	0.23 W
117	Hulst (hōōlst)	Neth. (Anvers In.)	51.17 N	4.3 E
143	Hulun (Hailar) (hōō'lōōn') (hī-lär')	Chn.	49.8 N	119.34 E
146	Hulutao (hōō'lōō-tä'ō)	Chn.	40.44 N	120.48 E
91	Humacao (ōō-mä-kä'ō)	P. R. (In.)	18.8 N	65.50 W
100	Humaitá (ōō-mä-ē-tä')	Braz.	7.30 S	63.0 W
102	Humaitá	Par.	27.1 S	58.30 W
134	Humansdorp (hōō'mäns-dôrp)	U. S. Afr.	34.2 S	24.47 E
134	Humbe (hōōm'bȧ)	Ang.	16.52 S	14.55 E
87	Humbermouth (hŭm'bēr-mŭth)	Can.	48.57 N	57.50 W
114	Humber (R.) (hŭm'bēr)	Gt. Brit.	53.35 N	0.20 W
81	Humble (hŭm'b'l)	Tex.	30.0 N	95.15 W
77	Humboldt (hŭm'bōlt)	Ia.	42.45 N	94.11 W
79	Humboldt	Kan.	37.47 N	95.27 W
79	Humbolt	Neb.	40.9 N	95.57 W
82	Humboldt	Tenn.	35.48 N	88.56 W
70	Humboldt B	Calif.	40.45 N	124.15 W
151	Humboldt B	Neth. N. Gui.	2.32 S	140.45 E
74	Humboldt R	Nev.	40.20 N	118.25 W
70	Humboldt R., East Fork	Nev.	41.0 N	115.25 W
70	Humboldt R., North Fork	Nev.	41.25 N	115.48 W
74	Humboldt Salt Marsh	Nev.	39.50 N	118.0 W
74	Humboldt Sink	Nev.	40.0 N	118.35 W
157	Hump, The Mt. (hŭmp)	N. Z. (In.)	45.46 S	170.37 E
75	Humphrey Peak (hŭm'frĭ)	Ariz.	35.20 N	111.40 W
73	Humphreys (hŭm'frĭz)	Calif. (Los Angeles In.)	34.25 N	118.26 W
120	Humpolec (hōōm'pō-lĕts)	Czech.	49.33 N	15.22 E
160	Humpy Bang (hŭm'pê băng')	Austl. (In.)	27.13 S	153.3 E
94	Humuya, R. (ōō-mōō'yä)	Hond.	14.35 N	87.40 W
108	Húnaflói (Fjord) (hōō'nä-flō'ĭ)	Ice.	65.45 N	21.0 W
144	Hunan (Prov.) (hōō'nän')	Chn.	27.24 N	111.14 E
143	Hunchun (hōōn'chōōn')	Chn.	42.50 N	130.22 E
127	Hunedoara (kōō'nĕd-wä'rȧ)	Rom.	45.45 N	22.53 E
120	Hungary (hŭŋ'gȧ-rĭ)	Eur.	47.0 N	19.15 E
159	Hungerford (hŭŋ'gēr-fērd)	Austl.	28.55 S	144.35 E
144	Hung L. (hōōng)	Chn.	29.45 N	112.58 E
147	Hŭngnam (hōōng'näm)	Kor.	39.49 N	127.37 E
144	Hung R	Chn.	25.8 N	106.50 E
146	Hungtze L. (hōōng'tzĕ')	Chn.	33.15 N	118.35 E
116	Hunmanby (hŭn'măn-bĭ)	Gt. Brit.	54.11 N	0.19 W
146	Hun R. (Yungting R.) (hōōn) (yōōng'tĭng')	Chn.	39.40 N	116.10 E
120	Hunsrück (Mts.) (hōōns'rûk)	Ger.	49.55 N	7.13 E
120	Hunte R. (hōōn'tē)	Ger.	52.50 N	8.29 E
160	Hunter I	Austl. (Tas. In.)	40.30 S	144.46 E
160	Hunters Is	Austl. (Tas. In.)	40.27 S	144.50 E
84	Huntingburg	Ind.	38.16 N	86.56 W
72	Huntingdon	Can. (Vancouver In.)	49.0 N	122.16 W
85	Huntingdon	Pa.	40.32 N	78.2 W
82	Huntingdon	Tenn.	36.1 N	88.25 W
116	Huntingdon County	Gt. Brit.	52.27 N	0.20 W
85	Huntington	Can.	45.6 N	74.4 W
84	Huntington	Ind.	40.55 N	84.28 W
84	Huntington	W. Va.	38.25 N	82.25 W
74	Huntington Beach	Calif.	33.40 N	118.0 W
74	Huntington Park	Calif.	33.58 N	118.15 W
156	Huntly	N. Z.	37.32 S	175.12 E
82	Huntsville	Ala.	34.44 N	86.36 W
85	Huntsville	Can.	45.21 N	79.14 W
79	Huntsville	Mo.	39.25 N	92.31 W
81	Huntsville	Tex.	30.44 N	95.34 W
71	Huntsville	Utah	41.16 N	111.46 W
93	Hunucmá (hōō-nōōk-mä')	Mex.	20.58 N	89.56 W
146	Hunyüan (hōōn'yû-än')	Chn.	39.40 N	113.47 E
151	Huan G. (hōō'ŏn)	N. Gui. Ter.	7.0 S	147.30 E
160	Huon R	Austl. (Tas. In.)	43.0 S	146.50 E
146	Hupeh (Prov.) (hōō'pȧ')	Chn.	31.25 N	114.20 E
55	Hurd, C. (hûrd)	Can.	45.10 N	81.12 W
77	Hurley (hûr'lĭ)	Wis.	46.27 N	90.11 W
84	Huron (hū'rŏn)	Ohio	41.23 N	82.36 W
76	Huron	S. D.	44.21 N	98.12 W
59	Huron, L	U. S.-Can.	45.0 N	82.30 W
75	Hurricane (hŭr'ĭ-kān)	Utah	37.11 N	113.20 W
96	Hurricane Flats	Ba. Is.	23.35 N	78.25 W
157	Hurunui R. (hōō-rōō-nōō'ê)	N. Z.	42.50 S	172.30 E
129	Husi (kōōsh')	Rom.	46.39 N	28.2 E
118	Huskvarna (hōōsk-vär'nȧ)	Swe.	57.48 N	14.15 E
72	Husted (hū'stĕd)	Colo. (Colo. Sprs. In.)	39.1 N	104.50 W
120	Husum (hōō'zōōm)	Ger.	54.28 N	9.3 E
78	Hutchinson (hŭch'ĭn-sŭn)	Kan.	38.2 N	97.56 W
77	Hutchinson	Minn.	44.54 N	94.21 W
89	Hutchinsons I	Ga. (Savannah In.)	32.6 N	81.6 W
146	Huto R. (hōō'tō')	Chn.	38.10 N	115.55 E
117	Hütteldorf (hût''l-dôrf)	Aus. (Wien In.)	48.12 N	16.15 E
156	Hutt R. (hŭt)	N. Z. (In.)	41.12 S	174.57 E
157	Huxley Mt. (hŭks'lĭ)	N. Z.	44.2 S	169.45 E
115	Huy (û-ē') (hû'ê)	Bel.	50.31 N	5.15 E
117	Huyton (hoi'tŭn)	Gt. Brit.	53.24 N	2.51 W
126	Hvar (I.) (khvär)	Yugo.	43.8 N	16.40 E
146	Hwahsien (hwä'hsyĕn')	Chn.	35.32 N	114.52 E
146	Hwaian (hwä'ê-än')	Chn.	33.38 N	119.12 E
146	Hwaijen (hwä-ê-jĕn')	Chn.	39.44 N	113.14 E
146	Hwaiking (hwä'ê-kĭng')	Chn.	35.6 N	112.59 E
146	Hwailu (hwä'ê-lōō')	Chn.	38.10 N	114.19 E
146	Hwai R. (hwä'ê)	Chn.	33.52 N	119.0 E
145	Hwaiyang Shan (Mts.) (hwī'yäng' shän')	Chn.	31.30 N	114.35 E
146	Hwaiyin (hwä'ē-yĭn')	Chn.	33.33 N	119.4 E
146	Hwaiyüan (hwä'ê-yü-än')	Chn.	32.57 N	117.8 E
144	Hwajung (hwä'jōōng')	Chn.	29.32 N	112.17 E
145	Hwangan (hwäng'än')	Chn.	31.18 N	114.33 E
144	Hwangchow (hwäng'chō')	Chn.	27.20 N	108.47 E
145	Hwangchow	Chn.	30.27 N	114.48 E
147	Hwang Hai (Yellow Sea) (hwäng' hä'ê)	Chn.	36.0 N	123.0 E
142	Hwang Ho (R.) (hwäng'hō')	Chn.	37.30 N	105.0 E
146	Hwanghsien (hwäng'hsyĕn')	Chn.	37.36 N	120.31 E
147	Hwangju (hwäng'jōō')	Kor.	38.44 N	125.48 E
144	Hwang L. (hwäng)	Chn.	29.37 N	113.28 E
145	Hwangmei (hwäng'mā')	Chn.	30.4 N	115.50 E
145	Hwangpei (hwäng'pā')	Chn.	30.52 N	114.11 E
144	Hwangping (hwäng'pĭng')	Chn.	26.49 N	107.44 E
145	Hwangpo R. (hwäng'pō)	Chn.	30.50 N	121.10 E
145	Hwang Shan (Mts.) (hwäng' shän')	Chn.	30.8 N	118.6 E
145	Hwangsha Shan (Mts.) (hwäng'-shä' shän')	Chn.	26.12 N	115.12 E
145	Hwangyen (hwäng'yĕn')	Chn.	28.37 N	121.13 E
142	Hwan Ho (R.) (hwän' hō')	Chn.	36.0 N	107.52 E
148	Hwanjen (hwän'jĕn')	Chn.	41.16 N	125.29 E
145	Hweichang (hwā'chäng')	Chn.	25.28 N	115.30 E
145	Hweichow (hwā'chō')	Chn.	29.52 N	118.23 E
145	Hweilai (hwā'lī')	Chn.	23.3 N	116.5 E
142	Hweili (hwā'ê-lĭ')	Chn.	26.45 N	102.16 E
144	Hweitung (hwā'tōōng')	Chn.	26.50 N	109.26 E
146	Hwokia (hwō'kyä')	Chn.	35.15 N	113.51 E
146	Hwokiu (hwō'kyōō')	Chn.	32.20 N	116.11 E
116	Hyde (hīd)	Gt. Brit.	52.27 N	2.4 W
117	Hyde Pk	Gt. Brit. (London In.)	51.30 N	0.10 W
141	Hyderabad (hī-dēr-ä-bäd')	India	17.15 N	78.30 E
141	Hyderabad	India	25.28 N	68.35 E
141	Hyderabad (State)	India	18.15 N	78.0 E
127	Hydra (I.) (ēdh'rä)	Grc.	37.20 N	23.30 E
123	Hyères (ē-âr')	Fr.	43.9 N	6.9 E
123	Hyères, Iles d' (Is.) (ēl' dyâr')	Fr.	43.0 N	6.10 E
148	Hyesanjin (hyĕ'sän-jĭn')	Kor.	41.24 N	128.10 E
72	Hygiene (hī-jĭ-ēn')	Colo. (Denver In.)	40.11 N	105.10 W
160	Hyland, Mt. (hī'lănd)	Austl. (In.)	30.10 S	152.25 E
84	Hymera (hī-mē'rȧ)	Ind.	39.13 N	87.19 W
71	Hyndman Peak (hīnd'măn)	Ida.	43.47 N	114.3 W
73	Hyrum (hī'rŭm)	Utah (Salt Lake City In.)	41.38 N	111.52 W

ăt; finăl; rāte; senâte; ärm; ȧsk; sofȧ; fâre; ch-choose; dh-as th in other; bē; êvent; bĕt; recĕnt; cratēr; g-go; gh-gutteral g; bĭt; ĭ-short neutral; rīde; k-gutteral k as ch in German ich;

Ialomita PRONOUNCING INDEX Iringa

Page	Name Pronunciation Region	Lat. °′	Long. °′
127	Ialomita R. (yä-lō-mēt'sȧ)..Rom.	44.40 N	26.40 E
121	Iasi (Jassy) (yä'shê)........Rom.	47.12 N	27.35 E
152	Iba (ē'bä)................Phil.	15.20 N	119.59 E
132	Ibadan (ê-bä'dän)..........Nig.	7.28 N	3.56 E
100	Ibagué (ê-bȧ-gā')............Col.	4.52 N	75.28 W
151	Ibahan (ê-bȧ-än').Phil. (Manila In.)	13.51 N	121.7 E
153	Ibajay (ê-bȧ-hī')............Phil.	11.48 N	122.11 E
149	Ibaraki (ē'bȧ-rä'kê) Jap. (Osaka In.)	34.49 N	135.34 E
127	Ibar R. (ē'bär)............Yugo.	43.4 N	20.53 E
100	Ibarra (ê-bär'rä)............Ec.	0.20 N	78.2 W
86	Iberville (ê-bâr-vēl') (ī'bĕr-vil) Can.	45.19 N	73.15 W
132	Ibi (ē'bê)..................Nig.	8.12 N	9.45 E
101	Ibitinga (ê-bê-tĭŋ'gȧ).......Braz.	21.40 S	48.58 W
125	Ibiza (ê-bē'thä)..............Sp.	38.55 N	1.25 E
125	Ibiza I......................Sp.	39.0 N	1.25 E
135	Ibo (ē'bō)..................Moz.	12.15 S	40.40 E
100	Ica (ē'kȧ)..................Peru	14.2 S	75.32 W
111	Icel (ê-chĕl')...............Tur.	36.28 N	34.0 E
108	Iceland (īs'lănd)..........Atl. O.	65.0 N	19.0 W
144	Ichang (ē'chäng')...........Chn.	25.28 N	112.40 E
144	Ichang.....................Chn.	30.43 N	111.10 E
146	Icheng (ē'chĕng)...........Chn.	32.17 N	119.11 E
149	Ichibusayama (Mt.) (ē'chê-bōō'sȧ-yä'mä).Jap.	32.18 N	131.4 E
149	Ichikawa (ē'chê-kä'wä) Jap. (Tokyo In.)	35.43 N	139.54 E
148	Ichinomiya (ē'chē-nō-mē'ya).Jap.	35.25 N	140.22 E
149	Ichinomiya.................Jap.	35.19 N	136.49 E
129	Ichnya (ĭch'nyä)........Sov. Un.	50.52 N	32.21 E
147	Ichŏn (ē'chŭn')............Kor.	38.30 N	126.52 E
146	Ichow (ē'chō')..............Chn.	35.5 N	118.16 E
101	Icó (ê-kô')................Braz.	6.28 S	38.58 W
100	Icutú, Mt. (ê-kōō-tōō')......Ven.	6.33 N	65.29 W
79	Idabel (ī'dȧ-bĕl)...........Okla.	33.53 N	94.48 W
76	Idagrove (ī'dȧ-grōv)..........Ia.	42.22 N	95.28 W
132	Idah (ē'dä)................Nig.	7.7 N	6.42 E
70	Idaho (State) (ī'dȧ-hō)......U. S.	45.0 N	115.10 W
71	Idaho Falls.................Ida.	43.30 N	112.1 W
75	Idaho Sprs.................Colo.	39.44 N	105.31 W
124	Idanha-a-Nova (ê-dän'yȧ-ä-nō'vȧ) Port.	39.58 N	7.13 W
133	Idfû (êd'fōō)................Eg.	24.59 N	32.46 E
150	Idi (ē'dê)................Indon.	4.59 N	97.46 E
131	Idkû (ēd'kōō)..........Eg. (In.)	31.18 N	30.20 E
116	Idle, R. (īd''l)..........Gt. Brit.	53.23 N	0.56 W
126	Idria (ē'drê-ȧ).............Yugo.	46.1 N	14.1 E
126	Iesi (yā'sê)..................It.	43.35 N	13.19 E
132	Iferouane (ēf'rōō-än').Fr. W. Afr.	19.30 N	8.30 E
132	Ifni (ēf'nê)..................Afr.	29.25 N	10.18 W
101	Igarapé-Mirim (ê-gä-rä-pâ'mê-rēɴ').Braz. (In.)	1.55 S	48.55 W
138	Igarka (ê-gär'kȧ)........Sov. Un.	67.29 N	86.34 E
112	Igharghar, Wadi (R.) (wä'dê ê-gär'gär).Alg.	32.30 N	6.5 E
132	Igidi (Sand Dunes) (ê-gē'dê)..Alg.	26.30 N	5.30 W
126	Iglesias (ê-glā'zê-äs)........Sard.	39.19 N	8.34 E
132	Igli (ê-glē')..................Alg.	30.30 N	2.15 W
101	Igrapiuna (ê-grä-pê-ōō'nȧ) Braz. (In.)	13.45 S	39.12 W
111	Igridir (ê-ghrê-dēr').........Tur.	37.50 N	30.50 E
111	Igridir, L...................Tur.	38.10 N	30.48 E
92	Iguala (ê-gwä'lä)...........Mex.	18.18 N	99.33 W
125	Igualada (ê-gwä-lä'dä)...Sp. (In.)	41.35 N	1.37 E
102	Iguassú, R. (ê-gwä-sōō').Arg.-Braz.	26.0 S	52.0 W
102	Iguassú Falls.........Arg.-Braz.	25.30 S	54.0 W
101	Iguatú (ê-gwä-tōō')........Braz.	6.28 S	39.28 W
152	Iguig (ē-gēg')..............Phil.	17.46 N	121.43 E
145	Ihing (ē'hĭng')..............Chn.	31.21 N	119.47 E
145	Ihwang (ē'hwäng')..........Chn.	27.28 N	116.3 E
149	Iida (ē'ê-dȧ)...............Jap.	35.38 N	137.52 E
110	Ii Joki (R.) (ē'yō'kĭ).........Fin.	65.28 N	27.0 E
149	Iizuka (ē'ê-zōō-kȧ)..........Jap.	33.38 N	130.42 E
132	Ijebu Ode (ê-jĕ'bōō ō'dâ).....Nig.	6.47 N	4.2 E
115	Ijsel Sea (ī'sĕl).............Neth.	54.15 N	5.0 E
119	Ikaalinen (ē'kä-lĭ-nĕn).......Fin.	61.48 N	22.58 E
127	Ikaria (I.) (ē-kä'ryȧ).......Grc.	37.35 N	26.10 E
149	Ikeda (ē'kâ-dä)..Jap. (Osaka In.)	34.50 N	135.25 E
127	Ikhtiman (êk'tê-män)........Bul.	42.26 N	23.49 E
149	Iki I. (ē'kê)...............Jap.	33.45 N	129.45 E
134	Ikoma (ê-kō'mä)............Tan.	2.12 S	34.47 E
152	Ilagan (ê-lä'gän)...........Phil.	17.8 N	121.53 E
143	Ilan (ē'län')...............Chn.	46.14 N	129.32 E
145	Ilan (ē'län)................For.	24.45 N	121.45 E
121	Ilawa (ê-lä'vȧ)..............Pol.	53.36 N	19.36 E
86	Ile-aux-Coudres, (I.) (ēl'-ō-kōōd'r') Can.	47.25 N	70.25 W
56	Ile des Chênes (ēl' dä chân') Can. (Winnipeg In.)	49.41 N	96.57 W
111	Ilek R. (ē'lyĕk).........Sov. Un.	51.0 N	54.10 E
111	Iletskaya Zashchita (ē-lyĕt'skä-yȧ zäs-chē'tȧ).Sov. Un.	51.8 N	55.5 E
117	Ilford (ĭl'fērd) Gt. Brit. (London In.)	51.34 N	0.4 E
114	Ilfracombe (ĭl-frȧ-kōōm').Gt. Brit.	51.10 N	4.10 W
99	Ilha Grande B. (ēl'yȧ grän'dĕ) Braz. (Rio de Janeiro In.)	23.12 S	44.30 W
99	Ilha Grande (I.) Braz. (Rio de Janeiro In.)	23.10 S	44.15 W
124	Ilhavo (ēl'yȧ-vô)...........Port.	40.36 N	8.40 W
101	Ilhéos (êl-yā'ôzh)..........Braz.	14.28 S	39.2 W
142	Ili (Qulja) (ê-lē') (kōōl'jä)...Chn.	43.55 N	81.0 E
53	Iliamna (ē-lê-ăm'nȧ)........Alsk.	59.45 N	154.0 W
52	Iliamna L..................Alsk.	59.30 N	155.0 W
53	Iliamna Vol.................Alsk.	60.10 N	153.0 W
110	Ilich R. (ê'l'ĭch)........Sov. Un.	62.35 N	57.30 E
153	Iligan B. (ê-lē'gän).........Phil.	8.25 N	124.5 E
152	Iligan Pt...................Phil.	18.20 N	122.20 E
139	Ilim R. (ê-lyêm')........Sov. Un.	57.0 N	103.30 E
138	Ilimsk (ê-lyêmsk').......Sov. Un.	56.45 N	103.45 E
152	Ilin I. (ê-lyēn')............Phil.	12.15 N	121.5 E

Page	Name Pronunciation Region	Lat. °′	Long. °′
129	Ilintsy (ê-lyênt'sĭ).......Sov. Un.	49.7 N	29.11 E
85	Ilion (ĭl'ĭ-ŭn)..............N. Y.	43.0 N	75.2 W
138	Ili R. (ê'l'ê)............Sov. Un.	44.0 N	77.0 E
114	Ilkeston (ĭl'kĕs-tŭn).....Gt. Brit.	52.55 N	2.20 W
116	Ilkley (ĭlk'lĭ)...........Gt. Brit.	53.55 N	1.49 W
100	Illampú (Mt.) (êl-yäm-pōō')..Bol.	15.58 S	68.30 W
153	Illana B. (êl-yä'nä).........Phil.	7.30 N	123.35 E
102	Illapeh (êl-yä'pâ)............Chl.	31.45 S	70.15 W
120	Iller R. (ĭl'er)..............Ger.	47.50 N	10.12 E
135	Illig (ēl'lêg)...............Som.	7.50 N	49.42 E
100	Illimani (Mt.) (ēl-yê-mä'nê)..Bol.	16.45 S	67.42 W
79	Illinois (State) (ĭl-ĭ-noi') (ĭl-ĭ-noiz') U. S.	39.40 N	90.0 W
88	Illinois and Michigan Canal Ill. (Chicago In.)	41.46 N	87.50 W
79	Illinois and Mississippi Canal..Ill.	41.25 N	89.40 W
79	Illinois R...................Ill.	40.0 N	90.0 W
123	Illkirch (êl'kĭrк)..............Fr.	48.32 N	7.45 E
124	Illora (ēl'yô-rä)..............Sp.	37.17 N	3.53 W
120	Ilmenau (ēl'mē-nou).........Ger.	50.42 N	10.56 E
128	Ilmen, L. (êl''mĕn'') (ĭl'mĕn) Sov. Un.	58.20 N	31.22 E
132	Ilo (ē'lô)...................Nig.	11.32 N	3.41 E
100	Ilo........................Peru	17.42 S	71.15 W
94	Ilobasco (ê-lô-bäs'kô)........Sal.	13.57 N	88.47 W
153	Iloc I. (ê-lŏk)...............Phil.	11.18 N	119.42 E
153	Iloilo (ē-lô-ē'lō)............Phil.	10.41 N	122.34 E
153	Iloilo Str...................Phil.	10.30 N	122.20 E
94	Ilopango, L. (ē-lô-päŋ'gō)....Sal.	13.40 N	89.0 W
132	Ilorin (ē-lô-rēn')............Nig.	8.33 N	4.32 E
128	Ilovai-Dmitrievsk (ê'lô-vī-d'mē'trê-ĕfsk).Sov. Un.	53.8 N	40.15 E
129	Ilskaya (ēl'skȧ-yȧ)......Sov. Un.	44.52 N	38.32 E
119	Ilukste (ê-lŏŏk'shtâ).....Sov. Un.	55.59 N	26.20 E
70	Ilwaco (ĭl-wā'kô)..........Wash.	46.18 N	124.2 W
149	Imabari (ē'mä-bä'rê)........Jap.	34.1 N	132.59 E
149	Imaichi (ē'mȧ-ē'chê).........Jap.	35.16 N	132.55 E
139	Iman (ê-män')...........Sov. Un.	45.59 N	133.35 E
110	Imandra, L. (ē-män'drȧ).Sov. Un.	67.40 N	32.30 E
148	Iman R. (ê-män').......Sov. Un.	45.52 N	135.0 E
135	Imbâba (ēm-bä'bȧ)...........Eg.	30.5 N	31.13 E
148	Imianpo (ēm'yän-pō').......Chn.	45.0 N	128.1 E
84	Imlay City (ĭm'lā).........Mich.	43.0 N	83.6 W
117	Immenbeck (ĭm'ĕn-bĕk) Ger. (Hamburg In.)	53.27 N	9.43 E
120	Immenstadt (ĭm'ĕn-shtät)....Ger.	47.34 N	10.13 E
126	Imola (ē'mô-lä)...............It.	44.21 N	11.41 E
126	Imotski (ê-môts'kê)........Yugo.	43.27 N	17.14 E
153	Impasugong (ĕm-pä-sōō'gông) Phil.	8.15 N	125.0 E
126	Imperia (êm-pā'rê-ä)..........It.	43.53 N	8.1 E
74	Imperial Beach (ĭm-pē'rĭ-ăl).Calif.	32.33 N	117.7 W
74	Imperial Valley.............Calif.	32.58 N	115.30 W
133	Impfondo (Desborderville) (ĭmp-fōn'dô) (dâ-bord'vēl').Fr. Eq. Afr.	1.41 N	18.2 E
141	Imphal (ĭmp'hŭl)..........India	24.45 N	93.58 E
127	Imroz (I.) (ĭm'rŏz)..........Tur.	40.8 N	25.50 E
153	Imuruan B. (ē-mōō-rōō'än)..Phil.	10.40 N	119.10 E
152	Imus (ē'mŏŏs)..............Phil.	14.25 N	120.57 E
153	Inabanga (ē-nä-bäŋ'gä)......Phil.	10.1 N	124.4 E
74	Inaja Ind. Res. (ê-nä'hä)...Calif.	32.55 N	116.45 W
132	In-Azaoua (ēn-ä-zou'ȧ).......Alg.	20.52 N	7.30 E
125	Inca (êŋ'kä)..................Sp.	39.42 N	2.55 E
102	Incahuasi (Mt.) (êŋ-kȧ-wä'sê) Arg.-Chl.	26.59 S	68.29 W
117	Ince (ĭns).Gt. Brit. (Liverpool In.)	53.32 N	2.36 W
111	Ince, C. (ĭn'jâ)..............Tur.	42.5 N	35.0 E
147	Inchŏn (Chemulpo) (ĭn'chŭn) (chê-mŭl'pō).Kor.	37.28 N	126.38 E
122	Incudine (Mt.) (ēn-kōō-dē'nâ) (ăɴ-kü-dēn').Cor. (In.)	41.55 N	9.15 E
118	Indals R. (ĭn'däls)..........Swe.	63.10 N	15.30 E
152	Indan (ēn-dän')..............Phil.	14.15 N	122.53 E
152	Indang (ēn'däng')...........Phil.	14.12 N	120.53 E
80	Inde (ēn'dâ)................Mex.	25.53 N	105.14 W
77	Independence (ĭn-dê-pĕn'dĕns).Ia.	42.28 N	91.52 W
79	Independence...............Kan.	37.14 N	95.42 W
79	Independence................Mo.	39.5 N	94.24 W
70	Independence...............Ore.	44.50 N	123.10 W
111	Inderskoe, L. (ên-dyĕr'skô-yĕ) Sov. Un.	48.30 N	52.0 E
141	India (ĭn'dĭ-ȧ)...............Asia	24.0 N	80.0 E
85	Indiana (ĭn-dĭ-än'ȧ)..........Pa.	40.38 N	79.10 W
84	Indiana (State).............U. S.	40.0 N	86.0 W
84	Indianapolis (ĭn-dĭ-ăn-ăp'ô-lĭs) Ind.	39.45 N	86.10 W
96	Indian Cays (Is.)...........Cuba	21.49 N	83.8 W
5	Indian O.....................	10.0 S	80.0 E
77	Indianola (ĭn-dĭ-ăn-ō'lȧ).......Ia.	41.21 N	93.32 W
82	Indianola..................Miss.	33.27 N	90.39 W
74	Indian Peak (Paiute) Ind. Res. (pī-ōōt').Utah	38.15 N	113.50 W
72	Indian R....Can. (Vancouver In.)	49.36 N	122.56 W
83	Indian R..............Fla. (In.)	28.25 N	80.53 W
85	Indian R..................N. Y.	44.10 N	75.40 E
139	Indigirka R. (ên-dê-gēr'kȧ) Sov. Un.	68.0 N	146.20 E
150	Indochina (ĭn-dô-chī'nȧ).....Asia	15.0 N	107.0 E
150	Indonesia (ĭn'dô-nē-zhȧ).....Asia	5.30 N	114.0 E
141	Indore (ĭn-dōr')............India	22.40 N	75.58 E
150	Indragiri R. (ĭn-drȧ-jē'rê)..Indon.	0.30 S	102.30 E
141	Indravari R. (ĭn-drŭ-vä'rê)..India	19.5 N	81.30 E
122	Indre (ăɴ'dr')................Fr.	47.15 N	1.40 W
118	Indre Sullen (I.) (ĭn'dhrĕ sōōl'ĕn) Nor.	61.8 N	4.56 E
141	Indus R. (ĭn'dŭs)...........Pak.	33.0 N	71.30 E
111	Inebolu (ê-nâ-bō'lōō)........Tur.	41.58 N	33.45 E
111	Inegöl (ê'nâ-gŭl)............Tur.	40.2 N	29.20 E
152	Infanta (ên-fän'tä)..........Phil.	15.49 N	119.54 E
152	Infanta.....................Phil.	14.44 N	121.39 E
124	Infantes (ên-fän'tâs)..........Sp.	38.45 N	3.1 W
93	Inferior, L. (ên-fâ-rê-ôr')....Mex.	16.17 N	94.44 W

Page	Name Pronunciation Region	Lat. °′	Long. °′
84	Ingersoll (ĭn'gēr-sŏl)........Can.	43.5 N	80.56 W
159	Ingham (ĭng'ăm)..........Austl.	18.45 S	146.5 E
73	Inglenook (ĭŋ'g'l-nŏŏk) Ala. (Birmingham In.)	33.34 N	86.46 W
153	Inglesia Pt. (êŋ-glā'sê-ȧ).....Phil.	8.30 N	117.30 E
116	Ingleton (ĭŋ'g'l-tŭn).....Gt. Brit.	54.9 N	2.27 W
160	Inglewood (ĭŋ'g'l-wŏŏd) Austl. (In.)	28.26 S	151.8 E
74	Inglewood.................Calif.	33.55 N	118.22 W
156	Inglewood..................N. Z.	39.9 S	174.15 E
139	Ingoda R. (ên-gō'dȧ)....Sov. Un.	51.45 N	113.0 E
120	Ingolstadt (ĭŋ'gôl-shtät).....Ger.	48.47 N	11.26 E
129	Ingul R. (ên-gōōl')......Sov. Un.	47.15 N	32.15 E
129	Ingulets R. (ên-gōōl'yĕts') Sov. Un.	47.10 N	33.0 E
129	Ingulskaya Kamenka (ên-gŏŏl'-skȧ-yȧ kȧ-mĕn'kȧ).Sov. Un.	48.16 N	32.30 E
111	Ingur R. (ên-gŏŏr')......Sov. Un.	42.45 N	42.0 E
134	Inhambane (ên-yäm-bä'nā)..Moz.	23.52 S	35.20 E
101	Inhambupe (ên-yäm-bōō'pä) Braz. (In.)	11.50 S	38.15 W
134	Inharrime (ên-yär-rē'mä)....Moz.	24.28 S	35.2 E
102	Inhaúma (ên-yä-ōō'mä) Braz. (In.)	22.52 S	43.17 W
124	Iniesta (ên-yās'tä)...........Sp.	39.27 N	1.44 W
144	Ining (ē'nĭng')..............Chn.	25.19 N	109.59 E
101	Inini (ē-nē'nē)............S. Am.	4.0 N	53.0 W
100	Inirida, R. (ē-nê-rē'dä).......Col.	2.30 N	69.30 W
114	Inishbofin (I.) (ĭn'ĭsh-bō-fĭn')..Ire.	53.39 N	10.10 W
114	Inishtrahull (I.) (ĭn'ĭsh-trä'hŭl) Ire.	55.25 N	7.10 W
114	Inishturk (I.) (ĭn'ĭsh-tûrk')...Ire.	53.45 N	10.5 W
153	Initao (ē-nê-tä'ō)...........Phil.	8.29 N	124.20 E
147	Inje (ĭn'yĕ).................Kor.	38.4 N	128.7 E
125	Inkermann (ĭŋ-kēr-mȧn).....Alg.	35.58 N	0.56 E
119	Inkeroinen (ĭn'kĕr-oi-nĕn)....Fin.	60.45 N	26.55 E
131	Inkisi R. (ên-kē'sē) Bel. Cong. (Brazzaville In.)	5.20 S	15.20 E
88	Inland (ĭn'lănd) N. Y. (Niagara Falls In.)	43.2 N	78.58 W
91	Inner Bras (I.) (ĭn'ēr-brä') St. Thomas (In.)	18.23 N	64.58 W
114	Inner Sd. (ĭn'ēr).........Gt. Brit.	57.25 N	6.5 W
120	Inn R. (ĭn).................Eur.	47.30 N	12.0 E
120	Innsbruck (ĭns'brŏŏk).......Aus.	47.10 N	11.24 E
149	Ino (ē'nô)..................Jap.	33.33 N	133.24 E
134	Inongo (ê-nôŋ'gō).....Bel. Cong.	1.50 S	18.32 E
121	Inowroclaw (ē-nô-vrŏts'läf)...Pol.	52.47 N	18.15 E
127	Inoz (Enos) (ĕn'ŏz) (ā'nôs)...Tur.	40.42 N	46.3 E
132	In-Salah (ēn-sȧ-lä')..........Alg.	27.18 N	2.25 E
75	Inscription House Ruin.....Ariz.	36.45 N	110.48 W
	Insterburg, see Tcherniakhovsk, Sov. Un.		
77	International Falls........Minn.	48.35 N	94.23 W
149	Inuyama (ē'nōō-yä'mä)......Jap.	35.23 N	136.58 E
157	Invercargill (ĭn-vēr-kär'gĭl)..N. Z.	46.25 S	168.22 E
159	Inverell (ĭn-vēr-ĕl')........Austl.	29.49 S	151.17 E
89	Invergrove (ĭn'vēr-grōv) Minn. (Minneapolis In.)	44.51 N	93.1 W
83	Inverness (ĭn-vēr-nĕs')..Fla. (In.)	28.50 N	82.20 W
114	Inverness.............Gt. Brit.	57.30 N	4.10 W
87	Inverness...................Can.	46.12 N	61.19 W
134	Inyangani (Mt.) (ên-yän-gä'nê) S. Rh.	18.17 S	32.47 E
74	Inyo Mts. (ĭn'yō)..........Calif.	36.55 N	118.8 W
117	Inzersdorf (ĭnt'sērs-dôrf) Aus. (Wien In.)	48.9 N	16.21 E
132	In Zize (Well) (ēn-zē'zĕ).....Alg.	23.29 N	2.30 E
127	Ioannina (Yannina) (yô-ä'nê-nȧ) (yä'nê-nȧ).Grc.	39.38 N	20.53 E
79	Iola (ī-ō'lȧ)................Kan.	37.55 N	95.24 W
72	Ione (ī-ō'nê)...Colo. (Denver In.)	40.8 N	104.49 W
84	Ionia (ī-ō'nĭ-ȧ)............Mich.	43.0 N	85.5 W
127	Ionian Is. (ī-ō'nĭ-ăn)........Grc.	38.45 N	20.50 E
127	Ionian Sea...............It.-Grc.	39.0 N	19.0 E
127	Ios (I.) (ĭ'ŏs)...............Grc.	36.45 N	25.18 E
110	Ioshkar Ola (Krasnokokshaisk) (yŏsh'kär ō'lä).Sov. Un.	56.35 N	47.50 E
77	Iowa (State) (ī'ô-wȧ).......U. S.	42.10 N	93.20 W
77	Iowa City...................Ia.	41.39 N	91.32 W
77	Iowa Falls..................Ia.	42.32 N	93.15 W
78	Iowa Park..................Tex.	33.57 N	98.38 W
77	Iowa R.....................Ia.	41.56 N	92.30 W
101	Ipameri (ē-pä-mâ-rē').......Braz.	17.45 S	48.10 W
144	Ipe (ē'pĕ)..................Chn.	25.13 N	108.19 E
100	Ipiales (ē-pê-ä'lâs)..........Col.	0.50 N	77.48 W
150	Ipoh (ĭ'pō)...............Malaya	6.25 N	101.0 E
121	Ipel R. (ê'pĕl)......Czech.-Hung.	48.6 N	19.20 E
159	Ipswich (ĭps'wĭch).........Austl.	27.40 S	152.59 E
115	Ipswich................Gt. Brit.	52.5 N	1.10 E
87	Ipswich............Mass. (In.)	42.41 N	70.50 W
76	Ipswich.....................S. D.	45.27 N	99.0 W
128	Iput R. (ê-pŏŏt')........Sov. Un.	52.40 N	31.46 E
100	Iquique (ê-kē'kā)............Chl.	20.5 S	70.1 W
100	Iquitos (ê-kē'tōs)...........Peru	3.45 S	73.0 W
102	Irajá (ê-rȧ-hä')........Braz. (In.)	22.51 S	43.19 W
140	Iran (Persia) (ē-rän').......Asia	33.0 N	55.0 E
150	Iran Mts. (ī'răn) (ē-rän')..Indon.	2.30 N	114.45 E
140	Iran, Plateau of (ē'rän').....Iran	32.0 N	59.0 E
140	Iranshahr (ē-rän-shär').....Iran	28.55 N	58.55 E
92	Irapuato (ē-rä-pwä'tō)......Mex.	20.40 N	101.20 W
140	Iraq (ē-räk')................Asia	32.0 N	43.30 E
101	Irará (ē-rȧ-rä')........Braz. (In.)	12.8 S	38.33 W
95	Irazú (Vol.) (ē-rä-zōō').....C. R.	9.59 N	83.53 W
137	Irbid (êr-bēd').........Jor. (In.)	32.33 N	35.49 E
138	Irbit (êr-bêt')...........Sov. Un.	57.40 N	63.10 E
134	Irebu (ē-rā'bōō).......Bel. Cong.	0.35 S	17.47 E
114	Ireland (īr'lănd)............Eur.	53.0 N	8.0 W
138	Irgiz (ĭr-gēz')..........Sov. Un.	48.35 N	61.15 E
138	Irgiz R.................Sov. Un.	49.30 N	60.20 E
147	Iri (ē'rê)....................Kor.	35.56 N	126.56 E
152	Iriga (ê-rē'gä)..............Phil.	13.25 N	123.24 E
134	Iringa (ê-rĭŋ'gä)............Tan.	7.45 S	35.38 E

ng-sing; ŋ-baŋk; ɴ-nasalized n; nŏd; cŏmmit; ōld; ôbey; ôrder; fōōd; fŏŏt; ou-out; s-soft; sh-dish; th-thin; pūre; ûnite; ûrn; stŭd; circŭs; ü-as "y" in study; '-indeterminate vowel.

Iriomote PRONOUNCING INDEX Japan

Page	Name Pronunciation Region	Lat. °′	Long. °′
148	Iriomote I. (ē'rē-ô-mō'tē) Ryukyu Is. (For. In.)	24.20 N	123.50 E
94	Iriona (ê-rê-ō'nä)...Hond.	15.57 N	85.7 W
101	Iriri, R. (ê-rē'rē)...Braz.	5.0 S	54.28 W
114	Irish Sea (ī'rĭsh)...Eur.	53.40 N	5.0 W
138	Irkutsk (ĭr-ko͝otsk')...Sov. Un.	52.30 N	104.20 E
117	Irlam (ûr'lăm) Gt. Brit. (Liverpool In.)	53.26 N	2.25 W
116	Irlam...Gt. Brit.	53.26 N	2.26 W
149	Iro C. (ē'rō)...Jap.	34.32 N	138.58 E
73	Irondale...Ala. (Birmingham In.)	33.33 N	86.43 W
73	Iron Mt...Calif. (Los Angeles In.)	34.21 N	118.14 W
77	Iron Mountain...Mich.	45.50 N	88.4 W
75	Iron Mountain...Utah	37.37 N	113.17 W
77	Iron River...Mich.	46.6 N	88.38 W
54	Ironside...Can. (In.)	45.30 N	75.44 W
84	Ironton...Ohio	38.32 N	82.42 W
77	Ironwood...Mich.	46.27 N	90.9 W
84	Iroquois R. (ĭr'ô-kwoi)...Ill.-Ind.	40.50 N	87.30 W
152	Irosin (ē-rō-sēn')...Phil.	12.42 N	124.2 E
129	Irpen R. (ĭr-pĕn')...Sov. Un.	50.20 N	30.10 E
141	Irrawaddy R. (ĭr-ȧ-wäd'ē)...Bur.	23.30 N	96.0 E
138	Irtysh R. (ĭr-tĭsh')...Sov. Un.	57.35 N	73.0 E
133	Irumu (ē-ro͞o'mo͞o)...Bel. Cong.	1.29 N	29.51 E
124	Irún (ē-ro͞on')...Sp.	43.20 N	1.48 W
73	Irvine (ûr'vĭn) Calif. (Los Angeles In.)	33.40 N	117.45 W
114	Irvine...Gt. Brit.	55.35 N	4.40 W
84	Irvine...Ky.	37.40 N	83.58 W
51	Irvington. Calif. (San Francisco In.)	37.32 N	121.57 W
88	Irvington...N. J. (New York In.)	40.44 N	74.15 W
117	Irwell R. (ûr'wĕl) Gt. Brit. (Liverpool In.)	53.32 N	2.17 W
153	Isabela (ē-sä-bā'lä)...Phil.	6.42 N	121.59 E
153	Isabela...Phil.	10.11 N	123.0 E
97	Isabela, C...Hai.	19.55 N	71.0 W
100	Isabela (I.)...Ec.	0.30 S	91.0 W
92	Isabel I. (ē-sä-bĕl')...Mex.	21.53 N	105.55 W
94	Isabella, Cordillera (Mts.)...Nic.	13.50 N	84.50 W
129	Isaccea (ē-säk'chä)...Rom.	45.16 N	28.28 E
108	Isafjördur (ēs'ä-fyûr-do͝or)...Ice.	66.8 N	23.15 W
133	Isangi (ē-säŋ'gē)...Bel. Cong.	0.51 N	24.13 E
131	Isangila (ē-säŋ-gē-lä') Bel. Cong. (Brazzaville In.)	5.22 S	13.31 E
126	Isarco R. (ē-sär'kō)...It.	46.35 N	11.30 E
152	Isarog Vol. (ē-sä-rōg')...Phil.	13.40 N	123.22 E
120	Isar R. (ē'zär)...Ger.	48.30 N	12.0 E
126	Ischia (I.) (ēs'kyä)...It.	40.44 N	13.54 E
149	Ise B. (ē'sĕ)...Jap.	34.44 N	136.44 E
126	Iseo, L. of (ē-zĕ'ō)...It.	45.42 N	10.4 E
123	Isère R. (ē-zâr')...Fr.	45.15 N	5.25 E
126	Isernia (ē-zĕr'nyä)...It.	41.37 N	14.32 E
140	Isfahan (ĭs-fä-hän')...Iran	32.44 N	51.45 E
127	Ishem (ĕsh"m)...Alb.	41.32 N	19.36 E
148	Ishigaki I. (ē'shē-gä'kē) Ryukyu Is. (For. In.)	24.24 N	124.12 E
138	Ishim (ĭsh-ēm')...Sov. Un.	56.10 N	69.15 E
138	Ishim R...Sov. Un.	54.0 N	67.40 E
148	Ishnomaki (ĭsh-nō-mä'kē)...Jap.	38.28 N	141.15 E
148	Ishnomaki B...Jap.	38.15 N	141.15 E
77	Ishpeming (ĭsh'pē-mĭng)...Mich.	46.30 N	87.40 W
127	Isker R. (ĭs'k'r)...Bul.	43.10 N	24.0 E
111	Iskilip (ēs'kĭ-lēp')...Tur.	40.45 N	34.35 E
124	Isla-Cristina (ĭs'lä-krē-stē'nä)..Sp.	37.14 N	7.21 W
153	Island B. (ī'lănd bā)...Phil.	9.6 N	118.10 E
55	Island L...Can.	53.30 N	94.30 W
87	Islands, B. of...Can.	49.10 N	58.20 W
156	Islands, B. of...N. Z.	35.12 S	174.10 E
52	Islands of the Four Mts...Alsk.	52.30 N	170.30 W
114	Islay (I.) (ī'lā)...Gt. Brit.	55.45 N	6.25 W
86	Isle au Haut (I.) (ēl ō ō')...Me.	44.2 N	68.38 W
114	Isle of Man...Gt. Brit.	54.10 N	4.40 W
122	Isle R. (ēl)...Fr.	45.0 N	0.10 E
77	Isle Royale (ĭl' roi-ăl')...Mich.	48.0 N	88.50 W
89	Isles, Lake of the (ilz) Minn. (Minneapolis In.)	44.57 N	93.19 W
75	Isleta (ēs-lā'tä) (ī-lē'tȧ)...N. M.	34.57 N	106.45 W
86	Isle Verte (ēl vĕrt')...Can.	48.1 N	69.19 W
131	Ismailia (ēs-mȧ-ēl'ē-ȧ) Eg. (Suez Can. In.)	30.35 N	32.18 E
131	Ismailia Canal...Eg. (In.)	30.25 N	31.40 E
131	Isna (ēs'nȧ)...Eg. (In.)	25.18 N	32.32 E
111	Isparta (ē-spär'tä)...Tur.	37.45 N	30.32 E
137	Israel (ĭz'rĭ-ĕl)...Asia (In.)	32.0 N	35.0 E
138	Issiq Kul (L.) (ĭ'sĭk kûl)..Sov. Un.	42.25 N	77.30 E
122	Issoire (ē-swär')...Fr.	45.31 N	3.15 E
122	Issoudun (ē-so͞o-däN')...Fr.	45.55 N	2.0 E
123	Issy-les-Moulineaux (ē-sē'-lâ-mo͞o-lē-nō').Fr. (In.)	48.48 N	2.16 E
111	Istanbul (Constantinople) (ē-stän-bo͞ol').Tur.	41.2 N	29.0 E
127	Istiaia (ĭs-tyī'yä)...Grc.	38.57 N	23.11 E
83	Istokpoga, L. (ĭs-tŏk-pō'gȧ) Fla. (In.)	27.23 N	81.15 W
129	Istovnoe (ĭs-tôf'nō-yĕ)...Sov. Un.	51.10 N	38.39 E
127	Istranca Mts. (ĭ-strän'jȧ)...Tur.	41.40 N	27.50 E
122	Istres (ēs'tr')...Fr.	43.30 N	4.59 E
126	Istrian Pen. (ĭs'trĭ-ăn)...Yugo.	45.15 N	14.0 E
149	Itabashi (ē'tȧ-bä'shē) Jap. (Tokyo In.)	35.45 N	139.42 E
99	Itaborahi (ē'tȧ-bō-rä'ē) Braz. (Rio de Janeiro In.)	22.48 S	42.49 W
101	Itacoatiara (ē-tȧ-kwȧ-tyȧ'rȧ) Braz.	3.5 S	58.28 W
102	Itaipu, L. de (ē-tī'po͞o).Braz. (In.)	22.57 S	43.2 W
101	Itaituba (ē-tȧ'ĭ-to͞o'bȧ)...Braz.	4.15 S	55.31 W
102	Itajahí (ē'tȧ-zhä-ē')...Braz.	26.52 S	48.40 W
135	Itala (ē-tä'lä)...Som.	2.45 N	46.12 E
135	Italian Somaliland...Africa	5.0 N	46.30 E
126	Italy (ĭt'ȧ-lē)...Eur.	42.50 N	12.50 E
81	Italy...Tex.	32.10 N	96.52 W
149	Itami (ē'tä'mē)..Jap. (Osaka In.)	34.46 N	135.26 E
101	Itaparica (ē-tȧ-pȧ-rē'kȧ).Braz. (In.)	12.53 S	38.40 W
101	Itaperuna (ē-tȧ-pȧ-ro͞o'nȧ)..Braz.	21.5 S	41.48 W
101	Itapicurú R. (ē-tȧ'pē-ko͞o-ro͞o') Braz.	4.0 S	44.12 W
101	Itapicurú-Mirim (mē-rēN')..Braz.	3.28 S	44.12 W
101	Itapira (ē-tȧ-pē'rȧ)...Braz.	20.30 S	51.18 W
102	Itararé (ē-tȧ-rȧ-rā')...Braz.	24.8 S	49.15 W
81	Itasca (ī-tăs'kȧ)...Tex.	32.9 N	97.10 W
77	Itasca, L...Minn.	47.14 N	95.11 W
99	Itatiaya Mt. (ē-tä-tē-ä'yä)..Braz.	22.29 S	44.47 W
152	Itbayat (ēt-bä-yät')...Phil. (In.)	20.45 N	121.52 E
84	Ithaca (ĭth'ȧ-kȧ)...Mich.	43.19 N	84.36 W
85	Ithaca...N. Y.	42.27 N	76.31 W
127	Ithake (I.) (ē'thä-kē)...Grc.	38.25 N	20.42 E
132	Itobe (ē-tō'bä)...Nig.	7.29 N	6.46 E
134	Itoko (ē-tō'kō)...Bel. Cong.	1.15 S	22.10 E
100	Itonama, R. (ē-tō-nä'mä)...Bol.	15.0 S	63.0 W
131	Itsa (ēt'sȧ)...Eg. (In.)	29.12 N	30.48 E
99	Itú (ē-to͞o') Braz. (Rio de Janeiro In.)	23.18 S	47.18 W
144	Itu (ē'to͞o')...Chn.	30.25 N	111.18 E
100	Ituango (ē-twäŋ'gō)...Col.	6.59 N	76.2 W
93	Itundujía (Santa Cruz) (ē-to͞on-do͞o-hē'ȧ).Mex.	16.51 N	97.39 W
143	Itung (ē'to͝ong')...Chn.	43.28 N	125.27 E
93	Iturbide (ē'to͞or-bē'dhȧ)...Mex.	18.25 N	92.54 W
92	Iturbide...Mex.	21.0 N	100.23 W
120	Itzehoe (ĭt'sē-hō)...Ger.	53.56 N	9.31 E
120	Itzling (ĭts'lĭng)...Aus.	47.50 N	13.2 E
82	Iuka (ī-ū'kȧ)...Miss.	34.48 N	88.11 W
128	Ivanovo (ē-vä'nô-vō)...Sov. Un.	57.1 N	40.59 E
128	Ivanovo Indust. Ter...Sov. Un.	56.48 N	40.40 E
128	Ivertsa R. (ē-vĕrt'sȧ)...Sov. Un.	57.20 N	34.50 E
132	Ivindo R. (ē-vĭn'dō)..Fr. Eq. Afr.	1.0 N	13.0 E
135	Ivohibe (ē-vō-hē-bā')...Madag.	22.15 S	46.52 E
89	Ivory (ī'vō-rĭ).Mo. (St. Louis In.)	38.32 N	90.17 E
132	Ivory Coast (Colony)..Fr. W. Afr.	7.0 N	6.0 W
126	Ivrea (ē-vrĕ'ä)...It.	45.27 N	7.52 E
148	Iwateyama (Mt.) (ē-wä-tĕ-yä'mä) Jap.	39.52 N	140.52 E
149	Iwaya (ē'wȧ-yȧ)..Jap. (Osaka In.)	34.36 N	135.2 E
149	Iwo, I. (ē'wō)...Jap.	30.47 N	130.16 E
92	Ixcateopán (ēs-kä-tä-ō-pän').Mex.	18.23 N	99.52 W
93	Ixhuatán (San Francisco) (ēs-hwä-tän').Mex.	16.22 N	94.28 W
93	Ixhuatlán (ēs-wät-län')...Mex.	20.40 N	98.0 W
92	Ixmiquilpan (ēs-mē-kēl'pän).Mex.	20.28 N	99.12 W
93	Ixtacalco (ēs-tä-käl'kō).Mex. (In.)	19.23 N	99.7 W
92	Ixtaccíhuatl, Cerro (Mt.) (ēs-täk-sē'hwät'l).Mex.	19.10 N	98.37 W
93	Ixtaltapec (Asunción) (ēs-täl-tĕ-pĕk').Mex.	16.30 N	95.1 W
93	Ixtapalapa (ēs'tä-pä-lä'pä) Mex. (In.)	19.22 N	99.6 W
93	Ixtapaluca (ēs'tä-pä-lo͞o'kä) Mex. (In.)	19.19 N	98.53 W
93	Ixtapan, R. (ēs-tä'pän').Mex. (In.)	19.35 N	98.57 W
93	Ixtenco (ēs-tĕŋ'kō)...Mex.	19.14 N	97.53 W
93	Ixtepec (San Jerónimo) (ēs-tĕ-pĕk') (sän hȧ-rō'nē-mō).Mex.	16.35 N	95.5 W
92	Ixtlahuaca (ēs-tlä-wä'kä)...Mex.	19.32 N	99.44 W
93	Ixtlán de Juárez (Villa Juárez) (ēs-tlän' dā hwä'räz).Mex.	17.20 N	96.30 W
92	Ixtlán del Rio (ēs-tlän'dĕl rē'ō) Mex.	21.4 N	104.22 W
145	Iyang (ē'yäng')...Chn.	28.33 N	117.28 E
138	Iya R. (ē'yä)...Sov. Un.	53.55 N	100.0 E
149	Iyo Sea (ē'yō)...Jap.	33.30 N	132.0 E
94	Izabal (ē'zä-bäl')...Guat.	15.24 N	89.11 W
94	Izabal, L. (Golfo Dulce) (gōl'fō do͞ol'sȧ).Guat.	15.30 N	89.10 W
94	Izalco (ē-zäl'kō)...Sal.	13.49 N	89.40 W
110	Izhevsk (ē-zhyĕfsk')...Sov. Un.	56.48 N	53.10 E
110	Izhma (ĭzh'mȧ)...Sov. Un.	65.0 N	54.0 E
110	Izhma R...Sov. Un.	64.15 N	53.30 E
122	Izieux (ē-zyû')...Fr.	45.28 N	4.25 E
129	Izmail (ēz-mȧ-ēl')...Sov. Un.	45.21 N	28.51 E
111	Izmir (Smyrna) (ĭz-mēr') (smûr'nȧ).Tur.	38.25 N	27.10 E
127	Izmir, G. of...Tur.	38.30 N	26.50 E
111	Izmit (ĭz-mēt')...Tur.	40.47 N	29.59 E
126	Izonzo, R. (ē-zŏn'zō)...It.	46.0 N	13.36 E
149	Izuhara (ē'zo͞o-hä'rä)...Jap.	34.12 N	129.16 E
149	Izu Shichitō (Is.) (ē'zo͞o shĭ-chē'tō).Jap.	34.0 N	139.30 E
129	Izyaslavl (ē'zyȧ-slăv'l)...Sov. Un.	50.8 N	26.51 E
129	Izyum (ē-zyo͞om')...Sov. Un.	49.9 N	37.18 E
124	Jabalón R. (hä-bä-lōn')...Sp.	38.45 N	3.35 W
120	Jablonec (yäb'lô-nyĕts)...Czech.	50.42 N	15.11 E
121	Jablunkov Pass (yäb'lo͞on-kôf) Czech.-Pol.	49.30 N	18.47 E
153	Jabonga (hä-bôŋ'gä)...Phil.	9.20 N	125.32 E
125	Jaca (hä'kä)...Sp.	42.35 N	0.31 W
94	Jacaltenango (hä-käl-tĕ-näŋ'gō) Guat.	15.39 N	91.41 W
99	Jacarépaguá (zhä-kä-rȧ'pȧ-gwä') Braz. (Rio de Janeiro In.)	22.58 S	43.24 W
120	Jáchymov (yä'chĭ-môf)...Czech.	50.22 N	12.50 E
81	Jacinto R. (hä-sēn'tō) (jȧ-sĭn'tō) Tex. (In.)	29.50 N	95.5 W
78	Jacksboro (jăks'bŭr-ō)...Tex.	33.13 N	98.10 W
82	Jackson (jăk'sŭn)...Ala.	31.30 N	87.54 W
74	Jackson...Calif.	38.21 N	120.47 W
82	Jackson...Ga.	33.18 N	83.56 W
84	Jackson...Ky.	37.34 N	83.23 W
81	Jackson...La.	30.50 N	91.12 W
84	Jackson...Mich.	42.17 N	84.27 W
77	Jackson...Minn.	43.38 N	94.59 W
82	Jackson...Miss.	32.17 N	90.12 W
84	Jackson...Ohio	39.4 N	82.42 W
82	Jackson...Tenn.	35.37 N	88.50 W
71	Jackson L...Wyo.	43.55 N	110.40 W
157	Jacksons B...N. Z.	43.55 S	168.45 E
82	Jacksonville...Ala.	33.53 N	85.47 W
83	Jacksonville...Fla.	30.20 N	81.40 W
79	Jacksonville...Ill.	39.44 N	90.13 W
81	Jacksonville...Tex.	31.58 N	95.18 W
83	Jacksonville Beach...Fla.	30.17 N	81.25 W
83	Jacksonville, South...Fla.	30.17 N	81.39 W
97	Jacmel (zhȧk-mĕl')...Hai.	18.13 N	72.33 W
101	Jacobina (zhä-kô-bē'nȧ)...Braz.	11.12 S	40.12 W
80	Jaco L. (hä'kō)...Mex.	27.50 N	103.55 W
86	Jacques Cartier (Tabletop), Mt. (zhȧk' kär-tyā').Can.	48.58 N	66.2 W
86	Jacquet R. (zhȧ-kĕ') (jăk'ĕt).Can.	47.57 N	66.0 W
101	Jacuhpey, R. (zhä-ko͞o-hē'pĕ) Braz. (In.)	12.0 S	39.30 W
100	Jaèn (hä-ān')...Ec.	5.32 S	78.45 W
124	Jaén...Sp.	37.46 N	3.48 W
137	Jaffa (yä'fä)...Pal.	32.3 N	34.44 E
141	Jaffna (jăf'nȧ)...Cey. (In.)	9.45 N	80.0 E
153	Jagna (häg'nä)...Phil.	9.39 N	124.22 E
99	Jaguari, R. (zhä-gwä'rē) Braz. (Rio de Janeiro In.)	22.42 S	47.30 W
101	Jaguaripe (zhä-gwä-rē'pä) Braz. (In.)	13.8 S	38.54 W
96	Jaguey Grande (hä'gwā grän'dā) Cuba	22.31 N	81.6 W
101	Jahú (zhä-ho͞o')...Braz.	22.15 S	48.31 W
97	Jaibo, R. (hä-ē'bō)...Cuba	20.8 N	75.15 W
141	Jaipur (jī'po͞or)...India	26.50 N	75.45 E
126	Jajce (yī'tsĕ)...Yugo.	44.20 N	17.18 E
141	Jajpur (jĭ'po͞or)...India	20.45 N	86.28 E
150	Jakarta (Batavia) (yä-kär'tä) (bȧ-tä'vĭ-ȧ).Indon.	6.16 S	106.48 E
151	Jako, Pulo (I.) (po͞o'lō yä'kō) Port. Tim.	8.31 S	127.29 E
110	Jakobstad (Pietarsaari) (yȧ'kôb-stȧdh).Fin.	63.40 N	22.45 E
92	Jala (hä'lä)...Mex.	21.7 N	104.24 W
93	Jalacingo (hä-lä-sĭŋ'gō)...Mex.	19.48 N	97.16 W
151	Jalajala (hä-lä-hä'lä) Phil. (Manila In.)	14.22 N	121.22 E
141	Jalalabad (jŭ-lä-lȧ-bäd') Afg. (Peshawar In.)	34.26 N	70.27 E
94	Jalan, R. (hä-län')...Hond.	14.20 N	86.20 W
94	Jalapa (hä-lä'pä)...Guat.	14.38 N	89.58 W
93	Jalapa de Diáz (San Felipe) (hä-lä'pȧ dä dē-äz') (sän fē-lē'pä).Mex.	18.3 N	96.55 W
93	Jalapa del Marqués (hä-lä'pȧ dĕl mär-kās').Mex.	16.30 N	95.28 W
93	Jalapa Enríquez (hä-lä'pȧ ĕn-rē'kāz).Mex.	19.32 N	96.55 W
92	Jalisco (hä-lēs'kō)...Mex.	21.26 N	104.55 W
92	Jalisco (State)...Mex.	20.30 N	103.20 W
123	Jallieu (zhȧ-lyû')...Fr.	45.35 N	5.20 E
124	Jalón R. (hä-lōn')...Sp.	41.30 N	1.30 W
92	Jalostotitlán (hä-lōs-tē-tlän').Mex.	21.14 N	102.26 W
93	Jalpa (häl'pä)...Mex.	18.12 N	93.3 W
92	Jalpa...Mex.	21.41 N	103.6 W
92	Jalpan (häl'pän)...Mex.	21.14 N	99.30 W
92	Jaltepec, R. (häl-tȧ-pĕk')...Mex.	17.22 N	95.20 W
93	Jaltipán (häl-tē-pän')...Mex.	17.58 N	94.42 W
92	Jaltocán (häl-tô-kän')...Mex.	21.9 N	98.31 W
88	Jamaica (jȧ-mā'kȧ) N. Y. (New York In.)	40.42 N	73.46 W
96	Jamaica...W. I.	18.10 N	77.10 W
88	Jamaica B..N. Y. (New York In.)	40.38 N	73.50 W
92	Jamay (hä-mī')...Mex.	20.16 N	102.42 W
133	Jamba (jäm-bä)...Bel. Cong.	3.3 N	24.5 E
127	Jambol (yȧm'bôl)...Bul.	42.27 N	26.30 E
101	Jambú Assú (zhäm-bo͞o' ä-so͞o') Braz. (In.)	1.4 S	47.41 W
55	James B. (jāmz)...Can.	53.30 N	80.30 W
72	James Cr...Colo. (Denver In.)	40.7 N	105.23 W
72	James I...Can. (Vancouver In.)	48.37 N	123.22 W
83	James, L...N. C.	35.35 N	81.55 W
97	James Pt...Ba. Is.	25.21 N	76.23 W
79	James R...Mo.	37.0 N	93.22 W
76	James R...S. D.-N. D.	44.55 N	98.28 W
85	James R...Va.	37.37 N	78.0 W
158	James Range...Austl.	24.15 S	133.30 E
72	Jamestown...Colo. (Denver In.)	40.7 N	105.24 W
85	Jamestown...N. Y.	42.7 N	79.15 W
76	Jamestown...N. D.	46.55 N	98.41 W
153	Jamiltepec (hä-mēl-tȧ-pĕk)..Mex.	16.17 N	97.50 W
153	Jamindan (hä-mēn-dän')...Phil.	11.25 N	122.30 E
141	Jamnagar (Navanagar) (jäm-nŭ'gŭr).India	22.15 N	70.5 E
141	Jamrud (jäm'ro͞od) Pak. (Peshawar In.)	34.0 N	71.21 E
141	Jamshedpur (jäm'shäd-po͞or) India	22.48 N	86.11 E
101	Jamunda, R. (zhä-mo͞on'dä).Braz.	1.30 S	58.30 W
125	Janda, Laguna de la (L.) (lä-go͞o-nä dä lä hän'dä).Sp. (In.)	36.17 N	5.51 W
160	Jandowae (jăn-dō-wä'ē) Austl. (In.)	26.46 S	151.6 E
124	Jándula R. (hän'do͞o-lä)...Sp.	38.30 N	3.55 W
77	Janesville (jānz'vĭl)...Wis.	42.41 N	89.0 E
	Janica, see Genitsa, Grc.		
153	Janiuay (hä-nē-wī')...Phil.	10.57 N	122.30 E
48	Jan Mayen (I.) (yän mī'ĕn) Grnld. Sea	71.0 N	8.0 W
118	Jannelund (yän'ĕ-lo͞ond)...Swe.	59.13 N	14.24 E
121	Jánoshalma (yä'nôsh-hôl-mô) Hung.	46.17 N	19.20 E
121	Janów Lubelski (yä'no͞of lŭ-bĕl'skĭ).Pol.	50.41 N	22.23 E
101	Januaria (zhä-nwä'rē-ä)...Braz.	15.28 S	44.28 W
146	Jaoyang (jä'ō-yäng')...Chn.	38.25 N	115.42 E
148	Japan (jȧ-păn')...Asia	36.0 N	138.0 E
148	Japan, Sea of...Asia	40.0 N	134.0 E

ăt; finȧl; rāte; senāte; ärm; ȧsk; sofȧ; fâre; ch-choose; dh-as th in other; bē; ēvent; bĕt; recĕnt; cratẽr; g-go; gh-guttural g; bĭt; ĭ-short neutral; rīde; K-guttural k as ch in German ich;

ng-sing; ŋ-baŋk; N-nasalized n; nŏd; cŏmmit; ōld; ŏbey; ôrder; fōōd; fŏŏt; ou-out; s-soft; sh-dish; th-thin; pūre; ūnite; ûrn; stŭd; circŭs; ü-as "y" in study; '-indeterminate vowel.

Juruá PRONOUNCING INDEX Kareima

Page	Name Pronunciation Region	Lat. °'	Long. °'
100	Juruá, R. (zhōō-rōō-ä') Braz.	6.0 S	67.45 W
133	Jur R. (jōōr) A. E. Sud.	7.0 N	28.0 E
146	Jushui R. (jōō'shwē') Chn.	32.50 N	114.55 E
120	Jüterbog (yü'tĕr-bōgh) Ger.	51.59 N	13.4 E
94	Jutiapa (hōō-tē-ä'pä) Guat.	14.16 N	89.55 W
94	Juticalpa (hōō-tē-käl'pä) Hond.	14.39 N	86.14 W
123	Juvisy sur Orge (zhü-vē-sē'sür ôrzh'). Fr. (In.)	48.41 N	2.22 E
92	Juxtlahuaca (Santiago) (hōōs-tlä-hwä'kä). Mex.	17.18 N	98.2 W
119	Jyväskylä (yü'vĕs-kü-lĕ) Fin.	62.14 N	25.46 E
150	Kabaena (I.) ((kä-bà-ā'nà). Indon.	5.15 S	122.0 E
134	Kabalo (kä-bä'lō) Bel. Cong.	6.5 S	26.50 E
134	Kabambare (kä-bäm-bä'rå) Bel. Cong.	4.52 S	27.45 E
129	Kabane (kä-bä'nyĕ) Sov. Un.	49.12 N	38.9 E
111	Kabardino-Balkaria (Reg.) (kå'bär-dē'nô bäl-kä'ryà). Sov. Un.	43.45 N	43.30 E
153	Kabasalan (kä-bä-sä-län') Phil.	7.47 N	122.47 E
149	Kabe (kä'bĕ) Jap.	34.32 N	132.29 E
134	Kabinda (kä-bēn'dä) Bel. Cong.	6.10 S	24.20 E
137	Kabir I. (kà-bēr') Red Sea (In.)	13.45 N	42.45 E
134	Kabompo R. (kà-bôm'pō) N. Rh.	13.50 S	24.0 E
134	Kabongo (kà-bông'ō) Bel. Cong.	7.50 S	25.22 E
152	Kabugao (kä-bōō'gä-ō) Phil.	18.3 N	121.10 E
141	Kabul (kä'bōōl) Afg.	34.31 N	69.0 E
141	Kabul R. Afg.-Pak.	34.30 N	70.30 E
141	Kachin Hills (Mts.) (kä'chēn) Bur.	26.15 N	96.0 E
129	Kadievka (kà-dĭ-yĕf'kà). Sov. Un.	48.28 N	38.31 E
138	Kadin (Nadym) R. (kä-dēn') Sov. Un.	65.20 N	73.20 E
110	Kadnikov (käd'nē-kôf) Sov. Un.	59.32 N	40.20 E
132	Kaduna (kä-dōō'nä) Nig.	10.30 N	7.30 E
147	Kaechŏn (kä'ĕ-chŭn) Kor.	39.40 N	125.58 E
132	Kaédi (kä-ā-dē') Fr. W. Afr.	16.25 N	13.32 W
155	Kaena Pt. (kä'ā-nä) Haw.	21.33 N	158.19 W
147	Kaesŏng (Kaijō) (kä'ĕ-sŭng) (kī'jō). Kor.	37.58 N	126.34 E
133	Kafia Kingi (kä'fē-å kĭŋ'gē) A. E. Sud.	9.21 N	24.30 E
134	Kafue (kä'fōō-å) N. Rh.	15.45 S	28.13 E
129	Kagalnik, R. (kä-gäl'nēk) Sov. Un.	47.2 N	39.25 E
134	Kagera, R. (kä-gā'rà) Tan.-Ug.	1.15 S	31.15 E
149	Kagoshima (kä'gô-shē'mà) Jap.	31.32 N	130.30 E
149	Kagoshima B. Jap.	31.15 N	130.40 E
117	Kagran (kä'grän). Aus. (Wien In.)	48.15 N	16.27 E
129	Kagul (kä-gōōl') Sov. Un.	45.48 N	28.16 E
77	Kahnipiminanikok L. (kä-nĭ-pĭ'mĭ-nä'nĭ-kôk). Can.	48.23 N	91.15 W
79	Kahoka (kà-hō'kà) Mo.	40.26 N	91.42 W
155	Kahoolawe (I.) (kä'hōō-lä'wē) Haw.	20.33 N	156.35 W
155	Kahuku Pt. (kä-hōō'kōō) Haw.	21.43 N	157.58 W
157	Kaiapoi (kä'ē-å-pō'ē) N. Z.	43.23 S	172.42 E
75	Kaibab Ind. Res. (kä'ē-bàb). Ariz.	36.58 N	112.40 W
144	Kaichow (kī'chō') Chn.	27.0 N	106.46 E
146	Kaichow Chn.	35.41 N	115.21 E
111	Kaidak G. (kī-däk') Sov. Un.	45.0 N	53.30 E
101	Kaieteur Falls (kī-ĕ-tōōr'). Br. Gu.	5.0 N	58.47 W
146	Kaifeng (kī'fĕng') Chn.	34.45 N	114.29 E
148	Kaiho (kī-hō') Chn.	43.32 N	129.36 E
145	Kaihwa (kī'hwä') Chn.	29.10 N	118.35 E
142	Kaihwa Chn.	23.28 N	104.32 E
147	Kaijō (Kaesŏng) (kī'jō') (kä'ĕ-sŭng). Kor.	37.58 N	126.34 E
156	Kaikohe (kä'ē-kō'hē) N. Z.	35.25 S	173.50 E
157	Kaikoura (kä-ē-kōō'rà) N. Z.	42.24 S	173.42 E
157	Kaikoura Ra. N. Z.	42.0 S	173.35 E
127	Kailaria (kī-lä'rĭ-à) Grc.	40.30 N	21.42 E
154	Kailua (kä'ē-lōō'ä) Haw.	19.38 N	155.59 W
156	Kaimanawa Ra. (kä'ē-mà-nä'wà) N. Z.	39.0 S	176.0 E
149	Kainan (kä'ē-nän') Jap.	34.10 N	135.12 E
138	Kainsk (kä-ēnsk') Sov. Un.	55.30 N	78.10 E
155	Kai o Kalohi (Chan.) (kä'ē ō' kä-lō'hē). Haw.	20.58 N	157.10 W
156	Kaipara Har. (kä'ē-pä'rä) N. Z.	36.25 S	174.30 E
147	Kaiping (kī-pĭng') Chn.	39.44 N	118.7 E
132	Kairouan (kĕr-ōō-äN') Tun.	35.43 N	10.2 E
129	Kairy Zapadnie (kīr'yē zä-päd"n-yĕ). Sov. Un.	46.57 N	33.42 E
	Kaisarieh, see Kayseri, Tur.		
117	Kaiser-Ebersdorf (kī'zĕr-ā'bĕrs-dôrf). Aus. (Wien In.)	48.10 N	16.28 E
120	Kaiserslautern (kī-zĕrs-lou'tĕrn) Ger.	49.27 N	7.47 E
146	Kaishow (kī'shō') Chn.	32.59 N	119.26 E
147	Kaishū (Haeju) (kī'shū) (hä'ĕ-jōō'). Kor.	38.2 N	125.42 E
156	Kaitaia (kä-ē-tä'ē-ä) N. Z.	35.7 S	173.20 E
157	Kaitangata (kī-täŋ-gä'tà) N. Z.	46.18 S	169.53 E
157	Kaitarau, Mt. (kä'ē-tä-rä'ōō) N. Z.	42.10 S	173.4 E
155	Kaiwi Chan. (kä'ē-wē) Haw.	21.15 N	157.35 W
148	Kaiyuan (kī'yōō-än') Chn.	42.52 N	123.58 E
52	Kaiyuh Mts. (kī-yōō') Alsk.	64.20 N	157.30 W
110	Kajaani (kä'yà-nē) Fin.	64.12 N	27.40 E
149	Kajiki (kä'jē-kē) Jap.	31.45 N	130.40 E
129	Kakhovka (kä-kôf'kà) Sov. Un.	46.48 N	33.27 E
133	Kakindu (kä-kĭn'dōō) Ug.	1.2 N	33.1 E
119	Käkisalmi (kĕ'kĭ-säl-mē) Fin.	61.3 N	30.6 E
131	Kalaa-kebira (kä'lä-ä-kĕ-bē'rà) Tun. (In.)	35.52 N	10.25 E
112	Kalaat (kà-là-ät') Tun.	35.50 N	8.23 E
132	Kalaba (kà-lä'bà) S. L.	9.52 N	11.27 W
111	Kalach (kà-làch') Sov. Un.	50.15 N	41.0 E
155	Ka Lae Pt. (kä-lä'å) Haw.	18.55 N	155.38 W
134	Kalahari Des. (kä-lä-hä'rē). Bech.	23.15 S	21.45 E
70	Kalama (kà-läm'à) Wash.	46.1 N	122.51 W
127	Kalamai (kä-lä-mī') Grc.	37.3 N	22.7 E
51	Kalama R. Wash. (Portland In.)	46.3 N	122.40 W
84	Kalamazoo (kăl-à-mà-zōō'). Mich.	42.20 N	85.38 W
84	Kalamazoo R. Mich.	42.30 N	85.50 W
129	Kalanchak (kä-län-chäk') Sov. Un.	46.16 N	33.13 E
155	Kalapana (kä-lä-pä'nä) Haw.	19.21 N	154.58 W
141	Kalat (kŭ-lät') Pak.	29.5 N	66.40 E
150	Kalautowa (kä-lä'ōō-tō'wà) Indon.	7.28 S	121.45 E
143	Kalgan (Chiangkiakow) (käl-gän') (chäng'kyä'kō'). Chn.	40.53 N	114.54 E
158	Kalgoorlie (kăl-gōōr'lē) Austl.	30.45 S	121.29 E
153	Kalian Pt. (käl-yän') Phil.	6.6 N	125.44 E
128	Kalikino (kä-lĭ-kē'nō) Sov. Un.	52.56 N	39.48 E
128	Kalinin (Iver) (kà'lē-nēn) Sov. Un.	56.51 N	35.57 E
121	Kaliningrad (Königsberg) (kà-lē-nēn'grät) (kû'nēks-bĕrgh). Sov. Un.	54.42 N	20.31 E
129	Kalinkovichi (kä-lēn-kô-vē'chē) Sov. Un.	52.7 N	20.20 E
70	Kalispel Ind. Res. (kăl-ĭ-spĕl') Wash.	48.25 N	117.17 W
71	Kalispell Mont.	48.12 N	114.20 W
121	Kalisz (kä'lēsh) Pol.	51.45 N	18.4 E
129	Kalitva R. (kä-lēt'vä) Sov. Un.	50.20 N	39.10 E
108	Kalix R. (kä'lēks) Swe.	66.50 N	22.45 E
134	Kalkfeld (kälk'fĕlt) S. W. Afr.	21.2 S	16.7 E
134	Kalkfontein (kälk'fōn-tān) S. W. Afr.	28.2 S	18.45 E
108	Kalkholmen (kälk'hôlm-ĕn) Swe.	64.42 N	21.15 E
117	Kalksburg (kälks'bōōrgh) Aus. (Wien In.)	48.8 N	16.15 E
118	Kalmar (käl'mär) Swe.	56.40 N	16.20 E
118	Kalmar Sd. Swe.	56.40 N	16.25 E
129	Kalmius R. (käl"myōōs). Sov. Un.	47.15 N	37.50 E
111	Kalmyk (Aut. Area) (käl"mōōk) (kăl'mŭk). Sov. Un.	46.0 N	46.0 E
121	Kalocsa (kä'lō-chä) Hung.	46.32 N	18.58 E
134	Kalomo (kä-lō'mō) N. Rh.	17.8 S	26.18 E
117	Kaltenleutgeben (käl'tĕn-loit' gä-bĕn). Aus. (Wien In.)	48.7 N	16.12 E
128	Kaluga (kå-lōō'gä) Sov. Un.	54.30 N	36.16 E
128	Kaluga (Dist.) Sov. Un.	54.36 N	35.24 E
118	Kalundborg (kà-lōōn'bôr'). Den.	55.40 N	11.6 E
121	Kalush (kä'lōōsh) Sov. Un.	49.2 N	24.23 E
121	Kaluszyn (kä-wōōsh'ĕn) Pol.	52.12 N	21.53 E
119	Kalvarija (käl-vä-rē'yà). Sov. Un.	54.23 N	23.12 E
128	Kalyazin (käl-yà'zēn) Sov. Un.	57.13 N	37.52 E
132	Kamabai (kä-mä-bä'ē) S. L.	9.15 N	11.57 W
148	Kamaishi (kä'mä-ē'shē) Jap.	39.16 N	141.54 E
149	Kamakura (kä'mä-kōō'rä) Jap.	35.19 N	139.34 E
138	Kama R. (kä'mà) Sov. Un.	55.28 N	51.0 E
134	Kambove (käm-bō'vĕ). Bel. Cong.	10.52 S	26.42 E
139	Kamchatka Mts. (kàm-chät'kà) Sov. Un.	60.0 N	165.0 E
139	Kamchatka Pen. Sov. Un.	56.0 N	160.0 E
127	Kamčik R. (käm'chĕk) Bul.	42.50 N	27.5 E
138	Kamen (kä'mĕn) Sov. Un.	53.50 N	81.20 E
	Kamenskoe, see Dneprodzerzhinsk, Sov. Un.		
129	Kamenka (kä-mĕŋ'kà) Sov. Un.	48.3 N	28.41 E
121	Kamenka Sov. Un.	50.6 N	24.22 E
129	Kamensk (kä'mĕnsk) Sov. Un.	48.22 N	40.15 E
110	Kamensk Sov. Un.	56.27 N	61.53 E
129	Kamenskoe, see Dneprodzerzhinsk, Sov. Un.		
120	Kamenz (kä'mĕnts) Ger.	51.15 N	14.5 E
149	Kameoka (kä'mā-ō'kä) Jap. (Osaka In.)	35.1 N	135.36 E
120	Kamienna Góra (kä-myĕn'nà gōō'rà). Pol.	50.47 N	16.2 E
120	Kamien Pomorski (kä'myĕn' pô-môr'skē). Pol.	53.57 N	14.48 E
51	Kamilche (kå-mĭ-lē'hē) Wash. (Seattle In.)	47.7 N	123.5 W
77	Kaministikwia R. (kä-mĭ-nĭ-stĭk'wĭ-å). Can.	48.22 N	89.30 W
138	Kamishlov (kä-mēsh'lôf). Sov. Un.	56.50 N	62.40 E
149	Kami Suwa (kä'mē sōō'wà) Jap.	36.3 N	138.8 E
54	Kamloops (kăm'lōōps) Can.	50.42 N	120.22 W
156	Kamo (kä'mō) N. Z.	35.42 S	174.17 E
133	Kampala (käm-pä'lä) Ug.	0.12 N	32.32 E
150	Kampar R. (käm'pär) Indon.	0.25 N	101.30 E
120	Kampen (kämp'ĕn) Neth.	52.32 N	5.54 E
150	Kampot (käm'pōt) Indoch.	10.37 N	104.10 E
120	Kamp R. (kämp) Aus.	48.35 N	15.23 E
155	Kamuela (kä-mōō-ā'lä) Haw.	19.58 N	155.30 W
148	Kamui C. (käm'wē) Jap.	43.15 N	140.20 E
129	Kamyshevatskaya (kä-mwēsh'ĕ-vät'skä-yà). Sov. Un.	46.24 N	37.54 E
111	Kamyshin (kä-mwēsh'ĭn). Sov. Un.	50.5 N	45.20 E
129	Kamyshnya (kä-mwēsh'n-yà) Sov. Un.	50.7 N	33.40 E
75	Kanab (kăn'ăb) Utah	37.2 N	112.31 W
149	Kanagawa (kä'nä-gä'wä) Jap. (Tokyo In.)	35.28 N	139.38 E
72	Kanaka Cr. (kà-năk'à) Can. (Vancouver In.)	49.15 N	122.25 W
149	Kanawa I. (kä'nà-wä) Jap.	33.30 N	139.20 E
84	Kanawha R. (kà-nô'wà) W. Va.	38.20 N	81.35 W
149	Kanazawa (kä'nà-zä'wä) Jap.	36.30 N	136.37 E
149	Kanazawa Jap. (Tokyo In.)	35.20 N	139.38 E
145	Kanchow (kän'chō) Chn.	25.52 N	114.25 E
142	Kanchow Chn.	38.45 N	100.58 E
141	Kandahar (kŭn-dŭ-här') Afg.	31.44 N	65.45 E
134	Kanda Kanda (kän'dà kän'dà) Bel. Cong.	5.40 S	23.32 E
110	Kandalaksha (kàn-dà-läk'shà) Sov. Un.	67.12 N	32.34 E
110	Kandalaksha B. Sov. Un.	66.25 N	34.30 E
119	Kandava (kän'dà-và) Sov. Un.	57.3 N	22.46 E
132	Kandi (käN-dē') Fr. W. Afr.	11.5 N	3.2 E
141	Kandy (kän'dē) Cey. (In.)	7.25 N	80.38 E
85	Kane (kān) Pa.	41.40 N	78.48 W
155	Kaneohe B. (kä-nā-ō'hä) Haw.	21.27 N	157.47 W
129	Kanev (kä-nyôf') Sov. Un.	49.45 N	31.26 E
140	Kangavar (kŭŋ'gà-vär) Iran	34.40 N	47.50 E
158	Kangaroo I. (kăŋ-gà-rōō') Austl.	35.50 S	137.10 E
147	Kangdong (käng'dŭng) Kor.	39.9 N	126.9 E
150	Kangean Is. (käŋ'gē-än) Indon.	7.0 S	115.45 E
148	Kanggye (käng'gyĕ) Kor.	40.58 N	126.36 E
147	Kanggyŏng (käng'yŭng) Kor.	36.10 N	127.1 E
147	Kanghwa (käng'hwà) Kor.	37.45 N	126.27 E
147	Kanghwa I. Kor.	37.45 N	126.28 E
147	Kangjin (käng'jĭn') Kor.	34.37 N	126.47 E
148	Kangkay (käng'kī') Kor.	40.59 N	120.40 E
147	Kangnŭng (käng'nōōng) Kor.	37.44 N	128.54 E
134	Kango (käN-gō') Fr. Eq. Afr.	0.12 N	10.6 E
147	Kangsŏ (käng'sŭ) Kor.	38.59 N	125.28 E
55	Kaniapiskau L. (kă-nĭ-ăp'ĭs-kô) Can.	54.15 N	69.15 W
55	Kaniapiskau R. Can.	56.30 N	68.30 W
110	Kanin Pen. (kà-nēn') Sov. Un.	68.10 N	45.0 E
79	Kankakee (kăŋ-kà-kē') Ill.	41.6 N	87.52 W
79	Kankakee R. Ill.	41.12 N	88.0 W
132	Kankan (käN-käN) (kän-kän') Fr. W. Afr.	10.22 N	9.17 W
147	Kankō (Hamhŭng) (käŋ'kō) (häm'hōōng). Kor.	39.58 N	127.32 E
83	Kannapolis (kăn-ăp'ō-lĭs) N. C.	35.30 N	80.38 W
149	Kannoura (kä'nō-ōō'rä) Jap.	33.34 N	134.17 E
132	Kano (kä'nō) Nig.	12.3 N	8.32 E
145	Kan R. (kän) Chn.	27.38 N	115.18 E
138	Kan R. Sov. Un.	56.15 N	95.0 E
78	Kansas (State) (kăn'zàs) U. S.	39.0 N	98.0 W
79	Kansas City Kan.	39.6 N	94.39 W
79	Kansas City Mo.	39.5 N	94.35 W
79	Kansas R. Kan.	39.5 N	95.40 W
147	Kansŏng (kän'sung) Kor.	38.38 N	128.29 E
142	Kansu (Prov.) (kän'sōō') Chn.	38.0 N	101.0 E
150	Kantang (kän'täng') Siam	7.27 N	99.30 E
146	Kanyü (kän'yü') Chn.	34.50 N	119.8 E
146	Kaocheng (kä'ō-chĕng') Chn.	38.4 N	114.48 E
148	Kaohsiung (kä'ōhsiung) (kä'ō-syōōng') For. (In.)	22.44 N	120.21 E
132	Kaolak (kä-ō-läk') Fr. W. Afr.	14.10 N	16.8 W
146	Kaotang (kä'ō-täng') Chn.	36.49 N	116.10 E
151	Kaouyao (kä'ō-ōō-yä'ō) Phil. (Manila In.)	14.17 N	121.9 E
146	Kaoyang (kä'ō-yäng') Chn.	38.49 N	115.42 E
146	Kaoyi (kä'ō-yē') Chn.	37.39 N	114.39 E
146	Kaoyu (kä'ō-yōō') Chn.	32.48 N	119.27 E
146	Kaoyuan (kä'ō-yōō-än') Chn.	37.8 N	118.7 E
146	Kaoyu L. Chn.	32.50 N	118.58 E
126	Kapela (Mts.) (kä-pā'lä) Yugo.	44.55 N	15.33 E
120	Kapfenberg (käp'fĕn-bĕrgh) Aus.	47.26 N	15.18 E
157	Kapiti I. (kä-pē'tē) N. Z.	40.50 S	174.55 E
121	Kaposvár (kô'pôsh-vär) Hung.	46.22 N	17.47 E
51	Kapowsin (kā'pō-sĭn) Wash. (Seattle In.)	46.59 N	122.14 W
148	Kapsan (käp'sän') Kor.	41.6 N	128.18 E
150	Kapuas Mts., Upper (kä'pōō-äs) Sar.-Indon.	1.30 N	112.15 E
150	Kapuas (R.) Indon.	0.30 N	112.0 E
111	Kapustin Yar (kä'pōōs-tēn yär') Sov. Un.	48.35 N	45.50 E
121	Kapuvár (kô'pōō-vär) Hung.	47.35 N	17.2 E
121	Kapyczynce (kä-pĭ-chĭn"tsĕ). Pol.	49.6 N	25.55 E
128	Karabanovo (kä-rà-bà-nō'vō) Sov. Un.	56.18 N	38.41 E
134	Karabib (kär'à-bĭb) S. W. Afr.	21.50 S	15.50 E
111	Karachai (Cherkess) (Aut. Reg.) (kå'rà-chī) (chĕr'kĕs). Sov. Un.	43.45 N	42.0 E
128	Karachev (kà-rà-chôf') Sov. Un.	53.7 N	34.58 E
141	Karachi (kŭ-rä'chē) Pak.	24.55 N	67.0 E
138	Karaganda (kà-rà-gän'dä) Sov. Un.	49.30 N	73.30 E
139	Karaginski I. (kà-rä-gēn'skĭ) Sov. Un.	59.0 N	164.0 E
	Karahissar, see Afyon-Karahisar, Tur.		
111	Kara Khobda R. (kä-rä kôb'dä) Sov. Un.	50.30 N	55.15 E
111	Kara Kichu G. (kä'rà kē'chōō) Sov. Un.	44.25 N	53.0 E
138	Karakol (kä-rä-kôl') Sov. Un.	42.25 N	78.15 E
142	Kara Korum (Ruins) (kä'rä kō'rōōm). Mong.	47.20 N	102.27 E
141	Karakorum Pass India	35.30 N	77.58 E
141	Karakorum Ra. India	35.45 N	77.0 E
111	Karaköse (kä-rä-kŭ'sĕ) Tur.	39.45 N	43.2 E
140	Kara Kum (Des.) (Qara Qum) (kä'rà kōōm). Sov. Un.	47.0 N	63.15 E
111	Karaman (kä-rä-män') Tur.	37.8 N	33.5 E
157	Karamea Bight (kà-rà-mē'à bīt) N. Z.	41.20 S	172.0 E
157	Karamea R. N. Z.	41.12 S	172.20 E
127	Kara Mts. (kä'rà) Yugo.	42.20 N	21.40 E
142	Kara Nor (L.) (kä'rä nōr') Chn.	40.37 N	94.34 E
142	Kara Nor (L.) Mong.	48.0 N	92.0 E
110	Kara R. Sov. Un.	68.45 N	65.30 E
138	Kara Sea Sov. Un.	72.30 N	62.0 E
138	Kara Str. Sov. Un.	70.30 N	58.0 E
95	Karata Lagoon (kä-rä'tä) Nic.	13.55 N	83.30 W
149	Karatsu (kä'rà-tsōō) Jap.	33.27 N	129.58 E
138	Karaul (kä-rä-ōōl') Sov. Un.	70.10 N	83.10 E
120	Karawankas (Mts.) (kä-rä-väŋ'kàs). Aus.	46.28 N	14.20 E
134	Karaz Mts. (kär'àz) S. W. Afr.	27.15 S	18.40 E
140	Karbala (kŭr'bà-lä) Iraq	32.45 N	44.5 E
121	Karcag (kär'tsäg) Hung.	47.18 N	20.57 E
127	Karditsa (kär-dē'tsä) Grc.	39.22 N	21.57 E
119	Kärdla (kĕrd'lä) Sov. Un.	59.0 N	22.46 E
133	Kareima (kä-rā'mà) A. E. Sud.	18.34 N	31.50 E

ăt; finăl; rāte; senāte; ärm; ȧsk; sofȧ; fâre; ch-choose; dh-as th in other; bē; ēvent; bĕt; recĕnt; cratēr; g-go; gh-gutteral g; bĭt; ĭ-short neutral; rīde; K-gutteral k as ch in German ich;

ng-sing; ŋ-baŋk; N-nasalized n; nŏd; cŏmmit; ōld; ōbey; ôrder; fōōd; fŏŏt; ou-out; s-soft; sh-dish; th-thin; pūre; ūnite; ûrn; stŭd; circŭs; ú-as "y" in study; '-indeterminate vowel.

Keyport PRONOUNCING INDEX **Kiskunhalas**

Page	Name Pronunciation Region	Lat. °′	Long. °′
88	Keyport (kē′pōrt). N. J. (N. Y. In.)	40.26 N	74.12 W
85	Keyser (kī′zēr)........... W. Va.	39.27 N	79.0 W
83	Key West (kē wĕst′).... Fla. (In.)	24.33 N	81.47 W
121	Kežmarok (kĕzh′mȧ-rôk) .. Czech.	49.8 N	20.27 E
139	Khabarovsk (ᴋä-bä′rôfsk) Sov. Un.	48.30 N	135.0 E
140	Khabis (ᴋä-bēs′)............ Iran	30.40 N	57.59 E
140	Khaburah (ᴋä-bōō′rä)...... Oman	23.52 N	57.30 E
140	Khaibar (ᴋī′bȧr)......... Sau. Ar.	25.45 N	39.29 E
142	Khaidik Gol (R.) (ᴋī′dêk gôl). Chn.	42.15 N	85.0 E
127	Khalkidike (Chalcidice) Pen. (kȧl-ᴋêd′ê-kĕ) (kăl-sĭd′ĭ-sê). Grc.	40.25 N	23.25 E
127	Khalkis (Chalcis) (ᴋȧl′kĭs) (kăl′sĭs). Grc.	38.27 N	23.38 E
110	Khalturin (ᴋäl′tōō-rēn).. Sov. Un.	58.32 N	48.58 E
137	Khan ez Zebib (ᴋän ĕz zē-bēb′) Jor. (In.)	31.29 N	36.2 E
126	Khania (Canea) (kä-nê′ȧ) (kä-nĕ′ä). Grc. (In.)	35.27 N	24.4 E
126	Khania, G. of............... Grc.	35.35 N	24.0 E
139	Khanka, L. (ᴋän′kȧ).... Sov. Un.	44.0 N	132.30 E
111	Khanskaya Stavka (Urda) (ᴋän′-skȧ′yȧ stäf′kȧ) (ōōr′dȧ). Sov. Un.	48.48 N	47.40 E
129	Kharkov (ᴋär′kôf)...... Sov. Un.	49.58 N	36.11 E
127	Kharmanlii (ᴋȧr-män′lê)..... Bul.	41.54 N	25.53 E
133	Khartoum (kär-tōōm′). A. E. Sud.	15.35 N	32.32 E
133	Khartoum North...... A. E. Sud.	15.40 N	32.34 E
127	Khaskovo (ᴋȧs′kô-vô)....... Bul.	41.56 N	25.32 E
139	Khatanga (ᴋȧ-täŋ′gȧ)... Sov. Un.	71.50 N	102.0 E
139	Khatanga R.............. Sov. Un.	72.0 N	102.30 E
139	Khatangski G........... Sov. Un.	74.0 N	110.0 E
129	Kherson (kĕr-sôn′)...... Sov. Un.	46.38 N	32.36 E
138	Kheta R. (ᴋĕ′tȧ)........ Sov. Un.	71.0 N	99.0 E
139	Khilok R. (ᴋê-lôk′)..... Sov. Un.	51.10 N	109.0 E
119	Khitola (ᴋê-tō′lȧ)....... Sov. Un.	61.12 N	29.44 E
143	Khingan Mts., Great (ᴋĭn-gän′) Chn.	48.30 N	120.0 E
143	Khingan Mts., Little......... Chn.	49.0 N	127.30 E
127	Khios (Chios) (kē′ŏs) (kī′ŏs) . Grc.	38.22 N	26.9 E
127	Khios (I.).................... Grc.	38.23 N	26.5 E
140	Khiva (ᴋē′vȧ)........... Sov. Un.	41.31 N	60.28 E
129	Khmelnik (ᴋmĕl′nĭk).... Sov. Un.	49.34 N	27.58 E
129	Khodorkov (ᴋô-dôr′kôf) . Sov. Un.	50.3 N	29.12 E
	Khodzhent, see Leninabad, Sov. Un.		
140	Khoi (koi).................. Iran	38.35 N	45.5 E
129	Khoiniki (ᴋoi-nē′kê)..... Sov. Un.	51.55 N	29.59 E
128	Kholm (ᴋôlm)........... Sov. Un.	57.9 N	31.8 E
148	Kholmsk (ᴋŭlmsk).......... Sakh.	47.2 N	142.2 E
150	Khong (ᴋŏng)........... Indoch.	14.4 N	105.37 E
111	Khoni (ᴋô′nê)........... Sov. Un.	42.20 N	42.30 E
150	Khonkaen (ᴋŏŋ′kä-ĕn′)..... Siam	16.35 N	102.46 E
111	Khoper R. (ᴋô′pēr)..... Sov. Un.	51.45 N	43.15 E
127	Khora (kō′rȧ)............... Grc.	37.44 N	26.55 E
126	Khora Sphakion (kō′rȧ sfä-kĭ-ōn′). Grc.	35.13 N	24.9 E
141	Khorog (ᴋôr′ôg)......... Sov. Un.	37.29 N	71.40 E
129	Khorol (ᴋô′rôl).......... Sov. Un.	49.48 N	33.18 E
129	Khorol R................ Sov. Un.	49.50 N	33.30 E
140	Khorramshahr (Mohammorah) (kô-räm′shär) (mô′hȧm-mô′rä) Iran	30.31 N	48.17 E
142	Khotan (Hotien) (ᴋō-tän′) (hō′tyĕn′). Chn.	37.2 N	79.52 E
142	Khotan Darya (R.) (ᴋō-tän′ där′yä). Chn.	38.30 N	80.50 E
129	Khotin (ᴋô′tên).......... Sov. Un.	48.31 N	26.30 E
140	Khurma (ᴋōōr′mȧ)...... Sau. Ar.	21.40 N	41.45 E
140	Khurramabad (ᴋōō-rä-mä-bäd′) Iran	36.59 N	50.31 E
121	Khust (ᴋōōst).......... Sov. Un.	48.11 N	23.18 E
111	Khvalinsk (ᴋvȧ-lĭnsk′)... Sov. Un.	52.28 N	48.0 E
141	Khyber Pass (kī′bēr).... Afg.-Pak.	34.9 N	71.10 E
144	Kiahwa (kyä′hwä′)......... Chn.	25.30 N	112.4 E
142	Kialing (R.) (kyä′lĭng′)...... Chn.	32.30 N	105.32 E
134	Kiambi (kyäm′bê)..... Bel. Cong.	7.28 S	27.58 E
79	Kiamichi R. (kyȧ-mē′chê)... Okla.	34.30 N	95.30 W
148	Kiamusze (Chiamussu) (kyȧ-mōō′sĕ) (kyȧ-mōō′sōō). Chn.	46.50 N	130.20 E
145	Kian (kyän)................ Chn.	27.3 N	114.43 E
152	Kiangan (kyäŋ′gän)......... Phil.	16.47 N	121.9 E
144	Kianghwa (kyäng′hwä′)..... Chn.	25.18 N	111.30 E
145	Kiangning (Nanking) (kyäng′nĭng′) (năn′kĭng′). Chn.	32.4 N	118.45 E
144	Kiangpei (kyäng′pā′)........ Chn.	29.45 N	106.35 E
146	Kiangpu (kyäng′pōō′)....... Chn.	32.2 N	118.33 E
145	Kiangshan (kyäng′shän′).... Chn.	28.47 N	118.45 E
145	Kiangsi (Prov.) (kyäng′sē′).. Chn.	27.52 N	115.38 E
145	Kiangsu (Prov.) (kyäng′sōō′). Chn.	31.30 N	120.5 E
144	Kiangtsin (kyäng′tsēn′)..... Chn.	29.12 N	106.18 E
145	Kiangyin (kyäng′yēn′)...... Chn.	31.50 N	120.16 E
110	Kianta, L. (kyȧn′tȧ).......... Fin.	65.0 N	28.15 E
146	Kiaochow (kyou′chō′)....... Chn.	36.18 N	120.2 E
146	Kiaochow B................. Chn.	36.8 N	120.11 E
146	Kiaomi (kyou′mē′).......... Chn.	36.22 N	119.47 E
146	Kiao R. (kyou).............. Chn.	36.50 N	119.34 E
142	Kiating (kyä′tĭng′).......... Chn.	29.31 N	103.51 E
144	Kiayu (kyä′yōō′)............ Chn.	29.56 N	113.45 E
127	Kičevo (kē′chĕ-vô)......... Yugo.	41.30 N	20.59 E
145	Kichow (kē′chō′)............ Chn.	30.2 N	115.19 E
146	Kichow...................... Chn.	40.2 N	117.21 E
146	Kichow...................... Chn.	37.42 N	115.37 E
77	Kickapoo R. (kĭk′ȧ-pōō)..... Wis.	43.20 N	90.50 W
132	Kidal (kê-dȧl′)....... Fr. W. Afr.	18.36 N	1.0 E
114	Kidderminster (kĭd′ēr-mĭn-stēr) Gt. Brit.	52.25 N	2.15 W
156	Kidnappers C. (kĭd′năp-ērz). N. Z.	39.40 S	177.7 E
116	Kidsgrove (kĭdz′grōv)... Gt. Brit.	53.5 N	2.15 W
120	Kiel (kēl).................... Ger.	54.19 N	10.10 E
77	Kiel......................... Wis.	43.52 N	88.3 W
120	Kiel B....................... Ger.	54.30 N	10.30 E
120	Kiel Canal................... Ger.	54.13 N	9.33 E
121	Kielce (kyĕl′tsĕ)............. Pol.	50.51 N	20.40 E

Page	Name Pronunciation Region	Lat. °′	Long. °′
117	Kieldrecht (kĕl′drĕᴋt) Bel. (Anvers In.)	51.18 N	4.10 E
145	Kienchang (kyĕn′chäng′).... Chn.	27.32 N	116.33 E
145	Kienchang.................. Chn.	29.9 N	115.32 E
144	Kienchow (kyĕn′chō′)....... Chn.	28.10 N	109.20 E
144	Kienli (kyĕn′lē′)............ Chn.	29.48 N	112.42 E
145	Kienning (kyĕn′nĭng′)....... Chn.	27.4 N	118.15 E
145	Kienping (kyĕn′pĭng′)....... Chn.	31.10 N	119.11 E
145	Kien R. (kyĕn).............. Chn.	26.40 N	117.8 E
144	Kienshih (kyĕn′shē′)......... Chn.	30.35 N	109.16 E
144	Kiensi (kyĕn′sē′)........... Chn.	27.0 N	105.52 E
145	Kienteh (kyĕn′tā′)........... Chn.	30.7 N	117.9 E
144	Kienyang (kyĕn′yäng′)...... Chn.	27.9 N	109.33 E
145	Kienyang................... Chn.	27.22 N	117.53 E
129	Kiev (kē′yĕf)........... Sov. Un.	50.28 N	30.31 E
132	Kiffa (kēf′ȧ).......... Fr. W. Afr.	16.53 N	10.47 W
134	Kigali (kê-gä′lê)....... Bel. Cong.	1.58 S	30.2 E
134	Kigoma (kê-gō′mä).......... Tan.	4.45 S	29.40 E
119	Kihnu I. (kē′nōō)....... Sov. Un.	58.8 N	24.0 E
146	Kihsien (kē′hsyĕn′).......... Chn.	34.31 N	114.54 E
135	Kihurio (kê-hōō′rê-ō)....... Tan.	4.28 S	38.5 E
149	Kii Chan. (kē′ê)............. Jap.	34.0 N	134.48 E
145	Kiirun (Chilung) (kē′ê-rōōn′) (chē′lŏŏng′). For.	25.6 N	121.45 E
135	Kijungu (kê-jŏŏn′gŏŏ)....... Tan.	5.23 S	37.18 E
144	Kikiang (kē′kyäng′)......... Chn.	28.56 N	106.38 E
134	Kikwit (kē′kwêt)...... Bel. Cong.	5.20 S	18.55 E
118	Kil (kêl).................... Swe.	59.29 N	13.16 E
155	Kilauea (kē-lä-ōō-ā′ä)...... Haw.	22.11 N	159.28 W
155	Kilauea Crater............. Haw.	19.27 N	155.15 W
84	Kilbourn (Wisconsin Dells) (kĭl′bŏŏrn). Wis.	43.37 N	89.45 W
148	Kilchu (kĭl′chŏŏ)........... Kor.	40.58 N	129.20 E
160	Kilcoy (kĭl′koi)....... Austl. (In.)	26.54 S	152.34 E
114	Kildare (kĭl-dār′)............. Ire.	53.5 N	6.55 W
135	Kilimanjaro Mt. (kĭl-ê-män-jä′rô) Tan.	3.5 S	37.15 E
134	Kilimatinde (kĭl-ê-mä-tĭn′dȧ). Tan.	5.47 S	34.55 E
135	Kilindini (kĭl-ên-dē′nê).... Kenya	4.5 S	39.36 E
119	Kilingi-Nomme (kē′lĭŋ-gê-nôm′mĕ). Sov. Un.	58.8 N	25.2 E
111	Kilis (kē′lês)................ Tur.	36.45 N	37.15 E
129	Kiliya (kē′lyȧ)........... Sov. Un.	45.27 N	29.19 E
114	Kilkenny (Cill Cainning) (kĭl-kĕn′ê) (kĭl ᴋä′nĭg). Ire.	52.39 N	7.15 W
127	Kilkis (kĭl′kĭs)............... Grc.	40.58 N	22.53 E
114	Killala (kĭ-lä′lȧ)............. Ire.	54.15 N	9.15 W
160	Killarney (kĭ-lär′nê)... Austl. (In.)	28.19 S	152.18 E
114	Killarney.................... Ire.	52.5 N	9.35 W
76	Killdeer (kĭl′dēr)........... N. D.	47.21 N	102.43 W
88	Kill van Kul (Inlet) (kĭl văn kŭl′) N. J.-N. Y. (In.)	40.39 N	74.6 W
114	Kilmarnock (kĭl mär′nŭk) Gt. Brit.	55.35 N	4.40 W
131	Kiloango (kĭ-lō-ăŋ′gō) Ang. (Brazzaville In.)	6.0 S	15.29 E
135	Kilosa (kē-lō′sȧ)............ Tan.	6.49 S	37.3 E
158	Kilroy Downs (kĭl′roi dounz′) Austl.	19.15 S	136.5 E
114	Kilrush (kĭl′rŭsh)............ Ire.	52.40 N	9.30 W
135	Kilwa (kēl′wä).............. Tan.	8.40 S	39.22 E
76	Kimball (kĭm-bȧl).......... Neb.	41.11 N	103.40 W
76	Kimball.................... S. D.	43.45 N	98.58 W
134	Kimberley (kĭm′bēr-lĭ). U. S. Afr.	28.42 S	24.46 E
158	Kimberleys (Reg.) (kĭm′bēr-lêz) Austl.	17.0 S	126.30 E
73	Kimberly.. Ala. (Birmingham In.)	33.47 N	86.49 W
116	Kimbolton (kĭm′bŭl-tŭn). Gt. Brit.	52.19 N	0.23 W
73	Kimbrel (kĭm′brĕl) Ala. (Birmingham In.)	33.18 N	87.3 W
145	Kimen (kē′mĕn′)........... Chn.	29.52 N	117.45 E
127	Kimolos (I.) (kē′mô-lôs)..... Grc.	36.48 N	24.35 E
131	Kimpanzou (kĭm-pän-zōō′) Fr. Eq. Afr. (Brazzaville In.)	4.23 S	15.10 E
128	Kimry (kĭm′rê).......... Sov. Un.	56.53 N	37.21 E
153	Kinabatangan R. (kê-nȧ-bȧ-täŋ′gȧn). N. Bor.	5.27 N	118.0 E
153	Kinapusan Is. (kê-nȧ-pōō-sän′) Phil.	5.12 N	120.36 E
84	Kincardine (kĭn-kär′dĭn)..... Can.	44.8 N	81.40 W
141	Kinchinjunga, Mt. (kĭn-chĭn-jŏŏŋ′gȧ). Nep.	27.38 N	88.15 E
146	Kinchow (kĭn′chō′).......... Chn.	39.8 N	121.38 E
81	Kinder (kĭn′dēr)............. La.	30.30 N	92.50 W
132	Kindia (kĭn′dê-ȧ)..... Fr. W. Afr.	10.1 N	12.58 W
134	Kindu (kēn-dōō′)...... Bel. Cong.	2.58 S	25.50 E
110	Kinel R. (kê-nĕl′′)....... Sov. Un.	53.25 N	51.2 E
110	Kinel-Cherkesskaya (kê-nĕl′′-chĕr-kĕs-kä′yȧ). Sov. Un.	53.32 N	51.32 E
128	Kineshma (kê-nĕsh′mȧ).. Sov. Un.	57.26 N	42.10 E
135	Kingani R. (kĭŋ-gä′nê)...... Tan.	6.40 S	38.45 E
144	Kingchow (kĭng′chō′)....... Chn.	30.21 N	112.0 E
74	King City.................. Calif.	36.12 N	121.8 W
78	Kingfisher (kĭng′fĭsh-ēr)..... Okla.	35.42 N	97.56 W
158	King George Sd........... Austl.	35.0 S	118.0 E
159	King I...................... Austl.	39.45 S	143.55 E
128	Kingisepp (kĭŋ-gê-sĕp′).. Sov. Un.	59.21 N	28.39 E
158	King Leopold Ra. (lē′ô-pōld) Austl.	16.45 S	125.0 E
75	Kingman (kĭng′măn)........ Ariz.	35.11 N	114.3 W
78	Kingman................... Kan.	37.37 N	98.8 W
144	Kingmen (kĭng′mĕn′)........ Chn.	31.2 N	111.55 E
145	Kingning (kĭng′nĭng′)....... Chn.	27.51 N	119.42 E
160	King R......... Austl. (Tas. In.)	42.10 S	145.40 E
144	Kingshan (kĭng′shän′)....... Chn.	31.2 N	112.57 E
115	Kings Lynn (kĭngz lĭn′).. Gt. Brit.	52.45 N	0.25 E
83	Kings Mountain........... N. C.	35.11 N	81.29 W
116	Kings Norton (nôr′tŭn).. Gt. Brit.	52.25 N	1.55 W
158	King Sd.................... Austl.	16.42 S	123.30 E
71	Kings Peaks................ Utah	40.47 N	110.25 W
83	Kingsport (kĭngz′pōrt)..... Tenn.	36.33 N	82.36 W
74	Kings R.................... Calif.	36.27 N	119.45 W

Page	Name Pronunciation Region	Lat. °′	Long. °′
158	Kingston (kĭngz′tŭn)....... Austl.	36.51 S	139.51 E
55	Kingston.................... Can.	44.10 N	76.44 W
114	Kingston.............. Gt. Brit.	51.25 N	0.19 W
96	Kingston.................... Jam.	17.59 N	76.49 W
85	Kingston................... N. Y.	41.58 N	74.0 W
157	Kingston................... N. Z.	45.18 S	168.45 E
85	Kingston.................... Pa.	41.16 N	75.52 W
51	Kingston..... Wash. (Seattle In.)	47.47 N	122.30 W
91	Kingstown (kĭngz′toun). St. Vincent	13.14 N	61.12 W
83	Kingstree (kĭngz′trē)........ S. C.	33.38 N	79.50 W
80	Kingsville (kĭngz′vĭl)........ Tex.	27.32 N	97.52 W
145	Kingtehchen (kĭng′tĕ′chĕn′) . Chn.	29.26 N	117.7 E
114	Kingussie (kĭn-yŏŏs′ê)... Gt. Brit.	57.5 N	4.5 W
54	King William I............. Can.	69.10 N	98.0 W
134	Kingwilliamstown (kĭng-wĭl′yŭmz-toun). U. S. Afr.	32.52 S	27.24 E
142	Kingyang (kĭng′yäng′)...... Chn.	36.2 N	107.55 E
144	Kingyuan (kĭng′yōō-än′).... Chn.	24.29 N	108.48 E
145	Kingyüan (kĭng′yû-än′)..... Chn.	27.38 N	118.43 E
146	Kingyün (kĭng′yûn′)........ Chn.	37.53 N	117.13 E
145	Kinhwa (kēn′hwä′)......... Chn.	29.8 N	119.42 E
150	Kinibalu, Mt. (kē-nê-bä′lōō) N. Bor.	6.0 N	116.35 E
145	Kinki (kēn′kē′)............. Chn.	27.56 N	116.44 E
146	Kinkiakow (kĭn′kyä-kō′).... Chn.	36.33 N	120.49 E
89	Kinlock Park (kĭn′lŏk) Mo. (St. Louis In.)	38.45 N	90.20 W
114	Kinnaird Hd. (kĭn-ȧrd′).. Gt. Brit.	57.40 N	1.50 W
149	Kinomoto (kē′nō-mō′tō)..... Jap.	33.53 N	136.5 E
149	Kinosaki (kē′nō-sä′kê)...... Jap.	35.37 N	134.47 E
145	Kin R. (kēn)............... Chn.	28.10 N	114.58 E
114	Kinsale (kĭn-sāl′)............ Ire.	51.40 N	8.30 W
114	Kinsale Harbor............. Ire.	51.35 N	8.30 W
114	Kinsale, Old Head of......... Ire.	51.35 N	8.30 W
146	Kinsha (kĭn′shä′)........... Chn.	32.7 N	120.59 E
146	Kinsiang (kĭn′syäng′)....... Chn.	35.4 N	116.17 E
78	Kinsley (kĭnz′lĭ)............ Kan.	37.55 N	99.25 W
83	Kinston (kĭnz′tŭn).......... N. C.	35.16 N	77.36 W
142	Kinta (kĭn′tä′).............. Chn.	40.4 N	99.0 E
132	Kintampo (kēn-täm′pō).... G. C.	8.4 N	1.38 W
131	Kinzila (kēn-zê-lȧ′)... Fr. Eq. Afr.	4.36 S	15.0 E
133	Kioga, L. (kē-ō′gȧ)........... Ug.	1.30 N	33.0 E
146	Kioshan (kyō′shän′)......... Chn.	32.51 N	113.53 E
78	Kiowa (kī′ô-wȧ)............ Kan.	37.1 N	98.29 W
79	Kiowa...................... Okla.	34.43 N	95.54 W
134	Kipembawe (kê-pĕm-bä′wȧ) . Tan.	7.45 S	33.23 E
81	Kirbyville (kŭr′bĭ-vĭl)....... Tex.	30.39 N	93.55 W
117	Kirchbach (kĭrᴋ′bäᴋ) Aus. (Wien In.)	48.17 N	16.13 E
117	Kirchsteinbek (kĭrᴋ′shtīn-bĕk) Ger. (Hamburg In.)	53.32 N	10.8 E
135	Kirdâsa (kĭr-dä′sȧ)........... Eg.	30.3 N	31.6 E
139	Kirenga R. (kê-rĕŋ′gȧ)... Sov. Un.	56.0 N	107.30 E
139	Kirensk (kē-rĕnsk′)...... Sov. Un.	57.45 N	108.15 E
138	Kirghiz (Aut. Rep.) (kĭr-gēz′) Sov. Un.	48.0 N	68.0 E
111	Kirghiz Steppe.......... Sov. Un.	48.45 N	56.0 E
142	Kirgis Nor (L.) (kĭr′gĭs nōr′) Mong.	49.10 N	93.15 E
143	Kirin (Chilin) (kĭ′rĭn) (chĭ-lĭn′) Chn.	43.50 N	126.36 E
149	Kirishima (Mt.) (kē′rê-shē′mȧ) Jap.	31.55 N	130.50 E
117	Kirkby (kûrk′bê) Gt. Brit. (Liverpool In.)	53.29 N	2.54 W
116	Kirkby-in-Ashfield (ăsh′fēld) Gt. Brit.	53.6 N	1.16 W
116	Kirkby Lonsdale (lŏnz′dāl) Gt. Brit.	54.12 N	2.36 W
114	Kirkcaldy (kēr-kô′dĭ).... Gt. Brit.	56.5 N	3.10 W
116	Kirkham (kûrk′ăm)..... Gt. Brit.	53.47 N	2.53 W
51	Kirkland (kûrk′lănd) Wash. (Seattle In.)	47.41 N	122.12 W
55	Kirkland Lake (kûrk′lȧnd)... Can.	48.10 N	80.0 W
111	Kirklareli (kêrk′lȧr-ĕ′lê)..... Tur.	41.45 N	27.12 E
79	Kirksville (kûrks′vĭl)........ Mo.	40.12 N	92.35 W
140	Kirkuk (kĭr-kōōk′).......... Iraq	35.29 N	44.29 E
114	Kirkwall (kûrk′wôl). Gt. Brit. (In.)	59.0 N	2.55 W
73	Kirkwood (kûrk′wŏŏd) Ga. (Atlanta In.)	33.46 N	84.18 W
79	Kirkwood (kûrk′wŏŏd)....... Mo.	38.34 N	90.25 W
120	Kirn (kêrn)................ Ger.	49.47 N	7.23 E
129	Kirovo (Zinove′vsk) (kêr′ō-vō) (zē-nô′vyĕfsk). Sov. Un.	48.31 N	32.15 E
110	Kirovsk (kê-rôfsk′)...... Sov. Un.	67.32 N	32.46 E
111	Kirsanov (kêr-sȧ′nôf).... Sov. Un.	52.40 N	42.40 E
111	Kirşehir (kêr-shĕ′hēr)....... Tur.	39.5 N	34.0 E
141	Kirthar Ra. (Mts.) (kĭr-tŭr) . Pak.	26.15 N	67.0 E
116	Kirton (kûr′tŭn)........ Gt. Brit.	53.29 N	0.35 W
134	Kiru, L. (kē-rōō′)...... Bel. Cong.	2.0 S	29.0 E
108	Kiruna (kē-rōō′nä).......... Swe.	67.50 N	20.15 E
149	Kiryu (kē′rĭ-ŏŏ)............ Jap.	36.20 N	139.20 E
128	Kirzhach (kêr-zhäᴋ′).... Sov. Un.	56.8 N	38.52 E
149	Kisabe (kē′sȧ-bā). Jap. (Osaka In.)	34.48 N	135.42 E
135	Kisaki (kē-sȧ′kē)........... Tan.	7.28 S	37.40 E
135	Kisanga Mts. (kē-säŋ′gä).... Moz.	12.30 S	38.30 E
149	Kisarazu (kē′sȧ-rȧ′zōō) Jap. (Tokyo In.)	35.24 N	139.55 E
134	Kisenyi (kē-sĕn′yē)... : Bel. Cong.	1.38 S	29.15 E
135	Kiserawe (kê-sȧ-rô′wā)...... Tan.	6.53 S	39.4 E
129	Kishinev (kê-shê-nyôf′).. Sov. Un.	47.2 N	28.52 E
149	Kishiwada (kē′shê-wä′dä).... Jap.	34.24 N	135.18 E
110	Kishtim (kēsh-tēm′)..... Sov. Un.	55.45 N	60.40 E
145	Kishui (kĭsh′wē′)........... Chn.	27.10 N	115.0 E
145	Kishui...................... Chn.	30.27 N	115.10 E
135	Kisiwani (kê-sê-wä′nê)...... Tan.	4.6 S	37.59 E
52	Kiska I. (kĭs′kȧ)........... Alsk.	52.20 N	175.45 E
121	Kiskörös (kĭsh′kû-rûsh).... Hung.	46.37 N	19.17 E
121	Kiskunfélegyháza (kĭsh′kŏŏn-fā′-lĕd-y′hä′zô). Hung.	46.43 N	19.51 E
121	Kiskunhalas (kĭsh′kŏŏn-hô′lôsh) Hung.	46.25 N	19.29 E

ăt; finăl; rāte; senâte; ärm; ȧsk; sofȧ; fâre; ch-choose; dh-as th in other; bē; ēvent; bĕt; recĕnt; cratēr; g-go; gh-gutteral g; bĭt; ĭ-short neutral; rīde; ᴋ-gutteral k as ch in German ich;

Kiskunmajsa PRONOUNCING INDEX **Kotabaro**

Page	Name Pronunciation Region	Lat. °′	Long. °′
121	Kiskunmajsa (kĭsh'kŏŏn-mī'shô) Hung.	46.30 N	19.45 E
111	Kislovodsk (kēs-lô-vôtsk') Sov. Un.	43.58 N	42.43 E
149	Kisogawa, R. (kē'sō-gä'wä) Jap.	35.28 N	137.15 E
121	Kispest (kĭsh'pĕsht) Hung.	47.28 N	19.12 E
126	Kissamos Kastelli (kē-sä'mōs käs-tĕl'ē) Grc.	35.28 N	23.39 E
132	Kissidougou (kē'sē-dōō'gōō) Fr. W. Afr.	9.20 N	10.15 W
83	Kissimmee (kĭ-sĭm'ē) Fla. (In.)	28.17 N	81.23 W
83	Kissimmee, L. Fla. (In.)	27.55 N	81.17 W
141	Kistna R. (kĭst'nȧ) India	16.15 N	76.0 E
108	Kistrand (kē'stränd) Nor.	70.30 N	25.5 E
121	Kisújszállás (kĭsh'ōō'y'-sä'läsh) Hung.	47.12 N	20.46 E
133	Kisumu (kē'sōō-mōō) Kenya	0.3 S	34.51 E
132	Kita (kē'tȧ) Fr. W. Afr.	13.9 N	9.30 W
142	Kitai (Kuchengtze) (kē'tī') (kōō'chĕng'tzē') Chn.	44.3 N	89.22 E
84	Kitchener (kĭch'ĕ-nēr) Can.	43.25 N	80.35 W
55	Kitchioh (kĭt'chĭ-ō') Chn.	22.50 N	115.40 E
134	Kitega (kê-tā'gȧ) Bel. Cong.	3.20 S	30.5 E
133	Kitgum (kĭt'gōōm) Ug.	3.22 N	33.2 E
75	Kitsil Ruin (kĭt'sĭl) Ariz.	36.46 N	110.32 W
149	Kitsuki (kēt'sōō-kē) Jap.	33.24 N	131.35 E
85	Kittaning (kĭ-tăn'ĭng) Pa.	40.50 N	79.32 W
86	Kittery (kĭt'ēr-ĭ) Me.	43.5 N	70.45 W
145	Kityang (kĭt'yäng') Chn.	23.33 N	116.9 E
120	Kitzingen (kĭt'zĭng-ĕn) Ger.	49.45 N	10.8 E
145	Kiukiang (kyōō'kyäng') Chn.	29.40 N	115.52 E
148	Kiuliencheng (kyōō'lyĕn-chĕng') Chn.	40.15 N	124.29 E
145	Kiulung R. (kyōō'lōōng') Chn.	25.0 N	117.24 E
150	Kiungchow (kyōōng'chō') Chn.	19.59 N	110.15 E
135	Kivale (kē-vä'lē) Kenya	4.11 S	39.28 E
144	Kiyang (kē'yäng') Chn.	26.28 N	111.46 E
138	Kizel (kē'zĕl) Sov. Un.	59.10 N	57.40 E
111	Kizil Irmak (R.) (kĭz'ĭl ĭr-mäk') Tur.	40.28 N	33.45 E
111	Kizlyar (kĭz-lyär') Sov. Un.	43.58 N	46.45 E
149	Kizu (kē'zōō) Jap.	34.44 N	135.46 E
149	Kizuki (kē'zōō-kē) Jap.	35.24 N	132.40 E
108	Kjölen Mts. (chû'lĕn) Swe.-Nor.	63.00 N	12.00 E
120	Kladno (kläd'nō) Czech.	50.9 N	14.6 E
120	Klagenfurt (klä'gĕn-fōōrt) Aus.	46.38 N	14.18 E
119	Klaipéda (Memel) (klī'pā-dȧ) (mā'mĕl) Sov. Un.	55.42 N	21.10 E
70	Klamath Falls (klăm'ăth) Ore.	42.12 N	121.48 W
70	Klamath L., Lower Ore.-Calif.	41.59 N	121.49 W
70	Klamath L., Upper Ore.	42.20 N	121.30 W
70	Klamath Mts. Ore.-Calif.	42.0 N	123.20 W
70	Klamath R. Ore.-Calif.	41.30 N	124.3 W
118	Klar R. (klär) Swe.	60.38 N	13.0 E
51	Klaskunine Cr. (kläs'kû-nīn) Ore. (Portland In.)	46.3 N	123.5 W
51	Klaskunine R. Ore. (Portland In.)	46.2 N	123.42 W
120	Klatovy (klä'tô-vē) Czech.	49.24 N	13.17 E
	Klausenberg, see Cluj, Rom.		
117	Klein-Machnow (klīn-mäĸ'nō) Ger. (Berlin In.)	52.24 N	13.14 E
128	Kletnya (klyĕt'nyȧ) Sov. Un.	53.18 N	33.11 E
128	Kletsk (klĕtsk) Sov. Un.	53.2 N	26.40 E
70	Klickitat R. (klĭk'ĭ-tăt) Wash.	45.50 N	121.5 W
128	Klimovichi (klē-mô-vē'chē) Sov. Un.	53.36 N	31.58 E
128	Klin (klēn) Sov. Un.	56.18 N	36.43 E
153	Kling (klĭng) Phil.	5.58 N	124.42 E
118	Klintehamn (klĕn'tē-häm) Swe.	57.24 N	18.12 E
128	Klintsy (klĭn'tsĭ) Sov. Un.	52.45 N	32.12 E
126	Ključ (klyōōch) Yugo.	44.33 N	16.47 E
121	Klobuck (kwō'bōōtsk) Pol.	50.53 N	18.58 E
120	Klodzko (klôd'skô) Pol.	50.27 N	16.38 E
108	Klofa-Jökull (Vatna-Jökull) (Glacier) (klō'fá-yû'kōōl) (vät'nȧ-yû'kōōl) Ice.	64.30 N	16.45 W
53	Klondike R. (klŏn'dīk) Can.	64.0 N	138.30 W
54	Klondike Reg. Can.	64.0 N	140.0 W
120	Klosterneuberg (klōs-tēr-noi'bōōrgh) Aus.	48.18 N	16.17 E
53	Kluane L. (klōō-ăn') Can.	61.15 N	139.0 W
121	Kluczborek (klōōch-bô'rĕk) Pol.	50.58 N	18.13 E
52	Klutina L. (klōō-tē'nȧ) Alsk. (In.)	61.40 N	146.7 W
128	Klyazma R. (klyäz'mȧ) Sov. Un.	56.1 N	40.10 E
139	Klyuchevskaya (Vol.) (klyōō-chĕf-skä'yȧ) Sov. Un.	56.10 N	160.55 E
51	Knappa (năp'ȧ) Ore. (Portland In.)	46.11 N	123.35 W
116	Knaresborough (nârz'bŭr-ô) Gt. Brit.	54.1 N	1.28 W
131	Kneiss I. (knĕ-ĕs') Tun. (In.)	34.22 N	10.17 E
127	Kneža (knyä'zhȧ) Bul.	43.29 N	24.3 E
76	Knife R. N. D.	47.11 N	102.0 W
52	Knight I. Alsk. (In.)	60.20 N	147.50 W
84	Knightstown (nīts'toun) Ind.	39.45 N	85.32 W
134	Kwilu R. (kwē'lōō) Fr. Eq. Afr.-Bel. Cong.	3.30 S	12.30 E
121	Knihinin (knê-hē'nĕn) Sov. Un.	48.57 N	24.45 E
126	Knin (knēn) Yugo.	44.3 N	16.14 E
120	Knittelfeld (knĭt''l-fĕlt) Aus.	47.14 N	14.49 E
157	Knobbs, The (Mt.) N. Z. (In.)	43.39 S	172.38 E
152	Knob Pk. (nŏb) Phil.	12.28 N	121.20 E
114	Knockmealdown Mts. (nŏk-mēl'doun) Ire.	52.15 N	8.0 W
116	Knottingley (nŏt'ĭng-lĭ) Gt. Brit.	53.42 N	1.14 W
117	Knowsley (nōz'lĭ) Gt. Brit. (Liverpool In.)	53.28 N	2.51 W
84	Knox (nŏks) Ind.	41.18 N	86.40 W
77	Knoxville (nŏks'vĭl) Ia.	41.18 N	93.5 W
82	Knoxville Tenn.	35.58 N	83.57 W
116	Knutsford (nŭts'fērd) Gt. Brit.	53.18 N	2.22 W
128	Knyaz, L. (knyäz) Sov. Un.	52.25 N	27.59 E
121	Knyszyn (knĭ'shĭn) Pol.	53.16 N	22.58 E
149	Kobayashi (kō'bȧ-yä'shē) Jap.	32.0 N	130.58 E
	Kobdo, see Chirgalantu, Mong.		
142	Kobdo R. (kôb'dō') Mong.	49.20 N	91.0 E
149	Kobe (kō'bĕ) Jap.	34.40 N	135.10 E
129	Kobelyaki (kō-bĕl-yä'kē) Sov. Un.	49.8 N	34.12 E
118	København (kû-b'n-houn') Den.	55.40 N	12.34 E
120	Koblenz (kō'blĕntz) Ger.	50.22 N	7.35 E
128	Kobozha R. (kô-bō'zhȧ) Sov. Un.	58.44 N	34.59 E
121	Kobrin (kō'brēn') Sov. Un.	52.13 N	24.23 E
52	Kobuk R. (kō'bŭk) Alsk.	67.0 N	160.0 W
111	Kobuleti (kô-bōō-lyā'tē) Sov. Un.	41.50 N	41.45 E
127	Kočane (kô'chä-nē) Yugo.	41.54 N	22.24 E
126	Kočevje (kô'chāv-yĕ) Yugo.	45.38 N	14.50 E
142	Kocha (Kuche) (kō'chä') (kōō'chē') Chn.	41.32 N	82.58 E
147	Kŏchang (kŭ'chäng') Kor.	35.44 N	127.56 E
120	Kocher R. (kôĸ'ēr) Ger.	49.10 N	9.45 E
149	Kochi (kō'chē) Jap.	33.35 N	133.30 E
53	Kodiak (kō'dyăk) Alsk.	57.40 N	152.30 W
53	Kodiak I. Alsk.	57.20 N	153.30 W
133	Kodok (ko'dŏk) A. E. Sud.	9.57 N	32.2 E
72	Koenig (kû'nĕg) Colo. (Denver In.)	40.23 N	104.57 W
151	Koepang (kōō'päng) Indon.	10.15 S	123.42 E
147	Koesan (kō'ĕ-san) Kor.	36.47 N	127.50 E
120	Koesfeld (kûs'fĕlt) Ger.	51.56 N	7.10 E
150	Koetaradja (kōō'tȧ-räd'jȧ) Indon.	5.29 N	95.23 E
132	Koforidua (kō-fô-rĭ-dōō'ȧ) G. C.	6.4 N	0.15 W
149	Kofu (kō'fōō') Jap.	35.41 N	138.32 E
149	Koga (kō'gȧ) Jap.	36.12 N	139.42 E
160	Kogarah (kō-gä'rȧ) Austl. (Sydney In.)	33.58 S	151.8 E
118	Köge (kû'gĕ) Den.	55.27 N	12.10 E
129	Kogilnik R. (kô-gēl-nēk') Sov. Un.	45.25 N	30.30 E
149	Kohana (kō'hȧ-nȧ) Jap. (Osaka In.)	34.49 N	135.21 E
141	Kohima (kô-ē'mȧ) India	25.45 N	94.15 E
156	Kohukohu (kô-hōō-kô-hōō') N. Z.	35.20 S	173.30 E
147	Kohŭng (kō'hōōng) Kor.	34.38 N	127.18 E
128	Koidanovo (koi-dȧ'nô-vô) Sov. Un.	53.40 N	27.8 E
127	Koinare (koi'nä-rĕ) Bul.	43.22 N	24.8 E
128	Koivisto (koi-vēs'tô) Sov. Un.	60.28 N	28.35 E
147	Kŏje I. (kŭ'jĕ) Kor.	34.57 N	128.37 E
121	Kojetin (kō'yĕ-tyēn) Czech.	49.21 N	17.19 E
147	Kojo (kō'jō') Kor.	38.50 N	128.20 E
138	Kokand (kô-känt') Sov. Un.	40.30 N	70.50 E
138	Kokchetav (kôk'chĕ-tȧf) Sov. Un.	53.25 N	69.20 E
119	Kokemäen R. (kô'kē-mȧ'ĕn) Fin.	61.20 N	22.9 E
134	Kokenap (kō'kē-năp) U. S. Afr.	31.28 S	18.28 E
128	Kokhma (kôĸ'mȧ) Sov. Un.	56.56 N	41.9 E
110	Kokkola (kô'kô-lȧ) Fin.	63.50 N	23.10 E
84	Kokomo (kō'kô-mō) Ind.	40.30 N	86.9 W
142	Koko Nor (L.) (kō'kō nôr) Chn.	37.0 N	100.0 E
151	Kokopo (kô-kô'pō) N. Gui. Ter.	4.22 S	152.27 E
138	Kokpektinskaya (kôk'pĕk-tēn'skȧ-yȧ) Sov. Un.	48.55 N	82.15 E
147	Koksan (kôk'sän) Kor.	38.47 N	120.39 E
72	Koksilah R. (kŏk'sē-lȧ) Can. (Vancouver In.)	48.39 N	123.45 W
55	Koksoak R. (kŏk'sô-ăk) Can.	58.0 N	69.0 W
147	Koksŭng (kôk'sōōng') Kor.	35.18 N	127.19 E
149	Kokubu (kō'kōō-bōō) Jap.	31.42 N	130.48 E
149	Kokubu Jap. (Osaka In.)	34.34 N	135.39 E
149	Kokura (kō'kōō-rä) Jap.	33.47 N	130.52 E
108	Kola (kō'lȧ) Sov. Un.	68.58 N	33.10 E
132	Kolahun (kō-lä'hōōn) Lib.	8.30 N	10.8 W
110	Kola Pen. (kō'lȧ) Sov. Un.	67.30 N	37.0 E
141	Kolar (kô-lär') India	13.15 N	77.59 E
	Kolberg, see Kolobrzeg, Pol.		
128	Kolchugino (kôl-chōō'gē-nô) Sov. Un.	56.16 N	39.28 E
118	Kolding (kŭl'dĭng) Den.	55.28 N	9.26 E
134	Kole (kō'lȧ) Bel. Cong.	3.20 S	22.43 E
110	Kolguev I. (kôl-gōō'yĕf) Sov. Un.	69.15 N	49.0 E
141	Kolhapur (kōl'hȧ-pōōr) India	16.45 N	74.2 E
120	Kolin (kō'lēn) Czech.	50.1 N	15.12 E
133	Kollo, Mt. (kōl'ō) Eth.	11.5 N	39.15 E
120	Köln (kûln) Ger.	50.57 N	6.57 E
121	Kolno (kôw'nô) Pol.	53.25 N	21.57 E
121	Kolo (kô'wô) Pol.	52.11 N	18.37 E
120	Kolobrzeg (kô-lôb'zhĕk) Pol.	54.9 N	15.35 E
128	Kolomna (kȧl-ôm'nȧ) Sov. Un.	55.5 N	38.49 E
121	Kolomyya (kō'lô-mē'yȧ) Sov. Un.	48.32 N	25.2 E
129	Kolosovka (kô-lô-sôf'kȧ) Sov. Un.	47.17 N	30.59 E
128	Kolpino (kôl'pē-nô) Sov. Un.	59.45 N	30.39 E
128	Kolpny (kôlp'nyē) Sov. Un.	52.12 N	36.52 E
128	Kolp R. (kôlp) Sov. Un.	59.25 N	35.40 E
139	Kolyma R. (kô-lē-mȧ') Sov. Un.	66.0 N	151.30 E
139	Kolymski Ridge (kô-lēm'skē) Sov. Un.	61.30 N	150.0 E
138	Kolyvan (kôl-ē-văn') Sov. Un.	55.25 N	82.50 E
137	Komandorskie Is. Sov. Un.	55.0 N	172.0 W
120	Komarno (kô'mär-nô) Czech.	47.47 N	18.8 E
121	Komárno (kô'mär'nô) Sov. Un.	49.37 N	23.43 E
121	Komárom (kô'mä-rôm) Hung.	47.44 N	18.6 E
134	Komatipoort (kō-mä'tē-pōrt) U. S. Afr.	25.25 S	31.55 E
149	Komatsu (kō-mät'sōō) Jap.	36.20 N	136.30 E
135	Kôm Bira (kôm' bē'ra) Eg.	30.5 N	31.8 E
110	Komi (Zyryan) (Aut. Ter.) (kō'mē) (zĭr'ĭ-ăn) Sov. Un.	64.0 N	55.0 E
132	Komodugu-Yobe R. (kō-mô-dōō'gōō-yō'bā) Nig.	12.52 N	11.0 E
127	Komotēnē (kô-mô-tē'nē) Grc.	41.7 N	25.23 E
150	Kompongthom (kŏm'pŏng-tŏm) Indoch.	12.38 N	104.41 E
129	Komrat (kôm-rät') Sov. Un.	46.17 N	28.39 E
139	Komsomolsk (kôm-sô-môlsk') Sov. Un.	50.45 N	137.5 E
111	Komsomol'tsa G. (kôm-sô-môl'tsȧ) Sov. Un.	45.30 N	54.15 E
142	Konche Darya (R.) (kōn'chĕ där'yä) Chn.	40.45 N	87.30 E
110	Konda R. (kôn'dȧ) Sov. Un.	60.25 N	63.50 E
134	Kondoa Irangi (kôn-dō'ȧ ē-räŋ'gē) Tan.	4.50 S	35.55 E
129	Konevskaya (kô-nyôf'skȧ-yȧ) Sov. Un.	46.5 N	38.56 E
132	Kong (kŏng) Fr. W. Afr.	9.7 N	4.36 W
132	Kong (Prov.) Fr. W. Afr.	9.30 N	4.30 W
135	Konge (kôŋ'gȧ) Tan.	5.51 S	37.53 E
147	Kongju (kŏng'jōō) Kor.	36.28 N	127.8 E
144	Kongmoon (kông'mōōn') Chn.	22.34 N	113.0 E
144	Kongmoon City Chn.	22.30 N	112.59 E
134	Kongolo (kôŋ'gō'lō) Bel. Cong.	5.18 S	26.57 E
118	Kongsberg (kŭngs'bĕrg) Nor.	59.40 N	9.39 E
118	Kongsvinger (kŭngs'vĭŋ-gēr) Nor.	60.12 N	12.0 E
	Königsberg, see Kaliningrad, Sov. Un.		
134	Koni Hill (kō'nē) Bel. Cong.	10.34 S	27.22 E
121	Konin (kô'nyēn) Pol.	52.11 N	18.15 E
127	Konitsa (kô'nyē'tsȧ) Grc.	40.4 N	20.45 E
127	Konjic (kôn'yēts) Yugo.	43.38 N	17.59 E
129	Konotop (kō-nô-tôp') Sov. Un.	51.13 N	33.13 E
121	Końskie (koin''skyĕ) Pol.	51.11 N	20.26 E
129	Konstantinov (kôn-stán-tē'nôf) Sov. Un.	49.46 N	27.12 E
129	Konstantinovka (kôn-stán-tē'-nôf-kȧ) Sov. Un.	47.49 N	31.11 E
129	Konstantinovka-Dmitrievka (kôn-stán-tē'nôf-kȧ-dmē'trē-yĕf'kȧ) Sov. Un.	48.33 N	37.39 E
120	Konstanz (Constance) (kôn'shtänts) (kŏn'stȧns) Switz.	47.39 N	9.11 E
132	Kontagora (kōn-tȧ-gō'rȧ) Nig.	10.30 N	5.30 E
132	Kontcha (kōn'chȧ) Cam.	8.0 N	12.20 E
111	Konya (kōn'yȧ) Tur.	37.52 N	32.30 E
160	Koonyum Range (kō-ŭn-yōōm') Austl. (In.)	28.30 S	153.12 E
158	Kooringa (Burra) (kō-ŭ-rĭŋ'gȧ) (bōōr'ȧ) Austl.	33.40 S	138.58 E
54	Kootenay L. (kōō'tē-nȧ) Can.	49.50 N	116.30 W
70	Kootenay Landing Can.	49.15 N	116.42 W
70	Kootenay R. U. S.-Can.	48.50 N	116.20 W
138	Kopal (kô-päl') Sov. Un.	45.20 N	79.0 E
118	Kopervik (kô'pĕr-vēk) Nor.	59.18 N	5.20 E
110	Kopeysk (kô-pāsk') Sov. Un.	55.6 N	61.37 E
118	Köping (chû'pĭng) Swe.	59.31 N	15.59 E
118	Kopparberg (kŏp'pȧr-bĕrgh) Swe.	59.52 N	15.0 E
126	Koprivnica (kô'prēv-nē'tsȧ) Yugo.	46.9 N	16.51 E
121	Kopychyntse (kô-pê-chēn'tsĕ) Sov. Un.	49.6 N	26.54 E
127	Korçë (Korica) (kôr'chĕ) (kô'rĭt-sȧ) Alb.	40.36 N	20.49 E
126	Korčula (I.) (kôr'chōō-lȧ) Yugo.	42.55 N	16.55 E
133	Kordofan Plat. (kôr-dô-făn') A. E. Sud.	11.30 N	30.30 E
147	Korea (Chosen) (kô-rē'ȧ) Asia	38.0 N	127.0 E
147	Korea B. Kor.	39.15 N	123.30 E
147	Korean Arch. Kor.	34.11 N	126.45 E
147	Korea Str. Kor.	34.35 N	129.0 E
132	Korhogo (kôr-hō'gō) Fr. W. Afr.	9.28 N	5.18 W
127	Korica (Korçë) (kô-rĭt'sȧ) (kôr'chĕ) Alb.	40.36 N	20.49 E
150	Korinchi, Mt. (kô-rĕn'chē) Indon.	1.45 S	101.21 E
127	Korinthos (Corinth) (kô-rēn'thôs) (kŏr'ĭnth) Grc.	37.55 N	22.55 E
149	Koriyama (kō'rê-yä'mä) Jap.	34.37 N	135.43 E
148	Koriyama Jap.	37.20 N	140.20 E
139	Korkodon R. (kôr'kô-dôn') Sov. Un.	63.30 N	153.0 E
120	Körmend (kûr'mĕnt) Hung.	47.2 N	16.35 E
126	Kornat (I.) (kôr-nät') Yugo.	43.45 N	15.20 E
120	Korneuburg (kôr'noi-bōōrgh) Aus.	48.22 N	16.20 E
129	Korocha (kô-rō'chȧ) Sov. Un.	50.50 N	37.11 E
135	Korogwe (kô-rō'gwĕ) Tan.	5.8 S	38.38 E
153	Koronadal (kô'rō-nȧ-däl') Phil.	6.7 N	125.2 E
129	Korop (kō'rôp) Sov. Un.	51.32 N	32.53 E
151	Koror (kō'rôr) Palau Is.	7.16 N	134.32 E
160	Kororoit Cr. (kō'rō-rō'ĕt) Austl. (Melbourne In.)	37.47 S	144.48 E
129	Korosten (kô'rôs-tĕn) Sov. Un.	50.58 N	28.40 E
129	Korostishev (kô-rôs'tē-shôf) Sov. Un.	50.20 N	29.0 E
129	Korotoyak (kô'rô-tô-yȧk') Sov. Un.	50.59 N	39.5 E
148	Korsakov (kôr'sȧ-kôf') Sakh.	46.38 N	142.45 E
119	Korsnäs (kôrs'nĕs) Fin.	62.45 N	21.10 E
118	Korsör (kôrs'ûr') Den.	55.18 N	11.7 E
133	Korti (kôr'tē) A. E. Sud.	18.10 N	31.33 E
129	Koryukovka (kôr-yōō-kôf'kȧ) Sov. Un.	51.45 N	32.22 E
120	Kóscian (kŭsh'tsyȧn) Pol.	52.5 N	16.37 E
121	Kościerzyna (kŭsh-tsyĕ-zhĕ'nȧ) Pol.	54.7 N	17.59 E
82	Kosciusko (kŏs-ĭ-ŭs'kō) Miss.	33.3 N	89.37 W
159	Kosciusko, Mt. Austl.	36.28 S	148.16 E
133	Kosha (kō'shä) A. E. Sud.	20.55 N	30.33 E
143	Koshan (kō'shän') Chn.	48.20 N	126.0 E
149	Koshiki Is. (kō-shē'kē) Jap.	31.45 N	129.45 E
121	Košice (kō'shē-tsĕ) Czech.	48.43 N	21.15 E
142	Koso Gol (L.) (kō'sō gōl') Mong.	51.0 N	100.30 E
147	Kŏsŏng (kŭ'sŭng) Kor.	34.58 N	128.20 E
121	Kossovo (kôs'sô-vô) Sov. Un.	52.45 N	25.12 E
126	Kostajnica (kôs'tä-ē-nē'tsȧ) Yugo.	45.14 N	16.33 E
133	Kosti (kôs'tē) A. E. Sud.	13.8 N	32.35 E
128	Kostroma (kôs-trô-mȧ') Sov. Un.	57.46 N	40.59 E
128	Kostroma (Dist.) Sov. Un.	58.12 N	41.50 E
128	Kostroma R. Sov. Un.	58.18 N	41.10 E
120	Kostrzyn (kôst'chēn) Pol.	52.35 N	14.39 E
120	Koszalin (kô-shä'lĭn) Pol.	54.11 N	16.10 E
120	Köszeg (kû'sĕg) Hung.	47.22 N	16.31 E
150	Kotabaro (kō'tȧ-bä'rō) Indon.	3.20 S	116.10 E

ng-sing; ŋ-baŋk; ɴ-nasalized n; nŏd; cŏmmit; ōld; ōbey; ôrder; fōōd; fŏŏt; ou-out; s-soft; sh-dish; th-thin; pūre; ūnite; ûrn; stŭd; circŭs; ü-as "y" in study; '-indeterminate vowel.

Page	Name Pronunciation Region	Lat. °′	Long. °′
149	Kotachi (kō'tä-chê) Jap. (Osaka In.)	34.38 N	135.39 E
134	Kota Kota (kō-tȧ kō'tȧ) Nya.	12.50 S	34.13 E
133	Kota R. (kō'tȧ) Fr. Eq. Afr.	6.0 N	22.0 E
127	Kotel (kō-tĕl') Bul.	42.53 N	26.26 E
129	Kotelevka (kô'tĕ-lyĕf'kȧ) Sov. Un.	50.2 N	34.42 E
139	Kotelni I. (kô-tyĕl'nê) Sov. Un.	75.10 N	140.0 E
110	Kotelnich (kô-tyĕl'nêch) Sov. Un.	58.20 N	48.20 E
120	Köthen (kû'tĕn) Ger.	51.46 N	11.58 E
119	Kotka (kŏt'kȧ) Fin.	60.28 N	27.0 E
110	Kotlas (kôt'lȧs) Sov. Un.	61.15 N	46.45 E
126	Kotor (kō'tôr) Yugo.	42.25 N	18.48 E
128	Kotorost R. (kō-tôr-ôst') Sov. Un.	57.16 N	39.40 E
120	Kottbus (kôt'bo͞os) Ger.	51.47 N	14.20 E
138	Kotul R. (kô-to͞ol') Sov. Un.	68.0 N	102.0 E
52	Kotzebue (kôt'sĕ-bo͞o) Alsk.	66.40 N	162.30 W
53	Kotzebue Sd. Alsk.	66.30 N	163.0 W
132	Kouandé (kwän-dā') Fr. W. Afr.	10.25 N	1.40 E
132	Koudougou (ko͞o-do͞o'go͞o) Fr. W. Afr.	12.7 N	2.15 W
132	Koulikoro (ko͞o-lê-kō'rō) Fr. W. Afr.	13.0 N	7.30 W
132	Koumbia (ko͝om'bê-ä) Fr. W. Afr.	11.36 N	13.3 W
133	Koundé (ko͞on-dā') Fr. Eq. Afr.	6.3 N	14.34 E
138	Kounrad (ko͞on'rät) Sov. Un.	46.59 N	75.0 E
132	Kouroussa (ko͞o-ro͞o'sä) Fr. W. Afr.	10.42 N	10.0 W
132	Koutiala (ko͞o-tê-ä'lä) Fr. W. Afr.	12.30 N	5.22 W
119	Kouvola (kō'o͝o-vô-lä) Fin.	60.45 N	26.45 E
110	Kovda, L. (kôv'dȧ) Sov. Un.	66.45 N	32.0 E
121	Kovel (kō'vĕl) Sov. Un.	51.12 N	24.43 E
119	Kovno (Kaunas) (kôv'nô) Sov. Un.	54.53 N	23.54 E
128	Kovrov (kôv-rôf') Sov. Un.	56.22 N	41.20 E
144	Kowloon (kō'lo͞on') Hong Kong	22.22 N	114.6 E
147	Kowŏn (kō'ŏn') Kor.	39.28 N	127.12 E
149	Koya (kō'yȧ) Jap. (Osaka In.)	34.47 N	135.23 E
52	Koyukuk R. (kô-yo͞o'ko͝ok) Alsk.	66.0 N	156.0 W
127	Kozanē (kô-zhä'nä) Grc.	40.17 N	21.50 E
129	Kozelets (kô'zĕ-lyĕts) Sov. Un.	50.53 N	31.5 E
128	Kozelsk (kô-zĕlsk') Sov. Un.	54.2 N	35.51 E
129	Kozhech (kô-zhĕch') Sov. Un.	50.35 N	27.12 E
121	Kozienice (kō-zyĕ-nē'tsĕ) Pol.	51.34 N	21.34 E
121	Koźle (kôzh'lĕ) Pol.	50.19 N	18.9 E
139	Kozlovskaya (kŏz-lôf'skȧ'yȧ) Sov. Un.	47.0 N	134.0 E
127	Kozlodui (kŭz'lô-dwē) Bul.	43.46 N	23.42 E
149	Kozushima (Seven Is.) (kō'zo͞o-shē'mȧ) Jap.	34.12 N	139.8 E
150	Kra Bin (krȧ bĕn) Siam	13.52 N	101.37 E
118	Kragerö (krä'gĕr-û) Nor.	58.53 N	9.25 E
127	Kragujevac (krä'go͞o'yĕ-vats) Yugo.	44.1 N	20.56 E
121	Kraków (krä'ko͝of) Pol.	50.5 N	19.59 E
127	Kraljevo (kräl'ye-vô) Yugo.	43.42 N	20.43 E
129	Kramatorskaya (krȧ-mȧ-tôr'skȧ-yȧ) Sov. Un.	48.45 N	37.32 E
118	Kramfors (kräm'fôrs) Swe.	62.55 N	17.50 E
126	Kranj (krȧn') Yugo.	46.15 N	14.23 E
129	Krasilov (krä'sê-lôf) Sov. Un.	49.41 N	27.1 E
119	Kràslava (kräs'lȧ-vä) Sov. Un.	55.52 N	27.12 E
120	Kraslice (kräs'lē-tsĕ) Czech.	50.19 N	12.29 E
121	Kraśnik (kräsh'nĭk) Pol.	50.54 N	22.14 E
129	Krasnoarmeisk (Yalta) (kräs'nô-ȧr-mä'ēsk) (yäl'tä) Sov. Un.	44.29 N	34.10 E
111	Krasnoarmeiskoe (kräs'nô-ȧr-mȧ'-skô-yĕ) Sov. Un.	48.30 N	44.30 E
129	Krasnodar (krȧs'nô-dȧr) Sov. Un.	45.3 N	39.0 E
139	Krasnoe (kräs'nô-yĕ) Sov. Un.	67.25 N	122.59 E
111	Krasnoe, L. Sov. Un.	64.0 N	173.30 E
129	Krasnograd (kräs'nô-grät) Sov. Un.	49.23 N	35.28 E
129	Krasnogrigorievka (kräs'nô-grê-gô-rê-yĕf'kä) Sov. Un.	47.40 N	34.31 E
110	Krasnokamsk (kräs-nô-kämsk') Sov. Un.	58.4 N	55.46 E
129	Krasnokutsk (krȧs-nô-ko͞otsk') Sov. Un.	50.2 N	35.5 E
111	Krasno-Polyanskoe (kräs'nô-pōl-yän'skō-yĕ) Sov. Un.	43.45 N	40.15 E
129	Krasnoselie (kräs'nô-sĕl'yĕ) Sov. Un.	48.54 N	32.21 E
110	Krasnoslobodsk (kräs'nô-slô-bôtsk') Sov. Un.	54.20 N	43.45 E
110	Krasnouralsk (kräs'nô-o͝o-rälsk') Sov. Un.	58.20 N	60.3 E
110	Krasnovishersk (kräs-nô-vê-shersk') Sov. Un.	60.25 N	57.6 E
111	Krasnovodsk (kràs-nô-vôtsk') Sov. Un.	40.0 N	53.10 E
138	Krasnoyarsk (kräs-nô-yȧrsk') Sov. Un.	56.10 N	93.0 E
128	Krasny (kräs'nê) Sov. Un.	59.44 N	30.6 E
142	Krasny (Khem Belder) (kräs'nê) (kĕm' bĕl-dĕr') Chn.	31.40 N	94.5 E
128	Krasny Kholm (kräs'nê κōlm) Sov. Un.	58.3 N	37.8 E
111	Krasnykut (krȧs-nê-ko͞ot') Sov. Un.	50.58 N	47.5 E
121	Krasnystaw (kräs-nê-stäf') Pol.	50.58 N	23.10 E
111	Krasny Sulin (kräs'nê so͞o-lēn') Sov. Un.	47.58 N	40.10 E
150	Kratié (krȧ-tyā') Indoch.	12.29 N	106.2 E
127	Kratovo (krä'tô-vô) Yugo.	42.4 N	22.11 E
127	Krdžali (k'rd'zhä-lē) Bul.	41.38 N	25.21 E
120	Krefeld-Uerdingen (krā'fĕlt-ür'dĭng-ĕn) Ger.	51.20 N	6.34 E
129	Kremenchug (krĕm'ĕn-cho͞ogh') Sov. Un.	49.4 N	33.29 E
121	Kremenets (krĕ-mĕn-yĕts') Sov. Un.	50.6 N	25.44 E
121	Kremennoe (krĕ-mĕn'ô-yĕ) Sov. Un.	49.3 N	38.9 E
120	Krems (krĕms) Aus.	48.26 N	15.35 E
128	Kresttsi (krâst'sê) Sov. Un.	58.12 N	32.24 E
119	Kretinga (krĕ-tĭŋ'gȧ) Sov. Un.	55.55 N	21.20 E
132	Kribi (krē'bê) Cam.	3.0 N	9.57 E
128	Krichev (krē'chôf) Sov. Un.	53.41 N	31.41 E
127	Kriekhankhi (krĭ-ĕ-κäŋ'κê) Grc.	38.13 N	23.17 E
118	Kristiansand (krĭs-tyȧn-sän'') Nor.	58.9 N	7.59 E
118	Kristianstad (krĭs-tyȧn-städ') Swe.	56.2 N	14.9 E
118	Kristiansund (krĭs-tyȧn-so͞on'') Nor.	63.8 N	7.45 E
119	Kristiina (Kristinestad) (krĭs'tē-nȧ) (krĭs-tē'nĕ-städh) Fin.	62.16 N	21.25 E
118	Kristinehamn (krês-tē'nĕ-häm') Swe.	59.18 N	14.7 E
119	Kristinestad (Kristiina) Fin.	62.16 N	21.25 E
127	Kriva-Palanka (krē-vȧ-pȧ-läŋ'kȧ) Yugo.	42.12 N	22.19 E
129	Krivoe Ozero (krē'vô-yĕ ô'zĕr-ô) Sov. Un.	47.58 N	30.17 E
129	Krivoi Rog (krê-voi' rôgh') Sov. Un.	47.56 N	33.21 E
126	Križevci (krē'zhĕv-tsĭ) Yugo.	46.2 N	16.32 E
126	Krk (I.) (k'rk) Yugo.	45.5 N	14.35 E
121	Krnov (k'r'nôf) Czech.	50.4 N	17.41 E
118	Kröderen (krû'dĕ-rĕn) Nor.	60.8 N	9.50 E
129	Krolevets (krô-lĕ'vyĕts) Sov. Un.	51.32 N	33.22 E
121	Kroměříž (krô'myĕr-zhēzh) Czech.	49.17 N	17.23 E
128	Kromi (krô'mê) Sov. Un.	52.44 N	35.41 E
139	Kronotskii, C. (krô'nôt'skĭ-ê) Sov. Un.	54.50 N	162.0 E
128	Kronshtadt (krōn'shtät) Sov. Un.	59.59 N	29.49 E
134	Kroonstad (krōn'shtät) U. S. Afr.	27.42 S	27.19 E
111	Kropotkin (krȧ-pôt'kĭn) Sov. Un.	45.28 N	40.35 E
121	Krosno (krôs'nô) Pol.	49.42 N	21.47 E
121	Krotoszyn (krô-tô'shĭn) Pol.	51.42 N	17.26 E
126	Krško (k'rsh'kô) Yugo.	45.58 N	15.29 E
127	Kruë (kro͞o'yĕ) Alb.	41.31 N	19.49 E
134	Kruger Natl. Park (kro͞o'gĕr) (krü'gĕr) U. S. Afr.	23.45 S	31.30 E
134	Krugersdorp (kro͞o'gĕrz-dôrp) U. S. Afr.	26.6 S	27.45 E
127	Kruševac (kro͞o'shĕ-vȧts) Yugo.	43.34 N	21.20 E
127	Kruševo (kro͞o-shĕ-vô) Yugo.	41.20 N	21.16 E
119	Krustpils (kro͞ost'pĕls) Sov. Un.	56.30 N	25.51 E
118	Krylbo (krŭl'bô) Swe.	60.7 N	16.13 E
129	Krym (Sov. Rep.) (krĭm) Sov. Un.	45.20 N	34.24 E
129	Krymskaya (krĭm'skȧ-yȧ) Sov. Un.	44.58 N	37.57 E
121	Krynki (krĭn'kê) Pol.	53.15 N	23.46 E
129	Kryukov (k'r'yo͞o-kôf') Sov. Un.	49.2 N	33.25 E
132	Ksar Smeidi (k'sär smā'ē-dê) Fr. W. Afr.	22.52 N	3.30 W
131	Ksour (k'so͞or) Tun. (In.)	35.53 N	9.0 E
131	Ksour Mts. Tun. (In.)	33.25 N	9.55 E
112	Ksour, Mts. of the Alg.	33.15 N	9.2 E
150	Kuala Lumpur (kwä'lä lo͞om-po͞or') Malaya	3.12 N	101.38 E
137	Kuala Pilah (pē'lȧ) Malaya (In.)	2.46 N	102.15 E
137	Kuala Sembrong (sĕm'brŏng) Malaya (In.)	2.29 N	103.35 E
146	Kuan (ko͞o'än') Chn.	39.28 N	116.14 E
111	Kuba (ko͞o'bȧ) Sov. Un.	41.10 N	48.32 E
111	Kuban R. (ko͞o-bȧn'') Sov. Un.	45.25 N	40.0 E
142	Kuche (Kocha) (ko͞o'chĕ') (kō'chä') Chn.	41.32 N	82.58 E
146	Kuchen (ko͞o'chĕn') Chn.	33.19 N	117.14 E
146	Kucheng (ko͞o'chĕng') Chn.	37.33 N	116.6 E
142	Kuchengtze (Kitai) (ko͞o'chĕng'-tzĕ') (kē'tī') Chn.	44.3 N	89.22 E
150	Kuching (ko͞o'chĭng) Sar.	1.30 N	110.26 E
149	Kuchi No Erabo (I.) (ko͞o'chê nō ĕr'ä-bō) Jap.	30.36 N	130.14 E
144	Kuchow (ko͞o'chō') Chn.	25.53 N	108.28 E
149	Kudamatsu (ko͞o'dȧ-mä'tso͞o) Jap.	34.1 N	131.52 E
150	Kudat (ko͞o-dät') N. Bor.	7.0 N	116.46 E
110	Kudenskoe, L. (ko͞o'dĕn-skô-yĕ) Sov. Un.	59.45 N	39.30 E
146	Kuen Lun Shan (Mts.) (ko͞o'ĕn lo͞on' shän') Chn.	37.6 N	121.20 E
142	Kuerhlei (Kurla) (ko͞o'ĕr-lā'ē) (ko͞or'lä) Chn.	41.30 N	86.10 E
146	Kufow (ko͞o'fō') Chn.	35.46 N	117.2 E
120	Kufstein (ko͞of'shtīn) Aus.	47.34 N	12.11 E
111	Kuibishev (Samara) (kwē'bĭ-shĕf) Sov. Un.	53.10 N	50.10 E
149	Kujusan (Mt.) (ko͞o'jo͞o-sän') Jap.	33.5 N	131.15 E
133	Kukawa (ko͞o-kä'wä) Nig.	12.58 N	13.38 E
127	Kukës (ko͞o'kĕs) Alb.	42.2 N	20.25 E
127	Kula (ko͞o'lȧ) Bul.	43.52 N	22.31 E
111	Kula Tur.	38.35 N	28.40 E
139	Kular Mts. (ko͞o-lär') Sov. Un.	69.25 N	131.0 E
119	Kuldiga (ko͞ol'dê-gȧ) Sov. Un.	56.58 N	21.58 E
110	Kulebaki (ko͞o-lĕ-bäk'ĭ) Sov. Un.	55.28 N	42.35 E
141	Kulhakangri, Mt. (ko͞ol-hȧ-käŋ'-grē) Bhu.	27.59 N	90.15 E
128	Kulikovo (ko͞o-lē'kô-vô) Sov. Un.	53.10 N	39.32 E
120	Kulmbach (ko͞olm'bäκ) Ger.	50.6 N	11.27 E
126	Kulpa R. (ko͞ol'pȧ) Yugo.	45.32 N	15.40 E
139	Kulskoe (ko͞ol'skô-yĕ) Sov. Un.	52.15 N	109.30 E
146	Kulu (ko͞o'lo͞o') Chn.	37.14 N	115.6 E
138	Kulunda (ko͞o-lo͞on'dȧ) Sov. Un.	52.36 N	78.55 E
138	Kulundinski, L. (ko͞o-lo͞on-dyĭn'skĭ) Sov. Un.	53.0 N	79.30 E
149	Kuma (ko͞o'mä) Jap.	33.21 N	130.55 E
149	Kumamoto (ko͞o'mȧ-mō'tô) Jap.	32.51 N	130.40 E
149	Kumano Sea (ko͞o-mȧ'nō) Jap.	33.40 N	136.30 E
127	Kumanovo (ko͞o-mä'nô-vô) Yugo.	42.8 N	21.40 E
111	Kuma R. (ko͞o'mä) Sov. Un.	45.6 N	46.0 E
157	Kumara (ko͞o-mä'rä) N. Z.	42.38 S	171.15 E
132	Kumasi (ko͞o-mä'sê) G. C.	6.48 N	1.33 W
132	Kumba (ko͝om'bȧ) Nig.	4.35 N	9.30 E
141	Kumbakonam (ko͝om'bŭ-kō'nŭm) India	10.50 N	79.28 E
147	Kŭmchŏn (ko͝om-chŭn') Kor.	38.10 N	126.29 E
147	Kŭmchŏn Kor.	36.7 N	128.7 E
147	Kŭmgangsan (Mts.) (ko͝om'gäng-sän) Kor.	38.39 N	128.7 E
147	Kŭmhwa (ko͝om'hwȧ) Kor.	38.18 N	127.29 E
147	Kŭmje (ko͝om'yĕ) Kor.	35.49 N	126.52 E
147	Kum R. (ko͝om) Kor.	36.7 N	126.53 E
147	Kŭmsan (ko͝om'sän') Kor.	36.6 N	127.29 E
147	Kŭmsŏng (ko͝om'sŭng') Kor.	38.25 N	127.36 E
148	Kunashiri I. (ko͞o'nä-shē'rê) Kur. Is.	44.15 N	145.50 E
119	Kunda (ko͞on'dȧ) Sov. Un.	59.31 N	26.35 E
137	Kuneitra (ko͞o-nā-ē'trȧ) Syr. (In.)	33.5 N	36.9 E
134	Kunene R. (ko͞o-nā'nĕ) Ang.-S. W. Afr.	16.30 S	15.15 E
118	Kungälv (kŭng'ĕlf) Swe.	57.53 N	12.0 E
144	Kungan (ko͞on'gän') Chn.	29.56 N	111.54 E
142	Kungchang (ko͝ong'chäng) Chn.	34.52 N	105.32 E
144	Kungcheng (ko͝ong'chĕng') Chn.	24.48 N	110.44 E
146	Kunghsien (ko͝ong'hsyĕn') Chn.	34.42 N	112.56 E
145	Kung R. (ko͝ong) Chn.	25.47 N	114.52 E
140	Kungrad (ko͞on-grät') Sov. Un.	43.15 N	59.5 E
118	Kungsbacka (kŭngs'bä-kȧ) Swe.	57.31 N	12.2 E
138	Kungur (ko͞oŋ-go͞or') Sov. Un.	57.30 N	57.0 E
159	Kunie (Isle of Pines) (ko͞on'yĕ) (kü-nyä') N. Cal.	22.30 S	167.30 E
142	Kunlun Mts. (ko͞on'lo͞on') Chn.	36.0 N	90.0 E
142	Kunming (Yunnanfu) (ko͞on'-mĭng') (yün'nän'fo͞o') Chn.	25.1 N	102.34 E
147	Kunsan (ko͞on'sän') Kor.	36.0 N	126.42 E
145	Kunshan (ko͞on'shän') Chn.	31.18 N	120.51 E
121	Kunszentmárton (ko͞on'sĕnt-mär-tōn') Hung.	46.49 N	20.19 E
128	Kuntsevo (ko͞on'tsĕ-vô) Sov. Un.	55.43 N	37.25 E
128	Kunya R. (ko͞on'yȧ) Sov. Un.	56.25 N	30.48 E
110	Kuopio (ko͞o-ô'pê-ô) Fin.	62.50 N	27.35 E
138	Kupino (Opalikha) (ko͞o-pĭ'nô) (ô-pä-lēk'ȧ) Sov. Un.	54.10 N	76.59 E
119	Kupiškis (ko͞o-pĭsh'kĭs) Sov. Un.	55.49 N	24.58 E
129	Kupyansk (ko͞op-yänsk') Sov. Un.	49.42 N	37.37 E
111	Kura R. (ko͞o'rä) Sov. Un.	41.20 N	45.40 E
149	Kurashiki (ko͞o'rä-shē'kê) Jap.	34.36 N	133.46 E
149	Kurayoshi (ko͞o'rä-yō'shê) Jap.	35.26 N	133.50 E
111	Kurdakly (ko͞ord'ȧ-klē) Sov. Un.	49.10 N	54.40 E
111	Kurdistan (Reg.) (kûrd'ĭ-stăn) Asia	37.40 N	43.50 E
149	Kure (ko͞o'rĕ) Jap.	34.15 N	132.32 E
129	Kuressaare (ko͞o'rĕ-sä'rĕ) Sov. Un.	58.16 N	22.30 E
138	Kurgan (ko͞or-gän') Sov. Un.	55.25 N	65.15 E
138	Kurgan Tyube (ko͞or-gän' tyo͞o'bĕ) Sov. Un.	37.45 N	68.55 E
137	Kuril Is. (ko͞o'rĭl) Sov. Un.	46.0 N	150.0 E
139	Kuril Str. Sov. Un.	50.50 N	156.40 E
121	Kurisches Haff (Sea) (ko͞o'rĭsh-ĕs häf') Pol.	55.5 N	21.0 E
141	Kurla (ko͞or'lä) India (Bombay In.)	19.4 N	72.53 E
142	Kurla (Kuerhlei) (kwĕr'lā') Chn.	41.30 N	86.10 E
133	Kurmuk (ko͞or'mo͝ok) A. E. Sud.	10.35 N	34.15 E
141	Kurnool (ko͞or-no͞ol') India	15.45 N	78.0 E
149	Kuro I. (ko͞o'rô) Jap.	30.50 N	129.55 E
157	Kurow (ko͞o'rou) N. Z.	44.44 S	170.30 E
119	Kuršenai (ko͞or'shȧ-nī) Sov. Un.	56.0 N	22.58 E
127	Kuršumlija (ko͞or'sho͞om'lĭ-yȧ) Yugo.	43.6 N	21.15 E
149	Kururi (ko͞o'ro͞o-rê) Jap. (Tokyo In.)	35.18 N	140.6 E
133	Kurusku (ko͞o-ro͞os-ko͞o') Eg.	22.32 N	32.21 E
147	Kurye (ko͞or'yĕ) Kor.	35.14 N	127.28 E
129	Kushchevskaya (ko͞osh-chôf'-skȧ-yȧ) Sov. Un.	46.33 N	39.36 E
128	Kurshinovo (ko͞or-shĭ'nô-vô) Sov. Un.	56.59 N	34.9 E
129	Kursk (ko͞orsk) Sov. Un.	51.45 N	36.9 E
129	Kursk (Dist.) Sov. Un.	51.25 N	36.0 E
134	Kuruman (ko͞o'ro͞o-män) U. S. Afr.	27.25 S	23.25 E
149	Kurume (ko͞o'ro͞o-mĕ) Jap.	33.27 N	130.30 E
138	Kushevatskoe (ko͞o-shĕ-vät'-skô-ye) Sov. Un.	65.10 N	65.30 E
146	Kushih (ko͞o'shĭ') Chn.	32.14 N	115.33 E
149	Kushikino (ko͞o'shĭ-kē'nō) Jap.	31.42 N	130.16 E
149	Kushimoto (ko͞o'shĭ-mō'tō) Jap.	33.29 N	135.47 E
148	Kushiro (ko͞o'shē-rō) Jap.	43.1 N	144.22 E
110	Kushka (ko͞osh'kȧ) Sov. Un.	35.15 N	62.37 E
111	Kushum R. (ko͞o-sho͞om') Sov. Un.	50.30 N	50.32 E
52	Kuskokwim B. (kŭs'kô-kwĭm) Alsk.	59.40 N	162.0 W
52	Kuskokwim R. Alsk.	61.20 N	160.0 W
147	Kusŏng (ko͞o'sŭng) Kor.	35.10 N	125.16 E
138	Kustanai (ko͞os-tȧ-nī') Sov. Un.	53.20 N	63.40 E
	Kustendje, see Constanta, Rom.		
111	Kütahya (kû-tä'hyȧ) Tur.	39.28 N	29.48 E
111	Kutais (ko͞o-tȧ-ēs) Sov. Un.	42.15 N	42.40 E
137	Kuteifé (ko͞o-tē-ē-fä') Syr. (In.)	33.54 N	36.40 E
145	Kutien (kū'tyĕn') Chn.	26.37 N	118.42 E
126	Kutina (ko͞o'tē-nȧ) Yugo.	45.27 N	16.49 E
120	Kutná Hôra (ko͞ot'nȧ hô'rȧ) Czech.	49.57 N	15.16 E
121	Kutno (ko͞ot'nô) Pol.	52.13 N	19.23 E
110	Kutno, L. Sov. Un.	65.15 N	31.30 E
121	Kuty (ko͞o'tê) Pol.	48.15 N	25.11 E
110	Kuusamo (ko͞o'sȧ-mô) Fin.	65.55 N	29.15 E
140	Kuwait (ko͞o-wĭt') Asia	29.30 N	47.45 E
149	Kuwana (ko͞o'wȧ-nȧ) Jap.	35.2 N	136.40 E
146	Kuyang (kū'yäng') Chn.	38.41 N	110.48 E
146	Kuyeh (ko͞o'yĕ') Chn.	35.24 N	116.8 E
138	Kuzkii I. (ko͞oz'kĭ-ê) Sov. Un.	72.45 N	79.4 E
111	Kuznetsk (ko͞oz-nyĕtsk') Sov. Un.	53.0 N	46.32 E

ăt; finăl; rāte; senâte; ärm; ȧsk; sofȧ; fâre; ch-choose; dh-as th in other; bē; êvent; bĕt; recĕnt; cratẽr; g-go; gh-gutteral g; bĭt; ĭ-short neutral; rīde; κ-gutteral k as ch in German ich;

ng-sing; ŋ-baŋk; N-nasalized n; nŏd; cŏmmit; ōld; ŏbey; ôrder; fōōd; fŏŏt; ou-out; s-soft; sh-dish; th-thin; pūre; ûnite; ûrn; stŭd; circŭs; ü-as "y" in study; '-indeterminate vowel.

Lambaréné PRONOUNCING INDEX **Lebanon**

Page	Name Pronunciation Region	Lat. °′	Long. °′
134	Lambaréné (läN-bá-rà-nā′) Fr. Eq. Afr.	0.45 S	10.10 E
100	Lambayeque (läm-bä-yā′kå) . Peru	6.30 S	79.59 W
82	Lambert (lăm′bērt) . . . . Miss.	34.13 N	90.18 W
85	Lambertville (lăm′bērt-vĭl) . . N. J.	40.22 N	74.56 W
153	Lambunao (läm-bōō-nä′ō) . . . Phil.	11.3 N	122.28 E
71	Lame Deer (lām dēr′) . . . . . . Mont.	45.37 N	106.40 W
124	Lamego (lä-mā′gō) . . . . Port.	41.6 N	7.38 W
74	La Mesa (lä mā′sä) . . . . Calif. (In.)	32.47 N	117.2 W
80	Lamesa . . . . Tex.	32.44 N	101.55 W
123	La Mesnil-Amelot (lä mâ-nēl′-à-mē-lō′) . Fr. (In.)	49.1 N	2.36 E
127	Lamia (lä-mē′à) . . . . Grc.	38.54 N	22.26 E
153	Lamitan (lä-mē′tän) . . . . Phil.	6.40 N	122.10 E
152	Lamon B. (lä-mōn′) . . . . Phil.	14.30 N	122.0 E
77	Lamoni (lȧ-mō′nĭ) . . . . Ia.	40.35 N	93.55 W
125	La Morella (Mts.) (lä mō-rä′lyä) Sp. (In.)	41.17 N	1.56 E
76	La Moure (lȧ mōōr′) . . . . N. D.	46.23 N	98.16 W
80	Lampasas (lăm-păs′ȧs) . . . . . . Tex.	31.4 N	98.10 W
80	Lampasas R. . . . . Tex.	31.20 N	98.10 W
80	Lampazos (läm-pä′zōs) . . . . . . Mex.	27.2 N	100.30 W
112	Lampedusa (I.) (läm-pȧ-dōō′sä) . It.	35.56 N	12.52 E
73	Lampo (lăm′pô) Utah (Salt Lake City In.)	41.40 N	112.27 W
135	Lamu (lä′mōō) . . . . Kenya	2.15 S	41.0 E
123	La Mure (lȧ mür′) . . . . Fr.	44.55 N	5.50 E
131	Lamy (lȧ-mē′) . . . . Tun. (In.)	36.30 N	8.25 E
155	Lanai (I.) (lä-nä′ē) . . . . Haw.	20.50 N	156.55 W
153	Lanao, L. (lä-nä′ō) . . . . Phil.	7.50 N	124.15 E
114	Lanark (lăn′ȧrk) . . . . Gt. Brit.	55.40 N	3.45 W
116	Lancashire Co. (lăŋ′kȧ-shĭr) Gt. Brit.	53.39 N	2.30 W
114	Lancaster (lăŋ′kȧs-tẽr) . . Gt. Brit.	54.5 N	2.50 W
84	Lancaster . . . . Ky.	37.36 N	84.34 W
87	Lancaster . . . . Mass. (In.)	42.27 N	71.40 W
86	Lancaster . . . . N. H.	44.30 N	71.35 W
85	Lancaster . . . . N. Y.	42.57 N	78.40 W
84	Lancaster . . . . Ohio	39.42 N	82.36 W
85	Lancaster . . . . Pa.	40.3 N	76.20 W
83	Lancaster . . . . S. C.	34.42 N	80.46 W
77	Lancaster . . . . Wis.	42.52 N	90.42 W
145	Lanchi (län′chē′) . . . . Chn.	29.10 N	119.35 E
142	Lanchow (län′chō) . . . . Chn.	36.6 N	103.50 E
134	Landana (län-dä′nä) . . . . Ang.	5.15 S	12.10 E
120	Landau (län′dou) . . . . Ger.	49.13 N	8.6 E
71	Lander (lăn′dẽr) . . . . Wyo.	42.49 N	108.43 W
122	Landerneau (läN-dĕr-nō′) . . . . . Fr.	48.28 N	4.12 W
122	Landes, The (Moorland) (läNd) . Fr.	44.30 N	1.0 W
122	Landevisau (läNd′vē-sō′) . . . . . Fr.	48.35 N	4.5 W
	Landsberg, see Gorzów, Pol.		
120	Lansberg (länts′bĕrgh) . . . . Ger.	52.44 N	15.13 E
114	Lands End . . . . Gt. Brit.	50.5 N	5.45 W
120	Lanshut (länts′hōōt) . . . . Ger.	48.32 N	12.8 E
118	Landskrona (låns-krōō′nå) . . . Swe.	55.51 N	12.49 E
82	Lanett (lȧ-nĕt′) . . . . Ala.	32.51 N	85.12 W
146	Lanfeng (län′fĕng′) . . . . Chn.	34.45 N	115.4 E
127	Langadia (läŋ-gä′dē-ȧ) . . . . Grc.	37.41 N	22.2 E
108	Langanes (Pt.) (läŋ′gȧ-nĕs) . . . Ice.	66.25 N	14.30 W
76	Langdon (lăng′dŭn) . . . . N. D.	48.45 N	98.22 W
122	Langeac (läN-zhäk′) . . . . Fr.	45.5 N	3.30 E
57	L'Ange Gardien (läNzh gȧr-dyăN′) Can. (Quebec In.)	46.55 N	71.7 W
117	Langenhorn (läng′ĕn-hôrn) Ger. (Hamburg In.)	53.39 N	10.0 E
120	Langensalza (läng-ĕn-zäl′tsä) . Ger.	51.7 N	10.40 E
118	Langesund (läng′ĕ-sōōn′) . . . . Nor.	58.59 N	9.2 E
118	Lang Fjord (läng′ fyôr′) . . . . . Nor.	62.43 N	7.50 E
108	Lang-Jökull (Glacier) (läng-yû′kōōl) . Ice.	64.45 N	20.30 W
83	Langley (lăng′lĭ) . . . . S. C.	33.30 N	81.52 W
51	Langley . . . . . . Wash. (Seattle In.)	48.2 N	122.25 W
72	Langley Prairie Can. (Vancouver In.)	49.6 N	122.40 W
120	Langnau (läng′nou) . . . . Switz.	46.57 N	7.47 E
122	Langogne (läN-gōn′y′) . . . . Fr.	44.43 N	3.51 E
122	Langon (läN-gôN′) . . . . Fr.	44.32 N	0.15 W
122	Langres (läN′gr′) . . . . Fr.	47.53 N	5.20 E
123	Langres, Plat. of . . . . Fr.	47.50 N	5.30 E
150	Langsa (läng′sȧ) . . . . Indon.	4.38 N	97.58 E
79	L'Anguille, R. (läN-gē′y′) . . . . Ark.	35.15 N	90.55 W
54	Lanigan (lăn′ĭ-gȧn) . . . . Can.	51.55 N	105.10 W
127	Lankhada (län-kä′dä) . . . . Grc.	40.43 N	23.6 E
122	Lannion (lä-nyôN′) . . . . Fr.	48.45 N	3.25 W
143	Lan R. (län) . . . . Chn.	41.30 N	117.10 E
121	Lan R. . . . . Sov. Un.	52.33 N	27.12 E
85	Lansdale (lănz′dāl) . . . . Pa.	40.17 N	75.18 W
88	Lansdowne (lănz′doun) Pa. (Philadelphia In.)	39.57 N	75.16 W
77	L'Anse (låns) . . . . Mich.	46.45 N	88.25 W
77	L'Anse Ind. Res. . . . . Mich.	46.45 N	88.22 W
85	Lansford (lănz′fērd) . . . . Pa.	40.47 N	75.48 W
144	Lanshan (län′shän′) . . . . Chn.	25.17 N	111.55 E
77	Lansing (lăn′sĭng) . . . . Ia.	43.22 N	91.15 W
84	Lansing . . . . Mich.	42.45 N	84.35 W
102	Lanús (lä-nōōs′) . . . . Arg. (In.)	34.42 S	58.23 W
126	Lanuse (lä-nōō′sȧ) . . . . Sard.	39.52 N	9.33 E
153	Lanuza B. (lä-nōō′zä) . . . . Phil.	9.20 N	126.5 E
132	Lanzarote (I.) (län-zȧ-rō′tä) Can. Is.	29.10 N	13.45 W
152	Laoag (lä-wäg′) . . . . Phil.	18.11 N	120.36 E
152	Laoang (lä-wäng′) . . . . Phil.	12.35 N	125.0 E
146	Lao-Chang R. (lä′ō chäng′) . . Chn.	37.30 N	115.52 E
150	Laoet (Laut) I. (lä′ōōt) . . . . Indon.	3.30 S	116.8 E
142	Lao Kay (lä′ō kä′ē) . . . . . . Indoch.	22.30 N	103.53 E
122	Laon (läN) . . . . Fr.	49.35 N	3.35 E
150	Laos (State) (lä′ōs) (lä-ōs′) Indoch.	18.30 N	104.30 E
153	Lapac I. (lä-päk′) . . . . Phil.	5.32 N	120.47 E
124	La Palma (lä päl′mä) . . . . Sp.	37.25 N	6.33 W
102	La Pampa (päm′pä) . . . . Arg.	37.0 S	66.0 W
153	Laparan I. (lä′pä-rän) . . . . Phil.	5.55 N	120.0 E
92	La Parrilla (lä pä-rēl′yä) . . . . Mex.	23.42 N	104.8 W
102	La Paz (lä päz′) . . . . Arg.	30.52 S	59.35 W
100	La Paz . . . . Bol.	16.29 S	68.3 W
94	La Paz . . . . Hond.	14.20 N	87.48 W
152	La Paz . . . . Phil.	17.40 N	120.40 E
84	Lapeer (lȧ-pēr′) . . . . Mich.	43.5 N	83.15 W
89	La Petit Pass I. ((lä pē-tē′ pås) La. (New Orleans In.)	30.6 N	89.24 W
92	La Piedad de Cabadas (lä pyå-dhädh′ dā kä-bä′dhäs) . Mex.	20.20 N	102.1 W
57	La Plaine (lȧ plän′) Can. (Montreal In.)	45.48 N	73.45 W
110	Lapland (lăp′lȧnd) . . . . Eur.	68.30 N	27.0 E
102	La Plata (lä plä′tä) . . . . Arg.	34.59 S	58.0 W
79	La Plata (lȧ plā′tȧ) . . . . Mo.	40.2 N	92.28 W
78	La Plata Pk. . . . . Colo.	39.0 N	106.27 W
90	La Playa (lä plä′yä) Cuba (Habana In.)	23.6 N	82.28 W
146	Lapo (lä′pō′) . . . . Chn.	39.24 N	121.31 E
125	Lä Pobla de Claramunt (lä pōb′lä dā klä-rä-mōōnt′) . Sp.	41.33 N	1.42 E
152	Lapog (lä-pōg′) . . . . Phil.	17.45 N	120.28 E
87	La Poile B. (lȧ pwäl′) . . . . Can.	47.45 N	58.20 W
77	La Pointe Ind. Res. (lȧ pwăNt′) . Wis.	46.30 N	90.40 W
124	La Pola (lä pō′lä) . . . . Sp.	42.51 N	5.40 W
84	La Porte (lȧ pōrt′) . . . . Ind.	41.37 N	86.44 W
81	La Porte . . . . Tex. (In.)	29.40 N	95.1 W
77	La Porte City . . . . Ia.	42.19 N	92.11 W
119	Lappeenranta (lä′pēn-rän′tä) . Fin.	61.5 N	28.6 E
57	Laprairie (lȧ-prâ-rē′) Can. (Montreal In.)	45.25 N	73.29 W
127	Lapsaki (läp′sȧ-kē) . . . . Tur.	40.19 N	26.42 E
125	La Puebla (lä pwā′blä) . . . . Sp.	39.46 N	3.1 E
124	La Puebla de Montalbán (lä pwā′blä dā mōnt-äl-bän′) . Sp.	39.52 N	4.21 W
100	La Punta (lä pōōn′tä) . . Peru (In.)	12.5 S	77.0 W
121	Lapusul R. (lä′pōō-shōōl) . . . Rom.	47.27 N	23.45 E
102	La Quiaca (lä kē-ä′kä) . . . . Arg.	22.0 S	65.35 W
140	Lar (lär) . . . . Iran	27.44 N	54.15 E
132	Larache (lä-räsh′) . . . . Mor.	35.9 N	6.5 W
71	Laramie (lăr′ȧ-mĭ) . . . . Wyo.	41.19 N	105.35 W
71	Laramie R. . . . . Wyo.-Colo.	41.15 N	105.40 W
125	L'Arba (lär′bä) . . . . Alg.	36.35 N	3.10 E
88	Larchmont (lärch′mŏnt) N. Y. (New York In.)	40.55 N	73.45 W
124	Laredo (lä-rā′dhō) . . . . Sp.	43.24 N	3.25 W
80	Laredo (lȧ-rā′dō) . . . . Tex.	27.30 N	99.30 W
153	Larena (lä-rā′nä) . . . . Phil.	9.14 N	123.36 E
122	La Réole (lȧ rȧ-ōl′) . . . . Fr.	44.35 N	0.1 W
122	Largentière (lär-zhäN-tyâr′) . . . Fr.	44.35 N	4.18 E
96	Largo Cay (I.) (lär′gō) . . . . Cuba	21.38 N	81.30 W
122	La Ricamarie (lȧ rē-kȧ-mȧ-rē′) . Fr.	45.20 N	4.20 E
76	Larimore (lăr′ĭ-môr) . . . . N. D.	47.54 N	97.37 W
126	Larino (lä-rē′nō) . . . . It.	41.47 N	14.53 E
102	La Rioja (lä rē-ō′hä) . . . . Arg.	29.25 S	66.58 W
102	La Rioja (State) . . . . Arg.	29.30 S	67.30 W
127	Larisa (lä′rē-sä) . . . . Grc.	39.36 N	22.25 E
73	Lark (lärk) Utah (Salt Lake City In.)	40.32 N	112.5 W
157	Larkins, Mt. (lär′kĭnz) . . . . . . N. Z.	44.52 S	168.38 E
113	Larnaca (lär′nȧ-kä) . . . . Cyp.	34.54 N	33.35 E
78	Larned (lär′nĕd) . . . . Kan.	38.11 N	99.7 W
124	La Robla (lä rō′blä) . . . . Sp.	42.48 N	5.36 W
125	La Roca (lä rō′kä) . . . . . . Sp. (In.)	41.35 N	2.20 E
122	La Rochelle (lȧ rō-shĕl′) . . . . . . Fr.	46.11 N	1.9 W
122	La Roche-sur-Yon (lȧ rôsh′-sûr-yôN′) . Fr.	46.40 N	1.25 W
124	La Roda (lä rō′dä) . . . . Sp.	39.12 N	2.9 W
97	La Romana (lä rō-mä′nä) . . . . . . Hai.	18.25 N	68.59 W
54	La Ronge, Lac (L.) (låk lȧ rôNzh′) Can.	55.12 N	105.0 W
158	Larrey, Pt. (lăr′ē) . . . . Austl.	20.0 S	119.0 E
72	Larson (lär′sŭn) Wash. (Vancouver In.)	48.45 N	122.25 W
122	Laruns (lȧ-răNs′) . . . . Fr.	42.58 N	0.28 W
118	Larvik (lär′vĕk) . . . . Nor.	59.5 N	10.2 E
124	La Sagra (Mt.) (lä sä′grä) . . . . Sp.	37.57 N	2.32 W
72	La Salle (lȧ sȧl′) . Colo. (Denver In.)	40.21 N	104.42 W
79	La Salle . . . . Ill.	41.18 N	89.5 W
85	La Salle . . . . N. Y.	43.5 N	78.57 W
78	Las Animas (läs ă′nĭ-mȧs) . . . Colo.	38.4 N	103.16 W
97	Las Cahobas (läs kä-ō′bȧs) . . . Hai.	18.48 N	71.57 W
94	Las Cañas (läs kän′yȧs) . . . . C. R.	10.27 N	85.7 W
90	Las Cascadas (läs käs-kä′däs) C. Z. (In.)	9.6 N	79.42 W
75	Las Cruces (läs krōō′sĕs) . . . N. M.	32.20 N	107.49 W
135	Las Dureh (läs dōō′rȧ) . . Br. Som.	10.7 N	45.55 E
97	La Selle Mts. (lä sĕl′) . . . . Hai.	18.22 N	72.3 W
123	La Seyne-sur-Mer (la sân′sur mêr′) Fr.	43.8 N	5.50 E
102	Las Flores (läs flō′rĕs) . . . . Arg.	36.5 S	59.2 W
99	Las Heras (läs ă′räs) Arg. (Buenos Aires In.)	34.54 S	58.54 W
142	Lashio (lăsh′ē-ō) . . . . Bur.	22.56 N	97.56 E
141	Lashkar (lŭsh′kŭr) . . . . India	26.10 N	78.15 E
135	Las Khoreh (läs kō′rȧ) . . Br. Som.	11.10 N	48.15 E
124	Las Marismas (Reg.) (mä-rēs′mäs) . Sp.	37.5 N	6.15 W
124	La Solano (lä sō-lä′nō) . . . . Sp.	38.56 N	3.14 W
132	Las Palmas (läs päl′mäs) . . Can. Is.	28.8 N	15.25 W
95	Las Palmas . . . . Pan.	8.5 N	81.23 W
95	Las Perlas (Pearl Lagoon) (läs pĕr′läs) . Nic.	12.20 N	83.41 W
151	Las Piñas (läs pē′nyäs) Phil. (Manila In.)	14.29 N	120.58 E
93	Las Rosas (Pinola) (läs rō′zäs) (pē-nō′lä) . Mex.	16.24 N	92.26 W
125	Las Rozas de Madrid (läs rō′thäs dā mä-dhrēdh′) . Sp.	40.29 N	3.53 W
135	Lassarat (lä-sä-rät′) . . . . Eth.	10.45 N	42.25 E
74	Lassen Pk. (lăs′ĕn) . . . . Calif.	40.30 N	121.39 W
74	Lassen Vol. Nat. Pk. . . . . Calif.	40.30 N	121.20 W
95	Las Tablas (läs tä′bläs) . . . . . . Pan.	7.47 N	80.17 W
134	Lastoursville (lȧs-tōōr-vēl′) Fr. Eq. Afr.	0.50 S	12.48 E
74	Las Vegas (läs vā′gäs) . . . . Nev.	36.11 N	115.9 W
78	Las Vegas . . . . N. M.	35.35 N	105.15 W
93	Las Vigas (läs vē′gäs) . . . . Mex.	19.37 N	97.3 W
100	Latacunga (lä-tä-kōōŋ′gä) . . . . Ec.	0.59 S	78.32 W
140	Latakia (Lattaquie) (lä-tä-kē′ä) (lȧ-tȧ-kē′) . Syr.	35.35 N	35.59 E
113	Latakia (Rep.) . . . . Syr.	35.10 N	36.0 E
122	La Teste (lȧ tĕst′) . . . . Fr.	44.40 N	1.8 W
79	Lathrop (lā′thrŭp) . . . . Mo.	39.33 N	94.20 W
126	Latium (Prov.) (lā′shŭm) . . . . . . It.	41.45 N	13.0 E
84	Latonia (lȧ-tō′nĭ-ȧ) . . . . Ky.	39.4 N	84.32 W
121	Latorica R. (lä′tō-rē-tsä) . Sov. Un.	48.30 N	22.40 E
52	Latouche (lȧ-tōōsh′) . . . Alsk. (In.)	60.5 N	148.0 W
123	La Tour du Pin (lȧ tōōr′ dü păN′) Fr.	45.33 N	5.27 E
122	La Tremblade (lȧ träN-blād′) . . Fr.	45.45 N	1.9 W
93	La Trinitaria (Zapaluta) (lä trē-nē-tä′rē-ä) (zä-pä-lōō′tä) . Mex.	16.7 N	92.2 W
160	Latrobe (lȧ-trōb′) . Austl. (Tas. In.)	41.12 S	146.25 E
85	Latrobe . . . . Pa.	40.22 N	79.18 W
140	Lattaquie (Latakia) (lȧ-tȧ-kē′) (lä-tä-kē′ä) . Syr.	35.35 N	35.59 E
55	La Tuque (lȧ tük′) . . . . Can.	47.25 N	72.58 W
119	Latvia (lăt′vĭ-ȧ) . . . . Sov. Un.	57.0 N	24.30 E
153	Laua-an (lä′wä-än′) . . . . Phil.	11.8 N	122.3 E
	Lauenburg, see Lebork, Pol.		
160	Launceston (lôn′sĕs-tŭn) Austl. (Tas. In.)	41.26 S	147.10 E
92	La Unión (lä ōō-nyōn′) . . . . Mex.	17.58 N	101.49 W
94	La Unión . . . . Sal.	13.18 N	87.50 W
125	La Unión . . . . Sp.	37.37 N	0.51 W
155	Laupahoehoe (lä′ōō-pä-hō′ē-hō-ē) Haw.	19.59 N	155.13 W
119	Laura (lou′rȧ) . . . . Sov. Un.	57.36 N	27.31 E
85	Laurel (lô′rĕl) . . . . Del.	38.33 N	75.39 W
85	Laurel . . . . Md.	39.5 N	76.52 W
82	Laurel . . . . Miss.	31.41 N	89.8 W
71	Laurel . . . . Mont.	45.40 N	108.47 W
83	Laurens (lô′rĕnz) . . . . S. C.	34.29 N	82.2 W
86	Laurentides Park (lô′rĕn-tĭdz) . Can.	47.40 N	71.20 W
126	Lauria (lou′rē-ä) . . . . It.	40.2 N	15.50 E
83	Laurinburg (lô′rĭn-bûrg) . . . . N. C.	34.46 N	79.28 W
77	Laurium (lô′rĭ-ŭm) . . . . Mich.	47.14 N	88.25 W
120	Lausanne (lō-zȧn′) . . . . Switz.	46.32 N	6.40 E
102	Lautaro (lou-tä′rō) . . . . Chl.	38.30 S	72.29 W
	Laut I., see Laoet I., Indon.		
150	Laut Is., Little . . . . Indon.	4.51 S	115.45 E
70	Lava Beds Nat. Mon. . . . . Calif.	41.45 N	121.30 W
81	Lavaca R. (lȧ-văk′ȧ) . . . . Tex.	29.15 N	96.50 W
124	Lavadores (lä-vä-dō′räs) . . . . . . Sp.	42.14 N	8.46 W
71	Lava Hot Springs . . . . Ida.	42.37 N	112.1 W
57	Laval (lȧ-vȧl′) . . Can. (Quebec In.)	47.1 N	71.13 W
122	Laval . . . . Fr.	48.5 N	0.45 W
119	Lavansaari I. (lä-vän-sä′rē) . . . Fin.	60.0 N	27.50 E
122	Lavaur (lȧ-vōr′) . . . . Fr.	43.40 N	1.50 E
122	Lavaveix-les-Mines (lȧ-vȧ-vĕ′-lā-mēn′) . Fr.	46.5 N	2.5 E
139	Lavdon R. (läv′dōn′) . . . . Sov. Un.	63.0 N	151.0 E
97	La Vega (lä vā′gä) . . . . Hai.	19.13 N	70.31 W
122	Lavelanet (lȧ-vē-lȧ-nĕ′) . . . . Fr.	42.56 N	1.51 E
126	Lavello (lä-vĕl′lō) . . . . It.	41.4 N	15.47 E
122	La Verdon (lȧ vĕr-dôN′) . . . . . . Fr.	45.33 N	1.5 W
73	La Verne (lȧ vûrn′) Calif. (Los Angeles In.)	34.6 N	117.46 W
158	Laverton (lā′vẽr-tŭn) . . . . . . Austl.	28.38 S	122.28 E
80	La Vibora (lä vē-bō′rä) . . . . . . Mex.	27.8 N	103.0 W
100	La Victoria (lä vēk-tō′rē-ä) . . Ven.	10.15 N	67.12 W
151	Lavongai (I.) (lä-vŏŋ-gä′ē) N. Gui. Ter.	2.30 S	150.15 E
82	Lavonia (lȧ-vō′nĭ-ȧ) . . . . Ga.	34.37 N	83.7 W
101	Lavras (lä′vräzh) . . . . Braz.	6.45 S	39.0 W
127	Lavrion (läv′rĭ-ŏn) . . . . Grc.	37.44 N	24.3 E
79	Lawrence (lô′rĕns) . . . . Kan.	38.58 N	95.14 W
86	Lawrence . . . . Mass.	42.41 N	71.11 W
157	Lawrence . . . . N. Z.	45.55 S	169.42 E
72	Lawrence . . Wash. (Vancouver In.)	48.52 N	122.17 W
84	Lawrenceburg (lô′rĕns-bûrg) . . Ind.	39.7 N	84.53 W
84	Lawrenceburg . . . . Ky.	38.2 N	84.56 W
82	Lawrenceburg . . . . Tenn.	35.14 N	87.20 W
82	Lawrenceville (lô-rĕns-vĭl) . . . . Ga.	33.37 N	83.58 W
84	Lawrenceville . . . . Ill.	38.45 N	87.44 W
83	Lawrenceville . . . . Va.	36.46 N	77.52 W
85	Lawsonia (lô-sō′nĭ-ȧ) . . . . Md.	37.58 N	75.50 W
78	Lawton (lô′tŭn) . . . . Okla.	34.35 N	98.24 W
137	Layang Layang (lä-yäng′ lä-yäng′) Malaya (In.)	1.49 N	103.33 E
56	Layland (lā′lănd) Can. (Winnipeg In.)	49.49 N	98.11 W
73	Layton (lā′tŭn) Utah (Salt Lake City In.)	41.4 N	111.59 W
119	Lazdijai (läzh′dē-yī′) . . . . Sov. Un.	54.12 N	23.30 E
153	Lazi (lä′zē) . . . . Phil.	9.8 N	123.39 E
117	Lea, R. (lē) . Gt. Brit. (London In.)	51.32 N	0.2 W
76	Lead (lēd) . . . . S. D.	44.21 N	103.46 W
78	Leadville (lĕd′vĭl) . . . . Colo.	39.14 N	106.19 W
55	Leaf R. (lēf) . . . . Can.	58.0 N	72.0 W
82	Leaf R. . . . . Miss.	31.25 N	89.20 W
81	League City (lēg) . . . . . . Tex. (In.)	29.31 N	95.5 W
84	Leamington (lĕm′ĭng-tŭn) . . . . Can.	42.5 N	82.37 W
114	Leamington . . . . Gt. Brit.	52.15 N	1.30 W
156	Leamington . . . . N. Z.	37.57 S	175.30 E
116	Leam, R. (lĕm) . . . . Gt. Brit.	52.19 N	1.18 W
54	Leaside (lē′sīd) . . . . Can. (In.)	43.42 N	79.22 W
79	Leavenworth (lĕv′ĕn-wûrth) . Kan.	39.18 N	94.55 W
70	Leavenworth . . . . Wash.	47.35 N	120.40 W
121	Leba (lā′bä) . . . . Pol.	54.44 N	17.34 E
113	Lebanon (lĕb′ȧ-nŭn) . . . . Asia	33.45 N	35.45 E

ăt; finȧl; rāte; senȧte; ärm; ȧsk; sofȧ; fâre; ch-choose; dh-as th in other; bē; ēvent; bĕt; recĕnt; cratẽr; g-go; gh-gutteral g; bĭt; ĭ-short neutral; rīde; K-gutteral k as ch in German ich;

Lebanon PRONOUNCING INDEX **Liegnitz**

Page	Name Pronunciation Region	Lat. °′	Long. °′
84	Lebanon . . . . . Ind.	40.1 N	86.31 W
84	Lebanon . . . . . Ky.	37.36 N	85.16 W
79	Lebanon . . . . . Mo.	37.41 N	92.44 W
86	Lebanon . . . . . N. H.	43.39 N	72.15 W
84	Lebanon . . . . . Ohio	39.25 N	84.12 W
70	Lebanon . . . . . Ore.	44.31 N	122.55 W
85	Lebanon . . . . . Pa.	40.20 N	76.25 W
82	Lebanon . . . . . Tenn.	36.12 N	86.17 W
113	Lebanon Mts. . . . . Syr.	34.10 N	35.50 E
133	Lebda (Homs) (lĕb′dȧ) (hōms) Libya	32.36 N	14.12 E
129	Lebedin (lyĕ′bĕ-dên) . . . . Sov. Un.	48.57 N	31.35 E
128	Lebedyan (lyĕ′bĕ-dyän′) . Sov. Un.	53.3 N	39.8 E
122	Le Blanc (lẽ blȧN′) . . . . . Fr.	46.38 N	1.1 E
122	Le Boncau (lẽ bôN-kō′) . . . . . Fr.	43.32 N	1.25 W
97	Le Borgne (lẽ bōrn′y′) . . . . . Hai.	19.51 N	72.30 W
121	Lębork (lăN-bo͝ork′) . . . . . Pol.	54.32 N	17.45 E
123	Le Bourget (lẽ bo͞or-zhĕ′) . Fr. (In.)	48.56 N	2.25 E
122	Le Bouscat (lẽ bo͞os-kȧ′) . . . . . Fr.	44.52 N	0.35 W
124	Lebrija (lȧ-brē′hä) . . . . . Sp.	36.55 N	6.5 W
102	Lebu (lā-bo͞o′) . . . . . Chl.	37.35 S	73.31 W
131	Le Cap (lẽ kȧp) Eg. (Suez Canal In.)	30.56 N	32.20 E
122	Le Cateau (lẽ kȧ-tō′) . . . . . Fr.	50.5 N	3.35 E
127	Lecce (lĕt′chā) . . . . . It.	40.21 N	18.10 E
126	Lecco (lĕk′kō) . . . . . It.	45.50 N	9.25 E
122	Le Chambon-Feugerolles (lẽ shäN-bôN′-fû-zhē-rōl′) . Fr.	45.25 N	4.20 E
93	Lechería (lȧ-chȧ-rē′ä) . . Mex. (In.)	19.37 N	99.11 W
120	Lech R. (lĕĸ) . . . . . Ger.	48.15 N	10.55 E
81	Lecomte (lē-kôNt′) . . . . . La.	31.6 N	92.25 W
122	Le Coteau (lẽ kō-tō′) . . . . . Fr.	46.2 N	4.8 E
122	Le Creusot (lẽ krû-zō′) . . . . . Fr.	46.49 N	4.25 E
122	Le Croisic (lẽ krwä-zēk′) . . . . . Fr.	47.18 N	2.30 W
121	Łęczyca (wăŋ-chĭ′tsä) . . . . . Pol.	52.3 N	19.13 E
124	Ledesma (lȧ-dĕs′mä) . . . . . Sp.	41.4 N	5.59 W
89	Lee (lē) . . . . La. (New Orleans In.)	30.1 N	89.57 W
77	Leech L. (lēch) . . . . . Minn.	47.10 N	94.20 W
82	Leeds (lēdz) . . . . . Ala.	33.33 N	86.31 W
114	Leeds . . . . . Gt. Brit.	53.45 N	1.30 W
76	Leeds . . . . . N. D.	48.17 N	99.25 W
116	Leeds and Liverpool Can. Gt. Brit.	53.54 N	2.10 W
116	Leek (lēk) . . . . . Gt. Brit.	53.6 N	2.1 W
120	Leer (lār) . . . . . Ger.	53.13 N	7.27 E
114	Lee, R. . . . . . Ire.	51.55 N	8.35 W
83	Leesburg (lēz′bûrg) . . . . . Fla.	28.49 N	81.53 W
85	Leesburg . . . . . Va.	39.7 N	77.35 W
79	Lees Summit (lēz) . . . . . Mo.	38.54 N	94.22 W
97	Lee Stocking I. . . . . . Ba. Is.	23.48 N	76.8 W
81	Leesville (lēz′vĭl) . . . . . La.	31.8 N	93.18 W
84	Leetonia (lē-tō′nĭ-ȧ) . . . . . Ohio	40.55 N	80.46 W
120	Leeuwarden (lā′wär-dĕn) . . . Neth.	53.11 N	5.47 E
158	Leeuwin, C. (lo͞o′wĭn) . . . . . Austl.	34.15 S	115.10 E
95	Leeward Is. (lē′wẽrd) . . W. I. (In.)	17.0 N	62.0 W
91	Leeward Is. . . . . . W. I.		
160	Lefevres Pen. (lẽ-fē′vẽrz) Austl. (Adelaide In.)	34.48 S	138.30 E
158	Lefroy, L. (lē-froi′) . . . . . Austl.	31.15 S	121.45 E
125	Leganes (lȧ-gä′nȧs) . . . . . Sp. (In.)	40.20 N	3.46 W
152	Legaspi (lȧ-gäs′pē) . . . . . Phil.	13.9 N	123.44 E
126	Leghorn (Livorno) (lĕg′hôrn) (lē-vôr′nō) . It.	43.33 N	10.20 E
126	Legnano (lȧ-nyä′nō) . . . . . It.	45.35 N	8.55 E
120	Legnica (lĕk-nĭt′sȧ) . . . . . Pol.	51.12 N	16.10 E
141	Leh (lā) . . . . . India	34.8 N	77.35 E
122	Le Havre (lẽ ȧv′r′) . . . . . Fr.	49.30 N	0.5 E
75	Lehi (lē′hī) . . . . . Utah	40.23 N	111.51 W
75	Lehman Caves Nat. Mon. (lē′mȧn) Nev.	39.0 N	114.13 W
120	Lehrte (lār′tē) . . . . . Ger.	52.22 N	9.58 E
155	Lehua (I.) (lā′ho͞o-ȧ) . . . . . Haw.	22.2 N	160.7 W
114	Leicester (lĕs′tẽr) . . . . . Gt. Brit.	52.40 N	1.10 W
116	Leicester Co. . . . . . Gt. Brit.	52.41 N	1.15 W
158	Leichhardt R. (lĭk′härt) . . . . Austl.	18.30 S	139.57 E
115	Leiden (lī′dĕn) . . . . . Neth.	52.10 N	4.30 E
116	Leigh (lē) . . . . . Gt. Brit.	53.30 N	2.32 W
117	Leigh-on-Sea Gt. Brit. (London In.)	51.32 N	0.38 E
118	Leikanger (lī′käŋ′gẽr) . . . . . Nor.	61.10 N	6.54 E
120	Leine R. (lī′nĕ) . . . . . Ger.	52.30 N	9.28 E
84	Leipsic (lĭp′sĭk) . . . . . Ohio	41.7 N	84.3 W
120	Leipzig (lĭp′tsĭĸ) . . . . . Ger.	51.20 N	12.20 E
124	Leiria (lā-rē′ä) . . . . . Port.	39.44 N	8.49 W
84	Leitchfield (lĕch′fēld) . . . . . Ky.	37.29 N	86.18 W
124	Leixoes (Matozinhos) (lā-shōŋzh′) (mä-tō-zēn′yōzh) . Port.	41.11 N	8.41 W
144	Leiyang (lā′yäng′) . . . . . Chn.	26.30 N	112.38 E
131	Le Kef (lẽ kĕf′) . . . . . Tun. (In.)	36.10 N	8.53 E
120	Lek R. (lĕk) . . . . . Neth.	51.57 N	5.20 E
118	Leksand (lĕk′sänd) . . . . . Swe.	60.45 N	15.0 E
82	Leland (lē′lȧnd) . . . . . Miss.	33.25 N	90.55 W
51	Leland . . . . . Wash. (Seattle In.)	47.53 N	122.53 W
120	Le Locle (lẽ lō′kl′) . . . . . Switz.	47.3 N	6.46 E
122	Le Lude (lẽ lüd′) . . . . . Fr.	47.38 N	0.10 E
102	Le Maire Str. (lẽ mâr′) . . . . . Arg.	55.0 S	65.0 W
122	Le Mans (lẽ mäN′) . . . . . Fr.	48.1 N	0.10 E
76	Le Mars (lē märz′) . . . . . Ia.	42.48 N	96.10 W
121	Lemberg (Lwów) (lĕm′bĕrgh) (lvo͞of) . Pol.	49.49 N	24.2 E
152	Lemery (lā-mā-rē′) . . . . . Phil.	13.52 N	120.55 E
120	Lemgo (lĕm′gō) . . . . . Ger.	52.1 N	8.54 E
71	Lemhi R. (lĕm′hī) . . . . . Ida.	45.0 N	113.40 W
71	Lemhi Ra. . . . . . Ida.	44.30 N	113.30 W
76	Lemmon (lĕm′ŭn) . . . . . S. D.	45.56 N	102.8 W
127	Lemnos (I.) (lĕm′nŏs) . . . . . Grc.	39.55 N	25.15 E
97	Le Mole (lẽ mōl′) . . . . . Hai.	19.49 N	73.22 W
74	Lemongrove (lĕm′ŭn-grōv) Calif. (In.)	32.44 N	117.2 W
95	Le Moule (lẽ mo͞ol′) . . . Guad. (In.)	16.20 N	61.22 W
94	Lempa, R. (lĕm′pä) . . . . . Sal.	13.30 N	88.40 W
118	Lemvig (lĕm′vēgh) . . . . . Den.	56.32 N	8.20 E
124	Lena (lā′nä) . . . . . Sp.	43.11 N	5.51 W

Page	Name Pronunciation Region	Lat. °′	Long. °′
118	Lena (lī′nä) . . . . . Swe.	60.0 N	17.42 E
139	Lena R. (lyĕ′nä) . . . . . Sov. Un.	60.0 N	119.0 E
101	Lençóes (lĕN-sôNs′) . . . . . Braz.	12.31 S	41.31 W
101	Lençóes . . . . . Braz.	22.50 S	49.1 W
111	Leninakan (lĕ-nyē-nȧ-kän′) Sov. Un.	40.45 N	43.50 E
138	Leninabad (Khodzhent) (lĕ-nyē-nȧ-bät′) (ĸôd-zhĕnt′) . Sov. Un.	40.20 N	69.40 E
128	Leningrad (lyĕ-nên-grät′) . Sov. Un.	59.55 N	30.20 E
128	Leninsk (lyĕ-nēnsk′) . . . . . Sov. Un.	56.43 N	37.32 E
138	Leninsk Kuznetski (lyĕ-nênsk′ ko͞oz-nyĕt′skĭ-ê) . Sov. Un.	54.30 N	86.40 E
140	Leninsk-Turkmenskii (lyĕ-nēnsk′-to͞ork-mĕn′skĭ-ê) . Sov. Un.	39.5 N	63.40 E
111	Lenkoran (lĕŋ-kō-rän′) . . . Sov. Un.	38.48 N	48.50 E
76	Lennox (lĕn′ŭks) . . . . . S. D.	43.22 N	96.52 W
83	Lenoir (lē-nōr′) . . . . . N. C.	35.55 N	81.33 W
82	Lenoir City . . . . . Tenn.	35.47 N	84.17 W
77	Lenox (lĕn′ŭks) . . . . . Ia.	40.52 N	94.32 W
122	Lens (läNs) . . . . . Fr.	50.28 N	2.50 E
120	Leoben (lȧ-ō′bĕn) . . . . . Aus.	47.23 N	15.9 E
97	Léogane (lā-ô-gän′) . . . . . Hai.	18.31 N	72.38 W
76	Leola (lē-ō′lȧ) . . . . . S. D.	45.43 N	98.55 W
116	Leominster (lĕm′stẽr) (lĕm′ĭn-stẽr) . Gt. Brit.	52.13 N	2.44 W
86	Leominster (lĕm′ĭn-stẽr) . . . Mass.	42.31 N	71.49 W
77	Leon (lē′ŏn) . . . . . Ia.	40.42 N	93.45 W
92	León (lā-ōn′) . . . . . Mex.	21.8 N	101.41 W
94	León . . . . . Nic.	12.27 N	86.53 W
153	Leon (lā′ōn′) . . . . . Phil.	10.46 N	122.23 E
124	León . . . . . Sp.	42.36 N	5.34 W
124	León (Prov.) . . . . . Sp.	41.30 N	5.50 W
131	Leona, Pt. (lā-ō′nä) Sp. Mor. (Gib. In.)	35.54 N	5.37 E
126	Leonforte (lā-ôn-fôr′tā) . . . . . It.	37.38 N	14.24 E
80	Leon R. (lē′ŏn) . . . . . Tex.	31.50 N	98.15 W
134	Leopold II, L. (lā′ô-pōld) Bel. Cong.	2.0 S	18.20 E
101	Leopoldina (lā-ô-pōl-dē′nȧ) . . Braz.	21.30 S	42.44 W
117	Leopoldsdorf (lā′ô-pōlts-dôrf′) Aus. (Wien In.)	48.7 N	16.24 E
134	Léopoldville (lā-ô-pōld-vēl′) Bel. Cong.	4.18 S	15.17 E
129	Leovo (lȧ-ō′vō) . . . . . Sov. Un.	46.30 N	28.13 E
124	Lepe (lā′pȧ) . . . . . Sp.	37.14 N	7.11 W
128	Lepel (lyĕ-pĕl′) . . . . . Sov. Un.	54.51 N	28.43 E
123	Le Perreux (lẽ pē-rû′) . . . . Fr. (In.)	48.50 N	2.30 E
57	L'Epiphanie (lā-pē-fȧ-nē′) Can. (Montreal In.)	45.51 N	73.29 W
120	Lepontine Alps (lē-pŏn′tĭn) . Switz.	46.27 N	8.54 E
122	Le Portel (lẽ pôr-tĕl′) . . . . . Fr.	50.41 N	1.35 E
86	Lepreau (lē-prō′) . . . . . Can.	45.8 N	66.28 W
138	Lepsinsk (lyĕp-sênsk′) . . . Sov. Un.	45.30 N	80.30 E
122	Le Puy (lẽ pwē′) . . . . . Fr.	45.0 N	3.55 E
123	Le Raincy (lẽ răN-sē′) . . . Fr. (In.)	48.53 N	2.31 E
126	Lercara (lĕr-kä′rä) . . . . . It.	37.42 N	12.34 E
80	Lerdo (lĕr′dō) . . . . . Mex.	25.34 N	103.30 W
133	Léré (lā-rā′) . . . . . Fr. Eq. Afr.	9.40 N	14.18 E
125	Lérida (lā′rê-dhä) . . . . . Sp.	41.38 N	0.36 E
93	Lerma (lĕr′mä) . . . . . Mex.	19.50 N	90.35 W
124	Lerma . . . . . Sp.	42.1 N	3.45 W
92	Lerma, R. . . . . . Mex.	20.13 N	100.40 W
85	Le Roy (lē roi′) . . . . . N. Y.	43.0 N	78.0 W
114	Lerwick (lĕr′ĭk) (lûr′wĭk) Gt. Brit. (In.)	60.10 N	1.10 W
122	Les Andelys (lā-zäN-dē-lē′) . . . . Fr.	49.15 N	1.30 E
123	Les Clayes (lā klā′) . . . . . Fr. (In.)	48.48 N	1.58 E
123	Les Essarts (lā zĕs-sär′) . . Fr. (In.)	48.44 N	1.54 E
127	Leshe (Alessio) (lĕshĕ) (ȧ-lā′sē-ō) Alb.	41.47 N	19.40 E
126	Lesina, L. of (lā′zê-nä) . . . . . It.	41.52 N	15.25 E
127	Leskovac (lĕs′kô-väts) . . . . . Yugo.	42.59 N	21.57 E
127	Leskovec (lĕs′kô-vyĕts) . . . . . Bul.	43.5 N	25.42 E
79	Leslie (lĕz′lĭ) . . . . . Ark.	35.49 N	92.32 W
123	Les Mesnil (lā mȧ-nēl′) . . Fr. (In.)	48.0 N	1.57 E
110	Lesnoy (lĕs′noi) . . . . . Sov. Un.	66.46 N	34.22 E
148	Lesogorsk (lyĕs′ô-gôrsk) . . . . Sakh.	49.25 N	142.12 E
122	Lesparre (lē-spär′) . . . . . Fr.	45.20 N	0.58 W
122	Les Sables d' Olonne (lā sȧ′bl′ dô-lŭn′) . Fr.	46.30 N	1.48 E
95	Les Saintes Is. (lā-săNt′) Guad. (In.)	15.52 N	61.38 W
91	Lesser Antilles (I.) (lĕs′ẽr ăn-tĭl′ēz) W. I.	15.0 N	62.0 W
54	Lesser Slave L. . . . . . Can.	55.28 N	115.45 W
88	Lester R. (lĕs′tẽr) Minn. (Duluth In.)	46.50 N	92.5 W
77	Le Sueur (lē so͞or′) . . . . . Minn.	44.27 N	93.54 W
120	Leszno (lĕsh′nō) . . . . . Pol.	51.55 N	16.35 E
122	Le Teil (lẽ tā′y′) . . . . . Fr.	44.35 N	4.48 E
54	Lethbridge (lĕth′brĭj) . . . . . Can.	49.45 N	112.50 W
129	Letichev (lyĕ-tê-chĕf′) . . . Sov. Un.	49.22 N	27.39 E
122	Le Tréport (lẽ trā-pôr′) . . . . . Fr.	50.2 N	1.25 E
121	Léva (Levice) (lā′vŏ) (lā′vĕt-sĕ) Hung.	48.13 N	18.37 E
127	Levadeia (lyĕ-vȧ-dhē′ȧ) . . . . . Grc.	38.26 N	22.51 E
123	Levallois-Perret (lē-väl-wȧ′-pĕ-rĕ′) Fr. (In.)	48.53 N	2.17 E
126	Levana (Mts.) (lȧ-vä′nä) . . . . . It.	45.21 N	7.10 E
108	Levanger (lĕ-väng′ẽr) . . . . . Nor.	63.38 N	11.8 E
114	Leven (lē′vĕn) . . . . . Gt. Brit.	56.15 N	3.0 W
116	Leven, R. . . . . . Gt. Brit.	54.12 N	3.3 W
158	Leveque, C. (lē-vĕk′) . . . . . Austl.	16.20 S	122.47 E
134	Leverville (lē-vā-vēl′) . . Bel. Cong.	5.15 S	18.45 E
121	Levice (lā′vĕt-sĕ) . . . . . Czech.	48.13 N	18.37 E
126	Levico (lā′vê-kō) . . . . . It.	46.2 N	11.19 E
122	Lévie (lĕ-vē′) . . . . . Cor.	41.40 N	9.10 E
122	Le Vigan (lẽ vē-gäN′) . . . . . Fr.	43.39 N	3.38 E
157	Levin (lĕv′ĭn) . . . . . N. Z.	40.32 S	175.17 E
55	Lévis (lā-vē′) (lē′vĭs) . . . . . Can.	46.50 N	71.13 W
127	Levkas (lyĕf-käs′) . . . . . Grc.	38.48 N	20.43 E
127	Levkas (I.) . . . . . Grc.	38.45 N	20.40 E

Page	Name Pronunciation Region	Lat. °′	Long. °′
121	Levoča (lā′vô-chȧ) . . . . . Czech.	49.2 N	20.39 E
83	Levy L. (lē′vĭ) . . . . . Fla.	29.31 N	82.20 W
89	Levy L. . . . . La. (New Orleans In.)	29.48 N	89.48 W
85	Lewes (lo͞o′ĭs) . . . . . Del.	38.46 N	75.12 W
114	Lewes . . . . . Gt. Brit.	50.55 N	0.0
54	Lewes R. . . . . . Can.	62.25 N	136.30 W
88	Lewis (lū′ĭs) N. Y. (Niagara Falls In.)	42.59 N	78.51 W
71	Lewis and Clark Cavern Nat'l. Mon. Mont.	45.50 N	111.42 W
51	Lewis and Clark R. Ore. (Portland In.)	46.6 N	123.53 W
82	Lewisburg (lū′ĭs-bûrg) . . . . . Tenn.	35.27 N	86.48 W
85	Lewisburg . . . . . W. Va.	37.50 N	80.25 W
114	Lewis, Butt of (C.) . . . . . Gt. Brit.	58.30 N	6.15 W
114	Lewis (I.) . . . . . Gt. Brit.	58.0 N	6.50 W
87	Lewisporte (lū′ĭs-pōrt) . . . . . Can.	49.15 N	55.2 W
71	Lewis Ra. . . . . . Mont.	48.10 N	113.10 W
70	Lewis R. . . . . . Wash.	46.3 N	122.10 W
70	Lewiston (lū′ĭs-tŭn) . . . . . Ida.	46.25 N	117.1 W
86	Lewiston . . . . . Me.	44.5 N	70.11 W
85	Lewiston . . . . . N. Y.	43.10 N	79.0 W
79	Lewistown (lū′ĭs-toun) . . . . . Ill.	40.24 N	90.9 W
71	Lewistown . . . . . Mont.	47.5 N	109.27 W
85	Lewistown . . . . . Pa.	40.37 N	77.30 W
84	Lexington (lĕk′sĭng-tŭn) . . . . . Ky.	38.2 N	84.31 W
87	Lexington . . . . . Mass. (In.)	42.27 N	71.13 W
82	Lexington . . . . . Miss.	33.7 N	90.3 W
79	Lexington . . . . . Mo.	39.10 N	93.52 W
78	Lexington . . . . . Neb.	40.45 N	99.45 W
83	Lexington . . . . . N. C.	35.48 N	80.16 W
82	Lexington . . . . . Tenn.	35.37 N	88.25 W
85	Lexington . . . . . Va.	37.47 N	79.27 W
72	Leyden (lā′dĕn) Colo. (Denver In.)	39.50 N	105.11 W
153	Leyte (lā′tā) . . . . . Phil.	11.22 N	124.30 E
153	Leyte G. . . . . . Phil.	10.50 N	125.28 E
153	Leyte (I.) . . . . . Phil.	10.50 N	124.50 E
114	Leyton (lā′tŭn) . . . . . Gt. Brit.	51.32 N	0.0
121	Lezajsk (lĕ′zhä-ĭsk) . . . . . Pol.	50.14 N	22.25 E
122	Lézignan (lā-zê-nyäN′) . . . . . Fr.	43.15 N	2.48 E
125	Lezirias (Reg.) (lā-zê-rē′äzh) Port. (In.)	38.54 N	8.57 W
129	Lgov (lgôf) . . . . . Sov. Un.	51.42 N	35.20 E
142	Lhasa (läs′ä) . . . . . Chn.	29.48 N	91.2 E
123	L'Hay (lä-ē′) . . . . . Fr. (In.)	48.47 N	2.22 E
151	Lian (lē-än′) . . . Phil. (Manila In.)	14.5 N	120.34 E
153	Lianga (lê-äŋ-gä′) . . . . . Phil.	8.38 N	126.6 E
153	Lianga B. . . . . . Phil.	8.36 N	126.10 E
142	Liangchow (lyäng′chō′) . . . . . Chn.	38.0 N	102.32 E
144	Liangshan (lyäng′shän′) . . . . . Chn.	30.47 N	107.55 E
151	Lian, R. . . . . . Phil. (Manila In.)	14.5 N	120.37 E
146	Liaochow (lyä′ō′chō′) . . . . . Chn.	37.6 N	113.24 E
143	Liao R. (lyä′ō) . . . . . Chn.	43.0 N	123.30 E
147	Liaotung Pen. . . . . . Chn.	40.10 N	122.50 E
143	Liaoyang (lyä′ō-yäng′) . . . . . Chn.	41.17 N	123.10 E
143	Liaoyüan (Chengchiatun) (lyä′ō-yü-än′) (chĕng′chyä′to͞on′) . Chn.	43.44 N	123.28 E
54	Liard (lê-är′) . . . . . Can.	60.13 N	123.32 W
54	Liard R. . . . . . Can.	59.30 N	125.0 W
153	Libacao (lê-bä-kä′ō) . . . . . Phil.	11.29 N	122.28 E
70	Libby (lĭb′ē) . . . . . Mont.	48.23 N	115.32 W
133	Libenge (lê-bĕŋ′gä) . . . . Bel. Cong.	3.33 N	18.36 E
78	Liberal (lĭb′ẽr-ȧl) . . . . . Kan.	37.3 N	100.56 W
120	Liberec (lē′bĕr-ĕts) . . . . . Czech.	50.46 N	15.4 E
132	Liberia (lī-bē′rĭ-ȧ) . . . . . Afr.	6.30 N	9.30 W
94	Liberia . . . . . C. R.	10.39 N	85.27 W
99	Libertad (lē-bĕr-tädh′) Ur. (Buenos Aires In.)	34.36 S	56.37 W
84	Liberty (lĭb′ẽr-tĭ) . . . . . Ind.	39.37 N	84.55 W
79	Liberty . . . . . Mo.	39.16 N	94.24 W
83	Liberty . . . . . S. C.	34.48 N	82.40 W
81	Liberty . . . . . Tex.	30.4 N	94.48 W
73	Liberty . Utah (Salt Lake City In.)	41.19 N	111.51 W
77	Libertyville (lĭb′ẽr-tĭ-vĭl) . . . . . Ill.	42.18 N	87.59 W
151	Libigan, R. (lê-bē′gän) Phil. (Manila In.)	13.56 N	121.24 E
152	Libmanan (lĭb-mä′nän) . . . . . Phil.	13.41 N	123.3 E
122	Libourne (lē-bo͞orn′) . . . . . Fr.	44.55 N	0.15 W
93	Libres (lē′brās) . . . . . Mex.	19.27 N	97.41 W
132	Libreville (lē-br′vēl′) . . Fr. Eq. Afr.	0.30 N	9.30 E
153	Libuganon R. (lē-bo͞o′gȧ-nōn′) Phil.	7.40 N	125.34 E
133	Libya (lĭb′ē-ȧ) . . . . . Afr.	28.0 N	18.0 E
133	Libyan Des. (lĭb′ē-ȧn) . . Eg.-Libya	28.0 N	25.0 E
133	Libyan Plat. . . . . . Eg.	30.30 N	26.30 E
102	Licancábur (Vol.) (lē-kän-kä′-bo͞or) . Chl.	22.38 S	67.50 W
126	Licata (lē-kä′tä) . . . . . It.	37.7 N	13.55 E
116	Lichfield (lĭch′fēld) . . . . . Gt. Brit.	52.41 N	1.49 W
144	Lichow (lē′chō′) . . . . . Chn.	29.36 N	111.24 E
117	Lichtenberg (lĭĸ′tĕn-bĕrgh) Ger. (Berlin In.)	52.31 N	13.28 E
117	Lichtenrade (lĭĸ′tĕn-rä-dȧ) Ger. (Berlin In.)	52.23 N	13.25 E
117	Lichterfelde, Gr. (lĭĸ′tẽr-fĕl-tȧ) Ger. (Berlin In.)	52.26 N	13.18 E
144	Lichwan (lĭch′wän′) . . . . . Chn.	30.16 N	108.34 E
84	Licking R. (lĭk′ĭng) . . . . . Ky.	38.25 N	84.0 W
126	Licosa (lē-kō′sä) . . . . . It.	40.15 N	14.53 E
135	Licungo R. (lê-koo͞ŋ′gō) . . . . . Moz.	16.30 S	37.0 E
121	Lida (lē′dȧ) . . . . . Sov. Un.	53.53 N	25.18 E
76	Lida L. . . . . . Minn.	46.36 N	95.59 W
160	Lidcombe (lĭd′kŭm) Austl. (Sydney In.)	33.52 S	151.3 E
76	Lidgerwood (lĭj′ẽr-wood) . . . N. D.	46.5 N	97.9 W
118	Lidköping (lēt′chû-pĭng) . . . . . Swe.	58.30 N	13.8 E
121	Lidzbark Warmiński (lĭts′bärk vär-mĭn′′skĭ) . Pol.	54.8 N	20.37 E
120	Liechtenstein (lĕĸ′tĕn-shtīn) . . Eur.	47.7 N	9.33 E
115	Liége (lê-äzh′) . . . . . Bel.	50.39 N	5.35 E
	Liegnitz, see Legnica, Pol.		

ng-sing; ŋ-baŋk; N-nasalized n; nŏd; cŏmmit; ōld; ôbey; ôrder; fo͞od; fo͝ot; ou-out; s-soft; sh-dish; th-thin; pūre; ůnite; ûrn; stŭd; circŭs; ü-as "y" in study; ′-indeterminate vowel.

ăt; fināl; rāte; senāte; ärm; àsk; sofá; fâre; ch-choose; ᵭh-as th in other; bē; évent; bĕt; recĕnt; cratēr; g-go; gh-gutteral g; bĭt; ĭ-short neutral; rīde; ᴋ-gutteral k as ch in German ich;

Llanelly PRONOUNCING INDEX **Luanginga**

Page	Name Pronunciation Region	Lat. °′	Long. °′
114	Llanelly (lȧ-nĕl'ĭ) . . . Gt. Brit.	51.42 N	4.10 W
124	Llanes (lyä'nȧs) . . . Sp.	43.26 N	4.45 W
80	Llano (lä'nō) (lyä'nō) . . . Tex.	30.45 N	98.40 W
78	Llano Estacado (Plain) (lä'nō ĕs-tä-kä'dō) . N. M.-Tex.	33.45 N	103.0 W
80	Llano R. . . . Tex.	30.40 N	99.5 W
92	Llera (lyā'rä) . . . Mex.	23.19 N	99.2 W
92	Llera, R. . . . Mex.	23.18 N	99.0 W
124	Llerena (lyā-rā'nä) . . . Sp.	38.15 N	6.1 W
114	Lleyn Pen. (lĭn) . . . Gt. Brit.	52.55 N	4.45 W
125	Llobregat R. (lyô-brĕ-gät') . . . Sp.	41.55 N	1.55 E
153	Llorente (lyō-rān'tā) . . . Phil.	11.24 N	125.32 E
125	Lluchmayor (lyōōch-mä-yôr') . . Sp.	39.28 N	2.54 E
102	Llullaillaco (Vol.) (lyōō-lyī-lyä'kō) Arg.-Chl.	24.45 S	68.40 W
145	Loan (lō'än') . . . Chn.	27.16 N	115.36 E
134	Loange R. (lô-äŋ'gä) . . . Bel. Cong.	6.15 S	19.45 E
134	Loango (lô-äŋ'gō) . . . Fr. Eq. Afr.	4.40 S	11.58 E
145	Lo-an R. (lō'än') . . . Chn.	28.56 N	116.48 E
102	Loa, R. (lō'ä) . . . Chl.	22.25 S	69.0 W
153	Loay (lō-ī') . . . Phil.	9.36 N	124.2 E
120	Löbau (lû'bou) . . . Ger.	51.7 N	14.41 E
134	Lobito (lô-bē'tō) . . . Ang.	12.15 S	13.37 E
152	Lobo (lō'bô) . . . Phil.	13.38 N	121.12 E
153	Loboc (lō'bôk) . . . Phil.	9.38 N	124.2 E
99	Lobos (lō'bôs) Arg. (Buenos Aires In.)	35.7 S	59.5 W
96	Lobos Cay (I.) . . . W. I.	22.21 N	77.36 W
93	Lobos I. . . . Mex.	21.26 N	97.13 W
100	Lobos Is. . . . Peru	6.30 S	79.59 W
120	Locarno (lô-kär'nō) . . . Switz.	46.11 N	8.46 E
144	Locheg (lō'chĕng') . . . Chn.	24.45 N	108.56 E
122	Loches (lôsh) . . . Fr.	47.9 N	1.0 E
83	Lochloosa, L. (lŏk-lō'sȧ) . . . Fla.	29.32 N	82.10 W
70	Lochsa R. (lŏk'sȧ) . . . Ida.	46.24 N	115.12 W
114	Lochy, Loch (L.) (lŏk lŏk'ĭ) Gt. Brit.	56.55 N	5.0 W
86	Lockeport (lŏk'pōrt) . . . Can.	43.45 N	65.5 W
83	Lockhart . . . S. C.	34.46 N	81.28 W
81	Lockhart . . . Tex.	29.53 N	97.40 W
85	Lock Haven (lŏk' hā-vĕn) . . . Pa.	41.6 N	77.37 W
84	Lockport (lŏk'pōrt) . . . Ill.	41.36 N	88.2 W
85	Lockport . . . N. Y.	43.11 N	78.41 W
82	Locust Fork (R.) (lō'kŭst) . . . Ala.	33.55 N	86.40 W
119	Lodeinoe Pole (lô'dâ-nô-yĕ pôl'yĕ) Sov. Un.	60.45 N	33.30 E
122	Lodève (lô-dĕv') . . . Fr.	43.42 N	3.17 E
78	Lodge Pole Cr. (lŏj'pōl) . Neb.-Wyo.	41.12 N	103.40 W
74	Lodi (lō'dī) . . . Calif.	38.7 N	121.18 W
126	Lodi (lô'dē) . . . It.	45.17 N	9.30 E
121	Lódz (wōōdzh) . . . Pol.	51.46 N	19.30 E
125	Loeches (lô-äch'ĕs) . . . Sp. (In.)	40.23 N	3.26 W
108	Lofoten Is. (lô'fō-tĕn) . . . Nor.	68.10 N	14.0 E
160	Loftus (lŏf'tŭs) . Austl. (Sydney In.)	34.3 S	151.3 E
160	Logan (lō'găn) . . . Austl. (In.)	27.45 S	153.6 E
84	Logan . . . Ohio	39.34 N	82.24 W
71	Logan . . . Utah	41.45 N	111.51 W
84	Logan . . . W. Va.	37.50 N	82.0 W
54	Logan, Mt. . . . Can.	60.48 N	140.28 W
73	Logan Pk. Utah (Salt Lake City In.)	41.43 N	111.43 W
160	Logan R. . . . Austl. (In.)	28.0 S	152.59 E
73	Logan R. Utah (Salt Lake City In.)	41.44 N	111.48 W
84	Logansport . . . Ind.	40.47 N	86.25 W
73	Loganville . . . Ga. (Atlanta In.)	33.50 N	83.54 W
133	Logone R. (lō-gō'nä) (lô-gôn') Fr. Eq. Afr.	10.0 N	15.40 E
132	Logoualé (lô-gwä-lā') . . Fr. W. Afr.	7.21 N	7.33 W
124	Logroño (lô-grō'nyō) . . . Sp.	42.27 N	2.25 W
124	Logrosán (lô-grô-sän') . . . Sp.	39.22 N	5.29 W
118	Lögstör (lûgh-stûr') . . . Den.	56.57 N	9.19 E
117	Lohe-Tonndorf (lō'hĕ-tōn'dôrf) Ger. (Hamburg In.)	53.35 N	10.8 E
122	Loire R. (lwȧr) . . . Fr.	47.55 N	2.0 E
122	Loir R. (lwȧr) . . . Fr.	47.40 N	0.25 E
100	Loja (lō'hä) . . . Ec.	4.2 S	79.3 W
124	Loja . . . Sp.	37.10 N	4.9 W
144	Lokchong (lôk'chông') . . . Chn.	25.13 N	112.50 E
129	Lokhvitsa (lôk-vēt'sȧ) . . . Sov. Un.	50.21 N	33.19 E
132	Lokoja (lô-kō'yä) . . . Nig.	7.57 N	6.41 E
117	Lokstedt (lôk'shtĕt) Ger. (Hamburg In.)	53.36 N	9.57 E
146	Loling (lō'lĭng') . . . Chn.	37.55 N	117.1 E
118	Lolland (I.) (lôl'än') . . . Den.	54.45 N	11.30 E
132	Lolo (lō'lō) . . . Cam.	3.15 N	10.38 E
133	Lol R. (lōl) . . . A. E. Sud.	9.0 N	28.0 E
127	Lom (lōm) . . . Bul.	43.48 N	23.12 E
134	Lomami R. (lô-mä'mê) . Bel. Cong.	5.0 S	25.3 E
99	Lomas B. (lō'mäs) Chl. (Magallanes In.)	52.35 S	69.0 W
102	Lomas de Zamora (lō'mäs dā zä-mō'rä) . Arg. (In.)	34.45 S	58.23 W
126	Lombardy (Prov.) (lŏm'bȧr-dĭ) . It.	45.15 N	9.30 E
151	Lomblen (I.) (lŏm-blĕn') . . . Indon.	8.20 S	123.45 E
150	Lombok (I.) (lŏm-bŏk') . . . Indon.	8.45 S	116.20 E
150	Lombok Str. . . . Indon.	8.30 S	115.45 E
132	Lomé (lō-mā') (lō'mä) . Fr. W. Afr.	6.11 N	1.12 E
134	Lomela (lô-mā'lä) . . . Bel. Cong.	2.20 S	23.40 E
134	Lomela R. . . . Bel. Cong.	1.12 S	22.0 E
80	Lometa (lô-mē'tȧ) . . . Tex.	31.10 N	98.25 W
133	Lomié (lô-mê-ā') . . . Cam.	3.12 N	13.35 E
114	Lomond, Lock (L.) (lŏk lō'mŭnd) Gt. Brit.	56.10 N	4.40 W
74	Lompoc (lŏm-pōk') . . . Calif.	34.38 N	120.30 W
121	Lomża (lôm'zhä) . . . Pol.	53.11 N	22.5 E
85	Lonaconing (lō-nȧ-kō'nĭng) . . . Md.	39.34 N	79.0 W
55	London (lŭn'dŭn) . . . Can.	43.2 N	81.30 W
117	London, Gt. Brit. (In.)		
114	London . . . Gt. Brit.	51.30 N	0.7 W
82	London . . . Ky.	37.7 N	84.7 W
84	London . . . Ohio	39.52 N	83.29 W
86	Londonderry (lŭn'dŭn-dĕr-ĭ) . Can.	45.29 N	63.37 W
114	Londonderry . . . N. Ire.	55.0 N	7.20 W
158	Londonderry, C. . . . Austl.	13.45 S	127.0 E
85	Lonely I. . . . Can.	45.34 N	81.26 W
72	Lonetree Res. (lōn'trē') Colo. (Denver In.)	40.20 N	105.7 W
134	Longa R. (lôŋ'gä) . . . Ang.	10.20 S	15.0 E
74	Long Beach . . . Calif.	33.47 N	118.11 W
85	Long Branch . . . N. J.	40.20 N	74.0 W
51	Long Branch . . Wash. (Seattle In.)	47.11 N	122.46 W
116	Long Eaton (ē'tŭn) . . . Gt. Brit.	52.54 N	1.17 W
117	Longfield (lông'fēld) . . . Gt. Brit.	51.24 N	0.18 E
160	Longford (lông'fērd) Austl. (Tas. In.)	41.37 S	147.7 E
114	Longford . . . Ire.	53.40 N	7.47 W
97	Long I. . . . Ba. Is.	23.20 N	75.9 W
86	Long I. . . . Can.	44.30 N	66.20 W
151	Long I. . . . N. Gui. Ter.	5.20 S	147.5 E
85	Long Is. . . . N. Y.	39.50 N	73.0 W
157	Long I. . . . N. Z.	47.13 S	167.28 E
88	Long Island City . . . N. Y. (In.)	40.46 N	73.54 W
85	Long Island Sd. . . . Conn.-N. Y.	41.10 N	72.30 W
123	Longjumeau (lôn-zhü-mō') Fr. (In.)	48.41 N	2.20 E
76	Longlake . . . S. D.	45.53 N	99.10 W
56	Long L. . . . Can. (Winnipeg In.)	50.6 N	97.57 W
86	Long L. . . . Me.	47.12 N	68.16 W
76	Long L. . . . N. D.	46.45 N	100.5 W
78	Longmont (lông'mŏnt) . . . Colo.	40.10 N	105.8 W
116	Longnor (lông'nôr) . . . Gt. Brit.	53.11 N	1.52 W
151	Longos (lôŋ'gōs) . Phil. (Manila In.)	14.20 N	121.33 E
76	Long Pine . . . Neb.	42.32 N	99.41 W
85	Long Pt. . . . Can.	42.33 N	80.5 W
87	Long Pt. . . . Can.	48.47 N	58.45 W
153	Long Pt. . . . Phil.	9.38 N	118.20 E
85	Long Point B. . . . Can.	42.40 N	80.10 W
77	Long Prairie . . . Minn.	45.56 N	94.50 W
87	Long Ra. . . . Can.	50.5 N	57.30 W
159	Longreach (lông'rēch) . . . Austl.	23.30 S	144.15 E
86	Long Reach (B.) . . . N. B.	45.30 N	66.0 W
116	Longridge (lông'rĭj) . . . Gt. Brit.	53.50 N	2.37 W
78	Longs Peak . . . Colo.	40.16 N	105.36 W
116	Longton (lông'tŭn) . . . Gt. Brit.	52.59 N	2.8 W
86	Longueuil (lôn-gû'y') . . . Can.	45.32 N	73.39 W
123	Longuyon (lôn-gwē-yôn') . . . Fr.	49.30 N	5.38 E
73	Longview (lông'vū) Ala. (Birmingham In.)	33.13 N	86.46 W
81	Longview . . . Tex.	32.29 N	94.45 W
70	Longview . . . Wash.	46.8 N	122.56 W
81	Longville (lông'vĭl) . . . La.	30.36 N	93.15 W
123	Longwy (lôn-wē') . . . Fr.	49.35 N	5.45 E
79	Lonoke (lō'nōk) . . . Ark.	34.47 N	91.52 W
123	Lons-le-Saunier (lôn-lē-sō-nyā') Fr.	46.40 N	5.30 E
152	Looc (lô-ōk') . . . Phil.	12.16 N	122.0 E
151	Looc B. . . . Phil. (Manila In.)	14.15 N	120.33 E
84	Loogootie (lō-gō'tē) . . . Ind.	38.42 N	86.57 W
83	Lookout, C. (lŏŏk'out) . . . N. C.	34.36 N	76.33 W
160	Lookout, Mt. . . . Austl. (In.)	30.25 S	152.35 E
153	Loon (lô-ōn') . . . Phil.	9.47 N	123.49 E
114	Loop Hd. . . . Ire.	52.35 N	9.55 W
122	Loos (lô-ōs') . . . Fr.	50.37 N	3.0 E
83	Loosahatchie R. (lō-zȧ-hă'chē) Tenn.	35.18 N	89.40 W
139	Lopatka, C. (lô-pät'kȧ) . . Sov. Un.	50.50 N	156.50 E
152	Lopez (lō'päz) . . . Phil.	13.53 N	122.15 E
72	Lopez . . . Wash. (Vancouver In.)	48.32 N	122.55 W
152	Lopez B. . . . Phil.	14.0 N	122.5 E
72	Lopez I. . . Wash. (Vancouver In.)	48.30 N	122.54 W
145	Loping (lō'pĭng') . . . Chn.	29.2 N	117.6 E
142	Lop Nor (L.) (lŏp nōr') . . . Chn.	40.0 N	90.0 E
133	Lopori R. (lō-pō'rē) . . . Bel. Cong.	1.30 N	21.0 E
124	Lora (lō'rä) . . . Sp.	37.40 N	5.31 W
84	Lorain (lō-rān') . . . Ohio	41.27 N	82.9 W
141	Loralai (lō-rŭ-lī') . . . Pak.	30.30 N	68.38 E
124	Lorca (lôr'kä) . . . Sp.	37.40 N	1.41 W
159	Lord Howe I. (hou) . . . Pac. O.	31.46 S	159.8 E
75	Lordsburg (lôrdz'bûrg) . . . N. M.	32.22 N	108.43 W
99	Lorena (lô-rā'nȧ) Braz. (Rio de Janeiro In.)	22.46 S	45.7 W
101	Loreta (lô-rā'tō) . . . Braz.	7.2 S	45.20 W
57	Lorette (lô-rĕt') . Can. (Quebec In.)	46.48 N	71.21 W
100	Lorica (lô-rē'kä) . . . Col.	9.5 N	75.45 W
122	Lorient (lō-rē'äN') . . . Fr.	47.48 N	3.12 W
114	Lorne, Firth of (lôrn) . . . Gt. Brit.	56.15 N	5.50 W
120	Lörrach (lûr'äk) . . . Ger.	47.37 N	7.40 E
73	Los Alamitos (lōs ăl-ȧ-mē'tōs) Calif. (Los Angeles In.)	33.49 N	118.4 W
102	Los Andes (State) (lōs än'dās) Arg.	25.0 S	67.30 W
99	Los Andes . . . Chl. (Valparaiso In.)	32.50 S	70.38 W
74	Los Angeles (lōs ăŋ'gĕl-ĕs) (lōs ăn'jĕl-ĕs) (lōs äŋ'hâ-lās) . Calif.	34.3 N	118.15 W
73	Los Angeles . . . Calif. (In.)		
102	Los Angeles (lōs äŋ'hâ-lās) . . . Chl.	37.20 S	72.29 W
74	Los Angeles Aqueduct . . . Calif.	35.0 N	118.12 W
73	Los Angeles R. Calif. (Los Angeles In.)	33.53 N	118.13 W
151	Los Baños (lōs bä'nyōs) Phil. (Manila In.)	14.12 N	121.15 E
124	Los Barrios (lōs bär'rē-ōs) . . . Sp.	36.11 N	5.29 W
150	Loser, Mt. (lōs'ĕr) . . . Indon.	3.42 N	97.20 E
74	Los Gatos (lōs gä'tōs) . . . Calif.	37.13 N	121.59 W
146	Loshan (lō'shän') . . . Chn.	32.15 N	114.25 E
80	Los Herreros (lōs ĕr-rā-rōs) . . Mex.	25.55 N	99.23 W
128	Losinoostrovskaya (lô'sê-nô-ôs-trôf'skȧ-yȧ) . Sov. Un.	55.51 N	37.41 E
97	Los Llanos (lōs lyä'nōs) . . . Hai.	18.36 N	69.30 W
73	Los Nietos (lōs nyā'tōs) Calif. (Los Angeles In.)	33.57 N	118.5 W
96	Los Organos Mts. (lōs ôr'gä-nōs) Cuba	22.40 N	83.12 W
96	Los Palacios (lōs pȧ-lä'sê-ōs) . Cuba	22.32 N	83.14 W
75	Los Pinos R. (lōs pē'nôs) Colo.-N. M.	37.0 N	107.35 W
92	Los Reyes (lōs rā'yĕs) . . . Mex.	19.29 N	102.29 W
95	Los Santos (lōs săn'tōs) . . . Pan.	7.56 N	80.24 W
124	Los Santos . . . Sp.	38.28 N	6.21 W
73	Lost Cr. Utah (Salt Lake City In.)	41.7 N	111.30 W
99	Los Toldos (lōs tōl'dōs) Arg. (Buenos Aires In.)	35.1 S	61.3 W
71	Los R. . . . Ida.	44.3 N	113.50 W
70	Lost R. . . . Ore.	42.7 N	121.30 W
71	Lost River Mts. . . . Ida.	44.20 N	113.50 W
102	Los Vilos (lōs vē'lōs) . . . Chl.	31.59 S	71.32 W
102	Lota (lō'tä) . . . Chl.	37.15 S	73.10 W
145	Lotien (lō'tyĕn') . . . Chn.	30.48 N	115.20 E
144	Loting (lō'tĭng') . . . Chn.	22.48 N	111.23 E
97	Lo Torro (Pk.) (lō tôr'rō) . . . Hai.	18.48 N	72.57 W
122	Lot R. (lō) . . . Fr.	44.30 N	0.55 E
122	Lötschen Tunnel (lût'shĕn) . Switz.	46.25 N	7.45 E
145	Lotung (lō'tōōng') . . . For.	24.41 N	121.46 E
	Lötzen, see Giżycko, Pol.		
150	Louangprabang (lōō-äng'-prä-bäng') . Indoch.	19.50 N	102.5 E
122	Loudon (lōō-dôn') . . . Fr.	47.2 N	0.1 E
82	Loudon (lou'dŭn) . . . Tenn.	35.44 N	84.23 W
84	Loudonville (lou'dŭn-vĭl) . . . Ohio	40.40 N	82.16 W
132	Louga (lōō'gä) . . . Fr. W. Afr.	15.33 N	16.20 W
114	Loughborough (lŭf'bŭr-ō) . Gt. Brit.	52.45 N	1.15 W
117	Loughton (lou'tŭn) Gt. Brit. (London In.)	51.39 N	0.3 E
57	Louisa (lōō-ē'zȧ) Can. (Montreal In.)	45.47 N	74.22 W
84	Louisa . . . Ky.	38.5 N	82.37 W
87	Louisburg (lōō'ĭs-bûrg) . . . Can.	45.55 N	60.0 W
83	Louisburg . . . N. C.	36.6 N	78.18 W
159	Louisiade Arch. (lōō-ē'zê-ăd) Pap. Ter.	11.0 S	153.30 E
79	Louisiana (lōō-ē-zê-ăn'ȧ) . . . Mo.	39.26 N	91 3 W
81	Louisiana (State) . . . U. S.	31.0 N	92.0 W
134	Louis Trichardt (lōō'ĭs trĭch'ärt) U. S. Afr.	22.58 S	29.58 E
78	Louisville (lōō'ĭs-vĭl) (lōō'ê-vĭl) Colo.	39.57 N	105.9 W
83	Louisville . . . Ga.	33.0 N	82.25 W
84	Louisville . . . Ky.	38.15 N	85.45 W
82	Louisville . . . Miss.	33.7 N	89.3 W
124	Loulé (lō-lā') . . . Port.	37.8 N	8.2 W
120	Louny (lō'nê) . . . Czech.	50.20 N	13.47 E
76	Loup City . . . Neb.	41.17 N	98.58 W
76	Loup R. (lōōp) . . . Neb.	41.20 N	98.0 W
76	Loup R., North . . . Neb.	41.50 N	99.30 W
122	Lourdes (lōōrd) . . . Fr.	43.7 N	0.3 W
134	Lourenço Marques (lō-rĕn'sô mär'kĕs) . Moz.	25.50 S	32.33 E
125	Loures (lō'rĕzh) . . . Port. (In.)	38.49 N	9.10 W
124	Lousa (lō'zȧ) . . . Port.	40.6 N	8.15 W
114	Louth (louth) . . . Gt. Brit.	53.20 N	0.0
115	Louvain (lōō-văN') . . . Bel.	50.51 N	4.40 E
72	Louviers (lōō-vyā') (lōō-vērz') Colo. (Denver In.)	39.29 N	105.0 W
122	Louviers (lōō-vyā') . . . Fr.	49.15 N	1.11 E
123	Louvres (lōōv'r') . . . Fr. (In.)	49.2 N	2.30 E
128	Lovat R. (lô-vát'y') . . . Sov. Un.	57.4 N	30.55 E
127	Loveč (lō'vĕts) . . . Bul.	43.8 N	24.40 E
73	Lovejoy (lŭv'joi) . Ga. (Atlanta In.)	33.27 N	84.18 W
78	Loveland (lŭv'lănd) . . . Colo.	40.24 N	105.6 W
72	Loveland and Greeley Ditch Colo. (Denver In.)	40.23 N	104.55 W
71	Lovell (lŭv'ĕl) . . . Wyo.	44.51 N	108.23 W
74	Lovelock (lŭv'lŏk) . . . Nev.	40.11 N	118.28 W
119	Loviisa (lô'vē-sä) . . . Fin.	60.28 N	26.11 E
4	Low (Tuamotu) Arch. (lō) (tōō-ä-mō'tōō) . Pac. O.	17.0 S	145.0 W
134	Lowa R. (lō'wä) . . . Bel. Cong.	1.15 S	27.15 E
75	Lowell (lō'ĕl) . . . Ariz.	31.26 N	109.53 W
84	Lowell . . . Ind.	41.17 N	87.25 W
86	Lowell . . . Mass.	42.40 N	71.20 W
84	Lowell . . . Mich.	42.57 N	85.20 W
73	Lowe, Mt. (lō) Calif. (Los Angeles In.)	34.14 N	118.7 W
54	Lower Arrow L. . . . Can.	49.50 N	118.1 W
76	Lower Brule Indian Res. (brü'lā) S. D.	44.7 N	99.58 W
156	Lower Hutt (hŭt) . . . N. Z. (In.)	41.12 S	174.55 E
70	Lower Klamath L. (klăm'ăth) Ore.-Calif.	41.59 N	121.49 W
70	Lower L. . . . Calif.-Nev.	51.14 N	120.3 W
74	Lower Otay Reservoir (ō'tā) Calif. (In.)	32.37 N	116.53 W
77	Lower Red L. . . . Minn.	47.57 N	95.0 W
115	Lowestoft (lō'stŏft) . . . Gt. Brit.	52.30 N	1.42 E
121	Lowicz (lō'vĭch) . . . Pol.	52.5 N	19.57 E
117	Lowton (lō'tŭn) Gt. Brit. (Liverpool In.)	53.28 N	2.34 W
85	Lowville (lou'vĭl) . . . N. Y.	43.47 N	75.28 W
93	Loxicha (San Agustin) (lô-zē'chä) (sän ä-gōōs-tēn') . Mex.	16.3 N	96.46 W
159	Loyalty Is. (loi'ăl-tê) . . . N. Cal.	21.0 S	167.30 E
144	Loyung (lō'yōōng') . . . Chn.	24.26 N	109.42 E
127	Loznica (lôz'nê-tsä) . . . Yugo.	44.31 N	19.15 E
129	Lozovatka (lô-zô-vät'kä) . Sov. Un.	48.3 N	33.16 E
129	Lozovaya (lô-zô-vä'yä) . . Sov. Un.	48.54 N	36.18 E
129	Lozovaya-Pavlovka (päv-lôf'kȧ) Sov. Un.	48.26 N	38.47 E
125	Lozoya, Can. of (Aqueduct) (lô-thō'yä) . Sp. (In.)	40.33 N	3.42 W
134	Lualaba-Congo R. . . . Bel. Cong.	4.30 S	26.30 E
134	Lualaba R. (lōō-ä-lä'bä) . Bel. Cong.	9.12 S	25.38 E
134	Luama R. (lōō-ä'mä) . . Bel. Cong.	4.30 S	28.15 E
134	Luanda (Dist.) (lōō-än'dä) . . . Ang.	9.15 S	15.45 E
134	Luanda (lōō-än'dä) . . . Ang.	8.47 S	13.15 E
134	Luanginga R. (lōō-än-gĭŋ'gä) Ang.-N. Rh.	14.10 S	22.0 E

ng-sing; ŋ-baŋk; N-nasalized n; nŏd; cŏmmit; ōld; ôbey; ôrder; fōōd; fŏŏt; ou-out; s-soft; sh-dish; th-thin; pūre; ûnite; ûrn; stŭd; circŭs; ü-as "y" in study; '-indeterminate vowel.

Luangwa PRONOUNCING INDEX Mackinaw

Page	Name Pronunciation Region	Lat. °′	Long. °′
134	Luangwa R. (lo͞o-äṉ'gwȧ)..N. Rh.	12.47 S	32.0 E
134	Luapula R. (lo͞o-ȧ-po͞o'lä) Bel. Cong.-N. Rh.	12.15 S	29.0 E
124	Luarca (lwär'kä)..............Sp.	43.34 N	6.35 W
121	Lubaczów (lo͞o-bä'cho͝of).....Pol.	50.8 N	23.8 E
120	Lubań (lo͞o'bän')............Pol.	51.7 N	15.17 E
119	Lubanas, L. (lo͞o'bȧ-nȧs).Sov. Un.	56.46 N	26.55 E
152	Lubang (lo͞o-bäng')..........Phil.	13.50 N	120.7 E
152	Lubang I..................Phil.	13.45 N	120.10 E
152	Lubang Is.................Phil.	13.45 N	120.25 E
152	Lubao (lo͞o-bä'ō)...........Phil.	14.56 N	120.36 E
121	Lubartów (lo͞o-bär'to͞of)......Pol.	51.27 N	22.36 E
121	Lubawa (lo͞o-bä'vä)..........Pol.	53.31 N	19.48 E
78	Lubbock (lŭb'ŭk)............Tex.	33.35 N	101.51 W
86	Lubec (lū'bĕk)..............Me.	44.50 N	67.2 W
120	Lübben (lüb'ĕn).............Ger.	51.57 N	13.52 E
120	Lübeck (lü'bĕk).............Ger.	53.53 N	101.41 E
120	Lübeck B...................Ger.	54.5 N	11.10 E
134	Lubilash R. (lo͞o-bē-lȧsh') Bel. Cong.	7.30 S	23.58 E
120	Lubin (lyo͝o'bĭn)............Pol.	51.24 N	16.13 E
121	Lublin (lyo͝o'blēn')..........Pol.	51.13 N	22.32 E
129	Lubny (lo͞ob'nē)........Sov. Un.	50.1 N	33.1 E
124	Lubrín (lo͞o-brēn')............Sp.	37.14 N	2.4 W
134	Lubudi R. (lo͞o-bo͞o'dē).Bel. Cong.	9.30 S	25.0 E
152	Lubungan (lo͞o-bo͞oŋ'gän)....Phil.	17.21 N	121.11 E
153	Lubungan (lo͞o-bo͞oŋ-gän)....Phil.	8.30 N	123.19 E
126	Lucca (lo͞ok'kä)..............It.	43.51 N	10.30 E
114	Luce B. (lūs)...........Gt. Brit.	54.45 N	4.40 W
152	Lucena (lo͞o-sä'nä)..........Phil.	13.56 N	121.37 E
124	Lucena (lo͞o-thā'nä)..........Sp.	37.25 N	4.29 W
125	Lucena de Cid (lo͞o-thā'nä dā thēdh').Sp.	40.8 N	0.19 W
121	Lučenec (lo͞o'chȧ-nyĕts)....Czech.	48.19 N	19.42 E
126	Lucera (lo͞o-châ'rä)...........It.	41.30 N	15.21 E
72	Lucerne (lû-sûrn') Colo. (Denver In.)	40.28 N	104.42 W
	Lucerne, see Luzern, Switz.		
120	Lucerne, L. of (lü-sĕrn') (lo͞o-tsĕrn').Switz.	46.59 N	8.30 E
146	Lucheng (lo͞o'chĕng')........Chn.	36.30 N	113.24 E
142	Luchow (lo͞o'chō')...........Chn.	20.0 N	105.20 E
144	Luchow (Liuchow).........Chn.	24.22 N	109.30 E
146	Lüchow (lü'chō')...........Chn.	31.51 N	117.9 E
71	Lucin (lû-sēn').............Utah	41.22 N	113.54 W
151	Lucipara Is. (lo͞o-sē-pä'rȧ)..Indon.	5.30 S	127.45 E
120	Luckenwalde (lo͞ok-ĕn-väl'dĕ).Ger.	52.6 N	13.9 E
141	Lucknow (lŭk'nou).........India	26.46 N	80.59 E
122	Luçon (lü-sôɴ')..............Fr.	46.28 N	1.11 W
94	Lucrecia Pt. (lo͞o-krā'sē-ȧ)...Cuba	21.4 N	75.36 W
120	Lüdenscheid (lü'dĕn-shīt).....Ger.	51.13 N	7.37 E
134	Lüderitz (lü'dēr-ĭts) (lü'dĕ-rĭts) S. W. Afr.	26.38 S	15.12 E
134	Lüderitz B..........S. W. Afr.	26.30 S	15.5 E
84	Ludington (lŭd'ĭng-tŭn)....Mich.	44.0 N	86.28 W
116	Ludlow (lŭd'lō)..........Gt. Brit.	52.22 N	2.43 W
89	Ludlow......Ky. (Cincinnati In.)	39.6 N	84.33 W
118	Ludvika (lo͞odh-vē'kȧ)......Swe.	60.10 N	15.11 E
120	Ludwigsburg (lo͞ot'vēks-bo͝orgh) Ger.	48.54 N	9.13 E
120	Ludwigshafen (lo͞ot'vēks-hä'fĕn) Ger.	49.28 N	8.25 E
120	Ludwigslust (lo͞ot'vēks-lo͞ost).Ger.	53.19 N	11.30 E
119	Ludza (lo͞od'zȧ)..........Sov. Un.	56.31 N	27.42 E
134	Luebo (lo͞o-ā'bō).......Bel. Cong.	5.20 S	21.20 E
134	Lufira R. (lo͞o-fē'rȧ)....Bel. Cong.	10.0 S	27.12 E
81	Lufkin (lŭf'kĭn)............Tex.	31.21 N	94.45 W
128	Luga (lo͞o'gȧ)...........Sov. Un.	58.42 N	29.52 E
120	Lugano (lo͞o-gä'nō).........Switz.	46.1 N	8.56 E
	Lugansk, see Vorichilovgrad, Sov. Un.		
128	Luga R...............Sov. Un.	59.4 N	29.20 E
116	Lugg R. (lŭg)............Gt. Brit.	52.9 N	2.42 W
135	Lugh (lo͞og).................Som.	3.47 N	42.38 E
126	Lugo (lo͞o'gō).................It.	44.25 N	11.54 E
124	Lugo (lo͞o'gō)................Sp.	43.1 N	7.33 W
127	Lugos (lo͞o'gōsh)...........Rom.	45.41 N	21.56 E
117	Lühe R. (lü'ĕ).Ger. (Hamburg In.)	53.30 N	9.33 E
146	Luho (lo͞o'hō')...............Chn.	32.22 N	118.48 E
134	Luilaka R. (lo͞o-ē-lä'kȧ).Bel. Cong.	1.52 S	21.0 E
144	Lui R. (lwē)..................Chn.	25.55 N	111.35 E
114	Luimneach (Limerick) (lĭm'nȧk) Ire.	52.38 N	8.58 W
151	Luisiana (lo͞o-ē-sē-ä'nä) Phil. (Manila In.)	14.12 N	121.35 E
99	Luján (lo͞o-hän') Arg. (Buenos Aires In.)	34.32 S	59.9 W
135	Lujenda R. (lo͞o-zhĕn'dȧ)....Moz.	12.15 S	37.30 E
134	Lukanga Swamp (lo͞o-käŋ'gȧ) N. Rh.	14.15 S	27.45 E
134	Lukenie R. (lo͞o-kā'nyȧ).Bel. Cong.	3.12 S	20.0 E
145	Lukfung (lo͞ok'fo͞ong').......Chn.	22.56 N	115.30 E
144	Luki (lo͞o'kē')...............Chn.	28.11 N	109.48 E
145	Lukiang (lo͞o'kyäng').........Chn.	31.15 N	117.19 E
135	Lukigura (R.) (lo͞o-kē-go͞o'rä).Tan.	6.0 S	37.54 E
134	Lukolele (lo͞o-kō-lā'lā)..Bel. Cong.	1.12 S	17.18 E
127	Lukovit (lo͞o'kō-vēt').......Bul.	43.12 N	24.9 E
121	Łuków (wo͞o'ko͞of)...........Pol.	51.56 N	22.23 E
134	Lukuga R. (lo͞o-ko͞o'gȧ).Bel. Cong.	5.55 S	28.15 E
108	Luleå (lo͞o'lĕ-ō)............Swe.	65.38 N	22.0 E
127	Lüleburgaz (lü'lĕ-bo͝or-gäs').Tur.	41.24 N	27.22 E
135	Luli (lúrio) (lo͞o'lē) (lo͞o'rē-ō).Moz.	14.9 S	38.0 E
81	Luling (lū'lĭng)............Tex.	29.41 N	97.38 W
134	Lulua bourg (lo͞o'lo͞o-ȧ-bo͞org') Bel. Cong.	6.15 S	22.25 E
134	Lulua R. (lo͞o'lo͞o-ȧ)....Bel. Cong.	7.0 S	22.30 E
72	Lulu I. (lū'lo͞o) Can. (Vancouver In.)	49.9 N	123.11 W
151	Lumban (lo͞om-bän') Phil. (Manila In.)	14.17 N	121.32 E
83	Lumber R................N. C.	34.50 N	79.20 W
82	Lumberton (lŭm'bēr-tŭn)...Miss.	31.0 N	89.27 W
83	Lumberton...............N. C.	34.36 N	78.59 W
134	Lumbira (lo͞om-bē'rȧ).......Tan.	9.32 S	34.10 E
72	Lummi I. (lŭm'ĭ) Wash. (Vancouver In.)	48.41 N	122.40 W
152	Luna (lo͞o'nȧ)..............Phil.	16.51 N	120.23 E
118	Lund (lŭnd)................Swe.	55.42 N	13.10 E
134	Lunda (Dist.) (lo͞on'dȧ).....Ang.	9.15 S	20.15 E
134	Lundi R. (lo͞on'dē)........S. Rh.	20.52 S	31.0 E
114	Lundy (I.) (lŭn'dē).....Gt. Brit.	51.10 N	4.40 W
120	Lüneburg (lü'nē-bo͝orgh).....Ger.	53.16 N	10.23 E
120	Lüneburger Heide (Moorlands) (lü'nĕ-bo͝or-gĕr hī'dĕ).Ger.	53.0 N	10.2 E
122	Lunel (lü-nĕl')................Fr.	43.40 N	4.9 E
86	Lunenburg (lo͞o'nĕn-bûrg)....Can.	44.25 N	64.15 W
87	Lunenburg..........Mass. (In.)	42.36 N	71.43 W
116	Lune, R. (lūn)..........Gt. Brit.	54.6 N	2.39 W
123	Luneville (lü-nȧ-vēl').........Fr.	48.38 N	6.30 E
144	Lungan (lo͞oŋ'gän')..........Chn.	23.12 N	107.48 E
134	Lunga R. (lo͞oŋ'gȧ).........N. Rh.	13.0 S	26.30 E
148	Lungchen (lo͞ong'chĕn).......Chn.	48.45 N	126.50 E
148	Lungchingtsun (lo͞ong'chĭng'tso͞on') Chn.	42.47 N	129.27 E
144	Lungchow (lo͞ong'chō')......Chn.	22.27 N	106.49 E
145	Lungchuan (lo͞ong'cho͞o-än').Chn.	26.38 N	113.54 E
144	Lungchüan (lo͞ong'chü-än')..Chn.	27.51 N	107.48 E
145	Lungchun (lo͞ong'cho͞on')....Chn.	24.4 N	115.0 E
134	Lunge Bungo R. (lŭn'gā bŭn'gō) Ang.-N. Rh.	13.20 S	22.0 E
142	Lungein-Bulan (lo͞oŋ'gän'-bo͞o-län').Mong.	47.42 N	105.4 E
145	Lungkang L. (lo͞ong'käng')..Chn.	29.55 N	116.8 E
143	Lungkiang (Tsitsihar) (lo͞ong'-kyäng') (tsēt-sē-här').Chn.	47.28 N	123.57 E
146	Lungkow (lo͞ong'kō')........Chn.	37.42 N	120.15 E
144	Lungli (lo͞ong'lē')...........Chn.	26.25 N	106.49 E
144	Lungmoon (lo͞ong'mo͞on')....Chn.	23.46 N	114.12 E
145	Lungnan (lo͞ong'nän')........Chn.	24.47 N	114.15 E
146	Lungping (lo͞ong'pĭng')......Chn.	37.26 N	114.54 E
144	Lung R. (lo͞ong)..............Chn.	24.35 N	108.20 E
144	Lungshan (lo͞ong'shän')......Chn.	29.22 N	109.3 E
145	Lungyen (lo͞ong'yĕn')........Chn.	25.10 N	116.50 E
145	Lungyu (lo͞ong'yo͞o')........Chn.	29.2 N	119.17 E
128	Luninets (lo͞o-nēn'yets)..Sov. Un.	52.14 N	26.49 E
153	Lun R. (lo͞on)...............Phil.	6.5 N	125.28 E
157	Lunsden (lŭnz'dĕn).........N. Z.	45.43 S	168.28 E
131	Luozi (lo͞o-ō'zē) Bel Cong. (Brazzaville In.)	4.55 S	14.7 E
143	Lupei (lo͞o'pī)................Chn.	44.35 N	121.0 E
143	Lupin (Manchouli) (lo͞o'pĭn') (män-cho͞o'lē).Chn.	49.34 N	117.28 E
133	Luqsor (lŭk'sôr)............Eg.	25.40 N	32.40 E
102	Luque (lo͞o'kä)..............Par.	25.15 S	57.30 W
85	Luray (lū-rā')................Va.	38.39 N	78.28 W
123	Lure (lür)....................Fr.	47.43 N	6.29 E
114	Lurgan (lûr'găn)..........N. Ire.	54.25 N	6.25 W
100	Lurigancho (lo͞o-rē-gän'chō) Peru (In.)	12.1 S	77.0 W
135	Lúrio (Luli) R. (lo͞o'rē-ō) (lo͞o'lē) Moz.	14.9 S	38.0 E
117	Lurup (lo͞o-ro͞op') Ger. (Hamburg In.)	53.35 N	9.52 E
134	Lusaka (lo͞o-sä'kȧ)........N. Rh.	15.27 S	28.17 E
134	Lusambo (lo͞o-säm'bō)..Bel. Cong.	4.52 S	23.30 E
135	Lushoto (lo͞o-shō'tō)..........Tan.	4.47 S	38.17 E
146	Lushun (Port Arthur) (lo͞o'shŭn) Chn.	38.51 N	121.7 E
76	Lusk (lŭsk).................Wyo.	42.47 N	104.28 W
126	Lussino (I.) (lo͞os-sē'nō)...Yugo.	44.35 N	14.24 E
126	Lussinpiccolo (lo͞os-sēn'pēk'kō-lō) Yugo.	44.31 N	14.29 E
81	Lutcher (lŭch'ēr)............La.	30.3 N	90.42 W
120	Lutherstadt (Wittenberg) (lo͞o'tēr-shtät) (vĭt'ĕn-bĕrk).Ger.	51.53 N	12.40 E
114	Luton (lū'tŭn)..........Gt. Brit.	51.55 N	0.20 W
121	Lutsk (lo͞otsk)..........Sov. Un.	50.45 N	25.20 E
82	Luverne (lū-vûrn')...........Ala.	31.42 N	86.16 W
76	Luverne...................Minn.	43.39 N	96.3 W
134	Luvua R. (lo͞o'vo͞o-ȧ)..Bel. Cong.	7.45 S	28.0 E
134	Luvungi (lo͞o-vo͞oŋ'gē).Bel. Cong.	2.53 S	28.58 E
82	Luxapallila R. (lŭk-sȧ-pôl'ĭ-lȧ).Ala.	33.35 N	88.0 W
123	Luxembourg (lŭk-sĕm-bûrg) (lük-säɴ-bo͞or') (lo͞ok-sĕm-bo͝orgh).Eur.	49.50 N	6.0 E
123	Luxeuil (lük-sû'y')............Fr.	47.50 N	6.20 E
90	Luyanó (lo͞o-yä-nō') Cuba (Habana In.)	23.7 N	82.20 W
90	Luyanó R....Cuba (Habana In.)	23.6 N	82.20 W
110	Luza R. (lo͞o'zȧ)........Sov. Un.	60.40 N	47.30 E
120	Luzern (lo͞o-tsĕrn')..........Switz.	47.3 N	8.17 E
120	Luzern, L. of...............Switz.	47.1 N	8.25 E
152	Luzon (I.) (lo͞o-zŏn')........Phil.	15.35 N	120.45 E
121	Lvov (lvo͞of)............Sov. Un.	49.49 N	24.2 E
146	Lwancheng (lwän'chĕng')....Chn.	37.57 N	114.42 E
146	Lwanchow (lwän'chō')........Chn.	39.50 N	118.43 E
139	Lyakhovskie (Is.) (lyȧ'kôf-skē) Sov. Un.	73.30 N	142.0 E
156	Lyall B. (lī'ăl)..........N. Z. (In.)	41.20 S	174.49 E
137	Lydda (lĭd'ȧ)..........Pal. (In.)	31.58 N	34.54 E
134	Lydenburg (lī'dĕn-bûrg).U. S. Afr.	25.8 S	30.25 E
117	Lydgate (lĭd'gāt) Gt. Brit. (Liverpool In.)	53.32 N	2.57 W
160	Lyell, Mt. (lī'ĕl)..Austl. (Tas. In.)	42.1 S	145.39 E
74	Lyell, Mt....................Calif.	37.44 N	119.17 W
85	Lykens (lī'kĕnz)..............Pa.	40.32 N	76.45 W
117	Lymm (lĭm) Gt. Brit. (Liverpool In.)	53.22 N	2.28 W
121	Lyna R. (lĭn'ȧ)...............Pol.	53.55 N	20.24 E
82	Lynch (lĭnch)................Ky.	36.57 N	82.56 W
85	Lynchburg (lĭnch'bûrg).......Va.	37.25 N	79.10 W
83	Lynches R. (lĭn'chĕz).......S. C.	34.10 N	80.10 W
70	Lynden (lĭn'dĕn)..........Wash.	48.56 N	122.28 W
86	Lyndonville (lĭn'dŭn-vĭl)......Vt.	44.32 N	72.0 W
86	Lynn (lĭn)..................Mass.	42.29 N	70.59 W
122	Lyon (lē-ôɴ')..................Fr.	45.45 N	4.50 E
72	Lyons (lī'ŭnz)..Colo. (Denver In.)	40.14 N	105.17 W
83	Lyons........................Ga.	32.8 N	82.17 W
88	Lyons..........Ill. (Chicago In.)	41.49 N	87.48 W
78	Lyons......................Kan.	38.21 N	98.12 W
76	Lyons......................Neb.	41.57 N	96.28 W
85	Lyons......................N. Y.	43.5 N	76.58 W
55	Lyon Str. (lī'ŭn)............Can.	62.48 N	81.30 W
118	Lyse Fjord (lü'sĕ fyōr')......Nor.	59.0 N	6.18 E
118	Lysekil (lü'sĕ-kĕl)...........Swe.	58.17 N	11.22 E
121	Lysogóry (Mts.) (wē-sō-go͞o'rē).Pol.	50.56 N	21.0 E
110	Lysva (lĭs'vȧ)..........Sov. Un.	58.5 N	57.49 E
116	Lytham (lĭth'ăm).......Gt. Brit.	53.44 N	2.58 W
157	Lyttelton (lĭt''l-tŭn)...N. Z. (In.)	43.35 S	172.44 E
157	Lyttelton, Port.......N. Z. (In.)	43.35 S	172.46 E
54	Lytton (lĭt'ŭn)...............Can.	50.9 N	121.25 W
128	Lyuban (lyo͞o'bän)......Sov. Un.	59.20 N	31.18 E
129	Lyubar (lyo͞o'bär).......Sov. Un.	49.56 N	27.46 E
128	Lyubertsi (lyo͞o'bĕr-tsē)..Sov. Un.	55.41 N	37.58 E
128	Lyubim (lyo͞o-bēm')......Sov. Un.	58.21 N	40.41 E
128	Lyudinovo (lyo͞o-dē-nô'vō) Sov. Un.	53.51 N	34.24 E
50	Ma'an (mä-än')..............Jor.	30.15 N	35.45 E
119	Maarianhamina (Mariehamn) (mä'rē-ȧn-hä'mē-nȧ) (mä-rē'ĕ-häm''n).Fin.	60.8 N	19.58 E
118	Maarvand (L.) (môr'vän)...Nor.	60.10 N	8.15 E
153	Maasin (mä-ä'sĭn)...........Phil.	10.8 N	124.51 E
115	Maastricht (mäs'trĭkt).....Neth.	50.50 N	5.40 E
81	Mabank (mā'bănk).........Tex.	32.22 N	96.7 W
151	Mabatan (mä-bä-tän') Phil. (Manila In.)	14.43 N	120.28 E
152	Mabini (mä-bē'nē)..........Phil.	13.44 N	120.56 E
153	Mabini.....................Phil.	9.51 N	124.31 E
151	Mabitao (mä-bē-tä'ō) Phil. (Manila In.)	14.27 N	121.30 E
73	Mableton (mā'b'l-tŭn) Ga. (Atlanta In.)	33.48 N	84.35 W
112	Mabrouk (mȧ-bro͞ok')........Alg.	29.20 N	0.20 E
132	Mabrouk............Fr. W. Afr.	19.30 N	1.15 W
151	Macabebe (mä-kä-bā'bā) Phil. (Manila In.)	14.54 N	120.38 E
86	McAdam (măk-ăd'ăm)......Can.	45.36 N	67.21 W
101	Macaé (mä-kä-ā')..........Braz.	22.18 S	41.50 W
153	Macajalar B. (mä-kä-hä-lär').Phil.	8.35 N	124.40 E
152	Macalelon (mä-kä-lā-lōn')...Phil.	13.45 N	122.8 E
79	McAlester (măk ăl'ĕs-tēr)...Okla.	34.56 N	95.45 W
160	Macalister (mă-kăl'ĭs-tēr) Austl. (In.)	27.4 S	151.3 E
133	Macalle (mä'kȧ-lä)..........Eth.	13.30 N	39.30 E
80	McAllen (măk-ăl'ĕn)........Tex.	26.12 N	98.14 W
101	Macapá (mä-kä-pä')........Braz.	0.1 S	51.1 W
150	Macassar Str. (Makasser) (mȧ-kăs'ăr).Indon.	2.0 S	118.30 E
80	McCamey (mȧ-kā'mĭ).......Tex.	31.7 N	102.15 W
144	Macau (mȧ-kä'o͞o)...........Chn.	22.7 N	113.10 E
101	Macau.....................Braz.	5.5 S	36.31 W
144	Macau......................Asia	22.7 N	113.10 E
82	McCaysville (mȧ-kāz'vĭl).....Ga.	34.57 N	84.21 W
114	Macclesfield (măk''lz-fēld) Gt. Brit.	53.15 N	2.10 W
116	Macclesfield Can........Gt. Brit.	53.15 N	2.7 W
151	MacCluer G. (mȧ-klo͞or') Neth. N. Gui.	2.15 S	132.30 E
83	McColl (mȧ-kôl')...........S. C.	34.38 N	79.32 W
82	McComb (mȧ-kōm').........Miss.	31.14 N	90.29 W
78	McCook (mȧ-ko͝ok').........Neb.	40.13 N	100.38 W
83	McCormick (mȧ-kôr'mĭk)...S. C.	33.55 N	82.18 W
47	McDonald (I.) (măk-dŏn'ăld) Ind. O.	53.0 S	72.45 E
158	Macdonald, L. (măk-dŏn'ăld) Austl.	23.30 S	128.30 E
158	Macdonnell Ranges (măk-dŏn'ĕl) Austl.	23.30 S	133.0 E
73	McDonough (măk-dŏn'ō) Ga. (Atlanta In.)	33.27 N	84.9 W
54	Macdougall, L. (măk-do͞o'găl) Can.	66.10 N	98.45 W
127	Macedonia (Prov.) (măs-ē-dō'nĭ-ȧ) Grc.	41.0 N	22.50 E
101	Maceió (mä-sȧ-yō')........Braz.	9.31 S	35.45 W
134	Macequece (mä-sȧ-kā'sȧ)....Moz.	19.2 S	32.45 E
126	Macerata (mä-châ-rä'tä)......It.	43.17 N	13.27 E
79	McGehee (mȧ-gē')...........Ark.	33.37 N	91.24 W
74	McGill (mȧ-gĭl')...............Nev.	39.25 N	114.47 W
77	McGregor (măk-grĕg'ēr).......Ia.	43.0 N	91.11 W
81	McGregor...................Tex.	31.25 N	97.24 W
146	Machang (mä'chäng')........Chn.	39.47 N	121.47 E
100	Machola (mä-chä'lä)..........Ec.	6.32 N	79.58 W
145	Macheng (mä'chĕng')........Chn.	31.10 N	114.56 E
86	Machias (mȧ-chī'ăs)..........Me.	44.42 N	67.27 W
127	Măcin (mȧ-chēn')............Rom.	45.14 N	28.9 E
76	McIntosh (măk'ĭn-tŏsh).....S. D.	45.55 N	101.21 W
160	Macintyre Cr. (măk'ĭn-tīr) Austl. (In.)	28.25 S	151.15 E
160	Macintyre R.........Austl. (In.)	29.0 S	150.50 E
159	Mackay (mȧ-kī')...........Austl.	21.7 S	149.5 E
71	Mackay......................Ida.	43.55 N	113.36 W
54	Mackay, L..................Can.	64.5 N	113.32 W
85	McKeesport (mȧ-kēz'pōrt)....Pa.	40.20 N	79.50 W
85	McKees Rocks (mȧ-kēz' rŏks).Pa.	40.26 N	80.3 W
82	McKenzie (mȧ-kĕn'zĭ)......Tenn.	36.8 N	88.31 W
53	Mackenzie B................Can.	69.20 N	136.30 W
54	Mackenzie, Dist. of..........Can.	63.35 N	115.0 W
53	Mackenzie Mts..............Can.	62.0 N	127.0 W
54	Mackenzie R................Can.	65.0 N	126.28 W
70	McKenzie R.................Ore.	44.7 N	122.40 W
77	Mackinac, Str. of (măk'ĭ-nô) (măk'ĭ-năk).Mich.	45.50 N	84.40 W
84	Mackinaw (măk'ĭ-nô)........Mich.	45.46 N	84.41 W
79	Mackinaw R..................Ill.	40.38 N	89.0 W

ăt; finăl; rāte; senâte; ärm; ȧsk; sofȧ; fâre; ch-choose; dh-as th in other; bē; ēvent; bĕt; recĕnt; cratēr; g-go; gh-gutteral g; bĭt; ĭ-short neutral; rīde; ĸ-gutteral k as ch in German ich;

McKinley PRONOUNCING INDEX Malinmore

Page	Name Pronunciation Region	Lat. °′	Long. °′
53	McKinley, Mt. (mȧ-kĭn'lĭ) . . Alsk.	63.0 N	151.0 W
50	McKinley Sea . . . Grnld.	84.0 N	15.0 W
79	McKinney (mȧ-kĭn'ĭ) . . . Tex.	33.10 N	96.21 W
54	Macklin (măk'lĭn) . . . Can.	52.18 N	109.48 W
76	McLaughlin (mȧk-lŏf'lĭn) . . . S. D.	45.49 N	100.47 W
79	McLeansboro (mȧ-klānz'bŭr-ô) . Ill.	38.6 N	88.31 W
134	Maclear (mȧ-klēr') . . . U. S. Afr.	31.4 S	28.21 E
54	Macleod (mȧ-kloud') . . . Can.	49.42 N	113.28 W
70	McLoughlin, Mt. (mȧk-lŏk'lĭn) Ore.	42.27 N	122.21 W
78	McMillan, L. (mȧk-mĭl'ȧn) . N. M.	32.40 N	104.17 W
51	McMillin (mȧk-mĭl'ĭn) Wash. (Seattle In.)	47.8 N	122.15 W
70	McMinnville (mȧk-mĭn'vĭl) . . Ore.	45.13 N	123.11 W
82	McMinnville . . . Tenn.	35.41 N	85.47 W
54	McMurray (mȧk-mŭr'ĭ) . . . Can.	56.42 N	111.19 W
51	McMurray . . . Wash. (Seattle In.)	48.19 N	122.14 W
81	McNary (mȧk-nâr'ê) . . . La.	31.0 N	92.33 W
51	McNeil I. (mȧk-nēl') Wash. (Seattle In.)	47.12 N	122.40 W
79	Macomb (mȧ-kōōm') . . . Ill.	40.26 N	90.39 W
82	Macon (mā'kŏn) . . . Ga.	32.49 N	83.39 W
82	Macon . . . Miss.	33.7 N	88.33 W
122	Mâcon (mä-kôn') . . . Fr.	46.20 N	4.50 E
79	Macon (mā'kŏn) . . . Mo.	39.44 N	92.29 W
54	McPherson (mȧk-fŭr's'n) . . . Can.	67.12 N	134.32 W
79	McPherson . . . Kan.	38.22 N	97.40 W
160	MacPhersons Range (mȧk-fŭr's'nz) . Austl. (In.)	28.23 S	153.0 E
160	Macquarie Har. (mȧ-kwŏr'ê) Austl. (Tas. In.)	42.15 S	145.20 E
47	Macquarie (I.) . . . Pac. O.	54.30 S	158.45 E
159	Macquarie R. . . . Austl.	31.30 S	147.38 E
134	Macquival (mä-kê-väl') . . . Moz.	17.45 S	36.45 E
82	McRae (mȧk-rā') . . . Ga.	32.3 N	82.57 W
83	McRoberts (mȧk-rŏb'ērts) . . . Ky.	37.13 N	82.39 W
74	Macuato, L. (mä-kwä'tô) . . . Mex.	32.25 N	115.25 W
135	Madagascar (măd-ȧ-găs'kȧr) Ind. O.	19.0 S	46.45 E
87	Madame I. . . . Can.	45.29 N	60.55 W
151	Madang (mä-däng') . . N. Gui. Ter.	5.12 S	145.42 E
132	Madaoua (mȧ-dou'ȧ) . . Fr. W. Afr.	14.3 N	6.0 E
85	Madawaska R. (măd-ȧ-wôs'kȧ) Can.	45.10 N	77.6 W
100	Madeira Falls (mä-dā'rä) . . . Braz.	9.15 S	64.45 W
132	Maderia I. . . . Madeira Is.	32.45 N	17.0 W
132	Madeira Is. . . . Atl. O.	33.0 N	16.30 W
100	Madeira, R. . . . Braz.	6.30 S	62.25 W
86	Madeleine, C. (măd'lĕn') . . . Can.	49.16 N	65.10 W
77	Madelia (mȧ-dē'lĭ-ȧ) . . . Minn.	44.4 N	94.22 W
77	Madeline I. (măd'ĕ-lĭn) . . . Wis.	46.50 N	90.40 W
74	Madera (mȧ-dā'rȧ) . . . Calif.	36.56 N	120.3 W
94	Madera (Vol.) . . . Nic.	11.27 N	85.32 W
79	Madill (mȧ-dĭl') . . . Okla.	34.4 N	96.46 W
131	Madimba (mä-dēm'bä) Bel. Cong. (Brazzaville In.)	4.52 S	15.19 E
82	Madison (măd'ĭ-sŭn) . . . Fla.	30.27 N	83.55 W
82	Madison . . . Ga.	33.36 N	83.29 W
89	Madison . . . Ill. (St. Louis In.)	38.41 N	90.10 W
84	Madison . . . Ind.	38.45 N	85.24 W
79	Madison . . . Kan.	38.7 N	96.8 W
86	Madison . . . Me.	44.46 N	69.52 W
76	Madison . . . Minn.	45.0 N	96.12 W
76	Madison . . . Neb.	41.50 N	97.27 W
83	Madison . . . N. C.	36.13 N	79.59 W
76	Madison . . . S. D.	44.1 N	97.6 W
77	Madison . . . Wis.	43.5 N	89.22 W
71	Madison Reservoir . . . Mont.	45.25 N	111.41 W
71	Madison R. . . . Mont.	45.10 N	111.44 W
84	Madisonville (măd'ĭ-sŭn-vĭl) . . Ky.	37.20 N	87.30 W
81	Madisonville . . . La.	30.27 N	90.11 W
81	Madisonville . . . Tex.	30.57 N	95.54 W
150	Madoera (Madura) (I.) (mä-dōō'rä) . Indon.	7.10 S	113.25 E
119	Madona (mä'dō'nä) . . . Sov. Un.	56.51 N	20.12 E
70	Mad R. . . . Calif.	49.39 N	123.45 W
140	Madraka, C. (mä-dräk'ä) . . . Oman	18.58 N	57.45 E
73	Madras (mȧ-drăs') Ga. (Atlanta In.)	33.26 N	84.43 W
141	Madras (Presidency) (mŭ-drŭs') (mȧ-drȧs') . India	15.30 N	80.0 E
141	Madras . . . India	13.5 N	80.15 E
102	Madre de Dios Arch. (mä'drā dā dê-ōs') . Chl.	50.30 S	75.0 W
100	Madre de Dios, R. . . . Bol.	12.0 S	68.0 W
92	Madre del Sur, Sierra (Mts.) (mä'drā dĕl sōōr') . Mex.	17.10 N	98.0 W
81	Madre, Laguna (L.) (lä-gōō'nä mä'drā) . U. S.-Mex.	25.0 N	97.35 W
152	Madre, Sierra (Mts.) . . . Phil.	17.0 N	122.15 E
92	Madre Occidental, Sierra (Mts.) (ôk-sê-dĕn-täl') . Mex.	22.0 N	104.35 W
92	Madre Oriental, Sierra (Mts.) (ō-rê-ĕn-täl') . Mex.	22.0 N	99.30 W
77	Madrid (măd'rĭd) . . . Ia.	41.54 N	93.48 W
124	Madrid (mä-dhrēdh') . . . Sp.	40.26 N	3.42 W
125	Madrid . . . Sp. (In.)		
125	Madrid (Prov.) . . . Sp. (In.)	40.30 N	3.45 W
124	Madridejos (mä-dhrê-dhä'hōs) . Sp.	39.28 N	3.31 W
73	Madsen (măd'sĕn) Utah (Salt Lake City In.)	41.40 N	112.6 W
141	Madura (mŭd'ōō-rŭ) . . . India	9.55 N	78.15 E
150	Madura (Madoera) (I.) (mä-dōō'rä) . Indon.	7.10 S	113.25 E
102	Madureira (mä-dōō-rā'rȧ) Braz. (In.)	22.53 S	43.20 W
149	Maebashi (mä-ĕ-bä'shê) . . . Jap.	36.25 N	139.2 E
125	Maella (mä-äl'yä) . . . Sp.	41.11 N	0.7 E
147	Maengsan (mä'ĕng-san') . . . Kor.	39.40 N	126.30 E
96	Maestra, Sierra (Mts.) (mä-äs'trä) . Cuba	20.5 N	76.30 W
134	Mafeking (mâf'ê-kĭng) . . U. S. Afr.	25.46 S	25.36 E
135	Mafia I. (mä-fē'ä) . . . Afr.	7.45 S	39.45 E
	Mafor, see Noemfoor (I.), Neth. N. Gui.		
125	Mafra (mäf'rȧ) . . . Port. (In.)	38.56 N	9.20 W
139	Magadán (mȧ-gȧ-dän') . . Sov. Un.	59.34 N	150.42 E
135	Magadi, L. (mä-gä'dê) . . . Kenya	1.50 S	36.15 E
134	Magadi (Natron) (nä'trŏn) . . Tan.	2.15 S	36.0 E
99	Magallanes (mä-gäl-yä'näs) Chl. (In.)		
102	Magallanes . . . Chl.	53.10 S	71.0 W
152	Magallanes . . . Phil.	12.49 N	123.50 E
151	Magallanes . . . Phil. (Manila In.)	14.13 N	120.42 E
100	Magangue (mä-gän'gä) . . . Col.	9.15 N	74.45 W
152	Magat R. (mä-gät') . . . Phil.	16.50 N	121.30 E
133	Magdala (mäg'dȧ-lä) . . . Eth.	11.23 N	39.29 E
99	Magdalena (mäg-dä-lā'nä) Arg. (Buenos Aires In.)	35.5 S	57.32 W
100	Magdalena . . . Bol.	13.30 N	63.45 W
93	Magdalena . . . Mex. (In.)	19.22 N	98.57 W
75	Magdalena . . . N. M.	34.7 N	107.16 W
100	Magdalena . . . Peru (In.)	12.5 S	77.4 W
151	Magdalena . . . Phil. (Manila In.)	14.13 N	121.30 E
100	Magdalena del Mar (dĕl mär') Peru (In.)	12.6 S	77.5 W
102	Magdalena I. . . . Chl.	44.30 S	73.0 W
92	Magdalena, L. . . . Mex.	20.50 N	104.0 W
100	Magdalena, R. . . . Col.	10.0 N	74.45 W
93	Magdalena, R. . . . Mex. (In.)	19.30 N	98.50 W
55	Magdalen Is. (măg'dȧ-lĕn) . . . Can.	47.30 N	61.45 W
120	Magdeburg (mäg'dĕ-bŏŏrgh) . Ger.	52.6 N	11.38 E
99	Magé (mä-zhā') Braz. (Rio de Janeiro In.)	22.40 S	43.3 W
149	Mage I. (mä'gĕ) . . . Jap.	30.44 N	130.48 E
102	Magellan, Str. of (mȧ-jĕl'ăn) . . Chl.	52.30 S	74.0 W
126	Magenta (mȧ-jĕn'tȧ) . . . It.	45.26 N	8.53 E
108	Magerö (I.) (mä'ghĕr-û) . . . Nor.	70.58 N	24.0 E
126	Maggiore, L. of (mäd-jō'rä) It.-Switz.	46.5 N	8.30 E
92	Magiscatzin (mä-kês-kät-zēn') Mex.	22.49 N	98.41 W
127	Maglaj (mȧ'glä-ê) . . . Yugo.	44.32 N	18.10 E
127	Maglic (mäg'lēch) . . . Yugo.	43.34 N	20.33 E
127	Maglie (mäl'yā) . . . It.	40.6 N	18.19 E
73	Magna (măg'nȧ) Utah (Salt Lake City In.)	40.43 N	112.6 W
110	Magnitogorsk (mäg-nyē'tô-gôrsk) Sov. Un.	53.10 N	59.10 E
79	Magnolia (măg-nō'lĭ-ȧ) . . . Ark.	33.15 N	93.14 W
82	Magnolia . . . Miss.	31.8 N	90.28 W
86	Magog (mȧ-gŏg') . . . Can.	45.15 N	72.10 W
86	Magpie L. (măg'pī) . . . Can.	51.0 N	64.43 W
86	Magpie R. . . . Can.	50.30 N	64.34 W
77	Magpie R. . . . Can.	48.12 N	84.40 W
137	Magra, Jebel El (Mts.) (jĕb'ĕl ĕl Măg'rä) . Pal. (In.)	30.35 N	35.0 E
134	Magude (mä-gōō'dȧ) . . . Moz.	25.3 S	32.37 E
141	Magwe (mŭg-wā') . . . Bur.	20.8 N	94.58 E
121	Magyaróvár (môd'yä-rō'vär) Hung.	47.50 N	17.17 E
135	Mahaddei (mä-häd'ā-ê) . . . Som.	2.55 N	45.28 E
133	Mahagi (mä-hä'gê) . . . Bel. Cong.	2.11 N	31.6 E
133	Mahalla (mȧ-häl'ȧ) . . . Eg. (In.)	30.59 N	31.10 E
135	Mahaly (mä-häl-ē') . . . Madag.	23.55 S	46.13 E
141	Mahanadi R. (mŭ-hä-nŭd'ê) . India	21.30 N	84.0 E
135	Mahanoro (mȧ-hȧ-nō'rō) . . Madag.	19.45 S	48.43 E
85	Mahanoy City (mä-hȧ-noi') . . . Pa.	40.48 N	76.10 W
135	Mahavavy R. (mä-hä-vä'vê) Madag.	17.0 S	46.5 E
133	Mahadera Maryam (mä'dȧ-rä mär'yȧm) . Eth.	11.40 N	38.2 E
131	Mahdia (mä-dē'ä) (mä'dê-ȧ) Tun. (In.)	35.31 N	10.52 E
141	Mahé (mä-ā') . . . India	11.45 N	75.29 E
135	Mahenge (mä-hĕŋ'gȧ) . . . Tan.	8.38 S	36.38 E
156	Mahia Pen. (mä-hē'ȧ) . . . N. Z.	39.10 S	177.55 E
76	Mahnomen (mô-nō'mĕn) . . . Minn.	47.19 N	95.58 W
125	Mahón (mä-ōn') . . . Sp.	39.55 N	4.15 E
86	Mahone B. (mȧ-hōn') . . . Can.	44.28 N	64.15 W
86	Mahone Bay . . . Can.	44.27 N	64.22 W
121	Mährisch Schönberg (Sumperk) (mâ'rĭsh shûn'bĕrk) (shŏŏm'pĕrk) Ger.	49.58 N	17.0 E
141	Mahul (mŭ'hōōl) India (Bombay In.)	19.0 N	72.54 E
133	Maidaguri (mä'ê-dä-gōō'rê) . . Nig.	11.58 N	13.12 E
140	Maidan-i-Naftun (mŭ-ê-dän'ē-näf-tōōn') . Iran	31.45 N	49.28 E
127	Maidos (Aci Abad) (mī'dōs) (ä'jē ä-bäd') . Tur.	40.11 N	26.21 E
115	Maidstone (mād'stŭn) . . . Gt. Brit.	51.15 N	0.31 E
149	Maiko (mī'kō') . . . Jap. (Osaka In.)	34.39 N	135.3 E
111	Maikop (mī'kôp) . . . Sov. Un.	44.35 N	40.8 E
140	Maimana (mī-mä-nä') . . . Afg.	35.58 N	64.47 E
86	Maine (State) (mān) . . . U. S.	45.8 N	69.25 W
156	Main Entrance (Chan.) . N. Z. (In.)	41.21 S	174.51 E
153	Mainit, L. (mä-ē'nĕt) . . . Phil.	9.27 N	125.32 E
114	Mainland (I.) . . . Gt. Brit. (In.)	60.15 N	1.20 W
89	Main Pass . . La. (New Orleans In.)	29.15 N	89.15 W
120	Main R. (mīn) . . . Ger.	50.0 N	10.0 E
135	Maintirano (mä'ēn-tê-rä'nō) Madag.	18.3 S	44.3 E
120	Mainz (mīnts) . . . Ger.	50.0 N	8.13 E
132	Maio I. (mä'yō) Cape Verde Is. (In.)	15.15 N	23.15 W
99	Maipo, R. (mī'pô) Chl. (Valparaiso In.)	33.40 S	70.40 W
102	Maipo (Vol.) . . . Arg.-Chl.	34.10 S	69.50 W
100	Maipures (mī-pōō'rȧs) . . . Ven.	5.15 N	67.32 W
153	Mairaira Pt. (mī-rī'rä) . . . Phil.	18.39 N	120.50 E
97	Maisí, C. (mī-sē') . . . Cuba	20.15 N	74.10 W
123	Maisons-Alfort (mā-zôn' ál-fôr') Fr. (In.)	48.47 N	2.26 E
123	Maisons-Laffitte (mā'zôn' lȧ-fēt') Fr. (In.)	48.56 N	2.9 E
135	Mait I. (māt) . . . Afr.	11.15 N	47.12 E
159	Maitland (māt'lȧnd) . . . Austl.	32.45 S	151.38 E
135	Maitland . . . U. S. Afr.	33.55 S	18.30 E
84	Maitland R. . . . Can.	43.50 N	81.28 W
149	Maizuru (mä-ĭ'zōō-rōō) . . . Jap.	35.25 N	135.15 E
133	Maji (mä'jê) . . . Eth.	6.9 N	35.33 E
125	Majorca (I.) (mȧ-jôr'kȧ) . . . Sp.	39.35 N	3.0 E
131	Majoura, Djebel (Mt.) (jĕb'ĕl mä-jōō'rä) . Tun. (In.)	34.40 N	9.20 E
135	Majunga (mȧ-jŭŋ'gä) . . . Madag.	15.40 S	46.20 E
70	Makah Indian Res. (mȧ-kô') Wash.	48.20 N	124.38 W
156	Makai (mȧ-kī') . . . N. Z.	38.32 S	175.55 E
	Makale, see Macalle, Eth.		
135	Makanya (mä-kän'yä) . . . Tan.	4.23 S	37.50 E
156	Makara R. (mä'kȧ-rä) . . N. Z. (In.)	41.15 S	174.44 E
110	Makariev (mȧ'kär-yôf) . . Sov. Un.	57.55 N	43.48 E
126	Makarska (mȧ'kär-skȧ) . . . Yugo.	43.17 N	17.4 E
150	Makasser (mȧ-käs'ĕr) . . . Indon.	5.9 S	119.30 E
150	Makasser (Macassar) Str. . Indon.	2.0 S	118.30 E
151	Makati (mä-kä'tê) Phil. (Manila In.)	14.34 N	121.2 E
129	Makeevka (Dmitrievsk) (mä-kĕ-yôf'kȧ) (d'mē'trê-yĕfsk) . Sov. Un.	48.2 N	37.55 E
111	Makhach-Kala (mäκ'äch-kä'lä) Sov. Un.	43.0 N	47.30 E
127	Makhlata (mäκ'lä-tä) . . . Bul.	43.27 N	24.16 E
129	Makhnovka (mäκ-nôf'kȧ) Sov. Un.	49.42 N	28.41 E
146	Makia R. (mä'kyä') . . . Chn.	37.50 N	117.6 E
121	Makó (mô'kō) . . . Hung.	46.13 N	20.31 E
132	Makokou (mȧ-kô-kōō') Fr. Eq. Afr.	0.40 N	12.40 E
121	Maków (mä'kōōf) . . . Pol.	52.52 N	21.7 E
141	Makri (mŭ-krī') . . . India	19.45 N	81.59 E
131	Maktar (mȧk-tȧr') . . . Tun. (In.)	35.53 N	9.20 E
149	Makurazaki (mä'kōō-rä-zä'kê) Jap.	31.16 N	130.18 E
138	Makushino (mȧ-kōō-shê'nô) Sov. Un.	55.15 N	67.30 E
149	Makuwari (mä'kōō-wä'rē) Jap. (Tokyo In.)	35.40 N	140.3 E
135	Makuyuni (mä-kōō-yōō'nê) . . Tan.	4.17 S	37.50 E
141	Malabar Coast (măl'ȧ-bär) . . India	11.0 N	75.30 E
131	Malabata, Pt. (mä'lä-bä'tä) Sp. Mor. (Gib. In.)	35.48 N	51.6 E
152	Malabon (mä-lä-bōn') . . . Phil.	14.24 N	120.58 E
153	Malabuyoc (mä-lä-bōō'yōk) . . Phil.	9.40 N	123.21 E
150	Malacca (mȧ-lăk'ȧ) . . . Malaya	2.17 N	102.16 E
150	Malacca (State) . . . Malaya	2.30 N	102.0 E
150	Malacca, Str. of . . . Indon.	2.30 N	101.30 E
71	Malad (mȧ-lăd') . . . Ida.	42.11 N	112.16 W
125	Maladetta (Reg.) (mä-lä-dĕt'tä) Sp.	42.32 N	0.45 E
124	Málaga (mä'lä-gä) . . . Sp.	36.43 N	4.25 W
124	Malága B. . . . Sp.	36.38 N	4.15 W
124	Malagón (mä-lä-gōn') . . . Sp.	39.12 N	3.51 W
159	Malaita I. (mȧ-lä'ê-tȧ) . Solomon Is.	9.0 S	161.0 E
133	Malakal (mä-lä-käl') . . . A. E. Sud.	9.38 N	31.47 E
123	Malakoff (mä-lȧ-kôf') . . . Fr. (In.)	48.48 N	2.18 E
153	Malampaya Sd. (mä-läm-pä'yä) Phil.	10.57 N	119.15 E
153	Malanao I. (mä-lä-nä'ō) . . . Phil.	9.28 N	118.37 E
134	Malanje (mȧ-läŋ'gä) . . . Ang.	9.28 S	16.22 E
153	Malanut B. (mä-lä-nōōt') . . . Phil.	9.18 N	118.0 E
95	Mala, Pt. (mä'lä) . . . Pan.	7.30 N	80.0 W
151	Malaraya Mt. (mä-lä-rä'yä) Phil. (Manila In.)	14.0 N	121.18 E
118	Mälar L. (mâ'lär) . . . Swe.	59.30 N	17.4 E
111	Malatya (mȧ-lä'tyä) . . . Tur.	38.25 N	38.18 E
128	Malaya Vishera (mȧ-lä'yȧ vê-shä'rä) . Sov. Un.	58.50 N	32.11 E
153	Malaybalay (mä-lī-bä'lī) . . . Phil.	8.3 N	125.7 E
150	Malay Pen. (mȧ-lā') (mā'lā) . Asia	7.0 N	100.0 E
150	Malaya (mȧ-lā'yȧ) . . . Asia	5.0 N	102.0 E
114	Mal B. (măl) . . . Ire.	52.50 N	9.30 W
158	Malbon (măl'bŭn) . . . Austl.	21.15 S	140.30 E
121	Malbork (mäl'bôrk) . . . Pol.	54.2 N	19.3 E
153	Malbul R. (mäl-bōōl') . . . Phil.	6.33 N	124.50 E
125	Malcabran R. (mäl-kä-brän') Port. (In.)	38.51 N	8.48 W
117	Malchow (mäl'kō) . Ger. (Berlin In.)	52.35 N	13.28 E
96	Malcolm B. (măl'kŭm) . . . Jam.	17.59 N	77.52 W
86	Malden (môl'dĕn) . . . Mass.	42.28 N	71.5 W
79	Malden . . . Mo.	36.32 N	89.57 W
4	Malden I. . . . Pac. O.	4.3 N	154.59 W
136	Maldive Is. (măl'dīv) . . . Ind. O.	5.0 N	73.0 E
102	Maldonado . . . Ur.	34.50 S	54.59 W
92	Maldonado, Pt. . . . Mex.	16.19 N	98.35 W
159	Malekula (Malikolo) I. (mä-lä-kōō'lä) (mäl-ê-kō'lō) . New Hebr.	16.20 S	167.30 E
122	Malesherbes (mȧl'zĕrb') . . . Fr.	48.19 N	2.25 E
70	Malheur L. (mȧ-lōōr') . . . Ore.	43.19 N	118.47 W
70	Malheur R. . . . Ore.	43.47 N	118.0 W
127	Malia, C. (mä'lĭ-ȧ) . . . Grc.	36.17 N	23.12 E
129	Malie Viski (mäl'yĕ vēs'kê) Sov. Un.	48.39 N	31.38 E
153	Maligay B. (mä-lē'gī) . . . Phil.	7.30 N	123.15 E
159	Malikolo (Malekula) I. (mäl-ê-kō'-lō) (mä-lä-kōō'lä) . New Hebr.	16.20 S	167.30 E
129	Malin (mä-lĕn') . . . Sov. Un.	50.46 N	29.11 E
92	Malinalco (mä-lê-näl'kō) . . . Mex.	18.58 N	99.29 W
92	Malinaltepec (mä-lê-näl-tâ-pĕk') Mex.	17.11 N	98.23 W
114	Malin Hd. (mă'lĭn) . . . Ire.	55.25 N	7.30 W
153	Malinao (mä-lē'nä-ō) . . . Phil.	11.38 N	122.18 E
135	Malindi (mä-lēn'dê) . . . Kenya	3.10 S	40.7 E
121	Malineč (mä'lê-nyĕts') . . . Czech.	48.30 N	19.41 E
115	Malines (mȧ-lēn') . . . Bel.	51.0 N	4.25 E
114	Malinmore Hd. (mă'lĭn-mōr) . . Ire.	54.40 N	8.50 W

ng-sing; ŋ-baŋk; N-nasalized n; nŏd; cŏmmit; ōld; ôbey; ôrder; fōōd; fŏŏt; ou-out; s-soft; sh-dish; th-thin; pūre; ûnite; ûrn; stŭd; circŭs; ü-as "y" in study; '-indeterminate vowel.

Page	Name Pronunciation Region	Lat. °′	Long. °′
129	Malinovka (mȧ-lê-nôf'kȧ). Sov. Un.	49.47 N	36.40 E
92	Malintzin, Cerro (Mt.) (mä-lênt-zēn'). Mex.	19.13 N	98.1 W
153	Malita (mä-lē'tä). Phil.	6.23 N	125.37 E
153	Malitbog (mä-lēt'bŏg). Phil.	10.9 N	125.0 E
153	Malitobug R. (mä-lē'tô-bōōg) Phil.	7.20 N	124.40 E
127	Malkara (mäl'kȧ-rȧ). Tur.	40.54 N	26.54 E
127	Malko-Trnova (mäl'kō-t'r'nô-vȧ) Bul.	41.57 N	27.29 E
114	Mallaig (măl'āg). Gt. Brit.	57.0 N	5.45 W
153	Mallawalle I. (mäl-ȧ-wäl'ā) N. Bor.	7.3 N	117.19 E
131	Mallawi (mȧ-lä'wê). Eg. (In.)	27.45 N	30.50 E
114	Mallow (măl'ō). Ire.	52.5 N	8.40 W
115	Malmédy (mȧl-mā-dē'). Bel.	50.25 N	6.0 E
134	Malmesbury (mämz'bēr-ĭ) U. S. Afr.	33.27 S	18.40 E
118	Malmköping (mälm'chû'pĭng) Swe.	59.8 N	16.40 E
118	Malmö (mälm'û). Swe.	55.35 N	13.0 E
139	Malmyzh (mȧl-mēzh'). Sov. Un.	49.55 N	136.50 E
110	Malmyzh. Sov. Un.	56.30 N	50.45 E
128	Maloarkhangelsk (mä'lô-ȧr-κän'gĕlsk). Sov. Un.	52.26 N	36.30 E
152	Malolos (mä-lō'lōs). Phil.	14.50 N	120.49 E
85	Malone (mȧ-lōn'). N. Y.	44.52 N	74.20 W
128	Maloyaroslavets (mä'lô-yä-rô-slä'vyĕts). Sov. Un.	55.1 N	36.29 E
116	Malpas (măl'pȧz). Gt. Brit.	53.1 N	2.46 W
100	Malpelo I. (mäl-pā'lō). Col.	4.1 N	81.30 W
86	Malpeque B. (môl-pĕk'). Can.	46.35 N	63.45 W
112	Malta (môl'tȧ). Medit. Sea	35.55 N	14.27 E
71	Malta. Mont.	48.21 N	107.50 W
134	Maltahohe (mäl'tä-hō'ē) S. W. Afr.	24.55 S	16.45 E
51	Maltby (môlt'bê) Wash. (Seattle In.)	47.47 N	122.7 W
116	Malton (môl'tŭn). Gt. Brit.	54.8 N	0.47 W
93	Maltrata (mäl-trä'tä). Mex.	18.49 N	97.15 W
153	Maluko (mä-lōō'kō). Phil.	8.20 N	125.0 E
79	Malvern (măl'vērn). Ark.	34.23 N	92.48 W
116	Malvern. Gt. Brit.	52.7 N	2.19 W
139	Maly Is. (mä'lĭ). Sov. Un.	74.0 N	141.0 E
93	Mamantel (mä-män-tĕl'). Mex.	18.31 N	91.5 W
153	Mambajao (mäm'bä'hä-ō). Phil.	9.14 N	124.43 E
151	Mamberamo (R.) (mäm-bȧ-rä'mō) Neth. N. Gui.	2.30 S	138.20 E
135	Mamboya (mäm-bō'yä). Tan.	6.16 S	37.13 E
152	Mamburao (mäm-bōō'rä-ō). Phil.	13.13 N	120.35 E
153	Mambusao (mäm-bōō'sä-ō). Phil.	11.26 N	122.36 E
122	Mamers (mȧ-mā'). Fr.	48.21 N	0.21 E
132	Mamfe (mäm'fē). Nig.	5.51 N	9.9 E
149	Mamibara (mä'mê-bä'rä). Jap.	32.41 N	131.11 E
82	Mammoth Cave (măm'ŏth). Ky.	37.12 N	86.5 W
82	Mammoth Cave Natl. Mon. Ky.	37.12 N	86.8 W
100	Mamoré, R. (mä-mô-rā'). Bol.	14.0 S	65.0 W
132	Mamou (mȧ-mōō'). Fr. W. Afr.	10.28 N	12.10 W
131	Mamoura, Ras (C.) (räs mä'mōō-rä'). Tun. (In.)	36.26 N	10.40 E
121	Mamry L. (mäm'rĭ). Pol.	54.7 N	21.43 E
138	Mamur (mä-mōōr'). Sov. Un.	56.7 N	103.2 E
140	Manama (mŭ-nä'mȧ). Bahrein I.	26.10 N	50.40 E
141	Manar (Mannar) (mŭ-när') Cey. (In.)	9.5 N	79.50 E
142	Manas R. (mȧ-näs'). Chn.	44.45 N	86.0 E
125	Manacor (mä-nä-kôr'). Sp.	39.34 N	3.12 E
94	Managua (mä-nä'gwä). Nic.	12.10 N	86.16 W
94	Managua, L. Nic.	12.20 N	86.20 W
156	Manaia (mä-nī'ä). N. Z.	39.32 S	174.8 E
153	Manamoc I. (mä-nä-mōk'). Phil.	11.18 N	120.41 E
135	Mananara R. (mä-nä-nä'rä) Madag.	23.0 S	47.15 E
135	Mananjari (mä-nän-zhä'rê) Madag.	21.15 S	48.18 E
101	Manáos (Manaus) (mä-nä'ōs) (mä-nä'ōōzh). Braz.	3.1 S	60.0 W
153	Manapla (mä-näp'lä). Phil.	10.57 N	123.8 E
157	Manapowri L. (mä-nä-pou'rê) N. Z.	45.28 S	167.30 E
85	Manassas (mȧ-năs'ȧs). Va.	38.45 N	77.30 W
83	Manatee (măn-ȧ-tē'). Fla. (In.)	27.29 N	82.34 W
101	Manaus (Manáos) (mä-nä'ōōzh) Braz.	3.1 S	60.0 W
135	Manawât (mä-nä-wät'). Eg.	29.55 N	31.14 E
156	Manawatu R. (mä-nä-wä'tōō) N. Z.	40.25 S	175.15 E
153	Manay (mä-nī'). Phil.	7.11 N	126.32 E
114	Man, Calf of (I.). Gt. Brit.	54.5 N	4.50 W
84	Mancelona (măn-sê-lō'nȧ). Mich.	44.50 N	85.7 W
124	Mancha Real (män'chä rā-äl'). Sp.	37.47 N	3.36 W
146	Mancheng (män'chĕng'). Chn.	39.3 N	115.13 E
85	Manchester (măn'chĕs-tēr). Conn.	41.46 N	72.28 W
82	Manchester. Ga.	32.51 N	84.37 W
114	Manchester. Gt. Brit.	53.30 N	2.15 W
77	Manchester. Ia.	42.30 N	91.29 W
84	Manchester. Ohio	38.42 N	83.38 W
87	Manchester. Mass. (In.)	42.34 N	70.46 W
86	Manchester. N. H.	43.0 N	71.30 W
116	Manchester Ship Canal. Gt. Brit.	53.22 N	2.33 W
143	Manchouli (Lupin) (män-chōō'lê) (lōō'pĭn'). Chn.	49.34 N	117.28 E
143	Manchuria (măn-chōō'rĕ-ȧ). Chn.	47.30 N	126.0 E
134	Manda (män'dä). Tan.	10.28 S	34.33 E
118	Mandal (män'däl). Nor.	58.2 N	7.28 E
141	Mandalay (măn'dȧ-lā). Bur.	21.59 N	95.59 E
118	Mandals R. (män'däls). Nor.	58.20 N	7.30 E
76	Mandan (măn'dăn). N. D.	46.51 N	100.55 W
133	Mandara Mts. (män-dä'rä). Cam.	10.30 N	14.30 E
153	Mandaue (män-dä'wä). Phil.	10.19 N	123.56 E
135	Mandera (män-dā'rä). Tan.	6.13 S	38.24 E
95	Mandinga (män-dĭŋ'gä). Pan.	9.32 N	79.4 W
127	Mandra (män'drä). Grc.	38.5 N	23.31 E
135	Mandritsara (män-drēt-sä'rä) Madag.	15.40 S	48.45 E
140	Mand Rud (R.) (mŭnd' rōōd'). Iran	28.15 N	52.30 E
99	Manduba Pt. (män-dōō'bȧ) Braz. (Rio de Janeiro In.)	24.2 S	46.17 W
127	Manduria (män-dōō'rē-ä). It.	40.23 N	17.39 E
141	Mandvi (mŭnd'vē). India	22.45 N	69.25 E
131	Manfalût (män-fȧ-lōōt'). Eg. (In.)	27.19 N	30.57 E
126	Manfredonia (män-frȧ-dô'nyä). It.	41.37 N	15.53 E
126	Manfredonia, G. of. It.	41.30 N	16.0 E
101	Mangabeiras, Serra das (Mts.) (sĕr'rȧ däzh mäŋ-gä-bā'ê-räzh). Braz.	9.30 S	46.30 W
141	Mangalore (mŭŋ-gŭ-lōr'). India	12.50 N	74.45 E
156	Mangari (män-gä'rē). N. Z. (In.)	36.57 S	174.48 E
152	Mangatarem (män'gȧ-tä'rĕm) Phil.	15.47 N	120.18 E
150	Mangkalihat, C. (mäng'kȧ-lē-hät') Indon.	1.2 N	119.2 E
96	Mangles Is. (mäŋ'gläs) (măŋ'g'lz). Cuba	22.5 N	82.35 W
135	Mangoky R. (män-gō'kē). Madag.	21.30 S	45.30 E
124	Mangualde (mäŋ-gwäl'dĕ). Port.	40.37 N	7.45 W
102	Mangueira, L. da (män-gā'ê-rȧ) Braz.	33.15 S	52.40 W
151	Mangulli (I.) (män-gōō-lē'). Indon.	1.50 S	126.0 E
78	Mangum (măŋ'gŭm). Okla.	34.52 N	99.31 W
79	Manhattan (măn-hăt'ăn). Kan.	39.11 N	96.34 W
73	Manhattan Beach Calif. (Los Angeles In.)	33.54 N	118.25 W
88	Manhattan (I.) N. Y. (New York In.)	40.48 N	73.58 W
135	Mania R. (män'yä). Madag.	20.0 S	46.20 E
101	Manicoré (mä-nê-kō-rā'). Braz.	5.45 S	61.15 W
4	Manihiki Is. (mä'nē-hē'kê). Pac. O.	10.23 S	161.1 W
55	Manikuagan R. (măn-ê-kwä'gȧn) Can.	51.30 N	68.30 W
152	Manila (mȧ-nĭl'ȧ). Phil.	14.35 N	121.0 E
151	Manila. Phil. (In.)		
152	Manila B. Phil.	14.40 N	120.50 E
111	Manisa (mä'nê-sä). Tur.	38.40 N	27.29 E
114	Man, Isle of. Gt. Brit.	54.10 N	4.40 W
84	Manistee (măn-ĭs-tē'). Mich.	44.4 N	86.20 W
84	Manistee R. Mich.	44.30 N	85.30 W
77	Manistique (măn-ĭs-tēk'). Mich.	45.58 N	86.15 W
77	Manistique L. Mich.	46.15 N	85.45 W
77	Manistique R. Mich.	46.13 N	85.59 W
54	Manitoba (Prov.) (măn-ĭ-tō'bȧ) Can.	55.10 N	98.0 W
54	Manitoba, L. Can.	50.45 N	98.30 W
78	Manitou (măn'ĭ-tōō). Colo.	38.53 N	104.56 W
77	Manitou I. Mich.	47.25 N	87.38 W
84	Manitou Is. Mich.	45.5 N	86.0 W
77	Manitou L. Can.	49.15 N	93.0 W
55	Manitoulin I. (măn-ĭ-tōō'lĭn). Can.	45.45 N	82.30 W
77	Manitowoc (măn-ĭ-tō-wŏk'). Wis.	44.5 N	87.39 W
100	Manizales (mä-nê-zä'lās). Col.	5.2 N	75.45 W
134	Manjacaze (man'yä-kä'zĕ). Moz.	24.45 S	34.0 E
140	Manjil (mŭn-jēl'). Iran	36.32 N	49.32 E
153	Manjuyod (män-hōō'yōdh). Phil.	9.40 N	123.9 E
78	Mankato (măn-kā'tō). Kan.	39.47 N	98.13 W
77	Mankato. Minn.	44.10 N	93.59 W
125	Manlleu (män-lyā'ōō). Sp.	42.0 N	2.17 E
160	Manly (măn'lĭ). Austl.	33.48 S	15.18 E
152	Manmanoc, Mt. (män-mä-nōk') Phil.	17.40 N	121.5 E
141	Mannar (Manar) (mȧ-när') Cey. (In.)	9.5 N	79.50 E
120	Mannheim (män'hīm). Ger.	49.30 N	8.28 E
77	Manning (măn'ĭng). Ia.	41.54 N	95.3 W
83	Manning. S. C.	33.41 N	80.12 W
85	Mannington (măn'ĭng-tŭn). W. Va.	39.33 N	80.26 W
160	Mann R. (măn). Austl. (In.)	29.42 S	152.5 E
97	Man of War B. Ba. Is.	21.3 N	73.40 W
97	Man of War Chan. Ba. Is.	22.45 N	75.51 W
151	Manokwari (mȧ-nŏk-wä'rê) Neth. N. Gui.	0.50 S	134.5 E
123	Manosque (mȧ-nôsh'). Fr.	43.51 N	5.50 E
125	Manresa (män-rä'sä). Sp.	41.44 N	1.50 E
55	Mansel I. (măn'sĕl). Can.	62.10 N	80.10 W
114	Mansfield (mănz'fēld). Gt. Brit.	53.10 N	1.10 W
81	Mansfield. La.	32.2 N	93.43 W
84	Mansfield. Ohio	40.47 N	82.32 W
70	Mansfield. Wash.	47.46 N	119.39 W
86	Mansfield Mt. Vt.	44.34 N	72.52 W
116	Mansfield Woodhouse. Gt. Brit.	53.10 N	1.11 W
133	Mansûra (män-sōō'rä). Eg.	31.2 N	31.11 E
100	Manta (män'tä). Ec.	1.0 S	80.33 W
153	Mantalingajan, Mt. (män-tä-lēŋ-gä'hän). Phil.	8.49 N	117.39 E
153	Mantangule I. (män-täŋ-gōō'lä) Phil.	8.10 N	117.10 E
122	Mantes (mäɴt'). Fr.	49.0 N	1.42 E
75	Manti (măn'tī). Utah	39.16 N	111.39 W
99	Mantiqueira, Serra da (Mts.) (sĕr'rä dä män-tê-kā'ê-rȧ) Braz. (Rio de Janeiro In.)	22.40 S	45.20 W
126	Mantova (Mantua) (män'tô-vä) (măn'tŭ-ȧ). It.	45.8 N	10.46 E
96	Mantua (män-tōō'ȧ). Cuba	22.17 N	84.16 W
126	Mantua (Mantova) (măn'tŭ-ȧ) (män'tô-vä). It.	45.8 N	10.46 E
73	Mantua (măn'tŭ-ȧ) Utah (Salt Lake City In.)	41.30 N	111.56 W
86	Manuan L. (mȧ-nōō'än). Can.	50.40 N	70.40 W
86	Manuan R. Can.	50.0 N	70.40 W
99	Manuel Rodriguez I. (mä-nōō-ĕl' rô-drē'gĕz). Chl. (Magallanes In.)	52.35 S	73.50 W
150	Manui Is. (mä-nōō'ē). Indon.	3.30 S	123.10 E
156	Manukau Entrance (mä-nōō-kä'ōō). N. Z. (In.)	37.3 S	174.33 E
156	Manukau Har. N. Z. (In.)	37.1 S	174.42 E
151	Manus (I.) (mä'nōōs). N. Gui. Ter.	2.0 S	146.45 E
81	Manvel (măn'vĕl). Tex. (In.)	29.27 N	95.22 W
135	Manyal Shiha (män-yäl' shē'hä) Eg.	29.57 N	31.13 E
131	Manyanga (män-yäŋ'gä) Bel. Cong. (Brazzaville In.)	4.55 S	14.28 E
111	Manych R. (mä-nĭch'). Sov. Un.	47.15 N	41.0 E
111	Manych Sea (Bolshoi Liman) (bôl'shô-ê lē'män). Sov. Un.	46.20 N	42.45 E
131	Manzala (män'zȧ-lȧ). Eg. (In.)	31.9 N	32.4 E
124	Manzanares (män-thä-nä'räs). Sp.	39.0 N	3.23 W
125	Manzanares Canal. Sp. (In.)	40.18 N	3.36 W
125	Manzanares R. Sp. (In.)	40.33 N	3.48 W
96	Manzanillo (män'zä-nēl'yō). Cuba	20.21 N	77.9 W
92	Manzanillo. Mex.	19.2 N	104.20 W
97	Manzanillo B. Hai.	19.42 N	71.52 W
92	Manzanillo B. Mex.	19.4 N	104.23 W
133	Mao (mä'ō). Fr. Eq. Afr.	14.9 N	15.12 E
93	Mapastepec (mȧ-päs-tȧ-pĕk') Mex.	15.25 N	92.55 W
151	Mapia Is. (mä'pē-ȧ). Pac. O.	1.0 N	134.25 E
80	Mapimi (mä-pê-mē'). Mex.	25.49 N	103.50 W
80	Mapimi, Bolson de (Depression) (bôl-sōn' dā mä-pê-mē'). Mex.	28.0 N	104.30 W
72	Maple Falls (mā'p'l) Wash. (Vancouver In.)	48.55 N	122.5 W
89	Maple Heights Ohio (Cleveland In.)	41.25 N	81.34 W
79	Maplewood (mā'p'l-wŏŏd). Mo.	38.37 N	90.19 W
117	Maplin Sands (măp'lĭn) Gt. Brit. (London In.)	51.35 N	0.55 E
153	Maqueda B. (mä-kā'dä). Phil.	11.30 N	125.0 E
152	Maqueda Chan. Phil.	13.45 N	124.4 E
134	Maquela do Zombo (mȧ-kā'lȧ dōō zôm'bōō). Ang.	6.2 S	15.13 E
77	Maquoketa (mȧ-kō-kê-tȧ). Ia.	42.4 N	90.39 W
77	Maquoketa R. Ia.	42.20 N	91.16 W
101	Maracá I. (mä-rä-kä'). Braz.	2.0 N	50.28 W
100	Maracaibo (mä-rä-kī'bō). Ven.	10.32 N	71.43 W
100	Maracaibo L. Ven.	9.30 N	71.30 W
132	Maradi (mȧ-rȧ-dē'). Fr. W. Afr.	13.33 N	7.10 E
131	Marâgha (mȧ-rä'gȧ). Eg. (In.)	26.42 N	31.37 E
101	Maragojipe (mä'rä-gô-zhē'pĕ) Braz. (In.)	12.46 S	38.55 W
151	Maragondon (mä'rä-gôn-dōn') Phil.	14.18 N	120.42 E
101	Marajó I. (mä-rä-zhō'). Braz.	1.0 S	50.30 W
153	Maramag (mä-rä'mäg). Phil.	7.44 N	125.1 E
135	Maramba (mä-räm'bä). Tan.	4.52 S	38.50 E
134	Marandellas (mä-rän-däl'äs) S. Rh.	18.15 S	13.30 E
101	Maranguape (mä-räŋ-gwä'pĕ) Braz.	3.58 S	38.43 W
101	Maranhão (Sao Luiz) (mä-rän-youɴ (souɴ lōō-ēzh'). Braz.	2.30 S	44.12 W
101	Maranhão (State). Braz.	5.0 S	45.0 W
159	Maranoa R. (mä-rä-nō'ä). Austl.	26.30 S	147.51 E
100	Marañon, R. (mä-rä-nyōn') Ec.-Peru	5.0 S	76.0 W
122	Marans (mä-räɴ'). Fr.	46.20 N	1.0 W
153	Maraob (mä'rä-ōb'). N. Bor.	5.25 N	119.0 E
101	Marapanim (mä-rä-päɴ-ēɴ'). Braz.	0.45 S	47.45 W
111	Maras (mä-räsh'). Tur.	37.40 N	36.55 E
150	Maratoea (Maratus) I. (mȧ-rä'tōō-ȧ) (mȧ-rä'tōōs). Indon.	2.15 N	118.35 E
	Maratus I., see Maratoea, Indon.		
92	Maravatio (mä-rä-vä'tê-ō). Mex.	19.53 N	100.24 W
124	Marbella (mär-bäl'yä). Sp.	36.32 N	4.52 W
158	Marble Bar. Austl.	21.15 S	119.30 E
87	Marblehead (mär'b'l-hĕd) Mass. (In.)	42.30 N	70.51 W
120	Marburg (mär'bŏŏrgh). Ger.	50.48 N	8.46 E
79	Marceline (mär-sê-lēn'). Mo.	39.44 N	92.56 W
115	Marche (märsh). Bel.	50.15 N	5.19 E
126	Marche (Prov.) (mär'kā). It.	43.30 N	13.0 E
124	Marchena (mär-chā'nä). Sp.	37.21 N	5.25 W
100	Marcheno (I.) (mär-chā'nō). Ec.	0.28 N	90.30 W
153	Marchesa B. (mär-chā'sä). N. Bor.	6.33 N	117.35 E
99	Marcos Paz (mär'kōs' päz) Arg. (Buenos Aires In.)	34.43 S	58.50 W
85	Marcus Hook (mär'kŭs hŏŏk). Pa.	39.47 N	75.27 W
85	Marcy, Mt. (mär'sê). N. Y.	44.8 N	73.57 W
102	Mar del Plata (mär dĕl plä'ta). Arg.	38.1 S	57.31 W
111	Mardin (mär-dēn'). Tur.	37.28 N	40.35 E
114	Maree, Loch (L.) (mȧ-rē'). Gt. Brit.	57.35 N	5.40 W
159	Maré I. (mȧ-rā'). N. Cal.	21.40 S	168.5 E
77	Marengo (mȧ-rĕŋ'gō). Ia.	41.47 N	92.3 W
122	Marennes (mȧ-rĕn'). Fr.	45.48 N	1.5 W
131	Mareotis, L. (mär-ê-ō'tĭs). Eg. (In.)	31.5 N	29.55 E
80	Marfa (mär'fȧ). Tex.	30.18 N	104.2 W
73	Margaret (mär'gȧ-rĕt) Ala (Birmingham In.)	33.39 N	86.30 W
100	Margarita I. (mär-gȧ-rē'tȧ). Ven.	11.0 N	54.0 W
115	Margate (mär'gāt). Gt. Brit.	51.21 N	1.21 E
138	Margelan (mär-gĕ'län'). Sov. Un.	20.20 N	71.50 E
153	Margosatubig (mär'gô-sä-tōō'bĕg) Phil.	7.33 N	123.10 E
110	Mari (Aut. Ter.) (mä'rê). Sov. Un.	56.35 N	48.20 E
86	Maria (mȧ-rē'ȧ). Can.	48.10 N	66.3 W
153	Maria (mä-rē'ä). Phil.	9.11 N	123.40 E
96	María Aguilar, Pt. (mä-rē'ä ä-gê-lär'). Cuba	21.45 N	80.0 W
92	María Cleofas I. (mä-rē'ä klā'ô-fäs). Mex.	21.17 N	106.13 W
118	Mariager (mä'rê-ägh'ēr). Den.	56.38 N	10.0 E
118	Mariager Fjord. Den.	56.42 N	10.15 E
160	Maria I. (mȧ-rī'ȧ). Austl. (Tas. In.)	42.37 S	148.6 E
92	María Madre I. (mä-rē'ä mä'drȧ). Mex.	21.35 N	106.32 W
92	Maria Magdalena I. (mä-rē'ä mäg-dä-lā'nä). Mex.	21.25 N	106.24 W

ăt; finăl; rāte; senâte; ärm; ȧsk; sofȧ; fâre; ch-choose; dh-as th in other; bē; êvent; bĕt; recĕnt; cratẽr; g-go; gh-gutteral g; bĭt; ĭ-short neutral; rīde; κ-gutteral k as ch in German ich:

Mariampole PRONOUNCING INDEX Mato Grosso

Page	Name Pronunciation Region	Lat. °′	Long. °′
119	Mariampole (mä-rê-äm-pô'le) (mä-rê-äm'pôl-y') . Sov. Un.	54.32 N	23.21 E
96	Marianao (mä-rê-ä-nä'ō) . . . . Cuba	23.4 N	82.28 W
90	Marianao, R. . . Cuba (Habana In.)	23.4 N	82.27 W
5	Mariana Is. (mä-rê-ä'nä) . . Pac. O.	16.0 N	145.0 E
79	Marianna (mā-rĭ-ăn'ȧ) . . . . . . Ark.	34.46 N	90.46 W
82	Marianna . . . . Fla.	30.46 N	85.16 W
120	Mariánské Lázně (mär'yȧn-skĕ' läz'nyĕ) . Czech.	49.58 N	12.42 E
71	Marias R. (mȧ-rī'ȧz) . . . . Mont.	48.25 N	111.50 W
95	Mariato Pt. (mä-rê-ä'tō) . . . . . Pan.	7.16 N	80.57 W
156	Maria van Diemer, C. (mȧ-rē'ȧ văn dē'mĕr) . N. Z.	34.27 S	172.36 E
118	Maribo (mä'rê-bô) . . . . Den.	54.47 N	11.28 E
153	Maribojoc (mä'rê-bô-yŏk') . . . Phil.	9.44 N	123.51 E
126	Maribor (mä'rê-bôr) . . . . Yugo.	46.34 N	15.36 E
127	Marica R. (mä'rêt-sȧ) . . . . Bul.	42.3 N	25.30 E
152	Maricaban I. (mä-rê-kä-bän') . Phil.	13.38 N	120.54 E
47	Marie Byrd Land (mȧ-rē' bûrd') Ant.	78.0 S	140.0 W
118	Mariefred (mä-rē'ĕ-frĭd) . . . . . Swe.	59.15 N	17.10 E
95	Marie Galante (I.) (mȧ-rē' gȧ-läNt') . Guad. (In.)	15.57 N	61.17 W
119	Mariehamn (Maarianhamina) (mä-rē'ĕ-häm''n) (mä'rê-än-hä'mê-nä) . Fin.	60.8 N	19.58 E
	Marienburg, see Malbork, Pol.		
117	Mariendorf (mä-rē'ĕn-dôrf) Ger. (Berlin In.)	52.26 N	13.24 E
117	Marienfelde (mä-rē'ĕn-fĕl'dē) Ger. (Berlin In.)	52.25 N	13.22 E
118	Mariestad (mä-rē'ĕ-städ') . . . . Swe.	58.41 N	13.48 E
82	Marietta (mā-rĭ-ĕt'ȧ) . . . . Ga.	33.57 N	84.34 W
84	Marietta . . . . Ohio	39.24 N	81.30 W
79	Marietta . . . . Okla.	33.54 N	97.8 W
72	Marietta . . Wash. (Vancouver In.)	48.48 N	122.35 W
97	Mariguana I. (mä-rē-gwä'nä) Ba. Is.	22.25 N	72.55 W
97	Mariguana Passage . . . . Ba. Is.	22.22 N	73.20 W
139	Mariinsk (mȧ-rē'ĭnsk) . . . Sov. Un.	51.45 N	140.20 E
138	Mariinsk . . . . Sov. Un.	55.50 N	87.40 E
151	Marikina (mä-rē-kē'nä) Phil. (Manila In.)	14.38 N	121.6 E
151	Marilao (mä-rê-lä'ō) Phil. (Manila In.)	14.46 N	120.56 E
124	Marin (mä-rēn') . . . . Sp.	42.23 N	8.41 W
152	Marinduque I. (mä-rên-dōō'kä) Phil.	13.20 N	122.0 E
84	Marine City (mȧ-rēn') . . . . . Mich.	42.45 N	82.30 W
77	Marinette (măr-ĭ-nĕt') . . . . . . Wis.	45.5 N	87.37 W
133	Maringa R. (mȧ-rĭŋ'gȧ) . Bel. Cong.	1.0 N	20.30 E
124	Marinha Grande (mä-rēn'yȧ grän'dĕ) . Port.	39.45 N	8.53 W
82	Marion (măr'ĭ-ŭn) . . . . Ala.	32.37 N	87.19 W
79	Marion . . . . Ill.	37.44 N	88.56 W
84	Marion . . . . Ind.	40.34 N	85.43 W
77	Marion . . . . Ia.	42.2 N	91.36 W
79	Marion . . . . Kan.	38.20 N	97.2 W
84	Marion . . . . Ky.	37.20 N	88.5 W
83	Marion . . . . N. C.	35.40 N	82.1 W
76	Marion . . . . N. D.	46.37 N	98.20 W
84	Marion . . . . Ohio	40.37 N	83.7 W
83	Marion . . . . S. C.	34.10 N	79.13 W
83	Marion . . . . Va.	36.50 N	81.32 W
160	Marion B. . . . . . . Austl. (Tas. In.)	42.45 S	147.55 E
159	Marion Reef . . . . Austl.	18.59 S	152.29 E
151	Mariquina R. (mä-rê-kē'nä) Phil. (Manila In.)	14.45 N	121.11 E
101	Maripanim (mä-rē-pän-ēN') Braz. (In.)	0.40 S	47.40 W
153	Maripipi I. (mä-rê-pê-pê') . . . Phil.	11.47 N	124.20 E
74	Mariposa R. (măr-ĭ-pō'sȧ) . . Calif.	37.13 N	120.35 W
127	Maritsa (Evros) R. (mä'rê-tsȧ) (ĕv'rôs) . Tur.	41.0 N	26.21 E
129	Mariupol (mä'rê-ŏŏ-pôl'y') Sov. Un.	47.6 N	37.34 E
152	Mariveles (mä-rê-vä'läs) . . . . . Phil.	14.27 N	120.29 E
151	Mariveles Mts. . Phil. (Manila In.)	14.31 N	120.23 E
118	Markaryd (mär'kä-rüd) . . . . . Swe.	56.30 N	13.37 E
79	Marked Tree . . . . Ark.	35.31 N	90.26 W
116	Market Bosworth (bŏz'wûrth) Gt. Brit.	52.37 N	1.23 W
116	Market Deeping (dēp'ĭng) . Gt. Brit.	52.40 N	0.18 W
116	Market Drayton (drā'tŭn) . Gt. Brit.	52.54 N	2.29 W
116	Market Harborough (här'bŭr-ô) Gt. Brit.	52.28 N	0.55 W
116	Market Rasen (rā'zĕn) . . . Gt. Brit.	53.23 N	0.21 W
116	Market Weighton (wā'tŭn) Gt. Brit.	53.52 N	0.40 W
139	Markha R. (mär'Kȧ) . . . . Sov. Un.	64.50 N	115.0 E
139	Markhakhanskoe (mär-Kȧ-Kän'-skô-yĕ) . Sov. Un.	60.40 N	123.40 E
47	Markham, Mt. (märk'ȧm) . . . . Ant.	82.59 S	160.30 E
129	Markova (mär'kô-vȧ) . . . Sov. Un.	49.31 N	39.32 E
139	Markovo (mär'kô-vô) . . . Sov. Un.	64.35 N	170.35 E
111	Marksshtadt (märks'shtät) Sov. Un.	51.40 N	46.48 E
81	Marksville (märks'vĭl) . . . . La.	31.7 N	92.5 W
120	Marktredwitz (märkt-rĕd'vēts) Ger.	50.1 N	12.5 E
86	Marlboro (märl'bŭr-ô) . . . . . Mass.	42.20 N	71.32 W
84	Marlette (mär-lĕt') . . . . Mich.	43.20 N	83.4 W
54	Marlile I. (mär'lĭl) . . . . Can.	62.42 N	91.30 W
81	Marlin (mär'lĭn) . . . . Tex.	31.18 N	96.54 W
85	Marlinton (mär'lĭn-tŭn) . . . W. Va.	38.14 N	80.10 W
78	Marlow (mär'lō) . . . . Okla.	34.39 N	97.57 W
123	Marly-le-Roi (mär-lē'lē-rwä') Fr. (In.)	48.51 N	2.6 E
122	Marmande (mȧr-mäNd') . . . . . . Fr.	44.30 N	0.10 E
127	Marmara I. (mär'mȧ-rȧ) . . . . . Tur.	40.35 N	27.40 E
111	Marmara, Sea of . . . . Tur.	40.45 N	28.30 E
76	Marmarth (mär'mȧrth) . . . . N. D.	46.18 N	103.57 W
125	Mar Menor (L.) (mär mā-nôr') . Sp.	37.45 N	0.45 W
126	Marmora (Mt.) (mär'mō-rä) . Sard.	40.0 N	9.19 E
93	Mar Muerto (L.) (mär mwĕr'tō) Mex.	16.10 N	94.12 W
122	Marne R. (märn) . . . . Fr.	49.0 N	3.30 E
133	Maroua (mär'wä) . . . . Cam.	10.33 N	14.21 E
100	Maroa (mä-rō'ä) . . . . Ven.	2.33 N	67.29 W
135	Maroantsetra (mȧ-rō-äŋ-tsä'trȧ) Madag.	15.20 S	49.48 E
123	Marolles (mȧ-rōl') . . . . Fr. (In.)	48.41 N	2.36 E
101	Maroni R. (mȧ-rō'nê) Fr. Gui.-Sur.	4.0 N	53.15 W
116	Marple (mär'p'l) . . . . Gt. Brit.	53.24 N	2.4 W
92	Marqués, R. del (rē'ō dĕl mär-käs') . Mex.	18.51 N	102.30 W
	Marquesas, see Marquises (Is.)		
83	Marquesas Keys (Is.) (mär-kē'zȧs) . Fla. (In.)	23.45 N	82.10 W
56	Marquette (mär-kĕt') Can. (Winnipeg In.)	50.4 N	97.45 W
77	Marquette . . . . Mich.	46.32 N	87.23 W
84	Marquette R. . . . . Mich.	43.55 N	86.0 W
81	Marquez (mär-käz') . . . . Mex.	29.0 N	105.7 W
81	Marquez . . . . Tex.	31.14 N	96.15 W
122	Marquise (mȧr-kēz') . . . . Fr.	50.49 N	1.41 E
4	Marquises (Is.) (mär-kēz') . Pac. O.	9.0 S	140.0 W
133	Marra, Jebel (Mts.) (jĕb'ĕl mär'ä) . A. E. Sud.	13.15 N	24.30 E
132	Marrakech (mȧr-rä'kĕsh) . . . . Mor.	31.50 N	8.0 W
160	Marrawah (mär'rȧ-wä) Austl. (Tas. In.)	40.54 S	144.43 E
158	Marre (măr'rē) . . . . Austl.	29.32 S	138.0 E
124	Marroqui, Pt. (mä-rō-kē') . . . . . Sp.	36.2 N	5.35 W
126	Marsala (mär-sä'lä) . . . . It.	37.48 N	12.28 E
113	Marsa Matrouh (mär'sȧ mä-trōō') Eg.	31.20 N	27.12 E
102	Mar, Serra do (Mts.) (sĕr'rȧ dōō mär') . Braz.	25.0 S	48.30 W
116	Marsden (märz'dĕn) . . . . . Gt. Brit.	53.36 N	155.0 W
122	Marseillan (mȧr-sâ-yäN') . . . . . . Fr.	43.20 N	3.30 E
123	Marseille (mȧr-sâ'y') . . . . Fr.	43.20 N	5.20 E
72	Marshall (mär'shȧl) Colo. (Denver In.)	39.57 N	105.14 W
84	Marshall . . . . Ill.	39.25 N	87.40 W
84	Marshall . . . . Mich.	42.18 N	84.56 W
76	Marshall . . . . Minn.	44.28 N	95.48 W
79	Marshall . . . . Mo.	39.6 N	93.11 W
81	Marshall . . . . Tex.	32.33 N	94.21 W
5	Marshall Is. . . . . Pac. O.	10.0 N	171.0 E
77	Marshalltown (mär'shȧl-toun) . Ia.	42.3 N	92.52 W
82	Marshallville (mär'shȧl-vĭl) . . . Ga.	32.28 N	83.58 W
87	Marshfield (märsh'fēld) Mass. (In.)	42.6 N	70.43 W
79	Marshfield . . . . Mo.	37.20 N	92.54 W
77	Marshfield . . . . Wis.	44.40 N	90.9 W
81	Marsh I. (märsh) . . . . La.	29.35 N	91.50 W
86	Mars Hill (märz' hĭl') . . . . Me.	46.32 N	67.55 W
51	Marshland (märsh'lȧnd) Ore. (Portland In.)	46.7 N	123.16 W
118	Marstrand (mär'stränd) . . . . . Swe.	57.55 N	11.34 E
81	Mart (märt) . . . . Tex.	31.33 N	96.50 W
150	Martaban, G. of (mär-tŭ-bän') Bur.	16.0 N	96.45 E
150	Martapoera (mär-tä-pōō'rä) Indon.	3.20 S	114.50 E
85	Marthas Vineyard I. (mär'thȧz vĭn'yȧrd) . Mass.	41.25 N	70.40 W
96	Marti (mär-tē') . . . . Cuba	22.58 N	80.55 W
120	Martigny (mär-tê-nyē') . . . . . Switz.	46.6 N	7.3 E
122	Martigues (mȧr-tēg') . . . . Fr.	43.24 N	5.0 E
82	Martin (mär'tĭn) . . . . Tenn.	36.20 N	88.47 W
127	Martina (mär-tē'nä) . . . . It.	40.42 N	17.20 E
51	Martinez (mär-tē'nĕz) Calif. (San Francisco In.)	38.1 N	122.7 W
55	Martin Falls (mär'tĭn) . . . . . . Can.	51.35 N	86.20 W
91	Martinique (mȧr-tê-nēk') . . . W. I.	14.45 N	61.0 W
51	Martins Bluff (mär'tĭnz) Wash. (Portland In.)	45.57 N	122.47 W
85	Martinsburg (mär'tĭnz-bûrg) W. Va.	39.27 N	77.58 W
84	Martins Ferry . . . . Ohio	40.5 N	80.45 W
84	Martinsville (mär'tĭnz-vĭl) . . . Ind.	39.25 N	86.27 W
83	Martinsville . . . . Va.	36.42 N	79.54 W
156	Marton (mär'tŭn) . . . . N. Z.	40.5 S	175.25 E
125	Martorell (mär'tō-rĕl') . . . Sp. (In.)	41.28 N	1.55 E
124	Martos (mär'tōs) . . . . Sp.	37.43 N	3.57 W
129	Martovaya (mȧr'tô-vä'yä) Sov. Un.	49.57 N	36.55 E
149	Marugame (mä'rōō-gä'mā) . . . Jap.	34.14 N	133.48 E
122	Marvejols (mȧr-vē-zhôl') . . . . . . Fr.	44.34 N	3.15 E
105	Mary (mä'rê) . . . . Sov. Un.	37.50 N	61.40 E
129	Maryanovskaya (mär'yä-nôf'skä-yä) . Sov. Un.	45.5 N	38.38 E
159	Maryborough (mā'rĭ-bŭr-ô) . Austl.	37.3 S	143.44 E
159	Maryborough . . . . Austl.	25.44 S	152.44 E
85	Maryland (State) (mĕr'ĭ-lȧnd) U. S.	39.0 N	76.30 W
114	Maryport (mā'rĭ-pōrt) . . . Gt. Brit.	54.45 N	3.25 W
70	Marys R. (mā'rĭz) . . . . Nev.	41.25 N	115.14 W
74	Marysville (mā'rĭz-vĭl) . . . . . . Calif.	39.8 N	121.36 W
86	Marysville . . . . Can.	45.59 N	66.38 W
79	Marysville . . . . Kan.	39.51 N	96.37 W
84	Marysville . . . . Ohio	40.13 N	83.23 W
51	Marysville . . . . Wash. (Seattle In.)	48.3 N	122.11 W
160	Maryvale (mā'rĭ-vāl) . . Austl. (In.)	28.4 S	152.14 E
79	Maryville (mā'rĭ-vĭl) . . . . Mo.	40.21 N	94.51 W
82	Maryville . . . . Tenn.	35.35 N	83.58 W
147	Masan (mä-sän') . . . . Kor.	35.12 N	128.34 E
151	Masantol (mä-sän-tōl') Phil. (Manila In.)	14.53 N	120.38 E
135	Mâ' sara Station (mä''sȧ-rä) . . Eg.	29.54 N	31.17 E
135	Masasi (mä-sä'sê) . . . . Tan.	10.25 S	38.0 E
94	Masaya (mä-sä'yä) . . . . Nic.	11.58 N	86.5 W
152	Masbate (mäs-bä'tä) . . . . Phil.	12.21 N	123.38 E
152	Masbate I. . . . . Phil.	12.20 N	123.30 E
132	Mascara (mäs'kä-rä) (mȧs-kȧ-rȧ') Alg.	35.30 N	0.5 E
82	Mascot (măs'kŏt) . . . . Tenn.	36.6 N	83.47 W
92	Mascota (mäs-kō'tä) . . . . Mex.	20.33 N	104.46 W
92	Mascota, R. de . . . . Mex.	20.35 N	104.50 W
57	Mascouche R. (mȧs-kōōsh') Can. (Montreal In.)	45.45 N	73.41 W
134	Maseru (măz'ēr-ōō) . . . . Bas.	29.19 S	27.30 E
116	Masham (măsh'ȧm) . . . . . Gt. Brit.	54.13 N	1.39 W
140	Mashhad (mŭsh-hŭd') . . . . Iran	36.20 N	59.30 E
133	Masindi (mä-sēn'dê) . . . . Ug.	1.42 N	31.40 E
114	Mask, Lough (L.) (lŏK mȧsk) . . Ire.	53.40 N	9.20 W
125	Masnou (mäs'nōō) . . . . . . Sp. (In.)	41.29 N	2.19 E
84	Mason (mā'sŭn) . . . . Mich.	42.34 N	84.28 W
80	Mason . . . . Tex.	30.45 N	99.14 W
77	Mason City . . . . Ia.	43.9 N	93.21 W
150	Ma Song (R.) (sŏng' mä') . Indoch.	20.30 N	105.0 E
51	Mason L. . . . . Wash. (Seattle In.)	47.20 N	122.57 W
72	Masonville (mā'sŭn-vĭl) Colo. (Denver In.)	40.30 N	105.14 W
140	Masqat (Muscat) (mȧs-kät') (mŭs-kăt') . Oman	23.35 N	58.38 E
125	Masquefa (mäs-kā'fä) . . Sp. (In.)	41.29 N	1.51 E
135	Masr el Atîga (Old Cairo) (mäz''r ĕl ȧ-tē'kȧ) . Eg.	30.1 N	31.15 E
126	Massa (mäs'sä) . . . . It.	44.2 N	10.8 E
86	Massachusetts (State) (măs-ȧ-chōō'sĕts) . U. S.	42.28 N	72.0 W
86	Massachusetts B. . . . . U. S.	42.25 N	70.15 W
126	Massafra (mäs-sä'frä) . . . . It.	40.35 N	17.6 E
126	Massa Maritima (mäs'sä mä-rē'tê-mä) . It.	43.3 N	10.54 E
133	Massaua (mäs-sä'wä) . . . . Erit.	15.36 N	14.28 E
85	Massena (mă-sē'nȧ) . . . . N. Y.	44.57 N	74.54 W
117	Massenhoven (mäs'ĕn-hō'vĕn) Bel. (Anvers In.)	51.12 N	4.38 E
133	Massenya (mä-sĕn'yä) . Fr. Eq. Afr.	11.28 N	16.10 E
54	Masset (măs'ĕt) . . . . Can.	54.2 N	132.4 W
122	Massif Central (Plat.) (mȧ-sēf' säN-trȧl') . Fr.	44.50 N	3.30 E
84	Massillon (măs'ĭ-lŏn) . . . . Ohio	40.50 N	81.32 W
134	Massinga (mä-sĭn'gä) . . . . Moz.	23.20 S	35.18 E
78	Massive, Mt. (mȧs'ĭv) . . . . . . Colo.	39.10 N	106.29 W
123	Massy (mȧ-sē') . . . . Fr. (In.)	48.45 N	2.17 E
160	Mastermans Range (măs'tēr-mȧnz) Austl. (In.)	20.10 S	150.50 E
157	Masterton (mȧs'tēr-tŭn) . . . . N. Z.	40.58 S	175.42 E
96	Mastic Pt. (măs'tĭk) . . . . . . Ba. Is.	25.5 N	78.0 W
149	Masude (mä-sōō'dȧ) . . . . Jap.	34.44 N	131.55 E
141	Masulipatam (mŭ-sōō'lē-pŭ-tŭm') India	16.8 N	81.8 E
121	Masuria (Reg.) (mȧ-zōō'rĭ-ȧ) . Ger.	53.45 N	21.25 E
134	Matadi (mȧ-tä'dê) . . . . . Bel. Cong.	5.47 S	13.35 E
101	Mata do São João (mä'tä dōō souN zhô-ouN') . Braz. (In.)	12.30 S	38.17 W
94	Matagalpa (mä-tä-gäl'pä) . . . . Nic.	13.9 N	85.41 W
81	Matagorda B. (măt-ȧ-gôr'dȧ) . Tex.	28.35 N	96.30 W
81	Matagorda I. . . . . Tex.	28.15 N	96.35 W
153	Matalom (mä-tä-lôm') . . . . . . Phil.	10.18 N	124.48 E
132	Matam (mä-täm') . . . . Fr. W. Afr.	15.42 N	13.21 W
156	Matamata (mä-tä-mä'tä) . . . N. Z.	37.47 S	176.4 E
80	Matamoros (mä-tä-mō'rôs) . . Mex.	25.32 N	103.14 W
81	Matamoros . . . . Mex.	25.52 N	97.30 W
92	Matamoros de Izúcar (mä-tä-mō'-rôs dā ē'zōō'kär) . Mex.	18.34 N	98.27 W
153	Matanal Pt. (mä-tä-näl') . . . . Phil.	6.37 N	122.19 E
55	Matane (mȧ-tăn') . . . . Can.	48.45 N	67.28 W
134	Matanga (mä-täŋ'gä) . . . . Ang.	7.32 S	17.28 E
53	Matanuska (mä-tä-nōōs'kȧ) . Alsk.	61.38 N	149.0 W
52	Matanuska R. . . . . Alsk. (In.)	61.50 N	148.15 W
102	Matanza (mä-tän'zä) . . . Arg. (In.)	34.42 S	58.32 W
96	Matanzas . . . . Cuba	23.1 N	81.39 W
97	Matanzas . . . . Hai.	19.19 N	69.47 W
96	Matanzas (State) (mä-tän'zäs) Cuba	22.47 N	81.10 W
96	Matanzas B. . . . . Cuba	23.5 N	81.34 W
102	Matanzas, R. . . . . Arg. (In.)	34.42 S	58.27 W
95	Matapalo, C. (mä-tä-pä'lō) . . C. R.	8.22 N	83.19 W
127	Matapan, C. (mȧ-tȧ-pän') . . . Grc.	36.22 N	22.30 E
86	Matapedia (mă-tȧ-pē'dĭ-ȧ) . . . Can.	48.0 N	66.56 W
86	Matapedia, L. . . . . Can.	48.34 N	67.35 W
86	Matapedia R. . . . . Can.	48.16 N	67.18 W
141	Matara (mä-tä'rä) . . . . . . Cey. (In.)	6.0 N	80.35 E
153	Matarinao B. (mä-tä-rê-nä'ō) Phil.	11.14 N	125.35 E
125	Mataró (mä-tä-rō') . . . . . . Sp. (In.)	41.33 N	2.27 E
156	Matata (mä-tä'tä) . . . . N. Z.	37.52 S	176.47 E
153	Matatindoc Pt. (mä-tä-tên-dŏk') Phil.	9.40 N	122.24 E
157	Mataura (mȧ-tou'rȧ) . . . . N. Z.	46.12 S	168.52 E
157	Mataura R. . . . . N. Z.	45.40 S	168.42 E
92	Matehuala (mä-tȧ-wä'lä) . . . . Mex.	23.38 N	100.38 W
126	Matera (mä-tä'rä) . . . . It.	40.40 N	16.36 E
131	Mateur (mȧ-tûr') . . . . . . Tun. (In.)	37.2 N	9.41 E
55	Matheson (măth'ĕ-sŭn) . . . . . . Can.	48.29 N	80.27 W
97	Mathewtown (măth'ū-toun) Ba. Is.	20.58 N	73.40 W
153	Mati (mä'tê) . . . . Phil.	6.58 N	126.14 E
72	Matia Is. (mȧ'tyä) Wash. (Vancouver In.)	48.45 N	122.50 W
153	Matiguid I. (mä-tê-gēd') . . . . Phil.	11.3 N	119.35 E
95	Matina (mä-tē'nä) . . . . C. R.	10.4 N	83.16 W
119	Matisi (mä'tē-sê) . . . . Sov. Un.	57.43 N	25.10 E
116	Matlock (măt'lŏk) . . . . . . Gt. Brit.	53.8 N	1.33 W
116	Matlock Bath . . . . Gt. Brit.	53.6 N	1.34 W
131	Matmata (mät-mä'tä) . . Tun. (In.)	33.33 N	9.58 E
101	Mato Grosso (State) (mät'ōō grōs'ōō) . Braz.	15.0 S	55.0 W
101	Mato Grosso, Plat. of . . . . Braz.	15.0 S	54.0 W

ng-sing; ŋ-baŋk; N-nasalized n; nŏd; cŏmmit; ōld; ôbey; ôrder; fōōd; fŏŏt; ou-out; s-soft; sh-dish; th-thin; pūre; ûnite; ûrn; stŭd; circŭs; ü-as "y" in study; '-indeterminate vowel.

Matozinhos PRONOUNCING INDEX Menzies

Page	Name Pronunciation Region	Lat. °′	Long. °′
124	Matozinhos (Leixoes) (mä-tô-zēn'yōzh). Port.	41.11 N	8.41 W
140	Matrah (mȧ-trä')..........Oman	23.35 N	58.36 E
129	Matrenki (mä-trĕŋ'kê)...Sov. Un.	51.27 N	38.39 E
72	Matsqui (măts'kê) Can. (Vancouver In.)	49.6 N	122.17 W
149	Matsudo (mät'sōō-dô) Jap. (Tokyo In.)	35.45 N	139.54 E
149	Matsué (mät'sōō-ĕ).........Jap.	35.29 N	133.2 E
149	Matsumoto (mät'sōō-mō'tô)..Jap.	36.14 N	138.0 E
149	Matsuyama (mät'sōō-yä'mȧ).Jap.	33.48 N	132.45 E
149	Matsuzaka (mät'sōō-zä'kȧ)...Jap.	34.34 N	136.33 E
55	Mattagami L. (mȧ-tȧ-gä'mê).Can.	50.0 N	77.28 W
85	Mattaponi R. (măt'ȧ-pô-nī')..Va.	37.45 N	76.35 W
55	Mattawa (măt'ȧ-wȧ)........Can.	46.16 N	78.13 W
86	Mattawin R. (măt'ȧ-wĭn)....Can.	46.55 N	73.30 W
120	Matterhorn (Mt.) (mät'ēr-hôrn) Switz.	45.58 N	7.38 E
79	Mattoon (mă-tōōn')..........Ill.	39.27 N	88.22 W
100	Maturín (mä-tōō-rēn').......Ven.	9.45 N	63.15 W
153	Matutum, Mt. (mä-tōō'tōōm) Phil.	6.20 N	125.7 E
102	Maua (mä'ōō-ä).......Braz. (In.)	22.42 S	43.10 W
152	Mauban (mä'ōō-bän')........Phil.	14.11 N	121.43 E
122	Maubeuge (mô-bûzh')........Fr.	50.20 N	3.50 E
85	Mauch Chunk (môk' chŭnk'). Pa.	40.52 N	75.45 W
117	Mauer (mou'ēr)...Aus. (Wien In.)	48.9 N	16.16 E
101	Maués (mä-ōō-āzh')........Braz.	3.31 S	57.32 W
155	Maui (I.) (mä'ōō-ē)........Haw.	20.45 N	156.20 W
122	Mauléon-Licharre (mō-lā-ôN'-lē-shär').Fr.	43.10 N	0.50 W
84	Maumee (mô-mē')............Ohio	41.35 N	83.39 W
84	Maumee B...........Mich.-Ohio	41.45 N	83.15 W
84	Maumee R............Ind.-Ohio	41.23 N	84.0 W
155	Mauna Kea (Vol.) (mä'ōō-nä kā'ä) Haw.	19.55 N	155.28 W
155	Mauna Loa (Vol.) (mä'ōō-nä lō'ä) Haw.	19.29 N	155.36 W
123	Maurecourt (mōr'kōōr')..Fr. (In.)	48.59 N	2.4 E
81	Maurepas L. (mō-rē-pä')......La.	30.15 N	90.30 W
132	Mauritania (Colony) (mô-rê-tā'nĭ-ȧ).Fr. W. Afr.	19.0 N	12.0 W
5	Mauritius (I.) (mô-rĭsh'ĭ-ŭs) Ind. O. (In.)	20.18 S	57.36 E
51	Maury I. (mô'rĭ) Wash. (Seattle In.)	47.22 N	122.27 W
77	Mauston (môs'tŭn)..........Wis.	43.45 N	90.5 W
93	Maxcanú (mäs-kä-nōō')......Mex.	20.36 N	89.59 W
	Maxim Gorki, see Gorki, Sov. Un.		
114	Maxwelltown (măks'wĕl-toun) Gt. Brit.	55.5 N	3.35 W
91	Mayagüez (mä-yä-gwāz') P. R. (In.)	18.10 N	67.15 W
144	Mayang (mä'yäng')..........Chn.	27.36 N	109.15 E
139	Maya R. (mä'yȧ)........Sov. Un.	58.0 N	135.20 E
97	Mayarí (mä-yä-rē')..........Cuba	20.40 N	75.41 W
97	Mayarí, R...............Cuba	20.32 N	75.40 W
120	Mayen (mī'ĕn)...............Ger.	50.18 N	7.13 E
122	Mayenne (mȧ-yĕn')............Fr.	48.20 N	0.30 W
122	Mayenne R....................Fr.	48.20 N	0.35 W
88	Mayfair (mā'fâr).Ill. (Chicago In.)	41.58 N	87.45 W
82	Mayfield (mā'fēld)..........Ky.	36.46 N	88.35 W
82	Mayfield Cr.................Ky.	36.55 N	88.50 W
51	Mayger (mā'gēr) Ore. (Portland In.)	46.9 N	123.6 W
160	Maylands (mā'lăndz) Austl. (Perth In.)	31.55 S	115.54 E
73	Maylene (mā-lēn') Ala. (Birmingham In.)	33.13 N	86.54 W
142	Maymyo (mī'myō')..........Bur.	22.25 N	96.30 E
87	Maynard (mā'nȧrd)...Mass. (In.)	42.26 N	71.26 W
72	Mayne I. (mān) Can. (Vancouver In.)	48.52 N	123.17 W
153	Mayo B. (mä'yō)............Phil.	6.56 N	126.20 E
83	Mayodan (mā-yō'dăn)......N. C.	36.25 N	79.59 W
53	Mayo L. (mā'ō).............Can.	63.45 N	135.0 W
54	Mayo Landing...............Can.	63.59 N	135.31 W
114	Mayo, Mts. of...............Ire.	54.10 N	9.40 W
152	Mayon Vol. (mä-yōn')......Phil.	13.15 N	123.40 E
156	Mayor I. (mā'ēr)..........N. Z.	37.17 S	176.15 E
135	Mayotte I. (mȧ-yôt')....Ind. O.	12.45 S	45.10 E
134	Mayoumba (mȧ-yōōm'bȧ) Fr. Eq. Afr.	3.13 S	10.42 E
80	Mayran, L. (mī-rän').......Mex.	25.45 N	102.45 W
84	Maysville (māz'vĭl)..........Ky.	38.38 N	83.46 W
85	Mayville (mā'vĭl)..........N. Y.	42.14 N	79.30 W
76	Mayville...................N. D.	47.31 N	97.18 W
77	Mayville....................Wis.	43.31 N	88.32 W
89	Maywood (mā'wŏŏd) Ill. (Chicago In.)	41.53 N	87.50 W
134	Mazabuka (mä-zä-bōō'kȧ).N. Rh.	16.0 S	27.48 E
132	Mazagan (mȧ-zȧ-gän')......Mor.	33.21 N	8.30 W
101	Mazaganópolis (mä-zä-gä-nō'pô-lēzh).Braz.	0.10 S	51.29 W
122	Mazamet (mȧ-zȧ-mĕ')........Fr.	43.30 N	2.20 E
80	Mazapil (mä-zä-pēl')........Mex.	24.40 N	101.30 W
141	Mazar-i-Sharif (mȧ-zär'-ē-shȧ-rēf') Afg.	36.44 N	67.28 E
124	Mazarón (mä-thä-rōn').......Sp.	37.36 N	1.18 W
101	Mazaruni R. (mä-zä-rōō'nē) Br. Gu.	6.0 N	59.30 W
94	Mazatenango (mä-zä-tâ-näŋ'gō) Guat.	14.31 N	91.31 W
92	Mazatlán (mä-zä-tlän').....Mex.	23.12 N	106.25 W
93	Mazatlán (San Juan) (sän hwän') Mex.	17.3 N	95.27 W
119	Mažeikiai (mȧ-zhā'kê-ī)..Sov. Un.	56.19 N	22.25 E
126	Mazzara del Vallo (mät-sä'rä dĕl väl'lō).It.	37.39 N	12.37 E
126	Mazzarino (mät-sä-rē'nō)......It.	37.18 N	14.12 E
134	Mbabane (m'bä-bä'nĕ).....Swaz.	26.22 S	31.12 E
133	M'Baïki (m'bȧ-ē'kê)..Fr. Eq. Afr.	3.58 N	17.58 E
134	M'Bigou (m-bê-gōō').Fr. Eq. Afr.	2.5 S	12.8 E
133	M'Bomu R. (m'bō'mōō) Bel. Cong.-Fr. Eq. Afr.	4.50 N	25.0 E
134	Mboukou (m-bōō-kōō').Fr.Eq.Afr.	4.28 S	12.12 E
132	M'Bout (m'bōō').....Fr. W. Afr.	16.2 N	12.32 W
135	Mbweni (m-bwā'nê)........Tan.	6.37 S	39.9 E
72	Mead (mēd)...Colo. (Denver In.)	40.14 N	105.0 W
74	Mead, L. (mēd)...........Nev.	36.10 N	114.40 W
78	Meade (mēd)...............Kan.	37.17 N	100.21 W
71	Meade Peak................Ida.	42.28 N	111.17 W
51	Meadowdale (mĕd'ō-dāl) Wash. (Seattle In.)	47.50 N	122.20 W
56	Meadows (mĕd'ōz) Can. (Winnipeg In.)	50.2 N	97.37 W
85	Meadville (mēd'vĭl)..........Pa.	41.40 N	80.10 W
84	Meaford (mē'fērd)..........Can.	44.36 N	20.39 W
159	Meandarra (mē-ăn-dȧ'rȧ)...Austl.	27.20 S	149.29 E
122	Meaux (mō)..................Fr.	49.0 N	2.52 E
93	Mecapalapa (mā-kä-pä-lä'pä) Mex.	20.30 N	97.54 W
87	Mecatina I. (mā-kȧ-tē'nȧ)...Can.	50.48 N	58.60 W
87	Mecatina R...............Can.	50.50 N	59.50 W
140	Mecca (mĕk'ȧ)..........Sau. Ar.	21.29 N	39.45 E
86	Mechanic Falls (mê-kăn'ĭk)...Me.	44.5 N	70.25 W
85	Mechanicsburg (mê-kăn'ĭks-bûrg) Pa.	40.15 N	77.2 W
85	Mechanicsville (mê-kăn'ĭks-vĭl) N. Y.	42.56 N	73.46 W
112	Mécheria (mā-shē-rē'ä)......Alg.	33.29 N	0.18 W
120	Mecklenburg (State) (mĕk'lĕn-bŏŏrgh).Ger.	53.35 N	12.5 E
150	Medan (mȧ-dän').........Indon.	3.37 N	98.38 E
116	Medden, R. (mĕd'ĕn)....Gt. Brit.	53.15 N	1.6 E
132	Médéa (mā-dā'ä)............Alg.	36.24 N	2.35 E
100	Medellín (mā-dhĕl-yēn').....Col.	6.1 N	75.47 W
93	Medellín....................Mex.	19.2 N	96.10 W
153	Medellín...................Phil.	11.8 N	123.59 E
131	Médenine (mā-dē-nēn').Tun. (In.)	33.23 N	10.25 E
87	Medfield (mĕd'fēld)...Mass. (In.)	42.11 N	71.18 W
87	Medford (mĕd'fērd)...Mass. (In.)	42.25 N	71.6 W
78	Medford....................Okla.	36.46 N	97.43 W
70	Medford....................Ore.	42.20 N	122.43 W
77	Medford....................Wis.	45.9 N	90.20 W
121	Medias (mĕd-yäsh')........Rom.	46.10 N	24.22 E
70	Medical Lake (mĕd'ĭ-kăl)...Wash.	47.34 N	117.40 W
71	Medicine L. (mĕd'ĭ-sĭn)....Mont.	48.27 N	104.25 W
71	Medicine Bow Ra. (bō).Wyo.-Colo.	41.0 N	106.8 W
71	Medicine Bow R...........Wyo.	42.0 N	106.30 W
54	Medicine Hat...............Can.	50.2 N	110.40 W
78	Medicine Lodge............Kan.	37.16 N	98.35 W
78	Medicine Lodge R.....Kan.-Okla.	37.10 N	98.34 W
140	Medina (mȧ-dē'nä)......Sau. Ar.	24.30 N	39.45 E
85	Medina (mê-dī'nȧ).........N. Y.	43.16 N	78.23 W
84	Medina.....................Ohio	41.8 N	81.51 W
124	Medina del Campo (mä-dē'nä dĕl käm'pō).Sp.	41.17 N	4.55 W
124	Medina de Rioseco (mā-dē'nä dā rê-ô-sā'kō).Sp.	41.53 N	5.4 W
80	Medina R. (mȧ-dē'nä).......Tex.	29.30 N	98.55 W
125	Medina-Sidonia (mā-dē'nä-sê-dō'nyä).Sp. (In.)	36.28 N	5.44 W
126	Mediterranean Sea (mĕd-ĭ-tĕr-ā'-nē-ăn).Eur.-Afr.-Asia	34.50 N	25.0 E
131	Medjerda Mts. (mĕ-jĕr'dȧ) Tun. (In.)	36.35 N	8.40 E
131	Medjerda, Oued (R.) (wĕd mĕ-jĕr'-dȧ).Tun. (In.)	36.32 N	9.0 E
131	Medjez-el-Bab (mĕ-jĕz'-ĕl-bȧb') Tun. (In.)	36.38 N	9.39 E
128	Medveditsa R. (mĕd-vyĕ'dê-tsȧ) Sov. Un.	50.30 N	44.30 E
129	Medvedovskaya (mĕd-vyĕ'dôf-skȧ-yȧ).Sov. Un.	45.28 N	38.58 E
110	Medvezhegorsk (mĕd-vyĕzh'-yĕ-gôrsk').Sov. Un.	62.54 N	34.27 E
139	Medvezhi Is. (mĕd-vyĕ'zhê) Sov. Un.	70.40 N	161.0 E
111	Medvezhie (mĕd-vyĕ'zhê-yĕ) Sov. Un.	45.45 N	41.28 E
129	Medvin (mĕd-vên')......Sov. Un.	49.22 N	30.48 E
87	Medway (mĕd'wā).....Mass. (In.)	42.8 N	71.23 W
117	Medway, R.Gt. Brit. (London In.)	51.22 N	0.29 E
128	Medyn (mĕ-dēn')........Sov. Un.	54.58 N	35.54 E
129	Medzhibozh (mĕd-zhê-bôzh') Sov. Un.	49.25 N	27.25 E
158	Meekatharra(mē-kȧ-thăr'ȧ).Austl.	26.28 S	118.30 E
75	Meeker (mēk'ēr)............Colo.	40.4 N	107.55 W
87	Meelpaeg L. (mēl'pȧ-ĕg).....Can.	48.15 N	56.35 W
120	Meerane (mā-rä'nē)..........Ger.	50.52 N	12.27 E
117	Meerdonck (mār'dônk) Bel. (Anvers In.)	51.16 N	4.9 E
141	Meerut (mē'rŏŏt)..........India	28.50 N	77.45 E
127	Megalopolis (mĕg-ȧ-lŏ'pô-lĭs).Grc.	37.22 N	22.8 E
55	Megantic (mê-găn'tĭk).......Can.	45.40 N	70.50 W
127	Megara (mĕg'ȧ-rȧ)...........Grc.	37.59 N	23.20 E
83	Meggett (mĕg'ĕt).............S. C.	32.44 N	80.16 W
51	Megler (mĕg'lēr) Wash. (Portland In.)	46.15 N	123.51 W
128	Meglino, L. (mȧ-glē'nô)..Sov. Un.	58.25 N	35.25 E
83	Meherrin R. (mê-hĕr'ĭn).......Va.	36.40 N	77.30 W
122	Mehun (mē-ŭN')................Fr.	47.10 N	2.15 E
117	Meiendorf (mī'ĕn-dôrf) Ger. (Hamburg In.)	53.37 N	10.9 E
144	Mei Ling (mā' lĭng')........Chn.	25.27 N	113.35 E
120	Meiningen (mī'nĭng-ĕn)......Ger.	50.34 N	10.25 E
145	Mei R. (mā'ē).................Chn.	23.45 N	115.35 E
120	Meiringen (mī'rĭng-ĕn).....Switz.	46.44 N	8.12 E
117	Meirreit (mī'rĭt).Bel. (Anvers In.)	51.21 N	4.35 E
120	Meiszen (mī'sĕn).............Ger.	51.10 N	13.27 E
144	Meitan (mā'tän')............Chn.	37.45 N	107.37 E
144	Meitsi Ling (Mts.) (mä'tsē lĭng') Chn.	25.7 N	112.7 E
102	Mejillones (mā-kē-lyō'nās)...Chl.	23.1 S	70.30 W
132	Meknés (mĕk'nĕs) (mĕk-nĕs').Mor.	34.0 N	5.33 W
150	Mekong R. (mē'kông') Indoch.-Siam	16.0 N	105.0 E
159	Melbourne (mĕl'bŭrn)......Austl.	37.47 S	144.58 E
160	Melbourne...........Austl. (In.)		
83	Melbourne.............Fla. (In.)	28.3 N	80.37 W
116	Melbourne............Gt. Brit.	52.49 N	1.26 W
79	Melcher (mĕl'chēr)..........Ia.	41.02 N	93.16 W
110	Melekess (mĕl-yĕ'kĕs)...Sov. Un.	54.15 N	49.35 E
128	Melenki (mĕ-lyĕŋ'kê)....Sov. Un.	55.20 N	41.41 E
126	Melfi (mĕl'fē)................It.	40.58 N	15.38 E
101	Melgaço (mĕl-gä'sōō).......Braz.	16.30 S	56.0 W
133	Melik, Wad el (R.) (wäd' ĕl mĕ-lēk').A. E. Sud.	17.0 N	30.0 E
132	Melilla (mā-lēl'yä)......Sp. Mor.	35.23 N	3.0 W
99	Melincué (mȧ-lēn-kwā') Arg. (Buenos Aires In.)	33.39 S	61.26 W
99	Melipilla (mȧ-lê-pē'lyä) Chl. (Valparaiso In.)	33.41 S	71.16 W
129	Melitopol (mā-lê-tô'pôl-y') Sov. Un.	46.49 N	35.22 E
131	Mellègue, O. (R.) (wäd mē-lĕg') Tun. (In.)	36.10 N	8.45 E
77	Mellen (mĕl'ĕn).............Wis.	46.19 N	90.39 W
118	Mellerud (mĕl'ĕ-rōōdh)......Swe.	58.42 N	12.27 E
120	Melo (mā'lō)..................Ur.	32.28 S	54.10 W
127	Melos (Milo) (I.) (mē'lŏs) (mē'lō) Grc.	36.42 N	24.27 E
112	Melrir, Chott (mĕl'rēr)......Alg.	34.30 N	6.30 E
87	Melrose (mĕl'rōz).....Mass. (In.)	42.27 N	71.4 W
77	Melrose....................Minn.	45.40 N	94.48 W
156	Melrose...............N. Z. (In.)	41.20 S	174.47 E
88	Melrose Park...Ill. (Chicago In.)	41.53 N	87.51 W
117	Melsele (mĕl'sĕ-lē) Bel. (Anvers In.)	51.13 N	4.16 E
134	Melsetter (mĕl-sĕt'ēr)......S. Rh.	19.50 S	32.47 E
116	Meltham (mĕl'thăm)....Gt. Brit.	53.35 N	1.51 W
116	Melton Mowbray (mĕl'tŭn mō'brȧ) Gt. Brit.	52.46 N	0.52 W
122	Melun (mē-lŭN')...............Fr.	48.35 N	2.41 E
131	Melusa (mā-lōō'sä) Sp. Mor. (Gib. In.)	35.42 N	5.23 E
133	Melut (mȧ-lōōt')......A. E. Sud.	10.30 N	32.11 E
81	Melville (mĕl'vĭl)..............La.	30.41 N	91.45 W
51	Melville.......Ore. (Portland In.)	46.2 N	123.51 W
159	Melville, C..................Austl.	14.8 S	144.38 E
153	Melville, C..................Phil.	7.48 N	117.0 E
158	Melville I..................Austl.	11.30 S	131.0 E
55	Melville, L..................Can.	54.2 N	59.0 W
55	Melville Pen.................Can.	67.50 N	84.30 W
50	Melville Sd..................Can.	73.30 N	10.50 W
160	Melville Water (L.) Austl. (Perth In.)	31.59 S	115.50 E
72	Melvin (mĕl'vĭn).Colo. (Denver In.)	39.37 N	104.50 W
121	Mélykút (mā'l'kōōt).........Hung.	46.13 N	19.23 E
135	Memba (mĕm'bȧ)..............Moz.	14.13 S	40.28 E
119	Memel (Klaipēda) (klī'pĕ-dȧ) Sov. Un.	55.42 N	21.10 E
121	Memel R. (mā'mĕl).....Sov. Un.	55.7 N	21.45 E
120	Memmingen (mĕm'ĭng-ĕn)...Ger.	47.49 N	10.11 E
131	Memphis (Ruins) (mĕm'fĭs) Eg. (In.)	29.50 N	31.15 E
79	Memphis.....................Mo.	40.27 N	92.11 W
82	Memphis....................Tenn.	35.7 N	90.5 W
78	Memphis.....................Tex.	34.43 N	100.32 W
86	Memphremagog L. (mĕm'frê-mā'gŏg).Can.	45.5 N	72.10 E
79	Mena (mē'nȧ)..................Ark.	34.35 N	94.10 W
129	Mena (mā-nä')..........Sov. Un.	51.31 N	32.11 E
151	Menado (mȧ-nä'dō).......Indon.	1.30 N	124.53 E
150	Menam Chao Bhraya (R.) (mȧ-näm' chä'ō brä'yȧ).Siam	15.0 N	100.17 E
150	Menam Nan (R.) (mȧ-näm' nän') Siam	18.0 N	100.30 E
80	Menard (mê-närd')..........Tex.	30.56 N	99.48 W
77	Menasha (mê-năsh'ȧ)........Wis.	44.12 N	88.26 W
122	Mende (mäNd)..................Fr.	44.30 N	3.30 E
111	Menderes (R.) (mĕn'dĕr-ĕs)...Tur.	38.10 N	29.0 E
151	Mendez Nuñez (mĕn'dĕz nōōn'yĕz) Phil. (Manila In.)	14.11 N	120.53 E
114	Mendip Hills (mĕn'dĭp)..Gt. Brit.	51.10 N	2.30 W
70	Mendocino, C. (mĕn'dô-sē'nō) Calif.	40.28 N	124.25 W
73	Mendon (mĕn'dŭn) Utah (Salt Lake City In.)	41.43 N	111.58 W
79	Mendota (mĕn-dō'tȧ)..........Ill.	41.34 N	89.6 W
89	Mendota.Minn. (Minneapolis In.)	44.53 N	93.10 W
77	Mendota, L.................Wis.	43.5 N	89.25 W
102	Mendoza (mĕn-dō'sä)........Arg.	32.50 S	68.45 W
102	Mendoza (State).............Arg.	35.15 S	68.30 W
146	Mengcheng (mĕng'chĕng')...Chn.	33.17 N	116.29 E
146	Meng Shan (Mts.) (mĕng' shän') Chn.	35.40 N	117.50 E
142	Mengtze (mĕng'tzĕ')..........Chn.	23.15 N	103.6 E
146	Mengyin (mĕng'yĭn')..........Chn.	35.47 N	117.54 E
76	Menno (mĕn'ô).................S. D.	43.14 N	97.33 W
77	Menominee (mê-nŏm'ĭ-nē)..Mich.	45.9 N	87.38 W
77	Menominee Ind. Res..........Wis.	45.0 N	88.40 W
77	Menominee R.........Mich.-Wis.	45.40 N	87.50 W
77	Menomonie..................Wis.	44.54 N	91.55 W
157	Menowai L. (mĕ-nō-wī')....N. Z.	45.50 S	167.25 E
150	Mentawai Is. (mĕn-tä-vī')...Indon.	2.0 S	99.30 E
123	Menton (mäN-tôN')..............Fr.	43.45 N	7.31 E
160	Mentone (mĕn-tō'nē) Austl. (Melbourne In.)	37.59 S	145.4 E
73	Mentone..Calif. (Los Angeles In.)	34.5 N	117.8 W
131	Menzala, L. (mĕn-zä'lȧ)..Eg. (In.)	31.15 N	32.0 E
110	Menzelinsk (mĕn'zyĕ-lênsk') Sov. Un.	55.45 N	53.2 E
158	Menzies (mĕn'zēz).........Austl.	29.47 S	121.10 E

ăt; finăl; rāte; senâte; ärm; ȧsk; sofȧ; fâre; ch-choose; dh-as th in other; bē; êvent; bĕt; recĕnt; cratēr; g-go; gh-gutteral g; bĭt; ĭ-short neutral; rīde; K-gutteral k as ch in German ich;

Meopham PRONOUNCING INDEX Minas de Ríotinto

Page	Name Pronunciation Region	Lat. °′	Long. °′
117	Meopham (mē-ŏp'ăm) Gt. Brit. (London In.)	51.22 N	0.22 E
80	Meoqui (mâ-ō'kē) Mex.	28.15 N	105.26 W
120	Meppel (mĕp'ĕl) Neth.	52.41 N	6.11 E
120	Meppen (mĕp'ĕn) Ger.	52.41 N	7.17 E
126	Merabelo, G. of (mâ-rä-bâ'lō) Grc.	35.15 N	25.55 E
79	Meramec R. (mĕr'á-mĕk) Mo.	38.20 N	90.50 W
126	Merano (mâ-rä'nō) It.	46.40 N	11.10 E
87	Merasheen I. (mē'rá-shēn) Can.	47.30 N	54.15 W
151	Merauke (mâ-rou'kā) Neth. N. Gui.	8.31 S	140.29 E
135	Merca (mĕr'kä) Som.	1.56 N	44.48 E
74	Merced (mẽr-sĕd') Calif.	37.17 N	120.30 W
102	Mercedario, Mt. (mĕr-sâ-dhä'rê-ō) Arg.	31.58 S	70.15 W
102	Mercedes (mĕr-sā'dhās) Arg.	29.15 S	58.10 W
102	Mercedes Ur.	33.28 S	58.0 W
80	Mercedes (mĕr-sē'dēs) Tex.	26.8 N	97.55 W
74	Merced R. Calif.	37.23 N	120.40 W
156	Mercer (mûr'sẽr) N. Z.	37.18 S	175.8 E
51	Mercer I. Wash. (Seattle In.)	47.33 N	122.13 W
88	Merchantville (mûr'chănt-vĭl) Pa. (Philadelphia In.)	39.57 N	75.3 W
57	Mercier (mĕr-syā') Can. (In.)	46.47 N	70.28 W
125	Mercier-Lacombe (mĕr-syā'-lá-kôNb') Alg.	35.15 N	0.12 W
137	Merdjeioun (mĕr-jâ-ōōn') Leb. (In.)	33.23 N	35.33 E
121	Merechanka R. (mâ'rá-chäŋ'ká) Sov. Un.	54.26 N	25.10 E
86	Meredith (mĕr'ê-dĭth) N. H.	43.35 N	71.35 W
129	Merefa (mâ-rĕf'á) Sov. Un.	49.48 N	36.3 E
94	Merendon, Sierra de (Mts.) (syâr'ä dā mâ-rĕn-dōn') Cen. Am.	15.15 N	88.55 W
143	Mergen (Nünkiang) (mĕr'gĕn) (nün'kyäng') Chn.	49.20 N	125.27 E
150	Mergui (mĕr-gē') Bur.	12.28 N	98.40 E
150	Mergui Arch. Bur.	11.30 N	98.15 E
93	Mérida (mā'rê-dhä) Mex.	20.57 N	89.37 W
153	Mérida Phil.	10.54 N	124.32 E
124	Mérida Sp.	38.55 N	6.20 W
100	Mérida Ven.	8.31 N	71.1 W
85	Meriden (mĕr'ĭ-dĕn) Conn.	41.32 N	72.48 W
82	Meridian (mê-rĭd'ĭ-ăn) Miss.	32.22 N	88.42 W
81	Meridian Tex.	31.55 N	97.38 W
102	Meriti (mâ-rē'tê) Braz. (In.)	22.47 S	43.17 W
119	Merikarvia (mā'rē-kàr'vê-ä) Fin.	62.45 N	21.30 E
80	Merkel (mûr'kĕl) Tex.	32.28 N	100.2 W
119	Merkine (mĕr'kĭ-nê) Sov. Un.	54.11 N	24.10 E
133	Merowi (mā-rô-wē') A. E. Sud.	18.30 N	31.55 E
77	Merrill (mĕr'ĭl) Wis.	45.11 N	89.40 W
87	Merrimac (mĕr'ĭ-măk) Mass. (In.)	42.50 N	71.5 W
86	Merrimack R. Mass.-N. H.	43.10 N	71.30 W
160	Merri Merri Cr. (mĕr'ê mĕr'ê) Austl. (Melbourne In.)	37.42 S	144.59 E
81	Merryville (mĕr'ĭ-vĭl) La.	30.46 N	93.35 W
120	Merseburg (mĕr'zĕ-bŏŏrgh) Ger.	51.21 N	11.59 E
160	Mersey R. (mûr'zê) Austl. (Tas. In.)	41.30 S	146.30 E
114	Mersey R. Gt. Brit.	53.15 N	2.50 W
111	Mersin (mĕr-sēn') Tur.	36.50 N	34.40 E
114	Merthyr Tydfil (mûr'thẽr tĭd'vĭl) Gt. Brit.	51.45 N	3.25 W
124	Mértola (mĕr'tô-lá) Port.	37.38 N	7.42 W
122	Méru (mā-rü') Fr.	49.15 N	2.9 E
133	Meru (mā'rōō) Kenya	0.2 N	37.36 E
115	Merxem (mĕrk'sĕm) Bel.	51.15 N	4.25 E
111	Merzifon (mĕr'zĕ-fōn) Tur.	40.50 N	35.32 E
75	Mesa (mā'sá) Ariz.	33.24 N	111.51 W
72	Mesa Colo. (Denver In.)	39.45 N	104.43 W
77	Mesabi Range Minn.	47.32 N	92.30 W
127	Mesagne (mā-sän'yâ) It.	40.34 N	17.49 E
75	Mesa Verde Natl. Park (mā'sä vĕr'dē) Colo.	37.15 N	108.30 W
78	Mescalero Apache Ind. Res. (mĕs-kä-lā'rō) N. M.	33.10 N	105.30 W
128	Meshchevsk (myĕsh'chĕfsk) Sov. Un.	54.18 N	35.19 E
	Meshed, see Mashhad, Iran.		
133	Meshraer Reg. (mĕsh'rá-ĕr) A. E. Sud.	8.28 N	29.19 E
75	Mesilla (mâ-sē'yä) N. M.	32.18 N	106.49 W
127	Mesolongion (mĕ-sô-lôŋ'gē-ôn) Grc.	38.23 N	21.27 E
	Mesopotamia, see Iraq.		
127	Messene (mĕ-sē'nē) Grc.	37.3 N	22.0 E
127	Messene, G. of Grc.	36.35 N	22.5 E
126	Messina (mĕ-sē'ná) It.	38.13 N	15.13 E
134	Messina U. S. Afr.	22.20 S	30.10 E
126	Messina, Str. of It.	38.15 N	15.37 E
123	Messy (mĕ-sē') Fr. (In.)	48.58 N	2.43 E
127	Mesta R. (mĕ-stá') Bul.	41.40 N	23.43 E
126	Mestre (mĕs'trā) It.	45.29 N	12.14 E
117	Meta (mā'tä) It. (Napoli In.)	40.38 N	14.23 E
86	Metabetchouan R. (mĕ-tá-bĕt-chōō-än') Can.	48.0 N	72.0 W
110	Metallist (mâ-tä-lêst') Sov. Un.	55.59 N	43.5 E
94	Metapa (Ciudad Dario) (mā-tä'pä) (syōō-dhädh' dä'rē-ō) Nic.	12.53 N	86.1 W
94	Metapán (mâ-tä-pän') Sal.	14.21 N	89.27 W
100	Meta, R. (mā'tä) Ven.-Col.	6.0 N	69.30 W
92	Metepec (mâ-tĕ-pĕk') Mex.	18.56 N	98.29 W
92	Metepec Mex.	19.16 N	99.35 W
70	Methow R. (mĕt'hou) (mĕt hou') Wash.	48.25 N	120.10 W
87	Methuen (mê-thū'ĕn) Mass. (In.)	42.43 N	71.11 W
55	Métis (mâ-tē') (mā-tĭs') Can.	48.32 N	68.0 W
86	Métis Beach Can.	48.39 N	68.3 W
127	Metković (mĕt'kô-vĭch) Yugo.	43.3 N	17.40 E
56	Metlakatla (mĕt-lá-kăt'lá) Can. (Prince Rupert In.)	54.21 N	130.28 W
79	Metropolis (mê-trŏp'ô-lĭs) Ill.	37.9 N	88.42 W
70	Metropolis Nev.	41.13 N	115.9 W
119	Metsäpirtti (mĕt'sĕ-pēr'tĭ) Fin.	60.35 N	30.34 E
83	Metter (mĕt'ẽr) Ga.	32.20 N	82.3 W
123	Metz (mĕtz) Fr.	49.9 N	6.10 E
92	Metztitlán (mĕtz-têt-län') Mex.	20.35 N	98.45 W
123	Meudon (mû-dôN') Fr. (In.)	48.48 N	2.14 E
123	Meulan (mû-läN') Fr. (In.)	49.0 N	1.54 E
122	Meung (măN') Fr.	47.52 N	1.49 E
115	Meuse, R. (mûz) (müz) Eur.	50.30 N	5.0 E
116	Mexborough (mĕks'bŭr-ô) Gt. Brit.	53.30 N	1.17 W
92	Mexcala, R. (mĕs-kä'lä) Mex.	17.55 N	99.0 W
81	Mexia (mâ-hē'ä) Tex.	31.41 N	96.28 W
74	Mexicali (mâk-sê-kä'lê) Mex.	32.38 N	115.30 W
86	Mexico (mĕk'sĭ-kō) Me.	44.35 N	70.31 W
92	Mexico (State) (mâk'sê-kō) Mex.	19.0 N	100.0 W
79	Mexico (mĕk'sĭ-kō) Mo.	39.9 N	91.51 W
90	Mexico N. A.	24.0 N	107.0 W
93	Mexico, D. F. Mex. (In.)	19.26 N	99.7 W
50	Mexico, G. of N. A.	25.0 N	90.0 W
92	Mexico, Plat. of Mex.	22.0 N	102.0 W
92	Mexticacán (mĕs'tê-kä-kän') Mex.	21.15 N	102.45 W
151	Meycauayán (mā'ê-kou-à-yän') Phil. (Manila In.)	14.45 N	120.56 E
85	Meyersdale (mī'ẽrz-dāl) Pa.	39.52 N	79.2 W
122	Méze (mâz) Fr.	43.25 N	3.35 E
110	Mezen (mâ-zĕn'y') Sov. Un.	65.50 N	44.25 E
110	Mezen R. Sov. Un.	65.0 N	46.0 E
128	Mezha R. (myā'zhà) Sov. Un.	55.50 N	32.15 E
129	Mezherichi (mâ-zhĕ-rē'chê) Sov. Un.	50.42 N	34.29 E
122	Mézières (mā-zyâr') Fr.	49.45 N	4.45 E
121	Mezökövesd (mĕ'zû-kû'vĕsht) Hung.	47.48 N	20.35 E
121	Mezötúr (mĕ'zû-tōōr) Hung.	47.0 N	20.36 E
92	Mezquital (mâz-kê-täl') Mex.	23.28 N	104.23 W
92	Mezquital, R. Mex.	23.33 N	104.20 W
92	Mezquitic (mâz-kê-tēk') Mex.	22.31 N	103.46 W
135	Mgera (m'gā'rä) Tan.	5.23 S	37.33 E
128	Mglin (m'glēn') Sov. Un.	53.2 N	32.51 E
135	Mhonda (m'hŏn'dä) Tan.	6.8 S	37.40 E
92	Miacatlán (mê'ä-kä-tlän') Mex.	18.45 N	99.21 W
153	Miagao (mê-ä-gä'ō) Phil.	10.38 N	122.14 E
93	Miahuatlán (San Andrés) (mê'ä-wä-tlän') Mex.	16.20 N	96.30 W
124	Miajadas (mê-ä-hä'däs) Sp.	39.10 N	5.52 W
75	Miami (mī-ăm'ĭ) Ariz.	33.23 N	110.54 W
84	Miami Fla. (In.)	25.46 N	80.12 W
79	Miami Okla.	36.53 N	94.51 W
78	Miami Tex.	35.41 N	100.38 W
83	Miami Beach Fla. (In.)	25.47 N	80.7 W
84	Miami R. Ohio	39.20 N	84.38 W
84	Miamisburg (mī-ăm'ĭz-bûrg) Ohio	39.40 N	84.18 W
145	Miaoli (mê-ou'lĭ) For.	24.34 N	120.48 E
121	Miastko (myäst'kô) Pol.	54.1 N	17.0 E
146	Miau-Tao I. (mē'ou'-tä'ō) Chn.	38.12 N	120.40 E
121	Michalovce (mē'κä-lôf'tsĕ) Czech.	48.45 N	21.55 E
87	Michel L. (mê-shĕl') (mĭch'ĕl) Can.	50.20 N	56.55 W
84	Michigan (State) (mĭsh'ĭ-găn) U. S.	44.0 N	85.0 W
84	Michigan City Ind.	41.42 N	86.54 W
84	Michigan, L. U. S.	44.0 N	87.0 W
77	Michipicoten Har. (mĕ-shĭ-pĭ-kō'-tĕn) Can.	47.59 N	84.51 W
55	Michipicoten I. Can.	47.50 N	85.32 W
77	Michipicoten R. Can.	47.56 N	84.28 W
92	Michoacán (State) (mê-chō-ä-kän') Mex.	19.0 N	102.0 W
128	Michurinsk (mĭ-chōō-rĭnsk') Sov. Un.	52.54 N	40.31 E
70	Midas (mī'dȧs) Nev.	41.15 N	116.48 W
134	Middleburg (mĭd'ĕl-bûrg) U. S. Afr.	31.29 S	25.0 E
115	Middleburg (mĭd'ĕl-bûrg) Neth.	51.32 N	3.35 E
118	Middelfart (mêd''l-fârt) Den.	55.30 N	9.44 E
96	Middle Bight (bīt) Ba. Is.	24.20 N	77.40 W
86	Middlebury (mĭd''l-bĕr-ĭ) Vt.	44.0 N	73.11 W
56	Middlechurch (mĭd''l-chûrch) Can. (Winnipeg In.)	49.58 N	97.4 W
80	Middle Concho R. (kŏn'chō) Tex.	31.22 N	101.0 W
134	Middle Congo (State) (kŏŋ'gō) Fr. Eq. Afr.	2.30 S	13.45 E
97	Middle Ground Ba. Is.	22.50 N	76.8 W
96	Middle Ground Ba. Is.	24.55 N	77.3 W
70	Middle L. Calif.-Nev.	41.25 N	120.3 W
76	Middle Loup R. (lōōp) Neb.	41.20 N	99.5 W
84	Middleport (mĭd''l-pōrt) Ohio	39.0 N	82.5 W
82	Middlesboro (mĭd''lz-bŭr-ō) Ky.	36.37 N	83.43 W
114	Middlesborough (mĭd''lz-brŭ) Gt. Brit.	54.35 N	1.15 W
86	Middleton (mĭd''l-tŭn) Can.	44.57 N	65.5 W
118	Middleton Gt. Brit.	53.33 N	2.11 W
87	Middleton Mass. (In.)	42.36 N	71.1 W
53	Middleton I. Alsk.	59.25 N	145.30 W
85	Middletown (mĭd''l-toun) Conn.	41.33 N	72.40 W
85	Middletown Del.	39.27 N	75.43 W
85	Middletown N. Y.	41.27 N	74.27 W
84	Middletown Ohio	39.30 N	84.27 W
116	Middlewich (mĭd''l-wĭch) Gt. Brit.	53.11 N	2.27 W
122	Midi d'Ossau, Pic du (Mt.) (pēk dü mê-dē' dôs-sō') Fr.	42.50 N	0.35 W
75	Midland (mĭd'lănd) Can.	44.43 N	79.54 W
72	Midland Colo. (Colo. Sprs. In.)	38.52 N	105.10 W
84	Midland Mich.	43.40 N	84.18 W
80	Midland Tex.	32.0 N	102.4 W
75	Midvale (mĭd'vāl) Utah	40.35 N	111.56 W
73	Midway (mĭd'wā) Utah (Salt Lake City In.)	40.31 N	111.29 W
4	Midway Is. Pac. O.	28.13 N	177.21 W
71	Midwest (mĭd-wĕst') Wyo.	43.37 N	106.15 W
111	Midye (mēd'yĕ) Tur.	41.35 N	28.8 E
135	Mie (mē'ä) Som.	9.54 N	49.30 E
121	Miechów (myĕ'κōōf) Pol.	50.22 N	20.2 E
120	Międzychód (myăN-dzŭ'κōōd) Pol.	52.36 N	15.54 E
121	Międzyrzec (myăN-dzû'zhĕts) Pol.	51.58 N	22.47 E
120	Międzyrzecz (myăN-dzû'zhĕch) Pol.	52.27 N	15.35 E
121	Mielec (myĕ'lĕts) Pol.	50.16 N	21.26 E
144	Mienyang (myĕn'yäng') Chn.	30.11 N	113.4 E
80	Mier (myâr) Mex.	26.27 N	99.10 W
124	Mieres (myā'rās) Sp.	43.15 N	5.45 W
92	Miery Noriega (myâr'ê nô-rê-ā'gä) Mex.	23.25 N	100.9 W
82	Mignon (mĭn'yŏn) Ala.	33.4 N	86.15 W
146	Mihsien (mĭ'hsyĕn') Chn.	34.29 N	133.20 E
149	Mi I. (mê) Jap.	34.48 N	131.8 E
125	Mijares R. (mē-hä'rȧs) Sp.	40.10 N	0.48 W
97	Mijo, Mt. (mē'hō) Hai.	18.58 N	71.9 W
149	Mikage (mē'kȧ-gȧ) Jap. (Osaka In.)	34.43 N	135.15 E
149	Mikawa, B. (mē'kä-wä) Jap.	34.45 N	137.10 E
135	Mikese (mê-kä'sȧ) Tan.	6.48 S	37.56 E
111	Mikhailov (mē-κä'ê-lôf) Sov. Un.	50.5 N	43.15 E
128	Mikhailov Sov. Un.	54.12 N	39.3 E
129	Mikhailovka (mê-κä'ê-lôf-kȧ) Sov. Un.	47.14 N	35.8 E
140	Mikhlaf (mêκ-läf') Sau. Ar.	17.37 N	45.16 E
149	Miki (mē'kê) Jap. (Osaka In.)	34.49 N	134.59 E
135	Mikindani (mê-kēn-dä'nê) Tan.	10.15 S	40.5 E
119	Mikkeli (mĕk'ĕ-lĭ) Fin.	61.44 N	27.16 E
120	Mikulov (mĭ'kōō-lôf) Ger.	48.47 N	16.38 E
149	Mikuni (mē'kōō-nê) Jap.	36.16 N	136.12 E
149	Mikura (mē'kōō-rä) Jap.	33.52 N	139.36 E
132	Mila (mē'lä) Alg.	36.30 N	6.15 E
77	Milaca (mê-lăk'ȧ) Minn.	45.46 N	93.39 W
152	Milagros (mē-lä'grōs) Phil.	12.14 N	123.31 E
126	Milan (Milano) (mĭl-ăn') (mê-lä'nō) It.	45.27 N	9.10 E
79	Milan (mī'lăn) Mo.	40.13 N	93.6 W
84	Milan Mich.	42.5 N	83.40 W
82	Milan Tenn.	35.55 N	88.47 W
126	Milano (Milan) (mê-lä'nō) (mĭl-ăn') It.	45.27 N	9.10 E
111	Milas (mê'läs) Tur.	37.20 N	27.45 E
126	Milazzo (mê-lät'sô) It.	38.13 N	15.15 E
76	Milbank (mĭl'băŋk) S. D.	45.14 N	96.38 W
159	Mildura (mĭl-dū'rȧ) Austl.	34.11 S	142.9 E
71	Miles City (mīlz) Mont.	46.25 N	105.49 W
85	Milford (mĭl'fẽrd) Conn.	41.12 N	73.5 W
85	Milford Del.	38.55 N	75.26 W
87	Milford Mass.	42.9 N	71.32 W
86	Milford N. H.	42.50 N	71.40 W
75	Milford Utah	38.25 N	113.1 W
114	Milford Haven Gt. Brit.	51.42 N	5.0 W
157	Milford Sd. N. Z.	44.35 S	167.52 E
112	Miliana (mêl-yä'nä) Alg.	36.20 N	2.7 E
158	Miling (mĭl'ĭng) Austl.	30.25 S	116.32 E
71	Milk R. Can.-Mont.	48.28 N	108.30 W
86	Mill Can.	44.10 N	64.39 W
122	Millau (mē-yō') Fr.	44.5 N	3.5 E
51	Millbrae (mĭl'brā) Calif. (San Francisco In.)	37.35 N	122.23 W
117	Millbrook (mĭl'brŏŏk) Gt. Brit. (Liverpool In.)	53.30 N	2.3 W
87	Millbury (mĭl'bĕr-ĭ) Mass. (In.)	42.12 N	71.45 W
74	Mill Cr. Calif.	40.9 N	121.55 W
82	Milledgeville (mĭl'ĕj-vĭl) Ga.	33.5 N	83.15 W
57	Mille Iles, R. des (rê-vyâr dā mē'y'ēl') Can. (Montreal In.)	45.40 N	73.45 W
77	Mille Lacs L. (mĭl lăk') Minn.	46.75 N	93.40 W
83	Millen (mĭl'ĕn) Ga.	32.48 N	81.57 W
76	Miller (mĭl'ẽr) S. D.	44.32 N	98.59 W
88	Miller Cr. Minn. (Duluth In.)	46.47 N	92.9 W
129	Millerovo (mĭl'ĕ-rô-vô) Sov. Un.	48.56 N	40.24 E
84	Millersburg (mĭl'ẽrz-bûrg) Ky.	38.18 N	84.10 W
84	Millersburg Ohio	40.38 N	81.56 W
85	Millersburg Pa.	40.34 N	76.58 W
86	Millerton (mĭl'ẽr-tŭn) Can.	46.55 N	65.37 W
87	Millertown (mĭl'ẽr-toun) Can.	48.48 N	56.30 W
72	Milliken (mĭl'ĭ-kĕn) Colo. (Denver In.)	40.19 N	104.52 W
86	Millinocket (mĭl-ĭ-nŏk'ĕt) Me.	45.40 N	68.43 W
87	Millis (mĭl'ĭs) Mass. (In.)	42.10 N	71.23 W
158	Millstream (mĭl'strēm) Austl.	21.40 S	117.0 E
86	Milltown (mĭl'toun) Can.	45.10 N	67.19 W
51	Milltown Wash. (Seattle In.)	48.18 N	122.21 W
51	Mill Valley Calif. (San Francisco In.)	37.53 N	122.31 W
79	Millville (mĭl'vĭl) Ark.	33.43 N	92.36 W
82	Millville Fla.	30.8 N	85.37 W
85	Millville N. J.	39.26 N	75.2 W
73	Millville. Utah (Salt Lake City In.)	41.41 N	111.49 W
160	Milmerran (mĭl'mē-rȧn) Austl. (In.)	27.56 S	51.21 E
135	Milnerton (mĭl'nẽr-tŭn) U. S. Afr.	33.53 S	18.29 E
76	Milnor (mĭl'nẽr) N. D.	46.17 N	97.26 W
86	Milo (mī'lō) Me.	45.17 N	69.0 W
127	Milo (Melos) (I.) (mī'lō) (mē'lŏs) Grc.	36.45 N	24.28 E
51	Milpitas (mĭl'pĭ-tȧs) Calif. (San Francisco In.)	37.26 N	121.55 W
82	Milton (mĭl'tŭn) Fla.	30.37 N	87.3 W
117	Milton Gt. Brit. (London In.)	51.21 S	0.43 E
87	Milton Mass. (In.)	42.16 N	71.3 W
157	Milton N. Z.	46.9 S	169.58 E
70	Milton Ore.	45.56 N	118.25 W
85	Milton Pa.	41.0 N	76.50 W
51	Milton Wash. (Seattle In.)	47.15 N	122.20 W
77	Milwaukee (mĭl-wô'kē) Wis.	43.2 N	87.55 W
125	Mina, Wadi (R.) (mē'nȧ) Alg.	35.30 N	0.40 E
149	Minakuchi (mē'nȧ-kōō'chē) Jap.	34.58 N	136.7 E
102	Minas (mē'näs) Ur.	34.28 S	55.15 W
86	Minas Basin (mī'nȧs) Can.	45.15 N	64.15 W
86	Minas Chan. Can.	45.15 N	64.45 W
124	Minas de Ríotinto (mē'näs dā rē-ō-tēn'tō) Sp.	37.42 N	6.35 W

ng-sing; ŋ-baŋk; N-nasalized n; nŏd; cŏmmit; ōld; ōbey; ôrder; fōōd; fŏŏt; ou-out; s-soft; sh-dish; th-thin; pūre; ûnite; ûrn; stŭd; circŭs; ü-as "y" in study; '-indeterminate vowel.

ăt; finăl; rāte; senāte; ârm; àsk; sofá; fâre; ch-choose; dh-as th in other; bē; ĕvent; bĕt; recĕnt; cratēr; g-go; gh-gutteral g; bĭt; ĭ-short neutral; rīde; ĸ-gutteral k as ch in German ich;

Moluccas PRONOUNCING INDEX Mormugão

Page	Name Pronunciation Region	Lat. °′	Long. °′
151	Moluccas (Spice Is.) (mô-lŭk'áz) Indon.	1.0 S	128.0 E
151	Molucca Sea............Indon.	0.15 N	126.0 E
157	Molyneux (mŭl'ĭ-nōōks)....N. Z.	46.23 S	169.45 E
135	Mombasa (mōm-bä'sä)....Kenya	4.0 S	39.40 E
148	Mombetsu (mōm'bĕt-sōō')...Jap.	44.27 N	143.4 E
135	Mombo (mōm'bō)..........Tan.	4.52 S	38.18 E
84	Momence (mō-mĕns')........Ill.	41.10 N	87.38 W
94	Momostenango (mô-môs-tā-näŋ'gô). Guat.	15.1 N	91.24 W
152	Mompog Pass (mōm-pōg')...Phil.	13.30 N	122.15 E
100	Mompos (mōm-pōs')........Col.	9.45 N	74.15 W
123	Monaco (mŏn'á-kō).........Eur.	43.44 N	7.24 E
126	Monaco...................Eur.	43.44 N	7.24 E
114	Monaghan (mŏn'á-găn)......Ire.	54.15 N	7.0 W
97	Mona Passage (mō'nä)......W. I.	18.0 N	68.45 W
131	Monastir (mōn-ås-tēr'). Tun. (In.)	35.47 N	10.42 E
127	Monastir (Bitolj) (mōn'ás-tēr') (bē'tōl-y'). Yugo.	41.2 N	21.22 E
129	Monastyrishche (mô-nás-tē-rēsh'-chå). Sov. Un.	48.58 N	29.49 E
128	Monastyrishche.........Sov. Un.	54.18 N	31.50 E
152	Moncada (mōn-kä'dä).......Phil.	15.43 N	120.34 E
125	Moncada y Reixach (mōnkä'dä ē rå-ēks-äch'). Sp. (In.)	41.28 N	2.11 E
101	Monção (moŋ-souN')........Braz.	3.28 S	45.12 W
124	Moncayo (Mt.) (mōn-kä'yō)..Sp.	41.46 N	1.49 W
110	Monchegorsk (mōn'chĕ-gôrsk) Sov. Un.	67.55 N	32.59 E
124	Monchique (môn-chē'kĕ)....Port.	37.19 N	8.34 W
124	Monchique, Serra de (Mts.) (sĕr'rä dā môn-chē'kĕ). Port.	37.20 N	8.35 W
80	Monclova (mōn-klō'vä).....Mex.	26.54 N	101.25 W
55	Moncton (mŭŋk'tŭn).......Can.	46.3 N	64.48 W
124	Mondego, C. (môn-dā'gōō)..Port.	40.12 N	8.55 W
124	Mondego R...............Port.	40.25 N	8.0 W
134	Mondombe (môn-dôm'bā) Bel. Cong.	0.45 S	23.6 E
124	Mondoñedo (môn-dô-nyā'dō)..Sp.	43.26 N	7.25 W
126	Mondovi (mōn-dô'vē')........It.	44.22 N	7.49 E
77	Mondovi (mōn-dō'vĭ)........Wis.	44.35 N	91.40 W
139	Monero R. (mô-nyĕr'ô)..Sov. Un.	67.30 N	104.0 E
79	Monett (mô-nĕt')...........Mo.	36.56 N	93.56 W
126	Monfalcone (mōn-fäl-kō'nä)..It.	45.59 N	13.31 E
122	Monfort (môN-fôr')..........Fr.	48.10 N	2.0 W
124	Monforte (mōn-fôr'tä)........Sp.	42.32 N	7.31 W
133	Mongala R. (mŏn-gäl'á). Bel. Cong.	2.30 N	20.30 E
133	Mongalla............A. E. Sud.	5.7 N	31.45 E
141	Monghyr (mōn-gēr')........India	25.15 N	87.0 E
142	Mongolia (mŏŋ-gō'lĭ-á)......Asia	46.30 N	105.0 E
133	Mongoumba (mŏŋ-gōōm'bá) Fr. Eq. Afr.	3.36 N	18.30 E
134	Mongu (mŏŋ-gōō')........N. Rh.	15.15 S	23.3 E
153	Monkayo (mōn-kä'yō)......Phil.	7.49 N	126.0 E
95	Monkey Pt. (mŭŋ'kĭ)........Nic.	11.38 N	83.40 W
94	Monkey River........Br. Hond.	16.21 N	88.32 W
134	Monkoto (mōn-kō'tō)..Bel. Cong.	1.50 S	20.55 E
73	Monmouth (mŏn'mŭth) Ala. (Birmingham In.)	33.44 N	86.45 W
114	Monmouth............Gt. Brit.	51.50 N	3.0 W
79	Monmouth..................Ill.	40.54 N	90.38 W
74	Mono L. (mō'nō)..........Calif.	38.0 N	119.0 W
84	Monon (mō'nŏn)...........Ind.	40.52 N	86.53 W
84	Monongah (mô-nŏŋ'gá)...W. Va.	39.26 N	80.13 W
85	Monongahela (mô-nōn-gá-hē'là) Pa.	40.12 N	79.58 W
85	Monongahela R.........W. Va.	39.30 N	80.10 W
127	Monopoli (mô-nô'pô-lê).......It.	40.56 N	17.17 E
125	Monóvar (mô-nō'vär)........Sp.	38.26 N	0.50 W
126	Monreale (mōn-rå-ä'lä)........It.	38.4 N	13.17 E
82	Monroe (mŭn-rō')...........Ga.	33.48 N	83.43 W
81	Monroe....................La.	32.30 N	92.7 W
84	Monroe..................Mich.	41.56 N	83.24 W
83	Monroe..................N. C.	34.39 N	80.33 W
75	Monroe..................Utah	38.38 N	112.10 W
70	Monroe..................Wash.	47.51 N	121.57 W
77	Monroe...................Wis.	42.35 N	89.39 W
79	Monroe City...............Mo.	39.38 N	91.42 W
83	Monroe, L.................Fla.	28.50 N	81.16 W
82	Monroeville (mŭn-rō'vĭl).....Ala.	31.32 N	87.20 W
74	Monrovia (mŏn-rō'vĭ-á).....Calif.	34.9 N	118.1 W
132	Monrovia..................Lib.	6.27 N	10.58 W
115	Mons (môN')................Bel.	50.29 N	3.55 E
101	Monsaraz (môŋ-sá-räzh') Braz. (In.)	0.55 S	48.35 W
86	Monson (mŏn'sŭn)..........Me.	45.17 N	69.28 W
118	Mönsterås (mŭn'stĕr-ōs')....Swe.	57.3 N	16.24 E
84	Montague (mŏn'tá-gū).....Mich.	43.27 N	86.22 W
53	Montague I................Alsk.	60.0 N	147.30 W
152	Montalban (mōnt-äl-bän')...Phil.	14.44 N	121.10 E
124	Montalegre (mōn-tä-lā'grĕ)..Port.	41.50 N	7.48 W
71	Montana (State) (mŏn-tăn'á). U. S.	46.48 N	109.10 W
124	Montánchez (mōn-tän'chāth)..Sp.	39.13 N	6.9 W
126	Montane R. (mōn-tä'nä)......It.	43.52 N	11.40 E
122	Montargis (môN-tár-zhē')......Fr.	47.59 N	2.42 E
122	Montataire (môN-tá-târ')......Fr.	49.18 N	2.28 E
122	Montauban (môN-tô-bäN')....Fr.	44.1 N	1.22 E
85	Montauk Pt. (mŏn-tôk')...N. Y.	41.5 N	71.52 W
122	Montbard (môN-bär')........Fr.	47.40 N	4.20 E
123	Montbéliard (môN-bā-lyár')...Fr.	47.32 N	6.48 E
81	Mont Belvieu (mŏnt bĕl'vū) Tex. (In.)	29.51 N	94.54 W
125	Montblanch (mōnt-blänch')...Sp.	41.21 N	1.7 E
122	Montbrison (môN-brē-zôN')...Fr.	45.35 N	4.9 E
122	Montcalm, Pic de (Mt.) (pēk dē môN-kàm'). Fr.	42.45 N	1.25 E
122	Montceau-les-Mines (môN-sō'lā-mēn'). Fr.	46.40 N	4.22 E
122	Montchanin-les-Mines (môN-chá-näN'lā-mēn'). Fr.	46.45 N	4.30 E
88	Montclair (mŏnt-klâr') N. J. (New York In.)	40.49 N	74.13 W
122	Mont-de-Marsan (môN-dē-mår-säN'). Fr.	43.55 N	0.30 W
121	Montdidier (môN-dē-dyā')....Fr.	49.41 N	2.35 E
100	Monteagudo (mōn'tå-ä-gōō'dhō) Bol.	19.48 S	64.2 W
101	Monte Alegre (mōn-tĕ à-lā'grĕ) Braz. (In.)	11.45 S	40.5 W
73	Montebello (mŏn-tê-bĕl'ō) Calif. (Los Angeles In.)	34.0 N	118.7 W
158	Monte Bello Is...........Austl.	20.30 S	115.35 E
97	Monte Cristi (mōn'tå krēs'tē). Hai.	19.51 N	71.40 W
97	Monte Cristi Mts...........Hai.	19.40 N	70.50 W
93	Montecristo (mōn'tå-krēs'tō) Mex.	17.44 N	91.45 W
126	Montecristo (I.)..............It.	42.20 N	10.19 E
92	Monte Escobedo (mōn'tå ĕs-kō-bā'dhō). Mex.	22.23 N	103.39 W
124	Montefrío (mōn-tå-frē'ō)......Sp.	37.20 N	4.1 W
96	Montego B. (mŏn-tē'gō)......Jam.	18.30 N	77.56 W
125	Montelavar (mōn-tē-lá-vär') Port. (In.)	38.51 N	9.20 W
126	Monteleone (mōn'tå-lå-ō'nä)...It.	38.41 N	16.7 E
122	Montélimar (môN-tā-lē-mār')..Fr.	44.35 N	4.46 E
90	Monte Lirio (mōn'tå lē'rē-ō) C. Z. (In.)	9.14 N	79.52 W
124	Montellano (mōn-tå-lyä'nō)...Sp.	37.0 N	5.34 W
77	Montello (mŏn-tĕl'ō)........Wis.	43.48 N	89.19 W
80	Montemorelos (mōn'tå-mô-rä'lōs) Mex.	25.13 N	99.50 W
124	Montemor-o-Novo (mōn-tĕ-môr'-ōō-nô'vōō). Port.	38.39 N	8.12 W
127	Montenegro (Crnagora) (Prov.) (mōn-tå-nē'grō) (mōn-tē-nē'grō) (tsĕr'nä-gô-rä). Yugo.	42.45 N	19.25 E
126	Montepulciano (mōn'tå-pōōl-chä'nō). It.	43.18 N	11.47 E
122	Montereau-faut-Yonne (môN-t'rō'-fō-yôn'). Fr.	48.25 N	3.0 E
74	Monterey (mŏn-tĕ-rā')......Calif.	36.35 N	121.52 W
82	Monterey.................Tenn.	36.8 N	85.18 W
74	Monterey B...............Calif.	36.50 N	122.5 W
100	Montería (mōn-tå-rē'ä)......Col.	8.30 N	76.0 W
80	Monterrey (mōn-tĕr-rā')....Mex.	25.42 N	100.20 W
126	Monte San Guiliano (mōn'tå sän jōōl-yä'nō). It.	38.2 N	12.36 E
70	Montesano (mŏn-tê-sä'nō)..Wash.	46.59 N	123.36 W
126	Monte Sant' Angelo (mōn'tå sän-tän' jå-lō). It.	41.42 N	15.59 E
123	Montesson (môN-tē-sôN'). Fr. (In.)	48.54 N	2.8 E
126	Montevarchi (mōn-tå-vär'kē)..It.	43.32 N	11.34 E
76	Montevideo (mŏn-tê-vĭd'ê-ō) Minn.	44.52 N	95.41 W
102	Montevideo (mōn'tå-vê-dhā'ō). Ur.	34.40 S	56.15 W
78	Monte Vista (mŏn'tê vĭs'tá). Colo.	37.34 N	106.9 W
83	Montezuma (mŏn-tê-zōō'má). Ga.	32.18 N	84.1 W
75	Montezuma Castle Natl. Mon. Ariz.	34.37 N	111.51 W
123	Montfermeil (môN-fĕr-mā'y') Fr. (In.)	48.53 N	2.35 E
123	Montgeron (môN-zhē-rôN') Fr. (In.)	48.42 N	2.27 E
82	Montgomery (mŏnt-gŭm'ĕr-ĭ). Ala.	32.21 N	86.18 W
160	Montgomery....Austl. (Tas. In.)	42.44 S	145.28 E
89	Montgomery. Ohio (Cincinnati In.)	39.14 N	84.21 W
84	Montgomery...............W. Va.	38.11 N	81.23 W
79	Montgomery City............Mo.	38.58 N	91.30 W
123	Monthyon (môN-tē-ôN')..Fr. (In.)	49.0 N	2.47 E
79	Monticello (mŏn-tĭ-sĕl'ō).....Ark.	33.36 N	91.48 W
82	Monticello..................Fla.	30.33 N	83.53 W
82	Monticello..................Ga.	33.19 N	83.43 W
84	Monticello..................Ind.	40.43 N	86.48 W
77	Monticello...................Ia.	42.16 N	91.11 W
82	Monticello..................Ky.	36.48 N	84.51 W
86	Monticello..................Me.	46.28 N	67.54 W
77	Monticello................Minn.	45.17 N	93.49 W
85	Monticello.................N. Y.	41.36 N	74.38 W
75	Monticello.................Utah	37.53 N	109.21 W
123	Montigny-les-Metz (môN-tēn-yē'-lā-mĕts'). Fr.	49.5 N	6.9 E
124	Montijo (môn-tē'hō)..........Sp.	38.55 N	6.36 W
95	Montijo, G. of..............Pan.	7.35 N	81.10 W
124	Montilla (mōn-tēl'yä)........Sp.	37.36 N	4.38 W
122	Montivilliers (môN-tē-vē-yā')..Fr.	49.35 N	0.11 E
86	Mont Joli (môN zhō-lē')....Can.	48.36 N	68.11 W
122	Montluçon (môN-lü-sôN')......Fr.	46.19 N	2.38 E
55	Montmagny (môN-män-yē'). Can.	46.58 N	70.33 W
57	Montmorency Falls (mŏnt-mô-rĕn'sĭ). Can. (Quebec In.)	46.53 N	71.10 W
123	Montmorency (môN'mô-räN-sē') Fr. (In.)	48.58 N	2.19 E
57	Montmorency R. (mŏnt-mô-rĕn'sĭ) Can. (Quebec In.)	47.0 N	71.12 W
122	Montmorillon (môN'mô-rê-yôN') Fr.	46.25 N	0.50 E
124	Montoro (môn-tō'rô)..........Sp.	38.1 N	4.22 W
71	Montpelier (mŏnt-pēl'yĕr)....Ida.	42.19 N	11.18 W
84	Montpelier..................Ind.	40.35 N	85.20 W
84	Montpelier.................Ohio	41.36 N	84.36 W
86	Montpelier..................Vt.	44.16 N	72.36 W
122	Montpellier (môN-pĕ-lyā')......Fr.	43.38 N	3.53 E
55	Montreal (mŏn-trê-ôl')......Can.	45.33 N	73.35 W
57	Montreal.............Can. (In.)		
57	Montreal, I. of. Can. (Montreal In.)	45.30 N	73.40 W
122	Montreuil (môN-trû'y')........Fr.	50.29 N	1.49 E
123	Montreuil-sous-Bois (môN-trû'y'-sōō-bwä'). Fr. (In.)	48.51 N	2.30 E
120	Montreux (môN-trû')......Switz.	46.26 N	6.56 E
75	Montrose (mŏn-trōz').......Colo.	38.28 N	107.52 W
114	Montrose.............Gt. Brit.	56.45 N	2.30 W
85	Montrose (mŏnt-rōz').........Pa.	41.49 N	75.48 W
123	Montrouge (môN-rōōzh'). Fr. (In.)	48.48 N	2.18 E
95	Montserrat (I.) (mŏnt-sĕ-răt') Le. Is. (In.)	16.45 N	162.12 W
86	Monts, Pointe des (pwăNt' dā môN'). Can.	49.19 N	67.22 W
72	Monument (mŏn'ū-mĕnt) Colo. (Colo. Sprs. In.)	39.5 N	104.52 W
72	Monument Cr. Colo. (Colo. Sprs. In.)	39.0 N	104.50 W
142	Monywa (mŏn'yōō-wä)......Bur.	21.55 N	95.12 E
126	Monza (mōn'tsä).............It.	45.35 N	9.15 E
125	Monzón (mōn-thōn').........Sp.	41.54 N	0.10 E
81	Moody (mōō'dĭ)............Tex.	31.19 N	97.20 W
160	Moonie R. (mōōn'ē)...Austl. (In.)	27.30 S	150.28 E
89	Moon Run...Pa. (Pittsburgh In.)	40.27 N	80.8 W
158	Moonta (mōōn'tá).........Austl.	34.4 S	137.35 E
158	Moora (mōōr'á)...........Austl.	30.32 S	116.2 E
117	Moorburg (môr'bōōrgh) Ger. (Hamburg In.)	53.29 N	9.56 E
71	Moorcroft (mōr'krôft)......Wyo.	44.27 N	104.58 W
117	Moore (mōr) Gt. Brit. (Liverpool In.)	53.21 N	2.38 W
158	Moore, L.................Austl.	29.50 S	117.40 E
89	Moore L..Minn. (Minneapolis In.)	45.5 N	93.14 W
84	Mooresville (mōrz'vĭl).......Ind.	39.36 N	86.26 W
83	Mooresville..............N. C.	35.34 N	80.48 W
117	Moorfleth (môr'flĕt) Ger. (Hamburg In.)	53.31 N	10.4 E
76	Moorhead (mōr'hĕd).......Minn.	46.52 N	96.45 W
82	Moorhead.................Miss.	33.27 N	90.32 W
160	Moorina (mōō-rē'nà) Austl. (Tas. In.)	41.6 S	147.58 E
117	Moorrege (mōr'ĕ-gĕ) Ger. (Hamburg In.)	53.40 N	9.40 E
86	Moosehead L. (mōōs'hĕd)....Me.	45.33 N	69.38 W
54	Moose Jaw (mōōs jô).......Can.	50.28 N	105.35 W
54	Moose L. (mōōs)...........Can.	54.0 N	100.15 W
86	Mooselookmeguntic L. (mōō-sĕ-lōōk-mê-gŭn'tĭk). Me.	44.55 N	70.45 W
55	Moose R..................Can.	51.0 N	81.0 W
55	Moosonee (mōō'sô-nê).......Can.	51.20 N	80.44 W
132	Mopti (mŏp'tē).........Fr. W. Afr.	14.30 N	4.3 W
52	Moquawkie (mô-kwô'kē) Alsk. (In.)	61.5 N	151.18 W
100	Moquegua (mô-kā'gwä).....Peru	17.15 S	71.0 W
121	Mor (mōr)...............Hung.	47.22 N	18.12 E
77	Mora (mō'rá)..............Minn.	45.53 N	93.17 W
78	Mora....................N. M.	35.57 N	105.17 W
124	Mora......................Sp.	39.43 N	3.45 W
125	Mora......................Sp.	41.6 N	0.37 E
141	Moradabad (mô-rä-dä-bäd'). India	28.45 N	78.30 E
72	Moraine, L. (mô-rān') Colo. (Colo. Sprs. In.)	38.48 N	104.50 W
135	Moramanga (mō-rä-mäŋ'gä) Madag.	18.45 S	48.10 E
97	Morant Pt. (mô-rănt')......Jam.	17.55 N	76.11 W
118	Morastrand (mō'rä-stränd)..Swe.	61.0 N	14.32 E
125	Morata de Tajuña (mô-rä'tä dā tä-hōō'nyä). Sp. (In.)	40.13 N	3.27 W
124	Moratalla (mō-rä-täl'yä)......Sp.	38.15 N	1.54 W
120	Morava R. (mô'rá-vä).....Czech.	49.15 N	17.29 E
127	Morava R.................Yugo.	43.30 N	21.45 E
120	Morava (Moravia) (Prov.) (mô'rá-vä) (mō-rā'vĭ-á). Czech.	49.25 N	17.15 E
121	Moravská Ostrava (mô'ráf-skä ôs'trá-vá). Czech.	49.49 N	18.17 E
101	Morawhanna (mô-rá-hwä'nà) Br. Gu.	8.12 N	59.32 W
114	Moray Firth (mŭr'å)....Gt. Brit.	57.40 N	3.40 W
118	Mörbylånga (mûr'bü-lōŋ'gà). Swe.	56.32 N	16.24 E
122	Morcenx (môr-säNs').........Fr.	44.1 N	0.51 W
76	Morden (môr'dĕn)..........Can.	49.15 N	98.4 W
160	Mordialloc (môr-dĭ-ăl'ŏk)...Austl.	38.0 S	145.5 E
76	Moreau R. (mô-rō')..........S. D.	45.12 N	102.0 W
116	Morecambe (mōr'kăm)..Gt. Brit.	54.4 N	2.52 W
114	Morecambe B..........Gt. Brit.	54.5 N	3.0 W
159	Moree (mō'rē)............Austl.	29.20 S	149.45 E
84	Morehead (mōr'hĕd)........Ky.	38.12 N	83.30 W
83	Morehead City............N. C.	34.43 N	76.43 W
79	Morehouse (mōr'hous).......Mo.	36.50 N	89.40 W
92	Morelia (mô-rā'lyä)........Mex.	19.42 N	101.11 W
125	Morella (mô-räl'yä)..........Sp.	40.37 N	0.7 W
92	Morelos (State) (mô-rā'lōs)..Mex.	18.40 N	99.0 W
92	Morelos...................Mex.	22.49 N	102.27 W
80	Morelos...................Mex.	28.25 N	100.52 W
124	Morena, Sierra (Mts.) (syĕr'rä mô-rā'nä). Sp.	38.25 N	5.0 W
75	Morenci (mô-rĕn'sĭ).........Ariz.	33.5 N	109.23 W
84	Morenci..................Mich.	41.44 N	84.8 W
54	Moresby I. (mōrz'bĭ)........Can.	52.30 N	132.0 W
72	Moresby I..Can. (Vancouver In.)	48.43 N	123.18 W
96	Mores I. (mōrz)..........Ba. Is.	26.18 N	77.35 W
160	Moreton B. (môr'tŭn). Austl. (In.)	27.12 S	153.12 E
160	Moreton I..........Austl. (In.)	27.10 S	153.23 E
123	Morez (mô-rĕ')...............Fr.	46.30 N	6.1 E
71	Morgan (môr'găn)..........Utah	41.10 N	111.41 W
81	Morgan City................La.	29.40 N	91.10 W
84	Morganfield (môr'găn-fēld)...Ky.	37.40 N	87.54 W
89	Morgan Har. La. (New Orleans In.)	29.50 N	89.15 W
159	Morgan, Mt...............Austl.	23.45 S	150.27 E
88	Morgan Park...Ill. (Chicago In.)	41.42 N	87.40 W
83	Morganton (môr'găn-tŭn)...N. C.	35.45 N	81.42 W
85	Morgantown (môr'găn-toun) W. Va.	39.38 N	79.57 W
149	Mori (mô'rē)...............Jap.	33.25 N	131.8 E
137	Morib (mô-rēb')....Malaya (In.)	2.47 N	101.27 E
149	Moriguchi (mō'rē-gōō'chē) Jap. (Osaka In.)	34.45 N	135.33 E
148	Morioka (mō'rē-ō'kà)........Jap.	39.45 N	141.13 E
139	Morkoka R. (mōr-kô'kà). Sov. Un.	65.0 N	112.0 E
122	Morlaix (môr-lĕ')............Fr.	48.37 N	3.50 W
141	Mormugão (mōr-mōō-gouN'). India	15.28 N	73.58 E

ng-sing; ŋ-baŋk; N-nasalized n; nŏd; cŏmmit; ōld; ôbey; ôrder; fōōd; fŏŏt; ou-out; s-soft; sh-dish; th-thin; pūre; ûnite; ûrn; stŭd; circŭs; ü-as "y" in study; '-indeterminate vowel.

Morne Diablotin PRONOUNCING INDEX Murraça

Page	Name Pronunciation Region	Lat. °'	Long. °'
95	Morne Diablotin (Mt.) (môrn dē-à-blô-tăN').Le. Is. (In.)	15.30 N	61.26 W
95	Morne Gimie (Mt.) (môrn' zhē-mē').Wind. Is.	13.52 N	61.2 W
151	Morobe (mô-rō'bā)...N. Gui. Ter.	7.53 S	147.32 E
132	Morocco (mô-rŏk'ō).........Afr.	32.0 N	6.0 W
132	Morocco, Spanish...........Afr.	35.0 N	5.0 W
128	Moroch R. (mô-rôch')...Sov. Un.	52.45 N	27.5 E
153	Moro G. (mō'rō)...........Phil.	7.0 N	123.0 E
135	Morogoro (mō-rō-gō'rō).....Tan.	6.47 S	37.43 E
92	Moroleón (mô-rō-lā-ōn')....Mex.	20.7 N	101.12 W
96	Morón (mô-rōn')..........Cuba	22.5 N	78.36 W
135	Morondava (mô-rōn-dá'vá) Madag.	20.15 S	44.18 E
124	Morón de la Frontera (mô-rōn' dā lä frôn-tā'rä).Sp.	37.7 N	5.26 W
152	Morong (mō'rông)..........Phil.	14.30 N	121.14 E
74	Morongo Indian Res. (mō-rôŋ'gō) Calif.	33.57 N	116.50 W
75	Moroni (mô-rō'nĭ)..........Utah	39.33 N	111.39 W
96	Morón Lagoon (mô-rōn')....Cuba	22.10 N	78.37 W
151	Morotai (I.) (mō-rō-tä'ē)...Indon.	2.15 N	128.30 E
111	Morozovskaya (mô'rô'-zôf-skà'yà) Sov. Un.	48.18 N	41.55 E
76	Morrill (mŏr'ĭl)..........Neb.	41.58 N	103.53 W
79	Morrilton (mŏr'ĭl-tŭn).......Ark.	35.9 N	91.42 W
101	Morrinhos (mô-rēn'yōzh)....Braz.	17.45 S	49.12 W
156	Morrinsville (mŏr'ĭnz-vĭl)...N. Z.	37.38 S	175.37 E
73	Morris (mŏr'ĭs) Ala. (Birmingham In.)	33.45 N	86.48 W
76	Morris..................Can.	49.20 N	97.30 W
79	Morris..................Ill.	41.22 N	88.25 W
76	Morris..................Minn.	45.36 N	95.52 W
73	Morris.Utah (Salt Lake City In.)	40.40 N	112.16 W
88	Morris Can......N. J. (N. Y. In.)	40.52 N	74.11 W
77	Morrison (mŏr'ĭ-sŭn).........Ill.	41.48 N	89.57 W
72	Morrison, Mt..Colo. (Denver In.)	39.40 N	105.13 W
82	Morristown (mŏr'ĭs-toun)...Tenn.	36.12 N	83.18 W
86	Morrisville (mŏr'ĭs-vĭl).......Vt.	44.32 N	72.36 W
90	Morro Castle (môr'ō) Cuba (Habana In.)	23.9 N	82.21 W
101	Morro do Champéo (môr-ōō dōō chäm-pā'ōō).Braz.	11.32 S	41.12 W
73	Morrow (mŏr'ō) Ga. (Atlanta In.)	33.34 N	84.20 W
111	Morshansk (môr-shànsk').Sov. Un.	53.10 N	41.55 E
118	Mors (I.) (môrs)...........Den.	56.48 N	8.45 E
122	Mortagne (môr-tän'y').......Fr.	48.32 N	0.35 E
126	Mortara (môr-tä'rä)..........It.	45.15 N	8.45 E
123	Morteau (môr-tō')............Fr.	47.5 N	6.38 E
88	Morton Grove (môr'tŭn grōv) Ill. (Chicago In.)	42.2 N	87.47 W
117	Mortsel (môr-sĕl').Bel. (Anvers In.)	51.10 N	4.28 E
122	Morvan Mts. (môr-väN')......Fr.	47.10 N	4.10 E
110	Morzhovets I. (môr'zhô-vyĕts') Sov. Un.	66.40 N	42.35 E
128	Mosalsk (mō-zàlsk').....Sov. Un.	54.28 N	34.58 E
70	Moscow (mŏs'kō)...........Ida.	46.44 N	117.0 W
128	Moscow (Moskva) (mŏs-kvä') Sov. Un.	55.45 N	37.36 E
128	Moscow (mŏs'kō) Sea...Sov. Un.	56.47 N	37.0 E
140	Moseirah (I.) (mô-sä'rä)....Oman	20.30 N	58.48 E
120	Mosel R. (mō'sĕl) (mô-zĕl)...Ger.	50.0 N	7.7 E
123	Moselle R. (mô-zĕl')..........Fr.	49.0 N	6.10 E
70	Moses L. (mō'zĕz)..........Wash.	47.9 N	119.10 W
157	Mosgiel (môs'gēl).....N. Z. (In.)	45.53 S	170.22 E
135	Moshi (mō'shē)..............Tan.	3.17 S	37.18 E
128	Moskva (Aut. Area) (mŏs-kvä') Sov. Un.	55.32 N	37.0 E
128	Moskva (Moscow)......Sov. Un.	55.45 N	37.36 E
128	Moskva R.............Sov. Un.	55.38 N	36.25 E
101	Mosqueiro I. (môs-kā'rōō) Braz. (In.)	1.7 S	48.25 W
95	Mosquito Cays (Is.) (mŏs-kē'tō) W. I.	14.35 N	82.40 W
95	Mosquito Coast (Reg.)......Nic.	12.40 N	83.45 W
95	Mosquito G................Pan.	9.20 N	81.10 W
118	Moss (môs)................Nor.	59.28 N	10.40 E
134	Mossámedes (mō-sä'mà-dĕs).Ang.	15.12 S	12.12 E
134	Mossámedes (Dist)..........Ang.	15.30 S	12.30 E
134	Mossel Bay (mŏs'ĕl)....U. S. Afr.	34.10 S	22.8 E
116	Mossley (mŏs'lĭ)........Gt. Brit.	53.31 N	2.3 W
101	Mossoró (mō-sô-rōō')........Braz.	5.10 S	37.28 W
82	Moss Point (môs)...........Miss.	30.25 N	88.33 W
120	Most (môst)...............Czech.	50.32 N	13.38 E
132	Mostaganem (mŏs'tà-gà-nĕm') Alg.	36.0 N	0.6 E
127	Mostar (môs'tär)............Yugo.	43.20 N	17.50 E
125	Mostoles (môs-tō'lās)...Sp. (In.)	40.19 N	3.52 W
117	Mostyn (mŏs'tĭn) Gt. Brit. (Liverpool In.)	53.19 N	3.17 W
140	Mosul (mō-sōōl')............Iraq	36.1 N	43.0 E
144	Mosün (mō'sün')...........Chn.	23.37 N	109.49 E
94	Motagua, R. (mô-tä'gwä)...Guat.	15.10 N	89.20 W
118	Motala (mô-tô'lä)..........Swe.	58.33 N	15.2 E
89	Mother L. (mŭdh'ēr) Minn. (Minneapolis In.)	44.54 N	93.14 W
114	Motherwell (mŭdh'ēr-wĕl) Gt. Brit.	55.48 N	4.0 W
156	Motiti I. (mô-tē'tē)........N. Z.	37.35 S	176.27 E
124	Motril (mô-trēl')............Sp.	36.45 N	3.30 W
157	Motueka (mô-tōō-ā'kä)......N. Z.	41.7 S	173.0 E
156	Motukorehu Chan. (mō-tōō-kō-rē'hū).N. Z. (In.)	36.50 S	174.53 E
156	Motukorehu I.........N. Z. (In.)	36.50 S	174.54 E
97	Mouchoir Bank (mōō-shwär') Ba. Is.	21.0 N	70.45 W
97	Mouchoir Passage.........Ba. Is.	21.9 N	70.55 W
122	Moulins (mōō-lăN')...........Fr.	46.35 N	3.20 E
150	Moulmein (mōl-mān')........Bur.	16.29 N	97.35 E
132	Moulouya R. (mōō-lōō'yà)...Mor.	34.0 N	3.40 W
82	Moultrie (mōl'trĭ)............Ga.	31.10 N	83.48 W
79	Mound City (mound)..........Ill.	37.6 N	89.10 W
79	Mound City...............Mo.	40.6 N	95.14 W
84	Moundsville (moundz'vĭl).W. Va.	39.57 N	80.55 W
123	Mounier, Mt. (mōō-nyā')......Fr.	44.10 N	6.57 E
138	Mountain Badakhshan (Gorno Badakhshan) (Aut. Ter.) (gôr'nô bà-dàk'shàn).Sov. Un.	38.50 N	73.0 E
79	Mountain Grove............Mo.	37.6 N	92.17 W
70	Mountain Home............Ida.	43.7 N	115.42 W
133	Mountain Nile (Bahr el Jebel) (R.) (bär ĕl jĕb'ĕl).Afr.	7.0 N	31.0 E
51	Mountain View Calif. (San Francisco In.)	37.24 N	122.5 W
79	Mountain View.............Mo.	37.0 N	91.47 W
83	Mount Airy (mount âr'ĭ)...N. C.	36.30 N	80.37 W
127	Mount Athos (Pen.) (ăth'ŏs).Grc.	40.15 N	24.15 E
77	Mount Ayr (âr)..............Ia.	40.43 N	94.12 W
84	Mount Carmel (kär'mĕl)......Ill.	38.26 N	87.45 W
85	Mount Carmel...............Pa.	40.48 N	76.25 W
84	Mount Clemens (klĕm'ĕnz)..Mich.	42.35 N	82.53 W
54	Mount Denis (dĕn'ĭs)...Can. (In.)	43.41 N	79.30 W
86	Mount Desert I. (dē-zûrt')...Me.	44.20 N	68.25 W
83	Mount Dora (dō'rà).........Fla.	28.46 N	81.38 W
84	Mount Forest...............Can.	43.38 N	80.46 W
158	Mount Gambier (găm'bēr)..Austl.	37.49 S	140.46 E
84	Mount Gilead (gĭl'ē-ăd).....Ohio	40.34 N	82.53 W
89	Mount Healthy Ohio (Cincinnati In.)	39.14 N	84.33 W
84	Mount Hope............W. Va.	37.55 N	81.12 W
158	Mount Isa (ī'zà)..........Austl.	20.59 S	139.35 E
72	Mount Lehman (lā'măn) Can. (Vancouver In.)	49.7 N	122.23 W
53	Mount McKinley Natl. Pk. (mà-kĭn'lĭ).Alsk.	63.20 N	150.0 W
84	Mount Morris (mŏr'ĭs).....Mich.	43.6 N	83.42 W
85	Mount Morris.............N. Y.	42.46 N	77.50 W
83	Mount Olive (ŏl'ĭv)........N. C.	35.12 N	78.4 W
70	Mount Olympic Natl. Park (ô-lĭm'pĭk).Wash.	47.55 N	123.30 W
73	Mount Pinson (pĭn'zŭn) Ala. (Birmingham In.)	33.41 N	86.42 W
77	Mount Pleasant (plĕz'ănt).....Ia.	40.58 N	91.33 W
84	Mount Pleasant.............Mich.	43.37 N	84.47 W
83	Mount Pleasant............S. C.	32.47 N	79.52 W
82	Mountpleasant.............Tenn.	35.32 N	87.12 W
81	Mount Pleasant............Tex.	33.8 N	95.0 W
75	Mount Pleasant............Utah	39.33 N	111.26 W
88	Mount Prospect (prŏs'pĕkt) Ill. (Chicago In.)	42.4 N	87.56 W
70	Mount Rainier Natl. Park (rà-nēr').Wash.	46.50 N	121.20 W
85	Mount Savage (săv'āj)......Md.	39.43 N	78.53 W
70	Mount Shasta (shăs'tà).....Calif.	41.17 N	122.15 W
79	Mount Sterling (stûr'lĭng).....Ill.	39.59 N	90.44 W
84	Mount Sterling..............Ky.	38.4 N	83.58 W
85	Mount Union...............Pa.	40.25 N	77.53 W
79	Mount Vernon (vûr'nŭn)......Ill.	38.17 N	88.55 W
84	Mount Vernon..............Ind.	37.56 N	87.53 W
79	Mount Vernon..............Mo.	37.7 N	93.46 W
85	Mount Vernon.............N. Y.	40.56 N	73.50 W
84	Mount Vernon.............Ohio	40.26 N	82.30 W
85	Mount Vernon...............Va.	38.43 N	77.5 W
70	Mount Vernon............Wash.	48.24 N	122.20 W
101	Moura (mō'rà)..............Braz.	1.32 S	61.33 W
124	Moura.....................Port.	38.7 N	7.27 W
114	Mourne Mts. (môrn)......N. Ire.	54.10 N	6.5 W
123	Moutières (mōō-tyâr')........Fr.	45.30 N	6.35 E
135	Mowbray (mō'brā).....U. S. Afr.	33.56 S	18.28 E
160	Mowbullan, Mt. (mō'bōō-lăn) Austl. (In.)	26.54 S	151.36 E
156	Mowlom Mt. (mō'lŏm).N. Z. (In.)	41.15 S	174.58 E
92	Moyahua (mō-yä'wä).......Mex.	21.19 N	103.17 W
133	Moyale (Fort Harrington) (mô-yä'-lä) (fŏrt hăr'ĭng-tŭn).Kenya	3.28 N	39.6 E
132	Moyamba (mô-yăm'bä)......S. L.	8.11 N	12.30 W
123	Moyeuvre (mô-yûv'r')........Fr.	49.17 N	6.5 E
70	Moyie R. (moi'yē)...........Ida.	49.0 N	116.12 W
100	Moyobamba (mō-yō-băm'bä) Peru	6.2 S	76.58 W
144	Moyün (mō'yün')..........Chn.	23.30 N	108.26 E
134	Mozambique (Portuguese East Africa) (mō-zăm-bēk').Afr.	18.15 S	35.0 E
134	Mozambique Chan.......Ind. O.	18.0 S	41.0 E
111	Mozdok (môz-dôk')......Sov. Un.	43.48 N	44.35 E
128	Mozhaisk (mô-zhà-ēsk')..Sov. Un.	55.31 N	36.3 E
129	Mozir (mô-zür')..........Sov. Un.	52.3 N	29.15 E
135	Mpera ('m-pä'rä)...........Tan.	6.50 S	38.43 E
134	Mponda ('m-pōn'dä)..........Nya.	14.22 S	35.8 E
134	Mporokoso('m-pō-rō-kō'sō).N.Rh.	9.31 S	30.12 E
135	Mpwapwa ('m-pwä'pwä).....Tan.	6.15 S	36.33 E
121	Mrągowo (mräŋ'gô-vô).......Pol.	53.52 N	21.18 E
135	Msangazi R. ('m-säŋ-gä'zē)..Tan.	5.43 S	38.40 E
132	M'sila (m'sē'là)............Alg.	35.45 N	4.32 E
128	Msta R. (m'stá')........Sov. Un.	58.29 N	32.25 E
128	Mstislavl (m'stē-släv''l)..Sov. Un.	54.1 N	31.42 E
113	Msus ('m-sōōs)..............Libya	31.22 N	21.13 E
135	Mtai ('m-tī')...............Tan.	4.29 S	38.14 E
135	Mtangata ('m-täŋ-gä'tà).....Tan.	5.14 S	39.3 E
135	Mtariça (Dom Luiz Filippe) ('m-tà-rē'sà) (dōN lōō-ēzh' fē-lēp'ē).Moz.	12.45 S	36.40 E
134	Mtengula ('m-tĕŋ-gōō'lä)....Moz.	12.40 S	34.50 E
134	Mtetwe Pan (Basin) ('m-tĕt'wē) Bech.	20.40 S	25.30 E
128	Mtsensk (m'tsĕnsk).....Sov. Un.	53.16 N	36.35 E
101	Muaná (mōō-à-nä')...Braz. (In.)	1.30 S	49.20 W
116	Much Wenlock (mŭch wĕn'lŏk) Gt. Brit.	52.35 N	2.33 W
114	Muck (I.) (mŭk)........Gt. Brit.	56.45 N	6.10 W
113	Muctar (El Mugtaa) (mōōk-tär') (ĕl mōōg-tä'à).Libya	30.25 N	18.42 E
101	Mucujé (mōō-kōō-zhā').....Braz.	13.2 S	41.28 W
148	Mudan R. (mōō'dän)........Chn.	45.0 N	129.33 E
79	Muddy Boggy Cr. (bôg'ĭ)...Okla.	34.30 N	96.12 W
74	Muddy R. (mŭd'ĭ)..........Nev.	36.55 N	114.45 W
77	Mud L....................Mich.	46.12 N	84.10 W
89	Mud L...Minn. (Minneapolis In.)	44.53 N	93.16 W
70	Mud L.....................Nev.	40.31 N	119.20 W
124	Mugía (mōō-κē'ä)...........Sp.	43.5 N	9.14 W
113	Muğla (mōōg'lä)............Tur.	37.15 N	28.25 E
120	Mühldorf (mül-dôrf)........Ger.	48.16 N	12.32 E
120	Mühlhausen (mül'hou-zĕn)...Ger.	51.13 N	10.25 E
119	Muhu (I.) (mōō'hōō)....Sov. Un.	58.36 N	23.15 E
51	Muir (mūr) Calif. (San Francisco In.)	37.59 N	122.7 W
74	Muir Woods Nat. Mon. (mūr).Calif.	37.53 N	122.35 W
147	Muju (mōō'jōō)..............Kor.	36.1 N	127.40 E
140	Mukalla (mŭ-kä'lä)........Aden	14.28 N	49.5 E
143	Mukden (Shenyang) (mōōk'dĕn) (shĕn'yäng').Chn.	42.1 N	123.28 E
139	Mukhtuya (mōōκ-tōō'yà) Sov. Un.	60.40 N	114.50 E
131	Mukimbungu (mōō'kēm-bōōŋ-gōō) Bel. Cong. (Brazzaville In.)	5.9 S	14.1 E
149	Mukogawa R. (mōō'kō-gä'wä) Jap. (Osaka In.)	34.52 N	135.18 E
149	Mukomachi (mōō'kō-mä'chē) Jap. (Osaka In.)	34.57 N	135.42 E
124	Mula (mōō'lä)..............Sp.	38.3 N	1.28 W
126	Mulat (I.) (mōō'lät).......Yugo.	44.15 N	14.50 E
82	Mulberry Fork (R.) (mŭl'bĕr-ĭ') Ala.	33.52 N	87.0 W
120	Mulde R. (mōōl'dĕ)........Ger.	51.10 N	12.47 E
92	Muleros (mōō-lā'rōs).......Mex.	23.45 N	103.59 W
87	Mulgrave (mŭl'grāv)........Can.	45.37 N	61.22 W
159	Mulgrave I.............Pap. Ter.	10.10 S	142.8 E
124	Mulhacén (Mt.) (mōōl-à-thān').Sp.	37.3 N	3.19 W
120	Mülheim (mül'hīm)..........Ger.	51.26 N	6.54 E
123	Mulhouse (mü-lōōz')..........Fr.	47.45 N	7.20 E
70	Mullan (mŭl'ăn)..............Ida.	47.27 N	115.47 W
150	Müller Mts. (mül'ēr).......Indon.	0.38 N	113.30 E
84	Mullet L. (mŭl'ĕt)..........Mich.	45.30 N	84.23 W
114	Mullets Pen................Ire.	54.10 N	10.0 W
114	Mull (I.) (mŭl)..........Gt. Brit.	56.30 N	6.0 W
114	Mullingar (mŭl-ĭn-gär')......Ire.	53.30 N	7.20 W
83	Mullins (mŭl'ĭnz)..........S. C.	34.12 N	79.14 W
94	Mullins River.....Br. Hond. (In.)	17.7 N	88.17 W
141	Multan (mōōl-tän').........Pak.	30.15 N	71.31 E
79	Mulvane (mŭl-vān')........Kan.	37.27 N	97.13 W
134	Mumbwa (mōōm'bwä)....N. Rh.	15.0 S	27.5 E
135	Muna el Amîr (mōō'nà ĕl à-mēr') Eg.	29.55 N	31.15 E
120	München (Munich) (mün'kĕn) (mū'nĭk).Ger.	48.8 N	11.35 E
147	Munchŏn (mōōn'chŭn)......Kor.	39.17 N	127.18 E
84	Muncie (mŭn'sĭ)............Ind.	40.10 N	85.25 W
159	Munda (mōōn'dà).....Solomon Is.	8.20 S	157.15 E
159	Mungana (mŭn-găn'à).....Austl.	17.8 S	144.15 E
159	Mungindi (mŭn-gĭn'dē).....Austl.	29.0 S	149.0 E
147	Mungyŏng (mōōŋ'yuŋ).......Kor.	36.44 N	128.6 E
134	Munhanga (mōōn-häŋ'gà)...Ang.	12.8 S	18.58 E
132	Muni (Prov.) (mōō'nē)...Sp. Gui.	1.30 N	10.30 E
120	Munich (münchen) (mū'nĭk) (mün-kĕn).Ger.	48.8 N	11.35 E
77	Munising (mū'nĭ-sĭng)......Mich.	46.24 N	86.39 W
121	Munkachevo (mōōn'kà-chĕ'vô) Sov. Un.	48.26 N	22.42 E
121	Munkács (Mukačevo)(mōōn'käch) (mōō'kà-chĕ'vô).Hung.	48.26 N	22.42 E
138	Munku Sardik (Mt.) (mōōn'kōō sär-dĭk').Sov. Un.	51.40 N	100.30 E
152	Muñoz (mōō-nyōth').........Phil.	15.43 N	120.54 E
99	Muñoz Gamero Pen. (mōōn'yōz gä-mä'rō).Chl. (Magallanes In.)	52.40 S	73.10 W
147	Munsan (mōōn'sän)..........Kor.	37.52 N	126.48 E
123	Munster (mün'stēr)...........Fr.	48.1 N	7.5 E
120	Münster (mün'stēr)..........Ger.	51.58 N	7.38 E
127	Muntenia (Prov.) (mōōn-tĕn'yà) Rom.	45.0 N	26.0 E
151	Muntinglupa (mōōn-tĭng-lōō'pä) Phil. (Manila In.)	14.25 N	121.3 E
150	Muntok (mōōn-tŏk')........Indon.	2.5 S	105.10 E
150	Muongsing (mōō'ŏng-sĭng') Indoch.	21.5 N	101.14 E
111	Muradiye (mōō-rä'dē-yĕ)....Tur.	38.58 N	43.45 E
129	Murafa (mōō-rä'fà).......Sov. Un.	50.1 N	35.17 E
126	Mura R. (mōō'rä)..........Yugo.	46.45 N	15.50 E
122	Murat (mü-rä').................Fr.	45.5 N	2.59 E
111	Murat R. (mōō-rät')...........Tur.	38.45 N	40.45 E
133	Murchison Falls (mûr'chĭ-sŭn).Ug.	2.15 N	31.46 E
158	Murchison R.................Austl.	26.30 S	116.30 E
124	Murcia (mōōr'thyà)............Sp.	38.0 N	1.8 W
124	Murcia (Prov.)...............Sp.	38.30 N	1.45 W
76	Murdo (mûr'dō)............S. D.	43.54 N	100.41 W
148	Muren R. (mōō'rĕn)..........Chn.	45.13 N	131.0 E
121	Mureşul R. (mōō'rĕsh-ōōl)..Rom.	46.20 N	23.43 E
122	Muret (mü-rĕ')................Fr.	43.28 N	1.19 E
82	Murfreesboro (mûr'frēz-bŭr-ō) Tenn.	35.51 N	86.24 W
140	Murghab R. (mōōr-gäb').Sov. Un.	37.0 N	62.30 E
160	Murgon (mûr'gŏn)..........Austl.	26.13 S	151.54 E
120	Müritz (mür'ĭts)..............Ger.	53.24 N	12.55 E
120	Müritz L.....................Ger.	53.25 N	12.42 E
110	Murmansk (mōōr-mänsk') Sov. Un.	68.50 N	33.10 E
110	Murom (mōō'rŏm)......Sov. Un.	55.30 N	42.0 E
148	Muroran (mōō'rō-rän)........Jap.	42.22 N	140.59 E
124	Muros (mōō'rōs)..............Sp.	42.47 N	9.5 W
149	Muroto C. (mōō'rō-tō)......Jap.	33.16 N	134.10 E
72	Murphy (mûr'fĭ) Colo. (Colo. Sprs. In.)	38.54 N	105.10 W
82	Murphy....................N. C.	35.6 N	84.2 W
79	Murphysboro (mûr'fĭz-bŭr-ō)..Ill.	37.46 N	89.21 W
121	Mur R. (mōōr)...............Aus.	47.10 N	14.20 E
134	Murraça (mōōr-rä'sà)........Moz.	17.52 S	35.12 E

ăt; finăl; rāte; senâte; ärm; àsk; sofà; fâre; ch-choose; dh-as th in other; bē; ēvent; bĕt; recĕnt; cratēr; g-go; gh-gutteral g; bĭt; ĭ-short neutral; rīde; κ-gutteral k as ch in German ich;

Murray PRONOUNCING INDEX Nasworthy

Page	Name Pronunciation Region	Lat. °′	Long. °′
82	Murray (mŭr'ĭ) Ky.	36.40 N	88.18 W
71	Murray Utah	40.40 N	111.54 W
55	Murray B Can.	47.47 N	70.17 W
59	Murray, L. S. C.	34.15 N	81.45 W
159	Murray R. Austl.	34.12 S	140.0 E
72	Murrayville. Can. (Vancouver In.)	49.5 N	122.37 W
159	Murrumbidgee R. (mŭr-ŭm-bĭd'jē) Austl.	34.30 S	145.42 E
141	Murshidabad (mōōr'shē-dä-bäd') India	24.5 N	88.29 E
151	Murua (Woodlark) (I.) (mōō'rōō-ȧ) (wŏŏd'lärk). Pap. Ter.	9.0 S	152.45 E
160	Murwillumbah (mŭr-wĭl-lŭm'bȧ) Austl. (In.)	28.19 S	153.21 E
120	Mürz R. (mürts) Aus.	47.47 N	15.40 E
133	Murzuch (mōōr'zōōk') Libya	25.58 N	14.12 E
133	Murzuch (Dunes) Libya	24.30 N	14.0 E
120	Mürzzuschlag (mürts'tsōō-shlägh) Aus.	47.37 N	15.41 E
111	Muş (mōōsh) Tur.	38.48 N	41.28 E
137	Musa (mōō'sȧ) Yem. (In.)	13.42 N	43.19 E
148	Musan (mōō'sän) Kor.	42.12 N	129.12 E
140	Muscat (Masqat) (mŭs-kăt') (mäs-kät'). Oman	23.31 N	58.38 E
77	Muscatine (mŭs-kȧ-tēn') Ia.	41.24 N	91.2 W
82	Muscle Shoals (mŭs''l shōlz'). Ala.	34.46 N	87.38 W
137	Musemir (mōō-sȧ-mēr'). Aden (In.)	13.29 N	44.49 E
158	Musgrave R. (mŭs'grāv) Austl.	26.10 S	131.45 E
134	Mushie (mŭsh'ē) Bel. Cong.	3.2 S	16.48 E
150	Musi R. (mōō'sē) Indon.	2.55 S	104.0 E
84	Muskegon (mŭs-kē'gŭn) Mich.	43.14 N	86.15 W
84	Muskegon Heights Mich.	43.10 N	86.18 W
84	Muskegon R. Mich.	43.20 N	86.0 W
84	Muskingum R. (mŭs-kĭŋ'gŭm) Ohio	39.55 N	82.0 W
79	Muskogee (mŭs-kō'gē) Okla.	35.44 N	95.22 W
85	Muskoka, L. (mŭs-kō'kȧ) Can.	45.5 N	79.30 W
87	Muskwaro L. (mŭsk-wä'rō). Can.	50.25 N	61.0 W
151	Mussau Is. (mōō-sä'ōō) N. Gui. Ter.	1.30 S	149.35 E
114	Musselburgh (mŭs''l-bŭr-ō) Gt. Brit.	55.55 N	3.0 W
71	Musselshell R. (mŭs''l-shĕl). Mont.	46.30 N	108.20 W
126	Mussolinia (mōōs'sō-lē'nē-ä). Sard.	40.45 N	8.32 E
111	Mustafakemalpaşa (Kemal Atatürk) (mōōs'tä-fä-kĕ-mäl'pä-shä'). Tur.	40.5 N	28.30 E
142	Mustagh Ata (Mt.) (mōōs-täk'ä-tä'). Chn.	38.22 N	75.0 E
81	Mustang Bayou (mŭs'tăng) Tex. (In.)	29.25 N	95.12 W
78	Mustang Cr. Tex.	36.0 N	102.30 W
81	Mustang I. Tex.	27.45 N	97.5 W
102	Musters, L. (mŭs'tērz) (mōōs-tĕrs') Arg.	45.30 S	68.30 W
95	Mustique I. (müs-tēk') Wind. Is. (In.)	12.52 N	61.12 W
148	Musu Pt. (mōō'sōō) Kor.	40.50 N	129.43 E
119	Mustvee (mōōst'vĕ-ĕ) Sov. Un.	58.50 N	26.56 E
134	Mutombo Mukulu (mōō-tôm'bō mōō-kōō'lōō). Bel. Cong.	8.0 S	23.58 E
102	Mutondo (mōō-tōn'dōō) Braz. (In.)	22.50 S	43.1 W
148	Mutsu B. (mōōt'sōō) Jap.	41.2 N	140.50 E
87	Mutton B. (mŭt''n) Can.	50.45 N	59.5 W
141	Muttra (mōōt'trȧ) India	27.25 N	77.45 E
149	Muya (mōō'yä) Jap.	34.13 N	134.34 E
138	Muyun Kum Desert (mōō-yōōn' kōōm'). Sov. Un.	44.40 N	72.0 E
80	Múzquiz (mōōz'kēz) Mex.	27.53 N	101.30 E
134	Mwanza (mwän'zä) Tan.	2.30 S	32.52 E
135	Mwatate (mwä-tä'tä) Kenya	3.22 S	38.18 E
134	Mwaya (mwä'yä) Tan.	9.35 S	33.52 E
134	Mweru, L. (mwā'rōō). Bel. Cong.	9.0 S	28.45 E
148	Myakonojo (myä'kō-nō'jō) Jap.	31.45 N	131.2 E
112	Mya, Wadi (R.) (wä'dē myä'). Alg.	29.45 N	3.30 E
142	Myingyan (myĭng-yŭn') Bur.	21.15 N	95.28 E
142	Myitkyina (myĭ'chē-nȧ) Bur.	25.29 N	97.21 E
121	Myjava (mû'ē-yȧ-vȧ) Czech.	48.45 N	17.33 E
127	Mykonos (I.) (mē'kō-nôs) Grc.	37.27 N	25.23 E
141	Mymensingh (mī-mŭn-sĭnk'). Pak.	24.45 N	90.20 E
114	Mynydd Bach (mŭ-nŭdh'bäk) Gt. Brit.	52.10 N	3.40 W
147	Myohyang Mt. (myō'hyäng). Kor.	40.1 N	126.20 E
108	Myrdals-Jökull (glacier) (mür'däls-yû'kōōl). Ice.	63.35 N	18.15 W
70	Myrtle Point (mûr't'l) Ore.	43.4 N	124.8 W
128	Myshkin (mēsh'kēn) Sov. Un.	57.47 N	38.25 E
141	Mysore India	12.17 N	76.32 E
141	Mysore (State) (mī-sōr') India	13.45 N	77.0 E
77	Mystic (mĭs'tĭk) Ia.	40.46 N	92.56 W
127	Mytilēnē (mĭt-ĭ-lē'nē) (mĭt-ĭ-lyē'nyē). Grc.	39.6 N	26.34 E
113	Mytilene (I.) Grc.	39.15 N	26.20 E
134	Mzimba ('m-zĭm'bä) Nya.	11.50 S	33.38 E
120	Naab R. (näp) Ger.	49.32 N	12.10 E
132	Naama (nä'ä-mȧ) Lib.	7.21 N	9.30 W
119	Naantali (nän'tȧ-lē) Fin.	60.30 N	22.1 E
153	Nabas (nä'bäs) Phil.	11.49 N	122.4 E
158	Nabberoo, L. (năb'ēr-ōō) Austl.	25.45 S	120.45 E
132	Nabeul (nä-bûl') Tun.	36.32 N	10.40 E
137	Nablus (Shekhem) (nä-blōōs') (shĕ'kĕm). Pal. (In.)	32.13 N	35.16 E
152	Nabua (nä'bwä) Phil.	13.24 N	123.22 E
94	Nacaome (nä-kä-ō'mȧ) Hond.	13.32 N	87.27 W
142	Na Cham (nä chäm') Indoch.	22.3 N	106.17 E
66	Naches R. (năch'ĕz) Wash.	46.50 N	120.50 W
120	Náchod (näk'ôt) Czech.	50.25 N	16.9 E
74	Nacimiento R. (nȧ-sĭ-myĕn'tō) Calif.	35.45 N	121.15 W
81	Nacogdoches (năk'ō-dō'chĕz). Tex.	31.37 N	94.40 W
80	Nadadores (nä-dä-dō'räs) Mex.	27.3 N	101.36 W
148	Nadan-Khatala-Alin (Mts.) (nä'dän-kä-tä'lä-ä-lēn'). Chn.	46.30 N	133.0 E
121	Nădlac (nŭd-läk') Rom.	46.9 N	20.45 E
121	Nadvornaya (näd-vōōr'nȧ-yȧ) Sov. Un.	48.36 N	24.30 E
138	Nadym (Kadin) R. (nȧ'dĭm) (kȧ'dĭn). Sov. Un.	65.20 N	73.20 E
118	Naestved (nĕst'vĭdh) Den.	55.11 N	11.46 E
152	Naga (nä'gä) Phil.	13.37 N	123.12 E
153	Naga Phil.	10.13 N	123.45 E
149	Nagahama (nä'gä-hä'mä) Jap.	33.32 N	132.28 E
149	Nagahama Jap.	35.25 N	136.15 E
149	Naga I. (nä'gä) Jap.	32.9 N	130.8 E
149	Nagano (nä'gä-nō) Jap.	36.44 N	138.3 E
148	Nagaoka (nä'gȧ-ō'kȧ) Jap.	37.25 N	138.59 E
148	Nagasaki (nä'gȧ-sä'kē) Jap.	32.45 N	129.50 E
149	Nagasu (nä'gäs-ōō) Jap.	33.31 N	131.22 E
152	Nagcarlan (näg-kär-län') Phil.	14.8 N	121.25 E
131	Nag Hamâdi (näg' hä-mä'dē) Eg. (In.)	26.2 N	32.12 E
111	Nagornogokarabakh (Aut. Area) (nȧ-gôr'nō-gō-kȧ'rȧ-bäk'). Sov. Un.	40.0 N	47.0 E
60	Nagor Rajasima (Korat) (nä-gōr' rä-jä-sē'mȧ) (kō-rät'). Siam	14.55 N	102.12 E
150	Nagor Sridharmarâj (nä-gōr' srē-dar'mŭ-räj'). Siam	8.27 N	100.0 E
149	Nagoya (nä'gō'yȧ) Jap.	35.11 N	136.58 E
141	Nagpur (näg'pōōr) India	21.15 N	79.12 E
152	Naguilian (nä-gwē-lē'än) Phil.	16.31 N	120.24 E
121	Nagykanizsa (nôd'y'-kô'nē-shô) Hung.	46.28 N	17.0 E
121	Nagykörös (nôd'y'-kû'rûsh). Hung.	47.2 N	19.47 E
148	Naha (nä'hä) Ryukyu Is. (In.)	26.10 N	127.44 E
150	Nahakam R. (nä'hä-käm). Indon.	0.20 S	116.0 E
87	Nahant (nȧ-hănt') Mass. (In.)	42.25 N	70.55 W
	Nāho, see Noho, Chn.		
125	Nahr-Ouassel (R.) (när'-wä-sĕl') Alg.	35.35 N	2.0 E
102	Nahuel Huapi, L. (nä'wâl wä'pē) Arg.	41.0 S	71.30 W
94	Nahuizalco (nä-wē-zäl'kō) Sal.	13.49 N	89.43 W
135	Nahya (nä'hyȧ) Eg.	30.3 N	31.8 E
152	Naic (nä'ĕk) Phil.	14.20 N	120.47 E
80	Naica (nä-ē'kä) Mex.	27.53 N	105.29 W
55	Nain (nīn) Can.	56.32 N	61.59 W
114	Nairn (nârn) Gt. Brit.	57.35 N	3.50 W
135	Nairobi (nī-rō'bē) Kenya	1.15 S	36.45 E
119	Naissaare (I.) (nī'sä-rĕ). Sov. Un.	59.32 N	24.32 E
135	Naivasha (nī-vä'shȧ) Kenya	0.43 S	36.23 E
96	Najasa R. (nä-hä'sä) Cuba	20.58 N	78.0 W
148	Najin (nä'jĭn) Kor.	42.12 N	130.18 E
140	Najran (nŭj-rän') (Reg.). Sau. Ar.	17.15 N	45.30 E
147	Naju (nä'jōō') Kor.	35.2 N	126.43 E
147	Nakadori I. (nä'kä-dō'rē) Jap.	32.56 N	129.4 E
149	Na Kaido (nä' kä'ē-dō) Jap. (Osaka In.)	34.42 N	135.39 E
148	Naka-Shiretoko, C. (nä'kä-shĭ-rē-tō'kō). Sakh.	46.5 N	143.28 E
149	Nakatsu (nä'käts-ōō) Jap.	33.31 N	131.12 E
111	Nakhichevan (nȧ-kē-chĕ-vän') Sov. Un.	39.12 N	45.28 E
129	Nakhichevan Sov. Un.	47.14 N	39.48 E
121	Naklo (näk'wō) Pol.	53.7 N	17.37 E
118	Nakskov (näk'skou) Den.	54.50 N	11.7 E
147	Naktong R. (näk'tŭng) Kor.	36.0 N	128.25 E
140	Nalchik (nȧl-chĕk') Sov. Un.	43.32 N	43.35 E
124	Nalon R. (nä-lōn') Sp.	43.20 N	5.50 W
112	Nalut (nä-lōōt') Libya	32.3 N	11.5 E
77	Namakan L. (nă'mȧ-kȧn). Minn.	48.27 N	92.35 W
140	Namakzar (Des.) (nŭ-mŭk-zär') Iran	30.15 N	58.45 E
134	Namaland (nä'mȧ-lănd). S. W. Afr.	26.15 S	18.0 E
138	Namangan (nȧ-män-gän') Sov. Un.	41.10 N	71.50 E
151	Namatanai (nä'mä-tȧ-nä'ē) N. Gui. Ter.	3.38 S	152.30 E
149	Namaze (nä'mȧ-zȧ) Jap. (Osaka In.)	34.49 N	135.19 E
75	Nambe Pueblo Ind. Res. (näm'bȧ pwĕb'lō). N. M.	35.53 N	106.0 W
147	Namchŏnjom (näm'chŭn-jŏm) Kor.	38.20 N	126.23 E
150	Namdinh (näm'dĕnk) Indoch.	20.29 N	106.10 E
147	Namhae (näm'hī') Kor.	34.51 N	127.53 E
147	Namhae I. Kor.	34.48 N	127.56 E
144	Namheung (näm'hĕ-ōōng') Chn.	22.49 N	109.26 E
134	Namib (Reg.) (nä-mēb') S. W. Afr.	24.30 S	14.45 E
145	Namkwan (näm'kwän') Chn.	27.12 N	120.20 E
145	Namoa I. (nä'mō-ȧ) Chn.	23.23 N	116.48 E
159	Namoi R. (năm'oi) Austl.	30.20 S	149.0 E
112	Namous, Wadi en (R.) (wä'dē ĕn nȧ-mōōs'). Alg.	31.30 N	0.27 W
70	Nampa (năm'pȧ) Ida.	43.35 N	116.34 W
108	Namsos (näm'sôs) Nor.	64.30 N	11.28 E
144	Namtow (näm'tō') Chn.	22.35 N	113.50 E
142	Nam Tso (Tengri Nor) (L.) (näm' tsō (tĕŋ'grē nôr'). Chn.	30.45 N	90.39 E
115	Namur (nä-mür') Bel.	50.28 N	4.50 E
134	Namutoni (nȧ-mōō-tō'nē) S. W. Afr.	18.55 S	17.2 E
147	Namwŏn (näm'wŭn') Kor.	35.24 N	127.22 E
144	Namyung (näm'yōōng') Chn.	25.15 N	113.58 E
70	Nanaimo (nȧ-nī'mō) Can.	49.8 N	123.58 W
148	Nanan (nä'näm') Kor.	41.42 N	129.41 E
144	Nanan (nän'nän') Chn.	25.31 N	113.52 E
160	Nanango (nä-năŋ'gō). Austl. (In.)	26.38 S	152.2 E
149	Nanao (nä'nä-ō) Jap.	37.0 N	136.59 E
145	Nanchang (nän'chäng') Chn.	28.37 N	115.46 E
145	Nanching (nän'chĭng') Chn.	24.34 N	117.27 E
144	Nanchow (nän'chō') Chn.	29.22 N	112.11 E
144	Nanchwan (nän'chwän') Chn.	29.9 N	107.6 E
123	Nancy (nän-sē') Fr.	48.41 N	6.10 E
141	Nanda Devi (nän'dȧ dā'vē) Mts. Chn.	30.27 N	80.20 E
148	Nanfaisan (Mt.) (nän'fī'sän'). Jap.	36.45 N	139.31 E
145	Nanfeng (nän'fĕng') Chn.	27.11 N	116.17 E
153	Nangalao I. (näŋ-gä-lä'ō) Phil.	11.27 N	120.11 E
153	Nangtud, Mt. (näng-tōōd'). Phil.	11.14 N	122.12 E
145	Nankang (nän'käng') Chn.	25.38 N	114.15 E
145	Nankang Chn.	29.23 N	115.54 E
145	Nanking (Kiangning) (nän'kĭng') (kyäng'nĭng'). Chn.	32.4 N	118.45 E
145	Nankodai-San (Mt.) (nän'kō'dī'-sän). For.	24.25 N	121.29 E
146	Nankung (nän'kōōng') Chn.	37.26 N	115.25 E
146	Nanlo (nän'lō') Chn.	36.5 N	115.28 E
158	Nannine (nă-nēn') Austl.	26.47 S	118.20 E
144	Nanning (nän'nĭng') Chn.	22.55 N	108.32 E
145	Nanning Chn.	30.56 N	118.20 E
146	Nanpi (nän'pĭ') Chn.	38.12 N	116.30 E
89	Nansemond R. (năn'sē-mŭnd) Va. (Norfolk In.)	36.53 N	76.29 W
144	Nan Shan (Mts.) (nän'shän'). Chn.	24.58 N	111.18 E
142	Nan Shan (Mts.) Chn.	38.30 N	98.30 E
145	Nansiang (nän'syäng') Chn.	31.13 N	121.21 E
149	Nantaisan (Mt.) (nän'tī-sän'). Jap.	36.47 N	139.30 E
144	Nantan (nän'tän') Chn.	24.57 N	107.30 E
123	Nanterre (nän-târ') Fr. (In.)	48.53 N	2.12 E
122	Nantes (nänt') Fr.	47.13 N	1.33 W
85	Nanticoke (năn'tĭ-kōk) Pa.	41.22 N	76.0 W
123	Nantua (nän'tü-ä) Fr.	46.10 N	5.38 E
85	Nantucket (I.) (năn-tŭk'ĕt). Mass.	41.15 N	70.5 W
145	Nantung (nän'tōōng') Chn.	32.0 N	120.53 E
116	Nantwich (nănt'wĭch) Gt. Brit.	53.4 N	2.31 W
144	Nan Yuek (Heng Shan) (Mts.) (nän' yōō-ĕk') (hĕng' shän). Chn.	26.55 N	111.48 E
125	Nao C. (nä'ō) Sp.	38.45 N	0.13 E
93	Naolinco (nä-ō-lēŋ'kō) Mex.	19.40 N	96.51 W
127	Naousa (nä'ōō-sȧ) Grc.	40.38 N	22.5 E
74	Napa (năp'ȧ) Calif.	38.19 N	122.19 W
85	Napanee (năp'ȧ-nē) Can.	44.15 N	77.0 W
156	Napier (nā'pĭ-ēr) N. Z.	39.30 S	176.55 E
126	Naples (Napoli) (nā'p'lz) (nä'pō-lē). It.	40.51 N	14.26 E
126	Naples, B. of It.	40.45 N	14.15 E
84	Napoleon (nȧ-pō'lē-ŭn) Ohio	41.24 N	84.10 W
81	Napoleonville (nȧ-pō'lē-ŭn-vĭl). La.	29.55 N	91.3 W
126	Napoli (Naples) (nä'pō-lē) It.	40.51 N	14.26 E
117	Napoli (Naples) It. (In.)		
100	Napo R. (nä'pō) Ec.	2.0 S	75.0 W
84	Nappanee (năp'ȧ-nē) Ind.	41.26 N	86.2 W
132	Nara (nä'rä) Fr. W. Afr.	15.7 N	7.30 W
149	Nara Jap.	34.44 N	135.46 E
158	Naracoorte (nȧ-rȧ-kōōn'tē). Austl.	36.59 S	140.42 E
128	Nara R. Sov. Un.	55.12 N	36.58 E
149	Narawa (nä'rȧ-wä) Jap. (Tokyo In.)	35.26 N	139.57 E
141	Narbada R. (nŭr-bŭd'ä) India	22.15 N	76.0 E
88	Narberth (när'bûrth) Pa. (Philadelphia In.)	40.0 N	75.16 W
122	Narbonne (nȧr-bôn') Fr.	43.11 N	3.0 E
127	Nardò (när-dō') It.	40.11 N	18.1 E
138	Nareny (nȧ-rĕn'y') Sov. Un.	53.15 N	102.59 E
121	Narew R. (nä'rĕf) Pol.	53.13 N	22.24 E
138	Narin (nȧ-rēn') Sov. Un.	41.25 N	76.0 E
153	Nariz Pt. (nä-rēth') Phil.	8.53 N	118.0 E
128	Narocz, L. (nä'rôch) Pol.	54.50 N	26.50 E
110	Narodnaya (nȧ-rôd'nȧ-yȧ) Sov. Un.	65.20 N	61.00 E
128	Naro-Fominsk (nä'rō-fô-mēnsk') Sov. Un.	55.23 N	36.45 E
124	Narón (nä-rōn') Sp.	43.31 N	8.9 W
151	Narotas (nä-rō'täs) Phil. (Manila In.)	14.40 N	120.56 E
160	Narrabeen (năr-ȧ-bĭn) Austl.	33.43 S	151.18 E
159	Narrabri (nä-rä'brē) Austl.	30.18 S	149.48 E
85	Narragansett B. (năr-ȧ-găn'sĕt) R. I.	41.20 N	71.20 W
159	Narrandera (nȧ-rȧn-dē'rȧ). Austl.	34.44 S	146.32 E
158	Narrogin (năr'ō-gĭn) Austl.	32.59 S	117.3 E
88	Narrows, The (Inlet) (năr'ōz) N. Y. (N. Y. In.)	40.37 N	74.3 W
119	Narva (nȧr'vȧ) Sov. Un.	59.22 N	28.8 E
152	Narvacan (när-vä-kän') Phil.	17.25 N	120.29 E
108	Narvik (när'vēk) Nor.	68.20 N	17.35 E
111	Naryan Mar (när'yän mär') Sov. Un.	67.38 N	53.0 E
138	Narym (nä-rēm') Sov. Un.	58.50 N	81.59 E
138	Narymskoe, Bolshoi (Sea) (bŏl'shôĭ-nä-rēm'skō-yĕ). Sov. Un.	49.15 N	84.35 E
138	Naryn R. (nȧ-rĭn') Sov. Un.	41.35 N	73.0 E
116	Naseby (nāz'bĭ) Gt. Brit.	52.23 N	0.59 W
157	Naseby N. Z.	45.2 S	170.10 E
86	Nashua (năsh'ū-ȧ) N. H.	42.45 N	71.30 W
79	Nashville (năsh'vĭl) Ark.	33.56 N	93.51 W
82	Nashville Ga.	31.13 N	83.17 W
79	Nashville Ill.	38.21 N	89.23 W
84	Nashville Mich.	42.37 N	85.4 W
82	Nashville Tenn.	36.10 N	86.49 W
77	Nashwauk (năsh'wôk) Minn.	47.22 N	93.10 W
127	Našice (nä'shē-tsĕ) Yugo.	45.29 N	18.6 E
121	Nasielsk (nä'syĕlsk) Pol.	52.36 N	20.51 E
141	Nasik (nä'sĭk) India	19.59 N	73.45 E
133	Nasir (nä-zēr') A. E. Sud.	8.32 N	33.2 E
55	Naskaupi (năs'kō-pĭ) Can.	54.0 N	61.30 W
153	Naso Pt. (nä'sō) Phil.	10.25 N	121.58 E
96	Nassau (năs'ō) Ba. Is.	25.4 N	77.22 W
151	Nassau Ra. (năs'ō) (nä'sou) Neth. N. Gui.	4.5 S	137.0 E
118	Nässjö (nĕs'shû) Swe.	57.39 N	14.41 E
152	Nasugbu (nȧ-sōōg-bōō') Phil.	14.5 N	120.38 E
80	Nasworthy, L. (năz'wûr-thē). Tex.	31.45 N	100.35 W

ng-sing; ŋ-baŋk; ɴ-nasalized n; nŏd; cŏmmit; ōld; ōbey; ôrder; fōōd; fŏŏt; ou-out; s-soft; sh-dish; th-thin; pūre; ûnite; ûrn; stŭd; circŭs; ü-as "y" in study; '-indeterminate vowel.

Natal PRONOUNCING INDEX **Newchurch**

Page	Name Pronunciation Region	Lat. ° ′	Long. ° ′
101	Natal (nä-täl') Braz.	5.45 S	35.15 W
134	Natal (Prov.) (nȧ-tăl')..U. S. Afr.	29.0 S	30.30 E
87	Natashkwan (nä-tăsh'kwăn). Can.	50.10 N	61.47 W
82	Natchez (năch'ĕz) Miss.	31.32 N	91.24 W
81	Natchitoches (năk'ĭ-tŏsh) (nȧch-ĭ-tŏsh'). La.	31.45 N	93.5 W
87	Natick (nā'tĭk) Mass. (In.)	42.17 N	71.21 W
71	National Bison Range Mont.	47.20 N	114.20 W
74	National City Calif. (In.)	32.40 N	117.7 W
160	National Park Austl.	34.4 S	151.3 E
160	National Park Austl.	34.6 S	151.5 E
101	Natividade (nä-tē-vē-dä'dĕ). Braz.	11.32 S	47.32 W
93	Natívitas (nä-tē'vē-täs). Mex. (In.)	19.15 N	99.5 W
150	Natoena (Natuna) I., Great (nä-tōō'nä). Indon.	4.0 N	108.0 E
150	Natoena (Natuna) Is. Indon.	3.0 N	108.30 E
150	Natoena (Natuna) Is., South Indon.	2.30 N	108.45 E
134	Natron (Magad) L. (nā'trŏn) (mä-gäd'). Tan.	2.15 S	36.0 E
131	Natrun, Wadi en (R.) (wä-dē ĕn nä'trōōn). Eg. (In.)	30.25 N	30.20 E
75	Natural Bridges Natl. Mon. Utah	37.21 N	109.48 W
158	Naturaliste, C. (năt-ů-rȧ-lĭst') Austl.	33.29 S	115.3 E
120	Nauen (nou'ĕn) Ger.	52.36 N	12.52 E
85	Naugatuck (nô'gȧ-tŭk) Conn.	41.27 N	73.6 W
93	Nauhcampatepen, Cerro (Mt.) (sĕr'ō nä'ōō-käm'pä-tā'pĕn). Mex.	19.28 N	97.8 W
152	Naujan (nä-ōō-hän') Phil.	13.18 N	121.17 E
152	Naujan, L. Phil.	13.9 N	121.20 E
120	Naumburg (noum'bŏŏrgh) Ger.	51.8 N	11.48 E
119	Naumiestis (nou'myĕs-tĭs) Sov. Un.	54.52 N	22.58 E
127	Nauplion (näf'plyē-ôn) Grc.	37.33 N	22.49 E
5	Nauru (I.) (nou'rōō) Pac. O.	0.25 S	166.57 E
93	Nautla (nä-ōōt'lä) Mex.	20.13 N	96.47 W
80	Nava (nä'vä) Mex.	28.25 N	100.45 W
124	Nava del Rey (nä-vä dĕl rā'ē). Sp.	41.21 N	5.4 W
124	Navahermosa (nä-vä-ĕr-mō'sä) Sp.	39.38 N	4.28 W
96	Navajas (nä-vä-häs') Cuba	22.41 N	81.19 W
75	Navajo Indian Reservation (năv'ȧ-hō). Ariz.-N. Mex.	36.0 N	110.0 W
75	Navajo Indian Reservation Ariz.-Utah	37.8 N	100.40 W
75	Navajo Natl. Mon. (năv'ȧ-hō) Ariz.	36.43 N	110.40 W
124	Nava, L. Sp.	42.4 N	4.40 W
125	Navalcarnero (nä-väl'kär-nā'rō) Sp. (In.)	40.18 N	4.2 W
124	Navalmoral de la Mata (nä-väl'mō-räl' dā lä mä'tä). Sp.	39.53 N	5.31 W
114	Navan (nă'vȧn) Ire.	53.40 N	6.42 W
	Navanagar, see Jamnagar, India		
102	Navarin I. (nä-vä-rēn') Arg.	55.10 S	67.40 W
124	Navarra (Prov.) (nä-vär'rä)...Sp.	42.40 N	1.30 W
81	Navasota (năv-ȧ-sō'tȧ) Tex.	30.24 N	96.5 W
81	Navasota R. Tex.	31.0 N	96.15 W
97	Navassa I. (nȧ-văs'ȧ) W. I.	18.25 N	75.2 W
124	Navia R. (nä-vē'ä) Sp.	43.10 N	6.55 W
97	Navidad Bank (nä-vē-dädh'). W. I.	20.0 N	68.53 E
6	Naviti (I.) (nä-vē'tē). Fiji Is. (In.)	17.9 S	177.21 W
6	NavuaMill (nä'vōō-ä). Fiji Is. (In.)	18.13 S	178.11 E
88	Navy I. (nā'vĭ) Can. (Niagara Falls In.)	43.3 N	79.1 W
141	Nawagai (nŭ-wŭ-gī') Pak. (Peshawar In.)	34.38 N	71.15 E
127	Naxos (I.) (năk'sŏs) Grc.	37.5 N	25.30 E
92	Nayarit (State) (nä-yä-rēt'). Mex.	21.40 N	104.40 W
92	Nayarit, Sierra de (Mts.) Mex.	23.0 N	105.0 W
124	Nazaré (nä-zä-rā') Port.	39.36 N	9.5 W
101	Nazareth (nä-zä-rĕt') Braz.	7.45 S	35.15 W
101	Nazareth Braz. (In.)	13.0 S	39.1 W
137	Nazareth (năz'ȧ-rĕth)...Pal. (In.)	32.42 N	35.16 E
80	Nazas (nä'zäs) Mex.	25.13 N	104.8 W
80	Nazas, R. Mex.	25.10 N	104.30 W
118	Naze, The (Lindesnes) (nāz) (lĭn'dĕs-nĕs). Nor.	58.0 N	7.6 E
111	Nazilli (nä-zĭ-lē') Tur.	37.50 N	28.25 E
138	Nazimovo (nä-zē'mô-fô). Sov. Un.	59.15 N	91.25 E
133	N'Délé (n'dā-lā')....Fr. Eq. Afr.	8.25 N	20.36 E
134	N'Djolé (n'dzhô-lā')..Fr. Eq. Afr.	0.12 S	10.45 E
134	Ndola (n'dō'lä) N. Rh.	13.0 S	28.43 E
114	Neagh, Lough (L.) (lŏk nā) N. Ire.	54.40 N	6.30 W
159	Neandara (nē-ȧn-dă'rȧ)....Austl.	27.20 S	149.29 E
127	Neapolis (nȧ-ŏp'ô-lĭs) Grc.	36.21 N	23.4 E
52	Near Is. (nēr) Alsk.	52.40 N	173.0 E
114	Neath (nēth) Gt. Brit.	51.38 N	3.49 W
137	Nebik (nĕb'ēk) Syr. (In.)	34.4 N	36.45 E
78	Nebraska (State) (nē-brăs'kȧ) U. S.	40.45 N	99.0 W
76	Nebraska City Neb.	40.42 N	95.52 W
81	Neches R. (nĕch'ĕz) Tex.	31.25 N	95.0 W
120	Neckar R. (nĕk'är) Ger.	49.8 N	9.10 E
102	Necochea (nā-kô-chā'ä) Arg.	38.30 S	58.40 W
99	Necol (nȧ-kōl') Arg. (Buenos Aires In.)	35.3 S	62.11 W
72	Nederland (nē'dēr-lȧnd) Colo. (Denver In.)	39.57 N	105.31 W
129	Nedrigailov (nĕ-drĭ-gī'lôf) Sov. Un.	50.49 N	33.50 E
87	Needham (nēd'ăm)....Mass. (In.)	42.17 N	71.14 W
74	Needles (nē'd'lz) Calif.	34.50 N	114.36 W
156	Neekes I. (Paketutu) (nēks) (pä-kȧ-tōō'tōō). N. Z. (In.)	36.58 S	174.45 E
77	Neenah (nē'nȧ) Wis.	44.10 N	88.28 W
140	Nefud (nĕ-fōōd') Sau. Ar.	28.45 N	41.0 E
141	Negapatam (neg'ȧ-pȧ-tăm'). India	10.38 N	79.50 E
77	Negaunee (nē-gô'nē) Mich.	46.31 N	87.35 W
127	Negoi (Mts.) (nā-goi') Rom.	45.32 N	24.35 E

Page	Name Pronunciation Region	Lat. ° ′	Long. ° ′
127	Negotin (nĕ'gô-tēn) Yugo.	44.13 N	22.34 E
141	Negrais, C. (nĕ'grīs) Bur.	16.0 N	94.10 E
124	Negreira (nā-grā'rä) Sp.	42.55 N	8.45 W
137	Negri Sembilan (State) (nā'grē sĕm-bē-län'). Malaya (In.)	2.45 N	102.0 E
124	Negro, C. (nā'grō) Mor.	35.41 N	5.18 W
95	Negro, Cumbre (Mt.) (kōōm'brā) Pan.	8.45 N	80.37 W
131	Negro, Mt....Sp. Mor. (Gib. In.)	35.39 N	5.43 E
102	Negro, R. Arg.	40.0 S	65.0 W
100	Negro R. (nā'grōō) Braz.	1.30 S	62.0 W
102	Negro, R. Braz.-Ur.	32.32 S	56.0 W
94	Negro, R. (nā'grō)....Hond.-Nic.	13.0 N	87.0 W
153	Negros (I.) (nā'grōs) Phil.	10.0 N	123.0 E
153	Negros, Cuernos de (Mt.) (kwĕr'nôs dā nā'grôs). Phil.	9.15 N	123.12 E
70	Nehalem R. (nē-hăl'ĕm) Ore.	45.60 N	123.30 W
51	Nehalem R....Ore. (Portland In.)	45.45 N	123.18 W
97	Neiba (nȧ-ē'bä) Dom. Rep.	18.28 N	71.22 W
97	Neiba B. Dom. Rep.	18.15 N	71.3 W
97	Neiba, Mts. of Dom. Rep.	18.38 N	71.33 W
71	Neihart (nī'härt) Mont.	46.55 N	110.41 W
146	Neihwang (nā'hwäng') Chn.	35.54 N	115.10 E
77	Neillsville (nēlz'vĭl) Wis.	44.35 N	90.35 W
120	Neisse R. (nīs'ĕ) Ger.-Pol.	51.30 N	14.50 E
100	Neiva (nȧ-ē'vä) (nā'vä) Col.	32.0 N	75.15 W
140	Nejd (năjd) Sau. Ar.	25.30 N	45.0 E
131	Nejila, Jebel (Mts.) (jĕb'ĕl nĕj'ĭ-lȧ). Eg. (In.)	26.40 N	32.30 E
77	Nekoosa (nē-kōō'sȧ) Wis.	44.19 N	89.53 W
118	Neksö (nĕk'sû) Den.	55.3 N	15.8 E
76	Neligh (nē'lĭg) Neb.	42.8 N	98.1 W
139	Nelkan (nĕl-kän') Sov. Un.	57.45 N	136.15 E
54	Nelson (nĕl'sŭn) Can.	49.30 N	117.2 W
116	Nelson Gt. Brit.	53.50 N	2.13 W
157	Nelson N. Z.	41.15 S	173.20 E
73	Nelson. Utah (Salt Lake City In.)	41.40 N	112.19 W
74	Nelson Cr. Nev.	40.20 N	114.40 W
53	Nelson I. Alsk.	60.30 N	164.30 W
54	Nelson R. Can.	56.0 N	96.48 W
84	Nelsonville (nĕl'sŭn-vĭl) Ohio	39.30 N	82.14 W
132	Néma (nā'mä) Fr. W. Afr.	16.45 N	7.0 W
121	Neman R. (nĕ'măn) Sov. Un.	53.39 N	22.10 E
88	Nemadji R. (nē-măd'jē) Wis. (Duluth In.)	46.40 N	92.4 W
120	Německý Brod (nyĕ'myĕt-skyĭ brōd'). Czech.	49.37 N	15.34 E
129	Nemirov (nyä-mē'rôf)...Sov. Un.	48.58 N	28.49 E
132	Nemours (nē-mōōr') Alg.	35.1 N	1.58 W
122	Nemours Fr.	48.17 N	2.40 E
119	Nemunas R. (nyĕ'mōō-nȧs) Sov. Un.	55.8 N	23.5 E
148	Nemuro (nā'mōō-rō) Jap.	43.15 N	145.30 E
148	Nemuro Str. Jap.	44.15 N	145.30 E
116	Nen, R. (nĕn) Gt. Brit.	52.18 N	0.39 W
114	Nenagh (nē'nȧ) Ire.	52.50 N	8.10 W
52	Nenana (nā-nä'nȧ) Alsk.	64.30 N	149.3 W
134	Neno (nā'nō) Nya.	15.27 S	34.40 E
79	Neodesha (nē'ō-dĕ-shô') Kan.	37.25 N	95.41 W
79	Neosho (nē-ō'shō) Mo.	36.53 N	94.23 W
79	Neosho R. Okla.	37.30 N	95.10 W
141	Nepal (nĕ-pôl') Asia	28.0 N	84.0 E
75	Nephi (nē'fī) Utah	39.43 N	111.50 W
122	Nérac (nā-räk') Fr.	44.8 N	0.20 E
160	Nerang (nĕ-răng')....Austl. (In.)	27.58 S	153.22 E
126	Nera R. (nā'rä) It.	42.40 N	12.47 E
139	Nerchinsk (nyĕr'chĕnsk). Sov. Un.	51.50 N	116.15 E
139	Nerchinski-Zavod (nyĕr'chĕn-skĭ-zȧ-vôt'). Sov. Un.	51.30 N	119.45 E
139	Nerchinski Mts. Sov. Un.	52.0 N	119.0 E
128	Nerekhta (nyĕ-rĕk'tȧ)...Sov. Un.	57.28 N	40.34 E
127	Neretva R. (nĕ'rĕt-vȧ) Yugo.	43.40 N	17.50 E
124	Nerja (nĕr'hä) Sp.	36.45 N	3.53 W
128	Nerl R. (nyĕrl) Sov. Un.	56.55 N	38.5 E
128	Nero, L. (nyĕ'rô) Sov. Un.	57.6 N	39.25 E
128	Nerusa R. (nyȧ-rōō'sȧ)..Sov. Un.	52.25 N	34.15 E
124	Nerva (nĕr'vä) Sp.	37.42 N	6.33 W
78	Ness City (nĕs) Kan.	38.26 N	99.55 W
114	Ness, Loch (lŏk nĕs)....Gt. Brit.	57.15 N	4.25 W
117	Neston (nĕs'tŭn)...Gt. Brit. (In.)	53.18 N	3.4 W
127	Nestos R. (näs'tôs) Grc.	41.15 N	24.40 E
121	Nesvich (nyĕsh'vyĕch)...Sov. Un.	53.12 N	26.41 E
120	Netherlands (nĕdh'ēr-lăndz). Eur.	52.20 N	5.50 E
150	Netherlands Borneo (nĕdh'ēr-lăndz bôr'nē-ō). Indon.	1.0 S	114.0 E
101	Netherlands Guiana (Surinam) (gē-ä'nȧ). S. A.	4.0 N	56.0 W
151	Netherlands New Guinea (gĭn'ē) New Guinea	4.0 S	138.0 E
151	Netherlands Timor (tē-mōr') Indon.	9.30 S	124.45 E
55	Netsalik L. (nĕt'sȧ-lĭk') Can.	66.30 N	71.30 W
120	Neubrandenburg (noi-brän'dĕn-bŏŏrgh). Ger.	53.33 N	13.15 E
120	Neuburg (noi'bŏŏrgh) Ger.	48.43 N	11.11 E
120	Neuchâtel (nû-shȧ-tĕl') Switz.	46.49 N	7.54 E
120	Neuchâtel, L. Switz.	46.54 N	6.51 E
117	Neuengamme (noi'ĕn-gäm'ĕ) Ger. (Hamburg In.)	53.27 N	10.13 E
123	Neufchâteau (nû-shä-tō') Fr.	48.25 N	5.42 E
122	Neufchâtel (nû-shȧ-tĕl') Fr.	49.42 N	1.28 E
117	Neugraben (noi'grä-bĕn) Ger. (Hamburg In.)	53.28 N	9.52 E
120	Neuhaldensleben (noi-häl'dĕns-lā'bĕn). Ger.	52.17 N	11.23 E
123	Neuilly (nû-yē') Fr. (In.)	48.52 N	2.17 E
117	Neukloster (noi'klōs-tēr) Ger. (Hamburg In.)	53.29 N	9.37 E
117	Neukölln (noi'kûln) Ger. (Berlin In.)	52.28 N	13.27 E
120	Neumarkt (noi'märkt) Ger.	49.17 N	11.29 E
120	Neumünster (noi'münstēr)...Ger.	54.4 N	9.59 E

Page	Name Pronunciation Region	Lat. ° ′	Long. ° ′
120	Neunkirchen (noin'kĭrk-ĕn)..Aus.	47.43 N	16.4 E
102	Neuquén (nĕ-ōō-kān') Arg.	38.59 S	68.1 W
102	Neuquén (Ter.) Arg.	39.0 S	70.30 W
102	Neuquén, R. Arg.	38.28 S	69.0 W
117	Neu-Rahlstedt (noi'-räl'shtĕt) Ger. (Hamburg In.)	53.36 N	10.9 E
120	Neu Ruppin (noi' rōō-pēn')..Ger.	52.56 N	12.47 E
83	Neuse R. (nūz) N. C.	35.20 N	78.0 W
120	Neusiedler L. (noi-zēd'lēr) Aus.-Hung.	47.46 N	16.41 E
120	Neustadt (noi'shtät) Ger.	50.20 N	11.8 E
120	Neustadt Ger.	54.7 N	10.48 E
120	Neustadt Ger.	49.22 N	8.8 E
	Neustettin, see Szczecinek, Pol.		
120	Neustrelitz (noi-strā'lĭts) Ger.	53.22 N	13.3 E
120	New Ulm (noi ōōlm') Ger.	48.23 N	10.2 E
120	Neuwied (noi'vēdt) Ger.	50.26 N	7.28 E
115	Neuzen (noi'sĕn) Neth.	51.20 N	3.50 E
77	Nevada (nē-vä'dȧ) Ia.	42.1 N	93.25 W
79	Nevada Mo.	37.50 N	94.21 W
74	Nevada (State) U. S.	39.8 N	117.0 W
74	Nevada City Calif.	39.16 N	121.3 W
100	Nevada de Mérida, Sierra (Mts.) (syĕr'rä nȧ-vä'dhä dā mä'rē-dhä). Ven.	9.0 N	70.0 W
74	Nevada, Sierra (Mts.) (nē-vä'dȧ) Calif.	36.0 N	118.40 W
124	Nevada, Sierra (Mts.) (syĕr'rä nä-vä'dhä). Sp.	37.0 N	3.10 W
102	Nevado de Cachi (Mt.) (nä-vä'dho dā kä'chē). Arg.	24.29 S	66.32 W
92	Nevado de Colima (Mt.) (nä-vä'dhō dā kō-lē'mä). Mex.	19.35 N	103.40 W
92	Nevado de Toluca (Mt.) (tô-lōō'kä). Mex.	19.8 N	99.41 W
128	Neva R. (nyĕ-vä') Sov. Un.	59.45 N	30.45 E
128	Nevel (nyĕ'vĕl) Sov. Un.	56.4 N	29.54 E
117	Nevendon (nĕv'ĕn-dŭn) Gt. Brit. (London In.)	51.36 N	0.30 E
139	Never (nē-vĕr') Sov. Un.	53.55 N	124.15 E
122	Nevers (nē-vâr') Fr.	47.0 N	3.10 E
102	Neves (nā'vĕzh) Braz. (In.)	22.52 S	43.6 W
127	Nevesinje (nĕ-vĕ'sĕn-yĕ)....Yugo.	43.15 N	18.8 E
95	Nevis (I.) (nē'vĭs)....Le. Is. (In.)	17.10 N	62.35 W
127	Nevrokop (nĕv'rō-kôp') Bul.	41.34 N	23.45 E
111	Nevsehir (nĕv-shĕ'hĕr) Tur.	38.35 N	34.40 E
110	Nevyansk (nĕv-yänsk')..Sov. Un.	57.25 N	60.10 E
84	Newago (nē-wā'gō) Mich.	43.25 N	85.50 W
84	New Albany (nū ôl'bȧ-nĭ)....Ind.	38.18 N	85.50 W
82	New Albany Miss.	34.28 N	89.0 W
101	New Amsterdam (ăm'stēr-dăm) Br. Gu.	6.15 N	57.30 W
51	Newark (nū'ērk) Calif. (San Francisco In.)	37.32 N	122.2 W
85	Newark Del.	39.41 N	75.47 W
114	Newark Gt. Brit.	53.5 N	0.50 W
85	Newark N. J.	40.45 N	74.10 W
85	Newark N. Y.	43.5 N	77.5 W
84	Newark Ohio	40.5 N	82.25 W
117	New Barnet (bär'nĕt) Gt. Brit. (London In.)	51.39 N	0.11 W
88	Newark B....N. J. (N. Y. In.)	40.41 N	74.8 W
85	New Bedford (bĕd'fērd)....Mass.	41.37 N	71.0 W
70	Newberg (nū'bûrg) Ore.	45.18 N	122.59 W
83	New Bern (bûrn) N. C.	35.6 N	77.3 W
82	Newbern Tenn.	36.7 N	89.16 W
77	Newberry (bĕr-ĭ) Mich.	46.22 N	85.30 W
83	Newberry S. C.	34.16 N	81.40 W
84	New Boston (bôs'tŭn) Ohio	38.47 N	82.56 W
80	New Braunfels (broun'fĕls)...Tex.	29.42 N	98.8 W
117	New Brighton (brī'tŭn) Gt. Brit. (Liverpool In.)	53.27 N	3.3 W
89	New Brighton Minn. (Minneapolis In.)	45.4 N	93.11 W
88	New Brighton N. Y. (In.)	40.39 N	74.5 W
157	New Brighton N. Z. (In.)	43.30 S	172.45 E
85	New Brighton Pa.	40.46 N	80.20 W
85	New Britain (brĭt''n) Conn.	41.40 N	72.48 W
151	New Britain (I.) (brĭt''n) N. Gui. Ter.	5.45 S	150.30 E
55	New Brunswick (Prov.) (brŭnz'wĭk). Can.	47.50 N	66.30 W
85	New Brunswick N. J.	40.28 N	74.28 W
84	Newburg (nū'bûrg) Ind.	37.58 N	87.26 W
79	Newburg Mo.	37.54 N	91.53 W
85	Newburgh N. Y.	41.30 N	74.1 W
114	Newbury (nū'bēr-ĭ)....Gt. Brit.	51.25 N	1.20 W
87	Newbury Mass.	42.48 N	70.52 W
86	Newburyport Mass.	42.49 N	70.55 W
159	New Caledonia (I.) (kăl-ē-dō'nĭ-ȧ). Pac. O.	21.30 S	165.30 E
86	New Carlisle (kär-līl') Can.	48.1 N	65.21 W
124	New Castile (Castilla La Nueva) (Prov.) (kăs-tēl') (käs-tēl'yä lä nwā'vä). Sp.	39.50 N	3.0 W
73	Newcastle (nū'kȧs'l) Ala. (Birmingham In.)	33.39 N	86.46 W
159	Newcastle Austl.	32.59 S	151.47 E
55	Newcastle Can.	47.8 N	65.32 W
85	New Castle Del.	39.38 N	75.36 W
116	Newcastle Gt. Brit.	53.1 N	2.14 W
114	Newcastle Gt. Brit.	54.55 N	1.37 W
84	New Castle Ind.	39.55 N	85.22 W
157	Newcastle N. Z.	44.42 S	169.15 E
84	New Castle Ohio	40.20 N	82.10 W
85	New Castle Pa.	41.0 N	80.22 W
78	Newcastle Tex.	33.12 N	98.45 W
76	Newcastle Wyo.	43.52 N	104.12 W
158	Newcastle Waters Austl.	17.12 S	133.14 E
117	Newchurch (nū'chûrch) Gt. Brit. (Liverpool In.)	53.27 N	2.31 W

ăt; finȧl; rāte; senȧte; ärm; ȧsk; sofȧ; fâre; ch-choose; dh-as th in other; bē; ēvent; bĕt; recĕnt; cratēr; g-go; gh-gutteral g; bĭt; ĭ-short neutral; rīde; ĸ-gutteral k as ch in German ich;

Newcomerstown PRONOUNCING INDEX Noatak

Page	Name Pronunciation Region	Lat. °′	Long. °′
84	Newcomerstown (nū'kŭm-ẽrz-toun) . Ohio	40.17 N	81.37 W
137	New Delhi (dĕl'hī) .... India	28.19 N	77.15 E
88	New Dorp (dŏrp) ..... N. Y. (In.)	40.35 N	74.8 W
76	Newell (nū'ĕl) .... S. D.	44.43 N	103.26 W
159	New England Plat. (nû ĭŋ'glănd) Austl.	30.0 S	152.0 E
87	Newfoundland (Prov.) (nû-fŭn'-lănd') (nū'fŭnd-lănd) (nû'found-lănd') . Can.	48.30 N	56.20 W
159	New Georgia I. (jôr'jĭ-ȧ) Solomon Is.	8.15 S	157.30 E
87	New Glasgow (glȧs'gō) ...... Can.	45.35 N	62.40 W
151	New Guinea, N. E. (Ter.) (gĭn'ē) . N. Gui. Ter.	5.0 S	144.0 E
151	New Guinea (Papua) (I.) (pă'po͞o-ȧ) . Pac. O.	6.0 S	142.0 E
151	New Guinea, Ter. of ...... Pac. O.	4.0 S	146.0 E
73	Newhall (nū'hôl) Calif. (Los Angeles In.)	34.22 N	118.32 W
86	New Hampshire (State) (hămp'shĭr) . U. S.	43.30 N	71.45 W
77	New Hampton (hămp'tŭn) .... Ia.	43.4 N	92.19 W
84	New Harmony (här'mô-nĭ) ... Ind.	38.9 N	87.56 W
160	New Haven (hāv''n) Austl. (Adelaide In.)	34.49 S	138.31 E
85	New Haven .... Conn.	41.18 N	72.58 W
84	New Haven .... Ind.	41.4 N	85.1 W
157	Newhaven .... N. Z.	46.27 S	169.43 E
159	New Hebrides (Is.) (hĕb'rĭ-dēz) Pac. O.	17.0 S	169.0 E
116	New Holland (hŏl'ănd) .. Gt. Brit.	53.42 N	0.21 W
83	New Holland .... N. C.	35.27 N	76.15 W
81	New Iberia (ī-bē'rĭ-ȧ) .... La.	30.0 N	91.50 W
117	Newington (nū-ĭng-tŭn) Gt. Brit. (London In.)	51.21 N	0.39 E
151	New Ireland (I.) (īr'lănd) N. Gui. Ter.	3.20 S	152.0 E
85	New Jersey (State) (jûr'zĭ) .. U. S.	40.0 N	74.30 W
85	New Kensington (kĕn'zĭng-tŭn) Pa.	40.35 N	79.45 W
79	Newkirk (nū'kûrk) .... Okla.	36.53 N	97.3 W
138	New Land (Novaya Zemlya) (nô'vä-yä zĕm-lyȧ') . Sov. Un.	74.0 N	57.0 E
84	New Lexington (lĕk'sĭng-tŭn) . Ohio	39.45 N	82.12 W
77	New Lisbon (lĭz'bŭn) .... Wis.	43.54 N	90.10 W
85	New London (lŭn'dŭn) ..... Conn.	41.20 N	72.8 W
79	New London .... Wis.	44.24 N	88.42 W
156	New Lynn (lĭn) .... N. Z. (In.)	36.55 S	174.41 E
79	New Madrid (măd'rĭd) ...... Mo.	36.35 N	89.32 W
117	New Malden (môl'dĕn) Gt. Brit. (London In.)	51.24 N	0.16 W
76	Newman Grove .... Neb.	41.46 N	97.45 W
83	Newman L. (nū'măn) .... Fla.	29.40 N	82.14 W
85	Newmarket (nū'mär-kĕt) .... Can.	44.3 N	79.28 W
84	New Martinsville (mär'tĭnz-vĭl) W. Va.	39.47 N	80.52 W
75	New Mexico (State) (mĕk'sĭ-kō) U. S.	34.45 N	107.30 W
116	New Mills .... Gt. Brit.	53.22 N	2.0 W
82	Newnan (nū'năn) .... Ga.	33.22 N	84.48 W
160	New Norfolk (nôr'fŏk) Austl. (Tas. In.)	42.46 S	147.5 E
81	New Orleans (ôr'lê-ănz) ...... La.	30.0 N	90.5 W
89	New Orleans .... La. (In.)		
84	New Philadelphia (fĭl-ȧ-dĕl'fĭ-ȧ) Ohio	40.30 N	81.27 W
156	New Plymouth (plĭm'ŭth) ... N. Z.	39.5 S	174.5 E
79	Newport (nū'pōrt) .... Ark.	35.35 N	91.16 W
160	Newport .... Austl.	37.51 S	144.53 E
114	Newport .... Gt. Brit.	50.40 N	1.20 W
114	Newport .... Gt. Brit.	51.35 N	3.0 W
116	Newport .... Gt. Brit.	52.46 N	2.22 W
84	Newport .... Ky.	39.4 N	84.30 W
86	Newport .... Me.	44.50 N	69.18 W
89	Newport . Minn. (Minneapolis In.)	44.52 N	93.0 W
86	Newport .... N. H.	43.25 N	72.10 W
85	Newport .... R. I.	41.27 N	71.20 W
82	Newport .... Tenn.	35.56 N	83.12 W
86	Newport .... Vt.	44.57 N	72.16 W
70	Newport .... Wash.	48.11 N	117.2 W
74	Newport Beach .... Calif.	33.37 N	117.56 W
85	Newport News .... Va.	36.57 N	76.26 W
116	Newport Pagnell (păg'nĕl) . Gt. Brit.	52.5 N	0.43 W
77	New Prague (prāg) .... Minn.	44.31 N	93.32 W
96	New Providence (I.) (prŏv'ĭ-dĕns) Ba. Is.	25.2 N	77.25 W
83	New R. (nū) .... Va.	36.50 N	80.58 W
84	New Richmond (rĭch'mŭnd) .. Ohio	38.57 N	84.17 W
77	New Richmond .... Wis.	45.8 N	92.31 W
81	New Roads .... La.	30.42 N	91.26 W
85	New Rochelle (rô-shĕl') ..... N. Y.	40.55 N	73.47 W
76	New Rockford (rŏk'förd) ... N. D.	47.41 N	99.9 W
114	New Ross (rôs) .... Ire.	52.25 N	6.55 W
139	New Siberian Is. (sī-bē'rĭ-ăn) Sov. Un.	75.30 N	145.0 E
83	New Smyrna (smûr'nȧ) ...... Fla.	29.2 N	80.56 W
159	New South Wales (State) ... Austl.	33.0 S	146.0 E
84	Newton (nū'tŭn) .... Ill.	39.0 N	88.10 W
77	Newton .... Ia.	41.42 N	93.1 W
79	Newton .... Kan.	38.3 N	97.21 W
87	Newton .... Mass. (In.)	42.20 N	71.12 W
82	Newton .... Miss.	32.18 N	89.10 W
85	Newton .... N. J.	41.5 N	74.48 W
83	Newton .... N. C.	35.40 N	81.13 W
81	Newton .... Tex.	30.50 N	93.46 W
116	Newton-in-Makerfield (nū'tŭn-ĭn-māk'ẽr-fēld) . Gt. Brit.	53.27 N	2.37 W
56	Newton Siding Can. (Winnipeg In.)	49.55 N	98.2 W
114	Newtownards (nū-t'n-ärdz') N. Ire.	54.35 N	5.40 W
77	New Ulm (ŭlm) .... Minn.	44.19 N	94.25 W
153	New Washington (wŏsh'ĭng-tŭn) Phil.	11.39 N	122.25 E
87	New Waterford (wô'tẽr-fẽrd) . Can.	46.15 N	60.5 W
54	New Westminster (wĕst'mĭn-stẽr) Can.	49.12 N	122.54 W
85	New York .... N. Y.	40.40 N	73.50 W
88	New York (yôrk) ..... N. Y. (In.)		
85	New York (State) .... U. S.	43.0 N	76.0 W
156	New Zealand (zē'lănd) .... Pac. O.	42.0 S	174.0 E
92	Nexapa, R. (nĕks-ä'pä) ..... Mex.	18.45 N	98.26 W
93	Nexquipayac (nĕs-kē-pä-yäk') Mex. (In.)	19.35 N	98.56 W
129	Nezhin (nyĕzh'ēn) ...... Sov. Un.	51.4 N	31.53 E
70	Nez Perce (nĕz' pûrs') .... Ida.	46.15 N	116.15 W
156	Ngakauranga ('n-gä-kou-räŋ'gȧ) N. Z. (In.)	41.15 S	174.49 E
134	Ngami, L. (n'gä'mē) .... Bech.	20.30 S	22.40 E
133	Ngaoundéré (n'gōn-dȧ-rā') .. Cam.	7.21 N	13.33 E
156	Ngaruawahia ('n-gä-ro͞o'ȧ-wä'hē-ä) N. Z.	37.40 S	175.13 E
156	Ngaruroro R. ('n-gä'ro͞o-rō'rō) N. Z.	39.30 S	176.22 E
156	Ngaurohoe (Vol.) ('n-gou-rō'hō-ĕ) N. Z.	39.10 S	175.38 E
131	Ngolo ('n-gō'lō) Fr. Eq. Afr. (Brazzaville In.)	4.47 S	14.30 E
135	Ngomeni ('n-gô-mā'nē) ...... Tan.	5.8 S	38.53 E
135	Ngong ('n-gông) .... Kenya	1.18 S	36.35 E
133	N'Guigmi ('n-gēg'mē) . Fr. W. Afr.	14.18 N	13.3 E
132	Nguru ('n-go͞o'ro͞o) .... Nig.	12.55 N	10.28 E
150	Nhatrang (nyä-träng') .... Indoch.	12.14 N	109.5 E
132	Niafunke (nyä-fo͝on'kĕ) Fr. W. Afr.	15.58 N	4.15 W
77	Niagara (nī-ăg'ȧ-rȧ) .... Wis.	45.46 N	88.3 W
55	Niagara Falls .... Can.	43.10 N	79.12 W
85	Niagara Falls .... N. Y.	43.5 N	79.2 W
88	Niagara Falls .... N. Y. (In.)		
88	Niagara-on-the-Lake Can. (Niagara Falls In.)	43.14 N	79.4 W
85	Niagara R. .... N. Y.	43.5 N	79.2 W
132	Niamey (nē-ä-mā') .... Fr. W. Afr.	13.40 N	2.3 E
133	Niangara (nē-äŋ-gä'rȧ) . Bel. Cong.	3.34 N	27.59 E
79	Niangua R. (nī-ăŋ'gwȧ) ...... Mo.	37.50 N	92.50 W
131	Niari R. (nyä-rē') Fr. Eq. Afr. (Brazzaville In.)	4.10 S	13.50 E
150	Nias I. (nē-äs') .... Indon.	1.0 N	97.40 E
118	Nibe (nē'bĕ) .... Den.	56.58 N	9.39 E
94	Nicaragua (nĭk-ȧ-rä'gwȧ) . Cen. Am.	12.50 N	85.0 W
94	Nicaragua, L. .... Nic.	11.30 N	85.30 W
126	Nicastro (nē-käs'trō) .... It.	38.58 N	16.19 E
123	Nice (nēs) .... Fr.	43.41 N	7.18 E
55	Nichikun L. (nĭch'ĭ-kŭn) .... Can.	53.15 N	70.40 W
96	Nicholas Chan. (nĭk'ô-lȧs) ... W. I.	23.20 N	80.0 W
84	Nicholasville .... Ky.	37.55 N	84.35 W
150	Nicobar, Great (I.) (nĭk-ô-bär') India	7.0 N	93.45 E
150	Nicobar Is. .... India	7.45 N	93.30 E
129	Nicoreşti (nē-kô-rĕsht'') .... Rom.	45.59 N	27.14 E
113	Nicosia (nē-kô-sē'ȧ) .... Cyp.	35.12 N	33.22 E
94	Nicoya (nē-kō'yä) .... C. R.	10.7 N	85.27 W
94	Nicoya, G. of .... C. R.	10.0 N	85.0 W
94	Nicoya Pen. .... C. R.	10.0 N	86.0 W
99	Nictheroy (Niteroi) (nĭk-tē-roi') (nē-tĕ-rō'ĭ) Braz. (Rio de Janeiro In.)	22.54 S	43.6 W
118	Nidaros (Trondheim) (nē'dȧ-rôs) (trôn'hâm) . Nor.	63.26 N	10.21 E
116	Nidd, R. (nĭd) .... Gt. Brit.	54.3 N	1.42 W
121	Nidzica (nē-jĕt'sȧ) .... Pol.	53.22 N	20.30 E
120	Nienburg (nē'ĕn-bo͝orgh) ..... Ger.	52.38 N	9.14 E
142	Nienchen Tangla (Mts.) (nyĕn'chĕn' tän'glä) . Chn.	30.0 N	90.0 E
117	Niendorf (nē'ĕn-dôrf) Ger. (Hamburg In.)	53.37 N	9.57 E
143	Nienkachow (nyĕn'kä-chō') Chn. (Shanghai In.)	31.9 N	121.29 E
117	Nienstedten (nēn'shtĕt-ĕn) Ger. (Hamburg In.)	53.33 N	9.51 E
160	Nietta (nĭ-ĕt'ȧ) .. Austl. (Tas. In.)	41.21 S	146.4 E
117	Nieuwkerken Waes (nē-kĕr'kĕn vä'ĕs) . Bel. (Anvers In.)	51.12 N	4.10 E
101	Nieuw Nickerie (nē-nē' kĕ-rē') . Sur.	5.45 N	57.0 W
92	Nieves (nyā'vȧs) .... Mex.	24.2 N	102.56 W
131	Nifîsha (nē-fēs'hȧ) Eg. (Suez Can. In.)	30.34 N	32.17 E
111	Nigde (nĭg'dĕ) .... Tur.	37.58 N	34.38 E
132	Nigeria (nī-jē'rĭ-ȧ) .... Afr.	9.0 N	8.0 E
132	Niger R. (nī'jẽr) . Fr. W. Afr.-Nig.	14.0 N	1.30 E
132	Niger, Ter. of the ..... Fr. W. Afr.	16.0 N	7.0 E
157	Nightcaps (nīt'kăps) .... N. Z.	45.57 S	168.3 E
148	Niigata (nē'ē-gä'tȧ) .... Jap.	37.50 N	139.7 E
155	Niihau (I.) (nē'ē-hä'o͞o) ..... Haw.	21.55 N	160.10 W
149	Niijima (I.) (nē'jē-mä) .... Jap.	34.25 N	139.15 E
149	Niimi (nē'mē) .... Jap.	34.59 N	133.29 E
148	Niitaka (Mt.) (nē'tä-kä) . For. (In.)	23.29 N	120.53 E
124	Níjar (nē'här) .... Sp.	36.56 N	2.11 W
120	Nijmegen (nī'mȧ-gĕn) ...... Neth.	51.50 N	5.52 E
149	Nikaido (nē'kī-dō) Jap. (Osaka In.)	34.37 N	135.48 E
128	Nikitinka (nē-kĭ'tĭn-kȧ) .. Sov. Un.	55.33 N	33.22 E
149	Nikko (nēk'kō) .... Jap.	36.45 N	139.38 E
129	Nikolaev (nē-kô-lä'yĕf) .. Sov. Un.	46.58 N	32.1 E
111	Nikolaevsk (nē-kô-lä'yĕfsk) Sov. Un.	50.2 N	45.30 E
139	Nikolaevsk .... Sov. Un.	53.20 N	140.35 E
120	Nikolsburg (Mikulov) (nē'kôls-bo͝org) (mĭ'ko͝o-lôf) . Czech.	48.47 N	16.38 E
110	Nikolsk (nē-kôlsk') ...... Sov. Un.	59.30 N	45.30 E
138	Nikolskoe (nē-kôl'skô-yĕ) . Sov. Un.	69.40 N	60.30 E
127	Nikopol (nē'kô-pŏl') .... Bul.	43.40 N	24.51 E
129	Nikopol .... Sov. Un.	47.35 N	34.25 E
127	Nikšić (nēk'shēch) .... Yugo.	42.46 N	18.59 E
133	Nile R. (nīl) .... Afr.	22.40 N	32.0 E
51	Niles (nīlz) Calif. (San Francisco In.)	37.35 N	121.59 W
88	Niles .... Ill. (Chicago In.)	42.1 N	87.48 W
84	Niles .... Mich.	41.50 N	86.17 W
84	Niles .... Ohio	41.13 N	80.47 W
88	Niles Center ..... Ill. (Chicago In.)	42.2 N	87.45 W
160	Nilumbik (nī-lŭm'bĭk) Austl. (Melbourne In.)	37.40 S	145.10 E
132	Nimba, Mt. (nĭm'bȧ) .. Fr. W. Afr.	7.45 N	8.30 W
122	Nimes (nēm) .... Fr.	43.50 N	4.22 E
133	Nimule (nē-mo͞o'lā) .... A. E. Sud.	3.40 N	32.9 E
150	Ninbinh (nēn-bēnᴋ') ..... Indoch.	20.15 N	106.5 E
159	Ninety Mile Beach .... Austl.	38.18 S	147.18 E
140	Ninevah (Ruins) (nĭn'ē-vȧ) .. Iraq	36.8 N	43.15 E
143	Ningan (nĭŋ'găn') .... Chn.	44.25 N	129.36 E
145	Ninghai (nĭng'hī') .... Chn.	29.18 N	121.26 E
146	Ninghai .... Chn.	37.24 N	121.34 E
146	Ningho (nĭng'hō') .... Chn.	39.26 N	117.33 E
145	Ninghwa (nĭng'hwä') .... Chn.	26.9 N	116.30 E
145	Ningkwo (nĭng'kwô') .... Chn.	30.58 N	118.43 E
145	Ningkwohsien (nĭng'kwô'syĕn') Chn.	30.37 N	118.59 E
142	Ninghsia (nĭng'syä') .... Chn.	38.27 N	106.6 E
142	Ninghsia (Prov.) .... Chn.	40.15 N	102.30 E
146	Ningling (nĭng'lĭng') .... Chn.	34.33 N	115.33 E
145	Ningpo (nĭng-pō') .... Chn.	29.53 N	121.34 E
144	Ningsiang (nĭng'syäng') ..... Chn.	28.17 N	112.12 E
146	Ningtsin (nĭng'tsĭn) .... Chn.	37.42 N	114.57 E
146	Ningtsin .... Chn.	37.50 N	116.39 E
146	Ningtsin L. .... Chn.	37.40 N	115.20 E
145	Ningtu (nĭng'to͞o') .... Chn.	26.27 N	115.44 E
143	Ningwu (nĭng'wo͞o') .... Chn.	39.15 N	112.10 E
145	Ningyang (nĭng'yäng') ...... Chn.	25.34 N	117.15 E
144	Ningyüan (nĭng'yü-än') ..... Chn.	25.37 N	111.47 E
142	Ningyüan .... Chn.	27.57 N	102.21 E
151	Ninigo Is. (nē-nē'gō) . N. Gui. Ter.	1.20 S	144.15 E
117	Ninkop (nēn'kŭp) Ger. (Hamburg In.)	53.31 N	9.47 E
78	Ninnescah R. (nĭn'ĕs-kä) .... Kan.	37.36 N	98.0 W
101	Nioaqua (nē-ô-ä'kwä) ..... Braz.	21.2 S	55.45 W
76	Niobrara R. (nī-ô-brâr'ȧ) .... Neb.	42.47 N	101.0 W
132	Nioro (nē-ō'rō) .... Fr. W. Afr.	15.23 N	9.27 W
122	Niort (nē-ôr') .... Fr.	46.20 N	0.28 W
97	Nipe B. (nē'pā) .... Cuba	20.48 N	75.40 W
97	Nipe, Sierra de (Mts.) ...... Cuba	20.28 N	75.48 W
55	Nipigon (nĭp'ĭ-gŏn) .... Can.	49.0 N	88.5 W
77	Nipigon B. .... Can.	48.55 N	88.0 W
55	Nipigon L. .... Can.	49.50 N	88.30 W
77	Nipigon R. .... Can.	49.12 N	88.20 W
86	Nipisiquit R. (nĭ-pĭ'sĭ-kwĭt) .. Can.	47.25 N	66.20 W
55	Nipissing, L. (nĭp'ĭ-sĭng) .... Can.	46.15 N	79.48 W
96	Niquero (nē-kā'rō) .... Cuba	20.1 N	77.36 W
140	Niriz, L. (nē-rēz') .... Iran	29.30 N	53.40 E
127	Niš (nēsh) .... Yugo.	43.17 N	21.53 E
124	Nisa (nē'sȧ) .... Port.	39.32 N	7.42 W
127	Nišava R. (nē'shȧ-vȧ) ...... Yugo.	43.13 N	22.20 E
140	Nishapur (nĭsh-ȧ-po͞or') ...... Iran	36.14 N	58.40 E
149	Nishino I. (nēsh'ē-nō) .... Jap.	36.5 N	133.5 E
149	Nishinomiya (nēsh'ē-nô-mē'yä) Jap. (Osaka In.)	34.45 N	135.20 E
149	Nishinoomote (nēsh'ē-nô-ô-mō'tō) Jap.	30.44 N	131.0 E
148	Nishi Notoro, C. (nē'shē nō'tô-rō) Sakh.	45.59 N	142.2 E
149	Nishio (nēsh'ē-ô) .... Jap.	34.51 N	137.3 E
79	Nishnabotna R. (nĭsh-nȧ-bŏt'nȧ) Ia.-Mo.	40.30 N	95.36 W
79	Nishnabotna R., East .... Ia.	41.05 N	95.15 W
79	Nishnabotna R., West .... Ia.	41.10 N	95.15 W
117	Nisida I. (nē'zê-dä) . It. (Napoli In.)	40.47 N	14.10 E
121	Nisko (nēs'kô) .... Pol.	50.30 N	22.7 E
51	Nisqually (nĭs-kwôl'ĭ) Wash. (Seattle In.)	47.4 N	122.41 W
70	Nisqually R. .... Wash.	46.50 N	122.20 W
118	Nissa R. (nĭs-sȧ) .... Swe.	56.58 N	13.10 E
118	Nisser L. (nĭs'ẽr) .... Nor.	59.14 N	8.29 E
129	Nistrul (Dnester, Dniester) R. (nēst'ro͝ol) . Sov. Un.	47.35 N	29.8 E
101	Niterói (nē-tĕ-rô'ĭ) .... Braz.	22.59 S	43.1 W
114	Nith (R.) (nĭth) .... Gt. Brit.	55.10 N	3.50 W
121	Nitra (nē'trȧ) .... Czech.	48.18 N	18.4 E
121	Nitra R. .... Czech.	48.25 N	18.8 E
84	Nitro (nī'trō) .... W. Va.	38.24 N	81.51 W
110	Nitva (nyĕt'vȧ) .... Sov. Un.	58.2 N	55.15 E
	Niuchwangcheng, see Yingkow, Chn.		
115	Nivelles (nē'vĕl') .... Bel.	51.37 N	4.20 E
122	Nivernais, Hills of the (nē-vĕr-nĕ') Fr.	47.10 N	3.30 E
72	Niwot (nī'wŏt) . Colo. (Denver In.)	40.7 N	105.10 W
81	Nixon (nĭk'sŭn) .... Tex.	29.17 N	97.45 W
111	Nizhne Chirskaya (nēzh'nyĕ chēr'skä-yȧ) . Sov. Un.	48.20 N	43.2 E
139	Nizhne Kamchatsk (käm-chätsk') Sov. Un.	56.20 N	161.40 E
139	Nizhne Kolymsk (kô-lēmsk') Sov. Un.	68.35 N	160.59 E
110	Nizhne Sergi (sĕr-gē) .... Sov. Un.	56.35 N	59.25 E
138	Nizhneudinsk (nēzh'nyĕ-o͞o-dēnsk') . Sov. Un.	54.55 N	99.15 E
129	Nizhnie Mayachki (nēzh'nyĕ mȧ-yäch'kĭ) . Sov. Un.	46.29 N	33.5 E
129	Nizhnie Serogazi (sā'rô-gä'zē) Sov. Un.	46.51 N	34.22 E
	Nizhni-Novgorod, see Gorki, Sov. Un.		
138	Nizhni Tagil (nēzh'nyē tȧ-gēl') Sov. Un.	57.50 N	59.55 E
118	Njurunda (nyo͞o-ro͝on'dȧ) .... Swe.	62.16 N	17.20 E
52	Noatak R. (nô-ȧ'tȧk) .... Alsk.	68.0 N	159.30 W

ng-sing; ŋ-baŋk; ɴ-nasalized n; nŏd; cŏmmit; ōld; ôbey; ôrder; fo͞od; fo͝ot; ou-out; s-soft; sh-dish; th-thin; pūre; ûnite; ûrn; stŭd; circŭs; ü-as "y" in study; '-indeterminate vowel.

Page	Name Pronunciation Region	Lat. °′	Long. °′
149	Nobeoka (nō-bȧ-ō'kȧ).......Jap.	32.36 N	131.40 E
84	Noblesville (nō'bl'z-vĭl)......Ind.	40.2 N	86.2 W
92	Nochistlán (nô-chēs-tlän')...Mex.	21.25 N	102.57 W
93	Nochixtlán (Asunción) (ä-sōōn-syōn').Mex.	17.27 N	97.13 W
79	Nodaway R. (nŏd'ȧ-wā)..Mo.-Ia.	40.30 N	95.4 W
151	Noemfoor (Mafor) (I.) (nōōm'fōr) (mä-fōr').Neth. N. Gui.	0.45 S	135.30 E
129	Nogaisk (nô-gīsk').......Sov. Un.	46.42 N	36.17 E
75	Nogales (nô-gä'lĕs).........Ariz.	31.21 N	110.56 W
93	Nogales....................Mex.	18.49 N	97.8 W
122	Nogent-en-Bassigny nô-zhäɴ'äɴ-bȧ-sē-nyē').Fr.	48.0 N	5.25 E
122	Nogent-le-Retrou (lĕ-rē-trōō').Fr.	48.21 N	0.50 E
123	Nogent-sur-Marne (sür-märn') Fr. (In.)	48.50 N	2.28 E
122	Nogent-sur-Seine (sür-sān')....Fr.	48.30 N	3.30 E
128	Noginsk (nô-gēnsk').....Sov. Un.	55.50 N	38.25 E
124	Nogueira (nô-gā'rä)..........Sp.	42.26 N	7.44 E
125	Nogueira Pallarisa R. (pä-lyä-rē'sä).Sp.	42.15 N	1.0 E
148	Noho (Bordo chan) (nô'hô') (bôr'dô' chän').Chn.	48.30 N	124.44 E
122	Noire Mts. (nwȧr)...........Fr.	48.5 N	3.50 W
122	Noirmoutier, Ile de (I.) (nwȧr-mōō-tyā').Fr.	47.0 N	2.15 W
123	Noisiel (nwȧ-zyĕl')......Fr. (In.)	48.51 N	2.37 E
123	Noisy-le-Grand (nwȧ-zē'-lē-gräɴ') Fr. (In.)	48.50 N	2.33 E
123	Noisy-le Sec (nwä'zē-lē sĕk') Fr. (In.)	48.53 N	2.27 E
149	Nojimi, C. (nō'jē-mē)........Jap.	34.55 N	139.55 E
54	Nokomis (nô-kō'mĭs)........Can.	51.31 N	105.10 W
79	Nokomis.....................Ill.	39.17 N	89.16 W
126	Nola (nô'lä)..................It.	40.55 N	14.33 E
83	Nolichucky R. (nŏl-ĭ-chŭk'ĭ).Tenn.	36.10 N	82.30 W
110	Nolinsk (nô-lēnsk')......Sov. Un.	57.30 N	49.55 E
77	Nomakagon R. (nō-mȧ-kā'gŏn) Wis.	45.55 N	91.50 W
149	Nomami C. (nō'mä-mē)......Jap.	31.28 N	130.15 E
52	Nome (nōm)..................Alsk.	64.25 N	165.30 W
150	Nong-Khây (nŏng-ᴋä'ē).....Siam	17.58 N	102.52 E
134	Nongoma (nŏn-gō'mȧ)..U. S. Afr.	27.52 S	31.40 E
143	Nonni R. (nŏn'ē)...........Chn.	47.30 N	123.57 E
72	Nooksack (nŏŏk'săk) Wash. (Vancouver In.)	48.56 N	122.19 W
72	Nooksack R. Wash. (Vancouver In.)	48.53 N	122.33 W
160	Noosa Hd. (nōō'sȧ)...Austl. (In.)	26.20 S	153.6 E
54	Nootka I. (nōōt'kȧ).........Can.	49.40 N	126.50 W
134	Nogui (nô-kē')..............Ang.	6.0 S	13.35 E
118	Nora (nô'rä)................Swe.	59.31 N	14.59 E
55	Noranda (nô-răn'dȧ)........Can.	48.25 N	79.10 W
79	Norborne (nôr'bôrn).........Mo.	39.16 N	93.38 W
73	Norco (nôr'kô) Calif. (Los Angeles In.)	33.56 N	117.34 W
73	Norcross (nôr'krôs) Ga. (Atlanta In.)	33.57 N	84.13 W
120	Norden (nôr'dĕn)...........Ger.	53.36 N	7.12 E
139	Nordenskjöld Sea (nôr'dĕn-shûl) Sov. Un.	74.30 N	126.0 E
120	Norderney (I.) (nôr'dĕr-nī).Neth.	53.43 N	7.15 E
118	Nord Fjord (nôr'fyôr).......Nor.	61.55 N	5.35 E
120	Nordhausen (nôrt'hau-zĕn)...Ger.	51.30 N	10.47 E
120	Nordhorn (nôrt'hôrn).......Ger.	52.26 N	7.3 E
51	Nordland (nôrd'lȧnd) Wash. (Seattle In.)	48.2 N	122.42 W
120	Nördlingen (nûrt'lĭng-ĕn)....Ger.	48.52 N	10.29 E
114	Nore, R. (nōr)..............Ire.	52.30 N	7.10 W
82	Norfield (nôr'fēld).........Miss.	31.24 N	90.18 W
87	Norfolk (nôr'fŏk).....Mass. (In.)	42.7 N	71.19 W
76	Norfolk....................Neb.	42.2 N	97.24 W
85	Norfolk.....................Va.	36.50 N	76.18 W
89	Norfolk...............Va. (In.)		
159	Norfolk I...............Pac. O.	29.8 S	168.8 E
92	Noria (nō'rē-ȧ)..............Mex.	23.31 N	106.15 W
138	Norilsk (nô-rēlsk').......Sov. Un.	69.20 N	82.28 E
79	Normal (nôr'mȧl)..............Ill.	40.31 N	88.59 W
54	Norman (nôr'măn)..........Can.	64.50 N	125.20 W
79	Norman.....................Okla.	35.13 N	97.26 W
156	Normanby..................N. Z.	39.33 S	174.15 E
87	Norman, C..................Can.	51.47 N	55.55 W
122	Normandy, Hills of (nôr'măn-dē) Fr.	48.40 N	0.10 W
159	Norman R. (nôr'măn)......Austl.	18.30 S	141.20 E
159	Normanton (nôr'mȧn-tŭn)..Austl.	17.38 S	141.0 E
116	Normanton............Gt. Brit.	53.41 N	1.25 W
54	Norman Wells..............Can.	65.17 N	126.45 W
158	Nornalup (nôr-năl'ŭp).....Austl.	34.45 S	116.47 E
148	Nor R. (nōr)................Chn.	47.2 N	133.0 E
118	Nörresundby (nû-rĕ-sōōn'bü).Den.	57.4 N	9.55 E
59	Norris L...................Tenn.	36.15 N	83.30 W
85	Norristown (nŏr'ĭs-town).....Pa.	40.8 N	75.20 W
118	Norrköping (nôr'chûp'ĭng)...Swe.	58.36 N	16.11 E
118	Norrköping B...............Swe.	58.35 N	16.55 E
118	Norrtälje (nôr-tĕl'yĕ).......Swe.	59.47 N	18.41 E
158	Norseman (nôrs'măn)......Austl.	32.12 S	121.55 E
86	North Adams (ăd'ămz).....Mass.	42.42 N	73.5 W
160	North Adelaide (ăd'ē-lād) Austl. (Adelaide In.)	34.54 S	138.37 E
158	Northam (nôr'dhăm)......Austl.	31.47 S	116.40 E
50	North America (ȧ-mĕr'ĭ-kȧ)		
91	North American Basin (Sea) Atl. O.	22.30 N	61.40 W
158	Northampton (nôr-thămp'tŭn) Austl.	28.47 S	114.40 E
114	Northampton...........Gt. Brit.	52.15 N	0.55 W
86	Northampton.............Mass.	42.20 N	72.40 W
85	Northampton................Pa.	40.42 N	75.30 W
116	Northampton Co........Gt. Brit.	52.21 N	1.0 W
87	North Andover (ăn'dô-vĕr) Mass. (In.)	42.42 N	71.7 W
153	North Balabac Str. (bä-lä'bäk) Phil.	8.10 N	117.0 E
73	North Baldy (bôl'dĭ) Calif. (Los Angeles In.)	34.22 N	117.46 W
84	North Baltimore (bôl'tĭ-môr).Ohio	41.12 N	83.40 W
54	North Battleford (băt''l-fērd).Can.	52.50 N	108.29 W
55	North Bay..................Can.	46.16 N	79.30 W
70	North Bend.................Ore.	43.23 N	124.15 W
86	North Berwick (bûr'wĭk).....Me.	43.19 N	70.45 W
96	North Bight (bĭt).........Ba. Is.	24.25 N	77.43 W
96	North Bimini I. (bĭ'mĭ-nē).Ba. Is.	25.46 N	79.17 W
150	North Borneo (bôr'nē-ō)..Borneo	5.30 N	117.0 E
87	Northboro (nôrth'bûr-ô) Mass. (In.)	42.19 N	71.38 W
86	Northbridge (nôrth'brĭj)....Mass.	42.10 N	71.40 W
97	North Caicos I. (kī'kôs)...Ba. Is.	1.57 N	72.0 W
87	North C....................Can.	47.0 N	60.25 W
156	North Cape.................N. Z.	34.21 S	173.2 E
108	North Cape.................Nor.	71.5 N	26.0 E
83	North Carolina (State) (kăr-ô-lī'nȧ).U. S.	35.40 N	78.50 W
84	North Channel..............Can.	46.5 N	83.0 W
114	North Channel.........Gt. Brit.	55.0 N	5.30 W
77	North Chicago (shĭ-kô'gō).....Ill.	42.19 N	87.51 W
80	North Concho R. (kŏn'chō)..Tex.	31.50 N	101.0 W
160	Northcote (nôrth'kôt) Austl. (Melbourne In.)	37.46 S	144.59 E
156	Northcote............N. Z. (In.)	36.50 S	174.48 E
76	North Dakota (State) (dȧ-kō'tȧ) U. S.	47.40 N	100.20 W
114	North Downs (dounz)...Gt. Brit.	51.15 N	0.20 E
83	Northeast Cape Fear R.....N. C.	34.45 N	77.55 W
89	Northeast Pass La. (New Orleans In.)	29.8 N	89.3 W
97	Northeast Pt.............Ba. Is.	24.38 N	75.40 W
97	Northeast Pt.............Ba. Is.	21.20 N	73.0 W
97	Northeast Pt.............Ba. Is.	22.45 N	73.51 W
96	Northeast Providence Channel (prŏv'ĭ-dĕns).Ba. Is.	25.42 N	77.0 W
120	Northeim (nôrt'hīm)........Ger.	51.42 N	10.0 E
117	Northenden (nôr'dhĕn-dĕn) Gt. Brit. (Liverpool In.)	53.24 N	2.15 W
71	Northern Cheyenne Ind. Res. (shī-ĕn').Mont.	45.30 N	106.40 W
114	Northern Highlands.....Gt. Brit.	57.20 N	5.0 W
114	Northern Ireland (īr'lănd) Gt. Brit.	55.0 N	7.0 W
139	Northern Land (Severnaya Zemlya).Sov. Un.	79.0 N	103.0 E
77	Northern Light L...........Can.	48.17 N	90.43 W
132	Northern Provinces.........Nig.	11.0 N	8.0 E
134	Northern Rhodesia (rô-dē'zhĭ-ȧ) Afr.	14.15 S	29.30 E
132	Northern Territories........G. C.	10.0 N	1.45 W
158	Northern Territory........Austl.	20.0 S	134.0 E
77	Northfield (nôrth'fēld).....Minn.	44.28 N	93.9 W
86	Northfield....................Vt.	44.10 N	72.39 W
115	North Foreland (fōr'lȧnd).Gt. Brit.	51.20 N	1.22 E
51	North Fork Reservoir Wash. (Portland In.)	46.1 N	122.27 W
80	North Franklin Park (frăŋ'klĭn) Tex.	31.55 N	106.30 W
160	North Fremantle (frē'măn-t'l) Austl. (Perth In.)	32.2 S	115.43 E
120	North Frisian I. (frĭzh'ȧn)...Ger.	54.40 N	8.30 E
156	North Havelock...........N. Z.	39.43 S	177.8 E
74	North I..............Calif. (In.)	32.40 N	117.13 W
156	North I...................N. Z.	38.0 S	174.0 E
84	North Judson (jŭd'sŭn)......Ind.	41.13 N	86.47 W
79	North Little Rock..........Ark.	34.46 N	92.16 W
84	North Manchester (măn'chĕs-tēr) Ind.	41.0 N	85.47 W
114	North Minch (Chan.)...Gt. Brit.	58.10 N	6.0 W
89	North Oakwood (ōk'wŏŏd) Va. (Norfolk In.)	36.55 N	76.15 W
117	North Ockendon (ŏk'ĕn-dŭn) Gt. Brit. (London In.)	51.32 N	0.18 E
73	North Ogden (ŏg'dĕn) Utah (Salt Lake City In.)	41.18 N	111.57 W
73	North Ogden Park Utah (Salt Lake City In.)	41.22 N	111.57 W
111	North Ossetia (Aut. Area) (ŏ-sē'shȧ).Sov. Un.	43.0 N	44.15 E
156	North Palmerston (päm'ēr-stŭn) N. Z.	40.18 S	175.38 E
89	North Pass. La. (New Orleans In.)	29.12 N	89.3 W
78	North Platte (plăt).........Neb.	41.09 N	100.46 W
58	North Platte R............U. S.	41.15 N	101.30 W
48	North Pole		
160	North Pt.....Austl. (Sydney In.)	33.49 S	151.19 E
95	North Pt............Barb. (In.)	13.20 N	59.37 W
84	North Pt..................Mich.	45.0 N	83.15 W
82	Northport (nôrth'pōrt).......Ala.	33.12 N	87.36 W
70	Northport.................Wash.	48.54 N	117.44 W
87	North Reading (rĕd'ĭng) Mass. (In.)	42.34 N	71.4 W
116	North Riding (borough) (rī'dĭng) Gt. Brit.	54.12 N	1.9 W
114	North Ronaldshay (I.) (rŏn'ăld-shȧ).Gt. Brit. (In.)	59.20 N	2.25 W
89	North St. Paul Minn. (Minneapolis In.)	45.0 N	93.0 W
73	North Salt Lake Utah (Salt Lake City In.)	40.51 N	111.56 W
118	North Sea................Atl. O.	55.20 N	3.0 W
88	North Shore Channel Ill. (Chicago In.)	42.5 N	87.40 W
160	North Sydney (sĭd'nē) Austl. (Sydney In.)	33.49 S	151.11 E
87	North Sydney..............Can.	46.12 N	60.15 W
72	North Table Mt. Colo. (Denver In.)	39.48 N	105.12 W
156	North Taranaki Bight (tȧ-rȧ-nä'kĭ bīt).N. Z.	38.50 S	174.30 E
85	North Tonawanda (tŏn-ȧ-wŏn'dȧ) N. Y.	43.2 N	78.54 W
56	North Transcona (trăns-kō'nȧ) Can. (Winnipeg In.)	49.55 N	97.0 W
75	North Truchas Peaks (trōō'chäs) N. M.	35.38 N	105.47 W
153	North Ubian I. (ōō-bē-än')..Phil.	6.9 N	120.28 E
114	North Uist (I.) (wĭst)...Gt. Brit.	57.40 N	7.20 W
86	Northumberland (nôr-thŭm'bēr-lȧnd).N. H.	44.33 N	71.32 W
86	Northumberland, (B.).......Can.	46.30 N	64.0 W
72	Northumberland Channel Can. (Vancouver In.)	49.12 N	123.55 W
159	Northumberland Is........Austl.	21.45 S	150.15 E
70	North Umpqua R. (ŭmp'kwȧ).Ore.	43.21 N	123.0 W
70	North Vancouver (văn-kōō'vēr) Can.	49.18 N	123.6 W
84	North Vernon (vûr'nŭn).....Ind.	39.3 N	85.42 W
158	North West C.............Austl.	21.50 S	114.10 E
96	Northwest Providence Channel (prŏv'ĭ-dĕns).Ba. Is.	26.10 N	78.20 W
158	North West Region........Austl.	24.0 S	117.30 E
54	Northwest Territories.......Can.	64.30 N	107.0 W
116	Northwich (nôrth'wĭch)..Gt. Brit.	53.15 N	2.31 W
83	North Wilkesboro (wĭlks'bûrô) N. C.	36.10 N	81.10 W
76	Northwood................N. D.	47.43 N	97.32 W
77	Northwood (nôrth'wŏŏd)......Ia.	43.28 N	93.12 W
71	North Wood Cr............Wyo.	44.10 N	107.30 W
114	North York Moors (nôrth yôrk mŏŏrz').Gt. Brit.	54.20 N	1.0 W
78	Norton (nôr'tŭn)...........Kan.	39.49 N	99.54 W
83	Norton......................Va.	36.57 N	82.37 W
52	Norton B..................Alsk.	64.30 N	161.30 W
52	Norton Sd.................Alsk.	64.0 N	163.0 W
73	Norwalk (nôr'wôk) Calif. (Los Angeles In.)	33.54 N	118.5 W
85	Norwalk..................Conn.	41.7 N	73.26 W
84	Norwalk..................Ohio	41.14 N	82.36 W
118	Norway (nôr'wā)...........Eur.	61.0 N	8.0 E
86	Norway.....................Me.	44.12 N	70.32 W
77	Norway...................Mich.	45.48 N	87.55 W
54	Norway House.............Can.	54.2 N	98.1 W
108	Norwegian Sea (nôr-wē'jăn) Atl. O.	65.40 N	1.30 E
87	Norwell (nôr'wĕl).....Mass. (In.)	42.10 N	70.47 W
85	Norwich (nôr'wĭch).......Conn.	41.31 N	72.4 W
115	Norwich (nôr'ĭch).......Gt. Brit.	52.40 N	1.20 E
85	Norwich (nôr'wĭch)........N. Y.	42.32 N	75.32 W
160	Norwood (nôr'wŏŏd) Austl. (Adelaide In.)	34.55 S	138.38 E
86	Norwood..................Mass.	42.12 N	71.11 W
83	Norwood..................N. C.	35.14 N	80.8 W
84	Norwood..................Ohio	39.10 N	84.25 W
151	Norzagaray (nôr'zä-gä-rä'ē) Phil. (Manila In.)	14.55 N	121.2 E
148	Noshap C. (nō'shäp')........Jap.	43.28 N	145.40 E
148	Noshiro (nō'shē-rô).........Jap.	40.11 N	140.2 E
134	Nosob R. (nô'sŏb).S. W. Afr.-Bech.	24.45 S	20.0 E
129	Nosovka (nô'sôf-kȧ).....Sov. Un.	50.56 N	31.34 E
135	Nossi Be (I.) (nô-sē'bā')..Madag.	13.15 S	48.15 E
135	Nossy-Vey (I.) (nô-sē'vā').Madag.	23.32 S	43.32 E
121	Noteć R. (nô'tĕch)..........Pol.	53.5 N	17.13 E
118	Notodden (nôt'ôd'n)........Nor.	59.35 N	9.18 E
149	Noto Pen. (nô'tō)...........Jap.	37.15 N	137.0 E
83	Notoway R. (nŏt'ô-wā).......Va.	36.52 N	77.30 W
87	Notre Dame B. (nō't'r dȧm').Can.	49.40 N	55.25 W
84	Nottawasaga B. (nŏt'ȧ-wȧ-sā'gȧ) Can.	44.40 N	80.30 W
55	Nottaway R. (nôt'ȧ-wā).....Can.	51.0 N	7.28 W
114	Nottingham (nŏt'ĭng-ăm).Gt. Brit.	52.55 N	1.10 W
116	Nottingham Co.........Gt. Brit.	53.8 N	1.0 W
131	Noual Sebkheten (L.) (sĕb'ᴋĕt-ĕn nōō-ȧl').Tun. (In.)	34.23 N	9.45 E
159	Nouméa (nōō-mā'ä)......N. Cal.	22.14 S	166.30 E
132	Noun, C. (nô-ōōn')......R. de O.	28.45 N	11.15 W
86	Nouvelle (nōō-vĕl')..........Can.	48.7 N	66.18 W
133	Nouvelle Anvers (nōō-vĕl' äɴ-vâr').Bel. Cong.	1.39 N	19.7 E
122	Nouzonville (nōō-zôɴ-vēl')....Fr.	49.48 N	4.48 E
101	Nova (nō'vȧ)..............Braz.	20.20 S	42.28 W
99	Nova Friburgo (nō'vȧ frē-bŏŏr'-gŏŏ).Braz. (Rio de Janeiro In.)	22.20 S	42.33 W
141	Nova Goa (nō'vȧ gō'ȧ).....India	15.25 N	74.5 E
134	Nova Lisboa (Huambo) (nō'vȧ lēzh-bô'ȧ).Ang.	12.45 S	15.47 E
126	Novara (nô-vä'rä).............It.	45.26 N	8.38 E
55	Nova Scotia (Prov.) (nō'vȧ skō'shȧ).Can.	45.0 N	64.0 W
127	Nova Varoš (nô'vȧ vä'rôsh).Yugo.	43.24 N	19.50 E
51	Novato (nô-vä'tō) Calif. (San Francisco In.)	38.5 N	122.32 W
129	Novaya Odessa (nô'vȧ-yȧ ô-dĕs'ä).Sov. Un.	47.18 N	31.47 E
129	Novaya Praga (nô'vȧ-yȧ prä'gȧ) Sov. Un.	48.34 N	32.55 E
129	Novaya Vodolaga (nô'vȧ-yȧ vô-dôl'ȧ-gȧ).Sov. Un.	49.42 N	35.51 E
139	Novaya Sibir I. (nô'vȧ-yȧ sē-bēr') Sov. Un.	75.15 N	148.0 E
138	Novaya Zemlya (New Land) (nô'vȧ-yȧ zĕm-lyȧ').Sov. Un.	74.0 N	57.0 E
127	Nova Zagora (nô'vȧ zä'gô-rȧ).Bul.	42.29 N	26.1 E
125	Novelda (nō-vĕl'dȧ)..........Sp.	38.24 N	0.45 W
151	Noveleta (nō-vȧ-lā'tä) Phil. (Manila In.)	14.26 N	120.51 E
121	Nové Mesto (nô'vĕ myĕs'tō) Czech.	48.47 N	17.49 E
121	Nové Zámky (nô'vĕ zäm'kē) Czech.	47.59 N	18.10 E

ăt; finăl; rāte; senâte; ärm; ȧsk; sofȧ; fâre; ch-choose; dh-as th in other; bē; ēvent; bĕt; recĕnt; cratēr; g-go; gh-gutteral g; bĭt; ĭ-short neutral; rīde; ᴋ-gutteral k as ch in German ich;

Page	Name Pronunciation Region	Lat. °′	Long. °′
128	Novgorod (nôv′gô-rŏt)...Sov. Un.	58.32 N	31.18 E
128	Novgorod (Dist.).......Sov. Un.	58.30 N	32.30 E
129	Novgorod-Seversk (syĕ′vĕrsk) Sov. Un.	52.1 N	33.16 E
126	Novi (nô′vē)................It.	44.45 N	8.49 E
129	Novi Bug (nô′vē bo͝og′)..Sov. Un.	47.41 N	32.30 E
129	Novie Senzhary (nô′vyĕ sĕn′zhȧ-rē).Sov. Un.	49.18 N	34.18 E
126	Novi Grad (nô′vē gråd′)....Yugo.	44.11 N	15.34 E
79	Novinger (nŏv′ĭn-jẽr).........Mo.	40.14 N	92.43 W
129	Novi Oskol (nô′vē ôs-kôl′) Sov. Un.	50.46 N	57.52 E
127	Novi Pazar (nô′vē pȧ-zär′)..Yugo.	43.7 N	20.31 E
127	Novi Sad (nô′vē säd′)......Yugo.	45.16 N	19.51 E
129	Novo-Aidar (nô′vô-ī-där′) Sov. Un.	48.57 N	38.59 E
129	Novo Belaya (nô′vô byĕ′lȧ-yȧ) Sov. Un.	49.52 N	39.29 E
129	Novo Belenkaya (nô′vô byĕl-ĕŋ′kȧ-yȧ).Sov. Un.	49.44 N	39.5 E
129	Novocherkassk (nô′vô-chĕr-kȧsk′) Sov. Un.	47.25 N	40.5 E
134	Novo Lisboa (Huambo) (nô′vo͞o lēzh bō′ȧ) (hwäm′bô).Ang.	12.45 S	15.47 E
126	Novo Mesto (nô′vô mās′tô).Yugo.	45.47 N	15.12 E
129	Novo Minskaya (nô′vô mēn′skȧ-yȧ).Sov. Un.	46.18 N	38.51 E
129	Novomirgorod (nô′vô-mēr′gô-rôt) Sov. Un.	48.46 N	31.42 E
129	Novomoskovsk (nô′vô-môs-kôfsk′) Sov. Un.	48.37 N	35.15 E
134	Novo Redondo (nô′vo͞o rå-dôn′do͞o) Ang.	11.13 S	13.54 E
129	Novorossiisk (nô′vô-rô-sēsk′) Sov. Un.	44.42 N	37.48 E
128	Novorshev (nô′vô-rzhôf′) Sov. Un.	57.2 N	29.18 E
127	Novo-selo (nô′vô-sĕ′lô).......Bul.	44.7 N	22.45 E
129	Novo Shcherbinovskaya (nô′vô shchĕr-bē-nôf′skȧ-yȧ).Sov. Un.	46.27 N	38.32 E
138	Novosibirsk (nô′vô-sē-bērsk′) Sov. Un.	55.10 N	82.59 E
128	Novosil (nô′vô-sēl′).....Sov. Un.	52.58 N	37.1 E
128	Novo Sokolniki (nô′vô sô-kôl′ṇē-kē).Sov. Un.	56.18 N	30.2 E
138	Novo-Turukhansk (nô′vô-to͞o-ro͞o-ᴋänsk′).Sov. Un.	65.55 N	88.30 E
129	Novo-Ukrainka (nô′vô-o͞o-krēn′kȧ).Sov. Un.	48.17 N	31.32 E
129	Novoukrainsk (nô′vô-o͞o-krēnsk′) Sov. Un.	48.28 N	31.30 E
111	Novouzensk (nô′vô-o͝o-zĕnsk′) Sov. Un.	50.32 N	48.12 E
128	Novozybkov (nô′vô-zēp′kôf) Sov. Un.	52.32 N	31.53 E
120	Nový Bydžov (nô′vē bē′jôf).Czech.	50.14 N	15.30 E
121	Nový Jičiń(nô′vē yē′chēn′).Czech.	49.36 N	18.1 E
79	Nowata (nô-wä′tȧ).........Okla.	36.43 N	95.37 W
120	Nowawes (nō′vä-vĕs′).......Ger.	52.23 N	13.4 E
121	Novogrodok (nō′vō-gro͝o′dôk) Sov. Un.	53.36 N	25.51 E
120	Nowa Sól (nô′vȧ sŭl′)........Pol.	51.49 N	15.41 E
121	Nowy Dwór (nô′vē dvo͝or′)...Pol.	52.27 N	20.47 E
121	Nowy Port (nô′vĭ po͝ort′).....Pol.	54.24 N	18.40 E
121	Nowy Sącz (nô′vē sôɴch′)....Pol.	49.38 N	20.43 E
121	Nowy Targ (nô′vē tärk′).....Pol.	49.29 N	20.1 E
82	Noxubee R. (nŏks′û-bē).Miss.-Ala.	33.0 N	88.28 W
124	Noya (nō′yä)..................Sp.	42.46 N	8.54 W
125	Noya R...............Sp. (In.)	41.27 N	1.45 E
122	Noyon (nwä-yôɴ′)............Fr.	49.37 N	3.0 E
133	Nubian Des. (no͞o′bĭ-ăn).A. E. Sud.	21.0 N	34.0 E
80	Nueces R. (nû-ā′sås).........Tex.	28.30 N	99.40 W
54	Nuelton L. (nwĕl′tŭn).......Can.	60.15 N	95.30 W
94	Nueva Armenia (nwā′vä är-mā′nē-ȧ).Hond.	15.50 N	86.40 W
96	Nueva Gerona (nwā′vä ᴋå-rō′nä) Isle of Pines	21.51 N	82.41 W
99	Nueva Palmira (nwä′vä päl-mē′-rä).Ur. (Buenos Aires In.)	33.52 S	58.23 W
94	Nueva San Salvador (Santa Tecla) (nwā′vä sän′ säl-vȧ-dōr′).Sal.	13.41 N	89.17 W
102	Nueve de Julio (nwā′vå dā ho͞o′lyô).Arg.	35.30 S	61.00 W
96	Nuevitas (nwā-vē′täs)......Cuba	21.34 N	77.16 W
96	Nuevitas B................Cuba	21.34 N	77.14 W
80	Nuevo Laredo (nwā′vō lä-rā′dhō) Mex.	27.29 N	99.30 W
80	Nuevo Leon (State) (nwā′vô lå-ōn′).Mex.	26.0 N	100.0 W
143	Nuichwangcheng (Yinkow) (nwē′chwäng-chĕng).Chn.	40.57 N	122.30 E
122	Nuits-St. George (nwē-săɴ zhôrzh′).Fr.	47.10 N	5.0 E
111	Nukha (no͞o′ᴋä)........Sov. Un.	41.15 N	47.12 E
52	Nulato (no͞o-lä′tō)..........Alsk.	64.40 N	158.15 W
125	Nules (no͞o′lås)..............Sp.	39.53 N	0.11 W
158	Nullarbor Plain (nŭ-lär′bôr).Austl.	30.45 S	130.40 E
158	Nullarbor Region..........Austl.	31.15 S	128.0 E
149	Numasu (no͞o′mä-so͞o).......Jap.	35.8 N	138.52 E
118	Nummedalslaagen (R.) (no͝om′ĕ-dȧls-lôgh′ĕn).Nor.	60.0 N	9.18 E
116	Nuneaton (nŭn′ē-tŭn)...Gt. Brit.	52.30 N	1.30 W
57	Nun I. (no͞on).Can. (Montreal In.)	45.28 N	73.33 W
54	Nunivak (no͞o′nĭ-văk).......Can.	68.15 N	135.20 W
53	Nunivak I...............Alsk.	60.5 N	166.30 W
143	Nünkiang (Mergen) (nün′kyäng′) (mĕr′gĕn).Chn.	49.20 N	125.27 E
126	Nuoro (nwô′rō)............Sard.	40.20 N	9.19 E
138	Nur Ata (no͞or′ ät′ä)....Sov. Un.	40.30 N	65.30 E
138	Nura R. (no͞o′rä)........Sov. Un.	50.0 N	74.0 E
120	Nürnberg (nürn′bĕrgh)......Ger.	49.27 N	11.5 E
97	Nurse Cay (I.)..........Ba. Is.	22.28 N	75.50 W
111	Nusaybin (no͞o′sī-bēn).......Tur.	37.5 N	41.10 E
141	Nushki (nŭsh′kē)...........Pak.	29.29 N	66.0 E
85	Nutter Fort (nŭt′ẽr)......W. Va.	39.14 N	80.18 W
53	Nutzotin Mts. (no͞ot′zô-tĭn) Alsk.-Can.	62.0 N	141.0 W
134	Nyangwe (nyäng′wå)..Bel. Cong.	4.15 S	26.15 E
134	Nyassa L. (nyä′sä)..........Afr.	12.0 S	34.30 E
134	Nyasaland (nyä′sä-lănd).....Afr.	13.0 S	34.0 E
132	Nyasso (nyä′sō)......Fr. W. Afr.	14.47 N	4.46 W
118	Nyborg (nü′bôr″)..........Den.	55.19 N	10.45 E
118	Nybro (nü′brô)..............Swe.	56.44 N	15.56 E
118	Nyhem (nü′hĕm).............Swe.	56.39 N	12.51 E
121	Nyíregyháza (nyē′rĕd-y′-hä′zä) Hung.	47.58 N	21.44 E
118	Nyköbing Fl. (nü′kû-bĭng)...Den.	54.45 N	11.54 E
118	Nyköbing S................Den.	55.55 N	11.40 E
118	Nyköbing...................Den.	56.46 N	8.48 E
118	Nyköping (nü′chû-pĭng).....Swe.	58.46 N	17.0 E
117	Nylen (nē′lĕn)...Bel. (Anvers In.)	51.10 N	4.40 E
134	Nylstroom (nĭl′strōm)..U. S. Afr.	24.42 S	28.18 E
159	Nymagee (nī-mȧ-gē′)......Austl.	32.2 S	146.19 E
160	Nymboida R. (nĭm-bô-ē′dȧ) Austl. (In.)	29.40 S	152.31 E
120	Nymburk (nêm′bo͝ork)....Czech.	50.11 N	15.2 E
77	Nymore (nī′mōr)..........Minn.	47.27 N	94.50 W
118	Nynäshamn (nü-nĕs-häm′n)..Swe.	58.54 N	17.58 E
159	Nyngan (nĭŋ′gȧn).........Austl.	31.33 S	147.12 E
120	Nyon (nē-ôɴ′).............Switz.	46.23 N	6.13 E
132	Nyong R. (nyông).........Cam.	3.35 N	11.0 E
120	Nýřany (nêr-zhä′nē)......Czech.	49.43 N	13.13 E
121	Nysa (nē′sȧ)................Pol.	50.28 N	17.20 E
129	Nystad (Uusikaupunki) (nü′ståd) (o͞o′sē-kou′po͝oŋ-kĭ).Fin.	60.49 N	21.28 E
139	Nyuya R. (nyo͞o′yȧ).....Sov. Un.	60.50 N	115.0 E
155	Oahu (I.) (ō-ä′ho͞o) (ō-ā′hû).Haw.	21.25 N	158.0 W
56	Oak Bluff....Can. (Winnipeg In.)	49.47 N	97.20 W
78	Oak Creek (ōk krēk′).......Colo.	40.18 N	106.57 W
74	Oakdale (ōk′dāl)...........Calif.	37.45 N	120.52 W
84	Oakdale....................Ky.	38.14 N	85.51 W
81	Oakdale....................La.	30.49 N	92.39 W
89	Oakdale......Pa. (Pittsburgh In.)	40.24 N	80.12 W
82	Oakdale...................Tenn.	35.59 N	84.32 W
116	Oakengates (ōk′ĕn-gāts)..Gt. Brit.	52.41 N	2.27 W
76	Oakes (ōks)...............N. D.	46.9 N	98.4 W
86	Oakfield (ōk′fēld)...........Me.	46.8 N	68.10 W
73	Oak Flat..Calif. (Los Angeles In.)	34.14 N	117.18 W
88	Oak Forest.....Ill. (Chicago In.)	41.36 N	87.44 W
116	Oakham (ōk′ăm).......Gt. Brit.	52.40 N	0.43 W
56	OakHammock.Can.(WinnipegIn.)	50.8 N	97.3 W
84	Oakharbor (ōk′här′bẽr)......Ohio	41.31 N	83.8 W
51	Oak Harbor...Wash. (Seattle In.)	48.17 N	122.38 W
77	Oak I.....................Wis.	46.55 N	90.45 W
74	Oakland (ōk′lănd).........Calif.	37.48 N	122.15 W
79	Oakland...................Kan.	39.4 N	95.40 W
76	Oakland...................Neb.	41.51 N	96.27 W
84	Oakland City...............Ind.	38.20 N	87.22 W
160	Oakleigh (ōk′lå) Austl. (Melbourne In.)	37.53 S	145.5 E
160	Oakley............Austl. (In.)	27.24 S	151.42 E
71	Oakley (ōk′lĭ)...............Ida.	42.14 N	113.53 W
78	Oakley....................Kan.	39.6 N	100.49 W
82	Oakman (ōk′măn)...........Ala.	33.42 N	87.22 W
89	Oakmont (ōk′mŏnt) Pa. (Pittsburgh In.)	40.31 N	79.51 W
79	Oak Park....................Ill.	41.53 N	87.43 W
81	Oakwood (ōk′wo͝od).........Tex.	31.38 N	95.50 W
157	Oamaru (ô-ä′mä-ro͞o).......N. Z.	45.7 S	171.2 E
160	Oatlands (ōt′lăndz) Austl. (Tas. In.)	42.19 S	147.23 E
75	Oatman (ōt′măn)...........Ariz.	35.3 N	114.23 W
93	Oaxaca (State) (wä-hä′kä)...Mex.	17.0 N	96.0 W
93	Oaxaca....................Mex.	17.4 N	96.43 W
93	Oaxaca, Sierra de (Mts.).....Mex.	16.20 N	97.20 W
149	Obama (ō′bȧ-mä)...........Jap.	35.30 N	135.44 E
114	Oban (ō′băn)..........Gt. Brit.	45.25 N	5.30 W
151	Obando (ō-bän′dō) Phil. (Manila In.)	14.43 N	120.55 E
86	Obatogamau L. (ō-bȧ-tō′găm-ô) Can.	49.35 N	74.30 W
135	Obbia (ôb′byä).............Som.	5.25 N	48.25 E
	Obdorsk, see Sale Khard, Sov. Un.		
120	Oberhausen (ō′bĕr-hou′zĕn)..Ger.	51.30 N	6.49 E
120	Oberhollabrünn (ō′bĕr-hō′la-brün) Aus.	48.34 N	16.4 E
78	Oberlin (ō′bẽr-lĭn)..........Kan.	39.48 N	100.31 W
84	Oberlin...................Ohio	41.17 N	82.12 W
123	Obernai (ô-bẽr-nĕ′)...........Fr.	48.30 N	7.30 E
138	Ob, G. of (ôp)..........Sov. Un.	69.0 N	73.30 E
101	Obidos (ō′bē-do͝ozh).........Braz.	1.59 S	55.30 W
148	Obihiro (ō′bē-hē′rō).........Jap.	42.55 N	143.12 E
151	Obi Is. (ō′bē)............Indon.	1.30 S	127.45 E
82	Obion R. (ô-bī′ŏn)..........Tenn.	36.10 N	89.20 W
82	Obion R., North Fork......Tenn.	36.26 N	88.40 W
82	Obion R., South Fork......Tenn.	36.5 N	88.45 W
151	Obira I. (ô-bē′rä).........Indon.	1.50 S	127.35 E
129	Obitochnaya, C. (ô-bē-tôch′nȧ-yȧ).Sov. Un.	46.31 N	36.8 E
135	Obock (ō-bŏk′)..........Fr. Som.	12.0 N	43.17 E
128	Obol R. (ô-bŏl′).........Sov. Un.	55.25 N	29.32 E
129	Oboyan (ô-bô-yän′).....Sov. Un.	5.12 N	36.18 E
138	Ob′ R. (ôp)............Sov. Un.	61.20 N	70.0 E
51	O′Brien (ô-brī′ĕn) Wash. (Seattle In.)	47.25 N	122.15 W
129	Obukhov (ō′bo͞o-ᴋôf)....Sov. Un.	50.7 N	30.35 E
83	Ocala (ô-kä′lȧ)...............Fla.	29.11 N	82.10 W
92	Ocampo (ô-käm′pō)........Mex.	22.50 N	99.20 W
100	Ocaña (ô-kän′yä)............Col.	8.0 N	73.30 W
124	Ocaña......................Sp.	39.57 N	3.30 W
100	Occidental, Cordillera (Mts.) (ôk-sē-dĕn-täl′).Col.	5.0 N	76.30 W
97	Ocean Bight............Ba. Is.	21.15 N	73.15 W
85	Ocean City.................Md.	38.20 N	75.7 W
85	Ocean City................N. J.	39.17 N	74.37 W
85	Ocean Grove..............N. J.	40.12 N	74.0 W
56	Oceanic (ō-shē-ăn′ĭk) Can. (Prince Rupert In.)	54.7 N	130.15 W
73	Ocean Park.Calif. (Los Angeles In.)	33.59 N	118.29 W
74	Oceanside (ō′shăn-sīd)......Calif.	33.10 N	117.21 W
82	Ocean Springs.............Miss.	30.25 N	88.49 W
89	Ocean View.....Va. (Norfolk In.)	36.57 N	76.15 W
129	Ochakov (ô-chä′kôf).....Sov. Un.	46.37 N	31.31 E
82	Ochlockonee R. (ŏk-lô-kō′nē) Fla.-Ga.	30.36 N	84.20 W
117	Ochsenwärder (ôk′sĕn-vâr′dẽr) Ger. (Hamburg In.)	53.29 N	10.6 E
82	Ocilla (ô-sĭl′ȧ)...............Ga.	31.36 N	83.18 W
118	Ockelbo (ôk′ĕl-bô)..........Swe.	60.54 N	16.39 E
82	Ocmulgee R. (ôk-mŭl′gē).....Ga.	32.40 N	83.35 W
121	Ocna-Sibiului (ōk′nȧ-sē-byo͞o′-lo͞o-ē).Rom.	45.53 N	24.3 E
127	Ocnele-Mari (ōk′nĕ-lĕ-mä′rē) Rom.	45.4 N	24.19 E
97	Ocoa B. (ô-kō′ȧ)......Dom. Rep.	18.25 N	70.38 W
82	Oconee R. (ô-kō′nē).........Ga.	33.0 N	83.10 W
77	Oconomowoc (ô-kŏn′ô-mô-wŏk′) Wis.	43.7 N	88.29 W
77	Oconto (ô-kŏn′tō)..........Wis.	44.54 N	87.52 W
77	Oconto Falls...............Wis.	44.53 N	88.10 W
77	Oconto R..................Wis.	45.5 N	88.22 W
94	Ocós (ô-kōs′)..............Guat.	14.33 N	92.12 W
94	Ocotal (ō-kô-täl′)...........Nic.	13.45 N	86.30 W
93	Ocotepec, Cerro (Mt.) (ô-kō-tå-pĕk′).Mex. (In.)	19.22 N	98.49 W
94	Ocotepeque (ô-kō-tå-pā′kå).Hond.	14.26 N	89.12 W
92	Ocotlán (ō-kô-tlän′)........Mex.	20.20 N	102.45 W
93	Ocotlán de Morelos (dā mô-rā′lōs).Mex.	16.48 N	96.41 W
93	Ocozingo (ô-kô-zĭŋ′gô)......Mex.	17.3 N	92.12 W
93	Ocozocoautla (ô-kō′zô-kwä-o͞o′tlä) Mex.	16.46 N	93.22 W
122	Octeville (ôkt′vēl′)...........Fr.	49.35 N	1.35 W
100	Ocumare del Tuy (ō-ko͞o-mä′rā del twē′).Ven.	10.2 N	66.45 W
108	Odádahraun (Plat.) (ō-dä′dhȧ-hroun′).Ice.	65.20 N	17.20 W
149	Odawara (ō′dȧ-wä′rä)........Jap.	35.15 N	139.10 E
118	Odda (ôdh-ȧ)...............Nor.	60.3 N	6.33 E
108	Oddi (ôdh′ē)................Ice.	63.43 N	20.20 W
76	Odebolt (ō′dē-bōlt)...........Ia.	42.20 N	95.15 W
124	Odemira (ō-då-mē′rȧ).......Port.	37.36 N	8.39 W
111	Ödemis (û′dĕ-mēsh).........Tur.	38.12 N	28.0 E
118	Odense (ō′dhĕn-sĕ)..........Den.	55.23 N	10.22 E
73	Odenville (ō′dĕn-vĭl) Ala. (Birmingham In.)	33.41 N	86.24 W
120	Oder R. (ō′dẽr).........Ger.-Pol.	51.50 N	15.43 E
80	Odessa (ô-dĕs′ȧ)............Tex.	31.51 N	102.21 W
129	Odessa (ô-dĕs′sä).......Sov. Un.	46.27 N	30.48 E
70	Odessa (ô-dĕs′ȧ)..........Wash.	47.20 N	118.42 W
124	Odiel R. (ō-dē-ĕl′)............Sp.	37.30 N	6.56 W
132	Odienné (ō-dē-ĕn-nā′)..Fr. W. Afr.	9.48 N	7.32 W
153	Odiongan (ō-dē-ôŋ′gän).....Phil.	12.24 N	121.59 E
125	Odivellas (ō-dē-vā′lyäs).Port. (In.)	38.48 N	9.10 W
121	Odobesti (ō-dô-bĕsh′t′).....Rom.	45.46 N	27.5 E
139	Odoma R. (ō′dô-mȧ)....Sov. Un.	59.45 N	138.0 E
80	O′Donnell (ō-dŏn′ĕl)........Tex.	32.57 N	101.50 W
121	Odorhei (ō-dôr-hā′)........Rom.	46.18 N	25.17 E
120	Odra (Oder) R. (ô′drȧ) (ō′dẽr).Pol.	52.3 N	15.0 E
101	Oeirás (wå-ē-räzh′).........Braz.	7.10 S	42.2 W
125	Oeirás..............Port. (In.)	38.42 N	9.19 W
117	Oeleghem (o͞o′lĕgh-ĕm) Bel. (Anvers In.)	51.13 N	4.36 E
120	Oelsnitz (ûl′snēts)..........Ger.	50.26 N	12.11 E
120	Oelsnitz...................Ger.	50.42 N	12.43 E
77	Oelwein (ōl′wīn).............Ia.	42.41 N	91.55 W
71	O′Fallon Cr. (ō-făl′ŭn).....Mont.	46.30 N	104.50 W
126	Ofanto R. (ô-fän′tō)..........It.	41.10 N	15.55 E
120	Offenbach (ôf′ĕn-bäᴋ).......Ger.	50.6 N	8.45 E
120	Offenburg (ôf′ĕn-bo͝orgh).....Ger.	48.27 N	7.57 E
108	Öfvertorneå (ûf′ĕr-tōr′nĕ-ô)..Swe.	66.18 N	23.35 E
149	Oga (ō′gȧ)......Jap. (Osaka In.)	34.49 N	135.6 E
149	Ogaki (ō′gä-kē).............Jap.	35.22 N	136.32 E
76	Ogallala (ō-gä-lä′lä).........Neb.	41.8 N	101.41 W
5	Ogasawara (Bonin) (Is.) (ô-gä′sȧ-wä′rȧ) (bō′nĭn).Pac. O.	28.0 N	141.30 E
132	Ogbomosho (ŏg-bô-mō′shō)..Nig.	8.7 N	4.9 E
77	Ogden (ŏg′dĕn)...............Ia.	42.1 N	94.1 W
71	Ogden.....................Utah	41.14 N	111.59 W
73	Ogden Pk. Utah (Salt Lake City In.)	41.12 N	111.53 W
73	Ogden R. Utah (Salt Lake City In.)	41.15 N	111.53 W
73	Ogden R., Middle Fork Utah (Salt Lake City In.)	41.18 N	111.44 W
73	Ogden R., North Fork Utah (Salt Lake City In.)	41.23 N	111.53 W
73	Ogden R., South Fork Utah (Salt Lake City In.)	41.16 N	111.40 W
85	Ogdensburg (ŏg′dĕnz-bûrg)..Can.	44.41 N	75.30 W
83	Ogeechee R. (ô-gē′chē).......Ga.	32.48 N	82.0 W
53	Ogilvie (ō′g′l-vĭ)............Can.	63.20 N	129.30 W
79	Oglesby (ō′g′lz-bĭ)............Ill.	41.16 N	89.4 W
126	Oglio R. (ōl′yō)..............It.	45.10 N	10.20 E
88	Ogontz (ō′gŏnts) Pa. (Philadelphia In.)	40.4 N	75.8 W
134	Ogowe R. (ō-gô-wā′)..Fr. Eq. Afr.	0.10 S	11.30 E
126	Ogulin (ō-go͞o-lēn′).........Yugo.	45.18 N	15.12 E
156	Ohakune (ô-hä′ko͞o-nē)......N. Z.	39.23 S	175.27 E
156	Ohariu R. (ô-hä′rē-o͞o)..N. Z. (In.)	41.14 S	174.45 E
156	Ohau B. (ō-hä′o͞o).....N. Z. (In.)	41.14 S	174.41 E
157	Ohau L....................N. Z.	44.15 S	169.55 E
156	Ohau Pt............N. Z. (In.)	41.14 S	174.40 E
84	Ohio (State) (ô′hī′ō)........U. S.	40.20 N	82.40 W
59	Ohio R...................U. S.	37.45 N	87.45 W

ng-sing; ŋ-baŋk; ɴ-nasalized n; nŏd; cŏmmit; ōld; ôbey; ôrder; fo͞od; fo͝ot; ou-out; s-soft; sh-dish; th-thin; pūre; ûnite; ûrn; stŭd; circŭs; ü-as "y" in study; ′-indeterminate vowel.

Ohoopee PRONOUNCING INDEX Orkla

Page	Name Pronunciation Region	Lat. °'	Long. °'
83	Ohoopee R. (ô-hōō'pē) . . . . Ga.	32.30 N	82.30 W
127	Ohrid (ō'krĕd) . . . . Yugo.	41.7 N	20.49 E
127	Ohrid, L. . . . . Yugo.-Alb.	41.0 N	20.45 E
156	Ohura (ô-hōō'rȧ) . . . . N. Z.	38.55 S	175.3 E
149	Oigawa R. (ō'ê-gä'wȧ) . . . . . . Jap.	35.10 N	138.10 E
85	Oil City . . . . Pa.	41.26 N	79.43 W
72	Oil Cr. . . . . . Colo. (Colo. Sprs. In.)	38.38 N	105.13 W
139	Oimekon (oi-mĕ-kôn) . . . . Sov. Un.	63.15 N	142.55 E
138	Oirat (Aut. Ter.) (oi-rät') . Sov. Un.	51.10 N	87.0 E
138	Oirat-Tura (Ulala) (tōō'rä) Sov. Un.	51.58 N	85.57 E
122	Oise R. (wäz) . . . . Fr.	49.25 N	2.40 E
148	Oita (ō'ê-tä) . . . . Jap.	33.14 N	131.35 E
117	Öjendorf (û'yĕn-dôrf) Ger. (Hamburg In.)	53.33 N	10.8 E
118	Öjer, L. (û'yĕr) . . . . Nor.	59.50 N	11.0 E
149	Oji (ō'jê) . . . . Jap. (Tokyo In.)	35.45 N	139.45 E
80	Ojinaga (ō-kê-nä'gä) . . . . Mex.	29.35 N	104.25 W
93	Ojitlán (San Lucas) (ō-kê-tlän') Mex.	18.4 N	96.23 W
92	Ojo Caliente (ō'kō käl-yĕn'tå) Mex.	21.52 N	100.43 W
92	Ojocaliente . . . . Mex.	22.38 N	102.14 W
96	Ojo del Toro, Pico (Pk.) (ō'kō dĕl tō'rō) . Cuba	19.57 N	77.29 W
156	Okahu (ō-kä'hōō) . . . . . N. Z. (In.)	36.51 S	174.50 E
134	Okakandja (ō-kȧ'kän'jȧ) S. W. Afr.	21.58 S	16.58 E
82	Okalona (ō-kȧ-lō'nȧ) . . . . Miss.	33.59 N	88.44 W
148	Okamoya (ō'kȧ-mō'yȧ) . . . . . . Jap.	36.0 N	138.0 E
54	Okanagan L. (ō'kȧ-näg'ȧn) . . Can.	50.0 N	119.30 W
70	Okanogan . . . . Wash.	48.30 N	119.35 W
70	Okanogan R. . . . . Wash.	48.30 N	119.30 W
132	Okano R. (ō'kä'nō) . . . Fr. Eq. Afr.	0.30 N	11.30 E
138	Oka R. (ô-kȧ') . . . . Sov. Un.	54.0 N	102.0 E
128	Oka R. . . . . Sov. Un.	54.52 N	39.40 E
82	Okatibbee Cr. (ō'kȧ-tĭb'ē) . . . Miss.	32.30 N	88.48 W
134	Okavango R. (ō'kä-väṇ'gō) . . . Afr.	18.0 S	20.50 E
134	Okavango Swamp . . . . Bech.	19.30 S	23.0 E
149	Okaya (ō'kȧ-yȧ) . . . . Jap.	36.4 N	138.1 E
149	Okayama (ō'kȧ-yä'mȧ) . . . . . . Jap.	34.40 N	133.51 E
149	Okazaki (ō'kȧ-zä'kê) . . . . Jap.	35.0 N	137.12 E
83	Okeechobee (ō-kê-chō'bē) Fla. (In.)	27.16 N	80.48 W
83	Okeechobee, L. . . . . Fla. (In.)	27.0 N	80.50 W
78	Okeene (ô-kēn') . . . . Okla.	36.7 N	98.19 W
83	Okefenokee Swamp (ō'kê-fê-nō'kê) Ga.	30.50 N	82.20 W
79	Okemah (ô-kē'mä) . . . . Okla.	35.25 N	96.18 W
139	Okhotsk (ô-kôtsk') . . . . Sov. Un.	59.25 N	143.20 E
139	Okhotsk, Sea of . . . . Sov. Un.	55.0 N	150.0 E
149	Oki I. (ō'kê) . . . . Jap.	36.15 N	133.15 E
149	Oki Is. . . . . Jap.	36.15 N	133.10 E
148	Okinawa I. (ō'kê-nä'wȧ) Ryukyu Is. (In.)	26.30 N	128.0 E
148	Okinawa Guntō (Is.) (ō'kê-nä'wȧ gōōn'tō') . Ryukyu Is. (In.)	26.30 N	128.0 E
148	Okinoerabu I. (ō-kē'nō-å-rä'bōō) Jap. (In.)	27.28 N	128.40 E
78	Oklahoma (State) (ŏ-klȧ-hō'mȧ) U. S.	35.50 N	97.30 W
79	Oklahoma City . . . . Okla.	35.28 N	97.31 W
83	Oklawaha R. (ŏk-lȧ-wô'hô) . . . Fla.	29.10 N	82.0 W
79	Okmulgee (ok-mŭl'gê) . . . . . . Okla.	35.36 N	95.58 W
79	Okolona (ō-kô-lō'nȧ) . . . . Miss.	33.59 N	88.41 W
149	Okushiri I. (ō'kōō-shē'rê) . . . . Jap.	42.15 N	139.30 E
73	Ola (ō'lȧ) . . . . Ga. (Atlanta In.)	33.26 N	84.3 W
155	Olaa (ō'lä'ä) . . . . Haw.	19.35 N	155.0 W
51	Olalla (ō-lä'lȧ) . Wash. (Seattle In.)	47.25 N	122.33 W
94	Olanchito (ō'län-chē'tō) . . . . Hond.	15.28 N	86.36 W
118	Öland (I.) (û-länd') . . . . Swe.	56.45 N	16.40 E
79	Olathe (ô-lā'thê) . . . . Kan.	38.53 N	94.49 W
102	Olavarría (ō-lä-vär-rē'ä) . . . . . Arg.	36.59 S	60.25 W
121	Olawa (ô-lä'vȧ) . . . . Pol.	50.57 N	17.17 E
96	Old Bahama Channel (bȧ-hā'mȧ) W. I.	22.20 N	77.40 W
116	Oldbury (ōld'bĕr-ĭ) . . . . . . Gt. Brit.	52.30 N	2.1 W
124	Old Castile (Castilla la Vieja) (Prov.) (kăs-tēl') (käs-tēl'yä lä vyā'hä) . Sp.	41.40 N	3.40 W
120	Oldenburg (State) (ōl'dĕn-bōōrgh) Ger.	52.55 N	8.3 E
120	Oldenburg . . . . Ger.	53.7 N	8.12 E
117	Oldenfelde (ōl'dĕn-fĕlt'ĕ) Ger. (Hamburg In.)	53.37 N	10.9 E
85	Old Forge (ōld fôrj) . . . . Pa.	41.20 N	75.48 W
114	Oldham (ōld'ăm) . . . . Gt. Brit.	53.30 N	2.10 W
89	Old Harbor Is. La. (New Orleans In.)	29.45 N	89.3 W
93	Old Providence I. . . . . W. I.	12.21 N	81.21 W
81	Old R. . . . . Tex. (In.)	29.52 N	94.50 W
86	Old Town . . . . Me.	44.57 N	68.40 W
85	Olean (ō-lê-ăn') . . . . N. Y.	42.5 N	78.25 W
121	Olecko (ô-lĕt'skô) . . . . Pol.	54.2 N	22.30 E
124	Oleiros (ō-lā'rōs) . . . . Sp.	43.20 N	8.20 W
139	Olekma R. (ô-lyĕk-mȧ') . . Sov. Un.	55.20 N	120.0 E
139	Olekminsk (ô-lyĕk-mênsk') Sov. Un.	60.30 N	120.40 E
139	Olenek R. (ô-lyĕ-nyôk') . . Sov. Un.	70.0 N	120.40 E
122	Oleron, Ile d' (ēl' dō lā-rôN') . . Fr.	46.0 N	1.20 W
125	Olesa de Montserrat (ô-lā'sä dā mōnt-sȧ-rät') . Sp. (In.)	41.32 N	1.53 E
121	Oleśnica (ô-lĕsh-nē'tsȧ) . . . . Pol.	51.12 N	17.23 E
139	Olga (ôl'gȧ) . . . . Sov. Un.	43.45 N	135.25 E
148	Olga B. . . . . Sov. Un.	43.43 N	135.10 E
129	Olgopol (ôl-gô-pôl'y') . . . Sov. Un.	48.11 N	29.26 E
124	Olhão (ōl-youN') . . . . Port.	37.1 N	7.51 W
134	Olifants R. (ŏl'ĭ-fănts) U. S. Afr.-Moz.	24.0 S	31.15 E
92	Olinalá (ô-lê-nä-lä') . . . . Mex.	17.45 N	98.48 W
73	Olinda (ô-lĭn'dȧ) Calif. (Los Angeles In.)	33.55 N	117.50 W
125	Oliva (ô-lē'vä) . . . . Sp.	38.55 N	0.7 W
124	Oliva de Jérez (ō-lē'vä dā hā'rĕth) Sp.	38.17 N	6.55 W
125	Olivães (ō-lê-văNsh') . . . Port. (In.)	38.46 N	9.6 W
84	Olive Hill (ŏl'ĭv) . . . . Ky.	38.17 N	83.10 W
124	Olivenza (ō-lê-vĕn'thä) . . . . Sp.	38.42 N	7.5 W
77	Olivia (ō-lĭv'ē-ȧ) . . . . Minn.	44.48 N	94.58 W
99	Olivos (ō-lē'vōs) Arg. (Buenos Aires In.)	34.31 S	58.30 W
129	Olkhovets (ôl'kô-vyĕts') . Sov. Un.	49.3 N	30.50 E
121	Olkusz (ôl'kōōsh) . . . . Pol.	50.16 N	19.40 E
100	Ollague (ô-lyä'gȧ) . . . . Chl.	21.2 S	68.15 W
116	Ollerton (ŏl'ēr-tŭn) . . . . . . Gt. Brit.	53.12 N	1.2 W
	Olmütz, see Olomouc, Czech.		
116	Olney (ŏl'nĭ) . . . . Gt. Brit.	52.9 N	0.42 W
88	Olney . . . . Ill.	38.45 N	88.6 W
51	Olney . . . . Ore. (Portland In.)	46.5 N	123.44 W
78	Olney . . . . Tex.	33.24 N	98.43 W
87	Olomanoshibo R. (ō'lô-mȧ'nô-shē'bō) . Can.	50.40 N	50.25 W
121	Olomouc (ô'lô-mōts) . . . . Czech.	49.36 N	17.14 E
122	Oloron-Ste. Marie (ō-lô-rôN'-săNt mȧ-rē') . Fr.	43.11 N	0.35 W
125	Olot (ô-lōt') . . . . Sp.	42.12 N	2.30 E
129	Olshanka (ôl'shȧŋ-kȧ) . . . Sov. Un.	48.12 N	30.50 E
129	Olshany (ôl'shȧn-ê) . . . . . Sov. Un.	50.2 N	35.52 E
121	Olsztyn (ôl'shtĕn) . . . . Pol.	53.46 N	20.27 E
120	Olten (ôl'tĕn) . . . . Switz.	47.21 N	7.53 E
127	Oltenia (Prov.) (ôl-tē'nyȧ) . . Rom.	44.25 N	23.35 E
127	Oltenița (ôl-tā'nĭ-tsȧ) . . . . Rom.	44.5 N	26.38 E
127	Oltul R. (ôl'tōōl) . . . . Rom.	44.30 N	24.10 E
153	Olutanga I. (ō-lōō-täng'ä) . . . Phil.	7.22 N	122.53 E
124	Olvera (ōl-vā'rä) . . . . Sp.	36.56 N	5.16 W
121	Olyka (ō-wē'kȧ) . . . . Sov. Un.	50.42 N	25.50 E
70	Olympia (ô-lĭm'pĭ-ȧ) . . . . Wash.	47.2 N	122.53 W
70	Olympic Mts. (ô-lĭm'pĭk) . . . Wash.	47.52 N	123.40 W
102	Olympio (ô-lĕm'pê-ōō) . Braz. (In.)	22.51 S	42.59 W
127	Olympus, Mt. (ô-lĭm'pŭs) . . . . Grc.	40.3 N	22.20 E
70	Olympus, Mt. . . . . Wash.	47.47 N	123.43 W
85	Olyphant (ŏl'ĭ-fănt) . . . . Pa.	41.27 N	75.39 W
139	Olyutorsk, C. (ô'lyōō-tôrsk) Sov. Un.	59.50 N	170.10 E
139	Olyutorskoe (ôl'yōō-tôr'skô-yĕ) Sov. Un.	60.25 N	168.20 E
149	Omae, C. (ō'mȧ-å) . . . . Jap.	34.35 N	138.14 E
114	Omagh (ō'mä) . . . . N. Ire.	54.35 N	7.25 W
76	Omaha (ō'mȧ-hä) . . . . Neb.	41.17 N	95.57 W
140	Oman (ô-män') . . . . Asia	22.0 N	58.30 E
40	Oman, G. of . . . . Asia	24.30 N	58.45 E
	Oman, Trucial, see Trucial Coast (Dist.), Sau. Ar.		
134	Omara R. (ō-mä'rä) Bech.-S. W. Afr.	21.45 S	22.30 E
134	Omaruru (ō-mä-rōō'rōō) . S. W. Afr.	21.28 S	15.55 E
126	Ombrone R. (ôm-brō'nä) . . . . . . It.	42.50 N	11.18 E
133	Omdurman (ŏm-dōōr-män') A. E. Sud.	15.40 N	32.30 E
93	Omealca (ō-mȧ-äl'kō) . . . . Mex.	18.43 N	96.47 W
92	Ometepec (ō'mȧ-tȧ-pĕk') . . . . Mex.	16.34 N	98.35 W
149	Omiya (ō'mē-yȧ) . . . . Jap.	35.57 N	139.38 E
94	Omoa (ô-mō'ä) . . . . Hond.	15.42 N	88.2 W
139	Omolon R. (ō-mô-lôn') . . . Sov. Un.	66.0 N	160.20 E
133	Omo R. (ō'mō) . . . . Eth.	6.30 N	36.30 E
94	Omotepe I. (ō-mô-tā'pȧ) . . . . . Nic.	11.30 N	85.35 W
77	Omro (ŏm'rō) . . . . Wis.	44.1 N	88.44 W
138	Omsk (ômsk) . . . . Sov. Un.	55.15 N	73.25 E
148	Omu (ō'mōō') . . . . Chn.	43.46 N	128.4 E
149	Omura (ō'mōō-rȧ) . . . . Jap.	32.56 N	129.58 E
149	Omuta (ō'mōō-tȧ) . . . . Jap.	33.2 N	130.26 E
110	Omutinsk (ô'mōō-tēnsk) . Sov. Un.	58.40 N	52.5 E
138	Ona (Biryusa) R. (ō-nȧ') (bēr'yōō-sȧ) . Sov. Un.	56.30 N	98.35 E
76	Onawa (ŏn-ȧ-wȧ) . . . . Ia.	42.4 N	96.5 W
84	Onaway (ŏn'ȧ-wā) . . . . Mich.	45.24 N	84.14 W
125	Onda (ŏn'dä) . . . . Sp.	39.57 N	0.14 W
121	Ondava R. (ōn'dȧ-vȧ) . . . . . Czech.	48.55 N	21.40 E
110	Onega (ô-nyĕ'gȧ) . . . . Sov. Un.	63.50 N	38.15 E
110	Onega B. . . . . Sov. Un.	64.30 N	36.30 E
110	Onega, L. . . . . Sov. Un.	61.35 N	35.30 E
110	Onega R. . . . . Sov. Un.	63.15 N	39.15 E
156	Onehunga (ō-nȧ-hōōn'gä) N. Z. (In.)	36.56 S	174.48 E
85	Oneida (ô-nī'dȧ) . . . . N. Y.	43.5 N	45.40 W
85	Oneida L. . . . . N. Y.	43.2 N	76.0 W
76	O'Neill (ō-nēl') . . . . Neb.	42.28 N	98.38 W
85	Oneonta (ō-nê-ŏn'tȧ) . . . . N. Y.	42.27 N	75.7 W
156	Onerahi (ō-nȧ-rä'hê) . . . . N. Z.	35.46 S	174.20 E
142	Ongin (ŏn'gĭn') . . . . Mong.	45.45 N	102.58 E
142	Ongin Gol (R.) (ŏn'gĭn gôl') . Mong.	45.42 N	103.30 E
147	Ongjin (ōōng'jĭn') . . . . Kor.	37.56 N	125.20 E
133	Onitsha (ô-nĭt'shȧ) . . . . Nig.	6.12 N	6.41 E
139	Onnekotan (I.) (ô-nȧ-kô'tän) . Jap.	49.0 N	154.45 E
149	Onomichi (ō'nô-mē'chê) . . . . . . Jap.	34.22 N	133.12 E
139	Onon R. (ô'nôn) . . . . Sov. Un.	50.30 N	115.0 E
158	Onslow (ŏnz'lō) . . . . Austl.	21.50 S	115.0 E
156	Onslow . . . . N. Z. (In.)	41.15 S	174.48 E
149	Ontake (Mt.) (ōn'tä-kē) . . . . . Jap.	35.55 N	137.30 E
70	Ontario (ŏn-tā'rĭ-ō) . . . . Ore.	44.3 N	116.59 W
73	Ontario . . . Calif. (Los Angeles In.)	34.4 N	117.39 W
55	Ontario (Prov.) . . . . Can.	50.15 N	89.0 W
85	Ontario, L. . . . . U. S.-Can.	43.35 N	77.30 W
125	Onteniente (ōn-tȧ-nyĕn'tä) . . . . Sp.	38.49 N	0.35 W
77	Ontonagon (ŏn-tō-năg'ŏn) . . . Mich.	46.51 N	89.18 W
158	Oodnadatta (ōōd'nȧ-dȧ'tȧ) . . Austl.	27.30 S	135.32 E
158	Ooldea (ōōl-dā'ȧ) . . . . Austl.	30.30 S	132.0 E
117	Oorderen (ōr'dĕr-ĕn) Bel. (Anvers In.)	51.18 N	4.21 E
82	Oostanaula R. (ōō-stȧ-nô'lȧ) . . . Ga.	34.25 N	85.5 W
138	Opalikha, see Kupino, Sov. Un.		
121	Opatów (ō-pä'tōōf) . . . . Pol.	50.47 N	21.25 E
121	Opava (ō'pȧ-vä) . . . . Czech.	49.56 N	17.52 E
118	Opdal (ôp'däl) . . . . Nor.	62.39 N	9.40 E
82	Opelika (ŏp-ê-lī'kȧ) . . . . Ala.	32.38 N	85.23 W
81	Opelousas (ŏp-ē-lōō'sȧs) . . . . . . La.	30.33 N	92.5 W
85	Opeongo L. (ŏp-ê-ôṇ'gō) . . . . . Can.	45.45 N	78.20 W
52	Ophir (ō'fēr) . . . . Alsk.	63.10 N	156.15 W
150	Ophir, Mt. (Talamau) (ō'fēr) (tä-lȧ-mä'ōō) . Indon.	0.15 N	99.50 E
94	Opico (ô-pē'kō) . . . . Sal.	13.49 N	89.23 W
55	Opinaka R. (ŏp-ĭ-nä'kȧ) . . . . . Can.	52.40 N	77.30 W
128	Opochka (ō-pôch'kȧ) . . . . Sov. Un.	56.42 N	28.40 E
121	Opoczno (ô-pôch'nô) . . . . Pol.	51.22 N	20.17 E
121	Opole (ô-pôl'å) . . . . Pol.	51.7 N	21.58 E
121	Opole . . . . Pol.	50.41 N	17.55 E
129	Oposhnya (ô-pôsh'nyȧ) . . Sov. Un.	49.57 N	34.33 E
156	Opotiki (ô-pō'tĭ-kê) . . . . N. Z.	38.0 S	177.20 W
82	Opp (ŏp) . . . . Ala.	31.17 N	86.17 W
156	Opunake (ō-pōō-nȧ'kê) . . . . . N. Z.	39.25 S	173.52 E
152	Oquendo (ô-kān'dō) . . . . Phil.	12.8 N	124.32 E
73	Oquirrh Mts. (ō'kwēr) Utah (Salt Lake City In.)	40.35 N	112.12 W
121	Oradea (ô-räd'yä) . . . . Rom.	47.3 N	21.55 E
108	Öraefa-Jökull (Mt.) (û'rĕf-å-yû'kōōl) . Ice.	64.5 N	16.40 W
132	Oran (ō-rän') (ō-răN') . . . . Alg.	35.45 N	0.38 W
102	Orán . . . . Arg.	23.10 S	64.20 W
79	Oran (ŏr'ăn) . . . . Mo.	37.4 N	89.39 W
159	Orange (ŏr'ĕnj) . . . . Austl.	33.18 S	149.5 E
74	Orange . . . . Calif.	33.48 N	117.51 W
85	Orange . . . . Conn.	41.16 N	73.2 W
88	Orange . . . . . . N. J. (New York In.)	40.46 N	74.14 W
81	Orange . . . . Tex.	30.6 N	93.43 W
83	Orangeburg (ŏr'ĕnj-bûrg) . . . . S. C.	33.30 N	80.50 W
96	Orange Cay (I.) . . . . Ba. Is.	24.56 N	79.7 W
76	Orange City . . . . Ia.	43.0 N	96.5 W
134	Orange Free State . . . . . . U. S. Afr.	28.20 N	26.40 E
88	Orange Grove. Md. (Baltimore In.)	39.15 N	76.45 W
83	Orange L. . . . . Fla.	29.25 N	82.10 W
151	Orange Range . . . . . . Neth. N. Gui.	4.30 S	140.0 E
134	Orange R. . . . . Afr.	28.49 S	18.0 E
85	Orangeville (ŏr'ĕnj-vĭl) . . . . Can.	43.55 N	80.2 W
94	Orange Walk . . . . . Br. Hond. (In.)	18.10 N	88.32 W
152	Orani (ō-rä'nê) . . . . Phil.	14.48 N	120.32 E
128	Oranienbaum (ō-rä'nê-ĕn-boum) Sov. Un.	59.53 N	29.43 E
120	Oranienburg (ō-rä'nê-ĕn-bōōrgh) Ger.	52.46 N	13.14 E
152	Oras (ō'räs) . . . . Phil.	12.9 N	125.27 E
152	Oras B. . . . . Phil.	12.10 N	125.30 E
127	Orăstie (ô-rŭsh'tyå) . . . . Rom.	45.50 N	23.12 E
126	Orbetello (ôr-bȧ-tĕl'lō) . . . . It.	42.26 N	11.14 E
124	Orbigo R. (ôr-bē'gō) . . . . Sp.	42.20 N	5.53 W
72	Orcas (ôr'kȧs) Wash. (Vancouver In.)	48.36 N	122.56 W
72	Orcas I. . . . Wash. (Vancouver In.)	48.40 N	122.55 W
100	Orchilla I. (ôr-chē'lyȧ) . . . . . . Ven.	11.45 N	66.15 W
76	Ord (ôrd) . . . . Neb.	41.35 N	98.55 W
124	Ordenes (ôr'dȧ-nās) . . . . Sp.	43.4 N	8.25 W
75	Ord Peak (ôrd) . . . . Ariz.	33.57 N	109.36 W
158	Ord R. . . . . Austl.	17.30 S	128.45 E
111	Ordu (ôr'dōō) . . . . Tur.	40.58 N	37.55 E
124	Orduña (ôr-dōō'nyȧ) . . . . Sp.	43.0 N	3.2 W
73	Ordway (ôrd'wā) Calif. (Los Angeles In.)	34.0 N	117.10 W
78	Ordway . . . . Colo.	38.13 N	103.46 W
111	Ordzhonikidze (Vladikavkaz) (ôrd'zhō-nĭ-kĭd'zĕ) (vlä-dĭ-käf'-käz) . Sov. Un.	43.5 N	44.32 E
129	Ordzhonikidze (Enakievo) (yĕ-nȧ-kyĕ'vô) . Sov. Un.	48.14 N	38.12 E
128	Ordzhonikidzegrad (Bezhitsa) (byĕ'shê-tsȧ) . Sov. Un.	53.18 N	34.15 E
118	Örebro (û'rē-brō) . . . . Swe.	59.16 N	15.11 E
77	Oregon (ŏr'ê-gŏn) . . . . Ill.	42.2 N	89.20 W
70	Oregon (State) . . . . U. S.	44.10 N	120.0 W
70	Oregon Caves Natl. Mon. . . . . Ore.	42.5 N	123.0 W
70	Oregon City . . . . Ore.	45.21 N	122.37 W
118	Öregrund (û'rĕ-grōōnd) . . . . . . Swe.	60.20 N	18.28 E
129	Orekhov (ôr-yĕ'kôf) . . . . . . Sov. Un.	47.33 N	35.50 E
127	Orekhovo (ôr'yĕ'kô-vô) . . . . . . Bul.	43.44 N	23.59 E
128	Orekhovo Zuevo (ôr'yĕ'kô-vô zōō'yĕ-vô) . Sov. Un.	55.47 N	38.59 E
128	Orel (ôr-yôl') . . . . Sov. Un.	52.56 N	36.5 E
128	Orel (Dist.) . . . . Sov. Un.	52.38 N	37.0 E
129	Orel R. . . . . Sov. Un.	49.5 N	34.40 E
75	Orem (ō'rĕm) . . . . Utah	40.16 N	111.46 W
120	Ore Mts. (ôr) . . . . Ger.	50.45 N	13.10 E
	Orenburg, see Chkalov, Sov. Un.		
124	Orense (ô-rĕn'sä) . . . . Sp.	42.19 N	7.51 W
118	Öresund (Sd.) (û'rē-sōōnd) . . . Eur.	55.32 N	12.35 E
157	Oreti R. (ō-rä'tē) . . . . N. Z.	46.10 S	168.15 E
75	Organ Pipe Cactus Natl. Mon. Ariz.	32.15 N	113.0 W
129	Orgeev (ôr-gyĕ'yĕf) . . . . . . Sov. Un.	47.22 N	28.49 E
124	Orgeval (ôrzh-väl') . . . . . . Fr. (In.)	48.55 N	1.58 E
100	Oriental, Cordillera (Mts.) (ō-rê-ĕn-täl') . Col.	3.0 N	74.0 W
96	Oriente (State) (ō-rê-ĕn'tȧ) . . Cuba	20.30 N	76.30 W
125	Orihuela (ô'rê-wā'lä) . . . . Sp.	38.6 N	0.56 W
110	Orihvesi, L. (ô'rĭ-vĕ-sĭ) . . . . Fin.	62.20 N	29.43 E
55	Orillia (ô-rĭl'ĭ-ȧ) . . . . Can.	44.32 N	79.42 W
51	Orillia . . . . Wash. (Seattle In.)	47.27 N	122.15 W
101	Orinoco, Delta of the (ô-rĭ-nō'kô) Ven.	9.30 N	61.30 W
100	Orinoco, R. . . . . Ven.-Col.	5.0 N	67.45 W
152	Orion (ô-rê-ōn') . . . . Phil.	14.37 N	120.34 E
126	Oristano, G. of (ô-rês-tä'nō) . . Sard.	39.50 N	8.30 E
93	Orizaba (ô-rê-zä'bä) . . . . Mex.	18.54 N	97.5 W
93	Orizaba (Vol.) . . . . Mex.	19.0 N	97.15 W
118	Orkedalen (ôr'kĕ-dä-lĕn) . . . . . Nor.	63.18 N	9.53 E
118	Örken (L.) (ûr'kĕn) . . . . Swe.	57.8 N	15.0 E
127	Orkhanie (ôr-kȧ'nyĕ) . . . . Bul.	42.54 N	23.38 E
142	Orkhon R. (ŏr-kôn') . . . . Mong.	49.0 N	105.0 E
118	Orkla R. (ôr'klä) . . . . Nor.	63.0 N	9.45 E

ăt; finăl; rāte; senâte; ärm; åsk; sofȧ; fâre; ch-choose; dh-as th in other; bē; êvent; bĕt; recĕnt; cratẽr; g-go; gh-gutteral g; bĭt; ĭ-short neutral; rīde; K-gutteral k as ch in German ich;

Orkney PRONOUNCING INDEX Paga

Page	Name Pronunciation	Region	Lat. °′	Long. °′
114	Orkney Is. (ôrk'nĭ)	Gt. Brit. (In.)	59.0 N	2.30 W
83	Orlando (ôr-lăn'dō)	Fla. (In.)	28.33 N	81.22 W
122	Orléans (ôr-lā-äN')	Fr.	47.55 N	1.57 E
84	Orleans (ôr-lēnz')	Ind.	38.40 N	86.27 W
86	Orleans I. (ôr-lâ-äN')	Can.	46.56 N	71.0 W
132	Orléansville (ôr-lâ-äN-vēl')	Alg.	36.14 N	1.20 E
153	Ormoc (ôr-mŏk')	Phil.	11.0 N	124.37 E
153	Ormoc B.	Phil.	10.58 N	124.35 E
83	Ormond (ôr'mŏnd)	Fla.	29.16 N	81.6 W
156	Ormondville (ôr'mŏnd-vĭl)	N. Z.	40.8 S	176.12 E
116	Ormskirk (ôrms'kērk)	Gt. Brit.	53.34 N	2.53 W
122	Orne R. (ôrn')	Fr.	49.0 N	0.30 W
121	Orneta (ôr-nyĕ'tä)	Pol.	54.6 N	20.10 E
118	Orn I. (ôrn)	Swe.	59.2 N	18.30 E
118	Örnskoldsvik (ûrn'skôlts-vēk)	Swe.	63.14 N	18.41 E
100	Orocué (ô-rô-kwā')	Col.	4.58 N	71.28 W
156	Orongorongo R. (ô-rôŋ-gô-rôŋ'gō)	N. Z. (In.)	41.23 S	174.56 E
114	Oronsay, Passage of (ō'rŏn-sâ)	Gt. Brit.	56.0 N	6.10 W
153	Oroquieta (ō-rô-kyā'tä)	Phil.	8.29 N	123.48 E
99	Oro, R. del (rē'ō dĕl ō'rō)	Chl. (Magallanes In.)	52.55 S	69.55 W
80	Oro, R. del	Mex.	25.58 N	105.30 W
126	Orosei, G. of (ō-rô-sā'ē)	Sard.	40.15 N	9.45 E
121	Orosháza (ô-rôsh-hä'sô)	Hung.	46.33 N	20.41 E
95	Orosi (Vol.) (ō-rō'sē)	C. R.	11.0 N	85.28 W
74	Oroville (ōr'ô-vĭl)	Calif.	39.31 N	121.33 W
70	Oroville	Wash.	48.54 N	119.27 W
117	Orrell (ŏr'ĕl)	Gt. Brit. (Liverpool In.)	53.32 N	2.40 W
84	Orrville (ôr'vĭl)	Ohio	40.50 N	81.48 W
118	Orsa (ōr'sä)	Swe.	61.9 N	14.38 E
123	Orsay (ôr-sĕ')	Fr. (In.)	48.41 N	2.11 E
128	Orsha (ôr'shà)	Sov. Un.	54.30 N	30.27 E
111	Orsk (ôrsk)	Sov. Un.	51.15 N	58.35 E
127	Orşova (ôr'shô-và)	Rom.	44.43 N	22.25 E
124	Ortegal C. (ôr-tâ-gäl')	Sp.	43.46 N	7.55 W
122	Orthez (ôr-tĕz')	Fr.	43.28 N	0.48 W
124	Ortigueria (ôr-tê-gā'ē-rä)	Sp.	43.41 N	7.50 W
51	Orting (ôrt'ĭng)	Wash. (Seattle In.)	47.5 N	122.12 W
126	Ortona (ôr-tō'nä)	It.	42.21 N	14.22 E
96	Ortonville (ôr'tŭn-vĭl)	Minn.	45.19 N	96.25 W
100	Oruro (ō-rōō'rō)	Bol.	17.58 S	67.3 W
126	Orvieto (ôr-vyâ'tō)	It.	42.43 N	12.7 E
118	Os (ôs)	Nor.	60.11 N	5.29 E
138	Osa (ô'sà)	Sov. Un.	53.30 N	103.59 E
77	Osage (ō'sāj)	Ia.	43.18 N	92.48 W
79	Osage City	Kan.	38.38 N	95.48 W
79	Osage Dam	Mo.	38.10 N	92.45 W
79	Osage R.	Mo.	38.12 N	93.0 W
149	Osaka (ō'sä-kä)	Jap.	34.32 N	135.30 E
149	Osaka	Jap. (In.)		
149	Osaka B.	Jap.	34.30 N	135.15 E
77	Osakis (ô-sā'kĭs)	Minn.	45.51 N	95.8 W
77	Osakis L.	Minn.	45.55 N	95.5 W
95	Osa Pen. (ō'sä)	C. R.	8.35 N	83.30 W
79	Osawatomia (ŏs-à-wăt'ô-mē)	Kan.	38.29 N	94.56 W
78	Osborne (ŏz'bŭrn)	Kan.	39.26 N	98.42 W
79	Osceola (ŏs-ē-ō'là)	Ark.	35.43 N	89.58 W
77	Osceola	Ia.	41.2 N	93.45 W
79	Osceola	Mo.	38.2 N	93.40 W
76	Osceola	Neb.	41.12 N	97.33 W
120	Oschatz (ō'shäts)	Ger.	51.17 N	13.6 E
120	Oschersleben (ôsh'ĕrs-lā-bĕn)	Ger.	52.2 N	11.13 E
84	Oscoda (ŏs-kō'dà)	Mich.	44.26 N	83.20 W
117	Osdorf (ôs'dôrf)	Ger. (Hamburg In.)	53.34 N	9.51 E
118	Ose L. (ōō'sē)	Nor.	61.12 N	11.55 E
128	Osetr R. (ô'sĕt'r)	Sov. Un.	54.25 N	38.25 E
84	Osgood (ŏz'gŏŏd)	Ind.	39.7 N	85.19 W
138	Osh (ôsh)	Sov. Un.	40.25 N	72.40 E
85	Oshawa (ŏsh'à-wà)	Can.	43.50 N	78.50 W
149	Oshima (I.) (ō'shē-mä)	Jap.	34.45 N	139.25 E
76	Oshkosh (ŏsh'kŏsh)	Neb.	41.22 N	102.20 W
77	Oshkosh	Wis.	44.0 N	88.30 W
121	Oshmyany (ôsh-myä'nĭ)	Sov. Un.	54.26 N	25.56 E
127	Osijek (ôs'ĭ-yĕk)	Yugo.	45.33 N	18.41 E
77	Osklaloosa (ŏs-kà-lōō'sà)	Ia.	41.18 N	92.38 W
118	Oskarshamn (ôs'kärs-häm'n)	Swe.	57.16 N	16.26 E
118	Oskarsström (ôs'kärs-strûm)	Swe.	56.49 N	12.59 E
128	Oskol R. (ôs-kôl')	Sov. Un.	50.40 N	37.50 E
118	Oslo (ôs'lō)	Nor.	59.57 N	10.42 E
153	Oslob (ôs-lōb')	Phil.	9.32 N	123.26 E
118	Oslo Fjord	Nor.	59.10 N	10.35 E
124	Osma (ōs'mä)	Sp.	41.34 N	3.3 W
119	Osmus (ôs'mŏŏs)	Sov. Un.	59.16 N	23.25 E
120	Osnabrück (ôs-nä-brük')	Ger.	52.16 N	8.3 E
102	Osorno (ō-sôr'nō)	Chl.	40.40 S	73.2 W
159	Osprey Reef (ŏs'prâ)	Austl.	13.45 S	146.38 E
85	Ossining (ŏs'ĭ-nĭng)	N. Y.	41.11 N	73.52 W
86	Ossipee (ŏs'ĭ-pē)	N. H.	43.40 N	71.8 W
128	Ostashkov (ôs-täsh'kôf)	Sov. Un.	57.7 N	33.5 E
84	Ostego (ŏs-tē'gō)	Mich.	42.29 N	85.45 W
115	Ostende (ôst-ĕn'dē)	Bel.	51.12 N	2.55 E
129	Oster (ōs'tĕr)	Sov. Un.	50.57 N	30.52 E
118	Öster Dal R. (ûs'tĕr däl)	Swe.	61.48 N	12.58 E
118	Öster Fjord (ûs'tĕr fyôr')	Nor.	60.38 N	5.30 E
118	Östersund (ûs'tĕr-sŏŏnd)	Swe.	63.11 N	14.40 E
118	Östhammar (ûst'häm'är)	Swe.	60.17 N	18.23 E
51	Ostrander (ŏs'trăn-dĕr)	Wash. (Portland In.)	46.11 N	122.53 W
121	Ostróda (ôs'trŏŏt-à)	Pol.	53.41 N	19.58 E
121	Ostróg (ôs-trôk')	Sov. Un.	50.19 N	26.30 E
129	Ostrogozhsk (ôs-trô-gôzhk')	Sov. Un.	50.53 N	39.4 E
121	Ostrolęka (ôs-trô-wôN'kà)	Pol.	53.4 N	21.36 E
129	Ostropol (ôs-trô-pôl')	Sov. Un.	49.49 N	27.31 E
127	Ostrov (ôs'trôv)	Rom.	44.56 N	28.11 E
128	Ostrov (ôs-trôf')	Sov. Un.	57.21 N	28.21 E
121	Ostrów (ôs'trŏŏf)	Pol.	51.39 N	17.49 E
121	Ostrów	Pol.	52.47 N	21.54 E
121	Ostrowiec (ôs-trô'vyĕts)	Pol.	50.56 N	21.24 E
121	Ostrów Lubelski (lōō'bĕl-skĭ)	Pol.	51.33 N	22.52 E
121	Ostrzeszów (ôs-tzhā'shŏŏf)	Pol.	51.26 N	17.56 E
127	Ostuni (ôs-tōō'nē)	It.	40.43 N	17.36 E
127	Osum R. (ō'sŏŏm)	Alb.	40.33 N	20.10 E
148	Osumi Is. (ō'sōō-mē)	Jap.	30.28 N	130.45 E
149	Osumi (Van Diemen) Str.	Jap.	30.55 N	131.0 E
124	Osuna (ô-sōō'nä)	Sp.	37.14 N	5.6 W
116	Oswaldtwistle (ŏz-wăld-twĭs''l)	Gt. Brit.	53.44 N	2.24 W
85	Oswegatchie R. (ŏs-wē-găch'ĭ)	N. Y.	44.15 N	75.10 W
79	Oswego (ŏs-wē'gō)	Kan.	37.11 N	95.8 W
85	Oswego	N. Y.	43.26 N	76.30 W
70	Oswego	Ore.	45.25 N	122.42 W
121	Oświęcim (ôsh-vyăN'tsyĭm)	Pol.	50.3 N	19.16 E
129	Otachi (ô-täch'')	Rom.	48.26 N	27.47 E
157	Otago Harbor (ô-tä'gō)	N. Z. (In.)	45.50 S	170.40 E
157	Otago Pen.	N. Z. (In.)	45.52 S	170.40 E
156	Otahuhu (ō-tä-hōō'hōō)	N. Z. (In.)	36.57 S	174.51 E
157	Otaki (ô-tä'kē)	N. Z.	40.40 S	175.10 E
156	Otari, Mt. (ô-tä'rē)	N. Z. (In.)	41.15 S	174.46 E
148	Otaru (ô'tà-rōō)	Jap.	43.10 N	140.59 E
148	Otaru B.	Jap.	43.28 N	141.0 E
157	Otautau (ô-tou'tou)	N. Z.	46.8 S	168.2 E
100	Otavalo (ō-tä-vä'lō)	Ec.	0.10 N	78.15 W
134	Otavi (ô-tä'vē)	S. W. Afr.	19.45 S	17.25 E
74	Otay (ō'tā)	Calif. (In.)	32.37 N	117.4 W
149	Otenjoyama (Mt.) (ō'tĕn-jô-yä'mä)	Jap.	36.22 N	137.38 E
119	Otepää (ô'tĕ-pâ)	Sov. Un.	58.4 N	26.32 E
156	Oterongu (ô-tà-rôŋ'gōō)	N. Z. (In.)	41.17 S	174.39 E
156	Oterongu B.	N. Z. (In.)	41.18 S	174.39 E
127	Othrys Mts. (ŏth'rĭs)	Grc.	39.0 N	22.30 E
157	Otira Pass (ô-tē'rá)	N. Z.	42.53 S	171.38 E
134	Otjiwarongo (ŏt-jê-wà-rôŋ'gō)	S. W. Afr.	20.27 S	16.32 E
116	Otley (ŏt'lĭ)	Gt. Brit.	53.54 N	1.41 W
126	Otočac (ō'tô-chàts)	Yugo.	44.50 N	15.16 E
153	Oton (ô-tōn')	Phil.	10.42 N	122.28 E
156	Otorohanga (ô-tō-rō-häŋ'gä)	N. Z.	38.8 S	175.12 E
127	Otranto (ô'trän-tô) (ō-trăn'tō)	It.	40.9 N	18.29 E
127	Otranto, C.	It.	40.6 N	18.32 E
127	Otranto, Str. of	It.	40.30 N	18.50 E
149	Otsu (ō'tsōō)	Jap.	35.2 N	135.52 E
117	Ottaiano (ôt-tä-yä'nō)	It. (Napoli In.)	40.51 N	14.29 E
118	Ottavand (L.) (ôt'tâ-vän)	Nor.	61.53 N	8.45 E
55	Ottawa (ŏt'à-wà)	Can.	45.30 N	75.44 W
54	Ottawa	Can. (In.)		
79	Ottawa	Ill.	41.21 N	88.50 W
79	Ottawa	Kan.	38.37 N	95.16 W
84	Ottawa	Ohio	41.2 N	84.4 W
55	Ottawa Is.	Can.	59.45 N	80.0 W
84	Ottawa Pt.	Mich.	44.15 N	83.25 W
55	Ottawa R.	Can.	46.30 N	78.30 W
75	Otter Cr. (ŏt'ĕr)	Utah	38.20 N	111.55 W
86	Otter Cr.	Vt.	43.55 N	73.13 W
118	Otter R. (ŏt'ĕr)	Nor.	59.15 N	7.30 E
76	Otter Tail L.	Minn.	46.24 N	95.38 W
135	Ottery (ŏt'ĕr-ĭ)	U. S. Afr.	34.5 S	18.31 E
93	Otumba (ô-tŭm'bä)	Mex.	19.41 N	98.47 W
77	Ottumwa (ô-tŭm'wà)	Ia.	41.0 N	92.22 W
159	Otway, C. (ŏt'wā)	Austl.	38.52 S	143.33 E
102	Otway Water	Chl.	53.0 S	71.30 W
121	Otwock (ôt'vôtsk)	Pol.	52.5 N	21.17 E
79	Ouachita Mts. (wŏsh'ĭ-tô)	Okla.-Ark.	34.30 N	94.30 W
59	Ouachita R.	Ark.	33.30 N	92.45 W
133	Ouada (Reg.) (wä'dä)	Fr. Eq. Afr.-A. E. Sud.	13.0 N	21.0 E
132	Ouagadougou (wä'gà-dōō'gōō)	Fr. W. Afr.	12.26 N	1.44 W
132	Ouahigouya (wä-ē-gōō'yä)	Fr. W. Afr.	13.36 N	2.27 W
132	Oualata (wä-lä'tä)	Fr. W. Afr.	17.11 N	6.48 W
132	Ouallèn (Well) (wäl-lân')	Alg.	24.40 N	1.10 E
97	Ouanaminthe (wä-nà-măNt')	Hai.	19.33 N	71.45 W
133	Ouanda Djalé (wän'dà jä-lā')	Fr. Eq. Afr.	9.0 N	22.48 E
132	Ouargla (wär'glä)	Alg.	32.0 N	5.21 E
132	Oudjda (ōōj-dä') (ōōj'dä)	Mor.	34.40 N	2.0 W
134	Oudtshoorn (outs'hōrn)	U. S. Afr.	33.35 S	22.11 E
132	Oued-Zem (wĕd-zĕm')	Mor.	33.2 N	5.45 W
133	Oueita (wä-ē-tä')	Fr. Eq. Afr.	17.40 N	20.27 E
133	Ouesso (wĕs-sô')	Fr. Eq. Afr.	1.32 N	16.0 E
132	Ouezzan (wĕ-zän')	Sp. Mor.	34.50 N	5.32 W
114	Oughter, Lough (L.) (lŏk ŏk'tĕr)	Ire.	54.0 N	7.30 W
132	Ouidah (wē-dä')	Fr. W. Afr.	6.28 N	2.2 E
112	Oulad Naïl, Mts. of the (ōō-làd' nà-ēl')	Alg.	34.30 N	3.0 E
122	Oullins (ōō-lăN')	Fr.	45.42 N	4.55 E
110	Oulu (ō'lōō)	Fin.	65.0 N	25.32 E
110	Oulu, L.	Fin.	64.25 N	27.30 E
110	Ounas R. (ō'näs)	Fin.	68.0 N	24.30 E
116	Oundle (ôn'd'l)	Gt. Brit.	52.28 N	0.28 W
133	Ounianga Kebir (ōō-nē-än'gà kē-bēr')	Fr. Eq. Afr.	19.2 N	20.17 E
75	Ouray (ōō-rā')	Colo.	38.2 N	107.39 W
124	Ourique (ō-rē'kĕ)	Port.	37.39 N	8.12 W
101	Ouro Preto (ō'rōō prā'tōō)	Braz.	20.28 S	43.30 W
160	Ouse R. (ōōz)	Austl. (Tas. In.)	42.15 S	146.50 E
114	Ouse, R.	Gt. Brit.	52.25 N	0.0
132	Outak-el-Had (ōō-tàk'-ĕl-hàd')	Mor.	33.25 N	3.38 W
55	Outarde R. (ōō-tàrd')	Can.	51.30 N	69.5 W
91	Outer Bras (I.) (bräs) (brä)	Vir. Is.	18.24 N	64.58 W
114	Outer Hebrides (Is.) (hĕb'rĭ-dēz)	Gt. Brit.	57.58 N	7.30 W
87	Outer I.	Can.	51.5 N	58.35 W
77	Outer I.	U. S.	47.3 N	90.25 W
124	Outes (ō-ōō'tās)	Sp.	42.51 N	8.55 W
134	Outjo (ōt'yō)	S. W. Afr.	20.6 S	16.12 E
122	Outreau (ōō-trō')	Fr.	50.41 N	1.38 E
102	Ovalle (ô-väl'yā)	Chl.	30.40 S	71.20 W
124	Ovar (ô-vär')	Port.	40.53 N	8.38 W
89	Overland (ō'vĕr-lănd)	Mo. (St. Louis In.)	38.42 N	90.21 W
129	Ovidiopol (ô-vê-dê-ô'pôl')	Sov. Un.	46.14 N	30.25 E
124	Oviedo (ō-vê-ā'dhō)	Sp.	43.22 N	5.51 W
129	Ovruch (ôv'rŏŏch)	Sov. Un.	51.19 N	28.51 E
149	Owada (ō'wä-dà)	Jap. (Tokyo In.)	35.44 N	140.6 E
85	Owasco, L. (ō-wăs'kō)	N. Y.	42.52 N	76.32 W
149	Owase (ō'wä-sä)	Jap.	34.4 N	136.11 E
89	Owasso L. (ō-wăs'sō)	Minn. (Minneapolis In.)	45.2 N	93.7 W
77	Owatonna (ō-wà-tŏn'à)	Minn.	44.5 N	93.12 W
85	Owego (ō-wē'gō)	N. Y.	42.6 N	76.17 W
77	Owen (ō'ĕn)	Wis.	44.57 N	90.32 W
55	Owen Sd.	Can.	44.40 N	80.57 W
84	Owensboro (ō'ĕnz-bŭr-ô)	Ky.	38.46 N	87.7 W
74	Owens L. (ō'ĕnz)	Calif.	36.25 N	117.45 W
74	Owens R.	Calif.	37.15 N	118.18 W
151	Owen Stanley Ra. (ō'ĕn stăn'lē)	Pap. Ter.	9.15 S	147.50 E
84	Owensville (ō'ĕnz-vĭl)	Ind.	38.27 N	87.40 W
79	Owensville	Mo.	38.19 N	91.30 W
84	Owenton (ō'ĕn-tŭn)	Ky.	38.34 N	84.55 W
132	Owerri (ô-wĕr'ē)	Nig.	5.28 N	7.0 E
71	Owl Cr. (oul)	Wyo.	43.42 N	108.40 W
84	Owosso (ô-wŏs'ō)	Mich.	42.0 N	84.12 W
70	Owyhee Reservoir (ô-wī'hē)	Ore.	43.25 N	117.20 W
70	Owyhee R.	Ore.	42.40 N	117.10 W
70	Owyhee R., South Fork	Ida.	42.18 N	116.53 W
93	Oxchuc (ôs-chōōk')	Mex.	16.49 N	92.23 W
82	Oxford (ŏks'fērd)	Ala.	33.36 N	85.50 W
86	Oxford	Can.	45.43 N	63.51 W
73	Oxford	Ga. (Atlanta In.)	33.37 N	83.53 W
114	Oxford	Gt. Brit.	51.45 N	1.15 W
87	Oxford	Mass. (In.)	42.7 N	71.52 W
84	Oxford	Mich.	42.52 N	83.16 W
79	Oxford	Miss.	34.22 N	89.31 W
157	Oxford	N. Z.	43.17 S	172.12 E
83	Oxford	N. C.	36.18 N	78.35 W
84	Oxford	Ohio	39.32 N	84.46 W
116	Oxford Co.	Gt. Brit.	52.6 N	1.24 W
73	Oxmoor (ŏks'mōōr)	Ala. (Birmingham In.)	33.26 N	86.51 W
74	Oxnard (ŏks'närd)	Calif.	34.12 N	119.11 W
149	Oyamazaki (ō'yä-mä-zä'kē)	Jap. (Osaka In.)	34.54 N	135.40 E
101	Oyapock, R. (ō-yà-pŏk')	Fr. Gui.-Braz.	2.30 N	52.30 W
147	Oye I. (ō'yà)	Jap.	32.28 N	130.20 E
132	Oyem (ô-yĕm) (ô-yăN')	Fr. Eq. Afr.	1.40 N	11.33 E
132	Oyo (ō'yō)	Nig.	7.57 N	3.58 E
123	Oyonnax (ô-yô-näks')	Fr.	46.18 N	5.40 E
160	Oyster B. (ois'tĕr)	Austl. (Tas. In.)	42.10 S	148.10 E
81	Oyster Bayou	Tex. (In.)	29.40 N	94.32 W
81	Oyster Creek	Tex. (In.)	29.15 N	95.30 W
97	Ozama R. (ô-zä'mä)	Dom. Rep.	18.40 N	69.50 W
82	Ozark (ō'zärk)	Ala.	31.28 N	85.28 W
79	Ozark	Ark.	35.29 N	93.48 W
79	Ozark Plat.	Mo.	37.10 N	93.0 W
79	Ozarks, L. of the	Mo.	38.13 N	93.7 W
128	Ozery (ô-zyô'rē)	Sov. Un.	54.52 N	38.34 E
126	Ozieri (ō-zyā'rē)	Sard.	40.35 N	9.1 E
123	Ozoir-la-Ferrière (ô-zwär'-lä-fĕr-ê-âr')	Fr. (In.)	48.46 N	2.40 E
121	Ozorków (ô-zôr'kŏŏf)	Pol.	51.58 N	19.20 E
93	Ozuluama (ō'zōō-lōō-ä'mä)	Mex.	21.35 N	97.52 W
134	Paarl (pärl)	U. S. Afr.	33.45 S	18.57 E
155	Paauilo (pä-ä-ōō'ē-lō)	Haw.	20.4 N	155.25 W
121	Pabianice (pä-byà-nē'tsĕ)	Pol.	51.40 N	19.23 E
100	Pacaraíma, Serra (Mts.) (sĕr'rà pä-kä-rä-ē'mà)	Ven.-Braz.	0.4 N	63.0 W
100	Pacasmayo (pä-käs-mä'yō)	Peru	7.0 S	79.30 W
144	Pachai (pä'chī')	Chn.	26.8 N	107.40 E
146	Pachow (pä'chō')	Chn.	39.13 N	116.21 E
142	Pachu (pä'chōō')	Chn.	39.45 N	78.40 E
92	Pachuca (pä-chōō'kä)	Mex.	20.8 N	98.43 W
51	Pacific (pà-sĭf'ĭk)	Wash. (Seattle In.)	47.15 N	122.15 W
74	Pacific Beach	Calif. (In.)	32.47 N	117.0 W
74	Pacific Grove	Calif.	36.36 N	121.55 W
154	Pacific O.			
73	Pacific Palisades	Calif. (Los Angeles In.)	34.3 N	118.32 W
153	Pacijan I. (pä-sē'hän)	Phil.	10.40 N	124.20 E
150	Padang (pä-däng')	Indon.	0.59 S	100.29 E
137	Padang I.	Indon. (In.)	1.10 N	102.20 E
84	Paden City (pā'dĕn)	W. Va.	39.34 N	80.56 W
120	Paderborn (pä-dĕr-bôrn')	Ger.	51.43 N	8.45 E
116	Padiham (păd'ĭ-hăm)	Gt. Brit.	53.48 N	2.19 W
92	Padilla (pä-dēl'yä)	Mex.	23.58 N	98.43 W
126	Padova (Padua) (pä'dô-vä) (păd'ū-à)	It.	45.25 N	11.50 E
81	Padre I. (pä'drā)	Tex.	27.0 N	97.23 W
126	Padua (Padova) (păd'ū-à) (pä'dô-vä)	It.	45.25 N	11.50 E
82	Paducah (pà-dū'kà)	Ky.	37.4 N	88.35 W
102	Pae I. (pä'â)	Braz. (In.)	22.59 S	43.5 W
148	Paektusan (Mt.) (pâk'tōō-sän')	Kor.	41.59 N	128.4 E
156	Paeroa (pä-à-rō'à)	N. Z.	37.22 S	175.43 E
151	Paete (pä-ā'tâ)	Phil. (Manila In.)	14.22 N	121.33 E
126	Pag (I.) (päg)	Yugo.	44.35 N	14.55 E
150	Paga I., North (pä'gä)	Indon.	2.35 S	100.0 E
150	Paga I., South	Indon.	3.0 S	100.25 E

ng-sing; ŋ-baŋk; N-nasalized n: nŏd; cŏmmit; ōld; ôbey; ôrder; fōōd; fŏŏt; ou-out; s-soft; sh-dish; th-thin; pūre; ûnite; ûrn; stŭd; circŭs; ū-as "y" in study; '-indeterminate vowel.

Pagosa Springs PRONOUNCING INDEX Parma

Page	Name Pronunciation Region	Lat. °′	Long. °′
75	Pagosa Springs (pá-gō'sá)...Colo.	37.16 N	107.2 W
151	Pagsanjan (päg-sän-hän') Phil. (Manila In.)	14.16 N	121.31 E
155	Pahala (pä-hä'lä)..........Haw.	19.11 N	155.29 W
156	Pahiatua (pä'hē-ä'tōō-ä)....N. Z.	40.27 S	175.50 E
140	Pahlevi (Enzeli) (pä'lĕ-vē') (ĕn'zĕ-lē).Iran	37.30 N	49.29 E
83	Pahokee (pá-hō'kē).....Fla. (In.)	26.47 N	80.39 W
119	Paide (pī'dĕ)...........Sov. Un.	58.54 N	25.32 E
119	Päijänne L. (pĕ'ē-yĕn-nĕ)....Fin.	61.35 N	25.30 E
110	Pai-Koi Range (pī-kō'ē)..Sov. Un.	69.10 N	62.30 E
155	Pailolo Channel (pä-ē-lō'lō)..Haw.	21.5 N	156.40 W
84	Painesville (pānz'vĭl)........Ohio	41.42 N	81.14 W
84	Paintsville (pānts'vĭl)........Ky.	37.50 N	82.50 W
146	Paisiang (pī'syäng')........Chn.	37.32 N	114.46 E
114	Paisley (pāz'lĭ)..........Gt. Brit.	55.50 N	4.29 W
100	Paita (pä-ē'tä).............Peru	5.10 S	81.2 W
153	Paitan B. (pä-ē-tän').....N. Bor.	6.50 N	117.20 E
74	Paiute Ind. Res. (pī-ūt')....Calif.	37.35 N	118.30 W
75	Paiute Ind. Res.............Utah	38.15 N	113.50 W
93	Pajápan (pä-hä'pän).........Mex.	18.15 N	94.42 W
156	Paketutu (Neekes I.) (pä-kĕ-tōō'-tōō) (nēks).N. Z. (In.)	36.58 S	174.45 E
150	Pakhoi (päk'hoi')..........Chn.	21.30 N	109.0 E
144	Paklow (päk'lō')...........Chn.	22.52 N	110.18 E
150	Paknambo (päk-näm'bō)....Siam	15.45 N	100.0 E
142	Pakokku (pä-kŏk'kōō).......Bur.	21.21 N	95.5 E
126	Pakrac (pä'kräts)..........Yugo.	45.26 N	17.13 E
121	Paks (pôksh).............Hung.	46.38 N	18.53 E
81	Palacios (pá-lä'syōs)........Tex.	28.43 N	96.12 W
125	Palafrugell (pä-lä-frōō-gĕl')...Sp.	41.55 N	3.4 E
123	Palaiseau (pá-lĕ-zō').....Fr. (In.)	48.42 N	2.15 E
125	Palamós (pä-lä-mōs')..........Sp.	41.51 N	3.7 E
152	Palanan B. (pä-lä'nän).......Phil.	17.12 N	122.25 E
152	Palanan Pt................Phil.	17.9 N	122.30 E
127	Palanka (pä'län-kä)........Yugo.	44.20 N	20.56 E
127	Palanka...................Yugo.	45.16 N	19.25 E
141	Palanpur (pä'lŭn-pōōr)......India	24.14 N	72.30 E
152	Palapag (pä-lä'päg)..........Phil.	12.33 N	125.7 E
134	Palapye (pá-läp'yĕ)..........Bech.	22.35 S	27.20 E
124	Palas de Rey (pä-läs' dā rā'ē)..Sp.	42.53 N	7.49 W
83	Palatka (pá-lăt'ká)..........Fla.	29.38 N	81.40 W
151	Palau Is. (pä-lä'ōō).......Pac. O.	7.30 N	134.35 E
152	Palaui I. (pä-lou'ē).........Phil.	18.32 N	122.9 E
152	Palauig (pä-lou'ēg)..........Phil.	15.26 N	119.55 E
152	Palauig Pt................Phil.	15.26 N	119.53 E
153	Palawan (I.) (pä-lä'wän).....Phil.	9.35 N	118.30 E
126	Palazzola (pä-lät'sô-lō)........It.	37.9 N	14.53 E
150	Palembang (pä-lĕm-bäng').Indon.	2.59 S	104.39 E
94	Palencia (pä-lĕn'sê-ä)......Guat.	14.42 N	90.22 W
124	Palencia....................Sp.	42.0 N	4.31 W
93	Palenque (pä-lĕŋ'kā).........Mex.	17.33 N	91.58 W
97	Palenque Pt.........Dom. Rep.	18.14 N	70.10 W
126	Palermo (pä-lĕr'mō)...........It.	38.7 N	13.23 E
137	Palestine (păl'ĕs-tīn)....Asia (In.)	32.0 N	35.0 E
81	Palestine..................Tex.	31.47 N	95.37 W
141	Paletwa (pŭ-lĕt'wä).........Bur.	21.12 N	92.50 E
94	Palín (pä-lēn')..............Guat.	14.24 N	90.42 W
74	Palisade (păl-ĭ-säd')........Nev.	40.38 N	116.12 W
72	Palisade Mt...Colo. (Denver In.)	40.26 N	105.19 W
88	Palisades, The (Park) (păl-ĭ-sādz') N. J. (N. Y. In.)	40.52 N	73.58 W
93	Palizada (pä-lê-zä'dä).......Mex.	18.17 N	92.3 W
141	Palk Str. (pôk)............India	10.0 N	79.30 E
157	Palliser B. (pôl'ĭ-sēr)........N. Z.	41.25 S	175.0 E
157	Palliser, C.................N. Z.	41.37 S	175.17 E
135	Palma (päl'mä)..........Moz.	10.43 S	40.25 E
125	Palma......................Sp.	39.34 N	2.39 E
125	Palma B....................Sp.	39.28 N	2.40 E
124	Palma del Río (päl'mä dĕl rē'ō) Sp.	37.42 N	5.18 W
132	Palma I. (päl'mä)........Can. Is.	28.45 N	17.50 W
102	Palmas (päl'mäs)...........Braz.	26.28 S	52.0 W
153	Palmas I..................Phil.	5.32 N	126.36 E
97	Palma Soriano (päl'mä sô-ré-ä'nō).Cuba	20.13 N	76.0 W
83	Palm Beach (päm bēch').Fla. (In.)	26.43 N	80.2 W
125	Palmela (päl-mā'lä)....Port. (In.)	38.34 N	8.54 W
51	Palmer (päm'ēr) Wash. (Portland In.)	45.33 N	122.7 W
72	Palmer Lake.Colo. (Colo. Sprs. In.)	39.8 N	104.55 W
89	Palmer L. Minn. (Minneapolis In.)	45.5 N	93.19 W
47	Palmer Pen..................Ant.	70.0 S	65.0 W
157	Palmerston (päm'ēr-stŭn)...N. Z.	45.30 S	170.43 E
159	Palmerville (päm'ēr-vĭl).....Austl.	16.5 S	144.14 E
83	Palmetto (păl-mĕt'ō)....Fla. (In.)	27.32 N	82.34 W
73	Palmetto.......Ga. (Atlanta In.)	33.31 N	84.41 W
97	Palmetto Pt.................Ba. Is.	25.10 N	76.10 W
126	Palmi (päl'mē)...............It.	38.22 N	15.52 E
100	Palmira (päl-mē'rä)..........Col.	3.30 N	76.28 W
96	Palmira....................Cuba	22.13 N	80.23 W
92	Palmito de la Virgen (I.) (päl-mē'-tō dā lä vēr-kĕn').Mex.	23.0 N	106.11 W
92	Palmito del Verde I. (päl-mē'tō dĕl vĕr'dā).Mex.	22.40 N	105.49 W
79	Palmyra (păl-mī'rá).........Mo.	39.46 N	91.31 W
140	Palmyra (Ruins)............Syr.	34.30 N	38.17 E
4	Palmyra I................Pac. O.	5.53 N	162.5 W
153	Palo (pä'lō)................Phil.	11.9 N	12.5 E
74	Palo Alto (pä'lō äl'tō).......Calif.	37.26 N	122.10 W
78	Paloduro Cr. (pä-lō-dōō'rō)..Tex.	36.25 N	101.5 W
80	Paloma, L. (pä-lō'mä)......Mex.	26.50 N	103.55 W
101	Palominos (I.) (pä-lō-mē'nōs) Peru (In.)	12.8 S	77.15 W
153	Palompon (pä-lôm-pōn').....Phil.	11.3 N	124.23 E
125	Palos C. (pä'lōs)..............Sp.	37.37 N	0.41 W
88	Palos Park (pä'lōs) Ill. (Chicago In.)	41.40 N	87.50 W
70	Palouse (pá-lōōz')...........Wash.	46.55 N	117.5 W
70	Palouse R..................Wash.	47.0 N	117.40 W
142	Palti, L. (Yamdok) (päl'tē) (yäm-dôk').Chn.	29.0 N	90.45 E

Page	Name Pronunciation Region	Lat. °′	Long. °′
111	Palu (pä-lōō')...............Tur.	38.48 N	40.8 E
152	Paluan (pä-lōō'än)...........Phil.	13.25 N	120.29 E
152	Pambuhan (päm-bōō'än)....Phil.	12.33 N	124.56 E
122	Pamiers (pá-myā')...........Fr.	43.8 N	1.35 E
142	Pamir (Highland) (pä-mēr') Sov. Un.-Chn.	38.0 N	73.50 E
83	Pamlico R. (păm'lĭ-kō).....N. C.	35.25 N	76.50 W
83	Pamlico Sd.................N. C.	35.20 N	76.0 W
78	Pampa (păm'pá)..............Tex.	35.33 N	100.55 W
151	Pampanga (Prov.) (päm-päŋ'gä) Phil. (Manila In.)	15.2 N	120.35 E
152	Pampanga R...............Phil.	15.20 N	120.55 E
102	Pampas (Reg.) (päm'päs)....Arg.	33.30 S	62.0 W
124	Pampilhosa (päm-pē-lyō'sá).Port.	40.21 N	8.25 W
100	Pamplona (päm-plō'nä)......Col.	7.10 N	72.45 W
124	Pamplona...................Sp.	42.48 N	1.39 W
85	Pamunkey R. (pá-mŭŋ'kĭ)....Va.	37.45 N	77.20 W
79	Pana (pā'ná)..................Ill.	39.24 N	89.5 W
153	Panabutan B. (pä-nä-bōō'tän) Phil.	7.35 N	122.7 E
127	Panagyuriste (pá-ná-gyōō'rêsh-tĕ) Bul.	42.29 N	24.11 E
95	Panama (păn-á-mä')....Cen. Am.	8.50 N	80.0 W
95	Panama...................Pan.	8.58 N	79.32 W
95	Panama, B. of.............Pan.	8.50 N	79.15 W
95	Panama Canal..............C. Z.	9.5 N	79.40 W
82	Panama City................Fla.	30.9 N	85.39 W
95	Panama, G. of..............Pan.	7.50 N	79.20 W
95	Panama, Isth. of............Pan.	9.30 N	79.55 W
153	Panaon I. (pä-nä-ōn')........Phil.	10.3 N	125.12 E
126	Panaria (I.) (pä-nä'rē-ä).......It.	38.39 N	15.4 E
126	Panaro R. (pä-nä'rō)...........It.	44.40 N	11.0 E
153	Panay (pä-nī')..............Phil.	11.34 N	122.48 E
153	Panay G...................Phil.	10.20 N	122.20 E
153	Panay (I.).................Phil.	11.10 N	122.30 E
153	Panay R...................Phil.	11.20 N	122.40 E
127	Pančevo (pän'chĕ-vô)......Yugo.	44.52 N	20.41 E
134	Panda (pän'dä')........Bel. Cong.	10.52 S	27.13 E
153	Pandan (pän-dän')..........Phil.	11.43 N	122.6 E
152	Pandan....................Phil.	14.2 N	124.10 E
153	Pandaras Pt. (pän-dä'räs)..N. Bor.	6.4 N	118.0 E
96	Pan de Guajaibon (Mt.) (pän dā gwä-jä-bōn').Cuba	22.41 N	83.27 W
95	Pando, Cerro (Mt.) (sĕr'rō pän'dō) Pan.	9.3 N	82.49 W
153	Panducan I. (pän-dōō'kän)..Phil.	61.7 N	120.40 E
138	Pandzh R. (pändzh).Sov. Un.-Afg.	37.0 N	71.25 E
119	Panevežys (pä'nyĕ-vāzh'ēs) Sov. Un.	55.44 N	24.20 E
133	Panga (päŋ'gä).........Bel. Cong.	1.51 N	26.40 E
135	Pangani (pän-gä'nē)..........Tan.	5.25 S	38.52 E
135	Pangani (Ruvu) R. (pän'gä'nē) (rōō'vōō).Tan.	5.0 S	38.6 E
151	Pangil (pän-gēl').Phil. (Manila In.)	14.25 N	121.32 E
150	Pangkalpinang (päng-käl'pē-näng').Indon.	2.5 S	106.5 E
153	Panglao (pän-glä'ô)..........Phil.	9.35 N	123.47 E
153	Panglao I..................Phil.	9.35 N	123.50 E
153	Panguil B. (pän-gēl')........Phil.	8.2 N	123.45 E
75	Panguitch (päŋ'gwĭch).......Utah	37.51 N	112.28 W
153	Pangutarang Group (Is.)....Phil.	6.20 N	120.30 E
153	Pangutarang I. (päŋ-gōō-tä'räng) Phil.	6.20 N	120.33 E
152	Paniqui (pä-nē'kē)..........Phil.	15.40 N	120.35 E
153	Panitan (pä-nē'tän)..........Phil.	11.28 N	122.45 E
150	Panjang R. (pän-yäng')......Indon.	1.0 N	102.15 E
117	Pankow (päŋ'kō).Ger. (Berlin In.)	52.35 N	13.24 E
156	Panmure (păn'mūr)...N. Z. (In.)	36.54 S	174.52 E
151	Pantar (I.) (pän'tär)........Indon.	8.20 S	124.15 E
112	Pantelleria (I.) (pän-tĕl-lä-rē'ä).It.	36.52 N	11.58 E
93	Pantepec (pän-tä-pĕk')........Mex.	17.10 N	93.0 W
123	Pantin (päN-tăN')........Fr. (In.)	48.53 N	2.24 E
124	Pantón (pän-tōn')............Sp.	42.31 N	7.36 W
153	Pantukan (pän-tōō'kän).....Phil.	7.8 N	125.54 E
92	Pánuco (pä'nōō-kô).........Mex.	22.4 N	98.11 W
92	Pánuco....................Mex.	23.27 N	105.54 W
80	Pánuco de Coronado (pä'nōō-kô dä kō-rō-nä'dhō).Mex.	24.31 N	104.20 W
92	Pánuco, R..................Mex.	22.7 N	98.10 W
140	Panwel R. (pän-wĕl') India (Bombay In.)	18.58 N	72.58 E
94	Panzós (pän-zós')...........Guat.	15.26 N	89.39 W
152	Paoay (pä-ô-ī')..............Phil.	18.4 N	120.31 E
144	Paoking (pou'kĭng')..........Chn.	27.6 N	111.20 E
126	Paola (pä-ô'lä)................It.	39.21 N	16.3 E
79	Paola (pā-ō'lá)...............Kan.	38.34 N	94.52 W
84	Paoli (pā-ō'lī)................Ind.	38.36 N	86.30 W
151	Paombong (pä-ôm-bông') Phil. (Manila In.)	14.51 N	120.45 E
75	Paonia (pā-ō'nyá)............Colo.	38.51 N	107.37 W
142	Paoning (pä'ô-nĭng')..........Chn.	31.33 N	105.58 E
145	Paoshan (pä'ô-shän')........Chn.	31.23 N	121.26 E
146	Paoti (pä'ô-tē')..............Chn.	39.44 N	117.15 E
146	Paoting (pä'ô-tĭng')..........Chn.	38.59 N	115.24 E
143	Paotowchen (pä'ô-tō'chĕn')..Chn.	40.33 N	110.2 E
144	Paosting (pä'ôs-tĭng')........Chn.	28.43 N	109.35 E
146	Paoying (pä'ô-yĭng')..........Chn.	33.13 N	119.19 E
146	Paoying L...................Chn.	33.0 N	119.15 E
121	Pápa (pä'pô)...............Hung.	47.18 N	17.28 E
75	Papago Ind. Res. (pä'pä-gō)..Ariz.	32.30 N	115.0 W
92	Papagayo Lagoon...........Mex.	16.45 N	99.45 W
92	Papagayo, R. (pä-pä-gä'yō).Mex.	17.8 N	99.30 W
93	Papaloapan, R. (pä'pä-lô-ä'pän) Mex.	18.20 N	95.50 W
93	Papalotla (pä-pä-lōt'lä).Mex. (In.)	19.34 N	98.51 W
93	Papalotla, R..........Mex. (In.)	19.35 N	98.55 W
93	Papantla (pä-pän'tlä).........Mex.	20.27 N	97.18 W
157	Papanui (pä'pä-nōō'ē).N. Z. (In.)	43.29 S	172.36 E
157	Papanui, Inlet.........N. Z. (In.)	45.51 S	170.43 E
156	Papatoetoe (pä-pä-tō'tō) N. Z. (In.)	36.58 S	174.51 E
120	Papenburg (päp'ĕn-bōōrgh)..Ger.	53.3 N	7.23 E

Page	Name Pronunciation Region	Lat. °′	Long. °′
142	Papien R. (pä'pyĕn').Chn.-Indoch.	23.0 N	101.45 E
125	Papiol (pä-pē-ōl')........Sp. (In.)	41.26 N	2.0 E
	Papua, see New Guinea (I.), Pac. O.		
151	Papua, Ter. of.......New Guinea	8.0 S	144.0 E
102	Paqueta I. (pä-kä'tä)..Braz. (In.)	22.45 S	43.6 W
101	Pará (State) (pä-rä').......Braz.	5.0 S	50.0 W
101	Pará........................Braz.	19.58 S	44.40 W
101	Para (Belém) (pä-rä') (bā-lĕN') Braz. (In.)	1.28 S	48.29 W
152	Paracale (pä-rä-kä'lä).......Phil.	14.17 N	122.47 E
101	Paracatú (pä-rä-kä-tōō')....Braz.	17.15 S	46.58 W
150	Paracel Is. (China) (pä-rä-sĕl') Indoch.	16.35 N	112.0 E
158	Parachilna (pá-rá-chĭl'ná)..Austl.	31.9 S	138.26 E
92	Paracho (pä-rä'chô).........Mex.	19.38 N	102.0 W
127	Paraćin (pá'rä-chēn).......Yugo.	43.49 N	21.25 E
73	Paradise (păr'á-dīs) Utah (Salt Lake City In.)	41.34 N	111.50 W
70	Paradise Valley..............Neb.	41.28 N	117.31 W
79	Paragould (păr'á-gōōld).....Ark.	36.3 N	90.29 W
100	Paraguano, Pen. of (pä-rä-gwä'nō) Ven.	11.45 N	70.0 W
101	Paraguassú, R. (pä'rä-gwä-sōō') Braz.	12.32 S	40.0 W
102	Paraguay (păr'á-gwā) (pä-rä-gwī') S. A.	24.0 S	57.0 W
102	Paraguay, R..................S. A.	22.30 S	57.50 W
101	Parahiba (State) (pä-rä-ē'bä).Braz.	7.0 S	36.30 W
99	Parahiba do Sul (pä-rä-ē'bä dōō sōōl').Braz. (Rio de Janeiro In.)	22.11 S	43.21 W
101	Parahiba (João Pessoa) (zhô-ouN' pĕ-sô'á).Braz.	7.3 S	34.55 W
99	Parahiba, R. Braz. (Rio de Janeiro In.)	22.20 S	43.45 W
90	Paraíso (pä-rä-ē'sō)....C. Z. (In.)	9.2 N	79.38 W
95	Paraíso.....................C.R.	9.50 N	83.53 W
93	Paraíso.....................Mex.	18.23 N	93.10 W
157	Parakanui, B. (pä'rä'kä-nōō'ē) N. Z. (In.)	45.45 S	170.39 E
132	Parakou (pá-rá-kōō')..Fr. W. Afr.	9.27 N	2.33 E
101	Paramaribo (pá-rá-mä'rē-bō).Sur.	5.45 N	55.15 W
122	Paramé (pä-rä-mā').............Fr.	48.41 N	1.55 W
139	Paramushiro (I.) (pä'rá-mōō-shē'rō).Jap.	50.30 N	156.0 E
102	Paraná (pä-rä-nä')..........Arg.	31.45 S	60.31 W
101	Paraná (State)..............Braz.	24.0 S	51.30 W
101	Paranaguá (pä-rä-ná-gwä')..Braz.	9.0 S	44.0 W
102	Paranaguá..................Braz.	25.30 S	48.30 W
101	Paranahiba R. (pä-rä-ná-ē'bá) Braz.	18.30 S	49.30 W
151	Paranaque (pä-rä-nä'kä) Phil. (Manila In.)	14.30 N	120.59 E
101	Paraná, R. (pä-rä-nä')......Braz.	13.0 S	47.0 W
102	Paraná, R....................S. A.	30.0 S	59.30 W
101	Pará, R. (pä-rä')..........Braz.	0.30 S	48.28 W
128	Para R.................Sov. Un.	53.56 N	41.0 E
99	Parati (pä-rä'tē) Braz. (Rio de Janeiro In.)	23.13 S	44.43 W
160	Parattah (pá-răt'á).Austl. (Tas.In.)	42.23 S	147.28 E
122	Paray-le-Monial (pá-rĕ'lē-mô-nyál').Fr.	46.27 N	4.18 E
120	Parchim (pär'kĭm)..........Ger.	53.24 N	11.51 E
121	Parczew (pär'chĕf)............Pol.	51.37 N	22.53 E
101	Pardo, R. (pär'dō)...........Braz.	15.15 S	40.30 W
120	Pardubice (pär'dōō-bĭt-sĕ)..Czech.	50.2 N	15.47 E
101	Parecis, Serra dos (Mts.) (sĕr'rá dōs pä-rá-sēzh').Braz.	12.30 S	61.0 W
124	Paredes de Nava (pä-rā'dās dā nä'vä).Sp.	42.12 N	4.40 W
126	Parenzo (pä-rĕnt'sō).......Yugo.	45.11 N	13.37 E
125	Parets (pä-räts')........Sp. (In.)	41.33 N	2.13 E
100	Paria, G. of (pä'rē-ä)...Trin. (In.)	10.30 N	61.36 W
75	Paria R. (păr-ē-á)...........Utah	37.15 N	111.55 W
80	Parida, R. de la (pä-rē'dä)...Mex.	26.30 N	104.40 W
100	Parima, Serra (Mts.) (sĕr'rá pä-rē'mä).Ven.-Braz.	3.0 N	64.30 W
100	Pariña Pt. (pä-rēn'yä)..........Ec.	4.45 S	81.15 W
101	Parintins (pä-rĭn-tĭNzh')....Braz.	2.45 S	56.33 W
79	Paris (păr'ĭs)...............Ark.	35.17 N	93.43 W
84	Paris......................Can.	43.13 N	80.24 W
122	Paris (pá-rē')..................Fr.	48.52 N	2.20 E
123	Paris...................Fr. (In.)		
84	Paris (păr'ĭs)..................Ill.	39.37 N	87.40 W
84	Paris.......................Ky.	38.14 N	84.16 W
79	Paris.......................Mo.	39.27 N	92.0 W
82	Paris.......................Tenn.	36.17 N	88.20 W
79	Paris.......................Tex.	33.39 N	95.33 W
95	Parita G. (pä-rē'tä).........Pan.	8.10 N	80.20 W
137	Parit Jawa (pä'rêt jä'vä) Malaya (In.)	1.57 N	102.39 E
75	Park City....................Utah	40.38 N	111.30 W
72	Parker (pär'kēr).Colo. (Denver In.)	39.31 N	104.45 W
76	Parker......................S. D.	43.24 N	97.9 W
75	Parker Dam..........Ariz.-Calif.	34.14 N	114.20 W
84	Parkersburg (pär'kērz-bûrg) W. Va.	39.16 N	81.32 W
77	Park Falls..................Wis.	45.56 N	90.28 W
117	Parkgate (pärk'gāt) Gt. Brit. (Liverpool In.)	53.19 N	3.6 W
51	Parkland (pärk'lănd) Wash. (Seattle In.)	47.8 N	122.26 W
81	Park Place..........Tex. (In.)	20.41 N	95.16 W
78	Park Range...................Colo.	40.45 N	106.35 W
77	Park Rapids.................Minn.	46.55 N	95.2 W
88	Park Ridge.....Ill. (Chicago In.)	42.1 N	87.50 W
76	Park River..................N. D.	48.22 N	97.43 W
160	Parkside (pärk'sīd) Austl. (Adelaide In.)	34.56 S	138.37 E
76	Parkston (pärks'tŭn).......S. D.	43.24 N	97.59 W
75	Park View..................N. M.	36.43 N	106.32 W
125	Parla (pär'lä)..........Sp. (In.)	40.14 N	3.35 W
126	Parma (pär'mä)................It.	44.47 N	10.20 E

ăt; finăl; rāte; senâte; ärm; ȧsk; sofá; fâre; ch-choose; dh-as th in other; bē; êvent; bĕt; recĕnt; cratēr; g-go; gh-gutteral g; bĭt; ĭ-short neutral; rīde; K-gutteral k as ch in German ich;

Parma PRONOUNCING INDEX Pen-y-ghent

Page	Name Pronunciation Region	Lat. °′	Long. °′
84	Parma....Ohio	41.24 N	81.45 W
101	Parnahiba (pär-nä-ē'bȧ).....Braz.	3.0 S	41.42 W
101	Parnahiba, R.....Braz.	4.0 S	42.50 W
127	Parnassus (Mt.) (pär-năs'ŭs). Grc.	38.31 N	22.37 E
119	Pärnu (pĕr'nōō).....Sov. Un.	58.22 N	24.30 E
119	Pärnu G.....Sov. Un.	58.15 N	24.20 E
119	Pärnu R.....Sov. Un.	58.30 N	24.55 E
159	Paroo R. (pä'rōō).....Austl.	30.0 S	144.7 E
127	Paros (pä'rôs) (pā'rŏs).....Grc.	37.4 N	25.10 E
127	Paros (I.).....Grc.	37.5 N	25.12 E
75	Parowan (păr'ô-wăn).....Utah	37.52 N	112.50 W
80	Parral (pär-räl').....Mex.	26.55 N	105.40 W
80	Parral, R.....Mex.	27.20 N	105.12 W
160	Parramatta (păr-ȧ-măt'ȧ) . . Austl.	33.48 S	150.59 E
160	Parramatta R. Austl. (Sydney In.)	33.50 S	151.4 E
80	Parras (pär-räs').....Mex.	25.28 N	102.8 W
73	Parrish (păr'ĭsh) Ala. (Birmingham In.)	33.43 N	87.18 W
86	Parrsborough (pärz'bŭr-ō) . . . Can.	45.26 N	64.19 W
53	Parry, C. (păr'ĭ).....Can.	70.0 N	123.38 W
85	Parry I.....Can.	45.15 N	80.10 W
50	Parry Is.....Can.	75.30 N	110.0 W
55	Parry Sound.....Can.	45.20 N	80.3 W
79	Parsons (pär's'nz).....Kan.	37.20 N	95.16 W
85	Parsons.....W. Va.	39.6 N	79.43 W
122	Parthenay (pȧr-t'-nĕ').....Fr.	46.39 N	0.15 W
126	Partinico (pär-tē'nê-kô).....It.	38.2 N	13.7 E
101	Parú, R. (pä-rōō').....Braz.	0.0	54.0 W
74	Pasadena (păs-ȧ-dē'nȧ).....Calif.	34.9 N	118.10 W
81	Pasadena.....Tex. (In.)	29.42 N	95.12 W
152	Pasaleng B. (pä-sä'lĕng).....Phil.	18.35 N	120.55 E
152	Pasay (pä'sä-ē).....Phil.	14.32 N	121.0 E
82	Pascagoula (păs-kȧ-gōō'lȧ) . . Miss.	30.21 N	88.33 W
82	Pascagoula R.....Miss.	30.50 N	88.45 W
121	Pascani (pȧsh-kän'').....Rom.	47.16 N	26.43 E
70	Pasco (păs'kō).....Wash.	46.13 N	119.7 W
160	Pascoe Vale (păs'kō vāl') Austl. (Melbourne In.)	37.44 S	144.55 E
100	Pasco, Nudo de (Mt.) (nōō'dô dā päs'kô) . Peru	10.45 S	76.29 W
120	Pasewalk (pä'zĕ-välk).....Ger.	53.31 N	14.1 E
148	Pashennaya (pȧsh'ĕn-nȧ-yȧ) Sov. Un.	47.47 N	134.48 E
139	Pashkova (pȧsh'kô-vȧ) . . Sov. Un.	48.59 N	130.59 E
129	Pashkovskaya (pȧsh-kôf'skȧ-yȧ) Sov. Un.	45.1 N	39.2 E
152	Pasig (pä'sĭg).....Phil.	14.34 N	121.5 E
151	Pasig R.....Phil. (Manila In.)	14.33 N	121.10 E
120	Pasing (pä'zĭng).....Ger.	48.8 N	11.27 E
94	Pasión, R. de la (pä-syōn') Guat. (In.)	16.33 N	90.20 W
127	Pašmakli (pȧsh'môk-lê).....Bul.	41.35 N	24.35 E
92	Paso de Sotos (pä'sō dā sō'tôs) Mex.	21.38 N	102.40 W
150	Pasoeroean (pȧ-sōō-rōō-än') Indon.	7.41 S	121.55 E
74	Paso Robles (pă'sō rō'blĕs) . . Calif.	35.37 N	120.43 W
85	Passaic (pă-sā'ĭk).....N. J.	40.52 N	74.8 W
88	Passaic R.....N. J. (New York In.)	40.53 N	74.15 W
86	Passamaquoddy B. (păs'ȧ-mȧ-kwŏd'ĭ) . Me.-Can.	45.5 N	66.58 W
134	Passa R. (pȧ-sä').....Fr. Eq. Afr.	2.0 S	13.32 E
120	Passau (päs'ou).....Ger.	48.34 N	13.27 E
82	Pass Christian (pȧs krĭs'tyĕn) Miss.	30.19 N	89.17 W
153	Passi (pȧs'ê).....Phil.	11.7 N	122.39 E
102	Passo Fundo (pä'sŏ fōōn'dōō) . Braz.	28.15 S	52.28 W
100	Pastaza, R. (päs-tä'zä).....Ec.	3.0 S	76.32 W
100	Pasto (päs'tō).....Col.	1.2 N	77.15 W
100	Pasto (Vol.).....Col.	1.0 N	77.15 W
152	Pasuquin (pä-sōō-kēn').....Phil.	18.20 N	120.37 E
119	Pasvalys (päs-vä-lēs') . . . . Sov. Un.	56.3 N	24.24 E
102	Patagones (pä-tä-gō'nās).....Arg.	40.50 S	62.58 W
102	Patagonia (Reg.) (păt-ȧ-gō'nĭ-ȧ) Arg.	47.0 S	69.30 W
153	Pata I. (pä'tä).....Phil.	5.48 N	121.10 E
88	Patapsco R. (pȧ-tăps'kō) Md. (Baltimore In.)	39.13 N	76.32 W
156	Patea (pȧ-tē'ȧ).....N. Z.	39.45 S	174.27 E
116	Pateley Bridge (pāt'lĭ) . . . Gt. Brit.	54.5 N	1.45 W
125	Paterna de Rivera (pä-tĕr'nä dā rē-vä'rä) . Sp. (In.)	36.31 N	5.51 W
126	Paternó (pä-tĕr-nô').....It.	37.34 N	14.52 E
85	Paterson (păt'ēr-sŭn).....N. J.	40.57 N	74.12 W
71	Pathfinder Reservoir (păth'fīn-dēr) Wyo.	44.22 N	106.55 W
141	Patiala (pŭt-ê-ä'lŭ).....India	30.16 N	76.17 E
141	Patna-Bankipore (pŭt'nŭ-băŋ'kē-pōr) . India	25.35 N	85.15 E
152	Patnanongan I. (pät-nä-nôŋ'gän) Phil.	14.48 N	122.12 E
153	Patnongon (pät-nôŋ-gōn') . . . Phil.	10.54 N	122.0 E
84	Patoka R. (pȧ-tō'kȧ).....Ind.	38.23 N	87.10 W
101	Patos (pä'tōzh).....Braz.	6.58 S	37.28 W
72	Patos I. (pä'tōs) Wash. (Vancouver In.)	48.48 N	122.57 W
102	Patos, Lagoa dos (L.) (lä'gō-ȧ dōzh pä'tōzh) Braz.	31.0 S	51.15 W
127	Patrai (Patras) (pä-trī') (pȧ-träs') Grc.	38.14 N	21.48 E
127	Patras (Patrai).....Grc.	38.14 N	21.48 E
127	Patras, G. of.....Grc.	38.15 N	21.35 E
101	Patrocinio (pä-trō-sē'nê-ōō) . Braz.	18.58 S	46.49 W
150	Pattani (păt'ȧ-nê).....Siam	6.56 N	101.15 E
86	Patten (păt''n).....Me.	45.59 N	68.28 W
81	Patterson (păt'ēr-sŭn).....La.	29.40 N	91.19 W
85	Patton (păt''n).....Pa.	40.41 N	78.42 W
95	Patuca Pt. (pä-tōō'kä).....Hond.	15.50 N	84.18 W
94	Patuca (R.).....Hond.	15.0 N	85.0 W
144	Patung (pä'tōōng').....Chn.	31.2 N	110.17 E
156	Patutahi (pä-tōō'tä-hē).....N.Z.	38.38 S	177.52 E
85	Patuxent R. (pȧ-tŭk'sĕnt) . . . Md.	39.0 N	76.45 W
92	Pátzcuaro (päts'kwä-rô).....Mex.	19.30 N	101.32 W
92	Pátzcuaro, L.....Mex.	19.35 N	101.33 W
94	Patzún (pät-zōōn').....Guat.	14.40 N	91.0 W
122	Pau (pō).....Fr.	43.18 N	0.21 W
84	Paulding (pôl'dĭng).....Ohio	41.8 N	84.37 W
101	Paulista (pou-lēs'tȧ).....Braz.	8.3 S	41.2 W
101	Paulo Affonso Falls (pou'lōō äf-fôN'sōō) . Braz.	9.28 S	38.15 W
79	Pauls Valley (pôlz).....Okla.	34.43 N	97.14 W
122	Pau R. (pō).....Fr.	43.10 N	0.10 W
155	Pauwela (pä-ōō-wä'lä).....Haw.	20.55 N	156.23 W
126	Pavia (pä-vē'ä).....It.	45.11 N	9.10 E
129	Pavoloch (pä-vô-lôch') . . . Sov. Un.	49.52 N	29.21 E
138	Pavlodar (pȧv-lô-dȧr') . . . Sov. Un.	53.15 N	77.10 E
129	Pavlograd (pȧv-lô-grȧt') . Sov. Un.	48.33 N	35.54 E
128	Pavlovsk (pȧv-lôfsk') . . . . Sov. Un.	53.2 N	30.24 E
129	Pavlovsk.....Sov. Un.	50.28 N	40.0 E
128	Pavlovski Posad (pȧv-lôf'skĭ pô-sȧt') . Sov. Un.	55.46 N	38.38 E
102	Pavuna (pä-vōō'nȧ) . . . Braz. (In.)	22.49 S	43.20 W
79	Pawhuska (pô-hŭs'kȧ).....Okla.	36.41 N	96.20 W
79	Pawnee (pô-nē').....Okla.	36.21 N	96.48 W
79	Pawnee City.....Okla.	40.6 N	96.9 W
84	Paw Paw (pô' pô).....Mich.	42.17 N	85.53 W
85	Pawtucket (pô-tŭk'ĕt).....R. I.	41.52 N	71.25 W
127	Paxos (I.) (păk'sôs).....Grc.	39.12 N	20.10 E
84	Paxton (păks'tŭn).....Ill.	40.28 N	88.5 W
71	Paxton.....Mont.	47.39 N	105.21 W
145	Payang (pä-yäng').....Chn.	29.5 N	116.40 E
148	Payen (pä'yĕn').....Chn.	46.0 N	127.29 E
70	Payette (pȧ-ĕt').....Ida.	44.5 N	116.56 W
70	Payette R., North Fork.....Ida.	44.20 N	116.5 W
70	Payette R., South Fork.....Ida.	44.9 N	115.45 W
55	Payne L. (pān).....Can.	60.5 N	73.0 W
77	Paynesville (pānz'vĭl).....Minn.	45.24 N	94.42 W
	Payo Obispo, see Ciudad Chetumal, Mex.		
102	Paysandú (pī-sän-dōō').....Ur.	32.25 S	58.1 W
75	Payson (pā's'n).....Utah	40.3 N	111.42 W
111	Pazar (pä'zär).....Tur.	41.15 N	41.0 E
127	Pazardžik (pä-zȧr-dzhĕk').....Bul.	42.11 N	24.19 E
79	Peabody (pē'bŏd-ĭ).....Kan.	38.9 N	97.7 W
86	Peabody.....Mass.	42.31 N	70.58 W
83	Peace Cr. (pēs).....Fla. (In.)	27.20 N	81.50 W
54	Peace R.....Can.	58.0 N	117.0 W
88	Peach Haven (pēch) N. Y. (Niagara Falls In.)	43.3 N	78.58 W
116	Peak, The (Mt.) (pēk) . . . Gt. Brit.	53.23 N	1.52 W
82	Pea R. (pē).....Ala.	31.27 N	86.0 W
81	Pearland (pûrl'ănd) . . . . Tex. (In.)	29.34 N	95.17 W
95	Pearl Lagoon.....Nic.	12.35 N	83.20 W
95	Pearl Lagoon (Las Perlas) (läs pĕr'läs) . Nic.	12.20 N	83.41 W
144	Pearl R. (Chu Kiang) (pûrl) (chōō' kyäng') . Chn.	22.38 N	113.38 E
82	Pearl R.....Miss.-La.	31.50 N	90.10 W
80	Pearsall (pēr'sôl).....Tex.	28.53 N	99.6 W
51	Pearson (pēr'sŭn) Wash. (Seattle In.)	47.42 N	122.39 W
48	Peary Land (pēr'ĭ).....Grnld.	82.0 N	40.0 W
78	Pease R. (pēz).....Tex.	34.10 N	99.40 W
78	Pease R. North.....Tex.	34.20 N	100.32 W
81	Peason (pēz''n).....La.	31.25 N	93.19 W
127	Peć (pĕch).....Yugo.	42.39 N	20.19 E
80	Pecan Bayou (pê-kăn').....Tex.	31.50 N	99.0 W
102	Pecanha (pȧ-kän'yȧ).....Braz.	18.30 S	42.40 W
77	Pecatonica R. (pĕk-ȧ-tŏn'ĭ-kȧ) . Ill.	42.18 N	89.30 W
110	Pechenga (pyĕ'chĕŋ-gȧ) . . Sov. Un.	69.33 N	31.12 E
110	Pechora B. (pyĕ-chô'rȧ) . . Sov. Un.	68.45 N	54.30 E
110	Pechora R.....Sov. Un.	66.0 N	52.30 E
72	Peckham (pĕk'ăm) Colo. (Denver In.)	40.17 N	104.45 W
80	Pecos (pā'kôs).....Tex.	31.26 N	103.30 W
80	Pecos R.....N. M.-Tex.	34.0 N	104.20 W
121	Pečs (pāch).....Hung.	46.3 N	18.14 E
102	Pedra da Gavea (Mt.) (pä'drȧ dä gä'vä-ȧ) . Braz. (In.)	23.0 S	43.17 W
93	Pedregal de San Angel (Mt.) (pā-drȧ-gäl' dā sän än'hāl) . Mex. (In.)	19.18 N	99.10 W
93	Pedregal R. (pā-drȧ-gäl') . . . Mex.	17.40 N	93.47 W
101	Pedro II (pā'drōō sȧ-gōōn'dōō) Braz.	4.28 S	41.28 W
94	Pedro Antonio Santos (Sta-Cruz Chico) (pā'drō än-tō'nê-ō sän'-tōs) (sän'tä krōōz' chē'kô) Mex. (In.)	18.50 N	88.15 W
96	Pedro Betancourt (pā'drô bä-täŋ-kōrt') . Cuba	22.41 N	81.26 W
96	Pedro Bluff (pē'drō blŭf) . . . . Jam.	17.50 N	77.45 W
90	Pedro Miguel (pä'drô mê-gāl') C. Z. (In.)	9.1 N	79.37 W
51	Pedro Valley (pē'drō) Calif. (San Francisco In.)	37.35 N	122.30 W
159	Peebinga (pê-bĭng'ȧ).....Austl.	34.52 S	140.52 E
114	Peebles (pē'b'lz).....Gt. Brit.	55.40 N	3.10 W
83	Peedee R. (pē-dē').....S. C.	34.10 N	79.33 W
85	Peekskill (pēks'kĭl).....N. Y.	41.17 N	73.56 W
157	Peel Mt. (pēl).....N. Z.	43.48 S	171.10 E
54	Peel R.....Can.	65.45 N	135.0 W
120	Peene R. (pā'nĕ).....Ger.	53.55 N	13.25 E
157	Pegasus B. (pĕg'ȧ-sŭs).....N. Z.	43.20 S	173.0 E
120	Pegnitz R. (pĕgh-nēts').....Ger.	49.32 N	11.30 E
125	Pego (pä'gō).....Sp.	38.51 N	0.8 W
150	Pegu (pĕ-gōō').....Bur.	17.15 N	96.29 E
150	Pegu Yoma (Mts.) (pĕ-gōō' yō'mä) Bur.	19.0 N	96.0 E
127	Pehčevo (pĕk'chĕ-vô).....Yugo.	41.43 N	22.58 E
145	Pehkow Shan (Mts.) (pĕ'kō shän') . Chn.	29.18 N	114.25 E
146	Pehtaiho (pĕ'tī'hō').....Chn.	39.50 N	119.30 E
146	Peihsien (pĕ'ê-hsyĕn').....Chn.	34.44 N	117.3 E
148	Peian (pĕ'ê-än').....Chn.	48.15 N	126.25 E
120	Peine (pī'nĕ).....Ger.	52.18 N	10.13 E
146	Peiping (Peking) (pĕ'ĭ-pĭng') (pē-kĭng') . Chn.	39.55 N	116.25 E
119	Peipsi (Chudskoe) L. (pĭp'sĭ) (chōōt'skô-yĕ) . Sov. Un.	58.40 N	27.30 E
146	Pei R. (pĕ'ĭ).....Chn.	39.30 N	116.58 E
144	Pei R.....Chn.	23.35 N	112.52 E
127	Peiraievs (Piraeus) (pĭ-rȧ-ĕfs') (pī-rē'ŭs) . Grc.	37.58 N	23.39 E
146	Peisha R. (pĕ'ĭ-shä').....Chn.	32.54 N	120.29 E
146	Peitang R. (pĕ'ĭ-täng').....Chn.	39.40 N	117.28 E
146	Peiyang R. (pĕ'ĭ-yäng').....Chn.	33.39 N	120.0 E
79	Pekin (pē'kĭn).....Ill.	40.34 N	89.38 W
88	Pekin . . . N. Y. (Niagara Falls In.)	43.10 N	78.54 W
146	Peking (Peiping) (pē-kĭng') (pĕ'ĭ-pĭng') . Chn.	39.55 N	116.25 E
126	Pelagosa Is. (pĕ-lȧ-gō'sä).....It.	42.22 N	16.20 E
82	Pelahatchee (pĕl-ȧ-hăch'ē) . . Miss.	32.18 N	89.48 W
123	Pelat, Mt. (pē-lȧ').....Fr.	44.15 N	6.45 E
84	Pelée I. (pē'lē).....Can.	41.55 N	82.30 W
95	Pelée, Mt. (pĕ-lā') . . . . Mart. (In.)	14.48 N	61.9 W
84	Pelee Pt. (pē'lē).....Can.	41.46 N	82.38 W
73	Pelham (pĕl'ăm) Ala. (Birmingham In.)	33.17 N	86.49 W
160	Pelham.....Austl. (In.)	26.23 S	150.20 E
82	Pelham.....Ga.	31.7 N	84.11 W
120	Pelhřimov (pĕl-rzhē-môf') . . Czech.	49.26 N	15.13 E
96	Pelican Har. (pĕl'ĭ-kăn) . . . . Ba. Is.	26.21 N	77.0 W
77	Pelican L.....Minn.	46.35 N	94.9 W
76	Pelican Rapids.....Minn.	46.35 N	96.5 W
110	Pelim R. (pyȧ-lēm') . . . . . Sov. Un.	60.45 N	62.50 E
77	Pella (pĕl'ȧ).....Ia.	41.25 N	92.52 W
120	Pellworm (I.) (pĕl'vôrm).....Ger.	54.30 N	8.38 E
81	Pelly (pĕl-ĭ).....Tex. (In.)	29.42 N	94.58 W
54	Pelly, L.....Can.	65.50 N	102.0 W
53	Pelly Mts.....Can.	61.20 N	131.30 W
54	Pelly R.....Can.	62.35 N	135.0 W
127	Peloponnesos (pĕl-ô-pô-nä'sôs) Grc.	37.30 N	22.40 E
102	Pelotas (pȧ-lō'tăzh).....Braz.	31.40 S	52.20 W
131	Pelusium (Tina) B. (pê-lūzh'ĭ-ŭm) (tē'nȧ) . Eg. (In.)	31.15 N	32.40 E
131	Pelusium (Tina), Plain of . Eg. (In.)	30.55 N	32.40 E
123	Pelvoux, Mt. (pĕl-vōō').....Fr.	44.55 N	6.22 E
83	Pelzer (pĕl'zēr).....S. C.	34.38 N	82.29 W
134	Pemba (pĕm'bȧ).....N. Rh.	16.33 S	27.26 E
135	Pemba I.....Zan.	5.10 S	39.45 E
76	Pembina (pĕm'bĭ-nȧ).....N. D.	48.58 N	97.14 W
76	Pembina R.....Can.-U. S.	49.0 N	98.10 W
116	Pembridge (pĕm'brĭj) . . . . Gt. Brit.	52.13 N	2.53 W
55	Pembroke (pĕm'brŏk).....Can.	45.45 N	77.31 W
114	Pembroke.....Gt. Brit.	51.40 N	4.57 W
87	Pembroke.....Mass. (In.)	42.4 N	70.48 W
124	Penafiel (pā-nȧ-fyĕl').....Port.	41.12 N	8.18 W
124	Peñafiel (pā-nyȧ-fyĕl').....Sp.	41.36 N	4.9 W
124	Peñalara (Mt.) (pā-nyȧ-lä'rä) . . Sp.	40.52 N	3.58 W
124	Penamacor (pā-nȧ-mȧ-kōr') . . Port.	40.11 N	7.11 W
150	Penang (State) (pê-năng') . Malaya	4.30 N	100.0 E
150	Penang I.....Malaya	5.21 N	100.15 E
152	Peñaranda (pä-nyä-rän'dä) . . Phil.	15.20 N	121.0 E
124	Peñaranda de Bracamonte (pā-nyȧ-rän'dä dā brä-kä-mōn'tā) . Sp.	40.54 N	5.13 W
125	Peña Roya (Mt.) (pä'nyä rō'yä) . Sp.	40.24 N	0.10 W
124	Peñas C. (pā'nyäs).....Sp.	43.40 N	5.51 W
78	Peñasco R. (pā-nyäs'kō) . . . N. M.	32.50 N	105.0 W
102	Peñas, G. of.....Chl.	47.30 S	75.0 W
144	Penchow (pĕn'chō').....Chn.	23.19 N	109.2 E
132	Pendembu (pĕn-dĕm'bōō) . . . S. L.	8.15 N	10.47 W
76	Pender (pĕn'dēr).....Neb.	42.8 N	96.41 W
72	Pender Is. . . Can. (Vancouver In.)	48.47 N	123.18 W
70	Pendleton (pĕn'd'l-tŭn).....Ore.	45.40 N	118.48 W
70	Pend Oreille L. (pŏn-dô-rā') (pĕn-dô-rĕl') . Ida.	48.12 N	116.30 W
70	Pend Oreille R.....Wash.-Ida.	48.30 N	117.17 W
101	Penedo (pȧ-nā'dōō).....Braz.	10.20 S	36.31 W
127	Peneios R. (pĕ-nē'ôs).....Grc.	39.35 N	22.10 E
85	Penetanguishene (pĕn'ē-tăŋ-gĭ-shēn') . Can.	45.46 N	79.46 W
144	Pengk (pĕŋk).....Chn.	30.48 N	105.55 E
146	Pengpu (pĕng'pōō').....Chn.	32.54 N	117.17 E
146	Pengshui (pĕng'shōō-ē').....Chn.	29.20 N	108.14 E
145	Pengtze (pĕng'tzĕ').....Chn.	29.56 N	116.42 E
160	Penguin (pĕŋ'gwĭn) Austl. (Tas. In.)	41.6 S	146.3 E
124	Peniche (pĕ-nē'chȧ).....Port.	39.22 N	9.23 W
116	Penistone (pĕn'ĭ-stŭn) . . . Gt. Brit.	53.32 N	1.39 W
92	Penjamillo (pĕn-hä-mēl'yō) . . Mex.	20.6 N	101.56 W
92	Pénjamo (pān'hä-mō).....Mex.	20.23 N	101.42 W
116	Penk, R. (pĕnk).....Gt. Brit.	52.45 N	2.5 W
116	Penkridge (pĕnk'rĭj) . . . . Gt. Brit.	52.43 N	2.7 W
126	Penne (pĕn'nä).....It.	42.27 N	13.55 E
141	Penner R. (pĕn'ēr).....India	14.30 N	79.0 E
114	Pennine Chain (Mts.) . . . Gt. Brit.	54.20 N	2.10 W
84	Pennsboro (pĕnz'bŭr-ō) . . . W. Va.	39.16 N	80.58 W
85	Pennsylvania (State) (pĕn-sĭl-vā'nĭ-ȧ) . U. S.	41.0 N	77.30 W
85	Penn Yan (pĕn yăn').....N. Y.	42.40 N	77.4 W
86	Penobscot B. (pē-nŏb'skŏt) . . . Me.	44.15 N	68.50 W
86	Penobscot R.....Me.	45.25 N	68.40 W
128	Peno, L. (pä'nô).....Sov. Un.	56.58 N	32.42 E
158	Penong (pê-nông').....Austl.	31.56 S	132.58 E
95	Penonome (pā-nō-nô-mā') . . . Pan.	8.28 N	80.17 W
82	Pensacola (pĕn-sȧ-kō'lȧ).....Fla.	30.25 N	87.13 W
82	Pensacola B.....Fla.	30.25 N	87.10 W
88	Pensauken Cr. (pĕn-sô'kĕn) Pa. (Philadelphia In.)	39.57 N	75.0 W
159	Pentecost I. (pĕn'tē-kŏst) New Hebr.	15.45 S	168.10 E
102	Pentia (pĕn-tē'ä) . . . . . Braz. (In.)	22.50 S	43.17 W
114	Pentland Firth (pĕnt'lănd) Gt. Brit. (In.)	58.40 N	3.0 W
116	Pen-y-ghent (Mt.) (pĕn-ĭ-gĕnt') Gt. Brit.	54.9 N	2.14 W

ng-sing; ŋ-baŋk; N-nasalized n; nŏd; cŏmmit; ōld; ôbey; ôrder; fōōd; fŏŏt; ou-out; s-soft; sh-dish; th-thin; pūre; ûnite; ûrn; stŭd; circŭs; ü-as "y" in study; '-indeterminate vowel.

Penza PRONOUNCING INDEX Pimal

Page	Name Pronunciation Region	Lat. °′	Long. °′
111	Penza (pĕn'zȧ) ... Sov. Un.	53.10 N	45.0 E
114	Penzance (pĕn-zăns') ... Gt. Brit.	50.5 N	5.35 W
120	Penzberg (pĕnts'bĕrgh) ... Ger.	47.43 N	11.20 E
139	Penzhina (pĕn-zhē'nȧ) ... Sov. Un.	63.15 N	168.59 E
139	Penzhina R. ... Sov. Un.	63.0 N	168.0 E
139	Penzhinskaya B. (pĕn-shēn'skȧ-yȧ) Sov. Un.	61.0 N	162.0 E
79	Peoria (pē-ō'rĭ-ȧ) ... Ill.	40.41 N	89.37 W
92	Peotillos (pā-ō-tēl'yōs) ... Mex.	22.30 N	100.34 W
96	Pepe, C. (pā'pā) ... Isle of Pines	21.28 N	83.3 W
87	Pepperell (pĕp'ẽr-ĕl) ... Mass. (In.)	42.40 N	71.36 W
127	Peqin (pĕ-kēn') ... Alb.	41.3 N	19.45 E
90	Pequiñi, R. (pȧ-kē'nyē) Pan. (C. Z. In.)	9.18 N	79.35 W
125	Perales R. (pā-rä'lās) ... Sp. (In.)	40.27 N	4.6 W
125	Perales de Tajuña (pā-rä'lās dā tä-hōō'nyä) . Sp. (In.)	40.13 N	3.21 W
86	Percé (pĕr-sā') ... Can.	48.31 N	64.15 W
117	Perchtoldsdorf (pĕrk'tōlts-dôrf) Aus. (Wien In.)	48.7 N	16.16 E
125	Perdido, Mt. (pĕr-dē'dō) ... Sp.	42.40 N	0.2 E
82	Perdido R. (pĕr-dī'dō) ... Ala.-Fla.	30.43 N	87.30 W
100	Pereira (pā-rā'rä) ... Col.	4.45 N	75.48 W
131	Perejil I. (pā-rȧ-ĸēl') Sp. Mor. (Gib. In.)	35.54 N	5.36 E
129	Perekop (pĕr-ȧ-kôp') ... Sov. Un.	46.8 N	33.42 E
129	Pereshchipino (pâ'rȧsh-chē'pē-nō) Sov. Un.	49.1 N	35.18 E
128	Pereslavskoe, L. (pȧ-rȧ släf'-skō-yĕ) . Sov. Un.	56.45 N	38.47 E
128	Pereslavl-Zalesskii (pȧ-rȧ-slàv''l-zȧ-lyĕs'kĭ-ē) . Sov. Un.	56.43 N	38.52 E
89	Peres, R. des (dā pâr') Mo. (St. Louis In.)	38.34 N	90.18 W
129	Pereyaslavl (pĕ-rȧ-yäs'lav'l) Sov. Un.	50.5 N	31.28 E
102	Pergamino (pĕr-gä-mē'nō) ... Arg.	33.58 S	60.40 W
76	Perham (pẽr'hăm) ... Minn.	46.36 N	95.32 W
55	Peribonka R. (pĕr-ĭ-bŏŋ'kȧ) .. Can.	51.0 N	71.30 W
122	Périgueux (pā-rē-gû') ... Fr.	45.11 N	0.45 E
137	Perim (I.) (pĕ-rēm') . Red Sea (In.)	12.39 N	43.26 E
95	Perlas Is. (pĕr'läs) ... Pan.	8.25 N	79.0 W
120	Perleberg (pĕr'lē-bĕrgh) ... Ger.	53.5 N	11.51 E
	Perm, see Molotov, Sov. Un.		
148	Permskoe (pĕrm'skō-yĕ) . Sov. Un.	43.43 N	135.1 E
101	Pernambuco (Recife) (pĕr-näm-bōō'kō) (rā-sē'fȧ) . Braz.	8.1 S	35.0 W
101	Pernambuco (State) ... Braz.	8.30 S	38.0 W
127	Pérnik (pĕr-nēk') ... Bul.	42.35 N	23.2 E
122	Péronne (pā-rôn') ... Fr.	49.57 N	2.55 E
93	Perote (pā-rō'tā) ... Mex.	19.34 N	97.14 W
122	Perpignan (pĕr-pē-nyäN') ... Fr.	42.42 N	2.55 E
125	Perregaux (pĕr-rē-gō') ... Alg.	35.35 N	0.5 E
73	Perris (pĕr'ĭs) Calif. (Los Angeles In.)	33.47 N	117.14 W
96	Perros B. (pā'rōs) ... Cuba	22.20 N	78.30 W
57	Perrot, Ile (pĕr'ŭt) Can. (Montreal In.)	45.23 N	73.55 W
82	Perry (pĕr'ĭ) ... Fla.	30.7 N	83.34 W
83	Perry ... Ga.	32.28 N	83.46 W
77	Perry ... Ia.	41.51 N	94.4 W
85	Perry ... N. Y.	42.55 N	78.0 W
79	Perry ... Okla.	36.17 N	97.18 W
73	Perry .. Utah (Salt Lake City In.)	41.28 N	112.3 W
84	Perrysburg (pĕr'ĭz-bûrg) ... Ohio	41.35 N	83.37 W
78	Perryton (pĕr'ĭ-tŭn) ... Tex.	36.24 N	100.48 W
79	Perryville (pĕr'ĭ-vĭl) ... Mo.	37.43 N	89.53 W
140	Persepolis (Ruins) (pẽr-sĕp'ō-lĭs) Iran	29.55 N	53.0 E
	Persia, see Iran		
140	Persian G. (pûr'zhȧn) ... Asia	26.30 N	52.45 E
158	Perth (pûrth) ... Austl.	31.47 S	116.0 E
160	Perth ... Austl. (In.)		
160	Perth ... Austl. (Tas. In.)	41.33 S	147.11 E
85	Perth ... Can.	44.53 N	76.15 W
114	Perth ... Gt. Brit.	56.25 N	3.25 W
85	Perth Amboy (pûrth ăm'boi) . N. J.	40.32 N	74.16 W
160	Perth Water (L.) . Austl. (Perth In.)	31.58 S	115.52 E
122	Pertuis (pĕr-tüē') ... Fr.	43.43 N	5.30 E
122	Pertuis Breton (B.) (pĕr-tüē' brē-tôN') . Fr.	46.20 N	1.30 W
79	Peru (pē-rōō') ... Ill.	41.19 N	89.9 W
84	Peru ... Ind.	40.47 N	86.3 W
100	Peru ... S. A.	10.0 S	75.0 W
126	Perugia (pā-rōō'jä) ... It.	43.17 N	12.23 E
129	Pervomaisk (pẽr-vō-mīsk') Sov. Un.	48.4 N	30.52 E
126	Pesaro (pā'zä-rō) ... It.	43.55 N	12.54 E
148	Pescadores Channel (pĕs-kȧ-dō'-rĕs) . For. (In.)	23.45 N	102.0 E
148	Pescadores Is. ... For. (In.)	23.40 N	119.35 E
93	Pescados, R. (pĕs-kä'dōs) ... Mex.	19.18 N	96.40 W
126	Pescara (pās-kä'rä) ... It.	42.26 N	14.12 E
126	Pescara R. ... It.	42.12 N	13.40 E
111	Peschani, C. (pås'chä-nĭ) . Sov. Un.	43.15 N	51.15 E
126	Pescia (pä'shä) ... It.	43.55 N	10.42 E
141	Peshawar (pĕ-shä'wŭr) ... Pak.	33.59 N	71.43 E
77	Peshtigo (pĕsh'tē-gō) ... Wis.	45.4 N	87.48 W
77	Peshtigo R. ... Wis.	45.25 N	88.20 W
128	Pesochenski (pȧ-sō-chĕn'skĭ-yĕ) Sov. Un.	54.4 N	34.17 E
124	Peso de Régua (pā-sōō dā rā'gwä) Port.	41.10 N	7.47 W
94	Pespire (pås-pē'rȧ) ... Hond.	13.38 N	87.22 W
101	Pesqueira (pĕs-kā'ē-rȧ) ... Braz.	8.15 S	36.32 W
80	Pesqueria, R. (pås-kȧ-rē'ȧ) .. Mex.	26.0 N	100.30 W
127	Peštera (pĕsh'tĕ-rȧ) ... Bul.	42.3 N	24.18 E
121	Pesterzsebet (pĕsht'ĕr-zhä'bĕt) Hung.	47.27 N	19.8 E
92	Petachalco B. (pā-tä-chäl'kō) . Mex.	17.58 N	102.5 W
74	Petaluma (pĕt-ȧ-lōō'mȧ) ... Calif.	38.14 N	122.39 W
92	Petatlán (pā-tä-tlän') ... Mex.	17.29 N	101.18 W
94	Petén (San Andres) L. (pȧ-tān') (sän än-drās') . Guat. (In.)	17.0 N	89.50 W
158	Peterborough (pē'tẽr-bŭr-ō) . Austl.	32.59 S	138.50 E
55	Peterborough ... Can.	44.15 N	78.29 W
114	Peterborough ... Gt. Brit.	52.35 N	0.15 W
116	Peterborough, Soke of ... Gt. Brit.	52.37 N	0.21 W
119	Petergof (pyĕ'tẽr-gôf) ... Sov. Un.	59.53 N	29.55 E
114	Peterhead (pē-tẽr-hĕd') .. Gt. Brit.	57.30 N	1.50 W
85	Peter Pt. ... Can.	43.50 N	77.8 W
53	Petersburg (pē'tẽrz-bûrg) ... Alsk.	56.45 N	133.0 W
79	Petersburg ... Ill.	40.0 N	89.51 W
84	Petersburg ... Ind.	38.30 N	87.15 W
83	Petersburg ... Va.	37.12 N	77.24 W
73	Peterson (pē-tẽr-sŭn) Utah (Salt Lake City In.)	41.7 N	111.46 W
143	Peter the Great B. . Sov. Un.-Chn.	42.30 N	132.0 E
138	Petimskoe (pȧ-tēm'skō-yĕ) Sov. Un.	74.20 N	84.30 E
86	Petitcodiac (pē-tē-kō-dyȧk') . Can.	45.56 N	65.11 W
85	Petite Nation R. (pē-tēt' nȧ-syôN') Can.	45.45 N	75.8 W
95	Petite Terre (I.) (pē-tēt' târ') Guad. (In.)	16.10 N	61.8 W
97	Petit Goave (pē-tē' gō-äv') ... Hai.	18.26 N	72.53 W
79	Petit Jean Cr. (pē-tē' zhäN') . Ark.	35.5 N	93.30 W
117	Petit Nethe R. (pē-tē'nât') Bel. (Anvers In.)	51.10 N	4.38 E
93	Petlalcingo (pĕ-tläl-sĕŋ'gō) .. Mex.	18.3 N	97.50 W
156	Petone (pē-tō'nē) ... N. Z. (In.)	41.14 S	174.53 E
99	Petorca (pā-tōr'kä) Chl. (Valparaiso In.)	32.14 S	70.59 W
99	Petorca, R. .. Chl. (Valparaiso In.)	32.20 S	71.20 W
84	Petoskey (pē-tŏs'kĭ) ... Mich.	45.23 N	85.58 W
89	Petre, Isle a (ēl ȧ pĕt'ẽr) La. (New Orleans In.)	30.9 N	89.9 W
127	Petrič (pā'trĭch) ... Bul.	41.23 N	23.12 E
75	Petrified Forest Natl. Mon. . Ariz.	34.55 N	109.37 W
129	Petrikovka (pyĕ'trē-kôf-kä) Sov. Un.	48.43 N	34.29 E
129	Petrikovo (pyĕ'trē-kô-vô) Sov. Un.	52.8 N	28.32 E
126	Petrinja (pā'trēn-yä) ... Yugo.	45.26 N	16.19 E
119	Petrokrepost (pyĕ'trô-krĕ-pôst') Sov. Un.	59.55 N	31.5 E
84	Petrolia (pē-trō'lĭ-ȧ) ... Mich.	42.52 N	82.10 W
101	Petrolina (pĕ-trō-lē'nȧ) ... Braz.	9.15 S	40.28 W
129	Petropavlovka (pyĕ'trô-päv'-lôf-kȧ) . Sov. Un.	48.27 N	36.21 E
138	Petropavlovsk (pyĕ-trô-päv'-lôfsk) . Sov. Un.	54.55 N	69.10 E
139	Petropavlovsk-Kamchatski (käm-chät'skĭ) . Sov. Un.	53.20 N	158.50 E
101	Petrópolis (pȧ-trô-pô-lēzh') .. Braz.	22.30 S	43.4 W
127	Petrosani (pā-trô-shän'') ... Rom.	45.24 N	23.23 E
111	Petrovsk (pyĕ-trôfsk') ... Sov. Un.	52.15 N	45.25 E
129	Petrovskaya (pyĕ-trôf'skȧ-yȧ) Sov. Un.	45.25 N	37.54 E
111	Petrovskoe (pyĕ-trôf'skō-yĕ) Sov. Un.	45.15 N	42.58 E
139	Petrovsk-Zabaikalski (pyĕ-trôfsk-zȧ-bī-käl'skĭ) . Sov. Un.	51.15 N	108.40 E
110	Petrozavodsk (pyā'trô-zȧ-vôtsk') Sov. Un.	61.45 N	34.20 E
119	Petseri (pĕt'sĕ-rē) ... Sov. Un.	57.48 N	27.40 E
88	Petty I. (pĕt'ĭ) N. J. (Philadelphia In.)	39.58 N	75.6 W
99	Peumo (pȧ-ōō'mō) Chl. (Valparaiso In.)	34.23 S	71.13 W
72	Peyton (pā'tŭn) Colo. (Colo. Sprs. In.)	39.2 N	104.29 W
88	Peyton ... Wis. (Duluth In.)	46.39 N	92.1 W
110	Peza R. (pyä'zȧ) ... Sov. Un.	65.35 N	46.35 E
122	Pézenas (pā-zē-nä') ... Fr.	43.25 N	3.25 E
120	Pforzheim (pfôrts'hīm) ... Ger.	48.53 N	8.42 E
127	Phanos (I.) (fä'nōs) ... Grc.	39.51 N	19.25 E
150	Phanrang (p'hän'räng') ... Indoch.	11.35 N	108.50 E
127	Pharsala (fär'sȧ-lȧ) ... Grc.	39.16 N	22.24 E
82	Phenix City (fē'nĭks) ... Ala.	32.29 N	85.1 W
	Philadelphia, see Amman, Jor.		
82	Philadelphia (fĭl-ȧ-dĕl'phĭ-ȧ) . Miss.	32.46 N	89.8 W
85	Philadelphia ... Pa.	40.0 N	75.10 W
88	Philadelphia ... Pa. (In.)		
127	Philiatra (fĭ-lē-ȧ'trȧ) ... Grc.	37.10 N	21.36 E
76	Philip (fĭl'ĭp) ... S. D.	44.4 N	101.37 W
132	Philippeville (fē-lēp'vēl') ... Alg.	36.58 N	6.58 E
152	Philippines (Is.) (fĭl'ĭ-pēnz) Pac. O.	12.0 N	122.0 E
151	Philippine Trough ... Pac. O.	9.30 N	127.0 E
127	Philippopolis (Plovdiv) (fĭl-ĭp-ŏp'ō-lĭs) (plôv'dĭf) . Bul.	42.8 N	24.42 E
71	Philipsburg (fĭl'ĭps-bûrg) ... Mont.	46.20 N	113.29 W
85	Philipsburg ... Pa.	40.54 N	78.12 W
85	Philippi (fĭ-lĭp'ĭ) ... W. Va.	39.9 N	80.3 W
77	Phillips (fĭl'ĭps) ... Wis.	45.41 N	90.22 W
78	Phillipsburg ... Kan.	39.45 N	99.19 W
85	Phillipsburg ... Pa.	40.42 N	75.10 W
117	Phlegrean Fields (flē-grē'ăn) It. (Napoli In.)	40.53 N	14.6 E
89	Phoebus (fē'bŭs) . Va. (Norfolk In.)	37.1 N	76.19 W
75	Phoenix (fē'nĭks) ... Ariz.	33.27 N	112.4 W
70	Phoenix ... Can.	49.4 N	118.35 W
89	Phoenix ... La. (New Orleans In.)	29.39 N	89.56 W
154	Phoenix Is. ... Pac. O.	4.0 S	172.0 W
85	Phoenixville (fē'nĭks-vĭl) ... Pa.	40.9 N	75.31 W
126	Piacenza (pyä-chĕnt'sä) ... It.	45.2 N	9.41 E
100	Piacoa (pyä-kō'ä) ... Ven.	8.31 N	62.2 W
117	Piano di Sorrento (pyä'nō dē sôr-rĕn'tō) . It. (Napoli In.)	40.38 N	14.24 E
126	Pianosa (I.) (pyä-nō'sä) ... It.	42.35 N	10.5 E
6	Pianosa I. ... It.	42.14 N	15.44 E
117	Pianura (pyä-nōō'rä) It. (Napoli In.)	40.52 N	14.11 E
153	Piapayungan Mt. (pyä-pä-yōōŋ'gän) . Phil.	7.39 N	124.32 E
121	Piatra-Neamt (pyä'trȧ-nä-ämts') Rom.	46.55 N	26.23 E
101	Piauhi (State) (pyou'ē) ... Braz.	7.0 S	42.30 W
101	Piauhi, Serra do (Mts.) (sĕr'rȧ dōō pyou'ē) . Braz.	9.30 S	43.15 W
126	Piave R. (pyä'vā) ... It.	45.47 N	12.20 E
126	Piazza Armerina (pyät'sä är-mȧ-rē'nä) . It.	37.24 N	14.23 E
133	Pibor R. (pē'bôr) .. A. E. Sud.-Eth.	7.30 N	33.0 E
91	Picara Pt. (pē-kä'rä) St. Thomas (In.)	18.23 N	64.56 W
82	Picayune (pĭk'ȧ-yōōn) ... Miss.	30.31 N	89.41 W
142	Pichan (Shanshan) (pē'chän') (shän'shän') . Chn.	42.40 N	90.4 E
79	Picher (pĭch'ẽr) ... Okla.	36.58 N	94.49 W
131	Pichon (pē-shôN') ... Tun. (In.)	35.39 N	9.41 E
93	Pichucalco (pē-chōō-käl'kō) . Mex.	17.30 N	93.5 W
77	Pickerel L. (pĭk'ẽr-ĕl) ... Can.	48.35 N	91.22 W
116	Pickering (pĭk'ẽr-ĭng) ... Gt. Brit.	54.14 N	0.46 W
73	Pico (pē'kō) Calif. (Los Angeles In.)	34.0 N	118.5 W
132	Pico I. (pē'kōō) ... Az. Is. (In.)	38.25 N	28.20 W
101	Picos (pē'kōzh) ... Braz.	7.2 S	41.32 W
77	Pic R. (pēk) ... Can.	49.0 N	86.7 W
85	Picton (pĭk'tŭn) ... Can.	44.2 N	77.10 W
157	Picton ... N. Z.	41.17 S	174.0 E
87	Pictou (pĭk-tōō') ... Can.	45.41 N	62.42 W
152	Piddig (pēd-dēg') ... Phil.	18.10 N	120.43 E
141	Pidurutalagala, Mt. (pē'dōō-rōō-tä'lȧ-gä'lȧ) . Cey. (In.)	7.5 N	80.45 E
93	Piedad (pyā-dhädh') ... Mex. (In.)	19.24 N	99.9 W
102	Piedade (pyā-dä'dē) ... Braz. (In.)	22.41 S	43.3 W
102	Piedade ... Braz. (In.)	22.53 S	43.19 W
82	Piedmont (pēd'mŏnt) ... Ala.	33.56 N	85.37 W
126	Piedmont (Prov.) ... It.	44.59 N	7.30 E
79	Piedmont ... Mo.	37.8 N	90.41 W
83	Piedmont ... S. C.	34.42 N	82.27 W
85	Piedmont ... W. Va.	39.30 N	79.3 W
124	Piedrabuena (pyā-drä-bwā'nä) . Sp.	39.2 N	4.10 W
97	Piedra Gran (Pk.) (pyā'drä grän') Cuba	20.1 N	75.41 W
80	Piedras Negras (pyā'dräs nā'gräs) Mex.	28.41 N	100.31 W
77	Pie I. (pī) ... Can.	48.15 N	89.5 W
119	Pieksämäki (pyĕk'sĕ-mĕ-kē) .. Fin.	62.17 N	27.15 E
124	Piélagos (pyā'lä-gōs) ... Sp.	43.23 N	3.56 W
110	Piels (pyĕls) ... Fin.	63.15 N	29.30 E
160	Pieman (Corinna) (pī'măn) (kō-rĭn'ȧ) . Austl. (Tas. In.)	41.45 S	145.20 E
76	Pierce (pẽrs) ... Neb.	42.12 N	97.31 W
85	Pierce ... W. Va.	39.13 N	79.32 W
76	Pierre (pēr) ... S. D.	44.22 N	100.20 W
123	Pierrefitte (pyâr-fēt') ... Fr. (In.)	48.57 N	2.22 E
123	Pierrelaye (pyâr-lā') ... Fr. (In.)	49.1 N	2.9 E
121	Pieštany (pyĕsh'tyȧ-nūĭ) ... Czech.	48.36 N	17.48 E
	Pietarsaari, see Jakobstad, Fin.		
134	Pietermaritzburg (pē-tẽr-mâr'ĭts-bûrg) (pyä'tẽr-mä'rēts-bōōrgh) U. S. Afr.	29.37 S	30.21 E
134	Pietersburg (pē'tẽrz-bûrg) . U. S. Afr.	23.55 S	29.20 E
134	Piet Retief (pēt rĕ-tēf') .. U. S. Afr.	27.2 S	30.49 E
126	Pieve di Cadore (pyā'vā dē kä-dō'rā) . It.	46.27 N	12.22 E
56	Pigeon Bluff .. Can. (Winnipeg In.)	50.11 N	96.59 W
56	Pigeon L. (pĭj'ŭn) Can. (Winnipeg In.)	49.57 N	97.36 W
77	Pigeon R. ... Can.-U. S.	48.0 N	89.55 W
89	Pig Eye L. Minn. (Minneapolis In.)	44.55 N	93.1 W
79	Piggott (pĭg'ŭt) ... Ark.	36.23 N	90.11 W
119	Pihkva (Pskov), L. (pē'kvȧ) (pskôf) . Sov. Un.	58.0 N	28.0 E
93	Pijijiapan (pē-ĸē-ĸē-ä'pän) .. Mex.	15.41 N	93.13 W
78	Pikes Peak (pīks) ... Colo.	38.50 N	105.3 W
88	Pikesville (pīks'vĭl) Md. (Baltimore In.)	39.22 N	76.43 W
72	Pikeview (pīk'vū) Colo. (Colo. Sprs. In.)	38.55 N	104.50 W
84	Pikeville (pīk'vĭl) ... Ky.	37.26 N	82.32 W
151	Pila (pē'lä) ... Phil. (Manila In.)	14.15 N	121.25 E
120	Pila (pē'lä) ... Pol.	53.8 N	16.42 E
99	Pilar (pē'lär) Arg. (Buenos Aires In.)	34.28 S	58.59 W
101	Pilar ... Braz.	14.43 S	49.32 W
102	Pilar ... Par.	26.50 S	58.28 W
152	Pilar ... Phil.	12.55 N	123.40 E
153	Pilar ... Phil.	11.28 N	123.0 E
152	Pilar ... Phil.	17.22 N	120.27 E
153	Pilar B. ... Phil.	11.30 N	123.40 E
99	Pilar, C. ... Chl. (Magallanes In.)	52.42 S	74.42 W
153	Pilas I. (pē'läs) ... Phil.	6.38 N	121.36 E
94	Pilas, Las (Vol.) (läs pē'läs) .. Nic.	12.32 N	86.42 W
98	Pilcomaya R. (pēl-kō-mä'yō) . S. A.	24.15 S	60.0 W
152	Pili (pē'lē) ... Phil.	13.33 N	123.17 E
121	Pilica R. (pē-lēt'sä) ... Pol.	51.30 N	20.0 E
151	Pililla (pē-lē'lyä) Phil. (Manila In.)	14.30 N	121.20 E
128	Pilka R. (pēl-kä') ... Sov. Un.	57.35 N	30.55 E
160	Pillar, C. (pĭl'ȧr) . Austl. (Tas. In.)	43.12 S	148.0 E
160	Pillinger (pĭl'ĭn-jẽr) Austl. (Tas. In.)	42.18 S	145.33 E
124	Piloña (pē-lō'nyä) ... Sp.	43.22 N	5.22 W
80	Pilon, R. (pē-lōn') ... Mex.	25.15 N	99.45 W
79	Pilot Cr. (pī'lŭt) ... Tex.	33.20 N	96.48 W
157	Pilot, Pt. ... N. Z. (In.)	45.46 S	170.42 E
79	Pilot Point ... Tex.	33.23 N	96.57 W
89	Pilottown .. La. (New Orleans In.)	29.11 N	89.15 W
	Pilsen, see Plzen, Czech.		
119	Pils Rauna, (pēls rou'nȧ) . Sov. Un.	57.20 N	25.32 E
119	Piltene (pĭl'tē-nĕ) ... Sov. Un.	57.16 N	21.42 E
92	Pimal, Cerro (sĕr'ō pē-mäl') . Mex.	22.58 N	104.18 W

ăt; finăl; rāte; senâte; ärm; ȧsk; sofȧ; fâre; ch-choose; dh-as th in other; bē; ēvent; bĕt; recĕnt; cratẽr; g-go; gh-gutteral g; bĭt; ĭ-short neutral; rīde; ĸ-gutteral k as ch in German ich;

Pimba PRONOUNCING INDEX **Polui**

Page	Name Pronunciation Region	Lat. °′	Long. °′
158	Pimba (pĭm′bȧ) Austl.	31.12 S	136.45 E
152	Pinamalayan (pē-nä-mä-lä′yän) Phil.	13.4 N	121.30 E
153	Pinamungajan (pē-nä-mo͞oŋ-gä′-hän). Phil.	10.15 N	123.35 E
111	Pinarbaşi (pē′när-bä′shĭ) Tur.	38.40 N	36.12 E
96	Pinar del Rio (State) (pē-när′ dĕl rē′ō). Cuba	22.30 N	83.40 W
96	Pinar del Rio Cuba	22.21 N	83.38 W
152	Pinatubo Mt. (pē-nä-to͞o′bō). Phil.	15.8 N	120.21 E
146	Pinchow (pĭn′chō′) Chn.	37.36 N	118.2 E
79	Pinckneyville (pĭnk′nĭ-vĭl) Ill.	38.5 N	89.22 W
121	Pińczów (pēn″cho͞of) Pol.	50.32 N	20.32 E
99	Pindamonhangaba (pēn-dȧ-mōn′-än-gä′bȧ) Braz. (Rio de Janeiro In.)	22.58 S	45.30 W
127	Pindus (pĭn′dŭs) Grc.	39.35 N	21.30 E
79	Pine Bluff Ark.	34.13 N	92.1 W
87	Pine, C. Can.	46.45 N	53.35 W
77	Pine City Minn.	45.49 N	92.59 W
72	Pine Cliffe (pīn′ klĭf) Colo. (Denver In.)	39.57 N	105.27 W
158	Pine Cr. Austl.	13.50 S	131.59 E
70	Pine Forest Ra. Nev.	41.45 N	118.40 W
110	Pinega (pē-nyĕ′gȧ) Sov. Un.	64.40 N	43.30 E
110	Pinega R. Sov. Un.	64.10 N	42.30 E
72	Pine Grove. Colo. (Denver In.)	39.25 N	105.19 W
83	Pine Is. Fla. (In.)	24.45 N	81.25 W
83	Pine I. Sd. Fla. (In.)	26.35 N	82.10 W
73	Pine Knot Calif. (Los Angeles In.)	34.14 N	116.55 W
76	Pine Ridge Ind. Res. S. D.	43.30 N	102.0 W
126	Pinerolo (pē-nā-rō′lō) It.	44.52 N	7.20 E
96	Pines, Isle of Cuba	21.40 N	82.44 W
159	Pines, Isle of (Kunie I.) (pīnz) (ko͞o′nyē) (kü-nyā′). N. Cal.	22.30 S	167.30 E
82	Pineville (pīn′vĭl) Ky.	36.45 N	83.33 W
81	Pineville La.	31.19 N	92.25 W
144	Pingchow (pĭng′chō′) Chn.	25.46 N	107.6 E
145	Pingho (pĭng′hō′) Chn.	24.17 N	116.53 E
145	Pinghu (pĭng′ho͞o′) Chn.	30.41 N	120.58 E
142	Pingkiang (pĭng′kyäng′) Chn.	28.40 N	113.25 E
144	Pingliang (pĭng′lyäng′) Chn.	35.27 N	106.35 E
144	Pinglo (pĭng′lō′) Chn.	24.33 N	110.35 E
150	Ping, Me (R.) (mē′ pĭng′) Siam	18.0 N	98.35 E
144	Pingnan (pĭng′nän′) Chn.	23.36 N	110.30 E
145	Pingnan Chn.	27.3 N	119.2 E
145	Pingshan (pĭng′shän′) Chn.	38.18 N	114.13 E
144	Pingsiang (pĭng′syäng′) Chn.	27.38 N	113.42 E
146	Pingting (pĭng′tĭng′) Chn.	37.48 N	113.36 E
146	Pingtu (pĭng′to͞o′) Chn.	36.47 N	119.53 E
143	Pingyan (pĭng′yän′) Chn.	36.0 N	111.30 E
145	Pingyang (pĭng′yäng′) Chn.	27.35 N	120.31 E
146	Pingyin (pĭng′yĭn′) Chn.	36.16 N	116.21 E
146	Pingyüan (pĭng′yü-än′) Chn.	37.6 N	116.20 E
144	Pingyueh (pĭng′yo͞o-ā′) Chn.	26.43 N	107.20 E
101	Pinheiro (pē-nyā′ro͞o). Braz. (In.)	1.20 S	48.28 W
124	Pinhel (pēn-yĕl′) Port.	40.45 N	7.5 W
125	Pinhel Novo (pēn-yĕl′ nō′vo͞o) Port. (In.)	38.38 N	8.54 W
150	Pini (I.) (pē′nē) Indon.	0.10 N	98.40 E
143	Pinkiang (Harbin) (pĭn′kyäng′) (här′bĭn). Chn.	45.40 N	126.31 E
74	Pinnacles Natl. Mon. (pĭn′ȧ-k′lz) Calif.	36.27 N	121.12 W
117	Pinnau, R. (pĭ-nou′) Ger. (Hamburg In.)	53.40 N	9.36 E
117	Pinneberg (pĭn′ĕ-bĕrgh) Ger. (Hamburg In.)	53.40 N	9.48 E
117	Pinner (pĭn′ẽr) Gt. Brit. (London In.)	51.36 N	0.24 W
93	Pinola (Las Rosas) (pē-nō′lä) (läs rō′zäs). Mex.	16.24 N	92.26 W
51	Pinole (pĭ-nō′lē) Calif. (San Francisco In.)	38.0 N	122.17 W
92	Pinos (pē′nōs) Mex.	22.16 N	101.36 W
125	Pinoso (pē-nō′sō) Sp.	38.24 N	0.59 W
124	Pinos-Puente (pē′nōs-pwān′tā). Sp.	37.15 N	3.45 W
92	Pinotepa Nacional (pē-nō-tā′pä nä-syō-näl′). Mex.	16.21 N	98.4 W
121	Pińsk (pēn′sk) Sov. Un.	52.7 N	26.7 E
121	Pinsk Marshes Sov. Un.	52.10 N	27.30 E
100	Pinta (I.) (pēn′tä) Ec.	0.31 N	90.45 W
125	Pinto (pēn′tō) Sp. (In.)	40.14 N	3.42 W
75	Pioche (pī-ō′chē) Nev.	37.57 N	114.28 W
126	Piombino (pyôm-bē′nō) It.	42.57 N	10.33 E
121	Piotrków (pyō′t′r-ko͞of) Pol.	51.23 N	19.44 E
82	Piper (pī′pẽr) Ala.	33.4 N	87.2 W
127	Piperi (I.) (pē′pĕr-ē) Grc.	39.18 N	24.19 E
75	Pipe Spring Natl. Mon. Ariz.	36.51 N	112.45 W
76	Pipestone (pīp′stōn) Minn.	44.0 N	96.18 W
77	Pipestone R. Can.	48.40 N	92.10 W
157	Pipikariti, Pt. (pē′pē-kä′rē-tē) N. Z. (In.)	45.48 S	170.47 E
86	Pipmakan L. (pĭp-mȧ-kän′). Can.	49.40 N	70.15 W
84	Piqua (pĭk′wȧ) Ohio	40.11 N	84.16 W
101	Piracicaba (pē-rä-sē-kä′bä). Braz.	22.31 S	48.2 W
127	Piraeus (Peiraievs) (pī-rē′ŭs) (pĕ′rā-ĕfs). Grc.	37.58 N	23.39 E
99	Pirahi (pē-rä′ē) Braz. (Rio de Janeiro In.)	22.38 S	43.55 W
126	Pirano (pē-rä′nō) Tr. F. Ter.	45.32 N	13.33 E
101	Pirapora (pē-rȧ-pō′rȧ) Braz.	17.28 S	44.58 W
102	Piratininga, L. de (pē-rä-tē-nĭŋ′gȧ) Braz. (In.)	22.56 S	43.4 W
120	Pirmasens (pĭr-mä-zĕns′) Ger.	49.12 N	7.35 E
120	Pirna (pĭr′nȧ) Ger.	50.58 N	13.52 E
151	Piroe (pē-ro͞o′) Indon.	2.59 S	128.18 E
127	Pirot (pē′rōt) Yugo.	43.9 N	22.34 E
75	Pirtleville (pûr′t′l-vĭl) Ariz.	31.24 N	109.33 W
129	Piryatin (pēr-yä-tēn′) Sov. Un.	50.14 N	32.31 E
126	Pisa (pē′sä) It.	43.43 N	10.24 E
100	Pisagua (pē-sä′gwä) Chl.	19.31 S	70.5 W
100	Pisco (pēs′kō) Peru	13.45 S	76.15 W
85	Piseco L. (pĭ-sā′kō) N. Y.	43.25 N	74.35 W
120	Pisek (pē′sĕk) Czech.	49.18 N	14.9 E
126	Pisino (pē-sē′nō) Yugo.	45.15 N	13.55 E
102	Pissis, Cerro (Vol.) (sĕr′rō pē-sēs′) Arg.	27.58 S	68.58 W
126	Pisticci (pēs-tē′chē) It.	40.23 N	16.33 E
112	Pistoia (pēs-tô′yä) It.	43.56 N	10.55 E
87	Pistolet B. (pĭs-tô-lā′) Can.	51.35 N	55.45 W
124	Pisuerga R. (pē-swĕr′gä) Sp.	42.0 N	4.23 W
100	Pitalito (pē-tä-lē′tō) Col.	2.2 N	75.47 W
4	Pitcairn I. (pĭt′kârn) Pac. O.	24.4 S	130.6 W
108	Piteå (pē′tĕ-ô′) Swe.	65.22 N	21.20 E
108	Pite R. (pē′tĕ) Swe.	65.52 N	20.0 E
127	Pitesti (pē-tĕsht″) Rom.	44.51 N	24.51 E
122	Pithiviers (pē-tē-vyā′) Fr.	48.12 N	2.18 E
70	Pit R. (pĭt) Calif.	41.30 N	120.55 W
117	Pitsea (pĭt′sē) Gt. Brit. (London In.)	51.34 N	0.30 E
147	Pitsuwo (pĭt-so͞o′wō′) Chn.	39.29 N	122.21 E
72	Pitt L. (pĭt). Can. (Vancouver In.)	49.25 N	122.33 W
72	Pitt R. Can. (Vancouver In.)	49.14 N	122.44 W
51	Pittsburg (pĭts′bûrg) Calif. (San Francisco In.)	38.2 N	121.53 W
74	Pittsburg Calif.	38.1 N	121.54 W
79	Pittsburg Kan.	37.24 N	94.42 W
81	Pittsburg Tex.	33.0 N	95.0 W
79	Pittsburg Tex.	33.01 N	94.58 W
85	Pittsburgh Pa.	40.27 N	79.57 W
89	Pittsburgh Pa. (In.)		
89	Pittsburg L. Ill. (St. Louis In.)	38.35 N	90.7 W
79	Pittsfield (pĭts′fēld) Ill.	39.37 N	90.47 W
86	Pittsfield Me.	44.46 N	69.28 W
85	Pittston (pĭts′tŭn) Pa.	41.18 N	75.46 W
160	Pittsworth (pĭts′wûrth) Austl. (In.)	27.42 S	151.39 E
100	Piura (pē-o͞o′rä) Peru	5.20 S	80.32 W
73	Placentia (plă-sĕn′shĭ-ȧ) Calif. (Los Angeles In.)	33.52 N	117.54 W
87	Placentia Can.	47.18 N	53.55 W
87	Placentia B. Can.	47.25 N	54.30 W
153	Placer (plä-thĕr′) Phil.	9.39 N	125.35 E
80	Placer Mex.	29.10 N	105.22 W
74	Placerville (plăs′ẽr-vĭl) Calif.	38.43 N	120.48 W
96	Placetas (plä-thā′täs) Cuba	22.17 N	79.39 W
85	Placid L. (plăs′ĭd) N. Y.	44.20 N	73.58 W
125	Pla del Panadés (plä dĕl pä-nä-dās′. Sp. (In.)	41.24 N	1.42 E
73	Plain (plān) Utah (Salt Lake City In.)	41.18 N	112.5 W
77	Plainesdale (plāns′dāl) Mich.	47.2 N	88.40 W
85	Plainfield (plān′fēld) N. J.	40.36 N	74.27 W
79	Plainview (plān′vū) Ark.	34.58 N	93.18 W
72	Plainview Colo. (Denver In.)	39.54 N	105.17 W
77	Plainview Minn.	44.9 N	92.10 W
76	Plainview Neb.	42.21 N	97.46 W
78	Plainview Tex.	34.12 N	101.41 W
78	Plainville (plān′vĭl) Kan.	39.12 N	99.18 W
84	Plainwell (plān′wĕl) Mich.	42.27 N	85.40 W
97	Plana (Flat) Cays (Is.) (plä′nä) Ba. Is.	22.37 N	73.35 W
81	Plano (plā′nō) Tex.	33.0 N	96.42 W
83	Plant City Fla. (In.)	28.2 N	82.7 W
81	Plaquemine (plăk′-mēn′) La.	30.17 N	91.13 W
153	Plaridel (plä-rē-dĕl′) Phil.	8.36 N	123.43 E
124	Plasencia (plä-sĕn′thē-ä) Sp.	40.2 N	6.5 W
110	Plast (plăsht) Sov. Un.	54.24 N	60.52 E
86	Plaster Rock (plås′tẽr rŏk) Can.	46.53 N	67.24 W
148	Plastun B. (plås-to͞on′). Sov. Un.	44.45 N	136.22 E
102	Plata, R. de la (dä lä plä′tä) Arg.-Ur.	35.0 S	57.0 W
126	Platani R. (plä-tä′nē) It.	37.28 N	13.40 E
72	Plateau Colo. (Denver In.)	39.26 N	104.53 W
97	Platform Pt. (plăt′fôrm) Hai.	19.36 N	73.22 W
92	Platón Sánchez (plä-tōn′ sän′chĕz) Mex.	21.16 N	98.18 W
76	Platte (plăt) S. D.	43.23 N	98.51 W
79	Platte R. Mo.	39.50 N	94.42 W
79	Platte R. Neb.	41.20 N	97.10 W
58	Platte R., North Neb.	42.0 N	104.0 W
72	Platteville (plăt′vĭl) Colo. (Denver In.)	40.12 N	104.50 W
77	Platteville Wis.	42.45 N	90.29 W
79	Platt Natl. Park (plăt) Okla.	34.30 N	96.58 W
79	Plattsburg (plăts′bûrg) Mo.	39.33 N	94.27 W
85	Plattsburg N. Y.	44.42 N	73.38 W
76	Plattsmouth (plăts′mŭth) Neb.	41.1 N	95.53 W
120	Plauen (plou′ĕn) Ger.	50.30 N	12.6 E
93	Playa Vicente (plä′yȧ vē-sĕn′tā) Mex.	17.50 N	95.50 W
93	Playa Vicente R. Mex.	18.0 N	95.42 W
79	Pleasant Hill (plĕz′ănt) Mo.	38.47 N	94.17 W
89	Pleasant L. Minn. (Minneapolis In.)	45.6 N	93.4 W
85	Pleasant, L. N. Y.	43.28 N	74.24 W
51	Pleasanton (plĕz′ăn-tŭn) Calif. (San Francisco In.)	37.39 N	121.53 W
79	Pleasanton Kan.	38.11 N	94.40 W
80	Pleasanton Tex.	28.57 N	98.30 W
157	Pleasant, Pt. N. Z.	44.20 S	171.0 E
156	Plenty, B. of (plĕn′tē) N. Z.	37.40 S	177.0 E
160	Plenty R. Austl. (Melbourne In.)	37.42 S	145.6 E
71	Plentywood (plĕn′tē-wo͝od). Mont.	48.47 N	104.32 W
128	Ples (plyĕs) Sov. Un.	57.26 N	41.32 E
86	Plessisville (plĕ-sē′vēl′) Can.	46.13 N	71.47 W
121	Pleszew (plĕ′zhĕf) Pol.	51.53 N	17.48 E
127	Pleven (plĕ′vĕn) Bul.	43.24 N	24.35 E
127	Plevlje (Pljevlja) (plyĕv′lyĕ) (plyĕv′lyä). Yugo.	43.21 N	19.22 E
121	Plock (pwôtsk) Pol.	52.33 N	19.42 E
123	Ploërmel (plô-ĕr-mĕl′) Fr.	47.55 N	2.25 W
127	Ploeşti (plô-yĕsht″) Rom.	44.56 N	26.1 E
127	Plomarion (plô-mä′rĭ-ŏn) Grc.	38.58 N	26.24 E
122	Plomb du Cantal (plôN′ dü käN-täl′). Fr.	45.0 N	2.51 E
121	Plónsk (pwôn′sk) Pol.	52.37 N	20.24 E
127	Plovdiv (Philippopolis) (plôv′dĭf) (fĭl-ĭp-ŏp′ō-lĭs). Bul.	42.8 N	24.42 E
93	Pluma Hidalgo (plo͞o′mä ē-däl′gō) Mex.	15.54 N	96.27 W
72	Plum Cr. Colo. (Denver In.)	39.29 N	105.0 W
72	Plummers (plŭm′ẽrz) Colo. (Denver In.)	40.36 N	105.1 W
119	Plunge (plo͞on′gā) Sov. Un.	55.56 N	21.47 E
114	Plymouth (plĭm′ŭth) Gt. Brit.	50.25 N	4.5 W
84	Plymouth Ind.	41.22 N	86.20 W
95	Plymouth Le. Is. (In.)	16.43 N	62.13 W
86	Plymouth Mass.	41.55 N	70.41 W
86	Plymouth N. H.	43.45 N	71.42 W
83	Plymouth N. C.	35.51 N	76.43 W
85	Plymouth Pa.	41.15 N	75.6 W
77	Plymouth Wis.	43.45 N	87.59 W
88	Plymouth Meeting Pa. (Philadelphia In.)	40.6 N	75.17 W
160	Plympton (plĭmp′tŭn) Austl. (Adelaide In.)	34.58 S	138.33 E
128	Plyusa R. (plyo͞o′sȧ) Sov. Un.	58.45 N	28.10 E
120	Plzeň (p′l′zĕn′) Czech.	49.46 N	13.23 E
150	Pnom Penh (p′nôm′ pĕn′). Indoch.	11.38 N	104.58 E
132	Pobé (pô-bā′) Fr. W. Afr.	6.48 N	2.32 E
125	Pobla de Lillet (pō′blä dā lē-lyĕt′) Sp.	42.16 N	1.57 E
79	Pocahontas (pō-kȧ-hŏn′tȧs). Ark.	36.15 N	91.1 W
77	Pocahontas Ia.	42.45 N	94.40 W
71	Pocatello (pō-kȧ-tĕl′ō) Ida.	42.51 N	112.27 W
128	Pochep (pô-chĕp′) Sov. Un.	52.56 N	33.29 E
110	Pochinki (pô-chēn′kē) Sov. Un.	54.40 N	44.50 E
128	Pochinok (pô-chē′nôk) Sov. Un.	52.44 N	32.25 E
146	Pochow (pō′chō′) Chn.	33.51 N	115.44 E
93	Pochutla (San Pedro) (pō-cho͞o′tlä) (sän pā′drō). Mex.	15.43 N	96.28 W
116	Pocklington (pŏk′lĭng-tŭn) Gt. Brit.	53.55 N	0.46 W
83	Pocolet R. (pō-kō-lĕt′) S. C.	35.0 N	81.50 W
85	Pocomoke City (pō-kō-mōk′). Md.	38.4 N	75.34 W
121	Podgaytsy (pôd′gä-ē-tsĭ). Sov. Un.	49.13 N	25.6 E
127	Podgorica (pôd′gô-rē-tsä) Yugo.	42.25 N	19.17 E
129	Podgornoe (pôd′gôr-nô-yĕ) Sov. Un.	50.26 N	39.31 E
121	Podkarpatska Rus (Ruthenia) (pôd′kär-pät-skä ro͞os′). Sov. Un.	48.28 N	23.20 E
120	Podmokly (pôd′mô-klē) Czech.	50.47 N	14.10 E
128	Podolsk (pô-dôl″sk) Sov. Un.	55.27 N	37.31 E
132	Podor (pô-dôr′) Fr. W. Afr.	16.35 N	15.3 W
129	Podvolochiska (pŭd-vō-lō-chĭs′kȧ). Sov. Un.	49.33 N	26.9 E
126	Poggibonsi (pōd-jē-bôn′sē) It.	43.27 N	11.12 E
139	Pogibi (pô′gē-bē) Sakh.	52.15 N	141.50 E
128	Pogodino (Gorki) (pô-gô′dē-nô) (gôr′kĭ). Sov. Un.	54.17 N	30.59 E
146	Pohai, Str. of (pō′hī′) Chn.	38.35 N	121.0 E
147	Pohang (pō′häng′) Kor.	36.2 N	129.23 E
146	Pohsing (pō′hsĭng′) Chn.	37.14 N	118.13 E
89	Point Comfort I. La. (New Orleans In.)	29.49 N	89.12 W
89	Pointe a la Hache (point′ á lȧ ȧsh′) La. (New Orleans In.)	29.35 N	89.48 W
91	Pointe à Pitre (pwăNt′ á pē-tr′) Guad.	16.15 N	61.30 W
57	Pointe aux Trembles (pwăNt′ ō träN′bl′). Can. (Montreal In.)	45.38 N	73.30 W
72	Point Roberts (point rŏb′ẽrts) Wash. (Vancouver In.)	48.59 N	123.5 W
57	Point Fortune (point fôr′tŭn) Can. (Montreal In.)	45.34 N	74.23 W
72	Point Grey (point grā′) Can. (Vancouver In.)	49.16 N	123.16 W
84	Point Pleasant W. Va.	38.50 N	82.8 W
122	Poissy (pwȧ-sē′) Fr.	48.55 N	2.1 E
122	Poitiers (pwȧ-tyā′) Fr.	46.35 N	0.20 E
122	Poitou Hills (pwȧ-to͞o′) Fr.	46.50 N	0.50 W
101	Pojuca, R. (pō-ho͞o′kä). Braz. (In.)	12.28 S	38.30 W
88	Pokegama (pô-kê-găm′ȧ) Wis. (Duluth In.)	46.39 N	92.9 W
145	Poklo (pŏk′lō′) Chn.	23.8 N	114.17 E
143	Pokotu (pō′kō-to͞o′) Chn.	48.37 N	122.0 E
128	Pokrov (pô′krôf) Sov. Un.	55.55 N	39.9 E
129	Pokrovskaya (pô-krôf′skä-yä) Sov. Un.	47.25 N	38.54 E
126	Pola (pō′lä) Yugo.	44.52 N	13.51 E
120	Poland (pō′lănd) Eur.	52.0 N	22.0 E
152	Polangui (pô-läŋ′gē) Phil.	13.18 N	123.29 E
128	Pola R. Sov. Un.	57.45 N	31.55 E
121	Polgár (pôl′gär) Hung.	47.53 N	21.9 E
143	Poli (pō′lĭ′) Chn.	45.50 N	130.40 E
126	Policastro, G. of (pō-lē-käs′trō). It.	39.55 N	15.35 E
123	Poligny (pō-lē-nyē′) Fr.	46.50 N	5.42 E
152	Polillo (pô-lēl′yō) Phil.	14.41 N	121.56 E
152	Polillo I. Phil.	14.50 N	121.55 E
152	Polillo Is. Phil.	14.50 N	122.12 E
152	Polillo Str. Phil.	15.0 N	121.42 E
126	Polistena (pō-lēs-tä′nä) It.	38.25 N	16.5 E
125	Pollensa (pōl-yĕn′sä) Sp.	39.53 N	3.1 E
153	Polloc Har. (pōl-yŏk′) Phil.	7.23 N	124.15 E
151	Polo (pō′lō). Phil. (Manila In.)	14.44 N	120.56 E
94	Polochic, R. (pō-lô-chēk′). Guat.	15.20 N	89.40 W
129	Polonnoe (pō′lô-nô-yĕ). Sov. Un.	50.7 N	27.31 E
128	Polotsk (pō′lôtsk) Sov. Un.	55.29 N	28.48 E
71	Polson (pōl′sŭn) Mont.	47.41 N	114.10 W
129	Poltava (pôl-tä′vä) Sov. Un.	49.36 N	34.35 E
129	Poltavka (pôl-täf′kä) Sov. Un.	47.31 N	32.27 E
119	Põltsamaa (põlt′sä-mä). Sov. Un.	58.40 N	26.0 E
138	Polui R. (pôl′wê) Sov. Un.	65.45 N	69.0 E

ng-sing; ŋ-baŋk; N-nasalized n; nŏd; cŏmmit; ōld; ôbey; ôrder; fo͞od; fo͝ot; ou-out; s-soft; sh-dish; th-thin; pūre; ûnite; ûrn; stŭd; circŭs; ü-as "y" in study; ′-indeterminate vowel.

Page	Name Pronunciation Region	Lat. °′	Long. °′
110	Polyarnoye (pôl'yár-nō-yĕ) Sov. Un.	69.10 N	33.30 E
127	Polygyros (pô-lê-yê-rōs') . . . . . Grc.	40.23 N	23.24 E
127	Polykhnitos (pō-lê-knē-tôs') . . Grc.	39.4 N	26.11 E
81	Polytechnic (pŏl-ĭ-tĕk'nĭk) . . . Tex.	32.45 N	97.18 W
124	Pombal (pôm-bäl') . . . . Port.	39.54 N	8.38 W
120	Pomerania (pŏm-ê-rā'nĭ-á) . . . . Pol.	53.55 N	16.0 E
118	Pomeranian Bay . . . . Ger.-Pol.	54.10 N	14.30 E
84	Pomeroy (pŏm'ẽr-oi) . . . . Ohio	39.4 N	82.2 W
70	Pomeroy . . . . Wash.	46.28 N	117.37 W
76	Pomme de Terre R. (pôm dē tĕr') Minn.	45.40 N	95.50 W
74	Pomona (pô-mō'ná) . . . . Calif.	34.3 N	117.43 W
114	Pomona (Mainland) . . . . . Gt. Brit.	59.0 N	2.50 W
83	Pompano (pŏm'pá-nō) . . Fla. (In.)	26.15 N	80.7 W
117	Pompeii (pŏm-pā'yê) It. (Napoli In.)	40.45 N	14.29 E
123	Pompey (pôɴ-pā') . . . . Fr.	8.48 N	6.9 E
76	Ponca (pŏn'ká) . . . . Neb.	42.35 N	96.41 W
79	Ponca City . . . . Okla.	36.43 N	97.6 W
91	Ponce (pōn'sā) . . . . P. R. (In.)	18.1 N	66.39 W
117	Ponders End (pŏn'dẽrz) Gt. Brit. (London In.)	51.39 N	0.3 W
141	Pondichery (pôɴ'dē-shā-rē') (pŏn-dĭ-shĕr'ê) . India	12.0 N	79.45 E
124	Ponferrada (pōn-fĕr-rä'dhä . . . . Sp.	42.34 N	6.36 W
100	Pongo de Manseriche (Falls) (pŏŋ'gō dā män-sā-rē'chā) . Ec.	4.30 S	77.30 W
110	Ponoi (pō'nô-ĭ) . . . . Sov. Un.	67.0 N	41.25 E
110	Ponoi R . . . . Sov. Un.	67.0 N	38.0 E
122	Pons (pôɴ) . . . . Fr.	45.35 N	0.35 W
153	Ponson I. (pōn-sōn') . . . . Phil.	10.44 N	124.32 E
132	Ponta Delgada (pōn'tá dĕl-gä'dá) Az. Is. (In.)	37.48 N	25.45 W
101	Ponta de Pedras (pôŋ'tá dā pā'dräzh) . Braz. (In.)	1.25 S	48.55 W
102	Ponta Grossa (pōn'tá grō'sá) . Braz.	25.10 S	50.15 W
123	Pont-à-Mousson (pôɴ'-tà-mōō-sôɴ') . Fr.	48.55 N	6.3 E
123	Pontarlier (pôɴ'tàr-lyā') . . . . . . Fr.	46.55 N	6.25 E
122	Pont-Audemer (pôɴ'-tōd'mâr') . Fr.	49.23 N	0.31 E
123	Pontault-Combault (pôɴ-tō'-kôɴ-bō') . Fr. (In.)	48.46 N	2.36 E
123	Pontcarré (pôɴ-kà-rā') . . . Fr. (In.)	48.47 N	2.42 E
81	Pontchartrain, L. (pôɴ-shàr-trăɴ') La.	30.10 N	90.10 W
101	Ponte (pōŋ'tĕ) . . . . Braz.	19.58 S	44.0 W
126	Pontedera (pōn-tā-dā'rä) . . . . . . It.	43.40 N	10.38 E
124	Ponte de Sor (pōŋ'tĕ dā sōr') Port.	39.15 N	8.4 W
116	Pontefract (pŏn'tê-frăkt) . Gt. Brit.	53.41 N	1.18 W
153	Pontevedra (pōn-tā-vā'drä) . . Phil.	11.28 N	122.50 E
124	Pontevedra . . . . Sp.	42.27 N	8.39 W
114	Ponthierville (pôɴ-tyā-vēl') Bel. Cong.	0.22 S	25.20 E
79	Pontiac (pŏn'tĭ-ăk) . . . . Ill.	40.53 N	88.36 W
84	Pontiac . . . . Mich.	42.40 N	83.18 W
150	Pontianak (pōn-tê-ä'nák) . . Indon.	0.5 S	109.28 E
117	Ponticelli (pōn-tê-chĕl'lē) It. (Napoli In.)	40.51 N	14.20 E
126	Pontine (Ponziane) Is. (pŏn'tĭn) (pōn-tsē-ä'nä) . It.	40.58 N	13.0 E
122	Pontivy (pôɴ-tê-vē') . . . . Fr.	48.5 N	2.58 W
122	Pont-l'Abbe (pôɴ-là-bā') . . . . . Fr.	47.53 N	4.11 W
123	Pontoise (pôɴ-twàz') . . . . . Fr. (In.)	49.2 N	2.6 E
82	Pontotoc (pŏn-tō-tŏk') . . . . Miss.	34.13 N	89.2 W
126	Pontremoli (pôn-trĕm'ô-lē) . . . . It.	44.21 N	9.55 E
122	Pont St. Esprit (pôɴ' săɴ tĕs-prē') Fr.	44.15 N	4.40 E
126	Ponza (I.) (pōn'tsä) . . . . It.	40.53 N	12.58 E
126	Ponziane (Pontine) Is. (pōn-tsē-ä'nä) (pŏn'tĭn) . It.	40.58 N	13.0 E
114	Poole (pōōl) . . . . Gt. Brit.	50.45 N	1.55 W
141	Poona (pōō'nŭ) . . . . India	18.30 N	73.45 E
100	Poopó L. (pō-ō-pô') . . . . Bol.	18.45 S	67.0 W
156	Poor Knights I . . . . N. Z.	35.30 S	174.45 E
100	Popayán (pō-pä-yän') . . . . Col.	2.18 N	76.45 W
71	Poplar (pŏp'lẽr) . . . . Mont.	48.6 N	105.10 W
79	Poplar Bluff . . . . Mo.	36.45 N	90.24 W
84	Poplar Plains . . . . Ky.	38.22 N	83.40 W
71	Poplar R . . . . Mont.	48.35 N	105.20 W
71	Poplar R., West Fork . . . . . . Mont.	48.50 N	106.10 W
82	Poplarville . . . . Miss.	30.51 N	89.32 W
92	Popocatepetl (Cerro) (pô-pô-kä-tä'pĕt'l) . Mex.	19.2 N	98.37 W
134	Popokabaca (pō'pô-kà-bä'kà) Bel. Cong.	5.40 S	16.47 E
93	Popotla (pô-pō'tlä) . . . . Mex. (In.)	19.27 N	99.10 W
129	Popovka (pô'pôf-kà) . . . . Sov. Un.	47.13 N	36.32 E
129	Popovka . . . . Sov. Un.	50.3 N	33.38 E
129	Popovka . . . . Sov. Un.	51.13 N	33.5 E
127	Popovo (pô'pô-vō) . . . . Bul.	43.19 N	26.13 E
117	Poppenbüttel (pôp'ĕn-büt-ĕl) Ger. (Hamburg In.)	53.40 N	10.5 E
88	Poquessing Cr. (pō-kwĕ'sĭng) Pa. (Philadelphia In.)	40.5 N	74.58 W
126	Po R. (pō) . . . . It.	44.55 N	10.30 E
141	Porbandar (pōr-bŭn'dŭr) . . . . India	21.38 N	69.37 E
99	Porcos, I. dos (dōzh pôr'kōzh) Braz. (Rio de Janeiro In.)	23.32 S	45.3 W
124	Porcuna (pôr-kōō'nä) . . . . Sp.	37.53 N	4.11 W
71	Porcupine Cr. (pôr'kū-pīn) . Mont.	48.30 N	106.30 W
52	Porcupine R . . . . Alsk.	67.0 N	143.0 W
126	Pordenone (pōr-dā-nō'nä) . . . . . . It.	45.57 N	12.38 E
128	Porechie (pô'ryĕch-yĕ) . . Sov. Un.	55.16 N	31.31 E
119	Pori (Björneborg) (pô'rê) (byûr'nē-bôrgh) . Fin.	61.30 N	21.48 E
108	Porjus (pôr'yōōs) . . . . Swe.	66.52 N	19.42 E
128	Porkhov (pôr'kôf) . . . . Sov. Un.	57.46 N	29.32 E
122	Pornic (pôr-nēk') . . . . Fr.	47.10 N	2.9 W
153	Poro I. (pō'rō) . . . . Phil.	10.40 N	124.27 E
148	Poronaysk (pô'rô-nīsk) . . . . . . Sakh.	49.13 N	143.4 E

Page	Name Pronunciation Region	Lat. °′	Long. °′
120	Porrentruy (pô-räɴ-trüē') . . Switz.	47.25 N	7.3 E
118	Porsgrund (pôrs'grōōn') . . . . . Nor.	59.8 N	9.40 E
100	Portachuelo (pôrt-ä-chwā'lō) . . Bol.	17.29 S	63.59 W
160	Port Adelaide (pôrt ăd'ê-lād) . Austl.	34.50 S	138.30 E
160	Port Adelaide R. Austl. (Adelaide In.)	34.49 S	138.31 E
85	Portage (pôr'tāj) . . . . Pa.	40.24 N	78.40 W
77	Portage . . . . Wis.	43.34 N	89.28 W
56	Portage Cr . . . Can. (Winnipeg In.)	50.5 N	98.16 W
54	Portage-la-Prairie (pôr'tāj-lä-prā'rĭ) . Can.	49.58 N	98.18 W
156	Port Albert . . . . N. Z.	36.18 S	174.28 E
124	Portalegre (pôr-tä-lā'grĕ) . . . . Port.	39.18 N	7.27 W
78	Portales (pôr-tä'lĕs) . . . . N. M.	34.11 N	103.21 W
134	Port Alfred (ăl'frĕd) . . . . U. S. Afr.	33.35 S	26.55 E
85	Port Allegany (ăl-ê-gā'nĭ) . . . . . Pa.	41.48 N	78.12 W
70	Port Angeles (ăn'jē-lĕs) . . . . Wash.	48.7 N	123.28 W
160	Port Arthur (är'thŭr) Austl. (Tas. In.)	43.9 S	147.50 E
55	Port Arthur . . . . Can.	48.30 N	89.10 W
	Port Arthur, see Lushun, Chn.		
81	Port Arthur . . . . Tex.	29.52 N	93.57 W
87	Port au Basque (pôr'tō bȧsk') Can.	45.30 N	59.10 W
158	Port Augusta (ô-gŭs'tá) . . . . Austl.	32.29 S	137.49 E
87	Port au Port B. (pôr'tō pōr') . . Can.	48.35 N	59.50 W
97	Port Au Prince (pôr'tō präɴs') Hai.	18.32 N	72.20 W
84	Port Austin (ôs'tĭn) . . . . Mich.	44.3 N	82.58 W
139	Port Ayan (á-yän') . . . . . . Sov. Un.	56.25 N	138.15 E
153	Port Barton (bär'tŭn) . . . . Phil.	10.30 N	119.10 E
134	Port Beaufort (bō'fẽrt) . U. S. Afr.	34.22 S	20.47 E
150	Port Blair (blâr) . . . . India	12.5 N	92.40 E
81	Port Bolivar (bŏl'ĭ-vȧr) . . . . . . Tex.	29.22 N	94.46 W
157	Port Chalmers (chä'mẽrs) . . . N. Z.	45.49 S	170.39 E
51	Port Chicago Calif. (San Francisco In.)	38.3 N	122.1 W
100	Port Chicama (chê-kä'mä) . . . Peru	7.45 S	79.28 W
84	Port Clinton (klĭn'tŭn) . . . . . . Ohio	41.30 N	82.57 W
85	Port Colborne (kōl'bôrn) . . . . . Can.	42.55 N	79.10 W
72	Port Coquitlam (kô-kwĭt'lăm) Can. (Vancouver In.)	49.15 N	122.46 W
51	Port Costa (kôs'tá) Calif. (San Francisco In.)	38.2 N	122.11 W
85	Port Dalhousie (dăl-hōō'zĭ) . . Can.	43.10 N	79.16 W
122	Port-de-Bouc (pôr-dē-bōōk') . . . Fr.	43.25 N	5.0 E
97	Port de Paix (pôr dē pĕ') . . . . Hai.	19.57 N	72.49 W
137	Port Dickson (dĭk'sŭn) Malaya (In.)	2.32 N	101.49 E
51	Port Discovery (dĭs-kŭv'ẽr-ĭ) Wash. (Seattle In.)	48.1 N	122.52 W
86	Port Elgin (ĕl'jĭn) . . . . Can.	46.3 N	64.6 W
134	Port Elizabeth (ê-lĭz'á-bĕth) U. S. Afr.	33.58 S	25.35 E
73	Porter (pōr'tẽr) Ala. (Birmingham In.)	33.37 N	87.4 W
82	Porterdale (pōr'tẽr-dāl) . . . . . Ga.	33.34 N	83.54 W
74	Porterville (pōr'tẽr-vĭl) . . . . . Calif.	36.4 N	119.4 W
132	Port Étienne (pôr' tā-tyĕn') Fr. W. Afr.	20.58 N	17.2 W
134	Port-Francqui (pôr-fräɴ-kē') Bel. Cong.	4.23 S	20.43 E
134	Port Gentil (pōr zhäɴ-tē') Fr. Eq. Afr.	0.40 S	8.46 E
82	Port Gibson (pôrt gĭb'sŭn) . . Miss.	31.57 N	91.0 W
132	Port-Gueydon (pôr-gā-dôɴ') . . Alg.	36.57 N	4.28 E
72	Port Guichon (pôrt gē-shôɴ') Can. (Vancouver In.)	49.5 N	123.6 W
160	Port Hacking (hăk'ĭng) . . . . Austl.	34.5 S	151.10 E
72	Port Hammond (hăm'ŭnd) Can. (Vancouver In.)	49.12 N	122.40 W
72	Port Haney (hā'nĭ) Can. (Vancouver In.)	49.13 N	122.35 W
132	Port Harcourt (här'kŭrt) . . . . Nig.	4.45 N	7.0 E
87	Port Hawkesbury (hôks'bẽr-ĭ) Can.	45.35 N	61.20 W
158	Port Hedland (hĕd'lănd) . . . Austl.	20.31 S	118.25 E
134	Port Herald (hĕr'ăld) . . . . Nya.	16.58 S	35.13 E
87	Port Hood (hōōd) . . . . Can.	46.0 N	61.31 W
85	Port Hope (hōp) . . . . Can.	43.56 N	78.10 W
84	Port Huron (hū'rŏn) . . . . Mich.	42.57 N	82.27 W
131	Port Ibrahim (ē-brä-hēm') Eg. (Suez Can. In.)	29.57 N	32.33 E
117	Portici (pôr'tê-chê) It. (Napoli In.)	40.49 N	14.20 E
159	Port Jackson (jăk'sŭn) . . . . . Austl.	33.49 S	151.14 E
85	Port Jervis (jûr'vĭs) . . . . N. Y.	41.25 N	74.41 W
72	Port Kells (kĕlz) Can. (Vancouver In.)	49.10 N	112.42 W
159	Portland (pōrt'lănd) . . . . Austl.	38.22 S	141.38 E
160	Portland . . . . Austl. (Tas. In.)	40.53 S	147.46 E
84	Portland . . . . Ind.	40.27 N	85.0 W
86	Portland . . . . Me.	43.40 N	70.15 W
84	Portland . . . . Mich.	42.52 N	84.58 W
70	Portland . . . . Ore.	45.30 N	122.37 W
51	Portland . . . . Ore. (In.)		
96	Portland Bight . . . . Jam.	17.50 N	77.6 W
114	Portland Bill . . . . Gt. Brit.	50.30 N	2.40 W
160	Portland, C . . . . . Austl. (Tas. In.)	40.43 S	147.57 E
156	Portland I . . . . N. Z.	39.18 S	177.53 E
96	Portland Pt . . . . Jam.	17.42 N	77.10 W
86	Portland, South . . . . Me.	43.38 N	70.13 W
81	Port Lavaca (lá-vä'ká) . . . . Tex.	28.37 N	96.38 W
157	Port Levy (lē'vĭ) . . . . . . N. Z. (In.)	43.38 S	172.51 E
158	Port Lincoln (lĭŋ'kŭn) . . . . . . Austl.	34.43 S	135.55 E
122	Port Louis (pôr'lōō-ē') . . . . Fr.	47.42 N	3 20 W
51	Port Ludlow (lŭd'lō) Wash. (Seattle In.)	47.55 N	122.41 W
132	Port-Lyautey (Kenitra) (lē-ô-tā') (kĕ-nē'trä) . Mor.	34.22 N	6.31 W
159	Port Macquarie (má-kwŏ'rĭ) . Austl.	31.25 S	152.55 E

Page	Name Pronunciation Region	Lat. °′	Long. °′
51	Port Madison (măd'ĭ-sŭn) Wash. (Seattle In.)	47.42 N	122.31 W
72	Port Mann (măn) Can. (Vancouver In.)	49.13 N	122.50 W
96	Port Maria (má-rī'á) . . . . Jam.	18.22 N	76.54 W
160	Port Melbourne (mĕl'bŭrn) Austl. (Melbourne In.)	37.50 S	144.54 E
86	Port Menier (pôr mē-nyā') . . . Can.	49.50 N	64.20 W
153	Port Misamis (mê-sä'mĭs) . . . Phil.	8.10 N	123.54 E
72	Port Moody (mōōd'ĭ) Can. (Vancouver In.)	49.17 N	122.50 W
151	Port Moresby (mōrz'bê) . Pap. Ter.	9.32 S	147.12 E
81	Port Neches (nĕch'ĕz) . . . . Tex.	30.0 N	93.58 W
54	Port Nelson (nĕl'sŭn) . . . . Can.	56.59 N	92.57 W
86	Portneuf (pôr-nûf') . . . . Can.	48.38 N	69.7 W
156	Port Nicholson (nĭk'ŭl-sŭn) N. Z. (In.)	41.17 S	174.48 E
134	Port Nolloth (nŏl'ŏth) . . U. S. Afr.	29.12 S	16.51 E
124	Pôrto (pōr'tōō) . . . . Port.	41.8 N	8.38 W
100	Porto Acre (pōr'tōō ä'krĕ) . . Braz.	9.30 S	67.33 W
102	Porto Alegre (pōr-tōō ä-lā'grĕ) Braz.	30.1 S	51.10 W
134	Porto Alexandre (pōr'tōō ä-lĕ-zhän'drĕ) . Ang.	15.55 S	11.47 E
135	Pôrto Amelia (pōr'tōō á-mā'lyá) Moz.	12.55 S	40.30 E
95	Portobelo (pôr'tô-bā'lō) . . . . . Pan.	9.33 N	79.40 W
135	Porto Durnford (Bur Gao) (pôr-tô dūrn'fôrd) (bōōr gou') . Som.	1.10 S	41.47 E
124	Pôrto de Mós (pōr'tōō dā mōzh') Port.	39.35 N	8.49 W
101	Porto de Pedras (pōr'tōō dā pā'dräzh) . Braz.	9.2 S	35.20 W
131	Porto-Farina (pōr'tô-fá-rē'nä) Tun. (In.)	37.10 N	10.10 E
126	Portoferraio (pōr'tô-fĕr-rä'yō) . . It.	42.47 N	10.21 E
101	Port of Spain . . . . Trin.	10.40 N	61.31 W
132	Porto Grande (pōr'tō grän'dā) C. V. Is. (In.)	16.52 N	25.58 W
126	Portogruaro (pōr'tô-grōō-ä'rō) . . It.	45.48 N	12.49 E
74	Portola (pôr'tō-lá) . . . . Calif.	39.46 N	120.30 W
102	Porto Murtinho (pōr'tōō mōōr-tēn'yōō) . Braz.	21.50 S	58.0 W
101	Porto Nacional (pōr'tōō ná-syô-näl') . Braz.	10.44 S	48.28 W
132	Porto-Novo (pōr'tô-nō'vō) Fr. W. Afr.	6.31 N	2.31 W
51	Port Orchard (ôr'chẽrd) Wash. (Seattle In.)	47.32 N	122.38 W
91	Porto Rico (Puerto Rico) (pôr'tō rē'kō) (pwĕr'tō rē'kō) . W. I. (In.)	18.0 N	66.0 W
132	Porto Santo I. (pōr'tōō säɴ'tōō) Madeira Is.	33.5 N	16.20 W
101	Porto Seguro (pōr'tōō sā-gōō'rōō) Braz.	16.28 S	39.14 W
126	Porto Torres (pōr'tō tôr'rĕs) . Sard.	40.49 N	8.55 E
122	Porto-Vecchio (Corsica) (pōr'tō-vĕk'ê-ō) . Fr. (In.)	41.35 N	9.15 E
100	Porto Velho (pōr'tōō väl'yōō) Braz.	8.45 S	63.45 W
100	Portoviejo (pôr'tô-vyā'hō) . . . . Ec.	1.0 S	80.20 W
114	Portpatrick (pôrt-păt'rĭk) . Gt. Brit.	54.50 N	5.5 W
157	Port Pegasus (pĕg'á-sŭs) . . . . N. Z.	47.13 S	167.45 E
159	Port Philip B. (fĭl'ĭp) . . . . . . Austl.	38.5 S	144.50 E
158	Port Pirie (pĭ'rê) . . . . Austl.	33.11 S	138.2 E
54	Port Radium (rā'dê-ŭm) . . . . . Can.	66.5 N	118.0 W
88	Port Richmond (rĭch'mŭnd) N. Y. (In.)	40.38 N	74.8 W
96	Port Royal (roi'ăl) . . . . Jam.	17.54 N	76.52 W
96	Port Sagua la Grande (sä'gwä lä grän'dā) . Cuba	22.55 N	80.4 W
134	Port St. Johns . . . . U. S. Afr.	31.37 S	29.31 E
133	Port Said (sä-ēd') . . . . Eg.	31.14 N	32.11 E
97	Port San Antonio (săn ăn-tō'nĭ-ō) Jam.	18.11 N	76.26 W
112	Port Say (pôr sà'ē) . . . . Alg.	35.3 N	2.15 W
134	Port Shepstone (shĕps'tŭn) U. S. Afr.	30.46 S	30.25 E
56	Port Simpson (sĭmp'sŭn) Can. (Prince Rupert In.)	54.34 N	130.25 W
114	Portsmouth (pôrts'mŭth) . Gt. Brit.	50.48 N	1.5 W
95	Portsmouth . . . . Le. Is. (In.)	15.34 N	61.28 W
86	Portsmouth . . . . N. H.	43.5 N	70.47 W
84	Portsmouth . . . . Ohio	38.45 N	83.0 W
85	Portsmouth . . . . Va.	36.47 N	76.20 W
133	Port Sudan (sōō-dän') . . . A. E. Sud.	19.32 N	37.6 E
150	Port Swettenham (swĕt'ĕn-hăm) Malaya	3.5 N	101.30 E
83	Port Tampa (tăm'pá) . . . Fla. (In.)	27.50 N	82.32 W
70	Port Townsend (tounz'ĕnd) . Wash.	48.8 N	122.48 W
124	Portugal (pōr'tū-găl) . . . . Eur.	40.0 N	8.0 W
124	Portugalete (pōr-tōō-gä-lā'tā) . . Sp.	43.18 N	3.3 W
	Portuguese East Africa, see Mozambique		
132	Portuguese Guinea (gĭn'ê) . . . . Afr.	12.0 N	15.0 W
	Portuguese West Africa, see Angola		
138	Port Ust-Eniseiski (ōōst'yĕ-nê-sā'-ĕsk-ĭ) . Sov. Un.	69.36 N	84.30 E
122	Port Vendres (pôr väɴ'dr') . . . . Fr.	42.32 N	3.5 E
117	Port Victoria Gt. Brit. (London In.)	51.26 N	0.42 E
159	Port Vila (vē'lä) . . . . . . New Hebr.	17.57 S	168.15 E
158	Port Wakefield (wāk'fēld) . . Austl.	34.13 S	138.12 E
77	Port Washington (wŏsh'ĭng-tŭn) Wis.	43.25 N	87.52 W
119	Porvoo (Borgå) (pôr'vō) (bôr'gōō) Fin.	60.26 N	25.44 E
102	Posadas (pō-sä'dhäs) . . . . Arg.	27.20 S	55.59 W
124	Posadas . . . . Sp.	37.49 N	5.7 W
144	Poseh (pō'sä') . . . . Chn.	23.58 N	106.45 E
	Posen, see Poznań, Pol.		
146	Poshan (pō'shän') . . . . Chn.	36.31 N	117.54 E

ăt; finăl; rāte; senāte; ärm; ȧsk; sofá; fâre; ch-choose; dh-as th in other; bē; ēvent; bĕt; recĕnt; cratẽr; g-go; gh-gutteral g; bĭt; ĭ-short neutral; rīde; ĸ-gutteral k as ch in German ich;

Poshekhono PRONOUNCING INDEX **Puerto Varas**

Page	Name Pronunciation Region	Lat. °′	Long. °′
128	Poshekhono-Volodarsk (pô-shyĕк'-ô-nô-vôl'ô-dàrsk). Sov. Un.	58.30 N	39.9 E
148	Posiet (pôs-yĕt'). Sov. Un.	42.46 N	130.47 E
148	Posiet, B. Sov. Un.	42.45 N	130.0 E
117	Posillipo C. (pô-sēl'lē-pō) It. (Napoli In.)	40.48 N	14.13 E
120	Poznań (pôz'nän'). Pol.	52.25 N	16.53 E
150	Poso, L. (pō'sō). Indon.	1.50 S	120.38 E
147	Posŏng (pō'sŭng'). Kor.	34.46 N	127.5 E
78	Post (pōst). Tex.	33.12 N	101.22 W
150	Postillion Is. (pŏs-tĭl'yŭn). Indon.	7.0 S	118.30 E
126	Postumia (pôs-tōō'myä). Yugo.	45.45 N	14.13 E
134	Potchefstroom (pŏch'ĕf-strōm) U. S. Afr.	26.42 S	27.4 E
79	Poteau (pô-tō'). Okla.	35.4 N	94.36 W
79	Poteau R. Okla.	35.0 N	94.36 W
80	Poteet (pô-tēt). Tex.	29.3 N	98.35 W
126	Potenza (pô-tĕnt'sä). It.	40.38 N	15.48 E
126	Potenza R. It.	43.17 N	13.20 E
157	Poteriteri, L. (pō-tĕ'rĭ-tĕ'rĭ). N. Z.	46.5 S	167.5 E
134	Potgieters Rust (pŏt'gē-tērz rüst') U. S. Afr.	24.13 S	28.57 E
111	Poti (pô'tē). Sov. Un.	42.10 N	41.40 E
85	Potomac R. (pô-tō'măk). Md.-Va.	39.10 N	77.30 W
100	Potosí (pō-tô-sē'). Bol.	19.31 S	65.45 W
79	Potosi (pô-tō'sĭ). Mo.	37.56 N	90.48 W
80	Potosí, R. (pō-tô-sē'). Mex.	25.0 N	99.45 W
153	Pototan (pô-tō'tän). Phil.	10.55 N	122.38 E
96	Potrerillo, Pico del (Pk.) (pō-trâ-rēl'yô). Cuba	21.55 N	80.2 W
94	Potrerillos (pō-trâ-rēl'yôs). Hond.	15.13 N	87.58 W
120	Potsdam (pôts'däm). Ger.	52.25 N	13.3 E
85	Potsdam (pŏts'dăm). N. Y.	44.40 N	74.38 W
116	Potteries, The (pŏt'ĕr-ĭz). Gt. Brit.	53.3 N	2.12 W
157	Potts, Mt. (pŏts). N. Z.	43.30 S	170.58 E
85	Pottstown. Pa.	40.15 N	75.40 W
85	Pottsville (pŏts'vĭl). Pa.	40.42 N	76.12 W
85	Poughkeepsie (pô-kĭp'sĭ). N. Y.	41.42 N	73.56 W
51	Poulsbo (pōlz'bōō) Wash. (Seattle In.)	47.44 N	122.38 W
116	Poulton-le-Fylde (pōl'tŭn-lē-fīld') Gt. Brit.	53.50 N	2.59 W
99	Pouso Alegre (pō'zōō ä-lā'grĕ) Braz. (Rio de Janeiro In.)	22.5 S	45.55 W
156	Poverty B. (pŏv'ĕr-tĭ). N. Z.	38.43 S	178.0 E
124	Póvoa de Varzim (pō-vō'ȧ dā vär'zēɴ). Port.	41.23 N	8.47 W
71	Powder R. (pou'dēr). Mont.-Wyo.	45.20 N	105.40 W
70	Powder R. Ore.	44.55 N	117.30 W
71	Powder R., South Fork. Wyo.	43.20 N	106.40 W
73	Powder Springs. Ga. (Atlanta In.)	33.52 N	84.41 W
71	Powell (pou'ĕl). Wyo.	44.45 N	108.45 W
97	Powell Pt. Ba. Is.	24.53 N	76.23 W
82	Powell R. Tenn.-Ky.	36.30 N	83.50 W
158	Powells Cr. (pou'ĕlz). Austl.	18.2 S	133.30 E
145	Poyang L. (pō'yäng). Chn.	29.4 N	116.15 E
89	Poydras (poi'drȧs) La. (New Orleans In.)	29.52 N	89.54 W
77	Poygan L. (poi'gȧn). Wis.	44.9 N	88.45 W
117	Poynton (poin'tŭn) Gt. Brit. (Liverpool In.)	53.21 N	2.7 W
127	Požarevac (pô'zhȧ'rĕ-vȧts). Yugo.	44.36 N	21.11 E
93	Pozas, Cerro (sĕr'ō pō'zäs) Mex. (In.)	19.24 N	99.22 W
127	Pozega (pô'zhĕ-gȧ). Yugo.	45.18 N	17.41 E
120	Poznań (Posen) (pôz'nän'') (pō'zĕn). Pol.	52.25 N	16.53 E
124	Pozoblanco (pô-thō-blăŋ'kō). Sp.	38.23 N	4.51 W
92	Pozos (pô'zōs). Mex.	22.5 N	100.51 W
125	Pozuelo de Alarcón (pô-thwā'lō dā ä-lär-kōn'). Sp. (In.)	40.27 N	3.50 W
126	Pozzuoli (pôt-swô'lē). It.	40.50 N	14.7 E
150	Prachin (prä'chēn). Siam	13.58 N	101.15 E
122	Prades (pråd). Fr.	42.35 N	2.25 E
73	Prado (prä'dō) Calif. (Los Angeles In.)	33.54 N	117.38 W
120	Praha (Prague) (prä'hȧ) (präg) Czech.	50.5 N	14.26 E
132	Praia (prä'yȧ). C. V. Is. (In.)	14.59 N	23.31 W
70	Prairie City (prâ'rĭ). Ore.	44.26 N	118.42 W
78	Prairie Dog Town Fork of Red R. Tex.	34.34 N	100.0 W
77	Prairie du Chien (prâ'rĭ dōō shēn') Wis.	43.2 N	91.9 W
57	Prairies, River des (rē-vyâr' dā prâ-rē'). Can. (Montreal In.)	45.35 N	73.40 W
128	Pra R. (prá). Sov. Un.	54.55 N	40.18 E
125	Prat del Llobregat (prät' dĕl lyō-brā-gät'). Sp. (In.)	41.19 N	2.5 E
126	Prato (prä'tō). It.	43.53 N	11.4 E
122	Prats-de-Mollo (prà-dē-mô-lō'). Fr.	42.25 N	2.35 E
78	Pratt (prăt). Kan.	37.37 N	98.43 W
82	Prattville (prăt'vĭl). Ala.	32.28 N	86.28 W
124	Pravia (prä'vē-ä). Sp.	43.29 N	6.9 W
121	Pravdinsk (Friedland) (präv'-dênsk) (frēd'länt). Sov. Un.	54.27 N	21.1 E
121	Pregel R. (prä'gĕl). Sov. Un.	54.38 N	21.25 E
125	Premiá de Mar (prā-mē-ä' dā mär'). Sp. (In.)	41.29 N	2.21 E
80	Premont (prē-mŏnt'). Tex.	27.20 N	98.10 W
73	Prenda (prĕn'dȧ) Calif. (Los Angeles In.)	33.55 N	117.22 W
120	Prenzlau (prĕnts'lou). Ger.	53.19 N	13.51 E
121	Přerov (przhĕ'rôf). Czech.	49.28 N	17.28 E
80	Presa de la Boquilla R. (prä'sä dä lä bô-kēl'yä). Mex.	27.32 N	105.30 W
116	Prescot (prĕs'kŭt). Gt. Brit.	53.26 N	2.48 W
75	Prescott. Ariz.	34.32 N	112.29 W
79	Prescott. Ark.	33.46 N	93.23 W
85	Prescott. Can.	44.42 N	75.32 W
56	Prescott I. Can. (Prince Rupert In.)	54.6 N	130.37 W
157	Preservation Inlet (prĕz-ēr-vā'-shŭn). N. Z.	46.5 S	166.40 E
76	Presho (prĕsh'ō). S. D.	43.56 N	100.2 W
101	Presidente Epitacio (prā-sē-dĕn'tĕ ā-pē-tä'syōō). Braz.	21.45 S	52.1 W
80	Presidio (prĕ-sĭ'dĭ-ō). Tex.	29.35 N	104.23 W
92	Presidio, R. (prā-sē'dē-ō). Mex.	23.50 N	105.50 W
121	Prešov (prĕ'shôf). Czech.	49.0 N	21.16 E
127	Prespa, L. (prĕs'pä). Yugo.-Alb.	40.55 N	21.5 E
86	Presque Isle (prĕsk' ēl'). Me.	46.31 N	67.57 W
117	Prestbury (prĕst'bēr-ē) Gt. Brit. (Liverpool In.)	53.17 N	2.9 W
114	Preston (prĕs'tŭn). Gt. Brit.	53.45 N	2.45 W
71	Preston. Ida.	42.4 N	111.53 W
77	Preston. Minn.	43.41 N	92.6 W
84	Prestonburg (prĕs'tŭn-bûrg). Ky.	37.38 N	82.50 W
160	Preston R. Austl. (Melbourne In.)	37.42 S	145.1 E
116	Prestwich (prĕst'wĭch). Gt. Brit.	53.31 N	2.18 W
99	Preto, R. (prā'tōō) Braz. (Rio de Janeiro In.)	22.30 S	43.55 W
134	Pretoria (prē-tō'rĭ-ȧ). U. S. Afr.	25.45 S	28.15 E
127	Preveza (prĕ'vȧ-zä). Grc.	38.57 N	20.45 E
72	Prevost I. (prē-vō') Can. (Vancouver In.)	48.50 N	123.23 W
52	Pribilof Is. (prĭ'bĭ-lôf). Alsk.	57.0 N	170.0 W
127	Priboj (prē'boi). Yugo.	43.34 N	19.33 E
120	Příbram (przhē'bräm). Czech.	49.42 N	14.0 E
75	Price (prīs). Utah	39.37 N	110.47 W
75	Price R. Utah	39.33 N	110.55 W
82	Prichard (prĭch'ērd). Ala.	30.44 N	86.7 W
124	Priego (prē-ā'gō). Sp.	37.26 N	4.11 W
119	Prienai (prē-ĕn'ī). Sov. Un.	54.37 N	23.58 E
134	Prieska (prē-ĕs'kȧ). U. S. Afr.	29.39 S	22.45 E
70	Priest L. (prēst). Ida.	48.35 N	116.50 W
126	Prijedor (prē'yĕ-dôr). Yugo.	44.58 N	16.43 E
111	Prikumsk (prē-kōōmsk'). Sov. Un.	44.50 N	44.10 E
127	Prilep (prē'lĕp). Yugo.	41.20 N	21.34 E
129	Priluki (prē-lōō'kē). Sov. Un.	50.35 N	32.21 E
78	Primero (prĭ-mē'rō). Colo.	37.7 N	104.44 W
129	Primorsko Akhtarskii (prē-môr' skô äк-tär'skĭ-ē). Sov. Un.	46.2 N	38.10 E
54	Prince Albert. Can.	53.12 N	105.35 W
54	Prince Albert Sd. Can.	70.15 N	117.0 W
55	Prince Edward I. (Prov.). Can.	46.30 N	63.15 W
5	Prince Edward Is. Ind. O.	46.36 S	37.57 E
85	Prince Edward Pen. Can.	44.0 N	77.15 W
54	Prince George. Can.	53.51 N	122.50 W
54	Prince of Wales, C. Alsk.	65.30 N	168.0 W
53	Prince of Wales I. Alsk.	55.25 N	133.0 W
159	Prince of Wales I. Pap. Ter.	10.44 S	142.8 E
54	Prince Rupert (roo'pērt). Can.	54.18 N	130.15 W
56	Prince Rupert. Can. (In.)		
159	Princess Charlotte B. (shär'lŏt) Austl.	14.0 S	144.0 E
47	Princess Martha Coast (mär'thȧ) Ant.	72.0 S	5.0 W
53	Princess Royal I. Can.	52.40 N	129.0 W
51	Princeton (prĭns'tŭn) Calif. (San Francisco In.)	37.30 N	122.29 W
79	Princeton. Ill.	41.22 N	89.28 W
84	Princeton. Ind.	38.22 N	87.35 W
82	Princeton. Ky.	37.6 N	87.53 W
77	Princeton. Mich.	46.18 N	87.31 W
79	Princeton. Mo.	40.24 N	93.34 W
77	Princeton. Minn.	45.35 N	93.34 W
85	Princeton. N. J.	40.21 N	74.39 W
83	Princeton. W. Va.	37.21 N	81.7 W
77	Princeton. Wis.	43.50 N	89.9 W
53	Prince William Sd. Alsk.	60.20 N	146.30 W
132	Principe I. (prēn'sē-pĕ). Afr.	1.40 N	7.28 E
70	Prineville (prĭn'vĭl). Ore.	44.18 N	120.50 W
72	Pring (prĭng) Colo. (Colo. Sprs. In.)	39.3 N	104.51 W
95	Prinzapolca (prēn-zä-pōl'kä). Nic.	13.20 N	83.34 W
95	Prinzapolca, R. Nic.	13.20 N	84.20 W
121	Pripyat (Pripet) R. (prē'pyȧt) (prĭ'pĕt). Sov. Un.	52.6 N	28.0 E
127	Priština (prēsh'tĭ-nä). Yugo.	42.38 N	21.10 E
78	Pritchett. Colo.	37.23 N	102.50 W
120	Pritzwalk (prēts'välk). Ger.	53.9 N	12.10 E
122	Privas (prē-väs'). Fr.	44.45 N	4.39 E
129	Privolnoe (prē'vôl-nô-yĕ). Sov. Un.	47.28 N	32.14 E
127	Prizren (prē'zrĕn). Yugo.	42.12 N	20.43 E
127	Prjepolje (p'r-yĕ'pôl-yĕ). Yugo.	43.22 N	19.21 E
117	Procida (prô'chē-dä) It. (Napoli In.)	40.46 N	14.2 E
117	Procida Channel. It. (Napoli In.)	40.47 N	14.3 E
77	Proctor (prŏk'tēr). Minn.	46.46 N	92.12 W
86	Proctor. Vt.	43.40 N	73.5 W
89	Proctor Pt. La. (New Orleans In.)	29.57 N	89.42 W
124	Proença-a-Nova (prô-ān'sä-ä-nō'vȧ). Port.	39.45 N	7.55 W
93	Progreso (prô-grā'sō). Mex.	21.16 N	89.40 W
80	Progreso. Mex.	27.29 N	101.5 W
127	Prokuplje (prô'kōōp'l-yĕ). Yugo.	43.14 N	21.38 E
141	Prome (prōm). India	18.45 N	95.15 E
126	Promontore, C. (prō'môn-tô'rā) Yugo.	44.46 N	13.55 E
73	Promontory Pt. (prŏm'ŭn-tô-rĭ) Utah (Salt Lake City In.)	41.13 N	112.26 W
128	Pronya R. (prô'nyä). Sov. Un.	54.5 N	39.40 E
101	Propriá (prō-prē-ä'). Braz.	10.15 S	36.48 W
129	Proskurov (prô-skōō'rôf). Sov. Un.	49.29 N	26.58 E
121	Prosna R. (prôs'ná). Pol.-Ger.	51.40 N	18.7 E
160	Prospect (prŏs'pĕkt) Austl. (Adelaide In.)	34.53 S	138.36 E
72	Prospect L. Colo. (Colo. Sprs. In.)	38.45 N	104.42 W
88	Prospect Park Pa. (Philadelphia In.)	39.51 N	75.19 W
160	Prospect Reservoir Austl. (Sydney In.)	33.49 S	150.53 E
70	Prosser (prŏs'ēr). Wash.	46.10 N	119.47 W
121	Prostějov (prôs'tyĕ-yôf). Czech.	49.28 N	17.8 E
160	Proston (prôs'tŭn). Austl. (In.)	26.12 S	151.32 E
129	Protoka R. (prôt'ô-kȧ). Sov. Un.	45.25 N	38.5 E
128	Protva R. (prôt'vä). Sov. Un.	55.5 N	36.35 E
127	Provadija (prō-väd'ē-yȧ). Bul.	43.12 N	27.28 E
54	Providence (prŏv'ĭ-dĕns). Can.	61.10 N	117.46 W
84	Providence. Ky.	37.25 N	87.48 W
85	Providence. R. I.	41.50 N	71.25 W
71	Providence. Utah	41.43 N	111.49 W
97	Providenciales I. (prō-vē-dĕn-sē-ä'läs) (prŏ-vĭ-dĕn'shălz). Ba. Is.	21.48 N	72.18 W
122	Provins (prô-văɴ'). Fr.	48.35 N	3.15 E
75	Provo (prō'vō). Utah	40.14 N	111.40 W
126	Prozor (prô'zôr). Yugo.	43.48 N	17.39 E
121	Prudnik (prōōd'nĭk). Pol.	50.19 N	17.33 E
120	Prüm (prüm). Ger.	50.13 N	6.25 E
119	Prunkkala (prōōŋk'ȧ-lȧ). Fin.	60.39 N	22.36 E
120	Prussia (State) (prŭsh'ȧ). Ger.	52.5 N	11.30 E
108	Prussia, East. Pol.-Sov. Un.	54.10 N	21.0 E
121	Pruszków (prōōsh'kōōf). Pol.	52.9 N	20.50 E
129	Prut R. (prōōt). Sov. Un.	46.35 N	28.15 E
121	Pruzhany (prōō-zhän'y'). Sov. Un.	52.33 N	24.28 E
79	Pryor (prī'ēr). Okla.	36.16 N	95.18 W
121	Prypeć (Pripet) R. (prĭ'pĕch) (prē'pyȧt) (prĭ'pĕt'). Sov. Un.	51.52 N	25.40 E
121	Przasnysz (pzhäs'nĭsh). Pol.	53.1 N	20.53 E
121	Przedbórz (pzhĕd'bōōzh). Pol.	51.4 N	19.53 E
121	Przemyśl (pzhĕ'mĭsh'l). Pol.	49.47 N	22.45 E
127	Psara (I.) (psä'rä). Grc.	38.35 N	25.35 E
129	Psel R. (psĕl). Sov. Un.	50.58 N	34.50 E
128	Pskov (pskôf). Sov. Un.	57.48 N	28.19 E
128	Pskov (Dist.). Sov. Un.	56.50 N	30.0 E
128	Pskov (Pikhva), L. (pĭк'vȧ) Sov. Un.	58.2 N	28.20 E
128	Ptich R. (p'tēch). Sov. Un.	53.14 N	28.15 E
126	Ptuj (ptōō'ē). Yugo.	46.26 N	15.51 E
137	Puah (pōō'ä). Indon. (In.)	1.39 N	102.30 E
147	Puan (pōō'än). Kor.	35.44 N	126.44 E
145	Pucheng (pōō'chĕng'). Chn.	28.0 N	118.20 E
144	Puchi (pōō'chē'). Chn.	29.42 N	113.45 E
143	Puchow (pōō'chō'). Chn.	34.53 N	110.29 E
146	Puchow. Chn.	35.51 N	115.42 E
153	Pucio Pt. (pōō'thyô). Phil.	11.46 N	121.51 E
121	Puck (pōōtsk). Pol.	54.42 N	18.23 E
110	Pudozh (pōō'dôzh). Sov. Un.	61.48 N	36.35 E
92	Puebla (State) (pwā'blä). Mex.	18.50 N	97.40 W
92	Puebla. Mex.	19.2 N	98.11 W
124	Puebla de Don Fadrique (dā dōn fä-drē'kā). Sp.	37.57 N	2.25 W
124	Puebla del Caramiñal (dĕl kä-rä-mē-nyäl'). Sp.	42.37 N	8.58 W
99	Pueblo (pwä'blō) Arg. (Buenos Aires In.)	34.6 S	61.26 W
78	Pueblo. Colo.	38.15 N	104.36 W
92	Pueblo Nuevo (pwā'blō nwā'vō) Mex.	23.22 N	105.22 W
124	Pueblo Nuevo. Sp.	38.18 N	5.16 W
93	Pueblo Viejo (pwā'blô vyā'hô) Mex.	22.10 N	97.51 W
73	Puente (pwĕn'tē) Calif. (Los Angeles In.)	34.2 N	117.58 W
124	Puenteareas (pwĕn-tā-ä-rā'äs). Sp.	42.9 N	8.31 W
124	Puente Ceso (pwĕn'tā thā'sō). Sp.	43.15 N	8.55 W
124	Puentedeume (pwĕn-tā-dhā-ōō'mā). Sp.	43.24 N	8.11 W
124	Puente-Genil (pwĕn'tā-hā-nēl'). Sp.	37.25 N	4.45 W
73	Puente Hills (pwĕn'tē hĭlz) Calif. (Los Angeles In.)	33.59 N	117.57 W
75	Puerco R. (pwĕr'kō). N. M.	35.15 N	107.5 W
142	Puerh (pōō'ĕr'). Chn.	22.59 N	101.7 E
100	Puerto Colombia (pwĕr'tô kô-lôm'bē-ä). Col.	10.59 N	75.0 W
93	Puerto Ángel (äŋ'hāl). Mex.	15.40 N	96.30 W
95	Puerto Armuelles (är-mōō-ā'lyās) Pan.	8.18 N	82.52 W
94	Puerto Barrios (bär'rē-ōs). Guat.	15.43 N	88.37 W
100	Puerto Bermudez (bĕr-mōō'dāz) Peru	10.5 S	74.58 W
100	Puerto Berrío (bĕr-rē'ō). Col.	6.28 N	74.30 W
100	Puerto Cabello (kä-bĕl'yō). Ven.	10.28 N	68.1 W
95	Puerto Cabezas (kä-bā'zäs). Nic.	14.2 N	83.25 W
102	Puerto Casado (kä-sä'dō). Par.	22.20 S	58.0 W
94	Puerto Castilla (käs-tēl'yō). Hond.	16.1 N	86.1 W
94	Puerto Cortés (kôr-täs'). Hond.	15.48 N	87.57 W
78	Puerto de Luna (dā lōō'nä). N. M.	34.49 N	104.35 W
92	Puerto de Maruata (dā mä-rōō-ä'tä). Mex.	18.13 N	103.6 W
102	Puerto Deseado (dā-sā-ä'dhō). Arg.	47.40 S	66.0 W
132	Puerto Grande (grän'dā) C. V. Is. (In.)	16.52 N	25.1 W
124	Puertollano (pwĕr-tôl-yä'nō). Sp.	38.42 N	4.6 W
102	Puerto Madryn (mä-drēn'). Arg.	42.45 S	65.2 W
100	Puerto Maldonado (mäl-dō-nä'dō) Peru	12.35 S	69.3 W
93	Puerto México (mā'ĸē-kō) (māk'sē-kō). Mex.	18.9 N	94.20 W
102	Puerto Montt (mônt). Chl.	41.29 S	72.59 W
100	Puerto Nutrias (nōō-trē-äs'). Ven.	8.2 N	69.12 W
96	Puerto Padre (pä'drā). Cuba	21.11 N	76.36 W
97	Puerto Plata (plä'tä). Dom. Rep.	19.47 N	70.41 W
153	Puerto Princesa (prēn-sā'sä). Phil.	9.44 N	118.44 E
125	Puerto Real (rā-äl'). Sp. (In.)	36.31 N	6.12 W
91	Puerto Rico (pwĕr'tô rē'kō) W. I. (In.)	18.0 N	66.0 W
102	Puerto San Julián (sän hōō-lyän') Arg.	49.17 S	67.59 W
102	Puerto Santa Cruz (sän'ta krōōz') Arg.	50.1 S	68.30 W
101	Puerto Suárez (swä'râz). Bol.	18.59 S	57.59 W
92	Puerto Vallarta (väl-yär'tä). Mex.	20.36 N	105.15 W
102	Puerto Varas (vär'äs). Chl.	41.20 S	73.0 W

ng-sing; ŋ-baŋk; ɴ-nasalized n; nŏd; cŏmmit; ōld; ōbey; ôrder; fōōd; fŏŏt; ou-out; s-soft; sh-dish; th-thin; pūre; ûnite; ûrn; stŭd; circŭs; ü-as "y" in study; '-indeterminate vowel.

Puerto Wilches PRONOUNCING INDEX Rajaburi

Page	Name Pronunciation Region	Lat. °′	Long. °′
100	Puerto Wilches (vēl′chĕs)....Col.	7.18 N	73.59 W
92	Puga (pōō′gä)..........Mex.	21.37 N	104.51 W
111	Pugachev (pōō′gȧ-chyôf).Sov. Un.	51.58 N	48.45 E
51	Puget I.......Wash. (Seattle In.)	46.10 N	123.23 W
70	Puget Sd..............Wash.	47.40 N	122.25 W
123	Puget-Théniers (pü-zhĕ′-tâ-nyā′) Fr.	43.55 N	6.55 E
125	Puigcerdá (pwēg-thĕr-dä′).....Sp.	42.26 N	1.55 E
153	Pujada B. (pōō-hä′dä)......Phil.	6.50 N	126.16 E
157	Pukaki, L. (pōō-kȧ′kĭ)......N. Z.	44.5 S	170.12 E
147	Pukchin (pŏŏk′chĭn′)........Kor.	40.12 N	125.44 E
156	Pukekohe (pōō-kê-hō′hȧ)....N. Z.	37.10 S	174.52 E
147	Pukhan R. (pŏŏk′hän′)......Kor.	38.10 N	127.52 E
146	Pukow (pōō′kō′)..........Chn.	32.8 N	118.38 E
100	Pulacayo (pōō-lä-kä′yō)......Bol.	20.28 S	66.44 W
153	Pulanduta Pt. (pōō-län-dōō′tä) Phil.	11.55 N	123.11 E
153	Pulangi R. (pōō-läŋ′gē).....Phil.	7.25 N	125.5 E
146	Pulantien (pōō′län′chĕn′)....Chn.	39.28 N	121.55 E
82	Pulaski (pû-lăs′kĭ).........Tenn.	35.12 N	87.3 W
83	Pulaski..................Va.	37.2 N	80.47 W
150	Pulau Kondor Is. (pōō-lou′ kôn-dōr′).Indoch.	8.45 N	106.38 E
121	Pulawy (pŏŏ-wä′vê)........Pol.	51.24 N	21.59 E
151	Pulilan (pōō-lē′län) Phil. (Manila In.)	14.55 N	120.48 E
88	Pullman (pŏŏl′măn) Ill. (Chicago In.)	41.42 N	87.36 W
71	Pullman..................Wash.	46.44 N	117.12 W
151	Pulo Cambing (I.) (pōō′lô käm′bĭng).Indon.	12.15 N	105.0 E
152	Pulog, Mt. (pōō′lôg)........Phil.	16.35 N	120.53 E
121	Pultusk (pōōl′tŏŏsk).........Pol.	52.43 N	21.6 E
71	Pumpkin Cr. (pŭmp′kĭn)...Mont.	45.40 N	105.50 W
141	Punaka (pōō-nŭk′ŭ)........Bhu.	27.29 N	89.55 E
100	Punata (pōō-nä′tä).........Bol.	17.31 S	66.1 W
92	Pungarabato (pōōŋ′gä-rä-bä′tō) Mex.	18.22 N	100.35 W
145	Puning (pōō′nĭng′)..........Chn.	23.24 N	115.56 E
141	Punjab (Prov.) (pŭn′jäb′)...India	30.45 N	73.30 E
100	Puno (pōō′nô)..............Peru	15.58 S	70.1 W
94	Punta Gorda (pōōn′tä gôr′dä) Br. Hond.	16.6 N	88.52 W
83	Punta Gorda (pŭn′tȧ gôr′dȧ) Fla. (In.)	26.55 N	82.3 W
95	Puntarenas (pōōnt-ä-rā′näs).C. R.	9.58 N	84.48 W
85	Punxsutawney (pŭnk-sŭ-tô′nê) Pa.	40.58 N	78.9 W
79	Purcell (pûr-sĕl′)..........Okla.	35.0 N	97.22 W
92	Purépero de Echaiz (pōō-rā′pâ-rō dâ ā-chä-ēz′).Mex.	19.55 N	102.2 W
117	Purfleet (pûr′flēt) Gt. Brit. (London In.)	51.29 N	0.14 E
78	Purgatoire R. (pûr-gȧ-twär′).Colo.	37.32 N	103.40 W
141	Puri (pōō′rê)..............India	19.45 N	85.50 E
97	Purial, Sierra de (Mts.) (pōō-rê-äl′).Cuba	20.15 N	74.35 W
100	Purificación (pōō-rê-fê-kä-syōn′) Col.	4.2 N	75.1 W
93	Purificación...........Mex. (In.)	19.31 N	98.48 W
92	Purificación...............Mex.	19.44 N	104.36 W
92	Purificación, R............Mex.	19.34 N	104.40 W
138	Pur R. (pōōr)..........Sov. Un.	66.0 N	78.0 E
147	Pusan (Fusan) (pōō′sän′) (fōō′sän′).Kor.	35.6 N	129.3 E
150	Pursat (pōōr-sät′).........Indoch.	12.28 N	103.45 E
92	Puruándiro de Calderón (pōō-rōō-än′dê-rō dā käl-dā-rōn′).Mex.	19.58 N	101.32 W
100	Purus R. (pōō-rōōzh′)......Braz.	5.0 S	63.0 W
153	Pusan Pt. (pōō-sän′)........Phil.	7.17 N	126.38 E
119	Pushkin (pōōsh′kĭn).....Sov. Un.	59.45 N	30.20 E
128	Pushkino (pōōsh′kê-nô)..Sov. Un.	56.1 N	37.51 E
121	Püspökladány (püsh′pû-klô′dän′) Hung.	47.18 N	21.9 E
99	Putaendo (pōō-tä-ĕn′dō) Chl. (Valparaiso In.)	32.39 S	70.46 W
146	Putai (pōō′tī′)............Chn.	37.21 N	118.7 E
123	Puteaux (pü-tō′).........Fr. (In.)	48.52 N	2.0 E
150	Puting, C. (poo-tĭng′).....Indon.	3.35 S	111.55 E
129	Putivl (pōō-tēv′l′).......Sov. Un.	51.20 N	33.52 E
93	Putla (pōō′tlä).............Mex.	17.2 N	97.57 W
85	Putnam (pŭt′năm).........Conn.	41.57 N	71.55 W
100	Putumayo, R. (pōō-tōō-mä′yō) Col.-Ec.	2.0 S	72.30 W
143	Putung (pōō′tŏŏng′) Chn. (Shanghai In.)	31.00 N	121.29 E
70	Puyallup (pū-ăl′ŭp).......Wash.	47.10 N	122.19 W
51	Puyallup R...Wash. (Seattle In.)	47.9 N	122.12 W
122	Puy-de-Carlitte (Pk.) (püē-dē-kär-lēt′).Fr.	42.35 N	1.55 E
122	Puy de Dome (Pk.) (püē′ dē dōm′) Fr.	45.45 N	3.0 E
147	Puyo (pōō′yô′)............Kor.	36.18 N	126.57 E
134	Pweto (pwā′tō).......Bel. Cong.	8.25 S	28.58 E
138	Pyasina R. (pyä-sē′nȧ)..Sov. Un.	72.30 N	88.0 E
111	Pyatigorsk (pyȧ-tê-gôrsk′) Sov. Un.	44.5 N	43.5 E
142	Pyinmana (pyên-mä′nŭ).....Bur.	19.45 N	96.15 E
72	Pylades Chan. (pī′lȧ-dēz) Can. (Vancouver In.)	49.6 N	123.42 W
147	Pyŏngchang (pyŭng′chäng′)..Kor.	37.22 N	128.24 E
147	Pyŏnggang (pyŭng′gäng′)....Kor.	38.25 N	127.18 E
147	Pyŏngtaek (pyŭng′tä′ĕk)....Kor.	37.0 N	125.5 E
147	Pyŏngyang (Heijō) (pyŭng′yäng′) (hā′jō).Kor.	39.1 N	125.44 E
74	Pyramid L. (pĭ′rȧ-mĭd)......Nev.	40.0 N	119.35 W
74	Pyramid Lake Indian Res...Nev.	40.0 N	119.35 W
122	Pyrenees (Mts.) (pĭr-ē-nēz′) Fr.-Sp.	42.50 N	1.0 E
101	Pyrenópolis (pê-rĕn-ō′pô-lêzh) Braz.	15.47 S	49.1 W
127	Pyrgos (pĭr′gōs)............Grc.	37.41 N	21.27 E

Page	Name Pronunciation Region	Lat. °′	Long. °′
120	Pyrzyce (pĕzhĭ′tsĕ).........Pol.	53.8 N	14.53 E
51	Pysht (pĭsht)..Wash. (Seattle In.)	48.12 N	124.7 W
140	Qain (kä′ēn)..............Iran	33.50 N	59.20 E
137	Qal′at ′Aneiza (käl′ät ȧ-nāz′ȧ) Jor. (In.)	30.28 N	35.50 E
137	Qal′at ed Dab′a (ĕd dȧb′ȧ) Jor. (In.)	31.37 N	36.2 E
137	Qal′at el Hasa (ĕl hä′sȧ).Jor. (In.)	30.52 N	35.53 E
133	Qallâbât (Gallabat) (kȧ-lä-bät′) (gȧ-lä-bät′).A. E. Sud.	12.58 N	36.6 E
140	Qamaran Is. (kȧ-mä-rän′)....Asia	15.30 N	42.30 E
131	Qantara (kän′tȧ-rȧ) Eg. (Suez Can. In.)	30.52 N	32.21 E
111	Qara Boghaz, G. of (kä′rȧ bō′gäz) Sov. Un.	41.15 N	54.10 E
140	Qara Chai R. (kä-rȧ chä′ē)...Iran	35.12 N	59.30 E
140	Qara Qum (Kara Kum) Des. (kä′rȧ kōōm′).Sov. Un.	47.0 N	63.15 E
142	Qara Shahr (Yenki) (kä′rȧ shär′) (yĕn′kē′).Chn.	42.2 N	86.28 E
142	Qargaliq (Yehcheng) (kär′gȧ-lēk) (yĕ′chĕng′).Chn.	37.28 N	79.41 E
140	Qasim (Reg.) (kä′sēm)...Sau. Ar.	26.30 N	43.30 E
137	Qasr el Azraq (käs″r ĕl äz′rȧk) Jor. (In.)	31.50 N	36.18 E
140	Qatar (Dist.) (kä′tȧr)....Sau.Ar.	25.30 N	51.15 E
140	Qatif (kä′têf)............Sau. Ar.	26.35 N	50.0 E
133	Qattara Depression (kä-tä′rä).Eg.	29.30 N	27.50 E
133	Qena (kā′nȧ)..............Eg.	26.15 N	32.42 E
131	Qift (kêft)...........Eg. (In.)	25.58 N	32.50 E
137	Qir Moav (El Kerak (kēr′mō′ȧv) (ĕl kĕ-räk′).Jor. (In.)	31.10 N	35.42 E
140	Qishm (kêsh″m)............Iran	26.55 N	56.15 E
140	Qishm I...................Iran	26.45 N	56.0 E
138	Qizil Qum (Kyzyl Kum) Des. (kĭ′zĭl kōōm′).Sov. Un.	44.0 N	64.0 E
140	Qizil Uzun (R.) (kĭz-ĭl ōō-zōōn′) Iran	37.30 N	48.15 E
132	Qnitra (Kenitra) (k′nē′trȧ) (kĕ-nē′trȧ).Mor.	34.22 N	6.31 W
142	Qomul (Hami) (kô-mōōl′) (hä′mē′).Chn.	42.47 N	93.29 E
157	Quail I. (kwāl)........N. Z. (In.)	43.37 S	172.43 E
160	Quaker Hill (kwā′kēr hĭl) Austl. (Sydney In.)	33.43 S	150.53 E
85	Quakertown (kwā′kēr-toun)...Pa.	40.27 N	75.21 W
78	Quanah (kwä′nȧ)...........Tex.	34 17 N	99.44 W
150	Quangngäi (kwäng′n′gä′ē) Indoch.	15.8 N	108.47 E
150	Quangtri (kwäng′trē′)....Indoch.	16.44 N	107.8 E
54	Qu′Appelle R. (kȧ-pĕl′)......Can.	50.30 N	103.0 W
157	Quarantine I. (kwär′ȧn-tēn) N. Z. (In.)	45.49 S	170.39 E
126	Quarnero, G. of (kwär-nȧ′rō) Yugo.	44.50 N	14.10 E
126	Quartú Sant Elena (kwär-tōō′ sänt a′lȧ-nä).Sard.	39.15 N	9.11 E
55	Quebec (kwê-bĕk′) (kâ-bĕk′).Can.	46.53 N	71.20 W
57	Quebec............Can. (In.)		
55	Quebec (Prov.).............Can.	51.30 N	70.0 W
120	Quedlinburg (kvĕd′lĕn-bōōrgh) Ger.	51.48 N	11.10 E
102	Queen Adelaide Arch. (ăd′ê-lād) Chl.	52.0 S	74.30 W
117	Queenborough (kwēn′bŭr-ô) Gt. Brit. (London In.)	51.25 N	0.44 E
158	Queen Channel............Austl.	14.45 S	129.30 E
72	Queen Charlotte Chan. (shär′lŏt) Can. (Vancouver In.)	49.23 N	123.18 W
54	Queen Charlotte Is.........Can.	53.0 N	132.30 W
54	Queen Charlotte Sd.........Can.	51.5 N	129.0 W
5	Queen Mary Coast..........Ant.	70.0 S	100.0 E
47	Queen Maud Land..........Ant.	75.0 S	10.0 E
47	Queen Maud Ra............Ant.	85.0 S	179.0 W
159	Queensland (State) (kwēnz′lănd) Austl.	22.45 S	144.0 E
88	Queenston (kwēnz′tŭn) Can. (Niagara Falls In.)	43.10 N	79.4 W
160	Queenstown (kwēnz′toun) Austl. (Tas. In.)	42.4 S	145.38 E
157	Queenstown...............N. Z.	45.2 S	168.42 E
	Queenstown, see Cobh, Ire.		
134	Quelimane (kā-lê-mä′nĕ)....Moz.	17.52 S	36.55 E
147	Quelpart (Cheju) I. (kwĕl′pärt) (chĕ′jōō′).Kor.	33.24 N	126.34 E
101	Queluz (kâ′lōōzh′)..........Braz.	20.32 S	43.58 W
96	Quemada (kā-mä′dhä)......Cuba	22.46 N	80.21 W
122	Quenilly (kā-nê-yē′).........Fr.	49.25 N	1.5 E
95	Quepos, Pt. (kā′pôs).........C. R.	9.23 N	84.11 W
134	Queque (kwĕ′kwĕ)..........S. Rh.	19.0 S	29.45 E
92	Querétaro (kâ-rā′tä-rō)......Mex.	20.36 N	100.23 W
92	Querétaro (State)...........Mex.	20.40 N	100.0 W
124	Quesada (kâ-sä′dhä)..........Sp.	37.53 N	3.3 W
54	Quesnel (kā-nĕl′)...........Can.	53.5 N	122.29 W
54	Quesnel L.................Can.	52.28 N	121.0 W
77	Quetico Park (kwĕ′tĭ-kô)....Can.	48.30 N	91.30 W
141	Quetta (Shal) (kwĕt′ä) (shäl).Pak.	30.20 N	67.12 E
94	Quezaltenango (kâ-zäl′tâ-näŋ′gō) Guat.	14.49 N	91.31 W
94	Quezaltepeque (kâ-zäl′tâ-pā′kâ) Guat.	14.40 N	89.26 W
151	Quezon (Prov.) (kä-zōn) Phil. (Manila In.)	14.30 N	121.40 E
151	Quezon City...Phil. (Manila In.)	14.38 N	121.2 E
100	Quibdo (kēb′dō)............Col.	5.32 N	76.32 W
122	Quiberon (kê-bē-rôɴ′)........Fr.	47.28 N	3.5 W
122	Quiberon Pen...............Fr.	47.30 N	3.5 W
94	Quiché (kē-shā′)..........Guat.	15.5 N	91.8 W
100	Quiciá (kê-sê-ä′)...........Braz.	7.29 S	66.29 W
51	Quilcene (kwĭl-sēn′) Wash. (Seattle In.)	47.49 N	122.52 W

Page	Name Pronunciation Region	Lat. °′	Long. °′
122	Quillan (kê-yäɴ′)............Fr.	42.55 N	2.15 E
54	Quill Lakes (kwĭl)..........Can.	51.48 N	104.30 W
99	Quillota (kēl-yō′tä) Chl. (Valparaiso In.)	32.53 S	71.16 W
102	Quilmes (kēl′mās)......Arg. (In.)	34.43 S	57.16 W
141	Quilon (kwê-lōn′).India (Cey. In.)	9.0 N	76.35 E
159	Quilpie (kwĭl′pê)..........Austl.	26.45 S	144.25 E
122	Quimper (kăɴ-pĕr′)...........Fr.	47.59 N	4.5 W
122	Quimperlé (kăɴ-pĕr-lā′).......Fr.	47.45 N	3.31 W
152	Quinabucasan Pt. (kē-nä-bōō-kä′sän).Phil.	14.7 N	123.21 E
70	Quinault Ind. Res. (kwê-nôlt′) Wash.	47.25 N	124.30 W
70	Quinault R...............Wash.	47.25 N	124.0 W
82	Quincy (kwĭn′sê)...........Fla.	30.35 N	84.36 W
79	Quincy.....................Ill.	39.55 N	91.24 W
86	Quincy (kwĭn′zê)..........Mass.	42.15 N	71.0 W
84	Quincy (kwĭn′sê)..........Mich.	41.57 N	84.53 W
51	Quincy.......Ore. (Portland In.)	46.7 N	123.10 W
151	Quingua (kĭng′wä) Phil. (Manila In.)	14.53 N	120.50 E
151	Quingua R.....Phil. (Manila In.)	14.55 N	120.45 E
150	Quinhon (kwĭ-nyôn′)......Indoch.	13.55 N	109.0 E
153	Quiniluban Is. (kê-nê-lōō-bän′) Phil.	11.25 N	120.50 E
70	Quinn R. (kwĭn)............Nev.	41.40 N	117.55 W
124	Quintana de la Serena (kēn-tä′nä dā lä sȧ-rā′nä).Sp.	38.44 N	5.40 W
124	Quintanar (kēn-tä-när′).......Sp.	39.36 N	3.2 W
94	Quintana Roo (kēn-tä′nä rô′ô) Mex.	19.30 N	88.30 W
92	Quiroga (kê-rō′gä)..........Mex.	19.40 N	101.27 W
124	Quiroga.....................Sp.	42.28 N	7.19 W
151	Quisao (kê-sä′ō).Phil. (Manila In.)	14.27 N	121.23 E
82	Quitman (kwĭt′măn)..........Ga.	30.47 N	83.33 W
82	Quitman...................Miss.	32.3 N	88.43 W
100	Quito (kē′tō)................Ec.	0.10 S	78.30 W
101	Quixadá (kê-shä-dä′)........Braz.	4.59 S	39.1 W
142	Qulja (Ili) (kōōl′jä) (ê-lē′)...Chn.	43.55 N	81.0 W
131	Qulusna (kōō-lōōs′nä)...Eg. (In.)	28.23 N	30.44 E
140	Qum (kōōm)................Iran	34.31 N	50.58 E
133	Qum Chalouba (kōōm shä-lōō′bä) Fr. Eq. Afr.	15.48 N	20.32 E
140	Qunfidha (Al Qunfidha) (kŭn′fēd′hȧ).Sau. Ar.	18.59 N	41.29 E
131	Qûs (kōōs)...........Eg. (In.)	25.54 N	32.46 E
133	Qusêr (kōō-sēr′)..............Eg.	26.2 N	34.18 E
120	Raab R. (räp)..............Ger.	46.58 N	15.50 E
110	Raahe (rä′ĕ).................Fin.	64.40 N	24.30 E
126	Rab (I.) (räb)............Yugo.	44.45 N	14.45 E
132	Rabat (rȧ-bät′)..............Mor.	34.6 N	6.51 W
151	Rabaul (rä′boul)....N. Gui. Ter.	4.10 S	152.18 E
140	Rabbath′Ammon (Amman) (rȧ-bät′äm′môn) (äm′män).Jor.	32.0 N	36.0 E
72	Rabbit Mt. (răb′ĭt) Colo. (Denver In.)	40.14 N	105.12 W
127	Rača (rä′chȧ)..............Yugo.	44.12 N	21.0 E
97	Raccoon Cay (I.).........Ba. Is.	22.22 N	75.48 W
77	Raccoon R....................Ia.	42.10 N	94.40 W
87	Race, C. (rās)...............Can.	46.37 N	53.10 W
137	Rachaya (rȧ-chä′yȧ)....Leb. (In.)	33.31 N	35.50 E
121	Rachov (rä′ĸôf)..........Sov. Un.	48.3 N	24.12 E
77	Racine (rȧ-sēn′)..............Wis.	42.44 N	87.48 W
121	Rădăuţi (rû-dû-ōōts″).......Rom.	47.52 N	25.54 E
116	Radcliffe (răd′klĭf)......Gt. Brit.	53.34 N	2.20 W
120	Radeberg (rä′dē-bĕrgh).......Ger.	51.7 N	13.55 E
83	Radford (răd′fērd)............Va.	37.7 N	80.35 W
118	Rad I. (räd)..................Nor.	60.42 N	5.0 E
114	Radnor Forest (răd′nēr)..Gt. Brit.	52.10 N	3.10 W
121	Radom (rä′dôm)..............Pol.	51.24 N	21.9 E
127	Radomir (rä′dô-mêr).........Bul.	42.33 N	22.58 E
121	Radomsko (rä-dôm′skô).......Pol.	51.4 N	19.27 E
129	Radomysl (rä-dô-mēsh″l) Sov. Un.	50.31 N	29.12 E
127	Radovište (rȧ′dô′vēsh-tĕ)...Yugo.	41.38 N	22.27 E
129	Radul (rȧ′dōōl)..........Sov. Un.	51.52 N	30.45 E
119	Radviliškis (rȧd′vê-lēsh′kês) Sov. Un.	55.49 N	23.32 E
121	Radzyń (räd′zên-y′)..........Pol.	51.47 N	22.43 E
83	Raeford (rā′fērd)...........N. C.	34.57 N	79.12 W
158	Raeside, L. (rā′sīd)........Austl.	29.15 S	121.45 E
54	Rae Str. (rā)................Can.	95.30 N	69.0 W
156	Raetihi (rä-ê-tē′hê)..........N. Z.	39.23 S	175.18 E
137	Rafa (rä′fä)............Eg. (In.)	31.5 N	34.10 E
102	Rafaela (rä-fä-ā′lä)...........Arg.	31.20 S	61.35 W
97	Rafael, C. (rä-fä-âl′)...Dom. Rep.	19.2 N	69.0 W
133	Rafai (rä-fī′).........Fr. Eq. Afr.	4.58 N	24.0 E
71	Raft R. (răft)................Ida.	42.10 N	113.28 W
152	Ragay (rä-gī′)...............Phil.	13.49 N	122.45 E
152	Ragay G.....................Phil.	13.45 N	122.35 E
156	Raglan (răg′lȧn).............N. Z.	37.47 S	174.57 E
121	Ragnit (rägh′nēt)........Sov. Un.	55.1 N	22.2 E
118	Ragunda (rä-gōōn′dä).......Swe.	63.7 N	16.18 E
127	Ragusa (Dubrovnik) (rä-gōō′sä) (dōō′brôv-nêk).Yugo.	42.39 N	18.9
88	Rahway (rô′wā) N. J. (New York In.)	40.37 N	74.16 W
141	Raichur (rä′ê-chōōr′).......India	16.17 N	77.29 E
75	Rainbow Bridge Natl. Mon. (rān′bō).Utah	37.4 N	110.57 W
117	Rainford (rān′fērd)......Gt. Brit.	53.30 N	2.47 W
117	Rainham (rān′ăm) Gt. Brit. (London In.)	51.32 N	0.12 E
70	Rainier (rā-nēr′)............Ore.	46.5 N	122.56 W
70	Rainier, Mt................Wash.	46.51 N	121.46 W
77	Rainy L. (rān′ê)......Can.-Minn.	48.37 N	93.0 W
77	Rainy R..............Can.-Minn.	48.37 N	94.0 W
141	Raipur (rä′ê-pōōr′)..........India	21.8 N	81.45 E
84	Raisin, R. (rā′zĭn).........Mich.	41.58 N	83.40 W
150	Rajaburi (rä′jŭ-bōō-rê′).....Siam	13.29 N	99.45 E

ăt; finăl; rāte; senâte; ärm; ȧsk; sofȧ; fâre; ch-choose; dh-as th in other; bē; êvent; bĕt; recĕnt; cratēr; g-go; gh-gutteral g; bĭt; ĭ-short neutral; rīde; ĸ-gutteral k as ch in German ich;

Rajahmundry PRONOUNCING INDEX **Reuss**

Page	Name Pronunciation Region	Lat. °′	Long. °′
141	Rajahmundry (räj-ŭ-mŭn'drē) India	17.0 N	81.50 E
150	Rajang R. (rä-jäng')........Sar.	2.0 N	112.45 E
141	Rajkot (räj'kōt)..........India	22.15 N	70.47 E
141	Rajputana (Agency) (räj-pōō-tä'nŭ).India	27.30 N	73.30 E
157	Rakaia R. (rȧ-kī'ä)........N. Z.	43.35 S	171.50 E
121	Rakhov (rä'κôf)........Sov. Un.	48.3 N	24.12 E
129	Rakitnoe (rȧ-kēt'nô-yě)..Sov. Un.	50.51 N	35.50 E
121	Rákospalota (rä'kôsh-pô'lô-tô) Hung.	47.34 N	19.11 E
128	Rakov (rä'kŏŏf)........Sov. Un.	53.59 N	27.0 E
120	Rakovnik (rä'kôv-nyêk)...Czech.	50.6 N	13.43 E
119	Rakvere (rȧk'vě-rě).....Sov. Un.	59.20 N	26.21 E
83	Raleigh (rô'lȧ)............N. C.	35.46 N	78.39 W
72	Ralston Cr. (rôls'tŭn) Colo. (Denver In.)	39.51 N	105.21 W
95	Rama (rä'mä).............Nic.	12.10 N	84.16 W
95	Rama, R..................Nic.	11.35 N	84.0 W
51	Ramapo......Wash. (Seattle In.)	48.8 N	123.40 W
123	Rambersvillers (räN-bĕr-vē-yā') Fr.	48.22 N	6.38 E
122	Rambouillet (räN-bōō-yĕ')....Fr.	48.38 N	1.48 E
128	Ramenskoe (rȧ'mĕn-skô-yĕ) Sov. Un.	55.34 N	38.10 E
137	Ramla (Er Ramle) (räm'lȧ) (ĕr räm'lĕ).Pal. (In.)	31.55 N	34.51 E
127	Râmnicul-Sărat (rûm'nê-kŏŏl-sû-rȧt').Rom.	45.23 N	27.5 E
127	Râmnicul-Vâlcea (rûm'nê-kŏŏl-vûl'chȧ-ȧ).Rom.	45.5 N	24.21 E
92	Ramos (rä'mōs)...........Mex.	22.49 N	101.55 W
80	Ramos Arizpe (rä'mōs ä-rēz'pȧ) Mex.	25.33 N	100.58 W
153	Ramos I...................Phil.	8.7 N	117.2 E
102	Ramos Mejía (rä'mōs mȧ-κē'ä) Arg. (In.)	34.39 S	58.34 W
80	Ramos, R. de.............Mex.	25.0 N	105.23 W
137	Rampah (räm'pä)....Indon. (In.)	1.47 N	101.26 E
53	Rampart (răm'pȧrt)........Alsk.	65.30 N	150.30 W
72	Rampart Ra. Colo. (Colo. Sprs. In.)	39.3 N	104.59 W
141	Rampur (räm'pōōr).......India	28.43 N	79.8 E
141	Rampur Boalia (räm'pōōr bô-ä'lē-ä).Pak.	24.20 N	88.40 E
150	Ramree I. (räm'rē')........Bur.	19.5 N	93.47 E
116	Ramsbottom (rămz'bŏt-ŭm) Gt. Brit.	53.39 N	2.19 W
114	Ramsey (răm'zē)........Gt. Brit.	54.18 N	4.20 W
115	Ramsgate (rămz'gāt)....Gt. Brit.	51.20 N	1.23 E
118	Ramsjö (räm'shû).........Swe.	62.12 N	15.41 E
151	Ramu R. (rä'mōō)...N. Gui. Ter.	4.30 S	144.30 E
150	Ranau, L. (rä-nä'ōō)......Indon.	4.50 S	103.55 E
102	Rancagua (rän-kä'gwä)......Chl.	34.10 S	70.55 W
122	Rance R. (räNs)............Fr.	48.15 N	2.10 W
141	Ranchi (rän'chē)..........India	23.20 N	85.29 E
99	Ranchos (rän'chōs) Arg. (Buenos Aires In.)	35.30 S	58.16 W
118	Randers (rän'ĕrs)..........Den.	56.28 N	10.2 E
83	Randleman (răn'd'l-măn)...N. C.	35.47 N	79.49 W
87	Randolph (răn'dôlf)...Mass. (In.)	42.10 N	71.2 W
76	Randolph..................Neb.	42.23 N	97.22 W
86	Randolph..................Vt.	43.55 N	72.41 W
87	Random I. (răn'dŭm).......Can.	48.10 N	53.45 W
118	Rands Fjord (räns'fyôr).....Nor.	60.35 N	10.15 E
128	Ranenburg (rä'nyĕn-bŏŏrk) Sov. Un.	53.14 N	39.58 E
156	Rangaunu B. (răŋ-gȧ-ōō'nŏŏ) N. Z.	34.50 S	173.12 E
86	Rangeley (rānj'lē)..........Me.	44.55 N	70.38 W
80	Ranger (rān'jēr)...........Tex.	32.27 N	98.41 W
157	Rangiora (räŋ'gē-ō'rȧ)......N. Z.	43.17 S	172.38 E
156	Rangitaiki R. (räŋ-gē-tī'kē)..N. Z.	38.30 S	176.40 E
157	Rangitata R. (räŋ-gē-tȧ'tȧ)..N. Z.	43.45 S	171.18 E
156	Rangitikei R. (răŋ-gē-tē'kȧ).N. Z.	40.0 S	175.32 E
156	Rangitoto (răŋ-gē-tō'tō) N. Z. (In.)	36.48 S	174.52 E
150	Rangoon (răŋ-gōōn')........Bur.	16.50 N	96.0 E
141	Rangpur (rŭng'pōōr)........Pak.	25.45 N	89.29 E
137	Rangsang (I.) (räng'säng') Indon. (In.)	1.0 N	102.55 E
141	Raniganj (rä-nē-gŭnj')......India	23.35 N	87.0 E
54	Ranken Inlet (răŋ'kĕn).....Can.	63.5 N	93.0 W
117	Rannersdorf (rän'ērs-dôrf) Aus. (Wien In.)	48.8 N	16.28 E
128	Ranova R. (rä'nô-vȧ)....Sov. Un.	53.50 N	40.5 E
88	Ransomville (răn'sŭm-vĭl) N. Y. (Niagara Falls In.)	43.14 N	78.54 W
117	Ranst (ränst)...Bel. (Anvers In.)	51.12 N	4.33 E
84	Rantoul (răn-tōōl')..........Ill.	40.19 N	88.9 W
160	Raoul, C. (rou'ŭl).Austl. (Tas. In.)	43.14 S	147.49 E
4	Rapa I. (rä'pä)..........Pac. O.	27.36 S	144.17 W
126	Rapallo (rä-päl'lô)............It.	44.21 N	9.12 E
4	Rapa Nui (Easter) I. (rä'pä nōō'ē).Pac. O.	27.0 S	109.17 W
99	Rapel, R. (rä-pål') Chl. (Valparaiso In.)	34.5 S	71.35 W
76	Rapid City (răp'ĭd).........S. D.	44.5 N	103.13 W
77	Rapid R...................Minn.	48.28 N	94.40 W
119	Rapla (räp'lȧ)..........Sov. Un.	59.1 N	24.48 E
85	Rappahannock R. (răp'ȧ-hăn'ŭk) Va.	38.10 N	77.10 W
152	Rapu-Rapu (rä-pōō-rä'pōō)..Phil.	13.12 N	124.9 E
152	Rapu-Rapu I...............Phil.	13.12 N	124.10 E
85	Raquette L. (răk'ĕt).......N. Y.	43.50 N	74.40 W
85	Raquette R................N. Y.	44.45 N	75.0 W
88	Raritan B. (răr'ĭ-tăn) N. J.-N. Y. (In.)	40.28 N	74.14 W
4	Rarotonga (I.) (rä'rô-tŏŋ'gȧ) Pac. O.	21.14 S	159.46 W
153	Rasa I. (rä'sä)............Phil.	9.14 N	118.27 E
133	Ras Dashan (Mt.) (räs dä-shän') Eth.	13.10 N	38.33 E
119	Raseiniai (rä-syā'nyī)....Sov. Un.	55.22 N	23.6 E
135	Ras Hafun (C.) (räs hä-fōōn') Som.	10.25 N	51.15 E
131	Rashîd (Rosetta) (rȧ-shēd') (rô-zĕt'ȧ).Eg. (In.)	31.23 N	30.25 E
129	Rashkovo (rȧsh'kô-vô) Sov. Un.-Rom.	47.57 N	28.50 E
127	Raška (räsh'kȧ)...........Yugo.	43.14 N	20.38 E
135	Ras Kiuyu (Pt.) (räs' kyōō'yōō) Zan.	4.53 S	39.53 E
137	Ras Seilan (räs' sê-län').Aden (In.)	13.4 N	45.25 E
111	Rasskazovo (räs-kä'sô-vô) Sov. Un.	52.35 N	41.50 E
120	Rastatt (rä-shtät)..........Ger.	48.53 N	8.12 E
135	Ras Upembe (Pt.) (räs' ōō-pĕm'bĕ) Zan.	5.26 S	39.43 E
81	Ratcliff (răt'klĭf)............Tex.	31.22 N	95.10 W
120	Rathenow (rä'tĕ-nō)........Ger.	52.36 N	12.20 E
114	Rathlin I. (răth'lĭn).......N. Ire.	55.15 N	6.15 W
121	Ratibor (rä'tê-bôr)..........Pol.	50.6 N	18.13 E
52	Rat Is....................Alsk.	52.0 N	177.30 W
78	Raton (rȧ-tōn')............N. M.	36.53 N	104.27 W
70	Rattlesnake Cr............Ore.	42.30 N	117.35 W
118	Rättvik (rĕt'vēk)...........Swe.	60.54 N	15.10 E
118	Raufoss (rou'fôs)..........Nor.	60.44 N	10.31 E
156	Raukumara Ra. (rou'kōō-mä'rȧ) N. Z.	38.0 S	177.50 E
119	Rauma (rä'ŏŏ-mȧ)..........Fin.	61.8 N	21.32 E
119	Rautilampo (rä'ŏŏ-tê-läm'pô).Fin.	62.38 N	26.51 E
121	Rava Russkaya (rä'vȧ rōōs'kä-yȧ) Sov. Un.	50.13 N	23.40 E
73	Ravenna (rȧ-vĕn'ȧ) Calif. (Los Angeles In.)	34.27 N	118.14 W
126	Ravenna (rä-vĕn'nä)..........It.	44.25 N	12.13 E
76	Ravenna (rȧ-vĕn'ȧ).........Neb.	41.01 N	98.52 W
84	Ravenna..................Ohio	41.10 N	81.20 W
120	Ravensburg (rä'vĕns-bŏŏrgh).Ger.	47.47 N	9.36 E
84	Ravenswood, W. (rā'vĕnz-wŏŏd) Va.	38.57 N	81.47 W
141	Rawalpindi (rä-wŭl-pên'dê)..Pak.	33.45 N	73.2 E
121	Rawa Mazowiecka (rä'vä mȧ-zô'vyĕt-skȧ).Pol.	51.46 N	20.17 E
156	Rawene (rȧ-wē'nê).........N. Z.	35.25 S	173.30 E
120	Rawicz (rä'vêch)............Pol.	51.37 N	16.50 E
71	Rawlins (rô'lĭnz)...........Wyo.	41.46 N	107.13 W
102	Rawson (rô'sŭn)............Arg.	43.20 S	65.15 W
116	Rawtenstall (rô'tĕn-stôl).Gt. Brit.	53.42 N	2.17 W
150	Raya, Mt. (rä'yȧ).......Indon.	0.38 S	112.29 E
87	Ray, C. (rā)...............Can.	47.35 N	59.18 W
117	Rayleigh (rā'lē) Gt. Brit. (London In.)	51.35 N	0.36 E
73	Raymond (rā'mŭnd) Ga. (Atlanta In.)	33.21 N	84.43 W
70	Raymond..................Wash.	46.42 N	123.44 W
81	Raymondville (rā'mŭnd-vĭl)..Tex.	26.30 N	97.45 W
81	Rayne (rān)..................La.	30.15 N	92.15 W
92	Rayón (rä-yōn')............Mex.	21.50 N	99.38 W
81	Rayville (rā-vĭl)..............La.	32.28 N	91.45 W
129	Razdelnaya (räz-dĕl'nä-yȧ) Sov. Un.	46.48 N	30.2 E
148	Razdolnoe (räz-dôl'nô-yĕ) Sov. Un.	43.38 N	132.0 E
127	Razgrad (räz'grȧt)..........Bul.	43.30 N	26.30 E
127	Razlog (räz'lôk).............Bul.	41.53 N	23.31 E
122	Ras, Pte. du (pwäNt dü rä')...Fr.	48.5 N	4.45 W
122	Ré, Ile de (ēl dē rā')..........Fr.	46.10 N	1.25 W
56	Reaburn (rā'bûrn) Can. (Winnipeg In.)	50.5 N	97.53 W
114	Reading (rĕd'ĭng).......Gt. Brit.	51.25 N	1.0 W
87	Reading............Mass. (In.)	42.32 N	71.6 W
84	Reading...................Mich.	41.47 N	84.47 W
84	Reading...................Ohio	39.16 N	84.28 W
85	Reading....................Pa.	40.22 N	75.56 W
100	Real, Cordilleras (Mts.) (rā-äl') Bol.	17.0 S	67.0 W
116	Rea, R. (rē)...........Gt. Brit.	52.24 N	2.28 W
148	Rebun I. (rē'bōōn)..........Jap.	45.25 N	141.0 E
126	Recanati (rā-kä-nä'tē)..........It.	43.26 N	13.33 E
158	Recherche, Arch. of the (rē-shârsh').Austl.	34.0 S	122.30 E
128	Rechitsa (ryĕ'chêt-sȧ)...Sov. Un.	52.21 N	30.25 E
101	Recife (Pernambuco) (rȧ-sē'fĕ) (pĕr-näm-bōō'kô).Braz.	8.1 S	35.0 W
120	Recklinghausen (rĕk'lĭng-hou-zĕn) Ger.	51.34 N	7.2 E
102	Reconquista (rā-kôn-kēs'tä)..Arg.	29.5 S	59.40 W
79	Rector (rĕk'tĕr)............Ark.	36.15 N	90.21 W
73	Redan (rê-dăn') (rĕd'ăn) Ga. (Atlanta In.)	33.44 N	84.8 W
74	Red Bluff..................Calif.	40.11 N	122.15 W
80	Red Bluff Reservoir...N. M.-Tex.	32.0 N	103.59 W
77	Redby (rĕd'bê)............Minn.	47.52 N	94.55 W
77	Red Cedar R...............Wis.	45.5 N	91.43 W
78	Red Cloud.................Neb.	40.5 N	98.31 W
54	Red Deer..................Can.	52.17 N	113.46 W
54	Red Deer R................Can.	51.0 N	109.30 W
70	Redding (rĕd'ĭng)..........Calif.	40.35 N	122.25 W
117	Reddish (rĕd'ĭsh) Gt. Brit. (Liverpool In.)	53.26 N	2.9 W
116	Redditch (rĕd'ĭch)......Gt. Brit.	52.19 N	1.56 W
76	Redfield (rĕd'fēld)..........S. D.	44.53 N	98.30 W
81	Red Fish Bar..........Tex. (In.)	29.31 N	94.5 W
87	Red Indian L...............Can.	48.45 N	56.50 W
76	Red Lake R...............Minn.	47.48 N	96.40 W
76	Red Lake Falls...........Minn.	47.53 N	96.18 W
77	Red Lake Ind. Res........Minn.	48.0 N	95.20 W
74	Redlands (rĕd'lăndz).......Calif.	34.4 N	117.13 W
85	Red Lion....................Pa.	39.54 N	76.34 W
71	Red Lodge................Mont.	45.12 N	109.15 W
51	Redmond (rĕd'mŭnd) Wash. (Seattle In.)	47.40 N	122.8 W
73	Red Mt....Ala. (Birmingham In.)	33.35 N	86.41 W
76	Red Oak......................Ia.	41.1 N	95.12 W
122	Redon (rē-dôN')..............Fr.	47.40 N	2.5 W
95	Redonda (I.) (rȧ-dōn'dä) Le. Is. (In.)	16.56 N	62.18 W
124	Redondela (rā-dhôn-dā'lä)....Sp.	42.16 N	8.36 W
124	Redondo (rȧ-dôn'dŏŏ)......Port.	38.39 N	7.31 W
51	Redondo (rê-dŏn'dō) Wash. (Seattle In.)	47.21 N	122.20 W
74	Redondo Beach............Calif.	33.47 N	118.25 W
76	Red River..........N. D.-Minn.	48.0 N	97.2 W
82	Red R....................Tenn.	36.35 N	87.5 W
79	Red R.....................U. S.	33.42 N	96.20 W
78	Red R., North Fork........Okla.	35.0 N	99.20 W
78	Red R., Salt Fork..........Okla.	34.51 N	100.0 W
71	Red Rock Cr..............Mont.	44.45 N	112.25 W
140	Red Sea................Asia-Afr.	20.0 N	39.0 E
132	Red Stony Des. (Hammada-el-Homra) (häm-ä-dä'ĕl-hôm'rä) Libya	29.30 N	12.0 E
71	Redwater Cr. (rĕd'wô-tĕr)..Mont.	47.35 N	105.40 W
77	Red Wing.................Minn.	44.33 N	92.32 W
74	Redwood City (rĕd'wŏŏd)...Calif.	37.28 N	122.16 W
77	Redwood Falls.............Minn.	44.31 N	95.4 W
84	Reed City (rēd)............Mich.	43.52 N	85.32 W
74	Reedley (rēd'lē)...........Calif.	36.36 N	119.28 W
77	Reedsburg (rēdz'bûrg).......Wis.	43.33 N	90.0 W
70	Reedsport (rēdz'pôrt)........Ore.	43.42 N	124.8 W
156	Reef Point (rēf)............N. Z.	35.10 S	173.5 E
157	Reefton (rēf'tŭn)...........N. Z.	42.3 S	171.55 E
82	Reelfoot L. (rēl'fŏŏt).......Tenn.	36.24 N	89.24 W
114	Ree, Lough (L.) (lŏκ' rē')......Ire.	53.30 N	8.0 W
74	Reese R. (rēs)..............Nev.	39.40 N	117.15 W
82	Reform (rê-fôrm')............Ala.	33.23 N	88.2 W
81	Refugio (rȧ-fōō'hyô) (rĕ-fū'jō) Tex.	28.19 N	97.15 W
120	Rega R. (rā'gȧ).............Ger.	53.45 N	15.15 E
120	Regen R. (rā'ghĕn)..........Ger.	49.14 N	12.40 E
120	Regensburg (rā'ghĕns-bŏŏrgh) Ger.	49.2 N	12.4 E
126	Reggio (rĕ'jô)................It.	44.41 N	10.38 E
126	Reggio Calabria (kä-lä'brê-ä)..It.	38.7 N	15.40 E
121	Reghin (rȧ-gēn')...........Rom.	46.47 N	24.43 E
54	Regina (rê-jī'nȧ)............Can.	50.29 N	104.40 W
90	Regla (räg'lä)..Cuba (Habana In.)	23.8 N	82.20 W
120	Regnitz R. (rĕgh'nĕts).......Ger.	49.30 N	10.58 E
124	Reguengos de Monsaraz (rȧ-gĕŋ'-gōzh dā mōn-sä-räzh').Port.	38.25 N	7.30 W
134	Rehoboth (rê-hō'bŏth)..S. W. Afr.	23.20 S	17.18 E
120	Reichenbach (rī'κĕn-bäκ)....Ger.	50.36 N	12.17 E
120	Reichenhall, Bad (bät rī'κĕn-häl) Ger.	47.43 N	12.52 E
83	Reidsville (rēdz'vĭl)........N. C.	36.21 N	79.39 W
122	Reims (răNs)................Fr.	49.17 N	4.0 E
77	Reinbeck (rīn'bĕk)...........Ia.	42.22 N	92.42 W
54	Reindeer L. (rān'dēr).......Can.	57.0 N	102.30 W
117	Reinickendorf (rī'nĭ-kĕn-dôrf) Ger. (Berlin In.)	52.34 N	13.20 E
124	Reinosa (rȧ-ê-nō'sä)..........Sp.	43.2 N	4.9 W
133	Rejaf (rĕ-jäf')..........A. E. Sud.	4.46 N	31.32 E
85	Relay (rē'lā)................Md.	39.13 N	76.43 W
51	Reliance (rê-lī'ăns) Ore. (Portland In.)	45.41 N	123.21 W
132	Relizane (rē-lē-zȧn')..........Alg.	35.47 N	0.4 E
96	Remedios (rā-mā'dhê-ōs)....Cuba	22.28 N	79.35 W
93	Remedios, R..........Mex. (In.)	19.30 N	99.8 W
123	Remiremont (rē-mēr-môN')....Fr.	48.1 N	6.38 E
120	Remscheid (rĕm'shīt).........Ger.	51.11 N	7.10 E
159	Rendova I. (rĕn'dô-vȧ).Solomon Is.	8.30 S	157.20 E
120	Rendsburg (rĕnts'bŏŏrgh)....Ger.	54.19 N	9.38 E
54	Renfrew (rĕn'frōō)..........Can.	45.28 N	76.58 W
137	Renggam (rĕng'gäm').Malaya(In.)	1.56 N	103.27 E
99	Rengo (rĕn'gō) Chl. (Valparaiso In.)	34.23 S	70.54 W
129	Reni (ran')............Sov. Un.	45.25 N	28.19 E
159	Renmark (rĕn'märk).......Austl.	34.10 S	140.43 E
159	Rennell I. (rĕn-nĕl')...Solomon Is.	11.45 S	160.15 E
122	Rennes (rĕn).................Fr.	48.19 N	1.41 W
74	Reno (rē'nō)...............Nev.	39.32 N	119.48 W
126	Reno R. (rā'nô)...............It.	44.30 N	11.17 E
85	Renovo (rê-nō'vō)............Pa.	41.20 N	77.45 W
84	Rensselaer (rĕn'sē-lâr).......Ind.	39.59 N	87.7 W
85	Rensselaer..................N. Y.	42.40 N	73.45 W
70	Renton (rĕn'tŭn)..........Wash.	47.27 N	122.15 W
77	Renville (rĕn'vĭl)..........Minn.	44.46 N	95.12 W
73	Republic (rê-pŭb'lĭk) Ala. (Birmingham In.)	33.27 N	86.54 W
70	Republic..................Wash.	48.39 N	118.45 W
78	Republican R.........Colo.-Neb.	40.5 N	98.50 W
159	Repulse B. (rê-pŭls').......Austl.	20.45 S	149.0 E
124	Requena (rȧ-kā'nä)..........Sp.	39.30 N	1.7 W
129	Reshetilovka (ryĕ'shĕ-tê-lôf-kȧ) Sov. Un.	49.34 N	34.1 E
140	Resht (rĕsht)...............Iran	37.20 N	49.46 E
117	Resina (rȧ-sē'nä)..It. (Napoli In.)	40.48 N	14.21 E
102	Resistencia (rā-sês-tĕn'syä)...Arg.	27.29 S	59.0 W
127	Reşita (rȧ'shê-tȧ)..........Rom.	45.17 N	21.55 E
54	Resolution..................Can.	61.2 N	113.50 W
55	Resolution I................Can.	61.45 N	65.0 W
157	Resolution I...............N. Z.	45.40 S	166.40 E
86	RestigoucheR.(rĕs-tê-gōōsh').Can.	47.30 N	67.35 W
151	Restinga, Pt. (rĕs-tĭŋ'gä) Phil. (Manila In.)	14.17 N	120.35 E
94	Retalhulen (rā-täl-ōō-lān')..Guat.	14.31 N	91.42 W
116	Retford (rĕt'fērd).......Gt. Brit.	53.19 N	0.57 W
122	Rethel (rē-tĕl')...............Fr.	49.35 N	4.21 E
126	Rethymnon (rā'thēm-nôn)...Grc.	35.21 N	24.29 E
5	Réunion (I.) (rā-ü-nyôN').Ind. O.	21.6 S	55.36 E
125	Reus (rā'ōōs)...............Sp.	41.9 N	1.5 E
120	Reuss R. (rois)............Switz.	47.17 N	8.23 E

ng-sing; ŋ-baŋk; N-nasalized n; nŏd; cŏmmit; ōld; ôbey; ôrder; fōōd; fŏŏt; ou-out; s-soft; sh-dish; th-thin; pūre; ûnite; ûrn; stŭd; circŭs; ü-as "y" in study; '-indeterminate vowel.

Page Name Pronunciation Region   Lat.°'   Long.°'

120 Reutlingen (roit'lĭng-ĕn).....Ger. 48.30 N 9.13 E
119 Reval (Tallinn) (rĕ-väl') (täl'ĕn)
 Sov. Un. 59.26 N 24.46 E
122 Revel (rĕ-vĕl').........Fr. 43.30 N 2.0 E
54 Revelstoke (rĕv'ĕl-stōk).....Can. 51.0 N 118.1 W
95 Reventazon, R. (rä-vĕn-tä-zōn')
 C. R. 10.10 N 83.30 W
87 Revere (rĕ-vēr')......Mass. (In.) 42.24 N 71.1 W
53 Revillagigedo (rä-vēl'yä-kĕ-kä'dō)
 Alsk. 55.30 N 131.30 W
90 Revilla Gigedo Is........Pac. O. 19.0 N 111.0 W
122 Revin (rĕ-văn')........Fr. 49.45 N 4.40 E
141 Rewah (rĕ'wä)......India 24.37 N 81.28 E
141 Rewaz (rä'wäz).India (Bombay In.) 18.47 N 72.56 E
73 Rex (rĕks)......Ga. (Atlanta In.) 33.35 N 84.16 W
71 Rexburg (rĕks'bûrg).......Ida. 43.49 N 111.49 W
80 Rey, L........Mex. 27.0 N 103.25 W
100 Reyes (rä'yĕs)......Bol. 14.2 S 67.2 W
74 Reyes, Pt........Calif. 38.0 N 123.0 W
95 Rey I. (rä'ē)........Pan. 8.24 N 78.54 W
108 Reykjanes (Pt.) (rä'kyä-nĕs)...Ice. 63.45 N 22.45 W
108 Reykjavik (rä'kyä-vēk)......Ice. 64.4 N 21.58 W
80 Reynosa (rā-ē-nō'sä)......Mex. 26.5 N 98.17 W
140 Rezaieh (Urmia) (rĕ-zī'ä)
 (ōōr'mē-ä).Iran 37.34 N 45.10 E
119 Rēzēkne (rä'zĕk-nĕ).....Sov. Un. 56.30 N 27.21 E
90 Rezende (rä-zĕnd'ĕ)
 Braz. (Rio de Janeiro In.) 22.30 S 44.27 W
129 Rezeni (ryĕzh'ē-nĭ).....Sov. Un. 47.43 N 28.54 E
120 Rheden (rā'dĕn)......Neth. 52.2 N 6.2 E
120 Rheine (rī'nĕ).......Ger. 52.16 N 7.26 E
120 Rheinland (Prov.) (rīn'länd).Ger. 50.24 N 6.46 E
77 Rhinelander (rīn'län-dēr)...Wis. 45.39 N 89.23 W
120 Rhine R. (rīn)........Eur. 50.0 N 8.16 E
137 Rhio (Bintan) (I.) (rē'ō)
 (bĭn'tän).Indon. (In.) 1.3 N 104.20 E
150 Rhio Arch........Indon. 0.40 N 104.20 E
137 Rhio Str.......Indon. (In.) 0.45 N 104.25 E
85 Rhode Island (State)
 (rōd ī'länd).U. S. 41.40 N 71.35 W
113 Rhodes (I.) (rōdz).....Grc. 36.15 N 28.0 E
127 Rhodope Mts. (rŏ'dô-pē)....Bul. 41.40 N 24.35 E
114 Rhondda (rŏn'dhä)....Gt. Brit. 51.40 N 3.30 W
122 Rhone R. (rōn)......Fr.-Switz. 44.50 N 4.45 E
114 Rhyl (rĭl)........Gt. Brit. 53.19 N 3.20 W
101 Riachão (rē-ä-choun')......Braz. 7.59 S 46.32 W
101 Riachão do Jacuhipe (rē-ä-choun'
 dōō kä-kōō-ē'pĕ).Braz. (In.) 11.51 S 39.20 W
73 Rialto (rē-äl'tō)
 Calif. (Los Angeles In.) 34.6 N 117.22 W
124 Rianjo (rē-än'hō).......Sp. 42.39 N 8.49 E
124 Riaza R. (rē-ä'thä)......Sp. 41.35 N 3.40 W
110 Ribachi Pen. (rē-bä'chē).Sov. Un. 69.45 N 32.50 E
124 Ribadavia (rē-bä-dhä'vē-ä)...Sp. 42.18 N 8.10 W
124 Ribadeo (rē-bä-dhā'ō)......Sp. 43.33 N 7.5 W
114 Ribble R. (rĭb''l)......Gt. Brit. 53.40 N 3.0 W
118 Ribe (rē'bĕ)........Den. 55.19 N 8.45 E
123 Ribeauville (rē-bō-vēl')....Fr. 48.10 N 7.18 E
124 Ribeira (rē-bā'rä)......Sp. 42.33 N 9.0 W
101 Ribeirão Preto (rē-bä-roun'
 prä'tōō).Braz. 21.10 S 47.45 W
78 Ribera (rē-bĕ'rä)......N. M. 35.23 N 105.26 W
100 Riberalta (rē-bä-räl'tä)....Bol. 11.0 S 65.59 W
77 Rib L........Wis. 45.21 N 90.11 W
139 Ribnoe (rēb'nô-yĕ).....Sov. Un. 72.45 N 106.0 E
112 Riçana, Er (ĕr rē-sä'nä)....Mor. 31.8 N 4.23 W
85 Rice L. (rīs).........Can. 44.10 N 78.8 W
89 Rice L....Minn. (Minneapolis In.) 44.55 N 93.14 W
77 Rice Lake........Wis. 45.30 N 91.43 W
53 Richard I. (rĭch'ĕrd)......Can. 69.20 N 134.0 W
85 Richardson Park (rĭch'ĕrd-sŭn)
 Del. 39.42 N 75.37 W
86 Richelieu R. (rĭsh'lyŭ')....Can. 45.30 N 73.15 W
75 Richfield (rĭch'fēld)......Utah 38.46 N 112.6 W
86 Richford (rĭch'fērd)......Vt. 45.0 N 72.40 W
79 Rich Hill........Mo. 38.6 N 94.12 W
86 Richibucto (rĭ-chĭ-bŭk'tō)..Can. 46.42 N 64.54 W
82 Richland (rĭch'lănd)......Ga. 32.6 N 84.41 W
77 Richland Center......Wis. 43.20 N 90.23 W
160 Richmond (rĭch'mŭnd)
 Austl. (Tas. In.) 42.46 S 147.36 E
74 Richmond........Calif. 37.58 N 122.22 W
86 Richmond........Va. 42.46 N 72.9 W
117 Richmond..Gt. Brit. (London In.) 51.27 N 0.19 W
84 Richmond........Ind. 39.50 N 84.55 W
84 Richmond........Ky. 37.45 N 84.20 W
79 Richmond........Mo. 39.16 N 93.59 W
157 Richmond........N. Z. 41.20 S 173.12 E
81 Richmond........Tex. 29.35 N 95.45 W
71 Richmond........Utah 41.55 N 111.50 W
85 Richmond........Va. 37.34 N 77.26 W
51 Richmond Beach
 Wash. (Seattle In.) 47.46 N 122.23 W
89 Richmond Heights
 Mo. (St. Louis In.) 38.37 N 90.17 W
88 Richmond Hill......N. Y. (In.) 40.43 N 73.52 W
160 Richmond Ra......Austl. (In.) 28.50 S 152.40 E
160 Richmond R......Austl. (In.) 28.45 S 152.57 E
82 Richten (rĭch'tĕn)......Miss. 31.20 N 88.57 W
84 Richwood (rĭch'wŏŏd)...W. Va. 38.14 N 80.32 W
138 Ridder (rĭ-dĕr')......Sov. Un. 50.30 N 83.20 E
85 Rideau L. (rē-dō')......Can. 44.40 N 76.20 W
51 Ridgefield (rĭj'fēld)
 Wash. (Portland In.) 45.48 N 122.45 W
88 Ridgefield Park..N. J. (N. Y. In.) 40.52 N 74.2 W
85 Ridgeley (rĭj'lē).......Va. 39.30 N 78.46 W
85 Ridgeway (rĭj'wā)......Pa. 41.25 N 78.43 W
96 Riding Rocks (rīd'ĭng)...Ba. Is. 25.14 N 79.10 W
120 Ried (rēd)........Aus. 48.13 N 13.29 E
120 Riesa (rē'zä)......Ger. 51.17 N 13.17 E
99 Riesco, Cordillera (Mts.)
 (rē-äs'kō).Chl. (Magallanes In.) 52.45 S 71.45 W

99 Riesco I........Chl. (Magallanes In.) 52.55 S 72.20 W
126 Rieti (rē-ā'tē)........It. 42.24 N 12.52 E
135 Riet Vley (L.) (rēt vlä).U. S. Afr. 33.50 S 18.30 E
75 Rifle (rī'f'l)........Colo. 39.33 N 107.46 W
119 Riga (rē'gä)........Sov. Un. 56.58 N 24.5 E
119 Riga, G. of........Sov. Un. 57.30 N 23.35 E
57 Rigaud (rē-gō').Can. (Montreal In.) 45.28 N 74.18 W
71 Rigby (rĭg'bē)........Ida. 43.40 N 111.55 W
121 Rika R. (rē'kä)......Sov. Un. 48.25 N 23.35 E
88 Rikers I. (rī'kērz)....N. Y. (In.) 40.47 N 73.53 W
116 Rillington (rĭl'ĭng-tŭn)..Gt. Brit. 54.10 N 0.41 W
100 Rimac, R. (rē-mäk')..Peru (In.) 12.2 S 77.6 W
121 Rimavská Sobota (rē'mäf-skä
 sŏ'bô-tä).Czech. 48.25 N 20.2 E
118 Rimbo (rēm'bōō)......Swe. 59.45 N 18.24 E
126 Rimini (rē'mē-nē)......It. 44.3 N 12.33 E
86 Rimouski (rē-mōōs'kē)....Can. 48.27 N 68.31 W
93 Rincón Antonio (rēn-kōn'
 än-tō'nyô).Mex. 16.53 N 95.2 W
92 Rincón de Romos (dā rō-mōs')
 Mex. 22.14 N 102.19 W
160 Ringarooma R. (rĭn'gä-rōō'mä)
 Austl. (Tas. In.) 41.3 S 148.0 E
118 Ringkōbing (rĭng'kŭb-ĭng)...Den. 56.6 N 8.15 E
118 Ringkōbing Fjord.......Den. 55.58 N 8.15 E
118 Ringsaker (rĭngs'äk-ēr)....Nor. 60.56 N 10.41 E
118 Ringsted (rĭng'stĕdh)....Den. 55.26 N 11.49 E
108 Ringvadsō (I.) (rĭng'vädhs-û).Nor. 69.55 N 19.5 E
100 Riobamba (rē'ō-bäm'bä)....Ec. 1.45 S 78.32 W
99 Rio Bonito (rē'ōō bō-nē'tōō)
 Braz. (Rio de Janeiro In.) 22.42 S 42.36 W
100 Rio Branco (rē'ōō brän'kōō).Braz. 9.59 S 67.50 W
99 Rio Claro (rē'ōō klä'rōō)
 Braz. (Rio de Janeiro In.) 22.26 S 47.33 W
102 Río Cuarto (rē'ō kwär'tō)..Arg. 33.15 S 64.20 W
101 Rio de Janeiro (rē'ōō dā
 zhā-nä'ē-rōō).Braz. 23.0 S 43.20 W
99 Rio de Janeiro.......Braz. (In.)
102 Rio de Janeiro.......Braz. (In.)
101 Rio de Janeiro (State)....Braz. 23.0 S 42.30 W
132 Rio del Rey (rē'ō dĕl rā'é)...Nig. 4.40 N 8.40 E
132 Rio de Oro (rē'ō dā ō'rō)....Afr. 25.0 N 13.30 W
102 Rio Gallegos (rē'ō gä-lā'gōs).Arg. 51.40 S 69.15 W
92 Río Grande (rē'ō grän'dä)..Mex. 23.52 N 103.2 W
80 Riogrande (rē'ō grän'dä)....Tex. 26.22 N 98.50 W
101 Rio Grande do Norte (State)
 (rē'ōō grän'dĕ dōō nôr'tĕ).Braz. 6.0 S 36.30 W
102 Rio Grande (rē'ōō grän'dĕ)..Braz. 32.10 S 52.15 W
102 Rio Grande do Sul (State).Braz. 29.0 S 53.0 W
95 Rio Grande (Matagalpa) R. (rē'ō
 grän'dä (mä-tä-gál'pä).Nic. 13.0 N 84.20 W
100 Ríohacha (rē'ō-ä'chä)....Col. 11.30 N 73.0 W
93 Rio Hondo (rē'ō ōn'dō).Mex. (In.) 19.26 N 99.15 W
122 Riom (rē-ôn')........Fr. 45.55 N 3.8 E
124 Rio Maior (rē'ōō mä-yôr')..Port. 39.17 N 8.53 W
102 Rio Negro (rē'ōō nä'grōō)...Braz. 26.8 S 49.58 W
102 Rio Negro (State) (rē'ō nä'grō)
 Arg. 39.45 S 66.0 W
126 Rionero (rē-ō-nā'rō)......It. 40.56 N 15.41 E
101 Rio Pardo (rē'ō pär'dō)...Braz. 15.58 S 42.28 W
100 Riosucio (rē'ō-sōō'syō)....Col. 5.20 N 75.58 W
101 Rio Verde (rē'ōō vĕr'dĕ)...Braz. 17.45 S 50.47 W
92 Rioverde (rē'ō-vĕr'dä)....Mex. 21.55 N 100.0 W
116 Ripley (rĭp'lĕ)......Gt. Brit. 53.3 N 1.25 W
82 Ripley........Tenn. 35.45 N 89.33 W
125 Ripoll (rē-pōl'')......Sp. 42.13 N 2.10 E
77 Ripon (rĭp'ŏn)......Gt. Brit. 54.8 N 1.31 W
77 Ripon........Wis. 43.50 N 88.50 W
133 Ripon Falls (Simliki R.)
 (sēm-lē'kē).Ug. 0.32 N 33.4 E
158 Ripon I. (rĭp'ŏn)......Austl. 20.15 S 119.0 E
160 Risdon (rĭz'dŭn)..Austl. (Tas. In.) 42.47 S 146.21 E
148 Rishiri I. (rē-shē'rē)....Jap. 45.10 N 141.12 E
84 Rising Sun........Ind. 38.58 N 84.52 W
122 Risle R. (rēl)........Fr. 49.5 N 0.40 E
118 Risör (rēs'ûr)........Nor. 58.44 N 9.14 E
119 Ristna (C.) (rēst'nä)...Sov. Un. 58.56 N 22.2 E
56 Ritchot (rĭch'ŏt)
 Can. (Winnipeg In.) 49.47 N 97.5 W
84 Rittman (rĭt'mǎn)......Ohio 40.58 N 81.47 W
70 Ritzville (rĭts'vĭl)......Wash. 47.7 N 118.23 W
97 Riva (rē'vä)......Dom. Rep. 19.10 N 69.54 W
126 Riva........It. 45.53 N 10.50 E
124 Rivadesella (rē'vä-dā-sāl'yä).Sp. 43.27 N 5.5 W
94 Rivas (rē'väs)........Nic. 11.26 N 85.52 W
123 Rive-de-Gier (rēv-dē-zhē-ā')..Fr. 45.32 N 4.37 E
102 Rivera (rē-vā'rä)........Ur. 31.0 S 55.36 W
132 River Cess (rĭv'er sĕs)....Lib. 5.45 N 9.50 W
73 Riverdale......Ga. (Atlanta In.) 33.33 N 84.25 W
88 Riverdale.....Ill. (Chicago In.) 41.39 N 87.37 W
157 Riverdale........N. Z. 45.53 N 168.45 E
73 Riverdale
 Utah (Salt Lake City In.) 41.11 N 111.59 W
82 River Falls........Ala. 31.21 N 86.33 W
77 River Falls........Wis. 44.52 N 92.38 W
88 River Forest.....Ill. (Chicago In.) 41.53 N 87.49 W
85 Riverhead........N. Y. 40.55 N 72.40 W
159 Riverina (Reg.) (rĭv-ēr-ē'nä).Austl. 35.0 S 146.0 E
82 River Junction......Fla. 30.42 N 84.50 W
84 River Rouge (rōōzh)....Mich. 42.20 N 83.5 W
74 Riverside........Calif. 33.58 N 117.22 W
88 Riverside.....Ill. (Chicago In.) 41.50 N 87.49 W
89 Riverside.....Mich. (Detroit In.) 42.21 N 82.56 W
157 Riverside........N. Z. 46.18 S 168.3 E
73 Riverton
 Utah (Salt Lake City In.) 40.31 N 111.57 W
85 Riverton........Va. 38.58 N 78.4 W
71 Riverton........Wyo. 43.1 N 108.23 W
73 Rivertown.....Ga. (Atlanta In.) 33.37 N 84.44 W
122 Riversaltes (rēv'zält')....Fr. 42.48 N 2.52 E
86 Rivière du Loup (rē-vyâr' dü lōō')
 Can. 47.49 N 69.33 W

57 Rivière Rouge (rē-vyâr' rōōzh')
 Can. (Montreal In.) 45.18 N 74.12 W
140 Riyadh (rē-yäd')......Sau. Ar. 24.45 N 46.45 E
151 Rizal (Prov.) (rē-zäl')
 Phil. (Manila In.) 14.40 N 121.10 E
111 Rize (rē'zĕ)........Tur. 41.0 N 40.32 E
127 Rizzuto, C. (rēt-sōō'tō).....It. 38.53 N 17.4 E
118 Rjukan (ryōō'kän)......Nor. 59.54 N 8.35 E
116 Roade (rōd)......Gt. Brit. 52.9 N 0.53 W
122 Roanne (rō-án')........Fr. 46.2 N 4.4 E
82 Roanoke (rō'á-nōk)......Ala. 33.8 N 85.22 W
83 Roanoke........Va. 37.17 N 79.57 W
83 Roanoke Rapids......N. C. 36.26 N 77.39 W
83 Roanoke R........Va. 36.33 N 77.0 W
94 Roatan (rō-ä-tän')......Hond. 16.18 N 86.32 W
94 Roatan I........Hond. 16.20 N 86.30 W
135 Robben I. (rŏb'ĕn)....U. S. Afr. 33.48 S 18.22 E
89 Robbinsdale (rŏb'ĭnz-dāl)
 Minn. (Minneapolis In.) 45.2 N 93.20 W
160 Robbins I. (rŏb'ĭnz)
 Austl. (Tas. In.) 40.40 S 144.57 E
72 Roberts, Pt. (rŏb'ērts)
 Wash. (Vancouver In.) 48.58 N 123.6 W
87 Robertson I. (rŏb'ērt-sŭn)...Can. 51.0 N 59.10 W
132 Robertsport (rŏb'ērts-pōrt)..Lib. 6.48 N 11.30 W
55 Roberval (rŏb'ēr-vál) (rō-bĕr-väl')
 Can. 48.35 N 72.14 W
84 Robinson (rŏb'ĭn-sŭn)......Ill. 39.4 N 87.46 W
87 Robinsons........Can. 48.15 N 58.45 W
54 Robson, Mt. (rŏb'sŭn).....Can. 53.2 N 118.15 W
81 Robstown (rŏbz'toun).....Tex. 27.47 N 97.40 W
117 Roby (rō'bē)
 Gt. Brit. (Liverpool In.) 53.24 N 2.52 W
125 Roca, C. (rō'kä)......Port. 38.47 N 9.30 W
101 Rocas (Is.) (rō'käs)......Braz. 3.55 S 33.45 W
102 Rocha (rō'chäs)......Braz. (In.) 22.50 S 43.3 W
102 Rocha........Ur. 34.30 S 54.15 W
114 Rochdale (rŏch'dāl)....Gt. Brit. 53.40 N 2.10 W
97 Roche à Bateau (rôsh ä bä-tō').Hai. 18.10 N 73.59 W
125 Roche, C. (rō'chä)....Sp. (In.) 36.18 N 6.9 W
122 Rochefort (rōsh-fôr')......Fr. 45.55 N 1.2 W
72 Roche Harbor (rōch)
 Wash. (Vancouver In.) 48.38 N 123.10 W
77 Rochelle (rō-shĕl')......Ill. 41.55 N 89.3 W
115 Rochester (rŏch'ĕs-tēr).Gt. Brit. 51.20 N 0.35 E
84 Rochester........Ind. 41.6 N 86.12 W
77 Rochester........Minn. 44.1 N 92.28 W
86 Rochester........N. H. 43.20 N 71.0 W
85 Rochester........N. Y. 43.8 N 77.35 W
117 Rochford (rŏch'fērd)
 Gt. Brit. (London In.) 51.35 N 0.43 E
85 Rockaway (rŏck'á-wā)....N. J. 40.54 N 74.35 W
88 Rockaway........N. Y. (In.) 40.36 N 73.46 W
88 Rockaway Beach...N. Y. (In.) 40.34 N 73.52 W
88 Rockaway Inlet....N. Y. (In.) 40.34 N 73.54 W
73 Rockcastle. Ala. (Birmingham In.) 33.15 N 87.14 W
71 Rock Cr........Mont. 48.42 N 107.0 W
71 Rock Cr........Mont. 46.25 N 113.40 W
70 Rock Cr........Ore. 45.30 N 120.5 W
70 Rock Cr........Wash. 47.5 N 117.50 W
81 Rockdale (rŏck'dāl)......Tex. 30.39 N 97.0 W
77 Rock Falls........Ill. 41.46 N 89.42 W
77 Rockford (rŏck'fērd)......Ill. 42.18 N 89.5 W
159 Rockhampton (rŏk-hämp'tŭn)
 Austl. 23.28 S 150.29 E
83 Rock Hill........S. C. 34.55 N 81.2 W
83 Rockingham (rŏk'ĭng-häm)..N. C. 34.56 N 79.46 W
116 Rockingham For......Gt. Brit. 52.32 N 0.39 W
54 Rockingham Station..Can. (In.) 44.41 N 63.39 W
79 Rock Island........Ill. 41.30 N 90.35 W
70 Rock Island Dam Site..Wash. 47.18 N 120.10 W
86 Rockland (rŏk'lănd)......Me. 44.6 N 69.8 W
87 Rockland......Mass. (In.) 42.8 N 70.55 W
142 Rock Mart (märt)......Ga. 34.0 N 85.3 W
84 Rockport........Ind. 37.52 N 87.3 W
87 Rockport......Mass. (In.) 42.38 N 70.37 W
79 Rockport........Mo. 40.25 N 95.30 W
81 Rockport........Tex. 28.2 N 97.3 W
76 Rock Rapids........Ia. 43.27 N 96.11 W
77 Rock R........Ill. 41.50 N 89.30 W
76 Rock R........Ia.-Minn. 43.22 N 96.10 W
97 Rock Sd.......Ba. Is. 24.52 N 76.10 W
157 Rocks Pt........N. Z. 40.55 S 172.8 E
80 Rocksprings........Tex. 30.1 N 100.12 W
71 Rock Springs........Wyo. 41.35 N 109.12 W
101 Rockstone (rŏk'stōn)....Br. Gu. 5.58 N 58.31 W
76 Rock Valley........Ia. 43.12 N 96.18 W
84 Rockville (rŏk'vĭl)......Ind. 39.46 N 87.14 W
85 Rockville Center......N. Y. 40.40 N 73.42 W
81 Rockwall (rŏk'wôl)......Tex. 32.55 N 96.26 W
77 Rockwell City (rŏk'wĕl)....Ia. 42.24 N 94.36 W
86 Rockwood (rŏk'wŏŏd).....Tenn. 35.52 N 84.42 W
71 Rocky Boys Ind. Res. (rŏk'ē)
 Mont. 48.15 N 109.55 W
78 Rocky Ford........Colo. 38.3 N 103.44 W
160 Rocky Hd......Austl. (Tas. In.) 40.50 S 143.20 E
83 Rocky Mount........N. C. 35.56 N 77.48 W
78 Rocky Mountain Natl. Park.Colo. 40.25 N 106.0 W
54 Rocky Mts........N. A. 50.0 N 114.0 W
73 Rocky Pt. Calif. (Los Angeles In.) 33.46 N 118.26 W
83 Rocky R........N. C. 35.20 N 80.40 W
89 Rocky River. Ohio (Cleveland In.) 41.28 N 81.50 W
131 Rôda (rō'dä)......Eg. (In.) 27.48 N 30.51 E
96 Rodas (rō'dhäs)......Cuba 22.18 N 80.34 W
117 Rodaun (rō'doun). Aus. (Wien In.) 48.7 N 16.16 E
116 Roden, R. (rō'dĕn)....Gt. Brit. 52.49 N 2.39 W
80 Rodeo (rō-dā'ō)......Mex. 25.10 N 104.34 W
122 Rodez (rō-dĕz')........Fr. 44.21 N 2.35 E
113 Rodi (rō'dhē)........Grc. 36.26 N 28.13 E
117 Roding, R. (rōd'ĭng)
 Gt. Brit. (London In.) 51.37 N 0.3 E

ăt; fĭnăl; rāte; senāte; ärm; ăsk; sofá; fâre; ch-choose; dh-as th in other; bē; ēvent; bĕt; recĕnt; cratēr; g-go; gh-gutteral g; bĭt; ĭ-short neutral; rīde; ĸ-gutteral k as ch in German ich;

Rodnei PRONOUNCING INDEX Ryazan

Page	Name Pronunciation	Region	Lat. °′	Long. °′
121	Rodnei Mts. (rôd'nĕ-ĕ)	Rom.	47.37 N	24.30 E
128	Rodniki (rôd'nê-kê)	Sov. Un.	57.7 N	41.45 W
102	Rodrigo de Freitas, L. (rô-drē'gŏŏ dā frā'ê-tàzh)	Braz. (In.)	22.58 S	43.12 W
5	Rodrigues (I.) (rô-drē'gĕs)	Ind. O.	19.57 S	63.15 E
158	Roebourne (rō'bŭrn)	Austl.	20.50 S	117.10 E
158	Roebuck B. (rō'bŭck)	Austl.	18.5 S	122.10 E
115	Roermond (rōōr'mônt)	Neth.	51.10 N	6.0 E
55	Roes Welcome (Str.) (rōz)	Can.	64.45 N	86.45 W
128	Rogachev (rôg'á-chyôf)	Sov. Un.	53.5 N	30.2 E
160	Rogans Hill (rō'gănz)	Austl. (Sydney In.)	33.44 S	150.59 E
127	Rogačica (rô'gä'chēt-sà)	Yugo.	43.47 N	19.1 E
79	Rogers (rŏj-ērz)	Ark.	36.18 N	94.8 W
84	Rogers City	Mich.	45.26 N	83.50 W
82	Rogersville (rŏj'ērz-vĭl)	Tenn.	36.23 N	83.2 W
100	Rogoaguado, L. (rō'gō-ä-gwä'dō)	Bol.	11.58 S	65.50 W
129	Rogovskaya (rô-gôf'skà-yà)	Sov. Un.	45.43 N	38.42 E
120	Rogoźno (rô'gôzh-nô)	Pol.	52.44 N	16.54 E
70	Rogue R. (rōg)	Ore.	42.35 N	123.0 W
121	Rohatin (rō-hä'tēn)	Sov. Un.	49.25 N	24.38 E
117	Rohrbeck (rōr'bĕk)	Ger. (Berlin In.)	52.32 N	13.2 E
118	Röikenviken (rûē'kĕn-vêk-ĕn)	Nor.	60.28 N	10.29 E
123	Roissy-en-France (rwä-sē'-än-fräNs')	Fr. (In.)	49.0 N	2.30 E
99	Rojas (rō'häs)	Arg. (Buenos Aires In.)	34.8 S	60.44 W
93	Rojo, C. (rō'hō)	Mex.	21.34 N	97.20 W
91	Rojo, C.	P. R. (In.)	17.50 N	67.12 W
148	Rokko C. (rŏk'kō)	Jap.	37.30 N	137.18 E
149	Rokugogawa R. (rō'kōō-gô-gä'wä)	Jap. (Tokyo In.)	35.36 N	139.36 E
120	Rokycany (rô'kĭ'tsà-nĭ)	Czech.	49.44 N	13.36 E
79	Rolla (rŏl'à)	Mo.	37.56 N	91.45 W
76	Rolla	N. D.	48.52 N	99.30 W
118	Rollag (rōō'lägh)	Nor.	59.54 N	8.35 E
159	Roma (rō'mà)	Austl.	26.29 S	148.45 E
126	Roma (Rome) (rō'mä) (rōm)	It.	41.45 N	12.15 E
87	Romaine (rō-mĕn')	Can.	50.15 N	60.39 W
55	Romaine R.	Can.	52.0 N	63.45 W
121	Roman (rō'män)	Rom.	46.57 N	26.55 E
137	Romani (rô-mä'nê)	Eg. (In.)	30.57 N	32.46 E
127	Romania (rō-mā'nê-à)	Eur.	45.0 N	25.0 E
83	Romano, C. (rō-mä'nō)	Fla. (In.)	25.51 N	81.40 W
96	Romano Cay (I.)	Cuba	22.10 N	77.52 W
122	Romans (rô-mäN')	Fr.	45.4 N	5.3 E
152	Romblon (rōm-blōn')	Phil.	12.34 N	122.15 E
152	Romblon I.	Phil.	12.33 N	122.16 E
82	Rome (rōm)	Ga.	34.15 N	85.10 W
126	Rome (Roma) (rōm) (rō'mä)	It.	41.45 N	12.15 E
85	Rome	N. Y.	43.14 N	75.30 W
84	Romeo (rō'mê-ō)	Mich.	42.50 N	83.0 W
117	Romford (rŭm'fērd)	Gt. Brit. (London In.)	51.35 N	0.11 E
117	Romiley (rŭm'ĭ-lê)	Gt. Brit. (Liverpool In.)	53.25 N	2.6 W
122	Romilly-sur-Seine (rô-mê-yē'-sür-sān')	Fr.	48.32 N	3.42 E
92	Romita (rō-mē'tä)	Mex.	20.54 N	101.32 W
129	Romny (rôm'nĭ)	Sov. Un.	50.46 N	33.31 E
118	Rōmō (I.) (rûm'û)	Den.	55.5 N	8.30 E
73	Romoland (rō'mō'lănd)	Calif. (Los Angeles In.)	33.45 N	117.10 W
122	Romorantin (rô-mô-räN-täN')	Fr.	47.25 N	1.45 E
71	Ronan (rō'năn)	Mont.	47.30 N	114.6 W
101	Roncador, Serra do (Mts.) (sĕr'rá dŏŏ rôn-kä-dôr')	Braz.	11.30 S	52.0 W
85	Ronceverte (rŏn'sê-vûrt)	W. Va.	37.45 N	80.30 W
135	Rondebosch (rŏn'dĕ-bŏsh)	U. S. Afr.	33.57 S	18.28 E
124	Rondo (rōn'dō)	Sp.	36.45 N	5.9 W
118	Rönne (rûn'ĕ)	Den.	55.5 N	14.42 E
118	Ronneby (rŏn'ĕ-bü)	Swe.	56.13 N	15.20 E
79	Roodhouse (rōōd'hous)	Ill.	39.28 N	90.20 W
115	Roosendaal (rō'zĕn-däl)	Neth.	51.35 N	4.30 E
75	Roosevelt (rōz''vĕlt)	Utah	40.17 N	109.58 W
75	Roosevelt Dam	Ariz.	33.40 N	111.12 W
47	Roosevelt (I.)	Ant.	79.30 S	162.0 W
75	Roosevelt L.	Ariz.	33.40 N	111.10 W
101	Roosevelt, R.	Braz.	10.0 S	60.30 W
158	Roper R. (rōp'ĕr)	Austl.	14.50 S	133.30 E
125	Roquetas (rō-kā'täs)	Sp.	40.50 N	0.31 E
101	Roraima Mt. (rô-rä-ē'mä)	Ven.-Br. Gu.	5.10 N	60.45 W
118	Röros (rûr'ôs)	Nor.	62.35 N	11.21 E
120	Rorschach (rōr'shäk)	Switz.	47.27 N	9.28 E
131	Rosa, C. (rō'sä)	Tun. (In.)	36.55 N	8.31 E
80	Rosales (rō-zä'läs)	Mex.	28.13 N	100.43 W
152	Rosales	Phil.	15.54 N	120.39 E
126	Rosa, Monte (Mt.) (mōn'tä rō'zä)	It.	45.56 N	7.51 E
92	Rosamorada (rō'zä-mō-rä'dhä)	Mex.	22.5 N	105.15 W
72	Rosa Mt. (rō'zä)	Colo. (Colo. Sprs. In.)	38.45 N	104.57 W
102	Rosario (rô-zä'rê-ō)	Arg.	33.0 S	60.45 W
101	Rosario (rô-zä'rê-ŏŏ)	Braz.	2.58 S	44.18 W
102	Rosario	Braz. (In.)	22.41 S	43.16 W
92	Rosario (rô-zä'rê-ō)	Mex.	23.0 N	105.51 W
152	Rosario	Phil.	13.50 N	121.12 E
151	Rosario	Phil. (Manila In.)	14.26 N	120.50 E
99	Rosario	Ur. (Buenos Aires In.)	34.18 S	57.23 W
96	Rosario Cay (I.)	Cuba	21.37 N	81.54 W
101	Rosario Oeste (rô-zä'rê-ŏŏ ô'ĕst'ĕ)	Braz.	14.45 S	56.28 W
72	Rosario Str.	Wash. (Vancouver In.)	48.35 N	122.45 W
125	Rosas, G. of (rō'zäs)	Sp.	42.10 N	3.10 E
51	Rosburg (rŏz'bûrg)	Wash. (Portland In.)	46.19 N	123.39 W
80	Roscoe (rôs'kō)	Tex.	32.27 N	100.38 W
114	Roscommon (rôs-kŏm'ŭn)	Ire.	53.40 N	8.10 W
95	Roseau (rô-zō')	Le. Is. (In.)	15.17 N	61.23 W
76	Roseau	Minn.	48.51 N	95.46 W
71	Rosebud Cr.	Mont.	45.50 N	106.30 W
76	Rosebud Ind. Res.	S. D.	43.10 N	100.42 W
70	Roseburg (rōz'bûrg)	Ore.	43.11 N	123.20 W
72	Rosedale (rōz'dāl)	Can. (Vancouver In.)	49.10 N	121.48 W
79	Rosedale	Kan.	39.4 N	94.39 W
82	Rosedale	Miss.	33.49 N	91.1 W
51	Rosedale	Wash. (Seattle In.)	47.19 N	122.39 W
88	Rosehill (rōz'hĭl)	Can. (Niagara Falls In.)	42.53 N	78.59 W
122	Rosendael (rô-zäN-däl')	Fr.	51.1 N	2.29 E
120	Rosenheim (rō'zĕn-hīm)	Ger.	47.51 N	12.6 E
117	Rosenthal (rō'zĕn-täl)	Ger. (Berlin In.)	52.36 N	13.23 E
131	Rosetta (Rashîd) (rô-zĕt'á) (rä-shēd')	Eg. (In.)	31.23 N	30.25 E
74	Roseville (rōz'vĭl)	Calif.	38.43 N	121.18 W
143	Rosham (rō-shàm)	Chn.	48.50 N	126.0 E
84	Rosiclare (rōz'ĭ-klâr)	Ill.	37.28 N	88.17 W
127	Rosiorii de Vede (rô-shôr'ê dĕ vĕ-dĕ)	Rom.	44.6 N	24.59 E
118	Roskilde (rôs'kêl-dĕ)	Den.	55.38 N	12.4 E
128	Roslavl (rôs'läv'l)	Sov. Un.	53.58 N	32.52 E
70	Roslyn (rŏz'lĭn)	Wash.	47.13 N	121.0 W
123	Rosny (rô-nē')	Fr. (In.)	48.52 N	2.29 E
160	Ross (rôs)	Austl. (Tas. In.)	42.3 S	147.31 E
51	Ross	Calif. (San Francisco In.)	37.57 N	122.32 W
157	Ross	N. Z.	42.52 S	170.54 E
126	Rossano (rô-sä'nō)	It.	39.34 N	16.39 E
55	Rosseau, L. (rôs-sō')	Can.	45.15 N	79.45 W
159	Rossel I. (rô-sĕl')	Pap. Ter.	11.30 S	154.0 E
56	Rosser (rôs'sēr)	Can. (Winnipeg In.)	49.59 N	97.29 W
86	Rossignol L. (rô-sê-nyôl')	Can.	44.20 N	65.5 W
54	Ross I.	Can.	54.15 N	98.15 W
70	Rossland (rôs'lănd)	Can.	49.4 N	117.47 W
129	Rossosh (rôs'sŭsh)	Sov. Un.	50.12 N	39.33 E
47	Ross Sea	Ant.	76.0 S	178.0 W
47	Ross Shelf Ice	Ant.	81.30 S	175.0 W
82	Rossville (rôs'vĭl)	Ga.	34.58 N	85.22 W
117	Rostherne (rôs'tērn)	Gt. Brit. (Liverpool In.)	53.21 N	2.24 W
120	Rostock (rôs'tŭk)	Ger.	54.5 N	12.6 E
129	Rostov (rôs-tôf')	Sov. Un.	47.12 N	39.42 E
128	Rostov	Sov. Un.	57.12 N	39.25 E
127	Rosul Pass (rô'zhōōl)	Rom.	45.32 N	24.17 E
108	Rös Water (L.) (rûs)	Nor.	65.48 N	14.0 E
72	Roswell (rôz'wĕl)	Colo. (Colo. Sprs. In.)	38.53 N	104.50 W
82	Roswell	Ga.	34.3 N	84.24 W
78	Roswell	N. M.	33.23 N	104.31 W
125	Rota (rō'tä)	Sp. (In.)	36.37 N	6.21 W
80	Rotan (rô-tăn')	Tex.	32.50 N	100.30 W
120	Rothenburg (rō'tĕn-bŏŏrgh)	Ger.	49.22 N	10.12 E
114	Rotherham (rŏdh'ēr-ăm)	Gt. Brit.	53.25 N	1.20 W
80	Rothesay	Can.	45.24 N	65.59 W
114	Rothesay (rôth'sâ)	Gt. Brit.	55.50 N	5.0 W
116	Rothwell (rôth'wĕl)	Gt. Brit.	53.44 N	1.29 W
152	Roti (I.) (rō'tê)	Indon.	10.45 S	123.0 E
122	Rotondo, Mt. (rô-tôn'dō)	Cor. (In.)	42.15 N	9.5 E
156	Rotorua (rō-tô-rōō'ä)	N. Z.	38.10 S	176.15 E
156	Rotorua L.	N. Z.	38.7 S	176.20 E
115	Rotterdam (rôt'ēr-däm')	Neth.	51.55 N	4.29 E
120	Rottweil (rōt'vīl)	Ger.	48.11 N	8.37 E
122	Roubaix (rōō-bĕ')	Fr.	50.41 N	3.10 E
122	Rouen (rōō-äN')	Fr.	49.25 N	1.5 E
89	Rouge, R. (rōōzh)	Mich. (Detroit In.)	42.19 N	83.10 W
115	Roulers (rô-lā')	Bel.	50.55 N	3.5 E
156	Round Back, Mt.	N. Z. (In.)	41.19 S	174.40 E
89	Round L.	Minn. (Minneapolis In.)	45.5 N	93.10 W
160	Round Mt.	Austl.	30.26 S	152.18 E
87	Round Pond	Can.	48.10 N	56.5 W
71	Roundup	Mont.	46.26 N	108.34 W
74	Round Valley Ind. Res.	Calif.	39.50 N	123.20 W
114	Rousay (I.) (rōō'zâ)	Gt. Brit. (In.)	59.5 N	3.0 W
160	Rous Hd. (rōōz)	Austl. (Perth In.)	32.3 S	115.44 E
55	Rouyn (rōōn)	Can.	48.17 N	79.5 W
110	Rovaniemi (rô'vá-nyĕ'mĭ)	Fin.	66.30 N	25.40 E
126	Rovato (rô-vä'tō)	It.	45.34 N	10.0 E
129	Rovenki (rô-vĕn'-kĭ')	Sov. Un.	48.4 N	39.41 E
129	Rovenki	Sov. Un.	49.55 N	38.55 E
126	Rovereto (rō-vā-rā'tō)	It.	45.54 N	11.3 E
126	Rovigno (Rovinj) (rô-vēn'yō) (rô-vēn')	Yugo.	45.5 N	13.38 E
126	Rovigo (rô-vē'gō)	It.	45.4 N	11.46 E
121	Rovno (rôv'nô)	Sov. Un.	50.36 N	26.16 E
129	Rovnoe (rôv'nô-yĕ)	Sov. Un.	48.11 N	31.43 E
87	Rowley (rou'lê)	Mass. (In.)	42.43 N	70.53 W
83	Roxboro (rŏks'bŭr-ō)	N. C.	36.23 N	78.58 W
157	Roxburgh (rŏks'bŭr-ô)	N. Z.	45.33 S	169.22 E
78	Roy (roi)	N. M.	35.55 N	104.11 W
73	Roy	Utah (Salt Lake City In.)	41.10 N	112.3 W
51	Roy	Wash. (Seattle In.)	47.1 N	122.33 W
96	Royal I. (roi'ăl)	Ba. Is.	25.32 N	76.50 W
84	Royal Oak	Mich.	42.29 N	83.11 W
84	Royalton (roi'ăl-tŭn)	Mich.	42.2 N	86.26 W
122	Royan (rwä-yäN')	Fr.	45.39 N	1.0 W
122	Roye (rwä)	Fr.	49.45 N	2.45 E
82	Royston (roiz'tŭn)	Ga.	34.17 N	83.9 W
116	Royton (roi'tŭn)	Gt. Brit.	53.34 N	2.7 W
121	Rožňava (rôzh'nyä-vá)	Czech.	48.40 N	20.32 E
111	Rtishchevo ('r-tĭsh'chĕ-vô)	Sov. Un.	52.12 N	43.45 E
135	Ruaha R. (rwä'hä)	Tan.	7.40 S	37.0 E
156	Ruahine Ra. (rōō-á-hē'nĕ)	N. Z.	40.0 S	176.10 E
134	Ruanda Urundi (Prov.) (rōō-än'dá ōō-rōōn'dê)	Bel. Cong.	2.45 S	30.0 E
156	Ruapehu (Vol.) (rōō'á-pā'hōō)	N. Z.	39.18 S	175.33 E
157	Ruapuke I. (rōō-á-pōō'kĕ)	N. Z.	46.47 S	168.28 E
140	Rub al Khali (Great Sandy Desert) (rŭb ăl kä'lê)	Sau. Ar.	20.0 N	52.0 E
129	Rubanovka (rōō-bä'nôf-kà)	Sov. Un.	47.0 N	34.10 E
125	Rubí (rōō-bê')	Sp. (In.)	41.29 N	2.2 E
117	Rübke (rüp'kĕ)	Ger. (Hamburg In.)	53.29 N	9.46 E
138	Rubtsovsk (rōōp-tsôfsk')	Sov. Un.	51.30 N	81.15 E
52	Ruby (rōō'bê)	Alsk.	64.40 N	155.30 W
74	Ruby L.	Nev.	40.10 N	115.27 W
71	Ruby R.	Mont.	45.25 N	112.10 W
134	Ruchugi (rōō-chōō'gê)	Tan.	5.13 S	30.20 E
128	Rudabkina (rōō-däp'kê-nà)	Sov. Un.	52.44 N	29.0 E
118	Rudkōbing (rōōdh'kûb-ĭng)	Den.	54.56 N	10.44 E
142	Rudok (rōō'dŏk)	Chn.	33.28 N	77.44 E
133	Rudolph, L. (rōō'dŏlf)	Kenya-Eth.	4.0 N	36.0 E
120	Rudolstadt (rōō'dôl-shtät)	Ger.	50.43 N	11.19 E
122	Ruelle (rü-ĕl')	Fr.	45.41 N	0.15 E
133	Rufāa (rōō-fä'ä)	A. E. Sud.	14.40 N	33.28 E
122	Ruffec (rü-fĕk')	Fr.	46.3 N	0.11 E
135	Rufiji R. (rōō-fē'jê)	Tan.	7.45 S	38.0 E
99	Rufino (rōō-fē'nô)	Arg. (Buenos Aires In.)	34.13 S	62.43 W
132	Rufisque (rü-fēsk')	Fr. W. Afr.	14.42 N	17.8 W
116	Rugby (rŭg'bê)	Gt. Brit.	52.22 N	1.15 W
76	Rugby	N. D.	48.22 N	100.0 W
116	Rugeley (rŭj'lê)	Gt. Brit.	52.46 N	1.56 W
120	Rügen (I.) (rü'ghĕn)	Ger.	54.26 N	13.25 E
	Rügenwalde, see Darlowo, Pol.			
119	Ruhno I. (rōō'nô)	Sov. Un.	57.48 N	23.15 E
120	Ruhr R. (rōōr)	Ger.	51.28 N	8.10 E
119	Rūjeena (rōō'yâ-nâ)	Sov. Un.	57.54 N	25.20 E
139	Rukhlovo (rōō-klô'vô)	Sov. Un.	53.55 N	123.59 E
134	Rukwa, L. (rōōk-wä')	Tan.	8.18 S	32.42 E
114	Rum (I.) (rŭm)	Gt. Brit.	57.0 N	6.20 W
127	Ruma (rōō'mà)	Yugo.	45.0 N	19.51 E
133	Rumbek (rŭm'bĕk)	A. E. Sud.	6.52 N	29.40 E
97	Rum Cay (I.)	Ba. Is.	23.40 N	74.51 W
86	Rumford (rŭm'fērd)	Me.	44.33 N	70.35 W
77	Rum R.	Minn.	45.25 N	93.20 W
157	Runanga (rōō-näŋ'gä)	N. Z.	42.22 S	171.15 E
156	Runaway, C. (rŭn'á-wâ)	N. Z.	37.30 S	178.3 E
116	Runcorn (rŭŋ'kôrn)	Gt. Brit.	53.20 N	2.44 W
72	Running Cr.	Colo. (Denver In.)	39.34 N	104.32 W
137	Rupat I. (rōō'pät)	Indon. (In.)	1.50 N	101.35 E
71	Rupert (rōō'pērt)	Ida.	42.37 N	113.41 W
55	Rupert R.	Can.	51.35 N	77.45 W
117	Ruschwedel (rōōsh'vä'dĕl)	Ger. (Hamburg In.)	53.27 N	9.33 E
127	Rusčuk (Russe) (rōōs'chŏŏk) (rōō'sĕ)	Bul.	43.50 N	25.59 E
77	Rush City	Minn.	45.40 N	92.59 W
78	Rush Cr.	Colo.	38.40 N	103.10 W
116	Rushden (rŭsh'dĕn)	Gt. Brit.	52.18 N	0.35 W
79	Rushville (rŭsh'vĭl)	Ill.	40.7 N	90.34 W
84	Rushville	Ind.	39.35 N	85.37 W
76	Rushville	Neb.	42.42 N	102.26 W
87	Rushy Pond (rŭsh'ĭ)	Can.	48.58 N	55.41 W
81	Rusk (rŭsk)	Tex.	31.48 N	95.10 W
73	Russ (rŭs)	Calif. (Los Angeles In.)	34.27 N	118.20 W
127	Russe (Rusčuk) (rōō'sĕ) (rōōs'chŏŏk)	Bul.	43.50 N	25.59 E
54	Russell (rŭs'ĕl)	Can.	50.48 N	101.1 W
78	Russell	Kan.	38.53 N	98.51 W
84	Russell	Ky.	38.30 N	82.45 W
156	Russell	N. Z.	35.17 S	174.10 E
72	Russell Gulch (gŭlch)	Colo. (Denver In.)	39.47 N	105.33 W
159	Russell I.	Solomon Is.	9.8 S	159.0 E
82	Russellville (rŭs'ĕl-vĭl)	Ala.	34.30 N	87.34 W
79	Russellville	Ark.	35.16 N	93.8 W
82	Russellville	Ky.	36.50 N	86.52 W
	Russia, see Soviet Union			
74	Russian R.	Calif.	38.55 N	123.10 W
81	Ruston (rŭs'tŭn)	La.	32.31 N	92.39 W
120	Rüstringen (rüs'trĭng-ĕn)	Ger.	53.32 N	8.6 E
129	Rutchenkovo (rōō-chĕn'kô-vô)	Sov. Un.	47.53 N	37.34 E
124	Rute (rōō'tā)	Sp.	37.20 N	4.21 W
74	Ruth (rōōth)	Nev.	39.16 N	114.59 W
121	Ruthenia (Podkarpatská Rus) (rōō-thē'nê-à)	Sov. Un.	48.28 N	23.20 E
88	Rutherford (rŭdh'ēr-fērd)	N. J. (N. Y. In.)	40.50 N	74.6 W
83	Rutherfordton (rŭdh'ēr-fērd-tŭn)	N. C.	35.22 N	81.58 W
86	Rutland (rŭt'lănd)	Vt.	43.35 N	73.0 W
116	Rutland Co.	Gt. Brit.	52.39 N	0.42 W
134	Rutshuru (rōōt-shōō'rōō)	Bel. Cong.	1.13 S	29.22 E
126	Ruvo (rōō'vô)	It.	41.6 N	16.30 E
135	Ruvu (Kingani) R. (rōō'vōō) (kĭŋ'gä'nĭ)	Tan.	6.40 S	38.45 E
135	Ruvu (Pangani) R. (päŋ-gä'nĭ)	Tan.	5.0 S	38.6 E
135	Ruvuma R. (rōō-vōō'mä)	Tan.-Moz.	11.15 S	38.15 E
140	Ruwanduz (rōō-wän-dōōz')	Iraq	36.38 N	44.40 E
133	Ruwenzori R. (rōō-wĕn-zō'rê)	Ug.	0.15 N	30.30 E
89	Ruxton (rŭks'tŭn)	Va. (Norfolk In.)	36.52 N	76.15 W
128	Ruza (rōō'zá)	Sov. Un.	55.42 N	36.11 E
121	Ruzhany (rōō-zhän'ĭ)	Sov. Un.	52.51 N	24.53 E
128	Ryazan (ryä-zän'')	Sov. Un.	54.38 N	39.42 E
128	Ryazan (Dist.)	Sov. Un.	54.8 N	40.0 E

ng-sing; ŋ-baŋk; N-nasalized n; nŏd; cŏmmit; ōld; ôbey; ôrder; fōōd; fŏŏt; ou-out; s-soft; sh-dish; th-thin; pūre; ûnite; ûrn; stŭd; circŭs; ü-as "y" in study; '-indeterminate vowel.

Ryazhsk PRONOUNCING INDEX St. John

Page	Name Pronunciation Region	Lat. °'	Long. °'
128	Ryazhsk (ryăzh'sk')......Sov. Un.	53.42 N	40.2 E
128	Rybinsk (rĭ'bĕnsk).......Sov. Un.	58.1 N	38.41 E
128	Rybinskoe Res. (rĭ-bĕn'skō-yĕ) Sov. Un.	58.30 N	38.30 E
121	Rybnik (rĭb'nĕk)............Pol.	50.6 N	18.33 E
129	Rybnitsa (rĭb'nēt-sȧ)........Rom.	47.45 N	28.59 E
114	Ryde (rīd).............Gt. Brit.	50.45 N	1.13 W
116	Rye, R. (rī)............Gt. Brit.	54.10 N	0.51 W
129	Rylsk (rêl''sk).........Sov. Un.	51.33 N	34.43 E
121	Rypin (rĭ'pĕn)...............Pol.	53.3 N	19.25 E
148	Ryukyu Is. (ryōō'kyōō') Pac. O. (For. In.)	24.40 N	126.10 E
121	Rzeszów (zhȧ'shōōf)..........Pol.	50.3 N	22.0 E
128	Rzhev ('r-zhĕf').........Sov. Un.	56.15 N	34.20 E
129	Rzhishchev ('r-zhĭsh'chĕf) Sov. Un.	49.58 N	31.2 E
120	Saale R. (sä'lĕ).............Ger.	51.0 N	11.51 E
120	Saalfeld (säl'fĕlt)............Ger.	50.38 N	11.20 E
72	Saanich Inlet (sä'nĭch) Can. (Vancouver In.)	48.38 N	123.30 W
120	Saarbrücken (zär'brük'ĕn)... Ger.	49.14 N	6.59 E
123	Saarebourg (sär'bōōrkh')......Fr.	48.45 N	7.5 E
119	Saaremaa (Ezel) (I.) (sä'rē-mä) (ĕt'sĕl)......Sov. Un.	58.26 N	22.36 E
112	Saar, Wadi (R.) (wä'dē sä'ăr). Mor.	34.12 N	2.30 W
102	Saavedra (sä-ȧ-vā'drä).......Arg.	37.45 S	62.20 W
95	Saba (I.) (sä'bä).....Le. Is. (In.)	17.38 N	63.14 W
127	Šabac (shä'bȧts)............Yugo.	44.45 N	19.43 E
125	Sabadell (sä-bä-dhȧl')....Sp. (In.)	41.32 N	2.6 E
97	Sabana de la Mar (sä-bä'nä dā lä mär'). Dom. Rep.	19.4 N	69.23 W
95	Sabana, R..................Pan.	8.40 N	78.5 W
93	Sabancuy (sä-bäŋ-kwē')......Mex.	18.58 N	91.6 W
97	Sabaneta (sä-bä-nā'tä). Dom. Rep.	19.28 N	71.23 W
150	Sabang (sä'bäng).........Indon.	5.52 N	95.26 E
126	Sabaudia (sȧ-bou'dē-ȧ).........It.	41.19 N	13.0 E
133	Sabderat (säb-dȧ-rät')........Erit.	15.28 N	36.41 E
79	Sabetha (sȧ-bĕth'ȧ)..........Kan.	39.55 N	95.48 W
119	Sabile (sä'bê-lĕ).........Sov. Un.	57.2 N	22.36 E
80	Sabinal (sȧ-bī'nȧl)...........Tex.	29.19 N	99.27 W
96	Sabinal Cay (I.) (sä-bē-näl'). Cuba	21.42 N	77.15 W
80	Sabinas Hidalgo (sä-bē'näs ē-däl'gō). Mex.	26.30 N	100.10 W
80	Sabinas, R. (sä-bē'näs)......Mex.	26.30 N	100.0 W
81	Sabine (sȧ-bēn')............Tex.	29.43 N	93.53 W
81	Sabine L...............La.-Tex.	29.50 N	93.50 W
47	Sabine, Mt..................Ant.	72.5 S	169.10 E
81	Sabine R...............La.-Tex.	31.31 N	93.35 W
134	Sabi R. (sä'bē).......Moz.-S. Rh.	21.17 S	34.0 E
152	Sablayan (säb-lä-yän').......Phil.	12.50 N	120.46 E
72	Sable (sā'b'l)..Colo. (Denver In.)	39.46 N	104.50 W
122	Sablé (sä-blā')...............Fr.	47.50 N	0.20 W
55	Sable, C. (sā'b'l)...........Can.	43.40 N	65.45 W
87	Sable I.....................Can.	43.55 N	60.0 W
86	Sable, Rivière du (rê-vyâr' dü sä'bl'). Can.	49.12 N	70.25 W
110	Sablia, Mt. (säp'lĭ-ȧ).....Sov. Un.	64.55 N	58.50 E
124	Sabor R. (sä-bōr')..........Port.	41.28 N	7.40 W
101	Sabral (sä-bräl')............Braz.	3.43 S	40.18 W
152	Sabtang I. (säb-täng'). Phil. (In.)	20.20 N	121.43 E
85	Sacandoga R. (să'kăn-dō'gȧ) N. Y.	43.20 N	74.18 W
125	Sacavem (sä-kä-vĕn')..Port. (In.)	38.48 N	9.6 W
125	Sacavem R...........Port. (In.)	38.51 N	9.8 W
126	Sacchia R. (säk'ê-ä)..........It.	44.35 N	10.46 E
77	Sac City (sŏk)................Ia.	42.25 N	94.59 W
147	Sachŏn (sä'chŭn')............Kor.	35.5 N	128.6 E
85	Sacketts Harbor (săk'ĕts)...N. Y.	43.55 N	76.6 W
86	Sackville (săk'vĭl)...........Can.	45.55 N	64.24 W
86	Saco (sô'kō).................Me.	43.31 N	70.28 W
86	Saco R.......................Me.	43.55 N	70.50 W
79	Sac R. (sôk).................Mo.	37.50 N	93.49 W
74	Sacramento (săk-rȧ-mĕn'tō). Calif.	38.35 N	121.30 W
80	Sacramento...................Mex.	27.3 N	101.45 W
80	Sacramento...................Mex.	25.45 N	103.21 W
58	Sacramento Mts.......N. M.-Tex.	32.0 N	104.30 W
74	Sacramento R................Calif.	38.15 N	121.35 W
134	Sá da Bandeira (sä' dȧ bän-dā'rȧ) Ang.	14.52 S	13.35 E
149	Sada C. (sä'dȧ)..............Jap.	32.46 N	133.0 E
149	Sadamotu (sä'dȧ-mō'tōō) Jap. (Tokyo In.)	35.20 N	139.54 E
135	Sadani (sȧ-dä'nē)............Tan.	6.2 S	38.46 E
117	Saddleworth (săd''l-wûrth) Gt. Brit. (Liverpool In.)	53.33 N	2.0 W
150	Sadec (sȧ-dĕk')............Indoch.	10.25 N	105.38 E
141	Sadiya (sŭ-dē'yä)...........India	27.55 N	95.40 E
148	Sado I. (sä'dō)...............Jap.	38.0 N	138.28 E
124	Sado R. (sä'dōō)............Port.	38.10 N	8.10 W
118	Saeby (sĕ'bü)................Den.	57.21 N	10.30 E
137	Safed (Zefath) (sä'fĕd) (zĕ'fŭt) Pal. (In.)	32.58 N	35.29 E
131	Saff (säf)..............Eg. (In.)	29.34 N	31.20 E
118	Säffle (sĕf'lĕ)...............Swe.	59.8 N	12.56 E
75	Safford (săf'fērd)............Ariz.	32.50 N	109.41 W
132	Safi (Asfi) (sä'fê) (äs'fê).....Mor.	32.34 N	9.12 W
135	Saft el Laban (säft ĕl lä'bän)..Eg.	30.2 N	31.10 E
149	Saga (sä'gä).................Jap.	33.16 N	130.18 E
149	Sagami S. (sä'gä'mê).........Jap.	35.2 N	139.20 E
77	Saganaga L. (sȧ-gȧ-nȧ'gȧ) Can.-Minn.	48.13 N	90.57 W
153	Sagay (sä-gī')................Phil.	9.6 N	124.44 E
153	Sagay........................Phil.	10.56 N	123.27 E
88	Sag Bridge (săg). Ill. (Chicago In.)	41.41 N	87.56 W
73	Saginaw (săg'ĭ-nô) Ala. (Birmingham In.)	33.14 N	86.47 W
84	Saginaw....................Mich.	43.27 N	83.57 W
84	Saginaw B..................Mich.	44.0 N	83.30 W
111	Sagiz (R.) (sä'gēz).......Sov. Un.	48.28 N	54.30 E
75	Saguache (sȧ-wăch') (sȧ-gwä'chê) Colo.	38.5 N	106.9 W
75	Saguache Cr..................Colo.	38.4 N	106.20 W
75	Saguaro Natl. Mon. (săg-wä'rō) Ariz.	32.8 N	110.33 W
55	Saguenay R. (săg-ē-nā')......Can.	48.30 N	71.0 W
125	Sagunto (sä-gōōn'tō)..........Sp.	39.40 N	0.17 W
129	Saguny (sä'gōō-nĭ).......Sov. Un.	50.38 N	39.41 E
132	Sahara (Desert) (sȧ-hä'rȧ)....Afr.	23.0 N	10.0 E
141	Saharanpur (sŭ-hä'rŭn-pōōr') India	29.58 N	77.31 E
92	Sahuayo (sä-wä'yō).........Mex.	20.3 N	102.42 W
132	Saida (sä'ê-dä)...............Alg.	34.49 N	0.5 E
113	Saida (Sidon) (sä'ê-dȧ) (sī'dŏn) Leb. (In.)	33.35 N	35.32 E
140	Saidabad (sä'ê-dȧ-bät')........Iran	29.31 N	55.45 E
150	Saigon (sȧ-ê-gôN') (sī-gŏn'). Indoch.	10.46 N	106.38 E
140	Saihut (sä'ê-hŭt)............Aden	15.17 N	51.29 E
149	Saijo (sä'ê-jō)................Jap.	33.55 N	133.12 E
149	Saiki (sä'ê-kê)...............Jap.	33.0 N	131.46 E
119	Saima, L. (sä'ĭ-mȧ)............Fin.	61.16 N	28.30 E
92	Sain Alto (sä-ēn' äl'tō)......Mex.	23.35 N	103.13 W
56	St. Adolphe (sănt ā'dŏlf) (săN' tȧ-dôlf'). Can. (Winnipeg In.)	49.40 N	97.5 W
122	St. Affrique (săN' tȧ-frēk')....Fr.	43.58 N	2.55 E
160	St. Albans (sănt ôl'bănz) Austl. (Melbourne In.)	37.45 S	144.48 E
114	St. Albans.............Gt. Brit.	51.45 N	0.20 W
86	St. Albans....................Vt.	44.49 N	73.8 W
84	St. Albans.................W. Va.	38.22 N	81.52 W
114	St. Albans Hd...........Gt. Brit.	50.30 N	2.0 W
122	St. Amand (săN' tȧ-mäN')......Fr.	50.30 N	3.40 E
122	St. Amand-Mont-Rond (săN' tȧ-mäN'-môN-rôN'). Fr.	46.45 N	2.30 E
95	St. Andrew (sănt ăn'drōō) Barb. (In.)	13.18 N	59.36 W
57	St. Andrews (ăn'drōōz) Can. (Montreal In.)	45.34 N	74.20 W
86	St. Andrews..................Can.	45.5 N	67.2 W
56	St. Andrews..Can. (Winnipeg In.)	50.3 N	97.0 W
114	St. Andrews.............Gt. Brit.	56.20 N	2.45 W
82	St. Andrews B................Fla.	30.15 N	85.45 W
87	St. Andrews Channel.........Can.	46.5 N	60.30 W
95	St. Andrews I...............W. I.	12.34 N	81.42 W
87	St. Ann B. (ăn)..............Can.	46.15 N	60.35 W
57	Ste. Annes (săNt'ăn') (sănt ăn') Can. (Montreal In.)	45.25 N	73.57 W
86	Ste. Anne de Beaupre (dē bō-prā') Can.	47.1 N	70.57 W
86	Ste. Anne de la Pocatière (dē lȧ pô-kȧ-tyȧr'). Can.	47.23 N	70.0 W
86	Ste. Anne R..................Can.	46.48 N	71.55 W
96	Ste. Anns B..................Jam.	18.26 N	77.14 W
57	St. Anselme (săN' tăN-sĕlm') Can. (Quebec In.)	46.37 N	70.58 W
126	St. Antioco (I.) (sänt' ăn-tē'ô-kō) Sard.	39.3 N	8.25 E
71	St. Anthony (sănt ăn'thō-nē). Ida.	43.59 N	111.42 W
57	St. Apollinaire (săN' tȧ-pôl-ê-nâr') Can. (Quebec In.)	46.37 N	71.31 W
83	St. Augustine (sănt ô'gŭs-tēn) Fla.	29.54 N	81.20 W
123	St. Avold (săN' tȧ-vôl').......Fr.	49.5 N	6.45 E
125	Ste. Barbe du Tlelat (sănt bärb' dü tlē-lȧ'). Alg.	35.34 N	0.25 W
87	St. Barbe Is. (sănt bärb')....Can.	50.12 N	55.45 W
86	St. Barthélemi (săN' bȧr-tā-lĕ-mē') Can.	46.11 N	73.8 W
95	St. Barthélemy (I.)....W. I. (In.)	17.55 N	62.50 W
157	St. Bathans, Mt. (sănt băth'ănz) N. Z.	44.43 S	169.47 E
114	St. Bees Hd. (sănt bēz' hĕd) Gt. Brit.	54.30 N	3.40 W
54	St. Boniface (bŏn'ĭ-fȧs).......Can.	49.57 N	97.1 W
123	St. Brice (săN' brēs')......Fr. (In.)	49.0 N	2.21 E
114	St. Brides B. (sănt brīdz'). Gt. Brit.	51.50 N	5.15 W
122	St. Brieuc (săN brê-û')..........Fr.	48.35 N	2.45 W
57	St. Canut (săN' kȧ-nü') Can. (Montreal In.)	45.43 N	74.5 W
86	St. Casimir (kȧ-zê-mēr')......Can.	46.38 N	72.14 W
57	Ste. Catherine (sănt kăth'ēr-ĭn) Can. (Quebec In.)	46.53 N	71.35 W
89	St. Catherine, L. La. (New Orleans In.)	30.8 N	89.44 W
95	St. Catherine, Mt..Wind. Is. (In.)	12.10 N	61.42 W
85	St. Catherines................Can.	43.10 N	79.13 W
122	St. Chamond (săN shȧ-môN')..Fr.	45.30 N	4.30 E
57	St. Charles (săN' shärl'). Can. (In.)	46.47 N	70.56 W
77	St. Charles (sănt chärlz').......Ill.	41.55 N	88.19 W
84	St. Charles..................Mich.	43.19 N	84.11 W
77	St. Charles..................Minn.	43.57 N	92.4 W
79	St. Charles....................Mo.	38.47 N	90.29 W
57	St. Charles R...Can. (Quebec In.)	46.53 N	71.22 W
122	St. Chély-d' Apcher (săN' shā-lē'-dȧp-shā'). Fr.	44.45 N	3.15 E
	St. Christopher, see St. Kitts (I.)		
84	St. Clair (sănt klâr)...........Mich.	42.50 N	82.30 W
157	St. Clair..................N. Z. (In.)	45.55 S	170.30 E
51	St. Clair......Wash. (Seattle In.)	47.2 N	122.43 W
55	St. Clair L...................Can.	42.28 N	82.30 W
84	St. Clair, L..............Mich.-Can.	42.35 N	82.30 W
84	St. Clair R..............Mich.-Can.	42.50 N	82.28 W
73	St. Clair Springs Ala. (Birmingham In.)	33.46 N	86.24 W
123	St. Claude (săN' klōd')..........Fr.	46.25 N	5.51 E
57	St. Clet (klā'). Can. (Montreal In.)	45.22 N	74.14 W
83	St. Cloud (sănt kloud')..Fla. (In.)	28.14 N	81.17 W
123	St. Cloud (săN' klōō')...Fr. (In.)	48.50 N	2.13 E
77	St. Cloud (sănt kloud')......Minn.	45.34 N	94.8 W
91	St. Croix (I.) (sănt kroi')....W. I.	17.45 N	64.45 W
86	St. Croix R................Me.-Can.	45.30 N	67.32 W
77	St. Croix R..............Minn.-Wis.	45.10 N	92.45 W
123	St. Cyr-l' École (săN' sēr'-lā-kôl') Fr. (In.)	48.47 N	2.7 E
57	St. Damien de Buckland (sănt dā'mê-ĕn dē bŭk'lănd) Can. (Quebec In.)	46.38 N	70.40 W
57	St. Damien Station (săN' dȧ-myăN'). Can. (Quebec In.)	46.36 N	70.43 W
114	St. Davids Hd. (sănt dā'vĭdz) Gt. Brit.	51.55 N	5.20 W
123	St. Denis (săN' dē-nē')...Fr. (In.)	48.56 N	2.22 E
112	St. Denis-du-Sig (săN' dē-nē'-dü-sēg'). Alg.	35.30 N	0.12 W
123	St. Dié (săN' dē-ā')............Fr.	48.18 N	7.0 E
122	St. Dizier (săN' dê-zyā')........Fr.	48.38 N	5.0 E
54	St. Elias, Mt. (sănt ê-lī'ăs)...Can.	60.15 N	140.45 W
122	Saintes (săNt)..................Fr.	45.42 N	0.40 W
122	St. Etienne (săN' tā-tyĕn')....Fr.	45.25 N	4.25 E
57	St. Eustache (săN' tû-stȧsh') Can. (Montreal In.)	45.34 N	73.53 W
56	St. Eustache..Can. (Winnipeg In.)	49.58 N	97.48 W
95	St. Eustatius (I.) (sănt û-stā'shŭs) Le. Is. (In.)	17.30 N	62.58 W
57	Ste. Famille (săNt' fȧ-mē'y') Can. (Quebec In.)	46.59 N	70.58 W
86	St. Felicien (săN' fā-lê-syăN'). Can.	48.38 N	72.28 W
57	St. Féréol (fa-rā-ôl') Can. (Quebec In.)	47.8 N	70.52 W
122	St. Florent-sur-Cher (săN' flô-răN'-sür-shâr'). Fr.	46.59 N	2.15 E
123	St. Flour (săN flōōr')............Fr.	45.1 N	3.10 E
79	St. Francis L. (sănt frăn'sĭs)..Ark.	35.40 N	90.25 W
85	St. Francis, L.................Can.	45.5 N	74.30 W
79	St. Francis R..................Ark.	36.30 N	90.10 W
86	St. Francis R..................Can.	45.46 N	72.10 W
57	St. François (săN' frăN-swä') Can. (Quebec In.)	46.55 N	70.42 W
57	St. François d'Orléans (dôr-lā-äN') Can. (Quebec In.)	47.1 N	70.49 W
56	St. François Xavier (zȧ-vyā') Can. (Winnipeg In.)	49.56 N	97.32 W
120	St. Gallen (sănt gäl'ĕn) (zänkt gäl'ĕn). Switz.	47.26 N	9.23 E
122	St. Gaudens (săN' gō-dăNs')...Fr.	43.7 N	0.45 E
79	Ste. Genevieve (sănt jĕn'ĕ-vēv) Mo.	37.58 N	90.2 W
159	St. George (sănt jôrj')........Austl.	28.0 S	148.35 E
86	St. George....................Can.	45.8 N	66.48 W
86	St. George (săN' zhôrzh')....Can.	46.9 N	70.41 W
83	St. George (sănt jôrj')........S. C.	33.11 N	80.35 W
75	St. George....................Utah	37.7 N	113.34 W
87	St. George B...................Can.	48.30 N	58.40 W
87	St. George, C..................Can.	48.29 N	59.15 W
82	St. George, C..................Fla.	29.35 N	85.4 W
102	St. George, G. of..............Arg.	46.0 S	67.0 W
52	St. George I..................Alsk.	56.30 N	169.30 W
87	St. Georges....................Can.	48.28 N	58.25 W
95	St. Georges.........Wind. Is. (In.)	12.3 N	61.46 W
114	St. Georges Chan....Gt. Brit.-Ire.	52.0 N	6.0 W
123	St. Germain, Fôret de (fô-rĕ' dē săN' zhĕr-măN'). Fr. (In.)	48.56 N	2.5 E
123	St. Germain-en-Laye (săN' zhĕr-măN'-äN-lā'). Fr. (In.)	48.53 N	2.6 E
57	St. Gervais (săN' zhĕr-vĕ') Can. (Quebec In.)	46.43 N	70.54 W
122	St. Gilles (săN' zhēl')...........Fr.	43.40 N	4.28 E
117	St. Gilles Waes (väs') Bel. (Anvers In.)	51.13 N	4.7 E
122	St. Girons (săN' zhē-rôN')......Fr.	43.0 N	1.9 E
120	St. Gotthard Tunnel (sănt gŏth'ȧrd) (săN' gô-tȧr'). Switz.	46.37 N	8.37 E
87	St. Gregory, Mt. (sănt grĕg'ēr-ê) Can.	49.25 N	58.12 W
160	St. Helena (hĕ-lē'nȧ)..Austl. (In.)	28.40 S	153.34 E
4	St. Helena (I.)...........Atl. O.	15.57 S	5.42 W
70	St. Helena....................Ore.	45.51 N	122.49 W
134	St. Helena B..........U. S. Afr.	32.45 S	18.5 E
114	St. Helens (sănt hĕl'ĕnz). Gt. Brit.	53.25 N	2.50 W
70	St. Helens, Mt............Wash.	46.12 N	122.12 W
160	St. Helens Pt....Austl. (Tas. In.)	41.16 S	148.22 E
122	St. Helier (sănt hĕl'yēr)..Gt. Brit.	49.10 N	2.5 W
57	St. Henry (hĕn'rê) Can. (Quebec In.)	46.42 N	71.4 W
57	St. Hubert (hū'bērt) Can. (Montreal In.)	45.31 N	73.24 W
86	St. Hyacinthe (săN' tē-ȧ-săNt') (sănt hī'ȧ-sĭnth). Can.	45.38 N	72.55 W
77	St. Ignace (sănt ĭg'năs).....Mich.	45.52 N	84.40 W
77	St. Ignace I...................Can.	48.45 N	87.55 W
86	St. Irénée (săN' tē-rȧ-nā')....Can.	47.33 N	70.13 W
57	St. Isidore (săN' tē-zê-dôr') (sănt ĭz'ĭ-dôr). Can. (Montreal In.)	45.19 N	73.40 W
77	St. James (sănt jāmz')......Minn.	43.58 N	94.35 W
79	St. James.......................Mo.	37.59 N	91.37 W
57	St. Janvier (săN' zhăN-vyā') Can. (Montreal In.)	45.44 N	73.55 W
86	St. Jean (săN' zhäN')..........Can.	45.18 N	73.17 W
122	St. Jean-d'Angély (săN zhäN'-däN-zhā-lē'). Fr.	45.55 N	0.32 W
122	St. Jean de Luz (dē lüz')........Fr.	43.25 N	1.39 W
57	St. Jean d'Orléans (dôr-lā-äN') Can. (Quebec In.)	46.56 N	70.54 W
85	St. Jerome (sănt jĕ-rōm') (săN zhā-rōm'). Can.	45.47 N	74.2 W
57	St. Joachim (sănt jō'ȧ-kĭm) Can. (Quebec In.)	47.4 N	70.50 W
117	St. Jobint Goor (săN' zhō-băN' gōr'). Bel. (Anvers In.)	51.18 N	4.34 E
70	St. Joe R. (sănt jō')..........Ida.	47.12 N	115.55 W
55	St. John (jŏn)..................Can.	45.18 N	66.10 W
78	St. John.......................Kan.	38.0 N	98.45 W
76	St. John......................N. D.	48.59 N	99.45 W

ăt; finăl; rāte; senȧte; ärm; ȧsk; sofȧ; fâre; ch-choose; dh-as th in other; bē; êvent; bĕt; recĕnt; cratēr; g-go; gh-gutteral g; bĭt; ĭ-short neutral; rīde; K-gutteral k as ch in German ich;

ng-sing; ŋ-baŋk; N-nasalized n; nŏd; cŏmmit; ōld; ōbey; ôrder; fōōd; fŏŏt; ou-out; s-soft; sh-dish; th-thin; pūre; únite; ûrn; stŭd; circŭs; ŭ-as "y" in study; '-indeterminate vowel.

Salmon PRONOUNCING INDEX Sanford

Page	Name Pronunciation Region	Lat. °′	Long. °′
71	Salmon (săm′ŭn)...........Ida.	45.10 N	113.55 W
72	Salmon Arm of Sechelt Inlet (sē′chĕlt). Can. (Vancouver In.)	49.39 N	123.45 W
70	Salmon Falls Cr...........Ida.	42.25 N	114.50 W
158	Salmon Gums (săm′ŭn gŭmz) Austl.	32.57 S	121.57 E
86	Salmon R................Can.	46.12 N	65.46 W
70	Salmon R................Ida.	45.28 N	115.40 W
85	Salmon R...........N. Y.-Can.	44.45 N	74.15 W
70	Salmon R., Middle Fork.....Ida.	44.50 N	114.46 W
70	Salmon R., South Fork......Ida.	44.20 N	114.30 W
70	Salmon River Mts..........Ida.	44.30 N	115.0 W
122	Salon-de-Province (sȧ-lôɴ′-dē-prô-väɴs′). Fr.	43.40 N	5.10 E
127	Salonika (Thessalonike) (sä-lô-nē′-kȧ) (thĕs′ȧ-lô-nē′kê). Grc.	40.35 N	22.55 E
121	Salonta (sä-lôn′tä).........Rom.	46.47 N	21.39 E
126	Salpi, L. (läʹgō dē säl′pê)......It.	41.23 N	16.3 E
111	Sal R. (sȧl).............Sov. Un.	47.15 N	42.0 E
111	Salsk (sälsk)...........Sov. Un.	46.30 N	41.35 E
102	Salta (säl′tä)..............Arg.	24.45 S	65.28 W
102	Salta (State)..............Arg.	24.0 S	63.30 W
73	Saltair (sôlt′âr) Utah (Salt Lake City In.)	40.46 N	112.9 W
97	Salt Cay (I.) (sôlt).........Ba. Is.	21.21 N	71.12 W
88	Salt Cr.........Ill. (Chicago In.)	41.50 N	87.53 W
80	Saltillo (säl-tēl′yō).........Mex.	25.25 N	101.0 W
137	Salt (sȧlt)............Jor. (In.)	32.2 N	35.44 E
132	Salt (El Juf) Desert (sȧlt) (ĕl jōōf′) Fr. W. Afr.	22.0 N	6.0 W
158	Salt L...................Austl.	24.15 S	113.40 E
158	Salt L...................Austl.	28.20 S	119.35 E
75	Salt Lake City............Utah	40.45 N	111.51 W
73	Salt Lake City........Utah (In.)		
158	Salt Lake Reg...........Austl.	27.15 S	121.0 E
158	Salt Lakes...............Austl.	29.15 S	131.0 E
99	Salto (säl′tō) Arg. (Buenos Aires In.)	34.14 S	60.13 W
102	Salto......................Ur.	31.29 S	58.2 W
101	Salto Grande de Paranápanema (säl′tō grän′dā dȧ pä-rä-nä′pä-nä′mä). Braz.	22.45 S	49.59 W
74	Salton Sea (sôlt′ŭn)........Calif.	33.20 N	115.50 W
132	Saltpond..................G. C.	5.15 N	1.1 W
75	Salt R....................Ariz.	33.30 N	111.35 W
79	Salt R....................Mo.	39.40 N	91.55 W
75	Salt River Ind. Res..........Ariz.	33.40 N	111.40 W
97	Saltrou (säl-trōō′)..........Hai.	18.13 N	71.58 W
118	Saltsjöbaden (sält′shû-bäd′ĕn) Swe.	59.15 N	18.21 E
72	Saltspring I.. Can. (Vancouver In.)	48.47 N	123.30 W
83	Saltville (sôlt′vĭl)...........Va.	36.51 N	81.46 W
160	Salt Water R. Austl. (Melbourne In.)	37.43 S	144.51 E
83	Saluda (sȧ-lōō′dȧ)..........S. C.	34.1 N	81.47 W
83	Saluda R..................S. C.	34.20 N	82.12 W
126	Saluzzo (sä-lōōt′sō)...........It.	44.37 N	7.30 E
101	Salvador (Baia) (säl-vä-dōr′) (bä-ē′ȧ). Braz. (In.)	13.0 S	38.30 W
94	Salvador (säl-vä-dôr′) (săl′vȧ-dôr) Cen. Am.	13.40 N	88.45 W
81	Salvador L..................La.	29.45 N	90.15 W
96	Salvador Pt..............Ba. Is.	24.27 N	77.45 W
92	Salvatierra (säl-vä-tyĕr′rä)..Mex.	20.14 N	100.53 W
124	Salvatierra..................Sp.	42.5 N	8.31 W
142	Salween R. (säl-wēn′)...Bur.-Chn.	25.0 N	98.45 E
111	Salyany (säl-yä′nĭ)......Sov. Un.	39.35 N	49.0 E
120	Salzburg (sälts′bōōrgh).......Aus.	47.48 N	13.1 E
120	Salzwedel (sälts-vä′dĕl).......Ger.	52.51 N	11.10 E
151	Samal (sä′mäl). Phil. (Manila In.)	14.45 N	120.28 E
63	Samales Group (Is.) (sä-mä′läs) Phil.	6.2 N	121.52 E
153	Samal I. (sä′mäl)...........Phil.	7.0 N	125.45 E
131	Samalut (sä-mä-lōōt′)...Eg. (In.)	28.18 N	30.43 E
97	Samaná (sä-mä-nä′)...Dom. Rep.	19.12 N	69.21 W
97	Samaná B............Dom. Rep.	19.8 N	69.25 W
97	Samaná, C...........Dom. Rep.	19.18 N	69.10 W
97	Samana (Atwood) Cay (I.) (ăt′wŏŏd). Ba. Is.	23.6 N	73.45 W
	Samara, see Kuibishev, Sov. Un.		
151	Samarai (sä-mä-rä′ê)....Pap. Ter.	10.38 S	150.42 E
129	Samara R..............Sov. Un.	48.45 N	35.30 E
110	Samara R..............Sov. Un.	53.8 N	51.30 E
152	Samar I. (sä′mär)...........Phil.	12.0 N	125.0 E
150	Samarinda (sä-mä-rēn′dä)..Indon.	0.29 S	117.8 E
138	Samarkand (sȧ-mȧr-känt′) Sov. Un.	39.40 N	67.0 E
138	Samarovo (sȧ-mȧ-rô′vô)..Sov. Un.	61.0 N	69.0 E
152	Samar Sea (sä′mär)..........Phil.	12.0 N	124.10 E
126	Samassu R. (sä-mäs′sōō)....Sard.	39.30 N	8.55 E
153	Samboan (säm-bō′än)........Phil.	9.32 N	123.20 E
149	Sambon Is. (säm′bōn)........Jap.	33.55 N	138.48 E
121	Sambor (säm′bôr)........Sov. Un.	49.30 N	23.12 E
115	Sambre, R. (säɴ′br′)..........Bel.	50.20 N	4.20 E
147	Samchŏk (säm′chŭk′).........Kor.	37.27 N	129.9 E
135	Same (sä′mä)...............Tan.	4.3 S	37.46 E
145	Samhopa (säm′hō′pä′).......Chn.	24.20 N	116.25 E
111	Sam, L. (sȧm)..........Sov. Un.	45.30 N	56.30 E
4	Samoa (Is.) (sä-mō′ȧ)....Pac. O.	13.42 S	172.0 W
127	Samokov (sä′mô-kôf)..........Bul.	42.20 N	23.33 E
125	Samora (sä-mô′rä).....Port. (In.)	38.56 N	8.53 W
127	Samos (I.) (sä′môs)..........Grc.	37.45 N	26.50 E
127	Samothrace (I.) (săm′ô-thrās). Grc.	40.25 N	25.35 E
152	Sampaloc Pt. (säm-pä′lōk)...Phil.	14.10 N	120.10 E
144	Samshui (säm′shwē′).........Chn.	23.12 N	112.48 E
118	Samsö (I.) (säm′sû)..........Den.	55.50 N	10.35 E
82	Samson (săm′sŭn)............Ala.	31.5 N	86.2 W
148	Samsu (säm′sōō′)............Kor.	41.16 N	128.1 E
111	Samsun (säm′sōōn′)..........Tur.	41.20 N	36.12 E
111	Samtredi (säm′trĕ-dê)...Sov. Un.	42.10 N	42.20 E
111	Samur R. (sä-mōōr′).....Sov. Un.	41.30 N	48.0 E
132	San (sän)............Fr. W. Afr.	13.35 N	4.41 W
140	San′a (sän′ä)..............Yem.	15.44 N	44.5 E
132	Sanaga R. (sä-nä′gä).......Cam.	4.30 N	12.0 E
93	San Agustín (Loxicha) (sän ä-gōōs-tēn′) (lô-kē′chä). Mex.	16.3 N	96.46 W
153	San Agustin, C............Phil.	6.17 N	126.12 E
98	San Ambrosio I. (sän äm-brō′zê-ō) Pac. O.	26.40 S	80.0 W
74	San Andreas (săn ăn′drê-ȧs). Calif.	38.10 N	120.42 W
93	San Andrés (sän än-drās′)...Mex.	18.59 N	97.32 W
93	San Andrés..........Mex. (In.)	19.33 N	99.13 W
93	San Andrés (Miahuatlán) (mē-ȧ-wät-län′). Mex.	16.20 N	96.36 W
94	San Andrés (Petén), L. (pā-tān′) Guat. (In.)	17.0 N	89.50 W
125	San Andrés de Palomar (dā pä-lō-mär′). Sp. (In.)	41.26 N	2.10 E
93	San Andrés Tuxtla (tōōs′tlä). Mex.	18.26 N	95.13 W
93	San Ángel (sän än′ĸäl). Mex. (In.)	19.21 N	99.11 W
80	San Angelo (săn ăn′jĕ-lō)....Tex.	31.27 N	100.26 W
102	San Antonio..................Chl.	33.31 S	71.32 W
151	San Antonio (sän än-tō′nê-ô) Phil. (Manila In.)	14.21 N	121.37 E
152	San Antonio...............Phil.	14.58 N	120.5 E
80	San Antonio (săn ăn-tō′nê-ô). Tex.	29.25 N	98.30 W
125	San Antonio Abad (sän än-tō′nyô ä-bädh′). Sp.	38.59 N	1.19 E
153	San Antonio B.............Phil.	8.38 N	117.35 E
81	San Antonio B..............Tex.	28.20 N	96.45 E
96	San Antonio, C............Cuba	21.55 N	84.55 W
99	San Antonio de Areco (sän än-tō′nyô dā ä-rä′kô) Arg. (Buenos Aires In.)	34.13 S	59.30 W
96	San Antonio de los Baños (dā lōs bän′yōs). Cuba	22.53 N	82.31 W
102	San Antonio de los Cobres (dā lōs kō′brās). Arg.	24.0 S	66.20 W
73	San Antonio, Mt. (săn ăn-tō′nĭ-ō) Calif. (Los Angeles In.)	34.17 N	117.39 W
152	San Antonio, Mt..............Phil.	13.20 N	122.0 E
102	San Antonio Oeste (sän än-tō′nyô ô-ĕs′tȧ). Arg.	40.45 S	64.50 W
74	San Antonio R............Calif.	36.0 N	121.15 W
81	San Antonio R..............Tex.	28.38 N	97.30 W
81	San Augustine (săn ô′gŭs-tēn). Tex.	31.33 N	94.7 W
80	San Bartolo (sän bär-tō′lō)...Mex.	24.42 N	103.11 W
93	San Bartolomé (sän bär-tô-lô-mā′). Mex.	16.21 N	92.34 W
126	San Bartolomeo (sän bär-tô-lô-mā′ō). It.	41.24 N	15.1 E
93	San Bartolo Naucalpán (sän bär-tō′lō nou-käl-pän′). Mex. (In.)	19.28 N	99.14 W
125	San Baudilio de Llobregat (sän bou-dē′lyō dā lyô-brä-gät′) Sp. (In.)	41.21 N	2.3 E
143	San-Beisa-Urgo (Kerulen) (sän-bā′ê-sȧ-ōōr′gō). Mong.	48.12 N	114.34 E
126	San Benedetto del Tronto (sän bā′nȧ-dĕt′tô dĕl trōn′tô). It.	42.57 N	13.52 E
81	San Benito (săn bĕ-nē′tō)....Tex.	26.7 N	97.37 W
74	San Benito R..............Calif.	36.40 N	121.20 W
93	San Bernabé (sän bĕr-nä-bā′) Mex. (In.)	19.19 N	99.15 W
93	San Bernardino (sän bĕr-när-dē′nô). Mex. (In.)	19.29 N	98.54 W
74	San Bernardino (săn bûr-när-dē′nô). Calif.	34.7 N	117.18 W
74	San Bernardino Mts.......Calif.	34.5 N	116.30 W
152	San Bernardino Str. (sän bĕr-när-dē′nô). Phil.	12.30 N	124.11 E
99	San Bernardo (sän bĕr-när′dô) Chl. (Valparaiso In.)	33.34 S	70.44 W
92	San Blas (sän bläs′)........Mex.	21.33 N	105.18 W
82	San Blas, C.................Fla.	29.40 N	85.22 W
95	San Blas, Cordillera de (Mts.) (kôr-dê-lyä′rä dā sän bläs′). Pan.	9.20 N	78.30 W
95	San Blas, G. of..............Pan.	9.30 N	79.0 W
93	San Borja, R. de (rē′ô dā sän bôr′hä). Mex.	19.21 N	99.17 W
88	Sanborn (săn′bŭrn) N. Y. (Niagara Falls In.)	43.8 N	78.54 W
80	San Buenaventura (sän bwā′nȧ-vĕn-tōō′rä). Mex.	27.6 N	101.30 W
101	San Caetano de Odivelas (sän kȧ-ȧ-tä′nōō dā ô-dê-vā′läzh) Braz. (In.)	0.42 S	48.5 W
93	San Carlos (sän kär′lōs).....Mex.	17.50 N	92.33 W
80	San Carlos..................Mex.	24.35 N	98.58 W
152	San Carlos..................Phil.	15.56 N	120.21 E
153	San Carlos..................Phil.	10.30 N	123.25 E
100	San Carlos..................Ven.	9.32 N	68.32 W
75	San Carlos Ind. Res........Ariz.	33.28 N	110.10 W
75	San Carlos Reservoir........Ariz.	33.12 N	110.25 W
95	San Carlos, R..............C. R.	10.40 N	84.20 W
92	San Carlos, R..............Mex.	24.18 N	99.10 W
126	San Cataldo (sän kä-täl′dō)....It.	37.29 N	13.59 E
122	Sancerre (säɴ-sâr′)............Fr.	47.20 N	2.51 E
97	Sanchez (sän′chĕz)....Dom. Rep.	19.13 N	69.38 W
152	Sanchez Mira (sän′chĕs mē′rä) Phil.	18.34 N	121.13 E
92	Sanchez Roman (Tlaltenango) (sän chĕz rō-män′) (tläl-tā-näŋ′gō) Mex.	21.48 N	103.25 W
92	San Ciro (sän sē′rō)........Mex.	21.39 N	99.49 W
124	San Clemente (sän klâ-mĕn′tä). Sp.	39.25 N	2.25 W
74	San Clemente I............Calif.	32.55 N	118.30 W
102	San Clemente, Mt............Chl.	46.35 S	73.28 W
153	Sanco Pt. (sän-kō′)..........Phil.	8.15 N	126.28 E
94	San Cristóbal (sän krēs-tō′bäl) Guat.	15.23 N	90.27 W
100	San Cristóbal................Ven.	7.45 N	72.10 W
93	San Cristóbal................Mex.	16.43 N	92.38 W
100	San Cristóbal (I.)............Ec.	0.59 S	89.30 W
93	San Cristóbal Ecatepec (ȧ-kä-tȧ-pĕk′). Mex.	19.36 N	99.2 W
159	San Cristoval (I.) (sän krēs-tō′väl) Solomon Is.	10.45 S	161.45 E
126	San Croce, C. (sän krō′chā)....It.	37.15 N	15.4 E
96	Sancti Spíritus (säŋk′tê spē′rê-tōōs). Cuba	21.55 N	79.27 W
149	Sanda (sän′dȧ)...............Jap.	34.53 N	135.14 E
150	Sandakan (sȧn-dä′kȧn) (sȧn-dä′kȧn). N. Bor.	5.51 N	118.0 E
153	Sandakan Har. (sȧn-dä′kȧn) N. Bor.	5.53 N	118.8 E
150	Sandalwood (Sumba) I. (săn′dăl-wŏŏd) (sōōm′bä). Indon.	9.45 S	120.0 E
114	Sanday (I.) (sănd′ā). Gt. Brit. (In.)	59.15 N	2.30 W
116	Sandbach (sănd′băch)...Gt. Brit.	53.8 N	2.22 W
72	Sand Cr....Colo. (Colo. Sprs. In.)	38.55 N	104.42 W
118	Sandefjord (sän′dĕ-fyôr′).....Nor.	59.8 N	10.13 E
80	Sanderson (săn′dĕr-sŭn).....Tex.	30.8 N	102.24 W
82	Sandersville (săn′dĕrz-vĭl)....Ga.	32.59 N	82.49 W
160	Sandgate (sănd′gāt).......Austl.	47.19 S	153.4 E
118	Sandhammar, C. (sänt′häm-mȧr) Swe.	55.22 N	14.10 E
77	Sand I....................Wis.	46.58 N	90.58 W
74	San Diego (săn dê-ā′gô).....Calif.	32.44 N	117.10 W
74	San Diego...........Calif. (In.)		
80	San Diego...................Tex.	27.47 N	98.14 W
92	San Diego de la Unión (sän dê-ā′gô dȧ lä ōō-nyōn′). Mex.	21.27 N	100.52 W
74	San Diego R...............Calif.	32.55 N	117.0 W
93	San Dieguito (sän dê-ȧ-gē′tô) Mex. (In.)	19.29 N	98.49 W
73	San Dimas (săn dĭ′mȧs) Calif. (Los Angeles In.)	34.7 N	117.49 W
92	San Dimas (sän dê-mäs′)....Mex.	24.7 N	105.57 W
73	Sand Mt...Ala. (Birmingham In.)	33.43 N	86.42 W
118	Sandnes (sänd′nĕs)...........Nor.	58.54 N	5.45 E
118	Sandoa (sän-dō′ȧ).....Bel. Cong.	9.40 S	23.0 E
121	Sandomierz (sän-dô′ myĕzh)..Pol.	50.39 N	21.45 E
126	San Donà di Piave (sän dô-nä′ dê pyä′vĕ). It.	45.38 N	12.33 E
160	Sandon Bluffs (săn′dŭn) Austl. (In.)	29.40 S	153.19 E
150	Sandoway (sän-dô-wī′)......Bur.	18.25 N	94.28 E
70	Sandpoint (sănd′point)......Ida.	48.16 N	116.33 W
160	Sandringham (săn′drĭng-ăm) Austl. (Melbourne In.)	37.57 S	145.0 E
79	Sand Springs..............Okla.	36.9 N	96.7 W
158	Sandstone (sănd′stōn)......Austl.	27.58 S	119.25 E
77	Sandstone...................Minn.	46.9 N	92.51 W
73	Sandtown (sănd′toun) Ga. (Atlanta In.)	33.43 N	84.34 W
84	Sandusky (săn-dŭs′kê).....Mich.	43.25 N	82.50 W
84	Sandusky....................Ohio	41.27 N	82.41 W
84	Sandusky R..................Ohio	41.10 N	83.10 W
89	Sandwich (sănd′wĭch) Mich. (Detroit In.)	42.18 N	83.3 W
159	Sandwich (Efate) I. (ĕ-fä′tȧ) New Hebr.	17.50 S	168.15 E
73	Sandy (sănd′ê) Utah (Salt Lake City In.)	40.35 N	111.54 W
159	Sandy C..................Austl.	24.30 S	153.15 E
160	Sandy C........Austl. (Tas. In.)	41.26 S	144.45 E
71	Sandy Cr..................Mont.	48.15 N	110.10 W
71	Sandy Cr...................Wyo.	42.5 N	109.35 W
158	Sandy Desert...............Austl.	19.30 S	130.30 E
88	Sandy Hook B. N. J. (New York In.)	40.26 N	74.2 W
85	Sandy Hook C. ....N. J.	40.27 N	74.0 W
87	Sandy I.....................Can.	51.10 N	58.25 W
87	Sandy L.....................Can.	49.15 N	56.50 W
72	Sandy Pt.. Wash. (Vancouver In.)	48.48 N	122.43 W
81	Sandy Point.........Tex. (In.)	29.22 N	95.27 W
102	San Estanislao (sän ĕs-tä-nēs-lä′ō) Par.	24.31 S	56.32 W
102	San Felipe (sän fâ-lē′pȧ).....Chl.	32.50 S	71.50 W
93	San Felipe...........Mex. (In.)	19.31 N	98.54 W
92	San Felipe..................Mex.	22.21 N	105.24 W
151	San Felipe.....Phil. (Manila In.)	14.36 N	121.1 E
100	San Felipe...................Ven.	10.20 N	68.45 W
99	San Felipe, B. Chl. (Magallanes In.)	52.45 S	70.0 W
96	San Felipe Cays (Is.).......Cuba	22.0 N	83.20 W
74	San Felipe Cr...............Calif.	33.10 N	116.0 W
75	San Felipe Ind. Res.........N. M.	35.25 N	106.25 W
93	San Felipe (Jalápa de Diáz) (hä lä′pä dā dē-äz′). Mex.	18.3 N	96.55 W
125	San Feliu de Guixols (sän fâ-lē′ōō dȧ gê-hôls′). Sp.	41.47 N	3.1 E
125	San Feliu de Llobregat (lyô-brä-gät′). Sp. (In.)	41.22 N	2.2 E
98	San Felix I. (sän fâ-lēks′)..Pac. O.	26.20 S	80.10 W
99	San Fernando (sän fĕr-nän′dô) Arg. (Buenos Aires In.)	34.25 S	58.35 W
73	San Fernando Calif. (Los Angeles In.)	34.17 N	118.27 W
102	San Fernando................Chl.	34.32 S	71.0 W
93	San Fernando................Mex.	16.53 N	93.11 W
80	San Fernando................Mex.	24.52 N	98.10 W
153	San Fernando................Phil.	10.10 N	123.42 E
152	San Fernando................Phil.	12.28 N	123.45 E
152	San Fernando................Phil.	15.4 N	120.42 E
152	San Fernando................Phil.	16.37 N	120.20 E
125	San Fernando...........Sp. (In.)	36.28 N	6.12 W
100	San Fernando de Apure (dā ȧ-pōō′rä). Ven.	7.45 N	67.28 W
100	San Fernando de Atabapo (ä-tä-bä′pô). Ven.	3.59 N	67.44 W
125	San Fernando de Henares (ā-nä′räs). Sp. (In.)	40.24 N	3.31 W
100	San Fernando, R............Mex.	25.0 N	98.20 W
83	Sanford (săn′fẽrd).......Fla. (In.)	28.46 N	81.17 W

ăt; finăl; rāte; senâte; ärm; ȧsk; sofȧ; fâre; ch-choose; dh-as th in other; bē; êvent; bĕt; recĕnt; cratẽr; g-go; gh-gutteral g; bĭt; ĭ-short neutral; rīde; ĸ-gutteral k as ch in German ich;

Sanford PRONOUNCING INDEX **San Sebastían**

Page	Name Pronunciation Region	Lat. °′	Long. °′
86	Sanford ... Me.	43.25 N	70.45 W
83	Sanford ... N. C.	35.27 N	79.10 W
52	Sanford, Mt ... Alsk. (In.)	62.10 N	144.10 W
102	San Francisco (sän frän-sēs'kô) Arg.	13.28 S	62.15 W
74	San Francisco (săn frăn-sĭs'kō) Calif.	37.45 N	122.27 W
51	San Francisco ... Calif. (In.)		
93	San Francisco (Ixhuatán) (sän frän-sēs'kô) (ēs-wä-tän'). Mex.	16.22 N	94.28 W
151	San Francisco .. Phil. (Manila In.)	14.39 N	121.0 E
94	San Francisco (Gotera) (gô-tā'rä) Sal.	13.47 N	88.7 W
74	San Francisco B ... Calif.	37.40 N	122.20 W
92	San Francisco de los Adames (sän frän-sēs'kô dā lōs ä-dä'mās). Mex.	22.25 N	102.14 W
92	San Francisco del Rincón (dĕl rēn-kōn'). Mex.	21.2 N	101.47 W
97	San Francisco de Macoris (dā mä-kō'rēs). Dom. Rep.	19.18 N	70.16 W
90	San Francisco de Paula (sän frän-sēs'kô dā pou'lä) Cuba (Habana In.)	23.4 N	82.16 W
75	San Francisco R ... Ariz.-N. M.	33.20 N	109.0 W
73	San Gabriel (săn gä-brē-ĕl') (gā'brē-ĕl). Calif. (Los Angeles In.)	34.6 N	118.7 W
92	San Gabriel ... Mex.	19.46 N	103.46 W
93	San Gabriel Chilac (chē-läk') Mex.	18.18 N	97.21 W
73	San Gabriel Mts. Calif. (Los Angeles In.)	34.23 N	118.0 W
73	San Gabriel R. Calif. (Los Angeles In.)	33.50 N	118.7 W
81	San Gabriel R ... Tex.	30.40 N	97.20 W
73	San Gabriel R., West Fork Calif. (Los Angeles In.)	34.15 N	117.57 W
79	Sangamon R. (săŋ'gá-mŭn) ... Ill.	40.0 N	89.50 W
133	Sanga R. (säŋ-gä) Fr. Eq. Afr.-Cam.	3.30 N	16.0 E
153	Sanga Sanga I. (säng-ä' säng-ä') Phil.	5.5 N	119.46 E
144	Sangchi (säng'chē') ... Chn.	29.20 N	109.57 E
74	Sanger (săng'ẽr) ... Calif.	36.42 N	119.33 W
120	Sangerhausen (säng'ẽr-hou-zĕn) Ger.	51.28 N	11.17 E
151	Sangihe (I.) (säŋ'gē-ē) ... Indon.	3.30 N	125.30 E
124	Sangüesa (säŋ-gwā'sä) ... Sp.	42.36 N	1.15 W
125	San Ginés de Vilasar (sän ĸē-nās' dā vē-lä-sär'). Sp. (In.)	41.30 N	2.19 E
117	San Giorgio a Cremona (sän jôr'jō ä krā-mō'nä). It. (Napoli In.)	40.49 N	14.20 E
117	San Giovanni a Teduccio (sän jō-vän'nē ä tā-dōō'chō) It. (Napoli In.)	40.49 N	14.19 E
126	San Giovanni in Fiore (sän jō-vän'nē ēn fyō'rā). It.	39.15 N	16.42 E
147	Sangju (säng'jōō') ... Kor.	36.24 N	128.10 E
124	Sangonera R. (säŋ-gō-nā'rä) ... Sp.	37.40 N	1.40 W
73	San Gorgonio Mt. (săn gôr-gō'nĭ-ō) Calif. (Los Angeles In.)	34.6 N	116.50 W
78	Sangre de Cristo Mts. (săŋ'grā dā krēs'tō). Colo.	37.40 N	105.40 W
126	Sangro R. (säŋ'grō) ... It.	42.0 N	14.20 E
83	Sanibel I. (săn'ĭ-bĕl) ... Fla. (In.)	26.27 N	82.5 W
93	San Ildefonso (sän ēl-dā-fōn'sō) Mex. (In.)	19.37 N	99.17 W
93	San Ildefonso (Villa Alta) (vēl'yä äl'tä). Mex.	17.20 N	96.10 W
152	San Ildefonso, C ... Phil.	16.3 N	122.2 E
124	San Ildefonso o la Granja (sän ēl-dā-fōn'sō ō lä grän'khä). Sp.	40.55 N	4.1 W
76	Sanish (sä'nĭsh) ... N. D.	47.59 N	102.32 W
153	San Isidro (sän ē-sē'drō) ... Phil.	11.23 N	124.21 E
73	San Jacinto (săn já-sĭn'tō) Calif. (Los Angeles In.)	33.47 N	116.58 W
95	San Jacinto (sän hä-sēn'tō) ... Nic.	11.30 N	83.48 W
152	San Jacinto ... Phil.	12.32 N	123.42 E
73	San Jacinto R. (săn já-sĭn'tō) Calif. (Los Angeles In.)	33.50 N	117.0 W
81	San Jacinto R ... Tex.	30.0 N	95.8 W
93	San Jerónimo (sän hā-rō'nē-mō) Mex. (In.)	19.20 N	99.13 W
93	San Jerónimo (Ixtepec) (ēs-tā-pĕk'). Mex.	16.35 N	95.5 W
100	San Jerónimo, Cerro (Mt.) (sän hā-rō'nē-mō). Peru (In.)	12.0 S	77.3 W
92	San Jerónimo de Juárez (dā hwä'rāz). Mex.	17.8 N	100.34 W
93	San Joaquín (sän hō-ä-kēn') Mex. (In.)	19.32 N	98.50 W
153	San Joaquin ... Phil.	10.36 N	122.9 E
74	San Joaquin R. (săn hwä-kēn') Calif.	37.30 N	121.10 W
101	San Jose (sän hō-sā') ... Bol.	17.30 S	60.30 W
74	San Jose (săn hō-zā') ... Calif.	37.20 N	121.55 W
95	San José (sän hō-sā') ... C. R.	9.58 N	84.4 W
94	San José ... Guat.	13.57 N	90.49 W
152	San José ... Phil.	12.21 N	121.3 E
152	San José ... Phil.	13.41 N	123.31 E
152	San José ... Phil.	13.51 N	121.7 E
152	San José ... Phil.	15.47 N	120.59 E
102	San José ... Ur.	34.25 S	56.45 W
153	San José de Buenavista (dā buā-nä-vēs'tä). Phil.	10.45 N	121.57 E
99	San José de la Esquina (dā lä ĕs-kē'nä). Arg. (Buenos Aires In.)	33.6 S	61.42 W
151	San José del Monte (sän hō-sā' dĕl mōn'tā). Phil. (Manila In.)	14.50 N	121.3 E
73	San Jose Hills (săn hō-zā') Calif. (Los Angeles In.)	34.4 N	117.50 W
95	San José I ... Pan.	8.17 N	79.7 W
75	San Jose R ... N. M.	35.15 N	107.55 W
99	San José, R. Ur. (Buenos Aires In.)	34.10 S	56.45 W
102	San Juan (sän hwän') ... Arg.	31.40 S	68.35 W
102	San Juan (State) ... Arg.	31.0 S	69.0 W
97	San Juan ... Dom. Rep.	18.48 N	71.14 W
93	San Juan (Guichicovi) (gē-chē-kō'vē). Mex.	16.59 N	5.5 W
93	San Juan (Mazatlán) (mä-zä-tlän'). Mex.	17.3 N	95.27 W
152	San Juan ... Phil.	16.40 N	122.20 E
91	San Juan ... P. R. (In.)	18.30 N	66.10 W
92	San Juan Bautista del Téul (sän hwän' bou-tēs'tä dĕl tā'ōōl). Mex.	21.32 N	100.35 W
91	San Juan, C ... P. R. (In.)	18.20 N	65.36 W
92	San Juan Capistrano (kä-pēs-trä'nō). Mex.	22.36 N	104.5 W
74	San Juan Cr. (săn hwän') ... Calif.	35.30 N	120.10 W
80	San Juan de Guadalupe (sän hwän dā gwä-dhä-lōō'pā). Mex.	24.38 N	102.43 W
80	San Juan del Mezquital (dĕl mĕz-kē-täl'). Mex.	24.20 N	103.20 W
151	San Juan del Monte (dĕl mōn'tā) Phil. (Manila In.)	14.37 N	121.2 E
95	San Juan del Norte (Greytown) (dĕl nôr'tā) (grā'toun). Nic.	10.56 N	83.46 W
95	San Juan del Norte B ... Nic.	11.10 N	83.40 W
92	San Juan de los Lagos (dā lōs lä'gōs). Mex.	21.16 N	102.17 W
92	San Juan del Río (dĕl rē'ō) .. Mex.	20.23 N	99.59 W
80	San Juan del Río ... Mex.	24.47 N	104.28 W
94	San Juan del Sur (dĕl sōōr') .. Nic.	11.15 N	85.53 W
125	San Juan de Vilasar (dā vē-lä-sär') Sp. (In.)	41.30 N	2.23 E
93	San Juan Evangelista (å-väŋ-ĸä-lēs'tä). Mex.	17.54 N	95.7 W
72	San Juan I. Wash. (Vancouver In.)	48.33 N	123.5 W
153	San Juanico Str. (sän hwä-nē'kō) Phil.	11.25 N	124.59 E
92	San Juanito I. (sän hwä-nē'tō) Mex.	21.43 N	106.38 W
75	San Juan Mts. (săn hwän') ... Colo.	37.40 N	107.10 W
93	San Juan, R. (sän hwän') ... Mex.	18.0 N	95.13 W
80	San Juan, R ... Mex.	26.0 N	99.12 W
94	San Juan, R ... Nic.-C. R.	10.50 N	84.15 W
75	San Juan R. (săn hwän') Utah-N. M.	37.15 N	110.20 W
80	San Juan Sabinas (sä-bē'näs). Mex.	27.55 N	101.17 W
96	San Juan y Martínez (ē mär-tē'nĕz) Cuba	22.12 N	83.48 W
102	San Justo (sän hōōs'tō). Arg. (In.)	34.31 S	58.33 W
132	Sankarani R. (sän'kä-rä'nē) Fr. W. Afr.	11.0 N	8.30 W
144	Sankiang (sän'kyäng') ... Chn.	26.41 N	109.2 E
134	Sankishia (sän-kē'shē-ä). Bel. Cong.	9.38 S	25.48 W
134	Sankuru R. (sän-kōō'rōō) Bel. Cong.	6.0 S	23.45 E
51	San Leandro (săn lē-ăn'drō) Calif. (San Francisco In.)	37.43 N	122.10 W
51	San Lorenzo (săn lō-rĕn'zō) Calif. (San Francisco In.)	37.41 N	122.8 W
94	San Lorenzo (sän lō-rĕn'zō). Hond.	13.25 N	87.12 W
95	San Lorenzo ... Pan.	8.18 N	82.8 W
124	San Lorenzo del Escorial (sän lō-rĕn'thō dĕl ĕs-kō-rē-äl'). Sp.	40.35 N	4.1 W
100	San Lorenzo I. (sän lō-rĕn'zō) Peru (In.)	12.6 S	77.14 W
125	Sanlúcar de Barrameda (sän-lōō'kär dā bär-rä-mā'dhä). Sp. (In.)	36.46 N	6.21 W
100	San Lucas (sän lōō'käs) ... Bol.	20.1 S	64.68 W
93	San Lucas ... Mex. (In.)	19.16 N	98.52 W
93	San Lucas (Ojitlán) (ō-ĸē-tlän') Mex.	18.4 N	96.23 W
102	San Luis (sän lōō-ēs') ... Arg.	33.20 S	66.20 W
102	San Luis (State) ... Arg.	34.0 S	66.0 W
97	San Luis ... Cuba	20.11 N	75.51 W
151	San Luis ... Phil. (Manila In.)	15.3 N	120.44 E
151	San Luis ... Phil. (Manila In.)	13.50 N	120.53 E
92	San Luis de la Paz (dā lä päz') Mex.	21.18 N	100.31 W
80	San Luis del Cordero (dĕl kôr-dā'rō). Mex.	25.25 N	104.20 W
74	San Luis Obispo (ō-bĭs'pō) .. Calif.	35.18 N	120.40 W
74	San Luis Obispo B ... Calif.	35.7 N	120.50 W
92	San Luis Potosí (pō-tō-sē') .. Mex.	22.9 N	100.58 W
92	San Luis Potosí (State) ... Mex.	22.40 N	100.50 W
74	San Luis Rey R. (rā'ē) ... Calif.	33.20 N	117.10 W
75	San Marcial (săn mär-shäl'). N. M.	33.42 N	106.59 W
126	San Marco (sän mär'kō) ... It.	41.43 N	15.38 E
94	San Marcos (sän mär'kōs) .. Guat.	14.57 N	91.48 W
92	San Marcos ... Mex.	16.46 N	99.28 W
93	San Marcos ... Mex. (In.)	19.18 N	98.52 W
80	San Marcos (săn mär'kōs) ... Tex.	29.53 N	97.55 W
81	San Marcos R ... Tex.	29.40 N	97.40 W
152	San Mariano (sän mä-rē-ä'nō) Phil.	17.0 N	121.59 E
126	San Marino (sän mä-rē'nō) ... Eur.	43.56 N	12.25 E
126	San Marino ... San Marino	43.56 N	12.25 E
102	San Martín (sän mär-tēn') Arg. (In.)	34.35 S	58.32 W
92	San Martín ... Mex.	21.24 N	98.39 W
93	San Martín (Vol.) ... Mex.	18.36 N	95.10 W
125	San Martín de la Vega (sän märtēn' dā lä vä'gä). Sp. (In.)	40.12 N	3.34 W
92	San Martín Hidalgo (ē-däl'gō) Mex.	20.27 N	103.56 W
102	San Martín, L ... Chl.-Arg.	48.45 S	72.40 W
74	San Mateo (săn mä-tā'ō) ... Calif.	37.32 N	122.19 W
125	San Mateo (sän mä-tā'ō) ... Sp.	40.26 N	0.8 E
151	San Mateo ... Phil. (Manila In.)	14.42 N	121.8 E
93	San Mateo (Etlatongo) (ĕ-tlä-tōŋ'gō). Mex.	17.1 N	97.1 W
102	San Matias, G. of (sän mä-tē'äs) Arg.	41.30 S	64.0 W
93	San Miguel (sän mê-gâl') ... Mex.	18.9 N	97.10 W
93	San Miguel ... Mex. (In.)	19.32 N	98.53 W
93	San Miguel ... Mex. (In.)	19.33 N	99.23 W
152	San Miguel ... Phil.	15.9 N	120.58 E
94	San Miguel ... Sal.	13.32 N	88.13 W
93	San Miguel (Sola de Vega) (sō'lä dā vā'gä). Mex.	16.30 N	96.58 W
93	San Miguel (Talea de Castro) (tä-lā'ä dā käs'trō). Mex.	17.22 N	96.15 W
94	San Miguel (Vol.) (sän mê-gâl'). Sal.	13.27 N	88.17 W
152	San Miguel B ... Phil.	13.50 N	123.10 E
92	San Miguel de Allende (dā ä-lyĕn'dā). Mex.	20.55 N	100.44 W
92	San Miguel de Mezquital (dĕl mĕz-kē-täl'). Mex.	24.17 N	103.27 W
92	San Miguel el Alto (ĕl äl'tō). Mex.	21.2 N	102.18 W
95	San Miguel G ... Pan.	8.20 N	78.20 W
74	San Miguel I ... Calif.	34.5 N	120.25 W
153	San Miguel I ... Phil.	7.45 N	118.32 E
75	San Miguel R. (săn mê-gĕl'). Colo.	38.12 N	108.25 W
145	Sanmun B. (sän'mōōn') ... Chn.	29.8 N	121.40 E
152	San Narciso (sän när-sē'sō) .. Phil.	13.33 N	122.32 E
152	San Narciso ... Phil.	15.1 N	120.5 E
152	San Nicolas (sän nē-kō-läs') .. Phil.	16.5 N	120.45 E
74	San Nicolas I. (săn nĭ'kō-lȧs). Calif.	33.15 N	119.30 W
123	Sannois (sȧ-nwä') ... Fr. (In.)	48.58 N	2.16 E
131	Sannûris (sän-nōō'rēs) ... Eg. (In.)	29.27 N	30.51 E
121	Sanok (sä'nôk) ... Pol.	49.32 N	22.12 E
93	San Pablo (sän pä'blō). Mex. (In.)	19.19 N	99.8 W
152	San Pablo ... Phil.	14.4 N	121.20 E
152	San Pablo ... Phil.	17.28 N	121.48 E
74	San Pablo B. (săn păb'lō) ... Calif.	38.5 N	122.30 W
95	San Pablo, R. (sän päb'lō) ... Pan.	8.10 N	81.15 W
152	San Pascual (sän päs-kwäl') .. Phil.	13.8 N	123.0 E
99	San Pedro (sän pā'drō) Arg. (Buenos Aires In.)	33.39 S	59.38 W
74	San Pedro (săn pē'drō) ... Calif.	33.45 N	118.25 W
93	San Pedro (sän pā'drō) ... Mex.	18.42 N	92.25 W
93	San Pedro ... Mex. (In.)	19.16 N	99.19 W
92	San Pedro (Amusgos) (ä-mōōs'gōs) Mex.	16.38 N	98.6 W
93	San Pedro (Pochutla) (pō-chōō'tlä) Mex.	15.43 N	96.28 W
102	San Pedro ... Par.	24.5 S	57.10 W
151	San Pedro (sän pä'drō) Phil. (Manila In.)	14.23 N	121.4 E
94	San Pedro ... Sal.	13.48 N	88.58 W
73	San Pedro B. (săn pē'drō) Calif. (Los Angeles In.)	33.44 N	118.13 W
153	San Pedro B. (sän pä'drō) ... Phil.	11.10 N	125.6 E
94	San Pedro del Norte (dĕl nôr'tā) Nic.	13.0 N	84.59 W
97	San Pedro de Macorís (dā mä-kō-rēs'). Dom. Rep.	18.28 N	69.18 W
125	San Pedro de Ribas (dā rē-bäs) Sp. (In.)	41.15 N	1.47 E
125	San Pedro de Ruidevitlles (dā rōō-ē'dhä-vēt'lyäs). Sp. (In.)	41.26 N	1.43 E
92	San Pedro Lagunillas (lä-gōō-nēl'yäs). Mex.	21.12 N	104.46 W
80	San Pedro las Colonias (läs kō-lō'nyäs). Mex.	25.45 N	103.0 W
75	San Pedro R. (săn pē'drō) ... Ariz.	32.30 N	110.30 W
96	San Pedro (sän pä'drō) ... Cuba	21.5 N	78.12 W
94	San Pedro, R ... Guat. (In.)	17.10 N	90.20 W
93	San Pedro R ... Mex.	17.40 N	91.8 W
92	San Pedro, R ... Mex.	22.16 N	105.0 W
80	San Pedro, R ... Mex.	28.10 N	105.30 W
94	San Pedro Sula (sōō'lä) ... Hond.	15.27 N	88.0 W
93	San Pedro y San Pablo (Teposcolula) (ē sän pä'blō) (tā-pō-skō-lōō'lä). Mex.	17.31 N	97.30 W
126	San Pietro (I.) (sän pyā'trō). Sard.	39.9 N	8.15 E
152	San Quintin (sän kēn-tēn') ... Phil.	15.59 N	120.47 E
121	San R. (sän) ... Pol.	49.50 N	22.53 E
102	San Rafael (sän rä-fä-äl') ... Arg.	34.29 S	68.29 W
74	San Rafael (săn rȧ-fĕl') ... Calif.	37.59 N	122.31 W
93	San Rafael (sän rä-fä-äl') Mex. (In.)	19.27 N	99.15 W
93	San Rafael ... Mex. (In.)	19.34 N	99.11 W
151	San Rafael (sän rä-fä-äl') Phil. (Manila In.)	14.59 N	120.56 E
75	San Rafael R. (săn rȧ-fĕl') ... Utah	39.0 N	110.40 W
95	San Ramón (sän rä-mōn') ... C. R.	10.7 N	84.30 W
153	San Remigio (sän rā-mē'hyō) Phil.	11.5 N	123.57 E
126	San Remo (sän rā'mō) ... It.	43.49 N	7.46 E
151	San Roque (sän rō'kȧ) Phil. (Manila In.)	14.29 N	120.52 E
124	San Roque ... Sp.	36.13 N	5.22 W
80	San Saba (săn sä'bȧ) ... Tex.	31.11 N	98.43 W
80	San Saba R ... Tex.	31.0 N	99.18 W
132	San Sabastián (sän sȧ-bäs-tē-än') Can. Is.	28.10 N	17.10 W
94	San Salvador (sän säl-vä-dōr'). Sal.	13.44 N	89.10 W
97	San Salvador (Watling) I. (săn săl'vȧ-dôr). Ba. Is.	24.0 N	74.0 W
132	Sansanné-Mango (sän-sȧ-nā'-mäɴ'gō). Fr. W. Afr.	10.30 N	0.28 E
125	San Saturnino de Noya (sän sä-tōōr-nē'nō dā nō'yä). Sp. (In.)	41.24 N	1.47 E
124	San Sebastian (sän sȧ-bäs-tyän') Sp.	43.19 N	1.59 W
93	San Sebastian (Tecomaxtlahuaca) (tā'kō-mäs-tlä-wä'kä). Mex.	17.41 N	96.56 W
117	San Sebastiano al Vesuvio (sän sä-bäs-tyä'nō äl vä-sōō'vē-ō) It. (Napoli In.)	40.50 N	14.25 E
125	San Sebastian de los Reyes (sän sä-bäs-tyän' dā lōs rä'yĕs). Sp. (In.)	40.33 N	3.39 W
93	San Sebastián Zinacatepec (zē-nä-kä-tä-pĕk'). Mex.	18.18 N	97.14 W

ng-sing; ŋ-baŋk; ɴ-nasalized n; nŏd; cŏmmit; ōld; ôbey; ôrder; fōōd; fŏŏt; ou-out; s-soft; sh-dish; th-thin; pūre; ûnite; ûrn; stŭd; circŭs; ü-as "y" in study; '-indeterminate vowel.

Sansego PRONOUNCING INDEX São Paulo

Page Name Pronunciation Region Lat. °′ Long. °′

126 Sansego (I.) (sän-sä'gô)....Yugo. 44.31 N 14.17 E
126 San Severo (sän sĕ-vâ'rō)......It. 41.41 N 15.23 E
151 San Simon (sän sē-mōn') Phil. (Manila In.) 15.0 N 120.45 E
117 San Strato (sän strä'tô) It. (Napoli In.) 40.48 N 14.12 E
74 Santa Ana (săn'tȧ ăn'ȧ)....Calif. 33.44 N 117.51 W
92 Santa Ana (sän'tä ä'nä).....Mex. 19.18 N 98.10 W
94 Santa Ana................Sal. 14.2 N 89.34 W
73 Santa Ana Mts............Calif. 33.50 N 117.37 W
74 Santa Ana R. (săn'tȧ ă'nȧ)..Calif. 33.55 N 117.35 W
117 Santa Anastasia (sän'tä ä-näs-tä'zē-ä).It. (Napoli In.) 40.52 N 14.24 E
80 Santa Anna (săn'tȧ ăn'ȧ)....Tex. 31.43 N 99.20 W
99 Santa Anna B. (sän'tä ä'nȧ) Braz. (Rio de Janeiro In.) 22.40 S 41.50 W
117 Sant' Agnello (sän tä-nyĕl'ō) It. (Napoli In.) 40.37 N 14.25 E
102 Sant' Anna do Livramento (sän tä'nȧ dŏŏ lê-vrä-mĕṇ'tōō).Braz. 30.40 S 55.32 W
101 Sant' Anna do Paranhiba (dŏŏ pä-rä-nä-ē'bȧ).Braz. 19.43 S 51.2 W
101 Santa Barbara (sän'tȧ bär'bä-rä) Braz. 19.59 S 43.28 W
74 Santa Barbara (săn'tȧ bär'bȧ-rȧ) Calif. 34.25 N 119.41 W
80 Santa Barbara............Mex. 26.47 N 105.49 W
153 Santa Barbara............Phil. 10.48 N 122.31 E
74 Santa Barbara Chan. (săn'tȧ bär'bȧ-rȧ).Calif. 34.13 N 120.0 W
74 Santa Barbara I..........Calif. 33.28 N 119.2 W
74 Santa Barbara Is.........Calif. 33.50 N 120.0 W
94 Santa Barbara, R. (sän'tä bär'bä-rȧ).Hond. 14.36 N 88.14 W
74 Santa Catalina I. (săn'tȧ kă-tȧ-lē'nȧ).Calif. 33.22 N 118.25 W
93 Santa Catarina (sän'tä kä-tä-rē'nȧ).Mex. (In.) 19.19 N 98.58 W
93 Santa Catarina........Mex. (In.) 19.29 N 98.46 W
80 Santa Catarina............Mex. 25.40 N 100.27 W
93 Santa Catarina (Yosonotú) (yō-sô-nô-tōō').Mex. 16.53 N 97.34 W
93 Santa Catarina, Cerro (Mts.) Mex. (In.) 19.20 N 99.0 W
102 Santa Catharina (State) (kä-tä-rē'nȧ).Braz. 27.0 S 51.0 W
74 Santa Clara (săn'tȧ klâ'rȧ)..Calif. 37.21 N 121.58 W
96 Santa Clara (sän'tä klä'rä)..Cuba 22.22 N 79.58 W
96 Santa Clara (State)........Cuba 22.20 N 80.30 W
92 Santa Clara..............Mex. 19.25 N 101.35 W
80 Santa Clara..............Mex. 24.27 N 103.20 W
94 Santa Clara (Vol.)..........Nic. 12.42 N 86.57 W
96 Santa Clara B............Cuba 23.5 N 80.55 W
93 Santa Clara Cuautitla (sän'tä klä'rȧ kwä'ōō-tē'tlä).Me. (In.) 19.43 N 99.4 W
78 Santa Clara Pueblo Ind. Res. (săn'tȧ klă'rȧ pwĕb'lō).N. M. 36.00 N 106.15 W
74 Santa Clara R. (săn'tȧ klă'rȧ) Calif. 34.23 N 118.50 W
125 Santa Coloma de Farnés (sän'tä kō-lō'mä dā fär-näs').Sp. 41.52 N 2.40 E
124 Santa Comba (sän'tä kōm'bä).Sp. 43.3 N 8.49 W
102 Santa Cruz (State) (sän'tä krōōz') Arg. 47.30 S 70.0 W
100 Santa Cruz................Bol. 17.45 S 63.32 W
101 Santa Cruz...............Braz. 19.58 S 40.15 W
74 Santa Cruz (săn'tȧ krōōz').Calif. 36.58 N 122.3 W
99 Santa Cruz (sän'tä krōōz') Chl. (Valparaiso In.) 34.38 S 71.24 W
94 Santa Cruz...............C. R. 10.17 N 85.37 W
92 Santa Cruz...............Mex. 20.38 N 101.1 W
80 Santa Cruz...............Mex. 25.48 N 105.25 W
153 Santa Cruz...............Phil. 6.50 N 125.25 E
152 Santa Cruz...............Phil. 13.28 N 122.1 E
152 Santa Cruz...............Phil. 14.17 N 121.25 E
152 Santa Cruz...............Phil. 15.46 N 119.54 E
152 Santa Cruz...............Phil. 17.5 N 120.28 E
93 Santa Cruz (Itundujia) (ē-tōōn-dōō-Kē'ä).Mex. 16.51 N 97.39 W
124 Santa Cruz de la Zarza (sän'tä krōōth' dā lä thär'thä).Sp. 39.58 N 3.9 W
96 Santa Cruz del Sur (sän'tä krōōz dĕl sōōr').Cuba 20.42 N 78.1 W
132 Santa Cruz de Tenerife (dā tā-nā-rē'fā).Can. Is. 28.32 N 16.14 W
74 Santa Cruz I.............Calif. 34.1 N 119.50 W
159 Santa Cruz Is. (sän'tä krōōz') Solomon Is. 11.0 S 166.0 E
102 Santa Cruz, R..............Arg. 50.20 S 70.30 W
126 Santa Eufemia, G. of (sän'tä â-ōō-fā'mê-ä).It. 38.50 N 16.10 E
125 Santa Eulalia del Río (sän'tä â-ōō-lä'lê-ä dĕl rē'ō).Sp. 38.59 N 1.30 E
102 Santa Fé (sän'tä fā').......Arg. 31.40 S 60.45 W
102 Santa Fé (State)............Arg. 30.0 S 61.0 W
96 Santa Fé........Isle of Pines 21.45 N 82.37 W
93 Santa Fé..........Mex. (In.) 19.23 N 99.11 W
75 Santa Fe (săn'tȧ fā')........N. M. 35.40 N 106.5 W
124 Santafé (sän'tä-fā')..........Sp. 37.11 N 3.42 W
92 Santa Inés Ahuatempán (ä-hwä-tĕm-pän').Mex. 18.25 N 98.1 W
102 Santa Inés I. (ê-näs')........Chl. 53.45 S 73.0 W
99 Santa Isabel (ê-zä-bĕl') Braz. (Rio de Janeiro In.) 23.19 S 46.15 W
132 Santa Isabel (ê-sä-bĕl')...Sp. Gui. 3.50 N 8.45 E
94 Santa Isabel, R............Guat. 16.0 N 89.40 W
96 Santa Lucia (sän'tä lōō-sē'ä).Cuba 21.21 N 77.32 W
152 Santa Lucia...............Phil. 17.8 N 120.28 E
96 Santa Lucia B.............Cuba 22.41 N 83.59 W
99 Santa Lucia, R. Ur. (Buenos Aires In.) 34.30 S 56.25 W

93 Santa Lucrecia (sän'tä lōō-krā'sê-ȧ).Mex. 17.26 N 95.0 W
101 Santa Luzia (sän-tȧ lōō-zē'ȧ).Braz. 16.18 S 47.58 W
93 Santa Margarita (Huitepec) (mär-gä-rē'tä) (wê-tȧ-pĕk').Mex. 16.54 N 95.43 W
102 Santa Maria (mä-rē'ȧ)........Braz. 29.35 S 53.40 W
74 Santa Maria (săn-tȧ mȧ-rē'ȧ) Calif. 34.58 N 120.29 W
126 Santa Maria (sän-tä mä-rē'ä)..It. 41.4 N 14.15 E
152 Santa Maria..............Phil. 14.48 N 120.58 E
151 Santa Maria...Phil. (Manila In.) 14.32 N 121.29 E
93 Santa María (Huazolotlitlán) (wä-zô-lô-tlê-tlän').Mex. 16.18 N 97.54 W
93 Santa María (Zaachila) (zä-ä-chē'lä).Mex. 16.57 N 96.45 W
93 Santa María Asunción (Tlaxiaco) (ä-sōōn-syōn') (tläk-sê-ä'kô) Mex. 17.15 N 97.40 W
124 Santa Maria, C.............Port. 36.57 N 7.55 W
96 Santa Maria Cays (Is.) (săn'tȧ mȧ-rē'ȧ kēz).Cuba 22.38 N 79.5 W
92 Santa María del Oro (sän'tä mä-rē'ä dĕl ō'rô).Mex. 21.17 N 104.36 W
92 Santa María de los Ángeles (dā lōs äŋ'Kā-läs).Mex. 22.15 N 103.18 W
92 Santa María del Río (dĕl rē'ō) Mex. 21.47 N 100.43 W
92 Santa María de Ocotán (dā ō-kō-tän').Mex. 22.56 N 104.30 W
127 Santa Maria di Leuca, C. dē lâ-ōō'kä).It. 39.47 N 18.22 E
132 Santa Maria I........Az. Is. (In.) 36.55 N 25.5 W
92 Santa María, R............Mex. 21.30 N 100.8 W
151 Santa Maria R.Phil. (Manila In.) 14.50 N 121.0 E
94 Santa María (Vol.)..........Guat. 14.45 N 91.34 W
100 Santa Marta (sän'tä mär'tä)..Col. 11.15 N 74.10 W
124 Santa Marta...............Sp. 38.39 N 6.38 W
74 Santa Monica (săn'tȧ mŏn'ĭ-kȧ) Calif. 34.1 N 118.28 W
73 Santa Monica Bay.........Calif. 34.57 N 118.28 W
73 Santa Monica Mts. Calif. (Los Angeles In.) 34.7 N 118.32 W
93 Santa Monica (sän'tä mō'nê-kä) Mex. (In.) 19.27 N 98.52 W
124 Santander (sän-tän-dâr')......Sp. 43.28 N 3.49 W
125 Santañy (sän-tän'yê)..........Sp. 39.22 N 3.6 E
74 Santa Paula (săn'tȧ pô'lȧ)..Calif. 34.22 N 119.4 W
101 Santa Philomena (sän'tä fê-lô-mä'nȧ).Braz. 9.0 S 45.45 W
101 Santarem (sän-tä-rĕṅ').Braz. (In.) 13.40 S 39.15 W
101 Santarem..................Braz. 2.28 S 54.32 W
124 Santarem.................Port. 39.14 N 8.42 W
125 Santarem (Prov.).......Port. (In.) 38.52 N 8.48 W
96 Santaren Chan. (sän-tä-rĕn').W. I. 23.50 N 79.30 W
75 Santa Rita (săn'tȧ rē'tȧ)...N. M. 32.47 N 108.4 W
151 Santa Rita (sän'tä rē'tä) Phil. (Manila In.) 15.2 N 120.32 E
90 Santa Rita Mt....Pan. (C. Z. In.) 9.19 N 79.47 W
74 Santa Rosa (săn'tȧ rō'zȧ)...Calif. 38.26 N 122.42 W
94 Santa Rosa (sän'tä rō'sä)..Guat. 14.22 N 90.15 W
94 Santa Rosa..............Hond. 14.42 N 88.48 W
93 Santa Rosa...............Mex. 18.48 N 97.12 W
78 Santa Rosa (săn'tȧ rō'sȧ)...N. M. 34.55 N 104.40 W
152 Santa Rosa (sän'tä rō'sä)...Phil. 14.18 N 121.7 E
102 Santa Rosa de Toay (tō'ī)...Arg. 36.40 S 64.20 W
84 Santa Rosa I. (săn'tȧ rō'zȧ).Calif. 33.55 N 120.10 W
74 Santa Rosa Ind. Res.......Calif. 33.30 N 116.42 W
80 Santa Rosalia (Camargo) (sän'tä rō-zä'lê-ȧ) (kä-mär'gō).Mex. 27.40 N 105.10 W
93 Santa Rosa, Monte (Mts.) (mōn'tä sän'tä rō'sȧ).Mex. (In.) 19.17 N 99.17 W
70 Santa Rosa Mts. (săn'tȧ rō'zȧ) Nev. 41.40 N 117.40 W
73 Santa Susana (săn'tȧ sōō-zä'nȧ) Calif. (Los Angeles In.) 34.17 N 118.43 W
73 Santa Susana Mts. Calif. (Los Angeles In.) 34.19 N 118.38 W
94 Santa Tecla (Nueva San Salvador) (sän'ta tĕk'la) (nwā'vä sän säl-vä-dôr').Sal. 13.41 N 89.17 W
74 Santa Ynez R. (săn'tȧ ē-nĕz') Calif. 34.37 N 120.10 W
74 Santa Ysabel Ind. Res. (săn-tȧ ĭ-zȧ-bĕl').Calif. 33.10 N 116.40 W
74 Santee (săn-tē')......Calif. (In.) 32.50 N 116.58 W
83 Santee Canal..............S. C. 33.20 N 80.12 W
83 Santee R..................S. C. 33.30 N 80.0 W
92 Santelmo, Pt. (sän-tĕl'mô)...Mex. 18.22 N 103.32 W
99 Santiago............Chl. (In.)
102 Santiago (sän-tê-ä'gô).......Chl. 33.28 S 70.45 W
100 Santiago (I.)...............Ec. 0.15 S 90.45 W
94 Santiago................Hond. 15.17 N 87.56 W
92 Santiago (Juxtlahuaca) (hōōs'tlä-wä'kȧ).Mex. 17.18 N 98.2 W
93 Santiago (Trejúpam) (trȧ-hōō'päm).Mex. 17.40 N 97.25 W
93 Santiago (Zacatepec) (zä-kä'tȧ-pĕk').Mex. 17.10 N 95.53 W
92 Santiago.................Mex. 19.48 N 99.5 W
95 Santiago..................Pan. 8.6 N 80.58 W
151 Santiago, C. (sän-tê-ä'gô) Phil. (Manila In.) 13.47 N 120.36 E
152 Santiago.................Phil. 16.41 N 121.32 E
124 Santiago..................Sp. 42.52 N 8.33 W
97 Santiago de Cuba (dā kōō'bȧ) Cuba 20.0 N 75.49 W
96 Santiago de las Vegas (dā läs vä'gäs).Cuba 22.58 N 82.24 W
102 Santiago del Estero (dĕl ĕs-tā'rō) Arg. 27.45 S 64.20 W
102 Santiago del Estero (State)...Arg. 28.0 S 63.30 W

97 Santiago de los Caballeros (dȧ lōs kä-bä-yä'rôs).Dom. Rep. 19.28 N 70.42 W
152 Santiago I..................Phil. 16.25 N 119.55 E
92 Santiago Ixcuintla (ês-kwēn'tlä) Mex. 21.48 N 105.12 W
80 Santiago Mts..............Tex. 30.0 N 103.30 W
80 Santiago Papasquiaro (pä-päs-kê-ä'rō).Mex. 25.3 N 105.25 W
73 Santiago Pk. Calif. (Los Angeles In.) 33.43 N 117.32 W
92 Santiago, R..............Mex. 21.20 N 104.20 W
93 Santiago Tuxtla (tōōs'tlä)...Mex. 18.27 N 95.18 W
80 Santiaguillo, L. (sän-tê-ä-gēl'yô) Mex. 24.50 N 104.50 W
93 Santiaguito (sän-tê-ä-gē'tō) Mex. (In.) 19.30 N 99.15 W
70 Santiam R. (săn'tyăm)......Ore. 44.50 N 122.50 W
125 Santi Petri Canal (sän'tê pä'trê) Sp. (In.) 36.24 N 6.11 W
124 Santisteban del Puerto (sän'tê-stâ-bän' dĕl pwĕr'tô).Sp. 38.16 N 3.11 W
101 Santo Amaro (sän'tōō ä-mä'rōō) Braz. (In.) 12.33 S 38.45 W
134 Santo Antonio (sän'tōō än-tō'nê-ōō).Ang. 6.5 S 12.23 E
101 Santo Antonio da Bôa Vista (dȧ bō'ȧ vēs'tȧ).Braz. 16.40 S 43.14 W
101 Santo Antonio de Balsas (dā bäl'zäzh).Braz. 7.0 S 45.59 W
96 Santo Domingo (sän'tô dō-mĭŋ'gô) Cuba 22.35 N 80.18 W
97 Santo Domingo (Ciudad Trujillo) (syōō-dhädh' trōō-hē'lyô) Dom. Rep. 18.28 N 69.53 W
152 Santo Domingo............Phil. 17.38 N 120.24 E
93 Santo Domingo (Tehuantepec) (tȧ-hwän'tȧ-pĕk').Mex. 16.20 N 95.14 W
93 Santo Domingo (Zanatepec) (zȧ-nä'tȧ-pĕk').Mex. 16.30 N 94.21 W
97 Santo Domingo Cay (I.) (sän-tô dô-mĭŋ'gô).Ba. Is. 21.42 N 75.45 W
124 Santo Domingo de la Calzada (dā lä käl-thä'dä).Sp. 42.26 N 2.57 W
124 Santoña (sän-tō'nyä).........Sp. 43.27 N 3.28 W
101 Santos (sän'tōzh)..........Braz. 23.58 S 46.18 W
152 Santo Tomás (sän'tô tô-mäs') Phil. 14.7 N 121.8 E
93 Santo Tomás (Tamazulápam) (tä-mä-zōō-lä'päm).Mex. 17.42 N 97.34 W
152 Santo Tomás..............Phil. 16.20 N 120.33 E
145 Santuao (sän'tōō-ä'ō).......Chn. 26.41 N 119.34 E
145 Santuao B.................Chn. 26.30 N 119.45 E
149 Sanuki (sä'nōō-kē) Jap. (Tokyo In.) 35.16 N 139.54 E
122 Sanvic (säN-vēk')............Fr. 49.31 N 0.10 E
94 San Vicente (sän vê-sĕn'tä)...Sal. 13.41 N 88.43 W
124 San Vicente de Alcántara (sän vê-thĕn'tä dā äl-kän'tä-rä).Sp. 39.23 N 7.9 W
125 San Vicente de Sarriá (dā sär-rē-ä').Sp. (In.) 41.24 N 2.7 E
126 San Vito (sän vē'tô)..........It. 45.54 N 12.51 E
75 San Xavier Ind. Res. (sän Kä-vyâr') (zăv'ĭ-ĕr).Ariz. 32.7 N 111.0 W
134 Sanyati R. (sän-yä'tê).....S. Rh. 17.30 S 29.15 E
101 São Carlos do Pinhal (souN kär'lōzh dŏŏ pê-nyäl').Braz. 22.1 S 47.59 W
101 São Domingos da Bôa Vista (souN dō-mĭŋ'gōsh dä bō'ȧ vēs'tȧ).Braz. (In.) 1.41 S 47.48 W
100 São Felipe (souN fâ-lē'pĕ)...Braz. 0.18 N 67.3 W
100 São Felipe...............Braz. 6.30 S 70.1 W
101 São Felix (souN fâ-lēks') Braz. (In.) 12.40 S 39.0 W
101 São Francisco (souN frăN-sēsh'kōō) Braz. 15.59 S 44.45 W
102 São Francisco.............Braz. 26.15 S 48.35 W
101 São Francisco, R...........Braz. 12.0 S 43.15 W
100 São Gabriel (gä-brē-ĕl').....Braz. 0.12 S 67.1 W
101 São Gonçalo (gōŋ-sä'lōō) Braz. (In.) 12.25 S 38.55 W
102 São Gonçalo de Niteroi (dȧ nē-tä-rōō'ī).Braz. (In.) 22.50 S 43.4 W
101 São João (souN zhô-ouN')...Braz. 5.30 S 48.58 W
101 São João d'el Rey (dĕl rē'ī)..Braz. 22.12 S 44.20 W
125 São João dos Lampas (souN' zhô-ouN' dōzh läN-päzh') Port. (In.) 38.53 N 9.24 W
99 São José dos Campos (souN zhô-zä' dōzh käN'pōzh) Braz. (Rio de Janeiro In.) 23.10 S 45.56 W
132 São Jorge I. (souN zhôr'zhĕ) Az. Is. (In.) 38.35 N 28.0 W
99 São Luiz (souN lōō-ēzh') Braz. (Rio de Janeiro In.) 23.8 S 45.12 W
101 São Luiz (Maranhão) (mä-rän-youN').Braz. 2.30 S 44.12 W
101 São Luis de Cáceres (souN lōō-ēzh' dä kä'sĕ-rĕzh).Braz. 16.2 S 57.45 W
101 São Manoel, R. (souN mä-nô-ĕl') Braz. 12.0 S 56.0 W
101 São Matheus (mä-tä'ŏŏzh)..Braz. 18.30 S 39.45 W
101 São Miguel (mê-gĕl')..Braz. (In.) 13.3 S 39.32 W
132 São Miguel I.........Az. Is. (In.) 37.45 N 25.30 W
97 Saona I. (sä-ō'nä)....Dom. Rep. 18.9 N 68.40 W
122 Saône R. (sōn)..............Fr. 46.10 N 4.50 E
102 Sao Nicolás (sä'ô nê-kô-läs')..Arg. 33.30 S 60.10 W
132 São Nicolão I. (souN' nē-kô-louN') C. V. Is. (In.) 16.36 N 24.15 W
101 São Paulo (pou'lōō).........Braz. 23.31 S 46.31 W
101 São Paulo (State)..........Braz. 22.0 S 49.0 W
São Paulo de Luanda, see Luanda, Angola

ăt; finăl; rāte; senâte; ärm; ȧsk; sofȧ; fâre; ch-choose; dh-as th in other; bē; êvent; bĕt; recĕnt; cratĕr; g-go; gh-gutteral g; bĭt; ĭ-short neutral; rīde; K-gutteral k as ch in German ich;

São Paulo de Olivença PRONOUNCING INDEX Sedgley

Page	Name Pronunciation Region	Lat. °′	Long. °′
100	São Paulo de Olivença (souN' pou'lōō dä ô-lê-vĕṇ'sȧ). Braz.	3.30 S	68.59 W
101	São Raymundo Nonato (souN' rä-ê-mōōn'dōō nô-nä'tōō). Braz.	9.0 S	42.29 W
101	São Roque (rō'kĕ)..........Braz.	5.3 S	35.30 W
99	São Sebastião (souN sä-bäs-tê-ouN') Braz. (Rio de Janeiro In.)	23.48 S	45.26 W
99	São Sebastião, Ilha de (I.) (ēl'yȧ dä souN' sä-bäs-tê-ouN') Braz. (Rio de Janeiro In.)	23.50 S	45.20 W
132	São Thiago I. (souN tê-ä'gōō) C. V. Is. (In.)	15.10 N	23.40 W
132	São Thomé (souN tô-mä') São Thomé I.	0.25 N	6.38 E
132	São Thomé I..............Afr.	0.15 N	6.35 E
101	São Vicente do Araguaia (vē-sĕn'tā dōō ä-rä-gwä'yȧ). Braz.	5.58 S	48.15 W
132	São Vicente I. (vê-sĕn'tā) C. V. Is. (In.)	16.50 N	25.0 W
132	Sapele (sä-pā'lā)..........Nig.	5.42 N	5.27 E
153	Sapian B. (sä-pê-än').......Phil.	11.31 N	122.36 E
128	Sapozhok (sä-pô-zhôk')..Sov. Un.	53.56 N	40.41 E
148	Sapporo (säp-pô'rô).........Jap.	43.2 N	141.16 E
128	Sapskoe (säp'skô-yĕ)....Sov. Un.	54.12 N	40.54 E
99	Sapucahi, R. (sä-pōō-kä'ē) Braz. (Rio de Janeiro In.)	22.40 S	45.40 W
102	Sapucaia I. (sä-pōō-kä'yä) Braz. (In.)	22.52 S	43.13 W
79	Sapulpa (sȧ-pŭl'pȧ)........Okla.	36.0 N	96.5 W
135	Saqqara Pyramids (sák-kär'ä).Eg.	29.52 N	31.12 E
153	Sara (sä'rä)................Phil.	11.14 N	123.1 E
127	Sarajevo (sä-rä-yĕv'ô) (sä-rä'yä-vô).Yugo.	43.50 N	18.26 E
101	Saramacca R. (sä-rä-mäk'kä).Sur.	5.0 N	56.0 W
85	Saranac L. (săr'ȧ-năk)......N. Y.	44.15 N	74.15 W
85	Saranac Lake.............N. Y.	44.22 N	74.6 W
102	Sarandi (sä-rän'dê).....Arg. (In.)	34.41 S	58.21 W
99	Sarandi....Ur. (Buenos Aires In.)	33.20 S	55.53 W
153	Sarangani B. (sä-rän-gä'nê)..Phil.	5.50 N	125.10 E
153	Sarangani I...............Phil.	5.27 N	125.28 E
110	Saransk (sȧ-ränsk')......Sov. Un.	54.8 N	45.10 E
102	Sarapuhi (sä-rä-pōō'ē).Braz. (In.)	22.45 S	43.17 W
102	Sarapuhi, R..........Braz. (In.)	22.44 S	43.20 W
138	Sarapul (sä-rä'pōōl')....Sov. Un.	56.30 N	53.50 E
148	Sarapulskoe (sä-rä-pōōl''skô-yĕ) Sov. Un.	48.55 N	136.12 E
83	Sarasota (săr-ȧ-sōtȧ)....Fla. (In.)	27.20 N	82.30 W
81	Saratoga (săr-ȧ-tō'gȧ)........Tex.	30.18 N	94.30 W
51	Saratoga Passage Wash. (Seattle In.)	48.6 N	122.30 W
85	Saratoga Springs..........N. Y.	43.5 N	73.8 W
111	Saratov (sä-rä'tôf)......Sov. Un.	51.30 N	45.55 E
153	Saravia (sä-rä'vyä)........Phil.	10.51 N	123.0 E
150	Sarawak (sä-rä'wäk)......Pac. O.	2.30 N	113.30 E
121	Sárbogárd (shär'bô-gärd)...Hung.	46.52 N	18.39 E
123	Sarcelles (sär-sĕl')......Fr. (In.)	48.59 N	2.23 E
126	Sardinia (I.) (sär-dĭn'ĭ-ȧ)........It.	40.0 N	9.0 E
72	Sardis (sär'dĭs) Can. (Vancouver In.)	49.8 N	121.58 W
82	Sardis...................Miss.	34.28 N	89.55 W
76	Sargent (sär'jĕnt)..........Neb.	41.39 N	99.22 W
122	Sariat (sä-rê-ä')..............Fr.	44.53 N	1.15 E
151	Sariaya (sä-rê-ä'yä) Phil. (Manila In.)	13.59 N	121.35 E
111	Sarikamiş (sä'rê-kä'mêsh)....Tur.	40.30 N	42.48 E
125	Sariñena (sä-rê-nyä'nä).......Sp.	41.47 N	0.10 W
147	Sariwŏn (sä'rê-wŭn')........Kor.	38.30 N	125.44 E
122	Sark (I.) (särk)..........Gt. Brit.	49.30 N	2.20 W
111	Şarkî-Karahisar (shär'kē-kä-rä'hĭ-sär').Tur.	40.12 N	38.30 E
127	Şarköy (shär'kû-ê)..........Tur.	40.38 N	27.8 E
102	Sarmiento, Mt. (sär-myĕn'tō).Chl.	54.30 S	70.58 W
55	Sarnia (sär'nê-ȧ)............Can.	42.58 N	82.27 W
121	Sarny (sär'nê).........Sov. Un.	51.17 N	26.39 E
127	Saronic G. (Aegina, G. of) (sȧ-rŏ'nĭk) (ê-jī'nȧ).Grc.	37.35 N	23.40 E
127	Saros, G. of (sä'rôs).........Tur.	40.30 N	26.30 E
121	Sárospatak (shä'rôsh-pô'tôk) Hung.	48.20 N	21.35 E
118	Sarpsborg (särps'bôrg)......Nor.	59.17 N	11.9 E
152	Sarrat (sär-rät')............Phil.	18.10 N	120.38 E
123	Sarreguemines (sär-gê-mēn')...Fr.	49.5 N	7.8 E
124	Sarria (sär'ê-ä)..............Sp.	42.46 N	7.25 W
94	Sarstoom, R. (sär-stoom') Guat.-Br. Hond.	15.53 N	89.20 W
122	Sartène (sär-tĕn').......Cor. (In.)	41.35 N	9.5 E
122	Sarthe R. (särt)..............Fr.	47.50 N	0.20 W
118	Sartor (Store Sotra) (I.) (sär'tôr) (stōō'rĕ sôt'rä).Nor.	60.18 N	5.8 E
148	Sartu (sär'tōō')............Chn.	46.30 N	125.12 E
120	Sárvár (shär'vär)...........Hung.	47.15 N	16.53 E
138	Sary Ishik-Otrau Des. (sä'rê ē'shêk-ō'trou).Sov. Un.	46.0 N	77.0 E
138	Sary-su (R.) (sä'rê-sōō).Sov. Un.	47.30 N	68.0 E
126	Sarzana (särt-sä'nä)..........It.	44.6 N	9.57 E
141	Sasaram (sŭs-ŭ-räm')........India	24.55 N	84.5 E
149	Sasayama (sä'sä-yä'mä)......Jap.	35.5 N	135.12 E
149	Sasebo (sä'sä-bô)............Jap.	33.15 N	129.45 E
117	Sasel (sä'sĕl)..Ger. (Hamburg In.)	53.39 N	10.6 E
127	Saseno (I.) (sä'sä-nô)........Alb.	40.30 N	19.17 E
54	Saskatchewan (Prov.) (săs-kăch'ê-wän).Can.	54.0 N	106.0 W
54	Saskatchewan R., North.....Can.	54.0 N	111.0 W
54	Saskatoon (săs-kȧ-tōōn').....Can.	52.12 N	106.44 W
119	Sasmaka (säs'mȧ-kȧ)....Sov. Un.	57.22 N	22.36 E
110	Sasovo (säs'ô-vô).......Sov. Un.	54.20 N	41.50 E
135	Sassabaneh (sä-sä-bä'nȧ).....Eth.	7.53 N	43.39 E
132	Sassandra R. (sás-sän'drá) Fr. W. Afr.	6.0 N	6.47 W
126	Sassari (säs'sä-rê).........Sard.	40.43 N	8.35 E
120	Sassnitz (säs'nêts)..........Ger.	54.32 N	13.36 E

Page	Name Pronunciation Region	Lat. °′	Long. °′
132	Satadougou (sä-tȧ-dōō-gōō') Fr. W. Afr.	12.34 N	11.26 W
148	Satano C. (sä'tä-nô).........Jap.	31.1 N	130.40 E
72	Satellite Channel (săt'ĕl-līt) Can. (Vancouver In.)	48.43 N	123.32 W
118	Säter (sĕ'tĕr)..............Swe.	60.21 N	15.43 E
83	Satilla R. (sȧ-tĭl'ȧ)..........Ga.	31.16 N	82.0 W
110	Satka (sät'kȧ).........Sov. Un.	55.10 N	58.59 E
121	Sátoraljaújhely (shä'tô-rô-lyô-ōō'yĕl').Hung.	48.24 N	21.39 E
121	Satu-Mare (sä'tōō-mä'rĕ)...Rom.	47.49 N	22.52 E
72	Saturna I. (sȧ-tûr'nȧ) Can. Vancouver In.)	48.48 N	123.9 W
118	Saude (sou'dĕ)............Nor.	59.40 N	6.21 E
140	Saudi Arabia (sȧ-ōō'dĭ ȧ-rā'bĭ-ȧ) Asia	25.0 N	43.0 E
84	Saugatuck (sô'gȧ-tŭk)......Mich.	42.42 N	86.10 W
84	Saugeen Pen. (sô'gēn).......Can.	44.50 N	81.10 W
84	Saugeen R.................Can.	44.10 N	81.2 W
85	Saugerties (sô'gēr-tēz).....N. Y.	42.7 N	73.57 W
141	Saugor (sä-gŭr') (sô-gōr')...India	23.42 N	78.35 E
73	Saugus (sô'gŭs) Calif. (Los Angeles In.)	34.25 N	118.33 W
87	Saugus............Mass. (In.)	42.28 N	71.1 W
77	Sauk Center (sôk).........Minn.	45.45 N	94.56 W
77	Sauk City..................Wis.	43.16 N	89.42 W
77	Sauk Rapids..............Minn.	45.36 N	94.8 W
77	Sauk R...................Minn.	45.35 N	94.45 W
55	Sault Ste. Marie (sōō sānt mȧ-rē') Can.	46.38 N	84.20 W
77	Sault Ste. Marie...........Mich.	46.29 N	84.18 W
88	Sault Ste. Marie.....Mich. (In.)		
97	Saumatre, L. (sô-māt'r')....Hai.	18.37 N	72.0 W
88	Saunders (sôn'dērz) Wis. (Duluth In.)	46.38 N	92.6 W
157	Saunders, C..........N. Z. (In.)	45.53 S	170.46 E
112	Saura, Wadi (R.) (wä'dê sä-ōō'rä).Alg.	29.0 N	1.48 W
134	Saurimo (sä-ōō-rē'mō).......Ang.	9.32 S	20.31 E
74	Sausalito (sô-sȧ-lē'tô)........Calif.	37.50 N	122.33 W
77	Savanna (sȧ-văn'ȧ)...........Ill.	42.5 N	90.9 W
83	Savannah...................Ga.	32.4 N	81.7 W
89	Savannah..............Ga. (In.)		
79	Savannah...................Mo.	39.57 N	94.50 W
82	Savannah.................Tenn.	35.13 N	88.16 W
89	Savannah Beach Ga. (Savannah In.)	32.0 N	80.51 W
83	Savannah R............Ga.-S. C.	33.30 N	82.0 W
96	Savanna la Mar (sȧ-văn'ȧ lä mär').Jam.	18.12 N	78.9 W
126	Sava R. (sä'vä)............Yugo.	45.5 N	18.0 E
150	Savargalok (sä-vär'gȧ-lôk').Siam	17.18 N	99.45 E
132	Savé (sȧ-vā')........Fr. W. Afr.	8.12 N	2.30 E
132	Savelou (sä-vê-lōō')...Fr. W. Afr.	8.0 N	2.2 E
122	Save R. (sàv)................Fr.	43.20 N	0.50 E
123	Saverne (sȧ-vĕrn')............Fr.	48.45 N	7.25 E
126	Savigliano (sä-vêl-yä'nô)......It.	44.37 N	7.39 E
124	Saviñao (sä-vên-yä'ô)..........Sp.	42.35 N	7.39 W
150	Savoe Is. (sä'vōō)........Indon.	10.30 S	121.55 E
126	Savona (sä-vō'nä)..............It.	44.17 N	8.30 E
119	Savonlinna (sä'vôn-lēn'nä)...Fin.	61.54 N	28.51 E
129	Savran (säv-rän').......Sov. Un.	48.7 N	30.4 E
150	Savu Sea (sä'vōō)..........Indon.	9.30 S	122.0 E
135	Sawākin (Suakin) (sŭ-wä'kên) (swä'kên).A. E. Sud.	19.3 N	37.20 E
80	Sawtooth Mt. (sô'tōōth).....Tex.	30.45 N	104.18 W
86	Sawyer L. (sô'yēr)...........Me.	45.5 N	70.59 W
132	Say (sä'ē)..........Fr. W. Afr.	13.12 N	21.12 E
138	Sayanski Mts. (sä-yän'skyĭ) Sov. Un.-Chn.	53.30 N	95.0 E
73	Sayre (sā'ēr).Ala. (Birmingham In.)	33.43 N	86.58 W
78	Sayre.....................Okla.	35.20 N	99.37 W
85	Sayre.......................Pa.	41.58 N	76.30 W
73	Sayreton (sā'ēr-tŭn) Ala. (Birmingham In.)	33.34 N	86.50 W
93	Sayula (sä-yōō'lä)..........Mex.	17.52 N	94.57 W
92	Sayula.....................Mex.	19.53 N	103.34 W
92	Sayula, L..................Mex.	19.56 N	103.32 W
85	Sayville (sā'vĭl)...........N. Y.	40.44 N	73.6 W
120	Sázava R. (sä'zȧ-vȧ).....Czech.	49.43 N	15.15 E
80	Scajaquada Cr. (skä-jȧ-kwä'dȧ) N. Y. (Niagara Falls In.)	42.55 N	78.51 W
51	Scappoose (skă-pōōs') Ore. (Portland In.)	45.56 N	122.52 W
54	Scarboro Junction (skär'bŭr-ô) Can. (In.)	43.44 N	79.14 W
84	Scarborough...........Gt. Brit.	54.18 N	0.25 W
113	Scarpanto (I.) (skär-pän'tō)..Grc.	35.40 N	27.10 E
89	Scarsdale (skärz'dāl) La. (New Orleans In.)	29.51 N	89.59 W
87	Scatari I. (skăt'ȧ-rê)........Can.	46.0 N	59.45 W
123	Sceaux (sō)............Fr. (In.)	48.46 N	2.17 E
135	Scebeli R. (shĕ'bȧ-lê).......Som.	1.5 N	43.28 E
115	Schaerbeek (skär'bāk).........Bel.	55.51 N	4.21 E
120	Schaffhausen (shäf'hou-zĕn).Switz.	47.43 N	8.38 E
115	Scheldt R. (skĕlt)............Bel.	50.50 N	3.30 E
85	Schenectady (skĕ-nĕk'tȧ-dê).N. Y.	42.48 N	73.56 W
117	Schenefeld (shĕ'nĕ-fĕlt) Ger. (Hamburg In.)	53.36 N	9.49 E
117	Schiffbek (shĭf'bĕk) Ger. (Hamburg In.)	53.32 N	10.6 E
117	Schilde (skĭl-dĕ).Bel. (Anvers In.)	51.14 N	4.35 E
123	Schiltigheim (shĕl'tĕgh-hīm)...Fr.	48.40 N	7.50 E
126	Schio (skē'ô)..................It.	45.43 N	11.22 E
120	Schleswig (shlĕs'vĕgh)........Ger.	54.31 N	9.33 E
120	Schleswig-Holstein (Prov.) (shlĕs'wĕgh-hōl'shtīn).Ger.	54.25 N	9.30 E
120	Schmalkalden (shmäl'käl-dĕn) Ger.	50.43 N	10.27 E
117	Schnelsen (shnĕl'sĕn) Ger. (Hamburg In.)	53.38 N	9.55 E
77	Schofield (skō'fēld).........Wis.	44.55 N	89.35 W

Page	Name Pronunciation Region	Lat. °′	Long. °′
117	Schöneberg (shû'nĕ-bĕrgh) Ger. (Hamburg In.)	52.29 N	13.17 E
117	Schooten (skō'tĕn) Bel. (Anvers In.)	51.15 N	4.30 E
160	Schouten I. (shōō'tĕn) Austl. (Tas. In.)	42.20 S	148.20 E
151	Schouten Is. (skou'tĕn) Neth. N. Gui.	1.0 S	136.0 E
115	Schouwen (I.) (skou'vĕn)...Neth.	51.45 N	3.55 W
120	Schramberg (shräm'bĕrgh)...Ger.	48.14 N	8.24 E
85	Schroon L. (skrōōn).........N. Y.	43.50 N	73.46 W
117	Schulau (shōō'lou) Ger. (Hamburg In.)	53.34 N	9.42 E
76	Schuyler (skī'lēr)...........Neb.	41.27 N	97.5 W
85	Schuylkill Haven (skōōl'kĭl)...Pa.	40.37 N	76.12 W
88	Schuylkill R. Pa. (Philadelphia In.)	39.59 N	75.12 W
120	Schwabach (shvä'bäk).......Ger.	49.20 N	11.0 E
120	Schwandorf (shvän'dôrf).....Ger.	49.19 N	12.8 E
150	Schwaner Mts. (skvän'ēr)..Indon.	1.30 S	111.30 E
120	Schwaz (shväts)..............Aus.	47.20 N	11.43 E
120	Schwechat (shvĕk'ät).......Aus.	48.8 N	16.28 E
120	Schwedt (shvĕt).............Pol.	53.3 N	14.16 E
120	Schweinfurt (shvīn'fōōrt)....Ger.	50.3 N	10.13 E
120	Schwenningen (shvĕn'ĭng-ĕn).Ger.	48.4 N	8.33 E
120	Schwerin (shvĕ-rēn')........Ger.	53.37 N	11.23 E
120	Schwerin, L..................Ger.	53.42 N	11.27 E
120	Schwyz (shvēts)...........Switz.	47.1 N	8.39 E
126	Sciacca (shê-äk'kä)............It.	37.30 N	13.5 E
133	Sciaradda (shȧ-räd'dä)......Eth.	7.20 N	36.29 E
114	Scilly I. (sĭl'ê)..........Gt. Brit.	49.55 N	6.25 W
84	Scioto R. (sī-ō'tō)...........Ohio	39.6 N	83.0 W
84	Sciotoville (sī-ō'tô-vĭl).......Ohio	38.45 N	82.46 W
87	Scituate (sĭt'ū-āt).....Mass. (In.)	42.12 N	70.45 W
71	Scobey (skō'bê)............Mont.	48.48 N	105.28 W
70	Scotia (skō'shȧ).............Calif.	40.29 N	124.5 W
114	Scotland (Division) (skŏt'lȧnd) Gt. Brit.	48.35 N	3.20 W
76	Scotland..................S. D.	43.9 N	97.42 W
83	Scotland Neck..............N. C.	36.8 N	77.24 W
86	Scotstown (skŏts'toun)......Can.	45.32 N	71.18 W
54	Scott, C. (skŏt)..............Can.	50.45 N	128.17 W
78	Scott City..................Kan.	38.28 N	100.53 W
73	Scottdale (skŏt'dāl) Ga. (Atlanta In.)	33.47 N	84.16 W
47	Scott (I.)...............Pac. O.	67.24 S	179.55 W
70	Scott, Mt.....................Ore.	42.56 N	122.1 W
47	Scott Ra......................Ant.	68.0 S	50.0 E
76	Scottsbluff (skŏts'blŭf)......Neb.	41.52 N	103.39 W
76	Scotts Bluff Natl. Mon.......Neb.	41.50 N	103.42 W
82	Scottsboro (skŏts'bŭr-ô).....Ala.	34.40 N	86.3 W
84	Scottsburg (skŏts'bûrg)......Ind.	38.41 N	85.47 W
160	Scottsdale (skŏts'dāl) Austl. (Tas. In.)	41.8 S	147.30 E
82	Scottsville (skŏts'vĭl)........Ky.	36.46 N	86.11 W
84	Scottville (skŏt'vĭl).........Mich.	43.59 N	86.19 W
85	Scranton (skrăn'tŭn)..........Pa.	41.24 N	75.42 W
76	Scribner (skrĭb'nēr).........Neb.	41.40 N	95.39 W
85	Scugog L. (skū'gôg)..........Can.	44.10 N	78.50 W
116	Scunthorpe (skŭn'thôrp).Gt. Brit.	53.36 N	0.38 W
127	Scutari (Shkoder) (skōō'tä-rê) (shkō'dûr).Alb.	42.3 N	19.31 E
127	Scutari, L............Alb.-Yugo.	42.10 N	19.20 E
51	Seabeck (sē'bĕck) Wash. (Seattle In.)	47.37 N	122.49 W
81	Seabrook (sē'brōōk)....Tex. (In.)	29.34 N	95.1 W
85	Seaford (sē'fērd)..............Del.	38.37 N	75.40 W
80	Seagraves (sē'grāvs).........Tex.	32.55 N	102.34 W
72	Sea I. (sē)..Can. (Vancouver In.)	49.12 N	123.10 W
73	Seal Beach (sēl) Calif. (Los Angeles In.)	33.45 N	118.5 W
97	Seal Cays (Is.).............Ba. Is.	21.11 N	71.42 W
81	Sealey (sē'lê)................Tex.	29.46 N	96.8 W
157	Seal Pt. (sēl)..........N. Z. (In.)	45.54 S	170.39 E
54	Seal R......................Can.	59.0 N	96.30 W
135	Sea Pt................U. S. Afr.	33.54 S	18.23 E
79	Searcy (sûr'sê)..............Ark.	35.14 N	91.43 W
73	Searles (sûrlz) Ala. (Birmingham In.)	33.18 N	87.18 W
86	Searsport (sērz'pōrt).........Me.	44.30 N	68.55 W
70	Seaside (sē'sīd)..............Ore.	45.59 N	123.55 W
70	Seattle (sê-ăt''l)...........Wash.	47.45 N	122.25 W
51	Seattle............Wash. (In.)		
51	Seaview (sē'vū) Wash. (Portland In.)	46.20 N	124.2 W
159	Seaview, Mt..................Austl.	31.20 S	152.5 E
86	Sebago L. (sê-bā'gō)..........Me.	43.50 N	70.38 W
74	Sebastopol (sê-bás'tô-pôl)...Calif.	38.26 N	122.51 W
126	Sebenico (Šibenik) (sĕ-bā'nê-kô) (shē'bē-nêk).Yugo.	43.44 N	15.54 E
121	Sebeşul (sā-bĕ'shōōl).......Rom.	45.57 N	23.33 E
150	Sebetik I. (sĕ-bĕ'tĭk)......N. Bor.	4.15 N	117.45 E
84	Sebewaing (sē'bê-wăng)....Mich.	43.45 N	83.26 W
128	Sebezh (syĕ'bĕzh)........Sov. Un.	56.16 N	28.31 E
120	Sebnitz (zĕb'nêts)............Ger.	51.0 N	14.14 E
84	Sebree (sê-brē')...............Ky.	38.37 N	87.31 W
83	Sebring (sē'brĭng)......Fla. (In.)	27.30 N	81.26 W
84	Sebring.....................Ohio	40.57 N	81.3 W
132	Sebu, Wadi (R.) (wäd'dê sä'bōō) Mor.	34.0 N	4.30 W
72	Sechelt (sē'chĕlt) Can. (Vancouver In.)	49.28 N	123.46 W
72	Sechelt Inlet.Can. (Vancouver In.)	49.36 N	123.50 W
157	Secretary I. (sĕk'rê-tȧ-rê)...N. Z.	45.12 S	166.55 E
141	Secunderabad (sē-kŭn'dēr-ä-bäd') India	17.30 N	78.29 E
72	Sedalia (sê-dā'lê-ȧ) Colo. (Denver In.)	39.27 N	104.58 W
79	Sedalia.......................Mo.	38.43 N	93.12 W
122	Sedan (sê-däN')...............Fr.	49.45 N	5.0 E
79	Sedan (sē-dăn')..............Kan.	37.7 N	96.10 W
116	Sedgley (sĕdj'lĭ)........Gt. Brit.	52.32 N	2.7 W

ng-sing; ŋ-baŋk; N-nasalized n; nŏd; cŏmmit; ōld; ôbey; ôrder; fōōd; fŏŏt; ou-out; s-soft; sh-dish; th-thin; pūre; ûnite; ûrn; stŭd; circŭs; ü-as "y" in study; '-indeterminate vowel.

Sedro-Woolley PRONOUNCING INDEX Sheenwater

Page	Name Pronunciation Region	Lat. °′	Long. °′
70	Sedro-Woolley (sē'drō-wŏŏl'ē) Wash.	48.30 N	122.15 W
119	Seduva (shĕ'dŏŏ-và) Sov. Un.	55.44 N	23.48 E
117	Seeburg (zā'bŏŏrgh) Ger. (Berlin In.)	52.31 N	13.7 E
117	Seegefeld (zā'gĕ-fĕlt) Ger. (Berlin In.)	52.34 N	13.6 E
112	Sefrou (sē-frōō') Mor.	33.42 N	4.45 W
153	Segama R. (sâ-gä'mä) N. Bor.	5.10 N	118.22 E
137	Segamat (sā'gà-màt) Malaya (In.)	2.31 N	102.48 E
149	Segawa (sē'gä'wä) Jap. (Osaka In.)	34.49 N	135.27 E
132	Segiet el-Hamra (R.) (sĕ-gyĕt' ĕl-häm'rà) R. de O.	26.40 N	11.30 W
110	Seg, L. (syĕgh) Sov. Un.	63.20 N	33.30 E
125	Segorbe (sâ-gōr'bā) Sp.	39.51 N	0.29 W
132	Ségou (sā-gōō') Fr. W. Afr.	13.30 N	6.23 W
124	Segovia (sâ-gō'vē-ä) Sp.	40.57 N	4.7 W
94	Segovia, R. (R. Coco or Wanks) (rē'ō kō'kō, rē'ō wänks) Hond.-Nic.	14.30 N	85.0 W
122	Segré (sē-grā') Fr.	47.40 N	0.52 W
125	Segre R. (sā'grā) Sp.	41.40 N	0.40 E
132	Séguéla (sā-gā-lä') Fr. W. Afr.	8.2 N	7.0 W
80	Seguin (sē-gēn') Tex.	29.35 N	97.58 W
124	Segura R. (sâ-gōō'rä) Sp.	38.25 N	2.0 W
129	Seim R. (sâ-ēm') Sov. Un.	51.19 N	33.0 E
119	Seinäjoki (sā'ē-nĕ-yō'kē) Fin.	62.47 N	22.46 E
123	Seine (sân) Fr. (In.)	48.46 N	2.25 E
122	Seine, B. of the Fr.	49.30 N	0.30 W
77	Seine R. Can.	49.0 N	91.0 W
122	Seine R. Fr.	48.25 N	3.0 E
147	Seishū (Chŏngju) (sī'shōō') (chŭng'jōō) Kor.	36.38 N	127.30 E
125	Seixal (sâ-ê-shäl') Port. (In.)	38.38 N	9.6 W
132	Sekondi (sĕ-kôn'dē) G. C.	4.58 N	1.42 W
137	Selangor (State) (sâ-län'gōr) Malaya (In.)	2.55 N	101.35 E
127	Selanovci (sĕl'á-nôf-tsĭ) Bul.	43.40 N	24.3 E
151	Selaroe (I.) (sâ-lä'rōō) Indon.	8.20 S	131.10 E
150	Selatan, C. (sâ-lä'tän) Indon.	4.14 S	114.44 E
120	Selb (zĕlp) Ger.	50.11 N	12.6 E
118	Selbu, L. (sĕl'bōō) Nor.	63.15 N	10.50 E
116	Selby (sĕl'bê) Gt. Brit.	53.47 N	1.3 W
116	Seldovia (sĕl-dō'vē-ȧ) Alsk.	59.25 N	151.30 W
139	Selegnyakh R. (sâ-lĕk-nyäk') Sov. Un.	67.25 N	141.0 E
139	Selemdzha R. (sâ-lĕmt-zhä') Sov. Un.	52.25 N	130.0 E
142	Selenga R. (sĕ-lĕŋ-gä') Mong.-Sov. Un.	49.30 N	104.0 E
123	Selestat (sē-lē-stä') Fr.	48.15 N	7.30 E
140	Seleucia (Ruins) (sē-lū'shĭ-ȧ) Iraq	33.0 N	44.30 E
132	Sélibaby (sâ-lê-bà-bē') Fr. W. Afr.	15.20 N	12.9 W
128	Seliger, L. (sĕl'ê-gĕr) Sov. Un.	57.18 N	33.0 E
128	Selizharovo (sâ'lê-zhä'rô-vô) Sov. Un.	56.49 N	33.28 E
54	Selkirk (sĕl'kûrk) Can.	50.12 N	96.59 W
54	Selkirk Can.	62.45 N	137.30 W
114	Selkirk Gt. Brit.	55.35 N	2.55 W
54	Selkirk Mts. Can.	50.48 N	117.30 W
133	Sella (sĕl'ä) Libya	28.25 N	17.50 E
131	Selloum, Djebel (Mts.) (jĕb'ĕl sĕl-lōōm') Tun. (In.)	35.0 N	8.55 E
139	Sellyakhskaya B. (sĕl-yäk'skä-yä) Sov. Un.	71.35 N	139.50 E
82	Selma (sĕl'mȧ) Ala.	32.24 N	87.0 W
74	Selma Calif.	36.33 N	119.37 W
83	Selma N. C.	35.33 N	78.17 W
134	Selukwe (sê-lŭk'wê) S. Rh.	19.42 S	30.3 E
70	Selway R. (sĕl'wā) Ida.	46.5 N	115.10 W
54	Selwyn L. (sĕl'wĭn) Can.	60.0 N	104.50 W
150	Semarang (sē-mä'räng) Indon.	7.5 S	110.28 E
131	Semellawia (sĕ-mĕ-lä'wê-ȧ) Eg. (In.)	30.45 N	31.30 E
133	Semendria (Smederevo) (sĕ-mĕn'drē-ä) (smĕ'dĕ-rĕ-vô) Yugo.	44.38 N	20.57 E
127	Semeni Devol R. (sā'mĕ-nê dä'vôl) Alb.	40.44 N	20.25 E
129	Semenovka (sĕ-myôn'ôf-kà) Sov. Un.	52.9 N	32.36 E
150	Semeru Mt. (Vol.) (sĕm'ĕr-ōō) Indon.	8.5 S	112.58 E
71	Seminoe Reservoir (sĕm'ĭ-nô) Wyo.	42.20 N	106.53 W
79	Seminole (sĕm'ĭ-nōl) Okla.	35.13 N	96.39 W
83	Seminole Ind. Res. Fla. (In.)	26.16 N	81.0 W
110	Semiostrovskaya (sĕ-mê-ôs'trôf-skä-yä) Sov. Un.	68.40 N	37.32 E
138	Semipalatinsk (sĕ'mê-pá-lá-tyĕnsk') Sov. Un.	50.25 N	80.20 E
153	Semirara I. (sä-mē'rä-rä) Phil.	12.3 N	121.23 E
153	Semirara Is. Phil.	11.55 N	121.33 E
138	Semiyarskaya (sĕ'mê-yär'skä-yä) Sov. Un.	50.59 N	78.25 E
133	Semliki R. (sĕm'lē-kē) Bel. Cong.-Ug.	1.30 N	30.30 E
127	Semlin (Zemun) (zĕm-lĕn') (zĕ'mōōn) Yugo.	44.50 N	20.25 E
120	Semmering Pass (sĕm'ĕr-ĭng) Aus.	47.38 N	15.50 E
82	Senatobia (sĕ-nà-tō'bê-ȧ) Miss.	34.36 N	89.58 W
148	Sendai (sĕn-dī') Jap.	38.17 N	140.55 E
70	Seneca (sĕn'ĕ-kȧ) Kan.	39.49 N	96.4 W
83	Seneca S. C.	34.40 N	83.0 W
85	Seneca Falls N. Y.	42.57 N	76.57 W
85	Seneca L. N. Y.	42.40 N	76.55 W
132	Senegal (Prov.) (sĕn-ĕ-gôl') Fr. W. Afr.	14.0 N	14.0 W
132	Senegal R. Fr. W. Afr.	15.30 N	13.0 W
120	Senftenberg (zĕnf'tĕn-bĕrgh) Ger.	51.32 N	14.1 E
126	Senigallia (sâ-nê-gäl'lyä) It.	43.43 N	13.11 E
126	Senj (sĕn') Yugo.	44.59 N	14.54 E
108	Senjen (I.) (sĕn'yĕn) Nor.	69.15 N	17.30 E
149	Senju (sĕn'jōō) Jap. (Tokyo In.)	35.45 N	139.48 E
122	Senlis (säN-lēs') Fr.	49.15 N	2.35 E
123	Senlisse (säN-lēs') Fr. (In.)	48.41 N	1.58 E
133	Sennār (sĕn-när') A. E. Sud.	13.33 N	33.31 E
133	Sennār Dam A. E. Sud.	13.33 N	33.31 E
128	Senno (syĕ'nô) Sov. Un.	54.47 N	29.42 E
122	Sens (säNs) Fr.	48.11 N	3.18 E
94	Sensuntepeque (sĕn-sōōn-tâ-pä'kâ) Sal.	13.53 N	88.33 W
127	Senta (sĕn'tä) Yugo.	45.55 N	20.5 E
125	Seo de Urgel (sā'ō dā ōōr-häl') Sp.	42.23 N	1.28 E
147	Seoul (kyŏngsŏng) (sōl') (kyŭng'sŭng') Kor.	37.34 N	127.0 E
157	Separation Pt. (sĕp-ȧ-rā'shŭn) N. Z.	40.45 S	173.0 E
99	Sepetiba B. (sâ-pâ-tē'bȧ) Braz. (Rio de Janeiro In.)	23.0 S	43.50 W
151	Sepik R. (sĕp-ēk') N. Gu. Ter.	4.2 S	143.0 E
82	Sequatchie R. (sê-kwăch'ê) Tenn.	35.26 N	85.20 W
51	Sequim (sē'kwĭm) Wash. (Seattle In.)	48.5 N	123.7 W
74	Sequoia (sê-kwoi'ȧ) Calif.	36.30 N	118.40 W
115	Seraing (sē-räN') Bel.	50.35 N	5.51 E
150	Serang (sâ-räng') Indon.	6.8 S	106.8 E
124	Serantes (sâ-rän'tās) Sp.	43.23 N	8.21 W
127	Serbia (Prov.) (sûr'bĭ-ȧ) Yugo.	43.40 N	20.40 E
111	Serdobsk (sĕr-dôpsk') Sov. Un.	52.28 N	44.20 E
119	Serdobol (sĕr'dô-bôl') Sov. Un.	61.44 N	30.42 E
121	Sered (sĕr'ĕd) Czech.	48.17 N	17.43 E
128	Sereda (sĕ'rā-dà) Sov. Un.	57.15 N	41.9 E
129	Seredina-Buda (sĕ-rā-dē'nà-bōō'dȧ) Sov. Un.	52.10 N	34.2 E
137	Seremban (sĕr-ĕm-bän') Malaya (In.)	2.44 N	101.55 E
102	Serena (sâ-rā'nä) Chl.	29.50 S	71.20 W
134	Serenje (sē-rĕn'yê) N. Rh.	13.9 S	30.47 E
135	Serenli (sâ-rĕn'lê) Som.	2.20 N	42.15 E
127	Seres (Serrai) (sĕr'ĕs) (sĕr'ĕ) Grc.	41.5 N	23.35 E
121	Seret R. (sĕr'ĕt) Sov. Un.	49.16 N	25.40 E
110	Sergievsk (sĕr-gē'yĕfsk) Sov. Un.	53.58 N	51.2 E
141	Seringapatam (sê-rĭŋ'gŭ-pŭ-täm') India	12.28 N	76.37 E
127	Seriphos (sê-rē'fôs) Grc.	37.8 N	24.31 E
127	Seriphos (I.) Grc.	37.10 N	25.30 E
101	Serjipe (State) (sĕr-zhĕ'pĕ) Braz.	11.0 S	37.15 W
124	Seron (sâ-rōn') Sp.	37.21 N	2.29 W
110	Serov (syĕ-rôf') Sov. Un.	59.40 N	60.40 E
134	Serowe (sĕ-rō'wĕ) Bech.	22.25 S	26.40 E
124	Serpa (sĕr'pȧ) Port.	37.56 N	7.36 W
128	Serpukhov (syĕr'pōō-kôf) Sov. Un.	54.55 N	37.25 E
127	Serrai (Seres) (sĕr'rĕ) (sĕr'ĕs) Grc.	41.5 N	23.35 E
131	Serrat, C. (sĕr-rät') Tun. (In.)	37.12 N	9.18 E
101	Serrinha (sĕr-rēn'yȧ) Braz. (In.)	11.39 S	38.58 W
101	Serro (sĕr'rô) Braz.	18.31 S	43.20 W
124	Serta (sĕr'tä) Port.	39.49 N	8.1 W
151	Serua (I.) (sĕ-rōō'ȧ) Indon.	6.28 S	130.1 E
126	Sesia R. (sâz'yä) It.	45.35 N	8.24 E
126	Sesto (sĕs'tô) It.	43.49 N	11.14 E
126	Sestri Levante (sĕs'trê lâ-vän'tä) It.	44.16 N	9.24 E
122	Sète (Cette) (sĕt) Fr.	43.25 N	3.45 E
132	Sétif (sâ-tēf') Alg.	36.18 N	5.22 E
149	Seto (sē'tô) Jap.	35.14 N	137.5 E
132	Settat (sĕt-ät') (sē-tà') Mor.	33.0 N	7.28 W
134	Sette-Cama (sĕ-tĕ-kä-mä') Fr. Eq. Afr.	2.29 S	9.45 E
116	Settle (sĕt''l) Gt. Brit.	54.4 N	2.16 W
96	Settlement Pt. (sĕt''l-mĕnt) Ba. Is.	26.42 N	79.0 W
125	Setúbal (sâ-tōō'bäl) Port. (In.)	38.32 N	8.54 W
125	Setúbal, B. of Port. (In.)	38.26 N	8.54 W
55	Seul, Lac (L.) (läk sûl) Can.	50.35 N	92.30 W
118	Sevalen (L.) (sĕ'vâ-lĕn) Nor.	62.16 N	10.28 E
129	Sevastopol (Akhiar) (syĕ-väs-tô'-pôl'') (äk'yär) Sov. Un.	44.35 N	33.32 E
86	Seven Islands Can.	50.12 N	66.23 W
149	Seven (Kozushima) Is. (kô-zōō'shē-mä') Jap.	34.12 N	139.8 E
72	Severance (sĕv'ĕr-ȧns) Colo. (Denver In.)	40.32 N	104.51 W
114	Severn (R.) (sĕv'ĕrn) Gt. Brit.	51.40 N	2.20 W
139	Severnaya Zemlya (Northern Land) (sĕ'vĕr-nà-yà zĕm'l-yä) Sov. Un.	79.0 N	103.0 E
160	Severn R. (sĕv'ĕrn) Austl. (In.)	29.23 S	151.20 E
55	Severn R. Can.	54.30 N	89.30 W
75	Sevier L. (sê-vēr') Utah	39.0 N	113.10 W
75	Sevier R. Utah	39.35 N	112.25 W
75	Sevier R., East Fork Utah	37.50 N	112.5 W
124	Sevilla (sâ-vēl'yä) Sp.	37.25 N	5.58 W
127	Sevlievo (sĕv'lyĕ-vô) Bul.	43.2 N	25.6 E
123	Sevran (sĕ-vräN') Fr. (In.)	48.56 N	2.33 E
122	Sèvre Niortaise R. (sâ'vr' nyôr-tâz') Fr.	46.20 N	0.50 W
122	Sèvre R. Fr.	47.5 N	1.15 W
129	Sevsk (syĕfsk) Sov. Un.	52.8 N	34.30 E
89	Sewall Pt. (sū'ăl) Va. (Norfolk In.)	36.57 N	76.19 W
52	Seward (sū'ărd) Alsk. (In.)	60.7 N	149.20 W
76	Seward Neb.	40.55 N	97.5 W
52	Seward Pen. Alsk.	65.20 N	163.0 W
89	Sewickly (sê-wĭk'lê) Pa. (Pittsburgh In.)	40.32 N	80.12 W
151	Sexmoan (sĕx-mō-än') Phil. (Manila In.)	14.57 N	120.33 E
93	Seybaplaya (sā-ē-bä-plä'yä) Mex.	19.40 N	90.41 W
5	Seychelles (Is.) (sā-shĕl') Ind. O.	5.20 S	55.10 E
108	Seydisfjördur (sā'dēs-fyûr-dōōr) Ice.	65.22 N	13.58 W
84	Seymour (sē'mōr) Ind.	38.57 N	85.52 W
77	Seymour Ia.	40.41 N	93.7 W
78	Seymour Tex.	33.35 N	99.15 W
72	Seymour Cr. Can. (Vancouver In.)	49.30 N	123.0 W
122	Sézanne (sā-zän') Fr.	48.40 N	3.42 E
126	Sezze (sĕt'sä) It.	41.30 N	13.3 E
121	Sfântul-Gheorghe (sfûn'tōōl-gyôr'gâ) Rom.	45.53 N	25.47 E
132	Sfax (sfäks) Tun.	34.47 N	10.46 E
115	's Gravenhage (The Hague) ('s Krä'vĕn-hä'Kĕ) (hāg) Neth.	52.5 N	4.20 E
131	Sguenaia (sgĕ-nĭ'ä) Sp. Mor. (Gib. In.)	35.40 N	5.52 W
47	Shackleton Shelf Ice (shăk''l-tŭn) Ind. O.	65.0 S	100.0 E
73	Shades Cr. (shādz) Ala. (Birmingham In.)	33.18 N	86.58 W
73	Shades Mt. Ala. (Birmingham In.)	33.17 N	86.57 W
138	Shadrinsk (shá-drĕnsk') Sov. Un.	56.15 N	63.35 E
140	Shagra (shăg'rä) Sau. Ar.	25.15 N	45.15 E
6	Shag Rocks Atl. O.	52.0 S	43.0 W
141	Shahjahanpur (shä-jŭ-hän'pōōr) India	27.45 N	79.58 E
140	Shahreza (shä-rä'zä) Iran	32.0 N	51.59 E
140	Shahrud (shä'rōōd) Iran	36.15 N	54.47 E
145	Shahsien (shä'hsyĕn') Chn.	26.23 N	117.41 E
89	Shaker Heights (shā'kĕr) Ohio (Cleveland In.)	41.29 N	81.32 W
111	Shakhova, C. (shä'kô-và) Sov. Un.	40.15 N	50.20 E
129	Shakhty (shäk'tē) Sov. Un.	47.43 N	40.12 E
146	Shakien (shä'kyĕn') Chn.	39.11 N	113.13 E
129	Shaknyal (shäk'nyäl) Sov. Un.	45.2 N	34.40 E
77	Shakopee (shăk'ô-pē) Minn.	44.46 N	93.30 W
138	Shakrizyabs (shà-krē-zyäps') Sov. Un.	39.15 N	66.45 E
141	Shal (Quetta) (shäl) (kwĕt'ä) Pak.	30.20 N	67.12 E
133	Shala, L. (shä'lä) Eth.	7.30 N	38.30 E
131	Shallufa (shäl'lōō-fä) Eg. (Suez Canal In.)	30.9 N	32.33 E
133	Shambe (shäm'bâ) A. E. Sud.	7.8 N	30.40 E
140	Sham, Jebel (Mt.) (jĕb'ĕl shäm') Oman	23.4 N	57.59 E
140	Shammar, Jebel (Mts.) (jĕb'ĕl shŭm'är) Sau. Ar.	27.15 N	41.30 E
	Shamo, see Gobi		
85	Shamokin (shȧ-mō'kĭn) Pa.	40.47 N	76.33 W
78	Shamrock (shăm'rŏk) Tex.	35.14 N	100.14 W
134	Shamva (shäm'vȧ) S. Rh.	17.27 S	31.33 E
146	Shangcheng (shäng'chĕng') Chn.	31.54 N	115.23 E
145	Shanghai (shäng'hī') Chn.	31.10 N	121.28 E
143	Shanghai Chn. (In.)		
145	Shanghang (shäng'häng') Chn.	24.59 N	116.12 E
146	Shangho (shäng'hō') Chn.	37.18 N	117.6 E
145	Shangkao (shäng'kou') Chn.	28.8 N	114.42 E
144	Shanglin (shäng'lĕn') Chn.	23.30 N	107.25 E
144	Shanglin Chn.	23.30 N	108.44 E
146	Shangshui (shäng'shwē') Chn.	33.41 N	114.35 E
146	Shangtsai (shäng'tsī') Chn.	33.16 N	114.14 E
144	Shangyü (shäng'yü) Chn.	25.59 N	114.5 E
145	Shangyu (shōōng'yōō') Chn.	29.58 N	120.58 E
146	Shanhaikwan (shän'hī'kwän') Chn.	39.59 N	119.30 E
146	Shanhsien (shän'hsyĕn') Chn.	34.50 N	116.4 E
73	Shannon (shăn'ŭn) Ala.	33.24 N	86.52 W
156	Shannon N. Z.	40.28 S	175.23 E
114	Shannon, R. Ire.	52.80 N	9.0 W
142	Shanshan (Pichan) (shän'shän') (pē'chän') Chn.	42.40 N	90.4 E
143	Shansi (Prov.) (shän'sē') Chn.	37.0 N	112.0 E
139	Shantar I. (shän'tär) Sov. Un.	55.0 N	137.30 E
146	Shantung (Prov.) (shän'tōōng') Chn.	36.10 N	118.10 E
146	Shantung Pen. Chn.	37.0 N	121.0 E
147	Shantung Pt. Chn.	37.25 N	122.38 E
145	Shaohing (shou'hĭng') Chn.	30.3 N	120.40 E
146	Shaopo (shou'-pō') Chn.	32.33 N	119.31 E
145	Shaowu (shou'wōō') Chn.	27.20 N	117.20 E
146	Sha R. (shä) Chn.	32.47 N	116.0 E
146	Sha R. Chn.	38.40 N	114.27 E
143	Sharasume (shä'rä-sōō'mä) Chn.	47.48 N	88.5 E
140	Shardjah (shär'jä) Sau. Ar.	25.20 N	55.29 E
133	Shari R. (shä-rē') Fr. Eq. Afr.	10.30 N	16.30 E
158	Shark B. Austl.	26.0 S	113.45 E
87	Sharon (shăr'ŏn) Mass. (In.)	42.7 N	71.10 W
84	Sharon Ohio	41.14 N	80.30 W
88	Sharon Hill Pa. (Philadelphia In.)	39.54 N	75.16 W
78	Sharon Springs Kan.	38.53 N	101.45 W
89	Sharpsburg (shärps'bûrg) Pa. (Pittsburgh In.)	40.30 N	79.55 W
144	Shasi (shä'sē') Chn.	30.18 N	112.5 E
70	Shasta, Mt. (shăs'tȧ) Calif.	41.25 N	122.12 W
110	Shatsk (shätsk) Sov. Un.	54.0 N	41.40 E
78	Shattuck (shăt'ŭk) Okla.	36.16 N	99.54 W
82	Shaw (shô) Miss.	33.35 N	90.47 W
77	Shawano (shȧ-wô'nô) Wis.	44.46 N	88.35 W
55	Shawinigan Falls (shô'nĭ-găn) Can.	46.42 N	72.40 W
79	Shawnee (shô-nē') Okla.	35.19 N	96.55 W
84	Shawneetown (shô'nē-toun) Ill.	37.42 N	88.8 W
72	Shawnigan L. (shô'nĭ-găn) Can. (Vancouver In.)	48.37 N	123.38 W
121	Shchara R. (shchä'rà) Sov. Un.	53.5 N	25.20 E
138	Shcheglovsk (shchĕg'lôfsk) Sov. Un.	55.30 N	85.55 E
128	Shchelkovo (shchĕl'kô-vô) Sov. Un.	55.53 N	38.2 E
129	Shcherbinovka (shchĕr-bē'nôf-kà) Sov. Un.	48.24 N	37.46 E
129	Shchetovo (shchĕ'tô-vô) Sov. Un.	48.10 N	39.9 E
129	Shchigry (shchē'grē) Sov. Un.	51.52 N	36.55 E
77	Sheboygan (shê-boi'gȧn) Wis.	43.45 N	87.42 W
77	Sheboygan Falls Wis.	43.45 N	87.50 W
86	Shediac (shĕ'dê-ăk) Can.	46.17 N	64.35 W
114	Sheelin, L. (shēl'ĭn) Ire.	53.45 N	7.20 W
88	Sheenwater (shēn'wô-tĕr) N. Y. (Niagara Falls In.)	43.0 N	79.0 W

ăt; finȧl; rāte; senâte; ärm; ȧsk; sofȧ; fâre; ch-choose; dh-as th in other; bē; êvent; bĕt; recĕnt; cratẽr; g-go; gh-gutteral g; bĭt; ĭ-short neutral; rīde; K-gutteral k as ch in German ich;

Sheepshead PRONOUNCING INDEX Siguiri

Page	Name Pronunciation Region	Lat. °′	Long. °′
88	Sheepshead B. (shēps'hĕd) N. Y. (In.)	40.35 N	73.57 W
115	Sheerness (shēr'nĕs) Gt. Brit.	51.25 N	0.45 E
82	Sheffield (shĕf'fēld) Ala.	34.45 N	87.42 W
114	Sheffield Gt. Brit.	53.20 N	1.30 W
137	Sheikh Sa'id (shāk sä'ēd) Yem. (In.)	12.40 N	34.30 E
146	Shehsien (shĕ'hsyĕn') Chn.	36.39 N	113.48 E
137	Shekhem (Nablus) (shĕ'kĕm) (nä-bloos') Pal. (In.)	32.13 N	35.16 E
144	Shekki (shĕk'kē') Chn.	22.32 N	113.18 E
144	Sheklung (shĕk'loong') Chn.	23.1 N	113.55 E
128	Sheksna R. (shĕks'nȧ) Sov. Un.	58.45 N	38.12 E
79	Shelbina (shĕl-bī'nȧ) Mo.	39.41 N	92.3 W
84	Shelburn (shĕl'bŭrn) Ind.	39.10 N	87.28 W
85	Shelburne Can.	44.3 N	80.8 W
86	Shelburne Can.	43.47 N	65.19 W
84	Shelby (shĕl'bē) Mich.	43.33 N	86.24 W
82	Shelby Miss.	33.57 N	90.47 W
71	Shelby Mont.	48.27 N	111.50 W
83	Shelby N. C.	35.16 N	81.34 W
84	Shelby Ohio	40.54 N	82.40 W
79	Shelbyville (shĕl'bē-vĭl) Ill.	39.24 N	88.48 W
84	Shelbyville Ind.	39.30 N	85.48 W
84	Shelbyville Ky.	38.10 N	85.14 W
82	Shelbyville Tenn.	35.30 N	86.28 W
76	Sheldon (shĕl'dŭn) Ia.	43.11 N	95.50 W
81	Sheldon Tex. (In.)	29.52 N	95.7 W
53	Shelikof Str. (shĕ'lē-kôf) Alsk.	58.30 N	153.30 W
89	Shell Beach La. (New Orleans In.)	29.52 N	89.41 W
70	Shelley (shĕl'lē) Ida.	43.21 N	112.8 W
89	Shell I. La. (New Orleans In.)	29.15 N	89.39 W
158	Shellborough (shĕl'bŭ-rō) Austl.	20.5 S	119.15 E
77	Shellrock R. (shĕl'rŏk) Ia.	43.20 N	93.10 W
51	Shellville (shĕl'vĭl) Calif. (San Francisco In.)	38.13 N	122.26 W
128	Shelon R. (shä'lôn) Sov. Un.	57.55 N	29.40 E
85	Shelton (shĕl'tŭn) Conn.	41.18 N	73.6 W
76	Shelton Neb.	40.48 N	98.42 W
70	Shelton Wash.	47.13 N	123.8 W
111	Shemakha (shĕ-mȧ-kä') Sov. Un.	40.40 N	48.40 E
76	Shenandoah (shĕn-ăn-dō'ȧ) Ia.	40.47 N	95.00 W
85	Shenandoah Pa.	49.48 N	76.12 W
85	Shenandoah Va.	38.32 N	78.34 W
85	Shenandoah Natl. Park Va.	38.37 N	78.20 W
85	Shenandoah R. Va.	39.0 N	78.5 W
135	Shenbâb (shĕn-bäb') Eg.	29.51 N	31.14 E
144	Shenchow (shĕn'chō') Chn.	28.19 N	110.2 E
133	Shendi (shĕn'dē) A. E. Sud.	16.45 N	33.28 E
146	Shenkiu (shĕn'kyōō') Chn.	33.13 N	115.7 E
110	Shenkursk (shĕn-koorsk') Sov. Un.	62.5 N	42.58 E
142	Shensi (Prov.) (shĕn'sē') Chn.	35.35 N	108.30 E
146	Shentseh (shĕn'tsĕ') Chn.	38.23 N	115.13 E
143	Shenyang (Mukden) (shĕn'yäng') (mook'dĕn) Chn.	42.1 N	123.28 E
129	Shepetovka (shĕ-pĕ-tôf'kȧ) Sov. Un.	50.9 N	27.2 E
87	Sherborn (shûr'bŭrn) Mass. (In.)	42.14 N	71.22 W
55	Sherbrooke (shûr'brook) Can.	45.23 N	71.46 W
116	Sherburn (shûr'bŭrn) Gt. Brit.	53.48 N	1.15 W
121	Shereshovo (shĕ-rĕsh'ō-vō) Sov. Un.	52.32 N	24.10 E
112	Shergui I. (shĕr'gwē) Medit. Sea	34.47 N	11.15 E
79	Sheridan (shĕr'ĭ-dăn) Ark.	34.18 N	92.21 W
70	Sheridan Ore.	45.7 N	123.22 W
71	Sheridan Wyo.	44.49 N	106.57 W
128	Sherikhovichi (shĕ-rĭ-kô'vē-chē) Sov. Un.	58.45 N	33.31 E
131	Sherki, Esh (R.) (ĕsh shĕr'kē) Eg. (In.)	30.50 N	31.17 E
73	Sherman (shûr'măn) Calif. (Los Angeles In.)	34.5 N	118.24 W
79	Sherman Tex.	33.38 N	96.36 W
120	's Hertogenbosch (sĕr-tō'ghĕn-bōs) Neth.	51.41 N	5.20 E
116	Sherwood Forest (shûr'wood) Gt. Brit.	53.11 N	1.6 W
114	Shetland Is. (shĕt'lănd) Gt. Brit. (In.)	60.30 N	1.20 W
76	Sheyenne R. (shī-ĕn') N. D.	47.30 N	98.0 W
84	Shiawassee R. (shī-ȧ-wôs'ē) Mich.	43.0 N	84.12 W
140	Shibam (shē'bäm) Aden	16.0 N	43.50 E
135	Shibeli R. (shē'bȧ-lē) Eth.	6.4 N	43.0 E
131	Shibîn el Kom (shē-bēn' ĕl kōm') Eg. (In.)	30.31 N	31.0 E
131	Shibîn el Qanâtir (shē-bēn' ĕl kȧ-nä'tēr) Eg. (In.)	30.18 N	31.20 E
149	Shibuya (shē'boo'yȧ) Jap. (Tokyo In.)	35.39 N	139.42 E
73	Shields (shēldz) Utah (Salt Lake City In.)	40.34 N	112.17 W
71	Shields R. Mont.	46.5 N	110.46 W
116	Shifnal (shĭf'năl) Gt. Brit.	52.40 N	2.21 W
142	Shigatse (shĭ'gä'tsĕ') Chn.	29.17 N	8.92 E
146	Shihcheng (shē'chĕng') Chn.	26.22 N	116.18 E
145	Shihchiu L. (shē'chē-ōō') Chn.	31.28 N	119.10 E
145	Shihma (shē'mä') Chn.	24.26 N	117.47 E
144	Shihmen (shē'mĕn') Chn.	29.27 N	110.58 E
145	Shihmen Chn.	30.33 N	120.23 E
144	Shihnan (shē'nän') Chn.	30.18 N	109.6 E
146	Shih R. (shē) Chn.	32.0 N	115.21 E
146	Shihshow (shē'shō') Chn.	29.43 N	112.10 E
147	Shihtao (shē'tä'ō) Chn.	36.55 N	122.20 E
144	Shihtsien (shē'tsyĕn') Chn.	27.32 N	108.10 E
141	Shikarpur (shē-kär'poor) Pak.	27.59 N	68.45 E
149	Shikoku (I.) (shē'kō'koo) Jap.	33.45 N	133.30 E
139	Shilka R. (shĭl'kȧ) Sov. Un.	53.0 N	119.0 E
141	Shillong (shēl-lông') India	25.38 N	91.59 E
149	Shimabara (shē'mä-bä'rä) Jap.	32.47 N	130.22 E
149	Shimada (shē'mä-dä) Jap.	34.49 N	138.12 E
149	Shimizu (shē'mē-zoo) Jap.	35.1 N	138.29 E
138	Shimki (shēm'kē) Sov. Un.	51.45 N	102.20 E
149	Shimoda (shē'mō-dȧ) Jap.	34.41 N	138.55 E
135	Shimoni (shē'mō-nē) Kenya	4.37 S	39.23 E
149	Shimonoseki (shē'mō-nō-sĕ'kē) (shē-mō-nō'sĕ-kĭ) Jap.	34.0 N	131.0 E
139	Shimushiru (I.) (shē'moo-shē'roo) Kur. Is.	47.15 N	152.0 E
149	Shinagawa (shē'nȧ-gä'wä) Jap.	35.34 N	139.43 E
149	Shingu (shĭn'goo) Jap.	33.43 N	135.59 E
149	Shinji, L. (shĭn'jē) Jap.	35.26 N	132.58 E
149	Shinjuku (shĭn'joo'koo) Jap. (Tokyo In.)	35.42 N	139.42 E
133	Shinko R. (shĭn'kō) Fr. Eq. Afr.	6.0 N	24.15 E
114	Shin, Loch (L.) (lŏk shĭn) Gt. Brit.	58.5 N	4.30 W
148	Shinomi C. (shē'nō'mē) Jap.	33.31 N	135.47 E
134	Shinyanga (shĭn-yäŋ'gä) Tan.	3.38 S	33.12 E
96	Ship Channel Cay. (I.) Ba. Is.	24.49 N	77.50 W
116	Shipley (shĭp'lē) Gt. Brit.	53.50 N	1.47 W
85	Shippensburg (shĭp'ĕnz-bûrg) Pa.	40.3 N	77.31 W
86	Shippigan I. (shĭp'ĭ-găn) Can.	47.48 N	64.36 W
86	Shipshaw R. (shĭp'shō) Can.	48.40 N	71.2 W
116	Shipston-on-Stour (shĭp'stŭn-ŏn-stour') Gt. Brit.	52.4 N	1.37 W
149	Shiranesan (Mt.) (shē'rä'nȧ-sän') Jap.	35.44 N	138.13 E
134	Shirati (shē-rä'tē) Tan.	1.15 S	34.3 E
140	Shiraz (shē-räz') Iran	29.32 N	52.31 E
134	Shire R. (shē'rā) Nya.-Moz.	16.0 S	34.45 E
148	Shiriya C. (shē'rē-yä) Jap.	41.22 N	141.22 E
72	Shirley (shûr'lē) Colo. (Colo. Sprs. In.)	38.54 N	104.39 W
87	Shirley Mass. (In.)	42.33 N	71.38 W
129	Shirokoe (shē'rō-kō-yĕ) Sov. Un.	47.39 N	33.15 E
144	Shiuchow (shū'chō') Chn.	24.56 N	113.2 E
144	Shiuhing (shū'hĭng') Chn.	23.5 N	112.24 E
75	Shivwits (Shebit) Ind. Res. (shĭv'wĭts) (shĕ'bĭt) Utah	37.10 N	113.45 W
149	Shizuki (shĭ'zoo-kē) Jap.	34.28 N	134.51 E
149	Shizuoka (shē'zoo'ōkȧ) Jap.	35.1 N	138.26 E
128	Shklov (shklôf) Sov. Un.	54.11 N	30.20 E
127	Shkodër (Scutari) (shkō'dûr) (skoo'tȧrē) Alb.	42.3 N	19.31 E
139	Shkotovo (shkō'tō-vō) Sov. Un.	43.20 N	132.30 E
70	Shoal Cr. (shōl) Ill.	38.45 N	89.30 W
84	Shoals (shōlz) Ind.	38.40 N	86.45 W
149	Shodo I. (shō'dō) Jap.	34.30 N	134.15 E
117	Shoeburyness (shoo'b'rĭ-nĕs') Gt. Brit. (London In.)	51.32 N	0.47 E
141	Sholapur (shō'lä-poor) India	17.45 N	75.59 E
149	Shomyo (shōm'yō) Jap.	34.23 N	131.9 E
77	Shorewood (shōr'wood) Wis.	43.5 N	87.55 W
117	Shorne (shōrn) Gt. Brit. (London In.)	51.25 N	0.26 E
73	Short Cr. Ala. (Birmingham In.)	33.33 N	87.6 W
71	Shoshone (shō-shōn'ē) Ida.	42.56 N	114.24 W
71	Shoshone Cavern Natl. Mon. Wyo.	44.30 N	109.0 W
71	Shoshone Ind. Res. Wyo.	43.6 N	109.0 W
71	Shoshone L. Wyo.	44.25 N	110.45 W
71	Shoshone R. Wyo.	44.35 N	109.0 W
129	Shostka (shôst'kȧ) Sov. Un.	51.51 N	33.31 E
145	Showchang (shō'chäng') Chn.	29.26 N	119.15 E
146	Shochang Chn.	35.57 N	115.50 E
146	Showchow (shō'chō') Chn.	32.34 N	116.42 E
146	Showkwang (shō'kwäng') Chn.	36.56 N	118.42 E
145	Showning (shō'nĭng') Chn.	27.32 N	119.17 E
146	Showyang (shō'yäng') Chn.	37.52 N	113.10 E
129	Shpola (shpô'lȧ) Sov. Un.	49.0 N	31.26 E
81	Shreveport (shrēv'pōrt) La.	32.30 N	93.46 W
114	Shrewsbury (shrooz'bēr-ĭ) Gt. Brit.	52.42 N	2.50 W
87	Shrewsbury Mass. (In.)	42.17 N	71.43 W
116	Shropshire (County) (shrŏp'shĕr) Gt. Brit.	52.39 N	2.45 W
114	Shropshire Hills, South Gt. Brit.	52.25 N	3.0 W
96	Shroud Cay (I.) (shroud) Ba. Is.	24.22 N	76.39 W
144	Shuanen (shoo'ä-nĕn') Chn.	30.3 N	109.4 E
142	Shufu (Kashgar) (shoo'foo') (käsh'gär) Chn.	39.28 N	76.2 E
72	Shukshan, Mt. (shook'shăn) Wash. (Vancouver In.)	48.50 N	121.36 W
142	Shuleh (Yangi Shahr) (shoo'lĕ') (yäŋ'gē shär') Chn.	41.22 N	80.25 E
129	Shulginka (shool'gĭn-kȧ) Sov. Un.	49.9 N	38.51 E
77	Shullsburg (shŭlz'bûrg) Wis.	42.35 N	90.15 W
146	Shulu (shoo'loo') Chn.	37.56 N	115.20 E
52	Shumagin Is. (shoo'mȧ-gēn) Alsk.	56.0 N	160.0 W
134	Shume (shoo'mȧ) Tan.	4.42 S	38.12 E
144	Shumkai (shoom'kī') Chn.	22.58 N	111.2 E
145	Shunan (shoo'nän') Chn.	29.40 N	119.5 E
145	Shungchang (shoong'chäng') Chn.	26.47 N	117.42 E
52	Shungnak (shŭng'nȧk) Alsk.	67.0 N	156.30 W
146	Shunking (shŭn'kĭng') Chn.	30.50 N	106.0 E
142	Shunning (shŭn'nĭng') Chn.	24.28 N	99.51 E
146	Shunteh (shŭn'tē') Chn.	37.5 N	114.40 E
146	Shunyi (shoon'yĭ') Chn.	40.8 N	116.49 E
146	Shu R. (shoo) Chn.	34.30 N	118.26 E
140	Shurab R. (shoo'räb) Iran	30.40 N	56.30 E
148	Shuri (shoo'rē) Ryukyu Is. (In.)	26.14 N	127.45 E
140	Shur R. (shoor) Iran	35.45 N	50.0 E
140	Shushtar (shoosh'tŭr) Iran	31.59 N	48.47 E
146	Shuvang (shoo'wäng') Chn.	34.5 N	118.52 E
128	Shuya (shoo'yȧ) Sov. Un.	56.52 N	41.25 E
148	Shwangcheng (shwän-chûng) Chn.	45.27 N	126.29 E
148	Siakhin, L. (sē-äk'hĭn) Chn.	45.17 N	132.34 E
145	Siakiang (syä'kyäng') Chn.	27.28 N	115.10 E
137	Siak R. (sē-äk') Indon. (In.)	0.57 N	101.30 E
137	Siaksriindrapoera (sē-äks'rĭ-ĕn'-drȧ-poo'rȧ) Indon. (In.)	0.45 N	102.3 E
141	Sialkot (sē-äl'kōt) Pak.	32.28 N	74.29 E
150	Siam (sī-ăm') Asia	16.0 N	102.30 E
150	Siam, G. of Siam-Indoch.	10.0 N	102.0 E
142	Sian (syän') Chn.	34.17 N	108.57 E
148	Sian Chn.	42.59 N	125.16 E
146	Siangho (syäng'hō') Chn.	39.44 N	116.59 E
144	Sianghsien (syäng'hsyĕn') Chn.	24.3 N	109.46 E
145	Siangshan (syäng'shän') Chn.	29.48 N	121.52 E
144	Siangsiang (syäng'syäng') Chn.	27.47 N	112.12 E
144	Siangtan (syäng'tän') Chn.	27.53 N	112.40 E
144	Siangyin (syäng'yĭn') Chn.	28.38 N	112.35 E
146	Siaoching R. (syä'ō-chĭng') Chn.	37.0 N	117.30 E
145	Siaofeng (syä'ō-fĕng') Chn.	30.30 N	119.37 E
148	Siaohaotze (syä'ō-hä'ō-tzĕ') Chn.	46.57 N	124.30 E
146	Siaohsien (syä'ō-hsyĕn') Chn.	34.11 N	117.3 E
145	Siao R. (syä'ō) Chn.	29.5 N	114.40 E
151	Siaoe (I.) (sē-ä'oo) Indon.	2.40 N	125.25 E
145	Siaoshan (syä'ō-shän') Chn.	30.10 N	120.16 E
153	Siargao I. (sē-är-gä'ō) Phil.	9.50 N	126.2 E
153	Siasi I. (sē-ä'sē) Phil.	5.32 N	120.52 E
127	Siatista (syä'tĭs-tȧ) Grc.	40.15 N	21.32 E
153	Siaton (sē-ä'tōn) Phil.	9.3 N	123.3 E
153	Siaton Pt. Phil.	9.2 N	123.2 E
119	Šiauliai (shē-ou'lē-ī) Sov. Un.	55.58 N	23.20 E
146	Siayi (syä'yĭ') Chn.	34.18 N	116.14 E
153	Sibalon (sē-bä-lōn') Phil.	10.47 N	122.1 E
153	Sibay I. (sē-bī') Phil.	11.50 N	121.28 E
126	Sibenik (Sebenico) (shē-bä'nēk) (sā-bā'nē-kō) Yugo.	43.44 N	15.54 E
138	Siberian Area (Reg.) (sī-bē'rĭ-ăn) Sov. Un.	60.0 N	90.0 E
150	Siberoet I. (sē'bȧ-root) Indon.	1.30 S	99.0 E
134	Sibiti (sē-bē-tē') Fr. Eq. Afr.	3.42 S	13.17 E
121	Sibiu (sē-bĭ-oo') Rom.	45.49 N	24.10 E
76	Sibley (sĭb'lē) Ia.	43.25 N	95.42 W
150	Siboga (sē-bō'gä) Indon.	1.50 N	98.50 E
153	Sibonga (sē-bôŋ'gä) Phil.	10.1 N	123.37 E
141	Sibsagar (sēb-sŭ'gŭr) India	26.50 N	94.37 E
153	Sibuguey B. (sē-boo-gā') Phil.	7.37 N	122.40 E
153	Sibuku B. (sē-boo'koo) Phil.	7.19 N	122.3 E
153	Sibutu I. (sē-boo'too) Phil.	4.47 N	119.28 E
153	Sibutu Passage Phil.	5.0 N	119.35 E
152	Sibuyan I. (sē-boo-yän') Phil.	12.25 N	122.35 E
152	Sibuyan Sea Phil.	12.30 N	122.40 E
152	Sicapoo, Mt. (sē-kä-poo') Phil.	18.1 N	120.51 E
143	Siccawei Cr. (sĭk'ȧ-wä'ē) Chn. (Shanghai In.)	31.9 N	121.24 E
126	Sicily (I.) (sĭs'ĭ-lē) It.	37.35 N	14.10 E
94	Sico, R. (sē'kō) Hond.	15.33 N	85.30 W
100	Sicuani (sē-kwä'nē) Peru	14.28 S	71.1 W
133	Sidamo (Division) (sē-dä'mō) Eth.	5.0 N	38.30 E
117	Sidcup (sĭd'kŭp) Gt. Brit. (London In.)	51.25 N	0.6 E
99	Side, R. (sē'dȧ) Chl. (Magallanes In.)	52.46 S	69.20 W
126	Siderno Marina (sē-dĕr'nō mä-rē'nä) It.	38.7 N	16.18 E
127	Siderokastron (sē-dhē-rō'kȧs-trōn) Grc.	41.13 N	23.26 E
126	Sideron, C. (sē-dhē-rōn') Grc.	35.19 N	26.20 E
132	Sidi-bel Abbès (sē'dē-bĕl ȧ-bĕs') Alg.	35.10 N	0.40 W
131	Sidi el Hani, Sebkra of (L.) (sĕb'-krȧ sē'dē ĕl hä'nē) Tun. (In.)	35.35 N	10.20 E
47	Sidley, Mt. (sĭd'lē) Ant.	77.25 S	129.0 W
72	Sidney (sĭd'nē) Can. (Vancouver In.)	48.39 N	123.24 W
71	Sidney Mont.	47.44 N	104.9 W
76	Sidney Neb.	41.9 N	103.0 W
84	Sidney Ohio	40.21 N	84.7 W
72	Sidney I. Can. (Vancouver In.)	48.38 N	123.18 W
137	Sidon (Saida) (sī'dŏn) (sä'ē-dȧ) Leb. (In.)	33.33 N	35.23 E
133	Sidra, G. of (sĕd'rȧ) Libya	31.30 N	18.0 E
117	Siebenhirten (sē'bĕn-hēr-tĕn) Aus. (Wien In.)	48.7 N	16.19 E
121	Siedlce (syĕd''l-tsĕ) Pol.	52.8 N	22.19 E
120	Siegburg (zĕg'boorgh) Ger.	50.49 N	7.12 E
120	Siegen (zē'ghĕn) Ger.	50.53 N	8.1 E
120	Sieg River (zĕg) Ger.	50.48 N	7.32 E
121	Siemiatycze (syĕm'yȧ'tē-chĕ) Pol.	52.26 N	22.52 E
150	Siemréap-Angkor (syĕm-rā'äp-ŭŋ'-kôr) Indoch.	13.25 N	103.59 E
126	Siena (sē-ĕn'ä) It.	43.19 N	11.21 E
146	Sienhsien (syĕn'hsyĕn') Chn.	38.20 N	115.59 E
145	Sienku (syĕn'koo') Chn.	28.51 N	120.42 E
145	Sienyu (syĕn'yoo') Chn.	25.18 N	118.38 E
121	Sieradz (syĕ'rädz) Pol.	41.35 N	18.44 E
124	Siero (syä'rō) Sp.	43.25 N	5.39 W
121	Sierpc (syĕrpts) Pol.	52.51 N	19.43 E
132	Sierra Leone (sē-ĕr'rä lā-ō'nā) Afr.	8.30 N	12.0 W
72	Siesse, Mt. (sē-ĕs') Can. (Vancouver In.)	49.2 N	121.35 W
117	Sievering (sē'vĕr-ĭng) Aus. (Wien In.)	48.15 N	16.19 E
146	Sifei R. (sē'fā'ē) Chn.	33.10 N	116.4 E
148	Sifeng (sē'fĕng') Chn.	42.50 N	128.30 E
51	Sifton (sĭf'tŭn) Wash. (Portland In.)	45.40 N	122.31 W
153	Sigaboy (sē-gȧ'boi) Phil.	6.37 N	126.5 E
153	Sigboye Passage (sĕg-bō'yȧ) Phil.	5.25 N	120.30 E
118	Sigdal (sĕgh'däl) Nor.	60.1 N	9.42 E
122	Sigean (sē-zhäN') Fr.	43.0 N	3.2 E
121	Sighet (sē-gāt') Rom.	47.57 N	23.54 E
121	Sighisoara (sē-gē-shwä'rä) Rom.	46.12 N	24.48 E
127	Sighitikos, G. of (sē-ghē'tē-kōs) Grc.	40.15 N	23.55 E
124	Sigüenza (sē-gwĕn'thä) Sp.	41.4 N	2.39 W
108	Siglufjördur (sĕgh'loo-fyûr-door) Ice.	66.10 N	18.50 W
111	Signakh (sĕg-näK') Sov. Un.	41.38 N	45.50 E
157	Signal Hill (sĭg'năl) N. Z. (In.)	45.51 S	170.35 E
77	Sigourney (sĭg'ĕr-nē) Ia.	41.19 N	92.11 W
100	Sigsig (sēg-sēg') Ec.	3.10 S	78.30 W
118	Sigtuna (sēgh-too'nȧ) Swe.	59.38 N	17.40 E
96	Siguanea B. (sē-gwä-nä'ä) Isle of Pines	21.40 N	83.0 W
132	Siguiri (sē-gē-rē') Fr. W. Afr.	11.31 N	9.2 W

ng-sing; ŋ-baŋk; N-nasalized n; nŏd; cŏmmit; ōld; ôbey; ôrder; fōōd; fŏŏt; ou-out; s-soft; sh-dish; th-thin; pūre; ûnite; ûrn; stŭd; circŭs; ü-as "y" in study; '-indeterminate vowel.

Sihwa PRONOUNCING INDEX Smederevo

Page	Name Pronunciation Region	Lat. °′	Long. °′
146	Sihwa (sē'hwä') Chn.	33.54 N	114.33 E
111	Siirt (sĭ-ērt') Tur.	38.2 N	42.2 E
142	Sikang (Prov.) (sĭ'käng') Chn.	29.45 N	98.0 E
132	Sikasso (sē-käs'sō) Fr. W. Afr.	11.20 N	5.36 W
79	Sikeston (sīks'tŭn) Mo.	36.52 N	89.35 W
139	Sikhota Alin (sē-kô'tȧ á-lēn') Sov. Un.	47.0 N	137.20 E
127	Sikinos (I.) (sĭ'kĭ-nōs) Grc.	36.42 N	25.7 E
121	Siklós (sĭ'klōsh) Hung.	45.52 N	18.19 E
92	Silacayoápam (sē-lä-kä-yō-ä'päm) Mex.	17.31 N	98.0 W
153	Silam (sē-läm') N. Bor.	4.59 N	118.12 E
153	Silam, Mt. N. Bor.	4.59 N	118.10 E
152	Silang (sē-läng') Phil.	14.13 N	120.58 E
92	Silao (sē-lä'ō) Mex.	20.56 N	101.25 W
153	Silay (sē-lī') Phil.	10.47 N	122.59 E
141	Silchar (sĭl-chär') India	24.45 N	92.45 E
83	Siler City (sī'lẽr) N. C.	35.44 N	79.28 W
120	Silesia (sĭ-lē'shȧ) Pol.	50.55 N	17.0 E
131	Siliana, Oued (R.) (wēd sē-lē-ä'nȧ) Tun. (In.)	36.10 N	9.25 E
72	Silica (sĭl'ĭ-kȧ) Colo. (Denver In.)	39.27 N	105.4 W
153	Silingan, Mt. (sĭ-lĭŋ'gän) Phil.	7.44 N	122.30 E
127	Silistra (sē-lēs'trȧ) Bul.	44.5 N	27.16 E
118	Siljan, L. (sēl'yän) Swe.	60.50 N	14.45 E
118	Silkeborg (sĭl'kĕ-bôr') Den.	56.9 N	9.34 E
131	Silla del Papa (Mt.) (sēl'yä dĕl pä'pä) Sp. (Gib. In.)	36.8 N	5.15 E
79	Siloam Sprs. (sī-lōm') Ark.	36.11 N	94.32 W
124	Sil R. (sēl) Sp.	42.25 N	7.0 W
81	Silsbee (sĭlz'bē) Tex.	30.20 N	94.10 W
73	Siluria (sĭ-lū'rĭ-ȧ) Ala. (Birmingham In.)	33.14 N	86.49 W
119	Šilute (shĭ-lōō'tȧ) Sov. Un.	55.21 N	21.11 E
51	Silvana (sĭl-vän'ȧ) Wash. (Seattle In.)	48.12 N	122.16 W
134	Silva Porto (Bihe) (sĭl'vȧ pôr'tōō) (bē-ā') Ang.	12.22 S	17.5 E
110	Silva R. (sĭl'vȧ) Sov. Un.	57.15 N	57.15 E
97	Silver Bank (sĭl'vẽr) Ba. Is.	20.35 N	69.40 W
97	Silver Bank Passage Ba. Is.	20.50 N	70.10 W
75	Silver City N. M.	32.46 N	108.19 W
75	Silver Cr. Ariz.	34.20 N	110.5 W
85	Silver Creek N. Y.	42.36 N	79.7 W
51	Silverdale (sĭl'vẽr-dāl) Wash. (Seattle In.)	47.38 N	122.43 W
70	Silver Mts. Ida.	43.15 N	116.50 W
72	Silver Pk. Can. (Vancouver In.)	49.8 N	121.30 W
75	Silverton (sĭl'vẽr-tŭn) Colo.	37.50 N	107.40 W
70	Silverton Ore.	45.1 N	122.48 W
124	Silves (sēl'vĕzh) Port.	37.14 N	8.22 W
70	Silvies R. (sĭl'vēz) Ore.	43.40 N	119.0 W
131	Silwa (sēl'wȧ) Eg. (In.)	24.42 N	32.59 E
153	Simaddel I. (sē'mȧ-dĕl) N. Bor.	6.40 N	117.25 E
150	Simalur I. (sē-mä'lōōr) Indon.	2.30 N	96.15 E
152	Simara I. (sē-mä'rȧ) Phil.	12.48 N	122.3 E
133	Simba (sĭm'bȧ) Bel. Cong.	0.32 N	23.4 E
85	Simcoe (sĭm'kō) Can.	42.48 N	80.20 W
55	Simcoe, L. Can.	44.15 N	79.35 W
129	Simferopol (Akmechet) (sēm-fĕ-rô'pôl') (äk-mĕch'ĕt) Sov. Un.	44.57 N	34.4 E
141	Simla (sĭm'lȧ) India	31.5 N	77.5 E
121	Simleul-Silvaniei (shēm-lā'ōōl-sēl-vä'nyĕ-ē) Rom.	47.15 N	22.46 E
119	Simola (sē'mô-lȧ) Fin.	60.55 N	28.10 E
93	Simojovel (sē-mō-hô-vĕl') Mex.	17.8 N	92.42 W
153	Simonoc I. (sē-mô-nôc') Phil.	4.54 N	119.49 E
120	Simplon Pass (sĭm'plŏn) (săN-plôN') Switz.	46.16 N	8.2 E
120	Simplon Tunnel Switz.-It.	46.16 N	8.8 E
54	Simpson (sĭmp'sŭn) Can.	61.50 N	121.31 W
77	Simpson I. Can.	48.45 N	87.41 W
54	Simpson Str. Can.	68.30 N	99.0 W
118	Simrishamn (sēm'rēs-häm'n) Swe.	55.33 N	14.20 E
81	Sims Bayou (sĭmz bī-yōō') Tex. (In.)	29.38 N	95.28 W
127	Sinaia (sĭ-nä'yȧ) Rom.	44.20 N	25.31 E
133	Sinai Pen. (sī'nī) Eg.	29.0 N	34.0 E
152	Sinait (sē-nä'ēt) Phil.	17.52 N	120.29 E
92	Sinaloa (State) (sē-nä-lō'ä) Mex.	23.0 N	105.50 W
140	Sinandij (sē-nän'dĕj) Iran	35.29 N	46.55 E
143	Sinanju (sĭ'nän-jōō') Kor.	39.36 N	125.37 E
148	Sinasan (sĭ'nä-sän') Kor.	42.37 N	130.20 E
100	Since (sēn'sȧ) Col.	9.15 N	75.15 W
100	Sincelejo (sēn-sȧ-lā'hō) Col.	9.15 N	75.28 W
145	Sinchang (sēn'chäng') Chn.	28.23 N	114.41 E
145	Sinchang Chn.	29.30 N	120.52 E
145	Sincheng (sēn'chĕng') Chn.	27.14 N	116.47 E
146	Sincheng Chn.	34.21 N	113.47 E
146	Sincheng Chn.	37.1 N	118.2 E
146	Sincheng Chn.	39.17 N	115.57 E
147	Sinchŏn (sin'chŭn) Kor.	38.22 N	125.29 E
156	Sinclair Head (C.) (sĭn-klâr') N. Z. (In.)	41.22 S	174.44 E
72	Sinclair I. Wash. (Vancouver In.)	48.38 N	122.41 W
153	Sindangan B. (sēn-däŋ'gän) Phil.	8.15 N	122.50 E
153	Sindangan Pt. Phil.	8.9 N	122.40 E
119	Sindi (sēn'dē) Sov. Un.	58.24 N	24.41 E
129	Sinelnikovo (sē'nyĕl-nē'kô'vō) Sov. Un.	48.18 N	35.33 E
124	Sines (sē'nȧzh) Port.	37.57 N	8.50 W
145	Sinfeng (sēn'fĕng') Chn.	25.22 N	114.30 E
133	Singa (sĭŋ'gȧ) A. E. Sud.	13.10 N	33.55 E
145	Singan R. (sĭŋ'gän') Chn.	29.43 N	118.35 E
150	Singapore (sĭŋ'gȧ-pōr') Malaya	1.14 N	103.55 E
137	Singapore I. Malaya (In.)	1.22 N	103.45 E
137	Singapore Str. Malaya (In.)	1.13 N	104.0 E
150	Singaradja (sĭŋ'gȧ-rä'jȧ) Indon.	8.17 S	115.5 E
150	Singkep I. (sĭng'kĕp) Indon.	0.30 S	104.30 E
144	Singling (sĭng'lĭng') Chn.	25.42 N	109.58 E
150	Singora (Songkhlâ) (sĭn-gō'rȧ) (sông'klä') Siam	7.8 N	100.35 E
146	Singtang (sĭng'täng') Chn.	38.31 N	114.30 E
142	Singu (sĭn'gŭ) Bur.	22.29 N	95.50 E
146	Sinho (sĭn'hō') Chn.	37.35 N	115.17 E
144	Sinhwa (sēn'hwä') Chn.	27.44 N	111.3 E
129	Sinie Lipyagi (sēn'ē-ĕ lēp'yä-gē) Sov. Un.	51.23 N	38.26 E
151	Siniloan (sē-nē-lō'än) Phil. (Manila In.)	14.26 N	121.31 E
142	Sining (sē'nĭng') Chn.	36.40 N	101.40 E
126	Sinj (sēn') Yugo.	43.2 N	16.39 E
145	Sinkan (sēn'kän') Chn.	27.42 N	115.24 E
142	Sinkiang (Prov.) (sĭn'kyäng') Chn.	40.15 N	85.0 E
146	Sinlo (sĭn'lō') Chn.	38.29 N	114.48 E
147	Sinmi I. (sĭn'mē) Kor.	39.34 N	124.53 E
148	Sinmin (sĭn'mĭn') Chn.	41.58 N	122.52 E
126	Sinni R. (sēn'nē) It.	40.10 N	16.22 E
144	Sinning (sĭn'nĭng') Chn.	22.0 N	108.0 E
144	Sinning Chn.	26.27 N	110.43 E
134	Sinoia (sĭ-noi'ȧ) S. Rh.	17.22 S	30.8 E
111	Sinop (sē-nōp') Tur.	42.0 N	35.10 E
146	Sinpei (sĭn'pā'ē) Chn.	34.26 N	118.6 E
145	Sin R. (sĭn) Chn.	28.34 N	116.44 E
146	Sin R. (sĭn) Chn.	35.8 N	116.30 E
146	Sinsiang (sĭn'syäng') Chn.	35.17 N	114.3 E
144	Sinti (sĭn'tē) Chn.	29.48 N	113.24 E
144	Sintien (sĭn'tyĕn') Chn.	25.51 N	112.4 E
81	Sinton (sĭn'tŭn) Tex.	28.2 N	97.30 W
125	Sintra (sēn'trȧ) Port. (In.)	38.48 N	9.23 W
146	Sintsai (sĭn'tsī') Chn.	32.45 N	114.54 E
147	Sinŭiju (sĭ'nōōĭ-jōō) Kor.	40.6 N	124.24 E
146	Sinyang (sĭn'yäng') Chn.	32.13 N	113.53 E
128	Sinyaya R. (sēn'yȧ-yȧ) Sov. Un.	56.42 N	28.20 E
145	Sinyü (sĭn'yü') Chn.	27.45 N	114.52 E
129	Sinyukha R. (sē'nyōō-kȧ) Sov. Un.	48.52 N	30.45 E
120	Sion (sē'ôN') Switz.	46.15 N	7.20 E
76	Sioux City (sōō) Ia.	42.30 N	96.22 W
76	Sioux Falls S. D.	43.33 N	96.42 W
127	Siphnos (I.) (sēf'nôs) Grc.	37.0 N	24.42 E
146	Siping (sē'pĭng') Chn.	33.23 N	113.57 E
127	Šipka Pass (shēp'kȧ) Bul.	42.3 N	25.19 E
150	Sipora (I.) (sē-pō'rȧ) Indon.	2.15 S	99.40 E
82	Sipsey R. (sĭp'sē) Ala.	33.10 N	87.48 W
92	Siqueros (sē-kā'rōs) Mex.	23.22 N	106.13 W
94	Siquia, R. (sē-kē'ä) Nic.	12.25 N	84.40 W
153	Siquijor (sē-kē-hôr') Phil.	9.12 N	123.32 E
153	Siquijor I. Phil.	9.10 N	123.35 E
144	Si R. (sē) Chn.	23.20 N	111.10 E
145	Si R. Chn.	26.10 N	117.38 E
126	Siracusa (Syracuse) (sē-rä-kōō'sä) (sĭr'ȧ-kūs) It.	37.5 N	15.17 E
131	Sirbon, L. (sẽr'bōn) Eg. (In.)	31.5 N	32.55 E
138	Sir Darya (Yaxartes) R. (sēr där'yȧ) (yăks-ăr'tēz) Sov. Un.	45.0 N	65.0 E
158	Sir Edward Pellew Group (Is.) (pĕl'ū) Austl.	15.40 S	137.0 E
118	Sire R. (sē'rĕ) Nor.	58.45 N	6.45 E
121	Siret (sĭ-rĕt') Rom.	47.58 N	26.2 E
127	Siret R. Rom.	45.30 N	27.40 E
140	Sirhan, Wadi (R.) (wä'dē sẽr'hän) Sau. Ar.-Jor.	30.20 N	37.45 E
139	Siriktakh R. (sē'rĭ-täk) Sov. Un.	65.20 N	141.0 E
87	Sir John H. Glover I. (glŭv'ẽr) Can.	48.45 N	57.45 W
133	Sirte (sûr'tē) (sēr'tä) Libya	31.10 N	16.32 E
119	Sirvintai (sẽr'vēn-tī) Sov. Un.	55.1 N	24.55 E
126	Sisak (sē'säk) Yugo.	45.29 N	16.21 E
93	Sisal (sē-säl') Mex.	21.8 N	90.1 W
110	Sisola R. (sē'sô-lȧ) Sov. Un.	61.0 N	50.20 E
74	Sisquoc R. (sĭs'kwŏk) Calif.	34.48 N	120.15 W
76	Sisseton (sĭs'tŭn) S. D.	45.40 N	97.3 W
123	Sisteron (sēst'rôN') Fr.	44.10 N	5.55 E
160	Sisters (Is.) Austl. (Tas. In.)	39.38 S	147.38 E
84	Sisterville (sĭs'tẽr-vĭl) W. Va.	39.30 N	81.0 W
125	Sitges (sēt-käs') Sp. (In.)	41.14 N	1.48 E
126	Sitia (sē'tĭ-ȧ) Grc. (In.)	35.10 N	26.7 E
53	Sitka (sĭt'kȧ) Alsk.	57.10 N	135.30 W
94	Sittee River (sĭt-tē') Br. Hond. (In.)	16.55 N	88.16 W
144	Siulam (syōō'läm') Chn.	22.38 N	113.10 E
145	Siuning (syōō'nĭng') Chn.	29.48 N	118.10 E
146	Siuwu (syōō'wōō') Chn.	35.14 N	113.28 E
147	Siuyen (syōō'yĕn') Chn.	40.16 N	123.11 E
111	Sivas (sē'väs) Tur.	39.45 N	36.58 E
111	Siverek (sē'vĕ-rĕk) Tur.	37.48 N	39.18 E
128	Siverskaya (sē'vẽr-skȧ-yȧ) Sov. Un.	59.16 N	30.3 E
121	Sivica R. (shē'vē-tsȧ) Pol.	49.0 N	23.53 E
133	Siwa Oasis (sē'wä) Eg.	29.15 N	25.30 E
95	Sixaola, R. (sē-kä-ō'lä) (sēk-sȧ-ō'lä) C. R.	9.34 N	83.0 W
88	Six Mile Cr. N. Y. (Niagara Falls In.)	43.14 N	78.59 W
118	Sjaelland (I.) (shĕl'län') Den.	55.30 N	12.0 E
127	Sjenica (syĕ'nē-tsȧ) Yugo.	43.16 N	20.1 E
108	Sjönstad (syûn'städ) Nor.	67.11 N	15.43 E
129	Skadovsk (skä'dôfsk) Sov. Un.	46.8 N	32.52 E
118	Skagen (skä'ghĕn) Den.	57.48 N	10.34 E
118	Skagen (The Skaw) (skô) Den.	57.44 N	10.38 E
118	Skagerrak (Str.) (skä-ghĕ-räk') Eur.	58.0 N	10.0 E
51	Skagit B. (skăg'ĭt) Wash. (Seattle In.)	48.19 N	122.30 W
70	Skagit W. Wash.	48.27 N	121.40 W
53	Skagway (skăg'wā) Alsk.	59.20 N	135.30 W
121	Skalat (skä'lät) Sov. Un.	49.26 N	25.58 E
118	Skaldervik (B.) (skäl'dẽr-vēk) Swe.	56.20 N	12.40 E
51	Skamania (skȧ-mā'nĭ-ȧ) Wash. (Portland In.)	45.37 N	122.3 W
51	Skamokawa (skȧ-mô-kô'wȧ) Wash. (Portland In.)	46.15 N	123.26 W
118	Skanderborg (skän'ẽr-bôr') Den.	56.3 N	9.55 E
85	Skaneateles (skăn-ĕ-ăt'lĕs) N. Y.	42.57 N	76.25 W
85	Skaneateles L. N. Y.	42.50 N	76.20 W
118	Skänninge (shĕn'ĭng-ĕ) Swe.	58.23 N	15.2 E
118	Skanör (skän'ûr) Swe.	55.23 N	12.50 E
127	Skantzoura (Is.) (skän'tsōō-rȧ) Grc.	39.3 N	24.5 E
118	Skara (skä'rȧ) Swe.	58.24 N	13.25 E
118	Skaw, The (Skagen) (skô) (skä'ghĕn) Den.	57.44 N	10.38 E
56	Skeena City (skē'nȧ) Can. (Prince Rupert In.)	54.14 N	129.46 W
54	Skeena R. Can.	54.30 N	129.0 W
108	Skellefteå (shĕl'ĕf-tē-ô') Swe.	64.45 N	20.55 E
108	Skellefte R. (shĕl'ĕ-ftē) Swe.	65.5 N	20.30 E
117	Skelmersdale (skĕl'mẽrz-dāl) Gt. Brit. (Liverpool In.)	53.33 N	2.48 W
118	Skern R. (skĕrn) Den.	55.58 N	8.35 E
114	Skerries (Is.) (skĕr'ēz) Gt. Brit.	53.25 N	4.35 W
127	Skiathos (I.) (skē'ȧ-thôs) Grc.	39.8 N	23.28 E
114	Skibbereen (skĭb'ẽr-ēn) Ire.	51.40 N	9.20 W
81	Skidmore (skĭd'môr) Tex.	28.16 N	97.40 W
118	Skien (skē'ĕn) Nor.	59.13 N	9.38 E
121	Skierniewice (skyĕr-nyĕ-vēt'sĕ) Pol.	51.56 N	20.12 E
52	Skilak L. (skĭl'ăk) Alsk. (In.)	60.25 N	150.35 W
72	Skinners (skĭn'ẽrz) Colo. (Colo. Sprs. In.)	38.47 N	104.45 W
116	Skipton (skĭp'tŭn) Gt. Brit.	53.58 N	2.0 W
118	Skive (skē'vĕ) Den.	56.33 N	9.0 E
108	Skjalfandá (R.) (skyäl'fänd-ô) Ice.	65.20 N	17.40 W
126	Skofja Loka (shkôf'yȧ lō'kȧ) Yugo.	46.10 N	14.18 E
121	Skole (skô'lĕ) Sov. Un.	49.2 N	23.32 E
127	Skopelos (I.) (skô'pȧ-lôs) Grc.	39.5 N	23.2 E
127	Skoplje (skôp'lyĕ) Yugo.	42.1 N	21.28 E
128	Skopin (skô'pēn) Sov. Un.	53.48 N	39.33 E
127	Skopo (skô'pō) Tur.	41.43 N	27.26 E
118	Skövde (shûv'dĕ) Swe.	58.24 N	13.50 E
139	Skovorodino (skô'vô-rô'dĭ-nô) Sov. Un.	53.55 N	123.59 E
86	Skowhegan (skou-hē'gȧn) Me.	44.46 N	69.44 W
126	Skradin (skrä'dēn) Yugo.	43.50 N	15.55 E
118	Skreia (skrā'ȧ) Nor.	60.38 N	10.58 E
118	Skudeneshavn (skōō'dĕ-nĕs-houn') Nor.	59.11 N	5.19 E
118	Skulerud (skōō'lĕ-rōōdh) Nor.	59.39 N	11.32 E
75	Skull Valley Ind. Res. (skŭl) Utah	40.25 N	112.45 W
77	Skunk R. (skŭnk) Ia.	41.16 N	92.20 W
77	Skunk R., North Ia.	41.30 N	92.40 W
119	Skuodas (skwô'dȧs) Sov. Un.	56.15 N	21.35 E
118	Skurup (skü'rōōp) Swe.	55.28 N	13.29 E
129	Skvira (skvē'rȧ) Sov. Un.	49.43 N	29.40 E
120	Skwierzyna (skvē-ĕr'zhĭ-nȧ) Pol.	52.35 N	15.31 E
114	Skye (I.) (skī) Gt. Brit.	57.25 N	6.20 W
102	Skyring Water (skī'rĭng) Chl.	52.35 S	72.0 W
127	Skyros (skē'rôs) Grc.	38.52 N	24.32 E
127	Skyros (I.) Grc.	38.50 N	24.35 E
118	Slagelse (slägh'ĕl-sĕ) Den.	55.25 N	11.19 E
150	Slamet, Mt. (Vol.) (slä'mĕt) Indon.	7.15 S	109.15 E
127	Slănic (slŭ'nĕk) Rom.	45.12 N	25.55 E
77	Slate Is. (slāt) Can.	48.40 N	87.0 W
79	Slater (slāt'ẽr) Mo.	39.13 N	93.2 W
127	Slatina (slä'tē-nä) Rom.	44.26 N	24.22 E
78	Slaton (slā'tŭn) Tex.	33.26 N	101.37 W
54	Slave R. (slāv) Can.	60.0 N	112.30 W
138	Slavgorod (slâf'gō-rôt) Sov. Un.	53.10 N	78.30 E
126	Slavonia (Prov.) (slȧ-vō'nĭ-ȧ) Yugo.	45.25 N	18.0 E
129	Slavuta (slȧ-vōō'tȧ) Sov. Un.	50.18 N	26.53 E
129	Slavyansk (sláv'yänsk') Sov. Un.	48.52 N	37.38 E
129	Slavyanskaya (sláv-yán'skȧ-yȧ) Sov. Un.	45.16 N	38.4 E
120	Slawno (sláv'nô) Pol.	54.21 N	16.39 E
76	Slayton (slā'tŭn) Minn.	43.59 N	95.34 W
116	Sleaford (slē'fẽrd) Gt. Brit.	53.0 N	0.24 W
77	Sleepy Eye Minn.	44.17 N	94.42 W
81	Slidell (slī-dĕl') La.	30.17 N	89.46 W
114	Sligo (slī'gō) Ire.	54.15 N	8.30 W
114	Sligo B. Ire.	54.20 N	8.40 W
138	Slinkina (slĭŋ'kē-nä) Sov. Un.	58.55 N	68.45 E
118	Slite (slē'tĕ) Swe.	57.41 N	18.50 E
133	Sliten (slĭt'ĕn) Libya	32.27 N	14.30 E
127	Sliven (slē'vĕn) Bul.	42.39 N	26.19 E
88	Sloan (slōn) N. Y. (Niagara Falls In.)	42.53 N	78.48 W
110	Slobodskoi (slô'bôt-skoi) Sov. Un.	58.45 N	50.10 E
127	Slobozia (slô-bō'zyȧ) Rom.	44.34 N	27.24 E
119	Sloka (slô'kȧ) Sov. Un.	56.57 N	23.40 E
121	Slonim (swō'nēm) Sov. Un.	53.4 N	25.19 E
133	Slonta (slŏn'tȧ) Libya	32.32 N	21.35 E
121	Slovakia (Slovensko) (Prov.) (slô-văk'ĭ-ȧ) (slô-vĕn'skô) Czech.	48.37 N	19.55 E
126	Slovenia (Prov.) (slô-vē'nĭ-ȧ) Yugo.	45.50 N	15.25 E
121	Slovensko (Slovakia) (Prov.) Czech.	48.37 N	19.55 E
128	Sluch R. (slōōch) Sov. Un.	52.40 N	27.20 E
121	Slucz R. (slōōch) Sov. Un.	51.10 N	26.47 E
126	Sluderno (slōō-dĕr'nô) It.	46.40 N	10.36 E
126	Slunj (slōōn') Yugo.	45.7 N	15.35 E
121	Slupca (swōōp'tsȧ) Pol.	52.16 N	17.52 E
121	Slupsk (slŭpsk) Pol.	54.27 N	17.3 E
128	Slutsk (slōōtsk) Sov. Un.	53.2 N	27.35 E
128	Slutsk Sov. Un.	59.43 N	30.24 E
114	Slyne Head (slīn) Ire.	53.25 N	10.10 W
79	Smackover (smăk'ô-vẽr) Ark.	33.22 N	92.41 W
131	Smala des Souassi ('s-mä'lȧ dā sōō-ä-sē') Tun. (In.)	35.22 N	10.28 E
117	Smay (smī) Bel. (Anvers In.)	51.10 N	4.3 E
127	Smederevo (Semendria) (smĕ'dĕ-rĕ-vô) (sĕ-mĕn'drĭ-ȧ) Yugo.	44.38 N	20.57 E

ăt; finȧl; rāte; senāte; ärm; ȧsk; sofȧ; fâre; ch-choose; dh-as th in other; bē; ēvent; bĕt; recĕnt; cratẽr; g-go; gh-gutteral g; bĭt; ĭ-short neutral; rīde; ᴋ-gutteral k as ch in German ich;

Smedjebacken PRONOUNCING INDEX Southern Rhodesia

Page	Name Pronunciation Region	Lat. °′	Long. °′
118	Smedjebacken (smĭ'tyĕ-bä-kĕn) Swe.	60.9 N	15.21 E
127	Smedovo (smĕ'dô-vô) Bul.	43.3 N	27.1 E
129	Smela (smyā'là) Sov. Un.	49.14 N	31.52 E
129	Smeloe (smyā'lô-ĕ) Sov. Un.	50.55 N	33.35 E
85	Smethport (smĕth'pōrt) Pa.	41.50 N	78.25 W
114	Smethwick (smĕdh'wĭk) Gt. Brit.	52.30 N	2.0 W
119	Smiltene (smĭl'tĕ-nĕ) Sov. Un.	57.26 N	25.54 E
78	Smith Center Kan.	39.46 N	98.47 W
160	Smithfield (smĭth'fēld) Austl. (Sydney In.)	33.51 S	150.55 E
83	Smithfield N. C.	35.30 N	78.20 W
71	Smithfield Utah	41.49 N	111.51 W
56	Smith I. (smĭth) Can. (Prince Rupert In.)	54.8 N	130.13 W
72	Smith I. . . Wash. (Vancouver In.)	48.19 N	122.50 W
84	Smithland (smĭth'lănd) Ky.	37.10 N	88.25 W
81	Smith Point Tex. (In.)	29.32 N	94.45 W
71	Smith R. Mont.	47.0 N	111.12 W
55	Smiths Falls (smĭths) Can.	44.51 N	76.0 W
87	Smith Sd. Can.	48.20 N	53.45 W
160	Smithton (smĭth'tŭn) Austl. (Tas. In.)	40.51 S	145.6 E
81	Smithville (smĭth'vĭl) Tex.	30.0 N	97.9 W
70	Smoke Creek Des. Nev.	40.40 N	119.40 W
79	Smoky Hill R. Kan.	38.44 N	99.0 W
53	Smoky R. Can.	55.0 N	118.30 W
118	Smölen (I.) (smûl'ĕn) Nor.	63.25 N	80.0 E
128	Smolensk (smô-lyĕnsk') Sov. Un.	54.45 N	32.1 E
128	Smolensk (Dist.) Sov. Un.	55.28 N	33.28 E
85	Smyrna (smûr'nȧ) Del.	39.18 N	75.38 W
73	Smyrna Ga. (Atlanta In.)	33.53 N	84.31 W
111	Smyrna (Izmir) (ĭz-mēr') Tur.	38.25 N	27.10 E
99	Smyth Canal (smĭth) Chl. (Magallanes In.)	52.30 S	73.25 W
77	Snake R. Minn.	45.50 N	93.15 W
70	Snake R. U. S.	44.35 N	117.15 W
70	Snake River Plains Ida.	43.15 N	113.25 W
96	Snap Pt. Ba. Is.	23.44 N	77.35 W
120	Sneek (snāk) Neth.	53.1 N	5.40 E
75	Sneffels Pk. (snĕf'ĕlz) Colo.	38.1 N	107.48 W
118	Snehetten (Mt.) (snĭ'hĕt-ĕn) Nor.	62.20 N	9.15 E
73	Snellville (snĕl'vĭl) Ga. (Atlanta In.)	33.52 N	84.1 W
121	Sniardwy L. (snyärt'vĭ) Pol.	53.45 N	21.45 E
70	Snohomish (snô-hō'mĭsh) Wash.	47.51 N	121.58 W
51	Snohomish (Tulalip) Ind. Res. (tōō'lȧ-lĭp) Wash. (Seattle In.)	48.8 N	122.20 W
70	Snohomish R. Wash.	47.40 N	121.50 W
129	Snovidovichi (snô'vê-dô-vê'chê) Sov. Un.	51.17 N	27.30 E
129	Snov R. (snôf) Sov. Un.	51.45 N	31.45 E
129	Snovsk (snôfsk) Sov. Un.	51.48 N	31.58 E
114	Snowdon, Mt. (snō'dŭn) Gt. Brit.	53.5 N	3.55 W
85	Snowhill (snō'hĭl) Md.	38.14 N	75.24 W
159	Snowy Mts. (snō'ē) Austl.	36.45 S	148.8 E
121	Snyatyn (snyä'tĭn) Sov. Un.	48.27 N	25.35 E
78	Snyder (snī'dẽr) Okla.	34.39 N	98.57 W
80	Snyder Tex.	32.43 N	100.55 W
73	Snyderville (snī'dẽr-vĭl) Utah (Salt Lake City In.)	40.42 N	111.32 W
116	Soar, R. (sōr) Gt. Brit.	52.48 N	1.16 W
133	Sobat R. (sō'bät) A. E. Sud.	9.0 N	32.30 E
128	Sobinka (sô-bĭŋ'kȧ) Sov. Un.	55.58 N	40.0 E
149	Sobosan (Mt.) (sō'bō-sän') Jap.	32.46 N	131.30 E
117	Soccayo (sô-kä'yô) It. (Napoli In.)	40.51 N	14.12 E
121	Sochaczew (sô-ĸä'chĕf) Pol.	52.14 N	20.18 E
142	Soche (Yarkand) (sō'chĕ) (yär-känt') Chn.	38.12 N	77.30 E
111	Sochi (sôch'ĭ) Sov. Un.	43.38 N	39.45 E
4	Société, Isles de la (Society Is.) (ĕl' dĕ lȧ sô-sē-ȧ-tā') (sō-sī'ĕ-tē) Pac. O.	16.30 S	152.0 W
146	Society B. Chn.	39.25 N	121.20 E
	Society Is, see Société, Is. de la		
56	Sockeye (sŏk'ī) Can. (Prince Rupert In.)	54.11 N	130.10 W
133	Socna (sôk'nȧ) Libya	29.7 N	15.47 E
93	Socoltenango (sô-kôl-tĕ-näŋ'gō) Mex.	16.17 N	92.18 W
93	Soconusco (sô-kô-nōōs'kō) Mex.	16.5 N	93.25 W
100	Socorro (sô-kôr'rō) Col.	6.12 N	73.45 W
75	Socorro N. M.	34.4 N	106.54 W
140	Socotra (I.) (sô-kō'trȧ) Ind. O.	12.30 N	54.0 E
124	Socuéllamos (sô-kōō-āl'yä-môs) Sp.	39.18 N	2.48 W
54	Soda Cr. (sō'dȧ) Can.	52.10 N	122.2 W
71	Soda Springs Ida.	42.39 N	111.37 W
118	Söderhamn (sû-dẽr-häm''n) Swe.	61.20 N	17.1 E
118	Söderköping (sû'dẽr-chû'pĭng) Swe.	58.30 N	16.15 E
118	Södertälje (sû-dẽr-tĕl'yĕ) Swe.	59.11 N	17.39 E
150	Soekaboemi (sōō'kä-bōō'mē) Indon.	6.58 S	106.59 E
150	Soekadana (sōō-kä-dä'nä) Indon.	1.15 S	109.59 E
150	Soemba (Sumba) (Sandalwood) I. (sōōm'bä) (sŭm'bȧ) Indon.	9.45 S	120.0 E
151	Soela Is. (sōō-lä') Indon.	1.50 S	126.0 E
150	Soembawa (sōōm-bä'wä) Indon.	8.35 S	117.25 E
150	Soembawa (Sumbawa) (I.) (sōōm-bä'wä) Indon.	8.45 S	118.0 E
150	Soerabaja (sōō-rä-bä'yä) Indon.	7.22 S	112.40 E
120	Soest (zōst) Ger.	51.35 N	8.5 E
134	Sofala (sô'fä-lä) Moz.	20.7 S	34.40 E
112	Sofeggin, Wadi (R.) (wä'dē sôf'ĕg-ĕn) Libya	31.22 N	14.0 E
127	Sofia (Sofija) (sô'fē-yȧ) (sô-fī'ȧ) Bul.	42.40 N	23.20 E
129	Sofievka (sô-fē'yĕf-kȧ) Sov. Un.	48.3 N	33.51 E
139	Sofiiskoe (sô-fēs'kô-ye) Sov. Un.	51.25 N	139.50 E
127	Sofija (Sofia) (sô'fē-yȧ) Bul.	42.40 N	23.20 E
149	Sogano (sō'gä-nô) Jap. (Tokyo In.)	35.35 N	140.9 E
118	Sogndal (sôghn'dȧl) Nor.	58.20 N	6.20 E
118	Sogndal Nor.	61.13 N	7.2 E
118	Sogne Fjord (sôgn'ĕ fyôrd) Nor.	61.8 N	6.0 E
153	Sogod (sō'gôd) Phil.	10.23 N	125.0 E
153	Sogod B. Phil.	10.20 N	124.55 E
128	Sogozha R. (sô'gô-zhȧ) Sov. Un.	58.30 N	39.0 E
153	Sohoton Pt. (sō-hō-tōn') Phil.	9.59 N	122.27 E
147	Sŏhŭng (sŭ'hōōng') Kor.	38.28 N	126.14 E
122	Soissons (swä-sôɴ') Fr.	49.25 N	3.20 E
121	Sokal (sô'käl') Sov. Un.	50.28 N	24.20 E
111	Söke (sû'kĕ) Tur.	37.45 N	27.25 E
132	Sokodé (sô-kô-dā') Fr. W. Afr.	8.58 N	1.4 E
121	Sokólka (sô-kōōl'kȧ) Pol.	53.23 N	23.31 E
132	Sokolo (sô-kô-lō') Fr. W. Afr.	14.52 N	6.9 W
121	Sokolów (sô-kô-wōōf') Pol.	52.25 N	22.14 E
132	Sokoto (sō'kô-tō) Nig.	13.9 N	5.15 E
132	Sokoto (Prov.) Nig.	12.30 N	7.0 E
93	Sola de Vega (San Miguel) (sō'lä dā vā'gä) (sän mê-gāl') Mex.	16.30 N	96.58 W
152	Solana (sō-lä'nä) Phil.	17.39 N	121.41 E
152	Solano (sō-lä'nō) Phil.	16.30 N	121.11 E
100	Solar Pt. (sō-lär') Peru (In.)	12.12 S	77.3 W
92	Soledad Díez Gutiérez (sô-lâ-dhädh' dē'äz gōō-tyâ'rĕz) Mex.	22.10 N	100.55 W
70	Soleduck R. (sōl'dŭk) Wash.	48.0 N	124.30 W
94	Solentiname Is. (sô-lĕn-tê-nä'mȧ) Nic.	11.10 N	85.0 W
128	Soligalich (sô-lê-gȧ-lēch') Sov. Un.	59.4 N	42.19 E
116	Solihull (sō'lĭ-hŭl) Gt. Brit.	52.25 N	1.46 W
110	Solikamsk (Ust-Usolka) (sô-lē-kȧmsk) (ōōst ōō'sŭl-kȧ) Sov. Un.	59.35 N	56.45 E
120	Solingen (zō'lĭng-ĕn) Ger.	51.10 N	7.4 E
138	Solitude (Uedineniya) I. (sŏl'ĭ-tōōd) (ōō'yĕ-dē'nyĕ-nē'yȧ) Sov. Un.	77.30 N	85.50 E
118	Sollefteå (sôl-lĕf'tĕ-ô) Swe.	63.9 N	17.14 E
125	Sóller (sō'lyĕr) Sp.	39.46 N	2.42 E
150	Solo (sō'lō) Indon.	7.38 S	110.40 E
150	Solok (sô-lôk') Indon.	0.45 S	100.44 E
94	Solola (sô-lō'lä) Guat.	14.45 N	91.12 W
159	Solomon Is. Prot. (sŏl'ô-mŭn) Pac. O.	9.0 S	159.0 E
78	Solomon R. Kan.	39.26 N	98.10 W
78	Solomon R., North Fork Kan.	39.38 N	99.25 W
78	Solomon R., South Fork Kan.	39.25 N	99.20 W
120	Solothurn (zō'lô-thōōrn) Switz.	47.13 N	7.32 E
110	Solovetskie I. (sô'lô-vyĕt'skĭ-yĕ) Sov. Un.	65.10 N	36.0 E
120	Soltau (sôl'tou) Ger.	52.59 N	9.50 E
128	Soltsy (sôl'tsê) Sov. Un.	58.5 N	30.11 E
113	Soluch (sō'lōōk) Libya	31.39 N	20.23 E
143	Solun (sô-lōōn') Chn.	46.39 N	120.47 E
85	Solvay (sŏl'vā) N. Y.	43.5 N	76.14 W
118	Sölvesborg (sûl'vĕs-bôrg) Swe.	56.4 N	14.35 E
110	Solvychegodsk (sôl'vê-chĕ-gôtsk') Sov. Un.	61.20 N	46.50 E
114	Solway Firth (sŏl'wā fûrth') Gt. Brit.	54.45 N	3.40 W
122	Somain (sô-măɴ') Fr.	50.20 N	3.15 E
127	Sombor (sôm'bôr) Yugo.	45.47 N	19.8 E
92	Sombrerete (sōm-brā-rā'tā) Mex.	23.39 N	103.37 W
82	Somerset (sŭm'ẽr-sĕt) Ky.	37.6 N	84.37 W
85	Somerset Pa.	40.1 N	79.5 W
86	Somersworth (sŭm'ẽrz-wûrth) N. H.	43.18 N	70.55 W
75	Somerton (sŭm'ẽr-tŭn) Ariz.	32.35 N	114.43 W
160	Somerton . . Austl. (Melbourne In.)	37.39 S	144.56 E
88	Somerton . . . Pa. (Philadelphia In.)	40.8 N	75.0 W
87	Somerville (sŭm'ẽr-vĭl) Mass.	42.25 N	71.5 W
82	Somerville Tenn.	35.14 N	89.22 W
81	Somerville Tex.	30.20 N	96.31 W
156	Somes I. (sōmz) N. Z. (In.)	41.15 S	174.52 E
121	Someşul R. (sô-mâ'shōōl) Rom.	47.20 N	23.46 E
147	Sŏmjin R. (sŭm'jĭn) Kor.	35.16 N	127.23 E
134	Somkele (sôm-kā'lâ) U. S. Afr.	28.19 S	32.4 E
117	Somma, Mt. (sôm'mä) It. (Napoli In.)	40.49 N	14.25 E
117	Somma Vesuviana (sôm'mä vā-zōō-vê-ä'nä) It. (Napoli In.)	40.53 N	14.26 E
122	Somme R. (sôm) Fr.	50.0 N	2.0 E
72	Sommers (sŭm'ẽrz) Colo. (Colo. Sprs. In.)	38.58 N	104.50 W
94	Somoto Grande (sô-mō'tō grän'dĕ) Nic.	13.35 N	86.37 W
124	Son (sōn) Sp.	42.43 N	8.59 W
95	Sona (sō'nä) Pan.	8.0 N	81.20 W
147	Sŏnchŏn (sŭn'chŭn) Kor.	39.48 N	124.55 E
118	Sönderborg (sûn''ẽr-bôrgh) Den.	54.55 N	9.48 E
120	Sondershausen (zōn'dẽrz-hou'zĕn) Ger.	51.17 N	10.45 E
126	Sondrio (sôn'drê-ō) It.	46.11 N	9.51 E
118	Sonfjället (Nat. Park) (sōn'fyĕl-ĕt) Swe.	62.20 N	13.28 E
147	Sŏngchŏn (sŭng'chŭn') Kor.	39.16 N	126.12 E
133	Songea (sôn-gā'ȧ) Tan.	10.43 S	35.40 E
147	Songhwa (sŭng'hwä') Kor.	38.23 N	125.7 E
148	Sŏngjin (sŭng'jĭn') Kor.	40.41 N	129.12 E
147	Sŏngju (sŭng'jōō') Kor.	35.57 N	128.15 E
150	Songkhlâ (Singora) (sông'klä') (sĭŋ-gō'rä) Siam	7.8 N	100.35 E
150	Song, Mt. (sông) Sar.	3.25 N	115.0 E
120	Sonneberg (sôn'ĕ-bĕrgh) Ger.	50.22 N	11.11 E
74	Sonora (sô-nō'rȧ) Calif.	37.58 N	120.22 W
90	Sonora (State) Mex.	31.55 N	113.20 W
80	Sonora Tex.	30.33 N	100.40 W
74	Sonora Pk. Calif.	38.20 N	119.38 W
141	Son R. (sōn) India	24.30 N	83.0 E
124	Sonseca (sôn-sā'kȧ) Sp.	39.43 N	3.57 W
100	Sonsón (sôn-sôn') Col.	5.32 N	75.32 W
94	Sonsonate (sōn-sô-nä'tä) Sal.	13.46 N	89.43 W
151	Sonsorol Is. (sŏn-sô-rōl') Pac. O.	4.40 N	130.20 E
150	Sontay (sôɴ-tī') Indoch.	21.8 N	105.28 E
145	Soochow (sōō'chō') Chn.	31.15 N	120.32 E
72	Sooke Basin (sōōk) Can. (Vancouver In.)	48.23 N	123.39 W
72	Sooke Har. . Can. (Vancouver In.)	48.22 N	123.43 W
72	Sooke L. . . . Can. (Vancouver In.)	48.33 N	123.42 W
143	Soping (sô'pĭng') Chn.	40.12 N	112.25 E
121	Sopot (sô'pôt) Pol.	54.26 N	18.33 E
120	Sopron (shôp'rôn) Hung.	47.42 N	16.33 E
126	Sora (sô'rä) It.	41.43 N	13.36 E
100	Sorato (Illampú) (Mt.) (sô-rä'tō) (ē-lyäm-pōō') Bol.	15.58 S	68.30 W
128	Sorat R. (sô-rát') Sov. Un.	57.8 N	29.20 E
124	Sorbas (sôr'bäs) Sp.	37.5 N	2.6 W
86	Sorel (sô-rĕl') Can.	46.1 N	73.7 W
160	Sorell, C. (sô-rĕl') Austl. (Tas. In.)	42.10 S	145.11 E
160	Sorell, L. Austl. (Tas. In.)	42.8 S	147.11 E
126	Soresina (sō-râ-zē'nä) It.	45.14 N	9.44 E
124	Soria (sō'rê-ä) Sp.	41.46 N	2.28 W
99	Soriano (sō-rê-ä'nō) Ur. (Buenos Aires In.)	33.25 S	58.21 W
110	Sormovo (sôr'mô-vô) Sov. Un.	56.28 N	43.35 E
108	Sorö (I.) (sōōr'ô) Nor.	70.35 N	22.15 E
101	Sorocaba (sō-rô-kä'bȧ) Braz.	23.30 S	47.30 W
129	Soroki (sô-rō'kĕ) Sov. Un.	48.8 N	28.18 E
121	Soroksár (shô'rôk-shär) Hung.	47.23 N	19.9 E
151	Sorong (sō-rông') Neth. N. Gui.	1.0 S	131.28 E
133	Soroti (sô-rō'tê) Ug.	1.57 N	33.34 E
124	Sor R. (sôr) Port.	39.10 N	8.5 W
124	Sorraia R. (sôr-rī'ȧ) Port.	38.58 N	8.30 W
126	Sorrento (sôr-rĕn'tō) It.	40.37 N	14.21 E
152	Sorsogon (sôr-sô-gōn') Phil.	12.59 N	124.0 E
152	Sorsogon B. Phil.	12.50 N	123.50 E
147	Sŏsan (sŭ'sän) Kor.	36.47 N	126.27 E
129	Sosika R. (sô'sê-kȧ) Sov. Un.	46.25 N	39.20 E
129	Sosna R. (sôs'nȧ) Sov. Un.	50.42 N	38.30 E
129	Sosnitsa (sôs-nê'tsȧ) Sov. Un.	51.31 N	32.29 E
121	Sosnowiec (sôs-nô'vyĕts) Pol.	50.16 N	19.10 E
123	Sospel (sôs-pĕl') Fr.	43.54 N	7.27 E
148	Sosunova, C. (sô-sōō-nôf'ȧ) Sov. Un.	46.30 N	138.22 E
110	Sosva R. (sôs'vȧ) Sov. Un.	63.15 N	63.30 E
93	Soteapan (sô-tā-ȧ'pän) Mex.	18.14 N	94.53 W
92	Soto la Marina (sō'tō lä mä-rē'nä) Mex.	23.46 N	98.12 W
93	Soto la Marina B. Mex.	23.46 N	96.47 W
92	Soto la Marina, R. Mex.	24.0 N	98.17 W
140	Soueida (sōō-ā'ê-dȧ) Syr.	32.33 N	36.33 E
91	Soufrière (Vol.) (sōō-frê-âr') Guad.	16.7 N	61.39 W
95	Soufrière (Vol.) Le. Is. (In.)	16.43 N	62.10 W
95	Soufrière (Vol.) Wind. Is. (In.)	13.20 N	61.12 W
112	Souk-Ahras (sōōk-ä-räs') Alg.	36.20 N	7.52 E
131	Souk-el-Arba (sōōk-ĕl-är'bä) Tun. (In.)	36.28 N	8.55 E
57	Soulanges Canal (sōō-läɴzh') Can. (Montreal In.)	45.19 N	74.5 W
127	Souphlion (sōōf'lĭ-ôn) Grc.	41.11 N	26.17 E
137	Sour (Tyre) (sōōr) (tīr) Leb. (In.)	33.18 N	35.15 E
134	Sources, Mont aux (môɴ' tō sōōrs') Bas.	28.46 S	28.53 E
101	Soure (sōr-ĕ) Braz. (In.)	0.40 S	48.32 W
124	Soure Port.	40.4 N	8.38 W
87	Souris (sōō-rē') Can.	46.20 N	62.17 W
54	Souris R. Can.	49.10 N	101.0 W
81	Sourlake (sour'lāk) Tex.	30.8 N	94.24 W
132	Sousse (sōōs) Tun.	35.52 N	10.32 E
122	Soustons (sōōs-tôɴ') Fr.	43.45 N	1.20 W
117	Southall (soudh''l) Gt. Brit. (London In.)	51.31 N	0.24 W
88	South Amboy (south' ăm'boi) N. J. (N. Y. In.)	40.29 N	74.18 W
98	South America		
114	Southampton (south-ămp'tŭn) Gt. Brit.	50.55 N	1.25 W
55	Southampton I. Can.	64.35 N	84.30 W
158	South Australia Austl.	30.0 S	135.0 E
97	South B. Ba. Is.	20.57 N	73.38 W
84	South Bend Ind.	41.40 N	86.18 W
70	South Bend Wash.	46.39 N	123.49 W
96	South Bight Ba. Is.	24.13 N	77.38 W
96	South Bimini I. (bē'mê-nê) Ba. Is.	25.42 N	79.18 W
97	South Bluff (Pt.) Ba. Is.	22.17 N	74.10 W
87	Southboro (south'bŭr-ô) Mass. (In.)	42.18 N	71.32 W
83	South Boston (bôs'tŭn) Va.	36.43 N	78.56 W
72	South Boulder Cr. (bōl'dẽr) Colo. (Denver In.)	39.57 N	105.23 W
86	Southbridge (south'brĭj) Mass.	42.5 N	72.5 W
157	Southbridge N. Z.	43.48 S	172.20 E
97	South Caicos I. (kī'kōs) Ba. Is.	21.31 N	71.31 W
157	South C. N. Z.	47.18 S	167.38 E
83	South Carolina (State) (kăr-ô-lī'nȧ) U. S.	34.10 N	81.0 W
116	South Cave Gt. Brit.	53.46 N	0.36 W
88	South Chicago (shĭ-kô'gō) Ill. (Chicago In.)	41.43 N	87.34 W
150	South China Sea Asia	15.0 N	115.0 E
76	South Dakota (State) (dȧ-kō'tȧ) U. S.	44.30 N	100.0 W
114	South Downs (dounz) Gt. Brit.	50.55 N	0.40 W
160	Southeast C. Austl. (Tas. In.)	43.39 S	146.51 E
89	Southeast Pass La. (New Orleans In.)	29.4 N	89.3 W
97	Southeast Pt. Ba. Is.	20.59 N	73.9 W
115	Southend-on-Sea (south-ĕnd') Gt. Brit.	51.32 N	0.42 E
157	Southern Alps (Mts.) N. Z.	43.30 S	170.20 E
158	Southern Cross Austl.	31.10 S	119.28 E
54	Southern Indian L. Can.	57.10 N	99.30 W
83	Southern Pines N. C.	35.8 N	79.22 W
132	Southern Provinces Nig.	7.0 N	5.30 E
134	Southern Rhodesia (rô-dē'zhĭ-ȧ) Afr.	19.0 S	30.0 E

ng-sing; ŋ-baŋk; ɴ-nasalized n; nŏd; cŏmmit; ōld; ôbey; ôrder; fōōd; fŏŏt; ou-out; s-soft; sh-dish; th-thin; pūre; ûnite; ûrn; stŭd; circŭs; ü-as "y" in study; '-indeterminate vowel.

Southern Territories PRONOUNCING INDEX Steblev

Page	Name Pronunciation Region	Lat. °'	Long. °'
132	Southern Territories (Div.)...Alg.	29.0 N	3.0 E
114	Southern Uplands (ŭp'lȧndz) Gt. Brit.	55.30 N	4.0 W
75	Southern Ute Ind. Res. (ūt) Colo.-N. M.	37.0 N	108.45 W
117	Southfleet (south'flēt) Gt. Brit. (London In.)	51.25 N	0.19 E
82	South Fulton...Tenn.	36.28 N	88.54 W
47	South Georgia (I.) (jôr'jȧ). Atl. O.	54.0 S	37.0 W
84	South Haven (hā'v'n)...Mich.	42.23 N	86.17 W
81	South Houston (hūs'tŭn) Tex. (In.)	29.40 N	95.13 W
85	Southington (sŭdh'ĭng-tŭn). Conn.	41.37 N	72.55 W
157	South Island...N. Z.	44.0 S	170.0 E
83	South Jacksonville...Fla.	30.17 N	81.39 W
76	South Loup R. (lo͞op)...Neb.	41.10 N	99.36 W
160	South Melbourne (mĕl'bŭrn) Austl. (Melbourne In.)	37.50 S	145.0 E
77	South Milwaukee (mĭl-wô'kē). Wis.	42.55 N	87.52 W
96	South Negril Pt. (nȧ-grēl')...Jam.	18.16 N	78.23 W
85	South Norfolk...Va.	36.44 N	76.16 W
117	South Ockendon (ŏk"n-dŭn) Gt. Brit. (London In.)	51.32 N	0.18 E
88	South Orange (ŏr'ĕnj) N. J. (New York In.)	40.45 N	74.16 W
47	South Orkney Is. (ôrk'nē). Atl. O.	60.30 S	45.0 W
111	South Ossetia (Aut. Area) (ō-sē'shȧ). Sov. Un.	42.20 N	44.30 E
86	South Paris (păr'ĭs)...Me.	44.12 N	70.35 W
73	South Pasadena (păs-ȧ-dē'nȧ) Calif. (Los Angeles In.)	34.7 N	118.10 W
89	South Pass. La. (New Orleans In.)	29.0 N	89.8 W
78	South Pease R. (pēz)...Tex.	34.10 N	100.20 W
160	South Perth (pûrth) Austl. (Perth In.)	31.58 S	115.52 E
82	South Pittsburgh (pĭts'bûrg). Tenn.	35.2 N	85.43 W
78	South Platte R. (plăt)..Colo.-Neb.	39.45 N	105.0 W
95	South Pt....Barb. (In.)	13.3 N	59.33 W
97	South Pt. (C. Verde)...Ba. Is.	22.50 N	74.54 W
84	South Pt....Mich.	44.52 N	85.18 W
89	South Point. La. (New Orleans In.)	30.9 N	89.52 W
47	South Polar Plateau...Ant.	87.0 S	2.0 W
47	South Pole		
151	Southport (south'pōrt)...Austl.	27.59 S	153.25 E
114	Southport...Gt. Brit.	53.38 N	2.55 W
83	Southport...N. C.	33.56 N	78.2 W
73	South R....Ga. (Atlanta In.)	33.38 N	84.7 W
83	South R....N. C.	34.50 N	78.30 W
114	South Ronaldshay (rŏn'ăld-sā) Gt. Brit.	58.48 N	3.0 W
77	South St. Paul...Minn.	44.52 N	93.2 W
72	South St. Vrains Cr. (sănt vrānz') Colo. (Denver In.)	40.10 N	105.20 W
4	South Sandwich Is. (sănd'wĭch) Atl. O.	58.30 S	26.0 W
51	South San Francisco Calif. (San Francisco In.)	37.39 N	122.25 W
54	South Saskatchewan R. (săs-kăch'ē-wăn). Can.	51.0 N	107.0 W
47	South Shetland Is. (shĕt'lȧnd) Atl. O.	62.0 S	58.0 W
114	South Shields (shēldz)...Gt. Brit.	55.0 N	1.25 W
76	South Sioux City (so͞o sĭt'ē)..Neb.	42.28 N	96.25 W
156	South Taranaki Bight (tä-rä-nä'kē). N. Z.	39.40 S	174.0 E
114	South Uist I. (wĭst)...Gt. Brit.	54.15 N	7.20 W
70	South Umpqua R. (ŭmp'kwä). Ore.	43.10 N	123.0 W
72	South Vancouver (văn-ko͞o'vẽr) Can. (Vancouver In.)	49.13 N	123.5 W
116	Southwell (south'wĕl)...Gt. Brit.	53.4 N	0.56 W
134	Southwest Africa...Afr.	22.0 S	17.0 E
160	South West C...Austl. (Tas. In.)	43.32 S	146.2 E
72	South Westminster (wĕst'mĭn-stẽr) Can. (Vancouver In.)	49.11 N	122.52 W
97	Southwest Pt....Ba. Is.	20.58 N	73.40 W
96	Southwest Pt....Ba. Is.	25.50 N	77.13 W
96	Southwest Pt....Ba. Is.	26.27 N	78.40 W
97	Southwest Pt....Ba. Is.	23.55 N	74.3 W
148	Soviet B. (sô-vyĕt')...Sov. Un.	49.0 N	140.15 E
121	Sovietsk (Tilsit) (sô-vyĕtsk') (tĭl'sĭt). Sov. Un.	55.3 N	21.54 E
139	Sovietskaia Gavan (sô'vyĕt-skä-yȧ gä-văn'). Sov. Un.	49.0 N	140.5 E
136	Soviet Union (sō-vĭ-ĕt')...Eurasia	55.0 N	70.0 E
116	Sow, R. (sou)...Gt. Brit.	52.49 N	2.9 W
93	Soyaltepec (sô-yäl-tȧ-pĕk')..Mex.	18.12 N	96.29 W
148	Soyami C. (sô-yä'mē)...Jap.	45.29 N	141.55 E
148	Soya Str. (sō'yä)...Sakh.-Jap.	45.45 N	142.0 E
128	Sozh R. (sôzh)...Sov. Un.	53.36 N	31.40 E
127	Sozopol (sôz'ô-pôl')...Bul.	42.15 N	27.45 E
115	Spa (spä)...Bel.	50.28 N	5.50 E
125	Spain (spān)...Eur.	40.30 N	4.0 W
	Spalato, see Split, Yugo.		
114	Spalding (spôl'dĭng)...Gt. Brit.	52.45 N	0.10 W
76	Spalding...Neb.	41.43 N	98.21 W
51	Spanaway (spăn'ȧ-wā) Wash. (Seattle In.)	47.6 N	122.27 W
120	Spandau (shpän'dou)...Ger.	52.33 N	13.10 E
85	Spangler (spăng'lẽr)...Pa.	40.40 N	78.48 W
75	Spanish Fork...Utah	40.7 N	111.40 W
132	Spanish Guinea (gĭn'ē)...Afr.	3.0 N	9.30 E
96	Spanish Town...Jam.	17.59 N	76.58 W
74	Sparks (spärks)...Nev.	39.33 N	119.45 W
88	Sparrows Pt. (spăr'ōz) Md. (Baltimore In.)	39.12 N	76.28 W
82	Sparta (spär'tȧ)...Ga.	33.16 N	82.58 W
127	Sparta (Sparte) (spär'tē)...Grc.	37.5 N	22.25 E
79	Sparta...Ill.	38.7 N	89.40 W
84	Sparta...Mich.	43.10 N	85.44 W
82	Sparta...Tenn.	35.55 N	85.27 W
77	Sparta...Wis.	43.57 N	90.48 E
83	Spartanburg (spär'tăn-bûrg). S. C.	34.57 N	81.57 W
127	Sparte (Sparta) (spär'tē) (spär'tȧ) Grc.	37.5 N	22.25 E
131	Spartel, C. (spär-tĕl') Tangier (Gib. In.)	35.46 N	5.6 E
126	Spartivento, C. (spär-tē-vĕn'tô). It.	37.55 N	16.5 E
126	Spartivento, C....Sard.	38.54 N	8.51 E
128	Spas Demensk (spȧs dyĕ-mĕnsk') Sov. Un.	54.24 N	34.2 E
128	Spas Klepiki (spȧs klĕp'ē-kē) Sov. Un.	55.9 N	40.9 E
139	Spassk (spȧsk)...Sov. Un.	44.40 N	132.50 E
128	Spassk...Sov. Un.	54.24 N	40.26 E
126	Spathi, C. (spä'thē)...Grc.	35.40 N	23.43 E
87	Spear, C. (spēr)...Can.	47.30 N	52.40 W
76	Spearfish (spēr'fĭsh)...S. D.	44.29 N	103.51 W
84	Spencer (spĕn'sẽr)...Ind.	39.16 N	86.48 W
79	Spencer...Ia.	43.9 N	95.6 W
83	Spencer...N. C.	35.42 N	80.25 W
85	Spencer...W. Va.	38.52 N	81.20 W
158	Spencer G....Austl.	33.55 S	137.22 E
157	Spenser Mts....N. Z.	42.10 S	172.45 E
127	Sperkheios R. (spĕr'ĸā-ŏs)...Grc.	38.52 N	22.20 E
114	Sperrin Mts. (spĕr'ĭn)...N. Ire.	54.55 N	6.50 W
114	Spey, (R.) (spā)...Gt. Brit.	57.20 N	3.20 W
120	Speyer (shpī'ẽr)...Ger.	49.19 N	8.25 E
126	Spezia (spāt'sē-ä)...It.	44.17 N	9.48 E
135	Sphinx (sfĭnks)...Eg.	29.59 N	31.8 E
151	Spice Is. (Moluccas) (spīs) (mō-lŭk'ȧz). Indon.	1.0 S	128.0 E
126	Spinazzolo (spē-nät'zō-lō)...It.	40.58 N	16.5 E
157	Spire Park, Mt. (spīr)...N. Z.	45.22 S	167.30 E
70	Spirit L. (spĭr'ĭt)...Ida.	47.57 N	116.53 W
77	Spirit Lake...Ia.	43.25 N	95.5 W
121	Spišská Nová Ves (spēsh'skä nō'vä vĕs). Czech.	48.57 N	20.33 E
117	Spital (spĭt'ăl) Gt. Brit. (Liverpool In.)	53.20 N	2.59 W
48	Spitsbergen (Svalbard) (spĭts'bûr-gĕn) (sväl'bärt). Arc. O.	79.0 N	16.0 E
120	Spittal (shpē-täl')...Aus.	46.48 N	13.30 E
126	Split (Spalato) (splēt) (spä'lä-tō). Yugo.	43.31 N	16.26 E
70	Spokane (spō-kăn')...Wash.	47.40 N	117.29 W
70	Spokane R....Wash.	47.45 N	118.0 W
126	Spoleto (spô-lā'tō)...It.	42.45 N	12.43 E
77	Spooner (spo͞on'ẽr)...Wis.	45.50 N	91.52 W
79	Spoon R. (spo͞on)...Ill.	40.45 N	90.10 W
127	Sporades (Is.) (spŏ'rȧ-dēz)...Grc.	37.40 N	26.40 E
127	Sporades, Northern (Is.)...Grc.	39.0 N	24.0 E
70	Sprague R. (sprāg)...Ore.	42.30 N	121.40 W
70	Sprague R., North Fork...Ore.	42.47 N	121.0 W
150	Spratly (Storm) I. (sprăt'lē)..Asia	8.39 N	111.51 E
83	Spray (sprā)...N. C.	36.31 N	79.45 W
120	Spree R. (shprā)...Ger.	51.45 N	14.20 E
120	Spremberg (shprĕm'bĕrgh)...Ger.	51.35 N	14.22 E
134	Springbok (sprĭng'bŏk). U. S. Afr.	29.39 S	17.51 E
88	Spring Brook N. Y. (Niagara Falls In.)	42.49 N	78.41 W
74	Spring Cr....Nev.	40.20 N	117.48 W
80	Spring Cr....Tex.	31.10 N	100.55 W
79	Springdale (sprĭng'dāl)...Ark.	36.11 N	94.8 W
78	Springer (sprĭng'ẽr)...N. M.	36.21 N	104.35 W
78	Springfield (sprĭng'fēld)...Colo.	37.25 N	102.37 W
79	Springfield...Ill.	39.47 N	89.38 W
84	Springfield...Ky.	37.43 N	85.12 W
86	Springfield...Mass.	42.5 N	72.35 W
77	Springfield...Minn.	44.15 N	94.59 W
79	Springfield...Mo.	37.14 N	93.17 W
84	Springfield...Ohio	39.56 N	83.48 W
70	Springfield...Ore.	44.1 N	123.1 W
82	Springfield...Tenn.	36.30 N	86.53 W
86	Springfield...Vt.	43.18 N	72.30 W
134	Springfontein (sprĭng'fŏn-tĭn) U. S. Afr.	30.18 S	25.41 E
86	Springhill (sprĭng-hĭl')...Can.	45.38 N	64.4 W
79	Spring R....Ark.-Mo.	36.25 N	91.32 W
56	Springstein (sprĭng'stīn) Can. (Winnipeg In.)	49.48 N	97.27 W
74	Spring Valley...Calif. (In.)	32.46 N	117.1 W
79	Springvalley...Ill.	41.19 N	89.14 W
77	Spring Valley...Minn.	43.41 N	92.22 W
73	Springville (sprĭng'vĭl) Ala. (Birmingham In.)	33.47 N	86.28 W
75	Springville...Utah	40.10 N	111.37 W
78	Spur (spûr)...Tex.	33.27 N	100.51 W
114	Spurn Hd. (spûrn)...Gt. Brit.	53.55 N	0.10 E
52	Spurr, Mt. (spûr)...Alsk. (In.)	61.20 N	152.10 W
72	Squamish (skwō'mĭsh) Can. (Vancouver In.)	49.42 N	123.11 W
126	Squillace, G. of (skwēl-lä'chä)..It.	38.45 N	16.40 E
127	Srbobran (s'r'bô-brän')...Yugo.	45.34 N	19.49 E
139	Sredne Kolymsk (s'rĕd'nyĕ kô-lēmsk'). Sov. Un.	67.20 N	154.55 E
121	Śrem (shrĕm)...Pol.	52.7 N	17.2 E
139	Sretensk (s'rĕ'tĕnsk)...Sov. Un.	52.15 N	117.20 E
141	Srinagar (srē-nŭg'ŭr)...India	34.7 N	74.45 E
121	Środa (shrô'dȧ)...Pol.	52.13 N	17.17 E
121	Staaken (shtäk'ĕn). Ger. (Berlin In.)	52.32 N	13.9 E
117	Stabroeck (stä'bro͝ok) Bel. (Anvers In.)	51.20 N	4.21 E
120	Stade (shtä'dĕ)...Ger.	53.36 N	9.29 E
118	Städjan (Mt.) (stĕd'yän)...Swe.	61.53 N	12.52 E
117	Stadlau (shtät'lou). Aus. (Wien In.)	48.13 N	16.27 E
108	Stadur (stä'do͝or)...Ice.	65.8 N	21.5 W
114	Stafford (stăf'fẽrd)...Gt. Brit.	52.50 N	2.10 W
78	Stafford...Kan.	37.57 N	98.37 W
116	Stafford Co....Gt. Brit.	52.50 N	2.0 W
117	Stahnsdorf (shtäns'dôrf) Ger. (Berlin In.)	52.23 N	13.13 E
123	Stains (stăɴ)...Fr. (In.)	48.57 N	2.23 E
129	Stalin (stä'lĕn)...Sov. Un.	47.59 N	37.48 E
141	Stalin, Mt....Sov. Un.	39.0 N	72.0 E
138	Stalinabad (Dyushambe) (stȧ-lēn-ȧ-bȧt') (dyo͞o-shäm'bĕ). Sov. Un.	38.45 N	68.50 E
111	Stalingrad (stȧ'lĕn-grȧt). Sov. Un.	48.40 N	44.30 E
138	Stalinsk (Kuznetsk) (stȧ'lĕnsk) (ko͞oz-nĕtsk'). Sov. Un.	53.55 N	87.10 E
121	Stallupönen (shtäl'o͞o-pû-nĕn) Sov. Un.	54.37 N	22.37 E
116	Stalybridge (stā'lē-brĭj)..Gt. Brit.	53.29 N	2.3 W
77	Stambaugh (stăm'bô)...Mich.	46.4 N	88.36 W
85	Stamford (stăm'fẽrd)...Conn.	41.3 N	73.34 W
116	Stamford...Gt. Brit.	52.38 N	0.28 W
80	Stamford...Tex.	32.56 N	99.49 W
116	Stamford Bridge...Gt. Brit.	53.59 N	0.54 W
117	Stammersdorf (shtäm'ẽrs-dôrf) Aus. (Wien In.)	48.18 N	16.25 E
79	Stamps (stămps)...Ark.	33.21 N	93.29 W
79	Stanberry (stăn'bĕr-ē)...Mo.	40.12 N	94.33 W
134	Standerton (stăn'dẽr-tŭn) U. S. Afr.	26.55 S	29.16 E
116	Standish (stăn'dĭsh)...Gt. Brit.	53.35 N	2.39 W
72	Standley L. (stănd'lē) Colo. (Denver In.)	39.53 N	105.7 W
84	Stanford (stăn'fẽrd)...Ky.	37.30 N	84.42 W
117	Stanford-le-Hope (lē-hōp') Gt. Brit. (London In.)	51.31 N	0.26 E
118	Stangvik Fd. (stäng'vĕk)...Nor.	62.54 N	8.27 E
127	Stanimaka (stä-nē-mä'kä)...Bul.	42.0 N	24.51 E
74	Stanislaus R. (stăn'ĭs-lō)...Calif.	37.47 N	121.0 W
121	Stanislav (stä-nē-släf')...Sov. Un.	48.54 N	24.44 E
160	Stanley (stăn'lē)..Austl. (Tas. In.)	40.45 S	145.16 E
54	Stanley...Can.	55.25 N	104.29 W
86	Stanley...Can.	46.18 N	66.45 W
76	Stanley...N. D.	48.18 N	102.22 W
77	Stanley...Wis.	44.57 N	90.55 W
102	Stanley...Falk. Is.	51.45 S	57.50 W
133	Stanley Falls...Bel. Cong.	0.15 N	25.30 E
134	Stanley Pool Bel. Cong.-Fr. Eq. Afr.	4.10 S	15.35 E
133	Stanleyville (stăn'lē-vĭl). Bel. Cong.	0.32 N	25.15 E
94	Stann Creek (stăn krēk) Br. Hond. (In.)	17.0 N	88.14 W
139	Stanovoi Mts. (stä-nô-vô'ĭ) Sov. Un.	56.30 N	135.0 E
160	Stanthorpe (stăn'thôrp) Austl. (In.)	28.37 S	151.58 E
73	Stanton (stăn'tŭn) Calif. (Los Angeles In.)	33.49 N	118.0 W
76	Stanton...Neb.	41.58 N	97.14 W
80	Stanton...Tex.	32.7 N	101.47 W
51	Stanwood (stăn'wo͝od) Wash. (Seattle In.)	48.15 N	122.21 W
117	Stapelfeld (shtä'pĕl-fĕlt) Ger. (Hamburg In.)	53.36 N	10.13 E
77	Staples (stā'p'lz)...Minn.	46.22 N	94.46 W
88	Stapleton (stā'p'l-tŭn). N. Y. (In.)	40.38 N	74.5 W
127	Stara Kanjiža (stä'rȧ kän'yĭ-zhȧ) Yugo.	46.5 N	20.2 E
128	Staraya Kazinka (stä'rȧ-yȧ kȧ'zĕn-kȧ). Sov. Un.	52.50 N	40.8 E
128	Staraya Russa (stä'rȧ-yȧ ro͞os'sȧ) Sov. Un.	57.59 N	31.21 E
127	Stara Zagora (stä'rȧ zä'gô-rȧ). Bul.	42.25 N	25.38 E
56	Starbuck (stär'bŭk) Can. (Winnipeg In.)	49.46 N	97.35 W
4	Starbuck (I.)...Pac. O.	5.37 S	155.53 W
120	Stargard (shtär'gärt)...Pol.	53.20 N	15.3 E
127	Stari Bečej (stä'rē bĕ'chā')..Yugo.	45.36 N	20.2 E
128	Staritsa (stä'rē-tsȧ)...Sov. Un.	56.29 N	34.59 E
83	Starke (stärk)...Fla.	29.57 N	82.7 W
78	Starkville (stärk'vĭl)...Colo.	37.6 N	104.33 W
82	Starkville...Miss.	33.27 N	88.49 W
129	Starobelsk (stä-rô-byĕlsk') Sov. Un.	49.17 N	38.57 E
128	Starobino (stä'rô-bē-nô'). Sov. Un.	52.46 N	27.28 E
128	Starodub (stä-rô-do͞op')..Sov. Un.	52.35 N	32.49 E
121	Starogard (stä'rô-gär')...Pol.	53.58 N	18.33 E
129	Staro Shcherbinovka (stä'rô shchĕr'bē-nôf'kȧ). Sov. Un.	46.37 N	38.37 E
129	Staroverovka (stä'rō-vyĕ-rôf'kȧ) Sov. Un.	49.32 N	35.44 E
114	Start Pt. (stärt)...Gt. Brit.	50.15 N	3.35 W
128	Stary Bykhov (stä'rē bĕĸ'ôf) Sov. Un.	53.32 N	30.15 E
129	Stary-Oskol (stä'rē-ôs-kôl') Sov. Un.	51.18 N	37.50 E
121	Stary Sacz (stä-rē sôɴch')...Pol.	49.34 N	20.37 E
128	Stary Seslavino (stä'rē sĕs-lä'vē-nô). Sov. Un.	53.11 N	40.21 E
120	Staszfurt (stäts'fo͞ort)...Ger.	51.53 N	11.33 E
121	Staszów (stä'sho͞of)...Pol.	50.33 N	21.11 E
85	State College...Pa.	40.48 N	77.56 W
102	Staten I. (stăt'ĕn)...Arg.	54.45 S	64.0 W
88	Staten Island...N. Y. (In.)	40.34 N	74.10 W
83	Statesboro (stāts'bŭr-ō)...Ga.	32.26 N	81.48 W
83	Statesville (stāts'vĭl)...N. C.	35.46 N	80.54 W
72	Statlu L. (stăt'lo͞o) Can. (Vancouver In.)	49.33 N	122.5 W
79	Staunton (stôn'tŭn)...Ill.	39.0 N	39.47 W
85	Staunton...Va.	38.10 N	79.5 W
118	Stavanger (stä'väng'ẽr)...Nor.	58.59 N	5.45 E
72	Stave Falls (stāv) Can. (Vancouver In.)	49.14 N	122.21 W
72	Stave L....Can. (Vancouver In.)	49.20 N	122.17 W
116	Staveley (stāv'lē)...Gt. Brit.	53.16 N	1.21 W
72	Stave R....Can. (Vancouver In.)	49.13 N	122.23 W
110	Stavropol (stäv'rô-pôl')..Sov. Un.	53.30 N	49.15 E
111	Stavropol...Sov. Un.	45.5 N	42.0 E
78	Steamboat Springs...Colo.	40.28 N	106.49 W
73	Stearn (stûrn) Calif. (Los Angeles In.)	33.53 N	117.48 W
129	Steblev (styĕp'lyôf)...Sov. Un.	49.23 N	31.4 E

ăt; finăl; rāte; senåte; ärm; ȧsk; sofȧ; fâre: ch-choose; dh-as th in other; bē; ēvent; bĕt; recĕnt; cratẽr; g-go; gh-guttural g; bĭt; ĭ-short neutral; rīde; ĸ-gutteral k as ch in German ich;

Page	Name Pronunciation Region	Lat. °'	Long. °'
77	Steel R. (stēl) Can.	49.0 N	86.51 W
85	Steelton (stēl'tŭn) Pa.	40.14 N	76.46 W
70	Steens Mts. (stēnz) Ore.	42.30 N	118.45 W
158	Steep Pt. Austl.	26.12 S	113.8 E
133	Stefanie (Chalbe), L. (stĕf-à-nē') (chäl'bȧ). Eth.	4.45 N	36.50 E
84	Steger (stē'gẽr) Ill.	41.26 N	87.38 W
120	Steiermark (Prov.) (shti'ẽr-märk) Aus.	47.15 N	15.0 E
51	Steilacoom (stêl'ȧ-kōōm) Wash. (Seattle In.)	47.10 N	122.36 W
120	Stein (shtīn) Aus.	48.25 N	15.33 E
117	Steinkirchen (shtīn'kēr-kĕn) Ger. (Hamburg In.)	53.34 N	9.36 E
117	Stekene (stĕk'ĕ-nĕ) Bel. (Anvers In.)	51.12 N	4.3 E
51	Stella (stĕl'ȧ). Wash. (Portland In.)	46.11 N	123.6 W
87	Stellarton (stĕl'ȧr-tŭn) Can.	45.32 N	62.41 W
88	Stemmers Run (stĕm'ẽrz) Md. (Baltimore In.)	39.20 N	76.28 W
120	Stendal (shtĕn'däl) Ger.	52.36 N	11.50 E
108	Stenkjaer (stĭn'kyĕr) Nor.	64.0 N	11.30 E
111	Stepanakert (styĕ'pän-à-kĕrt') Sov. Un.	39.50 N	46.40 E
129	Stepantsi (styĕp'än-tsė).. Sov. Un.	49.43 N	31.14 E
56	Stephens I. (stē'vĕnz) Can. (Prince Rupert In.)	54.10 N	130.45 W
160	Stephenson, Mt. (stē'vĕn-sŭn) Austl. (In.)	27.53 S	152.20 E
80	Stephenville (stē'vĕn-vĭl) Tex.	32.13 N	98.11 W
78	Sterling (stûr'lĭng) Colo.	40.37 N	103.14 W
77	Sterling Ill.	41.47 N	89.42 W
78	Sterling Kan.	38.13 N	98.12 W
87	Sterling Mass. (In.)	42.26 N	71.45 W
80	Sterling City Tex.	31.50 N	100.59 W
110	Sterlitamak (styĕr'lē-tȧ-mȧk') Sov. Un.	53.55 N	55.55 E
121	Šternberk (shtĕrn'bĕrk) Czech.	49.43 N	17.18 E
73	Sterrett (stĕr'ĕt) Ala. (Birmingham In.)	33.27 N	86.28 W
120	Stettin (Szczecin) (shtĕ-tēn') (shchĕ'tsĭn). Pol.	53.26 N	14.32 E
120	Stettiner Haff (Sea) (shtĕ'tē-nĕr häf). Ger.-Pol.	53.45 N	14.15 E
84	Steubenville (stū'bĕn-vĭl) Ohio	40.24 N	80.40 W
77	Stevens Point (stē'vĕnz) Wis.	44.31 N	89.32 W
71	Stevensville (stē'vĕnz-vĭl). Mont.	46.30 N	114.6 W
70	Steveston (stēvz'tŭn) Can.	49.5 N	123.8 W
99	Stewart I. (stū'ẽrt) Chl. (Magallanes In.)	54.55 S	71.20 W
157	Stewart I. N. Z.	47.0 S	168.0 E
54	Stewart R. Can.	63.30 N	138.0 W
86	Stewiacke (stū'wē-ăk) Can.	45.9 N	63.21 W
120	Steyr (shtīr) Aus.	48.2 N	14.24 E
117	Stifford (stĭf'ẽrd) Gt. Brit. (London In.)	51.30 N	0.18 E
53	Stikine Mts. (stĭ-kēn') Can.	59.0 N	129.0 W
54	Stikine R. (stĭ-kēn') Can..	57.30 N	131.30 W
51	Stilaguamish R. (stĭl-ȧ-gwä'mĭsh) Wash. (Seattle In.)	48.12 N	122.20 W
77	Stillwater (stĭl'wô-tẽr) Minn.	45.4 N	92.49 W
79	Stillwater Okla.	36.7 N	97.3 W
70	Stillwater R. Mont.	48.45 N	114.40 W
70	Stillwater R. Mont.	45.30 N	109.50 W
127	Štip (shtĭp) Yugo.	41.43 N	22.7 E
114	Stirling (stûr'lĭng) Gt. Brit.	56.5 N	3.55 W
118	Stjördalen (styûr'dä-lĕn) Nor.	63.27 N	10.58 E
73	Stockbridge (stŏk'brĭj) Ga. (Atlanta In.)	33.33 N	84.14 W
120	Stockerau (shtô'kĕ-rou) Aus.	48.24 N	16.12 E
86	Stockholm (stŏk'hōlm) Me.	47.5 N	68.10 W
118	Stockholm (stôk'hôlm') Swe.	59.20 N	18.0 E
114	Stockport (stŏk'pôrt) Gt. Brit.	53.25 N	2.10 W
74	Stockton (stŏk'tŭn) Calif.	37.56 N	121.18 W
114	Stockton Gt. Brit.	54.35 N	1.22 W
78	Stockton Kan.	39.26 N	99.16 W
117	Stockton Heath Gt. Brit. (Liverpool In.)	53.22 N	2.34 W
77	Stockton I. Wis.	46.55 N	90.35 W
118	Stöde (stû'dĕ) Swe.	62.28 N	16.38 E
114	Stoke-on-Trent (stōk-ŏn-trĕnt) Gt. Brit.	53.0 N	2.10 W
160	Stokes Pt. (stōks). Austl. (Tas. In.)	40.10 S	143.55 E
121	Stokhud R. (stô-ĸōōt') Sov. Un.	51.20 N	25.10 E
127	Stolac (stô'làts) Yugo.	43.4 N	17.59 E
120	Stolberg (shtôl'bĕrgh) Ger.	50.47 N	6.13 E
139	Stolbovoi I. (stôl-bô-voi'). Sov. Un.	74.0 N	136.0 E
121	Stolin (stô'lēn) Sov. Un.	51.53 N	26.50 E
116	Stone (stōn) Gt. Brit.	52.54 N	2.9 W
87	Stoneham (stōn'ăm) Mass. (In.)	42.28 N	71.6 W
114	Stonehaven (stōn'hā-v'n). Gt. Brit.	56.55 N	2.13 W
73	Stone Mountain. Ga. (Atlanta In.)	33.48 N	84.10 W
56	Stonewall (stōn'wôl) Can. (Winnipeg In.)	50.9 N	97.18 W
73	Stonewall Ga. (Atlanta In.)	33.35 N	84.33 W
82	Stonewall Miss.	32.8 N	88.46 W
85	Stonington (stōn'ĭng-tŭn) Conn.	41.20 N	71.56 W
74	Stony Cr. (stō'nē) Calif.	39.30 N	122.37 W
88	Stony Cr. Ill. (Chicago In.)	41.41 N	87.44 W
85	Stony Lake Can.	45.45 N	79.25 W
56	Stony Mountain Can. (Winnipeg In.)	50.5 N	97.13 W
108	Stora Lule R. (stōō'rä lōō'lĕ). Swe.	66.15 N	20.47 E
118	Stord I. (stôrd) Nor.	59.52 N	5.30 E
118	Storesotra (Sartor) (I.) (stô-rĕ-sô'trȧ) (sär'tôr). Nor.	60.18 N	5.8 E
118	Stor Fjord (stôr) Nor.	62.23 N	6.15 E
118	Stor L. Swe.	63.12 N	14.15 E
118	Stor L. Nor.	61.35 N	11.12 E
118	Stor R. Nor.	58.38 N	6.10 E
160	Storm B. (stôrm). Austl. (Tas. In.)	43.10 S	147.35 E

Page	Name Pronunciation Region	Lat. °'	Long. °'
150	Storm (Spratley) I. (sprăt'lē). Asia	8.39 N	111.51 E
77	Storm L. Ia.	42.40 N	95.10 W
77	Storm Mt. Colo. (Denver In.)	40.29 N	105.23 W
91	Stormy Pt. St. Thomas (In.)	18.22 N	65.0 W
114	Stornoway (stôr'nô-wā).. Gt. Brit.	58.15 N	6.20 W
121	Storozhinets (stô-rô'zhēn-yĕts) Sov. Un.	48.11 N	25.45 E
118	Storrsjö (stôr'shû) Swe.	62.50 N	13.2 E
118	Storvik (stôr'vēk) Swe.	60.37 N	16.31 E
89	Story (stō'rē). La. (New Orleans In.)	29.55 N	89.55 W
87	Stoughton (stō'tŭn) Mass. (In.)	42.7 N	71.5 W
77	Stoughton Wis.	42.55 N	89.14 W
114	Stour (R.) (stour) Gt. Brit.	50.55 N	2.0 W
116	Stourbridge (stour'brĭj).. Gt. Brit.	52.27 N	2.9 W
116	Stourport (stour'pōrt) Gt. Brit.	52.20 N	2.16 W
87	Stow (stō) Mass. (In.)	42.26 N	71.30 W
114	Strabane (strȧ-băn') N. Ire.	54.52 N	7.22 W
159	Stradbroke I. (străd'brōk).. Austl.	27.35 S	153.29 E
160	Strahan (strā'ăn). Austl. (Tas. In.)	42.8 S	145.19 E
120	Strakonice (strä'kô-nyė-tsĕ). Czech.	49.17 N	13.51 E
127	Straldža (sträl'dzhȧ) Bul.	42.35 N	26.38 E
120	Stralsund (shträl'sōōnt) Ger.	54.19 N	13.3 E
118	Strand (stränd) Nor.	59.4 N	6.0 E
72	Strandell (strănd'ĕl) Wash. (Vancouver In.)	48.55 N	122.21 W
114	Strangford, Lough (L.) (lŏĸ străng'fẽrd). N. Ire.	54.25 N	5.40 W
118	Strängnäs (strĕng'nĕs) Swe.	59.22 N	17.0 E
114	Stranraer (străn-rär') Gt. Brit.	54.50 N	5.0 W
123	Strasbourg (stràs-bōōr') Fr.	48.35 N	7.50 E
84	Stratford (străt'fẽrd) Can.	43.24 N	81.0 W
85	Stratford Conn.	41.8 N	73.8 W
117	Stratford.. Gt. Brit. (London In.)	51.33 N	0.1 W
156	Stratford N. Z.	39.20 S	174.15 E
77	Stratford Wis.	44.47 N	90.3 W
114	Stratford-on-Avon (ā'vŏn) Gt. Brit.	52.13 N	1.45 W
160	Strathfield (străth'fēld) Austl. (Sydney In.)	33.52 S	151.6 E
120	Straubing (strou'bĭng) Ger.	48.53 N	12.34 E
120	Strausberg (strous'bĕrgh) Ger.	52.36 N	13.52 E
73	Strawberry Utah (Salt Lake City In.)	41.7 N	111.49 W
72	Strawberry Hill Can. (Vancouver In.)	49.9 N	122.54 W
75	Strawberry R. Utah	40.5 N	111.0 W
80	Strawn (strôn) Tex.	32.34 N	98.28 W
121	Strážnice (strázh'nyė-tsĕ).. Czech.	48.55 N	17.20 E
79	Streator (strē'tẽr) Ill.	41.7 N	88.49 W
76	Streeter N. D.	46.39 N	99.22 W
127	Strehaia (strĕ-kä'yȧ) Rom.	44.36 N	23.11 E
116	Stretford (strĕt'fẽrd) Gt. Brit.	53.26 N	2.61 W
117	Stretton (strĕ'tŭn) Gt. Brit. (Liverpool In.)	53.20 N	2.34 W
151	Strickland R. (strĭk'lănd) Pap. Ter.	6.30 S	142.1 E
73	Stringers (strĭng'ẽrz) Utah (Salt Lake City In.)	40.45 N	111.45 W
126	Stromboli (Vol.) (strôm'bô-lē).. It.	38.47 N	15.3 E
118	Strömstad (strûm'städ) Swe.	58.58 N	11.8 E
82	Strong R. (strông) Miss.	32.0 N	89.53 W
114	Stronsay (I.) (strŏn'sā) Gt. Brit. (In.)	59.5 N	2.40 W
72	Strontia Sprs. (strŏn'shȧ) Colo. (Denver In.)	39.27 N	105.8 W
85	Stroudsburg (stroudz'bûrg) Pa.	40.59 N	75.13 W
127	Struma R. (strōō'mȧ) Bul.	42.0 N	23.2 E
127	Strumica (strōō'mĭ-tsȧ) Yugo.	41.26 N	22.39 E
84	Struthers (strŭdh'ẽrz) Ohio	41.2 N	80.37 W
121	Stry (strē) Sov. Un.	49.15 N	23.51 E
121	Stry R. Sov. Un.	49.10 N	23.45 E
127	Stryman, G. of (strē'măn) Grc.	40.40 N	23.50 E
120	Strzegom (stzhĕ'gôm) Pol.	50.58 N	16.20 E
121	Strzelce (stzhĕl'tsĕ) Pol.	50.30 N	18.20 E
121	Strzelin (stzhĕ'lĭn) Pol.	50.47 N	17.4 E
121	Strzelno (stzhăl'nô) Pol.	52.37 N	18.11 E
158	Stuart (Alice Sprs.) (stū'ẽrt). Austl.	23.38 S	133.50 E
83	Stuart Fla. (In.)	27.11 N	80.15 W
77	Stuart Ia.	41.31 N	94.19 W
72	Stuart Chan. Can. (Vancouver In.)	48.57 N	123.40 W
72	Stuart I... Wash. (Vancouver In.)	48.41 N	123.12 W
158	Stuarts Ra. Austl.	29.30 S	135.0 E
118	Struer (strōō'ẽr) Den.	56.29 N	8.36 E
150	Stungtreng (stōōng'trĕng') Indoch.	13.38 N	105.53 E
77	Sturgeon B. (stûr'jŭn) Wis.	44.51 N	87.21 W
77	Sturgeon R. Mich.	46.45 N	88.36 W
84	Sturgis (stûr'jĭs) Ky.	37.35 N	87.59 W
84	Sturgis Mich.	41.46 N	85.25 W
76	Sturgis S. D.	44.25 N	103.30 W
158	Sturt Cr. (stûrt) Austl.	19.30 S	128.0 E
79	Stuttgart (stŭt'gärt) Ark.	34.30 N	91.33 W
120	Stuttgart (shtōōt'gärt) Ger.	48.50 N	9.11 E
117	Styal (stī'ăl) Gt. Brit. (Liverpool In.)	53.21 N	2.14 W
121	Styr R. (stēr) Sov. Un.	51.3 N	25.30 E
133	Suakin (Sawakin) (swä'kēn) (sä-wä'kēn). A. E. Sud.	19.3 N	37.20 E
147	Suan (sōō'ăn) Kor.	38.42 N	126.21 E
143	Süanhwa (sü'ăn-hwä') Chn.	40.37 N	115.6 E
145	Suao (sōō'ou) For.	24.36 N	121.50 E
119	Subata (sōō'bȧ-tȧ) Sov. Un.	56.1 N	25.55 E
160	Subiaco (sōō-bē-ä'kō) Austl. (Perth In.)	31.57 S	115.50 E
152	Subic (sōō'bĭk) Phil.	14.53 N	120.14 E
152	Subic B. Phil.	14.40 N	120.12 E
127	Subotica (sōō'bô'tē-tsȧ) Yugo.	46.5 N	19.40 E
121	Suceava (sōō-chȧ-ä'vȧ) Rom.	47.39 N	26.17 E
121	Suceava R. Rom.	47.45 N	26.3 E
121	Sucha (sōō'ĸȧ) Pol.	49.43 N	19.38 E
146	Sucheng (sōō'chĕng') Chn.	31.29 N	116.55 E
93	Suchiapa (sōō-chē-ä'pä) Mex.	16.38 N	93.5 W

Page	Name Pronunciation Region	Lat. °'	Long. °'
94	Suchitoto (sōō-chē-tō'tō) Sal.	13.58 N	89.2 W
142	Suchow (sōō'chō') Chn.	39.40 N	98.28 E
146	Süchow (sü'chō') Chn.	34.13 N	117.18 E
146	Suchow (sōō'chō') Chn.	33.38 N	116.58 E
143	Suchow Cr... Chn. (Shanghai In.)	31.11 N	121.25 E
142	Süchow (Suifu) (swē'fōō') Chn.	28.53 N	104.37 E
72	Sucia Is. (sōō'sē-ȧ) Wash. (Vancouver In.)	48.46 N	122.54 W
114	Suck R. (sŭk) Ire.	53.15 N	8.15 W
100	Sucre (sōō'krā) Bol.	19.1 S	65.25 W
140	Sudair (sŭ-dä'ẽr) Sau. Ar.	25.50 N	45.30 E
132	Sudan (Reg.) (sōō-dän') Afr.	12.0 N	10.0 E
128	Suda R. (sōō'dȧ) Sov. Un.	59.0 N	37.0 E
55	Sudbury (sŭd'bĕr-ė) Can.	46.32 N	81.15 W
117	Sudbury... Gt. Brit. (London In.)	51.34 N	0.20 W
87	Sudbury Mass. (In.)	42.23 N	71.25 W
117	Süder Elbe (R.) (sü'der ĕl'bĕ) Ger. (Hamburg In.)	53.30 N	9.54 E
120	Sudetes (Mts.) (sōō-dē'tēz) Ger.	50.25 N	16.40 E
128	Sudogda (sōō'dôk-dȧ) Sov. Un.	55.58 N	40.51 E
128	Sudost R. (sōō-dôst') Sov. Un.	52.40 N	33.20 E
57	Sud, R. du (rē-vyâr' dü süd') Can. (In.)	50.0 N	70.45 W
129	Sudzha (sōōd'zhȧ) Sov. Un.	51.12 N	35.14 E
125	Sueca (swā'kä) Sp.	39.12 N	0.19 W
146	Suehfuchwang (swĕ'fōō-chwäng') Chn.	36.39 N	120.49 E
145	Suenping (swĕn'pĭng') Chn.	28.38 N	119.34 E
133	Suez (sōō-ĕz') Eg.	29.59 N	32.28 E
131	Suez Canal Eg. (In.)	30.36 N	32.21 E
133	Suez, G. of Afr.	29.0 N	30.0 E
85	Suffolk (sŭf'ŭk) Va.	36.40 N	76.35 W
79	Sugar Cr. (shōōg'ẽr) Ill.	40.25 N	89.15 W
84	Sugar Cr. Ind.	39.57 N	87.5 W
78	Sugar City Colo.	38.13 N	103.41 W
81	Sugarland Junction Tex. (In.)	29.30 N	95.31 W
72	Sugar Loaf Colo. (Denver In.)	40.0 N	105.27 W
102	Sugar Loaf (Mt.) Braz. (In.)	22.58 S	43.9 W
133	Suhâg (sōō-häg') Eg.	26.35 N	31.36 E
120	Suhl (zōōl) Ger.	50.37 N	10.42 E
145	Suian (sōō'ē-än') Chn.	29.32 N	118.53 E
145	Suichang (sōō'ē-chäng') Chn.	28.33 N	119.22 E
146	Suichow (sōō'ē-chō') Chn.	34.29 N	115.17 E
148	Suihwa (sōō'ē-hwä') Chn.	46.27 N	127.6 E
143	Suihwa Chn.	46.36 N	126.40 E
142	Suilai (sōō'ē-lī') Chn.	44.30 N	86.10 E
144	Suining (sōō'ē-nĭng') Chn.	26.28 N	109.49 E
144	Suining Chn.	30.32 N	105.40 E
146	Suining Chn.	33.53 N	118.4 E
99	Suipacha (swē-pä'chȧ) Arg. (Buenos Aires In.)	34.42 S	59.38 W
146	Suiping (sōō'ē-pĭng') Chn.	33.12 N	113.54 E
114	Suir, R. (sūr) Ire.	52.20 N	7.30 W
51	Suisun B. (sōō-ē-sōōn') Calif. (San Francisco In.)	38.5 N	122.3 W
142	Suiting (sōō-ē'tĭng) Chn.	31.5 N	107.38 E
142	Suiyan (Prov.) (sōō'ē-yän'). Chn.	41.30 N	108.30 E
144	Suiyang (sōō'ē-yäng') Chn.	27.52 N	107.10 E
128	Sukhinichi (sōō'ĸē'nē-chė) Sov. Un.	54.6 N	35.21 E
110	Sukhona R. (sōō-ĸô'nȧ).. Sov. Un.	59.40 N	42.30 E
111	Sukhum (sōō-ĸōōm') Sov. Un.	43.0 N	41.2 E
141	Sukkur (sŭk'ŭr) Pak.	27.40 N	68.55 E
149	Sukumo (sōō'kōō-mô) Jap.	32.58 N	132.43 E
151	Sulabesi (I.) (sōō-lä-bä'sē).. Indon.	2.15 S	126.0 E
94	Sulaco, R. (sōō-lä'kō) Hond.	14.57 N	87.30 W
141	Sulaiman Ra. (sōō-lä-ē-män'). Pak.	29.30 N	69.38 E
111	Sulak R. (sōō-läk') Sov. Un.	43.20 N	47.0 E
129	Sula R. (sōō-lä') Sov. Un.	50.35 N	33.20 E
153	Sulat (sōō'lät) Phil.	11.47 N	125.27 E
153	Sulauan Pt. (sōō-lou'än) Phil.	8.37 N	124.28 E
126	Sulet (I.) (sōō'lĕt) Yugo.	43.23 N	16.20 E
129	Sulina (sōō-lē'nä) Rom.	45.7 N	29.30 E
108	Sulitelma (Mt.) (sōō-lė-tyĕl'mȧ) Swe.	67.5 N	16.30 E
100	Sullana (sōō-lyä'nä) Peru	5.0 S	80.32 W
82	Sulligent (sŭl'ĭ-jĕnt) Ala.	33.53 N	88.9 W
72	Sullivan (sŭl'ĭ-vȧn) Can. (Vancouver In.)	49.7 N	122.48 W
72	Sullivan Colo. (Denver In.)	39.40 N	104.53 W
79	Sullivan Ill.	39.35 N	88.36 W
84	Sullivan Ind.	39.6 N	87.22 W
79	Sullivan Mo.	38.13 N	91.8 W
126	Sulmona (sōōl-mō'nä) It.	42.3 N	13.56 E
79	Sulphur (sŭl'fŭr) Okla.	34.31 N	96.58 W
79	Sulphur R. Ark.-Tex.	33.24 N	94.55 W
81	Sulphur Springs Tex.	33.8 N	95.36 W
80	Sulphur Springs Cr. Tex.	32.58 N	102.32 W
140	Sultanabad (sōōl-tän-ä-bäd'). Iran	28.15 N	55.29 E
92	Sultepec (sōōl-tȧ-pĕk') Mex.	18.45 N	99.52 W
153	Suluan I. (sōō-lōō'än) Phil.	10.44 N	125.58 E
153	Sulu Arch. (sōō'lōō) Phil.	5.30 N	121.0 E
142	Sulu Ho (R.) (sōō'lōō hō') Chn.	40.30 N	96.30 E
153	Sulu Sea Phil.	9.0 N	120.30 E
149	Suma (sōō'mä) Jap. (Osaka In.)	34.39 N	135.6 E
72	Sumas (sū'mȧs) Wash. (Vancouver In.)	49.0 N	122.16 W
72	Sumas L. Can. (Vancouver In.)	49.4 N	122.8 W
72	Sumas R.. Wash. (Vancouver In.)	48.57 N	122.15 W
150	Sumatra (I.) (sōō-mä'trȧ).. Indon.	1.0 S	102.0 E
150	Sumba (Soemba) (sŭm'bȧ) (sōōm'bȧ) (Sandalwood) I. Indon.	9.45 S	120.0 E
150	Sumbawa (Soembawa) (I.) (sōōm-bä'wä). Indon.	8.45 S	118.0 E
114	Sumburgh Pt. (sŭm'bŭr-ō) Gt. Brit. (In.)	59.55 N	1.20 W
121	Sümeg (shü'mĕg) Hung.	46.59 N	17.19 E
127	Šumen (shōō'mĕn) Bul.	43.15 N	26.55 E
149	Sumidagawa R. (sōō'mē-dä-gä'wä) Jap.	36.8 N	139.28 E

ng-sing; ŋ-baŋk; ɴ-nasalized n; nŏd; cŏmmit; ōld; ôbey; ôrder; fōōd; fŏŏt; ou-out; s-soft; sh-dish; th-thin; pūre; ůnite; ûrn; stŭd; circŭs; ü-as "y" in study; '-indeterminate vowel.

Sumidouro PRONOUNCING INDEX Taganrog

Page	Name Pronunciation Region	Lat. °′	Long. °′
99	Sumidouro (sōō-mē-dō'rōō) Braz. (Rio de Janeiro In.)	22.0 S	42.39 W
73	Sumiton (sŭm'ĭ-tŭn) Ala. (Birmingham In.)	33.45 N	87.3 W
149	Sumiyoshi (sōō'mē-yō'shē) Jap. (Osaka In.)	34.36 N	135.29 E
70	Summer L. (sŭm'ẽr) Ore.	42.50 N	120.50 W
86	Summerside (sŭm'ẽr-sīd) Can.	46.24 N	63.47 W
83	Summerton (sŭm'ẽr-tŭn) S. C.	33.37 N	80.22 W
83	Summerville (sŭm'ẽr-vĭl) S. C.	33.1 N	80.10 W
73	Summit (sŭm'ĭt) Calif. (Los Angeles In.)	34.20 N	117.25 W
70	Summit Lake Ind. Res. Nev.	41.35 N	119.15 W
75	Summit Pk. Colo.	37.18 N	106.42 W
157	Sumner (sŭm'nẽr) N. Z. (In.)	43.34 S	172.48 E
51	Sumner Wash. (Seattle In.)	47.12 N	122.14 W
157	Sumner Head N. Z. (In.)	43.34 S	172.48 E
121	Šumperk (shŏŏm'pĕrk) Czech.	48.58 N	17.0 E
82	Sumrall (sŭm'rôl) Miss.	31.25 N	89.33 W
83	Sumter (sŭm'tẽr) S. C.	33.56 N	80.20 W
129	Sumy (sōō'mĭ) Sov. Un.	50.55 N	34.48 E
147	Sunan (sōō'nän') Kor.	39.12 N	125.43 E
85	Sunbury (sŭn'bẽr-ē) Pa.	40.52 N	76.47 W
147	Sunchŏn (sōōn'chŭn') Kor.	39.26 N	125.56 E
147	Sunchŏn Kor.	34.58 N	127.30 E
144	Sunchow (sŭn'chō') Chn.	23.28 N	110.4 E
150	Sunda Is. (sōōn'dä) Ind. O.	10.0 S	115.0 E
118	Sundals Fjord (sōōn'däls) Nor.	62.50 N	8.10 E
118	Sundals L. Nor.	59.36 N	6.45 E
71	Sundance (sŭn'dăns) Wyo.	44.25 N	104.30 W
150	Sunda Trough Indon.	10.0 S	111.0 E
158	Sunday Str. Austl.	16.20 S	123.10 E
118	Sundbyberg (sōōn'bü-bĕrgh). Swe.	59.22 N	17.58 E
114	Sunderland (sŭn'dẽr-lănd) Gt. Brit.	54.55 N	1.25 W
150	Sundir Str. (sōōn'dẽr) Indon.	6.0 S	106.0 E
118	Sundsvall (sōōnds'väl) Swe.	62.26 N	17.16 E
82	Sunflower R. Miss.	33.0 N	90.35 W
143	Sungari R. (sōōn'gȧ-rē) Chn.	46.0 N	127.0 E
151	Sungay Mt. (sōōŋ-gä'ē) Phil. (Manila In.)	14.10 N	121.2 E
145	Sungfow (sōōng'fō') Chn.	31.5 N	114.44 E
144	Sungkan (sōōng'kän') Chn.	28.20 N	106.42 E
145	Sungki (sōōng'kē') Chn.	27.36 N	118.26 E
145	Sungkiang (sōōng'kyäng') Chn.	30.55 N	121.8 E
144	Sungtze (sōōng'tsě') Chn.	30.20 N	111.30 E
111	Sungurlu (sōōn'gōōr-lōō') Tur.	40.8 N	34.28 E
145	Sungyang (sōōng'yäng') Chn.	28.25 N	119.33 E
145	Sunhing (sōōn'hĭng') Chn.	22.48 N	112.8 E
146	Sunhsien (sōōn'hsyĕn') Chn.	35.41 N	114.53 E
144	Sunhwei (sōōn'hwī') Chn.	22.28 N	112.56 E
118	Sunne (sōōn'ĕ) Swe.	59.50 N	13.10 E
144	Sunning (sōōn'nĭng') Chn.	22.16 N	112.38 E
75	Sunnyside (sŭn'ĭ-sīd) Utah	39.34 N	110.22 W
70	Sunnyside Wash.	46.18 N	120.0 W
149	Suno C. (sōō'nō) Jap.	34.58 N	139.58 E
51	Sunol (sōō'nŭl) Calif. (San Francisco In.)	37.35 N	121.53 W
71	Sun R. Mont.	47.28 N	112.10 W
73	Sunset Beach Calif. (Los Angeles In.)	33.44 N	118.5 W
75	Sunset Crater Natl. Mon. Ariz.	35.40 N	111.30 W
160	Sunshine Austl. (Melbourne In.)	37.48 S	144.50 E
139	Suntar (sōōn-tär') Sov. Un.	62.10 N	117.30 E
119	Suojärvi (sōō'ô-yĕr'vē) Fin.	62.17 N	32.35 E
75	Superior (sū-pē'rĭ-ẽr) Ariz.	33.17 N	111.8 W
72	Superior Colo. (Denver In.)	39.57 N	105.10 W
78	Superior Neb.	40.2 N	98.4 W
77	Superior Wis.	46.44 N	92.4 W
71	Superior Wyo.	41.46 N	108.59 W
88	Superior B. Minn.-Wis. (Duluth In.)	46.45 N	92.5 W
77	Superior, L. U. S.-Can.	47.40 N	88.0 W
93	Superior, Laguna (lä-gōō'nä sōō-pā-rē-ōr'). Mex.	16.20 N	94.55 W
144	Süpu (sü'pōō') Chn.	27.53 N	110.13 E
120	Sur (sōōr) Oman	22.32 N	59.29 E
121	Šurany (shōō'rä-nû') Czech.	48.5 N	18.12 E
141	Surat (sōō'rŭt) (sōō-răt') India	21.5 N	72.46 E
128	Surazh (sōō-räzh') Sov. Un.	53.1 N	32.25 E
128	Surazh Sov. Un.	55.25 N	30.44 E
117	Surbiton (sûr'bĭ-tŭn) Gt. Brit. (London In.)	51.23 N	0.20 W
100	Surco (sōōr'kō) Peru (In.)	12.9 S	77.1 W
123	Suresnes (sü-rân') Fr. (In.)	48.51 N	2.13 E
122	Surgères (sür-zhâr') Fr.	46.8 N	0.50 W
138	Surgut (sōōr-gōōt') Sov. Un.	61.20 N	73.25 E
141	Suri (sōō'rē) India	23.46 N	87.48 E
153	Surigao (sōō-rē-gä'ō) Phil.	9.46 N	125.30 E
153	Surigao Str. Phil.	10.15 N	125.25 E
101	Surinam (Netherlands Guiana) (sōō-rē-näm') (gē-ăn'ȧ). S. A.	4.0 N	56.0 W
101	Surinam R. Sur.	5.0 N	55.2 W
160	Surrey (sŭr'ē) Austl. (Tas. In.)	41.26 S	145.40 E
149	Suruga B. (sōō'rōō-gä) Jap.	34.46 N	138.35 E
126	Susa (sōō'sä) It.	45.6 N	7.2 E
149	Susa Jap.	34.39 N	131.40 E
126	Sušak (sōō'shäk) Yugo.	45.17 N	14.28 E
149	Susaki (sōō'sä-kē) Jap.	33.22 N	133.15 E
74	Susanville (sōō'zăn-vĭl) Calif.	40.23 N	120.42 W
120	Sušice (sōō'shē-tsě) Czech.	49.14 N	13.31 E
53	Susitna (sōō-sĭt'nȧ) Alsk.	61.25 N	150.30 W
53	Susitna R. Alsk.	62.40 N	150.0 W
85	Susquehanna (sŭs'kwē-hăn'ȧ). Pa.	41.56 N	75.36 W
85	Susquehanna R. Pa.-N. Y.	41.35 N	76.0 W
86	Sussex (sŭs'ĕks) Can.	45.42 N	65.31 W
145	Susung (sōō'sōōng') Chn.	30.10 N	116.7 E
160	Sutherland (sŭdh'ẽr-lănd) Austl. (Sydney In.)	34.2 S	151.3 E
134	Sutherland U. S. Afr.	32.22 S	20.39 E
141	Sutley R. (sŭt'lĕj) Pak.	30.0 N	73.0 E
146	Sutsien (sōō'tsyĕn') Chn.	33.56 N	118.22 E
117	Sutton (sŭt''n) Gt. Brit. (London In.)	51.22 N	0.12 W
87	Sutton Mass. (In.)	42.9 N	71.46 W
117	Sutton at Hone (hōn) Gt. Brit. (London In.)	51.25 N	0.14 E
116	Sutton Coldfield (kōld'fēld) Gt. Brit.	52.34 N	1.49 W
116	Sutton-in-Ashfield (ăsh'fēld) Gt. Brit.	53.7 N	1.15 W
121	Suwalki (sōō-vou'kē) Pol.	54.5 N	22.56 E
82	Suwannee R. (sōō-wô'nē). Fla.-Ga.	30.0 N	83.0 W
147	Suwŏn (sōō'wŭn') Kor.	37.17 N	127.1 E
146	Suyi (sōō'yē') Chn.	33.1 N	118.27 E
128	Suzdal (sōōz'dȧl) Sov. Un.	56.25 N	40.28 E
48	Svalbard (Spitsbergen) (sväl'bärt) (spĭts'bûr-gĕn). Arc. O.	79.0 N	16.0 E
118	Svaneke (svä'nĕ-kĕ) Den.	55.7 N	15.9 E
108	Svappavaara (svä-pä-vä'rä) Swe.	67.37 N	21.20 E
129	Svatova Luchka (svä'tô-vȧ lōōch'kȧ). Sov. Un.	49.24 N	38.2 E
118	Svedala (svě'dä-lä) Swe.	55.28 N	13.29 E
118	Svegsman (sväks'män) Swe.	62.2 N	14.22 E
118	Svelvik (svĕl'vēk) Nor.	59.37 N	10.22 E
118	Svendborg (svĕn'bôrgh) Den.	55.3 N	10.35 E
51	Svensen (svĕn'sĕn) Ore. (Portland In.)	46.10 N	123.40 W
138	Sverdlovsk (svĕrd-lôfsk'). Sov. Un.	56.50 N	60.20 E
127	Svilajnac (svē'lä-ē-näts) Yugo.	44.13 N	21.12 E
127	Svilengrad (svēl'ĕn-grät) Bul.	41.45 N	26.11 E
110	Svir R. (svēr) Sov. Un.	60.50 N	34.30 E
128	Svisloch R. (svēs'lôᴋ) Sov. Un.	53.30 N	28.20 E
127	Svištov (svēsh'tôf) Bul.	43.35 N	25.20 E
	Svitavy, see Zwittau, Ger.		
121	Svobodny (svô-bôd'nĭ) Sov. Un.	51.25 N	128.20 E
108	Svolvaer (svôl'vĕr) Nor.	68.15 N	14.30 E
139	Svyatoi, C. (svyá'tô-ē) Sov. Un.	72.50 N	141.10 E
129	Svyentsyany (shvyĕn'tsyȧ-nĭ) Sov. Un.	55.8 N	26.10 E
145	Swabue (swä'bōō'ē) Chn.	22.47 N	115.19 E
116	Swadlincote (swŏd'lĭn-kōt) Gt. Brit.	52.47 N	1.34 W
159	Swain Reefs (swān) Austl.	22.0 S	152.0 E
83	Swainsboro (swānz'bŭr-ô) Ga.	32.36 N	82.20 W
134	Swakopmund (svä'kôp-mōōnt) (swä'kôp-mōōnd). S. W. Afr.	22.40 S	14.32 E
114	Swale, R. (swāl) Gt. Brit.	54.10 N	1.10 W
87	Swampscott (swômp'skŏt) Mass. (In.)	42.28 N	70.55 W
159	Swan Hill (swŏn) Austl.	35.21 S	143.33 E
158	Swanland (Reg.) (swŏn'lănd) Austl.	31.30 S	120.0 E
158	Swan R. Austl.	31.40 S	116.40 E
71	Swan R. Mont.	47.50 N	113.40 W
117	Swanscombe (swŏnz'kŏm) Gt. Brit. (London In.)	51.27 N	0.19 E
114	Swansea (swŏn'sē) Gt. Brit.	51.37 N	3.55 W
114	Swansea B. Gt. Brit.	51.35 N	3.50 W
156	Swanson (swŏn'sŭn) N. Z. (In.)	36.52 S	174.35 E
145	Swatow (swä'tō') Chn.	23.23 N	116.27 E
134	Swaziland (swä'zē-lănd) Afr.	26.30 S	31.30 E
118	Sweden (swē'dĕn) Eur.	60.0 N	15.0 E
71	Sweetgrass Cr. (swēt'grăs) Mont.	46.10 N	109.55 W
82	Sweetwater (swēt'wô-tẽr) Tenn.	35.36 N	84.29 W
80	Sweetwater Tex.	32.28 N	100.25 W
131	Sweetwater Canal Eg. (Suez Can. In.)	30.14 N	30.25 E
73	Sweetwater Cr. Ga. (Atlanta In.)	33.48 N	84.47 W
76	Sweetwater L. N. D.	48.12 N	98.48 W
74	Sweetwater Reservoir. Calif. (In.)	32.41 N	116.55 W
71	Sweetwater R. Wyo.	42.25 N	108.40 W
120	Świdnica (shvĭd-nē'tsä) Pol.	50.50 N	16.28 E
120	Świdwin (shvĭd'vĭn) Pol.	53.47 N	15.47 E
120	Świebodzice (shvyăɴ-bôd'jē-tsě) Pol.	50.52 N	16.17 E
120	Świebodzin (shvyăɴ-bôd'jēn). Pol.	52.16 N	15.36 E
121	Świecie (shvyăɴ'tsyě) Pol.	53.24 N	18.26 E
54	Swift Current Can.	50.18 N	107.47 W
116	Swift, R. Gt. Brit.	52.27 N	1.9 W
86	Swift R. Me.	44.45 N	70.41 W
114	Swindon (swĭn'dŭn) Gt. Brit.	51.35 N	1.50 W
	Swinemünde, see Świnoujście, Pol.		
120	Świnoujście (Swinemünde) (shvĭ-nĭ-ô-wēsh'chyě) (shvē'nĕ-mün-dĕ). Pol.	53.56 N	14.13 E
51	Swinomish Ind. Res. (swĭ-nō'mĭsh) Wash. (Seattle In.)	48.30 N	122.30 W
116	Swinton (swĭn'tŭn) Gt. Brit.	53.29 N	2.19 W
120	Switzerland (swĭt'zẽr-lănd) Eur.	46.40 N	8.0 E
128	Syas R. (syäs) Sov. Un.	59.30 N	33.30 E
77	Sycamore (sĭk'ȧ-mōr) Ill.	42.0 N	88.40 W
128	Sychevka (sē-chôf'kȧ) Sov. Un.	55.51 N	34.17 E
160	Sydenham (sĭd'ĕn-ăm) Austl. (Melbourne In.)	37.42 S	144.47 E
160	Sydenham Austl. (Sydney In.)	33.55 S	151.10 E
159	Sydney (sĭd'nē) Austl.	34.0 S	151.0 E
160	Sydney Austl. (In.)		
55	Sydney Can.	46.18 N	60.14 W
87	Sydney Mines Can.	46.15 N	60.15 W
133	Syene (Aswân) (sê-ā'nä) (ä-swän'). Eg.	24.7 N	32.58 E
110	Syktyvkar (Ust Sysolsk) (sük-tüf'kär) (ōōst sü-sôlsk'). Sov. Un.	61.40 N	50.45 E
82	Sylacauga (sĭl-ȧ-kô'gȧ) Ala.	33.9 N	86.14 W
118	Sylfjällen (Mt.) (sül'fyĕl-ĕn). Swe.	63.0 N	12.12 E
118	Sylling (sül'lĭng) Nor.	59.52 N	10.19 E
120	Sylt I. (sĭlt) Ger.	54.53 N	8.30 E
83	Sylvania (sĭl-vā'nĭ-ȧ) Ga.	32.44 N	81.38 W
82	Sylvester (sĭl-vĕs'tẽr) Ga.	31.32 N	83.52 W
126	Syracuse (Siracusa) (sĭr'ȧ-kūs) (sē-rä-kōō'sä). It.	37.5 N	15.17 E
78	Syracuse Kan.	37.57 N	101.45 W
85	Syracuse N. Y.	43.5 N	76.10 W
73	Syracuse. Utah (Salt Lake City In.)	41.5 N	112.7 W
140	Syria (sĭr'ĭ-ȧ) Asia	35.0 N	38.30 E
140	Syrian Des. Asia	31.0 N	40.0 E
127	Syros (I.) (sē'rôs) Grc.	37.25 N	24.55 E
111	Syzran (sêz-rän'') Sov. Un.	53.5 N	48.28 E
121	Szabadszállás (sô'bôd-sä'läsh) Hung.	46.52 N	19.14 E
120	Szamotuly (shȧ-mô-tōō'wê) Pol.	52.36 N	16.33 E
121	Szarvas (sôr'vôsh) Hung.	46.51 N	20.35 E
121	Szczebrzeszyn (shchě-bzhā'shĕn) Pol.	50.41 N	22.57 E
120	Szczecin (Stettin) (shchě'tsĭn) (shtě-tēn'). Pol.	53.26 N	14.32 E
120	Szczecinek (shchě'tsĭ-nĕk) Pol.	53.42 N	16.42 E
121	Szczuczyn (shchōō'chĕn) Pol.	53.33 N	22.17 E
121	Szczytno (shchĭt'nô) Pol.	53.33 N	20.59 E
144	Szecheng (sě'chĕng') Chn.	24.30 N	106.38 E
144	Szechow (sě'chō') Chn.	27.10 N	108.25 E
146	Szechow Chn.	33.29 N	117.48 E
144	Szechwan (Prov.) (sě'chwän'). Chn.	30.5 N	106.45 E
121	Szeged (sĕ'gĕd) Hung.	46.15 N	20.11 E
121	Székesfehérvár (sā'kĕsh-fĕ'hār-vär) Hung.	47.12 N	18.24 E
121	Szekszárd (sĕk'särd) Hung.	46.20 N	18.42 E
142	Szemao (sě'mä'ō) Chn.	22.40 N	101.2 E
144	Szenan (sě'nän') Chn.	27.55 N	108.15 E
144	Szengjen (sĕng'jĕn') Chn.	24.55 N	108.20 E
121	Szentendre (sĕnt'ĕn-drĕ) Hung.	47.40 N	19.4 E
121	Szentes (sĕn'tĕsh) Hung.	46.38 N	20.17 E
148	Szepingkai (sě'pĭng'kī') Chn.	43.26 N	124.15 E
146	Szeshui (sě'shōō'ē) Chn.	34.48 N	113.17 E
146	Szeshui Chn.	35.48 N	117.17 E
144	Szewui (sě'wōō'ē) Chn.	23.22 N	112.37 E
121	Szigetvár (sĭ'gĕt-vär) Hung.	46.5 N	17.50 E
121	Szolnok (sôl'nôk) Hung.	47.11 N	20.11 E
120	Szombathely (sôm'bôt-hĕl'). Hung.	47.13 N	16.35 E
120	Szprotawa (shprô-tä'vȧ) Pol.	51.34 N	15.32 E
121	Szydlowiec (shĭd-wô'vyĕts) Pol.	51.12 N	20.52 E
152	Taal (tä-äl') Phil.	13.51 N	120.55 E
152	Taal, L. Phil.	14.0 N	121.0 E
152	Taal, Vol. Phil.	14.1 N	121.0 E
152	Tabaco (tä-bä'kō) Phil.	13.21 N	123.42 E
151	Tabar Is. (tä'bär) N. Gui. Ter.	2.40 S	152.3 E
131	Tabarka (tä-bär'kä) Tun. (In.)	36.55 N	8.55 E
95	Tabasara, Serranía de (Mts.) (sĕr-rä-nē'ä dā tä-bä-sä'rä). Pan.	8.33 N	81.25 W
93	Tabasco (State) (tä-bäs'kō) Mex.	18.10 N	93.0 W
100	Tabatinga (tä-bä-tĭŋ'gä) Braz.	4.15 S	69.57 W
152	Tabayoc, Mt. (tä-bä-yōk') Phil.	16.41 N	120.53 E
124	Tabernas (tä-bĕr'näs) Sp.	37.3 N	2.22 W
102	Tablada (tä-blä'dhä) Arg. (In.)	34.42 S	58.31 W
152	Tablas Is. (tä'bläs) Phil.	12.20 N	122.0 E
152	Tablas Str. Phil.	12.30 N	121.45 E
135	Table B. U. S. Afr.	33.54 S	18.27 E
156	Table C. N. Z.	39.5 S	178.2 E
135	Table Mt. U. S. Afr. (Capetown In.)	33.58 S	18.27 E
86	Tabletop (Jacques Cartier) (Mt.) (zhäk kär-tyā'). Can.	48.58 N	66.2 W
124	Taboada (tä-bō-ä'dä) Sp.	42.43 N	7.45 W
90	Taboga I. (tä-bō'gä) C. Z. (In.)	8.47 N	79.33 W
153	Tabogon (tä-bō-gōn') Phil.	10.57 N	124.1 E
120	Tábor (tä'bôr) Czech.	49.25 N	14.40 E
134	Tabora (tä-bō'rä) Tan.	5.5 S	32.47 E
132	Tabou (tȧ-bōō') Fr. W. Afr.	4.30 N	7.26 W
140	Tabriz (tä-brēz') Iran	38.4 N	46.15 E
92	Tacámbaro de Codallos (tä-käm'-bä-rō dā kō-däl'yōs). Mex.	19.13 N	101.20 W
94	Tacaná (Vol.) (tä-kä-nä') Guat.	15.8 N	92.7 W
146	Tacheng (tä'chĕng') Chn.	38.49 N	116.26 E
144	Tachu (tä'chōō') Chn.	30.43 N	107.9 E
54	Tacla L. (tăk'lȧ) Can.	55.30 N	126.15 W
153	Tacloban (tä-klō'bän) Phil.	11.13 N	125.0 E
100	Tacna (tăk'nä) Chl.	17.45 S	69.45 W
70	Tacoma (tȧ-kō'mȧ) Wash.	47.15 N	122.30 W
85	Taconic Range (tȧ-kŏn'ĭk) N. Y.	42.0 N	73.40 W
88	Tacony (tȧ-kō'nē) Pa. (Philadelphia In.)	40.2 N	75.3 W
93	Tacotalpa (tä-kō-täl'pä) Mex.	17.37 N	92.50 W
102	Tacuarembo (tä-kwä-rĕm'bō) Ur.	31.50 S	56.10 W
93	Tacuba (tä-kōō'bä) Mex. (In.)	19.28 N	99.10 W
93	Tacubaya (tä-kōō-bä'yä) Mex. (In.)	19.24 N	99.13 W
149	Tada (tä'dä) Jap. (Osaka In.)	34.52 N	135.24 E
116	Tadcaster (tăd'kăs-tẽr) Gt. Brit.	53.53 N	1.15 W
132	Tademait Plat. (tä-dē-mä'ĕt). Alg.	28.30 N	3.0 E
135	Tadjoura (tȧd-zhōō'rä) Fr. Som.	11.50 N	42.52 E
149	Tadotsu (tä'dō-tsōō) Jap.	34.10 N	133.39 E
86	Tadoussac (tȧ-dōō-sȧk') Can.	48.9 N	69.43 W
138	Tadzhik (Aut. Rep.) (tät'zhĕk) Sov. Un.	39.0 N	71.0 E
147	Taebaeksanmaek (Mts.) (tī-bĭk'sän-mĭk'). Kor.	37.39 N	128.48 E
147	Taechŏn (tī'chŭn') Kor.	35.55 N	128.30 E
147	Taedong R. (tī-dŏng) Kor.	38.45 N	125.35 E
147	Taegu (Taikyū) (tī'gōō') (tī'kyōō'). Kor.	35.52 N	128.35 E
147	Taejŏn (tī'jŭn') Kor.	36.20 N	127.28 E
124	Tafalla (tä-fäl'yä) Sp.	42.31 N	1.40 W
137	Tafel (Et Tafila) (tä'fĕl) (ĕt tä'fē-lä). Jor. (In.)	30.50 N	35.37 E
137	Tafila (tä-fē'la) Jor. (In.)	30.50 N	35.37 E
132	Tafilelt Oasis (tä-fē'lĕlt) Mor.	31.15 N	4.15 W
125	Tafna R. (täf'nä) Alg.	35.25 N	1.0 W
74	Taft (tȧft) Calif.	35.9 N	119.28 W
129	Taganrog (tä-gän-rŏk') Sov. Un.	47.12 N	38.57 E
129	Taganrog, G. of Sov. Un.	47.5 N	39.0 E

ăt; finȧl; rāte; senâte; ärm; ȧsk; sofȧ; fâre; ch-choose; dh-as th in other; bē; ēvent; bĕt; recĕnt; cratẽr; g-go; gh-gutteral g; bĭt; ĭ-short neutral; rīde; ᴋ-gutteral k as ch in German ich;

Page	Name Pronunciation Region	Lat. °′	Long. °′
153	Tagapula I. (tä-gä-pōō-lä') Phil.	12.4 N	124.12 E
153	Tagbilaran (täg-bē-lä'rän) Phil.	9.38 N	123.52 E
151	Tagig (tä-hēg') Phil. (Manila In.)	14.32 N	121.4 E
112	Tagiura (tä-jōō'rä) Libya	32.55 N	13.19 E
126	Tagliamento R. (täl-yä-měn'tō) It.	46.0 N	12.54 E
153	Tagoloan (tä-gō-lō'än) Phil.	8.30 N	124.46 E
153	Tagoloan R. Phil.	8.21 N	125.0 E
153	Tagolo Pt. (tä-gō'lō) Phil.	8.42 N	123.24 E
153	Tagubud, Mt. (tä-gōō-bōōd') Phil.	7.20 N	126.11 E
159	Tagula Is. (tä'gōō-là) Pap. Ter.	11.30 S	153.15 E
153	Tagum (tä'gōōm) Phil.	7.19 N	125.44 E
153	Tagum R. Phil.	7.35 N	125.50 E
124	Tagus (Tajo) R. (tā'gŭs) (tä'hō) Sp.	39.50 N	5.0 W
132	Tahat, Mt. (tä-hät') Alg.	23.26 N	5.28 E
142	Tahcheng (Chuguchak) (tä'chěng') (chōō'gōō-chäk') Chn.	46.48 N	83.5 E
4	Tahiti (I.) (tä-hē'tē) (tä'ē-tē') Pac. O.	17.53 S	148.5 W
79	Tahlequah (tă-lĕ-kwä') Okla.	35.55 N	94.58 W
74	Tahoe, L. (tä'hō) Calif.-Nev.	39.2 N	120.0 W
132	Tahoua (tä'ōō-ä) Fr. W. Afr.	14.55 N	5.20 E
131	Tahta (tä'tä) Eg. (In.)	26.49 N	31.30 E
157	Tahunanui (tä'hōō-nä-nōō'ē) N. Z.	41.18 S	173.17 E
146	Taian (tī'än') Chn.	36.9 N	117.8 E
157	Taiaroa Head (tä'ē-à-rō'ä) N. Z. (In.)	45.47 S	170.45 E
145	Tai Chang R. (tī'chäng') Chn.	25.37 N	118.28 E
145	Taichow (tī'chō') Chn.	28.52 N	121.7 E
146	Taichow Chn.	32.28 N	119.53 E
145	Taichung (tī'chōōng) For.	24.15 N	120.43 E
146	Taierhchwang (tī'ĕr-chäng') Chn.	34.35 N	117.45 E
157	Taieri R. (tä-ē-ä'rē) N. Z.	45.30 S	170.12 E
140	Taif (tif) Sau. Ar.	21.10 N	40.50 E
138	Taiga (tä'ē-gà) Sov. Un.	56.0 N	85.40 E
139	Taigo, C. (tä'ē-gō) Sov. Un.	60.30 N	160.10 E
146	Taihang Shan (Mts.) (tī'häng'shän') Chn.	35.50 N	113.28 E
156	Taihape (tä'ē-hä'pä) N. Z.	39.42 S	175.45 E
148	Taihasen Mt. (tī'hä-sĕn') For. (In.)	24.29 N	121.15 E
146	Taihing (tī'hĭng') Chn.	32.9 N	119.59 E
145	Taiho (tī'hō') Chn.	26.46 N	114.37 E
145	Taihoku (Taipei) (tī'hō'kōō) (tī'pā') For.	25.1 N	121.30 E
146	Taiho Chn.	33.9 N	115.38 E
145	Taihu (tī'hōō') Chn.	30.26 N	116.12 E
146	Taikang (tī'käng') Chn.	34.9 N	115.3 E
147	Taikyū (Taegu) (tī'kyōō') (tī'gōō') Kor.	35.52 N	128.35 E
145	Tai L. (tī) Chn.	31.8 N	120.15 E
142	Tailagein Khara (Reg.) (tī'lä-gän' ĸä'rä) Chn.	43.30 N	106.0 E
144	Taileung (tī'lĕ-ōōng') Chn.	22.51 N	113.12 E
140	Taima (tä'ē-mä) Sau. Ar.	28.0 N	39.5 E
139	Taimyr I., Little (tä-ē-mēr') Sov. Un.	78.10 N	108.30 E
139	Taimyr, L. Sov. Un.	74.30 N	10.0 E
139	Taimyr Pen. Sov. Un.	75.30 N	105.0 E
138	Taimyr R. Sov. Un.	73.30 N	95.0 E
114	Tain (tān) Gt. Brit.	57.49 N	4.5 W
148	Tainan (tī'nän') For. (In.)	23.1 N	120.16 E
145	Taining (tī'nĭng') Chn.	26.55 N	117.0 E
145	Taipei (Taihoku) (tī'pā') (tī'hō'kōō) For.	25.1 N	121.30 E
144	Taiping (tī'pĭng') Chn.	22.28 N	107.32 E
145	Taiping Chn.	30.18 N	118.11 E
145	Taiping Chn.	31.36 N	118.28 E
146	Taiping Chn.	32.7 N	119.53 E
145	Taipu (tī'pōō') Chn.	24.27 N	116.29 E
148	Taira (tī'rä) Jap.	37.4 N	140.54 E
137	Tais (tä'ēs) Yem. (In.)	13.35 N	43.57 E
146	Tai Shan (Mt.) (tī' shän) Chn.	36.18 N	117.18 E
146	Tai Shan (Mts.) Chn.	36.25 N	117.25 E
138	Taishev (tī'shĕf') Sov. Un.	55.35 N	98.30 E
145	Taishun (tī'shōōn') Chn.	27.30 N	119.44 E
102	Taitao Pen. (tä-ē-tä'ō) Chl.	46.30 S	75.30 W
145	Taitsang (tī'tsäng') Chn.	31.24 N	121.0 E
148	Taitung (tī'tōōng') For. (In.)	22.46 N	121.5 E
	Taiwan, see Formosa		
146	Taiyi (tī'yē') Chn.	34.15 N	119.19 E
143	Taiyüan (tī'yü-än') Chn.	37.50 N	112.30 E
124	Tajo (Tagus) R. (tä'hō) (tā'gŭs) Sp.	39.50 N	5.0 W
94	Tajumulco (Vol.) (tä-hōō-mōōl'kō) Guat.	15.2 N	91.55 W
149	Takada (tä'kȧ-dȧ) Jap.	37.5 N	138.15 E
149	Takahashi (tä'kä'hä-shī') Jap.	34.48 N	133.35 E
149	Taka I. (tä'kä) Jap.	30.48 N	130.22 E
149	Takaido (tä'kä'ē-dō') Jap. (Tokyo In.)	35.39 N	139.36 E
157	Takaka (tä-kä'kä) N. Z.	40.52 S	172.48 E
149	Takamatsu (tä'kä'mä-tsōō') Jap.	34.14 N	134.0 E
149	Takamori (tä'kä'mō-rē') Jap.	32.50 N	131.8 E
148	Takao (tä'kä'ō) For. (In.)	22.44 N	120.21 E
149	Takaoka (tä'kä'ō-kä') Jap.	36.45 N	137.0 E
156	Takapuna (tä-kȧ-pōō'nȧ) N. Z. (In.)	36.48 S	174.46 E
149	Takasaki (tä'kät'sōō-kē') Jap.	36.19 N	139.1 E
149	Takata (tä'kȧ'tä) Jap.	35.7 N	133.42 E
149	Takatsuki (tä'kät'sōō-kē') Jap. (Osaka In.)	34.50 N	135.38 E
135	Takaungu (tä'kä'ōōŋ-gōō') Kenya	3.40 S	39.47 E
149	Takayama (tä'kä'yä'mä) Jap.	36.11 N	137.15 E
149	Takeda (tä'kĕ-dä) Jap.	32.60 N	131.25 E
149	Takefu (tä'kĕ-fōō) Jap.	35.51 N	136.10 E
144	Takhing (täk'hĭng') Chn.	23.10 N	111.42 E
133	Takkaze R. (täk'ȧ-zȧ) Eth.	13.45 N	38.30 E
142	Takla Makan (Des.) (tä'klȧ mä-kän') Chn.	39.20 N	83.0 E
132	Takoradi (tä-kō-rä'dē) G. C.	4.42 N	1.58 W
146	Taku (tä'kōō') Chn.	38.59 N	117.35 E
54	Taku R. (tä'kū) Can.	58.45 N	132.30 W
92	Tala (tä'lä) Mex.	20.39 N	103.40 W
153	Talacag (tä-lä-käg') Phil.	8.16 N	124.38 E
153	Talacogan (tä-lä-kō'gän) Phil.	8.30 N	125.40 E
95	Talamanca, Cordillera de (Mts.) (kôr-dēl-yä'rä dā tä-lä-mäŋ'kä) C. R.-Pan.	9.20 N	83.30 W
150	Talamau (Ophir) (Mt.) (tä-lä-mä'ōō) (ō'fēr) Indon.	0.15 N	99.50 E
134	Tala Mugongo (tä'lȧ mōō-gôŋ'gōō) Ang.	9.38 S	17.35 E
100	Talara (tä-lä'rä) Ec.	4.32 S	81.5 W
151	Talasea (tä-lä-sā'ä) N. Gui. Ter.	5.18 S	150.1 E
151	Talaud Is. (tä-lout') Indon.	4.15 N	126.45 E
124	Talavera de la Reina (tä-lä-vā'rä dā lä rā-ē'nä) Sp.	39.58 N	4.49 W
73	Talbert (tôl'bûrt) Calif. (Los Angeles In.)	33.42 N	117.58 W
135	Talbia (tàl'bĭ-à) Eg.	30.0 N	31.10 E
102	Talca (täl'kä) Chl.	35.28 S	71.45 W
102	Talcahuano (täl-kä-wä'nō) Chl.	36.45 S	73.1 W
138	Taldy-Kurgan (tàl'dĭ-kōōr-gän') Sov. Un.	45.10 N	78.25 E
93	Talea de Castro (San Miguel) (tä'lā-ä dā käs'trō) Mex.	17.22 N	96.15 W
122	Talence (tà-läɴs) Fr.	44.48 N	0.35 W
142	Tali (tä'lē) Chn.	25.51 N	100.10 E
151	Taliabu (I.) (tä-lē-ä'bōō) Indon.	1.45 S	124.45 E
153	Talibon (tä-lē-bôn') Phil.	10.9 N	124.19 E
146	Talienwan (tä'lyĕn-wän') Chn.	39.4 N	121.37 E
153	Talikud I. (tä-lē-kōōd') Phil.	6.55 N	125.42 E
152	Talim I. (tä-lēm') Phil.	14.20 N	121.13 E
151	Talin, Pt. (tä-lēn') Phil. (Manila In.)	13.59 N	120.32 E
153	Talisay (tä-lē'sī) Phil.	10.13 N	123.51 E
153	Talisay Phil.	10.43 N	122.59 E
152	Talisay Phil.	14.8 N	122.56 E
151	Talisay Phil. (Manila In.)	14.7 N	121.1 E
153	Talisayan (tä-lē-sä'yän) Phil.	8.59 N	124.53 E
53	Talkeetna (tàl-kēt'nä) Alsk.	62.20 N	150.0 W
52	Talkeetna Mts. Alsk. (In.)	62.10 N	149.0 W
82	Talladega (tăl-à-dē'gȧ) Ala.	33.27 N	86.7 W
82	Tallahassee (tăl-ȧ-hăs'ē) Fla.	30.26 N	84.18 W
82	Tallahatchie R. (tăl-ȧ-hăch'ē) Miss.	34.32 N	89.30 W
82	Tallapoosa (tăl-ȧ-pōō'sȧ) Ga.	33.45 N	85.17 W
82	Tallapoosa R. Ala.-Ga.	32.25 N	86.0 W
82	Tallassee (tăl'ȧ-sē) Ala.	32.31 N	85.55 W
119	Tallinn (Reval) (tàl'lēn) (rā'vàl) Sov. Un.	59.26 N	24.46 E
81	Tallulah (tă-lōō'lȧ) La.	32.25 N	91.11 W
129	Talnoe (tál'nō-yĕ) Sov. Un.	48.51 N	30.43 E
133	Talōdi (tä-lō'dē) A. E. Sud.	10.38 N	30.25 E
92	Talpa de Allende (täl'pä dā äl-yĕn'dā) Mex.	20.25 N	104.49 W
119	Talsi (tàl'sĭ) Sov. Un.	57.15 N	22.38 E
102	Taltal (täl-täl') Chl.	25.20 S	70.35 W
129	Taly (täl'ĭ) Sov. Un.	49.51 N	40.2 E
77	Tama (tā'mà) Ia.	41.57 N	92.35 W
156	Tamaki R. (tä-mä'kē) N. Z. (In.)	36.54 S	174.53 E
132	Tamale (tä-mä'lā) G. C.	9.24 N	0.50 W
77	Tamana Hill (Mt.) (tä-mä'nä) Trin. (In.)	10.29 N	61.12 W
129	Tamanskaya (tä-män'skà-yà) Sov. Un.	45.11 N	36.41 E
132	Tamanr'aset, Wadi (R.) (wä'dĭ tä-män-räs'sĕt) Alg.	22.15 N	2.30 E
85	Tamaqua (tȧ-mô'kwȧ) Pa.	40.45 N	75.57 W
160	Tamar R. (tā'mȧr) Austl. (Tas. In.)	41.20 S	147.3 E
114	Tamar, R. Gt. Brit.	50.35 N	4.15 W
125	Tamarite (tä-mä-rē'tä) Sp.	41.53 N	0.25 E
151	Tamata (tä-mä'tä) Phil. (Manila In.)	14.55 N	121.40 E
135	Tamatave (tä-mȧ-täv') Madag.	18.10 S	49.20 E
92	Tamaulipas (State) (tä-mä-ōō-lē'päs) Mex.	23.30 N	99.0 W
92	Tamazula de Gordiano (tä-mä-zōō'lä dā gôr-dē-ä'nō) Mex.	19.38 N	103.8 W
93	Tamazulápam (Santo Tomas) (tä-mä-zōō-lä'päm) (sän'tō tō-mäs') Mex.	17.42 N	97.34 W
92	Tamazunchale (tä-mä-zōōn-chä'lā) Mex.	21.17 N	98.46 W
132	Tambacounda (täm-bä-kōōn'dä) Fr. W. Afr.	13.52 N	13.45 W
150	Tambelan Is. (täm-bȧ-län') Indon.	0.38 N	107.0 E
159	Tambo (täm'bō) Austl.	25.0 S	146.20 E
128	Tambov (tàm-bôf') Sov. Un.	52.45 N	42.30 E
128	Tambov (Dist.) Sov. Un.	52.40 N	40.0 E
124	Tambre R. (täm'brā) Sp.	42.58 N	8.30 W
133	Tambura (täm-bōō'rä) A. E. Sud.	5.32 N	27.28 E
124	Tamega R. (tä-mā'gȧ) Port.	41.30 N	7.55 W
113	Tamel, Wadi (R.) (wä'dē täm'ĕl) Libya	30.30 N	16.18 E
116	Tame, R. (tām) Gt. Brit.	52.31 N	1.45 W
92	Tamesí, R. (tä-mȧ-sē') Mex.	22.40 N	98.40 W
132	Tamgak Mts. (täm-gäk') Fr. W. Afr.	19.10 N	8.40 E
112	Tamgrout (täm-grōōt') Mor.	30.12 N	5.47 W
93	Tamaihua (tä-mē-ä'wä) Mex.	21.16 N	97.28 W
92	Tamaihua Lagoon Mex.	21.30 N	97.27 W
146	Taming (tä'mĭng') Chn.	36.20 N	115.20 E
119	Tammela (täm'ĕ-lä) Fin.	60.50 N	23.44 E
119	Tammisaari (Ekenas) (tàm'ĭ-sä'rĭ) (ĕ'kĕn-ôs') Fin.	59.58 N	23.28 E
151	Tamon, R. (tä-mōn') Phil. (Manila In.)	14.18 N	120.47 E
131	Tampa (täm'pä) Bel. Cong. (Brazzaville In.)	4.45 S	15.23 E
72	Tampa (tăm'pȧ) Colo. (Denver In.)	40.8 N	104.27 W
83	Tampa Fla. (In.)	27.57 N	82.27 W
83	Tampa B. Fla. (In.)	27.40 N	82.35 W
119	Tampere (tàm'pĕ-rĕ) Fin.	61.30 N	23.46 E
93	Tampico (täm-pē'kō) Mex.	22.14 N	97.51 W
93	Tampico Alto (äl'tō) Mex.	22.7 N	97.50 W
140	Tamrida (tàm-rē'dȧ) Socotra	12.30 N	53.58 E
159	Tamworth (tăm'wûrth) Austl.	31.5 S	150.56 E
116	Tamworth Gt. Brit.	52.38 N	1.41 W
147	Tamyang (täm'yäng') Kor.	35.19 N	126.59 E
133	Tana, L. (tä'nä) Sov. Un.	12.0 N	37.15 E
149	Tanabe (tä-nä'bā) Jap.	33.45 N	135.28 E
52	Tanaga I. (tä-nä'gä) Alsk.	51.40 N	178.0 W
150	Tanahbala (I.) (tȧ-nä-bä'lä) Indon.	0.30 S	98.30 E
150	Tanahmasa (I.) (tȧ-nä-mä'sä) Indon.	0.10 S	98.30 E
158	Tanami (tȧ-nä'mē) Austl.	20.12 S	129.50 E
53	Tanana (tă'nȧ-nô) Alsk.	65.10 N	152.0 W
53	Tanana R. Alsk.	64.40 N	150.0 W
135	Tananarive (tȧ-nä-nä-rēv') Madag.	18.50 S	47.33 E
135	Tana R. (tä'nä) Kenya	0.30 S	39.42 E
108	Tana R. Nor.-Fin.	69.50 N	26.15 E
126	Tanaro R. (tä-nä'rō) It.	44.41 N	8.0 E
153	Tanauan (tä-nä'wän) Phil.	11.7 N	125.1 E
152	Tanauan Phil.	14.5 N	121.9 E
151	Tanay (tä-nä'ē) Phil. (Manila In.)	14.31 N	121.19 E
92	Tancanhuitz (tän-kän-wēts') Mex.	21.36 N	98.58 W
146	Tancheng (tän'chĕng') Chn.	34.47 N	118.23 E
148	Tanchŏn (tän'chŭn') Kor.	40.28 N	128.55 E
92	Tancítaro (tän-sē'tä-rō) Mex.	19.12 N	102.20 W
92	Tancítaro, Nudo de (Vol.) (nōō'dhō dä tän-cē'tä-rō) Mex.	19.12 N	102.23 W
93	Tancoco (tän-kō'kō) Mex.	21.18 N	97.46 W
153	Tandag (tän'däg) Phil.	9.3 N	126.12 E
102	Tandil (tän-dēl') Arg.	37.20 S	59.15 W
150	Tandjongbalei (tän'jông-bä'lā') Indon	2.58 N	99.45 E
150	Tandjongpandan (tän'jŏng-pän'-dän) Indon.	2.42 S	107.52 E
137	Tandjongpinang (tän'jŏng-pē'-näng) Indon. (In.)	0.54 N	104.28 E
153	Tandu (tän'dōō) Phil.	6.0 N	121.20 E
149	Tanega I. (tä'nȧ-gä') Jap.	30.30 N	130.59 E
132	Tanezrouft (Reg.) (tä'nĕz-rōōft) Alg.	24.0 N	0.30 E
135	Tanga (tăŋ'gȧ) Tan.	5.7 S	39.7 E
92	Tangancícuaro (täŋ-gän-sē'kwä-rō) Mex.	19.54 N	102.12 W
134	Tanganyika, L. (tăŋ-gän-yē'kȧ) Bel. Cong.-Tan.	6.30 S	29.45 E
134	Tanganyika Ter. Afr.	6.0 S	34.30 E
142	Tangar (täng'är) Chn.	36.52 N	101.14 E
120	Tangermünde (täŋ'ĕr-mün'dĕ) Ger.	52.33 N	11.57 E
132	Tangier (Neutral State) (tăn-jēr') Afr.	35.50 N	5.52 W
131	Tangier, B. of Sp. Mor. (Gib. In.)	35.46 N	5.14 E
81	Tangipahoa R. (tăn'jē-pȧ-hō'ȧ) La.	30.50 N	90.30 W
145	Tangki (täng'kē') Chn.	29.2 N	119.31 E
146	Tangku (täŋ'kōō') Chn.	39.5 N	117.39 E
142	Tangla Mts. (täng'lä') Chn.	32.30 N	93.0 E
146	Tang R. (täng) Chn.	39.0 N	114.47 E
146	Tangshan (täng'shän') Chn.	34.24 N	116.31 E
144	Tangyang (täng'yäng') Chn.	30.50 N	111.38 E
146	Tangyin (täng'yĭn') Chn.	35.52 N	114.34 E
148	Tangyuan (täng'wän') Chn.	46.50 N	129.55 E
153	Tanjay (tän-hä'ē) Phil.	9.30 N	123.11 E
141	Tanjore (tän-jōr') India	10.40 N	79.8 E
144	Tankiang (tän'kyäng') Chn.	26.18 N	107.59 E
159	Tanna I. (tän'ä) New Hebr.	18.25 S	169.20 E
143	Tann-bira R. (tän'-bē'rä) Chn.	47.0 N	128.35 E
142	Tannu Ola (Mts.) (tä'nōō ō'lä) Sov. Un.	50.30 N	95.0 E
142	Tannu Tuva (Dist.) (tä'nōō tōō'vä) Sov. Un.)	51.0 N	95.0 E
153	Tañon Str. (tän-yōn') Phil.	10.10 N	123.25 E
93	Tanquijo Reef (tän-kē'hō) Mex.	21.7 N	97.17 W
145	Tanshui (tän'shwē') For.	25.11 N	121.26 E
133	Tanta (tän'tä) Eg.	30.32 N	30.59 E
92	Tantoyuca (tän-tō-yōō'kä) Mex.	21.21 N	98.13 W
137	Tantura (tän-tōō'rä) Pal. (In.)	32.38 N	34.56 E
145	Tanyang (tän'yäng') Chn.	31.57 N	119.37 E
147	Tanyang Kor.	36.56 N	128.19 E
152	Tanza (tän'zä) Phil.	14.24 N	120.51 E
148	Taoan (tä'ō-än') Chn.	45.42 N	122.48 E
144	Taohsien (tä'ō-hsyĕn') Chn.	25.35 N	111.28 E
148	Taonan (tä'ō-nän') Chn.	45.27 N	122.31 E
145	Taoping (tä'ō-pĭng') Chn.	23.57 N	116.36 E
145	Tao R. (tä'ō) Chn.	25.12 N	114.32 E
126	Taormina (tä-ôr-mē'nä) It.	37.52 N	15.16 E
78	Taos (tä'ōs) N. M.	36.25 N	105.32 W
132	Taoudenni Oasis (tä'ōō-dĕ-nē' ō-ä'sĭs) Fr. W. Afr.	22.40 N	2.45 W
132	Taoulo (tä'ōō-lō) Lib.	6.30 N	8.48 W
132	Taourirt (tä-ōō-rērt') Alg.	26.52 N	0.8 E
144	Taoyuan (tä'ō-yōō-än') Chn.	28.52 N	111.11 E
146	Taoyüan (tä'ō-yü-än') Chn.	33.38 N	118.42 E
145	Taoyüan (tou'yü-än') For.	25.0 S	121.18 E
119	Tapa (tä'pȧ) Sov. Un.	59.12 N	25.55 E
101	Tapajoz, R. (tä-pȧ'zhōzh) Braz.	5.28 S	56.30 W
157	Tapanui (tä-pȧ-nōō'ē) N. Z.	45.55 S	169.18 E
101	Taperoá (tä-pä-rō-ä') Braz. (In.)	13.30 S	39.3 W
153	Tapiantana Group (Is.) (tä'pē-än-tä'nä) Phil.	6.18 N	122.0 E
156	Tapokopoko, Mt. (tä'pō-kō-pō'kō) N. Z. (In.)	41.23 S	174.59 E
148	Tappi C. (täp'ē) Jap.	41.10 N	140.25 E
141	Tapti R. (täp'tē) India	21.0 N	76.0 E
156	Tapu I. (tä-pōō') N. Z. (In.)	36.47 S	174.55 E
153	Tapul Group (Is.) (tä-pōōl') Phil.	5.35 N	120.50 E
153	Tapul I. Phil.	5.43 N	120.54 E

ng-sing; ŋ-baŋk; ɴ-nasalized n; nŏd; cŏmmit; ōld; ōbey; ôrder; fōōd; fŏŏt; ou-out; s-soft; sh-dish; th-thin; pūre; ûnite; ûrn; stŭd; circŭs; ü-as "y" in study; '-indeterminate vowel.

ặt: finặl; rāte; senằte; ärm; ặsk; sofᵅ; fâre; ch-choose; ᵭh-as th in other; bē; ĕvent; bĕt; recĕnt; cratẽr; g-go; gh-gutteral g; bĭt; ĭ-short neutral; rīde; к-gutteral k as ch in German ich;

Teodolina PRONOUNCING INDEX Timaru

Page	Name Pronunciation Region	Lat. °′	Long. °′
99	Teodolina (tā-ō-dō-lē'nȧ) Arg. (Buenos Aires In.)	34.10 S	61.36 W
92	Teoloyucan (tā'ō-lō-yōō'kän). Mex.	19.44 N	99.11 W
93	Teopisca (tā-ō-pēs'kä) . . . . . . Mex.	16.35 N	92.32 W
93	Teotitlán del Camino (tā-ō-tē-tlän' dĕl kä-mē'nō). Mex.	18.8 N	97.4 W
93	Tepalcapán (tā-päl-kä-pän') Mex. (In.)	19.37 N	99.12 W
92	Tepalcatepec (tā'päl-kä-tā'pĕk) Mex.	19.10 N	102.50 W
92	Tepalcingo (tā-päl-sēŋ'gō) . . . Mex.	18.35 N	98.50 W
92	Tepatitlán de Morelos (tā-pä-tē-tlän' dā mō-rā'los). Mex.	20.50 N	102.42 W
93	Tepeaca (tā-pȧ-ä'kä) . . . . Mex.	18.57 N	97.55 W
92	Tepecoacuilco de Trujano (tā'pȧ-kō'ä-kwēl'kō dā trōō-hä'nō). Mex.	18.15 N	99.30 W
92	Tepejí del Río (tā-pȧ-kē' dĕl rē'ō). Mex.	19.55 N	99.22 W
93	Tepelmeme (tā'pĕl-mā'mȧ) . . Mex.	17.50 N	97.25 W
93	Tepepan (tȧ-pā'pän) . . . Mex. (In.)	19.17 N	99.8 W
92	Tepetlaoxtoc (tā'pȧ-tlä'ōs-tōk') Mex.	19.34 N	98.49 W
93	Tepexpan (tȧ-pās'pän) . Mex. (In.)	19.37 N	98.56 W
92	Tepezalá (tā-pȧ-zä-lä') . . . . . . Mex.	22.12 N	102.11 W
92	Tepic (tā-pēk') . . . . Mex.	21.31 N	104.53 W
120	Teplice-Šanov (tĕp'lĭ-tsĕ-shä'nôf) Czech.	50.39 N	13.49 E
93	Teposcolula (San Pedro y San Pablo) (tā-pōs-kō-lōō'lä) (sän pä'drō ē sän pä'blō). Mex.	17.31 N	97.30 W
92	Tepoxtlán (tā-pōs-tlän') . . . . . Mex.	18.58 N	99.6 W
156	Te Puke (tā pōō'kȧ) . . . . N. Z.	37.45 S	176.23 E
93	Tequezquinahuac (tā'käz-kē-nä-wäk'). Mex. (In.)	19.29 N	98.49 W
92	Tequila (tȧ-kē'lä) . . . . Mex.	20.53 N	103.48 W
92	Tequisquiapan (tȧ-kēs-kē-ä'pän) Mex.	20.31 N	99.55 W
126	Teramo (tā'rä-mô) . . . . It.	42.39 N	13.40 E
124	Tera R. (tā'rä) . . . . Sp.	41.50 N	6.0 W
133	Terbu (tĕr'bōō) . . . . Libya	26.2 N	15.42 E
111	Tercan (tĕr'jän) . . . . Tur.	39.40 N	40.18 E
132	Terceira I. (tĕr-sā'rä) . Az. Is. (In.)	38.40 N	27.15 W
142	Terek Pass (tyĕ'rĕk) . Chn.-Sov. Un.	40.0 N	74.45 E
111	Terek R . . . . Sov. Un.	43.45 N	45.0 E
114	Terenure (tĕ'rĕ-nūr) . . . . Ire.	53.15 N	6.20 W
151	Teresa (tȧ-rā'sȧ) . Phil. (Manila In.)	14.35 N	121.14 E
101	Teresina (tĕr-ȧ-sē'nȧ) . . . . Braz.	5.2 S	42.45 W
99	Teresópolis (tĕr-ā-sô'pō-lēzh) Braz. (Rio de Janeiro In.)	22.25 S	42.59 W
110	Teriberka (tyĕr-ĕ-byôr'kȧ) Sov. Un.	69.9 N	35.11 E
119	Terioki (tyĕr'ĕ-ō'kĕ) . . . . . Sov. Un.	60.12 N	29.48 E
111	Terme (tĕr'mĕ) . . . . Tur.	41.10 N	37.2 E
141	Termez (tyĕr'mĕz) . . . . . . Sov. Un.	37.29 N	66.59 E
73	Terminal I. (tûr'mĭ-nȧl) Calif. (Los Angeles In.)	33.45 N	118.15 W
126	Termini (tĕr'mē-nē) . . . . It.	37.57 N	13.40 E
126	Termoli (tĕr'mô-lē) . . . . It.	42.0 N	15.0 E
151	Ternate (tĕr-nä'tā) . . . . Indon.	0.50 N	127.20 E
151	Ternate . . . . Phil. (Manila In.)	14.19 N	120.41 E
126	Terni (tĕr'nē) . . . . It.	42.35 N	12.40 E
116	Tern, R. (tûrn) . . . . Gt. Brit.	52.48 N	2.31 W
129	Terny (tĕrn'ĭ) . . . . Sov. Un.	50.58 N	33.57 E
125	Ter R. (târ) . . . . Sp.	41.58 N	2.30 E
126	Terracina (tĕr-rä-chē'nä) . . . . . . It.	41.17 N	13.13 E
126	Terranova (tĕr-rä-nô'vä) . . . . . . It.	37.4 N	14.14 E
126	Terranova . . . . Sard.	40.55 N	9.29 E
89	Terre aux Boeufs, Bayou (tĕr-ō bûf') . La. (New Orleans In.)	29.45 N	89.42 W
85	Terrebonne (tĕr-bŏn') . . . . Can.	45.42 N	73.40 W
81	Terrebonne B . . . . La.	29.10 N	90.30 W
84	Terre Haute (tĕr-ê hōt') . . . . . . Ind.	39.28 N	87.25 W
81	Terrell (tĕr'ĕl) . . . . Tex.	32.42 N	96.17 W
70	Terry (tĕr'ĭ) . . . . Mont.	46.47 N	105.19 W
120	Terschelling (I.) (tĕr-skĕl'ĭng) Neth.	53.24 N	5.20 E
124	Teruel (tȧ-rōō-ĕl') . . . . Sp.	40.21 N	1.7 W
127	Tešanj (tĕ'shän') . . . . Yugo.	44.35 N	17.59 E
93	Tesechoacán (tā'sȧ-chō-ȧ-kän') Mex.	18.10 N	95.40 W
148	Teshio R. (tĕsh'ē-ō) . . . . Jap.	44.32 N	142.15 E
148	Teshiodake (Mt.) (tĕsh'ē-ō-dä'kä) Jap.	44.2 N	142.58 E
54	Teslin (tĕs-lĭn) . . . . Can.	60.0 N	132.30 W
54	Teslin R . . . . Can.	61.0 N	134.0 W
142	Tes R. (tĕs) . . . . . Mong.-Sov. Un.	50.0 N	95.0 E
132	Tessaoua (tĕs-sä'ōō-ȧ) . Fr. W. Afr.	13.48 N	8.2 E
126	Testa del Gargano (Pt.) (tās'tä dĕl gär-gä'nō) . It.	41.48 N	16.13 E
114	Test, R. (tĕst) . . . . Gt. Brit.	51.10 N	1.20 W
134	Tete (tā'tĕ) . . . . Moz.	16.15 S	33.33 E
129	Teterev R. (tyĕ'tyĕ-rĕf) . . Sov. Un.	50.40 N	29.33 E
120	Teterow (tā'tĕ-rō) . . . . Ger.	53.46 N	12.33 E
127	Tetevene (tĕt'ĕ-vĕn') . . . . Bul.	42.55 N	24.15 E
129	Tetkino (tyĕt'kĕ-nō) . . . . . Sov. Un.	51.18 N	34.16 E
70	Teton R. (tē'tŏn) . . . . Mont.	47.55 N	111.50 W
127	Tetova (tā'tō-vȯ) . . . . Yugo.	42.1 N	21.0 E
110	Tetrina (tyĕ'trē-nȧ) . . . . . Sov. Un.	66.4 N	38.0 E
116	Tettenhall (tĕt'ĕn-hōl) . . . Gt. Brit.	52.35 N	2.10 W
132	Tetuán (tā-twän') . . . . Sp. Mor.	35.37 N	5.28 W
110	Tetyushi (tyĕt-yōō'shĭ) . . Sov. Un.	54.55 N	48.48 E
126	Tevere (Tiber) R. (tā'vȧ-rä) (tī'bēr) . It.	42.42 N	12.14 E
157	Tewaewae B. (tȧ-wä'ĕ-wä'ĕ) . N. Z.	46.15 S	167.30 E
160	Tewantin (tē-wôn'tĭn) . Austl. (In.)	26.19 S	153.1 E
87	Tewksbury (tūks'bēr-ĭ) Mass. (In.)	42.37 N	71.13 W
79	Texarkana (tĕk-sär-kăn'ȧ) . . . Ark.	33.25 N	94.1 W
79	Texarkana . . . . Tex.	33.25 N	94.3 W
80	Texas (State) (tĕk'sȧs) . . . . . . U. S.	31.0 N	100.0 W

Page	Name Pronunciation Region	Lat. °′	Long. °′
81	Texas City . . . . Tex.	29.24 N	94.55 W
92	Texcaltitlán (tās-käl'tē-tlän') . Mex.	18.53 N	99.49 W
93	Texcoco (tās-kō'kō) . . . . Mex. (In.)	19.31 N	98.53 W
93	Texcoco, L . . . . Mex. (In.)	19.28 N	99.0 W
93	Texcoco, R . . . . Mex. (In.)	19.28 N	98.48 W
120	Texel (I.) (tĕk'sĕl) . . . . Neth.	53.5 N	4.50 E
93	Texistepec (tĕk-sēs-tā-pĕk') . Mex.	17.52 N	94.48 W
92	Texmelucán (tās-mȧ-lōō'kän) Mex.	19.17 N	98.26 W
128	Teza R. (tā'zȧ) . . . . Sov. Un.	56.45 N	41.25 E
93	Teziutlán (tȧ-zē-ōō-tlän') . . . . Mex.	19.48 N	97.21 W
93	Tezonco (tȧ-zŏn'kō) . . . Mex. (In.)	19.19 N	99.4 W
92	Tezontepec (tȧ-zŏn-tȧ-pĕk') . Mex.	19.51 N	98.49 W
92	Tezontepec de Aldama (dā äl-dä'mȧ) . Mex.	20.11 N	99.25 W
54	Tha-anni R. (tȧ-ȧ'nĭ) . . . . Can.	60.15 N	96.0 W
	Thailand, see Siam		
150	Thakhoi (tȧ-koi') . . . . Siam	9.0 N	99.20 E
131	Thala (tä'lä) . . . . Tun. (In.)	35.34 N	8.51 E
156	Thames (tĕmz) . . . . N. Z.	37.7 S	175.35 E
156	Thames, Firth of . . . . N. Z.	37.5 S	175.25 E
117	Thames Haven Gt. Brit. (London In.)	51.31 N	0.30 E
84	Thames R . . . . Can.	42.40 N	81.50 W
114	Thames (R.) . . . . Gt. Brit.	51.35 N	1.0 W
156	Thames, R . . . . N. Z.	37.30 S	175.43 E
140	Thana R. (thä'nȧ) India (Bombay In.)	19.3 N	72.58 E
150	Thanh Hoa (tän'hō'ȧ) . . . . Indoch.	19.38 N	105.40 E
123	Thann (tän) . . . . Fr.	47.50 N	7.5 E
123	Thaon (tȧ-ôN) (tōn) . . . . Fr.	48.17 N	6.25 E
143	Thapingjau (tä'pĭng'jou') Chn. (Shanghai In.)	31.12 N	121.22 E
141	Thar (Indian) Des. (tŭr) . . . . India	27.30 N	72.0 E
159	Thargomindah (thär'gō-mĭn'dȧ) Austl.	27.58 S	143.59 E
127	Thasos (I.) (thä'sŏs) . . . . Grc.	40.40 N	24.38 E
91	Thatch Cay (I.) (thăch) Vir. Is. (In.)	18.22 N	64.52 W
79	Thayer (thâ'ĕr) . . . . Mo.	36.31 N	91.33 W
120	Thaya (Dyje) R. (tä'yȧ) (dē'yĕ) Czech.	48.50 N	15.55 E
127	Thebai (Thebes) (thē'vȧ) (thēbz) Grc.	38.21 N	23.18 E
133	Thebes (Ruins) (thēbz) . . . . Eg.	25.46 N	32.32 E
70	The Dalles (dălz) . . . . Ore.	45.35 N	121.11 W
127	Theologos (thȧ-ō'lō-gŏs) . . . . . Grc.	40.35 N	24.40 E
101	Theophilo Ottoni (tā-ōō-fē'lōō ôt-tō'nĭ) . Braz.	17.57 S	41.15 W
127	Thermaikos (Thessalonikē), G. of (thĕr-mä'ē-kŏs') (thĕs-sä-lō-nē'kē) . Grc.	40.10 N	22.50 E
70	Thermopolis (thēr-mŏp'ō-lĭs) . Wyo.	43.38 N	108.11 W
127	Thessalonikē (thĕs-sä-lō-nē'kē) Grc.	40.35 N	22.55 E
127	Thessalonikē (Thermaikos), G. of Grc.	40.10 N	22.50 E
127	Thessaly (Prov.) (thĕs'ȧ-lē) . . Grc.	39.40 N	22.20 E
86	Thetford Mines (thĕt'fērd) . . Can.	46.4 N	71.19 W
72	Thetis I. (thē'tĭs) Can. (Vancouver In.)	49.0 N	123.41 W
81	Thibodaux (tē-bō-dō') . . . . La.	29.47 N	90.49 W
76	Thief L . . . . Minn.	48.29 N	95.52 W
76	Thief R . . . . Minn.	48.22 N	96.0 W
76	Thief River Falls . . . . Minn.	48.6 N	96.11 W
122	Thiers (tyâr) . . . . Fr.	45.50 N	3.32 E
132	Thiès (tē-ĕs') . . . . Fr. W. Afr.	14.40 N	16.52 W
123	Thieux (tyû) . . . . Fr. (In.)	49.1 N	2.41 E
108	Thingvalla Water (tĭng-väl'ä) . Ice.	64.10 N	21.12 W
123	Thionville (tyôN-vēl') . . . . Fr.	49.25 N	6.5 E
116	Thirsk (thērsk) . . . . Gt. Brit.	54.13 N	1.20 W
118	Thisted (tēs'tĕdh) . . . . Den.	56.58 N	8.40 E
108	Thistil Fjord (tēs'tĕl fyôr') . . . Ice.	66.20 N	15.28 W
108	Thjórsá (R.) (tyûr'sȧ) . . . . Ice.	64.15 N	19.15 W
78	Thomas (tŏmȧs) . . . . Okla.	35.45 N	98.45 W
51	Thomas . . . . . . Wash. (Seattle In.)	47.21 N	122.15 W
85	Thomas . . . . W. Va.	39.10 N	79.30 W
96	Thomas B . . . . Ba. Is.	26.2 N	77.11 W
74	Thomas Cr . . . . Calif.	39.50 N	122.30 W
82	Thomaston (tŏm'ăs-tŭn) . . . . . . Ga.	32.53 N	84.18 W
82	Thomasville (tŏm'ȧs-vĭl) . . . . . Ala.	31.54 N	87.43 W
82	Thomasville . . . . Ga.	30.50 N	83.59 W
83	Thomasville . . . . N. C.	35.52 N	80.4 W
96	Thompson Cay (I.) . . . . Ba. Is.	25.24 N	77.54 W
70	Thompson Falls . . . . Mont.	47.36 N	115.20 W
53	Thompson R. (tŏmp'sŭn) . . . . Can.	51.0 N	120.30 W
72	Thompson R . . Colo. (Denver In.)	40.24 N	105.25 W
79	Thompson R . . . . Mo.-Ia.	40.25 N	93.47 W
83	Thomson (tŏm'sŭn) . . . . Ga.	33.28 N	82.29 W
159	Thomson R . . . . Austl.	24.0 S	143.20 E
123	Thonon-les-Bains (tō-nôN'-lȧ-băN') . Fr.	46.21 N	6.29 E
123	Thorigny (thō-rē-nyē') . . . Fr. (In.)	48.53 N	2.42 E
108	Thoris Water (L.) (tō'rēs) . . . . Ice.	64.12 N	18.50 W
114	Thornaby (thôr'nȧ-bē) . . . Gt. Brit.	54.33 N	1.20 W
72	Thornbrough Channel (thôrn'brŭ) Can. (Vancouver In.)	49.27 N	123.28 W
116	Thorne (thôrn) . . . . Gt. Brit.	53.37 N	0.58 W
117	Thornton (thôrn'tŭn) Gt. Brit. (Liverpool In.)	53.30 N	3.0 W
84	Thornton . . . . Ind.	40.6 N	86.36 W
88	Thorofare (thŭr'ō-fâr) N. J. (Philadelphia In.)	39.50 N	75.11 W
85	Thorold (thō'rōld) . . . . Can.	43.5 N	79.12 W
108	Thorshavn (tôrs-houn') . . . . . Faer.	62.1 N	6.45 W
122	Thouars (tōō-är') . . . . Fr.	47.0 N	0.15 W
115	Thourout (tōō-rōō') . . . . Bel.	51.5 N	3.5 E
85	Thousand Is . . . . N. Y.-Can.	44.15 N	76.10 W
127	Thrace (Prov.) (thrās) . . Grc.-Tur.	41.25 N	26.30 E
116	Thrapston (thrăp'stŭn) . . Gt. Brit.	52.23 N	0.31 W
71	Three Forks . . . . Mont.	45.54 N	111.35 W
160	Three Hammock I . . Austl. (Tas. In.)	40.24 S	144.55 E

Page	Name Pronunciation Region	Lat. °′	Long. °′
156	Three Kings I . . . . N. Z.	34.5 S	172.5 E
84	Three Oaks . . . . Mich.	41.48 N	86.40 W
132	Three Points, C . . . . G. C.	4.42 N	2.0 W
55	Three Rivers (Trois Rivieres) (trwä' rê-vyâr') . Can.	46.29 N	72.22 W
84	Three Rivers . . . . Mich.	41.58 N	85.40 W
88	Three Sisters Is. N. Y. (Niagara Falls In.)	43.5 N	79.4 W
88	Throgs Neck (thrŏgz) . . N. Y. (In.)	40.49 N	73.46 W
122	Thuir (tü-ēr') . . . . Fr.	42.35 N	2.45 E
120	Thun (tōōn) . . . . Switz.	46.46 N	7.36 E
77	Thunder B . . . . Can.	48.25 N	89.0 W
89	Thunderbolt . . Ga. (Savannah In.)	32.2 N	81.3 W
120	Thun, L . . . . Switz.	46.41 N	7.43 E
80	Thurber (thûr'bēr) . . . . Tex.	32.31 N	98.22 W
120	Thüringen (State) (tü'rĭng-ĕn) Ger.	51.4 N	11.4 E
114	Thurles (thûrlz) . . . . Ire.	52.45 N	7.45 W
151	Thursday I . . . . Pap. Ter.	10.35 S	42.10 E
114	Thurso (thŭr'sō) . . . . Gt. Brit. (In.)	58.35 N	3.30 W
47	Thurston Pen. (thûrs'tŭn) . . . Ant.	71.20 S	98.0 W
131	Thysville (tēs-vēl') Bel. Cong. (Brazzaville In.)	5.20 S	14.52 E
74	Tia Juana (tē'ȧ hwä'nȧ) Calif. (In.)	32.32 N	117.3 W
152	Tiaong (tē-ä-ŏng') . . . . Phil.	13.57 N	121.19 E
132	Tiaret (tyȧ-rĕ') . . . . Alg.	35.29 N	1.15 E
102	Tibaji (tē-bä'zhĭ) . . . . Braz.	24.29 S	50.29 W
126	Tiber (Tevere) R. (tī'bēr) (tā'vȧ-rā) . It.	42.42 N	12.14 E
137	Tiberias (tī-bē'rĭ-ăs) . . . . Pal. (In.)	32.48 N	35.30 E
133	Tibesti (Tu) (Reg.) (tē-bĕs'tē) (tōō) . Fr. Eq. Afr.	21.0 N	18.0 E
133	Tibesti Massif (Reg.) (mȧ-sēf') Fr. Eq. Afr.	20.10 N	17.30 E
142	Tibet (Dependency) (tĭ-bĕt') . Chn.	31.0 N	88.0 E
142	Tibet, Plat. of . . . . Chn.	32.15 N	90.0 E
152	Tibiao (tē-bē-ä'ō) . . . . Phil.	11.17 N	122.2 E
51	Tiburon (tē-bōō-rōn') Calif. (San Francisco In.)	37.52 N	122.26 W
97	Tiburon . . . . Hai.	18.20 N	74.23 W
97	Tiburon, C . . . . Hai.	18.23 N	74.28 W
95	Tiburon, C . . . . Pan.	8.40 N	77.20 W
152	Ticao I. (tē-kä'ō) . . . . Phil.	12.30 N	123.42 E
152	Ticao Pass . . . . Phil.	12.30 N	123.55 E
116	Tickhill (tĭk'ĭl) . . . . Gt. Brit.	53.26 N	1.6 W
126	Ticino R. (tē-chē'nō) . . . . It.	45.23 N	8.50 E
85	Ticonderoga (tī-kŏn-dēr-ō'gȧ) N. Y.	43.52 N	73.26 W
118	Tidaholm (tē'dȧ-hōlm) . . . . . . Swe.	58.10 N	13.55 E
116	Tideswell (tīdz'wĕl) . . . . . Gt. Brit.	53.17 N	1.47 W
133	Tidichi (Tousidé Pk.) (tê-dē'chê) (tōō-sē-dā') . Fr. Eq. Afr.	21.7 N	16.22 E
132	Tidikelt (Reg.) (tē-dē-kĕlt') . . Alg.	26.0 N	2.30 E
132	Tidjikdja (tē-jĭk'jä) . . . Fr. W. Afr.	18.34 N	11.26 W
143	Tiehling (tyă'lĭng) . . . . Chn.	42.50 N	123.32 E
125	Tielmes (tyȧl-mās') . . . . . . Sp. (In.)	40.15 N	3.20 W
146	Tienchang (tyĕn'chăng') . . . . . Chn.	32.42 N	118.57 E
144	Tienchu (tyĕn'chōō') . . . . Chn.	26.48 N	108.56 E
144	Tienho (tyĕn'hō') . . . . Chn.	24.48 N	108.49 E
143	Tienkaza (tyĕn'kä'zä') Chn. (Shanghai In.)	31.13 N	12.28 E
144	Tienkiang (tyĕn'kyăng') . . . . . Chn.	30.25 N	107.22 E
142	Tien, L. (tyĕn) . . . . Chn.	24.45 N	102.40 E
144	Tienmen (tyĕn'mĕn') . . . . Chn.	30.38 N	113.0 E
138	Tien Shan (Mts.) (tyĕn' shän') Sov. Un.-Chn.	43.0 N	80.0 E
145	Tientai (tyĕn'tī) . . . . Chn.	29.10 N	120.59 E
145	Tientang Shan (Mts.) (tyĕn'tăng' shän') . Chn.	31.10 N	116.8 E
146	Tientsin (tyĕn'tsĕn') . . . . Chn.	39.13 N	117.3 E
118	Tierp (tyĕrp) . . . . Swe.	60.21 N	17.30 E
102	Tierra del Fuego (State) (tyĕr'rä dĕl fwā'gō) . Arg.	54.30 S	67.30 W
124	Tiétar R. (tē-ā'tär) . . . . Sp.	40.5 N	5.30 W
101	Tieté, R. (tyā-tā') . . . . Braz.	21.15 S	50.0 W
84	Tiffin (tĭf'ĭn) . . . . Ohio	41.8 N	83.12 W
111	Tiflis (tĕf-lĕs') (tĭf'lĭs) . . . Sov. Un.	41.45 N	44.50 E
82	Tifton (tĭf'tŭn) . . . . Ga.	31.26 N	83.32 W
152	Tigaon (tē-gä'ōn) . . . . Phil.	13.37 N	123.30 E
95	Tiger Chan. (tī'gûr) . . . . Pan.	9.10 N	81.57 W
150	Tiger Is . . . . Indon.	6.45 S	121.10 E
134	Tiger Pt . . . . Ang.	16.30 S	11.42 E
86	Tignish (tĭg'nĭsh) . . . . Can.	46.58 N	64.2 W
140	Tigris R . . . . Asia	32.30 N	45.45 E
93	Tihuatlán (tē-wä-tlän') . . . . . . Mex.	20.43 N	97.33 W
142	Tihwa (Urumchi) (tē'hwä') (ōō-rōōm'chē) . Chn.	43.51 N	87.36 E
74	Tijuana (tē-hwä'nä) . . . . Mex.	32.32 N	117.1 W
102	Tijuca Pk. (tē-zhōō'kä) . Braz. (In.)	22.57 S	43.17 W
102	Tijucas Is. (tē-zhōō'kȧzh) Atl. O. (In.)	23.2 S	43.18 W
94	Tikal (Ruins) (tē-käl') . Guat. (In.)	17.12 N	89.36 W
111	Tikhoretsk (tē'kôr-yĕtsk') Sov. Un.	45.50 N	40.10 E
128	Tikhvin (tēk-vēn') . . . . . . Sov. Un.	59.37 N	33.38 E
140	Tikrit (tĭ-krēt') . . . . Iraq	34.38 N	43.45 E
120	Tilburg (tĭl'bûrg) . . . . Neth.	51.33 N	5.7 E
117	Tilbury (tĭl'bēr-ē) Gt. Brit. (London In.)	51.27 N	0.23 E
132	Tillabéry (tē-yȧ-bä-rē') Fr. W. Afr.	14.15 N	1.30 E
70	Tillamook (tĭl'ȧ-mŏŏk) . . . . Ore.	45.27 N	123.50 W
70	Tillamook B . . . . Ore.	45.30 N	124.0 W
51	Tillasana R. (tĭl-ȧ-săn'ȧ) Ore. (Portland In.)	46.8 N	123.33 W
118	Tillberga (tēl-bĕr'ghȧ) . . . . . . Swe.	59.39 N	16.34 E
121	Tilsit (Sovietsk) (tĭl'sĭt) (sô-vyĕtsk') . Sov. Un.	55.3 N	21.54 E
84	Tilsonburg (tĭl'sŭn-bûrg) . . . . Can.	42.51 N	80.57 W
129	Tim (tēm) . . . . Sov. Un.	51.38 N	37.2 E
157	Timaru (tĭm'ȧ-rōō') . . . . N. Z.	44.23 S	171.18 E

ng-sing; ŋ-baŋk; N-nasalized n; nŏd; cŏmmit; ōld; ôbey; ôrder; fōōd; fŏŏt; ou-out; s-soft; sh-dish; th-thin; pūre; ûnite; ûrn; stŭd; circŭs; ü-as "y" in study; '-indeterminate vowel.

Timbalier PRONOUNCING INDEX Torres Martinez

Page	Name Pronunciation Region	Lat. °′	Long. °′
81	Timbalier B. (tĭm'bȧ-lēr) La.	29.10 N	90.20 W
101	Timbó (tēṉ-bōō') Braz. (In.)	11.52 S	37.54 W
132	Timbo (tĭm'bō) Fr. W. Afr.	10.34 N	11.46 W
132	Timbuktu (Tombouctou) (tĭm-bŭk'tōō) (tôn-bōōk-tōō') Fr. W. Afr.	16.57 N	2.58 W
118	Time (tē'mĕ) Nor.	58.46 N	5.38 E
132	Timimoun (tē-mē-mōōn') Alg.	29.20 N	0.22 E
55	Timiskaming L. (tē-mĭs'kȧ-mĭng) Can.	47.0 N	79.0 W
121	Timişoara (tē-mĭsh-wä'rä) Rom.	45.45 N	21.15 E
127	Timişul R. (tē'mĭsh-ōōl) Rom.	45.42 N	21.20 E
55	Timmins (tĭm'ĭnz) Can.	48.28 N	81.21 W
132	Timmissao (Well) (tē-mē-sä'ō) Alg.	22.0 N	3.0 E
83	Timmonsville (tĭm'ŭnz-vĭl) S. C.	34.8 N	79.57 W
72	Timnath (tĭm'năth) Colo. (Denver In.)	40.32 N	104.59 W
127	Timok R. (tē'môk) Yugo.	43.40 N	22.18 E
151	Timor (tē-mōr') Indon.	10.0 S	124.0 E
151	Timor (I.) Ind. O.	9.15 S	125.0 E
151	Timor Laut Is. (tē-mōr' lout') Indon.	7.20 S	131.20 E
151	Timor, Portuguese Pac. O.	8.50 S	126.0 E
151	Timor Sea Ind. O.-Pac. O.	10.0 S	128.30 E
129	Timoshevskaya (tē-mō-shĕf'skȧ-yȧ) Sov. Un.	45.37 N	38.55 E
99	Timote (tē-mō'tā) Arg. (Buenos Aires In.)	35.12 S	62.4 W
75	Timpanogos Natl. Mon. (tĭm-pȧ-nō'gōs) Utah	40.28 N	111.45 W
81	Timpson (tĭmp'sŭn) Tex.	31.55 N	94.24 W
139	Timpton R. (têmp'tôn) Sov. Un.	57.30 N	126.25 E
131	Timsah, L. (tĭm'sä) Eg. (Suez Canal In.)	30.33 N	32.19 E
131	Tina (Pelusium) B. (tē'nȧ) (pē-lū'zhĭ-ŭm) Eg. (In.)	31.15 N	32.40 E
131	Tina (Pelusium), Plain of Eg. (In.)	30.55 N	32.40 E
152	Tinaca Pt. (tē-nä'kä) Phil.	5.33 N	125.20 E
97	Tina, Mt. (tē'nȧ) Dom. Rep.	18.43 N	70.41 W
132	Tindouf (tēn-dōōf') Alg.	27.35 N	7.41 W
124	Tineo (tē-nā'ō) Sp.	43.21 N	6.25 W
145	Tingchow (tĭng'chō') Chn.	25.45 N	116.9 E
146	Tingchow (tĭng'chō') Chn.	38.37 N	114.58 E
144	Tingfan (tĭng'fän') Chn.	26.5 N	106.25 E
160	Tingha (tĭn'gȧ) Austl. (In.)	29.58 S	151.12 E
145	Tinghai (tĭng'hī') Chn.	30.2 N	122.6 E
146	Tinghing (tĭng'hĭng') Chn.	39.20 N	115.38 E
146	Tingsiang (tĭng'syäng') Chn.	38.32 N	113.1 E
118	Tingsryd (tĭngs'rüd) Swe.	56.32 N	15.0 E
99	Tingua, Serra do (Mts.) (sĕr'rȧ dōō tēṉ'gwȧ) Braz. (Rio de Janeiro In.)	22.45 S	43.25 W
92	Tinguindín (tēn-gēn-dēn') Mex.	19.44 N	102.26 W
144	Tingyüan (tĭng'yü-än') Chn.	30.25 N	106.18 E
146	Tingyüan Chn.	32.31 N	117.32 E
101	Tinhare I. (tē-nyä'rĕ) Braz. (In.)	13.25 S	39.0 W
147	Tinnevelly (tĭn-ē-vĕl'ē) India	9.0 N	77.35 E
118	Tinn L. (tĕn) Nor.	59.50 N	9.0 E
118	Tinnosset (tĕn'nôs'sĕt) Nor.	59.42 N	9.2 E
102	Tinogasta (tē-nō-gäs'tä) Arg.	28.5 S	67.50 W
141	Tinsukia (tĭn-sōō'kĭ-ȧ) India	27.28 N	95.27 E
114	Tintagel Hd. (tĭn-tă'jĕl) Gt. Brit.	50.40 N	4.50 W
133	Tin Toumma Steppe (tĭn tōōm'ȧ) Fr. W. Afr.	16.0 N	14.0 E
94	Tipitapa R. (tē-pē-tä'pä) Nic.	12.7 N	85.57 W
84	Tippecanoe R. (tĭp-ē-kȧ-nōō') Ind.	41.0 N	86.45 W
114	Tipperary (tĭ-pē-rā'rē) Ire.	52.29 N	6.9 W
82	Tippo Bayou (tĭp'ō) Miss.	33.50 N	90.10 W
79	Tippo Bayou (Cr.) Miss.	33.55 N	90.07 W
116	Tipton (tĭp'tŭn) Gt. Brit.	52.32 N	2.4 W
84	Tipton Ind.	40.16 N	86.3 W
77	Tipton Ia.	41.48 N	91.9 W
127	Tiranë (tē-rä'nä) Alb.	41.18 N	19.50 E
126	Tirano (tē-rä'nō) It.	46.13 N	10.11 E
129	Tiraspol (tē-räs'pôl') Sov. Un.	46.51 N	29.40 E
111	Tire (tē'rĕ) Tur.	38.5 N	27.48 E
114	Tiree (I.) (tī-rē') Gt. Brit.	56.30 N	6.50 W
115	Tirlemont (tēr-l' môn') Bel.	50.49 N	4.59 E
120	Tirol (Prov.) (tē-rōl') Aus.	47.10 N	11.0 E
126	Tirso R. (tēr'sō) Sard.	40.15 N	9.0 E
127	Tisa R. (tē'sä) Yugo.	45.30 N	20.5 E
121	Tismenitsa (tĭsh-myĕ-nyē'tsȧ) Sov. Un.	48.53 N	24.53 E
121	Tisza R. (tē'sä) Hung.	47.45 N	20.42 E
100	Titicaca L. (tē-tē-kä'kä) Bol.-Peru	16.0 S	69.30 W
156	Titirangi (tē-tē-räṉ'gē) N. Z. (In.)	36.57 S	174.38 E
83	Titusville (tī'tŭs-vĭl) Fla. (In.)	28.37 N	80.47 W
85	Titusville Pa.	41.40 N	79.40 W
114	Tiverton (tĭv'ēr-tŭn) Gt. Brit.	50.55 N	3.30 W
126	Tivoli (tē'vō-lē) It.	41.57 N	12.48 E
152	Tiwi (tē'wē) Phil.	13.27 N	123.40 E
92	Tixtla de Guerrero (tēs'tlä dā gā-rā'rō) Mex.	17.36 N	99.25 W
93	Tizapán (tē-zä-pän') Mex. (In.)	19.20 N	39.12 W
150	Tizard Bank & Reefs (tĭz'ărd) Asia	10.30 N	114.30 E
132	Tizi-n-Tamjurt (Mt.) (tē'zē-'n-täm'jōōrt) Mor.	31.25 N	7.55 W
132	Tizi-Ouzou (tē'zē-ōō-zōō') Alg.	36.46 N	4.7 E
132	Tiznit (têz-nēt') Mor.	29.45 N	9.50 W
93	Tlacolula de Matamoros (tlä-kō-lōō'lä dā mä-tä-mō'rōs) Mex.	16.57 N	96.29 W
93	Tlacotálpan (tlä-kō-täl'pän) Mex.	18.37 N	95.40 W
92	Tlacotepec (tlä-kō-tā-pĕk') Mex.	17.39 N	99.56 W
93	Tlacotepec Mex.	18.40 N	97.39 W
92	Tlacotepec Mex.	19.12 N	99.40 W
93	Tlahuac (tlä-wäk') Mex. (In.)	19.16 N	99.0 W
92	Tlajomulco (tlä-hō-mōōl'kō) Mex.	20.28 N	103.28 W
92	Tlalchapa (tläl-chä'pä) Mex.	18.21 N	100.27 W
93	Tlalixcoyan (tlä-lēs'kō-yän') Mex.	18.50 N	96.5 W
93	Tlalnepantla (tläl-nā-pän'tlä) Mex. (In.)	19.32 N	99.12 W

Page	Name Pronunciation Region	Lat. °′	Long. °′
93	Tlalnepantla, R. Mex. (In.)	19.32 N	99.9 W
93	Tlaloc, Cerro (Mts.) (sĕr'rō tlä-lōk') Mex.	19.25 N	98.43 W
92	Tlálpam (tläl'päm) Mex.	19.16 N	99.10 W
92	Tlalpujahua de Rayón (tläl-pōō-hä'wä dā rä-yōn') Mex.	19.49 N	100.11 W
92	Tlaltenango (Sánchez Roman) (tläl-tā-näṉ'gō) (sän'chāz rō-män') Mex.	21.48 N	103.25 W
93	Tlaltenco (tläl-tĕṉ'kō) Mex. (In.)	19.18 N	99.1 W
92	Tlapa (tlä'pä) Mex.	17.30 N	98.37 W
93	Tlapacoyan (tlä-pä-kō'yän) Mex.	19.57 N	97.8 W
92	Tlapehuala (tlä-pä-wä'lä) Mex.	18.18 N	100.33 W
93	Tlapisahua (tlä-pē-sä'wä) Mex. (In.)	19.20 N	98.57 W
92	Tlatlaya (tlä-tlä'yä) Mex.	18.35 N	100.12 W
92	Tlaxcala (tläs-kä'lä) Mex.	19.18 N	98.13 W
92	Tlaxcala (State) Mex.	19.20 N	98.0 W
92	Tlaxco (tläs'kō) Mex.	19.37 N	98.6 W
93	Tlaxiaco (St. María Asunción) (tläk-sē-ä'kō) (sän'tä mä-rē'ä ä-sōōn-syōn') Mex.	17.15 N	97.40 W
132	Tlemçen (tlĕm-sĕn') Alg.	34.55 N	1.21 W
93	Tlilán (tlē-län') Mex.	19.35 N	99.20 W
71	Toand Range (tō'ănd) Nev.	40.50 N	114.10 W
97	Toa R. (tō'ä) Cuba	20.20 N	74.45 W
149	Toba (tō'bä) Jap.	34.28 N	136.50 E
97	Tobago (I.) (tō-bā'gō) Trin.	11.15 N	60.45 W
150	Toba, L. Indon.	2.35 N	98.50 E
124	Tobarra (tō-bär'rä) Sp.	38.36 N	1.41 W
138	Tobol R. (tō-bôl') Sov. Un.	55.0 N	65.0 E
138	Tobolsk (tō-bôlsk') Sov. Un.	58.15 N	68.30 E
133	Tobruk (tō-brōōk') Libya	32.0 N	24.0 E
101	Tocantins, R. (tō-kän-tēns') Braz.	3.30 S	49.32 W
82	Toccoa (tŏk'ō-ȧ) Ga.	34.35 N	83.20 W
149	Tochigi (tō'chē-gĭ) Jap.	36.24 N	139.48 E
102	Tocopilla (tō-kō-pēl'yä) Chl.	22.0 S	70.10 W
133	Tocra (tŏk'rȧ) Libya	32.30 N	20.33 E
116	Todmorden (tŏd'môr-dĕn) Gt. Brit.	53.43 N	2.6 W
54	Todmorden Can. (In.)	43.41 N	79.22 W
157	Toetoes B. (tō-ē-tō'ēz) N. Z.	46.37 S	168.40 E
149	Toge (tō'gȧ) Jap. (Osaka In.)	34.57 N	135.33 E
150	Togian (Turtle) (Is.) (tō'gē-än) (tûr't'l) Indon.	0.30 S	122.0 E
132	Togo (Reg.) (tō'gō) Fr. W. Afr.	8.30 N	0.1 E
83	Tohopekaliga L. (tō'hō-pē'kȧ-lī'gȧ) Fla. (In.)	28.10 N	81.20 W
149	Toi C. (tō'ē) Jap.	31.28 N	131.20 E
119	Toijala (toi'yȧ-lȧ) Fin.	61.15 N	23.50 E
148	Tokachi R. (tō-kä'chĭ) Jap.	42.59 N	143.0 E
121	Tokaj (tô'kô-ē) Hung.	48.7 N	21.25 E
157	Tokanui (tō-kȧ-nōō'ē) N. Z.	46.33 S	168.58 E
133	Tokar (tō'kär) A. E. Sud.	18.30 N	37.45 E
148	Tokara Guntō (Is.) (tō-kä'rä gōōn'tō') Jap.	29.40 N	129.45 E
148	Tokara Str. Jap.	30.5 N	130.0 E
111	Tokat (tō-kät') Tur.	40.15 N	36.32 E
147	Tŏkchŏn (tŭk'chŭn') Kor.	39.46 N	126.19 E
4	Tokelau (Union) Is. (tō-kē-lä'ōō) Pac. O.	9.0 S	172.0 W
138	Tokmak (tôk'mȧk) Sov. Un.	42.45 N	75.30 E
129	Tokmak Bolshoi (Sea) (bŏl'zhō-ĭ tôk'mȧk) Sov. Un.	47.15 N	35.46 E
148	Tokuno I. (tō-kōō'nō) Jap.	27.45 N	129.0 E
149	Tokushima (tō'kōō'shē-mä) Jap.	34.1 N	134.31 E
149	Tokuyama (tō'kōō'yä-mä) Jap.	34.2 N	131.50 E
149	Tokyo (tō'kē-ō) Jap.	35.40 N	139.45 E
149	Tokyo Jap. (In.)		
149	Tokyo B. Jap.	35.21 N	139.46 E
156	Tolaga B. (tō-lä'gȧ) N. Z.	38.20 S	178.25 E
143	Tola R. (tō'lä') Chn.	45.45 N	122.15 E
92	Tolcayuca (tōl-kä-yōō'kä) Mex.	19.55 N	98.55 W
77	Toledo (tō-lē'dō) Ia.	41.59 N	92.34 W
84	Toledo Ohio	41.40 N	83.30 W
70	Toledo Ore.	44.38 N	123.58 W
153	Toledo (tō-lā'dhō) Phil.	10.22 N	123.39 E
124	Toledo Sp.	39.53 N	4.2 W
100	Tolima (Vol.) (tō-lē'mä) Col.	4.32 N	75.30 W
92	Tolimán (tō-lē-män') Mex.	20.53 N	99.57 W
121	Tolmach (tôl-mäch') Sov. Un.	48.47 N	25.0 E
133	Tolmeta (tōl-mä'tä) Libya	32.41 N	21.0 E
126	Tolmezzo (tōl-mĕt'sō) It.	46.26 N	13.2 E
126	Tolmino (tōl'mē-nō) Yugo.	46.13 N	13.41 E
121	Tolna (tôl'nō) Hung.	46.25 N	18.47 E
150	Tolo, G. of (tō'lō) Indon.	2.0 S	122.30 E
153	Tolong (tō'lông') Phil.	9.22 N	122.49 E
153	Tolong B. Phil.	9.18 N	122.50 E
124	Tolosa (tō-lō'sä) Sp.	43.9 N	2.7 W
79	Toluca (tō-lōō'kȧ) Ill.	40.59 N	89.8 W
92	Toluca Mex.	19.17 N	99.40 W
143	Tolunnoerh (tō'lōōn-ōr') Chn.	42.20 N	116.25 E
120	Tölz, Bad (tûlts) Ger.	47.46 N	11.35 E
77	Tomah (tō'mȧ) Wis.	43.59 N	90.30 W
77	Tomahawk (tŏm'ȧ-hôk) Wis.	45.29 N	89.42 W
129	Tomakovka (tô-mä'kôf-kȧ) Sov. Un.	47.48 N	34.40 E
124	Tomar (tō-mär') Port.	39.36 N	8.25 W
121	Tomaszów Lubelski (tō-mä'shōōf lōō-bĕl'skĭ) Pol.	50.26 N	23.27 E
121	Tomaszów Mazowiecki (mȧ-zō'-vyĕt-skĭ) Pol.	51.33 N	20.0 E
93	Tomatlán (tō-mä-tlän') Mex. (In.)	19.19 N	99.6 W
92	Tomatlán Mex.	19.55 N	105.16 W
92	Tomatlán, R. de Mex.	20.0 N	105.10 W
101	Tombador, Serra do (Mts.) (sĕr'rȧ dōō tōm-bä-dôr') Braz.	12.30 S	57.30 W
82	Tombigbee R. (tŏm-bĭg'bē) Ala.-Miss.	32.20 N	88.0 W
132	Tombouctou (Timbuktu) (tôn-bōōk-tōō') (tĭm-bŭk'tōō) (tĭm-bŭk-tōō') Fr. W. Afr.	16.57 N	2.58 W

Page	Name Pronunciation Region	Lat. °′	Long. °′
75	Tombstone Ariz.	31.43 N	110.3 W
118	Tomelilla (tō'mĕ-lēl-lä) Swe.	55.32 N	13.57 E
124	Tomelloso (tō-mâl-lyō'sō) Sp.	39.9 N	3.1 W
150	Tomini (Gorontalo), G. of (tō-mē'nē) (gō-rōn-tä'lō) Indon.	0.0	122.0 E
124	Tomiño (tō-mēn'yō) Sp.	41.59 N	8.45 W
149	Tomioka (tō'mē-ō'kä) Jap.	32.30 N	130.4 E
138	Tom R. (tôm) Sov. Un.	55.0 N	87.0 E
138	Tomsk (tômsk) Sov. Un.	56.30 N	84.59 E
93	Tonalá (tō-nä-lä') Mex.	16.5 N	93.45 W
92	Tonalá Mex.	20.38 N	103.12 W
93	Tonalá R. Mex.	18.5 N	94.6 W
85	Tonawanda (tôn-ȧ-wŏn'dȧ) N. Y.	43.0 N	78.53 W
151	Tondano (tôn-dä'nō) Indon.	1.12 N	124.58 E
118	Tönder (tûn'nĕr) Den.	54.57 N	8.49 E
149	Tonegawa R. (tō'nȧ-gä'wä) Jap.	36.16 N	139.11 E
153	Tonejatan Pt. (tō-nȧ-hä'tän) Phil.	5.21 N	120.13 E
148	Tone R. (tō'nĕ) Jap.	36.0 N	139.50 E
4	Tonga Is. (tŏṉ'gȧ) Pac. O.	20.0 S	175.0 W
147	Tongchŏn (tông'chŭn') Kor.	38.54 N	127.54 E
147	Tongjosŏn Bay (tōōng'jō-sŭn) Kor.	39.30 N	128.30 E
147	Tongnae (tōōng'nȧ') Kor.	35.12 N	129.5 E
102	Tongoy (tōn-goi') Chl.	30.20 S	71.31 W
71	Tongue R. Mont.-Wyo.	45.15 N	106.45 W
129	Tongue of Arabat (Arabatskaya Strelka) (ä-rä-bät') (ä-rä-bät'skȧ-yä strĕl'kä) Sov. Un.	45.50 N	35.0 E
147	Tongyŏng (tông'yŭng') Kor.	34.50 N	128.26 E
92	Tonila (tō-nē'lä) Mex.	19.23 N	103.30 W
133	Tonj R. (tônj) A. E. Sud.	6.30 N	28.25 E
141	Tonk (tŏṉk) India	26.5 N	75.59 E
79	Tonkawa (tŏṉ'kȧ-wô) Okla.	36.42 N	97.18 W
153	Tonkil I. (tôn-kēl') Phil.	6.2 N	121.50 E
150	Tonkin (Prov.) (tŏn-kĕn') (tôn-kăn') Indoch.	21.30 N	105.0 E
150	Tonkin, G. of Indoch.	20.0 N	108.0 E
138	Tonkova (tôn'kō-vȧ) Sov. Un.	60.40 N	89.55 E
150	Tonlé Sap (L.) (tôn'lā săp') Indoch.	13.0 N	104.0 E
122	Tonneins (tô-năn') Fr.	44.25 N	0.20 E
122	Tonnerre (tō-nâr') Fr.	47.50 N	3.58 E
74	Tonopah (tō-nō-pä') Nev.	38.4 N	117.13 W
118	Tönsberg (tûns'bĕrgh) Nor.	59.18 N	10.24 E
75	Tonto Cr. (tôn'tô) Ariz.	33.55 N	111.15 W
75	Tonto Natl. Mon. Ariz.	33.38 N	111.9 W
93	Tonto, R. (tōn'tō) Mex.	18.30 N	96.40 W
72	Tonville (tŭn'vĭl) Colo. (Denver In.)	40.1 N	104.42 W
71	Tooele (tōō-ĕl'ē) Utah	40.31 N	112.19 W
160	Toongabbie (tōōṉ-găb'ē) Austl. (Sydney In.)	33.47 S	150.57 E
159	Toowoomba (tōō-wōōm'bȧ) Austl.	27.35 S	152.0 E
118	Topdals R. (tŏp'däls) Nor.	58.20 N	8.15 E
79	Topeka (tō-pē'kȧ) Kan.	39.3 N	95.40 W
110	Top, L. (tôp) Sov. Un.	65.45 N	31.30 E
127	Topola (tō'pō-lä) Yugo.	45.47 N	19.38 E
121	Topolčany (tō-pōl'chä-nü) Czech.	48.34 N	18.12 E
70	Toppenish (tŏp'ĕn-ĭsh) Wash.	46.21 N	120.21 W
146	To R. (tō) Chn.	33.50 N	116.30 E
87	Torbay (tôr-bā') Can.	47.39 N	52.45 W
84	Torch Lake Mich.	45.0 N	85.18 W
123	Torcy (tôr-sē') Fr.	48.51 N	2.38 E
118	Töreboda (tû'rĕ-bō'dä) Swe.	58.43 N	14.4 E
126	Torino (Turin) (tō-rē'nō) (tū'rĭn) It.	45.4 N	7.40 E
127	Torlak (tôr'lăk) Bul.	43.45 N	26.14 E
124	Tórmes R. (tōr'mās) Sp.	41.0 N	5.44 W
108	Torne R. (tōr'nĕ) Swe.	67.42 N	21.0 E
108	Torne Träsk (L.) (tōr'nĕ trĕsk) Swe.	68.18 N	19.20 E
110	Tornio (tōr'nĭ-ō) Fin.	65.52 N	24.10 E
124	Toro (tō'rō) Sp.	41.32 N	5.23 W
55	Toronto (tō-rŏn'tō) Can.	43.38 N	79.27 W
54	Toronto Can. (In.)		
84	Toronto Ohio	40.30 N	80.37 W
128	Toropets (tō'rō-pyĕts) Sov. Un.	56.31 N	31.39 E
125	Torote R. (tō-rō'tä) Sp. (In.)	40.35 N	3.26 W
118	Torp (tôrp) Swe.	62.31 N	16.3 E
118	Torpen (Åmot) (tôr'pĕn) (ô'môt) Nor.	61.7 N	11.18 E
114	Torquay (tôr-kē') Gt. Brit.	50.30 N	3.30 W
117	Torre Annunziata (tôr'rā ä-nōōn-tsē-ä'tä) It. (Napoli In.)	40.45 N	14.27 E
124	Torre de Cerredo (Mt.) (tôr'rā dā thā-rā'dhō) Sp.	43.13 N	4.52 W
126	Torre del Greco (tôr'rā dĕl grä'kō) It.	40.47 N	14.22 E
124	Torredonjimeno (tôr'rā-dōn-kē-mä'nō) Sp.	37.47 N	3.58 W
124	Torrejoncillo (tôr'rā-hōn-thē'lyō) Sp.	39.55 N	6.27 W
125	Torrejón de Ardoz (tôr-rā-hōn' dā är'dōth) Sp. (In.)	40.28 N	3.29 W
124	Torrelavega (tôr-rā'lä-vä'gä) Sp.	43.21 N	4.1 W
125	Torrellas de Foix (tôr-rā'lyäs dā fō-ēsh') Sp. (In.)	41.22 N	1.34 E
126	Torre Maggiore (tôr'rā mäd-jō'rā) It.	41.41 N	15.28 E
160	Torrens I. (tŏr'ĕnz) Austl. (Adelaide In.)	34.47 S	138.32 E
158	Torrens, L. Austl.	31.0 S	137.50 E
125	Torrente (tôr-rĕn'tā) Sp.	39.26 N	0.28 W
80	Torreón (tôr-rā-ōn') Mex.	25.33 N	103.25 W
125	Torre-Pacheco (tôr'rā-pä-chā'kō) Sp.	37.45 N	0.56 W
159	Torres Is. (tôr'rĕs) (tŏr'ĕz) New Hebr.	13.15 S	168.40 E
74	Torres Martinez Indian Res. (tôr'ĕz mär-tē'nĕz) Calif.	33.35 N	116.10 W

ăt; finăl; rāte; senâte; ärm; ȧsk; sofȧ; fâre; ch-choose; dh-as th in other; bē; êvent; bĕt; recĕnt; cratēr; g-go; gh-gutteral g; bĭt; ĭ-short neutral; rīde; k-gutteral k as ch in German ich;

Tôrres Novas PRONOUNCING INDEX Tsining

Page	Name Pronunciation Region	Lat. °′	Long. °′
124	Tôrres Novas (tôr'rězh nō'väzh) Port.	39.28 N	8.33 W
151	Torres Str. (tôr'rěs) Pap. Ter.	10.30 S	142.30 E
124	Torres Vedras (tôr'rězh vā'dräzh) Port.	39.6 N	9.15 W
125	Torrevieja (tôr-rā-vyā'hä) Sp.	37.58 N	0.40 W
152	Torrijos (tôr-rē'hōs) Phil.	13.19 N	122.4 E
85	Torrington (tŏr'ĭng-tŭn) Conn.	41.48 N	73.12 W
76	Torrington (tŏr'ĭng-tŭn) Wyo.	42.3 N	104.10 W
124	Torrox (tôr-rōsh') Sp.	36.46 N	4.0 W
118	Torsby (tôrs'bü) Swe.	60.7 N	12.59 E
118	Torshälla (tôrs'hěl-ä) Swe.	59.23 N	16.21 E
91	Tortola I. (tôr-tō'lä) W. I. (P. R. In.)	18.27 N	64.37 W
149	Totomi Sea (tō'tô-mê) Jap.	34.23 N	137.25 E
126	Tortona (tôr-tō'nä) It.	44.52 N	8.53 E
125	Tortosa (tôr-tō'sä) Sp.	40.49 N	0.34 E
97	Tortue Channel (tôr-tü') Hai.	20.0 N	72.50 W
97	Tortue I. Hai.	20.5 N	72.50 W
100	Tortuga I. (tôr-tōō'gä) Ven.	10.59 N	65.28 W
121	Toruń (tō'rōōn') Pol.	53.2 N	18.36 E
119	Tõrva (t'r'vȧ) Sov. Un.	58.0 N	25.54 E
114	Tory I. (tō'rê) Ire.	55.18 N	8.15 W
128	Torzhok (tôr'zhôk) Sov. Un.	57.2 N	34.56 E
149	Tosa Sea (tō'sä) Jap.	33.20 N	133.45 E
128	Tosno (tôs'nô) Sov. Un.	59.33 N	30.50 E
139	Tostakh R. (tôs'täĸ) Sov. Un.	67.0 N	137.50 E
111	Tosya (tôz'yȧ) Tur.	41.5 N	34.5 E
124	Totana (tō-tä'nä) Sp.	37.46 N	1.27 W
121	Tótkomlós (tōt'kŭm-lōs) Hung.	46.24 N	20.45 E
110	Totma (tôt'mȧ) Sov. Un.	59.58 N	42.45 E
94	Totonicapan (tô-tō-nê-kä'pän) Guat.	14.56 N	91.20 W
114	Tottenham (tŏt'ěn-ăm) Gt. Brit.	51.35 N	0.5 W
88	Tottenville (tŏt'ěn-vĭl) N. Y. (In.)	40.31 N	74.15 W
149	Tottori (tô'tô-rê') Jap.	35.30 N	134.14 E
132	Touat (Reg.) (tōō'ät) Alg.	27.15 N	0.30 W
132	Touggourt (tōō-gōōrt') (tōō-gōōr') Alg.	33.10 N	6.3 E
112	Touil (Chelif), Wadi (R.) (wä'dê tōō-ēl') (shȧ-lěf') Alg.	34.30 N	2.12 E
123	Toul (tōōl) Fr.	48.38 N	5.50 E
123	Toulon (tōō-lôɴ') Fr.	43.8 N	5.56 E
122	Toulouse (tōō-lōōz') Fr.	43.35 N	1.28 E
150	Toungoo (tŏ-ŏŏŋ-gōō') Bur.	19.0 N	96.28 E
150	Tourane (tōō-rän') Indoch.	16.5 N	108.7 E
122	Tourcoing (tōōr-kwăɴ') Fr.	50.45 N	3.5 E
122	Tournon (tōōr-nôɴ') Fr.	45.5 N	4.50 E
122	Tournus (tōōr-nü') Fr.	46.35 N	4.55 E
122	Tours (tōōr) Fr.	47.20 N	0.40 E
133	Tousidé Pk. (Tidichi) (tōō-sē-dā') (tê-dē'chê) Fr. Eq. Afr.	21.7 N	16.22 E
116	Tove, R. (tōv) Gt. Brit.	52.7 N	0.54 W
85	Towanda (tô-wän'dȧ) Pa.	41.47 N	76.28 W
116	Towcester (tou'stẽr) Gt. Brit.	52.7 N	0.59 W
100	Tower I. (tou'ẽr) Ec.	0.25 N	89.59 W
76	Towner (tou'nẽr) N. D.	48.20 N	100.22 W
87	Townsend (toun'zĕnd) Mass. (In.)	42.40 N	71.43 W
71	Townsend Mont.	46.18 N	111.31 W
158	Townsend Ra. Austl.	26.0 S	127.15 E
159	Townsville (tounz'vĭl) Austl.	19.14 S	146.45 E
85	Towson (tou'sŭn) Md.	39.20 N	76.38 W
150	Towuti L. (tô-wōō'tê) Indon.	2.15 S	121.30 E
80	Toyah (tô'yȧ) Tex.	31.20 N	103.48 W
149	Toyama (tō'yä-mä) Jap.	36.35 N	137.15 E
149	Toyama B. Jap.	37.0 N	137.5 E
144	Toyen Shan (Mts.) (tō'yĕn shän') Chn.	23.52 N	107.8 E
149	Toyohashi (tō'yô-hä'shê) Jap.	34.45 N	137.27 E
149	Toyonaka (tō'yô-nä'kȧ) Jap. (Osaka In.)	34.46 N	135.28 E
112	Tozeur (tô-zûr') Tun.	34.5 N	7.47 E
131	Tozeur Tun. (In.)	33.55 N	8.28 E
124	Trabancos R. (trä-bäŋ'kōs) Sp.	41.0 N	5.5 W
111	Trabzon (Trebizond) (tràb'zôn) (trĕb'ĭ-zŏnd) Tur.	40.58 N	39.45 E
72	Trachyte Mt. (trā'kīt) Colo. (Colo. Sprs. In.)	38.47 N	105.7 W
74	Tracy (trā'sê) Calif.	37.44 N	121.28 W
76	Tracy Minn.	44.14 N	95.37 W
82	Tracy City Tenn.	35.16 N	85.43 W
51	Tracyton (trā'sê-tŭn) Wash. (Seattle In.)	47.36 N	122.39 W
125	Trafalgar, C. (trăf-ăl-gär') (trä-fäl'gär) Sp. (In.)	36.11 N	6.2 W
70	Trail (trāl) Can.	49.6 N	117.42 W
157	Training Wall N. Z. (In.)	45.52 S	170.35 E
114	Tralee (trȧ-lē') Ire.	52.15 N	9.42 W
118	Trälleborg (trĕl'ĕ-bôrg) Swe.	55.22 N	13.8 E
118	Tranås (trän'ōs) Swe.	58.3 N	14.59 E
92	Trancoso (träŋ-kō'sō) Mex.	22.40 N	102.22 W
124	Trancoso (träŋ-kō'sōō) Port.	40.46 N	7.23 W
151	Trangan (I.) (träŋ'gän) Indon.	6.45 S	134.15 E
126	Trani (trä'nē) It.	41.17 N	16.24 E
111	Transcaucasian (Sov. Rep.) (trăns-kô-kăzh'ăn) Sov. Un.	41.30 N	45.30 E
56	Transcona (trăns-kō'nȧ) Can.	49.55 N	97.0 W
142	Trans-Himalaya Ra. (hĭ-mä'lȧ-yȧ) Chn.	30.15 N	85.0 E
121	Transilvania (Prov.) (trăn-sĭl-vā'nĭ-ȧ) Rom.	46.30 N	23.20 E
	Transjordan, see Jordan		
134	Transvaal (Prov.) (trăns-väl') U. S. Afr.	24.45 S	29.15 E
126	Trapani (trä'pä-nê) It.	38.1 N	12.32 E
123	Trappes (tràp) Fr. (In.)	48.46 N	2.0 E
126	Trasimeno, L. (trä-sê-mä'nō) It.	43.10 N	12.5 E
124	Tras os Montes (Mts.) (träzh' ōzh môn'täzh) Port.	41.35 N	7.0 W
124	Trasparga (trä-spär'gä) Sp.	43.12 N	7.49 W
120	Traun R. (troun) Aus.	48.12 N	14.8 E
120	Traunstein (troun'stīn) Ger.	47.53 N	12.38 E
84	Traverse City Mich.	44.45 N	85.40 W
76	Traverse L. (trăv'ẽrs) Minn.-S. D.	45.42 N	96.42 W
126	Travnik (träv'nēk) Yugo.	44.13 N	17.41 E
120	Třebíč (t'rzhĕ'bēch) Czech.	49.13 N	15.53 E
127	Trebinje (trȧ'bēn-yĕ) Yugo.	42.43 N	18.21 E
121	Trebišov (trĕ'bē-shôf) Czech.	48.37 N	21.43 E
111	Trebizond (Trabzon) (trĕb'ĭ-zŏnd) (tràb'zôn) Tur.	40.58 N	39.45 E
120	Třebon (t'rzhĕ'bôn') Czech.	49.0 N	14.45 E
122	Tréboul (trā-bōōl') Fr.	48.5 N	4.20 W
120	Třebová (t'rzhĕ'bô-vä) Czech.	49.54 N	16.25 E
159	Tregrosse Is. (trê-grōs') Austl.	17.30 S	151.0 E
102	Treinta y Tres (trȧ-ēn'tä ē trās') Ur.	33.20 S	54.20 W
122	Trélazé (trā-lȧ-zā') Fr.	47.28 N	0.30 W
102	Trelew (trē'lū) Arg.	43.15 S	65.25 W
114	Tremadoc B. (trê-mă'dŏk) Gt. Brit.	52.50 N	4.15 W
123	Tremblay-les-Gonesse (träɴ-blĕ'-lā-gô-nĕs') Fr. (In.)	48.58 N	2.32 E
121	Trembovla (trĕm-bôv'lä) Sov. Un.	49.18 N	25.43 E
126	Tremiti Is. (trȧ-mē'tē) It.	42.7 N	15.32 E
88	Tremont (trê-mŏnt') N. Y. (In.)	40.50 N	73.54 W
73	Tremonton (trê'mŏn-tŭn) Utah (Salt Lake City In.)	41.43 N	112.10 W
121	Trenčín (trĕn'chēn) Czech.	48.53 N	18.2 E
150	Trengganu (State) (trĕng-gä'nōō) Malaya	5.0 N	103.0 E
51	Trenholm (trĕn'hōlm) Ore. (Portland In.)	45.54 N	123.0 W
57	Trenholme Can. (Quebec In.)	46.45 N	71.35 W
116	Trent and Mersey Can. Gt. Brit.	53.0 N	2.10 W
126	Trentino (Prov.) (trĕn-tē'nô) It.	46.15 N	11.0 E
126	Trento (trĕn'tô) It.	46.4 N	11.9 E
153	Trento Phil.	8.2 N	126.3 E
55	Trenton (trĕn'tŭn) Can.	44.12 N	77.30 W
87	Trenton Can.	45.38 N	62.40 W
79	Trenton Mo.	40.5 N	93.36 W
85	Trenton N. J.	40.14 N	74.44 W
82	Trenton Tenn.	35.58 N	88.57 W
85	Trent R. (trĕnt) Can.	44.20 N	77.54 W
114	Trent (R.) Gt. Brit.	53.10 N	0.45 W
87	Trepassey (trê-păs'ê) Can.	46.45 N	53.21 W
102	Tres Arroyos (trās' är-rō'yōs) Arg.	38.25 S	60.20 W
112	Tres Forcas, C. (trās' fôr'kās) Mor.	35.30 N	3.5 W
92	Tres Marias Is. (trās' mä-rē'äs) Mex.	21.25 N	106.25 W
72	Tretheway (Fivemile) Cr. (trĕdh'-ĕ-wȧ) Can. (Vancouver In.)	49.38 N	122.12 W
126	Treviglio (trā-vē'lyô) It.	45.31 N	9.36 E
124	Trevino (trā-vēn'yō) Sp.	42.44 N	2.43 W
126	Treviso (trā-vē'zō) It.	45.40 N	12.14 E
141	Trichinopoly (trĭch-ĭ-nŏp'ō-lê) India	10.45 N	78.35 E
123	Triel (trē-ĕl') Fr. (In.)	48.58 N	2.0 E
120	Trier (trēr) Ger.	49.45 N	6.39 E
126	Trieste (trê-ĕs'tā) Tr. F. Ter.	45.38 N	13.45 E
126	Trieste Free Ter. Eur.	45.36 N	13.45 E
126	Trieste, G. of Tr. F. Ter.	45.35 N	13.35 E
124	Trigueros (trê-gā'rōs) Sp.	37.23 N	6.49 W
127	Trikhala (trē'ĸȧ-lȧ) Grc.	39.31 N	21.48 E
121	Trilessy (trē'lȧs-sê) Sov. Un.	50.0 N	29.44 E
129	Trincomalee (trĭŋ-kō-mȧ-lē') Cey. (In.)	9.5 N	80.50 E
72	Trincomali Chan. (trĭŋ-kō-mȧ-lē') Can. (Vancouver In.)	48.54 N	123.28 W
100	Trinidad (trē-nê-dhädh') Bol.	14.32 S	64.57 W
78	Trinidad (trĭn'ĭ-dăd) Colo.	37.10 N	104.31 W
96	Trinidad (trē-nê-dhädh') Cuba	21.48 N	79.59 W
99	Trinidad Ur. (Buenos Aires In.)	33.32 S	56.59 W
101	Trinidad (trĭn'ĭ-dăd) W. I.	10.27 N	61.18 W
98	Trinidad I. Atl. O.	20.20 S	29.40 W
96	Trinidad Mts. (trē-nê-dhädh') Cuba	21.55 N	79.52 W
87	Trinity (trĭn'ĭ-tê) Can.	48.20 N	53.25 W
81	Trinity Tex.	30.57 N	95.23 W
87	Trinity B. Can.	48.0 N	53.50 W
53	Trinity Is. Alsk.	56.20 N	154.30 W
70	Trinity R. Calif.	40.55 N	123.0 W
81	Trinity R. Tex.	31.30 N	95.43 W
79	Trinity R., West Fork of Tex.	33.25 N	98.0 W
126	Trino (trē'nô) It.	45.11 N	8.19 W
82	Trion (trī'ŏn) Ga.	34.33 N	85.19 W
133	Tripoli (trĭp'ō-lê) Libya	32.57 N	13.12 E
137	Tripoli (Tarabulus esh Sham) (tȧ-rä'bōō-lōōs ĕsh' shäm') Leb. (In.)	34.24 N	35.50 E
129	Tripolie (trê-pôl'yĕ) Sov. Un.	50.5 N	30.46 E
127	Tripolis (trĭ'pô-lĭs) Grc.	37.30 N	22.23 E
133	Tripolitania (Prov.) (trē-pō-lē-tä'-nyä) (trĭ-pŏ-lĭ-tā'nê-ȧ) Libya	31.15 N	13.30 E
76	Tripp (trĭp) S. D.	43.14 N	97.59 W
4	Tristan da Cunha (três-tän' dä kōōn'yȧ) Atl. O.	35.30 S	12.15 W
141	Trivandrum (trê-vŭn'drŭm) India (Cey. In.)	8.35 N	76.50 E
127	Trn (t'rn) Bul.	42.48 N	22.39 E
121	Trnava (t'r'nȧ-vȧ) Czech.	48.22 N	17.34 E
127	Trnovo (t'r'nô-vô) Bul.	43.5 N	25.7 E
151	Trobriand Is. (trō-brê-ănd') Pap. Ter.	8.30 S	151.5 E
126	Trogir (trô'gẽr) Yugo.	43.33 N	16.16 E
86	Trois Pistoles (trwä' pēs-tôl') Can.	48.7 N	69.10 W
55	Trois Rivières (Three Rivers) (trwä rê-vyâr') Can.	46.29 N	72.22 W
138	Troitsk (trô'ĕtsk) Sov. Un.	54.15 N	61.40 E
121	Troki (trō'kê) Sov. Un.	54.37 N	24.56 E
118	Troldheimen (Mts.) (trôl'hȧ-mĕn) Nor.	62.48 N	9.20 E
118	Trollhätten (trôl'hĕt-ĕn) Swe.	58.17 N	12.20 E
101	Trombetas, R. (trôm-bā'täzh) Braz.	0.0	56.45 W
108	Tromsö (trôm'sû) Nor.	69.35 N	19.0 E
102	Tronador, Mt. (trō-nä'dôr) Chl.-Arg.	41.15 S	71.59 W
118	Trondheim (Nidaros) (trôn'hàm) (nē'dhä-rôs) Nor.	63.26 N	10.21 E
118	Trondheims Fjord Nor.	63.26 N	10.10 E
118	Trosa (trô'sä) Swe.	58.54 N	17.29 E
111	Trotsk (trôtsk) Sov. Un.	53.0 N	49.35 E
128	Trotsk (Krasnogvardeisk) (kräs'-nô-gvär-däsk') Sov. Un.	59.38 N	30.6 E
72	Trout Cr. Colo. (In.)	39.3 N	105.7 W
70	Trout Cr. Ore.	42.15 N	118.30 W
51	Troutdale (trout'dāl) Wash. (Portland In.)	45.32 N	122.23 W
55	Trout L. Can.	51.15 N	93.15 W
55	Trout L. Can.	53.55 N	89.45 W
122	Trouville (trōō-vēl') Fr.	49.20 N	0.5 E
114	Trowbridge (trō'brĭj) Gt. Brit.	51.15 N	2.12 W
160	Trowulta (trō-wŭl'tȧ) Austl. (Tas. In.)	41.3 S	145.7 E
82	Troy (troi) Ala.	31.47 N	85.58 W
79	Troy Kan.	39.46 N	95.6 W
79	Troy Mo.	38.57 N	90.57 W
70	Troy Mont.	48.26 N	115.53 W
85	Troy N. Y.	42.46 N	73.42 W
83	Troy N. C.	35.22 N	79.54 W
84	Troy Ohio	40.2 N	84.15 W
122	Troyes (trwä) Fr.	48.18 N	4.5 E
127	Troy Ruins Tur.	39.58 N	26.15 E
127	Trstenik (t'r'stĕ-nĭk) Yugo.	43.34 N	21.0 E
128	Trubchevsk (trōōp'chĕfsk) Sov. Un.	52.35 N	33.48 E
140	Trucial Coast (Dist.) (trōō'shăl) Sau. Ar.	24.30 N	55.0 E
74	Truckee (trŭk'ê) Calif.	39.20 N	120.11 W
74	Truckee R. Calif.-Nev.	39.25 N	120.7 W
94	Trujillo (trōō-ĸē'yō) Hond.	15.56 N	85.58 W
100	Trujillo Peru	8.0 S	79.0 W
124	Trujillo Sp.	39.26 N	5.53 W
100	Trujillo Ven.	9.28 N	70.28 W
94	Trujillo B. Hond.	15.57 N	86.10 W
97	Trujin (trōō-ĸēn') Dom. Rep.	17.47 N	71.25 W
97	Trujin L. Dom. Rep.	17.45 N	71.24 W
79	Trumann (trōō'măn) Ark.	35.41 N	90.31 W
55	Truro (trōō'rō) Can.	45.20 N	63.32 W
114	Truro Gt. Brit.	50.15 N	5.5 W
73	Trussville (trŭs'vĭl) Ala. (Birmingham In.)	33.37 N	86.37 W
120	Trutnov (trōōt'nôf) Czech.	50.33 N	15.55 E
120	Trzcianka (tchyän'kȧ) Pol.	53.3 N	16.26 E
120	Trzebiatowo (tchĕ-byȧ'tōō-vô) Pol.	54.3 N	15.16 E
121	Trzebnica (tchĕ-bnĭ'tsȧ) Pol.	51.18 N	17.4 E
142	Tsaidam Swamp (tsī'däm) Chn.	37.0 N	95.0 E
83	Tsala Apopka L. (tsä'lȧ ă-pŏp'kȧ) Fla.	28.55 N	82.10 W
146	Tsangchow (tsäng'chō') Chn.	38.31 N	116.39 E
143	Tsangkapang (tsäng'kä-päng') Chn. (Shanghai In.)	31.10 N	121.29 E
146	Tsangkow (tsäng'kō') Chn.	36.9 N	120.21 E
142	Tsang Po (Brahmaputra) (tsäng'pō) (brä-mȧ-pōō'trȧ) Chn.-India	29.30 N	95.0 E
146	Tsaochow (tsä'ō-chō') Chn.	35.19 N	115.41 E
135	Tsaratanana, Mt. (tsä'rä-tä'nä-nä') Madag.	14.0 S	49.0 E
	Tsaritsin, see Stalingrad, Sov. Un.		
144	Tsengshing (tsĕng'shĭng') Chn.	23.14 N	113.48 E
143	Tsetsen-Khan-Kure (tsĕ'tsĕn-ĸän-kōō'rȧ) Mong.	47.30 N	110.50 E
134	Tshela (tshā'lȧ) Bel. Cong.	5.17 S	13.50 E
134	Tshikapa (tshê-kä'pȧ) Bel. Cong.	6.30 S	20.50 E
134	Tshilongo (tshê-lôŋ'gō) Bel. Cong.	10.28 S	26.5 E
139	Tshun Mt. (tshŏŏn) Sov. Un.	65.59 N	140.25 E
135	Tsiafajavona (Mt.) (tsē'ä-fȧ-yä-vō-nä') Madag.	19.20 S	47.18 E
145	Tsiahang (tsē'ä-häng') Chn.	24.3 N	115.49 E
135	Tsiandro (tsē-än-drō') Madag.	18.33 S	44.50 E
145	Tsianglo (tsĭ'äng-lō') Chn.	26.42 N	117.22 E
146	Tsienan (tsē'ĕn-än') Chn.	40.5 N	118.39 E
144	Tsienkiang (tsē'ĕn-kyäng') Chn.	23.38 N	109.7 E
144	Tsienkiang Chn.	30.24 N	112.40 E
145	Tsienshan (tsē'ĕn-shän') Chn.	30.37 N	116.34 E
145	Tsientang R. (tsē'ĕn-täng') Chn.	29.40 N	119.45 E
145	Tsienyün (tsē'ĕn-yün') Chn.	28.36 N	120.3 E
146	Tsiho (tsĭ'hō') Chn.	36.42 N	116.43 E
146	Tsimo (tsĭ'mō') Chn.	36.21 N	120.31 E
146	Tsinan (tsĭ'nän') Chn.	36.39 N	116.55 E
146	Tsingchang R. (tsĭng'chäng') Chn.	37.0 N	113.36 E
144	Tsingchen (tsĭng'chĕn') Chn.	26.25 N	106.17 E
146	Tsingcheng (tsĭng'chĕng') Chn.	37.9 N	117.47 E
144	Tsingchow (tsĭng'chō') Chn.	26.37 N	109.26 E
146	Tsingchow Chn.	36.46 N	118.34 E
146	Tsinghai (tsĭng'hī') Chn.	39.1 N	116.50 E
142	Tsinghai (tsĭng-hī') (Div.) Chn.	34.45 N	95.0 E
146	Tsingho (tsĭng'hō') Chn.	37.8 N	115.40 E
146	Tsinghsien (tsĭng'hsyĕn') Chn.	38.47 N	116.35 E
144	Tsingkiang (tsĭng'kyäng') Chn.	26.42 N	108.30 E
146	Tsingkiang Chn.	31.58 N	120.12 E
146	Tsingkiangpo (tsĭng'kyäng'pō') Chn.	33.37 N	119.2 E
142	Tsinling Shan (Mts.) (tsĭn'lĭng' shän') Chn.	34.0 N	107.0 E
145	Tsingliu (tsĭng'lē-ōō') Chn.	26.5 N	116.47 E
144	Tsingping (tsĭng'pĭng') Chn.	26.37 N	107.38 E
145	Tsingpu (tsĭng'pōō') Chn.	31.3 N	120.59 E
144	Tsing R. (tsĭng') Chn.	30.22 N	109.44 E
146	Tsingsing (tsĭng'sĭng') Chn.	38.5 N	114.3 E
146	Tsingtao (tsĭng'tä'ō) Chn.	36.4 N	120.19 E
145	Tsingteh (tsĭng'tĕ') Chn.	30.18 N	118.29 E
145	Tsingtien (tsĭng'tyĕn') Chn.	28.8 N	120.17 E
145	Tsingyang (tsĭng'yäng') Chn.	30.38 N	117.52 E
144	Tsingyün (tsĭng'yün') Chn.	23.44 N	112.58 E
146	Tsining (tsĭ'nĭng') Chn.	35.32 N	116.27 E

ng-sing; ŋ-baŋk; ɴ-nasalized n; nŏd; cŏmmit; ōld; ôbey; ôrder; fōōd; fŏŏt; ou-out; s-soft; sh-dish; th-thin; pūre; ûnite; ûrn; stŭd; circŭs; ü-as "y" in study; '-indeterminate vowel.

Tsinsien PRONOUNCING INDEX Tyler

Page	Name Pronunciation Region	Lat. °'	Long. °'
145	Tsinsien (tsĭn'syĕn')......Chn.	28.20 N	116.5 E
135	Tsiribihina R. (tsē'rē-bē-hē-nä') Madag.	19.43 S	45.0 E
146	Tsisia (tsĭ'syä')............Chn.	37.16 N	120.56 E
143	Tsitsihar (Lungkiang) (tsē-tsē-här') (lōōng'kyäng').Chn.	47.28 N	123.57 E
146	Tsitung (tsĭ'tōōng')........Chn.	37.6 N	117.24 E
146	Tsiyang (tsĭ'yäng')........Chn.	36.57 N	107.3 E
144	Tso (tsō)..................Chn.	22.45 N	107.41 E
146	Tsowhsien (tsō'hsyĕn')......Chn.	35.33 N	117.1 E
146	Tsowping (tsō'pĭng')........Chn.	36.54 N	117.41 E
149	Tsu (tsōō)..................Jap.	34.42 N	136.29 E
148	Tsugaru Str. (tsōō'gä-rōō')...Jap.	41.20 N	140.15 E
147	Tsu Is......................Jap.	34.17 N	129.20 E
134	Tsumeb (tsōō'mĕb)....S. W. Afr.	19.15 S	17.45 E
144	Tsungfa (tsōōng'fä')........Chn.	23.35 N	113.30 E
143	Tsunghochow (tsōōng'hō-chō') Chn. (Shanghai In.)	31.8 N	121.28 E
145	Tsungjen (tsōōng'jĕn')......Chn.	27.39 N	115.56 E
145	Tsung Ming I. (tsōōng'mĭng') Chn.	31.35 N	121.28 E
144	Tsungyang (tsōōng'yäng')...Chn.	29.32 N	113.54 E
144	Tsunyi (tsōōn'yē')..........Chn.	27.36 N	106.58 E
149	Tsuruga (tsōō'rōō-gä)........Jap.	35.40 N	136.2 E
149	Tsurugi, C. (tsōō'rōō-gē) Jap. (Tokyo In.)	35.8 N	139.40 E
149	Tsurugiyama (Mt.) (tsōō'rōō-gē'-yä-mä).Jap.	33.50 N	134.2 E
148	Tsuruoka (tsōō'rōō-ō'kä).....Jap.	38.45 N	139.52 E
149	Tsurusaki (tsōō'rōō-sä'kē)....Jap.	33.14 N	131.44 E
147	Tsushima Str. (tsōō'shē-mä').Jap.	33.53 N	129.20 E
149	Tsuwano (tsōō'wä-nō')........Jap.	34.28 N	131.48 E
149	Tsuyama (tsōō'yä-mä')........Jap.	35.2 N	134.0 E
142	Tsuyunga (tsōō'yōōng-ä')....Chn.	25.2 N	101.31 E
133	Tu (Tibesti) (Reg.) (tōō) (tē-bĕs'tē).Fr. Eq. Afr.	21.0 N	18.0 E
100	Tuaja (tōō-ä'hä)...............Col.	5.30 N	73.40 W
156	Tuakau (tōō'ä-kä'ōō)........N. Z.	37.16 S	17.50 E
4	Tuamotu (Low) Arch. (tōō-ä-mō'tōō) (lō).Pac. O.	17.0 S	145.0 W
152	Tuao (tōō-ä'ō)..............Phil.	17.44 N	121.26 E
95	Tuapi Lagoon (tōō-ä'pē)......Nic.	14.10 N	83.25 W
111	Tuapse (tōō'äp-sĕ)......Sov. Un.	44.5 N	39.10 E
124	Túa R. (tōō'ä)...........Port.	41.25 N	7.11 W
102	Tubarão (tōō-bä-rouN')......Braz.	28.30 S	49.2 W
153	Tubigon (tōō-bē'gōn).......Phil.	9.57 N	123.58 E
120	Tübingen (tü'bĭng-ĕn)........Ger.	48.33 N	9.2 E
4	Tubuai (Austral) Is. (tōō-bōō-ä'ē) (ôs'trăl).Pac. O.	23.0 S	150.0 W
153	Tuburan (tōō-bōō'rän)......Phil.	10.42 N	123.50 E
100	Tucacas (tōō-kä'käs)........Ven.	10.45 N	68.28 W
145	Tuchang (tōō'chäng').......Chn.	29.20 N	116.12 E
73	Tucker (tŭk'ēr)..Ga. (Atlanta In.)	33.51 N	84.13 W
75	Tucson (tōō-sŏn')............Ariz.	32.14 N	110.57 W
102	Tucumán (tōō-kōō-män')....Arg.	26.50 S	65.15 W
102	Tucumán (State)...............Arg.	27.0 S	65.30 W
78	Tucumcari (tōō'kŭm-kâr-ē).N. M.	35.10 N	103.43 W
124	Tudela (tōō-dhä'lä)..........Sp.	42.4 N	1.36 W
82	Tugaloo R. (tŭg'ă-lōō)..........Ga.	34.30 N	83.5 W
84	Tug Fork (R.) (tŭg)......W. Va.	37.40 N	82.15 W
153	Tugnug Pt. (tōōg-nōōg')....Phil.	11.20 N	125.37 E
152	Tuguegarao (tōō-gā-gä-rä'ō).Phil.	17.36 N	121.43 E
146	Tuhai R. (tōō'hī')..........Chn.	37.8 N	117.0 E
144	Tuhshan (tōōk'shän')........Chn.	25.49 N	107.24 E
73	Tujunga Cr. (tōō-jŭŋ'gä) Calif. (Los Angeles In.)	34.18 N	118.13 W
151	Tukangbesi Is. (tōō-käng-bā'sē) Indon.	5.30 S	124.0 E
144	Tukiang (tōō'kyäng').......Chn.	25.47 N	108.2 E
156	Tukituki R. (tōō'kē-tōō'kē).N. Z.	39.50 S	176.50 E
119	Tukums (tōō'kōōms)....Sov. Un.	56.58 N	23.10 E
134	Tukuyu (tōō-kōō'yä)........Tan.	9.15 S	33.38 E
51	Tukwila (tŭk'wĭ-lă) Wash. (Seattle In.)	47.28 N	122.16 W
92	Tula (tōō'lä)...............Mex.	20.4 N	99.21 W
92	Tula..........................Mex.	23.0 N	99.42 W
128	Tula (tōō'lä)...........Sov. Un.	54.12 N	37.39 E
128	Tula (Dist.).............Sov. Un.	53.40 N	37.30 E
159	Tulagi (I.) (tōō-lä'gē).Solomon Is.	9.6 S	160.20 E
51	Tulalip (tū-lă'lĭp) Wash. (Seattle In.)	48.4 N	122.18 W
70	Tulalip Ind. Res...........Wash.	48.5 N	122.25 W
92	Tulancingo (tōō-län-sĭŋ'gō)..Mex.	20.5 N	98.21 W
92	Tula, R. (tōō'lä)............Mex.	20.20 N	99.13 W
74	Tulare (tōō-lä'rā) (tŭ-lâr')..Calif.	36.12 N	119.21 W
74	Tulare Basin.................Calif.	36.5 N	119.50 W
75	Tularosa (tōō-lă-rō'ză).......N. M.	33.4 N	106.3 W
100	Tulcán (tōōl-kän')............Ec.	0.45 N	77.45 W
129	Tulcea (tōōl'chă)..............Rom.	45.8 N	28.49 E
129	Tulchin (tōōl'chĕn)......Sov. Un.	48.41 N	28.54 E
92	Tulcingo (tōōl-sĭŋ'gō)........Mex.	18.2 N	98.28 W
135	Tuléar (tōō-lā-är')........Madag.	23.15 S	43.38 E
74	Tule R. (tōō'lā)..............Calif.	36.7 N	119.20 W
74	Tule River Ind. Res.........Calif.	36.5 N	118.45 W
134	Tuli (tōō'lē)..................S. Rh.	21.55 S	29.10 E
78	Tulia (tōō'lĭ-ă).................Tex.	34.33 N	101.47 W
137	Tul Karm (Tel Kerem) (tōōl kärm) (tĕl kĕ-rĕm').Pal. (In.)	32.18 N	35.0 E
82	Tullahoma (tŭl-ă-hō'mă)...Tenn.	35.22 N	86.12 W
114	Tullamore (tŭl-ă-mōr')........Ire.	53.15 N	7.25 W
122	Tulle (tül).........................Fr.	45.15 N	1.45 E
123	Tullins (tü-lăN')...................Fr.	45.18 N	5.30 E
120	Tulln (tōōln).....................Aus.	48.20 N	16.2 E
86	Tulmistuk R. (tŭl-mĭs'tŭk)..Can.	50.10 N	67.49 W
92	Tulpetlac (tōōl-pă-tläk') Mex. (In.)	19.34 N	99.3 W
79	Tulsa (tŭl'să).................Okla.	36.9 N	95.59 W
142	Tulufan (Turfan) (tōō'lōō-fän') (tōōr-fän').Chn.	43.0 N	89.2 E
138	Tulun (tōō-lōōn').......Sov. Un.	54.30 N	100.30 E
93	Tulyehualco (tōōl-yă-wäl'kō) Mex. (In.)	19.15 N	99.1 W
75	Tumacacori Natl. Mon. (tōō-mä-kä'kō-rē).Ariz.	31.35 N	111.4 W
100	Tumaco (tōō-mä'kō)..........Col.	1.45 N	78.45 W
95	Tuma, R. (tōō'mä)............Nic.	13.13 N	85.10 W
152	Tumauini (tōō-mou-ē'nē)....Phil.	17.16 N	121.48 E
131	Tumba (tōōm'bä) Bel. Cong. (Brazzaville In.)	5.28 S	14.43 E
134	Tumba, L. (tōōm'bă)..Bel. Cong.	0.45 S	18.5 E
131	Tumba Mani (tōōm'bä mä'nē) Bel. Cong. (Brazzaville In.)	5.55 S	15.37 E
100	Tumbez (tōōm'bāz)............Ec.	3.45 S	80.29 W
92	Tumbiscatío (tōōm-bē-skä-tē'ō) Mex.	18.32 N	102.30 W
101	Tumeremo (tōō-mă-rā'mō)...Ven.	7.15 N	61.30 W
153	Tumindao I. (tōō-mĭn-dä'ō)..Phil.	4.43 N	119.24 E
133	Tummo (tōōm'mō)........Libya	22.40 N	14.19 E
132	Tummo Mts.................Libya	23.30 N	12.30 E
101	Tumuc-Humac Mts. (tōō-mōōk'-ōō-mäk').S. A.	2.0 N	54.0 W
51	Tumwater (tŭm'wô-tēr) Wash. (Seattle In.)	47.1 N	122.55 W
153	Tuna Pt. (tōō'nä)..........Phil.	6.23 N	124.3 E
96	Tunas de Zaza (tōō'näs dā zä'zä) Cuba	21.38 N	79.35 W
113	Tunbridge Wells (tŭn'brĭj wĕlz') Gt. Brit.	51.5 N	0.15 E
148	Tunchingcheng (tōōn'kĭng'chĕng') Chn.	44.6 N	129.6 E
127	Tundža R. (tōōnd'zhä)......Bul.	42.30 N	26.30 E
145	Tungan (tōōn'gän')..........Chn.	24.44 N	118.1 E
144	Tungan.........................Chn.	26.10 N	111.7 E
144	Tungan.........................Chn.	30.23 N	105.46 E
146	Tungan.........................Chn.	39.29 N	116.45 E
146	Tungchang (tōōng'chäng')...Chn.	36.23 N	115.56 E
144	Tungcheng (tōōng'chĕng')...Chn.	29.12 N	113.41 E
145	Tungcheng....................Chn.	31.3 N	116.55 E
142	Tungchow (tōōng'chō').......Chn.	34.50 N	109.50 E
146	Tungchow.....................Chn.	39.54 N	116.44 E
142	Tungchwan (tōōng'chwän')..Chn.	31.0 N	104.55 E
145	Tunghu (tōōng'hōō')........Chn.	29.50 N	119.42 E
145	Tunghu.........................Chn.	30.12 N	117.2 E
143	Tunghwa (tōōng'hwä')......Chn.	41.45 N	125.52 E
144	Tungjen (tōōng'jĕn')........Chn.	27.35 N	108.51 E
143	Tungkiang (tōōng'kyäng')...Chn.	47.35 N	132.41 E
144	Tungkun (tōōng'kōōn')......Chn.	23.0 N	113.44 E
143	Tungkwan (tōōng'kwän')....Chn.	34.55 N	110.30 E
146	Tungkwang (tōōng'kwäng')..Chn.	38.3 N	116.22 E
144	Tunglan (tōōng'län')........Chn.	24.30 N	107.20 E
144	Tungliang (tōōng'lyäng')....Chn.	29.58 N	106.5 E
148	Tungliaochen (tōōng'lyä'ō-chĕn') Chn.	43.26 N	122.0 E
145	Tungliu (tōōng'lyōō')........Chn.	28.31 N	114.3 E
146	Tungming (tōōng'mĭng')......Chn.	35.16 N	115.25 E
144	Tung R. (tōōng)...............Chn.	23.8 N	114.8 E
148	Tungpei (tōōng'pā)...........Chn.	48.0 N	126.50 E
145	Tungsan B. (tōōng'sän')......Chn.	23.50 N	117.32 E
145	Tungsan I......................Chn.	23.45 N	117.20 E
145	Tungshan (tōōng'shän')......Chn.	29.35 N	114.22 E
145	Tungsiang (tōōng'syäng')....Chn.	28.15 N	116.33 E
146	Tungtai (tōōng'tī')...........Chn.	32.49 N	120.14 E
144	Tungtao (tōōng'tä'ō)........Chn.	26.18 N	109.25 E
144	Tung Ting Hu (L.) (tōōng' tĕng' hōō').Chn.	29.0 N	112.15 E
144	Tungtse (tōōng'tsĕ')..........Chn.	28.0 N	106.42 E
139	Tungusk Ridge (tōōn-gōōsk') Sov. Un.	64.0 N	108.0 E
139	Tunguska R., Lower (tōōn-gōōs'kă).Sov. Un.	64.0 N	103.0 E
138	Tunguska R., Middle or Stony Sov. Un.	60.30 N	98.0 E
138	Tunguska R., Upper....Sov. Un.	58.30 N	97.0 E
146	Tung Wan, Gulf of (tōōng wän) Chn.	40.20 N	121.10 E
145	Tungyang (tōōng'yäng')......Chn.	29.15 N	120.11 E
143	Tunhwa (tōōn'hwä')..........Chn.	43.27 N	128.25 E
82	Tunica (tū'nĭ-kă).............Miss.	34.42 N	90.26 W
132	Tunis (tū'nĭs).................Tun.	37.0 N	10.10 E
131	Tunis, G. of..........Tun. (In.)	37.0 N	10.30 E
132	Tunisia (tū-nĭzh'ē-ă)..........Afr.	34.0 N	9.0 E
138	Tunka (tōōn'kä)..........Sov. Un.	51.50 N	103.10 E
85	Tunkhannock (tŭnk-hăn'ŭk)..Pa.	41.36 N	75.58 W
73	Tunnel (tŭn'ĕl) Calif. (Los Angeles In.)	34.19 N	118.30 W
157	Tunnel..........................N. Z.	43.34 S	172.44 E
160	Tunstall (tŭn'stăl) Austl. (Melbourne In.)	37.49 S	145.10 E
144	Tunting L. (tōōn'tĭng')......Chn.	29.8 N	112.20 E
74	Tuolumne R. (twô-lŭm'nē).Calif.	37.40 N	120.40 W
82	Tupelo (tū'pē-lō)..............Miss.	34.15 N	88.41 W
100	Tupiza (tōō-pē'zä)..............Bol.	21.28 S	65.30 W
85	Tupper Lake (tŭp'ēr).......N. Y.	44.15 N	74.28 W
102	Tupungato (Vol.) (tōō-pōōŋ-gä'tō) Arg.-Chl.	33.20 S	69.50 W
156	Turakirae, C. (tōō'rä-kē-rä'ā) N. Z. (In.)	41.26 S	174.56 E
110	Tura R. (tōō'rä)........Sov. Un.	58.45 N	62.0 E
100	Turbo (tōōr'bō)...............Col.	8.0 N	76.45 W
121	Turčiansky Svätý Martin (tōōr'chyän-skû' svä'tû' mär'tyĕn) Czech.	49.3 N	18.50 E
121	Turda (tōōr'dä).................Rom.	46.35 N	23.47 E
121	Turek (tōō'rĕk)....................Pol.	52.2 N	18.30 E
142	Turfan (Tulufan) (tōōr-fän') (tōō'lōō'fän').Chn.	43.0 N	89.2 E
138	Turgai (tōōr'gī).........Sov. Un.	49.40 N	63.30 E
111	Turhal (tōōr'hal)................Tur.	40.32 N	36.5 E
110	Türi (tü'rĭ)..............Sov. Un.	58.48 N	25.30 E
92	Turicato (tōō-rē-kä'tō)......Mex.	18.52 N	101.18 W
96	Turiguano I. (tōō-rē-gwä'nō).Cuba	22.18 N	78.40 W
126	Turin (Torino) (tū'rĭn) (tō-rē'nō) It.	45.4 N	7.40 E
110	Turinski (tōō-rĕn'skĭ)....Sov. Un.	59.50 N	60.15 E
121	Turka (tōōr'kă)..........Sov. Un.	49.8 N	23.1 E
140	Turkestan (Reg.) (tōōr-kĕ-stän') (tûr-kĕ-stăn').Sov. Un.	42.0 N	57.0 E
138	Turkestan...................Sov. Un.	43.20 N	68.25 E
142	Turkestan, Eastern.........Chn.	37.30 N	83.0 E
121	Túrkeve (tōōr'kĕ-vĕ)......Hung.	47.6 N	20.45 E
111	Turkey (tûrk'ē)............Eurasia	38.30 N	32.40 E
73	Turkey Cr.Ala. (Birmingham In.)	33.44 N	86.47 W
72	Turkey Cr.....Colo. (Denver In.)	39.35 N	105.15 W
77	Turkey R......................Ia.	43.0 N	91.40 W
140	Turkmen (Soviet Rep.) (tōōrk-mĕn').Sov. Un.	40.20 N	54.30 E
97	Turks I. Passage (tûrks)...Ba. Is.	21.25 N	71.25 W
97	Turks Is.....................Ba. Is.	21.25 N	71.5 W
119	Turku (Åbo) (tōōr'kōō) (ô'bō).Fin.	60.29 N	22.14 E
74	Turlock (tûr'lŏk)............Calif.	37.29 N	120.51 W
156	Turnagain, C. (tûrn'ă-gĕn)..N. Z.	40.28 S	176.40 E
94	Turneffe I. (tûr-nĕf'fē) Br. Hond. (In.)	17.20 N	87.52 W
96	Turner Sd. (tûr'nēr).......Ba. Is.	24.20 N	78.4 W
115	Turnhout (tûrn-hout').......Bel.	51.20 N	5.0 E
120	Turnov (tōōr'nôf)..........Czech.	50.35 N	15.12 E
127	Turnu Măgurele (tōōr'nōō mŭ-gōō-rĕ'ly').Rom.	43.43 N	24.50 E
127	Turnu-Severin (tōōr'nōō-sĕ-vĕ-rēn').Rom.	44.37 N	22.40 E
96	Turquino, Pico de (Mt.) (pē'kō dā tōōr-kē'nō).Cuba	19.58 N	76.49 W
140	Turt-Kul (tōōrt-kōōl')...Sov. Un.	41.37 N	61.15 E
81	Turtle B. (tûr't'l)......Tex. (In.)	29.47 N	94.41 W
76	Turtle Cr......................S. D.	44.40 N	98.38 W
89	Turtle I......S. C. (Savannah In.)	32.4 N	80.54 W
150	Turtle (Togian) Is. (tō'gē-än) Indon.	0.30 S	122.0 E
89	Turtle L..Minn. (Minneapolis In.)	45.6 N	93.10 W
76	Turtle Mts..................N. D.	48.50 N	100.10 W
127	Turtucaia (tōōr-tōō-kä'yä)...Bul.	44.2 N	26.36 E
156	Turua (tōō'rōō-ä)............N. Z.	37.17 S	175.35 E
121	Turya R. (tōōr'yä)......Sov. Un.	51.16 N	24.57 E
82	Tuscaloosa (tŭs-kă-lōō'să)....Ala.	33.11 N	87.35 W
126	Tuscany (Prov.) (tŭs'kă-nē)...It.	43.25 N	11.20 E
70	Tuscarora (tŭs-kă-rō'ră).....Nev.	41.18 N	116.15 W
88	Tuscarora Ind. Res. N. Y. (Niagara Falls In.)	43.10 N	78.57 W
79	Tuscola (tŭs-kō'lă)...............Ill.	39.47 N	88.18 W
82	Tuscumbia (tŭs-kŭm'bĭ-ă)....Ala.	34.43 N	87.42 W
82	Tuskegee (tŭs-kē'gē)..........Ala.	32.25 N	85.40 W
73	Tustin (tŭs'tĭn) Calif. (Los Angeles In.)	33.45 N	117.49 W
52	Tustumeno L. (tōōs-tōō-mē'nō) Alsk. (In.)	60.10 N	151.0 W
128	Tutayev (tōō-tă-yĕf')....Sov. Un.	57.53 N	39.34 E
116	Tutbury (tŭt'bēr-ē).....Gt. Brit.	52.52 N	1.41 W
141	Tuticorin (tōō-tē-kô-rĭn')....India	9.0 N	78.10 E
101	Tutoia (tōō-tō'yă)..........Braz.	2.35 S	42.20 W
120	Tuttlingen (tōōt'lĭng-ĕn).....Ger.	47.58 N	8.49 E
4	Tutuila (I.) (tōō-tōō-ē'lä).Pac. O.	14.19 S	170.50 W
82	Tutwiler (tŭt'wĭ-lēr).........Miss.	34.1 N	90.5 W
116	Tuxford (tŭks'fērd).....Gt. Brit.	53.14 N	0.54 W
93	Túxpan (tōōs'pän)............Mex.	20.57 N	97.24 W
93	Túxpan Reef..................Mex.	21.2 N	97.13 W
93	Túxpan R......................Mex.	20.55 N	97.40 W
92	Túxpan (tōōs'pän)............Mex.	19.30 N	103.18 W
92	Túxpan.........................Mex.	21.56 N	105.19 W
93	Tuxtepec (tōōs-tă-pĕk')......Mex.	18.5 N	96.8 W
93	Tuxtla Gutiérrez (tōōs'tlä gōō-tyâr'rĕs).Mex.	16.45 N	93.23 W
151	Tuy (tōō-ē')....Phil. (Manila In.)	14.2 N	120.40 E
124	Tuy...............................Sp.	42.3 N	8.40 W
139	Tuya R. (tōō'yä).........Sov. Un.	58.0 N	112.0 E
95	Tuyra, R. (tōō-ē'rä).........Pan.	8.0 N	77.30 W
144	Tuyün (tōō'yün')..............Chn.	26.13 N	107.22 E
111	Tuz L. (tōōz).....................Tur.	38.45 S	33.30 E
127	Tuzla (tōōz'lä)................Yugo.	44.33 N	18.47 E
118	Tvedestrand (tvĭ'dhĕ-stränd).Nor.	58.38 N	8.57 E
118	Tveitsund (tvăt'sōōnd)......Nor.	59.1 N	8.30 E
	Tver, see Kalinin, Sov. Un.		
128	Tver (Dist.) (tvĕr)......Sov. Un.	57.30 N	35.30 E
145	Twanfeng (twän'fĕng).......Chn.	30.36 N	114.48 E
114	Tweed (R.) (twēd)......Gt. Brit.	55.35 N	2.30 W
88	Twelve Mile Cr. N. Y. (Niagara Falls In.)	43.15 N	79.56 W
117	Twielenfleth (tvē'lĕn-flĕt) Ger. (Hamburg In.)	53.36 N	9.33 E
87	Twillingate (twĭl'ĭn-gāt).....Can.	49.40 N	54.49 W
87	Twillingate I..................Can.	49.35 N	54.45 W
51	Twin.........Wash. (Seattle In.)	48.9 N	123.56 W
71	Twin Bridges...............Mont.	45.33 N	112.18 W
71	Twin Falls......................Ida.	42.33 N	114.29 W
89	Twin Lakes Minn. (Minneapolis In.)	45.3 N	93.19 W
73	Twin Peaks Calif. (Los Angeles In.)	34.15 N	117.15 W
73	Twin Pks. (Mt.) Utah (Salt Lake City In.)	40.33 N	111.40 W
78	Two Butte Cr. (būt).......Colo.	37.40 N	102.28 W
77	Two Harbors...............Minn.	47.1 N	91.40 W
57	Two Mountains, L. of Can. (Montreal In.)	45.28 N	74.0 W
79	Two Prairie Bayou (Cr.).....Ark.	34.25 N	91.40 W
77	Two Rivers....................Wis.	44.9 N	87.35 W
121	Tyachevo (tyä'chĕ-vō)...Sov. Un.	48.1 N	23.42 E
129	Tyasmin R. (tyäs-mĭn')..Sov. Un.	49.10 N	32.25 E
89	Tybee I. (tī'bē).Ga. (Savannah In.)	32.0 N	80.53 W
89	Tybee R.......Ga. (Savannah In.)	31.58 N	80.56 W
89	Tybee Roads (Inlet) S. C.-Ga. (Savannah In.)	32.3 N	80.53 W
56	Tyee (tī'ē).Can. (Prince Rupert In.)	54.12 N	129.56 W
135	Tygerberg (tī'gēr-bûrg).U. S. Afr.	33.51 S	18.29 E
116	Tyldesley (tĭldz'lē)......Gt. Brit.	53.28 N	2.28 W
76	Tyler (tī'lēr)..................Minn.	44.18 N	96.8 W

ăt; finăl; rāte; senâte; ärm; åsk; sofă; fâre; ch-choose; dh-as th in other; bē; ėvent; bĕt; recĕnt; cratēr; g-go; gh-gutteral g; bĭt; ĭ-short neutral; rīde; K-gutteral k as ch in German ich;

Tyler PRONOUNCING INDEX Ust.Maiskaya

Page	Name Pronunciation Region	Lat. °′	Long. °′
81	Tyler....................Tex.	32.21 N	95.18 W
82	Tylertown (tī′lēr-toun).....Miss.	31.7 N	90.8 W
139	Tynda (tŏn′dȧ).........Sov. Un.	55.25 N	124.40 E
76	Tyndall (tĭn′dăl)..........S. D.	42.59 N	97.51 W
114	Tyne (R.) (tīn).........Gt. Brit.	54.55 N	2.10 W
114	Tynemouth (tīn′mŭth)..Gt. Brit.	55.0 N	1.30 W
118	Tynset (tün′sĕt)...........Nor.	62.18 N	10.48 E
137	Tyre (Sour) (tīr) (sōōr)..Leb. (In.)	33.17 N	35.11 E
118	Tyri Fjord (tü′rē)..........Nor.	60.2 N	10.10 E
139	Tyrma twür′mä)........Sov. Un.	50.30 N	131.10 E
127	Tyrnavos (têr′nȧ-vôs).......Grc.	39.30 N	22.11 E
73	Tyrone (tī-rōn′).Ga. (Atlanta In.)	33.28 N	84.36 W
75	Tyrone.................N. M.	32.38 N	108.22 W
85	Tyrone...................Pa.	40.42 N	78.15 W
126	Tyrrhenian Sea (tĭr-rē′nĭ-ȧn)...It.	40.0 N	12.0 E
119	Tyrvää (tür′vâ)............Fin.	61.20 N	22.52 E
138	Tyukalinsk (tyŏŏ-kȧ-lĭnsk′) Sov. Un.	55.55 N	71.30 E
139	Tyukyan R. (tyŏŏk′yȧn).Sov. Un.	65.30 N	117.0 E
111	Tyulenii Is. (tyŏŏ-lĕ′nĭ-ē).Sov. Un.	44.30 N	47.30 E
138	Tyumen (tyōō-mĕn′)....Sov. Un.	57.15 N	65.25 E
139	Tyungili R. (tyŏŏŋ′gē-lē).Sov. Un.	65.30 N	120.0 E
127	Tyurk-Arnautlar (tyŏŏrk-är-nout-lär′).Bul.	43.19 N	27.21 E
146	Tzechwan (tsŭch′wän′)......Chn.	36.44 N	118.1 E
144	Tzeli (tsŭ′lē′).............Chn.	29.10 N	110.52 E
146	Tzuchow (tsōō′chō′)........Chn.	36.20 N	114.33 E
144	Tzu R. (tsōō)..............Chn.	28.17 N	110.48 E
131	Uad Zaryon (wäd thär-yōn′) Mor. (Gib. In.)	35.43 N	5.34 E
100	Uaupes, R. (wä-ōō′pās).....Braz.	0.1 N	68.30 W
133	Ubangi R. (ōō-bäŋ′gē).......Afr.	3.0 N	18.30 E
133	Ubangi-Shari (Prov.) (ōō-bäŋ′gē-shä′rē).Fr. Eq. Afr.	6.30 N	21.30 E
99	Ubatuba (ōō-bȧ-tōō′bȧ) Braz. (Rio de Janeiro In.)	23.27 S	45.6 W
149	Ube (ōō′bā)...............Jap.	33.56 N	131.16 E
124	Úbeda (ōō′bȧ-dä)...........Sp.	38.1 N	3.21 W
101	Uberara (ōō-bȧ-rä′rȧ).......Braz.	19.45 S	48.0 W
138	Ubogan, L. (ŏŏ′bô-gȧn′).Sov. Un.	52.25 N	64.45 E
150	Ubol (ōō-bôl′)............Siam	15.15 N	104.50 E
134	Ubombo (ōō-bôm′bô)...U. S. Afr.	27.35 S	32.4 E
129	Ubort R. (ŏŏ-bôrt′).....Sov. Un.	51.25 N	27.53 E
124	Ubrique (ōō-brē′kȧ)..........Sp.	36.42 N	5.36 W
142	Ubsa Nor (L.) (ŏŏb′sȧ nōr′) Mong.	50.30 N	92.30 E
100	Ucayali, R. (ōō′kä-yä′lē)....Peru	6.30 S	75.3 W
115	Uccle (ü′kl′)...............Bel.	50.45 N	4.22 E
138	Uch Aral (ŏŏch′ ȧ-räl′)..Sov. Un.	46.15 N	81.10 E
149	Uchinoko (ōō′chē-nō′kô).....Jap.	33.30 N	132.39 E
149	Uchinoura (ōō′chē-nô-ōō′rȧ)..Jap.	31.16 N	131.3 E
148	Uchiura B. (ōō-chē-ōō′rä)....Jap.	42.15 N	140.45 E
142	Uch Turfan (Wushih) (ōōch′ tŏŏr-fän′) (wōō′shĭ′).Chn.	41.7 N	79.30 E
120	Ückermünde (ü′kĕr-mün-dĕ).Ger.	53.43 N	14.1 E
141	Udaipur (ŏŏ-dŭ′ē-pōōr).....India	24.30 N	73.45 E
129	Udai R. (ŏŏ-dī′)........Sov. Un.	50.30 N	32.35 E
139	Uda R. (ŏŏ′dȧ).........Sov. Un.	54.10 N	132.0 E
118	Uddevalla (ōōd′dĕ-väl-ȧ)....Swe.	58.22 N	11.57 E
135	Uddur (ōō-dōōr′)...........Som.	4.8 N	43.50 E
132	Udeni (ōō-dā′nē)............Nig.	8.1 N	8.9 E
110	Udima (ŏŏ′dē-mȧ).......Sov. Un.	61.7 N	46.30 E
126	Udine (ōō′dē-nȧ).............It.	46.4 N	13.13 E
139	Udskaya B. (ŏŏt′skä-yȧ).Sov. Un.	55.0 N	136.0 E
139	Udskii Ostrog (ŏŏt′skĭ-ē ôs-trôk′) Sov. Un.	54.30 N	134.30 E
149	Ueda (wā′dä)..............Jap.	36.20 N	138.15 E
159	Uea (I.) (ōō-ā′ä).........N. Cal.	20.30 S	166.45 E
133	Ueb Gestro R. (wĕb gĕs′tro)..Eth.	6.30 N	41.10 E
133	Uele R. (wā′lȧ)........Bel. Cong.	3.30 N	25.0 E
110	Ufa (ŏŏ′fȧ)............Sov. Un.	54.45 N	56.0 E
110	Ufa R..................Sov. Un.	55.30 N	56.30 E
134	Ugab R. (ōō′gäb)......S. W. Afr.	20.45 S	15.0 E
134	Ugala R. (ōō-gä′lä)..........Tan.	6.15 S	32.30 E
133	Uganda (ōō-gän′dä) (û-găn′dȧ).Afr.	2.0 N	32.30 E
52	Ugashik, L. (ōō′gȧ-shēk)....Alsk.	57.40 N	156.30 E
127	Ugerčin (ōō′gĕr-cēn).........Bul.	43.5 N	24.25 E
148	Uglegorsk (ōō-glĕ-gôrsk)....Sakh.	48.59 N	142.30 E
128	Uglich (ōōg-lēch′).......Sov. Un.	57.32 N	38.19 E
128	Uglovka (ōōg-lôf′kȧ)....Sov. Un.	58.13 N	33.30 E
128	Ugra R. (ōōg′rȧ)........Sov. Un.	54.50 N	34.30 E
121	Uherské Hradiště (ŏŏ-hĕr′skyĕ hrä-dēsh′tyĕ).Czech.	49.4 N	17.30 E
84	Uhrichsville (ū′rĭks-vĭl)......Ohio	40.25 N	81.21 W
147	Ŭiju (ŏŏ′ējōō)..............Kor.	40.12 N	124.32 E
111	Uil R. (ŏŏ-ēl′)..........Sov. Un.	48.58 N	54.0 E
73	Uintah (û-ĭn′tȧ) Utah (Salt Lake City In.)	41.8 N	111.55 W
71	Uintah Mts...............Utah	40.47 N	110.10 W
75	Uintah R.................Utah	40.23 N	110.0 W
147	Ŭisŏng (ŏŏ′ē-sŭng)..........Kor.	36.22 N	128.41 E
134	Uintenhage (ū′tĕn-hāg) ûē′tĕn-hä-ghĕ).U. S. Afr.	33.45 S	25.25 E
134	Ujiji (ōō-jē′jē)..............Tan.	4.55 S	29.42 E
149	Uji Yamada (ōō′jē yä′mä-dä).Jap.	34.28 N	136.44 E
141	Ujjain (ōō-jŭ′ēn)..........India	23.10 N	75.59 E
121	Ujpest (ōō′ē-pĕsht)........Hung.	47.34 N	19.7 E
110	Ukhta (ōōκ′tȧ).........Sov. Un.	65.25 N	31.15 E
74	Ukiah (ū-kī′ȧ)..............Calif.	39.8 N	123.14 W
119	Ukmergė (ŏŏk′mĕr-ghȧ)..Sov. Un.	55.18 N	24.46 E
129	Ukraine (Soviet Rep.) (ū′krān) Sov. Un.	49.30 N	34.0 E
149	Uku (I.) (ōōk′ōō)..........Jap.	33.15 N	129.8 E
138	Ulala (Oirat-Tura) (ŏŏ′lȧ-lȧ) (oi-rät′-tōō′rä).Sov. Un.	52.15 N	85.59 E
142	Ulan-Bator-Khoto (Urga) (ōō′län-bä′tôr-κô′tô) (ŏŏr′gä).Mong.	47.56 N	106.55 E
139	Ulan Ude (Verkhneudinsk) (ōō′län ōō′dȧ) (vĕr′κnyĕ-ōō-dĭnsk′) Sov. Un.	51.55 N	107.30 E
142	Ulankom (ōō-län-kōm′)....Mong.	50.12 N	92.10 E
142	Ulasutai (ōō′lyä-sŏŏ-tä′ē)...Mong.	47.50 N	96.50 E
151	Ulawun (Mt.) (ōō-lā′wŭn) N. Gui. Ter.	5.0 S	151.28 E
147	Ulchin (ōōl′chĕn′)..........Kor.	36.58 N	129.24 E
127	Ulčinj (Dulcigno) (ōōl′tsēn′) (dōōl-chēn′yô).Yugo.	41.56 N	19.12 E
143	Uldza R. (ōōl′dzä)........Mong.	49.0 N	113.15 E
134	Ulindi R. (ōō-lĭn′dē)...Bel. Cong.	2.40 S	27.0 E
128	Ulla (ŏŏl′ȧ).............Sov. Un.	55.13 N	29.12 E
114	Ullapool (ŭl′ȧ-pōōl).....Gt. Brit.	57.55 N	5.10 W
128	Ulla R. (ŏŏl′ȧ)..........Sov. Un.	54.56 N	28.55 E
124	Ulla R. (ōō′lä)...............Sp.	42.50 N	8.20 W
125	Ulldecona (ōōl′dā-kō′nä)......Sp.	40.37 N	0.27 E
147	Ullŭng (Utsuryō) I. (ōōl′lōōng′) (ōōt-sōō′ryō′).Kor.	37.29 N	130.52 E
147	Üllyul (ŏŏl′lyōōl′)..........Kor.	38.31 N	125.11 E
120	Ulm (ŏŏlm)................Ger.	48.24 N	9.59 E
47	Ulmer, Mt. (ŭl′mûr)........Ant.	77.30 S	86.0 W
118	Ulricehamn (ŏŏl-rē′sĕ-häm)..Swe.	57.48 N	13.26 E
147	Ulsan (ōōl′sän′)............Kor.	35.34 N	129.20 E
94	Ulúa, R. (ōō-lōō′ȧ)........Hond.	15.35 N	87.50 W
153	Ulugan B. (ōō-lōō′gän)......Phil.	10.10 N	118.45 E
111	Ulukisla (ōō-lōō-kēsh′lȧ).....Tur.	37.35 N	34.30 E
160	Ulverstone (ŭl′vēr-stŭn) Austl. (Tas. In.)	41.10 S	146.12 E
118	Ulvik (ōōl′vēk).............Nor.	60.35 N	7.0 E
110	Ul′yanovsk (ōō-lyä′nôfsk) Sov. Un.	54.12 N	48.25 E
78	Ulysses (ū-lĭs′ēz)...........Kan.	37.34 N	101.25 W
120	Ülzen (ült′sĕn).............Ger.	52.57 N	10.33 E
93	Umán (ōō-män′).............Mex.	20.53 N	89.38 W
129	Uman (ŏŏ-mȧn″).......Sov. Un.	48.44 N	30.12 E
129	Umanskaya (ŏŏ-män′skȧ-yȧ) Sov. Un.	46.19 N	39.20 E
70	Umatilla Ind. Res. (ū-mȧ-tĭl′ȧ) Ore.	45.37 N	118.40 W
153	Umayam R. (ōō-mȧ-yäm′)...Phil.	8.10 N	125.27 E
86	Umbagog L. (ŭm-bā′gôg) Me.-N. H.	44.45 N	71.2 W
151	Umbo (I.) (ŭm′bō)...N. Gui. Ter.	5.40 S	147.50 E
96	Umbrella Pt. (ŭm-brĕl′ȧ)....Jam.	18.30 N	77.56 W
126	Umbria (Prov.) (ŭm′brĭ-ȧ).....It.	42.55 N	12.35 E
108	Umeå (ŏŏ′mĕ-ô)............Swe.	63.48 N	20.20 E
108	Ume R. (ōō′mĕ)............Swe.	64.38 N	18.30 E
134	Umlalazi (ŏŏm-lȧ-lä′zĭ)..U. S. Afr.	28.57 S	31.45 E
52	Umnak I. (ōōm′nȧk)........Alsk.	53.20 N	168.0 W
52	Umnak Pass...............Alsk.	53.20 N	167.30 W
70	Umpqua R. (ŭmp′kwȧ)......Ore.	43.43 N	123.50 W
134	Umtali (ŏŏm-tä′lē)........S. Rh.	18.57 S	32.35 E
134	Umtata (ŏŏm-tä′tä)....U. S. Afr.	31.35 S	28.46 E
134	Umzinto (ŏŏm-zĭn′tô)...U. S. Afr.	30.10 S	30.40 E
52	Unalakleet (ū-nȧ-lȧk′lēt)....Alsk.	64.0 N	160.45 W
52	Unalaska (ū-nȧ-lȧs′kȧ).......Alsk.	53.50 N	166.25 W
52	Unalaska I..................Alsk.	53.30 N	166.30 W
126	Una R. (ōō′nȧ)............Yugo.	44.55 N	16.10 E
51	Uncas (ŭŋ′kȧs).Wash. (Seattle In.)	47.57 N	122.53 W
100	Uncia (ōōn′sē-ä).............Bol.	18.30 S	66.31 W
75	Uncompahgre Pk. (ŭn-kŭm-pä′grē).Colo.	38.3 N	107.25 W
75	Uncompahgre R............Colo.	38.25 N	107.48 W
128	Unecha (ŏŏ-nĕ′chȧ)......Sov. Un.	52.51 N	32.42 E
55	Ungava R. (ŭŋ-gȧ′vȧ).......Can.	59.40 N	67.30 W
145	Ungkung (ŏŏng′kōōng′).....Chn.	23.41 N	116.50 E
101	União (ōō-nē-ouɴ′)..........Braz.	9.2 S	36.0 W
93	Unidos, R. (ōō-nē′dōs)......Mex.	19.26 N	99.4 W
126	Unie (I.) (ōō′nyĕ).........Yugo.	44.37 N	14.13 E
52	Unimak Is. (ōō-nē-mȧk′)....Alsk.	54.40 N	164.0 W
52	Unimak Pass...............Alsk.	54.20 N	165.0 W
82	Union (ūn′yŭn)............Miss.	32.35 N	89.9 W
79	Union.....................Mo.	38.27 N	91.0 W
85	Union....................N. Y.	42.6 N	76.6 W
70	Union.....................Ore.	45.12 N	117.52 W
83	Union....................S. C.	34.42 N	81.40 W
51	Union........Wash. (Seattle In.)	47.21 N	123.6 W
73	Union City.....Ga. (Atlanta In.)	33.34 N	84.33 W
84	Union City.................Ind.	40.10 N	84.50 W
84	Union City...............Mich.	42.3 N	85.6 W
88	Union City..N. J. (New York In.)	40.47 N	74.2 W
85	Union City..................Pa.	41.54 N	79.50 W
82	Union City................Tenn.	36.25 N	89.3 W
96	Unión de Reyes (ōō-nē-ōn′ dā rā′ĕs).Cuba	22.45 N	81.33 W
92	Unión de San Antonio (sän än-tō′nyō).Mex.	21.8 N	58.0 W
92	Unión de Tula (tōō′lä)......Mex.	19.59 N	104.14 W
93	Unión Hidalgo (ē-däl′gō)....Mex.	16.28 N	94.50 W
4	Union (Tokelau) Is. (ūn′yŭn) (tō-kĕ-lou′).Pac. O.	9.0 S	172.0 W
	Union of Soviet Socialist Republics, see Soviet Union		
134	Union of South Africa.......Afr.	30.0 S	25.0 E
82	Union Point.................Ga.	33.37 N	83.7 W
82	Union Springs..............Ala.	32.9 N	85.43 W
82	Uniontown (ūn′yŭn-toun)....Ala.	32.27 N	87.31 W
85	Uniontown..................Pa.	39.55 N	79.43 W
79	Unionville (ūn′yŭn-vĭl)......Mo.	40.28 N	92.59 W
152	Unisan (ōō-nē′sän)..........Phil.	13.50 N	121.59 E
141	United Provinces (States)...India	27.0 N	80.0 E
58	United States.............N. A.	40.0 N	100.0 W
84	Universal (ū-nĭ-vûr′sȧl)......Ind.	39.37 N	86.29 W
124	Universales, Montes (Mts.) (mōn′tȧs ōō-nē-vĕr-sä′lȧs).Sp.	40.20 N	1.25 W
89	University City.Mo. (St. Louis In.)	38.40 N	90.20 W
160	Unley (ŭn′lē).Austl. (Adelaide In.)	34.57 S	138.37 E
147	Unsan (ōōn′sän)............Kor.	39.58 N	125.47 E
153	Unsang Pt. (ŏŏn′säng)....N. Bor.	5.26 N	119.14 E
114	Unst (I.) (ŏŏnst)...Gt. Brit. (In.)	60.45 N	1.30 W
111	Ünye (ün′yĕ)...............Tur.	41.10 N	37.18 E
110	Unzha R. (ŏŏn′zhȧ).....Sov. Un.	57.45 N	43.50 E
133	Uorra Hailu (vō′rä hä′ē-lōō)..Eth.	10.37 N	39.29 E
93	Upanapa, R. (ōō-pä-nä′pä)..Mex.	17.50 N	94.11 W
128	Upa R. (ŏŏ′pȧ).........Sov. Un.	53.58 N	36.40 E
100	Upata (ōō-pä′tä)...........Ven.	8.0 N	62.31 W
117	Upholland (ŭp-hŏl′ănd) Gt. Brit. (Liverpool In.)	53.32 N	2.42 W
151	Upig R. (ōō′pēg) Phil. (Manila In.)	15.3 N	121.0 E
134	Upington (ŭp′ĭng-tŭn)..U. S. Afr.	28.25 S	21.15 E
73	Upland (ŭp′lănd) Calif. (Los Angeles In.)	34.6 N	117.40 W
117	Upminster (ŭp′mĭn-stēr) Gt. Brit. (London In.)	51.33 N	0.15 E
155	Upolu Pt. (ōō-pô′lōō).......Haw.	20.17 N	155.50 W
79	Upper Alton (ôl′tŭn).........Ill.	38.55 N	90.8 W
54	Upper Arrow L............Can.	50.30 N	117.59 W
157	Upper Hutt (hŭt)..........N. Z.	41.7 S	175.5 E
70	Upper Klamath L. (klăm′ȧth).Ore.	42.20 N	121.30 W
70	Upper L...................Calif.	48.0 N	120.19 W
114	Upper Lough Erne (lŏκ ûrn) N. Ire.	54.14 N	7.32 W
77	Upper Red L..............Minn.	48.6 N	94.45 W
157	Upper Riccarton (rĭk′ȧr-tŭn) N. Z. (In.)	43.31 S	172.34 E
84	Upper Sandusky (săn-dŭs′kē) Ohio	40.50 N	83.22 W
116	Uppingham (ŭp′ĭng-ăm).Gt. Brit.	52.35 N	0.43 W
118	Uppsala (ōōp′sȧ-lä).........Swe.	59.53 N	17.40 E
87	Upton (ŭp′tŭn).......Mass. (In.)	42.10 N	71.36 W
116	Upton-on-Severn (sĕv′ērn) Gt. Brit.	52.4 N	2.13 W
149	Uraga (ōō′rȧ-gȧ′).Jap. (Tokyo In.)	35.15 N	139.38 E
149	Uraga Str.......Jap. (Tokyo In.)	35.12 N	139.45 E
138	Ural (Aut. Area) (ŏŏ-räl″) (ū′rôl) Sov. Un.	61.0 N	68.0 E
110	Ural Mts.............Sov. Un.	56.0 N	57.45 E
111	Ural R...............Sov. Un.	51.18 N	52.0 E
111	Uralsk (ŏŏ-rȧlsk′).......Sov. Un.	51.10 N	51.29 E
141	Uran (ōō-rän′).India (Bombay In.)	18.53 N	72.57 E
149	Urawa (ōō′rä-wä′)...........Jap.	35.50 N	139.40 E
129	Urazovo (ŏŏ-rȧ′zô-vô)...Sov. Un.	50.5 N	38.0 E
111	Urbakh (ŏŏr′bäκ).......Sov. Un.	51.12 N	46.55 E
84	Urbana (ûr-băn′ȧ)............Ill.	40.7 N	88.12 W
84	Urbana...................Ohio	40.6 N	83.46 W
126	Urbino (ōōr-bē′nô)............It.	43.44 N	12.37 E
139	Urchur R. (ŏŏr-chōōr′)...Sov. Un.	57.0 N	132.0 E
111	Urda (Khanskaya Stavka) (ŏŏr′dȧ) (κän′skȧ-yȧ stäf′kȧ).Sov. Un.	48.48 N	47.40 E
152	Urdaneta (ōōr-dä-nā′tä).....Phil.	15.59 N	120.35 E
138	Urdzhar (ŏŏrd-zhȧr′)....Sov. Un.	47.25 N	81.50 E
116	Ure, R. (ûr)............Gt. Brit.	54.8 N	1.30 W
111	Urfa (ŏŏr′fȧ)................Tur.	37.12 N	38.50 E
142	Urga (Ulan-Bator-Khoto) (ŏŏr′gä) (ōō′län-bä′tôr-κô′tô).Mong.	47.56 N	106.55 E
111	Urla (ŏŏr′lȧ)...............Tur.	38.25 N	26.55 E
140	Urmia (Rezaieh) (ŏŏr′mē-ä) (rĕ-zī′ȧ).Iran	37.34 N	45.7 E
148	Urmi R. (ŏŏr′mē).......Sov. Un.	48.40 N	134.0 E
117	Urmston (ûrmz′tŭŋ) Gt. Brit. (Liverpool In.)	53.27 N	2.21 W
128	Urod R. (ōō-rôt′).......Sov. Un.	56.44 N	41.5 E
128	Urshel (ŏŏr-shĕl′).......Sov. Un.	55.38 N	40.10 E
92	Uruapan (ōō-rōō-ä′pän).....Mex.	19.25 N	101.56 W
100	Urubamba, R. (ōō-rōō-bäm′bä) Peru	11.0 S	73.0 W
102	Uruguaiana (ōō-rōō-gwī-ä′nȧ) Braz.	29.45 S	57.10 W
102	Uruguay (ōō-rōō-gwī′) (ū′rōō-gwā) S. A.	32.45 S	56.0 W
102	Uruguay, R................S. A.	28.0 S	55.30 W
142	Urumchi (Tihwa) (ŏŏ-rōōm′chē) (tĭ′hwä′).Chn.	43.51 N	87.36 E
140	Urumlyeh (Urmia), L. (ŏŏ-rōōm′-′l-yȧ) (ŏŏr′mē-ä).Iran	37.45 N	45.30 E
160	Urunga (ōō-rŏŏŋ′gȧ).......Austl.	30.28 S	153.2 E
142	Urungu R. (ōō-rŏŏŋ′gōō′)....Chn.	46.15 N	88.30 E
139	Uruppu (I.) (ŏŏ-rōō′pōō).Kur. Is.	46.10 N	150.0 E
151	Urville, C. d′ (kāp dûr-vēl′) Neth. N. Gui.	1.23 S	137.42 E
111	Uryupinskaya (ŏŏr-yōō′pĭn-skä-yä).Sov. Un.	50.48 N	42.2 E
110	Urzhum (ŏŏr-zhŏŏm′)....Sov. Un.	57.5 N	50.0 E
127	Urziceni (ŏŏr-zē-chĕn″).....Rom.	44.42 N	26.31 E
111	Uşak (ōō′shȧk)..............Tur.	38.42 N	29.15 E
134	Usakos (ōō-sä′kōs).....S. W. Afr.	22.5 S	15.40 E
110	Usa R. (ŏŏ′sȧ)..........Sov. Un.	66.30 N	59.0 E
99	Useless B...Chl. (Magallanes In.)	53.30 S	69.50 W
149	Ushimado (ōō′shē-mä′dō)....Jap.	34.36 N	134.9 E
102	Ushuaia (ōō-shōō-ī′ä).........Arg.	54.50 S	68.28 W
111	Üsküdar (üs′kü′dȧr).........Tur.	41.0 N	29.10 E
128	Usman (ōōs-mȧn′)......Sov. Un.	52.1 N	39.40 E
138	Usol′e (ŏŏ-sô′lyĕ)........Sov. Un.	52.40 N	103.45 E
138	Usol′e................Sov. Un.	59.35 N	56.55 E
102	Uspallata Pass (ōōs-pä-lyä′tä) Arg.-Chl.	32.50 S	70.15 W
122	Ussel (üs′ĕl)..................Fr.	45.32 N	2.20 E
148	Ussuri (ōō-sōō′rē).......Sov. Un.	45.1 N	133.1 E
139	Ussuri R.........Chn.-Sov. Un.	47.0 N	134.0 E
138	Ust Abakanskoe (ōōst ȧ-bȧ-kän′-skô-yĕ).Sov. Un.	53.50 N	91.25 E
120	Usti (ōōs′tē)..............Czech.	50.40 N	14.1 E
126	Ustica (I.) (ōōs′tē-kä).........It.	38.42 N	13.10 E
129	Ustinovka (ŏŏs-tē′nôf-kä) Sov. Un.	47.59 N	32.29 E
120	Ustka (ōōst′kȧ).............Pol.	54.34 N	16.51 E
138	Ust Kamenogorsk (ŏŏst kȧ-mĕn′ô-gôrsk).Sov. Un.	50.0 N	82.35 E
110	Ust-Kulom (ŏŏst-kŏŏ′lŭm) Sov. Un.	61.40 N	53.45 E
142	Ust Kyakhta (Kyakhta) (ōōst kyäκ′tä).Sov. Un.	50.35 N	105.55 E
139	Ust Maiskaya (ŏŏst′ mī′skä-yä) Sov. Un.	60.30 N	134.30 E

ng-sing; ŋ-baŋk; ɴ-nasalized n; nŏd; cŏmmit; ōld; ôbey; ôrder; fōōd; fŏŏt; ou-out; s-soft; sh-dish; th-thin; pūre; ûnite; ûrn; stŭd; circŭs; ü-as "y" in study; ′-indeterminate vowel.

Ust-Medveditskaya PRONOUNCING INDEX Verdigris

Page	Name Pronunciation Region	Lat. °′	Long. °′
111	Ust-Medveditskaya (ōōst-mĕd-vyĕ-dēt'skȧ-yȧ). Sov. Un.	49.35 N	42.50 E
139	Ust Olemskoe (ō-lĕm'skô-yĕ) Sov. Un.	72.59 N	120.10 E
139	Ust Orda (ôr'dȧ) Sov. Un.	52.45 N	104.40 E
110	Ust-Sysolsk (Syktyvkar) (sē-sôlsk') (sĭk-tĭf-kär'). Sov. Un.	61.40 N	50.45 E
110	Ust-Tsylma (tsĭl'mȧ) Sov. Un.	65.29 N	52.28 E
140	Ust Urt Plat. (ōōst ōōrt). Sov. Un.	44.30 N	56.45 E
110	Ust-Usolka (Solikamsk) (ōō-sôl'kȧ) (sō-lĭ-kämsk'). Sov. Un.	59.35 N	56.45 E
139	Ust Yansk (yȧnsk) Sov. Un.	70.50 N	136.25 E
128	Ustyuzhna (ōōst-yōōzh'nȧ) Sov. Un.	58.48 N	36.21 E
149	Usuki (ōō'sōō-kē') Jap.	33.5 N	131.48 E
94	Usulatán (ōō-sōō-lä-tän') Sal.	13.22 N	88.24 W
93	Usumacinta, R. (ōō'sōō-mä-sēn'tō) Mex.	17.20 N	91.23 W
134	Usumbura (ōō-sōōm-bōō'rä) Bel. Cong.	3.22 S	29.22 E
75	Utah (State) (ū'tô) U. S.	39.0 N	111.50 W
75	Utah L. Utah	40.15 N	111.50 W
78	Ute Cr (ūt) N. M.	36.0 N	103.45 W
119	Uténa (ōō'tā-nä) Sov. Un.	55.31 N	25.40 E
135	Utete (ōō-tā'tȧ) Tan.	8.0 S	38.43 E
85	Utica (ū'tĭ-kȧ) N. Y.	43.7 N	75.13 W
124	Utiel (ōō-tyȧl') Sp.	39.35 N	1.13 W
94	Utila I (ōō-tē'lä) Hond.	16.6 N	86.56 W
149	Uto (ōō'tō') Jap.	32.45 N	130.43 E
120	Utrecht (ū'trĕkt) (ü'trĕkt) Neth.	52.5 N	5.9 E
124	Utrera (ōō-trā'rä) Sp.	37.12 N	5.46 W
118	Utsire (I.) (ōōt-sē'rĕ) Nor.	59.20 N	4.52 E
149	Utsunomiya (ōōt'sōō-nō'mē-yȧ') Jap.	36.31 N	139.47 E
147	Utsuryō (Ullŭng) I. (ōōt-sōō'ryō') (ōōl'lōōng'). Kor.	37.29 N	130.52 E
150	Uttara (ōō'tä-rä) Siam	17.35 N	102.50 E
116	Uttoxeter (ŭt-tŏk'sē-tēr). Gt. Brit.	52.54 N	1.52 W
91	Utuado (ōō-tōō-ä'dhō) P. R. (In.)	18.15 N	66.40 W
119	Uusikaupunki (Nystad) (ōō'sĭ-kou'pōōn-kĭ) (nü'städh). Fin.	60.49 N	21.28 E
80	Uvalde (ū-văl'dē) Tex.	29.13 N	99.48 W
134	Uvira (ōō-vē'rä) Bel. Cong.	3.28 S	29.3 E
149	Uwajima (ōō-wä'jē-mä) Jap.	33.15 N	132.31 E
87	Uxbridge (ŭks'brĭj) Mass. (In.)	42.4 N	71.38 W
100	Uyuni (ōō-yōō'nē) Bol.	19.29 S	66.48 W
138	Uzbek (Sov. Rep.) (ōōz-bĕk') Sov. Un.	40.30 N	69.0 E
111	Uzen R., Great (ōō-zĕn'). Sov. Un.	49.45 N	49.30 E
122	Uzès (ū-zĕs') Fr.	44.2 N	4.25 E
121	Uzhgorod (ōōzh'gō-rōt) Sov. Un.	48.38 N	22.19 E
129	Uzh R. (ōōzh) Sov. Un.	51.0 N	28.45 E
127	Užice (ōō'zhĭ-tsĕ) Yugo.	43.51 N	19.51 E
160	Uzunga (ōō-zōōŋ'gȧ) Austl. (In.)	30.27 S	153.3 E
127	Uzunköprü (ōō'zōōn'kû-prü). Tur.	41.15 N	26.41 E
118	Vaads (I.) (vôds) Nor.	61.58 N	5.5 E
134	Vaal R. (väl) U. S. Afr.	26.55 S	27.0 E
119	Vaasa (vä'sȧ) Fin.	63.5 N	21.40 E
121	Vac (väts) Hung.	47.47 N	19.10 E
97	Vache I. (väsh) Hai.	18.4 N	73.40 W
110	Vadsö (vädh'sû) Nor.	70.5 N	29.45 E
118	Vadstena (väd'stĭ'nȧ) Swe.	58.27 N	14.55 E
120	Vaduz (vä'dōōts) Liech.	47.9 N	9.32 E
110	Vaga R. (vä'gȧ) Sov. Un.	61.20 N	42.30 E
124	Vagos (vä'gōzh) Port.	40.33 N	8.41 W
121	Váh R. (väk) Czech.	49.16 N	18.40 E
110	Vaigach I. (vī-gȧch') Sov. Un.	70.0 N	59.30 E
138	Vakh R. (väk) Sov. Un.	60.30 N	82.10 E
119	Valaam (vȧ-lȧm') Sov. Un.	61.23 N	30.57 E
128	Valdai (väl-dī') Sov. Un.	57.58 N	33.12 E
128	Valdai Hills Sov. Un.	57.35 N	33.0 E
118	Valdemarsvik (väl'dĭ-märs-vēk') Swe.	58.12 N	16.41 E
125	Valdemorillo (väl-dȧ-mō-rēl'yō) Sp. (In.)	40.30 N	4.5 W
124	Valdepeñas (väl-dȧ-pān'yäs) Sp.	38.46 N	3.22 W
153	Valderrama (väl-dĕr-rä'mä) Phil.	11.0 N	122.7 E
72	Valdes I. (vàl'dĕs) Can. (Vancouver In.)	49.5 N	123.39 W
53	Valdez (văl'dĕz) Alsk.	61.5 N	146.5 W
102	Valdez Pen. (väl'dȧz) Arg.	42.30 S	64.0 W
125	Valdilecha (väl-dē-lä'chä). Sp. (In.)	40.17 N	3.18 W
102	Valdivia (väl-dē'vē-ä) Chl.	39.45 S	73.10 W
82	Valdosta (văl-dŏs'tȧ) Ga.	30.50 N	83.18 W
124	Valdoviño (väl-dō-vē'nō) Sp.	43.36 N	8.6 W
70	Vale (vāl) Ore.	43.59 N	117.15 W
101	Valença (vä-lĕN'sȧ) Braz. (In.)	13.20 S	39.6 W
99	Valença. Braz. (Rio de Janeiro In.)	22.13 S	43.44 W
124	Valença Port.	42.2 N	8.38 W
122	Valence (vȧ-läNs') Fr.	44.55 N	4.55 E
153	Valencia (vä-lĕn'syä) Phil.	9.37 N	124.13 E
124	Valencia (vä-lĕn'thē-ä) Sp.	39.25 N	7.15 W
125	Valencia Sp.	39.28 N	0.22 W
125	Valencia (Prov.) Sp.	39.30 N	0.40 W
100	Valencia (vä-lĕn'syä) Ven.	10.12 N	68.1 W
114	Valencia I. (vȧ-lĕn'shȧ) Ire.	51.55 N	9.25 W
122	Valenciennes (vȧ-läN-syĕn') Fr.	50.25 N	3.5 E
123	Valentigny (vȧ-läN-tē-nyē') Fr.	47.30 N	6.50 E
76	Valentine (văl'ĕn-tīn) Neb.	42.52 N	100.33 W
100	Valera (vä-lā'rä) Ven.	9.15 N	70.30 W
95	Valientes, C. (vä-lyĕn'tȧs) Pan.	9.10 N	81.55 W
71	Valier (vȧ-lēr') Mont.	48.17 N	112.15 W
127	Valjevo (väl'yȧ-vō) Yugo.	44.17 N	19.54 E
119	Valka (väl'kȧ) Sov. Un.	57.46 N	26.1 E
129	Valki (väl'kē) Sov. Un.	49.48 N	35.39 E
129	Valkovo (väl'kō-vō) Sov. Un.	45.25 N	29.36 E
124	Valladolid (väl-yä-dhō-lēdh') Sp.	41.40 N	4.41 W
123	Vallauris (vȧ-lō-rēs') Fr.	43.35 N	7.1 E
125	Vall de Uxó (väl dä ōō-kō') Sp.	39.50 N	0.15 W
125	Valldigna (väl-dēn'yä) Sp.	39.5 N	0.17 W
74	Valle, Arroyo del (ä-rō'yō dĕl väl'yȧ). Calif.	37.35 N	121.40 W
125	Vallecas (väl-yā'käs) Sp. (In.)	40.23 N	3.38 W
80	Valle de Allende (väl'yā dā äl-yĕn'dā). Mex.	26.55 N	105.25 W
92	Valle de Bravo (väl'yā dā brä'vō) Mex.	19.12 N	100.7 W
92	Valle de Santiago (väl'yā dā sän-tē-ä'gō). Mex.	20.23 N	101.11 W
100	Valledupar (väl'yā-dōō-pär'). Col.	10.2 N	73.30 W
100	Vallegrande (väl-yā-grän'dā). Bol.	18.33 S	64.15 W
153	Vallehermoso (väl'yȧ-ĕr-mō'sō) Phil.	10.19 N	123.19 E
74	Vallejo (väl-yä'hō) (vă-lā'hō) Calif.	38.6 N	122.15 W
102	Vallenar (väl-yȧ-när') Chl.	28.40 S	70.50 W
112	Valletta (väl-lĕt'ä) Malta	35.55 N	14.29 E
73	Valley Cr. (văl'ē) Ala. (Birmingham In.)	33.28 N	87.10 W
76	Valley City N. D.	46.56 N	98.0 W
79	Valley Falls Kan.	39.21 N	95.27 W
55	Valleyfield (văl'ē-fēld) Can.	45.18 N	74.0 W
97	Vallière (väl-yâr') Dom. Rep.	19.28 N	71.54 W
125	Valls (väls) Sp.	41.16 N	1.12 E
119	Valmiera (väl'myĕ-rä) Sov. Un.	57.34 N	25.25 E
72	Valmont (văl'mŏnt) Colo. (Denver In.)	40.2 N	105.12 W
122	Valognes (vȧ-lôn'y') Fr.	49.30 N	1.25 W
57	Valois (vȧ-lwä') Can. (Montreal In.)	45.27 N	73.48 W
127	Valona (Vlonë) (vä-lō'nä) (vlō'nȧ). Alb.	40.28 N	19.30 E
102	Valparaíso (väl'pä-rä-ē'sō) Chl.	33.0 S	71.40 W
84	Valparaiso (văl-pȧ-rā'zō) Ind.	41.28 N	87.2 W
92	Valparaíso (väl'pä-rä-ē'sō) Mex.	22.58 N	103.38 W
122	Valréas (vȧl-rā-ä') Fr.	44.25 N	4.59 E
151	Valsch, C. (välsh) Neth. N. Gui.	8.25 S	137.40 E
129	Valuiki (vȧ-lōō-ē'kē) Sov. Un.	50.13 N	38.5 E
73	Val Verde (văl vûr'dē) Calif. (Los Angeles In.)	33.50 N	117.15 W
124	Valverde (väl-vĕr'dä) Sp.	37.35 N	6.46 W
111	Van (vän) Tur.	38.32 N	43.18 E
79	Van Buren (văn bū'rĕn) Ark.	35.25 N	94.21 W
86	Van Buren Me.	47.9 N	67.58 W
84	Vanceburg (văns'bûrg) Ky.	38.36 N	83.20 W
70	Vancouver (văn-kōō'vēr) Can.	49.16 N	123.5 W
56	Vancouver Can. (In.)		
70	Vancouver Wash.	45.37 N	122.40 W
70	Vancouver I. Can.	48.52 N	124.0 W
79	Vandalia (văn-dā'lĭ-ȧ) Ill.	38.57 N	89.6 W
79	Vandalia Mo.	39.17 N	91.30 W
158	Van Diemen, C. (văn dē'mĕn) Austl.	11.5 S	130.29 E
158	Van Diemen G. Austl.	12.0 S	132.0 E
73	Vandiver (văn'dĭ-vēr) Ala. (Birmingham In.)	33.28 N	86.31 W
108	Vandö (I.) (vänd'û) Nor.	70.10 N	19.45 E
118	Väner, L. (vĕ'nēr) Swe.	59.0 N	13.0 E
118	Vänersborg (vĕ'nērs-bôr') Swe.	58.23 N	12.18 E
135	Vanga (väŋ'gä) Kenya	4.38 S	39.10 E
117	Vange (văn'jē) Gt. Brit. (London In.)	51.33 N	0.28 E
111	Van, L. (vän) Tur.	38.45 N	43.0 E
84	Van Lear (văn lēr') Ky.	37.45 N	82.50 W
122	Vannes (vàn) Fr.	47.40 N	2.45 W
84	Van Wert (văn wûrt') Ohio	40.50 N	84.38 W
72	Van Zandt (văn zănt') Wash. (Vancouver In.)	48.48 N	122.12 W
118	Vara (vä'rä) Swe.	58.18 N	12.56 E
126	Varallo (vä-räl'lō) It.	45.46 N	8.16 E
108	Varanger Fjord (vä-räng'gĕr fyôr'). Nor.	69.55 N	30.30 E
126	Varano, L. of (vä-rä'nō) It.	41.53 N	15.45 E
126	Varaždin (vä'räzh'dĕn) Yugo.	46.19 N	16.21 E
126	Varazze (vä-rät'sā) It.	44.22 N	8.37 E
118	Varberg (vär'bĕrg) Swe.	57.6 N	12.16 E
127	Vardar R. (vär'där) Yugo.	41.33 N	22.0 E
118	Varde (vär'dĕ) Den.	55.38 N	8.30 E
118	Varde R. Den.	55.45 N	8.40 E
110	Vardö (värd'û) Nor.	70.25 N	31.0 E
119	Varena (vä-rā'nä) Sov. Un.	54.16 N	24.32 E
57	Varennes (vȧ-rĕn') Can. (In.)	45.41 N	73.25 W
127	Vareš (vä'rĕsh) Yugo.	44.11 N	18.21 E
126	Varese (vä-rā'sā) It.	45.48 N	8.50 E
119	Varkaus (vär'kous) Fin.	62.20 N	27.57 E
119	Varklāni (värk'lä-nē) Sov. Un.	56.36 N	26.48 E
127	Varna (vär'nȧ) Bul.	43.12 N	27.56 E
118	Värnamo (vĕr'nȧ-mō) Swe.	57.10 N	14.3 E
120	Varnsdorf (värns'dôrf) Czech.	50.55 N	14.35 E
83	Varnville (värn'vĭl) S. C.	32.51 N	81.4 W
126	Varoš (vä'rōsh) Yugo.	44.37 N	17.23 E
119	Värtsilä (vĕrt'sē-lĕ) Fin.	62.10 N	30.40 E
129	Varvaropolie (vär'vär'ō-pō-lyĕ) Sov. Un.	48.37 N	38.35 E
124	Vascongadas (Prov.) (väs-kōn-gä'däs). Sp.	43.5 N	2.35 W
110	Vashka R. (vȧsh'kȧ) Sov. Un.	64.15 N	47.20 E
51	Vashon (văsh'ŭn) Wash. (In.)	47.26 N	122.27 W
51	Vashon I. Wash. (In.)	47.25 N	122.30 W
140	Vasht (väsht) Iran	28.17 N	61.2 E
129	Vasilkov (vȧ-sĕl'-kôf') Sov. Un.	50.10 N	30.21 E
121	Vaslui (väs-lōō'ē) Rom.	46.39 N	27.43 E
84	Vassar (văs'ēr) Mich.	43.23 N	83.35 W
99	Vassouras (väs-sō'räzh) Braz. (Rio de Janeiro In.)	22.25 S	43.41 W
118	Västanfors (vĕst'än-fôrs) Swe.	59.59 N	15.50 E
118	Västerås (vĕs'tĕr-ôs) Swe.	59.38 N	16.30 E
118	Västervik (vĕs'tĕr-vēk) Swe.	57.46 N	16.38 E
126	Vasto (väs'tō) It.	42.6 N	14.41 E
138	Vasyugan R. (vȧs-yōō-gȧn') Sov. Un.	59.20 N	78.0 E
127	Vathy (vä-thē') Grc.	37.45 N	26.59 E
126	Vatican City (Città del Vaticano) (văt'ĭ-kăn sĭt'ē) (chē-tȧ' dĕl vä-tē-kä'nō). It.	41.53 N	12.28 E
126	Vaticano, C. (vä-tē-kä'nō) It.	38.37 N	15.50 E
108	Vatna-Jökull (Klofa-Jökull) (Glacier) (vät'nȧ-yû'kōōl) (klō'fȧ-yû'kōōl). Ice.	64.30 N	16.45 W
121	Vatra Dornei (vät'rȧ dôr'nȧ') Rom.	47.23 N	25.30 E
118	Vätter, L. (vĕt'ĕr) Swe.	58.20 N	14.30 E
85	Vaudreuil (vō-drû'y') Can.	45.24 N	74.2 W
78	Vaughn (vôn) N. M.	34.36 N	105.13 W
51	Vaughn Wash. (Seattle In.)	47.21 N	122.46 W
123	Vaujours (vō-zhōōr') Fr. (In.)	48.56 N	2.35 E
118	Vaxholm (väks'hôlm) Swe.	59.25 N	18.20 E
118	Växjö (vĕks'shû) Swe.	56.53 N	14.48 E
118	Veblungsnaes (vĭb'lōōngs-nĕs) Nor.	62.33 N	7.44 E
119	Vecgulbene (vĕts'gōōl'bĕ-nĕ) Sov. Un.	57.9 N	26.49 E
90	Vedado (vā-dhä'dhō) Cuba (Habana In.)	23.9 N	82.24 W
72	Vedder Crossing (vĕd'ēr) Can. (Vancouver In.)	49.5 N	121.58 W
127	Vedea R. (vȧ'dyȧ) Rom.	44.20 N	24.45 E
84	Veedersburg (vē'dērz-bûrg) Ind.	40.5 N	87.16 W
51	Vega (vä'gȧ) Wash. (Seattle In.)	47.7 N	122.42 W
93	Vega de Alatorre (vä'gä dā ä-lä-tōr'rā). Mex.	20.2 N	96.40 W
97	Vega Real (Mts.) (vä'gä rā-äl') Hai.	19.20 N	70.40 W
108	Vegen (I.) (vĕ'ghĕn) Nor.	65.37 N	11.55 E
99	Veinticinco de Mayo (vȧ-ēn'tē-sēŋ'kō dā mä'yō) Arg. (Buenos Aires In.)	35.23 S	60.10 W
125	Vejer de la Frontera (vā-kĕr' dā lä frōn-tā'rä). Sp. (In.)	36.15 N	5.57 W
118	Vejle (vī'lĕ) Den.	55.40 N	9.30 E
120	Vejprty (vā'p'r-tĭ) Czech.	50.29 N	13.3 E
126	Velebit Mts. (vā'lĕ-bēt) Yugo.	44.25 N	15.20 E
127	Veles (vĕ'lĕs) Yugo.	41.42 N	21.49 E
124	Vélez Blanco (vā'lāth blän'kō). Sp.	37.42 N	2.5 W
124	Vélez de la Gomera I. (dā lä gō-mä'rä). Sp. Mor.	35.12 N	4.18 W
124	Vélez-Málaga (vā'lāth-mä'lä-gä) Sp.	36.47 N	4.5 W
124	Vélez Rubio (vā'lāth rōō'bē-ō). Sp.	37.39 N	2.5 W
127	Velika Kikinda (vĕ'lĭ-kä kē-kēn'dä). Yugo.	45.48 N	20.29 E
128	Velikaya R. (vȧ-lē'kȧ-yȧ). Sov. Un.	57.30 N	28.10 E
127	Veliki Beckerek (vĕ'lĭ-kĭ bĕch'kā-rĕk). Yugo.	45.22 N	20.25 E
128	Velikie Luki (vȧ-lē'kyē lōō'kē) Sov. Un.	56.19 N	30.32 E
110	Veliki Ustyug (vȧ-lē'kĭ ōōs-tyōōg'). Sov. Un.	60.45 N	46.15 E
128	Velikoe (vȧ-lē'kō-yĕ) Sov. Un.	57.18 N	39.45 E
128	Velikoe, L. Sov. Un.	55.12 N	40.8 E
128	Velikoe, L. Sov. Un.	56.58 N	36.35 E
121	Veliky Bockov (vâl-ē'kē bôch'kôf). Sov. Un.	47.59 N	24.2 E
128	Velizh (vâ'lēzh) Sov. Un.	55.37 N	31.10 E
120	Velké Meziříčí (vĕl'kä mĕzh'r-zhĭ-chĭ). Czech.	49.22 N	16.1 E
159	Vella Lavella I. (väl'yä lä-väl'yä) Solomon Is.	7.45 S	156.30 E
126	Velletri (vĕl-lā'trē) It.	41.42 N	12.47 E
141	Vellore (vĕl-lōr') India	12.46 N	79.8 E
115	Velsen (vĕl'sĕn) Neth.	52.28 N	4.40 E
110	Velsk (vĕlsk) Sov. Un.	61.5 N	42.10 E
122	Venaco (vā-nä'kō) Cor. (In.)	42.30 N	9.22 E
92	Venado (vā-nä'dō) Mex.	22.55 N	101.5 W
123	Vence (väNs) Fr.	43.45 N	7.5 E
122	Vendôme (väN-dōm') Fr.	47.45 N	1.5 E
125	Vendrell (vĕn-drāl') Sp.	41.14 N	1.31 E
126	Venetian Alps (Mts.) (vē-nē'shăn ălps). It.	46.5 N	12.30 E
128	Venev (vĕn-ĕf') Sov. Un.	54.19 N	38.10 E
126	Venezia (Prov.) (vā-nāt'sē-ä) It.	45.50 N	12.0 E
126	Venezia (Venice) (vĕn'ĭs) It.	45.26 N	12.20 E
100	Venezuela (vĕn-ē-zwē'lȧ) S. A.	8.0 N	65.0 W
100	Venezuela, G. of Ven.	11.30 N	71.0 W
73	Venice (vĕn'ĭs) Calif. (Los Angeles In.)	33.58 N	118.27 W
89	Venice Ill. (St. Louis In.)	38.40 N	90.10 W
126	Venice (Venezia) (vā-nāt'sē-ä). It.	45.26 N	12.20 E
89	Venice La. (New Orleans In.)	29.17 N	89.22 W
126	Venice, G. of It.	45.20 N	13.0 E
119	Venta R. (vĕn'tȧ) Sov. Un.	57.4 N	21.45 E
126	Ventimiglia (vĕn-tē-mēl'yä) It.	43.47 N	7.37 E
85	Ventnor (vĕnt'nēr) N. J.	39.20 N	74.30 W
119	Ventspils (vĕnt'spēls) Sov. Un.	57.24 N	21.36 E
74	Ventura (vĕn-tōō'rȧ) Calif.	34.17 N	119.19 W
100	Ventuari, R. (vĕn-tōō-ä'rē) Ven.	5.0 N	66.28 W
124	Vera (vā'rä) Sp.	37.14 N	1.51 W
93	Veracruz (vā-rä-krōōz') Mex.	19.10 N	96.10 W
92	Veracruz (State) Mex.	19.0 N	96.20 W
141	Veraval (vĕr'ŭ-väl) India	21.10 N	70.12 E
129	Verbki (vĕrp'kĭ) Sov. Un.	48.37 N	35.52 E
126	Vercelli (vĕr-chĕl'lē) It.	45.18 N	8.25 E
57	Verchères (vĕr-shâr') Can. (In.)	45.47 N	73.21 W
132	Verde, C. (vûrd) (vĕr'dȧ) Fr. W. Afr.	14.42 N	12.30 W
97	Verde C. (South Pt.) Ba. Is.	22.50 N	74.52 W
97	Verde, Cay (I.) Ba. Is.	22.3 N	75.11 W
152	Verde I. (vĕr'dȧ) Phil.	13.33 N	121.4 E
120	Verden (fĕr'dĕn) Ger.	52.57 N	9.15 E
75	Verde R. (vûrd) Ariz.	34.5 N	111.40 W
93	Verde, R. (vĕr'dȧ) Mex.	16.20 N	97.10 W
92	Verde, R. Mex.	21.2 N	102.43 W
92	Verde, R. Mex.	21.40 N	99.46 W
79	Verdigris R. (vûr'dē-grēs) Okla.	36.40 N	95.34 W

ăt; finăl; rāte; senâte; ärm; ȧsk; sofȧ; fâre; ch-choose; dh-as th in other; bē; ēvent; bĕt; recĕnt; cratēr; g-go; gh-gutteral g; bĭt; ĭ-short neutral; rīde; K-gutteral k as ch in German ich;

ng-sing; ŋ-baŋk; N-nasalized n; nŏd; cŏmmit; ōld; ôbey; ôrder; fōōd; fŏŏt; ou-out; s-soft; sh-dish; th-thin; pūre; ūnite; ûrn; stŭd; circŭs; ū-as "y" in study; '-indeterminate vowel.

Vincent PRONOUNCING INDEX Wallisville

Page	Name Pronunciation Region	Lat. °′	Long. °′
82	Vincent (vĭn'sĕnt) ... Ala.	33.22 N	86.24 W
108	Vindeln (vĭn'dĕln) ... Swe.	64.10 N	19.45 E
108	Vindel R. (vĭn'dĕl) ... Swe.	65.16 N	18.0 E
141	Vindhya Range (vĭnd'yä) ... India	22.45 N	77.30 E
85	Vineland (vīn'lănd) ... N. J.	39.30 N	75.3 W
150	Vinh (vên'y') ... Indoch.	18.17 N	105.52 E
124	Vinhais (vēn-yä'ēzh) ... Port.	41.50 N	7.1 W
150	Vinhlong (vên-y'lŏng') ... Indoch.	10.18 N	106.5 E
73	Vinings (vī'nĭngz) Ga. (Atlanta In.)	33.52 N	84.28 W
79	Vinita (vĭ-nē'tȧ) ... Okla.	36.37 N	95.8 W
127	Vinkovci (vēn'kôv-tsê) ... Yugo.	45.17 N	18.48 E
129	Vinnitsa (vê'nêt-sȧ) ... Sov. Un.	49.12 N	28.31 E
77	Vinton (vĭn'tŭn) ... Ia.	42.10 N	92.0 W
81	Vinton ... La.	30.12 N	93.35 W
83	Vinton ... Va.	37.18 N	79.54 W
127	Vir (vêr) ... Yugo.	42.15 N	19.5 E
152	Virac (vê-räk') ... Phil.	13.34 N	124.13 E
119	Virbalis (vêr'bȧ-lês) ... Sov. Un.	54.38 N	22.52 E
79	Virden (vûr'dĕn) ... Ill.	39.27 N	89.45 W
122	Vire (vēr) ... Fr.	48.50 N	0.50 W
77	Virginia (vẽr-jĭn'yȧ) ... Minn.	47.31 N	92.32 W
85	Virginia (State) ... U. S.	37.0 N	78.0 W
74	Virginia City ... Nev.	39.18 N	119.39 W
91	Virgin Is. (vûr'jĭn) ... W. I.	18.25 N	65.0 W
75	Virgin R. ... Nev.	36.25 N	114.20 W
119	Virmo (vĭr'mô) ... Fin.	60.42 N	21.59 E
123	Viroflay (vê-rô-flĕ') ... Fr. (In.)	48.47 N	2.12 E
77	Viroqua (vĭ-rō'kwȧ) ... Wis.	43.35 N	90.52 W
126	Virovitica (vê-rô-vē'tê-tsȧ) ... Yugo.	45.49 N	17.24 E
119	Virrat (vĭr'ät) ... Fin.	62.15 N	23.50 E
118	Virserum (vĭr'sĕ-rŏŏm) ... Swe.	57.22 N	15.36 E
119	Virts, L. (vĭrts) ... Sov. Un.	58.14 N	26.0 E
126	Vis (vês) ... Yugo.	43.4 N	16.11 E
126	Vis (I.) ... Yugo.	43.3 N	16.10 E
74	Visalia (vĭ-sā'lĭ-ȧ) ... Calif.	36.20 N	119.18 W
152	Visayan Is. (vê-sä'yän) ... Phil.	11.0 N	124.0 E
153	Visayan Sea ... Phil.	11.30 N	123.45 E
118	Visby (vĭs'bü) ... Swe.	57.39 N	18.21 E
127	Višegrad (vē'shĕ-gräd) ... Yugo.	43.46 N	19.20 E
124	Viseu (vê-zȧ'ōō) ... Port.	40.39 N	7.55 W
121	Vishnevets (vēsh'nĕ-vyĕts) Sov. Un.	49.55 N	25.46 E
128	Vishnii Volochek (vēsh'nyĭ vôl-ô-chĕk') . Sov. Un.	57.35 N	34.36 E
118	Viske R. (vĭs'kĕ) ... Swe.	57.33 N	12.40 E
119	Viski (vēs'kĭ) ... Sov. Un.	56.2 N	26.46 E
127	Visoko (vē'sô-kô) ... Yugo.	43.59 N	18.11 E
126	Viso, Mt. (vē'zō) ... It.-Fr.	44.40 N	7.5 E
127	Vistonis, L. (vês'tô-nĭs) ... Grc.	41.3 N	25.8 E
127	Vistritsa (Aliakmon) R. (vês'trē-tsȧ) (ä-lê-äk'mōn) . Grc.	40.20 N	22.10 E
121	Vistula (Wisla) R. (vĭs'tû-lȧ) (vēs'wȧ) . Pol.	51.4 N	21.50 E
153	Vitali I. (vē-tä'lē) ... Phil.	7.20 N	122.22 E
127	Vitanovac (vê'tä'nô-vȧts) ... Yugo.	43.43 N	20.47 E
128	Vitebsk (vē'tyĕpsk) ... Sov. Un.	55.11 N	30.11 E
126	Viterbo (vê-tĕr'bō) ... It.	42.15 N	12.7 E
7	Viti Levu (I.) (vē'tê lā'vōō) Fiji Is.	17.48 S	178.0 E
139	Vitim (vē'têm) ... Sov. Un.	59.25 N	112.40 E
139	Vitim R. ... Sov. Un.	56.0 N	115.50 E
101	Vitoria (vê-tō'rê-ä) ... Braz.	20.15 S	40.28 W
124	Vitoria ... Sp.	42.51 N	2.39 W
126	Vitré (vê-trā') ... Fr.	48.10 N	1.10 W
122	Vitry-le-Francois (vê-trē'-lē-fräɴ-swȧ') . Fr.	48.45 N	4.35 E
126	Vittorio (vê-tô'rê-ô) ... It.	45.59 N	12.19 E
151	Vitu Is. (vē'tōō) ... N. Gui. Ter.	4.50 S	149.13 E
124	Vivero (vê-vā'rō) ... Sp.	43.39 N	7.37 W
81	Vivian (vĭv'ĭ-ȧn) ... La.	32.51 N	93.59 W
141	Vizagapatam (vê-zŭg'ȧ-pȧ-tŭm') India	17.45 N	83.15 E
127	Vize (vē'zĕ) ... Tur.	41.34 N	27.47 E
141	Vizianagram (vē-zê-ȧ-nŭ'grȧm') India	18.0 N	83.30 E
126	Vizzini (vêt-sē'nê) ... It.	37.12 N	14.44 E
115	Vlaardingen (vlär'dĭng-ĕn) ... Neth.	51.55 N	4.20 E
111	Vladikavkaz (Ordzhonikidze) (vlȧ-dê-käf-käz') (ôrd'zhô-nê-kē'dzĕ) Sov. Un.	43.5 N	44.32 E
128	Vladimir (vlȧ-dyē'mĕr) ... Sov. Un.	56.8 N	40.22 E
139	Vladimiro Aleksandrovskoe (vlȧ-dyē'mē-rô ä-lyĕk-sän-drôf'skô-yĕ) . Sov. Un.	42.45 N	132.59 E
121	Vladimir Volynsk (vlä-dyē'mĕr vô-lēnsk') . Sov. Un.	50.49 N	24.20 E
139	Vladivostok (vlȧ-dê-vôs-tôk') Sov. Un.	43.15 N	131.50 E
127	Vlasenica (vlä'sĕ-nêt'sȧ) ... Yugo.	44.12 N	18.58 E
127	Vlasotince (vlä'sô-tên-tsĕ) ... Yugo.	42.57 N	22.7 E
127	Vlčedrma (v'l'chĕd'r-mȧ) ... Bul.	43.41 N	23.26 E
120	Vlieland (I.) (vlē'länt) ... Neth.	53.16 N	4.57 E
115	Vlissingen (Flushing) (vlĭs'sĭng-ĕn) Neth.	51.35 N	3.35 E
127	Vlonë (Valona) (vlō'nā) (vȧ-lō'nä) Alb.	40.28 N	19.30 E
120	Vltava R. (v'l'tȧ-vȧ) ... Czech.	49.14 N	14.24 E
110	Vodl, L. (vôd''l) ... Sov. Un.	62.15 N	37.0 E
151	Vogelkop Pen. (fō'gĕl-kôp) Neth. N. Gui.	1.30 S	133.0 E
156	Vogeltown (vō'gĕl-toun) . N. Z. (In.)	41.19 S	174.47 E
126	Voghera (vô-gā'rä) ... It.	44.59 N	9.1 E
135	Vohémar (vô-ā-mär') ... Madag.	13.30 S	50.3 E
123	Voiron (vwȧ-rôɴ') ... Fr.	45.22 N	5.38 E
123	Voisins-le-Bretonneux (vwȧ-săɴ'-lē-brĕ-tôn-nû') . Fr. (In.)	48.0 N	2.3 E
129	Volchansk (vôl-chänsk') . Sov. Un.	50.17 N	36.57 E
129	Volchya R. (vôl-chyä') . Sov. Un.	49.35 N	34.35 E
129	Volegotsulovo (vô-lĕ-gôt'sŏŏ-lô-vō) Sov. Un.	47.28 N	29.52 E
111	Volga R. (vôl'gä) ... Sov. Un.	51.45 N	47.0 E
119	Volkhov (vôl'κôf) ... Sov. Un.	59.52 N	32.21 E
128	Volkhov R. (vôl'κôf) ... Sov. Un.	59.0 N	31.48 E
110	Volkivisk (vôl-kē-vêsk') ... Sov. Un.	53.9 N	24.28 E
117	Volksdorf (fôlks'dôrf) Ger. (Hamburg In.)	53.39 N	10.10 E
128	Vologda (vô'lôg-dȧ) ... Sov. Un.	59.11 N	39.51 E
128	Volokolamsk (vô'lô-kô-lämsk') Sov. Un.	56.2 N	35.59 E
129	Volokopovka (vô'lô-kô-pôf'kȧ) Sov. Un.	50.28 N	37.49 E
127	Volos (vô'lôs) ... Grc.	39.21 N	22.58 E
127	Volos, G. of ... Grc.	38.15 N	23.0 E
128	Volozhin (vô'lô-zhên) ... Sov. Un.	54.6 N	26.32 E
111	Volsk (vôl'sk) ... Sov. Un.	52.0 N	47.30 E
132	Volta R. (vôl'tȧ) ... G. C.	8.30 N	0.45 W
99	Volta Redonda (vōl'tä rā-dôn'dä) Braz.	22.30 S	44.7 W
126	Volterra (vôl-tĕr'rä) ... It.	43.23 N	10.53 E
126	Voltri (vōl'trē) ... It.	44.26 N	8.45 E
126	Volturno R. (vôl-tōōr'nô) ... It.	41.12 N	14.30 E
127	Volvi, L. (vôl'vê) ... Grc.	40.38 N	23.30 E
119	Võõbsu (vŭb'sōō) ... Sov. Un.	58.5 N	27.31 E
128	Vop R. (vôp) ... Sov. Un.	55.15 N	32.52 E
118	Vordingborg (vôr'dĭng-bôr') ... Den.	55.0 N	11.55 E
110	Vorkuta (vôr-kōō'tȧ) ... Sov. Un.	67.31 N	64.0 E
129	Vorochilovgrad (Lugansk) (vô-rô-chĭ'lôf-gräd) . Sov. Un.	48.35 N	39.19 E
119	Vorms I. (vôrms) ... Sov. Un.	59.0 N	23.15 E
129	Voronezh (vô-rô'nyĕzh) ... Sov. Un.	51.40 N	39.10 E
128	Voronezh R. ... Sov. Un.	52.15 N	39.21 E
119	Voronovo (vô'rô-nô-vô) ... Sov. Un.	54.9 N	25.19 E
129	Vorontsovo-Gorodishche (vô-rônt'sô-vô-gô-rôd-êsh'chĕ) . Sov. Un.	49.18 N	31.26 E
110	Voronya R. (vô-rô'nyȧ) ... Sov. Un.	68.30 N	35.30 E
139	Voroshilov (vô-rô-shĭ'lôf) . Sov. Un.	43.35 N	131.59 E
119	Võru (vŭ'rōō) ... Sov. Un.	57.51 N	27.1 E
122	Vosges (Mts.) (vōzh) ... Fr.	48.20 N	7.10 E
118	Voss (vôs) ... Nor.	60.40 N	6.25 E
110	Votkinsk (vôt-kēnsk') ... Sov. Un.	54.0 N	57.10 E
124	Vouga R. (vō'gȧ) ... Port.	40.45 N	8.0 W
122	Vouziers (vōō-zyā') ... Fr.	49.25 N	4.40 E
127	Voyutsa R. (vô'yōō-tsȧ) ... Alb.	40.20 N	20.0 E
110	Vozhe, L. (vôzh'yĕ) ... Sov. Un.	60.30 N	39.0 E
129	Voznesensk (vôz-nyĕ-sĕnsk') Sov. Un.	47.33 N	31.23 E
117	Vracene (vrȧ-sĕ'nĕ) Bel. (Anvers In.)	51.13 N	4.12 E
127	Vranje (vrän'yĕ) ... Yugo.	42.33 N	21.54 E
127	Vratca (vrät'tsȧ) ... Bul.	43.12 N	23.32 E
127	Vrbas (v'r'bäs) ... Yugo.	45.35 N	19.42 E
126	Vrbas R. ... Yugo.	44.40 N	17.10 E
120	Vrchlabi (v'r'chlä-bê) ... Czech.	50.37 N	15.37 E
117	Vremde (vrĕm'dĕ) . Bel. (Anvers In.)	51.11 N	4.31 E
127	Vršac (v'r'shȧts) ... Yugo.	45.16 N	21.18 E
121	Vrutky (vrōōt'kê) ... Czech.	49.8 N	18.54 E
134	Vryburg (vrī'bûrg) ... U. S. Afr.	26.58 S	24.42 E
134	Vryheid (vrī'hīt) ... U. S. Afr.	27.48 S	30.46 E
121	Vsetín (fsĕt'yēn) ... Czech.	49.21 N	18.1 E
96	Vuelta Abajo (Mts.) (vwĕl'tä ā-bä'hō) . Cuba	22.15 N	83.55 W
135	Vugha (vōō'gȧ) ... Tan.	4.55 S	38.20 E
127	Vukovar (vōō'kô-vär) ... Yugo.	45.20 N	19.0 E
126	Vulcano (I.) (vōōl-kä'nô) ... It.	38.23 N	14.57 E
110	Vyatka (vyȧt'kȧ) ... Sov. Un.	58.35 N	49.35 E
110	Vyatka R. ... Sov. Un.	59.25 N	51.30 E
128	Vyazma (vyȧz'mȧ) ... Sov. Un.	55.11 N	34.19 E
110	Vyazniki (vyȧz'nê-kê) ... Sov. Un.	56.12 N	42.10 E
119	Vyborg (vwē'bôrk) ... Sov. Un.	60.44 N	28.42 E
121	Výškov (vêsh'kôf) ... Czech.	49.17 N	17.0 E
120	Vysoké Myto (vû'sô-kā mû'tô) Czech.	49.57 N	16.9 E
128	Vysokovo Nekrasovo (vê-sô'-kô-vô nĕk-rȧ'sô-vô) . Sov. Un.	56.13 N	36.32 E
110	Vytegra (vû'tĕg-rȧ) ... Sov. Un.	61.0 N	36.30 E
120	Waal R. (väl) ... Neth.	51.53 N	5.26 E
84	Wabash (wô'băsh) ... Ind.	40.48 N	85.50 W
77	Wabasha (wä'bȧ-shô) ... Minn.	44.24 N	92.2 W
84	Wabash R. ... Ill.-Ind.	39.15 N	87.30 W
121	Wąbrzeźno (vôŋ-bzĕzh'nô) ... Pol.	53.17 N	18.58 E
83	Waccamaw R. (wăk'ȧ-mô) ... S. C.	33.45 N	79.3 W
82	Waccassassa B. (wă-kȧ-să'sȧ) . Fla.	29.0 N	83.0 W
81	Waco (wā'kō) ... Tex.	31.35 N	97.7 W
149	Wadayama (wä'dä'yä-mä) ... Jap.	35.16 N	134.49 E
133	Wadelai (wä-dĕ-lä'ê) ... Ug.	2.36 N	31.30 E
77	Wadena (wŏ-dē'nȧ) ... Minn.	46.26 N	95.6 W
83	Wadesboro (wādz'bŭr-ô) ... N. C.	34.59 N	80.5 W
135	Wadi Digla (R.) (wä'dê dēg'lȧ) . Eg.	29.57 N	31.24 E
133	Wādi Halfa (wä'dê häl'fä) A. E. Sud.	21.57 N	31.25 E
125	Wadi Sli (R.) (wä'dê slē') ... Alg.	35.40 N	1.10 E
135	Wadi Tih (R.) (wä'dê tē') ... Eg.	29.58 N	31.21 E
83	Wadley (wŏd'lê) ... Ga.	32.53 N	82.24 W
133	Wad Medani (wäd mĕ-dä'nê) A. E. Sud.	14.25 N	33.30 E
121	Wadowice (vȧ-dô'vēt-sĕ) ... Pol.	49.53 N	19.31 E
84	Wadsworth (wŏdz'wŭrth) ... Ohio	41.2 N	81.44 W
54	Wager B. (wā'jĕr) ... Can.	65.45 N	90.30 W
159	Wagga Wagga (wôg'ȧ wôg'ȧ) Austl.	35.6 S	147.25 E
76	Wagner (wăg'nẽr) ... S. D.	43.5 N	98.18 W
79	Wagoner (wăg'ŭn-ẽr) ... Okla.	35.57 N	95.23 W
78	Wagon Mound ... N. M.	36.0 N	104.42 W
121	Wągrowiec (vôŋ-grô'vyĕts) ... Pol.	52.47 N	17.13 E
133	Wahat el Dakhla (Oasis) (wä-hät' ĕl däk'lä) . Eg.	25.45 N	28.50 E
133	Wahat el Kharga (Oasis) (κär'gä) Eg.	25.26 N	30.36 E
155	Wahiawa (wä-hē-ä'wä) ... Haw.	21.30 N	158.3 W
72	Wahl (wŏl) . Wash. (Vancouver In.)	48.50 N	122.22 W
72	Wahleach L. (wä'lĭch) Can. (Vancouver In.)	49.13 N	121.37 W
76	Wahoo (wä-hōō') ... Neb.	41.13 N	96.38 W
76	Wahpeton (wô'pê-tŭn) ... N. D.	46.17 N	96.36 W
155	Waialeale, Mt. (wä'ê-ä-lā'ä-lā) Haw.	22.5 N	159.31 W
155	Waialua (wä'ê-ä-lōō'ä) ... Haw.	21.34 N	158.8 W
155	Waianae (wä'ê-ȧ-nä'ā) ... Haw.	21.25 N	158.9 W
157	Waiau R. (wä'ê-ä'ōō) ... N. Z.	45.50 S	167.40 E
157	Waiau-uha (Dillon) R. (wä'ê-ä'ōō-ōō'hä) (dĭl'ŭn) . N. Z.	42.38 S	173.0 E
145	Waichow (wī'chō) ... Chn.	23.10 N	114.24 E
120	Waidhofen (vīd'hôf-ĕn) ... Aus.	47.58 N	14.47 E
156	Waiheki I. (wä'ê-hā'kē) ... N. Z.	36.48 S	175.8 E
151	Waigeo (I.) (wä-ê-gā'ô) Neth. N. Gui.	0.15 N	131.0 E
156	Waihi (wä'ê-hē) ... N. Z.	37.22 S	175.52 E
157	Waihola (wä'ê-hō'lä) ... N. Z.	46.2 S	170.8 E
156	Waikara, L. (wä'ê-kä'rä) ... N. Z.	38.45 S	177.10 E
156	Waikato R. (wä'ê-kä'tō) ... N. Z.	38.20 S	175.50 E
156	Waikomiti (wä-ê-kô-mē'tê) N. Z. (In.)	36.54 S	174.39 E
157	Waikouaiti (wä-ê-kō-ōō-ä'ê-tê) N. Z.	45.37 S	170.42 E
155	Wailuku (wä'ê-lōō'kōō) ... Haw.	20.55 N	156.31 W
157	Waimakariri R. (wä'ê-mä'kä-rē'rê) N. Z.	43.27 S	172.30 E
155	Waimanalo (wä-ê-mä'nä-lô) . Haw.	21.19 N	157.43 W
157	Waimate (wä'ê-mä'tȧ) ... N. Z.	44.43 S	171.5 E
155	Waimea (wä-ê-mā'ä) ... Haw.	21.57 N	159.39 W
141	Wainganga R. (wä-ēn-gŭŋ'gä) India	21.0 N	79.40 E
150	Waingapoe (wä'ên-gä'pōō) . Indon.	9.38 S	120.8 E
156	Wainuiomata R. (wä'ê-nōō'ē-ō-mä'tä) . N. Z. (In.)	41.22 S	174.56 E
156	Waipa R. (wä'ê-pä) ... N. Z.	37.50 S	175.12 E
155	Waipahu (wä'ê-pä'hōō) ... Haw.	21.20 N	157.2 W
157	Waipapa Pt. (wä'ê-pä'pä) ... N. Z.	42.10 S	175.58 E
157	Waipara (wä-ê-pä'rä) ... N. Z.	43.3 S	172.47 E
156	Waipawa (wä-ê-pä'wä) ... N. Z.	39.53 S	176.42 E
156	Waipukurau (wä'ê-pōō'kōō-rä'ōō) N. Z.	40.0 S	176.35 E
157	Wairarapa, L. (wä'ê-rä-rä'pä) N. Z.	41.10 S	175.18 E
157	Wairau R. (wä'ê-rä'ōō) ... N. Z.	41.37 S	173.30 E
156	Wairoa (wä'ê-rō'ä) ... N. Z.	39.3 S	177.22 E
156	Wairoa R. ... N. Z.	36.8 S	174.0 E
157	Waitaki (wä'ê-tä'kē) ... N. Z.	44.57 S	171.8 E
157	Waitaki, R. ... N. Z.	44.45 S	170.35 E
156	Waitara (wä'ê-tä'rä) ... N. Z.	39.0 S	174.15 E
156	Waitemata Chan. (wä'ê-tȧ-mä'tä) N. Z. (In.)	36.49 S	174.50 E
156	Waitemata Har. ... N. Z. (In.)	36.51 S	174.43 E
66	Waitsburg (wāts'bûrg) ... Wash.	46.16 N	118.10 W
156	Waiuku (wä'ê-ōō'kōō) ... N. Z.	37.15 S	174.45 E
149	Wajima (wä'jê-mȧ) ... Jap.	37.24 N	136.52 E
134	Waka (wä'kä) ... Bel. Cong.	0.40 S	20.10 E
148	Wakamatsu (wä-kä'mät-sōō) . Jap.	37.29 N	139.59 E
149	Wakamatsu ... Jap.	33.55 N	130.44 E
149	Wakasa B. (wä'kȧ-sȧ) ... Jap.	35.45 N	135.40 E
157	Wakatipu L. (wä-kä-tē'pōō) . N. Z.	45.10 S	168.45 E
149	Wakayama (wä-kä'yä-mä) ... Jap.	34.10 N	135.15 E
78	Wakeeney (wô-kē'nê) ... Kan.	39.0 N	99.54 W
114	Wakefield (wāk'fēld) ... Gt. Brit.	53.40 N	1.30 W
87	Wakefield ... Mass. (In.)	42.30 N	71.4 W
77	Wakefield ... Mich.	46.29 N	89.55 W
76	Wakefield ... Neb.	42.16 N	96.51 W
83	Wake Forest ... N. C.	35.58 N	78.30 W
5	Wake (I.) (wāk) ... Pac. O.	19.11 N	166.31 E
149	Wakimachi (wä'kê-mä'chê) ... Jap.	34.5 N	134.10 E
148	Wakkanai (wä'kä-nä'ê) ... Jap.	45.25 N	141.40 E
134	Wakkerstroom (vȧk'ẽr-strōm) (wăk'ẽr-strōōm) . U. S. Afr.	27.21 S	30.11 E
127	Walachia (Prov.) (wŏ-lä'kĭ-ȧ) (wô-lā'chĭ-ȧ) . Rom.	44.45 N	25.0 E
88	Walbridge (wôl'brĭj) Wis. (Duluth In.)	46.37 N	92.14 W
120	Walbrzych (väl'bzhûκ) ... Pol.	50.46 N	16.16 E
120	Walcz (välch) ... Pol.	53.16 N	16.27 E
86	Waldoboro (wôl'dô-bŭr-ô) ... Me.	44.6 N	69.21 W
70	Waldo L. (wôl'dō) ... Ore.	43.45 N	122.10 W
72	Waldron (wôl'drŭn) Wash. (Vancouver In.)	48.42 N	123.2 W
72	Waldron I. Wash. (Vancouver In.)	48.43 N	123.2 W
114	Wales (Div.) (wālz) ... Gt. Brit.	52.30 N	3.30 W
159	Walgett (wôl'gĕt) ... Austl.	30.1 S	148.10 E
47	Walgreen Coast (wôl'grên) ... Ant.	73.0 S	98.0 W
82	Walhalla (wŏl-hăl'ȧ) ... Ga.	34.46 N	83.4 W
117	Walkden (wôk'dĕn) Gt. Brit. (Liverpool In.)	53.31 N	2.24 W
72	Walker (wôk'ẽr) Colo. (Denver In.)	40.16 N	104.57 W
77	Walker ... Minn.	47.5 N	93.36 W
86	Walker L. ... Can.	50.17 N	67.12 W
74	Walker L. ... Nev.	38.40 N	118.45 W
74	Walker R. ... Nev.	39.9 N	119.10 W
74	Walker River Ind. Res. ... Nev.	39.0 N	118.52 W
74	Walker River Range ... Nev.	38.40 N	119.0 W
71	Walkerville (wôk'ẽr-vĭl) ... Mont.	46.2 N	112.33 W
160	Walkerville . . Austl. (Adelaide In.)	34.53 S	138.38 E
89	Walkerville Junction Mich. (Detroit In.)	42.19 N	82.57 W
141	Walkeshwar (wŭ'kĕsh-wär) India (Bombay In.)	18.56 N	72.48 E
70	Wallace (wŏl'ȧs) ... Ida.	47.28 N	115.55 W
160	Wallangarra (wŏl-ăŋ-găr'ȧ) Austl. (In.)	28.54 S	151.55 E
158	Wallaroo (wŏl-ȧ-rōō') ... Austl.	33.56 S	137.37 E
114	Wallasey (wŏl'ȧ-sê) ... Gt. Brit.	53.25 N	3.5 W
70	Walla Walla (wŏl'ȧ wŏl'ȧ) ... Wash.	46.4 N	118.21 W
86	Wallingford (wŏl'ĭng-fẽrd) ... Vt.	43.30 N	72.55 W
117	Wallington (wŏl'ĭng-tŭn) Gt. Brit. (London In.)	51.21 N	0.10 W
81	Wallisville (wŏl'ĭs-vĭl) . . Tex. (In.)	29.50 N	94.45 W

ăt; finăl; rāte; senâte; ärm; ȧsk; sofȧ; fâre; ch-choose; dh-as th in other; bē; êvent; bĕt; recĕnt; cratẽr; g-go; gh-gutteral g; bĭt; ĭ-short neutral; rīde; κ-gutteral k as ch in German ich;

Wallowa PRONOUNCING INDEX Welty

Page	Name	Pronunciation	Region	Lat. °'	Long. °'
70	Wallowa	(wŏl'ō-wȧ)	Ore.	45.34 N	117.32 W
70	Wallowa Mts.		Ore.	45.8 N	117.15 W
70	Wallowa R.		Ore.	45.30 N	117.30 W
112	Wallsend	(wôlz'ĕnd)	Gt. Brit.	55.0 N	1.32 W
88	Walmore	(wôl'mōr)	N. Y. (Niagara Falls In.)	43.7 N	78.57 W
114	Walney (I.)	(wôl'nē)	Gt. Brit.	54.5 N	3.15 W
73	Walnut	(wôl'nŭt)	Calif. (Los Angeles In.)	34.0 N	117.52 W
75	Walnut Canyon Natl. Mon.		Ariz.	35.10 N	111.30 W
78	Walnut Cr.		Kan.	38.27 N	99.20 W
51	Walnut Creek		Calif. (San Francisco In.)	37.54 N	122.3 W
73	Walnut Grove		Ga. (Atlanta In.)	33.44 N	83.52 W
79	Walnut R.		Kan.	37.35 N	97.0 W
79	Walnut Ridge		Ark.	36.5 N	90.57 W
87	Walpole	(wôl'pōl)	Mass. (In.)	42.8 N	71.15 W
86	Walpole		N. H.	43.5 N	72.25 W
114	Walsall	(wôl'sôl)	Gt. Brit.	52.35 N	2.0 W
78	Walsenburg	(wôl'sĕn-bûrg)	Colo.	37.37 N	104.48 W
83	Walterboro	(wôl'tēr-bŭr-ō)	S. C.	32.52 N	80.40 W
78	Walters	(wôl'tērz)	Okla.	34.21 N	98.19 W
87	Waltham	(wôl'thăm)	Mass. (In.)	42.23 N	71.14 W
114	Walthamstow	(wôl'tăm-stō)	Gt. Brit.	51.35 N	0.5 W
85	Walton	(wôl'tŭn)	N. Y.	42.11 N	75.7 W
116	Walton-le-Dale	(lē-dāl')	Gt. Brit.	53.44 N	2.40 W
117	Walton-on-the-Hill		Gt. Brit. (Liverpool In.)	53.28 N	2.57 W
134	Walvis B.	(wôl'vĭs)	S. W. Afr.	22.53 S	14.25 E
134	Walvis Bay		S. W. Afr.	22.55 S	14.30 E
77	Walworth	(wôl'wŭrth)	Wis.	42.32 N	88.35 W
133	Wamba		Bel. Cong.	2.12 N	28.3 E
134	Wamba R.	(wăm'bȧ)	Bel. Cong.	6.45 S	17.45 E
79	Wamego	(wŏ-mē'gō)	Kan.	39.13 N	96.17 W
135	Wami R.	(wä'mē)	Tan.	6.13 S	38.0 E
145	Wanan	(wä'nän')	Chn.	26.44 N	114.12 E
145	Wanchih	(wän'chĭ')	Chn.	31.5 N	118.35 E
143	Wanchuan	(wän'chōō-än')	Chn.	41.0 N	114.35 E
147	Wando	(wän'dō')	Kor.	34.18 N	126.46 E
120	Wandsbek	(vänts'bĕk)	Ger.	53.35 N	10.4 E
156	Wanganui	(wôŋ'gȧ-nōō'ē)	N. Z.	39.55 S	175.3 E
156	Wanganui R.		N. Z.	39.30 S	175.5 E
148	Wangching	(wäng'chĕng)	Chn.	43.20 N	129.30 E
120	Wangeroog (I.)	(väŋ-gē-rōg')	Neth.	53.47 N	7.55 E
145	Wangkiang	(wäng'kyäng')	Chn.	30.9 N	116.45 E
146	Wangtu	(wäng'tōō')	Chn.	38.47 N	115.1 E
144	Wanhsien	(wän'hsyĕn')	Chn.	31.4 N	108.32 E
134	Wankie	(wăŋ'kē)	S. Rh.	18.35 S	26.30 E
94	Wanks, R. (Coco or Segovia)	(wăŋks) (kō'kō; sē-gō'vē-ä)	Hond.-Nic.	14.30 N	85.0 W
157	Wanoka L.	(wȧ-nō'kȧ)	N. Z.	44.30 S	169.12 E
145	Wansai	(wän'sī')	Chn.	27.57 N	114.10 E
84	Wapakoneta	(wä'pȧ-kō-nĕt'ȧ)	Ohio	40.34 N	84.12 W
77	Wapello	(wŏ-pĕl'ō)	Ia.	41.12 N	91.13 W
85	Wappingers Falls	(wŏp'ĭn-jērz)	N. Y.	41.36 N	73.55 W
77	Wapsipinicon R.	(wŏp'sĭ-pĭn'ĭ-kŏn)	Ia.	42.11 N	91.30 W
141	Warangal	(wŭ'răŋ-gȧl)	India	17.59 N	79.40 E
158	Warburton (R.), The	(wŏr'bûr-tŭn)	Austl.	27.30 S	138.30 E
117	Warden	(wôr'dĕn)	Gt. Brit. (London In.)	51.25 N	0.53 E
141	Wardha	(wŭr'dȧ)	India	20.45 N	78.32 E
141	Wardha R.		India	20.30 N	78.30 E
156	Ward I.	(wôrd)	N. Z. (In.)	41.18 S	174.53 E
84	War Eagle		Ky.	37.32 N	81.56 W
120	Waren	(vä'rĕn)	Ger.	53.32 N	12.42 E
160	Warialda	(wôr-ē-ăl'dȧ)	Austl. (In.)	29.34 S	150.36 E
56	Wark Channel	(wârk)	Can. (Prince Rupert In.)	54.25 N	130.10 W
156	Warkworth	(wärk'wûrth)	N. Z.	36.25 S	174.40 E
141	Warli	(wŭr'lē)	India (Bombay In.)	19.2 N	72.49 E
134	Warmbad	(värm'bäd) (wôrm'băd)	S. W. Afr.	28.28 S	18.41 E
70	Warm Springs Reservoir		Ore.	43.40 N	118.17 W
120	Warnemünde	(vär'nē-mün-dē)	Ger.	54.11 N	12.4 E
73	Warner	(wôr'nēr)	Utah (Salt Lake City In.)	40.32 N	112.20 W
70	Warner Range		Calif.-Ore.	41.50 N	120.15 W
120	Warnow R.	(vär'nō)	Ger.	53.50 N	11.57 E
135	Warraq el Arab	(wä'răk ĕl är'ăb)	Eg.	30.6 N	31.13 E
159	Warrego R.	(wôr'ē-gō)	Austl.	28.0 S	145.50 E
79	Warren	(wŏr'ĕn)	Ark.	33.36 N	92.4 W
84	Warren		Ind.	40.42 N	85.25 W
76	Warren		Minn.	48.11 N	96.45 W
84	Warren		Ohio	41.15 N	80.55 W
51	Warren		Ore. (Portland In.)	45.50 N	122.51 W
85	Warren		Pa.	41.50 N	79.7 W
73	Warren		Utah (Salt Lake City In.)	41.17 N	112.8 W
79	Warrensburg	(wŏr'ĕnz-bûrg)	Mo.	38.46 N	93.43 W
56	Warrenton	(wŏr'ĕn-tŭn)	Can. (Winnipeg In.)	50.8 N	97.32 W
83	Warrenton		Ga.	33.25 N	82.40 W
51	Warrenton		Ore. (Portland In.)	46.10 N	123.55 W
85	Warrenton		Va.	38.45 N	77.50 W
132	Warri	(wär'ē)	Nig.	5.32 N	5.41 E
82	Warrington	(wŏr'ĭng-tŭn)	Fla.	30.21 N	87.17 W
114	Warrington		Gt. Brit.	53.25 N	2.35 W
73	Warrior	(wôr'yēr)	Ala. (Birmingham In.)	33.49 N	86.49 W
159	Warrnambool	(wôr'năm-bōōl)	Austl.	38.23 S	142.31 E
77	Warroad	(wôr'rōd)	Minn.	48.55 N	95.18 W
159	Warrumbungle Ra.	(wôr'ŭm-bŭŋ-g'l)	Austl.	31.35 S	149.45 E
79	Warsaw	(wôr'sô)	Ill.	40.21 N	91.25 W
84	Warsaw		Ind.	41.13 N	85.50 W
85	Warsaw		N. Y.	42.47 N	78.10 W
83	Warsaw		N. C.	35.0 N	78.7 W
121	Warsaw (Warszawa)	(vär-shä'vȧ)	Pol.	52.14 N	21.0 E
116	Warsop	(wôr'sŭp)	Gt. Brit.	53.12 N	1.9 W
121	Warszawa (Warsaw)	(vär-shä'vȧ)	Pol.	52.14 N	21.0 E
121	Warta	(vär'tȧ)	Pol.	51.42 N	18.38 E
120	Warta R.		Pol.	52.44 N	15.20 E
159	Warwick	(wŏr'ĭk)	Austl.	28.10 S	152.5 E
114	Warwick		Gt. Brit.	52.15 N	1.40 W
85	Warwick		R. I.	41.38 N	71.22 W
116	Warwick County		Gt. Brit.	52.21 N	1.30 W
71	Wasatch Range	(wô'săch)	Utah	41.35 N	11.30 W
70	Wasco	(wăs'kō)	Ore.	45.35 N	120.43 W
77	Waseca	(wŏ-sē'kȧ)	Minn.	44.5 N	93.29 W
86	Washburn	(wŏsh'bŭrn)	Me.	46.45 N	68.10 W
77	Washburn		Wis.	46.41 N	90.53 W
71	Washburn, Mt.		Wyo.	44.50 N	110.24 W
82	Washington	(wŏsh'ĭng-tŭn)	Ga.	33.43 N	82.45 W
84	Washington		Ind.	38.38 N	87.10 W
79	Washington		Ia.	41.18 N	91.40 W
79	Washington		Kan.	39.48 N	97.4 W
79	Washington		Mo.	38.34 N	91.0 W
83	Washington		N. C.	35.33 N	77.3 W
85	Washington		Pa.	40.10 N	80.20 W
70	Washington (State)		U. S.	47.25 N	120.38 W
84	Washington Court House		Ohio	39.34 N	83.27 W
1	Washington, D. C.		U. S.	38.55 N	77.0 W
84	Washington Heights		Mich.	42.23 N	85.15 W
4	Washington (I.)		Pac. O.	4.43 N	160.25 W
77	Washington I.		Wis.	45.24 N	86.55 W
51	Washington, L.		Wash. (Seattle In.)	47.37 N	122.17 W
86	Washington, Mt.		N. H.	44.15 N	71.20 W
72	Washington Sd.		Wash. (Vancouver In.)	48.35 N	123.0 W
79	Washita R.	(wŏsh'ĭ-tô)	Tex.-Okla.	35.5 N	98.20 W
51	Washougal	(wŏ-shōō'gȧl)	Wash. (Portland In.)	45.35 N	122.21 W
51	Washougal R.		Wash. (Portland In.)	45.38 N	122.16 W
115	Wash, The	(wŏsh)	Gt. Brit.	53.0 N	0.30 E
121	Wasilków	(vȧ-sēl'kōōf)	Pol.	53.12 N	23.13 E
52	Wasilla	(wŏ-sĭl-ȧ)	Alsk. (In.)	61.35 N	149.25 W
89	Wassaw Sd.	(wŏs'sô)	Ga. (Savannah In.)	31.56 N	80.58 W
131	Wasta	(wăs'tȧ)	Eg. (In.)	29.20 N	31.14 E
85	Waterbury	(wô'tēr-bĕr-ē)	Conn.	41.32 N	73.2 W
86	Waterbury		Vt.	44.21 N	72.46 W
97	Water Cay (I.)		Ba. Is.	23.0 N	75.45 W
83	Wateree R.	(wô'tēr-ē)	S. C.	34.20 N	80.45 W
160	Waterford		Austl. (In.)	27.41 S	153.10 E
114	Waterford	(wô'tēr-fērd)	Ire.	52.15 N	7.5 W
160	Waterhouse I.	(wô'tēr-hous)	Austl. (Tas. In.)	40.47 S	147.39 E
91	Water I.	(wô'tēr)	Vir. Is. (In.)	18.19 N	64.57 W
84	Waterloo	(wô-tēr-lōō')	Can.	43.27 N	80.39 W
86	Waterloo		Can.	45.21 N	72.32 W
79	Waterloo		Ill.	38.19 N	90.9 W
77	Waterloo		Ia.	42.30 N	92.20 W
85	Waterloo		N. Y.	42.55 N	76.52 W
117	Waterloo Seaforth	(sē'fôrth)	Gt. Brit. (Liverpool In.)	53.28 N	3.3 W
73	Waterman Mt.	(wô'tēr-măn)	Calif. (Los Angeles In.)	34.20 N	117.55 W
72	Waters	(wô'tērz)	Colo. (Colo. Sprs. In.)	38.51 N	105.9 W
71	Waterton-Glacier Intl. Peace Park	(wô'tēr-tŭn-glā'shûr)	U. S.-Can.	48.50 N	114.0 W
71	Waterton Lakes Natl. Park		Can.	49.5 N	114.0 W
87	Watertown	(wô'tēr-toun)	Mass. (In.)	42.22 N	71.11 W
85	Watertown		N. Y.	43.58 N	75.56 W
76	Watertown		S. D.	44.55 N	97.5 W
77	Watertown		Wis.	43.13 N	88.42 W
82	Water Valley		Miss.	34.9 N	89.39 W
86	Waterville	(wô'tēr-vĭl)	Me.	44.34 N	69.38 W
77	Waterville		Minn.	44.12 N	93.32 W
70	Waterville		Wash.	47.37 N	120.5 W
85	Watervliet	(wô'tēr-vlēt')	N. Y.	42.46 N	73.46 W
72	Watkins	(wŏt'kĭnz)	Colo. (Denver In.)	39.45 N	104.35 W
85	Watkins		N. Y.	42.22 N	76.52 W
144	Watlam	(wät'lăm')	Chn.	22.48 N	110.12 E
97	Watling (San Salvador) I.	(wŏt'lĭng) (săn săl'vȧ-dôr)	Ba. Is.	24.1 N	74.0 W
78	Watonga	(wŏ-tŏŋ'gȧ)	Okla.	35.51 N	98.26 W
122	Watrelos	(vȧ-tr'-lō')	Fr.	50.41 N	3.11 E
133	Watsa	(wät'sä)	Bel. Cong.	2.59 N	29.32 E
84	Watseka	(wŏt-sē'kȧ)	Ill.	40.46 N	87.42 W
73	Watson	(wŏt'sŭn)	Ala. (Birmingham In.)	33.38 N	86.53 W
54	Watson Lake		Can.	60.6 N	128.46 W
74	Watsonville	(wŏt'sŭn-vĭl)	Calif.	36.55 N	121.47 W
72	Wattenberg	(wŏt'ĕn-bērg)	Colo. (Denver In.)	40.1 N	104.50 W
73	Watts	(wŏts)	Calif. (Los Angeles In.)	33.56 N	118.15 W
133	Wau	(wä'ōō)	A. E. Sud.	7.40 N	28.0 E
76	Waubay	(wô'bā)	S. D.	45.19 N	97.18 W
83	Wauchula	(wô-chōō'lȧ)	Fla. (In.)	27.33 N	81.47 W
77	Waukegan	(wô-kē'găn)	Ill.	42.22 N	87.50 W
77	Waukesha	(wô'kē-shô)	Wis.	43.0 N	88.15 W
77	Waukon	(wô'kŏn)	Ia.	43.15 N	91.29 W
77	Waupaca	(wô-păk'ȧ)	Wis.	44.21 N	89.4 W
77	Waupun	(wô-pŭn')	Wis.	43.36 N	88.42 W
78	Waurika	(wô-rē'kȧ)	Okla.	34.9 N	97.59 W
77	Wausau	(wô'sô)	Wis.	44.58 N	89.38 W
77	Wausaukee	(wô-sô'kē)	Wis.	45.23 N	87.59 W
84	Wauseon	(wô'sē-ŏn)	Ohio	41.30 N	84.13 W
77	Wautoma	(wô-tō'mȧ)	Wis.	44.4 N	89.18 W
77	Wauwatosa	(wô-wȧ-tō'sȧ)	Wis.	43.4 N	88.0 W
95	Wava	(wä'vä)	Nic.	14.0 N	83.58 W
158	Wave Hill	(wāv)	Austl.	17.15 S	131.10 E
115	Waveney R.	(wāv'nē)	Gt. Brit.	52.30 N	1.30 E
156	Waverley	(wā'vēr-lē)	N. Z.	39.45 S	174.40 E
77	Waverly		Ia.	42.45 N	92.28 W
82	Waverly		Tenn.	36.5 N	87.47 W
84	Wawasee L.	(wô-wô-sē')	Ind.	41.24 N	85.42 W
81	Waxahachie	(wăk-sȧ-hăch'ē)	Tex.	32.23 N	96.50 E
83	Waycross	(wā'krŏs)	Ga.	31.11 N	82.23 W
82	Wayland	(wā'lănd)	Ky.	37.26 N	82.49 W
87	Wayland		Mass. (In.)	42.22 N	71.22 W
76	Wayne	(wān)	Neb.	42.14 N	97.2 W
83	Waynesboro	(wānz'bŭr-ō)	Ga.	33.6 N	82.3 W
85	Waynesboro		Pa.	39.55 N	80.12 W
85	Waynesboro		Va.	38.5 N	78.50 W
85	Waynesburg	(wānz'bûrg)	Pa.	39.54 N	80.12 W
82	Waynesville	(wānz'vĭl)	N. C.	35.29 N	82.59 W
78	Waynoka	(wā-nō'kȧ)	Okla.	36.35 N	98.51 W
143	Wayun	(wä'yōōn')	Chn.	49.1 N	130.1 E
117	Wealdstone	(wēld'stŭn)	Gt. Brit. (London In.)	51.36 N	0.21 W
114	Weald, The	(wēld)	Gt. Brit.	51.0 N	0.1 E
78	Weatherford	(wĕ-dhēr-fērd)	Okla.	35.32 N	98.42 W
81	Weatherford		Tex.	32.45 N	97.49 W
116	Weaver R.	(wē'vēr)	Gt. Brit.	53.12 N	2.31 W
70	Weaverville	(wē'vēr-vĭl)	Calif.	40.44 N	122.56 W
79	Webb City	(wĕb)	Mo.	37.9 N	94.26 W
86	Webster	(wĕb'stēr)	Mass.	42.5 N	71.52 W
76	Webster		S. D.	45.20 N	97.30 W
81	Webster		Tex. (In.)	29.32 N	95.7 W
77	Webster City		Ia.	42.28 N	93.48 W
79	Webster Grove		Mo.	38.35 N	90.20 W
85	Webster Springs		W. Va.	38.28 N	80.22 W
47	Weddell Sea	(wĕd'ĕl) (wĕd-dĕl')	Atl. O.	73.0 S	45.0 W
117	Wedel	(vā'dĕl)	Ger. (Hamburg In.)	53.35 N	9.42 E
117	Wedeler Au (R.)	(vā'dē-lēr ou')	Ger. (Hamburg In.)	53.36 N	9.45 E
86	Wedgeport	(wĕj'pōrt)	Can.	43.45 N	66.0 W
114	Wednesbury	(wĕd''nz-bŭr-ē)	Gt. Brit.	52.35 N	2.2 W
116	Wednesfield	(wĕd''nz-fēld)	Gt. Brit.	52.36 N	2.4 W
70	Weed	(wēd)	Calif.	41.25 N	122.21 W
121	Węgorapa R.	(vôŋ-gô'rȧ-pä)	Pol.	42.25 N	22.3 E
121	Węgorzewo	(vôŋ-gô'zhĕ-vô)	Pol.	54.14 N	21.40 E
121	Węgrów	(vôŋ'grōōf)	Pol.	52.23 N	22.3 E
121	Wehlau	(vā'lou)	Sov. Un.	54.37 N	21.16 E
143	Weichang	(wā'chäng')	Chn.	42.20 N	117.48 E
120	Weiden	(vī'dĕn)	Ger.	49.42 N	12.8 E
117	Weidling	(vīd'lĭng)	Aus. (Wien In.)	48.17 N	16.19 E
146	Weihaiwei	(wā'hī-wā')	Chn.	37.32 N	122.2 E
142	Weihsi	(wā'hsē')	Chn.	27.20 N	99.32 E
146	Weihsien	(wā'hsyĕn')	Chn.	36.46 N	119.7 E
146	Weihwei	(wā'hwā')	Chn.	35.20 N	114.21 E
120	Weilheim	(vīl'hīm')	Ger.	47.50 N	11.6 E
144	Weilnan (Saining)	(wāl'nän') (sī'nĭng')	Chn.	23.4 N	111.24 E
120	Weimar	(vī'mär)	Ger.	50.59 N	11.18 E
120	Weinheim	(vīn'hīm)	Ger.	49.36 N	8.39 E
146	Wei R.	(wā'ē)	Chn.	36.10 N	115.17 E
160	Weir R.	(wēr)	Austl. (In.)	27.50 S	150.22 E
84	Weirton	(wēr'tŭn)	Ohio	40.27 N	80.37 W
70	Weiser	(wē'zēr)	Ida.	44.15 N	116.59 W
70	Weiser R.		Ida.	44.30 N	116.45 W
120	Weiszenburg	(vīs'sĕn-bōōrgh)	Ger.	49.4 N	11.20 E
120	Weiszenfels	(vīs'sĕn-fĕls)	Ger.	51.12 N	11.58 E
117	Weiszensee	(vīs'sĕn-sā)	Ger. (Berlin In.)	52.34 N	13.27 E
140	Wejh	(wĕj)	Sau. Ar.	26.25 N	36.40 E
121	Wejherowo	(vā'-hĕ-rō'vô)	Pol.	54.36 N	18.14 E
73	Welby	(wĕl'bē)	Utah (Salt Lake City In.)	40.35 N	111.59 W
83	Welch	(wĕlch)	W. Va.	37.24 N	81.38 W
72	Weld Can.	(wĕld)	Colo. (Denver In.)	40.34 N	104.35 W
83	Weldon	(wĕl'dŭn)	N. C.	36.25 N	77.36 W
79	Weldon R.		Ia.-Mo.	40.25 N	93.35 W
79	Weleetka	(wē-lēt'kȧ)	Okla.	35.18 N	96.9 W
159	Welford	(wĕl'fērd)	Austl.	25.8 S	143.38 E
85	Welland	(wĕl'ănd)	Can.	43.0 N	79.10 W
114	Welland (R.)		Gt. Brit.	52.35 N	0.30 W
87	Wellesley	(wĕlz'lē)	Mass. (In.)	42.17 N	71.17 W
158	Wellesley Is.		Austl.	16.45 S	139.30 E
116	Wellingborough	(wĕl'lĭng-bŭr-ō)	Gt. Brit.	52.18 N	0.42 W
158	Wellington	(wĕl'lĭng-tŭn)	Austl.	35.19 S	139.22 E
72	Wellington		Can. (Vancouver In.)	49.6 N	123.52 W
116	Wellington		Gt. Brit.	52.42 N	2.30 W
79	Wellington		Kan.	37.15 N	97.25 W
157	Wellington		N. Z.	41.17 S	174.47 E
156	Wellington		N. Z. (In.)		
84	Wellington		Ohio	41.10 N	82.12 W
78	Wellington		Tex.	34.51 N	100.14 W
102	Wellington I.		Chl.	49.15 S	74.30 W
160	Wellington, Mt.		Austl. (Tas. In.)	42.53 S	147.11 E
77	Wells	(wĕlz)	Minn.	43.45 N	93.41 W
70	Wells		Nev.	41.8 N	115.0 W
85	Wellsboro	(wĕlz'bŭ-rō)	Pa.	41.46 N	77.18 W
84	Wellsburg	(wĕlz'bûrg)	W. Va.	40.14 N	80.38 W
100	Wells I.		Peru (In.)	12.7 S	77.14 W
158	Wells, L.		Austl.	26.45 S	123.15 E
84	Wellston	(wĕlz'tŭn)	Ohio	39.8 N	82.37 W
79	Wellsville	(wĕlz'vĭl)	Mo.	39.3 N	91.34 W
85	Wellsville		N. Y.	42.9 N	77.57 W
84	Wellsville		Ohio	40.37 N	80.42 W
71	Wellsville		Utah	41.38 N	111.56 W
120	Wels	(vĕls)	Aus.	48.10 N	14.1 E
114	Welshpool	(wĕlsh'pōōl)	Gt. Brit.	52.52 N	3.5 W
72	Welty		Colo. (Denver In.)	40.20 N	105.2 W

ng-sing; ŋ-baŋk; N-nasalized n; nŏd; cŏmmit; ōld; ôbey; ôrder; fōōd; fŏŏt; ou-out; s-soft; sh-dish; th-thin; pūre; ûnite; ûrn; stŭd; circŭs; ü-as "y" in study; '-indeterminate vowel.

Wem PRONOUNCING INDEX **Wilhelmina**

Page	Name Pronunciation Region	Lat. °′	Long. °′
116	Wem (wĕm)............Gt. Brit.	52.52 N	2.44 W
146	Wenan (wĕn'än')...........Chn.	39.2 N	116.29 E
71	Wenatchee (wê-năch'ê)....Wash.	47.24 N	120.19 W
145	Wenchow (wĕn'chō')........Chn.	28.1 N	120.38 E
145	Wenchow B...............Chn.	27.55 N	121.4 E
87	Wenham (wĕn'ăm)....Mass. (In.)	42.36 N	70.53 W
146	Wenhsien (wĕn'hsyĕn')......Chn.	34.56 N	113.9 E
100	Wenman I. (wĕn'măn).......Ec.	1.30 N	91.45 W
116	Wenning R. (wĕn'ĭng)...Gt. Brit.	54.7 N	2.30 W
146	Wen R. (wĕn)..............Chn.	36.1 N	116.50 E
142	Wensuh (Aqsu) (wĕn'sōō') (äκ'sōō').Chn.	41.40 N	80.5 E
115	Wensum, R. (wĕn'sŭm)..Gt. Brit.	52.40 N	1.30 E
146	Wenteng (wĕn'tĕng')........Chn.	37.12 N	121.59 E
116	Went, R. (wĕnt)........Gt. Brit.	53.39 N	1.6 W
159	Wentworth...............Austl.	34.5 S	141.54 E
116	Weobley (wē'ô-blê)......Gt. Brit.	52.9 N	2.53 W
134	Wepener (wē'pĕn-ēr) (vā'pĕn-ēr) U. S. Afr.	29.41 S	27.2 E
120	Werdau (vĕr'dou)...........Ger.	50.44 N	12.22 E
120	Wernigerode(vĕr-nê-gē-rō'dĕ).Ger.	51.51 N	10.47 E
120	Werra R. (vĕr'ä)............Ger.	50.51 N	10.0 E
120	Wertach R. (vĕr'täκ)........Ger.	48.15 N	10.45 E
120	Wesel (vā'zĕl)..............Ger.	51.39 N	6.38 E
120	Wesermünde (vā'zĕr-mün-dĕ).Ger.	53.32 N	8.36 E
120	Weser R. (vā'zĕr)...........Ger.	52.23 N	9.0 E
120	Weser Canal...............Ger.	52.18 N	9.0 E
80	Weslaco (wĕs-lā'kō).........Tex.	26.9 N	98.0 W
85	Weslemkoon L. (wĕs'lĕm-kōōn) Can.	45.3 N	77.26 W
158	Wessel Is. (wĕs'ĕl).........Austl.	11.30 S	136.30 E
76	Wessington Springs (wĕs'ĭng-tŭn) S. D.	44.6 N	98.33 W
51	West (wĕst)...Ore. (Portland In.)	46.4 N	123.55 W
77	West Allis (ăl'ĭs)............Wis.	43.0 N	87.59 W
88	West Arlington (är'lĭng-tŭn) N. J. (N. Y. In.)	40.47 N	74.8 W
89	West B....La. (New Orleans In.)	29.6 N	89.21 W
81	West B....................Tex.	29.15 N	95.0 W
77	West Bend.................Wis.	43.26 N	88.11 W
87	Westboro (wĕst'bŭr-ô).Mass. (In.)	42.16 N	71.37 W
87	West Boylston (boil'stŭn) Mass. (In.)	42.22 N	71.47 W
84	West Branch...............Mich.	44.18 N	84.12 W
116	West Bridgford (brĭj'fērd).Gt. Brit.	52.56 N	1.8 W
86	Westbrook (wĕst'brŏŏk)......Me.	43.42 N	70.21 W
77	Westby (wĕst'bê)...........Wis.	43.39 N	90.51 W
97	West Caicos I. (kä-ē'kōs)..Ba. Is.	21.40 N	72.28 W
85	West Chester (chĕs'tēr).......Pa.	38.58 N	75.36 W
83	West Columbia.............S. C.	33.58 N	81.5 E
81	West Columbia.............Tex.	29.9 N	95.36 W
81	West Cote Blanche B. (kōt blănch).La.	29.40 N	91.45 W
89	Westcott (wĕst'kŭt) Minn. (Minneapolis In.)	44.50 N	93.6 W
77	West Des Moines (dē-moin')..Ia.	41.34 N	93.41 W
77	West Des Moines R..........Ia.	43.30 N	94.52 W
88	West Duluth (dŏŏ-lōōth') Minn. (Duluth In.)	46.45 N	92.10 W
85	Westerly (wĕs'tēr-lê)........R. I.	41.20 N	71.50 W
158	Western Australia.........Austl.	25.0 S	120.00 E
114	Western Downs.........Gt. Brit.	51.0 N	2.0 W
85	Western Port...............Md.	39.32 N	79.5 W
88	Western Springs.Ill. (Chicago In.)	41.49 N	87.54 W
84	Westerville (wĕs'tēr-vĭl).....Ohio	40.8 N	82.58 W
120	Westerwald (Reg.) (vĕs'tĕr-väld) Ger.	50.45 N	8.7 E
120	Westfalen (State) (vĕst-fä'lĕn).Ger.	51.50 N	7.40 E
85	Westfield (wĕst'fēld).......N. Y.	42.20 N	70.38 W
108	West Fd....................Nor.	67.40 N	14.0 E
87	Westford (wĕst'fērd)..Mass. (In.)	42.35 N	71.27 W
79	West Frankfort (frăŋk'fŭrt)...Ill.	37.55 N	88.56 W
120	West Frisian Is.............Neth.	53.22 N	4.57 E
72	Westham (wĕst'ăm) Can. (Vancouver In.)	49.5 N	123.9 W
114	West Ham (wĕst hăm)...Gt. Brit.	51.30 N	0.5 E
72	Westham I..Can. (Vancouver In.)	49.5 N	123.10 W
85	West Hartford (härt'fērd)..Conn.	41.44 N	72.44 W
114	West Hartlepool (här't'l-pōōl) Gt. Brit.	54.40 N	1.0 W
79	West Helena (hĕl'ĕ-nȧ)......Ark.	34.32 N	91.38 W
88	West Hoboken (hō'bō-kĕn) N. J. (New York In.)	40.46 N	74.2 W
117	Westhoughton (wĕst'hô-tŭn) Gt. Brit. (Liverpool In.)	53.33 N	2.32 W
96	West Indies (ĭn'dēz)........N. A.		
145	West Kienning (kyĕn'nĭng').Chn.	26.47 N	116.42 E
118	West Kirby (kûr'bê)....Gt. Brit.	53.22 N	3.10 W
84	West Lafayette (lä-fȧ-yĕt')...Ind.	40.27 N	86.57 W
79	West Liberty................Ia.	41.31 N	91.18 W
70	West Linn (lĭn).............Ore.	45.22 N	122.37 W
117	Westmalle (vĕst-mäl') Bel. (Anvers In.)	51.18 N	4.40 E
73	Westminster (wĕst'mĭn-stēr) Calif. (Los Angeles In.)	33.45 N	118.0 W
72	Westminster...Colo. (Denver In.)	39.50 N	105.3 W
85	Westminster................Md.	39.37 N	77.58 W
82	Westminster...............S. C.	34.40 N	83.6 W
72	West Monument Cr. (mŏn'ū-mĕnt).Colo. (Colo. Sprs. In.)	38.58 N	104.55 W
116	Westmorland Co. (wĕst'môr-lănd) Gt. Brit.	54.14 N	2.45 W
57	Westmount (wĕst'mount) Can. (Montreal In.)	45.31 N	73.55 W
88	West New Brighton (brī'tŭn) N. Y. (In.)	40.58 N	74.7 W
87	West Newbury (nū'bēr-ê) Mass. (In.)	42.48 N	71.0 W
88	West New York N. J. (New York In.)	40.48 N	74.0 W
77	West Nishnabotna R. (nĭsh-nȧ-bŏt'nȧ).Ia.	41.15 N	95.27 W
89	West Norfolk (nôr'fŏk) Va. (Norfolk In.)	36.52 N	76.21 W
87	Weston (wĕs'tŭn).....Mass. (In.)	42.21 N	71.17 W
84	Weston..................W. Va.	39.0 N	80.30 W
114	Weston-super-Mare (sū'pēr-mā'rê) Gt. Brit.	51.20 N	2.55 W
88	West Orange (ŏr'ĕnj) N. J. (New York In.)	40.47 N	74.15 W
73	Westover (wĕst'ô-vēr) Ala. (Birmingham In.)	33.20 N	86.32 W
83	West Palm Beach......Fla. (In.)	26.42 N	80.4 W
84	West Park.................Ohio	41.26 N	81.50 W
79	Westplains (wĕst-plānz').....Mo.	36.43 N	91.51 W
86	West Pt...................Can.	49.53 N	64.34 W
87	West Pt...................Hai.	18.56 N	73.18 W
82	West Point.................Ga.	32.53 N	85.10 W
82	West Point................Miss.	33.36 N	88.39 W
76	Westpoint (wĕst'point)......Neb.	41.51 N	96.41 W
85	West Point...............N. Y.	41.26 N	74.0 W
85	West Point.................Va.	37.32 N	76.48 W
114	Westport (wĕst'pōrt).........Ire.	53.45 N	9.32 W
157	Westport..................N. Z.	41.48 S	171.47 E
51	Westport.....Ore. (Portland In.)	46.8 N	123.23 W
114	Westray (I.) (wĕs'trȧ) Gt. Brit. (In.)	59.15 N	2.55 W
116	West Riding (Borough) (rīd'ĭng) Gt. Brit.	53.54 N	2.3 W
89	West St. Paul Minn. (Minneapolis In.)	44.54 N	93.4 W
97	West Sand Spit..........Ba. Is.	21.22 N	72.9 W
115	West Scheldt R. (skĕlt).....Neth.	51.25 N	3.40 E
72	Westsound (wĕst'sound) Wash. (Vancouver In.)	48.38 N	122.58 W
84	West Terre Haute (tĕr-ê hōt').Ind.	39.28 N	87.28 W
77	West Union.................Ia.	42.58 N	91.48 W
89	Westview (wĕst'vû) Pa. (Pittsburgh In.)	40.31 N	80.2 W
87	Westville (wĕst'vĭl).........Can.	45.35 N	62.45 W
84	Westville..................Ill.	40.3 N	87.39 W
88	Westville..N. J. (Philadelphia In.)	39.52 N	75.8 W
84	West Virginia (State) (vēr-jĭn'ĭ-ȧ).U. S.	39.0 N	80.30 W
74	West Walker R. (wôk'ēr) Calif.-Nev.	38.20 N	119.25 W
85	West Warwick (wŏr'ĭk).....R. I.	41.40 N	71.30 W
73	West Weber (wĕb'ēr) Utah (Salt Lake City In.)	41.15 N	112.5 W
74	Westwood (wĕst'wŏŏd).....Calif.	40.18 N	121.3 W
87	Westwood...........Mass. (In.)	42.13 N	71.13 W
151	Wetar (I.) (wĕt'ár)........Indon.	7.45 S	126.15 E
54	Wetaskiwan (wĕ-tăs'kê-wŏn).Can.	53.3 N	113.28 W
116	Wetherby (wĕdh'ēr-bê)..Gt. Brit.	53.55 N	1.23 W
135	Weti (wā'tê)...............Zan.	5.3 S	39.44 E
82	Wetumpka (wê-tŭmp'kȧ)....Ala.	32.33 N	86.13 W
120	Wetzlar (vĕts'lär)...........Ger.	50.33 N	8.31 E
151	Wewak (wȧ-wäk')....N. Gui. Ter.	3.45 S	143.30 E
79	Wewoka (wê-wō'kȧ)........Okla.	35.7 N	96.30 W
114	Wexford (wĕks'fērd).........Ire.	52.20 N	6.30 W
86	Weymont (wā'mŏnt)........Can.	47.55 N	73.48 W
114	Weymouth (wā'mŭth)...Gt. Brit.	50.37 N	2.30 W
86	Weymouth.................Mass.	42.15 N	70.59 W
156	Whakatane (whä-kä-tä'nā)..N. Z.	37.55 S	177.5 E
96	Whale Cay (I.) (hwāl).....Ba. Is.	25.24 N	77.48 W
96	Whale Cay Channels......Ba. Is.	26.42 N	77.13 W
156	Whale I...................N. Z.	37.50 S	177.2 E
135	Whale Rock...........U. S. Afr.	33.49 S	18.23 E
117	Whaley Bridge (hwā'lê) Gt. Brit. (Liverpool In.)	53.20 N	1.59 W
156	Whangarei (hwăŋ'gär-ê)....N. Z.	35.43 S	174.20 E
156	Whangarei Harbor.........N. Z.	35.52 S	174.35 E
143	Whangpu R. (whäng'pōō') Chn. (Shanghai In.)	31.12 N	121.30 E
114	Wharfe (R.) (hwôr'fê)...Gt. Brit.	53.55 N	1.30 W
81	Wharton (hwôr'tŭn)........Tex.	29.19 N	96.7 W
77	What Cheer.................Ia.	41.23 N	92.21 W
72	Whatcom, L. (hwät'kŭm) Wash. (Vancouver In.)	48.46 N	122.13 W
71	Wheatland (hwēt'lănd).....Wyo.	42.4 N	104.56 W
71	Wheatland Reservoir.......Wyo.	41.52 N	105.30 W
76	Wheaton (hwē'tŭn)........Minn.	45.48 N	96.29 W
72	Wheat Ridge..Colo. (Denver In.)	39.46 N	105.5 W
78	Wheeler Natl. Mon. (hwē'lēr) Colo.	37.53 N	106.47 W
75	Wheeler Pk................Nev.	38.56 N	114.15 W
84	Wheeling (hwēl'ĭng)......W. Va.	40.3 N	80.43 W
116	Whernside (Mt.) (hwērn'sīd) Gt. Brit.	54.13 N	2.25 W
117	Whetstone (hwĕt'stŭn) Gt. Brit. (London In.)	51.38 N	0.11 W
51	Whidbey I. (hwĭd'bê) Wash. (Seattle In.)	48.10 N	122.40 W
134	Whimo (hwē'mô)...........Tan.	3.50 S	32.36 E
82	Whistler (hwĭs'lēr)..........Ala.	30.46 N	88.10 W
85	Whitby (hwĭt'bê)...........Can.	43.50 N	78.58 W
114	Whitby.................Gt. Brit.	54.30 N	0.40 W
116	Whitchurch (hwĭt'chûrch) Gt. Brit.	53.58 N	2.40 W
157	Whitcombe Pass (hwĭt'kōm).N. Z.	43.12 S	171.0 E
87	White B...................Can.	50.0 N	56.40 W
87	White Bear B..............Can.	47.40 N	57.20 W
89	White Bear L. Minn. (Minneapolis In.)	45.5 N	92.59 W
89	White Bear Lake Minn. (Minneapolis In.)	45.5 N	93.0 W
81	White Castle................La.	30.11 N	91.10 W
157	Whitecliff (whĭt'klĭf).......N. Z.	43.27 S	171.55 E
84	White Cloud..............Mich.	43.35 N	85.45 W
76	White Earth R............N. D.	48.20 N	102.45 W
77	Whiteface R..............Minn.	47.10 N	92.20 W
117	Whitefield Gt. Brit. (Liverpool In.)	53.33 N	2.17 W
86	Whitefield................N. H.	44.22 N	71.38 W
71	Whitefish.................Mont.	48.23 N	114.21 W
77	Whitefish Bay.............Wis.	43.5 N	87.89 W
77	Whitefish B...............Mich.	46.35 N	84.45 W
88	Whitefish I. Can. (Sault Ste. Marie In.)	46.31 N	84.21 W
77	White Fish R.............Mich.	46.0 N	86.53 W
79	White Hall..................Ill.	39.26 N	90.24 W
84	Whitehall (hwīt'hôl).......Mich.	43.23 N	86.20 W
85	Whitehall.................N. Y.	43.33 N	73.26 W
114	Whitehaven (hwīt'hā-vĕn) Gt. Brit.	54.35 N	3.32 W
54	Whitehorse................Can.	60.35 N	134.59 W
114	White Horse Hills.......Gt. Brit.	51.30 N	1.40 W
156	White I...................N. Z.	37.30 S	177.13 E
138	White (Belii) I. (byȧl'ĭ-ê).Sov. Un.	73.20 N	71.0 E
77	White L...................Can.	48.50 N	85.35 W
85	White L...................Can.	45.16 N	76.32 W
81	White L....................La.	29.45 N	92.30 W
74	White Mountain Pk........Calif.	37.37 N	118.12 W
86	White Mts.................N. H.	44.20 N	71.15 W
76	Whitemouth L. (hwīt'mŭth).Can.	49.14 N	95.38 W
133	White Nile (Bahr el Abyad) (R.) (bär ĕl ä-byäd').A. E. Sud.	13.0 N	32.45 E
77	White Otter L. (ŏt'ēr).......Can.	49.10 N	91.55 W
53	White Pass...........Alsk.-Can.	59.50 N	135.30 W
74	White Pine Pk.............Nev.	38.55 N	115.30 W
85	White Plains..............N. Y.	41.2 N	73.48 W
79	White R..............Ark.-Mo.	35.56 N	92.0 W
77	White R...................Can.	48.40 N	85.40 W
75	White R..................Colo.	40.8 N	108.55 W
84	White R...................Ind.	39.10 N	86.51 W
76	White R..................S. D.	43.46 N	101.20 W
78	White R...................Tex.	34.10 N	101.40 W
86	White R....................Vt.	43.45 N	72.45 W
70	White R..................Wash.	47.5 N	121.50 W
84	White R., East Fork........Ind.	38.45 N	86.10 W
72	White Rock.Can. (Vancouver In.)	49.1 N	122.48 W
128	White Russia (Soviet Rep.) Sov. Un.	53.30 N	29.30 E
80	White Sands Natl. Mon....N. M.	32.45 N	106.15 W
110	White Sea..............Sov. Un.	66.0 N	40.0 E
99	Whiteside Canal Chl. (Magallanes In.)	53.55 S	70.20 W
88	Whitestone (hwīt'stōn).N. Y. (In.)	40.47 N	73.49 W
71	White Sulphur Springs.....Mont.	46.33 N	110.53 W
83	Whiteville (hwīt'vĭl)........N. C.	34.18 N	78.43 W
77	Whitewater................Wis.	42.50 N	88.44 W
83	Whitewater B..........Fla. (In.)	25.15 N	80.57 W
71	Whitewater Cr............Mont.	48.50 N	107.40 W
76	Whitewater L..............Can.	49.16 N	100.20 W
79	Whitewright (hwīt'rīt).......Tex.	33.31 N	96.24 W
84	Whiting (hwīt'ĭng)...........Ind.	41.42 N	87.28 W
87	Whitman (hwĭt'măn)..Mass. (In.)	42.5 N	70.56 W
83	Whitmire (hwĭt'mīr)........S. C.	34.31 N	81.39 W
74	Whitney, Mt. (hwĭt'nê).....Calif.	36.33 N	118.18 W
73	Whittier (hwĭt'ĭ-ēr) Calif. (Los Angeles In.)	33.59 N	118.2 W
159	Whitsunday I. (hwĭt's'n-dā).Austl.	20.8 S	148.52 E
82	Whitwell (hwĭt'wĕl)........Tenn.	35.12 N	85.32 W
116	Whitworth (hwĭt'wŭrth).Gt. Brit.	53.40 N	2.10 W
72	Whonnock (hwŏn'nŭk) Can. (Vancouver In.)	49.10 N	122.30 W
158	Whyalla (hwī-ăl'ȧ).........Austl.	33.2 S	137.35 E
72	Whytecliff (hwīt'klĭf) Can. (Vancouver In.)	49.22 N	123.16 W
84	Wiarton (wī'ȧr-tŭn).........Can.	44.45 N	81.10 W
79	Wichita (wĭch'ĭ-tô).........Kan.	37.41 N	97.21 W
78	Wichita Falls...............Tex.	33.54 N	98.29 W
78	Wichita Mts..............Okla.	34.55 N	98.50 W
78	Wichita R.................Tex.	33.45 N	99.10 W
114	Wick (wĭk).............Gt. Brit.	58.25 N	3.10 W
157	Wickcliffe B. (wĭk'klĭf).N. Z. (In.)	45.50 S	170.46 E
117	Wickford (wĭk'fērd) Gt. Brit. (London In.)	51.37 N	0.31 E
114	Wicklow (Cill Mantain) (wĭk'lō) (kĭl män'tān).Ire.	53.0 N	6.5 W
114	Wicklow Mts. (wĭk'lō).......Ire.	53.0 N	6.20 W
72	Widefield (wīd'fēld) Colo. (Colo. Sprs. In.)	38.45 N	104.44 W
84	Widen (wī'dĕn)..........W. Va.	38.26 N	80.54 W
116	Widnes (wĭd'nĕs).......Gt. Brit.	53.21 N	2.45 W
121	Wieliczka (vyĕ-lēch'kȧ)......Pol.	49.58 N	20.7 E
121	Wieluń (vyĕ'lōōn')...........Pol.	51.12 N	18.33 E
120	Wien (Vienna) (vēn) (vê-ĕn'ä).Aus.	48.14 N	16.20 E
117	Wien (Vienna).........Aus. (In.)		
120	Wiener Neustadt (vē'nĕr noi'shtät).Aus.	47.48 N	16.15 E
121	Wieprz (vyĕpzh)............Pol.	51.0 N	23.10 E
81	Wiergate (wēr'gāt)..........Tex.	31.2 N	93.43 W
121	Wierzbnik (vyāzh'bnêk)......Pol.	51.3 N	21.6 E
120	Wiesbaden (vēs'bä-dĕn)......Ger.	50.5 N	8.14 E
114	Wigan (wĭg'ăn)..........Gt. Brit.	53.30 N	2.38 W
82	Wiggins (wĭg'ĭnz)..........Miss.	30.53 N	89.9 W
114	Wight, Isle of (wīt)......Gt. Brit.	50.40 N	1.20 W
114	Wigtown (wĭg'tŭn)......Gt. Brit.	54.52 N	4.25 W
114	Wigtown B.............Gt. Brit.	54.50 N	4.10 W
72	Wigwam (wĭg'wôm) Colo. (Colo. Sprs. In.)	38.32 N	104.38 W
79	Wilber (wĭl'bēr)............Neb.	40.28 N	96.59 W
79	Wilburton (wĭl'bēr-tŭn).....Okla.	34.55 N	95.18 W
159	Wilcannia................Austl.	31.32 S	143.25 E
102	Wilde (wīld)...........Arg. (In.)	34.41 S	58.19 W
73	Wildomar (wĭl'dô-mär) Calif. (Los Angeles In.)	33.36 N	117.17 W
77	Wild Rice R.........Minn.-N. D.	47.17 N	96.5 W
72	Wilds (wīldz)..Colo. (Denver In.)	40.25 N	105.10 W
85	Wildwood (wīld'wŏŏd)......N. J.	38.58 N	74.52 W
78	Wiley (wī'lê)..............Colo.	38.7 N	102.42 W
108	Wilhelmina (vêl-hĕl-mē'nä)..Swe.	64.37 N	16.42 E
151	Wilhelmina, Mt. (vêl-hĕl-mē'nȧ) Neth. N. Gui.	4.5 S	138.36 E

ăt; finăl; rāte; senâte; ärm; ȧsk; sofȧ; fâre; ch-choose; dh-as th in other; bē; êvent; bĕt; recĕnt; cratēr; g-go; gh-gutteral g; bĭt; ĭ-short neutral; rīde; κ-gutteral k as ch in German ich;

Wilhelmsburg PRONOUNCING INDEX **Wukao**

Page	Name Pronunciation Region	Lat. °′	Long. °′
117	Wilhelmsburg (vĕl'hĕlms-bŏŏrgh) Ger. (Hamburg In.)	53.30 N	10.0 E
120	Wilhelmshaven (vĕl-hĕlms-hä'fĕn) Ger.	53.31 N	8.9 E
85	Wilkes-Barre (wĭlks'-băr-ē)....Pa.	41.14 N	75.52 W
47	Wilkes Land (wĭlks)........Ant.	71.0 S	126.0 E
89	Wilkinsburg (wĭl'kĭnz-bûrg) Pa. (Pittsburgh In.)	40.26 N	79.53 W
70	Willamette R. (wĭ-lăm'ĕt)....Ore.	44.35 N	123.15 W
70	Willamette R., Middle Fork..Ore.	43.55 N	123.10 W
70	Willapa B. (wĭ-lăp'ȧ) (wĭl'ȧ-pȧ) Wash.	46.40 N	124.5 W
84	Willard (wĭl'ȧrd)..........Ohio	41.3 N	82.47 W
73	Willard.Utah (Salt Lake City In.)	41.24 N	112.2 W
75	Willcox (wĭl'kŏks)..........Ariz.	32.13 N	109.51 W
100	Willemstad (vĭl'ĕm-stät)....W. I.	12.5 N	68.59 W
116	Willenhall (wĭl'ĕn-hôl)...Gt. Brit.	52.35 N	2.4 W
114	Willesden (wĭlz'dĕn).....Gt. Brit.	51.30 N	0.15 W
158	William Creek (wĭl'yăm)....Austl.	28.45 S	136.15 E
75	Williams (wĭl'yămz)..........Ariz.	35.17 N	112.11 W
82	Williamsburg (wĭl'yămz-bûrg).Ky.	36.43 N	84.12 W
85	Williamsburg...............Va.	37.15 N	76.40 W
96	Williams I.............Ba. Is.	24.39 N	78.28 W
83	Williamson (wĭl'yăm-sŭn)...N. C.	35.52 N	77.4 W
84	Williamson.............W. Va.	37.40 N	82.15 W
85	Williamsport (wĭl'yămz-pōrt).Md.	39.36 N	77.48 W
85	Williamsport...............Pa.	41.13 N	77.2 W
75	Williams R................Ariz.	34.14 N	113.50 W
83	Williamston (wĭl'yămz-tŭn)..S. C.	34.36 N	82.29 W
160	Williamstown (wĭl'yămz-toun) Austl.	37.49 S	144.50 E
84	Williamstown...........W. Va.	39.22 N	81.30 W
85	Willimantic (wĭl-ĭ-măn'tĭk).Conn.	41.40 N	72.10 W
81	Willis (wĭl'ĭs)..............Tex.	30.25 N	95.28 W
159	Willis Is...................Austl.	16.15 S	150.8 E
76	Williston (wĭl'ĭs-tŭn).......N. D.	48.8 N	103.39 W
74	Willits (wĭl'ĭts)............Calif.	39.26 N	123.21 W
77	Willmar (wĭl'mär).........Minn.	45.7 N	95.2 W
84	Willoughby (wĭl'ō-bē).......Ohio	41.39 N	81.22 W
89	Willoughby B...Va. (Norfolk In.)	36.57 N	76.18 W
71	Willow Creek (wĭl'ō).......Mont.	48.45 N	111.30 W
70	Willow Cr..................Ore.	45.35 N	119.55 W
70	Willow Cr..................Ore.	44.10 N	117.40 W
134	Willowmore (wĭl'ō-mōr).U. S. Afr.	33.18 S	23.29 E
74	Willows (wĭl'ōz)...........Calif.	39.31 N	122.12 W
88	Willow Springs..Ill. (Chicago In.)	41.44 N	87.52 W
79	Willow Springs.............Mo.	37.0 N	91.57 W
81	Wills Point (wĭlz)...........Tex.	32.42 N	96.2 W
117	Wilmarsdonck (vĕl'märz-dŏnk) Bel. (Anvers In.)	51.17 N	4.22 E
77	Wilmette (wĭl-mĕt').........Ill.	42.4 N	87.43 W
73	Wilmington (wĭl'mĭng-tŭn) Calif. (Los Angeles In.)	33.47 N	118.18 W
85	Wilmington................Del.	39.44 N	75.32 W
87	Wilmington..........Mass. (In.)	42.33 N	71.10 W
83	Wilmington...............N. C.	34.14 N	77.57 W
84	Wilmington................Ohio	39.21 N	83.49 W
89	Wilmington I..Ga. (Savannah In.)	32.0 N	80.58 W
89	Wilmington R.Ga. (Savannah In.)	32.0 N	81.0 W
84	Wilmore (wĭl'mōr)...........Ky.	37.50 N	84.40 W
116	Wilmslow (wĭlmz'lō).....Gt. Brit.	53.20 N	2.14 W
117	Wilryck (vĕl'rĭk).Bel. (Anvers In.)	51.10 N	4.23 E
79	Wilson (wĭl'sŭn)............Ark.	35.34 N	90.3 W
83	Wilson....................N. C.	35.43 N	77.56 W
79	Wilson....................Okla.	34.9 N	97.26 W
72	Wilson Cr..Colo. (Colo. Sprs. In.)	38.40 N	105.11 W
77	Wilson I..................Can.	48.44 N	87.29 W
82	Wilson L...................Ala.	34.48 N	87.30 W
73	Wilson Mt.Calif. (Los Angeles In.)	34.14 N	118.4 W
71	Wilson Peak................Utah	40.47 N	110.48 W
159	Wilson's Promontory.......Austl.	39.5 S	146.12 E
73	Wilsonville.Ala. (Birmingham In.)	33.14 N	86.29 W
76	Wilton (wĭl'tŭn)...........N. D.	47.9 N	100.47 W
158	Wiluna (wĭ-lōō'nȧ).........Austl.	26.32 S	120.18 E
114	Wimbledon (wĭm'b'l-dŭn) Gt. Brit.	51.25 N	0.10 W
84	Winamac (wĭn'ȧ-măk).......Ind.	41.5 N	86.40 W
73	Winchester (wĭn'chĕs-tẽr) Calif. (Los Angeles In.)	33.43 N	117.4 W
114	Winchester.............Gt. Brit.	51.5 N	1.20 W
70	Winchester.................Ida.	46.13 N	116.38 W
84	Winchester.................Ky.	37.59 N	84.12 W
87	Winchester...............Mass.	42.27 N	71.8 W
86	Winchester...............N. H.	42.45 N	72.25 W
84	Winchester................Ohio	39.0 N	84.50 W
82	Winchester...............Tenn.	35.11 N	86.7 W
85	Winchester.................Va.	39.10 N	78.12 W
85	Windber (wĭnd'bẽr)..........Pa.	40.15 N	78.48 W
76	Wind Cave Natl. Park......S. D.	43.33 N	103.29 W
82	Winder (wĭn'dẽr)...........Ga.	33.58 N	83.43 W
114	Windermere (wĭn'dẽr-mẽr) Gt. Brit.	54.25 N	2.55 W
85	Windham (wĭnd'ăm).......Conn.	41.44 N	2.6 W
134	Windhoek (vĭnt'hōōk)..S. W. Afr.	22.33 S	17.10 E
77	Windom (wĭn'dŭm).........Minn.	43.52 N	95.5 W
159	Windora (wĭn-dō'rȧ).......Austl.	25.29 S	142.40 E
71	Wind R. (wĭnd)............Wyo.	43.25 N	109.15 W
71	Wind River Ra..............Wyo.	43.0 N	109.30 W
55	Windsor (wĭn'zẽr)...........Can.	45.5 N	64.14 W
55	Windsor....................Can.	42.18 N	82.50 W
78	Windsor...................Colo.	40.27 N	104.54 W
114	Windsor...............Gt. Brit.	51.25 N	0.35 W
79	Windsor....................Mo.	38.32 N	93.29 W
83	Windsor...................N. C.	35.59 N	76.57 W
86	Windsor....................Vt.	43.30 N	72.25 W
97	Windward Chan. (wĭnd'wẽrd) W. I.	19.50 N	73.50 W
91	Windward Is................W. I.	13.0 N	61.30 W
95	Windward Is.........W. I. (In.)		
73	Wineville (wīn'vĭl) Calif. (Los Angeles In.)	34.2 N	117.32 W
79	Winfield (wĭn'fēld)..........Kan.	37.14 N	97.0 W
88	Winfield Junction.....N. Y. (In.)	40.44 N	73.54 W
144	Wingsun (wĭng'sōōn').........Chn.	22.52 N	109.2 E
55	Winisk R. (wĭn'ĭsk).........Can.	54.32 N	87.0 W
80	Wink (wĭŋk).................Tex.	31.48 N	103.9 W
132	Winneba (wĭn'ē-bȧ)........G. C.	5.28 N	0.38 W
77	Winnebago (wĭn-ē-bā'gō)...Minn.	43.47 N	94.8 W
77	Winnebago, L..............Wis.	44.0 N	88.25 W
70	Winnemucca (wĭn-ē-mŭk'ȧ)..Nev.	40.59 N	117.43 W
86	Winnepesaukee, L. (wĭn'ē-pē-sô'kē).N. H.	43.40 N	71.25 W
76	Winner (wĭn'ẽr)............S. D.	43.22 N	99.51 W
77	Winnetka (wĭ-nĕt'kȧ).........Ill.	42.5 N	87.43 W
71	Winnett (wĭn'ĕt)..........Mont.	47.1 N	108.20 W
81	Winnfield (wĭn'fēld)..........La.	31.55 N	92.39 W
77	Winnibigoshish L. (wĭn'ĭ-bĭ-gō'shĭsh).Minn.	47.25 N	94.10 W
54	Winnipeg (wĭn'ĭ-pĕg)........Can.	49.47 N	97.15 W
56	Winnipeg............Can. (In.)		
54	Winnipeg L................Can.	53.0 N	97.0 W
54	Winnipegosis(wĭn'ĭ-pē-gō'sĭs).Can.	51.42 N	99.59 W
54	Winnipegosis, L............Can.	52.40 N	99.58 W
81	Winnsboro (wĭnz'bŭr-ō)......La.	32.8 N	90.43 W
83	Winnsboro.................S. C.	34.22 N	81.6 W
81	Winnsboro..................Tex.	32.57 N	95.18 W
77	Winona (wĭ-nō'nȧ)........Minn.	44.3 N	91.38 W
82	Winona....................Miss.	33.28 N	89.43 W
86	Winooski (wĭ-nōōs'kē)........Vt.	44.31 N	73.11 W
116	Winsford (wĭnz'fẽrd)....Gt. Brit.	53.11 N	2.30 W
75	Winslow (wĭnz'lō)..........Ariz.	35.1 N	110.43 W
51	Winslow.....Wash. (Seattle In.)	47.37 N	122.32 W
85	Winsted (wĭn'stĕd)........Conn.	41.55 N	73.5 W
116	Winster (wĭn'stẽr).......Gt. Brit.	53.8 N	1.38 W
73	Winston (wĭn'stŭn) Ga. (Atlanta In.)	33.43 N	84.50 W
83	Winston-Salem (sā'lĕm)....N. C.	36.5 N	80.14 W
83	Winter Garden.........Fla. (In.)	28.32 N	81.34 W
83	Winter Haven.........Fla. (In.)	28.2 N	81.43 W
83	Winter Park..........Fla. (In.)	28.36 N	81.20 W
80	Winters (wĭn'tẽrz)..........Tex.	31.59 N	99.58 W
77	Winterset (wĭn'tẽr-sĕt)........Ia.	71.19 N	94.1 W
120	Winterthur (vĭn'tẽr-tōōr)...Switz.	47.30 N	8.42 E
86	Winthrop (wĭn'thrŭp)........Me.	44.19 N	70.0 W
87	Winthrop.............Mass. (In.)	42.22 N	70.59 W
77	Winthrop..................Minn.	44.32 N	94.20 W
159	Winton....................Austl.	22.14 S	143.0 E
157	Winton (wĭn'tŭn)..........N. Z.	46.8 S	168.20 E
117	Winwick (wĭn'wĭk) Gt. Brit. (Liverpool In.)	53.25 N	2.36 W
71	Wiota (wī-ō'tȧ)............Mont.	48.7 N	106.14 W
116	Wirksworth (wûrks'wûrth) Gt. Brit.	53.5 N	1.35 W
114	Wisbech (wĭz'bĕch)......Gt. Brit.	52.40 N	0.10 E
85	Wisconisco (wĭs-kŏn-ĭs'kō)....Pa.	40.35 N	76.43 W
77	Wisconsin (State) (wĭs-kŏn'sĭn) U. S.	44.40 N	89.40 W
77	Wisconsin Dells............Wis.	43.38 N	89.45 W
77	Wisconsin R................Wis.	44.10 N	89.54 W
77	Wisconsin Rapids..........Wis.	44.23 N	89.48 W
76	Wishek (wĭsh'ĕk)...........N. D.	46.16 N	99.34 W
121	Wisla (Vistula) R. (vēs'wȧ) (vĭs'tū-lȧ).Pol.	51.4 N	21.50 E
121	Wisloka R. (vēs-wô'kȧ)......Pol.	49.50 N	21.23 E
101	Wismar (wĭz'mȧr)........Br. Gu.	5.58 N	58.15 W
120	Wismar (vĭs'mär)...........Ger.	53.54 N	11.26 E
76	Wisner (wĭz'nẽr)...........Neb.	42.0 N	96.54 W
88	Wissahickon Cr. (wĭs-ȧ-hĭk'ŭn) Pa. (Philadelphia In.)	40.3 N	75.13 W
123	Wissembourg (vē-sȧɴ-bōōr')...Fr.	49.1 N	7.59 E
134	Wissmar Pool (L.) (vĭs'mär) Bel. Cong.	3.12 S	17.20 E
114	Witham (R.) (wĭdh'ăm).Gt. Brit.	53.0 N	0.10 W
114	Withernsea (wĭdh'ẽrn-sē).Gt. Brit.	53.40 N	0.5 E
117	Withington (wĭdh'ĭng-tŭn) Gt. Brit. (Liverpool In.)	53.26 N	2.13 W
82	Withlacoochee R. (wĭth-lȧ-kōō'-chē).Fla.	31.0 N	83.18 W
117	Wittenau (vĭt'ē-nou) Ger. (Berlin In.)	52.36 N	13.20 E
	Wittenberg, see Lutherstadt, Ger.		
120	Wittenberge (vĭt-ĕn-bĕr'gē)..Ger.	53.0 N	11.43 E
120	Wittlich (vĭt'lĭĸ)...........Ger.	49.58 N	6.53 E
120	Wittstock (vĭt'shtôk).........Ger.	53.11 N	12.26 E
135	Witu (wē'too).............Kenya	2.18 S	40.28 E
121	Wkra (Dzialdowka) R. (f'krȧ) (dzhäl-dōōf'kȧ).Pol.	52.50 N	20.48 E
121	Wloclawek (vwô-tswä'vĕk)...Pol.	52.38 N	19.6 E
121	Wlodawa (vwô-dä'vȧ).........Pol.	51.33 N	23.33 E
121	Wloszczowa (vwôsh-chô'vä)..Pol.	50.51 N	19.58 E
87	Woburn (wōō'bŭrn) (wō'bŭrn) Mass. (In.)	42.28 N	71.9 W
120	Wolfenbüttel (vôl'fĕn-büt-ĕl).Ger.	52.10 N	10.31 E
85	Wolf I. (wōōlf).............Can.	44.10 N	76.25 W
88	Wolf L.....Ill.-Ind. (Chicago In.)	41.40 N	87.32 W
82	Wolf R.............Tenn.-Miss.	35.5 N	89.40 W
77	Wolf R.....................Wis.	44.50 N	88.38 W
71	Wolf Point................Mont.	48.6 N	105.40 W
86	Wolfville (wōōlf'vĭl).........Can.	45.5 N	64.21 W
120	Wolgast (vôl'gäst)...........Ger.	54.4 N	13.45 E
158	Wollall (wōōl'ôl)............Austl.	19.45 S	120.58 E
54	Wollaston L. (wōōl'ăs-tŭn)..Can.	58.15 N	103.30 W
159	Wollongong (wōōl'ŭn-gŏng).Austl.	34.24 S	150.54 E
121	Wolomin (vô-wō'mēn).........Pol.	52.19 N	21.15 E
116	Wolstanton (wōōl-stăn'tŭn) Gt. Brit.	53.2 N	2.13 W
114	Wolverhampton (wōōl'vẽr-hămp-tŭn).Gt. Brit.	52.35 N	2.10 W
116	Wolverton(wōōl'vẽr-tŭn).Gt. Brit.	52.4 N	0.48 W
117	Wommelghem (vŏm'ĕl-gĕm) Bel. (Anvers In.)	51.12 N	4.31 E
147	Wŏnju (wŭn'jōō')............Kor.	37.21 N	127.57 E
147	Wŏnsan (Genzan) (wŭn'sän') (gĕn'zän).Kor.	39.10 N	127.26 E
159	Wonthaggi (wŏnt-hăg'ē)....Austl.	38.37 S	145.33 E
76	Wood (wōōd)..............S. D.	43.28 N	100.24 W
76	Woodbine (wōōd'bīn).........Ia.	41.45 N	95.42 W
70	Woodburn (wōōd'bûrn).......Ore.	45.9 N	122.51 W
88	Woodbury (wōōd'bĕr-ē) N. J. (Philadelphia In.)	39.50 N	75.9 W
117	Woodchurch (wōōd'chûrch) Gt. Brit. (Liverpool In.)	53.23 N	3.6 W
117	Woodford (wōōd'fẽrd) Gt. Brit. (London In.)	51.36 N	0.1 E
117	Wood Green Gt. Brit. (London In.)	51.36 N	0.8 W
51	Woodinville (wōōd'ĭn-vĭl) Wash. (Seattle In.)	47.45 N	122.10 W
89	Wood L..Minn. (Minneapolis In.)	44.52 N	93.16 W
74	Woodland (wōōd'lănd).....Calif.	38.40 N	121.48 W
56	Woodland....Can. (Winnipeg In.)	50.12 N	97.40 W
51	Woodland...Wash. (Portland In.)	45.53 N	122.45 W
72	Woodland Park Colo. (Colo. Sprs. In.)	38.59 N	105.4 W
151	Woodlark (Murua) (I.) (wōōd'-lärk) (mōō'rōō-ȧ).Pap. Ter.	9.0 S	152.45 E
158	Woodroffe, Mt. (wōōd'rŭf)..Austl.	26.0 S	132.0 E
83	Woodruff (wōōd'rŭf)........S. C.	34.44 N	82.2 W
73	Woods Cross Utah (Salt Lake City In.)	40.53 N	111.55 W
84	Woodsfield (wōōdz'fēld).....Ohio	39.45 N	81.9 W
158	Woods, L. (wōōdz)........Austl.	17.50 S	133.30 E
77	Woods, L. of the......Can.-Minn.	49.10 N	94.40 W
73	Woodstock (wōōd'stŏk) Ala. (Birmingham In.)	33.13 N	87.9 W
55	Woodstock.................Can.	46.1 N	67.37 W
84	Woodstock.................Can.	43.8 N	80.50 W
77	Woodstock..................Ill.	42.20 N	88.28 W
85	Woodstock..................Va.	38.54 N	78.29 W
86	Woodsville (wōōdz'vĭl).....N. H.	44.9 N	72.0 W
160	Woodville (wōōd'vĭl) Austl. (Adelaide In.)	34.53 S	138.33 E
82	Woodville..................Miss.	31.6 N	91.18 W
156	Woodville..................N. Z.	40.20 S	175.55 E
81	Woodville...................Tex.	30.47 N	94.25 W
73	Woodward (wōōd'wẽrd) Ala. (Birmingham In.)	33.25 N	86.57 W
78	Woodward.................Okla.	36.26 N	99.25 W
73	Woolsey (wōōl'sē) Ga. (Atlanta In.)	33.22 N	84.24 W
157	Woolston (wōōl'stŭn)..N. Z. (In.)	43.32 S	172.43 E
117	Woolton (wōōl'tŭn) Gt. Brit. (Liverpool In.)	53.22 N	2.52 W
117	Woolwich (wōōl'ĭj) Gt. Brit. (London In.)	51.29 N	0.2 E
86	Woonsocket (wōōn-sŏk'ĕt)...R. I.	42.0 N	71.31 W
76	Woonsocket................S. D.	44.4 N	98.16 W
84	Wooster (wōōs'tẽr).........Ohio	40.49 N	81.56 W
145	Woosung (wōō'sōōng')........Chn.	31.21 N	121.30 E
114	Worcester..............Gt. Brit.	52.10 N	2.10 W
86	Worcester................Mass.	42.15 N	71.50 W
134	Worcester.............U. S. Afr.	33.39 S	19.22 E
116	Worcester Co..........Gt. Brit.	52.19 N	2.15 W
114	Workington (wûr'kĭng-tŭn) Gt. Brit.	54.35 N	3.30 W
116	Worksop (wûrk'sŏp) (wûr'sŭp) Gt. Brit.	53.18 N	1.7 W
71	Worland (wûr'lănd)........Wyo.	44.1 N	107.57 W
120	Worms (vōrms).............Ger.	49.37 N	8.21 E
81	Wortham (wûr'dhăm).........Tex.	31.46 N	96.28 W
114	Worthing (wûr'dhĭng)...Gt. Brit.	50.50 N	0.25 W
84	Worthington (wûr'dhĭng-tŭn).Ind.	39.6 N	87.0 W
76	Worthington..............Minn.	43.38 N	95.35 W
73	Worthville (wûrth'vĭl) Ga. (Atlanta In.)	33.22 N	83.54 W
150	Wowoni I. (wō-wō'nē).....Indon.	4.0 S	123.0 E
116	Wragby (răg'bē).........Gt. Brit.	53.17 N	0.19 W
139	Wrangel I. (răŋ'gĕl).....Sov. Un.	70.45 N	180.0 E
53	Wrangell.................Alsk.	56.25 N	132.30 W
53	Wrangell, Mt..............Alsk.	62.5 N	144.0 W
114	Wrath, C. (răth)........Gt. Brit.	58.35 N	5.0 W
78	Wray (rā)..................Colo.	40.5 N	102.15 W
116	Wreak, R. (rēk).........Gt. Brit.	52.44 N	1.0 W
159	Wreck Reef (rĕk)...........Austl.	22.15 S	155.30 E
116	Wrekin, The (Mt.) (rĕk'ĭn).Gt. Brit.	52.40 N	2.33 W
83	Wrens (rĕnz)...............Ga.	33.13 N	82.23 W
87	Wrentham (rĕn'thăm).Mass. (In.)	42.3 N	71.20 W
114	Wrexham (rĕk'săm).....Gt. Brit.	53.0 N	2.55 W
120	Wriezen (vrē'tsĕn)............Ger.	52.44 N	14.6 E
153	Wright (rīt).................Phil.	11.47 N	125.2 E
89	Wrights R. (rīts) S. C. (Savannah In.)	32.6 N	80.58 W
83	Wrightsville (rīts'vĭl).........Ga.	32.43 N	82.43 W
54	Wrigley (rĭg'lē)..............Can.	63.20 N	124.15 W
121	Wroclaw (Breslau) (vrô'tsläv) (brĕs'lou).Pol.	51.7 N	17.2 E
121	Wrzésnia (vzhăsh'nyȧ)......Chn.	52.18 N	17.33 E
120	Wschowa (vĭsh'kō-vȧ).......Pol.	51.47 N	16.19 E
146	Wuan (wōō'ăn')..............Chn.	36.46 N	114.18 E
145	Wuchang (wōō'chăng')......Chn.	30.32 N	114.10 E
148	Wuchang....................Chn.	44.50 N	127.12 E
145	Wuchanghsien (wōō'chăng'hsyĕn') Chn.	30.22 N	114.45 E
146	Wucheng (wōō'chĕng')......Chn.	37.8 N	115.53 E
146	Wuchih (wōō'chĭ')...........Chn.	35.3 N	113.28 E
146	Wuching (wōō'chĭng')........Chn.	39.32 N	116.51 E
144	Wuchow (wōō'chō')..........Chn.	23.28 N	111.20 E
144	Wuchwan (wōō'chwän')......Chn.	28.22 N	108.2 E
144	Wufeng (Changlo) (wōō'fĕng') (chăng'lō').Chn.	30.18 N	110.35 E
146	Wuho (wōō'hō')..............Chn.	33.8 N	117.50 E
146	Wuhsien (wōō'hsyĕn')........Chn.	38.6 N	113.26 E
145	Wuhu (wōō'hōō')............Chn.	31.20 N	118.23 E
144	Wukang (wōō'käng')..........Chn.	26.40 N	110.25 E
145	Wukang.....................Chn.	30.33 N	119.57 E
146	Wukao R. (wōō'kä'ō).........Chn.	36.35 N	120.13 E

ng-sing; ŋ-baŋk; ɴ-nasalized n; nŏd; cŏmmit; ōld; ôbey; ôrder; fōōd; fŏŏt; ou-out; s-soft; sh-dish; th-thin; pūre; ûnite; ûrn; stŭd; circŭs; ü-as "y" in study; '-indeterminate vowel.

Wuki PRONOUNCING INDEX Yŏngchŏn

Page	Name Pronunciation Region	Lat. °'	Long. °'
146	Wuki (wōō'kĭ') Chn.	38.16 N	114.56 E
146	Wukiang (wōō'kyäng') Chn.	38.10 N	115.21 E
146	Wukiao (wōō'kyä'ō) Chn.	37.45 N	116.23 E
148	Wukon R. (wōō'kôn') Chn.	46.27 N	130.27 E
145	Wu Kung Shan (Mts.) (wōō' kōōng' shän'). Chn.	27.0 N	115.40 E
148	Wulachieh (wōō'lä-kē'ä) Chn.	44.4 N	126.30 E
145	Wuning (wōō'nĭng') Chn.	29.10 N	114.43 E
95	Wuonta (wōō-ôn'tä) Nic.	13.31 N	83.32 W
75	Wupatki Natl. Mon. (wōō-păt'kĭ) Ariz.	35.45 N	111.35 W
145	Wuping (wōō'pĭng') Chn.	25.3 N	115.54 E
120	Wuppertal (vŏŏp'ēr-täl) Ger.	51.16 N	7.10 E
	Wu R., see Yu R., China.		
144	Wu R. Chn.	29.20 N	107.42 E
145	Wu R. Chn.	28.6 N	120.25 E
120	Württemberg (State) (vür'tĕm-bĕrgh). Ger.	48.35 N	9.20 E
120	Würzburg (vürts'bŏŏrgh) Ger.	49.48 N	9.56 E
120	Wurzen (vŏŏrt'sĕn) Ger.	51.23 N	12.45 E
144	Wushan (wōō'shän') Chn.	31.10 N	109.45 E
142	Wushih (Uch Turfan) (wōō'shĭ') (ōōch' tōōr-fän'). Chn.	41.7 N	79.30 E
145	Wusih (wōō'sĭ') Chn.	31.32 N	120.18 E
142	Wusu (Kweitun) (wōō'sōō') (kwā'tōōn'). Chn.	44.29 N	84.28 E
145	Wusueh (wōō'sōō'ĕ) Chn.	29.46 N	115.52 E
	Wusung, see Woosung, China.		
146	Wutai (wōō'tī') Chn.	38.46 N	113.23 E
146	Wutai Shan (Mts.) (shän') Chn.	39.5 N	113.30 E
146	Wutaishan (Mt.) Chn.	38.47 N	113.47 E
146	Wuting (wōō'tĭng') Chn.	37.32 N	117.32 E
145	Wuwei (wōō'wā') Chn.	31.17 N	117.52 E
145	Wuyi (wōō'yē') Chn.	28.53 N	119.52 E
146	Wuyi Chn.	37.56 N	115.53 E
146	Wuyi Chn.	32.15 N	118.27 E
145	Wuyuan (wōō'yōō-än') Chn.	29.17 N	117.50 E
143	Wuyun (wōō-yün') Chn.	49.5 N	130.1 E
159	Wyalong (wī'ă-lông) Austl.	33.55 S	147.16 E
84	Wyandotte (wī'ăn-dŏt) Mich.	42.12 N	83.10 W
73	Wyatt (wī'ăt) Ala. (Birmingham In.)	33.41 N	87.4 W
114	Wycombe (wĭ'kŭm) Gt. Brit.	51.40 N	0.50 W
116	Wye, R. (wī) Gt. Brit.	53.13 N	1.42 W
79	Wymore (wī'mōr) Neb.	40.9 N	96.39 W
135	Wynberg (wĭn'bĕrg) U. S. Afr.	33.59 S	18.25 E
158	Wyndham (wĭnd'ăm) Austl.	15.30 S	128.10 E
157	Wyndham N. Z.	46.30 S	168.50 E
117	Wyneghem (vī'nĕ-gĕm) Bel. (Anvers In.)	51.14 N	4.31 E
79	Wynne (wĭn) Ark.	35.13 N	90.47 W
79	Wynne Wood Okla.	34.37 N	97.10 W
79	Wynona (wī-nō'nȧ) Okla.	36.33 N	96.19 W
160	Wynyard (wĭn'yērd) Austl. (Tas. In.)	41.0 S	145.43 E
71	Wyoming (State) (wī-ō'mĭng). U. S.	41.05 N	105.30 W
71	Wyoming Ra. Wyo.	42.40 N	110.40 W
160	Wyreema (wī-rē'mȧ). Austl. (In.)	27.36 S	151.54 E
116	Wyre Forest (wīr) Gt. Brit.	52.26 N	2.26 W
116	Wyre, R. Gt. Brit.	53.51 N	2.57 W
121	Wysokie Mazowieckie (vê-sô'kyĕ mä-zô-vyĕts'kyĕ). Pol.	52.56 N	22.43 E
121	Wyszków (vêsh'kŏŏf) Pol.	52.36 N	21.28 E
83	Wytheville (wĭth'vĭl) Va.	36.57 N	81.6 W
96	Xagua Bank (sä'gwä) Cuba	21.40 N	81.0 W
127	Xanthē (ksän'thē) Grc.	41.8 N	24.53 E
84	Xenia (zē'nĭ-ȧ) Ohio	39.43 N	83.55 W
127	Xerokhorios (I.) (ksê-rô-kô'rĭ-ôs) Grc.	39.10 N	23.59 E
92	Xicotencatl (sē-kô-tĕn-kät'l) Mex.	23.0 N	98.56 W
92	Xilitla (sê-lē'tlä) Mex.	21.23 N	99.2 W
101	Xingú, R. (zhĕŋ-gōō') Braz.	3.0 S	52.15 W
93	Xochaque (sō-chä'kä). Mex. (In.)	19.25 N	98.56 W
92	Xochihuehuetlán (sō'chē-wā'-wĕ-tlän'). Mex.	17.55 N	98.33 W
93	Xochimilco (sō-chē-mēl'kō) Mex. (In.)	19.16 N	99.6 W
93	Xochinahuac (sō-chē-nä-wäk') Mex. (In.)	19.30 N	99.11 W
93	Xochitepec (sō-chē-tä-pĕk') Mex. (In.)	19.15 N	99.8 W
93	Xocoyahualco (sō-kô-yä-wäl'kō) Mex. (In.)	19.31 N	99.13 W
139	Yablonovoi Ridge (Mts.) (yä'blô-nô-voi'). Sov. Un.	53.30 N	115.0 E
121	Yablonitsa Pass (yä-blô-nē'tsä) Sov. Un.	48.22 N	24.23 E
142	Yachow (yä'chō') Chn.	29.56 N	102.50 E
142	Yachu (Yalung Ho) (R.) (yä'chōō') (yä'lōōng' hō'). Chn.	30.0 N	101.6 E
51	Yacolt (yă'kōlt) Wash. (Portland In.)	45.52 N	122.24 W
100	Yacuiba (yä-kōō-ē'bä) Bol.	21.58 S	64.0 W
83	Yadkin R. (yăd'kĭn) N. C.	35.40 N	80.20 W
129	Yagotin (yä'gô-tēn) Sov. Un.	50.17 N	31.45 E
96	Yaguajay (yä-guä-hä'ē) Cuba	22.17 N	79.18 W
92	Yahualica (yä-wä-lē'kä) Mex.	21.9 N	102.57 W
93	Yahuatengo (yä-wä-tĕŋ gō) Mex. (In.)	19.38 N	98.54 W
129	Yaila Range (yä'ê-lä) Sov. Un.	44.50 N	34.30 E
93	Yajalón (yä-hä-lōn') Mex.	17.17 N	92.10 W
70	Yakima (yăk'ĭ-mȧ) Wash.	46.36 N	120.30 W
70	Yakima R. Wash.	46.45 N	120.21 W
149	Yaku I. (yä'kōō) Jap.	30.15 N	130.30 E
139	Yakut (Aut. Rep.) (yȧ-kōōt') Sov. Un.	65.0 N	125.0 E
53	Yakutat (yăk'ōō-tăt) Alsk.	59.35 N	139.48 W
139	Yakutsk (yȧ-kōōtsk') Sov. Un.	62.0 N	129.50 E
93	Yalálag (Villa Hidalgo) (yä-lä'läg) (vēl'yä ē-dăl'gō). Mex.	17.12 N	96.11 W
72	Yale (yāl). Can. (Vancouver In.)	49.33 N	121.25 W
84	Yale Mich.	43.8 N	82.46 W
79	Yale Okla.	36.7 N	96.43 W
51	Yale Wash. (Portland In.)	45.58 N	122.19 W
83	Yale, L. Fla.	28.55 N	81.45 W
133	Yalinga (yä-lĭŋ'gȧ) Fr. Eq. Afr.	6.50 N	23.27 E
82	Yalobusha R. (yă-lô-bŏŏsh'ȧ). Miss.	33.47 N	89.30 W
148	Yal R. (yäl) Chn.	48.0 N	122.35 E
129	Yalta (Krasnoarmeisk) (yäl'tȧ) (kräs-nô-är-mâsk'). Sov. Un.	44.29 N	34.10 E
142	Yalung Ho (Yachu) (R.) yä'lōōng' hō') (yä'chōō'). Chn.	30.0 N	101.6 E
147	Yalu R. (yä'lōō') Chn.-Kor.	40.10 N	124.30 E
138	Yalutorovsk (yä-lōō-tô'rôfsk) Sov. Un.	56.40 N	66.25 E
149	Yamabe (yä'mȧ-bȧ) Jap. (Osaka In.)	34.59 N	135.23 E
149	Yamada (yä'mȧ-dȧ) Jap.	33.36 N	133.40 E
148	Yamagata (yä-mȧ'gä-tȧ) Jap.	38.14 N	140.21 E
149	Yamaguchi (yä-mȧ'gōō-chê). Jap.	34.11 N	131.30 E
138	Yamal Pen. (yä-mäl') Sov. Un.	71.0 N	71.0 E
97	Yamasa (yä-mä'sä) Dom. Rep.	18.47 N	70.2 W
149	Yamasaki (yä'mȧ'sä-kê) Jap.	35.1 N	134.32 E
149	Yamatogawa R. (yä-mȧ-tô'gȧ-wä) Jap. (Osaka In.)	34.36 N	135.33 E
151	Yamdena (I.) (yäm-dā'nä). Indon.	7.30 S	131.30 E
142	Yamdok (Palti), L. (yȧm'dôk') (päl'tē). Chn.	29.0 N	90.45 E
142	Yamethin (yŭ-mē'thĕn) Bur.	20.15 N	96.28 E
152	Y'ami I. (ê-ä'mê) Phil. (In.)	21.5 N	121.58 E
159	Yamma Yamma, L. (yăm'ȧ yăm'ȧ). Austl.	26.30 S	141.30 E
78	Yampa R. (yăm'pȧ) Colo.	40.28 N	107.10 W
139	Yamsk (yȧmsk) Sov. Un.	59.35 N	154.0 E
159	Yanac (yăn'ăk) Austl.	36.9 S	141.29 E
149	Yanagawa (yä-nä'gä-wä) Jap.	33.11 N	130.23 E
139	Yana R. (yä'nȧ) Sov. Un.	68.0 N	134.10 E
141	Yanaon (yȧ'nȧ'ôN') India	16.44 N	82.12 E
144	Yanfa (yän'fä') Chn.	25.14 N	113.10 E
146	Yangcheng (yäng'chĕng') Chn.	33.51 N	113.38 E
146	Yanhchow (yäng'chō') Chn.	32.26 N	119.23 E
147	Yangdŏk (yäng'dŭk') Kor.	39.9 N	126.54 E
142	Yangihissar (Yingkisha) (yäŋ'gê-hĭs'är) (yĭng'kĭ-shä'). Chn.	39.2 N	75 37 E
142	Yangi Shahr (Shuleh) (yäŋ'gê shär') (shōō'lă'). Chn.	41.22 N	80.25 E
146	Yangku (yäng'kōō') Chn.	36.8 N	115.53 E
143	Yangkyung (yäng'kyōōng') Chn. (Shanghai In.)	31.11 N	121.31 E
144	Yangli (yäng'lē') Chn.	22.52 N	107.19 E
147	Yangpyŏng (yäng'pyŭng') Kor.	37.29 N	127.29 E
144	Yangshan (yäng'shän') Chn.	24.27 N	112.23 E
146	Yangsin (yäng'sĭn') Chn.	37.46 N	117.28 E
144	Yangso (yäng'sō') Chn.	24.40 N	110.24 E
143	Yangtze Kiang (R.) (yäng'tsĕ kyăng'). Chn.	30.0 N	116.30 E
144	Yangtze Kiang (Great R.) Chn.	30.10 N	108.0 E
142	Yangtze Kiang (Dichu) (R.) (dē'chōō'). Chn.	33.0 N	97.30 E
146	Yangwu (yäng'wōō') Chn.	35.1 N	114.11 E
147	Yangyang (yäng'yäng') Kor.	38.4 N	128.38 E
51	Yankton (yănk'tŭn) Ore. (Portland In.)	45.52 N	122.52 W
76	Yankton S. D.	42.53 N	97.23 W
127	Yannina (Ioannina) (yä'nê-nä) (yô-ä'nê-nä). Grc.	39.38 N	20.53 E
129	Yanushpol (yȧ-nōōsh'pôl') Sov. Un.	49.53 N	28.12 E
133	Yao (yä'ō) Fr. Eq. Afr.	13.0 N	17.36 E
132	Yaoundé (yȧ-ōōn-dā') Cam.	3.58 N	11.40 E
5	Yap (I.) (yăp) Pac. O.	9.30 N	138.10 E
97	Yaque del Norte, R. (yä'kȧ dĕl nôr'tȧ). Dom. Rep.	19.40 N	71.8 W
97	Yaque del Sur, R. (dĕl sōōr') Dom. Rep.	18.40 N	71.8 W
97	Yaque, Pico del (Mt.) (pē'kō dĕl yä'kȧ). Dom. Rep.	19.2 N	70.58 W
159	Yaraka (yȧ-răk'ȧ) Austl.	24.50 S	144.5 E
110	Yaransk (yä-ränsk') Sov. Un.	57.15 N	47.50 E
133	Yarda (yär'dȧ) Fr. Eq. Afr.	18.30 N	19.13 E
148	Yarigadake (Mt.) (yä-rē-gä'dä-kĕ) Jap.	36.28 N	137.35 E
142	Yarkand (Soche) (yär-känt') (sō'chē'). Chn.	38.12 N	77.30 E
55	Yarmouth (yär'mŭth) Can.	43.57 N	66.5 W
160	Yarra, R. (yăr'ȧ) Austl. (Melbourne In.)	37.50 S	144.57 E
160	Yarraville (yăr'ȧ-vĭl) Austl. (Melbourne In.)	37.49 S	144.53 E
160	Yarra Yarra Cr. (yăr'ȧ yăr'ȧ) Austl. (Melbourne In.)	37.45 S	145.5 E
110	Yarro-to, L. (yȧ'rô-tô'). Sov. Un.	68.30 N	71.30 E
128	Yartsev (yärt'sĕf) Sov. Un.	55.2 N	32.40 E
100	Yarumal (yä-rōō-mäl') Col.	6.32 N	75.32 W
119	Yaschuny (yäsh'chōō-nĭ). Sov. Un.	54.27 N	25.20 E
121	Yaselda R. (yä-syŭl'dȧ). Sov. Un.	52.15 N	25.55 E
121	Yasenya (yȧ'sê-nyä) Sov. Un.	48.17 N	24.22 E
97	Yateras (yä-tä'räs) Cuba	19.59 N	74.58 W
79	Yates Center (yāts) Kan.	37.53 N	95.44 W
55	Yathkyed L. (yȧth-kī-ĕd') Can.	62.45 N	97.32 W
149	Yatsugatake (Mt.) (yät'sōō-gä'-tä-kä). Jap.	35.58 N	138.22 E
149	Yatsushiro (yät'sōō'shē-rô). Jap.	32.30 N	130.35 E
141	Yatung (yä'tōōng') India	27.28 N	88.59 E
147	Yatushiro B. (yä'tōō'shē-rô). Jap.	32.23 N	130.27 E
92	Yautepec (yä-ōō-tä-pĕk') Mex.	18.53 N	99.4 W
121	Yavaruv (yä-vä'rōōf) Sov. Un.	49.56 N	23.23 E
149	Yawata (yä'wä-tä) Jap.	33.47 N	130.48 E
149	Yawata Jap.	34.50 N	135.40 E
149	Yawatahama (yä'wä'tä'hä-mä) Jap.	33.25 N	132.25 E
138	Yaxartes (Sir Darya) R. (yăks-är'-tēz) (sēr där'yä). Sov. Un.	45.0 N	65.0 E
82	Yazoo City (yă'zōō) Miss.	32.50 N	90.25 W
82	Yazoo R. Miss.	33.0 N	90.20 W
88	Yeadon (yē'dŭn) Pa. (Philadelphia In.)	39.56 N	75.15 W
124	Yecla (yā'klä) Sp.	38.36 N	1.8 W
142	Yehcheng (Qargaliq) (yĕ'chĕng') (kär'gä-lĭk). Chn.	37.28 N	79.41 E
114	Yell (I.) (yĕl) Gt. Brit. (In.)	60.40 N	1.5 W
54	Yellowknife (yĕl'ō-nīf) Can.	62.28 N	114.42 W
73	Yellowleaf Cr. (yĕl'ō-lēf) Ala. (Birmingham In.)	33.17 N	86.35 W
146	Yellow R. (Hwang Ho) (hwäng' hō'). Chn.	36.0 N	115.58 E
82	Yellow R. Fla.	31.0 N	85.32 W
73	Yellow R. Ga. (Atlanta In.)	33.47 N	84.4 W
147	Yellow Sea (Hwang Hai) (hwäng' hī'). Chn.	36.0 N	123.0 E
71	Yellowstone L. (yĕl'ô-stōn). Wyo.	44.25 N	110.25 W
71	Yellowstone Natl. Park Wyo.	44.45 N	110.40 W
71	Yellowstone R. Mont.-N. D.	46.0 N	107.0 W
51	Yelm (yĕlm). Wash. (Seattle In.)	46.57 N	122.36 W
139	Yelovka (Elovka) (yĕ-lôf'kȧ) Sov. Un.	56.59 N	160.45 E
124	Yéltes R. (yāl'tĕs) Sp.	41.0 N	6.30 W
132	Yelwa (yĕl'wä) Nig.	8.58 N	9.46 E
140	Yemen (yĕm'ĕn) Asia	15.0 N	44.15 E
142	Yenan (yĕn'än') Chn.	36.35 N	109.35 E
140	Yenbo (yĕn'bō) Sau. Ar.	24.0 N	38.10 E
146	Yencheng (yĕn'chĕng') Chn.	33.20 N	120.5 E
146	Yencheng Chn.	33.35 N	113.57 E
143	Yenchi (Chultzuchien) (yĕn'chĭ') (chōōl'tzōō-chyĕn'). Chn.	43.0 N	129.32 E
145	Yenchow (yĕn'chō') Chn.	29.36 N	119.36 E
146	Yenchow Chn.	35.43 N	116.53 E
132	Yendi (yĕn'dē) G. C.	9.28 N	0.2 E
127	Yenişehir (yĕ-nê-shĕ'hĭr) Tur.	39.59 N	26.11 E
142	Yenisei R. (yĕ-nê-sĕ'ê) Chn.	52.30 N	95.0 E
138	Yenisei (Enisei) R. Sov. Un.	61.30 N	90.0 E
142	Yenki (Qara Shahr) (yĕn'kĭ') (kä'rȧ shär'). Chn.	42.2 N	86.28 E
146	Yenling (yĕn'lĭng') Chn.	34.11 N	114.17 E
72	Yennadon (yĕn'ȧ-dŭn) Can. (Vancouver In.)	49.15 N	122.35 W
145	Yenping (yĕn'pĭng') Chn.	26.38 N	118.3 E
146	Yen R. (yĕn) Chn.	33.50 N	119.20 E
146	Yenshan (yĕn'shän') Chn.	38.15 N	117.4 E
52	Yenta R. (yĕn'tȧ) Alsk. (In.)	61.40 N	150.35 W
146	Yentsing (yĕn'tsĭng') Chn.	35.7 N	114.24 E
158	Yeo, L. (yō) Austl.	27.27 S	124.20 E
114	Yeovil (yō'vĭl) Gt. Brit.	50.55 N	2.50 W
74	Yerington (yĕ'rĭng-tŭn) Nev.	38.58 N	119.10 W
123	Yerres (yĕr') Fr. (In.)	48.42 N	2.30 E
123	Yerres R. Fr. (In.)	48.42 N	2.30 E
147	Yesan (yĕ'sän') Kor.	36.41 N	126.51 E
124	Yeste (yĕs'tȧ) Sp.	38.22 N	2.19 W
122	Yeu d' Ile (yŭ dēl') Fr.	46.40 N	2.20 W
140	Yezd (yĕzd) Iran	31.59 N	54.20 E
146	Yichow (yĭ'chō') Chn.	39.29 N	115.17 E
146	Yihsien (yĭ-shyĕn') Chn.	34.45 N	117.45 E
146	Yingcheng (yĭng'chĕng') Chn.	30.54 N	113.23 E
146	Yingchow (yĭng'chō') Chn.	32.55 N	115.46 E
146	Yingchow Chn.	39.35 N	113.20 E
142	Yingkisha (Yangihissar) (yĭng'kĭ-shä') (yäŋ'gĭ-hĭs'är). Chn.	32.2 N	75.37 E
143	Yingkow (Niuchwangcheng) (yĭng'kō') (nyōō'chwäng'chĕng') Chn.	40.40 N	122.12 E
148	Yingpan (yĭng'pän') Chn.	41.59 N	124.27 E
146	Ying R. (yĭng) Chn.	33.12 N	115.0 E
145	Yingshan (yĭng'shän') Chn.	30.45 N	115.43 E
146	Yingshang (yĭng'shäng') Chn.	32.37 N	116.11 E
146	Yingtak (yĭng'täk') Chn.	24.9 N	113.6 E
144	Yinkiang (yĭn'kyäng') Chn.	28.5 N	108.29 E
146	Yi, R. (yĭ) Chn.	34.50 N	118.20 E
99	Yi, R. (rē'ō yē') Ur. (Buenos Aires In.)	33.15 S	57.0 W
144	Yiyang (yĭ'yäng') Chn.	28.33 N	112.2 E
81	Yoakum (yō'kŭm) Tex.	29.17 N	97.9 W
144	Yochih (yō'chĭ') Chn.	30.39 N	106.26 E
144	Yochow (yō'chō') Chn.	29.21 N	112.46 E
82	Yocona R. (yō-kō'nȧ) Miss.	34.10 N	89.42 W
149	Yodo (yō'dō). Jap. (Osaka In.)	34.54 N	135.42 E
149	Yodogawa R. (yō'dō'gä-wä) Jap. (Osaka In.)	34.48 N	135.36 E
152	Yog Pt. (yōg) Phil.	14.6 N	124.13 E
54	Yoho Natl. Park (yō'hō) Can.	51.0 N	116.0 W
94	Yojoa, L. (yô-hō'ä) Hond.	14.50 N	88.0 W
147	Yŏju (yŭ'jōō') Kor.	37.17 N	127.38 E
82	Yokahockany Cr. (yôk-ȧ-hŏk'ȧ-nê) Miss.	33.0 N	89.35 W
79	Yokahockany R. Miss.	33.15 N	89.25 W
149	Yokkaichi (yō'kä'ē-chê) Jap.	35.1 N	136.32 E
149	Yokohama (yō'kō-hä'mȧ) (yō-kō'hä'mä'). Jap.	35.22 N	139.37 E
149	Yokosuka (yō-kō'sōō-kä) Jap.	35.17 N	139.41 E
149	Yokota (yō-kō'tä) Jap. (Tokyo In.)	35.24 N	140.2 E
132	Yola (yō'lä) Nig.	9.18 N	12.26 E
95	Yolaina, Cordillera de (Mts.) (yō-lä-ē'nä). Nic.	11.45 N	84.25 W
82	Yolande (yō-lăn'dē) Ala.	33.18 N	87.12 W
149	Yonago (yō'nä-gō) Jap.	35.25 N	133.20 E
147	Yŏnan (yŭ'nän') Kor.	37.55 N	126.9 E
147	Yŏnchŏn (yŭn'chŭn') Kor.	38.6 N	127.5 E
148	Yonezawa (yō'nĕ'zȧ-wä) Jap.	37.52 N	140.2 E
147	Yŏngam (yŭn'gäm) Kor.	34.38 N	126.42 E
147	Yŏngbyŏn (yŭng'byŭn') Kor.	34.49 N	125.48 E
147	Yŏngchŏn (yŭng'chŭn') Kor.	35.58 N	128.56 E

ăt; finăl; rāte; senâte; ärm; åsk; sofȧ; fâre; ch-choose; dh-as th in other; bē; ėvent; bĕt; recĕnt; cratẽr; g-go; gh-gutteral g; bĭt; ĭ-short neutral; rīde; ᴋ-gutteral k as ch in German ich;

Yŏngdŏk PRONOUNCING INDEX Zhmerinka

Page	Name Pronunciation Region	Lat. °′	Long. °′
147	Yŏngdŏk (yŭng'dŭk')........Kor.	36.25 N	129.22 E
147	Yŏnghŭng (yŭng'ho͞ong')....Kor.	39.32 N	127.15 E
147	Yŏnghŭng Bay............Kor.	39.15 N	127.30 E
147	Yŏngil Bay (yŭng'ĭl)........Kor.	36.4 N	129.27 E
147	Yŏngju (yŭng'jo͞o')........Kor.	36.50 N	128.37 E
147	Yongsan (yŏng'sän')........Kor.	37.32 N	126.59 E
147	Yŏngyang (yŭng'yäng')......Kor.	36.40 N	129.7 E
147	Yŏngyu (yŭng'yo͞o')........Kor.	39.18 N	125.36 E
85	Yonkers (yŏŋ'kẽrz)........N. Y.	40.57 N	73.53 W
122	Yonne R. (yôn)..............Fr.	48.10 N	3.20 E
149	Yono (yō'nō)....Jap. (Osaka In.)	34.55 N	135.30 E
73	Yorba (yôr'bä) Calif. (Los Angeles In.)	33.52 N	117.48 W
82	York (yôrk)................Ala.	32.28 N	88.18 W
158	York......................Austl.	31.50 S	116.50 E
160	York..........Austl. (Tas. In.)	41.9 S	146.46 E
114	York..................Gt. Brit.	53.55 N	1.5 W
76	York......................Neb.	40.52 N	97.35 W
85	York........................Pa.	39.58 N	76.42 W
83	York......................S. C.	34.59 N	81.4 W
159	York, C...................Austl.	10.45 S	142.25 E
50	York, C..................Grnld.	76.0 N	68.0 W
116	York Co..............Gt. Brit.	54.0 N	1.30 W
55	York Factory..............Can.	56.58 N	92.31 W
114	Yorkshire Wolds (Hills) (yôrk'shĭr). Gt. Brit.	54.0 N	0.30 W
54	Yorkton (yôrk'tŭn).........Can.	51.13 N	102.31 W
81	Yorktown (yôrk'toun).......Tex.	28.58 N	97.30 W
85	Yorktown...................Va.	37.12 N	76.32 W
94	Yoro (yō'rô)..............Hond.	15.8 N	87.4 W
74	Yosemite Natl. Park (yô-sĕm'ĭ-tê) Calif.	37.55 N	119.40 W
149	Yoshida (yō'shê-dȧ).........Jap.	34.39 N	132.41 E
149	Yoshinogawa R. (yō'shê-nō'gȧ-wä) Jap.	34.3 N	133.50 E
149	Yoshiwara (yō-shê'wä'rä')....Jap.	35.11 N	138.41 E
149	Yosii (yō'sē-ē)..............Jap.	33.25 N	130.45 E
93	Yosonotú (Santa Catarina) (yô-sō-nô-to͞o') (sän'tä kä-tä-rē'nä). Mex.	16.53 N	97.34 W
147	Yŏsu (yŭ'so͞o')..............Kor.	34.45 N	127.45 E
145	Yotsing (yŏt'sĭng')..........Chn.	28.9 N	120.55 E
114	Youghal (yo͞o'ôl) (yôl).......Ire.	51.45 N	7.50 W
114	Youghal B...................Ire.	51.55 N	7.50 W
89	Youghiogheny R. (yôk-yô-gā'nê) Pa. (Pittsburgh In.)	40.20 N	79.52 W
133	Youkadouma (yo͞o-kȧ-do͞o'mä) Cam.	3.28 N	15.2 E
145	Youngfeng (yō'o͝ong'fĕng')...Chn.	27.17 N	115.18 E
51	Youngs R. (yŭngz) Ore. (Portland In.)	46.8 N	123.48 W
88	Youngstown (yŭngz'toun) N. Y. (Niagara Falls In.)	43.15 N	79.3 W
84	Youngstown...............Ohio	41.5 N	80.40 W
111	Yozgat (yôz'gȧd)...........Tur.	39.50 N	34.48 E
115	Ypres (ē'pr')................Bel.	50.50 N	2.50 E
84	Ypsilanti (ĭp-sĭ-lăn'tĭ)......Mich.	42.14 N	83.37 W
70	Yreka (wī-rē'kȧ)...........Calif.	41.43 N	122.38 W
159	Ysabel I. (ē'zȧ-bĕl)...Solomon Is.	8.0 S	159.0 E
80	Ysleta (êz-lĕ'tȧ)............Tex.	31.42 N	106.18 W
122	Yssingeau (ē-săN-zhō')........Fr.	45.10 N	4.10 E
118	Ystad (ü'städ)...............Swe.	55.25 N	13.49 E
118	Ytre Sullen (I.) (ü'trĕ so͞o'lĕn). Nor.	61.2 N	4.50 E
144	Yuanan (yo͞o'ä-nän')........Chn.	31.3 N	111.29 E
144	Yuanchow (yo͞o'än-chō').....Chn.	27.18 N	109.22 E
145	Yüanchow (yü'än-chō').....Chn.	27.37 N	114.16 E
144	Yüankiang (yü'än-kyäng')...Chn.	28.45 N	112.8 E
145	Yüanlin (yü'än-lĭn')..........For.	23.58 N	120.34 E
144	Yuan R. (yo͞o'än')..........Chn.	28.32 N	110.15 E
145	Yuan R....................Chn.	27.40 N	114.50 E
142	Yuan R..........Chn.-Indoch.	22.30 N	103.55 E
145	Yüanshan (yü'än-shän')......Chn.	28.13 N	117.41 E
146	Yuanshih (yü'än-shĭ')........Chn.	37.50 N	114.33 E
149	Yuasa (yo͞o'ȧ-sȧ)...........Jap.	34.2 N	135.10 E
74	Yuba City (yo͞o'bȧ)........Calif.	39.8 N	121.38 W
132	Yubi, C. (yo͞o'bê).......R. de O.	28.0 N	12.52 W
73	Yucaipa (yŭ-kȧ-ē'pȧ) Calif. (Los Angeles In.)	34.4 N	117.3 W
93	Yucatan (yo͞o-kä-tän')......Mex.	20.45 N	89.0 W
90	Yucatan, Channel of....Cen. Am.	21.30 N	86.30 W
75	Yucca House Natl. Mon. (yŭk'ȧ) Colo.	37.14 N	108.42 W
144	Yücheng (yü'chĕng')........Chn.	25.30 N	113.16 E
146	Yücheng...................Chn.	36.56 N	116.31 E
146	Yüchow (yü'chō')...........Chn.	34.9 N	113.29 E
146	Yüchow....................Chn.	39.50 N	114.28 E
127	Yugoslavia (Serb-Croat-Slovene-State) (yo͞o-gô-slä-vĭ-ȧ). Eur.	43.0 N	20.0 E
110	Yug R. (yo͝ok)..........Sov. Un.	60.0 N	46.0 E
145	Yuhang (yo͞o'häng').........Chn.	30.18 N	119.55 E
144	Yuhsien (yo͞o'hsyĕn')........Chn.	26.58 N	113.4 E
145	Yuhwan I. (yo͞o'hwän')......Chn.	28.2 N	121.20 E
145	Yuhwanting (yo͞o'hwän-tĭng') Chn.	28.10 N	121.12 E
145	Yukan (yo͞o'kän')...........Chn.	28.43 N	116.40 E
128	Yukhnov (yo͝oK'nôf).....Sov. Un.	54.45 N	35.12 E
145	Yuki (yo͞o'kê')..............Chn.	26.12 N	118.3 E
144	Yuking (yo͞o'kĭng')..........Chn.	27.9 N	107.39 E
54	Yukon (Ter.) (yo͞o'kŏn).....Can.	63.0 N	136.0 W
52	Yukon R...................Alsk.	65.20 N	151.0 W
142	Yulin (yo͞o'lĭn')............Chn.	38.15 N	109.34 E
74	Yuma (yo͞o'mä).............Ariz.	32.41 N	114.37 W
78	Yuma......................Colo.	40.7 N	102.44 W
97	Yuma B............Dom. Rep.	18.20 N	68.35 W
142	Yümen (yü'mĕn')............Chn.	40.9 N	97.2 E
97	Yuna R. (yo͞o'nä')....Dom. Rep.	79.8 N	70.0 W
145	Yungan (yo͞on'gän')..........Chn.	23.37 N	115.5 E
145	Yungan....................Chn.	25.51 N	117.20 E
142	Yungchang (yo͝ong'chäng')..Chn.	25.8 N	99.10 E
144	Yungchang (yo͝ong'chäng')..Chn.	29.35 N	105.33 E
146	Yüncheng (yün'chĕng')......Chn.	35.33 N	116.2 E
144	Yungchow (yo͝ong'chō')......Chn.	26.10 N	111.29 E
145	Yungchun (yo͝ong'cho͞on')...Chn.	25.20 N	118.12 E
144	Yungchwan (yo͝ong'chwän').Chn.	29.33 N	105.54 E
144	Yungfu (yo͝ong'fo͞o')........Chn.	24.58 N	109.59 E
145	Yungfu....................Chn.	25.44 N	118.43 E
144	Yungfu R..................Chn.	24.35 N	109.50 E
144	Yunghing (yo͝ong'hĭng')....Chn.	26.4 N	112.41 E
144	Yungkang (yo͝ong'käng')....Chn.	22.56 N	108.1 E
145	Yungkang..................Chn.	28.56 N	120.3 E
144	Yungming (yo͝ong'mĭng')....Chn.	25.14 N	111.18 E
144	Yungning..................Chn.	26.53 N	113.40 E
144	Yungshun (yo͝ong'sho͞on')....Chn.	28.57 N	109.44 E
144	Yungsin (yo͝ong'sĭn')........Chn.	27.0 N	113.55 E
144	Yungsui (yo͝ong'swē')......Chn.	28.37 N	109.15 E
145	Yungting (yo͝ong'tĭng')......Chn.	24.47 N	116.33 E
144	Yungting..................Chn.	28.58 N	110.21 E
146	Yungting R. (Hun R.) (yo͝ong'tĭng'). Chn.	39.40 N	116.10 E
144	Yungtsong (yo͝ong'tsông')...Chn.	25.58 N	108.59 E
144	Yungyün (yo͝ong'yün')......Chn.	24.28 N	113.18 E
145	Yunho (yo͞on'hō')...........Chn.	28.5 N	119.34 E
145	Yün Ling (Mts.) (yün lĭng)..Chn.	27.55 N	117.45 E
144	Yünmeng (yün'mĕng')......Chn.	31.0 N	113.32 E
142	Yünnan (Prov.) (yün'nän')..Chn.	24.0 N	102.0 E
144	Yunnan (Prov.) (yo͞on'nän'). Chn.	23.52 N	106.10 E
	Yünnanfu, see Kunming, Chn.		
142	Yünnan, Plat. of..........Chn.	25.45 N	103.0 E
146	Yunping (yo͞on'pĭng')........Chn.	39.57 N	118.51 E
146	Yun R. (Grand Canal) (yo͞on). Chn.	35.50 N	116.10 E
145	Yunsiao (yo͞on'syou')........Chn.	23.59 N	117.8 E
144	Yun Wu Shan (Mts.) (yo͞on' wo͞o' shän'). Chn.	26.5 N	107.10 E
144	Yünyang (yün'yäng')........Chn.	31.10 N	109.2 E
143	Yünyang (yün'yäng')........Chn.	33.0 N	110.56 E
144	Yüping (yü'pĭng')...........Chn.	27.10 N	108.35 E
144	Yu R. (yo͞o)................Chn.	23.23 N	107.45 E
149	Yura (yo͞o'rä)...............Jap.	34.18 N	134.55 E
92	Yurécuaro (yo͞o-rā'kwä-rô)..Mex.	20.19 N	102.15 W
128	Yur'ev (yo͞o'ryĕf).......Sov. Un.	56.31 N	39.41 E
110	Yurievets (yo͞o'ryĕ-vyĕts) Sov. Un.	57.15 N	43.0 E
100	Yurimaguas (yo͞o-rê-mä'gwäs) Peru	5.58 S	76.2 W
92	Yuriria (yo͞o'rê-rē'ä)........Mex.	20.12 N	101.7 W
92	Yuriria, L.................Mex.	20.15 N	101.5 W
94	Yuscarán (yo͞os-kä-rän')....Hond.	13.55 N	86.53 W
145	Yushan (yo͞o'shän').........Chn.	28.40 N	118.18 E
146	Yüshih (yü'shê')............Chn.	34.25 N	114.18 E
146	Yutai (yo͞o'tī')..............Chn.	34.54 N	116.28 E
146	Yütien (yü'tyĕn')............Chn.	39.53 N	117.38 E
142	Yutien (Keriya) (yo͞o'tyĕn') (kĕ'rê-yä). Chn.	36.32 N	81.20 E
145	Yutsien (yo͞o'tsyĕn')........Chn.	30.13 N	119.30 E
145	Yütu (yü'to͞o')..............Chn.	25.52 N	115.10 E
102	Yuty (yo͞o-tē')..............Par.	26.45 N	56.20 W
154	Yuyang (yo͞o'yäng')..........Chn.	28.53 N	108.39 E
145	Yüyao (yü'you')..............Chn.	30.4 N	121.10 E
110	Yuzha (yo͞o'zhȧ)........Sov. Un.	56.40 N	42.10 E
148	Yuzhno-Sakhalinsk (yo͞ozh'nô-sä-Kä-lĭnsk'). Sakh.	46.55 N	142.42 E
120	Yverdon (ê-vĕr-dôN')......Switz.	46.46 N	6.40 E
132	Yvette R. (ē-vĕt')......Fr. (In.)	48.42 N	2.15 E
122	Yvetot (ēv-tō')..............Fr.	49.38 N	0.45 E
93	Zaachila (Santa Maria) (sä-ä-chē'-lȧ) (sän'tä mä-rē'ä). Mex.	16.57 N	96.45 W
120	Zaandam (zän'dȧm).........Neth.	52.57 N	4.50 E
120	Ząbkowice (zaNb'kô-vē'tsĕ)...Pol.	50.45 N	16.47 E
121	Zabrze (zäb'zhĕ)............Pol.	50 18 N	18.48 E
94	Zacapa (sä-kä'pä)..........Guat.	14.57 N	89.31 W
93	Zacapoaxtla (sä-kä-pō-äs'tlä) Mex.	19.53 N	97.35 W
92	Zacapú (sä-kä-po͞o')........Mex.	19.45 N	101.45 W
92	Zacatecas (sä-kä-tā'käs).....Mex.	22.46 N	102.33 W
92	Zacatecas (State)...........Mex.	23.0 N	103.0 W
94	Zacatecoluca (sä-kä-tȧ-kô-lo͞o'kä) Sal.	13.30 N	88.50 W
92	Zacatelco (sä-kä-tĕl'kō).....Mex.	19.13 N	98.13 W
93	Zacatepec (Santiago) (sä-kä-tȧ-pĕk') (sän-tê-ä'gô). Mex.	17.10 N	95.53 W
93	Zacatlán (sä-kä-tlän')......Mex.	19.56 N	97.57 W
92	Zacoalco de Torres (sä-kô-äl'kô dā tōr'rĕs). Mex.	20.13 N	103.33 W
92	Zacualpán (sä-ko͝o-äl-pän')..Mex.	18.43 N	99.46 W
92	Zacualtipán (sä-ko͝o-äl-tē-pän') Mex.	20.38 N	98.38 W
128	Zadonsk (zä-dônsk').....Sov. Un.	52.23 N	38.57 E
120	Zagan (zhä'gän')............Pol.	51.36 N	15.19 E
119	Žagere (zhä'gĕ-rā)......Sov. Un.	56.22 N	23.15 E
132	Zaghouan (zȧ-gwäN')........Tun.	36.28 N	10.3 E
131	Zaghouan, Djebel (Mt.) (jĕb'ĕl zȧ-gwäN'). Tun. (In.)	36.20 N	10.9 E
127	Zagora (zä'gô-rȧ)...........Grc.	39.28 N	23.3 E
128	Zagorsk (zä-gôrsk')......Sov. Un.	56.18 N	38.7 E
126	Zagreb (zä'grĕb)...........Yugo.	45.49 N	15.58 E
131	Zahara (thä-ä'rä)...Sp. (Gib. In.)	36.9 N	5.11 E
140	Zahedan (Duzdab) (zä'hȧ-dän) (do͝oz'däb). Iran	29.32 N	60.34 E
137	Zahlé (zä-lā')..........Leb. (In.)	33.45 N	35.52 E
140	Zaindeh Rud (R.) (zä'ēn-dĕ ro͞od'). Iran	32.30 N	51.32 E
138	Zaisan Nor (L.) (zī'sȧn nôr) Sov. Un.	48.0 N	84.0 E
124	Zájar R. (thä'ghär)..........Sp.	38.55 N	5.20 W
127	Zaječar (zä'yĕ-chär')........Yugo.	43.53 N	22.16 E
138	Zakarovskoe (Bakhty) (zä-Kä'rôf-skô-yĕ) (bȧK'tê). Sov. Un.	46.58 N	82.50 E
121	Zakopane (zȧ-kô-pä'nĕ)......Pol.	49.18 N	19.57 E
127	Zakynthos (zȧ'kên-thôs).....Grc.	37.47 N	20.53 E
127	Zakynthos (Zante) (I.) (zän'tĕ) Grc.	37.45 N	20.48 E
120	Zalaegerszeg (zŏ'lô-ĕ'gĕr-sĕg) Hung.	46.50 N	16.47 E
124	Zalamea de la Serena (thä-lä-mā'ä dā lä sā-rā'nä). Sp.	38.37 N	5.39 W
124	Zalamea la Real (lä rā-äl')....Sp.	37.42 N	6.40 W
121	Zalău (zȧ-lŭ'o͞o)............Rom.	47.11 N	23.4 E
134	Zambezi R. (zȧm-bā'zê)......Afr.	18.0 S	27.0 E
153	Zamboanga (säm-bô-äŋ'gä)..Phil.	6.54 N	122.5 E
121	Zambrów (zäm'bro͝of)........Pol.	52.58 N	22.16 E
92	Zamora (sä-mō'rä).........Mex.	19.59 N	102.15 W
124	Zamora (thä-mō'rä)..........Sp.	41.31 N	5.45 W
121	Zamość (zä'môshch).........Pol.	50.43 N	23.15 E
93	Zanatepec (Santo Domingo) (sä-nä-tȧ-pĕk') (sän-tô dō-mĭŋ'gô). Mex.	16.30 N	94.21 W
84	Zanesville (zānz'vĭl)........Ohio	39.56 N	82.2 W
127	Zante (Zakynthos) (I.) (zän-tĕ) (zä'kên-thôs). Grc.	37.45 N	20.48 E
135	Zanzibar (I.) (zăn'zĭ-bär).....Afr.	5.30 S	39.30 E
135	Zanzibar...................Zan.	6.5 S	39.13 E
112	Zanzur (zän-zo͞or').........Libya	32.53 N	13.3 E
132	Zaouri, Wad (R.) (zä'o͝o-rê)..Alg.	29.30 N	1.30 W
102	Zapala (zä-pä'lä)...........Arg.	38.50 S	70.2 W
93	Zapaluta (La Trinitaria) (sä-pä-lo͞o'tä) (lä trē-nê-tä'rê-ä). Mex.	16.7 N	92.2 W
80	Zapata (sä-pä'tä)...........Tex.	26.52 N	99.19 W
96	Zapata Pen...............Cuba	22.18 N	81.30 W
96	Zapata Swamp............Cuba	22.23 N	81.15 W
94	Zapatero I. (sä-pä-tā'rō).....Nic.	11.45 N	85.50 W
92	Zapopan (sä-pō'pän)........Mex.	20.43 N	103.22 W
129	Zaporozh'e (zä-pô-rôzh'yĕ) Sov. Un.	47.45 N	35.11 E
92	Zapotiltic (sä-pô-têl-tēk')....Mex.	19.37 N	103.23 W
92	Zapotitlán (sä-pô-tê-tlän')...Mex.	17.18 N	98.49 W
93	Zapotitlán...........Mex. (In.)	19.18 N	99.2 W
93	Zapotitlán, C..............Mex.	18.33 N	94.48 W
92	Zapotlanejo(sä-pô-tlä-nā'hô). Mex.	20.37 N	103.5 W
133	Zaqaziq (zä-kȧ-zēk')........Eg.	30.33 N	31.32 E
126	Zara (Zadar) (dzä'rä) (zä'där) Yugo.	44.7 N	15.4 E
92	Zaragoza (sä-rä-gō'sä)......Mex.	23.58 N	99.48 W
80	Zaragoza..................Mex.	26.7 N	103.26 W
80	Zaragoza..................Mex.	28.28 N	100.54 W
125	Zaragoza (thä-rä-gō'thä)......Sp.	41.39 N	0.52 W
128	Zaraisk (zä-rä'êsk)......Sov. Un.	54.46 N	38.56 E
119	Zarasai (Ežerēnai) (zä-rä-sī') (ĕ-zhĕ-rā-nī'). Sov. Un.	55.44 N	26.17 E
102	Zarate (zä-rä'tā)...........Arg.	34.15 S	59.0 W
132	Zaria (zä'rê-ä)..............Nig.	11.8 N	7.45 E
120	Zary (zhä'rê)...............Pol.	51.38 N	15.7 E
139	Zashiversk(zȧ'shĭ-vĕrsk'). Sov.Un.	67.0 N	143.50 E
121	Zastavna (zȧs-täf'nȧ)....Sov.Un.	48.32 N	25.50 E
120	Zatec (zhä'tĕts)...........Czech.	50.19 N	13.32 E
139	Zavitaya (zä'vê-tä'yȧ)...Sov. Un.	50.15 N	129.40 E
133	Zawia (zä'wê-ä)...........Libya	32.38 N	12.51 E
121	Zawiercie (zȧ-vyĕr'tsyĕ)......Pol.	50.28 N	19.25 E
96	Zaza R. (zȧ'zȧ)............Cuba	21.58 N	79.20 W
121	Zbarazh (zbä-räzh').....Sov. Un.	49.39 N	25.48 E
121	Zbruch R. (zbro͝och).....Sov. Un.	49.15 N	26.15 E
121	Zdolbunov (zdôl-bo͞o'no͝of) Sov. Un.	50.31 N	26.16 E
121	Zduńska Wola (zdo͞on''skä vō'lȧ) Pol.	51.36 N	18.56 E
137	Zebdany (zĕb'dȧ-nê)....Syr. (In.)	33.44 N	36.4 E
115	Zeebrugge (zā'bro͝og'gĕ)......Bel.	51.20 N	3.10 E
160	Zeehan (zē'ăn)...Austl. (Tas. In.)	41.54 S	145.24 E
160	Zeehan, Mt......Austl. (Tas. In.)	42.0 S	145.15 E
84	Zeeland (zē'lănd)..........Mich.	42.50 N	86.2 W
137	Zefath (Safed) (zĕ-făt') (sȧ-fēd') Pal. (In.)	32.58 N	35.29 E
120	Zehdenick (tsā'dĕ-nêk)......Ger.	52.59 N	13.20 E
117	Zehlendorf (tsā'lĕn-dôrf) Ger. (Berlin In.)	52.26 N	13.15 E
133	Zeila (zā'lä)............Br. Som.	11.15 N	43.26 E
120	Zeitz (tsīts)................Ger.	51.3 N	12.7 E
121	Zelechów (zhĕ-lĕ'Ko͝of).......Pol.	51.47 N	21.54 E
120	Zella-Mehlis (tsȧl'ȧ-mā'lês)...Ger.	50.40 N	10.39 E
131	Zembra I. (zĕm'brä)...Tun. (In.)	37.8 N	10.40 E
133	Zémio (zā-myō').....Fr. Eq. Afr.	5.2 N	25.11 E
93	Zempoala, Pt. (sĕm-pô-ä'lä)..Mex.	19.27 N	96.19 W
93	Zempoatlépetl (Mt.) (sĕm-pô-ä-tlā'pĕt'l). Mex.	17.15 N	95.57 W
120	Zemsz (zhĕmsh).............Pol.	51.48 N	14.57 E
127	Zemun (Semlin) (zĕ'mo͞on) (sĕm'lĭn). Yugo.	44.50 N	20.25 E
127	Zenica (zĕ'nêt-sä).........Yugo.	44.10 N	17.54 E
140	Zenjan (zĕn-jän')...........Iran	36.32 N	48.32 E
129	Zenkov (zĕn-kôf')......Sov. Un.	50.12 N	34.22 E
127	Žepče (zhĕp'chĕ)..........Yugo.	44.25 N	18.1 E
120	Zerbst (tsĕrbst).............Ger.	51.57 N	12.3 E
137	Zerga (zēr'gă).........Jor. (In.)	32.5 N	36.6 E
139	Zeya (zȧ'yȧ)............Sov. Un.	53.45 N	127.15 E
139	Zeya R..................Sov. Un.	53.0 N	127.30 E
111	Zeytun (zā-to͞on')...........Tur.	37.55 N	36.50 E
124	Zêzere R. (zĕ'zȧ-rĕ).........Port.	40.0 N	7.58 W
121	Zgierz (zgyĕzh).............Pol.	51.51 N	19.26 E
137	Zgorta (zgôr'tȧ).......Leb. (In.)	34.21 N	35.52 E
129	Zgurovka (zgo͞o'rôf-kä)..Sov. Un.	50.32 N	31.43 E
129	Zhadov (zhȧ'dôf).......Sov. Un.	52.2 N	32.50 E
69	Zhelaniya, C. (zhĕ'lä-nĭ-yȧ) Sov. Un.	76.45 N	69.0 E
121	Zhidachuv(zhê-dä'cho͝of). Sov. Un.	49.22 N	24.11 E
139	Zhigalovo (zhê-gä'lô-vô). Sov. Un.	54.50 N	105.10 E
139	Zhigansk (zhē-gȧnsk')...Sov. Un.	66.40 N	123.30 E
129	Zhitomir (zhê'tô'mêr)....Sov. Un.	50.15 N	28.40 E
128	Zhizdra (zhêz'drȧ)......Sov. Un.	53.46 N	34.44 E
128	Zhizhitskoe, L. (zhê-zhēt'skô-yĕ) Sov. Un.	56.10 N	31.15 E
129	Zhmerinka (zhmyĕ'rêŋ-kȧ) Sov. Un.	49.3 N	28.8 E

ng-sing; ŋ-baŋk; N-nasalized n; nŏd; cŏmmit; ōld; ôbey; ôrder; fo͞od; fo͝ot; ou-out; s-soft; sh-dish; th-thin; pūre; ûnite; ûrn; stŭd; circŭs; ü-as "y" in study; '-indeterminate vowel.

ăt; fĭnăl; rāte; senâte; ärm; ásk; sofà; fâre; ch-choose; dh-as th in other; bē; ĕvent; bĕt; recĕnt; cratēr; g-go; gh-gutteral g; bĭt; ĭ-short neutral; rīde; ĸ-gutteral k as ch in German icĥ;